ENCYCLOPEDIA OF
Consumer Brands

ENCYCLOPEDIA OF CONSUMER BRANDS

VOLUME I
CONSUMABLE PRODUCTS

VOLUME II
PERSONAL PRODUCTS

VOLUME III
DURABLE GOODS

ENCYCLOPEDIA OF
Consumer
Brands

VOLUME 1

Consumable

Products

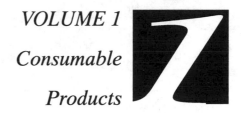

Editor   JANICE JORGENSEN

St James Press

Detroit   London   Washington D.C.

STAFF

Janice Jorgensen, *Editor*

Sonia Benson, Nicolet V. Elert, Mary Ruby, *Associate Editors*
Suzanne M. Bourgoin, Kevin Hillstrom, Paula Kepos, *Contributing Editors*
Marilyn Allen, *Editorial Associate*
Michael J. Tyrkus, *Assistant Editor*

Peter M. Gareffa, *Senior Editor*

Mary Beth Trimper, *Production Director*
Shanna Heilveil, *Production Assistant*
Cynthia Baldwin, *Art Director*
Mark C. Howell, *Graphic Designer*

Victoria B. Cariappa, *Research Manager*
Jeanne Gough, *Permissions Manager*

∞™ This book is printed on acid-free paper that meets the minimum requirements of American National Standard for Information Sciences—Permanence Paper for Printed Library Materials, ANSI Z39.48-1984.

Library of Congress Catalog Card Number 93-37940
A CIP catalogue record for this book is available from the British Library.
ISBN 1-55862-336-1

Printed in the United States of America
Published simultaneously in the United Kingdom

I⊤P™

The trademark **ITP** is used under license.

10 9 8 7 6 5 4 3 2 1

ADVISERS

Martin Boddy
Information Officer
ICI Group Headquarters, London, England

Linda Golden
Professor of Marketing
University of Texas, Austin

Pamela K. Jenkins
Librarian/Business Specialist
Kansas City Public Library, Kansas City, Missouri

Paul Kirner
Vice President/Executive Art Director
J. Walter Thompson, Detroit, Michigan

Jeanette M. Mueller-Alexander
Reference Librarian/Business Subject Specialist
Hayden Library, Arizona State University, Tempe

BRAND CATEGORIES COVERED IN THE ENCYCLOPEDIA

VOLUME I: CONSUMABLE PRODUCTS
Food
Pet Food
Non-Alcoholic Beverages
Alcoholic Beverages
Tobacco

VOLUME II: PERSONAL PRODUCTS
Apparel and Accessories
Cosmetics and Fragrances
Health and Beauty Aids
Household Cleaning and Paper Products
Miscellaneous Household Products
Over the Counter Drugs
Stationary and Office Supply

VOLUME III: DURABLE GOODS
Appliances
Automobiles and Related Products
Computers, Electronics, and Office Equipment
Home Furnishings and Building Supplies
Musical Instruments
Photographic Equipment
Sporting Goods
Toys

CONTENTS

Preface xiii
Index to Brand Names 657
Index to Companies and Persons 665
Index to Advertising Agencies 673
Index to Brand Categories 675
Notes on Contributors 679

Volume I: Consumable Products

PREFACE

Encyclopedia of Consumer Brands provides substantive information on products that have been leaders in their respective brand categories and have had decided impact on American business or popular culture. Often considered "household words," the featured products have become integral parts of the lives of American consumers, and many have gone on to achieve international recognition.

The *Encyclopedia*'s three volumes highlight approximately 600 of the most popular brands in America. Coverage in each book emphasizes brands that have been prominent since 1950 and are now on the market, with a few inclusions of instructive debacles such as the Edsel. Younger products that have experienced profound success or have notably influenced their industry are also included. With thousands of new products being introduced to the market each year—and only a handful of them still in existence five years after their launch—much can be learned from the stories behind prominent brands, whose success depends on an elusive combination of careful research, quality development, market savvy, advertising prowess, and precise timing. The *Encyclopedia* is intended for use by students, librarians, job seekers, advertising and business people, and others who want to learn more about the historical and modern development of brands most significant to American culture.

Inclusion Criteria

Brands included in the series were selected by the editor and advisory board members, who chose brands possessing a combination of elements: top sales and leading market share in their field, strong public recognition, and longevity. Many top selling brands and market share leaders were discovered through listings found in trade journals, advertising periodicals, and industry and business publications; Gale Research's *Market Share Reporter* and *Business Rankings Annual* also aided in identifying leading brands. The editor and advisory panel selected brands from a wide range of categories, but because of the increasingly vast number of brand names on the market, some significant products inevitably were left out.

St. James Press does not endorse any of the brand names or companies mentioned in this book. Brands that appear in the *Encyclopedia* were selected without reference to the wishes of their parent companies, who have in no way endorsed their brands' entries. Parent companies were given the opportunity to participate in the compilation of the articles by providing first-hand research and reading their entries for factual inaccuracies. We are indebted to many of these companies for their comments and corrections. We also thank them for allowing the use of their logos and other art work for identification purposes. All brand names mentioned in the *Encyclopedia* are trademarks or registered trademarks of their respective parent companies.

Focus

The focus regarding a particular brand name varies from entry to entry. When an individual *product* has found significant success in the market place, that one product is featured in its own entry (e.g. Twinkies, Scotch Tape, or Mustang). When a *brand name* or *trademark* is placed on a wide range of products in different brand categories (e.g. Pillsbury, Calvin Klein, or Sony), that brand name or trademark is the focus of the entry, and discussion of most or all of the products on which that brand name appears will ensue.

Because companies choose to market their products using a variety of tactics—which can include capitalizing on an existing brand name by placing it on new products, or creating new brand names while still emphasizing the company name—a consistent rule of thumb for determining the focus of each of the *Encyclopedia*'s entries was sometimes challenging to establish. The responsibility of deciding the focus of each article rested with the editor, advisory board members, and writers and researchers. Please refer to the Index to Brand Names to identify products that have been either historically chronicled in full or merely mentioned within the series.

Entry Format

An array of special features is included in the entries, which have been designed for quick research and interesting reading.

● **Attractive page design** incorporates textual subheads, making it easy to pinpoint specific information.

● **Easy-to-locate data sections** provide an "At a Glance" overview of brand history, sales and market share (when available), major competitors to the brand, advertising information, and the address and phone number of the brand's parent company.

● **Informative essays** trace how a product originated and was first marketed, how it evolved as a product and developed commercially, and how it fares today compared with its competitors and its own past history. Current coverage encompasses today's changing markets and marketing strategies, the impact of a global economy, and future projections, as well as any controversies associated with the product such as trade name disputes, false advertising claims, and safety, ethical, and environmental issues.

● **Current brand logos or photos** have been included with most entries to further enhance your appreciation of the brand; some entries include historical illustrations as well.

● **Sources for additional information** provide the reader with suggested further reading on the brand; these sources, also used to compile the entries, are publicly accessible materials such as magazines, general and academic periodicals, books, and annual reports, as well as material supplied by the brands' companies.

Helpful Indexes

Encyclopedia of Consumer Brands includes cumulative indexes to Brand Names, Companies and Persons, Advertising Agencies, and Brand Categories that make it easy to locate not only featured brand names but pertinent brand names, companies, people, and advertising agencies mentioned within each article.

ENCYCLOPEDIA OF

Consumer
Brands

A&W®

Legend has it that root beer gained its name—over the original choice of "root tea"—as part of a scheme to lure alcohol drinkers. In fact, the beverage's name refers to the brewing process that is used to make root beer, as opposed to fermentation, which is used to make wine, beer, and other spirits. The term "beer," as it turns out, helped boost the popularity of the beverage in its early years. While similar concoctions were brewed in Europe and South America, the first root beers in colonial America were made from molasses, water, yeast, and a variety of herbs, including vanilla, licorice, cinnamon, bruised birch, and sassafras bark. Root beer remained a home brew until 1876, when Theodore Hires developed an extract suitable for brewing root beer at soda fountains.

Brand Origins

The history of the A&W Root Beer, a product of A&W Brands, Inc., begins with Roy Allen, who made a living buying, repairing, and selling hotels in the southwestern United States. One day Allen became acquainted with an elderly gentleman at the soda fountain of one of his hotels near Tucson, Arizona. The man offered Allen a recipe for root beer that he urged Allen to commercialize, saying, "You can make a fortune with a five cent root beer."

The next stop for the nomadic Allen was Lodi, California. At the time, 1919, World War I was coming to an end, and novelties and new products were gaining popularity. Many food stand owners had taken to erecting hot-dog-, hamburger-, and pickle-shaped buildings to attract customers. Since the passage of Prohibition laws had made alcoholic beverages illegal, Allen figured it would be clever to build a soft drink stand for his root beer recipe, fashioning it as an old saloon, complete with a bar and sawdust floor.

The store opened its doors on June 20, 1919, to a celebration of returning World War I soldiers and was a tremendous success. Allen immediately opened a second concession stand in nearby Stockton, California. Unable to keep up with demand, he formed a partnership with an employee, Frank Wright, and opened five more outlets in Sacramento under the simple banner "Root Beer." After taking over the refreshment stand of a large theater in Sacramento, Allen set up another outlet in a converted carnival wagon. Opening two root beer stands in Houston in 1922, Allen first introduced "A&W" as the brand name of his root beer.

Automobiles were becoming commonplace in the early 1920s, and without air conditioning, people were anxious to get out of their houses. Entire families would often pile into the car for a spin and head for the well-lighted streets of downtown. There they spotted the A&W stand, which Allen had equipped with "tray boys" who delivered customers' orders directly to car windows. Thus was born the famous A&W drive-in, an informal gathering place for a cool refreshing mug of root beer.

In 1924, encouraged by the popularity of his root beer and drive-ins, Allen bought out Frank Wright and began laying plans for expansion throughout northern California. Allen decided, however, to sell the franchises for A&W restaurants in California, Oregon, Washington, Nevada, and Arizona to Lewis Reed and H. C. Bell, who changed the name of the outlets to Reed & Bell Root Beer. Allen, meanwhile, relocated to Salt Lake City, where he started the A&W business over again.

Early Marketing Strategy

Allen sold franchises for A&W throughout the United States—except the five states where Reed & Bell controlled the franchises—creating the first nationwide chain. One of the first to sign was Willard Marriott, who built his Marriot Hotel empire on a successful A&W business in Washington, D.C.

Allen established precise franchise agreements that, among other things, stipulated the color and design of A&W outlets, the use of handled, 10-ounce mugs, and even the amount of ice over the coils through which the root beer flowed. He invariably discovered that some franchisees were cutting corners by watering down the extract or otherwise failing to respect their contracts. In response, he usually bought out their interest, with the belief that it took only one bad operator to give all A&W franchises a negative image.

Many A&W outlets were unaffected by the Great Depression of the 1930s, but many more struggled with dwindling sales volume. Assuming it would give people another reason to visit an A&W, Allen encouraged those who wanted to sell food to do so. Despite the Depression, A&W continued to grow. In 1933 the company had more than 170 outlets. By 1936, however, when Allen moved the business to Santa Monica, sales growth had finally stagnated. Business picked up again in 1938, and by 1941 the company boasted more than 260 outlets throughout the United

AT A GLANCE

A&W brand root beer founded in 1919 in Lodi, CA, by Roy Allen and sold exclusively at A&W restaurants; A&W Root Beer formula and business sold to Gene Hurtz, who formed A&W Root Beer Company; sold in 1963 to J. Hungerford Smith Company, which was purchased in 1966 by United Fruit Company; United Fruit acquired by United Brands Company, 1970; A&W Root Beer first bottled in 1971; A&W division sold by United Brands and renamed A&W Brands, Inc., 1986. Sugar Free A&W Root Beer introduced in 1974; renamed Diet A&W, 1987.

Performance: *Market share*—30% (top share) of root beer category.

Major competitor: Hires; also, Barq's and Dad's.

Advertising: *Agency*—Della Femina McNamee, New York, NY. *Major campaign*—Great Root Bear mascot.

Addresses: *Parent company*—A&W Brands, Inc., 709 Westchester Avenue, White Plains, NY 10604; phone: (914) 397-1700; fax: (914) 993-0538.

States. With the eruption World War II in the following year, many A&W outlets suffered shortages of employees, extract, and sugar. While some were able to survive by closing one day a week, 80 were forced to close.

Business rebounded after 1945, when Reed and Bell's contract expired, and all the franchises in the five western United States reverted to Allen and the A&W name. The availability of GI loans made it possible for hundreds of returning servicemen to apply for A&W franchises, which contributed to tremendous growth. By 1947 virtually all the stands that had closed were back in operation. But in June of 1950, with A&W now expanded to more than 450 outlets, Allen sold the business and retired to care for his wife, who had become ill.

Brand Development

Allen sold the A&W business to Gene Hurtz, a Nebraska businessman. Hurtz, however, never maintained a corporate staff numbering more than four, which caused considerable hardship for the growing number of franchisees. Hurtz left most of the chain's promotion to individual restaurants, a decision that did not endear him to store operators. Still, by 1960, the chain—now with franchises throughout Canada—had grown to more than 1,900 restaurants.

After 13 often difficult years, Hurtz sold the A&W Root Beer Company to the J. Hungerford Smith Company, which had manufactured the root beer extract since 1919. But Hungerford was itself acquired by the United Fruit Company in 1966. United Fruit, meanwhile, merged with the AMK Corporation in 1970 to form United Brands Company. While ultimate ownership in A&W was changing hands, promotion of the A&W brand turned to the restaurant "concept." The root beer-only stands had disappeared shortly after the war. Now, promotion was based on the outlet itself, rather than the root beer.

The A&W outlet-centered marketing strategy changed drastically in 1970, when United Brands established a new franchise agreement under which individual operators could purchase all supplies from A&W International, rather than from approved

suppliers. The new royalty system caught on slowly, as it was somewhat less advantageous for franchisees. It did, however, standardize the nationwide system to a greater degree.

Also in the 1970s United Brands proposed bottling A&W Root Beer for the first time. The first cans of the product hit the market in San Diego and Phoenix and cleared the way for a national roll-out. With the growing popularity of diet drinks, United Brands developed Sugar Free A&W Root Beer in 1974. By 1976 both versions of A&W Root Beer had grown to surpass even industry leader Hires in market share. The creation of a beverage unit in effect marked the divorce of the root beer from the restaurant chain. Still built around the classic root beer, though, the restaurants became separately administered, merely serving as outlets for the root beer.

In 1980 United Brands enlisted independent bottlers to take over production of A&W Root Beer from the few food brokers who had handled the brand. By mainstreaming the root beer as a major bottler brand, United made A&W an attractive acquisition target. Held briefly by a consortium from 1983 to 1985, A&W Brands, Inc., was taken over by its management in 1986 and taken public the following year.

Brand Extensions

While the bottled version of A&W Root Beer may be considered an extension of the actual drive-in, the root beer itself has given rise to variations. The use of A&W Root Beer in the root beer float—a restaurant favorite—inspired the production of canned A&W Root Beer brewed specifically for homemade floats. A true extension, however, is the sugar-free line, introduced in 1974 and added to the restaurant menu shortly afterward. Sugar Free A&W Root Beer was reformulated in 1987, using NutraSweet, and reintroduced as Diet A&W. The brand accounts for about one-third of A&W's total root beer sales volume.

In 1986 the company introduced A&W Cream Soda and its diet equivalent. By 1989 even these brands, which had no connection to the drive-ins other than the A&W name, became the nation's top-selling cream soda brands, with more than 40 percent of the segment's market share.

Packaging

From its earliest days, A&W used the classic "arrow" logo, essentially an arrow placed over a circular emblem containing the A&W name and the words "ice cold." The company's colors, extended to buildings as well as mugs and paper wrappers, are a deep orange, dark brown, and white. In addition, A&W Root Beer was not available in anything but the characteristic heavy, frosted mug until 1971, when the company began selling its root beer in cans.

The introduction of canning presented several problems for A&W, including the formula of the root beer. Classical root beers had a shelf life of only seven minutes. Even A&W's, drawn from a fountain, was subject to some settling. These problems, however, were easily corrected, but the canned product retained a different, slightly metallic taste.

Advertising

Advertising for A&W Root Beer is very low-key, with almost no television or other mass media purchases. Promotion of the brand consists mainly of point-of-purchase displays. A&W had experimented with a number of advertising themes, particularly during the 1960s. Oddly, because the business was centered around restaurant franchises, advertising did not include taglines or mass media copy but, rather, symbols. The first to be tried, and only briefly, was the comic strip character Dennis the Menace, who was featured with A&W products on banners and packaging. Adopting the popular cartoon icon was intended to counterbalance McDonald's restaurants' clown, Ronald, who was supported by a truly massive television advertising budget.

Discontinuing its use of Dennis the Menace in its advertising, A&W created another animated character, the Great Root Bear, in 1974. The bear, who perhaps unavoidably bore a slight resemblance to Yogi Bear, was promoted as a mascot, like Ronald McDonald. Publicity people in Great Root Bear suits attended the openings of new restaurants and were featured prominently in charity functions and visits to children's hospitals.

Health Claims

In the early days of root beer—and, in fact, all root- and herb-brewed concoctions—the beverage was believed to have some medicinal value. Thought to "tone up" the system, root beer was for many years considered a tonic. A&W, however, never marketed its root beer with any such claims. While the precise formula for the root beer is proprietary, consumers can be certain that sassafras is no longer an ingredient; the root had been labeled a carcinogen and banned by the U.S. Government during the late 1950s.

Performance Evaluation

In spite of the troublesome and often confusing changes in ownership that have thrown A&W's brand development off track from time to time, the brand is an unparalleled success. As a soft drink, A&W Root Beer competes with such major brands as Coca Cola, Pepsi and 7-Up. As a root beer, however, its appeal is decidedly different. Root beer drinkers rarely choose between a cola and a root beer, but instead choose among the various root beer brands. As a result, A&W controls only 1.5 percent of the soft drink market but remains the number one brand of root beer in the United States, holding more than 30 percent of the root beer category. This formidable rise—accomplished in only five years—was achieved mainly by leveraging the established A&W drive-in identity.

Future Predictions

A&W has proven successful even without huge promotional campaigns and flashy television spots. Therefore, barring spirited attempts by such competitors as Barq's, Hires, and Dad's to wrest back some market share, it is unlikely that A&W will take a higher profile than it has.

A&W Root Beer benefits from a very solid reputation for quality that can no doubt be traced back to the brand's founder, Roy Allen. Much of the strength of A&W Root Beer is built upon its legacy as a drive-in drink and its relation to the unique preparations of the A&W drive-in menu items. As long as the A&W restaurant—franchises of which now exist in such countries as Hong Kong, Singapore, Malaysia, Guam, Indonesia, and Japan—remain popular, the root beer is likely to retain its top position in the market.

Further Reading:

"An American Tradition, The History of A&W," A&W Brands, Inc.

Enkema, L. A., *Root Beer,* Indianapolis, IN: Hurty-Peck & Company.

"Extracting the Secrets of Root Beer," *Encounters,* July/August, 1991.

"History of A&W," A&W Brands, Inc., press release.

"Milestones in the History of A&W Restaurants, Inc.," A&W Brands, Inc.

"Remembrances of Roy Allen, A&W's Founder" *A&W News Dispenser,* July-August, 1973.

"The Roots of Root Beer," *Pittsburgh Press,* January 8, 1989.

—John Simley

ABSOLUT®

ABSOLUT VODKA

Absolut vodka leads the imported vodka category in the United States with a market share nearing 65 percent. Produced in Sweden by V&S Vin & Sprit AB, Absolut was introduced in the United States in 1979. Due to a strong marketing campaign by its U.S. distributor, Carillon Importers Ltd., Absolut immediately began edging out competitors in the imported vodka market. In 1986 Absolut became the top seller in its category, ousting Stolichnaya vodka. The growth of Absolut sales continued, and by 1993 Absolut began threatening the U.S. domestic market's share of the billion dollar industry.

Early History

Distilling vodka was already a centuries-old tradition in Sweden in the 19th century when businessman Lars Olson Smith worked to enhance the process at his Stockholm distillery. His improved method, labeled a "purified tenfold" distilling system, produced *Absolut rent brannvin* (absolutely pure vodka). Although Smith's process was improved upon in subsequent years, the name Absolut and a portrait of Smith appear on all bottles of Absolut Vodka.

Introduction in the United States

The U.S. vodka market had been stagnant for some time when Carillon Importers introduced Absolut in 1979, and easy success seemed unlikely. A $65,000 market research program initiated in 1978 predicted that Absolut would fail because, among other things, the bottle lacked the usual paper label and a neck long enough for bartenders to grab. During its first year in the United States, Carillon sold only 150,000 cases of Absolut.

Industry sales slumped even further in the 1980s due to growing concerns over alcohol abuse and drunk driving, but, largely because of its vigorous marketing strategy, Absolut sales soared. Between 1983 and 1984 alone, the vodka's revenues rose 65 percent. Within ten years of Absolut's introduction in the United States, sales jumped to almost 1.5 million cases. And within five more years, sales reached more three million cases, not only beating out all other imported vodkas in the United States, but threatening the lesser priced U.S. domestic vodka market as well.

Product Innovations

Flavoring vodka has been a tradition in Sweden for more than 400 years. Absolut began bottling this tradition in 1986 with the introduction of Absolut Peppar, vodka flavored with natural jalapeno and paprika. In August of 1988, Absolut Citron, flavored with lemon and hints of lime, mandarin orange, and grapefruit, was introduced. Sales grew quickly, and soon Absolut Citron was among the top five imported vodkas; by 1993 Absolut Citron was the third most popular imported vodka in most of the United States. Absolut Kurant, flavored with northern European black currant berries in accordance with an age-old Swedish custom, was put on the market in early 1993.

Marketing

Industry analysts credit Carillon President Michel Roux with Absolut's success. Roux, a transplant from the Cognac region of France, became Carillon's first salesperson in 1970 and worked his way up to president by 1982. Possessing a personal, progressive style of marketing, he positioned Absolut to suit his tastes.

Distinguishing Absolut from its competitors proved an interesting challenge in the early years. By legal definition, vodka is a "neutral spirit, without distinctive character, aroma, taste or color." Thus, image building was a key ingredient to Absolut's success. The image Roux sought to create for Absolut was that of a premium, upscale product consumed by a progressive group of consumers on the cutting edge of taste and fashion. Carillon's parent company, Grand Met/IDV, gave Roux free reign to direct marketing in his own manner. This sometimes resulted in uncustomary corporate tactics such as hiring feminist Gloria Steinem as the keynote speaker at an annual sales meeting in 1983; Roux hoped that his sales force would become better attuned to the mind-set and buying habits of women in the 1980s. Overall, Roux's tactics resulted in continuous growth of Absolut sales.

By 1985 Absolut was "just rocking and rolling and creating all kinds of stir in the market place," gushed *Market Watch* magazine. More important, it was pushing Stolichnaya vodka out of its top position in the import category and was on its way to developing an image that would win praise and awards from marketing experts.

AT A GLANCE

Absolut brand of vodka founded in 1879 in Sweden by V&S Vin & Sprit; Absolut vodka introduced in the United States in 1979; distributed in the United States by Carillon Importers Ltd.; by 1986, Absolut was the top seller in the imported vodka category.

Performance: *Market share*—Nearly 65% (top share) of imported vodka category. *Sales*—Approximately three million cases per year.

Major competitor: Monsieur Henri Wines' Stolichnaya; also, Palace Brands' Finlandia.

Advertising: *Agency*—TBWA Advertising, New York, NY, 1980—. *Major campaign*—Numerous print ads featuring the Absolut Vodka bottle, including works by commissioned artists.

Addresses: *Parent company*—V&S Vin & Sprit AB, Formansvagen 19, S-100 72 Stockholm, Sweden; phone: 8 7447000; (U.S. distributor) Carillon Importers Ltd., Glenpointe Centre West, Teaneck, NJ 07666-6897; phone: (201) 836-7799. *Ultimate parent company*—(Of Carillon Importers, Ltd.) Grand Met/IDV, 11-12 Hanover Square, London W1Q 1DP, England; phone: 71 6297488.

Award-Winning Advertising

Absolut's advertising campaign, first introduced in 1980, not only set it apart from its competitors, it actually re-invigorated the imported vodka market. TBWA, a New York City advertising agency, invented the first ad, an image of the clear glass bottle with a halo and the pun, "Absolut Perfection." Another featured a martini glass leaning toward a bottle of Absolut with the caption, "Absolut Attraction."

Over the years, the campaign has undergone innumerable transformations, but the format, a pun of the name Absolut, has remained the same. *Forbes* hailed the campaign as "absolutly (sic) ingenious," while *Sales and Marketing Management* cited it as "a classic example of marketing artistry in action." The long-running campaign has won two Kelly awards for advertising from the Magazine Publishers of America and in 1990 earned the prestigious Grand Effie Award from the American Marketing Association. Upon presenting its award, the American Marketing Association lauded Absolut's campaign for "being able to support a continuing 30 to 40 percent annual sales growth while maintaining a fresh, exciting look to the advertising—always the same yet always different."

Absolut Art

Initially, Absolut sought to project a cool, clean image in its advertising. But in 1985 its image was jazzed up with the first in what was to become a long line of artistic commissions. According to Roux, as quoted in *Forbes,* pop artist Andy Warhol approached him and said, "I'd like to make a painting of Absolut. I love the product, the packaging. I even use it as a perfume." Carillon paid $65,000 for Warhol's bright, splashy rendition of an Absolut bottle. The painting was transformed into print ads with the simple caption, "Absolut Warhol." Almost overnight, this $65,000 commission created a strong new image for Absolut and linked it to the sophisticated urban art crowd.

The following year, Warhol recommended that his protege, artist Keith Haring, create a portrait of the Absolut bottle. Haring's painting presented a completely different image and interpretation of the Absolut bottle, yet the ad's format was not altered; this time it featured the phrase "Absolut Haring." Since then Carillon has gone on to commission work from more than 300 artists, most of whose pieces have been incorporated into Absolut's enduring print ad design.

While Absolut frequently commissioned work from a number of well-established artists, the company also actively sought out artists considered "young or emerging in the national arts scene," providing them with greater visibility at a time when government and foundation support for the arts was in decline. Absolut cornered the imported vodka market, and sometimes the payoff to artists was also big. Artist Romero Britto, for example, saw his sales double in the year that Absolut commissioned him, and the price of his paintings went from the $5,000 to $25,000 range to $9,000 to $40,000.

All original commissioned art is owned by Carillon, which from time to time opens its gallery to the public. The original Warhol rendition of the Absolut bottle is said to be worth $350,000, and a signed lithograph remains in the permanent collection at the Whitney Museum of American Art in New York City. But as Roux said in 1991, "They are not an investment. They're advertising." Lest one forget the fact, small print at the bottom of each ad provides a toll-free number and ordering information.

Different Strokes for Different Folks

Through careful placement of advertising, Carillon and TBWA have been able to mold Absolut's image to please wildly different audiences. Some print ads were tailored to regions: "Absolut Manhattan" contained an aerial view of Central Park, reshaped to resemble an Absolut bottle; and "Absolut L.A." presented a view of a swimming pool in the shape of the bottle. An ad captioned "Absolute Merger" appeared in issues of *Forbes* magazine; "Absolut Centerfold" was featured in *Playboy*. The June 1991 issue of the *New Yorker* contained a series of editorial cartoons along the Absolut theme, plus an official entry form for the Absolut Vodka Cartoon Contest. Winning entries were then run in future issues of the magazine.

Beginning in 1990, Carillon began featuring in its ads a series of commissioned art focusing on specific themes. "Absolut Glasnost," a 31-page full-color insert of contemporary Russian art appeared in the June 1990 issue of *Interview* magazine. Earlier that year, "Absolut Americana," a commissioned series of American folk art, was run in *Country Home Magazine*. In 1991 the "Absolut Heritage" collection of paintings and sculptures by African-American artists was featured in the June issue of *Black Enterprise* magazine. Other series include "Absolut Southwest" and "Absolut Artists of the Nineties." "Absolut Statehood," a $350 million, two-year advertising program began running in *USA Today* in 1993, displays commissioned art from 51 U.S. artists presenting their vision of their home states, plus the District of Columbia, and, of course, the Absolut bottle.

Other Commissions

Roux received praise from the business community for mixing marketing with arts support in a new way. "I like art," Roux told a reporter in *Sales and Marketing Management* in 1992, "and I think art needs a lot of support in this country. You go to a small country like Belgium or Luxembourg and there's a lot of government support of the arts there. But here, we really have very little. So it's up to corporations to help out. Of course, there's a commercial side to all this, creating in the public consciousness a specific image for Absolut.''

Absolut's support for the arts extends to classical music, ballet, modern dance, and furniture and fashion design. The vodka has sponsored concerts of new American music at the Lincoln Center in New York City as well as concerts by such world-renowned composers as Brazilian Carlos Jobim. Carillon also began a series

Absolut Kurant joined Absolut's popular line of flavored vodkas in 1993.

in the late 1980s entitled ''Absolut Fashion,'' which ran in *Elle* magazine and showcased ten couture fashion designs incorporating the Absolute name or bottle. ''Absolut Design'' commissioned work from nine furniture designers and ran in national magazines in 1992. A playful variation on the furniture design theme also ran that year in *Metropolis* magazine. Entitled ''Absolut Cutouts,'' the ad featured scaled-down versions of furniture designed by Eliav Nissan in realistic cut-outs. Readers could clip and assemble the chairs, tables and beds to create their own ''Absolut bedroom and Absolut dining room.''

Advertising Innovations

Other advertising innovations include a recording of Jobim's music on a clear, floppy 33 rpm record. This record was then inserted into magazines and placed over an image of the Absolut bottle etched with the words ''Absolut Song, Music of Brazil.'' The record served as an advertisement both for the vodka and for Jobim's Carnegie Hall concert sponsored by Absolut. In 1990

Absolut became the first brand to incorporate a full-page, four-color hologram in its national magazine advertising. The following year Absolut created possibly another first, a cardboard jigsaw puzzle entitled ''Absolut Puzzle,'' which debuted in the February issue of *New York* magazine. Readers of *Mirabella* magazine received a free gift of Absolut stockings by designer Christian Roth. The stockings, which appeared in 1992, were printed with a black-and-white crossword puzzle design containing the words Absolut Vodka. And, in the July 1993 issue of *Interview,* readers could clip a stylish gift bag designed by one of four artists.

Competition and Performance Appraisal

Although total liquor sales in the United States declined 2.5 percent in 1988, imported vodka sales grew 20 percent. For the most part, Absolut was responsible for the growth, and in 1989 four top liquor marketers introduced new products into the imported vodka market, hoping to ride the coattails of Absolut's popularity.

Monsieur Henri Wines had been the premier importer of vodka before Stolichnaya was toppled by Absolut in 1985. In an attempt to regain some of its lost market, Monsieur Henri introduced Stolichnaya Cristall, a top-quality vodka priced about six dollars higher than Absolut. Also in 1989, Seagrams began distributing Wyborowa, a Polish vodka marketed as a high-end product. Wyborowa followed the introduction of Buckingham Wine's Denaka vodka from Denmark and Brown-Forman's ICY vodka from Iceland.

Brown-Forman predicted that import vodka sales would double by 1994, creating room for a number of competitors. By the end of 1989, ten new premium imported vodkas flooded the market. Industry experts, noting Absolut's innovative advertising campaign, rightfully predicted that gaining any substantial market share would be difficult for other importers. ''We made [the premium imported vodka] category,'' Roux told *Advertising Age* in 1989, ''and we were expecting [new competition]—that's life.'' As its advertising campaign soared to new creative heights and won industry awards, Absolut's sales came close to three million cases per year.

Throughout its history, the Absolut brand of vodka has, as a result of Carillon Importers' efforts, built a tradition of arts sponsorship that has paid off in high sales. Starting with a small market of urban intellectuals and artists, Carillon has been able to expand its advertising and market to include a variety of audiences and interests. With the ''Absolut Statehood'' series in *USA Today,* the vodka seemed to be working its way toward mainstream America. Asked to predict the end result of the two-year, $350 million campaign, Roux responded in a David S. Wachsman Associates, Inc., press release, ''We hope it will encourage other companies to make or to increase their own commitments to the arts.''

Further Reading:

Brown, Christie, ''Absolutely Ingenious,'' *Forbes,* April 15, 1991, p. 128.

David S. Wachsman Associates, Inc., press releases, November 1992; December 1992.

Drucker, Mindy, ''Absolut Integrity,'' *Target Marketing,* June 1992, p. 10.

Dunkin, Amy, ''What Stirs the Spirit Makers: Vodka, Vodka, Vodka,'' *Business Week,* June 12, 1989, p. 54.

Gervey, Gay, ''Carillon Scores With Profits on the Rocks,'' *Advertising Age,* May 27, 1985, p. 4.

Hager, Bruce, "Michel Roux: The Absolut Truth," *Business Week,* August 27, 1990, p. 58.

Levine, Joshua, "Absolut Marketing," *Forbes,* December 11, 1989, p. 282.

"Sales and Marketing Management's 1992 Marketing Achievement Awards," *Sales and Marketing Management,* August 1992, p. 40.

Winters, Patricia, "Vodka on the Docks: Importers Pour Into U.S. Market as Sales Boom," *Advertising Age,* March 20, 1989.

—Maura Troester

ALMADEN®

Almaden has achieved firsts as a wine producer in several note-worthy categories: it is the oldest California winery, the largest premium wine producer, the inventor of the popular grenache rosé vintage, and the initiator of bag-in-the-box packaging in the United States. Almaden has proven to be an expert at marketing its popular Mountain Red and Mountain White generic jug wines to the average consumer. A workhorse in production, Almaden was a formidable power in the wine business up to the beginning of the 1980s, selling more than 13 million cases—approximately 15 million gallons of wine—annually.

Owning three large production sites and an expansive 6,000 acres of vineyards, Almaden created more than 50 different vintage types, from apéritifs to dessert and sparkling wines. Once the appeal of the fashionable grenache rosé abated in the late 1980s, however, Almaden was stricken with the label of just another jug-wine maker. It was sold to liquor giant Heublein Inc. in 1987 by National Distillers and Chemical Corporation, which had purchased Almaden in 1967. The brand joined a growing roster of other Heublein labels, including Inglenook, Christian Brothers, Beaulieu Vineyard Wines, Rutherford Estate, and T.J. Swann. Most of Almaden's winery facilities and cellars were sold by Heublein under the ownership of England's Grand Metropolitan PLC. Throughout its history, Almaden has successfully positioned itself as a producer of lower-priced varietals and bulk wines.

Brand Origins

Almaden owns California's oldest winery, which was founded by two French immigrants, Charles Lefranc and Étienne Thée, in 1852 at Los Gatos in Santa Clara County. Bordering San Jose's urban sprawl, the Almaden vineyards stand on the location of the original winery. The first wine maker in the United States to till *Vitis vinifera,* a species of grapevine brought over from Europe by Lefranc and known to make the world's best wines, Almaden is named after a California quicksilver mining town and is a Moorish term meaning "the mine." A California state historical landmark seven miles south of the winery reads: "In 1852 Charles Lefranc made the first commercial planting of fine European wine grapes in Santa Clara County and founded Almaden Vineyards." Almaden grapes, cultivated from the rocky soil at the base of the Santa Cruz Mountains, were of a unique character, atypical of other varietal wines.

Charles Lefranc married Étienne Thée's daughter in 1880 and acquired control of Almaden Vineyards, cultivating 130 additional acres in Santa Clara County. Transplanted vines from the Burgundy, Bordeaux, Champagne, and the Rhone Valley areas of France thrived in California soil. After Thée's death, Paul Masson, another French citizen from Burgundy, assisted Lefranc at the winery. Masson became Lefranc's son-in-law, eventually leaving Almaden to organize his own winery. By the turn of the century, Almaden was producing 100,000 gallons of wine a year.

Disbanded during Prohibition, Almaden began producing wine again when San Francisco financier Louis Benoist, an oenophile and gourmet, purchased it in 1941. Benoist was president of the investment firm Lawrence Warehouse, but throughout the 1960s he devoted all his time and energy to the commercial success and expansion of the Almaden winery. Benoist hired renowned wine connoisseur and distributor Frank Schoonmaker and wine master Oliver Goulet as advisers. Under this management team, Almaden dedicated itself to creating top-quality varietals.

Early Marketing Strategy

Benoist became serious about marketing Almaden's products to the public when he hired Peter Jurgens as sales manager in 1951. Jurgens held wine tastings conducted by representatives of the California Wine Advisory Board for select groups, including the academic society at the University of California at Los Angeles, museum-affiliated groups, and doctors' associations. In the words of William A. Dieppe, president and chief executive officer of Almaden from 1969 to 1982, the wine tastings "were immensely successful."

For the wine tastings, Schoonmaker and artist Oscar Fabrés designed colorful take-home pamphlets explaining how each wine tasted and outlining the history of the Almaden winery. Before state-enforced price regulations, the cost of the wine label was also printed. According to Dieppe, "We spent a lot of money on the wine tastings because I felt the need for advertising per se was not nearly so great as the need to get directly to the consumer."

In addition to wine tastings, Almaden worked on increasing the visibility of its premium vintages in major grocery store chains. In the 1950s winegrower E&J Gallo had become a major force with which Almaden had to compete in the supermarket arena. Instead of grabbing key end stands in front of the store near check-out

AT A GLANCE

Almaden brand of wine founded in 1852 in Santa Clara County, CA, by Étienne Thée and Charles Lefranc; brand sold to National Distillers and Chemical Corporation, 1967; purchased in 1987 by Heublein Inc., which was acquired by Grand Metropolitan PLC the same year. Numerous varieties of red, rosé, and white wines are sold under the Almaden label.

Performance: *Market share*—2.9% of domestic wine category. *Sales*—$179.1 million.

Major competitor: Sutter Home Winery Inc.'s Sutter Home; also, E. & J. Gallo Winery's Carlo Rossi and Gallo.

Advertising: *Agency*—McCann-Erickson, New York, NY, 1987—. *Major campaign*—Celebrity spokeswoman Catherine Oxenberg introducing Almaden Golden Champagne in television commercials.

Addresses: *Parent company*—Heublein Inc., 16 Munson Road, Farmington, CT 06034; phone: (203) 240-5000; fax: (203) 674-9082. *Ultimate parent company*—Grand Metropolitan PLC, 11-12 Hanover Square, London W1Q 1DP, England; phone: 71 6297488.

counters, Almaden, hoping to establish an association between its vintages and various food products, displayed its premium wines in bins set up in the delicatessen section.

Having increased the visibility of its premium wines, Almaden took an aggressive approach to introducing its generic "mountain wines" to the Southern California market. Consisting of a blend of good varietals, the mountain wines allowed Almaden to compete and eventually overtake Paul Masson varieties as leaders in the lower-priced, premium wine market. "We were able to compete against Paul Masson originally mostly because here we were with this ninety-nine-cent premium wine, cork-bottled and everything else," commented Dieppe in the book *Almadén Is My Life.*

Almaden was the first winery to concentrate on restaurants and eventually acquired up to 150 distributors covering the entire United States. Almaden salespeople started a rigorous training program for its distributors, educating them about Almaden products. The winery printed wine lists for restaurants dominated by Almaden labels and accented with the bright sketches of Oscar Fabrés. People were encouraged to bring the wine lists home; many would later buy Almaden wines. During the years from 1955 to 1956, the cost of generating the wine lists was just $25 per 100 copies.

Greatest Commercial Success

In the early 1960s there was a tremendous supply of grenache grapes—used primarily to make port wine—in California. Schoonmaker decided Almaden could produce a slightly sweet, yet dry wine, helping to conquer in the minds of the consumer the "dry wine as sour" impression. Modeled after the Tavel rosé from France's Rhone Valley, Almaden created grenache rosé, which became a best-seller in the 1960s. Almaden's mass-produced pink wine became the most popular rosé of its kind, and according to William Dieppe, "it was probably the most successful single wine product in the country" for strictly table wines.

Marketing and Expansion of Products

The success of grenache rosé allowed Almaden to market its wines nationally. Ads designed with Fabrés artwork could be found in *Gourmet* magazine as well as in the *New Yorker.* Back labels on bottles of premiums and varietals stylishly described the wines' vintages. Schoonmaker initiated another "first" for Almaden by editing a newsletter called *News from the Vineyards,* in which stories about the general history of wine were highlighted with recipes. It was Schoonmaker's intent to convince readers of what he considered the perfect partnership: food and wine. Meanwhile, Almaden continued to push its diversified product line into restaurants.

Production grew in the 1960s, taking advantage of the wine boom in the United States. In 1962 Almaden hired chemist Al Huntsinger, formerly employed by the Charles Krug winery, to make vast amounts of quality generic and mountain wines "absolute in their continuity," according to Dieppe. Oliver Goulet continued on as wine master of the fine varietal and premium lines. To increase production of its top varietal wines, Almaden expanded into San Benito County, including the hillsides of Paicines and Cienega. Grapes used to make Almaden Pinot Noir, Cabernet Sauvignon, Gewürztraminer, Chardonnay, and Johannisberg Riesling were cultivated. Vineyard properties were later acquired in Monterey County, pioneering grape-growing in southern California. At the end of the 1960s, Almaden owned approximately 6,000 acres, more vineyards than any other U.S. winery.

Innovations in Packaging and Labeling

Prior to National Distillers and Chemical Company's purchase of Almaden in June of 1967, Almaden bottled its mountain wines in half-gallon and gallon bottles topped with a metal screw cap. The decision was made in 1966 to change to "private-molded" bottles fashioned after the stoneware receptacles featured in the artwork of Omar Khayyam—"a teardrop glass container," explained Dieppe. The glass-handled jug Almaden created was cork sealed with a bulb-top that could be easily screwed on and off without a corkscrew. Sales of the bulb-top jug soared.

In addition, Almaden "ponies," six-and-a-half ounce wine bottles, became extremely popular on commercial airline flights. Passengers could slip the ponies, which could be opened with a standard bottle opener, quite easily into their purses or handbags, taking them home for later consumption. There were four ponies in all: red (burgundy or claret), white (chablis or rhine), pink (rosé or zinfandel), and until 1951, golden (sweet semillon). Madrone Vineyards were the inventors of the privately molded pony.

Almaden was the first U.S. winery to market its varietals in "bag-in-the-box" packaging, which had gained popularity in Europe in the 1980s. The pouch container packaging was used primarily in mega-casks of 18 liters sold to such institutions as restaurants, hotels, and hospitals. Begun in Australia by the Scholle firm, bag-in-the-box pouch containers eliminated the problem of oxidation. The wine is withdrawn from the bag by an outside spigot attached to the cardboard box. As the bag deflates, air is prevented from getting to the wine and souring it.

In the summer of 1991 Almaden targeted its bag-in-the-box to individual consumers, debuting 14 varietals in four-liter pouches called winecasks. Freshness, portability, and convenience were the container's marketed virtues. According to *Beverage World,* the winecask was part of Almaden's "It's a Matter of Taste" promotional campaign and retailed between $9 and $13.

Shifted Marketing Focus

As the popularity of its hugely successful grenache rosé fell, Almaden slipped in sales. This led to its sale in 1987 to liquor giant Heublein Inc., which in turn came under the ownership of Grand Metropolitan of London. Almaden carried more than 50 table, dessert, and apéritif wines and brandies, ranging from generic jugs to high-quality varietals under three labels: the best vintages of a particular year were bottled under the prestigious Charles Lefranc Cellars label; sparkling wines and lower-priced champagnes were part of the Le Domaine label; generics and lower-priced varietals fell under the vast Almaden label.

Heublein closed some of Almaden's facilities and most of its vineyards in order to consolidate production. Almaden's original 135-year-old winery in San Jose was closed, and production was moved to Heublein's large all-purpose facility in Madera. The second half of the 1980s and the early 1990s saw a concentration on low-priced varietals, such as white zinfandel and white barbera, as well as several generics, including blush chablis and blush rhine.

International Ventures

Almaden has also ventured into the international market. Establishing two vineyards in Brazil, Almaden planted the first rootings in 1974 and eventually boasted 90,000 rootings. Since valuable Brazilian acreage was reserved for banana plants, the vineyards—producing grapes for red, rosé, and white wines—had to be tilled at an elevation of more than 800 feet. Almaden President William Dieppe was convinced that Brazil, predominantly a red-wine-drinking country, would become avid white-wine-drinkers, just as white jug wines bearing the Almaden label had become "*the* beverage, to the cost of the liquor business."

Almaden also became active in the import-export business. Under Dieppe's presidency, Almaden increased its activity in the import business in 1977 by acquiring European franchises. Lines from Italy and France were included as well as Taylor Ports and Spain's "Guff Gordon." Imports were part of the Charles Lefranc Cellars label, which kept them intentionally distinct from Almaden. In 1982 a chardonnay was introduced under the Caves Laurent Perrier label, part of a joint venture with Laurent Perrier of France. Almaden fulfilled the role as maker and sales distributor of the product.

Having once owned the Frederick William Company, Almaden also obtained a foothold in England, exporting cabernet sauvignon, sauvignon blanc, semillon, and pinot noir. Exports to buyers in other countries were also pursued, including the navy and Kikkoman food chain in Japan as well as distributors in Switzerland, Germany, Italy, and the Alsace region of France. Almaden even had representation in Fauchon, one of Paris's most esteemed food stores.

Later Brand Development and Promotions

Offering an extensive portfolio of wine varieties, Almaden could change products in a given geographical region of the country based on what sold best. Like other wine producers, Almaden experimented with the low-alcohol, light wine market. Health concerns of consumers and the highly publicized drinking-and-

driving issue fostered the increasing popularity of low-alcohol vintages. Almaden's was the lowest alcohol volume brand at 7.1 percent, followed by Paul Masson at 7.4 percent. Almaden debuted its newest light line, Almaden Light White Zinfandel, in January of 1992, joining the ranks of the already established light blush and light chablis vintages. According to *Market Watch,* "all contain 35 percent less alcohol and 25 percent fewer calories than standard still wine." The light wine is promoted as the ideal companion to salads, "Perfect for today's Light Style."

Supported by more than $4 million in advertising expenditures—perhaps the largest advertising campaign for the brand in its history—Almaden Golden Champagne was released in November of 1985. Combined with a reasonable price, a stylish package, and a celebrity spokeswoman—television's *Dynasty* star Catherine Oxenberg—Almaden debuted the new product in video-styled TV commercials.

In the spring of 1989 Almaden debuted five wines under the Blossom Hill label. The premium line, comprised of chardonnay, cabernet sauvignon, white zinfandel, sauvignon blanc, and gamay beaujolais, was packaged in 1.5 liter bottles. According to Almaden's marketing director Michael Jacobson, as reported in *Marketing & Media Decisions,* the premium line was aimed at the average consumer. "These wines do not require an education in wine tasting to enjoy," Jacobson explained. Promotions for the premium line included radio advertisements touting Almaden as "The wine you don't have to learn to love."

In October of 1992 red zinfandel was added as an Almaden varietal. Michael Jacobson was quoted in *Market Watch* as saying, "There's a strong demand for varietal wines, and red zinfandel is among the most popular." According to the Impact Databank, sales in 1991 of "domestic and imported Red Zinfandel reached 900,000 nine-liter-case shipments, a 12.5 percent increase over the year earlier."

Performance Appraisal

Almaden produced 150,000 cases of wine in 1954, five million cases in 1973, and 13 million cases in the early 1980s. At its peak, Almaden was the largest premium wine brand and was ranked third in volume production. The establishment of distributors in the neglected Midwest and South contributed to the winery's meteoric growth, as did heavy radio and magazine advertising. According to Dieppe, consistency in presentation, or "salesmanship," was strictly obeyed by everyone at Almaden. "All of the emphasis on the timetable was everybody do and say the same thing at the same time so that it's the greatest possible impact on the trade as well as the consumer." In 1990 Almaden was the third-best-selling brand at $190 million. The following year, though, Almaden's place fell to number five with total retail sales at $179.1 million.

Future Predictions

Mid-priced premium wines have appeared as the wine market's new wave of "superbrands." *Adweek's Marketing Week* reported in 1991 that "workhouse 'generics' such as Carlo Rossi, Gallo, Almaden and Inglenook are fast becoming relics." Increased competition from the superbrands, coupled with the fact that consumers are drinking less but choosing better wines due to health concerns and more sophisticated tastes, supports expansion into the mid-priced varietal market. Almaden's addition of red zinfandel in late 1992 to its varietal line was designed to accommodate changing consumer preferences. According to Dieppe, the "hardest decision" that he ever made during his presidency at Almaden was choosing to market "volume to the masses." If premium- and vintage-labeled varietals gain mass-market appeal, as their generic jug-wine predecessors had, the future for Almaden may once again be bright.

Further Reading:

"Almaden Light White Zinfandel," *Market Watch,* January/February 1992, p. 93.

"Almaden Red Zinfandel," *Market Watch*, October 1992, p. 63

Bird, Laura, "Losing Ground, Vintners Till New Soil," *Adweek's Marketing Week,* Superbrands 1991, p.60.

"Creating A Mass Market For Wine," *Business Week,* March 15, 1982, pp. 108-110, 118.

Dieppe, William A., *Almadén Is My Life,* edited by Ruth Teiser, Berkeley, CA: The Regents of the University of California, September 1985.

Dougherty, Philip H., "Almaden Reassigned To McCann-Erickson," *New York Times,* April 13, 1987, sec. D, p. 11.

"Heublein to Buy Almaden Vineyards," *New York Times,* January 7, 1987, sec. D, p. 4.

"It's in the Bag," *Beverage World,* July 1991, p. 10.

Johnson, Hugh, *Modern Encyclopedia of Wine,* third edition, New York, NY: Simon & Schuster, 1991.

Prial, Frank, with Rosemary George & Michael Edwards, *The Companion to Wine,* Mirabel Books Ltd., 1992.

Roby, Norman S. and Charles E. Oelken, *The New Connoisseurs' Handbook of California Wines,* Chicago, IL: Alfred A. Knopf, 1992, p. 115.

"Seagram Sells; Heublein to Close Almaden Plants," *Wines & Vines,* April 1987, p. 18.

"Wine-by-the-Box," *Beverage World,* August 1990, p.16.

"Wine Unveiled," *Beverage World,* November 1985, p. 33.

—Kim Tudahl

ALPO®

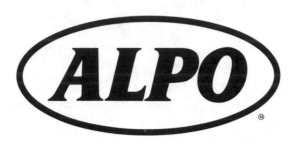

Alpo was the top-selling canned dog food in the nation from the late 1960s until it was pushed into second place in 1991 by its chief competitor, Kal Kan Pedigree. Until 1989, Alpo Pet Foods, Inc. was the only major pet food marketer that did not also have a cat food line. However, the American trend toward higher cat ownership than dog ownership instigated diversification within the company. Alpo Cat Food, a 28-item line that took five years to develop, debuted with the largest advertising campaign in pet food history. Within the year, Alpo Cat Food was lauded as the most successful new pet food to be introduced within the past decade. The canned cat food swiftly rose to be the fifth most popular brand of 1990. During that same year, the dry cat food took its position as number eight. The cat food line was credited with restoring some of the company's market share and securing its place as a major pet food manufacturer.

In order to remain competitive in a mature industry that was experiencing little growth, Alpo embarked on a major development program both before and after the introduction of its cat food line. The program included the creation of record numbers of new products, reformulations of existing products to suit the different needs and interests of pets and their owners, product line extensions, and new items obtained through acquisitions of other pet food companies. The newly developed products focused on owners' interests in providing pets with healthy foods and reflected contemporary human trends by pampering pets with gourmet cuisine.

Brand Origins

Pre-packaged pet foods were first sold during the 1920s. The foods were chiefly cereal-based and sold through mail order and specialty outlets. In 1936, a young entrepreneur by the name of Robert Hunsicker began to make a new type of dog food, one that contained 100 percent meat. Working out of a rented basement in Allentown, Pennsylvania, Hunsicker created a meat loaf, wrapped it in cellophane, and named it K-9 Health Foods for Dogs. He delivered it door-to-door to his customers' homes. The following year, Hunsicker moved his small company to a rented garage. At this site he began to make his first canned food, an all-meat product called All-Pro. Hunsicker charged 15 cents per can and sold it through kennels and veterinarians in Pennsylvania's Lehigh Valley.

In the next two decades, All-Pro dog food underwent changes in brand name, distribution, and location. In 1944, the name was changed to Alpo. In 1949, the brand obtained its first supermarket distribution in Philadelphia. In 1958, the company moved three miles west of Allentown—where it is still based—and expanded distribution to the northeast. By 1965, Alpo was in national distribution, and by the end of the 1960s it was the nation's leading brand of canned dog food.

Developments in Dog Food

Over the years, dog food manufacturers have recognized that most dog owners treat their pets like members of the family. Many owners want the same things for their pets that they want for themselves. Changes in owners' personal interests and preferences are often reflected by changes they make in the lives of their pets. Two such shifts in interest affecting the pet food industry in recent years have been a higher focus on health and a desire for upscale specialty products. To meet consumers' changing tastes, Alpo introduced a series of products that addressed specific pet health issues and extended its line to include premium pet food products.

For owners of overweight dogs, and for those who simply prefer to reduce the calories in their dogs' diets, as in their own, to avoid obesity and its health risks, Alpo introduced Alpo Lite in 1989. The food contained 25 percent fewer calories than regular Alpo and was aimed at the 40 percent of American dogs presumed to be overweight. Alpo Lean, a product with 33 percent less fat and 15 percent fewer calories than leading dry dog foods, followed in 1992. For owners who were concerned about health risks associated with the use of chemical additives in foods, Alpo reformulated its Beef Flavored Dinner, a dry food originally introduced in 1970. The new version, distributed in 1992, contained only natural ingredients. Similarly, Alpo Premium canned dog food was repackaged with new flavors and in new sizes.

Alpo was actually following a trend that had begun as far back as the 1970s when small food companies were marketing scientifically formulated pet foods promoted for their health value. The major retail outlets for the small companies were veterinarians, health food stores, and pet shop boutiques. In contrast, the main outlets for Alpo pet foods were supermarkets and grocery stores. But the scientific food trend proved to be so popular with pet owners that by 1990 the specialty outlets had obtained an estimated 20 percent of total pet food sales compared to 5 percent in 1980.

As early as 1985, Alpo began to design foods geared to dogs with specific needs. In 1985, the company introduced canned puppy food because young dogs' needs differ from those of adult dogs. In 1992, the company introduced Alpo Protein Plus, a product with a 20 percent protein content designed for energetic, active dogs. Protein Plus contained no artificial colors or flavors, appealing to dog owners who prefer only natural ingredients in their dogs' diets.

Buying upscale, premium products for pets was a trend among members of the so-called yuppie generation during the economically booming 1980s, before the decade's recession started to take hold. In 1991, Alpo introduced a line of gourmet dog food in a sauce and called it Prime Cuts. The canned food consisted of chunks in gravy that have the appearance of human food. According to an Alpo spokesperson, "Prime Cuts look and smell more like human stew than dog food."

Introducing a gourmet item was an effort to regain the brand's market share from erosion due to specialty outlet sales of dog and cat foods. However, premium brands were the first to slide in sales during the recession, and the major manufacturers had to slash prices to retain market share. Pet owners found that super-premium products were only a few pennies higher than premium brands.

Alpo had also been introducing different types of snacks throughout the years. The company bought the rights to the Liv-A-Snaps treat line and began selling the product in the 1970s. In 1983, Alpo Jerky Style Premium Dog Treats and Alpo Beef Bite Dog Treats were introduced, two products obtained with the acquisition of The Reward Co. Subsequent snacks included Alpo Snaps dog treats, Alpo Beef Biscuits (which replaced Alpo Stew Biscuits), Alpo Rawhide Chews, and Alpo Biscuits and Bones. Pet food makers called these items premium treats because they are meat-based rather than cereal-based and, when calculated on a per-pound basis, can be as costly as filet mignon.

Developments in Cat Food

The decision to enter the cat food business was based on the trend of declining dog ownership. Smaller households, smaller homes, more single households, and more working women meant that the lower maintenance cat was often preferred to the dog. The Pet Food Institute reported that in 1991 there were 53.3 million dogs owned by 37 million households, and 62.4 million cats owned by 30 million households. While the average household owned 1.4 dogs, the average household owned two cats.

Alpo's initial cat food line consisted of 16 flavors and two size varieties of canned food and four sizes of dry cat food. Canned Alpo Premium was followed in 1990 by dry Alpo Gourmet Dinner. In 1992, Alpo created a new category, pet beverages. Dairy Cat was a drink intended for lactose-intolerant cats. In that year the company also introduced its special Urinary pH Formula, which relieves urinary tract disorders in cats.

Premium cat foods were another casualty of the recession because they were promoted more as indulgences than as nutritional products and therefore became logical corners to cut in tight budgets. To keep cat owners from choosing less expensive brands, many cat food manufacturers engaged in the same kind of price wars that dog food manufacturers had entered.

Product Varieties

The manufacturers of Alpo have sought to satisfy the needs and interests of pet owners by giving them choices in the types and sizes of pet foods. Canned dog foods include Alpo regular, lite, senior, protein plus, puppy, and premium chunks and gravy. Dry dog foods include regular, lite, senior, and puppy. Debbie Kelly-Ennis, director of marketing, explained Alpo's strategy in reference to product varieties: "The Alpo name has a tremendous amount of equity. And we have that equity in one brand name spanning the three key segments of dog food, wet, dry and snacks."

Dry dog food was initially promoted as more convenient, as well as less expensive per pound than canned foods. Many owners also believe that dry foods are healthy for teeth and gums, more nutritious, and easier to use than some canned food. Based on material from the Pet Food Institute Fact Sheet of 1992, all brands of dry dog foods accounted for about 50 percent of total dog food sales, canned dog foods accounted for about 29 percent, and dog treats for about 12 percent. Canned cat food accounted for 56 percent of total cat food sales, dry cat food accounted for 39 percent, and cat treats for a little more than 1 percent.

Advertising Innovations

Advertising pet food requires a unique approach because the buyer of the product is not the actual consumer. Owners buy pet foods on the basis of what they believe their pets need and want. Advertising must appeal to the pet owner, yet the products must satisfy the needs of the particular dog or cat. Franklin W. Krum, president of Alpo, told Richard W. Anderson of *Business Week* in 1988, "Nimble marketing is the key to this business in which the buyer usually doesn't evaluate the product himself. If the dogs pushed the shopping carts, we wouldn't have to spend $35 million a year in ads."

Within a year of Krum's statement, Alpo's advertising budget doubled as it launched its new cat food, using the comic strip cat Garfield to kick off the campaign. Alpo allocated a $70 million ad budget for the cat food line, the largest introductory budget in pet food history. In addition, there were other promotions such as free-standing inserts offering free products, trade promotions, and mailings to veterinarians.

Alpo also promoted its products through spokespersons who were well-known celebrities or experts in their field. In 1975,

A vehicle used to transport Alpo dog food.

Lorne Greene, the TV actor of the popular *Bonanza* series, became Alpo's spokesperson. In 1982, Joan Embery, good will ambassador for the San Diego Zoo, became Alpo's new spokesperson.

Another $90 million in advertising was targeted in 1992 to recapture market share. The previous year, Alpo lost its position as the nation's leading pet food manufacturer. The company's advertising budget had been cut by 64 percent as part of an overall decline in media spending by parent company, Grand Met.

Alpo Sues for False Ads

Alpo and rival Ralston Purina have been locked in litigation for several years over the issue of false advertising. According to Steven W. Colford in *Advertising Age,* Alpo filed a suit in 1985 against Purina for its advertising campaign claiming that Purina Puppy Chow dog food could prevent or heal joint disease in a young dog. The statement was based on unsound data, but, according to the U.S. District Court findings, Purina continued the ad campaign even after it learned its research was faulty. With Purina drawing customers with its claims of having a remedy to this common and very painful ailment in dogs, Alpo was forced to mount an expensive ad campaign for its new puppy food in response to the ads of its rival. Purina retaliated against Alpo's lawsuit by filing a countersuit.

The court reached a decision in 1991, requiring Purina to pay a total of $12 million in total damages. The district judge allocated the damages as $3.5 million for the cost of the response advertising campaign launched by Alpo in an effort to maintain its market share, $4.5 million for revenue lost by Alpo due to the delay in going national with its puppy food, and $4 million in damages.

According to an Alpo spokesperson, as of the spring of 1993 the case was still in litigation.

Performance Appraisal

Alpo hit the million dollar mark in pet food sales in 1957 and just six years later achieved $100 million in sales. The company's market share steadily increased as new products were introduced. In 1989, the company was estimated to have a 6.9 percent market share and by 1991 it had moved up to 9.5 percent, largely because of its cat food business.

Overall, Alpo ranked as the sixth largest pet food manufacturer in 1991, and in subsequent years as well. Sales of its canned dog food led the way with a market share of 22.8 percent until Kal Kan Foods' Pedigree captured the larger share of 23.7 percent in 1991. The cat food line moved quickly as a front-runner. In 1990, just one year after it was introduced, Alpo Premium Cat Food had 9 percent of the canned cat food market, ranking in fifth place. The dry cat food, Alpo Gourmet Dinner, had a 5 percent share in 1990 and ranked in eighth place. Most of the other products had a smaller market share but still ranked high. Alpo Regular Dinner had a 5.5 percent market share in 1990 and ranked third. This dry dog food was outpaced by two brands manufactured by Alpo's chief competitor. The dry Alpo puppy food had less than 1 percent market share but it still ranked third in this category. By 1993 Alpo treats held a 6.5 percent market share in the treat category with the largest share of the 2.2 percent belonging to Liv-A-Snaps. In addition, the Prime Cuts line experienced a total share of 5.7 percent in the canned category. Alpo had high hopes for the cat food line and anticipated that it would reach 40 percent of the pet food business with its expanded product line.

Further Reading:

"Alpo Builds Presence in Cat Food—at a Cost," *Wall Street Journal,* October 12, 1990, p. B 1.

"Alpo Cat Food Gets $70M Start," *Advertising Age,* August 21, 1989, p. 3 and 63.

"Alpo Eats into Cat Food Market," *Advertising Age,* October 1, 1990, p. 51.

Alpo Petfoods, Company Background and History, The Weightman Group, Philadelphia, 1993.

Anderson, Karen, "Pet Needs," *Supermarket Business,* September, 1990, pp. 169-170.

Anderson, Richard W., "Now Alpo Wants to Dish It Out to Kitty," *Business Week,* September 19, 1988, pp. 165-166.

Colford, Steven W., "$12 Million Bite," *Advertising Age,* December 2, 1991, p. 4.

Gibson, Richard, "Pet-Food Shoppers Watch Their Pennies," *Wall Street Journal,* October 22, 1992, p. B1.

"Grand Met Shifts; It Will Keep Alpo," *New York Times,* May 25, 1990, p. D3.

Laura Klepacki, "A New Breed of Chow: Supermarkets See Health-Oriented Pet Foods as a Way of Trading Up to Higher Margins," *Supermarket News,* January 6, 1992, p. 13.

Liesse, Julia, "$90M Backs Alpo Run for No. 1," *Advertising Age,* January 4, 1991, p. 20.

"100 Leading National Advertisers," *Advertising Age,* September 23, 1992, pp. 31-32.

"The 1992 Supermarket Sales Manual," *Progressive Grocer,* July, 1992, p. 84.

Noble, Barbara Presley, "Will the American Pet Go for Haute Cuisine?," *New York Times,* December 16, 1990, p. F5.

"Pet Food Institute Fact Sheet, 1992," Pet Food Institute, Washington D.C.

''Putting Natural Food in the Pet Bowl,'' *New York Times,* August 12, 1991, p. D3.

''What's Next? Freeing the Inner Kitten?,'' *Business Week,* July 6, 1992, p. 42.

—Dorothy Kroll

ARM & HAMMER®

The Arm & Hammer baking soda brand, in the yellow box with the famous red and blue trademark image, has been produced since 1867. Arm & Hammer baking soda is a widely recognized product in the United States—the box used today is nearly identical to packaging utilized well over a century ago—that is used by consumers for baking, cleaning, deodorizing, and as a dentifrice; and by industrial manufacturers for baking, pharmaceuticals, animal feed additives, and fire extinguishing.

Business Beginnings

As early as 1839 Dr. Austin Church, a practicing physician who dabbled in chemistry as a hobby, was producing "saleratus," or bicarbonate of soda. In a letter to his wife, Nancy Dwight, who was visiting family in South Hadley, Massachusetts, Church mentioned that he wanted to sell the product on which he had been experimenting since 1834. Thus Nancy's younger brother John Dwight heard of a business opportunity. The brothers-in-law became partners, naming the business John Dwight & Company, and began manufacturing baking soda in 1846 from the kitchen of Dwight's Massachusetts farmhouse. Eventually the business was moved to New York City, where the two families lived together and established a strong bond during their early years in Brooklyn.

The partners leased land just west of 10th Avenue at 25th Street. In a shack on the property, Church refined his processing of bicarbonate of soda, while Dwight worked on selling the product in the city. Several British firms sold competing products at the time, causing the partners to explore new markets for their baking soda. New York, however, remained the obvious place to fuel growth. In 1847 Church and Dwight looked to expand; investor John R. Maurice stepped in, becoming a partner and remaining with the company until 1881.

When both Church and Dwight expressed the wish to bring their sons into the business in the mid-1860s, Maurice objected vehemently. Church decided to resign from the company in 1865, though the families of Dr. Church and Mr. Dwight remained friends, even after the former established his own competing firm, Church & Company, in 1867.

Austin Church had good reason to want to hire his sons—both men had experience running successful businesses. While Elihu D. Church oversaw an axe-handle factory, James A. Church owned the Vulcan Spice Mills. In addition, the now-familiar Arm & Hammer logo—a picture of a man's arm wielding a hammer just before striking an anvil, representing the Roman god Vulcan, a blacksmith skilled in forging weapons—was originally used by James Church. The trademark was adopted for use with one of several brands of baking soda that Church & Company originally sold. It soon became clear, however, that the Arm & Hammer brand was the most popular choice, and the other brands were abandoned. In 1878 Arm & Hammer baking soda was patented; Dr. Church died the following year.

By 1876 John Dwight had begun to sell his baking soda under the Cow brand name in an almost identical packaging style, and both companies competed keenly, but courteously, in the bicarbonate of soda business for 29 years. Though Arm & Hammer eventually gained nearly universal recognition, the Cow brand continued to be preferred in a few East Coast markets. Descendants of the founders decided to unite the two businesses in 1896 as Church & Dwight Company.

Innovations

The combined efforts of Church and Dwight resulted in a number of advances. While Dr. Church was still with John Dwight & Company, the partners distinguished their product from competitors by packaging the baking soda by hand in paper bags, rather than the barrels used at the time by most manufacturers to ship dry goods. Customers looked for the red-labeled soda on the shelf, rather than in an open—and unhygienic—keg.

Building on the idea of individual packages of baking soda, John McCrodden, an employee of John Dwight & Company in the 1880s, invented an automatic filling machine while he was head of the packing department. The machine increased productivity and improved upon the strict standards to which the company held itself.

Meanwhile, at Church & Company, Captain Albert Stearns designed a machine that aided in the wrapping of baking soda packages. Employees wrapped boxes at a rate of 1,000 per day, per person. After use of the new machine began in 1885, the rate jumped to 15,000 packages a day per employee. With the help of such technological advancements, by the time Church & Dwight Company was formed, Arm & Hammer led the baking soda business in sales.

AT A GLANCE

Arm & Hammer brand of baking soda was started in South Hadley, MA, in 1839 by Dr. Austin Church, who sold bicarbonate of soda in Rochester, New York; with brother-in-law John Dwight, manufacture of baking soda began in 1846; firm named John Dwight & Company; in 1867 Austin Church resigned, establishing Church & Company with sons James A. and Elihu D. Church in Brooklyn and introducing Arm & Hammer logo; 1876, Dwight begins selling Cow Brand; Arm & Hammer brand patented in 1878; Dr. Austin Church dies the next year; 1896, descendants merged the two companies to form Church & Dwight; 1903, John Dwight dies.

Performance: *Market share*—90% of consumer market; 65% of industrial market (baking, pharmaceutical, animal feed, and fire extinguisher companies).

Major competitor: Generic baking soda producers; also Colgate-Palmolive Company, Procter & Gamble Company, and Unilever PLC household products.

Advertising: *Agency*—Partners & Shevack, New York, NY; *Major campaign*—Stresses trademark recognition, emphasizing specific uses of the multiple-use product in separate, focussed campaigns.

Address: *Parent company*—Church & Dwight Co., Inc., 469 North Harrison St., Princeton, NJ 08540; phone: (609) 683-5900; fax: (609) 279-7301.

Early Advertising Strategies

While partners, Austin Church and John Dwight recognized early on the benefits of distinguishing their product from the competition. Salesmen for the young company travelled the American country by foot, horse, horse-and-buggy, and rail. "Wherever a new town sprang up, a John Dwight & Company salesman would be among its first commercial visitors," related William J.P. Cullen in *The Story of Church & Dwight Company*. Carriages were decorated with plumes, flags, and bells; the horse drawing the buggy was covered with a blanket with the lettering, "Dwight's Soda, Cow Brand." Some salesmen went so far as to blow a bugle to get attention.

Once the packages were on the shelves, the baking soda became easily visible in its red wrapping. In addition, the founder's wives compiled and tested recipes enclosed in the package; Mrs. Dwight's "Gold Cake" and "Silver Cake" were popular. Also, leaflets dispensed gave information on the many uses of baking soda, a promotional tactic continued by Church & Dwight 150 years later. In 1888 Church & Company began distributing trading cards with colored birds pictured on the front and descriptive information on the back, enclosing one in every box of baking soda. Even after the Church & Dwight merger, the cards were produced for decades.

Shortly after the turn of the century, Church & Dwight created a mailing list from telephone books and post office information, and began sending out free cookbooks. By 1916 more than two million pieces of mail issued from company offices annually. The steady cookbook following, which built on the audience gained from the recipes offered in earlier years, led the company to set up a test kitchen in 1932. Located in Syracuse, New York—site of one of the company's largest suppliers—a full-time home economist developed and tested recipes under the name of "Martha Lee Anderson" for seven years.

Baking Soda's Many Uses

The early practice of promoting the versatility of baking soda with leaflets stating, "Arm & Hammer Brand Soda should be in 1) Your Kitchen, 2) Your Laundry, 3) Your Nursery, 4) Your Medicine Chest, 5) Your Barn and Your Dairy," would eventually become the backbone of Church & Dwight's advertising strategy.

In addition, the company formally established a health education program in 1922, preparing a variety of pamphlets, and advertising its findings. By 1927 Church & Dwight was advertising in 11 national magazines, and baking soda was listed in the American Dental Association's original list of approved products in 1931.

Through the 1930s baking soda for baking purposes was less in demand. As more shoppers bought cake and biscuit mixes, which saved them time and contained all the necessary dry ingredients, baking soda sales became dependent on alternate uses of the utilitarian powder. By 1955 Arm & Hammer's many household uses were promoted in 24 magazines, two syndicated shopping columns, and via radio. With J. Walter Thompson, the company planned 28 radio spots during Child Dental Health Week in 1959, letting the consumer know that baking soda had been recommended by generations of dentists. Church & Dwight switched to the Charles W. Hoyt Co. advertising agency in October of that year, but continued the theme of versatility, mainly in print ads which were deemed more appropriate for giving examples of how to use Arm & Hammer baking soda.

Updated Marketing

While Church & Dwight admitted that its bicarbonate of soda had no direct competitors—an executive was quoted as saying in the November 9, 1964, *Advertising Age* that he doubted "the government would be concerned about a product that has only increased in price from 5¢ to 7¢ in over 100 years"— the product was experiencing declining sales. However, a turnaround began with the 1961 arrival of Dwight Church Minton, the fifth generation to run the company, who was later named chairman of the board. With his Stanford University MBA, Minton wanted to diversify, while expanding the company's established consumer base and boosting sales to industrial sectors. He was not afraid to do things differently, and one of those things was marketing, which had previously been viewed as a general management task. In 1968 the first vice president of marketing, Edward B. Gellert, was appointed.

Gellert went after a younger market segment, aiming at 18-to-35-year-olds who might not be aware of the Arm & Hammer brand. He considered the relative smallness of Church & Dwight a distinct advantage, allowing rapid development of ideas into production. Rather than take the traditional approach and highlight the many uses of baking soda in a single ad, clever print ads were developed with ad agency Ross Roy of New York, aimed at specific uses. One showed an Arm & Hammer box, flattened to display all sides, with the copy, "Get a suggestion box for your family." A simple line-drawing of feet had the caption, "Oh, your aching feet. Treat 'em to a baking soda foot bath." In another, a close-up sketch of teeth featured the words, "Baking soda gives you the fairest smile of them all." Taking this strategy a step further, Gellert determined that separate uses of Arm & Hammer baking soda should be focussed on at different times of the year, since, as he pointed out in the September 2, 1968, *Advertising Age*, Arm & Hammer was "competing with just about everybody."

Robert A. Davies, who would later become president and chief operating officer, succeeded Gellert as vice president of marketing in 1969. At that point Church & Dwight began planning test television commercials, and by 1972, working with ad agency Kelly, Nason Inc., the company launched a highly successful campaign. After years of pushing the seemingly unending uses of baking soda, Church & Dwight zoomed in on one specific use—baking soda as a refrigerator deodorizer, with the suggestion that the box be replaced every three months—and sales shot up, while ad spending doubled to $2 million from the previous year's budget. As an August 15, 1974, *Forbes* story stated, "Thanks to Americans' compulsive fear of offensive smells and the fact that baking soda really does absorb them, about 70% of the nation's refrigerators now contain that familiar package." The article also maintained, however, that most corporate income came not from baking soda sales, but from a $12-million investment portfolio that, according to Dwight Minton, "the old gentlemen put aside to provide for the possibility of building a plant."

Minton's drive to try new products and enter new markets was underestimated, though. By 1974 Church & Dwight had pioneered a nonphosphate (nonpolluting) laundry detergent. In an *Advertising Age* story of September 20, 1982, Burton B. Stanier, group business manager of Church & Dwight at the time, said of the Arm & Hammer laundry detergent success, "We had a $25 million business almost overnight." Church & Dwight went from a $15.6 million company in 1969 to a $57.9 million firm in 1974.

Competition in Line Extensions

Church & Dwight ran into several legal tangles in the mid-1970s. The Sacramento County district attorney filed suit in August 1975, charging that television and newspaper advertising for the use of baking soda to balance the chlorine and pH balance in swimming pools was false and misleading. A Church & Dwight attorney offered to produce substantiation of the firm's claims, but the suit was dropped within two days of the company's meeting with the California district attorney.

A year later, Church & Dwight was on the offensive, suing Helene Curtis in Rochester, New York's district court. Both companies had new baking soda deodorants on the market. Church & Dwight claimed that the Helene Curtis product, Arm in Arm, infringed on its trademark and that the package was purposely given the same color scheme as Arm & Hammer products to confuse the consumer. The June 30, 1976, *Chemical Week* story reported that Helene Curtis charged Church & Dwight with advertising its Arm & Hammer brand name "in a manner intended to reinforce its attempted monopolization of the consumer market for baking soda and relevant consumer submarkets in that it has . . . succeeded in creating an identity in the public mind between baking soda and C&D," and asked that the Arm & Hammer trademark be nullified. Helene Curtis also charged that Allied Chemical, a soda ash supplier, conspired with Church & Dwight; Allied stated its sales to Church & Dwight comprised only eight percent of its annual revenue. The case was decided in Church & Dwight's favor. A 1979 settlement of $2 million was one of the largest amounts recorded for a trademark infringement in U.S. legal history.

Re-entering Dental Care

In the early 1980s Church & Dwight focussed again on baking soda's usefulness as a dentifrice, placing ads in *People* magazine,

stating that Arm & Hammer pure baking soda was proven to remove plaque. The outlook for Arm & Hammer's success was lukewarm since Colgate-Palmolive Company—with a 1982 advertising budget of nearly $30 million—failed with Peak, a baking soda toothpaste introduced several years earlier.

Undaunted, Church & Dwight followed up by introducing its own baking soda toothpaste in 1988 to compete for a share in the specialty toothpaste category which comprised approximately seven percent of the general toothpaste market. By 1990 Arm & Hammer's baking soda toothpaste commanded five percent of the $1 billion-plus general toothpaste market. Striving to double its share, the company introduced a gel toothpaste, backing the new product with a $7 million television budget and the aid of ad agency Partners & Shevack.

Arm & Hammer increased its toothpaste share to eight percent by the end of 1991, placing it at a respectable number five in the segment. Hoping to build on its success, Church & Dwight rolled out a new tartar control Dental Care, the first product of its kind on the market.

Environment

Church & Dwight had a history of commitment to environmental causes long before it was fashionable, although the company did not begin to promote this fact until the 1990s. An early example was the wildlife trading cards Church & Company enclosed in each box of soda, encouraging public education in conservation. In addition, Arm & Hammer baking soda has been packaged in boxes made from recycled paper since 1907. The product itself is an inorganic salt which occurs naturally in mineral deposits. Church & Dwight reinforces this in its packaging with the phrase "the standard of purity" underneath the trade name. In the lower left corner are the words "pure, safe & natural since 1846."

More recently, research in the early 1990s demonstrated the successful use of blends of sodium bicarbonate to reduce the lead content in drinking water, in addition to reducing acidity in lake water suffering the effects of acid rain, enabling the lake to retain recreational use quality. Scientific tests also determined that sodium bicarbonate blends serve as non-toxic paint removers and can reduce acid gas from smokestack emissions.

In 1990 Church & Dwight finally began to promote its Arm & Hammer brand as an environmentally safe product. In addition, the company planned to increase its corporate recognition through various programs coinciding with Earth Day 1991. Among a number of initiatives sponsored by Church & Dwight, National Public Radio received a grant to hire environmental reporters. The company also funded "Home Safe Home," a supermarket-based education program for shoppers using "environmental information centers" which were placed at the end of aisles to display Arm & Hammer brand and other environmentally safe products and pamphlets.

Outlook

Church & Dwight's goals for the 21st century are twofold. First, the company plans to license the Arm & Hammer trademark through co-branding with other well-known companies. Second, the company, in business for a century and a half, joined many other American firms in seeking growth in the global marketplace. In the early 1990s Arm & Hammer had full distribution only in the

U.S. and Canada, with limited outlets in Mexico. However, the company was arranging to launch baking soda overseas, with other strong brands, including Arm & Hammer toothpaste, to follow. "Moving into overseas markets," wrote Riccardo A. Davis in the August 17, 1992, *Advertising Age,* "will put Church & Dwight into heightened competition with major oral-care and household product marketers such as Proctor & Gamble Co., Unilever and Colgate-Palmolive Co." The Arm & Hammer brand, unlike many competing products, has a century and a half of strong business behind it; the challenge is for Church & Dwight to use that history to its advantage.

Further Reading:

"Arm & Hammer Mixes Its Own," *Adweek's Marketing Week,* July 4, 1988, p. 3.

"Arm & Hammer Soda Sales Zoom after Single-Use Ad," *Advertising Age,* September 18, 1972, p. 48.

"Baking Soda Ads Mislead, Cal. Suit Says," *Advertising Age,* August 18, 1975, p. 2.

Bird, Laura, "Arm & Hammer Stakes Its Name on the Environment," *Adweek's Marketing Week,* November 19, 1990, p. 4.

Byrne, Harlan S. "Church & Dwight Co. Scores Big with Brand-Name Pull," *Barron's,* December 10, 1990, p. 49.

"Church & Dwight Print Ads to Tell Multiple-Use Story," *Advertising Age,* December 14, 1959, p. 3.

"Church & Dwight Pushes Baking Soda as a Dentifrice," *Advertising Age,* February 16, 1959, p. 86.

Cullen, William J. P., *The Story of Church & Dwight Company,* New York: Church & Dwight, 1937.

Dagnoli, Judann, "Toothpaste Battle," *Advertising Age,* October 21, 1991, p. 3.

Davis, Riccardo D., "Arm & Hammer Seeks Growth Abroad," *Advertising Age,* August 17, 1992, p. 3 +.

Environmental Initiatives, New Jersey: Church & Dwight Co., Inc., 1992.

"Flexing Muscles over Trademarks," *Chemical Week,* June 30, 1976, p. 22.

Giges, Nancy, "Arm & Hammer Enters Dentifrice War," *Advertising Age,* June 14, 1982, p. 3.

"A Heritage of Commitment, New Jersey: Church & Dwight Co., Inc., 1992.

Honomichl, Jack J., "The Ongoing Saga of 'Mother Baking Soda,'" *Advertising Age,* September 20, 1982, p. M2 +.

Lazarus, George, "Arm & Hammer Ups Its Toothpaste Ante," *Adweek's Marketing Week,* September 24, 1990, p. 50.

"New Campaign by Church & Dwight Tells Versatility," *Advertising Age,* November 9, 1964, p. 6.

"Profitable Pairing," *Barron's,* September 6, 1982, p. 37.

Revett, John, "Church & Dwight Steps Up Ad Budget for New Round of Marketing Activity," *Advertising Age,* September 2, 1968, p. 30.

"A Smell-Less Story," *Forbes,* August 15, 1974, p. 29.

—Frances E. Norton

AUNT JEMIMA®

The beaming face of Aunt Jemima is one of the world's most powerful and enduring trademarks. This fictional Southern cook can claim many firsts: she was the first trademark to be given a human face, the first to be portrayed by a human actor, and she sold the first ready-mix food of any kind. Aunt Jemima's hold on the American consciousness has proved so strong that she is the subject of scholarly studies analyzing her roots in the stereotypical "mammy" image of the Old South and her evolution into the modern, gracious Southern hostess she symbolizes today. Skillfully managed and promoted, the Aunt Jemima brand remains the world's most popular pancake mix and represents approximately $300 million annually in sales of mixes, syrups, and frozen foods for her parent company, Quaker Oats.

The First Ready-Mix

Aunt Jemima was "born" in St. Joseph, Missouri, a city which boomed as a grain milling capital in the mid-nineteenth century. Then overproduction, along with the slowing of western migration, caused hard times for the flour mills; many were sold at a loss or shut down entirely. It was thus that the Pearl Milling Company came to be acquired in 1889 by Charles G. Underwood, a veteran of the milling business, and his friend Chris L. Rutt, an editorial writer for the *St. Joseph Gazette.* Their goal was to create a unique product that would use a great deal of flour, giving their company a competitive advantage over its rivals, who sold only plain flour.

In those days, pancakes were considered tricky to make with consistent quality. The two entrepreneurs set out to invent a self-rising flour mix that would allow even an inexperienced cook to make good pancakes every time it was used. Neither Underwood nor Rutt had any cooking expertise, so they were excellent candidates to test a formula intended to be foolproof. After several weeks of experimentation, they settled on a particular blend of wheat flour, corn flour, phosphate of lime, soda, and salt, to which milk was added just before cooking. For an objective judgement on their recipe they served up a batch of pancakes to Purd Wright, the town librarian and a man known for his candor. When Wright gave his approval, Underwood and Rutt mixed the first commercial batch of their invention, totalling about 210 pounds. It was sold in brown paper sacks adorned only with the bald description "self-rising pancake flour." The sacks sat on store shelves for many weeks, largely untouched. Consumers of the day had never heard of a convenience food product, and they found the concept baffling and suspicious.

Trademark Origins

Rutt realized that a good name and image were crucial to successful marketing, and he began searching for a symbol with enough appeal to sweep away consumer mistrust of his revolutionary product. Inspiration came when the vaudeville team of Baker and Farrell visited St. Joseph in the fall of 1889. The hit of their show was "Aunt Jemima," a cakewalk performed in blackface, with Baker wearing the red bandanna and apron associated with the black Southern mammy stereotype. The whole town was humming the tune, and Rutt realized that by appropriating the Aunt Jemima name and image, he could capitalize on both the immediate popularity of Baker and Farrell's act and on the more enduring tenets of the mammy myth, including the notions that mammy was a great cook and a warm, friendly household helper.

The sacks of generic "self-rising pancake flour" were replaced by "Aunt Jemima's Pancake Flour," in bags decorated with a grinning caricature of vaudevillian Baker in his mammy makeup and kerchief. Sales picked up a little, but the Pearl Milling Company's financial resources were already running dangerously low. Rutt and Underwood took a booth at the New Era Exposition in St. Joseph to familiarize the public with their product, but it was too late. The Pearl Milling Company folded soon after the Exposition.

Rutt returned to the *St. Joseph Gazette,* but Underwood persevered, forming the Aunt Jemima Manufacturing Company and enlisting his brother Bert to handle the financial end of his new venture. Bert Underwood registered the Aunt Jemima trademark in 1890, thereby accomplishing the only real success of the Aunt Jemima Manufacturing Company, which quickly collapsed. At this point, Charles Underwood decided that the security of a steady paycheck was preferable to the dreams and uncertainties of the entrepreneurial life. He sold his rights to the Aunt Jemima brand to the R.T. Davis Milling Company and took a regular job with that organization. The company's owner, R.T. Davis, used his 50 years of milling experience to improve the Aunt Jemima formula. He added rice flour and corn sugar to enhance the flavor and texture of the pancakes, and simplified preparation by using powdered milk in the mix so that only water needed to be added.

AT A GLANCE

Aunt Jemima brand pancake flour first marketed in 1889 by the Pearl Milling Company, owned by Chris L. Rutt and Charles G. Underwood, St. Joseph, MO; Aunt Jemima trademark registered in 1890 by the Aunt Jemima Manufacturing Company, founded by Charles and Bert Underwood; trademark rights sold to R.T. Davis Milling Company in the early 1890s; R.T. Davis Milling Company went bankrupt, 1900; reorganized in 1903 as the Aunt Jemima Mills Company; sold January 15, 1926, to the Quaker Oats Company.

Performance: *Market share*—20% (top share) of total breakfast syrup category; 12% (top share) of light breakfast syrup category; 21% (top share) of pancake mix category. *Sales*—$124 million in breakfast syrups; $59.8 million in pancake mixes.

Advertising: *Agency*—(mixes and syrups) J. Walter Thompson, Chicago, IL. *Major campaign*—Actresses portraying Aunt Jemima, a legendary cook from the Deep South.

Addresses: *Parent company*—The Quaker Oats Company, Quaker Tower, 321 North Clark St., Chicago, IL, 60610; phone: (312) 222-7111.

Jemima Comes to Life

Four years had passed since the mix had become available, but sales were still sluggish. The general public continued to believe that pancake-making was a complex art and that any food created for the sake of convenience must be second-rate. R.T. Davis showed his faith in his newly acquired Aunt Jemima mix by betting his whole business on one extravagant publicity stunt that cost $10,000 to stage—enough to drive his company into bankruptcy if the promotion failed to dramatically boost sales. He obtained space at the 1893 World's Columbian Exposition in Chicago, held to commemorate the four hundredth anniversary of the voyage of Christopher Columbus. There he constructed the world's largest flour barrel, measuring 24 feet long, 16 feet in diameter, and 12 feet across at the end. The interior was decorated in the style of a homey Southern parlor. Visitors to the Exposition would be able to come inside, relax, learn about the product, and sample Aunt Jemima's pancakes.

The key element in this plan was a living Aunt Jemima who would charm her guests, cook for them, and, Davis hoped, win their trust. Prior to the opening of the Exposition, Davis alerted his contacts in the food industry to be on the lookout for a black woman who could exemplify Southern hospitality, who had sufficient poise to demonstrate the pancake mix repeatedly in front of large crowds, and who had enough acting talent to play the role of the fictional Aunt Jemima. Davis was betting that if consumers believed that Aunt Jemima was a real person and that the mix was a long-guarded secret from a famous Southern kitchen, they would eagerly buy the convenience product.

A Chicago food wholesaler named Charles Jackson discovered the perfect Aunt Jemima. Her name was Nancy Green, and she was employed as a cook for one of the city's prominent citizens, Judge Walker. Born a slave in 1835 in Montgomery, Kentucky, Green was an outstanding cook whose specialty just happened to be pancakes. This attractive, outgoing woman accepted the job of bringing Aunt Jemima to life.

On May 1, 1893, President Grover S. Cleveland welcomed the first of over a million visitors to the World's Columbian Exposition. The giant flour barrel was publicized by lapel pins bearing the likeness of Aunt Jemima and the slogan, "I'se in town, honey!" Outside the barrel stood Nancy Green, dressed in the Aunt Jemima costume. She captivated the crowd with folk songs, stories of her fictional past as Aunt Jemima (many of them drawn from her own real-life experiences) and, of course, her delicious pancakes. Thanks in large measure to Green's winning personality and her skillful impersonation of a wise old cook from the Deep South, the R.T. Davis flour barrel became the sensation of the Exhibition. Crowds followed Green whenever she left her post, clamoring for her autograph and cooking tips. Special details of police were assigned to the display to keep the throngs moving through. By the end of the Exhibition, Green had flipped over one million pancakes; she was honored with a special medal proclaiming her the Pancake Queen.

The exhibit, and later promotional campaigns created by Davis, are considered classics of the marketing industry. Well aware of the value of Nancy Green's charisma, Davis signed her to a lifetime contract as the living Aunt Jemima. He published a souvenir booklet written by Purd Wright—the one-time St. Joseph librarian and taste tester who had become his advertising manager—entitled *The Life of Aunt Jemima, the Most Famous Colored Woman in the World*. Salesmen crisscrossed the country with it, arranging personal appearances at stores, fairs, and charity events for Aunt Jemima. The public began to see Aunt Jemima as a celebrity and her arrival in any town was anticipated for weeks. Through her masterful cooking demonstrations and charming ways, Green made countless friends for the Aunt Jemima brand and legitimized the idea of cooking shortcuts, paving the way for a whole new era of convenience in the food industry.

Various premiums extended the appeal of Aunt Jemima. When the original paper sacks were replaced by cardboard cartons, Aunt Jemima paper dolls were printed on the new boxes. The dolls were so popular that they led to another offer destined to become one of the most successful in merchandising history. For one box top and twenty-five cents, pancake eaters could own an Aunt Jemima rag doll. Demand for these was so great that a whole family was created, including Uncle Mose and twins Diana and Wade. In exchange for four cents in stamps, consumers also received a copy of a book entitled *The Life History of Aunt Jemima and Her Pickaninny Dolls*.

Company Reorganization

The R.T. Davis Company went into bankruptcy after its founder's death in 1900. Robert Clark, the former general manager, reorganized it in 1903 as the Aunt Jemima Mills Company. Under Clark's direction, the brand broke all of its own sales records. The advertising of that era emphasized the mystique of Southern hospitality. "Years ago, Aunt Jemima refused to tell anyone how she mixed her batter. In those days, only her old master and his guests could enjoy her pancakes," stated one advertisement, quoted in the book *Getting It Right the Second Time*. By 1910, the name Aunt Jemima was known in every state. In fact, it had become so popular that several other companies had tried to steal sales by copying the trademark. The Aunt Jemima Mills brought suits against these imitators that were consistently upheld in court.

With World War I came disaster. Wheat flour was rationed and the company's wartime blend proved unacceptable to the public; sales plunged. When the original recipe was restored, an advertising campaign was launched to renew the public's fascination with the legend and lore of Aunt Jemima. James Webb Young of the J. Walter Thompson advertising agency—still the lead agency for the Aunt Jemima account—created a series of advertisements depicting dramatic highlights of the life of Aunt Jemima. Beginning in the fall of 1919, readers of national magazines learned of the night Aunt Jemima served pancakes to the stunned survivors of a riverboat fire; how she saved her master, Colonel Higbee, from capture by distracting the Union soldiers with her pancakes; and how after the war, Yankee businessmen sought her out and persuaded her to come North to make her magical pancake batter available to the entire world. Each advertisement was illustrated

Aunt Jemima's portrait, as it appeared in earlier days.

with a four-color illustration by N.C. Wyeth. Nancy Green, who had remained under contract as Aunt Jemima, served as the model for Wyeth's paintings; her likeness replaced the mammy caricature on the product's packaging in 1917.

Sale to Quaker Oats

Still more troubles arose in 1920. A commodity market collapse caused the Aunt Jemima Mills Company, and many others, to suffer tremendous losses. Clark tried to rescue his business by attracting new investors, but the burden of debt was overwhelming. Even the revival of the Aunt Jemima rag doll premium could not bring in enough sales to offset the company's losses. The shareholders of the Aunt Jemima Mills retained Clark as president, but gave all real control to a three-man committee led by George E. Porter, the new chairman of the board. On January 15, 1926, the committee authorized the sale of the Aunt Jemima Mills to the Quaker Oats Company for a sum of 4.2 million dollars.

Quaker's marketing department quickly expanded Aunt Jemima's distribution. Previously available primarily in metropolitan areas, the pancake flour mix was now sold in retail stores everywhere. Before long the annual volume of the business was higher than it had been during the peak years for Aunt Jemima Mills, and for a decade after the acquisition by Quaker, the Aunt

Jemima brand experienced strong, steady growth. The new management continued to employ Nancy Green as goodwill ambassador for Aunt Jemima until her death in 1923. For a decade after her death, there was no living Aunt Jemima, but when the Great Depression set in, Quaker decided to combat the morbid economic climate by hiring another actress to recreate Green's role. Hundreds auditioned for the part. The final choice was Anna Robinson, a massive woman with a sweet face. Like Nancy Green, she made her debut at a spectacular trade show, the Chicago Century of Progress Exhibition of 1933.

From the 1933 exhibition and on into the age of television, Anna Robinson captivated America with her version of Aunt Jemima. Like Green, she appeared at fairs and charity events, but she was also photographed in glamorous locations such as New York City's Stork Club, 21, and the Waldorf. There she served pancakes to the leading celebrities of the day. The advertisements featuring these photos were among the most widely read of the time. Anna Robinson's face became universally identified with Aunt Jemima, and the brand image using Nancy Green's face was replaced by one featuring Robinson's darker, heavier features. The new painting, by Haddon Sundblom, was used for many years. When Robinson died in 1951, the role of Aunt Jemima was filled by Edith Wilson. She portrayed Aunt Jemima on radio and television and in personal appearances until 1966, and her face replaced Robinson's as the trademark. Other women portrayed Aunt Jemima in various settings, the most famous being Aylene Lewis, hostess at the Aunt Jemima Kitchen built at Disneyland in 1955. That restaurant became so popular that within a decade of its opening, it was rebuilt to accommodate its huge patronage.

Civil Rights Bring Changes

Quaker continued to market Aunt Jemima novelties to keep the brand highly visible and appealing. In addition to countless lapel buttons, advertising trade cards, recipe cards, and advertising stamps, the Quaker Oats Company distributed some four million sets of Aunt Jemima and Uncle Mose salt and pepper shakers, 150,000 copies of an Aunt Jemima cookie jar, and one million plastic Aunt Jemima syrup pitchers. But as the civil rights movement took hold, the image of the jolly, compliant black servant became increasingly anachronistic. Objections began to be voiced that Aunt Jemima novelty items and the brand image itself perpetuated virulent stereotypes of blacks. Accordingly, premium items were discontinued and the company ceased to sponsor a living Aunt Jemima.

In 1968, Quaker Oats responded to threats of a boycott by redesigning the Aunt Jemima trademark portrait. Edith Wilson's face was replaced by a composite, and in the process, Aunt Jemima shed more than 100 pounds, traded in her bandanna for a streamlined headband, and became about forty years younger. She was given another makeover in honor of her one hundredth birthday. In April 1989 the new Aunt Jemima was revealed. Her headrag was completely gone, replaced by a fluffy, gray-streaked hairstyle. Pearl earrings and a lace collar gave her a new elegance. All that remained of the stereotypical Aunt Jemima was her sparkling smile.

Performance Appraisal

By the summer of 1989 the new face was on the forty-plus products in the Aunt Jemima line, which is one of the strongest brand names in the Quaker Oats Company. The name competes in three categories: pancake mixes, frozen foods and breakfast syrups. According to Quaker's annual report, the ongoing strategy for the entire product line is to maintain market shares, increase profitability for existing lines, and to seek out new marketing opportunities by creating products that address current consumer needs. A good illustration of this strategy can be seen in the company's syrup line. In addition to regular Aunt Jemima syrup, Aunt Jemima Lite and ButterLite syrups were created to appeal to consumers searching for a lighter, lower-calorie food. These brands have continued to grow since their introduction. In 1991, Aunt Jemima ButterRich was offered to tempt the more indulgent consumer. The total market share of Aunt Jemima syrups in fiscal year 1992 represented 20 percent of the $620 million breakfast syrup category, in which Aunt Jemima is a perennial leader. The pancake mix market is considered mature, but Aunt Jemima continues to dominate sales in that category, increasing mix volume, operating income, and market share in fiscal 1991.

The Aunt Jemima frozen breakfast line includes waffles, french toast, pancakes, batter, and Aunt Jemima Homestyle Breakfast Entrees. In 1991, Quaker Oats created a separate division to develop and market these and other frozen products. Aunt Jemima frozen product sales grew that year by 22 percent and volume increased by eight percent, but volume and market share both dropped in 1992, due to intense pressure in the frozen breakfast category—the fastest-growing division of the frozen foods market. The high-tech food processing and marketing techniques of the modern Quaker Oats Company are a far cry from the old paper sacks of "self-rising pancake flour," but even today, Aunt Jemima's good-humored face still represents delicious treats served with style.

Further Reading:

Campbell, Hannah, *Why Did They Name It . . . ?*, New York: Fleet Publishing, 1954, pp. 40-42.

Erickson, Julie Liesse, "Aunt Jemima Makeover," *Advertising Age,* May 1, 1989, p. 8.

——, "Quaker Oats is Shedding New Light on Aunt Jemima," *Wall Street Journal,* April 28, 1989, p. A4.

——, "Aunt Jemima Trademark to Get 1990s Makeover," *Jet,* May 15, 1989.

Gershman, Michael, *Getting It Right the Second Time,* Reading, MA: Addison-Wesley, 1990, pp. 202-206.

Harrison, John Thorton, *The History of the Quaker Oats Company,* Chicago: The University of Chicago Press, 1933, p. 242.

Kern-Foxworth, Marilyn, "Plantation Kitchen to American Icon: Aunt Jemima," *Public Relations Review,* Fall 1990, pp. 55-67.

McCauley, Lucy A., "The Face of Advertising," *Harvard Business Review,* November-December 1989, pp. 155-159.

Marquette, Arthur F., *Brands, Trademarks, and Good Will: The Story of the Quaker Oats Company,* New York: McGraw-Hill, 1957, pp. 137-158.

Morgan, Hal, *Symbols of America,* New York: Penguin, 1986.

The Quaker Chronicle, Chicago: The Quaker Oats Company, 1991.

The Quaker Oats Company Annual Report, Chicago: The Quaker Oats Company, 1991, 1992.

—Joan Goldsworthy

BACARDI®

Bacardi rum, a product of Bacardi & Company Limited, is the world's most popular brand of rum. Positioned successfully after years of advertising and careful quality control, Bacardi is produced in several countries and sold worldwide. Because of its origins in Cuba and its association with the tropical casino resort lifestyle, Bacardi has a reputation as the premium party mixer. Straight or mixed, Bacardi Rum has a distinctive flavor and is often asked for by name.

Brand Origins

The original Bacardi Rum was invented by Don Facundo Bacardi y Maso, who was born in Sitges, Spain, in 1816. After immigrating with his family to a Catalan colony in Cuba at the age of 14, Bacardi prospered as a wine importer and merchant. At age 27, he married the daughter of a French Bonapartist fighter and raised four children.

A leader in his community of Santiago de Cuba and still a wine trader, Bacardi tried numerous times to produce a lighter, mellower rum than the common harsh varieties favored by buccaneers and Spanish adventurers. Made from molasses, a by-product of sugarcane processing, rum is produced by fermenting a pinpoint of yeast in molasses and continually transferring the culture to larger vats as it grows. At the time, Cuba was one of the largest sugar-producing areas in the world; sugar had been introduced by Christopher Columbus on his second voyage to the New World in 1494. With tons of cheap molasses at his disposal, Bacardi labored many years trying to develop a smoother, more refined rum.

Having perfected the art of rum making, Bacardi produced the liquor only in small quantities for his own personal consumption. But after serving the drink to house guests, he was asked to produce it commercially. Bacardi purchased for $3,500 a small tin-roof distillery in Santiago that was equipped with an arcane cast-iron pot still, fermenting tanks, and aging barrels and was populated by a hoard of fruit bats. On February 4, 1862, Bacardi went into business.

Assisted by his three sons, Bacardi kept his production process a family secret. His wife, Doña Amilia, suggested that the new enterprise should have a trademark emblem. After much thought, she recommended a logo containing a representation of the distillery's bats. The bat insignia remains on bottles of Bacardi to this day.

The Bacardi distillery had been operating for several years when the family encountered difficulties with Spanish colonial authorities for its support of the Cuban independence movement. For his activities, Emilio Bacardi, the eldest son, who handled the company's business operation, was later exiled to a Mediterranean island off the coast of Spanish Morocco for four years. Upon his return to Cuba, however, he was gratified to learn that the family rum had been awarded a gold medal of recognition at the Philadelphia International exposition of 1876.

A few years later, Don Facundo retired from the operation, leaving his sons and his son-in-law, Enrique Schueg y Chassin, in charge of the enterprise. Schueg brought additional family capital to the operation, allowing it to expand production and win additional awards in Barcelona in 1888, Paris in 1889, and Chicago in 1893.

The Bacardi Rum operation suffered again during the late 1890s with the second exile of Emilio Bacardi; this time he was accompanied by Enrique Schueg. A mysterious explosion aboard the U.S. battleship *Maine* touched off the Spanish-American War, which ended in Cuban independence. Emilio returned to Cuba and was elected mayor of Santiago; in 1906 he was elected to the Cuban Senate. Despite these disruptions, the quality of the rum produced by Bacardi remained high and production volume increased. The family continued to expand the operation by purchasing additional tracts of sugarcane cropland.

International Growth

In 1910, after building out the operation as much as possible in Cuba, Emilio Bacardi returned to Spain. In Barcelona, the company established its first overseas bottling facility, from which it could more easily distribute its products throughout Europe. The Spanish operation demonstrated that Bacardi Rum could be distilled and bottled anywhere in the world.

In 1931 Bacardi established a factory in Mexico. Nearly destroyed by a worldwide economic depression, however, the facility was kept in operation only by the personal intervention of José M. Bosch, a son-in-law of Enrique Schueg. Bosch, confident that conditions would improve, bolstered sales efforts in Mexico and succeeded in making the small operation profitable.

AT A GLANCE

Bacardi brand of rum founded in 1862 in Cuba by Don Facundo Bacardi y Maso, president of Compañia Ron Bacardi, S.A.; incorporated as Bacardi Corporation, 1919; company reconstituted as Bacardi & Company Limited, 1960. Bacardi Rum formally introduced to export markets, 1910. Bacardi & Company Limited remains in private hands, owned and operated by descendants of Don Facundo Bacardi.

Performance: *Market share*—(Bacardi Rum) 4.8% (top share) of liquor category; (Bacardi Breezers) 2.5% of liquor category. *Sales*—$490 million.

Major competitor: Myers' Rum; also, Mount Gay Rum.

Advertising: *Agency*—Lintas, New York, NY, 1992—. *Major campaign*—The slogan "Bacardi Rum, the mixable one" in numerous applications to establish the use of Bacardi in mixed drinks.

Addresses: *Parent company*—Bacardi & Company Limited, P.O. Box N-4880, Nassau, Bahamas; phone: (809) 362-1271. (U.S. distributor) Bacardi Imports, Inc., 2100 Biscayne Blvd., Miami, FL 33137; phone: (305) 573-8511.

Whatever opportunities there may have been for Bacardi Rum in the United States, though, had been destroyed in 1920 with the enactment of Prohibition. Finally, on December 5, 1933, the U.S. Congress repealed the nationwide ban on alcohol. José Bosch was subsequently dispatched to New York City to arrange for the import and distribution of Bacardi Rum in the United States. More than 80,000 cases of the company's rum were sold in 1934 alone.

The import duty on Bacardi Rum was nearly one dollar per bottle. Bosch, however, reasoned that if the rum were manufactured in the United States, it would be exempt from the import duty. Rather than choosing a location in Florida, whose swampy Everglades could not support sugar production, Bosch turned his attention to Puerto Rico, an American possession since the Spanish-American War. Because Puerto Rico was technically American soil, rum produced there could be sent to Miami and New York City without restriction. In 1935 Bosch established a Bacardi facility in Old San Juan until a larger facility across the bay in Cataño could be completed. To handle the increasing volumes of Puerto Rican and Cuban Bacardi Rum imported into the United States, the company set up a distribution arm, Bacardi Imports, Inc., in New York City on March 11, 1944.

The Cuban Revolution in 1959 led to the confiscation of major enterprises by the Cuban government under the country's leader, Fidel Castro. The Bacardi operation, valued at $76 million in 1960, was essentially lost. After the government tried unsuccessfully to seize the valuable Bacardi trademark, the company's shareholders reconstituted the company—previously known as Compañia Ron Bacardi, S.A., then Bacardi Corporation—as Bacardi & Company Limited, with headquarters in the Bahamas. A second operation, Bacardi International Limited, was subsequently established in Bermuda to handle worldwide sales, distribution, marketing, and customer services.

Bacardi Rum eventually came to be manufactured in the Bahamas, Brazil, Martinique, Mexico, Panama, Puerto Rico, Trinidad, Canada, and Spain. The company also maintains bottling facilities in Australia, New Zealand, Austria, France, Germany, Switzerland, the United Kingdom, and the United States. In addition, the company's rum is sold in more than 175 countries throughout the world.

Early Marketing Strategy

Because Bacardi was a relatively small Cuban concern in its early days, little attention was initially given to the notion of promoting the rum in America. Unfamiliar with advertising, Bacardi built its reputation in the United States not through a genuine marketing strategy, but by word of mouth. Americans visiting Cuba invariably discovered the rum and returned to United States with stories about a marvelous new libation. Even Pan American Airways, which began flights to Cuba in the 1920s, proclaimed in an early advertisement, "Fly Pan Am to Cuba and you can be bathing in Bacardi in hours."

An American engineer mining copper in Cuba's Sierra Maestra mountains began experimenting with various mixers for Bacardi, and tried combining the rum with lime juice and crushed ice. Favoring the concoction, he shared his invention with others. As the new icy cocktail swept Cuba, it was given the name Daiquiri, for the Cuban town in which it was said to have originated. Later, an American army lieutenant, intent on jazzing up his simple glass of Coca-Cola, splashed a healthy shot of Bacardi into the bubbly drink, giving birth to the Cuba Libre. This drink was later popularized by the U.S. pop music group the Andrews Sisters with their recording of the song "Rum & Coca-Cola."

Advertising

The earliest advertisements for Bacardi, beginning in 1933, played heavily upon the Cuban origins of Bacardi, incorporating about as much Spanish as the average American knew. Ads featured an actor asking, "Have you tried, señor, old-fashioned á la Cuba?," and another responding, "Si, si, señor, this is the way to mix that Bacardi Cocktail." The advertising strategy during the period from 1933 to 1943 centered on establishing brand superiority, its tropical appeal, and the Bacardi Cocktail.

Beginning in 1944, Bacardi began to emphasize extended usage of its rum in other drinks and in new circumstances. This campaign became especially important in 1947, when, after a long absence, whiskey once again became available in the United States. Even with this effort, however, rum sales collapsed, falling 47 percent in one year.

During the 1950s, Bacardi continued to position its rum as the highest-quality product. Added to this, however, was a new message aimed at quieting consumer concerns over the caloric content of alcohol. In one 1953 ad, a Bacardi Daiquiri was shown to have less calories than a glass of milk. The company also began segmentation campaigns, featuring the first ads targeted at blacks and hispanics. In 1956 the company made history by running the first liquor ad featuring a woman; she encouraged homemakers to try serving a Daiquiri with dinner.

In the 1960s, again fearing displacement by cheaper rums as mixers, Bacardi noted, "The original Daiquiri was made with Bacardi (the best still are!)." To forestall the growing popularity of other "white goods," such as vodka, the company's advertising emphasized the mixability and versatility of Bacardi in core drinks, including highballs. As a result of the campaign, which featured the tagline "Enjoyable always and all ways," Bacardi registered 10 percent annual growth during the decade and broke into the top ten in sales for all distilled spirits brands.

Ads during the 1970s mainstreamed the Bacardi brand as an essential party mixer. Bacardi was featured in joint promotions with Schweppes' tonic water, 7UP, Pepsi, Canada Dry Ginger Ale, Perrier, Dr. Pepper and, of course, Coca-Cola. The strategy during this period was to make Bacardi the biggest-selling distilled spirit in the United States. Further emphasizing usage and demographic targeting, Bacardi achieved its goal, surpassing Smirnoff vodka. Sales increased from 2.6 million cases in 1970 to 7.2 million cases in 1979.

In vogue with socially responsible advertising, Bacardi also began running spots that invited people to drink responsibly. One ad showed a series of soda bottle caps, fruit slices, a Bacardi cap, and a steering wheel, and read, "Bacardi rum mixes with everything. Except driving." The company continued to build on its proven themes into the 1980s, revived the diet drink mixer campaign, and began to push its brand, principally the premium brand, Añejo.

Brand Development

Competitors tried on several occasions to dilute the value of the Bacardi name and rob some of the value of the brand. Some of these competitors implored consumers to use their rum when making a "Bacardi Cocktail," a term which had begun to mean a drink made with any kind of rum. Eager to protect the unique value of the Bacardi brand, the company challenged others for the right to use the name. In a 1936 New York State Supreme Court case, it was decided that only Bacardi Rum may be used to make a Bacardi Cocktail.

In a separate case in 1940, parties opposed to Bacardi sued to prevent the company from using its name on the rum it produced in Puerto Rico, claiming that it was fundamentally different from the rum produced in Cuba. Finding no merit in the complaint, U.S. Chief Justice Evans Hughes wrote, "Bacardi has always been made according to definite secret processes . . . and enjoys an excellent reputation."

Later efforts to promote more versatile applications of Bacardi Rum led the company to several discoveries. Bacardi recognized that many consumers loved fruity drinks but didn't like to go to all the trouble of mixing them. The company floated several brand extensions in the 1980s, including Bacardi Tropical Fruit Mixers and Bacardi Breezers—a direct challenge to successful wine cooler brands. In addition, in an attempt to build premium brands, Bacardi began special promotions of its premium Añejo brand, Premium Black (Bacardi's first dark rum), and Amber Label (an intermediate dark rum).

Performance Appraisal

Bacardi, the world's most popular rum, has achieved its position not through rapid and therefore potentially unstable growth, but through many decades of careful, planned expansion and, above all, unwavering attention to product quality. The Bacardi brand name carries an outstanding reputation as a proven 100-year-old premium product. An intensive scientific approach to marketing, begun in the 1960s, has allowed the company to further refine the value of its trademark.

The company's brand extensions are well positioned to meet competition across the spirits market. Bacardi Light (Silver Label) is an alternative to gin and vodka, and Bacardi Dark (Amber Label) and Bacardi Premium Black are targeted at whiskey and bourbon drinkers. Añejo competes in the upscale brown spirits category, while Gold Reserve is aimed at brandy and cognac drinkers.

In addition, further enhancing Bacardi & Company Limited's competitiveness, the relative price of Bacardi Rum has fallen over the years as a result of higher production efficiencies. Adjusted for inflation, a bottle that cost $5 in 1978 should be priced closer to $15 in the early 1990s. Sold at about eight dollars, however, the brand is affordable to a large segment of consumers.

Future Growth

Entering the 1990s, the Bacardi & Company Limited promised to build upon the successful advertising strategies of its past, emphasizing the value of Bacardi Rum relative to its competition. Perhaps the greatest threat to Bacardi comes from within. Structurally divided into a loose confederation of five companies, Bacardi is controlled by more than 250 family shareholders who have recently scuffled for control of the Bacardi empire. These turf battles, however, have yet to seriously endanger the Bacardi operation and the production of one of the world's most popular liquors, Bacardi Rum.

Further Reading:

Bacardi company history, Bacardi & Company Limited.

"Bacardi," *World's Greatest Brands,* Wiley, 1992.

DeGeorge, Gail, "Yo, Ho, Ho, and a Battle for Bacardi," Business Week, April 16, 1990.

"Divide and Conquer," *Market Watch,* July-August 1980.

Lazarus, George, "A Rum for the Money," *Marketing Week,* March 9, 1987.

Levin, Gary, "Bacardi Stirs up Megabrand Strategy," *Advertising Age,* June 3, 1992.

"Our History in Advertising," Bacardi & Company Limited.

Youman, Nancy, "Bacardi Mixers get Sales Punch from Coke Foods," *Marketing Week,* June 1, 1987.

—John Simley

BAILEYS IRISH CREAM®

Baileys Original Irish Cream, a distinctive blend of Irish whiskey and cream with hints of chocolate and vanilla, created the world cream liqueur market when it was introduced in 1974. In 1979, after establishing itself in Europe and Australia, Baileys began trade in the United States, which became its largest market. By 1983, *Harper's Bazaar* hailed Baileys as "the largest-selling liqueur—cream or otherwise—in the world." Jean DuBois of Paddington Corp., Baileys' U.S. distributor, told *Advertising Age* that Baileys' success can be attributed to its ability to make "alcohol taste good." Despite the introduction of over three dozen competitors into the United States since 1979, Paddington has maintained Baileys' market share in part by inundating the media with the largest advertising budget of any competitor. Baileys continued to hold the leading international liqueur brand market share in 1992.

Irish Origins

The exact origins of Baileys Original Irish Cream are not clear, but all the stories agree on Baileys' Irishness. Anna Sobczynski, writing in *Advertising Age,* attributed the origins of Baileys in 1974 to David Dand, at that time the managing director of R&A Bailey & Co., a Dublin distillery. Dand wanted to create a "truly Irish" product, she noted, and spent four years trying to combine Irish whiskey with cream without curdling the cream. However, Keith McCarthy-Morrogh, assistant managing director of Gilbeys of Ireland, told *Time* that their chemists made Baileys to sell as a low-alcohol, Irish-ingredient beverage for "people who don't like to get sloshed." R&A Bailey & Co. credits its own extensive international market research and a recognition of the need to change from a purely domestic company to an international exporter of Irish products as the inspiration for Baileys' recipe. No matter who concocted the first batch, the secret of Baileys' creamy consistency is the ultrapasteurization and homogenization of cream, processes that make the fat globules very small, allowing the alcohol to surround and preserve the cream for up to eighteen months without need for refrigeration or preservatives.

By using Irish workers, Irish whiskey, and Irish cream, Baileys contributes significantly to Ireland's economy. Basing 90 percent of its production in Ireland, in 1992 R&A Bailey employed 400 people to work on the manufacture, marketing, and sales of Baileys. The Midleton and Carbery Distilleries in Cork make Baileys' whiskey and Irish spirits. In 1992 Baileys consumed 33

percent of Ireland's total liquid milk production, demanding 40 million gallons of milk to be made into double cream. R&A Bailey & Co. reported in 1992 that their product accounted for 80 percent of Ireland's cream liqueur exports, almost half of all Irish beverage exports, and one percent of Ireland's total exports.

A Taste of Success

Baileys' early success in the U.S. market surprised market analysts, for the product was introduced at the same time that "cows"—frothy alcoholic drinks containing imitation cream— were going out of fashion. Upon their introduction, Baileys and other cream liqueurs were labelled as an expensive variation of the "cows." The trend forecasters, however, completely misread the public's appetite for the product: Baileys' cases were depleted within months. Paddington vice-president of marketing Robert Suhr told *Advertising Age* that Baileys' creamy, delicious taste convinces 50 percent of those who sample it to take a bottle home. Baileys' taste—which *Newsweek* likened to a "high-octane milkshake" and "chocolate milk with a little nip"—is still considered the reason for the brand's success.

A number of studies have attempted to account for the quick and continued success of cream liqueurs. Cream liqueur sales were low in bars, but the market's high profits were explained by reports in *Advertising Age*, which found that 80 percent of cream liqueur consumption occurs in the home, and in *Newsweek*, which discovered that consumption of the product is rapid; a bottle of Baileys is often empty 48 hours after it is opened. Sobczynski noted that Baileys appeals to both men and women in all demographic sectors, and attracts moderate drinkers with its low (17 percent) alcohol content, less than half the alcohol of other spirits. Creams have truly integrated themselves into the cordial market. Generally served alone, in coffee, or over ice cream, cream liqueurs have also found a prominent place in specialty drinks in restaurants and bars. One entrepreneur even used Baileys Irish Cream to produce her own gourmet ice cream.

Baileys Attracts Imitators

After Baileys' successful 1979 U.S. introduction, many competitors hurried to take part in the booming new market for cream liqueurs. Many distillers skipped elaborate product rollouts to quickly take in the promising profits. Baileys' first competitor, a Bacardi product named O'Darby Irish Cream Liqueur, advertised

AT A GLANCE

Baileys Original Irish Cream created in 1974 by R&A Bailey & Co., Dublin, Ireland; marketed in the United States after 1979; brand extensions include Baileys Original Irish Light Cream in the U.S. market and Baileys Gold in the Japanese market.

Performance: *Market share*—84% (top share) of world cream liqueur market in 1992.

Major competitor: O'Darby Irish Cream Liqueur; also Emmets Ireland's Cream Liqueur, O'Shortal's Pub Cream, St. Brendan's Irish Cream Liqueur, and Carolans Finest Irish Cream Liqueur.

Advertising: *Agency*—Lowe & Partners, New York City, 1993—. *Major campaign*—"Baileys raises the art of the everyday" (1992; Berenter, Greenhouse, and Webster agency).

Addresses: *Parent company*—R&A Bailey & Co., Western Estate, Dublin, Ireland 12; phone: (01) 569222; fax: 508977. *Ultimate parent company*—International Distillers and Vintners Group (IDV). *Ultimate ultimate parent company*—Grand Metropolitan PLC., 20 St. James's Square, London SW1Y 4RR; phone: (071) 321 6000.

itself in 1980 as "The cream of the Irish cream liqueurs." Later that same year, Renfield Importers introduced Carolans Finest Irish Cream Liqueur, which claimed to be the "richest, freshest, creamiest, Irishest taste in all the world." Emmets Ireland's Cream Liqueur, sold by "21" Brands, was not advertised but was sold at half of Baileys' price in an attempt to appropriate a chunk of the cream liqueur market. The producer of St. Brendan's Irish Cream Liqueur took the opposite track, spending millions of dollars in advertising to find profits in a price niche above Baileys. St. Brendan's rollout theme in 1984 was "The price is high, but the taste is heaven." Acknowledging that Baileys had the "lion's share" of the cream liqueur market, Thomas Kaminsky, president and chief executive officer of Saint Brendan's Irish Imports, emphasized to *Advertising Age* that their product is made with real Irish whiskey.

"There are very nice profits to be made" in the cream liqueur market, George J. Bull, chief executive of International Distillers & Vintners Ltd., told *Business Week,* "but it's the major players who will emerge with the strong brands." Baileys certainly meets that criteria for success, for it is part of one of the world's largest food and beverage companies, Grand Metropolitan PLC. England-based Grand Metropolitan owns Burger King, Pillsbury, and Häagen-Dazs ice cream, as well as many other food producers around the world. Its alcohol unit, International Distillers and Vintners (IDV), controls some of the top selling liquors in the world, including Baileys and Absolut Vodka. IDV oversees all of Baileys operations as owner of R&A Baileys in Ireland and Baileys' U.S. distributor, the Paddington Corp. Clearly, Baileys has the corporate backing to absorb the substantial luxury taxes on its product, and to support the large advertising budget required for success in a highly competitive market. Indeed, Paul Bensinger, executive vice-president of Park, Bensinger & Co., said in *Advertising Age*: "Several million dollars a year spent on advertising. That's what's going to give cream liqueurs staying power."

Baileys' 60 percent market share in 1981 was built by an advertising budget that topped nine million dollars, according to *Newsweek.* Since no competitor came close to Baileys' advertising

budget, no competitor claimed much more than a fraction of Baileys' sales. Smaller companies gave up trying to directly compete with Baileys. Brian O'Byrne of Irish Distillers International told *Newsweek* that "we tried to go head to head, but it was a mistake. We'll never be a Baileys." Gary Levi, vice-president and group brand manager at Glenmore Distillers, marketer of a Baileys' competitor, Dowland's Greensleeves, told Sobczynski that "Everybody's No. 2. There is no clear cut No. 2." By 1989, "Baileys [was] the leader by about 10 to 1," a salesman at Young's Market Co., a distributor of wines and spirits, related to the Sacramento *Business Journal.*

From its introduction, Baileys' advertising budget remained out of proportion to the number of cases sold. Paddington's DuBois explained in *Advertising Age* why the budget was so high: "I want to reach the consumer with Baileys first. If he tries another product and decides 'I don't like it,' it's harder for me to persuade him to try mine." R&A Bailey & Co. noted that Baileys' aggressive advertising takes advantage of every outlet available to support its image. In 1992 Baileys spent $60 million promoting its product, concentrating $30 million in Europe.

Penetrating a Global Market

Baileys' popularity outpaced its production capability for ten years after the product's introduction to the United States. Forecasts for Baileys' sales were a modest 15,000 cases in November 1974, when Baileys introduced Europe to cream liqueur. But the brand's popularity pushed sales up to 600,000 cases by 1978. Its popularity upon introduction to the U.S. market in 1979 still surpassed Baileys' initial sales estimates, and their stock was depleted within months, according to *Harper's Bazaar.* Because production continued to lag behind demand throughout the 1980s, Baileys was only sold in 750ml bottles. By the early 1990s, however, Baileys was available in a wider variety of sizes. Taking advantage of increased production capabilities, Baileys' sales reached an astonishing 3.8 million cases in 1992. *Impact,* an industry newsletter, ranked Baileys as the 15th largest selling spirit brand in the world in 1992, despite the fact that cream liqueurs account for only 3.8 percent of all liquor sales.

Baileys is marketed wherever it is not prohibited by law or religion. Sold in 167 markets throughout the world in 1992, Baileys' sales were most heavily concentrated in Europe, with 53 percent of its sales, and the Americas, which accounted for 39.5 percent of Baileys sales, according to the company's own statistics. R&A Bailey & Co. also noted that "this roughly corresponds to the spread of most spirit brands in world terms." The company reported their top markets to be the United States, Spain, Germany, the United Kingdom, Canada, France, Australia, and Italy.

Staying on Top

Baileys has maintained its lead in the competitive cream liqueur market through aggressive and sometimes unpredictable marketing and advertising. Conventional wisdom holds that consistent advertising maintains market share because it promotes brand recognition. However, Baileys has switched themes many times over the years, often in rapid succession. During its first year in the United States, Baileys' theme switched from "The impossible cream" to "Taste the magic" when U.S. distribution switched from Austin Nichols and Co. to the Paddington Corp. But Paddington continued to search for new ways to garner greater profits by setting itself apart from the liquor advertisements of its look-alikes.

In 1984, Paddington sought a growth promoting theme to replace "Taste the magic." According to *Advertising Age,* the 1984 advertising campaign was designed to achieve Paddington's five-year goal of doubling Baileys' sales. In January the first advertisements of the new "Baileys brings you closer" campaign showed a group of young married couples enjoying Baileys and each other above the caption, "What started out as an open house, ended up with a small circle of friends and a bottle of Baileys." Writing in *Advertising Age,* Carol Nathanson-Moog, a psychologist who specializes in advertising, described the setting of the Baileys' ad as a "very secure, very comfortable, nonthreatening psychological place to be." The "small circle of friends," however, is discriminating about who they've chosen as mates and about who they've chosen to share their Baileys.

By November 1984, the theme was changed to the less personal "It must be magic," with advertisements showing the Baileys product crossing the sea in an Irish airliner and, during the Christmas season, aboard Santa's sleigh. One such ad depicted an Aer Lingus plane with its trademark shamrock on the tail. The copy, positioned next to a mid-size photo of the box and bottle, read, "Not so long ago, it would cost you $1,000 for a bottle of Baileys. You would have had to fly all the way to Ireland to get it. Now, just a few years after it was imported, more Baileys is bought & served & shared & given than any other liqueur in the world. Baileys. It must be magic." These advertisements seemed to confirm the story suggested by Sobczynski that American consumers travelling abroad before Baileys was introduced into the United States developed a taste for it, brought it home with them, and inadvertently created Baileys' largest market. The beginning of the new year began yet another new theme, "To know it is to love it."

Along with the theme switches in the early 1980s, Baileys' vice-president of marketing, Chuck Nardizzi, who came from promotion-minded Pepsi-Cola, channeled some of Baileys' advertising dollars into promotional efforts to secure new sales, according to *Advertising Age.* Photo enlargement offers with a purchase, discounts on Irish crystal, and samplings of Baileys at the Shopping Center Network's travelling food and beverage festival invited people to try Baileys. Also, in the summer of 1985, a joint effort with Canada Dry promoted Baileys as more than a drink for chilly days. Promotional efforts did not boost Baileys' profits as expected, however, and were abandoned by 1989. Roger Slone, senior-vice-president of marketing at Paddington, commented in the *Wall Street Journal* that Baileys' promotion deals and discounts damaged Baileys' premium quality image: "We found we were cannibalizing longer-term business for the sake of short-term volume gains." Premium products cannot afford to train consumers to shop by comparing prices; premium products stay competitive by training consumers to identify with their brand's quality image.

Early in 1991, the Berenter, Greenhouse, and Webster advertising agency created advertisements showing Baileys being poured into a glass, allowing the consumer to imagine Baileys' creamy flavor, a technique that *Beverage World* called "sampling with the eyes." By 1992, Baileys' advertising emphasized its premium image, stating that Baileys "raised the art" of anything from "the holidays" to "the everyday." The autumn and December advertisements featured handwritten notes describing how Baileys

made an occasion more special or magical. One ad depicted a couple sitting in a pile of leaves drinking Baileys with the caption "Baileys raises the art of the everyday." The large handwritten note read: "Raking leaves wasn't exactly the way I wanted to spend Sunday afternoon. But after Linda brought out the Baileys and coffee, I warmed up to the idea immediately." In early 1993, Baileys moved its advertising to the Lowe & Partners agency in New York City.

Minor Marketing Problem

Baileys has, for the most part, been very carefully marketed. The state of Washington brought trouble for Baileys when it tried to save money by buying Baileys and other spirits from both U.S. and European distributors, a practice called parallel marketing, according to Don Duncan of the *Seattle Times.* This parallel market practice saved the state $2.6 million dollars between 1985 and 1988. All Planet Exports Ltd. imported Baileys' European formula Irish Cream, and sold twelve-bottle cases to Washington for prices up to 20 percent lower than the price Paddington charged for Baileys' U.S. formula Irish Cream. Both the U.S. and European brands were marketed at the same time. The only difference between the two formulas is that the U.S. formula is made with real vanilla while the European formula contains artificial vanilla. Customers made no complaints about the difference in ingredients but in 1988 the U.S. government decided to enforce a labeling law that required the European formula Baileys to be labeled as "imitation liqueur." News of the impending label prompted Paddington to consider a lawsuit because, according to Don Duncan, the institution of such a label on the European formula Baileys could conceivably have negative image repercussions on Paddington's U.S. formula. To avoid labelling, which Paddington saw as "trademark infringement," it swapped the state its U.S. formula for the unsold European formula in the state's warehouse. Washington stopped buying Baileys on the parallel market and relied solely on Paddington for Baileys purchases into the 1990s.

Growth and Innovation

R&A Bailey & Co. called Baileys a "very buoyant and growing brand" in 1992, and hoped to continue Baileys' growth through marketing strategies that touch the consumer, cooperation between international and local brand managers, and the infiltration of new markets. South America is one area Baileys wishes to expand into in the early 1990s. In addition, the introduction of new Baileys products is also expected to promote growth. Baileys Original Irish Light Cream, which is lower in fat and calories than the Original formula, targeted a new market in the United States. The Japanese market was introduced to Baileys Gold, a cream liqueur made with Irish malt whiskey. These new products, coupled with Baileys Original Irish Cream, are expected to secure Baileys leading position, to open new markets, and to foster growth well into the 1990s.

Further Reading:

"Baileys Brew: Leprechauns' Delight," *Time,* February 22, 1982, p. 48.

"Baileys Creams the Competition," *Newsweek,* March 21, 1983, p. 62.

Bertrand, Kate, "Consumers Join the Paddington Generation," *Advertising Age,* July 18, 1985, pp. 34-35.

Colford, Steven W., "Hispanic TV Stations Under Fire: Coalition Wants End to Liquor Spots," *Advertising Age,* October 12, 1987, p. 12.

Duncan, Don, "Why Some Liquor Is So Pricey," *Seattle Times,* February 19, 1991, p. 1.

Dunkin, Amy, "In Sales, Liquor Isn't Quicker," *Business Week,* June 22, 1987, pp. 120-121.

Fitch, Mike, "Tellus Industries Aims to Drown Its Woes with O'Shortal's Pub Cream," *Business Journal* (Sacramento), December 25, 1989, sec. 1, p. 4.

Fried, Eunice, "Cream Liqueurs," *Black Enterprise,* July, 1986, p. 81.

Garfield, Peter, "The New Allure of Liqueurs: Or Are They Cordials?," *Changing Times,* December, 1983, pp. 56-58.

Grand Metropolitan PLC Annual Report, London: Grand Metropolitan, 1992.

Greenberg, Madeline, and Emanuel Greenberg, "Creams at the Top," *Harper's Bazaar,* September, 1983, pp. 252, 257.

Jervey, Gay, "Baileys Ads Tout Success," *Advertising Age,* November 8, 1984, pp. 3, 39.

——, "St. Brendan's to Touch Off Irish Conflict," *Advertising Age,* August 2, 1984, p. 1, 37.

Jones, Deborah Lee, "Creams of the Crop Keep Sprouting," *Advertising Age,* August 15, 1983, pp. M22-24.

King, Thomas R., "Marketing," *Wall Street Journal,* May 24, 1989.

Levine, Josh, "Baileys Irish Cream Faces New Crop," *Advertising Age,* September 8, 1980, pp. 2, 80.

Marks, Debra, "Profit Increase Posted by Grand Metropolitan; Drinks Operation Leads Way as Company Shows Gain of 6.9% for the First Half," *Wall Street Journal,* May 15, 1992, sec. A, p. 11.

Mouflier, Sylvia, "Breaking the Glass Ceiling," *Manitoba Business,* August 1991, p. 34.

Nathanson-Moog, Carol, "Brand Personalities Undergo Psychoanalysis," *Advertising Age,* July 26, 1984, p. 18.

Rackham, Anne, "Begosh, Don't Let Erin Go Blah," *Los Angeles Business Journal,* March 16, 1992, sec. 1, p. 1.

Sobczynski, Anna, "Which Cream Will Rise to the Top?," *Advertising Age,* July 27, 1981, p. S36.

"Top 20 Spirit Brands Worldwide-1992," *Impact,* January, 1993.

—Sara and Tom Pendergast

BAKER'S®

Baker's, owned by Kraft General Foods, Inc., is the oldest brand of chocolate made in the United States. Introduced in 1780, the brand name has become virtually synonymous with squares of unsweetened and semi-sweet chocolate used to prepare brownies, cakes, and other desserts. Products bearing the Baker's brand name include German's Sweet Chocolate Bar, Semi-Sweet Chocolate Chips, and Angel Flake Coconut. The success of Baker's can be traced in part to its reputation for using high-quality ingredients and processing techniques.

Brand Origins

Cacao, the plant from which chocolate is derived, was first cultivated at least 3,000 years ago in Central America. The Aztec Indians, for example, used the plant's cocoa beans for currency, as well as for making chocolatl, a drink in which crushed beans were mixed with vanilla, spices, honey, or water and then made foamy with a wooden beater. They believed that chocolatl was an aphrodisiac and provided them with strength and wisdom.

The first Europeans to taste chocolate were Spanish explorers of the Western World. Christopher Columbus was offered chocolatl on a trip in 1502. Hernán Cortés, after his conquests of Central America, returned to Spain in 1528 with a supply of cocoa beans. By the 1600s the drink, now sweetened with sugar, began to spread across Europe, eventually becoming popular among the nobility and served in expensive, fashionable chocolate houses. Like the Aztecs, Europeans came to believe that chocolate was nourishing as well as an aphrodisiac. Heavily taxed in most countries, chocolate was a precious commodity.

Although chocolate was available in the British colonies as early as the 1600s, the first American chocolate business did not begin until 1755, when sea captains from Massachusetts sailed to the West Indies to trade cargos of fish for cocoa beans. The beans were then sold to apothecaries, who would grind the chocolate by mortar and pestle and sell it as a medicine. Many American colonists were convinced of chocolate's restorative powers. Some believed, for example, that a cup of chocolate after a large breakfast would aid in digestion.

With chocolate favored as a medicine, it is not surprising that the founder of the Baker's brand of chocolate, James Baker, was a physician. A resident of Dorchester, Massachusetts, he initially entered the chocolate business after meeting John Hannon, a recent Irish immigrant, in the fall of 1764. Hannon, a chocolate maker, complained that the colonies did not have a chocolate mill, and Baker decided it would be a good idea to provide capital for such a project. Soon they bought kettles and other equipment and rented a space in a local grist and sawmill along the Neponset River. The water-powered mill was located in the center of Dorchester.

Opened in 1765, the new business was the first to mill chocolate in the North America. It sold ground chocolate to be used in drinks or medicines, and cocoa beans brought in by customers were ground for a fee. In 1768 the operations were moved to another mill, also in Dorchester, that was owned by Baker's brother-in-law, Edward Preston. By the 1770s Hannon's company was advertising a money-back guarantee: "Hannon's Best Chocolate. . . . Warranted pure, and ground exceeding fine. . . . If the Chocolate does not prove good, the Money will be returned." Baker, however, was also experimenting with another chocolate business. In 1772 he rented part of a local paper mill, hired a relative of the mill's owner to help with the operations, and by July 2 had made his first sale of chocolate.

With his factory earning a decent profit, Hannon sailed off in 1779 for the West Indies, where he planned to buy cocoa beans. What happened on the voyage is not known, but Hannon, who likely died at sea, was never heard from again. By 1780 the mill came under the full control of Baker. That year, with the help of Preston, Baker began producing the first chocolate under the brand name Baker's.

Product Development

Sales of Baker's chocolate grew rapidly despite the establishment of other chocolate factories in the United States. Company records suggest that Baker's mill was exceptionally efficient at grinding chocolate. Baker, moreover, benefited from increasing demand for the product, a development that led former U.S. President Thomas Jefferson to forecast that the "superiority of chocolate, both for health and nourishment, will soon give it the same preference over tea and coffee in America which it has in Spain."

Despite its rapid growth, the company remained a family-run enterprise for more than 100 years. Baker's son Edmund entered the business in 1791, and in 1804, when the founder retired,

AT A GLANCE

Baker's brand of chocolate founded in 1780 in Dorchester, MA, by James Baker; business named Walter Baker & Co. in 1824, when the founder's grandson, Walter Baker, took over operations; incorporated as Walter Baker & Co., Ltd., in 1895; acquired in 1927 by Postum Company, which was renamed General Foods Corporation in 1929; General Foods purchased by Philip Morris Companies, Inc., 1985; General Foods merged with another Philip Morris subsidiary, Kraft, Inc., to become Kraft General Foods, Inc., 1989.

Major competitor: Hershey's chocolate products; also, Nestlé.

Advertising: *Agency*—Grey Advertising, New York, NY, 1990—. *Major campaign*—"One Bowl Recipes," featuring easily prepared dishes made with a Baker's product.

Addresses: *Parent company*—Kraft General Foods, Inc., 250 North St., White Plains, NY 10625; phone: (914) 335-2500. *Ultimate parent company*—Philip Morris Companies, Inc., 120 Park Avenue, New York, NY 10017; phone: (212) 880-5000.

Edmund took over the operations. When Edmund himself retired in 1824, the factory was handed down to his son Walter, who renamed the business Walter Baker & Co. Trained as a lawyer, Walter Baker oversaw great expansion in the company's production, which by the 1830s had reached more than 750 pounds of chocolate per day. Indicative of its widespread sales, Baker's chocolate was by 1833 the only packaged and branded food sold in Abraham Lincoln's country store in Salem, Illinois.

During the nineteenth century innovations from Europe forced important changes in the way Walter Baker & Co. made its chocolate. When cocoa beans were ground in Baker's mill, the result was a rich, bitter chocolate—called chocolate liquor—that contained slightly more than 50 percent of a fat known as cocoa butter. Because of the fat content, chocolate liquor made drinks that tended to be oily unless another substance, such as potato starch, was added. Coenraad van Houten, a Dutch chemist, developed a screw press in 1828 that was able to force about two-thirds of the cocoa butter out of the chocolate liquor. The pressed cake that remained was then pulverized into a dry powder. This powder, called cocoa, made a much lighter chocolate beverage that was soon in demand throughout both Europe and the United States. Van Houten's cocoa was further enhanced by treating it with alkali—a process called Dutching—which made the product darker, more soluble, and mellower in flavor.

Van Houton's successful techniques, however, left Baker's and other chocolate manufacturers with a new problem. What could be done with the excess cocoa butter? The answer came from Fry & Sons, a British company that in 1847 combined cocoa butter, chocolate liquor, and sugar to make the first chocolate for eating. From this incarnation came a variety of other chocolate products. One of the most important, milk chocolate, made with the addition of dry milk, was developed by Swiss chocolatier Daniel Peter in 1876.

Despite developments in the production of chocolate, many competitors of Walter Baker & Co. failed to change their manufacturing techniques. In 1851 a study in the British medical journal *Lancet* reported that of 50 commercial "cocoas" tested, 90 percent were mixed with starch, lead pigment, or other fillers. Walter Baker, however, continued to make a pure chocolate and also began to experiment with new products. In 1840, for example, the company introduced Spiced Cocoa Sticks, wrapped in tinfoil and sold at two cents a piece.

In the remaining years of the 1800s the company introduced additional Baker's products and gained even wider distribution. By 1844 Walter Baker & Co. was making Homeopathic Chocolate, which was sold especially to invalids. As early as 1850, gold miners in California were drinking chocolate, made "in one minute only" with Baker's cocoa paste. In 1852, the year Walter Baker died, the company introduced one of its most enduring products, German's Sweet Chocolate, made with both cocoa butter and chocolate liquor. It was named after the product's developer, Samuel German, who began with the company as Walter Baker's coachman.

Walter Baker was succeeded in 1852 by his brother-in-law Sidney Williams, and then in 1854 by his nephew Henry L. Pierce. Pierce ran the company until it was incorporated as Walter Baker & Company, Ltd., in 1895. In the intervening years the company's products gained international recognition. Baker's chocolate and cocoa won prizes at the 1867 Paris Exposition, and in the 1870s they received the highest awards at both the Vienna Exposition and the Philadelphia Centennial. Pierce also began to take advantage of new machinery. The company, for example, started to sell its products in vending machines beginning in 1891, and three years later chocolate wrapping machines were installed at Baker's mills.

When Pierce decided to incorporate the business in 1895, he reportedly told his secretary, "They say corporations have no soul, but they outlive men, and I have done what I think best for the business and for everyone." The restructuring did not seem to hurt the company—which now employed more than 400 workers—as the turn of the century brought "the largest trade in history of the Walter Baker chocolate business," according to a company publication.

The early twentieth century was a time of great change and growth for Walter Baker & Co., Ltd. During this period the company's major products included Baker's Premium No. 1 Chocolate, Baker's Breakfast Cocoa, and Baker's Vanilla Cocoa. New equipment helped the company keep pace with growing demand. Electric refrigeration, allowing chocolate to be produced even in warm weather, was introduced in 1907. In addition, an electric truck, bought by Walter Baker & Co. in 1909, initiated the replacement of horses with mechanical transport. The company purchased its first gasoline-powered truck in 1914.

After World War I the sales of Baker's products benefited from the country's growing consumption of cocoa. Approaching 100,000 tons in 1916, U.S. consumption of cocoa increased to some 200,000 tons in 1928. Such growth made Walter Baker & Co., Ltd., as well as other producers of chocolate and cocoa, a more attractive takeover target. In 1927 Walter Baker & Co., Ltd., was, in fact, acquired by Postum Company, a firm that two years later was renamed General Foods Corporation.

An Enduring Trademark

The history of Baker's famous trademark, La Belle Chocolatière (which is French for "the beautiful chocolate girl"), can be traced to the mid-eighteenth century, although more than one version of its origin has been recorded. According to some accounts, in 1745 Prince Ditrichstein of Austria visited a Vienna chocolate shop, where he had come to sample a cup of chocolate, the city's fashionable new drink. Although presumably impressed with the chocolate, the prince immediately fell in love with his waitress, Anna Baltauf, and later that year they were married. For a wedding present he had the noted Swiss painter Jean Etienne Liotard paint Baltauf in her shop uniform.

More than a century later, in 1862, Baker president Henry Pierce was visiting Germany and saw Liotard's portrait of Anna Baltauf, which was known as *La Belle Chocolatière,* in the Dresden Gallery. Enthralled with the picture, he began to use it on company products after he returned to the United States, and in 1883 La Belle Chocolatière became the official trademark of Baker's chocolate. Although still displayed prominently on Baker's products, the image has been altered to make it seem more contemporary.

Advertising

Since throughout much of Baker's history chocolate was thought to have medicinal value, products bearing the Baker's label were advertised as promoting health. For example, an 1870 advertisement featuring a robed woman embracing a cornucopia of Baker's chocolate claimed that Baker's products were "an excellent diet for children, invalids, and persons in health; allay, rather than induce, the nervous excitement attendant upon the use of tea or coffee, and are recommended by the most eminent physicians." A quarter of a century later, these claims about Baker's chocolate were impressively confirmed in an 1896 advertisement printed in *Ladies' Home Journal* that quoted various medical publications. The ad quoted the *Dominion Medical Monthly* as saying, "pure cocoa acts as a gentle stimulant, and invigorates and corrects the action of the digestive organs, furnishing the body with some of the purest elements of nutrition. The firm of Walter Baker & Co., Ltd. . . . put up one of the few really pure cocoas, and physicians are quite safe in specifying their brand."

Purity was also a notable selling point for food manufacturers in the nineteenth century. Many people were concerned, sometimes justifiably, that mass-produced food products contained unsavory ingredients or were manufactured in unsanitary conditions. To help combat any doubts about its own operation, Walter Baker & Co. ran an advertisement in a 1899 issue of *Ladies' Home Journal* illustrating its workers and chocolate machines. One picture showed a chocolate machine run by three men wearing aprons, and another featured numerous women wrapping Baker's chocolate.

Recipe books were also a common marketing strategy for food companies in the late 1800s. Walter Baker & Co. hired noted cooking teacher Maria Parloa to prepare a collection of recipes using Baker's cocoa and chocolate. The cookbook was offered to the public at no cost. By 1912 it was in such demand that it was already in its 27th edition, and more than 250,000 copies were printed of this edition alone. Two years later French and German language editions were introduced. The company built on this success by inviting its customers to enter Baker's chocolate recipe contests.

During World War I the company was a major supplier of chocolate to the Allied forces. To emphasize its support of the war effort, Walter Baker & Co. produced a ten-pound coating chocolate with the marking W.T.W., which stood for "Win the war."

Attempts were also made to establish an association between Baker's Cocoa and soldiers in Europe. An appealing print advertisement illustrated four cheerful U.S. soldiers seated at a restaurant table beneath a reproduction of the portrait La Belle Chocolatière and being served by a modern-day chocolate waitress. Below the drawing a caption read, "Somewhere the boys are drinking a Baker's Cocoa toast to mothers, fathers, wives or sweethearts. Delicious as dreams of home."

After the war Walter Baker & Co. continued to emphasize in its advertising the purity of its products. A 1926 ad in *Country Life,* for example, boasted that Baker's Breakfast Cocoa "is made without the use of chemicals and that no artificial flavoring or coloring is added." The advertisement featured a fair-skinned woman whose golden hair was surrounded by a ring of flowers. Other postwar advertisements were directed toward children, the group increasingly associated with cocoa drinking. Beneath a winter scene of a small girl pulling a sled and a boy carrying a black-and-white dog, a 1923 blurb read, "Sweet childish days, that were as long as twenty days are now. And not the least of their pleasures is a steaming cup of delicious Baker's Cocoa." In addition, a 1929 ad reminded mothers that Baker's

A December, 1926, advertisement for Baker's Breakfast Cocoa.

Cocoa's "smooth chocolate flavor appeals to *your* children, just as it did to you when you were a little girl. . . . Serve it to your youngsters often."

The acquisition of the Baker's brand by General Foods Corporation did not change the strategy of using of recipes in advertising. In the late 1930s customers were still offered a free cookbook, *Baker's Famous Chocolate Recipes,* and recipes continued to be printed in magazines. In the February 1937 issue of *Ladies' Home*

Journal, a Baker's advertisement provided a recipe for a bitter-sweet tier cake and a bittersweet frosting using squares of Baker's Unsweetened Chocolate. The advertisement warned, ''But don't expect *perfection* . . . unless you make them this way . . . *with famous Baker's Chocolate!*'' It went on to read, ''So why risk disappointment when, for only a few cents more, you can buy the world's finest, richest chocolate.''

Recipes, in fact, became the dominant marketing strategy for the Baker's brand for much of the twentieth century. In 1949 the company used recipes to encourage sales of a new quick-cooking cocoa—4-in-1 Sweet Cocoa Mix—that could be made into hot cocoa in just two minutes. Like regular cocoa, the product could also be used to make frosting and such desserts as fudge. More than 40 years later, in the early 1990s, Baker's recipe-centered advertising was focused on the ''One Bowl Recipes,'' a variety of recipes that were printed in magazines and on packages of Baker's products.

Baker's Products

General Foods Corporation, the parent company of Baker's chocolate, was purchased in 1985 by Philip Morris Companies, Inc., a corporation best known as a producer of cigarettes. In 1989 Philip Morris combined General Foods with another recent acquisition, Kraft, Inc., to form a widely diversified food company called Kraft General Foods, Inc. As a result, Baker's chocolate, once the primary offering of a small company, had become one of many products of a giant multinational corporation.

The Baker's products, made in Dover, Delaware, since 1964, had undergone major changes by the early 1990s. Baker's Cocoa, for more than a century one of the best-selling products sold under the Baker's name, was discontinued in 1967. A number of new products were introduced, however, including Baker's Semi-Sweet REAL Chocolate Chips, Baker's Milk Chocolate Chips, and Baker's Semi-Sweet Chocolate-Flavored Chips (made with palm oil and low fat cocoa processed with alkali). Baker's German's Sweet Chocolate Bar was still a major product, and Baker's Unsweetened Baking Chocolate Squares and Semi-Sweet Baking Chocolate Squares continued to dominate their category of the chocolate market. The Baker's name was also used for the first time on a non-chocolate item—Baker's Angel Flake Coconut, which had been purchased by the Postum Company in 1927. Competing brands were largely products of Hershey's and Nestlé, the country's other major chocolate producers.

The sales of Baker's products have always been linked to the United States' overall demand for chocolate. Health trends have an impact on this demand, although chocolate, no longer considered medicinal, has not yet been shown to be a cause of any serious health problem, especially when eaten in moderation. The outlook for Baker's chocolate was likely to be most dependent upon the ability of Kraft General Foods to maintain the brand's long, enviable reputation for purity and high-quality ingredients.

Further Reading:

Morton, Marcia and Frederic, *Chocolate: An Illustrated History,* New York, NY: Crown Publishers, 1986.

''Postum Seeking Baker Co.,'' *New York Times,* May 27, 1927, p. 32.

''Sues Over Trade-Mark: Walter Baker & Co., Inc., Charges Misuse by Rival Cocoa Firm,'' *New York Times,* October 30, 1930, p. 39.

—Thomas Riggs

BANQUET®

The history of Banquet frozen foods extends from the formative years of commercial food refrigeration well into the modern microwave age, where it became a leader in frozen foods. When Finis M. Stamper began marketing eggs and poultry in 1898, he could never have anticipated the boom in refrigeration science and veritable explosion in fast-food consumption that would eventually have his chicken, along with other foods, prepared, wrapped, frozen, packaged, and distributed to a multibillion dollar marketplace bearing the Banquet label. After substantial growth in the sixties, the F. M. Stamper Company, Inc. was acquired in 1970 by RCA Corporation. That year the company, renamed Banquet Foods Corporation, initiated unprecedented growth with its two-pound box of fried chicken, an item that proved so successful that a 17-piece retail box followed in 1977. When ConAgra, Inc., bought the brand from RCA in 1980, Banquet had grown substantially, but was not yet a market leader. With a strategy of unusually low profit margins and high-efficiency management, ConAgra introduced 55 new products, many under the Banquet name, and quadrupled Banquet's operating profits by 1986. By 1992, Banquet, along with ConAgra's other frozen food brands, was a market leader, holding 27 percent of a $5.5 billion market. Yet violent price wars between frozen food giants put a general damper on 1992 profits, calling on creative strategies for continued success.

Brand Origins

Banquet's long and varied history is characterized by the central importance of poultry. In 1898, Finis M. Stamper, a schoolteacher in Randolph County, Missouri, established an egg and poultry distribution business to augment his income. Operations centered around a barn, supply came from nearby farms, and distribution remained local, with the exception of small, express rail shipments of live poultry to St. Louis, Kansas City, and occasionally Chicago. Low prices and high quality products proved profitable, enabling Stamper to expand operations. In 1903, he moved production to a new, state-of-the-art plant in Moberly, Missouri. The facility occupied an entire city block and combined multiple operations: feeding and watering of up to 20,000 birds on one level; picking, candling, and cold storage on another. The business's dressed poultry was easily distributed due to Moberly's centrality along several rail lines.

Further business growth was accompanied by diversification. Following the 1909 establishment of a plant in Carrollton, Missouri, the company, operating as a proprietorship, was finally incorporated in 1912 as the F. M. Stamper Company, Inc. The following year, the Moberly plant opened a creamery, producing an average of one million pounds of butter annually. Additional plants were opened in Macon, Missouri, in 1917, and in Milan, Missouri, in 1925. Innovations in refrigerated rail transportation contributed to expanded business in egg processing. Centrally produced eggs could be separated, frozen, and shipped long distances: egg whites to bakeries and yolks to mayonnaise processors. The company also diversified into animal and poultry feeds and established the Stamper Feed Mill in Moberly in 1928. By the onset of World War II, the company was producing ready-to-cook poultry, frozen and dehydrated eggs, poultry and animal feeds, milk, butter, and ice cream.

War and Chicken Rations

In 1941, Stamper began production of dehydrated eggs, a lightweight, nutritional and long-lasting food supplement, for the allied troops fighting in World War II. At peak production, ten million eggs a day were reduced to one-quarter their original mass and shipped overseas. In 1943, Stamper expanded the menu, producing canned chicken products for American military C-rations, or canned field rations. After the war, the company refurbished its canning machinery and introduced canned chicken bearing the "Banquet" label. The timing was right, as consumption of canned foods had nearly doubled since 1941. Fred A. Stare, president of the National Canners Association, estimated in 1946 that Americans would consume over 500 million cases of canned foods and vegetables alone and an additional 175 million cases of canned fish, meats, poultry, and milk. C-rations had evolved from field rations to grocery store chicken rations, launching the Banquet brand into the packaged grocery business with a head start.

Early Marketing Strategies

The rise in canned goods coincided with an equally dramatic increase in frozen goods in the 1940s and 1950s, as refrigeration technology made possible distribution as well as retail and home storage. As early as 1929, *Ladies Home Journal* predicted the replacement of the corner grocery with an integrated store, combining grocery, meat and fish markets, and a delicatessen. The journal predicted that "One whole side of the store would be devoted to foods in low-temperature refrigerated cases." Since frozen foods could be packaged in waxed paper cartons during the metal shortages of the war, they represented a popular alternative to canned goods and used up relatively few ration points. Such availability, paired with the growing emphasis on speed and practicality on the part of working women, contributed to the rise of frozen food. Once the war was over, the availability of metal and advances in metallurgy, along with high-speed stamping equipment, made possible the mass production of disposable aluminum containers. By 1946, more than 400 items were being frozen by over 500 packers, amounting to about eight percent of total grocery sales, according to a 1946 *New York Times* article. Demand was so high that the market could hardly accommodate it: in 1946, leading trade associations—like the National American Wholesale Grocers Association and the New York State Food Merchants Association—struggled to establish merchandising structures to regularize profits, in anticipation of large chain operations in the field; and retailers hardly had the room to properly store the new cold merchandize. According to 1946 trade estimates, 100,000 new selling cases were required in retail stores alone, and their immediate availability did not seem promising.

By 1953, Stamper had geared up to enter the bustling arena, with Missouri locations in Moberly, Macon, Milan, Marshall, Carrollton, Stanberry, St. Joseph, Booneville and St. Louis, as well as in Memphis, Tennessee. In 1953, the company produced its first frozen food item, Banquet chicken pies, followed 3 years later by the first Banquet frozen dinner of fried chicken. The success of these items led to consolidation and growth. The company withdrew from the milk, butter and ice cream business, closing its Moberly creamery. In 1954, it opened a plant in Wells, Minnesota and, in 1958, it moved corporate headquarters to St. Louis, with better access to financial, legal and marketing support.

Withdrawing from egg processing in 1963, the company began unprecedented expansion of its frozen product line.

Television and the 1960s

By 1965, the F. M. Stamper company offered 53 different products, 90 percent of which had been developed since 1950. A 1964 *Printers' Ink* article remarked that frozen-foods departments were the largest single source of new products in supermarkets. In order successfully to support new items, producers increasingly relied on comprehensive advertising. Television became the preferred medium, as demonstrated by figures from the six-year period from 1958 to 1963: newspapers' percentage changes in frozen-foods ad dollars were down 35 percent, magazines were up 120 percent, network TV up 311 percent, and spot TV up 130 percent, according to *Printers' Ink*. Riding the wave, Banquet used television for the first time in a series of 1966 commercials referring playfully to the eating extravaganzas of King Henry VIII, among other themes. That same year, Stamper introduced the "Buffet Supper" label, acquired Bright Foods, and opened a new plant in Turlock, California. Crowning its 1960s growth, the company acquired the Batesville, Arkansas, broiler business of J. K. Southerland Company, anticipating Banquet's future dependence on poultry.

Corporate Growth

In 1970, F. M. Stamper Co. merged with RCA Corporation and changed its name to Banquet Foods Corporation. Its alliance with the communications giant promised the extra support for an increasingly competitive frozen foods industry. Results were positive: that same year, Banquet introduced its two-pound box of fried chicken, which would prove the company's largest selling item. Such success precipitated continued growth, with special attention to poultry. In 1973, the company established a plant in Sellston, Ohio. That same year it introduced its "Man-Pleaser" large-size dinners which, by 1978, were available in eight varieties: Mexican-Style, Salisbury Steak, Turkey, Western Brand, Chopped Beef, Fried Chicken, Meat Loaf, and Veal Parmesan. In 1975, the company purchased Madelia, Minnesota-based Royal Pantry Foods and added frozen bread dough to its expanding repertoire. Fried chicken success prompted the 1976 purchase of the Whitworth Hatchery and Poultry Farm, Inc., in Lavonia, Georgia, and Greenville, South Carolina, and the 1976 introduction of a 17-piece box of chicken to expand on the success of its smaller predecessor. In addition, the company opened its St. Louis County Research Center, a high-tech facility with seven laboratories and a pilot processing plant, in 1977. By 1978, Banquet was producing over 100 different products.

Banquet's growth pattern under RCA turned into a veritable growth spurt after ConAgra, Inc., bought the brand in September of 1980. A brief overview of ConAgra's success story helps explain the subsequent success of Banquet. Until 1974, when Charles Harper left the Pillsbury Company to head ConAgra, the company was a troubled and little known agricultural commodities business, producing feed, flour, and poultry. When Harper first joined, ConAgra "was basically bankrupt," according to William Leach, an analyst with Donaldson, Lufkin & Jenrette, Inc. "They were caught speculating in the futures markets the wrong way," Leach told the *New York Times*. That year alone, the company lost $12 million. But Harper helped set the business on the right course, slashing inventories, selling off idle real estate and unprofitable businesses, and tightening commodity trading guidelines.

Harper also began an acquisitions spree that turned the company into a diversified food powerhouse by the mid-1980s. Between 1974 and 1990, ConAgra negotiated over 100 acquisitions, placing the company at every step along "the food chain," as Harper described it, from seed planting to retail frozen foods sales. Sales rose from $633.6 million in 1974 to about $7 billion in 1987 and over $20 billion by 1990, positioning ConAgra as the number two food company in the United States, after Kraft General Foods. Nor could the company's stock appreciation be easily rivaled: a $1,000 stake in ConAgra in 1974 would have yielded $221,704 in 1991, reflecting a compound annual growth rate of 37.4 percent.

Banquet factored prominently into ConAgra's rapid growth. In 1980, ConAgra bought the frozen food company from RCA, which had been trying to sell it for $250 million. A cyclical depression in the broiler business, however, made the sale particularly difficult, and ConAgra was able to buy Banquet for a mere $50 million—capitalizing on its understanding of commodity cycles. At the time, many investors feared that ConAgra was neglecting primary interests in commodities in order to make a last-ditch attempt to enter the packaged food market, already dominated by Pillsbury and General Mills, among others. Harper insisted that primary emphasis was not on packaged food at all, but rather on Banquet's lesser-known poultry producing operations, which would increase ConAgra's chicken capacity by one-third, according to *Business Week*. With its acquisition of Banquet, Conagra would strengthen its commodity-based strategy. In 1990, the company sold 1.3 billion pounds of chicken, accounting for $1.5 billion in sales, according to the *New York Times*.

The Banquet acquisition yielded more than growth in the poultry market, for ConAgra's frozen foods sales also increased dramatically. With the acquisition of Banquet, Harper recruited the president of Campbell Soup Company's Swanson frozen-foods division, John B. Phillips, to overhaul the brand. Phillips revamped Banquet by eliminating low-price promotions so it would sell on its own merits as a mid-priced dinner. He also redesigned packaging and introduced dozens of new products, ranging from chicken nuggets to chicken patties. The plan worked, with profits tripling by 1983; quadrupling, to $40 million by 1986; and soaring to $700 million by 1991. In 1982, Phillips's position as head of the Banquet unit was filled by Philip Fletcher. As if to underline the importance of the Banquet segment, Harper eventually hand-picked Fletcher to succeed him as president and chief executive officer of ConAgra in 1992.

Brand Development

By 1986, ConAgra had added 55 new or restaged products to its frozen foods line, including the four-item Banquet Mexican Dinners, Side Dishes for One (four-item, single-serving portions), Banquet All White Meat Chicken Platters, Flavored Chicken Nuggets, and a Banquet Gourmet line, among others. ConAgra's Armour, Banquet, Light & Elegant, and Singleton brands had risen to third place in the frozen dinner market, holding a 14.9 percent share and following only Nestlé's 25 percent share (Stouffer's and Lean Cuisine) and Campbell's 22 percent share (Swanson and Le Menu).

In 1985, Charles Harper suffered a heart attack that provided the impetus for yet further business growth: the conception of ConAgra's most successful product, Healthy Choice, nutritional frozen dinners, in late 1989. Not only did the new line generate record sales—$150 million in its first year—but reinforced over-

all frozen food operations, including Banquet's. A 1990 *Forbes* article described a "new Mike Harper," dedicated to healthier processed foods. "We in the food industry," said Harper, "didn't believe bad eating was our fault, because we didn't believe there was a market for healthy foods. Well, we were wrong." In addition to the company's development of other brands, it modified the Banquet line by reducing salt content.

Health marketing was just one of several strategies to stimulate growth in the 1990s. Banquet also targeted the nearly $250-million children's market with its 1990 introduction of Banquet's Kid Cuisine, frozen meals including a "fun pack" of games and puzzles and instructions for achieving a balanced diet. Banquet had to compete against Tyson Foods, Inc., which introduced a line called Looney Tunes, supported by a $15-million media plan relying primarily on television and drawing on the popularity of established cartoon characters. Banquet's strategy, on the other hand, focused on education and lower pricing. In addition to "fun packs" enclosed in each package, ConAgra called on over 4,000 elementary schools nationwide, sending them teaching kits with a teacher's guide, worksheets, and games that demonstrated how to make a complete meal. The Banquet meals also sold for 20 percent less than Tyson's. By 1991, Kid Cuisine reported $75 million in sales, outpacing Looney Tunes three to one.

All of Banquet's lines, including Kid Cuisine, depended on more general marketing efforts as well. Microwave compatibility was one important factor. When microwave ovens reached the mass market in the 1970s, the company (like its competition) developed convenient packages accommodating microwave as well as conventional cooking methods. In 1992, ConAgra acquired Golden Valley Microwave Foods, Inc., a leader in foods primarily for microwave preparation. In efforts to address environmental concerns, the company also began a joint venture with Du Pont chemical company to develop and market polyactides, polymers made from lactic acid, that exhibited degradabililty in laboratory tests and promised alternative recycling possibilities for late 1994, when the material would be commercially available.

More direct promotional efforts have included sponsorship of racing car events such as the "Banquet Foods 300K" at the Sears Point International Raceway in 1989. And in 1992, Banquet promoted a high-quality cassette of "Country Music's Rising Stars," offered free with proofs-of-purchase and through Sunday newspaper inserts. In addition to the cassette, consumers were invited to vote for their favorite Rising Star by dialing 1-900-COUNTRY for a 50-cent fee. "Banquet and country music are a natural combination because they both stand for traditional American ideals such as family, value and a wholesome lifestyle," explained Dave Lunghino, vice president of marketing for Banquet, in a 1992 *Business Wire* interview.

International Market

Until the early 1990s, Banquet played a marginal role in international markets, primarily because its parent company had failed to develop an overseas market. Truxton Morrison, president and chief operation officer of ConAgra International, explained in *Forbes* that "the first thing ConAgra needed to do was build a secure house here in the U.S." Its main competitor in packaged food, Kraft, got one-third of its sales overseas, however. Marc C. Particelli, head of the consumer-goods consulting practice at Booz, Allen & Hamilton, Inc., forecasted that "those two giants are going to be slugging it out for a long time," in a 1991 *Business*

Week article. By 1992, ConAgra was gearing up: ConAgra International had trading offices in 23 nations, extensive merchandizing facilities and transportation assets in the United States, and processing facilities in the U.S., Asia, Australia, Canada, Europe and Latin America.

Performance Appraisal

While Banquet was a prominent brand under RCA's ownership in the 1970s, its growth stagnated. Few new products were launched between 1970 and 1980, and sales were falling. The 1980 ConAgra acquisition resulted in a growth explosion: annual operating income more than doubled to $25 million from 1980 to 1984, and then grew 100 percent to top $700 million by 1991. In 1986, ConAgra held 4.9 percent of the frozen dinner market group; by 1992, its share had risen to 27 percent. In a 1990 *New York Times* article titled, "ConAgra Who?" Leach summarized the company's skill: "They just have this knack for buying things cheap and improving them."

Banquet was one of those "things." By 1992, however, the frozen foods industry was entrenched in a price war that threatened all its contenders. According to analyst Bonnie Wittenburg of Dain Bosworth, Inc., prices for frozen dinners and entrees were 30 percent below the same period of the previous year. In the 1992 *Forbes* article, Harper called the situation "a grubby fight," exacerbated by "bloodthirsty price discounting." It is a fight that Harper would, for the most part, leave to his successor, Philip Fletcher, who would have to live up to a legacy that set more people feasting on Banquet (and its ConAgra kin) than any other frozen foods.

Further Reading:

"Advertisers Fight Economic Woes," *Advertising Age,* November 3, 1986, p. 54.

Bagot, Brian, "What's Up, Kids?," *Marketing & Media Decisions,* May, 1990, pp. 49-52.

"Canned Food Use Gains," *New York Times,* December 5, 1946, p. 45.

"ConAgra: Buying a Frozen-Food Maker to Get at Its Chickens," *Business Week,* December 1, 1980, p. 124.

"Country Music Association and Banquet Foods Join for Promotion," *Business Wire,* October 19, 1992.

" 'Drawbacks' of Glass-Door Cabinets Only Psychologists' Myths," *Quick Frozen Foods,* August, 1965, pp. 87-88.

Hall, Trish, "How a Heart Attack Changed a Company," *New York Times,* February 26, 1992, p. C6.

"History of Banquet," *Quick Frozen Foods,* October, 1978, pp. 54-57.

Ivey, Mark, "How ConAgra Grew Big," *Business Week,* May 18, 1987, p. 87.

"Keen Competition Due in Frozen Food," *New York Times,* September 7, 1946, p. B1.

Lubove, Seth, "I Hope My Luck Holds Out," *Forbes,* July 20, 1992, p. 114.

Murray, William D. "Rudd Wins Banquet Foods 300K," *United Press International Sports News,* June 11, 1989.

Sanchagrin, Ted, "Frozen Foods Generate Sales Heat," *Printer's Ink,* December 11, 1964, pp. 37-40.

Shapiro, Eben, " 'ConAgra Who?' Seeks Mainstream Success," *New York Times,* June 13, 1990, p. D1.

Therrien, Lois, "ConAgra Turns Up the Heat in the Kitchen," *Business Week,* September 2, 1991, pp. 58-60.

Weiner, Steve, "How Josie's Chili Won the Day," *Forbes,* February 5, 1990, p. 57.

—Kerstan Cohen

BARNUM'S ANIMALS® CRACKERS

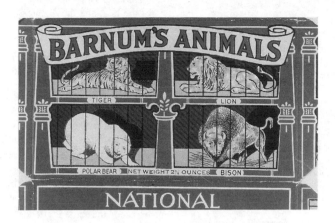

Nabisco's Barnum's Animals Crackers brand of cookies has been part of just about everyone's childhood in America and various other parts of the world. Since 1902, when the National Biscuit Company started producing and marketing them, these mildly sweet animal-shaped cookies have been packaged in a circus-wagon box topped with a string. They were originally called Barnum's Animals, a name derived from P. T. Barnum, the popular circus-owner and showman. Since Barnum's Animals came onto the market during the Christmas season, the National Biscuit Company executives thought a colorful five-cent carton of crackers would be a great holiday attraction. The string attached to the box was initially designed to allow Barnum's Animals Crackers to be hung from the Christmas tree.

Barnum's Animals Crackers became such a standard treat for children that they have received a good share of free publicity from the arts and media over the years. In 1935 Shirley Temple sang the well-known song, "Animal Crackers in My Soup," in the movie *Curly Top*. Writer and editor Christopher Morley also paid tribute to the product in one of his children's poems, which began: "Animal crackers and cocoa to drink / That is the finest of suppers, I think; / When I am grown up and can have what I please, / I think I shall always insist upon these."

Bakeries Unite

The history of the Barnum's Animals Crackers brand is intertwined with that of its parent company, Nabisco Food Groups, and with the origins of mass produced baked goods. During the late 1800s, as railroads grew and city populations mushroomed, America was changing from a mostly rural economy to an urban one. Businesses united into large organizations, often thus achieving unprecedented success. Factories prospered as high birth and immigration rates contributed to a consumer demand that frequently outstripped supply.

Bakeries could be found in every city and most towns. But bakery packaging, distribution, and promotion were limited. Horse-and-wagon deliveries restricted territories, and keeping perishables fresh was virtually impossible. In fact, most foods, and crackers in particular, came out of barrels and boxes in local grocery stores. By the late 1880s, a committee of prominent western U.S. bakery owners realized they had to change with the times. The cracker barrel that had become a symbol of the general store tradition was on its way to obsolescence. Even though assembly line production was not yet born, these bakers were frustrated by their lack of production, quality, and standardization. They saw huge businesses being formed in other industries and so decided to unite in their own organization of bakers.

The bakers enlisted the aid of Chicago attorney Adolphus Green. Under Green's guidance, numerous bakeries from Chicago, Milwaukee, St. Louis, New Orleans, Kansas City, and other cities joined to form the American Biscuit and Manufacturing Company in 1890. About a block away from Green's Chicago law office, attorney William H. Moore also was speculating in, and offering advice to, business owners looking to consolidate into one large organization. Moore met with bakers from New York and New England. He too organized a corporation in 1890; it was named the New York Biscuit Company. For a time, the two bakery companies competed with each other, although they had divided up their markets, roughly between the Northeast and the Midwest.

After years of competition, the New York Biscuit Company found itself in a weakened position, and Green felt the time had come to overtake his neighbor. New York Biscuit, with a new board of directors, wanted an end to the warfare between the two organizations, and began efforts to unite the eastern and western companies. Thus, the National Biscuit Company was established in 1898. Green became legal counsel, chair of the board, and acting chief executive. The new company brought together more than 100 bakeries across the country.

Brand Origins

Green was determined to launch the National Biscuit Company's reputation by combining "top of the barrel" quality with recognizable brand names. He started with the soda cracker Uneeda and packaged it in airtight, moisture-proof waxed paper. This new "In-er-seal" packaging created a sensation, and since the National Biscuit Company had few competitors, sales skyrocketed. After succeeding with other imaginative products, National Biscuit Company turned its sights to animal crackers.

The United States had begun importing animal-shaped cookies from England in the late 1800s. As the demand for fancy baked goods grew, bakers began making "animals" in America. Hetfield & Ducker in Brooklyn and Vandeveer & Holmes Biscuit Company in New York produced these slightly sweet crackers, also sometimes called "circus crackers." They eventually became

AT A GLANCE

Barnum's Animal Crackers brand of cookies founded in 1902 by the National Biscuit Company under the name Barnum's Animals; name changed to Barnum's Animals Crackers in 1948. National Biscuit Company changed name to Nabisco, Inc., 1971; merged with Standard Brands Incorporated to form Nabisco Brands, Inc., 1981; Nabisco Brands merged in 1985 with R. J. Reynolds Industries, Inc., which changed its name to RJR Nabisco, Inc. in 1986.

Addresses: *Parent company*—Nabisco Foods Group, 7 Campus Drive, Parsippany, NJ 07054; phone: (201) 682-7100. *Ultimate parent company*—RJR Nabisco, Inc., 1301 Avenue of the Americas, New York, NY 10019; phone: (212) 258-5600.

one of the New York Biscuit Company's staple products. By 1898, when the New York Biscuit Company merged with American Biscuit to form the National Biscuit Company (later frequently called NBC), animal crackers were a standard commodity for the company.

Advertising Innovations

Green made sure all his company's products were popular not only in certain regions, but across the entire country. The National Biscuit Company advertised Barnum's Animals Crackers so aggressively—spending $7 million in 10 years-—that grocery stores had no choice but to stock the company's merchandise in response to consumer demand. One of the first advertisements for Barnum's Animals Crackers proclaimed: "A cracker lion cannot roar, / And wouldn't if he could; / But kiddies like him all the more / Because he tastes so good."

After moving the executive offices to New York in 1906, all departments of the National Biscuit Company were also relocated there in subsequent years. The complex of buildings soon became the biggest baking center in the world. Depending on the day and the direction of the wind, one could smell Vanilla Wafers, Marshmallow Fancies, Fig Newton Cakes, or Barnum's Animals Crackers. Green turned this situation into a public relations opportunity by opening a special visitors' gallery where the public could view bakery operations.

By the 1920s, a system of National Biscuit Company bakeries and sales agencies operated across the nation. Green had died at the age of 74 in 1917, and thirty-nine year old Roy E. Tomlinson, a 15-year National Biscuit Company veteran, was asked by Moore to succeed as president. He quickly showed that, unlike Green, he valued the opinions of others, guiding the company efficiently through the shortages of World War I years, and promoting it's products effectively when radio provided a new medium. The National Biscuit Company adopted the name Nabisco in the 1940s, since its initials could be confused with those of the National Broadcasting Company; however, the National Biscuit Company did not formally become Nabisco until 1971.

Product Changes

In 1945, Tomlinson turned the company presidency over to 25-year National Biscuit Company veteran, assistant general counsel George H. Coopers. Coopers gathered young, energetic leaders for Nabisco, and declared an open season on company policy in an unprecedented letter to employees. The old, conservative ways of

doing things were to be forgotten, and policy decisions were to be "dictated by your common sense, sound judgement, observance of the law, and the dictates of your conscience." Coopers tackled mechanization and expansion to improve baking techniques by spending more than $200 million in 12 years. This was epitomized by a new research laboratory in Fair Lawn, New Jersey. Here product lines were expanded, production methods were modernized, and packaging was improved.

By this time, Barnum's Animals Crackers had been a reliable profit maker for years. They were exported to about 70 foreign countries. More than five million pounds were sold annually. But since Coopers demanded crucial examination of all areas of production, no product went without scrutiny. A young scientist in the company's Fair Lawn laboratory spent hours studying ways to improve the efficiency of baking animal crackers, a method that had been the same for decades. Until this time, animal shapes were stamped out of a dough sheet by a cutter. This produced outlines with little sophistication, making it difficult to distinguish between the various animals. A different type of die—an engraved metal device used to cut out and impress a design— was proposed and accepted. In 1958, production methods were changed to improve the crackers' visual details. Rotary dies were installed, allowing bakers to engrave details onto each cracker, creating much more intricate designs. Appeal and sales increased.

Brand Development

In 1948, the brand name was changed to Barnum's Animals Crackers, its name today. Throughout the years, the number and variety of animals caged inside the colorful little box have changed. In early years, children would encounter a variety of animals among their Barnum's Animals Crackers. They included the tiger, elephant, bear, hippopotamus, rhinoceros, polar bear, horse, sheep, dog, lion, jaguar, bison, and bull. But since the brand's origins in 1902, there have been 37 different animals represented by Barnum's Animals Crackers, with new species replacing certain of the old ones. Hyenas and gorillas, for example, have replaced dogs and jaguars. The boxes are produced in three colors—red, blue, and yellow—with a different variety of animals in each. In the early 1990s each Barnum's Animals Crackers package contained 22 crackers with 17 types of animal: the bear (sitting and walking), bison, camel, cougar, elephant, giraffe, gorilla, hippopotamus, hyena, kangaroo, lion, monkey, rhinoceros, seal, sheep, tiger, and zebra.

Performance Appraisal

In the early 1990s Barnum's Animals Crackers were produced by Nabisco Brands in the Fair Lawn, New Jersey bakery. More than 40 million packages are sold each year, both in the United States and by export to 17 foreign countries. They are baked on a 300-foot long traveling band oven for about four minutes at the rate of 12,000 per minute. The rotary dies are still used today. Some 20 miles of string is used on the box tops in a single production shift. This runs to nearly 6,000 miles of string a year. Although Barnum's Animals Crackers are not as prevalent in stores or as popular as certain other Nabisco brands, such as the Oreo cookie, the unique circus-wagon box and string will continue to catch the eyes of children for years to come.

Further Reading:

Cahn, William, *Out of the Cracker Barrel: The Nabisco Story, from Animal Crackers to Zuzus,* New York: Simon & Schuster, 1969.

Donahue, Christine, "At RJR Nabisco, New Owner KKR Is Already Wielding the Knife," *Adweek's Marketing Week,* August 21, 1989, p. 4.

Fact Sheet, New York: RJR Nabisco, Inc.

Grayson, Melvin J. *42 Million a Day: The Story of Nabisco Brands,* East Hanover, NJ: Nabisco Brands, Inc., 1986.

History of Barnum's Animals Crackers, East Hanover, NJ: Nabisco Brands, Inc.

"Nabisco Brands, Inc.," *International Directory of Company Histories,* Detroit: St. James Press, pp. 542-544.

"Nabisco's Blitz Advertising," *Business Week,* September 27, 1976, pp. 95, 98.

RJR Nabisco 1991 Annual Report to Shareholders, volumes 1 and 2, New York: RJR Nabisco, Inc., 1992.

—Anne C. Hughes

BASS® ALE

Bass Ale, a high quality pale ale, has been brewed since 1777 in Burton on Trent, a town in west central England. With a copper color and a strong hop flavor, it is the flagship brand for a variety of beers produced by Bass Brewers Ltd., the brewery's parent company. Bass Ale has been exported to the United States for more than 100 years. It is the largest imported ale and features in the top 12 U.S. imports, outgrowing the import market from 1989 to 1993. It has continued to be widely distributed and, reflecting its high price, viewed among the finest of the world's major beer brands. Carling Black Label, a lager brewed by Bass PLC, is the company's best-selling beer and the top-selling brand in Britain.

Brand Origins

Burton on Trent, the home of Bass Ale, has a brewing history going back almost 1,000 years. The town's first ale was brewed by monks of Burton Abbey, which was established by the Earl of Mercia in 1002. The monks sold their ale to local families and travelers. In 1545 the abbey was closed down, and its brewery was taken over by Sir William Paget, secretary to King Henry VIII. The ale from the Burton brewery had gradually gained wide respect, and by the 16th century, the area was famous for its ale. This success resulted not only from careful brewing but also from the special properties of the town's water. Drawn from wells above the ground's gravel beds, this water was rich in calcium and magnesium salts, making it particularly suitable for brewing.

The town's first truly commercial brewery, established by Benjamin Printon in the early 18th century, came to Burton on Trent to take advantage of this water, as did many others that soon followed. The water's reputation for brewing was so great that in the 19th century a brewery located in northern England had the water shipped by train to its operations. It was in Burton on Trent that William Bass, the owner of a transport company, decided to open a brewery in 1777. To do so, he bought a plot of land with an existing malt house and other brewing operations. Living just outside the gateway of his brewery, Bass produced a few hundred barrels of ale in his first year, and by 1785 production rose to 800 barrels (28,800 gallons). From this modest start the Bass brewery would help establish Burton on Trent as one of Britain's brewing capitals.

Early Development

When William Bass died in 1787, his son, Michael Thomas Bass, took over the brewery. Under the new leadership the Bass brewery expanded its export trade, especially to Russia and eastern Europe. By 1800 the Bass brewery was producing about 2,000 barrels (72,000 gallons) of beer annually, more than half for export. Within England, Bass Ale was sold most heavily in the surrounding area of Burton on Trent and in the large cities of London, Liverpool, and Manchester. For export, casks were shipped up the Trent river to the North Sea and eventually to the Baltic, and along the way its beer was sold in the ports of the German states, Russia, and Finland.

With the rise in production came a similar increase in the size of Bass's operations. Even so, the brewery was still dependent on rather rudimentary equipment and techniques of 1800 England. Without electricity, for example, power for the brewery was generated by the muscle of humans and horses. Moreover, because beer had to be fermented at a cool temperature, all production was limited to the months of October through April.

Of concern to the early Bass brewery was the acquisition of fine barley and hops, which, along with water, are the main ingredients of most beer, whether ale or lager. Good quality barley was bought from local farms, but the brewery purchased its hops from faraway Kent and Worcester farmers. With these ingredients the Bass brewery made ales that were exceptionally strong, dark, and sweet, with the taste of hops especially pronounced.

New Markets in the 19th Century

With so much of its ale exported to foreign markets, the Bass brewery became dependent on a stable political climate in Europe. This stability was shaken with the military conquests of Napoleon's French troops. When Napoleon issued his Berlin Decree of 1806, Bass and other Burton breweries lost their access to Baltic ports. As a result, some of Bass's competing breweries in Burton on Trent went out of business, and Bass's own sales were seriously damaged.

Although Napoleon's armies were eventually defeated, Bass was not able to recover its sales in the Baltic. Instead, it found itself looking for new world markets, a search that led the brewery to the new British possession of India, where thousands of British soldiers, British administrators, and their families were in need of

AT A GLANCE

Bass brand of ale founded in 1777 in Burton on Trent, England, by William Bass, president of Bass & Co.; became a registered trademark, 1876; brewery incorporated and company named changed to Bass, Ratcliffe & Gretton Ltd., 1888; company name changed (as a result of mergers) to Bass, Mitchells & Butler, 1961; company renamed Bass Charrington, 1967; company name changed to Bass PLC, 1983.

Major competitor: Foster's; also Guinness, Heineken.

Advertising: *Agency*—Weiss, Whitten, Carroll, Stagliano Inc., New York, NY. *Major campaign*—"Bass helps you get to the bottom of it all," emphasizing that Bass is to be savored, not quaffed.

Addresses: *Parent company*—Bass Brewers Limited, 137 High St., Burton on Trent DE14 1JZ, England; phone: (011 02) 83-511-1000. *Ultimate parent company*—Bass PLC, 20 North Audley Street, London W1Y 1WE, England; phone: (011 44) 71-409-1919.

a cool beverage to combat India's oppressive summer heat. Bass's solution, East India Pale Ale, was a light, sparkling, and mildly bitter beer. Strongly hopped to ward off infective agents, the ale was also brewed with a high gravity (in brewing, a measure of density), that allowed it to continue maturing while it was shipped to India. Later shortened to India Pale Ale and then simply to I.P.A., this type of ale was also produced by other Burton brewers, such as Worthington & Company.

The success of India Pale Ale in the early 19th century brought new fortune to the Bass brewery, and by this time it is thought that Bass Ale was also being exported to the United States. In 1827, the year Michael Thomas Bass II took over brewing operations, Bass & Co.'s India Pale Ale gained even greater fame when a ship carrying 300 Bass casks wrecked in the Irish Sea. Casks recovered from the ship were sold at an auction in Liverpool, and these casks, distributed over various parts of England, acquainted new customers with the exceptional ale of the Bass brewery.

Another important influence on Bass production was a new form of transportation—the railroads. The first railway reached Burton on Trent in 1839, and within the next four decades a number of other railways followed, connecting the town to major markets across Great Britain. The railroads, combined with increased sales to foreign markets, sent Bass production skyrocketing, from 10,000 barrels in 1832 to 60,000 in 1847, 100,000 in 1850, 400,000 in 1863, and nearly 1,000,000 in 1877, the 100th year of the Bass brewery. Bass had become Britain's largest brewing company. By 1884, when Michael Bass II died, the 145-acre operation, employing more than 2,000 people, was the largest of the world's ale brewers.

The popularity of Bass Ale was highlighted by the brewery's protection of its famous symbol, the red triangle (which was originally a shipping mark). Although officially used by the brewery since 1855, it was not until the passage of the British government's Trade Marks Registration Act of 1875 that Bass had a means to safeguard its symbol. According to company lore, on the eve of the act's introduction in 1876, an employee of the Bass brewery spent the night waiting on the steps of the appropriate registrar's office, thus ensuring that the red triangle would be the first trade mark to be registered in Britain. The employee was also

able to register the red diamond used on the brewery's Burton Ale and the brown diamond printed on its porter and stout.

20th-Century Production

In 1900 Bass Ale was sold throughout Europe, in Asia, and in North America. In the United States, for example, Bass Ale was one of the beverages sold on Union Pacific railroad. As the century unfolded, however, Bass was to find growing competition in its home market and increasingly in British pubs, or "public houses," where the majority of British beer consumption took place.

In the early 20th century most British breweries owned a chain of pubs in order to guarantee distribution of their products. Bass, in contrast, relied on what was called the "free-trade system," in which the brewery sold ale to distributors, who would then sell the product to pubs requesting it. With its enviable reputation, Bass was able to compete using this system, but only for awhile, as changes in British habits were soon brought on by World War I, the temperance movement, and new taxation on alcohol. Instead of spending an evening at a pub, customers increasingly found leisure in the new activities of the 20th century, such as films and radio. Brewing companies who owned chains were able to bring some of their customers back by upgrading their pubs, but Bass, without such a network, continued to lose business as the independent pubs selling Bass Ale failed to make similar changes.

Attempting to boost sales through acquisitions, Bass bought several breweries, including long-time competitor Worthington & Company. The Depression of the 1930s, however, brought greater financial strain to Bass, and the brewery found itself cutting production. Fighting back, Bass introduced a new brand, Blue Triangle, which was a pasteurized version of its tradition ale, and by the late 1950s it had also bought shares in the breweries William Hancock & Company and Wenlock Brewery Company.

In the 1960s Bass began a series of mergers and acquisitions that would greatly expand its brands of beer, as well as enter the company in new businesses, such as hotels. In 1961 the brewery, then called Bass, Ratcliffe & Gretton Ltd., merged with Mitchells & Butler, a regional brewer, to become Bass, Mitchells & Butler. In 1967 it merged with Charrington United Breweries, the owner of numerous pubs and a producer of spirits, soft drinks, and a variety of beer brands, including Carling Black Label. The merger resulted in a strong, diversified beverage company called Bass Charrington, which in 1983 changed its name to Bass PLC. Continued diversification led to the acquisition of hotels (such as the Holiday Inn chain), betting shops, and other businesses. As a result of these mergers, Bass PLC became Britain's largest brewer, producing not only Bass Ale and Carling Black Label but also such brands as Lemot, Tennent's, Worthington, Stones, and Barbican (a nonalcoholic beer). By the early 1990s overall sales for the brewing operations reached £1.59 billion, or about $2.3 billion, and Carling Black Label, with annual sales of 75 million gallons, was Britain's best-selling beer.

Advertising

Bass Ale, labeled as Bass & Co.'s Pale Ale, has a small but solid market in the United States. Throughout the 1980s, sales of Bass Ale steadily increased in the United States, and by the late 1980s more than 2.3 million cases were sold annually. Important in advertising Bass Ale has been the company's famous trade mark, the red triangle. Positioned in the center of the bottle's label, the triangle has been a simple reminder of the company's long history and its dedication to quality brewing. Also marked on the label have been the initials I.P.A., referring to its earlier name, India Pale Ale.

Because of its high price, Bass Ale has been advertised in the United States as a beverage to be savored, not merely to slake a thirst, the kind of ale over which an important issue or weighty matter might be considered. In fact, according to market studies, typical drinkers of Bass Ale do think of themselves as more intellectual than the average person. To lure such customers, Bass began an advertising campaign in the early 1990s featuring famous writers and thinkers. For example, a printed advertisement placed in American transit stations displayed a black-and-white picture of German philosopher Friedrich Nietzsche. The poster asked commuters, "Why does man exist?"—in a general sense, the question Nietzsche sought to answer—and then asserted, "Bass helps you get to the bottom of it all." Other advertisements featured D.H. Lawrence and Mark Twain.

This advertising campaign was also a gentle reminder of the company's distinguished history and the association it has had with noted artists and writers. Monet, for example, included two bottles of Bass Ale in his famous painting *The Bar at the Folies Bergères,* and a number of still lifes by Picasso feature the Bass label. Rudyard Kipling and Lord Tennyson cited Bass Ale in their writing.

Brand Outlook

Bass Ale is one of many beer brands exported by Bass Export, the company responsible for all beer exporting for parent Bass PLC. The lowering of international trade barriers with other European countries and with the United States could benefit business.

In 1990 the parent company had 85 percent of its sales in Britain, five percent in the rest of Europe, and eight percent in North America. Within Britain, Bass Ale on draft (Draught Bass) was the best selling cask ale in the expanding premium ale niche market.

In the United States Bass Ale is more expensive than Budweiser, the U.S. market leader. The company points to its "provenance, high quality image, and more interesting flavor profile" as a reason Bass Ale is able to achieve a price premium. Bass Ale, therefore, continues to compete with other premium priced imports as well as domestic microbrew ales.

Further Reading:

"Bass Chairman Says Firm Recaptured Beer Sales Declines," *Wall Street Journal,* January 24, 1992, p. B5A.

Bass of Burton on Trent: Brewers Since 1777, London: Bass PLC.

Bass PLC Annual Report 1992, London: Bass PLC, 1992.

"Bass to Split its Operations," *New York Times,* June 26, 1989, p. D10.

"Brewer Says it is Studying Ways to Expand Overseas," *Wall Street Journal,* December 3, 1992, p. 10.

"Brits' New Love for Cans Keeps Bass at High Speed," *Beverage Industry,* June 1991, p. 30.

Feder, Barnaby J., "Caution Rules Bass Brewery," *New York Times,* February 16, 1983, pp. D1, D3.

Jackson, Michael, *The New World Guide to Beer,* Philadelphia: Running Press, 1988, pp. 160-63.

Larson, Christine, "Bass Toasts Great Thinkers, Not Big Drinkers," *Adweek,* January 21, 1991, p. 4.

Prokesch, Steven, "Britain's Evolving Beverage Industry," *New York Times,* March 29, 1992, p. F15.

The Story of Bass, London: Bass PLC.

Winters, Patricia, "Import Fight Looms: Sales Drop Leads to Share War," *Advertising Age,* May 29, 1989, pp. 3, 50.

—Thomas Riggs

BECK'S®

Beck's Beer, produced by Brauerei Beck & Co. of Bremen, Germany, and distributed in the United States by Dribeck Importers of Greenwich, Connecticut, is the most widely recognized German beer in the world. Sold in 140 countries, its cases proclaim, "Found on Five Continents." Even in its highly competitive home market in Germany, Beck's claims the highest brand awareness and largest distribution of any beer. Beck's held third place in the imported beer market in the United States throughout the 1980s, achieving a market share of 8.6 percent by 1990. In addition to Beck's popular lager beer, the company also produces Beck's Light, Beck's Dark, and the nonalcoholic malt beverage Haake-Beck for the export market. Its advertising campaigns in the United States have targeted the young and sophisticated imported beer drinker, stressing that Beck's is "The Number One Imported German Beer in Your Town, America, and the World."

Origin of Brewery

Brauerei Beck & Co. was established in 1553 in Bremen, a city-state located on a major port on the Weser River. Bremen was an important member of the Hanseatic League, a powerful federation formed by German merchants in the Middle Ages for trading and defense, and Bremen's merchant class was pivotal in controlling Northern European shipping and commerce for two centuries.

One of the largest exports out of the Bremen harbor in the Middle Ages was beer from the city's three hundred–plus breweries. As early as the thirteenth century this beer was exported to Scandinavia, England, and Holland, and in 1489 the city's breweries had formed the Bremen Brewers' Society to regulate the production and export of the beverage. Little is known about the original founding family Beck, but they were probably wealthy merchants granted a brewing license by the Bremen city council. None of the family's ancestors are involved in the company today.

As demand for Bremen beers grew in foreign markets, competition increased, and only the Bremen brewers whose products consistently withstood long sea journeys survived. Over the years Brauerei Beck altered the chemical formulation of its beer to produce a heavy barley ale that survived the rigors of the trade routes. For hundreds of years, until the modern brewing age began in the 19th century, this type of ale was Beck's standard product.

By 1870 only thirty breweries of the original 350 members of the Brewer's Society remained in Bremen. Brauerei Beck & Co.

came into existence in its current form in 1921. By then in the hands of prominent Bremen burger Lueder Rutenberg, the company had earlier taken over two other local breweries, Bierbrauerei Wilhelm Remmer and Hemelinger Aktienbrauerei, and in that year formed a cooperative agreement with a third, the Brauerei C. H. Haake & Co. Beck's and Haake divided control of the market, with Brauerei Beck & Co. agreeing to produce beer under the brand name of Beck's for the export market, while Haake-Beck Brauerei AG would sell its products under the names Haake-Beck, Remmer, and Hemelinger in the domestic German market. The two firms later merged, becoming the largest privately owned brewery in Germany. Today Brauerei Beck & Co. is the last brewer remaining in the city of Bremen, and is a publicly held company. In addition to brewing Beck's for export, the company produces a variety of beers for the German market, including Haake-Beck Pils, Haake-Beck Kreuesen-Pils, and Remmer Light. Although there are several thousand breweries producing regional beers, Beck's is one of the few that can claim distribution throughout all of the reunified Germany. Dribeck Importers, Inc., was formed in 1964 as a subsidiary of Brauerei Beck & Co. to import Beck's into the United States.

Global Tastes Differ

To compete in a world market, Beck's attempted to appeal to the widest range of tastes while still adhering to German brewing standards; as a result, the beer Beck's produces for the American market is lighter and thinner than its German cousins. By definition, it is a lager, a light-colored, bottom-fermented product with a moderate head. The introduction of lager beers (lager being German for "to store") was spurred by technological developments, including research into yeast cultures and fermentation as well as the invention of refrigeration. In a bottom-fermented beer, the yeast sinks to the bottom, which makes for a clearer beer that is less likely to sour, but which needs to be stored and cooled longer than top-fermented ales. Beck's, like the other major German breweries, began producing lager beers late in the 19th century.

Product Lines

The beers produced under the Beck's label, in addition to the flagship lager, include Beck's Dark, Beck's Light, and Haake-Beck. Beck's Dark has long held the top spot among dark beers in the United States. The forerunner of Beck's Light was Dribeck's

Light, which appeared on the market in the early 1980s as light beers grew in popularity. However, confusion resulted when "dry" beers from Japan appeared a few years later. Dribeck's Light was discontinued, but reintroduced in a new formula and packaging as Beck's Light in 1991. Haake-Beck, a nonalcoholic malt beverage, first appeared in 1989 and was targeted toward fitness-minded consumers.

The alcohol content of Beck's is 4 percent by weight and 5 percent by volume, which is comparable to other imported brands such as Heineken and St. Pauli Girl. In its advertising Beck's has cited the Reinheitsgebot, or Purity Law, enacted by the Bavarian Court of Duke Wilhelm IV in 1516. Considered the first consumer protection statute, the law specified that only malted barley, yeast, hops, and water could be used in beer brewed in Germany for the German market. German beer exporters stress this law in citing the long tradition of excellence of German beers, but not all brew their export beer in compliance with it. All of Beck's beers, according to the company's literature, contain only hops grown in the nearby Tettnag and Hallertau regions, water from Geest-area springs and the reservoirs of the Harz mountains, and a particular strain of yeast cultivated for decades by the brewmasters at the Bremen plant.

Inroads into the East

The fall of the Berlin Wall in 1989 opened up a huge new market of consumers for German companies. Beer brewed in the former East Germany by state-owned breweries was poor in quality due to a shortage of raw materials and antiquated machinery. Frequently adulterated with corn or rice, East German beer required additives to enhance shelf-life and therefore did not meet Reinheitsgebot standards. Shortly after trade between the two Germanies was reinstituted, Beck's began selling its products in the former East German states and achieved remarkable gains in sales, due in part to the novelty of West German beer among consumers there. In April 1991 Brauerei Beck & Co. acquired the Rostocker Brauerei VEB, a formerly state-owned company in Rostock, a port on the Baltic Sea. Although Beck's had to invest heavily to upgrade the brewery's equipment, it gave the company an excellent position from which to target the East German market, brewing a new and improved Rostocker for East German consumers. In addition, the geographical location of the newly acquired brewery permitted easier access for exports of Beck's to

areas within the former Soviet Union. By 1992 Beck's products were sold in most of the former Eastern Bloc countries.

Packaging

Beck's has long reaped the benefits of efficient and sturdy packaging of its beer for overseas markets. Originally, the bottles were covered in straw and sent abroad on ships in wooden crates. Today the beer appears in a shouldered green glass bottle with a red and silver label. The green glass helps to protect the beer from potentially damaging ultraviolet rays that could affect its quality. Beck's standard lager is available in the United States in 12-ounce bottles or cans sold in six-packs and cases, 21.6-ounce bottles, or 13.2-gallon barrels for draft sales. The 21.6-ounce bottle was introduced in retail outlets in 1990 and a few years later in on-premise locations.

A Centuries-Old Trademark

Throughout the years, Beck's logo has used an old-fashioned key in various sizes and positions. The key was taken from Bremen's coat of arms, which was used by the city as early as 1366. Beck's logo eventually began incorporating the entire coat of arms, which is found both on the oval label as well as on the foil neck covering. The predominant colors of the logo are red, green, black, and silver.

Technical Innovations

Beer, because of the nature of its chemical character, had until modern times a relatively short shelf life. Beck's has continually invested in state-of-the-art brewing facilities, applying technological innovations to improve product quality. For instance, Beck's had managed to greatly reduce the oxygen count of its product to give it a longer shelf life. Beck's was also one of the first breweries to use the modern keg. These have been improved by using stainless steel containers as well as a hygienic tap system that helps lengthen the amount of time beer can be stored and reduces the risk involved in pouring draft beers.

Marketing Strategies

Originally, import beers in the United States were marketed toward immigrants who sought a taste of the old country. However, as subsequent generations drew farther away from their ethnic origins and the average consumer became more sophisticated, advertising agencies began courting a younger, more affluent beer drinker. An increase in on-premise alcohol consumption in the late 1970s and 1980s also helped fuel the popularity of imported beers, with bar and restaurant patrons exhibiting a greater willingness to test unfamiliar products. Beck's has sought to position itself as part of a centuries-old tradition of German brewing excellence, stressing both the company's longevity and the quality of their product.

Current Advertising

Beck's current advertising account in the United States is held by Messner Vitere Berger McNamee Schmetterer-Euro RSCG, formerly Della Femina McNamee of New York City. Della Femina won the Beck's account in 1973. Beck's spends $10 to 14 million dollars a year on advertising; the amount is uncertain because participants in this highly competitive market do not like to disclose exact media expenditure figures. A campaign that began in 1991 promotes Beck's as "The Number One German

Beer in Your Town, America, and the World.'' A humorous 1991 commercial for Beck's highlighted the cultural exchange between Germany and America: Germany gave America Beck's, while the United States has exported products such as the Chia Pet, a small clay statue that sprouts vegetation when watered. However, in most cases the campaign has positioned Beck's as a serious choice of imported beer in an upscale setting. Seasonal promotions are also used to reinforce the television ads at both on-premise and retail points of purchase. Oktoberfest promotions run in the fall, for instance, and Alpine-type leprechauns are used to promote Beck's near St. Patrick's Day in March.

The Haake-Beck advertising campaign is the domain of the Connecticut-based firm CSA. The current campaign relates the nonalcoholic malt beverage to an athletic lifestyle with the slogan ''The Haake-Beck Body.''

Performance Appraisal

Import beers continued to grow in popularity among consumers throughout the 1980s. American beer drinkers had grown increasingly sophisticated since the mid-seventies, and a well-traveled and status-conscious baby boomer made an excellent imported beer consumer. By 1987 import beers accounted for five percent of total beer sales in the United States. Beck's held the third-place slot in the import category with a market share of 8.4 percent for that year. As the top-selling German import, it followed Dutch-owned Heineken beer and the upstart Corona from Mexico. The only other German beer that held a significant segment of the market was St. Pauli Girl, which hovered near the bottom of the top ten imports throughout the 1980s. St. Pauli Girl is brewed in Germany by a subsidiary of Brauerei Beck & Co, but is not distributed in the United States through Dribeck. The Beck's label saw overall growth of 12.5 percent from 1980 to 1990.

However, by 1990 beer sales had begun to slump, due in part to an increased awareness among the general public of the ill effects of alcohol. This trend toward moderation in alcohol consumption was felt most directly by import brewers, while a weakened U.S. dollar also made it difficult for foreign companies such as Brauerei Beck to keep prices low. Competition in the beer market became fierce as consumers' palates became more discriminating. Domestic breweries such as Anheuser-Busch began to go after the more sophisticated beer drinker with the introduction of premium lines. Microbreweries, pioneered in California, Colorado, and other

states, began springing up across the country, and import brands were forced to compete with these American regional brews. By the late 1980s many imports, including Beck's, had lost a few percentage points in market share. Beck's responded to this trend by gearing marketing strategies toward the promising segment of off-premise beer purchases, introducing the 21.6-ounce bottle and the nonalcoholic Haake-Beck.

Future Growth

Beck's centuries-old position as the major German exporter of beer has given the brewery the financial stability necessary to compete in both new and old markets. Brauerei Beck & Co.'s 1991-92 annual report projected that the new market in the former East Germany would provide the greatest opportunity for expansion and profit, and the inroads that the company has made into Eastern Europe has helped offset the decrease in import sales by its Dribeck subsidiary in the United States. The company has also benefited from holdings of glass container manufacturing concerns and a bottling concession with Coca-Cola, Inc. Brauerei Beck & Co. is also likely to benefit from a uniting of Europe's economic markets with the implementation of the Maastricht Treaty. In all likelihood Beck's will continue to promote itself throughout the world as the beer of choice for quality minded beer drinkers.

Further Reading:

Anderson, Will, *From Beer to Eternity: Everything You Always Wanted to Know About Beer,* Lexington, MA: Stephen Greene Press, 1987.

''Beck's Counts Itself Among German Gems,'' *New York Times,* November 21, 1992, p. D19.

Brauerei Beck & Co. Annual Report, 1991/92, Bremen, Germany: Brauerei Beck & Co., 1992.

''Bulging Beck's,'' *Food and Beverage Marketing,* April, 1992, p. 43.

Dennis, Darienne L., ''How About a Beer?,'' *Fortune,* August 1, 1988, p. 8.

Fahey, Alison, ''Party Hardly,'' *Adweek's Brandweek,* October 26, 1992, pp. 24-25.

Finch, Christopher, *Beer: A Connoisseur's Guide to the World's Best,* New York: Abbeville Press, 1989.

Hemphill, Gary A., ''Imports: A Taste of Reality,'' *Beverage Industry,* September, 1989, pp. 1-26.

Jackson, Michael (ed.), *The World Guide to Beer,* New York: Prentice-Hall, 1977.

—Carol Brennan

BENSON & HEDGES®

Benson & Hedges brand cigarettes, in their assorted low-tar and deluxe forms, were the ninth most popular cigarette among American smokers, according to a 1993 *Wall Street Journal* report. This despite the fact that the cigarette industry—dominated by about half-a-dozen brands in the early 1950s—has since deluged smokers with more than 200 brands and styles. The proliferation of brands, combined with a decline in smokers and shift in demographics, has caused a steady decline in the brand's market share during the past decade, from five percent in 1983 to 3.1 percent in 1992. However, distinctive packaging, clever advertising and a focused marketing effort continued to support Benson & Hedges' sophisticated image and position the brand as a premium smoke.

Philip Morris Companies, Inc., owner of the Benson & Hedges brand since 1954, is credited with pioneering the 100-millimeter cigarette when it introduced Benson & Hedges 100s in 1965. (However, a 1965 *Wall Street Journal* story stated that American Tobacco Co. debuted a cigarette "of similar length" under the Pall Mall banner.) Benson & Hedges product-line extensions include: Little Filter cigars, 1964; 100s, 1965; 100 Lights, a low-tar version, 1977; 100s Deluxe Ultra Lights, 1982; 100s King Size, in de-nicotine and menthol, 1990; and Special Kings, 1992.

Brand Origins

Richard Benson and William Hedges began marketing their special tobacco blends in London, England, in 1873. In 1899, the duo established Benson & Hedges Inc., a branch of their hand-rolled cigarette company, in New York City. The firm was incorporated in 1907. The first New York City Benson & Hedges shop, located on Fifth Avenue, specialized in home delivery of special blends. It was there, according to a 1961 *Printers' Ink* report, that the brand's "genteel tradition" was established, with customers being received in morning coats and served tea on teakwood inlaid tables during afternoon calls. It was not until 1932 that Benson & Hedges Inc. ventured into machine-made cigarettes with a new brand the cigarette marketer christened Parliament. In 1954, Philip Morris Inc. acquired both brands when Benson & Hedges Inc. became a consolidated subsidiary of Philip Morris in an exchange of stock.

Linking Brand Image to Packaging

In 1958, Philip Morris selected the advertising firm of Doyle Dane Bernbach to handle the Benson & Hedges account. The agency was brought on to develop a campaign around product improvements, namely an improved tobacco blend and a redesigned filter system. Doyle Dane Bernbach was convinced that the typical "new and improved" ad campaign strategy would not generate enough consumer interest. So the agency focused on providing Benson & Hedges customers—already identified as buyers of premium brands, as evidenced by their willingness to pay seven cents more than most cigarette buyers—with something different. That "something" turned out to be the cigarette's package. Rather than the conventional flip-top box, Benson & Hedges

cigarettes were packaged in a slide-compartment box that resembled a cigarette case. The box was wrapped in a sliding cellophane wrapper bearing the Benson & Hedges logo that, when removed, left no trace. Dubbed the "disappearing logo" by Philip Morris marketing executives, this innovation was just the beginning of a new design aimed at solidifying the Benson & Hedges distinctive, premium image.

Drawing from the work of research agencies and an industrial designer, Philip Morris continued to modify the Benson & Hedges package. The old Benson & Hedges crest was modernized and the basic colors—gold and blue—were downplayed in favor of simulated wood paneling. To add a touch of elegance, the brand's name was spelled out in extended capitals—in red on white textured paper—to achieve a "calling card" effect. A six-month market test of the newly packaged brand indicated that Benson & Hedges sales surged 26 percent over the national average during the test period, according to *Printers' Ink*. The cigarette marketer attributed the results directly to the new packaging, pointing out that the package was tested without benefit of any additional advertising support or added sales drives.

Early Advertising Strategies

The tobacco industry has been described as a brand industry; consumers buy brands without paying much attention to which company manufactures the brand. As a result, image creation has long dominated the industry's advertising. Following the introduction of its distinctive package, Benson & Hedges developed a brand advertising campaign aimed at creating an image of prestige and quality by associating the product with interesting art objects. Such ads pictured the Benson & Hedges pack surrounded by rare curios, many of which were found only after hours of browsing through New York antique shops. The four-color ads, which ran in major national magazines such as *Time, Newsweek* and the *New Yorker,* drew "unexpected reader response," according to *Printers' Ink*. A spokesman for Doyle Dane, the agency which created the campaign, told *Printers' Ink* that the agency received hundreds of letters following an ad that depicted the Benson & Hedges pack in the midst of rare medals. The ad identified the medals in print "so fine that many people would have to strain to read it," the spokesman said. Yet readers wrote in asking all kinds of questions, including whether or not a certain medal had been identified correctly. Ads in the series, which also included the Benson & Hedges pack surrounded by 19th century toy soldiers, carried the tag line "Pay more . . . get more."

After several years of establishing the desired image, the Benson & Hedges brand turned to whimsical, offbeat advertising and promotions with appeal to upscale consumers—those who were willing to pay a little extra for the brand and its image. One of its most memorable television advertising campaigns was developed to promote the Benson & Hedges 100s line. Launched in 1965, Benson & Hedges 100s were described by the *Wall Street Journal* as "one of the longest and more expensive national brands available." At the time, most king-sized cigarettes were 85

AT A GLANCE

Benson & Hedges brand cigarettes founded in 1873 in London, England, by Richard Benson and William Hedges; introduced to the U.S. market in 1899 when Benson and Hedges established Benson & Hedges Inc., in New York City; incorporated 1907; merged with Philip Morris Inc. (now Philip Morris Companies, Inc.) in 1954.

Performance: *Market share*—3.1 percent of cigarette category.

Major competitor: Philip Morris's Marlboro; also R. J. Reynolds' Winston, Salem, Doral, and Camel; Lorillard's Newport; Brown & Williamson's Kool and GPC-Approved.

Advertising: *Agency*—Leo Burnett, Chicago, IL, 1991—. *Major campaign*—"Oh the disadvantages . . . "; "For people who like to smoke"; "Get the Edge . . . The Smooth Edge."

Addresses: *Parent company*—Philip Morris Companies, Inc., 120 Park Ave., New York, NY 10017; phone: (212) 880-5000.

millimeters long. Benson & Hedges 100s were 100 millimeters long—18 percent longer than king-sized and 40 percent longer than regular brands. The brand was launched in 100 cities and backed by a series of television commercials featuring the hazards of smoking an extra-long cigarette. TV spots carrying the tag line, "Oh, the disadvantages," depicted Benson & Hedges smokers with their extra-long cigarettes getting caught in elevator doors, igniting beards, and popping balloons. The advantage of the 100s, according to the ads, was value: smokers got more for their money—purportedly three to five more puffs.

The Wells, Rich, Greene agency created the campaign, suggesting that it intentionally steered clear of making any claims about taste. "The company eschews talking of taste in the commercials," an article in *Advertising Age* stated. "An announcer notes a lot of other filter brands dwell on this feature and asks, if one more taste claim were made for the 100s, 'Would you buy it?' " In 1966, Mary Wells of Wells, Rich, Greene told *Advertising Age,* "We try to keep a sense of proportion about the things we say about a product, and we think the sophisticated consumer is grateful for this. We try to use utmost theatrical skill in presenting our statements. . . . We try to produce sweet, lovable, friendly commercials. We think people respond to friendliness."

The first "Oh, the disadvantages" campaign ran on high-profile CBS network programming, including shows that were popular at the time, such as *The Red Skelton Show, Jackie Gleason Show, Hogan's Heroes, Friday Night at the Movies,* and *CBS Evening News with Walter Cronkite.* A print campaign using the same theme ran in national publications such as *Life, Look, Sports Illustrated, The Saturday Evening Post,* and *National Observer.* The campaign was later modified to feature the names of persons who got extra puffs. For instance, one spot featured Charles Moss, a member of the Wells, Rich, Greene creative team, who got "five extra puffs." Three years after the campaign was introduced, the agency played off its popularity with a new campaign: "Introducing disadvantages, without the disadvantages," designed for the new Benson & Hedges 85mm cigarette. According to a 1968 *Advertising Age* report, Philip Morris was the first tobacco marketer to take a brand which was successful in the 100mm market and place it additionally in the 85mm market.

Popular Promotions

By the 1960s, cigarette smoking had been linked to a number of health problems, including lung cancer. As a result, in 1971, cigarette advertising on television was banned and tobacco marketers began relying more heavily on a combination of print and outdoor advertising and direct mail and promotions. In the same year, Philip Morris, in conjunction once again with Wells, Rich, Greene, launched a novel promotion dubbed the Benson & Hedges 100s Sweepstakes. The sweepstakes proved so popular that it was still running 15 years later, with only minor adaptations. To enter the sweepstakes, consumers filled out an entry blank, indicating the prizes they were interested in, and included two bottom panels from Benson & Hedges cigarette packs. While the concept of a sweepstakes was not necessarily unique, it was the prize list that hooked consumers. For instance, consumers could win 100 pounds of spicy meatballs, 100 singing telegrams, 100 pairs of argyle socks and 100 bushels of apples, or they might choose a 100-square inch color television, 100 pieces of china or 100 hours at Cypress Gardens. Winners always had the option of trading their prize for $200 cash. When the contest was first launched, a Wells, Rich, Greene agent told *Advertising Age* that "the promotion is designed to capture the same warmth and empathetic spirit which has characterized Benson & Hedges advertising in the past. It also offers the reader some fun things to consider, he added, 'not the usual, run of the mill prizes.' "

The popular 100s Sweepstakes ran in leading national magazines such as *Ebony, Ladies Home Journal, Life,* and *Look.* It also evolved to mirror changes in the product. In 1982 the Benson & Hedges line was extended to include Benson & Hedges Deluxe Ultra Lights, and the brand was repositioned as a "deluxe" product. Although Philip Morris executives toyed with the idea of abandoning the sweepstakes at this point, they instead opted to reposition the sweepstakes. The contest took on a "classy new look with fancier graphics and higher value prizes," according to *Advertising Age.* Prizes were upgraded to include 100 inches of mink coat, 100 bottles of French champagne, 100 pieces of sushi in Tokyo and 100 mysteries on the Orient Express.

Slipping Market Share

The popularity of Benson & Hedges peaked in 1983 when the brand owned five percent of the cigarette market, according to a 1986 *Advertising Age* report. The number five brand in 1986, it had slipped to number nine in 1992, with 3.1 percent of the market, according to analyst John C. Maxwell Jr., of Wheat First Securities in Richmond, Virginia. The decade-long decline in the popularity of Benson & Hedges may be attributed only in part to the general decline in the number of smokers. The brand's positioning—as an upscale product—shares in the blame. The upscale cigarette market began shrinking when health concerns prompted the educated and affluent to abandon smoking. "In the days of controversy over the potential health effects of smoking, the more affluent and educated a smoker is, the more likely that smoker is to quit," *Advertising Age* wrote in 1986. That trend has continued, resulting in more emphasis in the industry on value and generic brands which appeal to the less affluent smoker.

Despite its upscale image, the Benson & Hedges 100s line has always been promoted as a "more for your money" product—more puffs than the 85 millimeter smoke. However, when the demographics of smokers shifted, it began to make less sense to combine the messages of value and prestige in one package. In 1992, David E. R. Dangoor, Philip Morris senior vice-president of marketing, told the *New York Times* that in the 100-millimeter market segment, Benson & Hedges "is fighting a no-win game" because smokers buy 100-millimeter cigarettes to save money, and there are just too many lower-priced brands offering a similar product. The brand was further weakened by its aging consumer base. "It is the price-conscious, older person, most likely female, who buys value cigarettes," noted Dangoor, "and 100s are the ultimate value."

Throughout a decade of declining interest, Benson & Hedges continued efforts to appeal to upscale smokers as well as to broaden its appeal to younger smokers. One of its more memorable efforts was a campaign, launched in 1988, that attracted widespread attention despite its failure to shore up the brand's market share. The campaign, another brainchild of Wells, Rich, Greene, generated interest more because of what it didn't say, than what it did. "The idea," wrote an *Advertising Age* contributor, "was to re-establish Benson & Hedges' upscale, top-shelf image," through the creation of a series of print ads containing scenes depicting "a frame from a story in progress—a story for which the reader is supplied insufficient data."

The most written-about of the ads depicted a young man, dressed only in pajama bottoms, interrupting a stylish brunch attended by five well-dressed women and an older man. Readers were left to speculate on who was who, and what they were doing. And speculate they did. According to the *Wall Street Journal*—which did some speculating of its own—the agency, as well as magazines such as *Adweek* and *Advertising Age*, were inundated with letters asking questions and offering suggestions. *Advertising Age* received 411 responses to its request for interpretations. The agency never volunteered critical information for this or any of the other similar scenes in the ad series, explaining to the *Wall Street Journal* that "We're trying to avoid cliches."

Strategies for the 1990s

After years of success with the Benson & Hedges 100s line, followed by a decade of waning interest, Philip Morris in 1992 devised an ambitious strategy to switch loyal Benson & Hedges 100s smokers to the new, 85-millimeter Benson & Hedges Special King. According to the *New York Times,* Benson & Hedges Special King would become the second-most advertised cigarette—after Philip Morris' Marlboro brand—between August and December of 1992. "In magazines alone, print advertisements, replete with the brand's longtime luxury imagery—'In short, America's premium cigarette' is the punny pitch—will run from one to seven times in 58 publications ranging from *Genre,* for gay men, to *Playboy,* for straight men, to *Esquire* for men who would rather read Norman Mailer than think about sex." Philip Morris continued its efforts on behalf of its Special Kings into 1992, with

a new campaign designed by Leo Burnett of Chicago. The ads featured ominous images of snakes and bees alongside the similarly colored pack of cigarettes. The tagline—"Get the Edge . . . The Smooth Edge"—promoted both the brand and the "Take the Edge Off Collection" of Benson & Hedges clothing. Burnett's ads appeared in national magazines and in bus shelter billboards in large cities.

Though the Special Kings launch marked a new direction for the Benson & Hedges brand, Philip Morris said it will continue to stand by its most popular line—the 100s—though perhaps back it with less advertising support. "We want to stabilize the 100s as much as possible, and build incremental volume through introducing the brand into the new segment," Dangoor told the *New York Times.* In 1992, Philip Morris offered 100s consumers mail-in coupons for merchandise from a "Signature Collection."

Further Reading:

Alsop, Ronald, "Our Theory: He's the Ad's Creator, and He's Been Given the Day Off," *Wall Street Journal,* April 14, 1988, p. B1.

"Benson & Hedges Ads Offer a Sweepstake Per Millimeter," *Advertising Age,* August 30, 1971, p. 16.

"Benson & Hedges 85 TV Ads Trade on Success of B&H 100s," *Advertising Age,* March 4, 1968, p. 2.

"Benson & Hedges is Butt of TV Spots Kidding Long Cigarette," *Advertising Age,* August 29, 1966, p. 26.

"Benson & Hedges to Be 1st Big Hit Since Tareyton: Wells," *Advertising Age,* November 28, 1966, p. 24.

Dagnoli, Judann and Jon Lafayette, "B&H Account May Move," *Advertising Age,* November 2, 1990, p. 2.

Dagnoli, Judann, "Tobacco Giants Dig Deeper into Promotion," *Advertising Age,* May 23, 1988, p. 2.

Elliot, Stuart, "Benson & Hedges Shrinks in a Bid to Regain Growth," *New York Times,* August 27, 1992, p. D18.

Gloede, William F., "PM Hedges Benson Bet with Review," *Advertising Age,* June 16, 1986, p. 3.

Kinkead, Gwen, "The Still-Amazing Cigarette Game," *Fortune,* September 3, 1984, p. 70.

LeRoux, Margaret, "Benson & Hedges Lights up Cultural Barometer," *Advertising Age,* May 2, 1985, p. 16.

"Philip Morris is Introducing Extra-Long, Expensive Cigarette," *Wall Street Journal,* September 30, 1965, p. 7.

"Philip Morris Keeps Smoking," *Advertising Age,* November 19, 1990, p. 20.

"Philip Morris Seeks New Brand Image for Benson & Hedges, *Printers' Ink,* April 18, 1958, p. 15.

Shapiro, Eben, "Marlboro Smokers Defect to Discounters," *Wall Street Journal,* January 13, 1993, p. B1.

Skenazy, Lenore, "B&H Bedtime Stories," *Advertising Age,* May 9, 1988, p. 102.

—Katherine J. Paul

BERINGER®

The Beringer brand, owned by Wine World, Inc., graces approximately fourteen varietal table wines and is the seventh best-selling brand in the $8 billion wine industry. The brand originated in the heart of the Napa Valley region of northern California in the late 1800s and has been consistently pleasing the American palate ever since. As a classic California-bred, Beringer is known for its opulent fruitiness and flavorful complexity.

Brand Origins

The Beringer brand was created in 1876 when two German brothers, Frederick and Jacob Beringer, purchased and bonded a ranch in St. Helena, California, a town located in the heart of the Napa Valley. According to corporate folklore, it was Frederick—the younger of the two brothers—who took an interest in wine-making. Growing up near Meissen in the southeastern part of Germany, Frederick was aware that many European winemakers were leaving their homelands and moving to the west coast of the United States in search of the mild coastal temperatures and rich, fertile lands they heard so much about. Charles Krug, a German winemaker from the same southeastern region of Germany, emigrated to California in the early 1850s and established a winery two miles north of what was to become the Beringer estate. Frederick followed him and convinced Krug to hire him as assistant winemaker for the newly established Krug winery. In that position, he learned about the merits of his new homeland in the Napa Valley as well as the finer details about growing grapes in the region. Most importantly, he polished his skills as a wine-master and developed a keen sense of what creates a fine wine.

Frederick worked for Krug for nearly twenty years but never lost sight of his ultimate goal: owning his own winery. In 1872, his dream came closer to being realized when a ranch two miles south of the Krug estate appeared for sale. Frederick purchased the estate in 1875 with a large financial contribution from his older brother, Jacob. The following year, in 1876, the Beringer Vineyards were bonded and Beringer wine was born. At the time of purchase, the ranch had several poor-quality vineyards planted on site. Frederick's first goal was to plant the necessary vineyards and dig the tunnels and wine cellars required for wine production. Because this took a number of years to accomplish, it was the early 1880s before Beringer wine reached full-scale production.

Frederick's attention to his company piqued his brother Jacob's interest. As a result, Jacob decided he wanted to play a larger role in the family business, and he packed his belongings and his family and made the long trek from Germany to Napa Valley. Once living on the estate, Jacob hired Chinese laborers to construct the Rhine House, a huge manor house which, for many years, served as the home of the Beringer family. Still standing, the Rhine House is a beautiful, ornate example of Victorian architecture. Winery visitors tour the home as well as the extensive wine cellars beneath. The magnificent structure stands as the symbol of Beringer wines and—emblazoned in gold embossing—decorates the label of every bottle of Beringer wine. Although no longer a family home, Beringer still uses the wine cellars for aging the estate's private reserve wines.

Brand Development

The primary goal of the Beringer Winery was to produce a high quality wine that met the taste specifications of wine-loving Americans. For many years, Beringer accomplished this goal as its wines steadily gained popularity and earned respect on American tabletops. American wine critics, too, grew to respect the Beringer label as the brand gained notoriety among customers and connoisseurs alike.

After nearly a century of production, however, Beringer wines began to lose momentum and respect among wine-lovers. Descendants of the Beringer brothers owned and ran the winery throughout the 1960s and into the early 1970s. They watched in desperation as Beringer wines steadily lost market share and sales dwindled. The problems of the winery were attributed to the strategic stagnation common within long-time family-owned businesses. After nearly 100 years of direction by the same group of people, the company was in dire need of new equipment, upgraded vineyards, novel insight, and an infusion of fresh blood.

Stagnation was a common problem in the wine industry during the 1960s. From the time European winemakers began emigrating to the United States until the mid-1960s, most wine estates were family-owned businesses. The Beringer family, like so many of its competitors, failed to maintain the winery's vines in the condition required for successful production. As a result, quite a few Beringer wine vintages were produced with very poor guidance and direction. In 1971, Beringer Wine found its savior. Nestlé Foods Corporation, a Swiss-owned food conglomerate, purchased the estate from the Beringer family. Known world-wide for its vast presence in the food industry, Nestlé had never competed in the wine industry, and the Beringer acquisition marked the company's flagship entrant.

The Nestlé Strategy

From the first day of the purchase, Nestlé had a clear vision for Beringer: to rekindle the popularity of the brand among American wine drinkers. Typical of European parent companies, however, Nestlé took a very long-term view of Beringer's situation. Nestlé's strategy was to give the Beringer the financial support, the manpower, the expertise, and the time—ten to fifteen years—the winery required to orchestrate a turnaround. Such a turnaround, the company knew, could only be accomplished from the ground up, and it often took many years to re-establish a brand in the eyes of consumers and wine critics.

Nestlé's first step in the wine industry was to establish an independent subsidiary, which the company named Wine World, Inc. This subsidiary functioned as a decentralized, independent profit center. For the first several years of operation, Beringer was Wine World's only brand. The company's plan was to focus its attention and its resources on this single brand until it regained the

AT A GLANCE

Beringer brand of wine founded in 1876 in St. Helena, CA, by brothers Frederick and Jacob Beringer; in 1971, Nestlé Foods Corporation purchased the winery and made it part of their newly-created subsidiary, Wine World, Inc.

Performance: Market share—2.1% (seventh-largest share) of the U.S. wine category. *Sales*—$171.4 million.

Major competitor: Sutter Home; also, E & J Gallo Winery's Carlo Rossi, Gallo, and Reserve Cellars brands; Canandaigua Wine Co.'s Richards Wild Irish Rose; Heublein's Almaden.

Advertising: Agency—Fran Huelse Advertising, San Francisco, CA.

Addresses: Parent company—Wine World, Inc., 1000 Pratt, St. Helena, CA 94574; phone: (707) 963-7115; fax: (707) 963-5054. *Ultimate parent company*—Nestlé Foods Corporation, 100 Manhattanville Rd., Purchase, NY 10577; phone: (914) 251-3000. *Ultimate ultimate parent company*—Nestlé USA Inc., 800 N. Brand Blvd., Glendale, CA 91203; phone: (818) 549-6000; fax: (818) 549-6952.

popularity and strength it had lost during the 1960s. In the early 1980s, Wine World began to realize the success it forecast for Beringer. Although Beringer still ranked behind such brands as Gallo, Carlo Rossi, Almaden, and Inglenook, the brand gradually began to gain strength and climb in market share.

Having realized its top priority—pushing Beringer to success—Wine World could then turn its attention and resources to secondary goals. The next order of business was to expand its presence in the industry by purchasing additional vineyards. In the late 1980s, Wine World acquired the Santa Barbara, California-area vineyards of Chateau Souberverain and Meridian Vineyards. Both estates were situated southwest of the Napa Valley, and the temperate ocean breezes produced grapes with enough distinction and diversity to give the parent company greater breadth in the industry.

The 1980s saw the entire wine industry expand dramatically. As the 1990s approached, however, U.S. wine consumption dropped some 3 percent overall and some 9 percent in certain categories. As a result, quite a few market entrants began to fail. Fortunately, Beringer Vineyards was not among the failures. Nestled in the mid- to premium-price range, the brand found itself in a category which was suddenly gaining popularity among consumers. By 1991, the brand was firmly established as the seventh-leading wine brand with sales of $171.4 million.

In 1993, Wine World, Inc. marketed a wide assortment of varietals under the Beringer brand, including the following: an estate chardonnay; a Knights Valley cabernet sauvignon; a Knights Valley sauvignon blanc; a Napa Valley fumé blanc; a North Coast red zinfandel; a Johannesburg reisling; a gewürztraminer; a chenin blanc; a French columbard; a gamay beaujolais; a grey reisling; a white zinfandel; a white cabernet sauvignon; a cabernet port; and a late-harvest reisling. In addition, Beringer also mass produced two reserve wines, a Napa Valley reserve chardonnay and a Napa Valley reserve cabernet sauvignon. Finally, the Beringer estate produced three private reserve wines marketed under the Chabot Vineyards label. With only 2,000 cases of each produced each year, these premium wines were available in very limited quantities. Each was distinguishable by the intense flavor of similar fine wines.

Future Predictions

According to Jim Beckman in *Beverage World*, Beringer's future will depend on its ability to balance its state-of-the-art technology with the traditional values and practices of winemaking. Staying at the top of the wine industry requires the ability to keep up with increasing market demand, yet maintain a high-quality, premium product typical of small, privately-held wineries. Beringer's role as a leader in the industry means that it will continue to invest heavily in research and technology to improve the growing, harvesting, and aging processes.

According to the *Beverage World* "Beverage Market Index," U.S. wine consumption dropped 6.8 percent in 1992. While some market experts cite a dwindling fondness for wine among Americans, many more experts blame the laggard sales figures on increases in the federal excise taxes that went into effect in January of 1991. The strength and diversity of Beringer's parent company gives the brand the flexibility and freedom to endure the cyclical nature of the wine industry. Frederick and Jacob Beringer would be proud of what their small company has become.

Further Reading:

Beckman, Jim, "The Best of Both Worlds," *Beverage World*, March, 1990, pp. 62-64.

Bird, Laura, "Losing Ground, Vinters Till New Soil," *Adweek's Marketing Week Superbrands*, 1991, p. 60.

Boyd, Gerald D., "Regional Wines," *Restaurant Hospitality*, March, 1992, pp. 108-118.

Sfiligoj, Eric, "The Beverage Market Index for 1992," *Beverage World*, May, 1992, pp. 30-41.

—Wendy Johnson Bilas

BETTY CROCKER®

The calm, confident countenance of Betty Crocker has graced advertisements for General Mills, Inc., food products for more than 60 years. No mere corporate symbol, Betty has one of the highest recognition factors in the United States. In fact, when consumers were asked in 1989 to link name credibility with product endorsement, Betty Crocker was ranked number one in nearly every age category, leaving a raft of real-life celebrities in her wake.

Betty Crocker's reputation was built over years of strategic positioning and awareness of the times. Even before the Betty Crocker image was created, General Mills—then known as the Washburn Crosby Company—was marketing a full line of flour. Though the line was successful, Washburn Crosby executives didn't realize just how popular the products had become until 1921, when they sponsored a jigsaw-puzzle contest. Thousands of women entered, and along with their entries came scores of questions about baking. It occurred to company managers that a Home Service outreach program might answer questions while promoting its products; furthermore, an identifiable name might gain awareness of a such a program. "The two most significant factors . . . behind the creation of Betty Crocker," according to a General Mills company document, "were the philosophy and doctrine of sincere, helpful home service and the belief that the company's Home Service contract with homemakers should be personalized and feminized."

Advertising manager James A. Quint is credited with first using the name Betty Crocker as a signature on General Mills Home Service activities. The surname "Crocker" was a tribute to a retired company director and secretary, William Crocker; "Betty" was considered a friendly sounding nickname. The idea didn't catch on immediately, since the staffs running the cooking demonstrations often preferred using their own names.

But at Washburn Crosby, Betty was very much a group project. One worker, Florence Lindeberg, employed her handwriting skills to sign Betty's name to official correspondence; dozens of staff members provided answers to consumer questions; and a local woman, Blanche Ingersoll, became the speaking voice of Betty Crocker in 1924, when Washburn Crosby's radio station, WCCO, began a Home Service show out of Minneapolis. This cooking series became the *Betty Crocker Cooking School of the Air*, which was created primarily to promote General Mills' Gold Medal flour.

From Minneapolis to Buffalo, then finally nationwide, the radio show picked up momentum and fans. It was one of the premier series on the fledgling NBC Radio network. The program found its longest-running Betty Crocker voice in Betty Lutz, who was featured on the broadcast from 1927 until 1948. Something in Betty's homespun, common-sense approach appealed to listeners; when General Mills opened registration to Betty Crocker cooking schools, more than 1.1 million people entered their names between 1924 and 1948.

Betty had her competitors, of course. Rival General Foods Inc. broadcast its own *Magazine of the Air* in the late 1920s and early 1930s. In those days, General Foods had a much larger advertising budget: the company was able to broadcast up to five hours a week, as opposed to General Mills' three 15-minute Betty Crocker segments a week. But *Magazine of the Air* didn't have the staying power of Betty Crocker; despite its higher budget, it folded within a decade, a victim of poor sales returns.

Early Marketing Strategy

General Mills credits Betty's early success to the slow, steady rise of her reputation. In 1930 the company conducted a test in two radio markets to assess its trademark's appeal. The test involved "an entirely different kind of Betty Crocker patterned on the former actress and, at the time, promoter of cosmetics, Edna Wallace Hopper," a company history noted. "Betty Crocker was given the fast, staccato, excited, high-pressure style of Edna Wallace Hopper in the experiment. Fortunately, the findings were not positive and Betty remained her own self. In a couple of years, Edna Wallace Hopper had completely faded from the scene while Betty Crocker kept growing slowly but surely." By 1940 Betty was a national phenomenon, as evidenced by her cooking show, which at the time was the longest-running radio series.

Radio provided an initial means for establishing familiarity with the Betty Crocker name. Other early marketing efforts worked equally well. Betty Crocker coupons, introduced in 1929, were inserted into Gold Medal flour bags and could be redeemed to provide savings on Oneida flatware. The precursor of the Betty Crocker cookbook appeared soon after; published in the Depres-

AT A GLANCE

Betty Crocker brand founded in 1921 to promote Gold Medal flour and other baking products for Washburn Crosby Company, which later became General Mills; the Betty Crocker brand appears on more than 200 food items and cooking accessories, including Bisquick, Pop Secret, Nature Valley, SuperMoist, and Potato Buds.

Major competitor: Procter & Gamble's Duncan Hines baking mixes; also, Pillsbury baking mixes, Unilever's Sunkist fruit snacks and ConAgra's Orville Redenbacher popcorn.

Advertising: Agency—DDB Needham, Chicago, IL. Major campaign—"Betty's got it."

Addresses: Parent company—General Mills, Inc., 1 General Mills Blvd., Minneapolis, MN 55426; phone: (612) 540-2311; fax: (612) 540-4925.

sion-era 1930s, Betty Crocker booklets offered advice to struggling families on how to prepare healthy meals with limited resources, including government relief foods. The publication gained acclaim from both nutritionists and social workers. General Mills would repeat the favor during World War II, when a Betty Crocker show, *Your Nation's Rations,* and the *Your Share* booklet provided suggestions for innovative ways to prepare rationed food.

Throughout the 1930s and 1940s, General Mills expanded its baking line and routinely used the Betty Crocker name to advertise its new products. One of the most well-known brands, Bisquick baking mix, is still found on shelves today. Bisquick was concocted almost by accident when in 1931 an executive in the Sperry Division of General Mills ordered biscuits in the dining car of Southern Pacific Lines. Those light, flaky, and sweet biscuits were like nothing he had eaten before. The train's chef had premixed all the dry ingredients to save time, and in doing so revolutionized the preparation process by just adding milk and baking—thus producing biscuits within 15 minutes.

The Sperry team set out to duplicate, then mass-produce the premix biscuit recipe. The task was a daunting one: the proportions of each ingredient needed to blend exactly lest an inexperienced cook try to add more flour or shortening. Finally, Betty Crocker's name was added to the Bisquick package in 1947. Bisquick came to be used as a base for everything from biscuits to pancakes to pizza crust.

Quality Breeds Variety

Betty Crocker had always stood for quality in the minds of consumers, but during the first half of the twentieth century, convenience foods were not associated with good eating. All that changed in 1947, when the first Betty Crocker cake mixes hit America's shelves. The debut mix was labeled Ginger Cake but would soon evolve into Gingerbread Cake and Cookie Mix. Devil's Food Layer Cake and Party Layer Cake Mix—products that offered an alternative to the time-consuming process of baking a cake from scratch—soon followed.

The early mixes bearing the Betty Crocker label eventually yielded more than 130 cooking and baking products. Betty Crocker's name appears on various incarnations of such well-

known brands as SuperMoist cake mix, Creamy Deluxe frosting, Potato Buds instant mashed potatoes, Pop Secret popcorn, and two of the budget-stretcher's staples, Hamburger Helper and Tuna Helper. Expanding even further, the Betty Crocker name was later licensed by General Mills to a line of cooking-related utensils, including small appliances, cutlery, and even kitchen clocks. By distancing the name strictly from food, the brand extension "represents the modernization of Betty Crocker," noted image consultant Clive Chajet in a *Marketing Week* piece. "The classic Midwestern housewife image is no longer appropriate for everyone."

The Changing Face of Tradition

The Betty Crocker image, however, has certainly proven its staying power. Betty Crocker had already been established through written and spoken words, but for her first 15 years of life, she lacked one thing—a face. That was remedied in 1937, when the first Betty Crocker character likeness appeared on General Mills products. Neysa McMein, a New York portrait artist, won the task of creating a look to match the reputation of a can-do homemaker. McMein blended the features of several Home Service staffers, ending up with a stylish matronly woman with blue

A rendering of Betty Crocker as she appeared in 1936.

eyes and gray-streaked hair. She wore a red suit with a white ruffle around the neck (all subsequent Bettys would repeat this red-with-white theme). Though her expression seems slightly stern compared to her more smiley reincarnations, this Betty would boast the longest reign, from 1936 to 1955.

When it was time to update Betty's look in 1955, several well-known artists, including famed painter Norman Rockwell, were invited to submit ideas. Hilda Taylor's portrait of a softly smiling, slightly younger woman-in-red was voted the favorite by 1,600 women who participated in the judging. Ten years later, a new portrait reflected women's more prominent role in society. This Betty, created by Joe Bowler, could work in any company in 1965—she wore a crisp business suit adorned by a string of pearls. Bowler updated Betty again just three years later, letting her hair down a bit, and replacing the pearls with a white scarf.

By 1972 Betty continued her evolution as a woman who means business: artist Jerome Ryan gave her the look of a corporate go-getter. But General Mills, sensing that their character was moving away from the traditional image of a homemaker, restyled Betty for 1980, adding a few years to her in the tradition of early portraits, costuming her in a dress' neckline as opposed to a suit, but retaining the woman-for-all-seasons appeal. As times changed, however, and attitudes shifted, another portrait was introduced in 1986 and remained in through the early 1990s. As envisioned by artist Harriet Perchik, the thirty-something Ms. Crocker is younger than her predecessors, and sports a dress-for-success red suit highlighted by an oversized white bow.

Betty Crocker's face stopped appearing on General Mills consumer products in the early 1970s. By that time, just her name, appearing within a large wooden-spoon logo, was enough to prompt most shoppers' consideration. By the early 1990s any combination of the name, portrait, and spoon logo was being utilized for various marketing and communication efforts.

Though by the late twentieth century it was a mature brand, Betty Crocker in some ways became more popular than ever. Betty Crocker cookbooks are dependable bestsellers in their category, they have been published since 1950 under nearly 200 different titles, including *Betty Crocker's Boys and Girls Cookbook; Betty Crocker's Eat and Lose Weight; Betty Crocker's Low-Fat, Low-Cholesterol Cookbook; and Betty Crocker's Old-Fashioned Cookbook*. In addition, the Betty Crocker recipe magazine is a supermarket checkout favorite. Most important, sales of Betty Crocker-branded foods and accessories continued to rise impressively, to the point where in the early 1990s, the baking mixes ranked number 15 among all food brands. General Mills continued to turn out 20 to 50 new Betty Crocker products each year.

Betty Crocker's TV Career

Television has no doubt helped cement consumer recognition of the Betty Crocker brand name. The successful format of radio's *Betty Crocker Cooking School of the Air* lent itself naturally to the emerging video medium. In 1950 CBS premiered *The Betty Crocker Television Show*, "virtually a half-hour TV commercial," Jim Hall commented in his book *Mighty Minutes: An Illustrated History of Television's Best Commercials*. The show brought Betty's character to life. Portrayed by actress Adelaide Hawley, Betty Crocker "performed in CBS's first color television commercial, where she concocted a 'mystery fruitcake,'" according to Hall. "She also baked up confections on two ABC daytime shows in 1952, *Betty Crocker Star Matinee* and *Bride and Groom*. In the latter show, she interviewed newlyweds back from their honeymoon and coached the brides on the preparation of their husbands' favorite dishes. Through the remainder of the decade, Adelaide Hawley appeared in chatty TV ads, greeting viewers brightly: 'Hello, everybody! Once again, it's time for us to talk about "something different" to help you drive that old monster, monotony, right out of your kitchen window.'"

By the 1980s the tone of advertising had of course shifted—Betty Crocker products were seen as high-quality, easy-to-prepare meals and desserts suitable for consumers' busy lifestyles. "You sweet talker, Betty Crocker," was one jingle used in a commercial featuring upscale men and women enjoying fresh-looking baked goods.

An Attitude of Confidence

The spirit of forward movement began in the offices of General Mills. A 1991 *Fortune* article described how the "boring" traditional Betty Crocker line had been given a morale—and sales—boost by its then-division president, Dave Murphy. Murphy worked on fostering creativity and confidence—and his efforts paid off. "Murphy's enthusiasm . . . has invigorated Betty Crocker," *Fortune*'s Patricia Sellers reported. "Sales volume has increased more than 10 percent for two years straight, and the recent quarter's 24 percent rise brought responses like 'stunning' and 'shocking' from Wall Street."

Sellers also detailed the most recent big success stories: "Betty Crocker's Nature Valley is crunching Quaker Oats in granola snacks. Its Pop Secret popcorn is outselling ConAgra's Orville Redenbacher. And the volume of Bugles, those cone-shaped corn chips you munched at parties 20 years ago, was up 37 percent last year because of improved distribution, better packaging, and a new ranch flavor." Betty Crocker entered the age of high technology in 1992 when it offered a series of recipes on computer disc.

Naturally, Betty Crocker's rivals have also risen to the challenge. As Sellers continued, the cake-mix line "has taken a lickin' since [Procter & Gamble's] Duncan Hines brought cutthroat pricing to the frostings market eight years ago." After years of can-you-top-this price slashing with Duncan Hines, Betty Crocker fought back by beating its rival to market with "low-calorie frosting and . . . brought out a successful premium-priced icing that comes with packets of dinosaur, teddy bear, or turbo-racer candies to sprinkle on Junior's birthday cake. Frosting volume was up 13 percent [in 1990], and in August Murphy raised most prices above Duncan Hines's for the first time since early 1989."

One other Betty Crocker product has benefitted from recent innovation. General Mills had entered the fruit snack market in 1983 with Fruit Roll-ups, "those sheets of sugary goo that peel off pieces of coated paper," as Sellers described it. Rival Unilever unveiled Sunkist fruit bits that kids liked better, the article continued. "Betty Crocker retaliated with gummy fruit pieces called Thunder Jets, Berry Bears and Shark Bites." Unfortunately, rising production costs made introducing these new products difficult. So General Mills attempted a comeback of the original Fruit Roll-up. An idea Murphy liked, multicolored roll-ups, was dismissed by many in the operation. "But the marketers persisted," Sellers recounted, "and in a project called Operation Roadkill, they walked into the plant themselves and threw Garfields—fruity shapes of the cartoon cat—into production lines. The giant rollers crushed the cats, creating crude versions of rainbow-colored roll-ups. Theses Crazy Color Roll-ups hit supermarkets recently, and the volume of Roll-ups is rising for the first time since 1984."

One secret to Betty Crocker's continuing success, Betty Crocker Products President Jeff Rotsch told Sellers, is that the company has built careful profiles of the people who buy their products. For the Hamburger Helper dishes, for instance, a typical user is "a married female homemaker with three-plus kids and a Ford Escort. She is not good in the kitchen but wants to be." Rotsch added, "We've cut our market research organization in half over the past five years and actually improved our success because we know our consumer."

Further Reading:

Applebaum, Cara, "Spreading Betty's Name Around," *Adweek's Marketing Week,* March 25, 1991.

General Mills company document.

Hall, Jim, *Mighty Minutes: An Illustrated History of Television's Best Commercials,* New York, NY: Harmony Books, 1984, pp. 47-48.

Sellers, Patricia, "A Boring Brand Can Be Beautiful," *Fortune,* November 18, 1991, p. 169.

—Susan Salter

BIRDS EYE®

Birds Eye, owned by Kraft General Foods, Inc., is the most important brand name in the history of the frozen food industry. Clarence "Bob" Birdseye was single-handedly responsible for every major early breakthrough in the development of the methods and technology that made freezing a viable way of preserving food without sacrificing too much taste or quality. Though the idea of preserving food by freezing had existed for countless generations, Birdseye invented the process that paved the way toward the creation of a gigantic industry. Birdseye sold the Birds Eye brand name before it had achieved significant commercial success. By that time, however, the course had been set for the explosion of frozen food products that occurred later in the twentieth century, a course along which such obstacles as public resistance and legal constraints on frozen foods had to be overcome.

Brand Origins

Clarence Birdseye was born in Brooklyn, New York, in 1886. After studying biology for three years at Amherst College in Massachusetts, Birdseye left the school in 1910 and began working at a series of summer jobs with the U.S. Biological Survey of the Department of Agriculture. There he enhanced his knowledge of biology. Birdseye worked as a naturalist in the southwestern United States and then spent several years in Labrador in the Canadian Arctic as a fur trader and trapper. It was during this period that he observed methods used to freeze freshly caught fish. After being pulled from the icy waters, the fish were allowed to air dry in the extreme cold; in this way, the fish would freeze solid almost immediately. Fish frozen in this way could be thawed and eaten months later without losing its fresh taste.

When Birdseye returned from the Canadian Arctic in 1917, he began experimenting with ways to quick-freeze foods mechanically. He speculated that it was the speed of the freezing that made the techniques he observed in Labrador superior to conventional cold storage, which robbed food of much of its flavor. He tested a method that involved immersing meat, fish, and vegetables in brine that circulated at about −45 degrees Fahrenheit. Birdseye received a patent for his quick-freezing process in 1921, and in 1923 he established Birdseye Seafoods, Inc., in New York.

Initial Setbacks

The idea of commercial frozen foods originally met with resistance on several fronts. Retailers were reluctant to invest in the specialized refrigeration equipment that frozen products required. Restaurant owners, irked by the prospect of competition from cheaper foods that could be prepared at home, spread claims that frozen food was unhealthy. The American public itself was quick to dismiss Birdseye's "frosted food," associating it with cold-storage products, notorious for their poor quality. In the face of such resistance, Birdseye's original company quickly went bankrupt.

In 1924 three new backers, including well-known financier Whetmore Hodges, put up $160,000 to launch Birdseye's next venture, General Seafoods Corporation in Gloucester, Massachusetts, a leading fishing port. By this time, Birdseye had developed his revolutionary "belt froster," a 40-foot monster weighing 20 tons. The belt froster was essentially a machine that placed packages of fish between two metal surfaces chilled to sub-zero temperatures. By 1927 Birdseye was experimenting with other types of food, especially produce, and he had organized General Foods Company as a holding company for General Seafoods stock and belt froster patents.

The results produced by the belt froster were excellent; foods froze more quickly, and quality was preserved. The financial results of the new products were less impressive however, and by the winter of 1928, most of the 1.6 million pounds of frozen seafood the company had warehoused the previous summer remained in stock. Neither retailers nor consumers had yet been persuaded of the convenience or quality of the products.

Early Marketing Strategy

With the failure of his frozen foods to capture the public's fancy, Birdseye was in need of capital by late 1928 for the company to have any chance of surviving. He realized that one of his biggest problems was the lack of a useful distribution system. Therefore he sought backing from companies that had strong marketing networks already in place. After numerous refusals from many leading food-processing companies, meat packers, and canneries, Birdseye finally hooked up with the Postum Company. Postum was established in 1895 as makers of a cereal beverage and two years later introduced one of the earliest ready-to-eat breakfast cereals, Grape-Nuts. Later the company had absorbed several well-established independent food companies, including the makers of Maxwell House Coffee.

In 1929 Postum bought out Birdseye's General Foods Company lock, stock, and barrel, purchasing everything from patent rights on the quick-freeze process to the Birds Eye trademark itself. The sale price was $22 million, $20 million for the patents and $2 million for the company's assets. The $20 million figure was among the highest prices ever paid for patents up to that time. The name of the company was immediately changed to General Foods Corporation.

Following the purchase, General Foods concocted a 40-week-long marketing push more ambitious than any that had come before. The campaign approached the problem of breaking down consumer resistance to frozen foods from several angles. First, new Birds Eye storage cases were installed at no cost in ten stores in Springfield, Massachusetts. Free samples of chicken, steak, fish, and strawberries were offered in these stores by an army of demonstrators. Hundreds of potential customers were interviewed in their homes to determine what could win them over. Birds Eye representatives spoke at women's clubs, home economics classes, and other gatherings to preach the nutritional merits of frozen food.

Despite 40 weeks of feverish proselytizing backed by conventional advertising, the campaign was only partly successful. Following the official introduction of the Birds Eye products on March 6, 1930, only 75,000 pounds of the 600,000-pound food stockpile were sold.

First Commercial Success

Between 1929 and 1933 Birds Eye developed a full line of products, built the first frozen food laboratories, and developed super-insulated railroad cars and a special fleet of Birds Eye fishing trawlers. In spite of these advances, little progress was made breaking through the wall of consumer and retailer attitudes. The nearly 23 million pounds of food processed by Birds Eye were sold through only 532 retail outlets, primarily in New England.

During the next few years, General Foods made two significant moves aimed at broadening the base of frozen food users. First, a

new, less expensive freezer case was developed in 1934. Birds Eye was able to rent the new equipment to retailers at a reasonable cost on a monthly basis. This made the company's products available in stores where the cost of buying freezers had previously been prohibitive.

The other, more important move was a total shift in marketing strategy. The focus of sales efforts was abruptly switched away from individual consumers and families toward large institutions such as hospitals, hotels, schools, and steamships. The advantages of this approach were numerous. Purchase sizes were much greater, and large numbers of people were exposed to the products at a time. The institutions benefitted from the convenience of preparation and more compact size the Birds Eye packages afforded. Some early customers included the Childs restaurant chain, the employee lunchrooms of the Chase National Bank, and the Waldorf-Astoria Hotel. The Waldorf in particular multiplied the credibility of Birds Eye as a quality product, and by 1937 Birds Eye turned its first ever profit.

Birds Eye finally began to reach a nationwide market around the onset of World War II. As greater numbers of American women became involved in the war effort, the value of food that took less time to prepare became increasingly apparent. General Foods executives were able to convince government officials that frozen foods, packaged in paper, were economically sounder to produce than canned goods. They argued that the 2,600 tons of steel required for the canning of 20 million pounds of vegetables would be better used elsewhere in the war machine. The government agreed to put quick-frozen foods on the lists of available foods posted in food stores throughout the country. Meanwhile, the palates of soldiers overseas were growing accustomed to the best quality frozen vegetables available. This would help generate an all-time high demand for frozen foods upon the soldiers' return home.

Technological Innovations

Clarence Birdseye was above all an inventor. With over 350 patents to his credit, it is no surprise that Birdseye invented virtually every piece of equipment that made frozen foods a viable industry. In his early days in the fish business, Birdseye was one of the first merchants to pack his fish with dry ice in insulated cartons, shipping it as far west as Chicago. It was the high cost and unreliability of this method that first led him to experiment with quick-freezing. Before unveiling his groundbreaking "belt froster," Birdseye had already developed a filleting machine capable of processing haddock fillets for packaging. Next came the original belt froster. This 20-ton giant consisted of two endless moving belts made of a nickel alloy that, by removing heat from the packages simultaneously from the top and bottom, greatly speeded up the freezing process.

The standard plate freezer that was still being used in many operations decades later was also invented by Birdseye. The plate freezer operated on the same principle as the belt froster. In the original freezer, one side of the moving belt was sprayed with a calcium chloride brine at 40 degrees below zero Fahrenheit while the other side touched the product. Either whole or packaged fish could be frozen this way.

In 1939 Birdseye introduced the "gravity froster." The gravity froster was designed for quick-freezing products individually. Using a series of hollow freezer plates containing ammonia attached to a revolving central shaft, items such as peas could be processed in a way that resulted in a batch of free-flowing frozen units.

One of the most important innovations that took place at Birds Eye was developed by Donald K. Tressler, a leading food technologist who went to work for the company shortly after the buyout by General Foods. Prior to about 1930, Birdseye had achieved great success with fish, but still found that vegetables acquired an off-flavor when frozen. Tressler was able to solve this problem by "blanching." Blanching meant immersing the vegetables in hot water, but not long enough to cook them. This halted the activity of certain enzymes, thus more effectively preserving flavor. This discovery led to an explosion of new products, and plate freezers were shipped to several General Foods plants that canned lima beans, peas, and mushrooms so that production of Birds Eye frozen vegetables could begin.

Brand Development

With the newfound popularity of frozen foods after World War II, competition increased. New brands were launched by canning and packaging companies that had previously served Birds Eye as co-packers. Farm cooperatives and meat packing firms also entered the market. Birds Eye began to build more of its own packing plants and to absorb new subsidiaries in response. As the proliferation of frozen meat companies continued, Birds Eye focused increasingly on the frozen vegetable market. Eventually, technological capabilities throughout the industry began to level off, robbing Birds Eye of the main edge it once held over the competition. Birds Eye answered this challenge by creating new combinations of vegetables and relying on the quality of the new recipes that were being developed at the General Foods Kitchens.

Birds Eye continued to advertise aggressively, maintaining its image as the brand with "the extra measure of flavor." By 1958, approximately $1.7 million was spent annually on advertising for Birds Eye products; nearly all of the ads appeared in newspapers. By the early 1960s, television was added, bringing the Birds Eye advertising budget up to nearly $4 million, second only to Swanson among frozen food brands. In 1963 General Foods also commissioned a study on the economics of frozen foods, the McKinsey Birds Eye study. Product diversification continued during this period, with the introduction of a line of boil-in-bag vegetables, a concept that had been established earlier by Green Giant.

In November of 1963, Birds Eye began marketing Awake, an orange-flavored synthetic concentrated beverage. Awake seized 12 percent of the total processed beverage market by the following year, but generated controversy in the industry. Because it was a synthetic product, Awake was not susceptible to price fluctuations due to Florida's weather or orange harvest.

Birds Eye had great success with its new line of International Recipe Vegetables introduced in 1970. This line of products consisted of different combinations of vegetables, some with specially seasoned sauces, designed to simulate the foods of various countries. Among the cuisines offered were Spanish, Danish, Mexican, Japanese, Bavarian, and Hawaiian. The International Recipe line was Birds Eye's most successful new line of prepared vegetables up to that time.

In 1986 General Foods introduced Birds Eye DeLuxe, developed in an attempt to tap into the trend among consumers toward higher quality, more upscale choices in prepared foods. The line included such entries as artichoke hearts, baby carrots, and sugar snap peas. Birds Eye DeLuxe was marketed as a premium product, costing from 50 cents to a dollar more per package than the more conventional products. The DeLuxe line was packaged in gold to distinguish it from the silver-packaged regular vegetables. General Foods also emphasized the upscale nature of the DeLuxe products in television advertising, which showed the product with black and gold china and glasses of white wine on a black marble table contrasted with the image of a very plain-looking meal of peas with chicken and mashed potatoes. In the early 1990s Birds Eye Easy Recipes—which consisted of vegetable mixes and sauce to be combined with meat to create entire meals—was added to the product line.

International Market

In the United Kingdom, the Birds Eye brand is owned by Unilever PLC, a large British corporation involved primarily in the manufacture of consumer goods. Founded in 1894 as Lever Brothers Ltd., Unilever owns such well-known brands as Ragu Foods, Inc., Thomas J. Lipton, Inc., Elizabeth Arden Co., and Calvin Klein Cosmetics Co. Unilever took over the British operations of Birds Eye in 1943 and by the late 1950s dominated Great Britain's frozen food market. In fact, as late as 1958, Birds Eye was the only frozen food brand in that country that advertised. This domination of the British market was made possible in part by working in tandem with Speedy Prompt Delivery (SPD), another Unilever subsidiary. SPD's total of 42 depots in 1958 was nearly twice as many as were available to Birds Eye's nearest competitors, Ross Foods and Findus Ltd.

In the 1960s the proliferation of new chain-store brands in England began to chip away at the market share held by Birds Eye. The trend continued throughout the 1970s, resulting in a gross deficit for the brand in 1977, and no net gain the following year. Birds Eye's share of the frozen food market in Great Britain fell from about 32 percent to 18 percent between the late 1970s and early 1980s. In 1981 Birds Eye merged with Walls, another frozen food subsidiary of Unilever.

Status in the Early 1990s

In 1985 General Foods was purchased for $5.6 billion by the tobacco conglomerate Philip Morris Companies, Inc. Philip Morris went on to acquire Kraft in 1988 for $12.9 billion. The two food companies were grafted into one giant subsidiary, Kraft General Foods, Inc., which upon its creation became the second-largest food producer in the world, behind only Nestlé. In 1991 food accounted for approximately half of Philip Morris's $56 billion in operating revenue, about $4.3 billion more than was made in tobacco sales. With these developments, Birds Eye became part of perhaps the world's most impressive list of venerable brand names under a single corporate umbrella.

It will most likely be a long time, if ever, before the Birds Eye brand name disappears from the public consciousness. It is unlikely, however, that it will ever quite regain the position it held several decades ago in the frozen food world. With the dawn of the microwave age, the number of frozen prepared foods on the market has grown at a rate that no single line of products could hope to keep pace with. Newer and fancier products that boast special qualities such as low-calorie and low-price sophistication seem to arise constantly. Nevertheless, by continuing to appeal to the tastes of the American majority, Birds Eye is likely to hold its position as an important force in the frozen vegetable arena.

Further Reading:

Cleary, David Powers, *Great American Brands,* New York, NY: Fairchild Publications, 1981, pp. 7-12.

Furman, Phyllis, "Upscale Line Extensions are Looking Golden," *Advertising Age,* May 4, 1987, p. S-22.

Geroski, Paul, and Tassos Vlassopoulos, "The Rise and Fall of a Market Leader: Frozen Foods in the U.K.," *Strategic Management Journal,* vol. 12, 1991, pp. 467-478.

Gershman, Michael, *Getting It Right the Second Time,* Reading, MA: Addison-Wesley, 1990.

"Hawaiian Vegetables for Birds Eye Line," *Quick Frozen Foods,* November 1970, p. 49.

Martin, Sam, "Clarence Birdseye: The Man and His Achievements," *Quick Frozen Foods,* March 1980, pp. 39-60 and 78.

Philip Morris Companies, Inc., Annual Report, 1991.

Sanchagrin, Ted, "Frozen Foods Generate Sales Heat," *Printers' Ink,* December 11, 1964, pp. 27-29.

Sherman, Stratford P., "How Philip Morris Diversified Right," *Fortune,* October 23, 1989, pp. 120-28.

—Robert R. Jacobson

BISQUICK®

Bisquick

Bisquick brand baking mix, a product of the Sperry Division of General Mills, has helped cooks in America make an ever-changing and growing variety of foods for over half a century. A Sperry sales executive discovered the concept for this revolutionary product in 1930 in a rather unusual place—the dining car of a train. The discovery led to the creation of the nation's first prepared convenience mix and changed the course of baking forever. General Mills' President D. D. Davis coined the name for the new product that made it possible to make biscuits quick. Bisquick remains a household word in America. Packaged in familiar yellow and blue boxes, Bisquick is the country's premier baking mix.

A Pleasant Surprise

In 1930, there were no prepared baking mixes on the market. If you wanted to bake a cake, muffins, pie crust, biscuits, or hot rolls, you had to measure, sift, and mix all the ingredients yourself. One night, Sperry employee Carl Smith boarded a Southern Pacific Railroad train traveling from Portland to San Francisco. Hungry, Smith headed for the dining car, even though it was well past the dinner hour. He did not expect to get a hot meal, especially one served with hot, fresh biscuits, but within minutes he had a pleasant surprise. The waiter served him a palatable meal and a plate of piping hot biscuits.

After his meal, Smith went into the galley to compliment the chef and to ask him how he was able to produce delicious hot biscuits so quickly. The secret turned out to be an idea apparently the chef's own. The chef premixed the lard, flour, baking powder, and salt for the dough and stored it in the icebox. Whenever he needed to bake biscuits, especially in a bind, he merely had to add milk to finish the dough and produce delicious, flaky biscuits.

The Right Formula

The idea of a mass-produced biscuit mix intrigued Smith, so he turned it over to the Sperry chief chemist. The research chemists faced tremendous problems that the chef on the Southern Pacific, who made a limited quantity of his mix and stored it in the icebox, did not have to worry about. They needed to formulate a mixture of flour and shortening that would not go rancid on grocers' shelves and that had a leavening agent that would retain its power. The mixture also had to be tolerant in the hands of inexperienced

homemakers and yet make biscuits as good as, or better than, homemade.

The chemists went to work to find solutions to these problems. The answer turned out to be a little known fat imported from Italy called sesame oil. The oil had a peculiar affinity for flour and stayed sweet under most circumstances. Sesame oil, since replaced by newer discoveries, was the key ingredient that allowed the introduction of Bisquick in 1931 as the nation's first prepared mix. Many of the technologies developed for Bisquick would later be used in the first cake mixes.

A New Company's Unique Product

The vast research and development program that made it possible for Sperry chemists to develop Bisquick had only been in place a short time. In 1928, while many American industries had pooled resources, plants, and marketing facilities, the milling industry was still largely a localized one dominated by small operators. The number of Minneapolis millers had declined due to mergers, but it was not until James Ford Bell became president of the Washburn Crosby Co. that the merger of a number of leading U.S. flour milling firms took place.

The Washburn Crosby Co. had a long history of milling innovations. Cadwallader Colden Washburn's mills experimented with "new-process" milling, a system of air currents and sieves to separate flour from bran; with porcelain and steel rollers, instead of stones, to grind the grain; and with belts instead of wheels to drive the mill. All of these experimental systems became standards for American mills.

Bell did for the distribution side of the milling industry what Washburn did for the production side. Bell was an acknowledged leader in operational, management, and marketing developments who had studied the situation facing millers. Besides the unpredictability of wheat crops, he saw glaring inconsistencies among millers in their pricing, shipping, and marketing practices. The inconsistencies became apparent at the consumer level and were a detriment to the entire industry.

Bell presented his idea for a solution in 1928 to the Washburn Crosby board of directors: a merger of reputable millers, located in strategic wheat-growing and wheat-consuming areas across the

AT A GLANCE

Bisquick brand of baking mix founded in 1931 by Carl Smith, a sales executive of the Sperry Division of General Mills, Inc., who discovered the "instant mix" idea in 1930 in the dining car of a train; Bisquick name coined by General Mills' president D. D. Davis.

Performance: *Market share*—Top share of $140 million baking mix category.

Advertising: *Agency*—DDB Needham, Chicago, IL, mid-1950s--. *Major campaign*—"You've Got It Made with Bisquick."

Addresses: *Parent company*—General Mills, Inc., One General Mills Blvd., P.O. Box 1113, Minneapolis, MN 55440; phone: (612) 540-2311.

country into a single organization. The Washburn Crosby Co. was the first of twenty-seven operating companies to integrate to become the largest miller in the world, General Mills, Inc. The 1950s brought an expansion of General Mills into foreign countries, and by 1992 the company had operations in Canada, minority ownership in flour milling joint ventures in Latin America, and export and technology activities.

Many of the ideas and names consumers take for granted resulted from the organization of General Mills, including Bisquick, Gold Medal flour, Betty Crocker, Wheaties, and Brown 'N Serve Rolls. While never a real person, Betty Crocker came to symbolize General Mills' continuing tradition of service to consumers. Her origin stems from a predicament arising from a special promotion in 1921 for Gold Medal flour. The Washburn Crosby Co. offered consumers a pincushion resembling a flour sack if they correctly completed a jigsaw puzzle of a milling scene. Thousands of responses flooded into the company's office. The advertising department created Betty Crocker to give personal answers to the questions that came with responses. The surname chosen for her honored a recently retired company director, while her first name was chosen simply for its friendliness. Women employees submitted sample Betty Crocker signatures. The distinctive signature selected remained in use into the 1990s.

Over the years, Betty Crocker continued to help consumers and to promote an expanding number of products. Betty Crocker consumer education activities encompassed books, magazines, special services, and, for 24 years, the Betty Crocker Cooking School of the Air radio program. Betty Crocker first appeared in print ads in the 1920s, and her first package appearance was on Softasilk cake flour in 1937. The familiar red spoon that bears the Betty Crocker signature replaced the Betty Crocker face on packaging during the mid-1960s. More than two hundred products, including Bisquick, carry the Betty Crocker spoon.

"Impossible Pie"

Early advertisements promised that Bisquick "Makes Anybody a Perfect Biscuit Maker." However, consumers soon discovered that Bisquick could be used to make more than biscuits. Cooks developed recipes for meat pies, coffee cakes, pancakes, nutbreads, shortcakes, dumplings, cookies, waffles, muffins, cobblers and yeast bakings. Bisquick was later categorized as a variety baking mix and advertised with the slogans, "Bisquick,

Bride's Best Bet;" "The Flower of the Flour;" "Stop Baking Risk, Use Bisquick;" and "A World of Baking in a Box." In 1992, the brand's slogan was "You've Got It Made with Bisquick."

The versatility of Bisquick emerged in the 1960s in a popular idea generated at the community level: "Impossible Pie." Pie makers blend Bisquick and other ingredients, pour the combination into a pie plate, and bake it. The combination does the "impossible" by making its own crust. It all began when Impossible Coconut Pie made the rounds of potluck suppers and family get togethers. The recipe became very popular as it passed by word of mouth and through newspaper recipe exchanges. The idea caught on and cooks developed Impossible Pie recipes from main dishes to desserts.

To commemorate Bisquick's 50th anniversary in 1980, General Mills formed the Bisquick Recipe Club. Some 440,000 consumers nationwide joined the club the first year and became recipients of a quarterly newsletter, special offers on kitchen accessories, and Betty Crocker cookbooks. The club encouraged members to share their Bisquick recipes and tips with each other. The world's largest peach shortcake was made using Bisquick at the 1981 South Carolina Peach Festival. The five-layer shortcake measured 25.5 feet in diameter and contained more than four tons of Bisquick and nine tons of peaches. General Mills discontinued its recipe club in late 1985 to chart the brand on a new and different course.

Brand Improvements and Outlook

General Mills' headquarters is in Golden Valley, Minnesota, no more than 10 miles from where C. C. Washburn constructed his first flour mill and worked to improve the quality of flour meal. Focusing on that tradition of quality, the company views their commitment to responding to consumers' changing needs and the ever-changing environment as essential to the company's future and growth. A direct result of this company policy was that market research and continual product testing have led to ongoing improvements in Bisquick's successful formula over the years. Lighter, fluffier and better-tasting baked goods was the aim of each improvement.

New Bisquick, introduced in the 1960s, replaced regular Bisquick. The new formula contained additional shortening and sugar, and used an entirely new leavening system. Soft wheat flour replaced the hard wheat flour in the former product. At the same time, General Mills modernized the Bisquick package, while retaining the familiar yellow and blue colors. Responding to concerns of health conscious consumers about the quantity of fat in their diets, General Mills introduced Bisquick Reduced Fat for national distribution early in 1993. For several years Bisquick has led the baking mix category, enjoying consistent volume gains. As General Mills continues its commitment to consumer needs, and cooks test the versatility of Bisquick in the kitchen, there is little doubt that Bisquick will endure.

Further Reading:

Bisquick—Baking at Its Best, Minneapolis: General Mills, Inc., January, 1989.

Byrne, Harlan S., "General Mills: Paced by Gains in Cereals' Market Share, It Exceeds Growth Targets," *Barron's,* April 20, 1992, pp. 47-48.

Campbell, Hannah, *Why Did They Name It . . . ?,* New York: Fleet Publishing, 1964, pp. 16-20.

General Mills Annual Report, Minneapolis: General Mills, Inc., 1992.

General Mills: Historical Highlights, Minneapolis: General Mills, Inc., November, 1989.

Moskowitz, Milton, Robert Levering and Michael Katz, editors, *Everybody's Business: A Field Guide to the 400 Leading Companies in America,* New York: Doubleday, 1990, pp. 13-15.

Sharp, Harold S., *Advertising Slogans of America,* Metuchen, NJ: Scarecrow Press, 1984, p. 53.

The Story of Betty Crocker, Minneapolis: General Mills, Inc., July, 1992.

—*Doris Morris Maxfield*

BORDEN® DAIRY

Eagle Brand condensed milk was first produced in 1853 by Gail Borden, the founder of the present giant dairy industry, and is the oldest commercial dairy product still on the market. Gail Borden in turn became the "father of the modern dairy industry" because of his exceptional attention to hygienic practices in milk production long before the germ theory was ever propounded. So firm was the foundation he laid that Borden, Inc., has long ranked as the largest dairy company in the nation.

Brand Origins

Any meaningful discussion of Borden dairy products and its initial market entry, condensed milk, inevitably returns to the dynamic founder of the company, Gail Borden. The world's first successful processor of condensed milk in the 1850s, Borden enjoyed a long and varied career prior to his entry in the dairy business. A surveyor, farmer, schoolteacher, businessman, journalist, and one of the founding fathers of the Lone Star State, Borden was also keenly interested in healthy living and wholesome foods. He experimented with condensing foods, especially meat, to retard spoilage, and was successful to the point where his "meat biscuit" (concentrated meat extract baked with flour in the form of a biscuit) was bought in huge quantities by the California gold seekers in 1849. Borden even travelled to London in 1851 to receive a gold medal for his newfangled meat product at the International Exposition. On the voyage back, discouraged by the generally tepid reception his product had received in his own country, Borden was further dismayed at the numerous illnesses and deaths suffered by infants aboard. Their deaths had resulted from drinking tainted milk from cows that, housed in filthy, undernourished conditions in the ship's hold, had taken sick. If wholesome, pure milk could be made to last indefinitely without spoiling, Borden reasoned, many young lives could be nourished and saved.

First Commercial Success

Temporarily shelving his condensed meat project, Borden was determined to experiment with preserving milk. If he succeeded, the market for milk would be far greater and more profitable than for meat. Back in the United States, he proceeded to tinker with ways to keep milk from spoiling, starting with the obvious method of boiling it. This treatment prolonged its freshness for a few hours, but left an unpleasant and unmarketable aftertaste. A native

of New York state, Borden recalled how Shakers in a nearby community had condensed fruit and other foods by means of a vacuum kettle that kept air out, used less heat than required for boiling, and resulted in a superior condensed product that would not spoil for a lengthy period. He traveled to New Lebanon, New York, to learn from the Shakers firsthand, and soon was sufficiently adept at the practice to conduct his experiments with milk, to the skepticism of many Shakers. After considerable trial and error, Borden produced the world's first condensed milk in 1853.

Undaunted by the universal skepticism and rejection of his first patent request, Borden eventually was able to convince an intrigued New York banker and wholesale grocer—Jeremiah Milbank—to lend him the capital to start his own business. In 1857 the New York Condensed Milk Company was established in a modest building in New York City. The founder and president of the new company went about the streets of the city with a pushcart loaded with 40-quart cans of condensed unsweetened milk (the sweetened version would come later), available at 25 cents a quart.

While New Yorkers were won over to the condensed milk, it might never have achieved national renown had it not been for the outbreak of the Civil War. Almost immediately after the conflict began, the federal government purchased all of Gail Borden's output, a state of affairs that continued throughout the war. Borden condensed milk accompanied Union soldiers on their marches, and was considered a boon for wounded and ill soldiers in field hospitals. Mary Lincoln even served Borden condensed milk in the White House, inadvertently advertising the product to Gail Borden's advantage. The commercial success of Borden's first milk product was assured. In 1866 Borden affixed the name "Eagle Brand " to the new milk product in recognition of that well-known symbol of the United States. This was done as a "hands off" warning to competitors marketing inferior products under the Borden name.

Early Marketing Strategy

Introduced in a day and age before national advertising, Borden's condensed milk undoubtedly would not have gained such quick recognition outside of its limited region had the Civil War not succeeded in making condensed milk a staple. Marketing was not ignored, however. Prior to the Civil War, *Leslie's Illustrated Weekly* attacked the common "swill milk" garnered from cows that were housed in distillery stables and fed fermented mash. Armed with a superior product, Gail Borden tried to make the most of this development and ran his first advertisements for his milk to further distinguish it from its inferior competition. Borden condensed milk remained a regional product, however.

Borden's marketing strategy after the conclusion of the Civil War was centered on advertising the extreme cleanliness and hygiene of his milk processing plants, noting his insistence that farmers boil their milking utensils twice daily and that women plant workers wear caps. This strategy worked. Even when competitors emerged in the post-Civil War years, Borden's Eagle Brand condensed milk had a reputation for "purity" and healthfulness that no other rival could match.

Utilizing a marketing strategy that factored in geographic expansion, Gail Borden actively sought a location for a new plant outside of the New York City region situated on a railroad line. In 1894 the company made its first acquisition: the Elgin Condensed Milk Company in Elgin, Illinois, which Borden had helped form in 1865. This would become the biggest condensed milk facility in the United States.

Perhaps sensing the tougher business climate that would follow the Civil War, Gail Borden decided as early as 1864 to market Borden condensed milk in small individual containers, which would also have the effect of making it more affordable and easier for grocers to store. Years after his death, in 1891, "evaporated" Eagle Brand milk cans were marketed in distinctively decorated cans, side by side with Eagle Brand condensed milk. The eye-catching appearance of the can, which sported a portrait of a huge, defiant eagle, remained unchanged until well into the twentieth century, making it a familiar trademark from coast to coast.

Advertising Innovations

Borden had an advantage over many products, since few consumers had to be convinced about the nutritious benefits of milk consumption. Nonetheless, by the turn of the century, Eagle Brand condensed and evaporated milk, as well as Borden's fresh milk, were advertised in the standard household magazines, in trams, and on billboards. Borden dairy products received a tremendous boost during and especially after World War I. Once again the federal government bought huge quantities of Borden's milk and after the war, until the early 1920s, Eagle Brand condensed and evaporated milk was used to feed millions of starving people from the Pyrenees to Siberia. Radio came into its own as well during this time, and The Borden Company (which adopted the name in

1919, retaining it until 1968, when it became simply Borden, Inc.) supplemented its traditional advertising avenues with advertisements broadcast on the new medium.

Many people identify Borden with its trademark, a portrait of Elsie the Cow's kindly face bordered by the petals of a daisy. In 1936 advertisements in the form of color cartoons of Elsie the Cow, aimed at extolling milk's healthfulness, were featured in leading medical journals. Two years later, using radio as an advertising medium, a "letter" written by Elsie was read to listeners, resulting in Elsie's first fan mail.

From that point on, there was no stopping Elsie. At the 1939 World's Fair in New York City, a live Elsie, sponsored by Borden, was one of the biggest crowd pleasers (at the 1940 World's Fair, Elsie would have her own boudoir, complete with "portraits" of her forebears on the walls). Thereafter Elsie traveled the length and breadth of the country in a specially fitted railroad car, appearing at charitable causes and special events. A touch of sensationalism was in order now and then, as when the live Elsie gave birth to her calf, Beulah, who became Elsie's inseparable companion on her travels until a second calf, Beauregard, was born.

When Elsie and her family were featured in advertising during and after the war years, they assumed thoroughly human characteristics, standing on two legs, wearing clothes, and speaking. In the era of television, however, the Borden company reduced the role of Elsie in its advertising strategy. Elsie the Cow receded into the background, although her trademark continued to appear on Borden dairy products. Elsie was deemed useful only in selling dairy products. By then, Borden had transformed itself into a business empire, a leading producer of chemicals, adhesives, and other industrial products, as well as a wide range of non-dairy foods. Instead of Elsie, a catchy slogan, introduced in 1939, "If It's Borden - It's Got To Be Good," was put into widespread use as a replacement for the ubiquitous cow and a standard for all Borden products.

This was not to be the end of Elsie, however. A Borden survey of young mothers, conducted in 1970, revealed that Elsie the Cow symbolized to them wholesomeness and nostalgia for a better, simpler era. Elsie the Cow, tailored to the growing preoccupation with healthy eating, returned.

Since that time, the company's emphasis on the Elsie logo has waxed and waned. Hurt by the recession of the early 1990s, which spelled declining sales and intensified competition, Borden's advertisers have been working on a revival of Elsie the Cow for the same reasons given by the young mothers in 1970: she personifies quality, purity, and nostalgia for the good old days. A major marketing campaign was launched to reestablish Elsie as the spokescow for Borden dairy products. The campaign also involved Elmer and the calves, nicknamed "Bea" and "Beau."

Company Development

Until 1875, Gail Borden's New York Condensed Milk Company (which changed its name in 1899 to Borden Condensed Milk Company) produced only Eagle Brand condensed milk. In 1875 fresh milk was sold for the first time, followed in 1892 by canned evaporated milk. Judging by the purchase of Elgin Condensed Milk Company in 1894, the company's main emphasis was still on condensed and evaporated milk, sold primarily under the Eagle Brand name.

In the late 1920s Borden embarked on a period of radical restructuring and diversification. In only two years, more than 100 companies were acquired. By the 1990s, dairy products accounted for only 25 percent of company sales. Product diversification at Borden began in 1928 when the company entered the ice cream business wholeheartedly by purchasing two of the country's leading ice cream companies. One year after its ice cream acquisitions, Borden entered into the cheese business. Several years later, in 1933, the company became the first to market Vitamin D fortified milk commercially. Ten years later, Gail Borden Signature Quality milk, a multivitamin fortified milk, was introduced. In addition to its product diversification in the dairy business, Borden diversified in non-dairy businesses as well, while an increasing proportion of its sales were derived from abroad. Today Borden remains a market leader in ice cream and other frozen dessert products, and continues as a U.S. leader in the dairy industry.

International Growth

According to a recent statement of the Chairman and CEO of Borden, Inc., A.S. D'Amato, international markets will be increasingly important for American food companies. In 1992 30 percent of Borden, Inc.'s revenue derived from overseas sales, although much of that total was gathered from its non-dairy business. Only 15 percent of Borden's international sales in 1992 came from its dairy holdings.

As far back as the late 1920s, joint ventures and international sales have played an important role in Borden's history. Borden's powdered milk, KLIM, currently ranks as the second most popular milk powder in the world, sold in more than 80 countries. In a recently concluded joint venture agreement with a Chinese dairy concern to produce powdered milk, the Chinese were reminded by Borden that it had sold KLIM milk powder in China in the 1920s, and would thus merely be reintroducing it.

Future Predictions

With a solid name in the dairy industry, Borden, Inc. is expected to continue to be a U.S. leader in the production of dairy products. It is the oldest dairy company in the United States still in operation, and continues to hold its position as the largest dairy producer in the country. Borden has proven a resilient company as well, weathering setbacks in the past, only to rebound.

Further Reading:

Borden 1992 Annual Report, New York, NY: Borden, Inc., 1993.

''Borden Buys German Chain (Kamps GmbH),'' *Supermarket News,* November 9, 1992, p. 42.

''Borden Plans Restructuring, Aims to Boost Dairy Brands,'' *Supermarket News,* November 9, 1992, p. 38.

''Churn at Borden: Elsie's Ad Billings are at Stake,'' *Adweek,* September 7, 1992, p. 1.

Collins, James H., *The Story of Condensed Milk,* Borden, Inc., 1922.

''Elsie the Borden Cow,'' Columbus, OH: Borden Inc., 1992.

''Gail Borden and the Illinois Condensing Company,'' *Historic Illinois,* August 1991, pp. 1-3, 11.

''Grey Will be Big Winner in Borden Ad Realignment,'' *Adweek,* November 9, 1992, p. 3.

''A History of Borden, Inc.,'' Columbus, OH: Borden Inc., 1992.

McKinley, James P., ''Borden Forms Joint Venture to Produce Milk Powder in China,'' *Business Wire,* October 6, 1992.

Wade, Mary Dodson, *Milk, Meat Biscuits, and the Terraqueous Machine: The Story of Gail Borden,* Austin, TX: Eakin Press, 1987.

''With Elsie as Mascot, Borden Inc. Hopes to Revitalize its Whole Stable of Brands,'' *Wall Street Journal,* September 3, 1992, p. B1.

—Sina Dubovoj

BRACH'S®

Brach's is the brand name for the biggest-selling line of general-line candies in the United States, making the low-profile, privately owned E. J. Brach Corporation of Oakbrook Terrace, Illinois, the third-largest confectioner in the country, behind Mars, Inc., and the Hershey Foods Corporation. Brach manufactures an extensive variety of hard candies, mints, toffees, caramels, and chocolates, which are sold in distinctive pink- and purple-striped packages or in bulk from "Pick-A-Mix" displays in retail stores. Brach's red and white Starlight Mints are the best-selling hard candy mint in the United States. Brach also is the top maker of candy corn, jelly beans, and other holiday favorites, including the heart-shaped "conversation mints" sold for Valentine's Day.

In the mid 1960s Brach's accounted for as much as two thirds of all general-line candies sold in the United States. The company, however, suffered serious financial problems in the 1980s that were attributed to poor brand management. Sales, which had once topped $700 million, fell as low as $470 million, with the company losing an estimated $200 million between 1987 and 1990. In 1992, although sales were estimated at $600 million, the company's two-million square-foot plant in Chicago was operating at 50 percent capacity. There was speculation within the industry that Brach would be sold to a larger company with a full line of candies.

In 1991 Peter N. Rogers, who was president of the E. J. Brach Corporation from 1990 to 1992, told *U.S. Distribution Journal* that the Brach's name was "trusted and is perceived as a quality brand." Rogers conceded, however, that Brach's was "not totally contemporary." "In a very broad sense, it's an old fashioned brand," he said. "It's the kind of product that mother had at home. . . . We've got to get a more contemporary product profile and we don't have enough kid-oriented items. We have to rejuvenate the brand."

Brand Origins

Emil J. Brach was a German immigrant who went to work for Chicago candy maker Bunte Brothers & Spoehr in 1881. In 1904 Brach left the company to open his own retail candy store, which he called the "Palace of Sweets," on the north side of Chicago. At the rear of the store he began making caramels, which proved to be so popular that Brach and two of his sons were soon selling caramels to department stores throughout Chicago. It wasn't until

1958 that E. J. Brach & Sons introduced the ever popular Pick-A-Mix concept. Consumers were able to buy their choice of individually wrapped hard candies by the pound. Pix-A-Mix displays were especially popular during holiday seasons, when Brach traditionally did most of its promotion.

From 1966 until 1987 E. J. Brach was owned by American Home Products. During that time it captured about two-thirds of the general-line candy market in the United States. In 1987 the company was purchased for $750 million by Jacobs Suchard AG, a Swiss chocolate and coffee conglomerate looking to expand distribution of its upscale Suchard and Tobler brands of candy in the United States. That purchase almost proved disastrous for Brach.

A Different Brach under Jacobs Suchard

In 1989, *Advertising Age* writer Julie Liesse Erickson reported on the changes at Brach; in an article headlined "Suchard Arms Brach's to Fight Candy Giants," Erickson reported that the new owners had "installed a new management and sales staff, hired a new ad agency, introduced new product packaging and even moved to a new headquarters." Erickson noted that one of the first moves by the new management was to "slash the number of Brach's products" by eliminating package varieties. For example, although the company still sold its popular Starlight Mints, the peppermint favorites came in 4 package sizes instead of 27.

Tom Snyder, then senior vice president of marketing, told *Advertising Age:* "We're trying to take the equity and strength of the brands and people to make this a company of the '90s." Jacobs Suchard also dropped the holiday promotions that had been such a big part of Brach's marketing strategy since the company's early days. And, although "Brach's" remained the brand name, the company name was changed to Jacobs Suchard USA, Inc.

Reaction to the changes among retailers turned into a nightmare for Jacobs Suchard. Many analysts agree that brand loyalty is notoriously weak for general-line candies, and many retailers—apparently upset by the loss of package variety and promotional support—turned to Brach's competitors. Among the beneficiaries of Brach's marketing gaffe were the Farley Candy Co., the country's second-largest maker of general-line candies, the similar-sounding Brock Candy Co., and Sathers, Inc., which had already

AT A GLANCE

Brach's brand of candy founded by German immigrant Emil J. Brach, who opened a retail candy store in Chicago, IL, in 1904, making caramels that the Brach family sold to area department stores; E. J. Brach & Sons Corporation purchased by American Home Products, 1966; company purchased by Jacobs Suchard AG, 1987, and E. J. Brach & Sons Corporation renamed Jacobs Suchard USA, Inc.; Swiss billionaire Klaus Jacobs retained ownership of the company's U.S. candy operations when Philip Morris Companies, Inc., bought most of Jacobs Suchard's holdings, 1990; company name later changed to E. J. Brach Corporation.

Performance: *Sales*—$600 million.

Major competitor: Mars, Inc.'s brands of candy and Hershey Foods Corporation's brands of candy; also general-line candy manufacturers Farley Candy Co., Brock Candy Co., and Sathers, Inc.

Advertising: *Agency*—Slack Brown & Myers, Inc., Chicago, IL, 1993—. *Major campaign*—In-store holiday displays; trade advertising.

Addresses: *Parent company*—E. J. Brach Corporation, One Tower Lane, Oakbrook Terrace, IL 60181-4644; phone: (708) 572-1600.

made inroads when it was chosen to supply the K-Mart chain of discount stores. By the end of 1989 Brach's sales had plummeted 20 percent, and the company reported its third straight year of sizable losses. *Forbes* reported in 1991 that Jacobs "just didn't understand the U.S. market."

Dragged down by the trouble with its U.S. subsidiary, profits at the parent company also fell ten percent in 1989; in 1990 the financially weakened Jacobs Suchard AG was purchased by the Philip Morris Companies, Inc. Philip Morris, however, reportedly insisted that the Brach candy operation not be included in the deal, and Klaus Jacobs retained ownership.

The Brach name experienced another setback in 1990 when the company threatened to close its Chicago plant and eliminate 2,700 jobs unless it received an exemption from federal import quotas on world price sugar. The U.S. Food and Drug Administration refused, and Brach was forced to lay off nearly 1,000 workers at that site to make it economically feasible. Judith Crown in *Crain's Chicago Business* criticized the company in an editorial in July of 1990: "After stamping its feet and whining about its dire need for an exemption from U.S. government quotas . . . Brach's now tacitly admits that its investment in the Chicago plant is too enormous to jettison, and it wants to stay—even though the exemption was denied. . . . As we see it, Brach's credibility is shot."

Restoring Credibility

Shortly after Philip Morris bought most of Jacobs Suchard, Klaus Jacobs visited the Oakbrook Terrace headquarters of the Brach's candy operation and promised to let local management run the company. In September of 1990 Jacobs brought in Peter Rogers, former president of the Curtiss Candy Company, to run the firm, which had been without a president since a management layoff in April. *Forbes* reported that Rogers "quickly decided the

way to fix this business was to restore the formula that had made it successful before Jacobs stepped in." One of the first decisions was to change the name of the company to the E. J. Brach Corporation.

The company also brought back many of the package varieties that had been discontinued, and returned to its use of in-store holiday promotions. By 1991, the product line, which Jacobs Suchard had wanted to rename and cut to 300, was back up to 1,300 items. In 1991 Brach featured Bugs Bunny in several promotions and introduced a line of Looney Tunes-licensed cartoon character candies. At Halloween of that year the company introduced new candies such as Gummi Mummies and Gummi Creatures of the Night, chewy, fruit-flavored candies in the shapes of bats, rats, spiders, and snakes.

Advertising and Marketing Innovations

Traditionally, Brach has done little consumer advertising, a practice stemming from the days when the Brach family delivered caramels to Chicago department stores; the company targeted the retailers, who then sold the candy to the consumer as its principal customers. Most of Brach's advertising efforts were focused on store promotions and displays. Rogers once described the approach as being "a candy resource" to the retail food industry. He told *U.S. Distribution Journal* that Brach's role was to "help the retailer merchandise Easter and . . . Halloween and other 'traditional' seasons and help the retailer create non-seasonal events."

Brach has also developed new products to better market its candy. In 1992 the company introduced Brach's Rocks, a dinosaur-themed jelly-centered candy aimed at kids, and T.D.'s Peanut Chocolate candies with chocolate shells, available in 18 National Football League team colors. In 1993 Brach introduced Fun Factory candy centers, featuring individually wrapped candies that kids could select by the cupful from colorful 3-D displays. Brach also advertised heavily in retail trade publications, stressing how its in-store displays encouraged impulse buying.

In 1992 about 75 percent of Brach's candies were sold through grocery stores. The company, however, was attempting to gain a bigger presence in other market channels, including convenience stores.

Further Reading:

"Brach's Easter Candy Promotion Soars to New Heights," *U.S. Distribution Journal*, October 15, 1990, p. 47.

"Brach's New Guardian," *U.S. Distribution Journal*, July 1991, pp. 48-50.

"Bugs Pounds the Pavement in Brach's Halloween Promotion," *U.S. Distribution Journal*, May 15, 1991, p. 44.

Crown, Judith, "Brach Fails to Mint a Revival," *Crain's Chicago Business*, September 7, 1992, p. 3.

E. J. Brach Corporation . . . A Rich Heritage of Quality, Oakbrook Terrace, IL: E. J. Brach Corporation, January 24, 1991.

"E. J. Brach Taps Peter Rogers," *U.S. Distribution Journal*, October 1990, p. 8.

Erickson, Julie Liesse, "Suchard Arms Brach's to Fight Candy Giants," *Advertising Age*, February 1989, pp. 22-23.

Feldman, Amy, "Arrogance Goeth Before a Fall," *Forbes*, September 30, 1991, pp. 82-83.

Fink, Laurie, "Sweet Success," *Corporate Report Minnesota*, March 1992, pp. 28-32.

Koeppel, Dan, ''Brach Regroups and Rediscovers Its Roots,'' *Adweek's Marketing Week,* July 23, 1991, p. 8.

''Restoring Credibility at Brach,'' *Crain's Chicago Business,* July 23, 1990, p. 16.

Superbrands 1992: America's Top 2,000 Brands (supplement to *Adweek* magazines), 1992, p. 86.

''USDA Urges Denial of Brach Exemption,'' *Crain's Chicago Business,* April 9-15, 1990, p. 1.

—Dean Boyer

BREYERS®

For more than a century, the Breyers name has been synonymous with high-quality, all-natural ice cream. Produced according to a strict "Pledge of Purity" and marketed at a price most Americans can afford, it is the top-selling frozen desserts brand in the United States. When, in the late 1980s, dozens of low-calorie, low-fat frozen desserts flooded the market, Breyers responded by introducing its own "light" ice milk and yogurt products. Within a short time, these accounted for more than one-quarter of the company's frozen dessert business. Owned for many years by Kraft General Foods, Inc., before being purchased in 1993 by Unilever—producer of Klondike bars and Good Humor ice cream—Breyers retains its popularity based on the rigorous standard of quality and wholesomeness established by its original founders. In a business dominated by regional brands, Breyers is the only ice cream distributed in all 50 states.

Brand Origins

The Breyers brand was created in 1866, when Philadelphia grocer and confectioner William A. Breyer began producing ice cream made from rich cream, cane sugar, fruits, nuts, berries, and other natural flavorings in the kitchen of his home and selling it to his neighbors. So pleased were his neighbors with the product that the news soon spread, and within a few months Breyer was selling his "mighty good ice cream" from a horse-drawn wagon in the streets of Philadelphia, the sound of a large brass dinner bell announcing his arrival. During his first year in business, he sold 1,000 gallons of homemade ice cream.

By 1882 the enterprise had grown so large that Breyer decided to open a retail ice cream store, with a manufacturing area in the rear and a soda fountain in the front where he could wait on customers. He died that same year, at the height of his success, leaving his widow, Louisa, and their two sons, Henry W. and Fred Breyer, to develop the business. Demand for the product continued to grow, and before long, two more stores had sprung up in northeast Philadelphia, one operated by Fred, the other by Henry.

In order to ensure a continuing supply of fine-quality dairy products, the Breyer family purchased the quantities they needed direct from local farmers and set up a network of company-owned and operated creameries to carry out the processing. The first of these was established in Hancock, Pennsylvania, in 1900. As new flavors were introduced, the company opened its own fruit-processing plants. Early in the product's history, the family relied on word-of-mouth advertising by satisfied customers, but by the early 1900s, newspaper ads and large billboards, as well as generous free samples, helped to spread the message. By this time, Philadelphia had gained a reputation as the ice cream capital of the United States, with longstanding brands such as Abbott's and Bassett's offering rigorous competition on the local level.

Although the name "Breyers" had been emblazoned on William A. Breyer's original delivery wagon, it was not until the 1890s that a logo was developed to accompany it. Sometime after 1894, Henry W. Breyer came up with the idea of using the picture of a briar leaf—"briar" being a pun on the family name—as a recognizable trademark. Reproductions of his hand-penned sketch later appeared on all packaging and in all advertisements for the brand, along with the famous "Pledge of Purity."

William Breyer believed from the beginning that his homemade ice cream owed its immense popularity to the pure, high-quality ingredients it contained. Upon his death, he passed his ideal of quality on to his sons. Sometime later, Henry Breyer formalized this commitment by writing a Breyers Pledge of Purity. Various versions of the following pledge, signed by Henry Breyer, have appeared on the company's packaging ever since: "I pledge that Breyers ice cream has never contained adulterants, gums, gelatins, powders or fillers, extracts or artificial flavorings of any nature. Real cream, granulated sugar and pure flavorings are used to make Breyers ice cream. The old-fashioned kind." Henry took over full responsibility of the enterprise in 1907, following the death of his brother, Fred, and in 1908 incorporated it as the Breyer Ice Cream Company. He is considered the company's official founder.

Growth of Manufacturing and Distribution

In 1896 Henry and Fred Breyer established the first wholesale manufacturing facility for Breyers ice cream. Located in a converted warehouse on East Somerset Street in Philadelphia, it featured new, mechanical freezers in place of the slower, hand-cranked ones commonly used in the industry. Nine years later, the company became the first major ice cream manufacturer to substitute brine, a revolutionary and efficient freezing agent, for ice and salt in the freezing process.

By 1904, Breyers Ice Cream had outgrown its east Somerset Street manufacturing facility, and a new, larger plant was opened

AT A GLANCE

Breyers brand of frozen desserts founded in 1866 in Philadelphia, PA, by William A. Breyer; brand later developed by his son, Henry W. Breyer, who in 1908 established the Breyer Ice Cream Company; in 1926 the Breyer Ice Cream Company was acquired by the National Dairy Products Company (NDPC), which later became a part of Kraft, Inc.; in 1989, after its purchase by Philip Morris Companies, Inc., Kraft, Inc., merged with another subsidiary, General Foods Corporation, to become Kraft General Foods, Inc.; in 1993 Kraft sold its ice cream business, which included the Breyers brand, to Unilever.

Performance: *Market share*—Top share of frozen desserts category. *Sales*—Estimated $341 million (according to *Dairy Foods* magazine).

Major competitor: Dreyer's Grand and Edy's Grand ice cream brands; also Kraft General Foods' Sealtest brand.

Advertising: *Agency*—Young & Rubicam, New York, NY. *Major campaign*—Product-focused imagery reinforcing that Breyers' unique taste results from its all-natural ingredients, using the slogan, "The Difference Is Real."

Addresses: *Parent company*—Unilever United States, Inc., 390 Park Ave., New York, NY 10022; phone: (212) 888-1260; fax (212) 752-6365. *Ultimate parent company*—Unilever PLC/Unilever N.V.

on Cumberland Street. Ten years later, in 1914, the company's annual output of ice cream had reached one million gallons. During the early years, when distribution was limited to Philadelphia and its suburbs, the product was delivered by horse-drawn wagons. By the early 1920s, however, the demand for Breyers ice cream had grown so much that Henry Breyer decided to set up a network of distributors and retailers in New York City, Newark, New Jersey, and Washington, D.C. He arranged for the product to be packed in tubs of ice and salt and shipped by trolley freight, railway, boat, and auto express to distant locations. Soon afterwards he opened what was then the world's largest ice cream manufacturing facility on Woodland Avenue in Philadelphia, followed by one in Long Island City, New York, and another in Newark. In 1926 Broadway heralded the opening of the Long Island plant with an enormous, lighted billboard advertising Breyers ice cream. Members of the public were also invited to tour the new facilities.

In 1926, ten years before the death of Henry Breyer, the Breyer Ice Cream Company was acquired by the National Dairy Products Corporation (NDPC), a large organization formed following the merger of Hydrox Corporation of Chicago and Rieck-McJunkin Dairy Company of Pittsburgh. Among the many other products marketed by the NDPC were Breakstone's cottage cheese and Sealtest ice cream. The organization quickly expanded the distribution of Breyers ice cream throughout the northeast and mid-Atlantic states. It remained a regional brand until 1970, when the NDPC, which in 1969 changed its name to the Kraftco Corporation to reflect its international scope and broader product line, introduced Breyers ice cream to selected southeastern markets, including Georgia and Florida. Then, in 1984, the product was launched in Kansas City, Missouri, marking its official arrival west of the Mississippi River. The following year it appeared on supermarket shelves in Iowa, Oklahoma, Nebraska, Western Kansas, the Pacific Northwest, and Northern California. Until 1987,

when a Knudsen ice cream plant owned by the Kraft Dairy Division added Breyers to its production line, all western markets were supplied with ice cream manufactured at the company's plant in Memphis, Tennessee.

Brand Development

Although the Breyer Ice Cream Company founded its business on traditional vanilla ice cream with real vanilla bean specks, other flavors, such as chocolate, strawberry, coffee, and butter pecan, were quickly added to the product line. Over the years, flavors have come and gone according to changes in consumer tastes. In October of 1976 Kraftco Corporation, a holding company consisting of a string of semi-autonomous divisions, became Kraft, Inc. The following year, Kraft expanded the Breyers product line, launching Breyers all-natural (non-frozen) yogurt on a national level.

During the 1980s a growing emphasis on healthy, low-fat foods on the part of American consumers prompted frozen dessert manufacturers to introduce a wide variety of low-calorie and fat-free products, such as ice milk, light ice cream, and frozen yogurt. According to the Food Marketing Institute's 1990 consumer survey, between 1989 and 1990 alone, grocery store frozen dessert sales increased 8.7 percent due to the popularity of low-fat and fat-free entries, such as ice milk and frozen yogurt. Although ice cream continued to lead the field, reduced-fat alternatives helped to bring back health-conscious consumers who had abandoned dairy desserts in the 1970s and 80s. Breyers light ice milk, containing one-third less butterfat than ice cream, was introduced in 1988, followed by Breyers frozen yogurt in 1990. The company launched a line of frozen snacks or novelties in 1992. Breyers ice cream was originally packaged in small pint and half-pint containers. During the 1920s, quart-size packages were introduced. Half-gallon containers appeared in the 1950s.

Innovations in Marketing and Advertising

In preparation for the entry of Breyers ice cream into the large and potentially lucrative western market in the mid-1980s, Kraft, Inc., turned to the New York marketing firm of Gerstman and Meyers, Inc., to design a new, eye-catching package that, according to Skip Wollenberg in the *Washington Post,* would be "good enough to eat." Breyers, he wrote, "had long been a leader in premium ice cream in the Northeast, but its packaging was drawing so many imitators that the design was melting into the crowd in the frozen dessert case." The new design took the traditional color photograph of a tempting scoop of ice cream and superimposed it against a bold, black background, replacing the familiar white package that many private-label manufacturers had imitated. The green briar leaf trademark was moved from the upper left-hand corner of the package to the lower right, and the Breyers name was emblazoned across the top to help distinguish it from other brands. (During 1991, the year Breyers ice cream celebrated its 125th anniversary, a special red anniversary ribbon was added.) Breyers frozen yogurt appears in a royal blue package, while ice milk comes in a gradated black container.

Despite the product's bold, new look, Southern California proved a difficult battleground. As soon as the product arrived on supermarket shelves, it faced a powerful adversary in the form of Dreyer's Grand ice cream, the West Coast's leading premium brand. (According to the International Ice Cream Association, the term "premium" was once used to describe ice creams with a higher level of butterfat than so-called "regular" brands, but now refers only to higher priced products. Breyers and Dreyer's are both considered premium ice creams, while the newer "gourmet" entries, such as Häagen-Dazs and Ben and Jerry's, are referred to as "superpremium" ice creams.) In 1986 the Oakland-based Dreyer's (marketed as Edy's in the East) claimed 15 percent of all ice cream sales in Southern California. In an effort to capture consumers and overcome the confusion stemming from the similarity of the two brand names, Breyers launched a statewide TV advertising campaign emphasizing the product's attributes. According to Denise Gellene in the *Los Angeles Times,* one commercial went so far as to picture a carton of Breyers ice cream alongside a Dreyer's carton—a tactic which, according to former Breyers marketing executive Scott Wallace, was intended to "help show the difference." Although Dreyer's objected, claiming the commercial suggested that Dreyer's was not all natural, Breyers maintained that the ad merely pointed out that Dreyer's, unlike Breyers, contained ingredients such as corn syrup and food dyes. "We suggested that consumers read the labels," Wallace told Gellene in the *Los Angeles Times.* "It's not something they would ordinarily do." Spokesmen for Dreyer's claimed, according to Gellene, that during the first few months of the campaign, the Breyers ads actually helped increase sales of Dreyer's, as confused shoppers purchased what they mistakenly thought was Breyers.

Since 1866, the leading marketing strategy of Breyers ice cream has been its famous "Pledge of Purity." The brand's key advertising slogans, "The all-natural ice cream" and "All natural since 1866," have appeared on packages and in newspaper, TV, and radio ads for decades. During the mid-1980s, earnest TV spokesman Fred Newman urged viewers to "read the label" and understand what the brand contained versus what it did not. Breyers mint chocolate chip ice cream, for example, is white, not green, he pointed out, adding that some brands use green coloring because people think mint should be green. The campaign's tag line was that Breyers offered "nothing but real enjoyment." In the early 1990s actress Bernadette Peters described Breyers products as "so real you can taste it." Although many brands claim to contain only natural ingredients, stabilizers and emulsifiers, such as carrageenan, are often overlooked. According to company marketing managers, Breyers has a stricter definition of "all-natural" than other ice creams.

Over the years, Breyers ice cream has benefitted from a considerable amount of informal, if high-profile, publicity. In the early 1960s, for example, First Lady Jacqueline Kennedy made news by specifically requesting Breyers pistachio ice cream for a White House party. Although the flavor was not in season at the time, Breyers opened a special production line to supply it. Then, in 1991, in an effort it described as "Operation Dessert Storm," Breyers arranged to have 180 gallons of mint chocolate chip ice cream shipped to General Norman Schwarzkopf and his troops in the Saudi Arabian desert, having learned from an interview in *People* magazine that the General counted it among his favorite things (the company deliberately did not promote this shipment to the public). Breyers ice cream gained additional followers in the

early 1990s when it became affiliated with San Francisco's Pier 39 tourist attraction and with the Dallas Cowboys football team.

Performance Appraisal

During the early 1980s, a variety of new, superpremium ice creams captured the palates of many prosperous and discriminating consumers eager for rich, exotic flavor regardless of butterfat content or chemical additives. By the end of the decade, however, there were signs that all-natural, less-expensive premium brands, such as Breyers, were coming back into fashion even among more privileged consumers. "Yuppies are scooping up 60 percent less Häagen-Dazs than they were in 1985," wrote Faye Rice in *Fortune.* "Now they're into Breyers, which is cheaper ($1.69 a pint vs. $2.19 for Häagen-Dazs) and lower in calories (160 per four-ounce serving vs. Häagen-Daz's 270)." In 1992 total sales of Breyers ice cream were estimated at $341 million. Its significant share of the category made it the undisputed leader in the $9.5 billion U.S. frozen dessert market. The category includes superpremium products as well as low-fats, non-fats, ice milks, and frozen yogurts. In 1989, following the purchase of Kraft, Inc., by Philip Morris Companies, Inc., and the merger of Kraft with Philip Morris subsidiary General Foods Corporation, Breyers became a registered trademark of Kraft General Foods, Inc. In 1993 Kraft sold Breyers and its entire line of ice cream to Unilever.

Further Reading:

The American Way: A History of Breyers Ice Cream, Morton Grove, IL: Kraft General Foods Archives Department, 1956.

Breyers Calling: A Century of Fine Ice Cream, Morton Grove, IL: Kraft General Foods Archives Department, 1966.

A Brief History of Kraft General Foods, Northfield, IL: Kraft General Foods, 1992.

Dairy Foods, August 1991, p. 51.

DeNitto, Emily, "Unilever's Big Scoop Heats Ice Cream Market," *Advertising Age,* September 13, 1993, p. 3.

Gellene, Denise, "Battle Over Shelf Space Heating Up for Makers of Premium Ice Cream," *Los Angeles Times,* April 28, 1986, business section, part 4, p. 1.

Gellene, Denise, "Breyers' Attempt to Scoop Dreyer's Breeds Confusion," *Los Angeles Times,* June 19, 1986, business section, part 4, p. 1.

The History of Breyers Ice Cream, Northfield, IL: Kraft General Foods, June 1991.

History of Kraft General Foods—Timeline, Morton Grove, IL: Kraft General Foods Archives Department, January 1993.

The Latest Scoop, International Ice Cream Association, 1992.

"Low-Fat Frozen Desserts: Better for You Than Ice Cream?," *Consumer Reports,* August 1992, p. 483.

Peterson, Jonathan and Nancy Rivera Brooks, "Philip Morris Offering $11.8 Billion for Kraft," *Los Angeles Times,* October 18, 1988, part 1, p. 1.

Rice, Faye, "Yuppie Spending Gets Serious," *Fortune,* March 27, 1989, p. 149.

Wollenberg, Skip, "Food Marketers Find Packaging a Key to Success," *Washington Post,* April 5, 1987. p. H7.

—Caroline Smith

BUDWEISER®

The Budweiser brand is the top selling beer worldwide. In the United States, nearly 25 percent of all beers sold carry the Budweiser logo. The Budweiser family of beers—Budweiser, Bud Light, and Bud Dry—account for about a third of U.S. beer sales. Initially introduced in 1876, Budweiser became the first successful national beer brand. For over a century, Budweiser has been brewed with the same traditional process and concentration on quality. Although the times and marketplace have changed dramatically since Budweiser's initial introduction, Budweiser has continued to adapt with effective advertising and marketing, making Budweiser the world's "King of Beers" for more than 35 years.

Brand Origins

In 1852 George Schneider opened the Bavarian Brewery in south St. Louis, Missouri. Within five years his business failed and was purchased by a group of local businessmen who launched a major expansion financed by a loan from Eberhard Anheuser, a prosperous soap manufacturer. By 1860, however, the brewery had failed again. Anheuser, to protect his investment, bought out the other creditors and became a reluctant brewery owner. He renamed the business the Anheuser & Co. Bavarian Brewery.

The brewery was only marginally successful until Anheuser's son-in-law, Adolphus Busch, agreed to join the firm. In 1864 Busch began work as a salesman for the brewery while maintaining his own wholesale supply business. By 1869 Busch had decided to concentrate on the brewery business, selling his interest in the wholesale company and becoming a full partner in E. Anheuser & Co.

As a partner, Busch became increasingly responsible for the operation of the brewery. Unschooled in the brewing trade at that point, Busch undertook a series of trips to Europe to learn the art of brewing and examine what European brewers were doing. Having honed his knowledge of the industry, he slowly began to turn E. Anheuser & Co. from a nondescript local brewery into an industry leader. Through a combination of shrewd, showy marketing techniques and the introduction of pioneering technological innovations, he increased production within ten years from 6000 barrels to more than 38,000.

Busch sought to make the brewery the first in America with a national presence, its product recognized and acknowledged from

coast to coast. In 1870, collaborating with his good friend Carl Conrad, Adolphus created a new beer brand—Budweiser. This product would become the country's first national beer. The smooth, light, naturally carbonated beer was created from a process that included a step known as kraeusening, meaning that it was fermented twice.

Early Marketing Strategy

After its introduction in 1876, Budweiser soon received many honors in Europe and the U.S. at various world fairs. The great success of the beer was not strictly attributable to its taste, however. Budweiser was pasteurized, a new process at the time, which allowed Budweiser to be shipped long distances without losing its flavor. Busch invested in a fleet of refrigerated railroad cars, a first in the beer industry, and began to market the beer nationally.

Busch once again relied on his salesmanship and personally promoted the beer in city after city. His flair for personally selling his beer, as well as his ability to devise effective national promotions, led to Budweiser's success as America's first national beer brand. Propelled by Budweiser's sales, the brewery's production by 1888 exceeded half-a-million barrels.

Brewing Quality

Budweiser has been brewed in the same manner for over a century. Anheuser-Busch Companies, Inc. believes that the quality of its beers is the most important benefit the company offers consumers and the key reason for Budweiser's success. Anheuser-Busch's brewing quality laboratory, the first one used by a U.S. brewer, ensures the quality of its products. In addition, August A. Busch III, chairman of the board and president of Anheuser-Busch, personally oversees daily output from the company's 13 breweries.

Budweiser contains more barley malt than any major competitor. A much higher percentage of the premium two-row barley malt is used in brewing Budweiser, giving the beer its smoother taste. In addition, during the secondary fermentation process, Anheuser Busch adds a feature not utilized by any of the world's major brewers, the beechwood aging process. Despite the substantial added cost of the traditional beechwood aging, Anheuser-Busch believes it gives its beers a superior taste.

AT A GLANCE

Budweiser brand of beer founded in 1876 in St. Louis, MO; initially brewed by E. Anheuser Co.'s Brewing Association; brand developed by Adolphus Busch and Carl Conrad; company name changed to Anheuser-Busch Brewing Association in 1879, Anheuser-Busch, Inc. in 1919, and Anheuser-Busch Companies, Inc., in 1979; Budweiser Light introduced in 1982, with name change to Bud Light in 1984; Bud Dry introduced in 1990.

Performance: *Market share*—(Budweiser) 24.1% of U.S. market (top brand share); (Bud Light) 7.1% of U.S. market; (Bud Dry) 1.4% of U.S. market.

Major competitor: Miller Brewing Co.'s brands of beer; also Stroh Brewing Co. and Coors Brewing Co.'s brands of beer.

Advertising: *Agency (for Budweiser)*—D'Arcy Masius Benton & Bowles, St. Louis, MO, 1915—. *Major campaign (for Budweiser)*—"Proud to Be Your Bud." *Agency (for Bud Light)*—DDB Needham, Chicago, IL, 1982—. *Major campaign (for Bud Light)*—"Make it a Bud Light." *Agency (for Bud Dry)*—DDB Needham, Chicago, IL, 1990—. *Major campaign (for Bud Dry)*—"Why Ask Why—Try Bud Dry."

Addresses: *Parent company*—Anheuser-Busch, Inc., 1 Busch Place, St. Louis, MO 63118-1852; phone: (314) 577-2000. *Ultimate parent company*—Anheuser-Busch Companies, Inc., 1 Busch Place, St. Louis, MO 63118-1852; phone: (314) 577-2000.

The brewing differences between Budweiser, Bud Light, and Bud Dry are primarily in the added grains. Budweiser uses rice, while Bud Light and Bud Dry contain selected grains. In addition, Budweiser and Bud Light are both kraeusened, but Bud Dry is brewed with a special dry brew process and cold-filtered packaged draft technology.

Notable Advertising

"This Bud's For You" remains one of Budweiser's most memorable advertising slogans. The campaign began in 1979 and came to symbolize life in America so effectively that a display highlights it at the Smithsonian Institution. This slogan was eventually replaced by "Nothing Beats a Bud" and, most recently, the "Proud to be your Bud" slogan.

The Bud Bowl advertising campaign, aired with the Super Bowl broadcast since 1989, has ranked among the most recalled ads featured during the game. The ad parodies the on-going game with helmeted bottles of Bud family beers competing in their own animated football game. Exceptionally strong January sales each year have been attributed to this advertising campaign.

To support Budweiser's light beer name change in 1984 from Budweiser Light to Bud Light, the "Gimme A Light" campaign was launched. Featuring unexpected light sources, such as train headlights and flaming hoops, the ads served to remind consumers to ask for their light beer by name—Bud Light. The campaign helped the brand's sales expand at four times the rate of the overall light beer category.

Spuds McKenzie, a dog featured in a series of commercials, served as Bud Light's memorable "party animal." In 1987, the year the campaign was nationally advertised, Bud Light posted a 20 percent sales increase. But the marked success of the campaign

grew criticism for attracting under-age drinkers to the brand. In 1988 Spuds began making appearances in Anheuser-Busch's "Know When to Say When" drinking moderation program.

Bud Dry was launched in 1990 with the "Why Ask Why? Try Bud Dry" campaign. The campaign was selected as the best of the year by the American Bartender's Association, and helped Bud Dry achieve phenomenal sales success in its first year of introduction.

Notable Marketing Efforts

One of Budweiser's most widely recognized symbols is the famous Budweiser Clydesdale team. The original Clydesdale team was presented to August A. Busch, Sr., to celebrate the end of Prohibition in 1933. To thank Al Smith, the former governor of New York, for his persistent work in opposing Prohibition and seeking its repeal, Busch sent the Clydesdale team and two cases of beer to New York on April 7, 1933. The Budweiser Clydesdales high-stepped their way up Fifth Avenue to the Empire State Building, attracting a crowd elated with the anticipation of the repeal of Prohibition. There, with thousands looking on, Governor Smith was presented with two cases of Budweiser. The publicity surrounding the event made the Budweiser Clydesdale team famous and created a continual stream of requests for their appearance. Three teams of horses are now used. They travel approximately 90,000 miles across the country every year, creating goodwill and promoting the Budweiser brand.

To effectively market Budweiser to its targeted consumer base, defined as all adult beer drinkers, Anheuser-Busch invests heavily in sports promotions and sponsorships. The Budweiser brand sponsors the Miss Budweiser hydroplane, the Budweiser King Indy car, the Budweiser King Top Fuel Dragster, and the Budweiser/Junior Johnson Ford NASCAR car. The Bud Light brand sponsors the Bud Light Powerboat racing team. In addition to specific cars and boats, the Budweiser brands sponsor many sporting tournaments and events, including skiing, bowling, horse racing, pool, darts, trap and skeet shooting, triathlons, surfing, volleyball, and water-skiing.

Brand Expansion

In the late 1970s and early 1980s, Anheuser-Busch watched Miller Lite quickly account for the top share of the light beer market—at the time the only growing segment of the industry. Although Anheuser-Busch had launched two light beers to compete with Miller Lite, Miller remained on top. In an effort to capitalize on the success of Budweiser, Anheuser-Busch launched Budweiser Light (later renamed Bud Light) in May of 1982 after 13 months of test marketing. As a product line extension of the popular Budweiser brand, Bud Light quickly climbed in market share. As of 1992 Bud Light was the third-largest selling brand in the industry.

Anheuser-Busch was determined not to be relegated to a follower position as the next beer trend appeared. Dry beer was created in Japan to offer consumers an alternative to the traditional "sweet" beer taste. Anheuser-Busch envisioned the primary benefits of this new product to the U.S. market to be the lack of an aftertaste, as well as the slightly lower calorie content compared with a traditional beer. As Anheuser-Busch's first premium-priced dry beer, Bud Dry was nationally rolled out in April 1990. The product is unique in that it is the only cold-filtered dry beer. The beer's packaging was designed to be as unique as its taste, and featured the first vertical label in the beer industry.

Although the Budweiser flagship brand has suffered from some degree of sales cannibalization with each of these product introductions, the expanded Budweiser family benefited from accumulated sales growth. Further expansion of the Budweiser family, however, would pose greater risks, notes Robert Weinberg, an industry consultant. In *Financial World* he was quoted, "You don't want the message to change from 'This Bud's For You' to 'Which Bud's for you?'"

The Competition

The top five selling beers in 1992 were Budweiser (24.1 percent market share), Miller Lite (9.7), Bud Light (7.1), Coors Light (6.7), and Busch (5.2). Budweiser's closest rival, Miller Lite, represented less than half the king's market share, and as of 1992 was losing share to Budweiser's closest family member, Bud Light. Bud Light's ability to gain market share at the expense of Miller Lite and at a greater rate than Coors Light reflects the continued strength of the Budweiser brand family.

International Market

In 1981 Anheuser-Busch established an international licensing and marketing subsidiary in order to effectively expand sales in the global market. Through the support of this organization, Budweiser has become not only the number one selling beer in the United States, but the world as well. The brand is brewed in Japan, South Korea, Ireland, Canada, and the United Kingdom through licensing or contract agreements, and exported to more than 60 other countries. 1992 marked the seventh consecutive year of double-digit growth for Anheuser-Busch's international division, and 1993 has thus far been marked by new business alliances with Kirin in Japan, Modelo in Mexico, and Peroni in Italy.

Performance

Budweiser has reigned as the world's top-selling beer brand for more than 35 years, although some years during that time have been rougher than others. While the industry volume as a whole has increased three percent from 1987 to 1992, Budweiser has lost about five percent. A 3.1 percent volume drop was experienced between 1991 and 1992. Anheuser-Busch cites the 1991 federal excise tax increase and recessionary pressures as the short-term influences on Budweiser's volume decline. As the economic picture brightens, Anheuser-Busch expects Budweiser, along with its other premium priced brands, to bounce back. Meanwhile, Anheuser-Busch is aggressively pursuing marketing as the manner in which to stem further decline, pumping the ad budget for all of its premium beers. Industry analyst Robert Weinberg noted in *Forbes* that he was unaware of a declining brand regaining market share without lowering its price. Anheuser-Busch is also protecting share with sales discounts, but this method is very expensive. The proliferation of brands in the market may have cost Budweiser some of its "premium" image. Not only has the Budweiser family expanded, but Anheuser-Busch's beer offerings have grown from five brands in 1980 to 16 in 1992. By finely segmenting the market and targeting specific consumer groups with particular brands, it has become more difficult for one beer, "Budweiser," to appeal to everyone.

Budweiser's best protection may come from its distribution chain, the strongest in the industry. Currently, a network of ap-

proximately 900 independently owned and operated wholesalers distribute Anheuser-Busch's products. Anheuser-Busch closely attends to its distributors and has built a loyal relationship with the network. The vast majority of Anheuser-Busch distributors will only handle Anheuser-Busch's products, making it very difficult for lesser competitors to make inroads into the company's sales ground.

Market Trends

Beer consumption in the United States could, at best, be expected to grow at a rate of 0.5 percent, according to First Boston analyst Martin Romm, quoted in *Financial World*. This stagnant growth rate was expected due to several legal and demographic changes. On the legal front, tougher drunk driving law enforcement, a 21-year-old legal drinking age, and increased excise taxes have all contributed to flattening consumption patterns. In addition, the aging population and resulting increase in interest in health issues has reduced overall alcohol consumption. By the early 1990s, light beer accounted for almost one-third of beer consumption. Non-alcohol and light beers are expected to be the high growth categories for the beer industry.

Future Opportunities

Budweiser is the primary brand of beer Anheuser-Busch markets internationally. Although the brand has achieved great success as the top selling beer in the world, the focus for expanding the brand's sales remains on the international front. The worldwide market is seen as the major opportunity for growth within the next 10 to 20 years. As of 1992, most of Budweiser's international sales were through licensee agreements, where Anheuser-Busch has little direct control over the marketing and distribution efforts for the brand. In an effort to recapture that important element of control to truly conquer international markets, Anheuser-Busch formed a subsidiary specifically to develop the market in Europe. The United Kingdom was the first major European market for which the subsidiary assumed direct control of the brand's marketing and distribution. In 1993 the company announced the formation of a joint venture sales and marketing company, 90-percent owned by Anheuser-Busch and intended to provide the company with total sales and marketing control in one of its largest markets. David Goldman, an industry analyst, pointed out in *Financial World* another rich source of international growth—Central and South America, where youthful markets, increasing beer consumption, and a particularly weak competitive environment could be a boon for Budweiser and other Anheuser-Busch brands.

Further Reading:

"Anheuser-Busch Achieves Record First Quarter Sales and Earnings," *P.R. Newswire,* April 22, 1992.

"Anheuser-Busch Boosts Share of Beer Market," *Reuter Business Report,* January 19, 1993.

Anheuser-Busch Companies Fact Book, St. Louis: Anheuser-Busch Companies, 1992-1993.

Anheuser-Busch Companies, Inc., Annual Report, St. Louis: Anheuser-Busch Companies, 1991.

Beckett, Jamie, "Winning at Advertising—Knowing When to Say When," *San Francisco Chronicle,* March 23, 1992, p. B3.

"Brand Scorecard," *Advertising Age,* July 20, 1992, p. 20.

"Bud Dry Arrives," *Food and Beverage Marketing,* May, 1990, p. 98.

Fucini, Joseph J., and Suzy Fucini, *Entrepreneurs: The Men and Women Behind Famous Brand Names and How They Made It,* Boston: G. K. Hall & Co., 1985, pp. 19-22.

Gershman, Michael, *Getting It Right the Second Time,* Reading, PA: Addison-Wesley, 1990, pp. 207-210.

The History of Anheuser-Busch Companies—A Fact Sheet, St. Louis: Anheuser Busch Companies, 1991.

Morris, Kathleen, "The Dog Days of August," *Financial World,* January 5, 1993, p. 32.

Norman, James R., "Beer Barrel Blues," *Forbes,* June 22, 1992, p. 98.

Palmer, Thomas, "Is This 'Dry' for You?" *Boston Globe,* April 16, 1990, p. 57.

"Send in the Sales Force," *Sales and Marketing Management,* March 14, 1983, p. 56.

Teinowita, Ira, "A-B Turns Up Heat Under U.K. Marketing," *Advertising Age,* July 20, 1992, p. 38.

Teinowita, "A-B Gains in Beer Share, Thanks to Hot Bud Light," *Advertising Age,* January 4, 1993, p. 2.

—Louise L. Groden

BUSCH®

Busch Beer is the top-selling beer brand in the popular-priced segment and ranks fifth in overall beer market share. By offering the market a quality beer at a relatively low price, Anheuser-Busch Companies, Inc. has secured a leadership position in the popular-priced market segment. The success of the brand prompted the launch of a light version of the original Busch in 1989. Together the Busch beers account for roughly seven percent of total beer sales.

For more than 35 years Anheuser-Busch has been the industry leader. The strength of its marketing and distribution systems, and its commitment to quality, has led to powerful market positions for all of the company's beer products. As of 1992, sales of Anheuser-Busch beers constituted 45 percent of the total market volume. The Anheuser-Busch beer brand family also includes Budweiser, Bud Light, Michelob, Natural Light, King Cobra, Carlsberg, Elephant Malt Liquor, and O'Doul's.

Brand Origins

Adolphus Busch was born in 1839 as the second youngest of 22 children. His father, a prosperous German businessman, owned a wholesale supply company that afforded Adolphus Busch valuable insight into business methods and allowed him to be educated in some of Europe's finest schools. Busch pursued his own success and immigrated from Germany to the United States at the age of 18. Within two years, with the help of an inheritance, he started his own wholesale brewery supply company in St. Louis. Through his business dealings, he met Eberhard Anheuser, the owner of a struggling local brewery. In 1861 Busch married Anheuser's daughter, Lilly. Anheuser encouraged Busch to become involved in the management of his brewery, then named E. Anheuser & Co. In 1864 Busch began working at the brewery and for a while continued to manage his own wholesale business as well. In 1869 Busch sold his wholesale business and successfully concentrated his efforts on improving the fortunes of his father-in-law's brewery. Busch's salesmanship and marketing ability proved superior. Within ten years of Busch joining the brewery, sales volume more than tripled.

The tremendous turnaround had been accomplished without any substantial changes to the product, however, and Busch realized further growth of the business couldn't be accomplished without improving the beer. Busch embarked on an extensive study of European brewing techniques, and joined efforts with his friend Carl Conrad to develop a unique premium beer. Their efforts resulted in the Budweiser beer, introduced in 1876. As the first nationally distributed beer, it ultimately rose to become the world's "King of Beer." In 1896 Busch introduced Michelob as a "connoisseur's" beer, available only on draft at finer hotels, restaurants, and taverns. By 1901, these successful product introductions had spurred the brewery's growth to more than one million barrels of annual production.

Busch's efforts did not go unrewarded. In 1879, the company was renamed Anheuser-Busch Brewing Association, and upon the death of Anheuser, Busch became president of the company in 1880. By the time of his own death in 1913, he had become one of the richest men in the country. Although not the original owner of the firm, Busch is recognized as the patriarch of Anheuser-Busch. In 1955, when the company sought to further expand its product offering, the brand name honored the person responsible for Anheuser-Busch's success—"Busch."

Busch beer was introduced in 1955 and became Anheuser-Busch's first entrant into the popular priced market segment. Initially, the brand was not made available nationally; it instead began as a regional beer in the Midwest and slowly expanded its geographic distribution. As of 1993, the brand was available in 46 states and Washington, D.C.

Brewing Quality

Anheuser-Busch has maintained a commitment to quality brewing for more than a century, and its popularly-priced Busch family of beers is no exception. Busch is brewed using only quality natural ingredients. Busch and Busch Light use corn as a beer adjunct to give the brews their milder and characteristic tastes. The Busch beers differ from the competition because they are fermented using a beechwood aging process—a process not utilized by any other major brewer in the world. The added cost of this process has not swayed Anheuser-Busch to forgo it even in this lower priced market segment. Anheuser-Busch claims the added quality and taste afforded by beechwood aging gives its beers a distinct competitive advantage. To ensure consistent taste and quality, Busch beers are rigorously monitored through Anheuser-Busch's quality control program, which the company touts as the toughest in the industry.

AT A GLANCE

Busch brand of beer founded in 1955 in St. Louis, Missouri, by Anheuser-Busch Inc.; company name changed to Anheuser-Busch Companies, Inc., in 1979; Busch Light introduced in 1989.

Performance: *Market Share*—(Busch) 5.4% of U.S. market; (Busch Light) 2.5% of U.S. market.

Major competitor: Miller Brewing Co.'s brands of beer; also Stroh Brewing Co. and Coors Brewing Co.'s brands of beer.

Advertising: *Agency*—DDB Needham, Chicago, IL, 1977— (Busch), 1989— (Busch Light). *Major campaign*—"Mountain Man" (for Busch and Busch Light); "Head for the Mountains" (for Busch only).

Addresses: *Parent company*—Anheuser-Busch, Inc., 1 Busch Place, St. Louis, MO 63118-1852; phone: (314) 577-2000. *Ultimate parent company*—Anheuser-Busch Companies, Inc., 1 Busch Place, St. Louis, MO 63118-1852; phone (314) 577-2000.

Notable Advertising

Anheuser-Busch introduced the brand's successful "Head for the Mountains" campaign in 1979. The campaign was sparked by Anheuser-Busch's president and chairman of the board, August A. Busch III. He believed the allure of the American cowboy best reflected the values he wanted projected on the Busch brand. The tremendous success of the ad campaign has led to numerous variations on the western theme for Busch beer over the years.

The "mountain man" campaign, introduced in 1991, was the first advertising effort that supported both Busch and Busch Light beers. This campaign delivered a more contemporary message in an effort to appeal to the younger light beer consumer.

Anheuser-Busch defines the target market for the Busch brand as males, as that audience segment consumes 75 percent of all beer sold. Its not surprising, then, that Anheuser-Busch utilizes sports as a means to reach its target audience. Busch regularly sponsors the broadcasts of professional and collegiate sports events. In addition, the brand directly sponsors two sporting events. Busch is the official beer of the National Association of Stock Car Auto Racing (NASCAR) circuit and frequently offers promotions related to NASCAR events. Busch also sponsors the Busch World Cup Tour, a five-city jet-ski tour.

Brand Expansion

Busch Light was among the fastest-growing major brands in 1992. Introduced in May 1989 as a response to Miller's successful introduction of packaged draft beer, Busch Light was Anheuser-Busch's first packaged draft beer. Previously, Anheuser-Busch had been vocal about its opposition to packaged drafts, but Anheuser-Busch feared leaving Miller unchallenged given its evolving success with packaged draft beer products. Miller had succeeded in promoting its first cold-filtered draft product, Miller Genuine Draft. Introduced in 1986, it had risen to a 3.6 percent share by 1992. Miller was testing Lite Genuine Draft in 1989, and another successful Miller entry could have cornered the draft market segment. History had taught Anheuser-Busch that leaving Miller unchallenged could cost precious market share.

Miller had successfully introduced the first light beer in 1974. Anheuser-Busch waited until 1984 to enter the light beer arena. As of 1992, Miller Lite had retained the top light beer market share. Although both Miller products remain successful, Busch Light quickly gained market share as a popularly priced alternative. Busch Light is brewed utilizing cold-filtering brewing technology that results in a taste that is lighter and brisker than Busch. As of 1992, Busch Light was ranked as the number two popular-priced light beer, behind Anheuser-Busch's Natural Light brand, and the fifth ranked beer in the overall light beer category. As a packaged draft, it ranked second only to Miller Genuine Draft.

Performance

At a time of stagnant growth for the beer industry, Busch has outpaced the market. While the industry volume has increased less than three percent from 1987 to 1992, the Busch brand has grown more than 20 percent. Busch Light has also experienced a consistent rise since its introduction. From 1990, the first year Busch Light was marketed to all areas selling the original Busch beer, to 1992, its sales volume has increased more than 80 percent, ranking it as the 11th best-selling beer overall.

The popular-priced segment accounts for approximately 17 percent of U.S. beer sales. The strength of the popular-priced category has been linked with recessionary pressures and beer price increases fueled by the doubling of the federal excise tax enacted in 1991. Because of trends in this price segment, having a strong entrant is important. The current strong position of the Busch brand is expected to continue to give Anheuser-Busch the flexibility to respond to changes in the economic environment while maintaining a strong market presence.

The popular-priced market segment leader is the Busch family of beers at 6.9 percent of the overall beer market. Its closest competitors include Miller Brewing Company's Milwaukee's Best brand, Stroh Brewing Company's Old Milwaukee product, and Coors Brewing Co., with its Keystone brands.

Market Trends

Overall beer consumption in the United States is predicted to remain flat, with anticipated growth at less than one percent in the long-term, according to market analyst Emmanual Goldman, quoted in *Beverage World*. Several demographic and legal factors have influenced this trend. The 21-year-old drinking age, continued tougher drunk driving laws, and the doubling of the federal excise tax have all worked to limit beer sales and flatten the market. Demographically, the aging of the U.S. population and the associated increased emphasis on health concerns, coupled with a renewed trend toward moderation, has worked to further reduce alcohol consumption.

The lower alcohol content of beer presented the beer industry with some product development opportunities. Light beer and non-alcohol beer have been the fastest growing beer product categories. Since Miller Lite's introduction in 1974, light beers have constituted the industry's most dramatic area of growth, amounting to one third of the industry's sales by 1992. By 1992, Anheuser-Busch, with successful entrants at every price point, had achieved a 40 percent share of the light beer market. Non-alcohol beers have not yet evolved into a significant share of the overall market, but major increases are expected as higher percentages of beer drinkers enter the 35-year-old and up market segment, commonly regarded as the customer base most receptive to non-alcohol beer entries.

As competitors have reacted to the changing consumption trends and pursued opportunities for share growth, more product introductions with less extensive market testing have appeared. Expecting consumers to be more apt to try extensions of brands they are already familiar with, most of these product introductions since the 1980s have been extensions of existing brands. The risk, however, with the introduction of too many brand extensions is that consumers become more willing to switch products, resulting in diminished brand loyalty. Cannibalization of the main brand is another concern. If only current brand users begin to use the extension, then the brewer hasn't gained in overall market share and the extension hasn't been a worthwhile effort. Despite analysts' concerns, this hasn't been a problem for the Busch beers. The two products together have benefited from combined sales growth.

Future Opportunities and Predictions

Since the domestic market is expected to remain flat, international expansion is expected to be the major growth opportunity in the next 10 to 20 years. As of 1992 the Busch brand was only marketed in the United States and Canada; however, Anheuser-Busch has pursued the international market with its top selling Budweiser brand since 1981. As of 1992, Anheuser-Busch had acquired slightly more than 10 percent of the world's beer market. As Anheuser-Busch increases its international presence, it may seek to market Busch overseas.

Whether or not Busch remains a domestic brand, it will surely continue to be an important member in Anheuser-Busch's beer brand family. The tremendous success of the brand has increased Anheuser-Busch's market share and reach. With the strength of the Anheuser-Busch organization behind it and the market presence it has already achieved, the Busch brand has a solid foundation for continuing market prominence and product evolution.

Further Reading:

Anheuser-Busch Companies Fact Book, St. Louis: Anheuser-Busch Companies, 1992-1993.

"Anheuser-Busch Inc. Introduces Busch Light in Florida," *Business Wire,* January 17, 1990.

Anheuser-Busch Marketing Fact Sheet, St. Louis: Anheuser-Busch Companies, June 1992.

Barrett, Jean T., "Cold Gold," *Marketing & Media Decisions,* March, 1990, p. 62.

"Brand Scorecard," *Advertising Age,* July 20, 1992, p. 20.

Busch Media Information Package, St. Louis: Fleishman-Hillard, Inc., 1992-1993.

Fisher, Lawrence M., "All About Beer," *New York Times,* July 21, 1991.

Fucini, Joseph J., and Suzy Fucini, *Entrepreneurs: The Men and Women Behind Famous Brand Names and How They Made It,* Boston: G.K. Hall & Co., 1985, pp. 19-22.

Gibson, Richard, "Anheuser-Busch to Buy 18% Stake in Mexican Brewer," *Wall Street Journal,* March 23, 1993, p. B3.

The History of Anheuser-Busch Companies—A Fact Sheet, St. Louis: Anheuser-Busch Companies, 1991.

Leib, Jeffery. "New Busch Beer Has Miller Hopping," *Denver Post,* March 21, 1990, p. C1.

"Light Beers Continue Growth in Brewing Industry," *Business Wire,* January 29, 1993.

Prince, Greg, "Questions Brewing," *Beverage World,* February, 1991, p. 34.

Ryan, Nancy, "Brewers Tap New Brands to Put Fizz into Flat Sales," *Chicago Tribune,* June 10, 1991, p. C1.

Sellers, Patricia, "How Busch Wins in a Doggy Market," *Fortune,* June 22, 1987, pp. 99-111.

Teinowitz, Ira, "A-B Gains in Beer Share, Thanks to Hot Bud Light," *Advertising Age,* January 4, 1993, p.2.

Teinowitz, "A-B Pours Another with Busch 'Draft,'" *Advertising Age,* April 17, 1989, p. 3.

Teinowitz, "A-B Turns Up Heat Under U.K. Marketing," *Advertising Age,* July 20, 1992, p. 38.

Teinowitz, "Busch Brands Pair Up in Ads," *Advertising Age,* February 4, 1991, p. 6.

Teinowitz, "Busch Warms Up to Draft," *Advertising Age,* September 19, 1988, p.3.

Teinowitz, "Coors Uncaps Popular-Price Keystone," *Advertising Age,* July 10, 1989, p. 1.

Teinowitz, "Michelob Enlists in Draft Battle," *Advertising Age,* April 1, 1991, p. 1.

Teinowitz, "Miller Will Go With Genuine Draft Light," *Advertising Age,* January 22, 1990, p. 51.

Teinowitz, "Premium Beers Fall Flat," *Advertising Age,* February 3, 1992, p. 4.

—Louise L. Groden

BUTTERBALL®

Butterball Turkey had a modest beginning in America's heartland. Swift & Company, an Illinois-based meat producer, began selling turkeys around 1900 under the brand name of Swift Premium. Throughout the first half of the twentieth century, turkey was marketed primarily as a commodity with little, if any, differentiation among brands, and the bird Swift sold during this period was a far cry from the tender, juicy poultry we know today. The dark meat, infused throughout with tough tendons, was difficult both to slice and to eat, and the white meat tended to become dry and chewy when baked. These characteristics also made it difficult to sell. During the 1953 holiday season, retailers were selling the birds at a two-cent-per-pound loss. That year, however, marked a transition in the turkey industry. In 1953, Swift began an aggressive pursuit of a new broad-breasted breed of turkey which promised an end to tough pin feathers and a greater proportion of tender white to tough dark meat. Through its company hatcheries, Swift began to research and breed turkeys with this genetic makeup.

Simultaneously, Swift realized several important advances in operating procedures. Company researchers found that it was possible to remove all pin feathers by increasing the temperature of the sterilizing bath, or "scald water." In addition, company researchers learned to produce brighter skin color through a process of rapid freezing, and they developed a process for removing all leg tendons. The result was a smooth, appealing-looking turkey which was easier to carve and, ultimately, to eat. Swift knew it must find a way to capitalize on these achievements. The company's plan was to create the industry's first consumer franchise through a new, differentiated brand of turkey. Using the classic marketing tools of advertising and promotion, Swift introduced the Butterball brand turkey in 1954.

The Butterball Name

First, company marketing executives wanted to find a name for their new product which would dramatize the difference between the Swift-marketed turkey and other commodity-level turkeys of the day. Defined in the dictionary as "a fat, chubby person," the word "butterball" suggested the plumpness, meatiness, and tenderness that Swift wanted to communicate. As a common expression of the 1950s, however, company officials were skeptical they could register and protect the term as a trademark. At the time, usage—rather than registration—was the most important factor in trademark rights, and Swift's strategy was to use the name Butterball for one or two years, then attempt to register it. As a safety precaution, the company used the words "Swift Premium" in combination with Butterball upon the new brand's introduction.

In 1954, Swift began a program of market research on the Butterball name. First appearing on store promotional materials as a "feeler," the Butterball name was gradually phased into packaging, and finally, into advertising. The initial television commercial ran on Arlene Francis's "Today Show." The television campaign was successful in its goal of generating interest among turkey consumers, but it also brought claims of trademark infringement. The first claim was from a Kansas City retail firm which had a Missouri registration and clear prior rights to the Butterball name. Eventually, Swift settled this case for $5,000 and allowed the small retail firm to market its poultry under the Butterball name in the Kansas City area provided it was preceded by the name "Klein's." It was never used.

The second claim was made by the inventor of the Jiffy Margarine Bag, a man who received a one-quarter-cent-per-pound royalty on nearly every pound of margarine sold in the United States at the time. With his recently-acquired margarine wealth, the man purchased an Ohio farm owned by Ida Walker. Mrs. Walker owned the trademark rights to the name Butterball for sandwiches, eggs, ice cream, cheese, and butter. In an attempt to prove evidence of usage, the inventor shipped an occasional box of Butterball-labeled poultry to a friend in New York who owned a restaurant. Swift negotiated a $1,000 per year licensing agreement with the inventor. As time went on, however, the inventor became increasingly demanding and unhappy with the licensing arrangements. Eventually, Swift purchased the rights to use the Butterball name on all poultry and poultry products.

Product Innovations

At Butterball turkey's inception in 1954, the most important differentiating factor was the product itself. During that year, Swift produced its turkeys in 36 factories. (Today, Butterball turkeys are processed in only four modern and highly efficient state-of-the-art plants.) Butterball turkeys endured a stringent production process, from the eggs in the incubators through the frozen turkeys in retail stores. Every step of the process was carefully studied and planned by poultry experts who paid careful attention to each detail. The entire turkey operation underwent a constant cycle of research, refinement, and production.

From the beginning, much of Swift's research has been consumer-driven. The company developed large-scale research projects to find out what customers and retailers wanted in turkey products. In response to the findings of those projects, Swift carefully engineered its turkey production to meet market demands. As a result, Butterball turkeys were able to carry a premium price successfully. In 1954, the leg tendons were removed from the drumsticks. No other turkey producer pulled leg tendons from turkeys destined for whole-bird sale, and today, this innovation is still a Butterball exclusive.

In 1955, Swift developed a new method of shaping its turkeys. First, a hand-cutter snipped the tail to form a loop, or bar strap, into which the turkey's legs were neatly tucked. Second, the wing tips were cracked and bent toward the breast. The overall result was a plumper-, rounder-, meatier-looking bird. This new shape gave birth to the term "butterballing" throughout the poultry industry. This new method of shaping the turkeys also led to other product improvements. The tail loop eliminated the need for skewers and/or trussing during baking. The bent wing tips no longer punctured the plastic outer packaging, and fewer tears in the protective bags meant less freezer burn.

AT A GLANCE

Butterball brand of turkey founded in 1954 in Downers Grove, IL, by Swift & Company; company merged with Eckrich to become Swift-Eckrich; later merged with competitor Armour to become Armour Swift-Eckrich, 1991.

Major competitor: Honeysuckle White brand turkey.

Advertising: *Agency*—Puskar Gibbon Chapin, Dallas, TX, 1992—.

Addresses: *Parent company*—Armour Swift-Eckrich, 2001 Butterfield Rd., Downers Grove, IL 60515; phone: (708) 512-1000.

Swift pioneered a process of liquid freezing in three plants in 1959. This method of freezing gave Butterball turkeys brighter skin color and led to more uniform freezing. By 1965, all Swift turkey plants were equipped with the liquid freeze.

Market research told Swift that consumers found the white breast meat to be dry. In response to these findings, Swift initiated an intense research project to develop a juicy, moist, and tender Butterball turkey. It took nearly ten years to develop a method for deep-basting the turkeys. During the holiday season of 1967, Swift began to test-market its Deep Basted Butterball turkey in the Tampa, Florida area. The product was an instant success. Although at the time Armour was distributing a self-basting turkey, Swift was the first company to market the product nationwide. By the holiday season of 1968, Deep Basted Butterball turkeys were available in all U.S. markets.

Originally, Swift introduced its basting material into the breast meat through the turkey's skin. This, however, gave rise to patent-infringement concerns, and Swift subsequently developed its own method of deep basting without puncturing the skin. Leaving the skin intact led to several other advances: the turkey was assured of browning evenly, and the basting material could not escape through holes in the skin during roasting. In 1985, Swift returned to its original method of injecting its turkeys through the skin. Technology, however, allowed the company to do this effectively by improved needle patterns and carefully planned placement and injections.

The basting material itself was a significant part of Butterball's strategic history. From the beginning, all Butterball turkeys were basted with an exclusive vegetable oil mixture. Swift developed the formula after extensive research. The final product enhanced the moistness and juiciness of the white meat and produced a much richer flavor than commonly-used water and broth solutions. Swift, like many other manufacturers, basted its turkeys to exactly 3 percent of each turkey's weight. Several producers basted to 5.5 percent; some did not baste at all. According to company experts, Swift's process yielded the optimal outcome. Anything less created an underbasted, dry bird; anything over 3 percent produced a greasy, overbasted bird.

Armour, once a Swift competitor, basted its turkeys with a creamy butter mixture. While this butter mixture sounded appealing, taste tests revealed that consumers preferred the taste of Butterball's vegetable oil mixture. Moreover, Armour's butter mixture was more expensive to manufacture. While Swift was selling its turkeys profitably at a price of 49 cents per pound,

Armour found it necessary to charge between 55 cents and 59 cents per pound to earn a profit.

Throughout the 1960s and early 1970s, it was clear that the Butterball turkey was superior, both in terms of popularity and technology, to its competition. In the early 1970s, Swift began to turn its attention to improving the convenience of its product. In 1972, a survey showed that consumers found it difficult to lift cooked turkeys from the roasting pans to the serving platters. That year, Swift introduced its Turkey Lifter. This simple concept catapulted Butterball's popularity among housewives. With the convenient lifter, a homemaker could simply use the two handy loops to move the turkey from its roasting pan. For the next twenty years, this lifter was a Butterball exclusive.

Next, Swift addressed the issue of giblets and necks. Like many other turkey manufacturers, Swift packaged the giblets and necks in paper bags and placed them in the body cavities of the frozen birds. Consumer research, however, indicated that these bags were messy and hard to handle. In response to this problem, Swift began using special plastic bags—one for the giblets and one for the neck—which could be removed before or after the turkey was defrosted. Furthermore, Swift printed convenient easy-to-follow cooking directions and carving illustrations on the giblet bags.

In 1975, Swift developed yet another Butterball exclusive. That year, the company created a comprehensive booklet outlining everything a cook needed to know about serving a Butterball turkey. The booklets were encased in plastic pouches and packaged with all Butterball turkeys. A homemaker could easily remove the pouch without thawing the turkey. The booklet told her everything she needed to know about thawing, roasting, and carving a bird. This development eliminated the need for Swift to print such directions on the plastic giblet bags.

In 1976, Swift introduced the size-selector handle. Printed in various colors, the plastic handles served two purposes: first, they made Butterball turkeys easy to lift and handle and second, they indicated to the shopper at a glance the weight of the turkey. This made it easier for shoppers to locate the size turkeys that best suited their needs. In addition, the color-coded handles made it easy for retailers to organize and stock their cases.

The Talk-Line is Butterball's latest and most famous innovation. This toll-free phone number allows thousands upon thousands of consumers to call the company and talk to home economists trained to answer all their questions about preparing the perfect holiday meal. This highly successful program handles over 100,000 consumer questions each holiday season.

Product Packaging

Butterball packaging, likewise, has gone through quite a few phases. When the brand was originally created, Butterball turkeys were marketed in a clear plastic bag. In 1956, Swift turned to a translucent, cream-colored bag which gave the birds more eye appeal. A gold color was added to the label in 1964, and the word Butterball was given prominence over "Swift Premium " for the first time.

In addition, the company placed yellow vexar netting with loop handles around the plastic film bags. DuPont produced Butterball's netting through an extrusion process. Swift obtained two-year exclusive rights to the product from DuPont which gave the company a head-start in terms of packaging. The new packaging method earned Swift a commendation from *Printers Ink Magazine*. The purpose of this netting was threefold: it protected the turkey, it made it easier for the retailer and consumer to lift the turkey, and it gave the entire package a classier, more distinctive look. The latter point helped Swift to combat the checkerboard design of its closest competitor—Ralston Purina.

Successful Marketing Strategies

At the brand's modest beginning in 1954, Swift launched a two-pronged marketing strategy. First, the company targeted a campaign toward the housewife to convince her that a Butterball turkey could guarantee a successful meal. Second, the company targeted retailers to assure them that Butterball turkeys could be sold at premium prices thereby generating profit for the retailers.

Since the first campaign in the mid-1950s, advertising has been a strong component of Butterball's marketing strategy. Under the direction of New York-based advertising agency McCann-Erickson, the first Butterball ad hit the media in the form of a double-page-spread in the November 1956 edition of *Life Magazine.* As luck would have it, this ad appeared immediately following the settlement of Swift's trademark infringement suit. The public impact was tremendous, and 1956 marked the first of Butterball's "sold out" years.

In 1957, the famous "Grace" campaign struck the national media and ran successfully for the next five years. Appearing in national magazines and on outdoor billboards, the ad portrayed a family saying grace before a holiday meal. Swift's goal was to establish a "classy" image in the minds of consumers, but the campaign also drew letters and comments from all over the country complimenting Swift on its religious theme. Interestingly, the famous "grandfather" was not a grandfather nor model at all; he was just the elevator operator at McCann Erickson's headquarters. For the first five years, Butterball ads ran without national opposition from competitors. In the early 1960s, however, Ralston Purina gave Swift its first challenge with its "Honeysuckle White" brand turkey.

With the poultry industry integrating rapidly, Ralston entered the business to ensure a market for its already-strong feed business. The company was a strong, experienced marketer of breakfast cereal, dog food, and other consumer food products, and it applied the same professionalism and strength to its new turkey business unit. Claiming its Honeysuckle White had more white meat, Ralston hit the airwaves with an expensive television campaign. The results were alarming to Swift. Consumer research revealed that viewers had a much higher level of recall from the Ralston ads, and many more people remembered Honeysuckle White's claim of "more white meat." Clearly, Swift was "praying" for a strong Butterball image while Ralston was giving consumers concrete reasons to buy a Honeysuckle White turkey.

Swift developed an immediate counter-attack. Research showed that consumers favored white and dark meat equally, but they all demanded tenderness. Hence, Butterball's new advertising tag line became "tender as its name." Initially, this ad ran in conjunction with the "grace" ad. In time, the new theme replaced "grace" entirely except in point-of-sale materials.

Ralston Purina continued to saturate the media with its sizeable advertising budget, but Swift refused to succumb to the challenge. In a dramatic decision to expand its advertising campaign, Swift increased television coverage promoting whole turkeys from the holiday season through Easter. By moving to entire networks, Butterball targeted 95 percent of the television sets in the United States. Swift reinforced this television campaign by systematically placing newspaper ads in particularly promising local markets. The frequency and strength of the Butterball image allowed Swift to solidify the brand/quality relationship in the minds of consumers.

Advertising and promotion continued to be mainstays of the Butterball marketing strategy into the 1990s. By positioning Butterball as a "special occasion" turkey, Swift labels its brand as high quality. Butterball campaigns evoke positive emotional responses from consumers by guaranteeing successful meals and relating that success to the warmth and emotions of happy family gatherings.

Future Directions

Since 1954, Butterball turkey has consistently been among the best-selling brands of turkey on the market, and its sales have skyrocketed in the 1990s. While Swift attributes the brand's success to superior product quality, other factors have certainly influenced the Butterball phenomenon. Consumers in the 1990s are increasingly concerned with finding good tasting, nutritious food, and many are finding that low-fat, low-calorie turkey is the answer. According to the National Turkey Federation, the average American will eat 30 pounds of turkey in 1993, up 17 pounds from 1988, and the sale of turkey parts grew 85 percent from 1982 to 1987. This trend shows no sign of fading in the near future, and for that reason—along with its continued aggressive marketing strategy—Butterball's success into the late 1990s is assured.

Further Reading:

The Butterball Story, Downers Grove, IL: Swift-Eckrich, 1990.

Freeman, Kris, "By Popular Demand: More Poultry Picks!," *Restaurants and Institutions*, April 22, 1992, pp. 38-68.

History of Innovations and Product Improvements, Downers Grove, IL: Swift-Eckrich, 1990.

"Last Minute News: Butterball Turkey Moves to Puskar," *Advertising Age*, October 12, 1992, p.8.

Ryan, Nancy Ross, "Keeping Abreast of Turkey," *Restaurants and Institutions*, June 10, 1992, pp. 35-44.

—*Wendy Johnson Bilas*

CADBURY'S®

The name of Cadbury has been virtually synonymous with chocolate in the United Kingdom almost since the day in 1824 that John Cadbury opened a small grocery in Birmingham, England, and began selling cocoa and a personally-produced chocolate for drinking. Nearly 170 years later, Cadbury Limited, with its distinctive logo and purple and gold corporate colors, is the number one chocolate confectioner in a country with one of the highest per-capita consumption rates of chocolate in the world.

In 1992 Cadbury Ltd., a subsidiary of international candy and soft-drink giant Cadbury Schweppes PLC, owned 13 of the 30 best selling chocolate confectionery brands in the United Kingdom, including Cadbury's Dairy Milk, the first milk chocolate made in England, and Cadbury's Roses, a twist-wrap assortment introduced in 1938. Cadbury claimed a 31.9 percent share of the £2.9 billion British chocolate market, with approximately 25 percent going to each of its two largest competitors, Nestlé-Rowntree and Mars, Inc.

Cadbury also had a strong brand presence in former British territories such as India, where it enjoyed about a 70 percent share of the chocolate market in the early 1990s. In fact, the connection between Cadbury and chocolate was so strong in India that cocoa trees were known as Cadbury trees. As David Wellings, Cadbury Schweppes confectionery group managing director, told *Marketing* in 1991, "Cadbury is a business that has extended worldwide wherever Brits have been."

The company has a limited presence elsewhere, however, including the rest of Europe, where it had claimed a nine percent share of the chocolate market in the early 1990s, and the United States, where the Hershey Foods Corporation held the franchise on the Cadbury name. In 1991 a Lander Associates ImagePower survey found Cadbury's to be the third most recognized brand name in the United Kingdom, but practically unknown in continental Europe.

Cadbury Schweppes made a move on the U.S. market in 1978, when it bought Connecticut-based Peter Paul, which owned the popular Mounds and Almond Joy brands of chocolate bars. Ten years later, however, Cadbury Schweppes sold its U.S. operations to chocolate industry powerhouse Hershey Foods. Dominic Cadbury, great-grandson of the company's founder and Cadbury Schweppes confectionery group chief executive officer, told *Advertising Age* magazine in 1991, " . . . in the end (we) judged that

our best route was to franchise our business to Hershey. That delivered a lot more value that we were able to see looking ahead in an all-out contest with Hershey and Mars." Under the licensing agreement, Hershey Foods manufactured, marketed, and distributed Mounds, Almond Joy, and York Peppermint Pattie candies, along with Cadbury-branded products, including Cadbury's Dairy Milk, Fruit & Nut, Caramello, Creme Eggs, Roast Almond, Mini Eggs, and Krisp.

Early History

When John Cadbury opened his grocery in 1824, chocolate for eating was still two decades away, but an often-bitter chocolate drink had been stylish in Europe for almost 200 years and cocoa was widely used in cooking. The sale of cocoa and drinking chocolate began as a sideline for Cadbury, but by 1831 John Cadbury and his brother Benjamin were manufacturing both products in a warehouse in Birmingham.

Although a Cadbury company history indicates that the Cadburys began making "French eating chocolate" in 1842, other sources credit J.S. Fry & Sons of Bristol, in 1847, with being the first English firm to make chocolate for eating. Regardless, by 1849 the Cadbury family was selling eating chocolate from still larger quarters in Birmingham. (Cadbury Brothers Ltd would eventually acquire J.S. Fry & Sons in 1919.)

In 1853 the Cadbury brothers received a Royal Warrant to provide chocolate and cocoa products to Queen Victoria. Cadbury Ltd. continued as confectioner to the English monarchy into the 1990s, creating special chocolate assortments to commemorate coronations and other royal events. One of the most popular Cadbury assortments was created to celebrate the coronation of King George V. In 1986 Cadbury's created a Milk Tray tin to celebrate the marriage of Prince Andrew and Sarah Ferguson.

"Absolutely Pure-Therefore Best"

John and Benjamin Cadbury dissolved their partnership in 1860, with John retaining ownership of the company. A second generation of Cadbury brothers, Richard and George, took over in 1861 when their father, John, retired. This second generation of Cadburys struggled to keep the business going until 1866, when they set about learning a process for producing a better quality cocoa that had been developed in Holland almost 40 years earlier.

AT A GLANCE

Cadbury brand founded in 1847 by John and Benjamin Cadbury; Cadbury Brothers incorporated as Cadbury Brothers Limited in 1899; introduced Cadbury's Dairy Milk brand in 1905; Cadbury's Milk Trays introduced in 1915; Cadbury's Flake created in 1920; Cadbury Brothers Limited merged with Schweppes Limited in 1969 to become Cadbury Schweppes PLC; entered into licensing agreement with Hershey Foods Corporation in 1988, wherein Hershey manufactures and distributes Cadbury products in United States.

Performance: *Market share (United Kingdom)*—31.9% (top share) of UK chocolate market. *Sales (United Kingdom)*— £925.1 million.

Major competitor: Nestlé-Rowntree's chocolate brands; Mars, Inc.'s chocolate brands.

Addresses: *Parent company*—Cadbury Limited, P.O. Box 12, Bournville, Birmingham UK; phone: 021-458-2000. *Ultimate parent company*—Cadbury Schweppes PLC, 1-4 Connaught Place, London W2 EX2, United Kingdom; phone: (01) 262 1212.

Up until the 1860s, most cocoa had been blended with starchy fillers to absorb excess cocoa butter. John Cadbury had used potato starch and sago flour. But in Holland, Richard and George Cadbury learned how to extract the cocoa butter from the cocoa beans. This allowed them to produce a less fatty, unadulterated cocoa. The Cadburys soon began advertising their cocoa as "Absolutely Pure-Therefore Best." This Dutch process also created an abundant supply of cocoa butter, which could be used in making a creamier chocolate for eating. From the mid-1860s on, the Cadburys introduced several new styles of eating chocolate, including chocolate cremes—fruit flavored centers covered with chocolate. Richard, a talented artist, designed the first decorated boxes for the company's fancy chocolate assortments, some of which bore his own paintings.

By 1899 Cadbury Brothers had become a private limited company, Cadbury Brothers Ltd, and employed more than 2,600 people at its Bournville facility. Bournville was a factory town whose name was deliberately created to sound French since the best chocolate in the late nineteenth century came from France.

Cadbury's Dairy Milk

In 1905 Cadbury Brothers Ltd. introduced Cadbury's Dairy Milk, which was to become the most successful molded chocolate in UK history and the basic ingredient for many other Cadbury products. Almost 90 years later, Dairy Milk was one of the world's most famous brand names and the company's leading chocolate bar by revenue. As Patricia Magee wrote in *Candy Industry* magazine in 1989, "Children literally grow up with Dairy Milk and it remains a household product throughout their adult lives."

Milk chocolate is created by blending chocolate liquor (the mash created by roasting and grinding cocoa beans) with additional cocoa butter and milk or milk product. Prior to 1900, most companies, including Cadbury Brothers, used powdered milk, and the milk chocolate was coarse and dry by modern standards. Around the turn of the century, however, Swiss confectioners began using condensed milk, which produced a much smoother and tastier product. At Cadbury, George Cadbury, Jr., was put in charge of developing a milk chocolate to compete with the Swiss product.

By 1904, Cadbury had developed a recipe using full-cream, condensed milk, resulting in a chocolate that contained more milk than any previous product. The company considered three names: Jersey, Highland Milk, and Dairy Maid. Dairy Maid eventually became Dairy Milk. Not long afterwards, Dairy Milk chocolate began to outsell foreign brands in England.

Initially, Dairy Milk came in a pale mauve wrapper with red script. The distinctive purple and gold wrapper that eventually came to represent Cadbury's official livery was adopted in 1920. From the start, Cadbury touted the nutritional value of its Dairy Milk chocolate, but it wasn't until 1928 that the company introduced the slogan "glass and a half of full cream milk in every half pound." After more than 60 years, the simple drawing of two glasses of milk being poured into a Dairy Milk chocolate bar remains one of the longest running campaigns in British advertising. The design was officially incorporated into the Dairy Milk wrapper in the late 1970s.

Dairy Milk is also used to make Cadbury's Chocolate Buttons, Milk Tray, Spira, and Fruit & Nut and Whole Nut chocolate bars. In 1992 Cadbury introduced Dairy Milk Tasters, a nugget-sized version of Cadbury's most popular product.

In the late 1980s and early 1990s Cadbury was also beginning to license Dairy Milk for use outside the confectionery market. Two of the earliest associations were with a chocolate drink marketed by Premier Brands and cakes marketed by Manor Bakeries. In 1990 Cadbury announced that Birds Eye Wall would produce an ice cream bar covered with Dairy Milk and sold in a purple wrapper. In the early 1990s Dairy Milk chocolate was being made in ten countries in addition to the United Kingdom.

Cadbury's Creme Eggs

Cadbury created its first chocolate Easter eggs in 1875. They were made of dark chocolate with a smooth surface and filled with small candies. By 1893 Cadbury was selling 19 varieties of Easter eggs, many with elaborate chocolate piping and decorative confectionery flowers. The popularity of chocolate Easter eggs soared after the introduction of Dairy Milk chocolate in 1905. While small eggs and novelties were made for children, Cadbury created ornate chocolate eggs, often packed in fancy, decorated cardboard boxes for adults.

Cadbury introduced its first cream-filled chocolate eggs in 1923, but it wasn't until 1971 that the company began making its famous Cadbury's Creme Eggs, which quickly came to dominate the Easter market. At one time, Cadbury claimed 95 percent of the market for cream-filled eggs in the United Kingdom. Although that figure had fallen to about 70 percent in the 1990s, Cadbury still sold more than 200 million Creme Eggs in the United Kingdom alone in 1992. The company was also the acknowledged world leader in cream-filled Easter eggs, exporting another 150 million, primarily to the United States and Canada.

Cadbury's Creme Eggs were wrapped in a distinctive blue, red, and yellow foil with a chick motif to signify the coming of Easter. (In the United States, the chick was replaced by an Easter bunny.) What really set Cadbury's Creme Eggs apart, however, was a center that was made to resemble a real egg. Inside a shell of chocolate was a sugary yellow "yolk" surrounded by a white candy cream. Cadbury shipped its Creme Eggs only between Christmas and Easter; however, many retailers stocked up so they could satisfy their customers throughout the year.

In 1985 Cadbury launched a light-hearted advertising campaign that focused on the different ways people eat Creme Eggs. According to Cadbury, "Everyone has his or her own technique, including the 'Nibbler' (who nibbles the chocolate round and round), the 'Sucker' (who bites the top off and sucks the centre out) and even the 'Chunky Eater' (who can demolish a Creme Egg in one go!)" Five Creme Egg cars and a Creme Egg hot-air balloon also traveled the United Kingdom between Christmas and Easter in the 1980s and early 1990s. In 1992 Creme Eggs was the company's third best-selling brand between January and Easter, behind Cadbury's Dairy Milk and Cadbury's Roses.

Cadbury's Milk Tray

Introduced in 1915, Cadbury's Milk Tray was an assortment of chocolates designed for everyday and everyone. It abandoned the plush, frilly packaging that clearly positioned other assortments for special occasions and priced many average chocolate buyers out of the market. By the 1930s the Milk Tray assortment, named because it was delivered to retailers on trays of five half-pound boxes, was outselling its fancier competitors in the United Kingdom. It was still the best-selling assortment in the United Kingdom in the early 1990s.

Beginning in the 1960s, Milk Tray packaging became increasingly elegant, featuring a white orchid on the traditional Cadbury purple background. Even fancier boxes were available for special occasions. Milk Tray was "re-launched" in 1989 with a new swirl-design box. Cadbury, though, continued to avoid the elaborate decorations of many other assortments.

Cadbury's Flake

In 1920 Cadbury created Flake, advertised as "the Crumbliest, Flakiest Milk Chocolate in the World." Flake consisted of tissue-thin layers of milk chocolate, creating a flavorful chocolate bar that required a special twist-wrapped package. In addition to catching the falling flakes of milk chocolate, the twist-wrap also forced chocolate lovers to give their full attention to the task at hand.

From the moment of its introduction, Cadbury's Flake was promoted as a chocolate bar of indulgence, especially for young women. Advertisements showed young women enjoying Flake in a variety of fantasy or risque settings, from poppy fields and Gypsy caravans to luxurious bathrooms. In later years, television commercials for Flake were shot in romantic settings around the world. Flake, which was manufactured in Dublin, Ireland, was also popular as a topping or ingredient for creative cooks. A product known as 99 Flake was sold to bakeries and ice cream makers.

Cadbury's Crunchie

Originally introduced in 1929 by J.S. Fry & Sons, then a subsidiary of Cadbury Limited, Crunchie was one of the oldest brands of chocolate bar still on the market in 1993. Crunchie consisted of a honeycomb bar covered with milk chocolate. It was renamed "Cadbury's Crunchie" in 1981, and was one of Cadbury's leading brands in the "countline" market—chocolate that is sold by count rather than by weight.

Although the largest market for Cadbury's Crunchie was the United Kingdom, which gobbled down nearly 190 million Crunchies in 1990, it was also produced in some of Cadbury's overseas factories. The honeycomb center is the same everywhere, but the chocolate coating varies according to each country's chocolate laws. The nature of the Crunchie bar also presents a packaging challenge. Because the honeycomb becomes soft if exposed to moisture, the wrapper has to be airtight.

Cadbury's Wispa

Wispa, Cadbury's first all-chocolate countline since Flake was introduced 60 years earlier, was considered the confectioner's success story of the 1980s, essential to Cadbury's reversal of a 20-year decline in market share.

In the 1970s, chocolate eaters in the United Kingdom, especially young adults, were beginning to buy more countline products. Consumers were also looking for "lighter" products. Wispa, with an aerated milk chocolate center filled with thousands of tiny air bubbles, was developed in response to this new snack market.

Cadbury began test marketing Wispa in 1981. The company underestimated the response and was unable to satisfy the demand, even in the test-markets. Wispa was withdrawn from the market and, according to *Fortune*, let word leak to its competitors that the introduction had been a flop. Secretly, however, the company began building a new chocolate plant especially for Wispa to handle the anticipated demand from a nationwide debut. Wispa was back nationally by 1983, but not until after one of its major competitors, Nestle-Rowntree, whose KitKat bar is the best selling brand in the United Kingdom, had introduced its own textured candy bar, Aero.

Wispa was re-launched in dramatic fashion. The publicity push included a stunt in which six parachutists, each carrying a giant Wispa bar, landed at a soccer stadium and then hurried off on motorcycles to deliver Wispa to the Lord Mayor of Newcastle. It also was promoted with one of the most extensive advertising campaigns in British history, marked by Cadbury's first use of television celebrity endorsements. In 1986 Wispa took first prize in the UK Marketing Awards. But as popular as Wispa would become, Aero, with a one-year head start, outsold it throughout the rest of the 1980s and into the early 1990s.

New Products for the 1990s

The most popular brand in the United Kingdom, Rowntree's KitKat, was introduced in 1935, and Cadbury's best seller, Dairy Milk, was introduced in 1905. But between 1987 and 1992, more than 150 new chocolate confectionery products were launched in the United Kingdom alone, an average of more than one new chocolate product every two weeks. Ten of the top 50 brands in the United Kingdom in 1992 had been introduced since 1980, including Cadbury's Wispa, Twirl, Spira, and Strollers.

Twirl, two fingers of Cadbury's Flake dipped in Dairy Milk, was introduced over a period of several years because of capacity at the company's plant in Northern Ireland, where it had grown in popularity since first being produced in 1985. By 1990, however, Twirl was available nationally.

Spira, which had been test marketed with the name Rollers, was also launched nationwide in 1990. Spira consisted of two hollow twists of Dairy Milk chocolate with a "cartwheel" interior, making it look somewhat like a licorice stick. It was Cadbury's first chocolate bar to use extrusion technology. Instead of pouring liquid chocolate into molds, chocolate is forced through a spiral-shaped tube. The chocolate is then supercooled so it sets quickly and keeps its shape.

Cadbury's Strollers product, introduced in 1991, was a bagged assortment of biscuit, caramel, and raisin centers covered in milk chocolate. Historically, products such as Strollers have been sold as individual varieties, or as "selflines"—bags of either biscuit, caramel, or raisin centers. The Strollers package was the first "selfline" to offer a variety of tastes and textures in the same bag. Unlike other Cadbury "selfline" products that were designed to appeal to children, such as Mini Eggs and Dairy Milk Buttons, Strollers were targeted at the adult market.

Branding Strategy

Many of Cadbury's chocolate products have enjoyed strong, individual brand recognition. Dairy Milk, Creme Eggs, and Wispa, for example, were well-known brands in the United Kingdom. Since 1952, however, Cadbury has positioned its corporate name prominently on all its products. The company made certain that the public was aware that the products were "Cadbury's Dairy Milk" and "Cadbury's Creme Eggs," with "Cadbury's" printed in the company's distinctive script lettering. This corporate branding represented a significantly different strategy than the approach used by Cadbury's principal competitors, Nestle-Rowntree and Mars.

The first move towards establishing such a consistent corporate identity came in 1911, when the company registered its Cadbury Tree symbol, a stylistic drawing of a cocoa tree interwoven with the Cadbury name. The Cadbury Tree was imprinted on aluminum foil candy bar wrappers and various assortment boxes, catalogs, and promotional items. It was used until 1939, and then again briefly after World War II.

When Cadbury introduced Milk Tray in 1915, it chose purple for the packaging. Five years later, it began using purple and gold for the company's flagship brand, Dairy Milk. Those colors were firmly in place as the corporate colors by the early 1920s.

The Cadbury script was introduced in 1921, based on the signature of William A. Cadbury. Originally the script was very elaborate and was used on the sides of the company's trucks. Later its use was extended to sales catalogs, the corporate seal on the company's stationary, and special assortment boxes. In 1952 Cadbury began using the script to identify all its chocolate bars.

In 1928 Cadbury launched a poster and press campaign advertising a "Glass and a Half of Full Cream Milk in every half pound" of its Dairy Milk chocolate. Included in that campaign was a drawing of two glasses of milk, one full and one half full, which eventually became an integral part of the Dairy Milk wrapper. In the 1960s, the "glass and a half" drawing became part of the complete Cadbury corporate logo, which also included the line, "The first name in chocolate."

Entering the 1990s, the company was reinforcing its branding by redesigning several of its product packages to incorporate the purple and gold corporate colors. Cadbury also was trading on the link that research showed existed between the Cadbury name and family values in the United Kingdom through high-profile corporate sponsorships. In 1992 the company announced a three-year sponsorship to raise money for the Save the Children Fund. The company also operated Cadbury's World, a company museum and major tourist attraction in the United Kingdom, to reinforce the corporate brand.

Further Reading:

"A brandstand view of chocolate," *The Economist*, April 30, 1988, p. 63.

"A hit British candy aims to bubble in the U.S.," *Fortune*, April 29, 1985, p. 196.

Blodgett, Timothy, "Cadbury Schweppes: More than chocolate and tonic," *Harvard Business Review*, January-February 1983, p. 134-144.

"Brand Power and Determination," *Directors & Boards*, Fall 1991, p. 26-30.

"Cadbury and Phillip Morris: Sh-h-h-h, you know who," *The Economist*, June 30, 1990, p. 68.

"Cadbury's Dairy Milk Chocolate," Birmingham, UK: Cadbury Limited, 1987.

"Cadbury's sweet charity," *Marketing*, May 14, 1992, p. 18-19.

"Chocolate Market Review of 1992," Birmingham, UK: Cadbury Limited, 1993.

"The Development of Cadbury Design & Packaging," Birmingham, UK: Cadbury Limited, 1989.

"The Development of Easter and Easter Eggs," Birmingham, UK: Cadbury Limited, 1991.

"Global goodies," *Forbes*, January 28, 1985, p. 104-105.

"Global potential sweet to Cadbury," *Advertising Age*, Oct. 28, 1991, p. S1.

Gofton, Ken, "Cadbury's sweet charity," *Marketing*, May 14, 1992, p. 18-19.

Hoggan, Karen, "Cadbury breaks its mould to widen base," *Marketing*, March 15, 1990, p 3.

Johnson, Mike, "Cadbury conquers the world . . . ," *Marketing*, January 24, 1991, p. 20-21.

Magee, Patricia L., "Cadbury defends top spot with chocolate brands," *Candy Industry*, October 1989, pp. 29-34.

Morton, Frederic, *Chocolate, An Illustrated History*, New York: Crown Publishers, 1986.

"Setting Their Sites on the Public," *Advertising Week*, November 22, 1990, pp. 29-30.

Simpson, Rachel, "Chocolate Wars: Lines of Attack," *Marketing*, April 20, 1989.

"The Story of Cadbury Limited," Birmingham, UK: Cadbury Limited, 1987.

"Sweet Dreams Are Made of This," *Management Today*, September 1989, pp. 74-78.

"This Chocolate Isle," *Time*, April 26, 1963, p. 85.

Wentz, Laurel, "Global potential sweet to Cadbury," *Advertising Age*, October 28, 1991, p. S-1.

"When, where and how to test market," *Harvard Business Review*, May-June 1975, p. 96-105.

—Dean Boyer

CAMEL®

Introduced in 1913, Camel was the first nationally branded cigarette in the United States and, prior to the introduction of filtered cigarettes, it waged a fierce battle for top billing in the competitive U.S. cigarette market, first with Lucky Strikes and Chesterfields, and later with Marlboro and Pall Mall. Camel led cigarette sales for 41 of its first 50 years. The brands success, especially among working class smokers, helped to make its manufacturer, R.J. Reynolds Tobacco Company, into one of the largest consumer products companies in the world. Careful marketing that highlighted the brand's superior quality tobacco and encouraged recognition helped Camel gain international recognition. Despite declining sales in the face of a changing American cigarette market after World War II, Camel maintains a respectable position in the market.

Brand Origins

Richard Joshua Reynolds started in the tobacco business in 1875, producing cut-plug chewing tobacco in Winston-Salem, North Carolina. Reynolds was locked in a competitive war with his arch-competitor, James Buchanan Duke, whose American Tobacco Company introduced machine-made cigarettes in 1884. Reynolds sold his company to American Tobacco after Duke threatened to destroy him with predatory pricing. By 1910, Duke controlled over 80 percent of the American tobacco market, prompting the U.S. government to break up the American Tobacco Company on antitrust grounds. Reynolds regained his company in 1911 and decided to challenge the American Tobacco Company's dominance in the cigarette market.

A growing market for manufactured cigarettes was emerging in the early twentieth century, although many smokers continued to "roll their own." Reynolds noted that, of the 50 or so brands of tobacco available, all were made from straight Virginia tobacco or the stronger, more aromatic Turkish varieties. Reynolds decided a market existed for a blended cigarette that combined the favorable characteristics of both kinds of tobaccos. In 1913, Reynolds developed four brands for market testing: Reyno, a straight Virginia brand; Osman, a pure Turkish blend; Red Kamel, a Turkish brand with filters made from cork; and Camel, an experimental brand. Camel contained a blend of Virginia burley and bright tobaccos, Turkish varieties for a more distinctive taste and aroma, and sweetening agents. The name Camel was meant to emphasize the exotic, middle-eastern origin of the tobaccos.

Early Marketing Strategy

Cigarette manufacturers of the 1910s had to overcome varying tobacco quality and low product differentiation if they were to gain customers. In order to spur brand loyalty, many manufacturers included premiums or coupons with their brands. It was believed that this strategy encouraged the consumer to repeatedly purchase only one brand, collecting enough coupons to receive a free package, or some other premium. Reynolds chose different marketing strategies, however, pricing the Camel brand below competitors, 10 cents for a package of 20, as opposed to 15 cents on competing brands. Moreover, the Camel package carried an highly effective tagline: "Don't look for premiums or coupons, as the cost of the tobaccos blended in Camel Cigarettes prohibits the use of them." The simple 21-word statement indicated to the consumer that this was a superior quality brand, despite its lower price. The consumer was led to believe that Camel was so distinctive that it did not need to rely on premiums to establish a loyal following.

Packaging

At the time Reynolds was developing the Camel brand, the Barnum and Bailey Circus made a stop in Winston-Salem. Included in the show was a curious dromedary named Old Joe. Reynolds dispatched his stenographer, R. C. Haberkern, to the circus with a camera. The employee returned with a photograph of the animal, from which Reynolds had a sketch artist create a rendering that included palm trees and pyramids. The image illustrated the oriental origin of the Turkish leaf, even though there are no pyramids in Turkey. While the Red Kamel package displayed a trotting camel, and Osman featured an elder Ottomanesque figure, the Camel package featuring Old Joe was more modern and distinctive. The package design caused a visual association with mature, cured tobacco leaf, and led people to think of Camel as an exotic, superior quality product.

Advertising

Camel thoroughly outsold the other brands in market tests. This inspired Reynolds to circumvent the regional wholesale network, and go directly into national distribution. Camel was introduced nationally late in 1913 in a massive storm of advertising, including a two-page spread in the popular *Saturday Evening Post*. Camel was the first cigarette brand to be sold and promoted

AT A GLANCE

Camel brand cigarettes introduced in 1913 by R.J. Reynolds Tobacco Company in order to test the acceptance of a cigarette that blended both Virginia and Turkish tobacco; was the top selling brand in the United States from 1913 to 1929, and from 1935 to 1960.

Performance: *Market share*—4.2% of 1992 cigarette category.

Major competitor: Phillip Morris Companies Inc.'s Marlboro; also Lorillard Tobacco Company's Newport and R. J. Reynolds Tobacco Co.'s Winston, Salem, and Doral.

Advertising: *Agency*—Mezzina/Brown, Inc., New York, NY. *Major campaign*—"I'd walk a mile for a Camel"; Old Joe.

Addresses: *Parent company*—R.J. Reynolds Tobacco Company, 401 N. Main St., Winston-Salem, NC 27102; phone: (919) 741-5000. *Ultimate parent company*—RJR Nabisco, Inc., 1301 Avenue of the Americas, New York, NY 10019; phone: (212) 258-5600; fax: (212) 969-9173.

nationally. In 1914, sales of Camel stood at $425 million. The following year, sales exploded to $2.3 billion, and by 1917, sales exceeded $11 billion. In 1920, two years after R. J. Reynolds died, sales of Camel topped $20 billion, and the brand accounted for half of all cigarette sales in the United States.

In 1920, Camel introduced one of the most distinctive advertising campaigns in American history. That year, a golfer asked a spectator for a Camel cigarette, and commented "I'd walk a mile for a Camel." The man he asked happened to be an advertising agent for the brand, who knew a good slogan when he heard one. The message, expressive and to the point, reinforced the value image Reynolds had established with its "no coupons" advisory. "I'd walk a mile for a Camel" was aggressively repeated in advertising for more than 30 years from that point, and was used occasionally into the 1970s.

Competitors responded to the rise of the Camel brand with creative and well-funded advertising campaigns. Through heavy promotion and sponsorship, American Tobacco's Lucky Strike brand overtook Camel in 1929. In 1931 Reynolds introduced cellophane package wrapping to preserve freshness, but this failed to stimulate sales. By 1933, Liggett & Myers' Chesterfields forced Camel into third place. During the Depression, however, all manufactured brands suffered at the hands of discount brands and a popular resurgence of roll-your-own cigarettes. Finally, Reynolds decided to take a lesson from its competitors, and launched another massive promotional campaign. In 1934 more than 80 percent of the company's net earnings were dedicated to the advertising and promotion of Camel. By the following year, Camel had regained the number one position in the market.

Health Claims

In an attempt to build market share, cigarette manufacturers began to emphasize use of their products by more diverse types of people. Liggett & Myers portrayed "nice girls" in its advertising, conditioning the public for wider social acceptance of smoking. American Tobacco pushed odd claims such as, "For men who know tobacco, it's Luckies two to one," and "It's toasted" (virtually all brands were flue-cured, or "toasted"). Reynolds, recognizing the public's growing concern with the relationship

between smoking and poor health, decided to portray athletes with the Camel brand, making spurious claims about its wholesome, healthy qualities. Baseball players, lifeguards, and tennis players claimed, "Camels never get on my nerves." By featuring these images during prime-time sports broadcasts, Reynolds built such a strong reputation for Camel that, when the health scare erupted after World War II, Camel sales were barely affected.

The most immediate beneficiaries of the health scare (which took the form of magazine exposes) were filtered brands. Increasingly, these brands targeted Camel's healthy image with claims of their own. Filters, long disdained by smokers concerned with taste, were soon regarded as necessary safety features. The Federal Trade Commission put an end to all health claims in cigarette advertising in 1955, noting that such claims could not be scientifically proven.

International Growth

Camel prospered in international markets after being popularized in Europe during World War I by American GIs, who were provided with Camel cigarettes as part of their rations. During World War II, packages of Camel were again provided to American soldiers, who were reputed to be better paid and better cared for than other soldiers. Camel came to represent the freedom and affluence of Americans, an image that was powerfully reinforced after the war by the influence of Hollywood and its legions of glamorous, cigarette-smoking movie stars. American cigarette manufacturers continued to expand their market overseas into the 1990s, reported *Business Week,* and in 1991 Camel was sold in over 135 countries. However, the domestic market continued to provide the vast majority of Reynold's tobacco profits.

Brand Development

Without the ability to play upon its health claims, and with a general decline in popularity of unfiltered brands, Reynolds was largely powerless to reverse slowing sales of Camel. The company remained true to the Camel formula, hoping to keep loyal the legions of people who had made the brand number one. A differently blended king-size variation called Cavalier failed to generate interest, and filters were deemed distasteful to true tobacco lovers. In 1954, Reynolds decided to involve itself in the growing market for king-size filtered brands, introducing Winston. Aimed at stemming the rapid growth of competing filtered brands, Winston was promoted without health claims, promising only full flavor. To ensure that Camel smokers did not defect to filtered brands from other manufacturers, Winston was introduced as being from "the makers of Camels." In 1956, Reynolds created the first filtered king-size menthol brand, called Salem. While continuing to preserve the Camel image, Reynolds promoted Salem with fresher, green packaging, creating an outdoorsy image of nature.

Camel, however, continued to lose ground as smokers deserted unfiltered "straight" brands in favor of the filtered Marlboro, Winston, Benson & Hedges, and other brands. Straight brands lost popularity because they were not capable of preventing unsightly tobacco particles from getting on smokers' teeth, they were very strong, and they were increasingly associated with an older generation of smokers. Reynolds finally introduced a new filtered Camel brand in 1966. Subsequent brand extension led to boxed and soft-pack lights and 100-millimeter variations.

Performance Appraisal

Although Reynolds continued to emphasize the quality of the tobaccos blended in Camel, consumers grew disinterested. The depressing news for smokers about the relationship between tobacco and severe health problems succeeded in weaning many over to filtered brands. These brands, which masked much of the character of the tobaccos, made it difficult for manufacturers to promote their brands based on tobacco quality. Increasingly, brand loyalty had to be built on images. Marlboro established itself as a rough-hewn cowboy brand, Virginia Slims afforded an image of elegance and exclusivity, and low-tar Carlton gained a reputation for being for the smoker who is trying to quit. Camel, while remaining true to its quality heritage, remained the cigarette of blue-collar working men. And few people wanted to be so closely associated with this average Joe.

As part of an interim advertising campaign in late 1987, a 13-year old characterization of Old Joe from a French campaign was reintroduced to celebrate the brand's 75th anniversary. The tired old animal was portrayed as a younger character wearing a leather flight jacket and Ray-Ban sunglasses. Reynolds promoted its spokescamel as a ''smooth character,'' playing pool in hipster bars. Through heavy promotion, the newly cool Old Joe aimed at winning over a younger audience. But the campaign worked too well, complained critics. According to *Adweek* columnist Richard Morgan, one study found that 51 percent of children between the ages of three and six could identify the Old Joe character. Believing that such a high recognition rate encouraged underage smoking, the Surgeon General of the United States and the American Medical Association called for an end to the advertising. A Reynolds spokeswoman countered their complaints, noting that ''People don't respond to dog-food commercials unless they have dogs. By the same token, they don't respond to cigarette advertising unless they already smoke.'' The campaign was also criticized for what some took to be the subliminal representation of male genitalia in the cartoon depiction of Old Joe.

Future Predictions

As straight brands dropped in popularity, the original version of Camel continued to lose market share. However, with the elimination of broadcast advertising of cigarettes in 1971, a premium value was placed on established brand identities. As a result, Reynolds continues to extend the Camel name to variations of the brand, highlighting the popularity of Old Joe, and concentrating much of their promotional efforts on sponsoring athletic events.

Further Reading:

Cleary, David Powers, *Great American Brands,* New York: Fairchild Publications, 1981, pp. 40-52.

Dagnoli, Judann, ''Groups Smoking Over Camel Ad,'' *Advertising Age,* July 17, 1989, p. 49.

Gershman, Michael, *Getting It Right the Second Time,* Reading, MA: Addison Wesley, 1990, p. 38.

Hoover's Handbook, Austin, TX: Reference Press, 1991.

''Lots of Puffing But Less Profit in New Markets Overseas,'' *Business Week,* May 3, 1993, p. 132.

Morgan, Hal, *Symbols of America,* New York: Viking, 1986, p. 90.

Morgan, Richard, ''Is Old Joe Taking Too Much Heat?,'' *Adweek,* March 16, 1992, p. 44.

—John Simley

CAMPBELL'S® SOUP

For nearly a century, the familiar red and white label on cans of Campbell's Soups has represented quality and convenience. Open the cupboard in just about any American household and you'll find the icon of popular culture that was immortalized by Andy Warhol. From the gold medallion won for excellence in 1900, to the once-cherubic, now-hip Campbell Kids, Campbell's is an extraordinarily well-known power brand.

Brand Origins

Campbell's Soups were developed in the 1890s by Dr. John T. Dorrance, a chemist from Philadelphia. Dorrance earned his Ph.D. at the University of Gottingen in Germany, then stayed on in Paris to learn about French cooking, especially soup making. Meanwhile, Dr. Dorrance's uncle, Arthur, was a partner in Joseph Campbell's Camden, New Jersey, canning company.

The Jos. Campbell Preserve Co. was created in 1869 by Joseph Campbell, a fruit merchant, and Abram Anderson, an ice box manufacturer. Anderson's conservatism clashed with Campbell's interest in promotion, and in 1876 Anderson left to be replaced by Arthur Dorrance. That same year Campbell preserves won a medal at the 1876 Centennial Exposition. By 1897 the Jos. Campbell Preserve Co. had an established reputation for packing tomatoes, vegetables, salad dressings, jellies, mince meat, and condiments. Arthur Dorrance assumed the presidency of the company upon Mr. Campbell's death, and offered his young nephew a salary of seven dollars per week to work with him at the Campbell company.

Dr. John T. Dorrance turned down offers of professorships from Cornell, Columbia, and Bryn Mawr to work with his uncle in the canning industry, not because of the lucrative salary his uncle offered, but becuase he had developed an idea while studying in the kitchens of Paris. He believed that condensed canned soup would be a very attractive product for three basic reasons: it was less expensive to ship, it took up less shelf space, and it was infinitely more convenient. Campbell's tomato soup was introduced in 1897 and was instantly popular: a woman could heat a can of Campbell's as quickly and easily as she could brew a cup of tea. And at just 10 cents a can, Campbell's Soup cost one-third as much as ready-to-eat soup.

Early Marketing Strategy

The distinctive red and white label—inspired by Cornell University's school colors—was introduced in 1898, and soon a full-fledged advertising campaign was underway. Created in-house, the campaign consisted of trolley car cards that carried an image of the product and a rhyme: "We blend the best with careful pains, in skillful combination. And everything we make contains our business reputation."

In 1899 it cost Campbell $4,200 to put posters on one-third of New York's trolley cars. Within just three years the program had expanded to 378 cities, and by 1902 Campbell was purchasing 45,000 cards per month. The company was the target of many printers nationwide.

One such printer approached Campbell with an idea for new product representatives. The "round roly-polies" drawn by his wife, Grace G. Drayton, appealed to turn-of-the-century women who believed that chubbiness equaled health in children, and the now-infamous Campbell twins became strong "spokes-urchins" for the company. Then as now, advertising was aimed at women; children have been the primary consumers of soup, and marketing schemes have centered on their mothers as the primary food purchasers. Campbell used the relatively new concept of the advertising campaign to great advantage by connecting the branded product with new household technologies like gas and electric stoves. Emphasis on the unique qualities of the Campbell's brand was achieved through the use of the Campbell Kids as representatives and the rhymes to push what one executive called the "Soup Idea."

Proud of his product, Dr. Dorrance entered Campbell's 21 varieties of condensed soups in a contest at the Paris Exposition of 1900. The products won a gold medal of excellence, a medal that replaced the 1876 insignia and has remained an important part of the product's iconography.

First Commercial Success

Quality, convenience, and value—not to mention the popularity of the Campbell Kids—catapulted the soups to national distribution by 1911. That same year, Dr. John Dorrance was selected general manager of the company, a position on par with chief executive officer. He accumulated enough stock in Campbell to acquire it outright by 1915. In the first decades of the twentieth

AT A GLANCE

Campbell's brand of soup was founded by Dr. John T. Dorrance of the Jos. Campbell Preserve Company in Camden, NJ, 1897; company name changed to Campbell Soup Company in 1922.

Performance: *Market share*—76.5%. *Sales*—$3.9 billion.

Major competitor: Progresso.

Advertising: *Agency*—Backer, Spielvogel, Bates, Inc., New York, NY. *Major campaign*—"M'mm, m'mm, good!"

Addresses: *Parent company*—Campbell Soup Company, Campbell Place, P.O. Box 29D, Camden, NJ 08103-1799; phone: (609) 342-4800.

century, Campbell joined a small group of technologically advanced companies whose new machinery and processes enabled dramatic increases in output. Such companies as the Campbell Soup Company—so named in 1922—H.J. Heinz, Quaker Oats, and Procter & Gamble required massive customer bases to capitalize on their production capabilities. Campbell developed a highly successful centralized organization to coordinate national sales and marketing.

By the time Dr. Dorrance died in 1930, the Campbell advertising budget for soup had grown to $3 million per year, the largest in the United States. John was succeeded by his brother, Arthur C. Dorrance, who died in 1946 and was eventually followed by John T. Dorrance, Jr., son of the soup's originator.

Grace Drayton drew the Campbell Kids for twenty years. The Campbell twins drove cars and flew planes in the early twentieth century. They sold Liberty Bonds during World War I, danced the Charleston during the "Roaring Twenties," served as air-raid wardens during World War II, and were soon singing the "M'mm, m'mm good!" jingle that so many Americans have come to recognize. Although the Kids were deemed too cheerful for the bleak years of the Great Depression and by the end of World War II were seen as "old-fashioned and obsolete," they were resurrected in the 1950s, when the company could reach 50 percent of all American households just by sponsoring "Lassie" on TV.

Campbell's national advertising strategy worked well for many decades, and the brand's market share peaked in 1952 at 82.9 percent. The 1950s were a turning point in company history and in the success of the brand. 1954 marked the end of an era: the last Dorrance family member to lead the company died and Campbell went public. Although the Dorrance's kept a controlling interest in the company, some observers maintained that the move freed Campbell from a conservative, even "paternalistic" company culture that had begun to have an adverse affect on the brand.

Market Segmentation

Campbell put out a line of soups that was manufactured and promoted in the same way nation-wide for most of the 20th century. But in the early 1980s new leadership, market segmentation, regional consumer research, and a 14-year decline in soup sales led to changes in Campbell products and in the ways they were presented. Gordon McGovern's rise to the position of chief executive officer of Campbell in 1981 constituted the first time a marketing professional led the organization. In his first three years at the helm, McGovern more than doubled the adver-

tising budget and reorganized the company into 50 autonomous units. He also strove to focus on the consumer by, among other things, doing his family's shopping and encouraging his managers to do the same. In 1982 McGovern was named "Adman of the Year" by *Advertising Age* for his efforts to change Campbell into an aggressive, market-driven company.

Demographic shifts in the 1980s demanded changes in advertising strategies. The over-65 age group overtook the 13-to-19 age group for the first time in American history in 1980, and more than half of all households had only one or two members. Upper-income households were growing 3.5 times faster than total households, and nearly half of adult meal-planners were dieting or avoiding salt, sugar, calories, chemicals, cholesterol, and/or additives.

Americans' tastes were changing, too: more people ate chicken and more people prepared ethnic foods. From 1973 to 1980 per capita soup consumption declined 11.5 percent. Under these circumstances, traditional, national marketing plans gave way to

The Campbell's Soup Kids have represented the brand since the turn of the 20th century.

regional schemes, and Campbell Soup led the revolution. McGovern emphasized the three major marketing factors facing Campbell in a 1985 *Management Review* interview: "healthy food, working women, and microwave ovens."

Advertising Innovations

The company reorganized its central marketing structure and switched to a regional strategy in 1986. By 1991 Campbell had 22 sales and marketing regions, each with its own sales manager, a group of brand managers, and a sales force. The company began to concentrate on growing minority groups, even hiring separate agencies to appeal to the various segments of the population. Media choices also changed dramatically—rather than concentrating almost exclusively on network television, Campbell began to devote more funding to radio, newspaper, magazine, outdoor posters, cable TV, and other outlets. In addition, Campbell went farther than any other consumer goods company in its efforts to regionalize marketing, and in a 1989 survey of 75 chief executives, corporate presidents, and marketing directors, it was rated America's most innovative consumer goods company.

In 1980 Campbell launched its "Soup is Good Food" campaign, which boosted red & white soup sales by 2.6 percent in just two years. The campaign quoted a federal study that found that subjects who ate more soup and dairy products were in the study's most nutritionally healthy group. The soup-eaters also consumed fewer sugary foods and drinks and took in the fewest calories.

But the nutritional claims made in Campbell's ads were questioned by consumer groups, most notably the Council of Better Business Bureaus' National Advertising Division and the Center for Science in the Public Interest. Their complaints were based on the fact that Campbell had neglected to mention most condensed soups' high sodium content and that the soup was not necessarily a causative factor in good health. Campbell cut the nuritional claims from its ads in 1984, but continued with the "Soup is Good Food" theme until 1988, when the company revived the "m'mm, m'mm good!" tag line after a ten-year hiatus.

Competition

Despite leadership in regionalized advertising, in the 1980s the Campbell's brand came under fire from such companies as Progresso, which had been targeting ethnic and specialty markets for decades. Private label, or generic, soups had also cut into Campbell's market share, which declined from more than 80 percent in the 1970s to near 60 percent by the late 1980s.

Research showed that 74 percent of American adults remembered "m'mm, m'mm good," so the motto was trotted out again in 1988. The Campbell Kids also reappeared. This time the twins brought along new multicultural friends who asked, "What kind of Campbell's Kid are you?" to help the company recoup its share of the stagnant prepared soup market.

Campbell also opened a line of competitive fire with a new dry soup line and new microwaveable soups. The company challenged Thomas J. Lipton Inc.'s Cup-A-Soup with five varieties of Campbell's Cup, and soon garnered a 17 percent share of the Lipton-dominated dry soup market. In an effort to jump-start sales in the canned soup arena, Campbell introduced new value-added Gold Label and Golden Classics soups. In an appeal to the increasingly segmented market, Campbell introduced new products within the soup category like: Chunky, Soup-for-One, Low Sodium, Home Cookin', Special Request, and Microwaveable Soups.

Led by McGovern, the company continued to try to develop a new product for each market segment until the 1990s, when mounting evidence showed that the successful spin-offs like Healthy Request were eating into red & white market shares. McGovern also came under fire for gambling millions on new product development when pre-tax pofit margins dropped to 8 percent—2 percent lower than the industry average. He resigned in 1989 and was replaced by David Johnson, who took many cost-cutting measures to raise profits. Johnson invested more money in consumer research on basic lines like red & white soups to take advantage of United Product Code data and to fine-tune regional marketing strategies.

Future Growth

In addition to stressing market research, Johnson has also made a huge push for international expansion. In 1988 Campbell took its first tentative steps in that direction with the acquisition of Great

Britain's Freshbake Foods Group PLC. The effort fell flat, however, since the British were not particularly fond of the brand.

Johnson's attempt proved difficult, but he was eventually successful in taking over the Australian company Arnotts Ltd. Through Arnotts, Johnson hoped to reach Asian markets with soup and other Campbell products. While intense marketing efforts are underway for this and other foreign markets Campbell hopes to penetrate, some industry analysts feel the company may be tardy in its move toward foreign growth. Not only is Campbell trying to tap markets which may be unused to convenience foods, they are arriving behind their competitors. Such rivals as Knorr, Nestlé, and H.J Heinz have already garnered market share in the countries Campbell is trying to target.

However, with stagnant domestic growth, Campbell has little alternative than to forge ahead. Indeed, the company has even had some small successes. By creating new soups that cater to regional tastes, Campbell has made inroads in Mexico and Hong Kong. In addition, by stressing the fact that fresh ingredients are used in Campbell's soups, the company has won ten percent of the powdered soup dominated category in Argentina. So, while Campbell has encountered some recent difficulties, their soup continues to be "m'mm, m'mm good." The familiar red and white cans should still be seen on grocers' shelves, not only in the United States, but around the world, for years to come.

Further Reading:

Abernathy, Chris A., "Company Study: Building Networks of Small Brands," *Journal of Consumer Marketing*, v. 8, Spring 1991, pp. 25-30.

Barach, Arnold B., *Famous American Trademarks*, Washington, DC: Public Affairs Press, 1971, pp. 29-30.

"Campbell is Bubbling, But for How Long?" *Business Week*, June 17, 1991, pp. 56-57.

"Campbell Soup Claims Boil Over at NAD," *Advertising Age*, v. 55, September 17, 1984, pp. 14, 87.

"Campbell Rated Nation's Most Innovative Company," *Marketing News*, v. 23, February 27, 1989, p. 6.

Cleary, David Powers, *Great American Brands: The Success Formulas That Made Them Famous*, New York: Fairchild Publications, 1981, pp. 53-59.

Dagnoli, Judann, "Campbell vs. Lipton: Dry-soup War Brewing," *Advertising Age*, v. 58, August 3, 1987, p. 1.

"Healthy Soups Cut in at Campbell," *Advertising Age*, v.6, April 6, 1992, p. 12.

"Campbell Ups Ad $: 30% Boost to Restore Brand Power," *Advertising Age*, v. 62, July 1, 1991, p. 1+.

Diffily, Anne Hinman, "Gordon McGovern: A Marketing-Oriented President Stirs up on Old Company," *Management Review*, v. 74, August 1985, pp. 17-19.

Dugas, Christine, and Mark N. Vamos, "Marketing's New Look: Campbell Leads a Revolution in the Way Consumer Products Are Sold," *Business Week*, January 26, 1987, pp. 64-69.

Ecklund, Christopher S., "Campbell Soup's Recipe for Growth: Offering Something for Every Palate," *Business Week*, December 24, 1984, pp. 66-67.

"Progresso Cooks Up a Challenge to Campbell," *Business Week*, January 21, 1985, pp. 120-121.

Fucini, Joseph H. and Suzy, *Entrepreneurs: The Men and Women Behind Famous Brand Names and How They Made It*, Boston: G.K. Hall & Co., 1985, p. 179.

Henson, Sharon, "Case 20: Campbell Soup Company," *Strategic Management Concepts and Cases*, Arthur A. Thompson, Jr. and A. J. Strickland III, eds., Homewood, IL: BPI/Irwin, 1990, pp. 656-677.

"M'm! M'm! BAD! Trouble at Campbell Soup," *Business Week,* September 25, 1989, pp. 68-70.

Morgan, Hal, *Symbols of America,* Penguin, 1986.

"The National Business Hall of Fame," *Fortune,* v. 123, March 11, 1991, p. 102.

Norris, Eileen, "Segmentation Heats Up Soup Market," *Advertising Age,* October 13, 1986, p. 30.

Saportio, Bill, "The Fly in Campbell's Soup," *Fortune,* v. 117, May 9, 1988.

"Soup Maker Bets Future on Monitoring Technological, Consumption Changes," *Marketing News,* v. 18l, October 12, 1984, p. 44.

"Soup Researcher Defends Ad Claims by Citing Federal Data," *Marketing News,* v. 18, February 3, 1984.

Strasser, Susan, *Satisfaction Guaranteed: The Making of the American Mass Market,* New York: Pantheon Books, 1989, pp. 52-53, 94-95, 116-117.

Weber, Joseph, "From Soup to Nuts and Back to Soup," *Business Week,* November 5, 1990, pp. 114 + .

Weber, Joseph, "Campbell: Now it's M-M-Global," *Business Week,* March 15, 1993, pp. 52-54.

—April S. Dougal

CANADA DRY®

Canada Dry brand of ginger ale dominates the ginger ale segment of the soft drink market with more than one third of sales. For almost 90 years, the Canada Dry trademark has represented the refreshing coolness of the icy north. Since the 1920s, when the beverage was a favorite mixer with "bathtub gin," Canada Dry has been positioned as an adult soft drink. The brand also carries the top club soda/seltzer, the second most popular tonic water, and the fourth most popular bottled water. By the early 1990s, Cadbury Beverages Inc., the brand's parent company, boasted lemon and cranberry flavored ginger ales, and Canada Dry had become the number eight soft drink in the United States.

Brand Origins

Canada Dry was invented in 1904 by John J. McLaughlin, a Toronto, Ontario, chemist and soda fountain supplier. Traditional ginger ale recipes produced dark brown drinks with a sharp ginger flavor. McLaughin's drink was lighter in color and flavor, hence the original name Canada Dry Pale Ginger Ale. The originator designed a logo featuring the outline of North America on a shield and added a crown to suggest the beverage's superiority over its competitors.

J.J. McLaughlin, Ltd. began to ship the beverage to New York City in 1919 and opened its first Canada Dry plant in the United States that same year. The drink was immediately popular in the United States. It was introduced to the United States during the prohibition of alcoholic beverages under the 18th Amendment to the Constitution. Bottled soft drinks, especially dry ginger ales, benefitted from the absence of beer and liquors from the legal market. Ginger ales also gained popularity during this period as a mixer that masked the taste of underground liquor or "bathtub gin." In addition, the 1920s saw increased marketing efforts by bottlers, which boosted soft drink consumption.

In 1923 Canada Dry was purchased from J.J. McLaughlin by P.D. Saylor and Associates for $1 million. The owners named the new company Canada Dry Ginger Ale, Inc. and purchased additional plants in Hudson, New York and Maywood, Illinois. After an extensive advertising campaign that first coined the phrase "down from Canada came tales of a wonderful beverage," the drink was shipped from those plants to customers nationwide. Canada Dry soon became a leader in the soft drink industry.

Distribution Innovations

Intense competition in the 1930s precluded changes in distribution, and Canada Dry became a pioneer in the revolution that led to local distribution centers. Prior to the late 1930s, beverage producers built their own plants and distributed the products individually. But in 1938 Canada Dry and another ginger ale producer announced plans to franchise their products. Under the new arrangement, Canada Dry provided the extract, the formula, and the quality controls; the bottlers handled the manufacturing and distribution in local markets. The franchise gave local bottlers permission to package and distribute Canada Dry beverages for a fee. That way, the owner of the brand would not have to build plants, and local distributors would benefit from greater selection. Canada Dry helped establish this industry standard that has led to cooperation among brands in the international arena. As early as 1936, a Lima, Peru, bottler was licensed to manufacture and sell Canada Dry beverages.

World War II controls and rationing slowed soft drink sales that had been growing substantially since the beginning of the 1940s. But as America entered active participation in the war, virtually everything the bottlers utilized came under controls and rationing—bottles, gasoline, tires, trucks, coolers, vending machines, and even sugar. Soft drinks were in high demand at military training centers, therefore some ration adjustments were made to allow for production to meet those requirements.

In the 1950s, frozen concentrated juices offered new competition for the soft drink industry. Another threat to soft drinks was the "crusading" food movement whose followers campaigned against items consumed for pleasure and enjoyment. The crusaders focused especially on products sweetened with sugar. Since few of the claims against soft drinks were based in fact, industry-wide efforts to publicize the fairly innocent nature of soft drinks were successful.

Focus on Adult Market

Canada Dry was acquired by Dr. Pepper in February of 1982, and the new parent increased the product's advertising budget 20 percent to $15 million. Young & Rubicam, Dr. Pepper's agency, took over the Canada Dry account from Grey Advertising and moved to promote Canada Dry club soda as "the perfect diet soft drink." The advertisements used the signature, "Aren't you ready

AT A GLANCE

Canada Dry brand of ginger ale founded in 1904 by John J. McLaughlin; originally produced by J. J. McLaughlin, Ltd. in Toronto, Ontario; first distributed to United States in 1919 in New York; brand purchased by P.D. Saylor and Associates in 1923; acquired by Dr. Pepper in 1982; later owned by RJR Nabisco; acquired by Cadbury Schweppes plc in 1986.

Performance: *Market share*—34 percent (top share) of ginger ale category.

Major competitor: Schweppes, Faygo.

Advertising: *Agency*—Foote, Cone & Belding, Chicago, IL, 1986—. *Major campaign*—"Less sweet. What a refreshing idea."

Addresses: *Parent company*—Cadbury Beverages Inc., 6 High Ridge Park, P.O. Box 3800, Stamford, CT 06905-0800; phone: (203) 329-0911; fax: (203) 968-7653. *Ultimate parent company*—Cadbury Schweppes plc, 25 Berkeley Sq., London W1X 6HT, England.

for Canada Dry?'' and were aimed at 18 to 49-year-olds, whose tastes were supposedly turning to less sweet, more healthy beverages. The company set a five-year goal of placing Canada Dry in the top ten of soft drinks.

A 1983 ginger ale push gave Canada Dry a 35 percent share of that segment and a 1.1 percent share of the total $9.8 billion soft drink market. The emerging interest in healthy products prompted Canada Dry to promote diet ginger ale in the early 1980s. At the same time, the brand hoped to profit from the rapidly expanding diet segment with its club soda. Longtime Canada Dry spokesman Louis Jourdan was joined by an attractive, weight-conscious young woman who extolled "the perfect diet soft drink's" lack of calories, saccharine, and sugar. A refund program utilized a check signed by Louis Jourdan. Canada Dry seltzer was hyped with a "seltzerbrate" campaign, and the brand's mixers enjoyed renewed advertising attention. The "mix with the best" campaign also featured couponing.

In 1983 Canada Dry utilized its first network radio advertising effort to promote ginger ale as an adult soft drink, becoming the exclusive sponsor of Daryl Hall and John Oates' 107-city U.S. tour. The rock-and-roll tour, which featured two network radio concerts, focused on Canada Dry's target age group of 18- to 34-year-olds. A special promotion on the Fourth of July weekend was especially profitable to local bottlers. That weekend, a three-hour concert was broadcast in 200 cities nationwide. The radio program featured seven minutes of Canada Dry advertisements on one of the most popular soft drink weekends of the year.

By the late 1980s, Canada Dry had firmly positioned itself in the adult beverage market with the slogan "For when your tastes grow up." Young & Rubicam set the product apart from other soft drinks, whose advertising depicted active teens. Television ads featured a young couple in romantic but tame home situations.

International Market

Although Canada Dry was locked out of the United States cola competition early on in the game, the international market held out more potential for growth. The brand was acquired by Cadbury Schweppes plc in 1986. Cadbury Schweppes, a growing international conglomerate, gained control of Canada Dry's line of mixers and ginger ale for U.S. sales. Young & Rubicam retained Canada Dry's $12 million advertising account for three more years, when the business was awarded to Foote, Cone & Belding's Chicago office. As part of Cadbury Schweppes' "beverage stream," Canada Dry is positioned for growth worldwide. The conglomerate holds 16 percent of the beverage market in France and is well positioned in the rest of Europe. While the U.S. soda market reaches saturation, analysts see the international soft drink business as a consumer growth industry, with room for three major competitors: Coca-Cola, Pepsi, and Cadbury Schweppes.

Despite its time-tested name and image, the brand is positioned in the "New Age" group of beverages. The category includes flavored mineral waters, tonic waters, and seltzers (which happen to be several of the brand's strengths). New Age beverage sales rose 18 percent in 1991, from $640 million in 1990 to $757.2 million. An aging U.S. population's preoccupation with fitness and consumers' quest for alternate beverages have combined to fuel the category's extraordinary growth.

The "change of pace" soft drinks introduced by Canada Dry include lemon and cranberry ginger ales and plain, lemon-citrus, and raspberry sparkling waters. In 1991 Canada Dry's ginger ale sales alone grew 8.2 percent on the introduction of flavored varieties to 50 percent of the United States and parts of Canada. The brand's sales increased by over 66 percent between 1991 and 1992, moving it from the 10th to the 8th most popular soft drink. Canada Dry's combination of old and new positions it as a vital brand for the 1990s and beyond.

Further Reading:

"Beyond the Water's Edge: The International Soft Drink Roundtable," *Beverage World*, January 31, 1991, p. 10.

Delaney, Tom, "Schweppes Guzzles Canada Dry: Coke Getting a Piece, Pepsi Getting Nothing," *AdWeek*, May 19, 1986, pp. 1, 6.

Flatow, Jennifer, "The Beverage World Top 50," *Beverage World*, July 1991, pp. 19, 22, 24.

Giges, Nancy, "Canada Dry, Pepsi-Cola Make Major Revamps," *Advertising Age*, December 13, 1971, p. 10.

Grimm, Matthew, "Another Not-so-sweet Pitch from Canada Dry," *AdWeek's Marketing Week*, June 8, 1992, p. 9.

Hume, Scott, "FCB sparkles," *Advertising Age*, July 17, 1989, p. 47.

Liff, Mark, "How One Campaign Worked," *Advertising Age*, November 7, 1983, p. M-48.

Mahoney, David, "How the Sparkle Turned to a Fizzle," *Advertising Age*, March 7, 1988, pp. 36, 39.

Pendleton, Jennifer, "Canada Dry Pins Hopes on Ginger Ale, Water Lines," *Advertising Age*, September 20, 1982, pp. 2, 92.

Riley, John J. *A History of the American Soft Drink Industry: 1807-1957*, Washington, D.C.: American Bottlers of Carbonated Beverages, 1958.

Sfiligoj, Eric, "Alive and Fizzing," *Beverage World*, August 1992, pp. 28-32. Wentz, Laurel, "Global Potential Sweet to Cadbury," *Advertising Age*, October 28 1991.

—*April S. Dougal*

CANADIAN MIST®

IMPORTED

CANADIAN MIST.

Canadian Mist began as a small, obscure brand in the mid-1960s introduced by Barton Brands, Inc., but a consumer shift to lighter whiskeys, combined with heavy advertising of the product, quickly increased the whiskey's popularity. The brand began as a blend of Canadian whiskeys bought and blended by Barton Brands. It was made from corn and barley malt and aged in mellowed, charred oak barrels.

Brand Origins

Barton Brands had started as a vender of whiskey to bottlers and vendors for resale under private labels, but by the 1960s it was forging its own brands. Whiskey was the firm's primary product, accounting for 90 percent of sales, and the company's products in this area were primarily heavier, bourbon whiskeys such as Kentucky Gentleman and Barton Reserve. Canadian Mist was introduced in very limited quantities in the mid-1960s so that the firm would have an entry in the lighter, Canadian whiskey category.

By 1966 the popularity of Canadian whiskey was soaring in the United States as consumers turned away from heavier, darker bourbon whiskeys toward the lighter brands. Lester S. Abelson, president of Barton Brands, Inc., decided to win part of that pie for his company by ratcheting up production of Canadian Mist. He was joined in that goal by marketing director Jerry Adler. Adler joined the company in 1966 and immediately restructured it, organizing the marketing staff along brand management lines and conducting the firm's first national consumer studies. These revealed that Canadian whiskeys were the fastest growing in the United States. As a result, the firm selected Canadian Mist as its potential top brand. It developed marketing plans, prototype advertisements, and special carton display cases and counter displays for Canadian Mist.

A new distillery was needed for volume production. Construction began at a site in Collingwood, Ontario, in 1966. Collingwood was in the depressed Georgia Bay area, making the project eligible for assistance from the Canadian government. The site also offered pure Lake Huron water, grain storage elevators on the harbor, and an ample, trained work force. Corn was grown in the area to the south, ensuring a steady, inexpensive supply of that vital ingredient.

Early Marketing Strategy

Advertising and image-building for the brand began in key markets in 1967. The distillery became operational in May 1967. It was extremely efficient, with almost full automation. Canadian Mist became Barton's first national brand when it was introduced in 1967, and the whiskey quickly became the firm's top seller. Market research showed that the product appealed more to blend drinkers than to Canadian whiskey drinkers, so it was marketed against leading American blends rather than Canadian whiskeys. Sales for 1968 reached $9.8 million.

Most of Barton's other products were not growing, and in 1968 the firm decided to phase out less profitable products and concentrate on its best prospects. As part of this campaign, the firm gave Canadian Mist a huge infusion of advertising, spending $2 million, an amount that matched what the company spent on all its other brands combined. The brand's promotion budget grew from $71,400 in 1965 to almost $2.5 million in 1970, while sales soared from its first-year level of 55,000 cases. The firm sold 229,000 cases of Canadian Mist in 1968, 470,000 in 1969, and close to 700,000 in 1970. The brand's 1970 sales of $37 million were over 25 percent of Barton's total, making it the firm's leading brand. Canadian Mist was the fastest growing brand in the Canadian whiskey category, the fastest growing segment of the liquor market. Nevertheless, it was still virtually unknown. To increase its visibility, Barton launched the brand's first national advertising campaign in mid-1970, with advertisements in *Life* and *Playboy* magazines.

Change in Parent Company

Despite the early success and growing promise of Canadian Mist, Barton sold it to Brown-Forman in 1971. Brown-Forman offered $34 million for the brand and its distillery, and since that was more than Barton Brands itself was worth, the company decided to sell. It was one of the first times a major liquor brand was sold separately to another company. The purchase price was considered high by some analysts, given that Canadian Mist was still a small, poorly distributed brand.

Brown-Forman, based in Louisville, Kentucky, was one of the oldest U.S. liquor firms, founded in 1870. Its success was based on growing or buying premium brands and heavily promoting them, charging prices high enough to entice customers to purchase pres-

AT A GLANCE

Canadian Mist brand of whiskey founded in the mid-1960s by Barton Brands, Inc.; bought by Brown-Forman Corp. in 1971; Canadian Mist brand currently part of Brown-Forman Beverage Company.

Performance: *Market share*—18.1% (top share) of U.S.-bottled Canadian whiskey category. *Sales*—$305.8 million.

Major competitor: Seagram's VO Canadian Whiskey.

Advertising: *Agency*—Altschiller Reitzfeld, 1992—. *Major campaign*—"Canada At Its Best" (McCann-Erickson advertising agency).

Addresses: *Parent company*—Brown-Forman Beverage Company, P.O. Box 1080, Louisville, Kentucky 40210-1091; phone: (502) 585-1100. *Ultimate parent company*—Brown-Forman Corporation, 850 Dixie Hwy., Louisville, Kentucky 40210-1091; phone: (502) 585-1100; fax: (502) 774-7833.

tige brands and pay for the advertising such brands require. Though the firm's leading brands, such as Jack Daniel's whiskey, were still growing, the market for bourbons was generally shrinking and the firm was diversifying. The popularity of Canadian whiskey was rising as consumers turned to lighter spirits and even soft drinks. Brown-Forman therefore saw Canadian Mist as an important piece of its long-term strategy. It hoped to use the brand to challenge the leading Canadian whiskey, Seagram's Seven Crown, a medium-priced blend.

Brown-Forman priced Canadian Mist in the mid-range. The product was distilled in Canada, then shipped in stainless-steel tank cars to Louisville, where it was watered down to 80 proof, then bottled. This method saved about 30 cents a bottle in taxes, savings not garnered by Seagram's VO Canadian Whiskey and Canadian Club, which were bottled in Canada. Canadian Mist was also bottled when it was four years old, compared with six years for some premium Canadian brands. Brown-Forman claimed that modern production methods, such as keeping the aging whiskey warm, made the additional aging unnecessary. It also made Canadian Mist less expensive to make. Brown-Forman could therefore undersell its competitors while still spending heavily on advertising.

Advertising Strategy

The McCann-Erickson advertising firm was hired. It set up a branch office in Louisville to coordinate communications between Brown-Forman and its main office in New York. Brown-Forman immediately increased advertising on Canadian Mist, bringing it up to the firm's standard 14 percent ad to sales ratio. Brown-Forman's market research showed that drinkers of rival Canadian whiskeys did not particularly associate those brands with Canada. So in addition to pushing Canadian Mist's light color and smooth taste, the firm began positioning Canadian Mist as the most Canadian of the Canadian whiskeys. It began the theme, "Canada at its Best," which appeared in every Canadian Mist ad for over 20 years, an unusually long period of consistency in advertising. Two ads were produced each year showing a bottle of Canadian Mist positioned against dramatic photographs of the Canadian Rockies. The snow, streams, and lakes of the mountains reinforced the brand's claim to lightness and smoothness. Models were deliberately left out of the scene because it was felt they were a distrac-

tion; executives wanted the Canadian Mist bottle itself to stand for the freshness of Canada.

Meanwhile, the Brown-Forman sales force began working on distributors, getting the brand into stores. To further encourage consumers to try it, the firm promoted Canadian Mist's lower price for the only time in its advertising history. Though it was consistently priced at about $2 a bottle lower than rivals like Canadian Club and Seagram's VO, thereafter Brown-Forman touted it only as a premium brand, leaving its lower price as a "pleasant surprise" to be discovered at the liquor store.

By 1974 Canadian Mist was selling at the rate of 1.75 million cases a year. At that point, the brand had shifted into its next advertising phase. It still used photographs of the Canadian Rockies, but Brown-Forman had learned more about Canadian Mist drinkers. Whiskey was one of many alcoholic beverages they drank, depending on the occasion. So Canadian Mist was touted as the liquor to drink when they wanted a whiskey.

In 1974 Brown-Forman set up a brand management system for all of its brands. It saw this as the best means of positioning its brands in the intensely competitive distilled spirits market. The move gave the manager of Canadian Mist, as well as managers of the firm's other brands, control over everything from packaging to advertising and promotion. Bud Ballard was named senior brand manager of Canadian Mist. One of his earliest moves was to hire Burrell Public Relations Inc. in Chicago to work on an ad campaign to attract African-American consumers to Canadian Mist. A series of people-oriented ads was developed that depicted elegantly dressed black couples with mist eddying around their feet. The logo read, "Misting. Misting is settling for nothing but the best." The campaign worked. By 1984 African-Americans accounted for 25 percent of Canadian Mist sales.

Canadian Mist sales continued to grow as competitor sales were leveling off or falling. In 1977 sales reached 2 million cases, in 1979 2.5 million cases. The advertising campaign moved into new phases. First, social drinking was featured, with two glasses pictured in the ads with the caption, "Share some tonight." Then quality was pushed more strongly than ever as Canadian Mist sales moved up on those of Seagram's VO and Canadian Club. The phrase "Canada at its best" became more prominent.

Magazine ads were placed to precisely reach the brand's audience, men and woman 21 to 54 years old, at a ratio of 60 percent men to 40 percent women. Men were targeted through advertising in such magazines as *Outdoor Life*, *Field and Stream*, and *Inside Sports*. Men and women were reached using *People*, *Sports Illustrated*, *Time*, and *Newsweek*. Canadian Mist was also advertised in black magazines like *Dawn* and *Ebony*. Because Brown-Forman was such a large advertising buyer, it could split its ads to target geographic areas. So, for example, Canadian Mist was not advertised in Minnesota, where Windsor Canadian whiskey was deemed too strong to challenge. Outdoor advertising was also used, particularly in larger cities like Chicago and St. Louis, and in densely populated states such as California.

In 1983 Canadian Mist sales increased 5.5 percent to become the best-selling Canadian whiskey in the United States, passing Seagram's VO Canadian Whiskey. This goal was achieved despite a liquor industry downturn that came on the tail end of a recession. Advertising spending was running at about $10 million a year, down slightly from the previous year because of the cost of coupons. Canadian Mist's competitors were heavily promoting their brands through the use of discount coupons, and Brown-Forman responded in kind, taking money from advertising to pay for the coupons.

In 1988 the "Misting" campaign was replaced by a "Mist Behavin' " campaign. The new campaign still showed African-Americans in elegant attire, but rather than sitting and looking at the viewer, they were engaged in playful flirtation. In 1989 the "Canada At Its Best" campaign was updated to include "North American Wildlife," moose and reindeer striding majestically through pools of water or mountain meadows.

Canadian Mist's sales growth slowed as the 1990s began and the overall liquor market continued to shrink. Nonetheless, the brand was the number eight liquor brand in 1991, selling nearly 3.3 million cases. Canadian Club, the second-place Canadian whiskey, sold 2.1 million cases.

In October 1992 Brown-Forman named Altschiller Reitzfeld, based in New York, the lead advertising firm for Canadian Mist.

Further Reading:

"Barton Brands Enjoys Profitable Blend of New and Upgraded Lines," *Barron's,* June 8, 1970.

"Brown-Forman to Buy Barton's Canada Business," *Wall Street Journal,* May 21, 1971.

Fromson, Brett Duval, "Keeping It All in the Family," *Fortune,* September 25, 1989.

"Little Giant," *Forbes,* October 15, 1974.

"Not Everybody Drinks Rum, White Wine or Perrier," *Marketing and Media Decisions,* Spring 1984.

O'Connor, John J., "B-F Ready to Pour It On," *Advertising Age,* August 10, 1988.

"One Drink at a Time," *Sales Management,* October 1, 1970.

—Scott M. Lewis

CAP'N CRUNCH®

Quaker Oats Company's Cap'n Crunch Cereal was introduced in 1963 and has steadily held the position as the second highest-selling presweetened cereal since 1965. The cereal's namesake has remained the focal point of advertising efforts over the years as well. The white-haired Cap'n graces the bright red box with his portly and jovial figure, decked out in a blue admiral's uniform and hat.

Brand Origins

During the 1940s, Quaker's Minneapolis-based competitor General Mills began experimenting with a cartoon-character approach to advertising its cereals. It enlisted the help of Disney World, among other organizations, for creative ideas. During this same decade Quaker, stolidly carrying its unsweetened, healthy cereals such as Quick Oats, Puffed Oats, and Puffed Rice, worked on a new product. The company put a sugar coated Puffed Rice on the market in 1950, which did not farewell.

Despite this initial unsuccessful foray into sugared cereals, Quaker made another all-out effort to enter the profitable presweetened market in the late 1950s. From market research Quaker discovered that children younger than ten preferred crunchy cereals to those with flakes (which tended to get soggy). At the time, according to industry standards, new cereals were developed in-house. The product ideas were then forwarded to merchandising departments for naming, packaging, promotion and marketing.

As Arthur Marquette summed up in *Brands, Trademarks, and Goodwill,* "The most successful cereal of the decade reversed that order. The idea for the new cereal was first hatched and then a cereal was cooked up to meet the specifications marketing men drew up." The Quaker advertising team pictured a character to represent their cereal; according to Marquette, the company designed "a trademark strong in juvenile appeal; a salty, bumbling old sea captain." This captain was to be surrounded by a close group of pals, not exclusively humans. Quaker named their cereal Cap'n Crunch, creating a unity of trademark and product description.

It was only after all this creative work that Quaker manufactured a corn-oats derived nugget, which was then toasted and coated with sugar. The cereal stayed crisp in milk. With the first stage of a big project complete, Quaker approached outside agencies to further develop the idea into a television advertising campaign.

Advertising Development

At this time, General Mills was searching for advertising shine as well. When the Disney connection didn't pan out, General Mills went to Jay Ward, a Harvard MBA real estate man who dabbled in creative work on the side. In 1959 Jay Ward met cartoon writer Bill Scott, a cowriter for the *Mr. Magoo* show, who was looking for a chance to further explore his talent. The two formed Jay Ward Productions, creating the television series *Rocky and his*

Friends (with the famous characters Bullwinkle and Dudley Do-Right) in their first year.

With General Mills, Ward produced the first animated commercials for Cheerios, Cocoa Puffs, Trix, and other cereals, which aired in 1959. But Scott went a bit too far with the humor, alienating some General Mills executives. In stepped Quaker, with its crunchy cereal all ready to go. Jay Ward Productions, along with heavy-hitters Disney and Hanna-Barbera, were just some of many agencies Quaker approached to help market its new product. Bill Scott developed characters and wrote commercials. Al Burus worked on drawings. Burus is credited by Ward's animation director Bill Hurtz for naming the ship the captain sailed (the Guppy) and for creating Cap'n Crunch's nemesis, the pirate Jean La Foote. Another key character the Ward team developed was Seadog, the Cap'n's buddy.

The Cap'n's Debut

Cap'n Crunch debuted in September, 1963; the commercials test marketed in six cities. As described by Jim Hall in *Mighty Minutes,* "In his first appearance, the Guppy's skipper, with his white walrus mustache and blue Napoleonic hat, assured his viewers that the Quaker cereal 'has to be good because they named it after me!' " The first series of commercials also featured the slogan "It's got corn for crunch, oats for punch, and its stays crunchy even in milk." Sailing along with the Cap'n were a crew of half-pints: four children with realistic, endearing traits. There was pony-tailed Brunnhilde, bespectacled Alfie, gap-toothed Dave, and the speechless little Carlyle. And always, the popular Seadog.

The best-executed episode, according to author Jim Hall, was "Breakfast Aboard the Guppy," in which the ship is invaded by cross-country bicyclists and Martians, to name a few characters. "But no one," states Hall, "was as voracious as a pirate named Jean La Foote, who conspired throughout the series to steal the Guppy's precious cereal cargo." The Jay Ward style—mixing mature satire with sophisticated messages—was a great hit with children and adults alike.

Plant production could not keep up with the immediate surge in sales of Quaker's first sweetened-cereal hit. Stores in the test markets could not stay stocked. Preparing for national distribution, Quaker built a plant devoted to Cap'n Crunch production in Cedar Rapids, Iowa. By 1965, Cap'n Crunch rose to the number-two position in presweetened cereal sales nationally. The cereal was the top seller in New York and Chicago and outsold 55 competitors. Soon fans grouped into "Crunch clubs" in various locations across the United States.

Cap'n Crunch Cousins

Riding the crest of popularity, Quaker commissioned Jay Ward Productions to create other cereal characters. As America raced to the moon in the 1960s, the propeller-headed alien Quisp arrived on

AT A GLANCE

Cap'n Crunch brand of cereal founded in 1963 by Quaker Oats Company. Quaker advertising team first created Cap'n character and named cereal, then Quaker developed cereal.

Performance: *Market share*—3% of cold cereal market (number two selling presweetened cereal). *Sales*—$250 million.

Major competitor: General Mills's Cocoa Puffs, Count Chocula, Frankenberry.

Advertising: *Agency*—Bayer Bess Vanderwarker, Chicago, IL. *Major campaign*—"Who's the real Cap'n?"; "Where's the Cap'n?" campaign of 1985 which elicited public participation in a man-hunt for a missing person, Cap'n Horatio Crunch.

Addresses: *Parent company*—Quaker Oats Company, P. O. Box 9001, 321 North Clark Street, Chicago, IL 60610; phone: (312) 222-7111.

the cereal scene. As with Cap'n Crunch and his nemesis LaFoote, Quisp was confronted by a hard-hat superhero named Quake.

Oddly enough, General Mills apparently had not been intimidated by Quaker's success with Cap'n Crunch in the mid-1960s. Instead, General Mills's own advertising agency (Dancer, Fitzgerald, Sample) sought to use characters developed by Ward Productions years after Cap'n Crunch was introduced. But after Quaker's second generation of Ward characters gained popular support, General Mills was nonchalant no longer. All the cereal manufacturers noticed that Ward Productions was onto something with its rivalry theme in cereal characters.

By the early 1970s, General Mills struck back with a number of cereals developed around a monster theme. Count Chocula, Frankenberry, and Booberry performed their own version of the Cap'n Crunch-Pirate LaFoote and Quisp-Quake sparring. Count Chocula and Frankenberry maintained their popularity for decades afterward.

Cap'n Crunch Spinoffs

Beginning in the 1970s a host of cereals designed by Quaker capitalized on the Cap'n Crunch theme. The Crunchberry Beast surfaced with Crunch Berries, featuring strawberry flavored nuggets that were mixed with the original cereal. Then came Smedley the elephant with Peanut Butter Crunch. Other characters represented less popular versions: Jean La Foote offered Cinnamon Crunch, Wilma the white whale spouted Vanilly Crunch, Chockle the Blob pushed Choco Crunch. Punch Crunch appeared with the other cereals, but it was not strongly identified with any particular character.

As stated in a company source, the last animated character Jay Ward developed for the Quaker Oats Company was King Vitamin in 1970. Within a few years, the now-confident sweetened cereal producer decided to use a live spokesperson instead, and thus ended the reign of Ward's cartoon character in Quaker advertising. The animation of Cap'n Crunch and his host of characters led to a 22-year working relationship between Jay Ward Productions and Quaker Oats, resulting in more than 500 commercials.

Sweet Cereal?

In 1979 studies revealed that the sugar content was as high as 57 percent in some cereals; even the venerable Post Raisin Bran was culpable, with sugar totalling 32 percent by weight. By the early 1980s the public voiced its desire that nutrition as well as entertainment be considered by cereal producers. Some zealous reformers even campaigned to get advertisements pulled from the Saturday morning television slot.The commotion had no effect on cereal sales. But manufacturers did discover that while sales to children comprised a huge 25 percent chunk of the market, adults were buying the other 75 percent. With that in mind, producers began to gear products for family consumption.

With institutions such as the American Cancer Society stressing the benefits of whole grains and fiber, experts predicted a decline in the popularity of presweetened cereal. But the bottom line was that sweet cereals kept selling. Cap'n Crunch's popularity was not affected, and Quaker's newcomer, Choco Crunch, also sold well. Heavily sweetened cereals, it seemed, were here to stay. A reporter noted in a 1984 issue of *Advertising Age,* "The convenience of Quaker Oats Co.'s Choco Crunch, compared with Quaker Oats hot cereal, is what makes it acceptable to busy parents." In the October 1986 *Consumer Reports,* Cap'n Crunch was ranked—along with one other cereal—at the very bottom of cereals studied due to high sugar content. The same magazine judged Cap'n Crunch in the lowest category of nutritional quality in a 1988 article devoted to the subject. These results did not move Cap'n Crunch from its number two spot in the presweetened cereal category, however.

Where's Cap'n?

The Cap'n Crunch brand, undaunted by such studies, moved right along—off the supermarket shelves and into consumers' kitchens. A popular campaign launched in 1981 centered on the disappearance of the barefoot pirate LaFoote. As reported by William Robinson, president of a Chicago marketing services agency, in the October 10, 1985 *Advertising Age,* 25 million calls reached the 800 telephone number set up for the "Find LaFoote" promotion.

In 1985 Cap'n Crunch brand managers Jerry Perkins, Tom Feitel, and ad agency Backer & Spielvogel's Ray Rhamey staged one of the largest missing-person searches—this time for Cap'n Horatio Crunch himself. Golin/Harris Communications handled the public relations for the Quaker campaign budgeted at $18 million. One million dollars was offered as a cash prize, to be split by however many contestants guessed correctly.

In an unusual move, Quaker shipped boxes of Cap'n Crunch, Crunch Berries, Peanut Butter Crunch and Choco Crunch with a blank space and question mark where the captain's face appeared. Clues were given via "detective kits" in three separate boxes of the cereal. The campaign culminated with a two-minute television commercial, run on the Saturday 9:30-10:30 a.m. slot, which explained the captain's disappearance.

In a related promotion, a double-acrostic was delivered through the "Crunch Chronicle", which was stuffed into student publications. The puzzle was offered as a special sweepstakes for college-age fans. Cap'n Crunch enjoyed a substantial following among the age group, since many had been born the same year the Cap'n was introduced, and had grown up with the brand.

The "Where's Cap'n?" campaign—inspired by and designed for the 22-year-old brand, succeeded on a number of fronts. It reached its main objective, which was to build awareness of the brand among children ages six through twelve. The promotion also introduced a modern world for the aging captain. A related bonus was the sprouting of Crunch clubs in various college campuses. Most importantly, during the promotion dollar sales of Cap'n Crunch cereal increased by 50 percent.

Experiments

In the 1990s Quaker tried promotions linked with educational materials. The company's "Who's the Real Cap'n?" campaign was joined with a packet demonstrating exercises in visual discrimination, logical reasoning, and following directions. The tie-in with Lifetime Learning Systems of Fairfield, Connecticut reached an estimated 93 percent of public and private schools nationwide. While Quaker considered the possible negative effects the promotion might have on parents or teachers, Lifetime Learning Systems stated that many teachers welcomed any extra assistance provided by major corporations. A spokeswoman for the National Congress of Parents and Teachers stated in the *Wall Street Journal* that her group's guidelines on school programming outlined that corporate involvement "must be structured to meet an identified educational need, not a commercial motive."

Quaker veered off the beaten path to try a few other products including Cap'n Crunch cookies and an instant drink called Cap'n Crunch's Ship Shake. A new version of the Cap'n crunch cereal emerged in the late 1980s, complete with red and green nuggets— a special holiday version called Christmas Crunch. Other variations on the theme emerged as well; Triple Crunch offered three 6-ounce bags of regular Cap'n Crunch, Crunch Berries, and Peanut Butter Crunch in one box. Cap'n Crunch line extensions did well, considering they all tasted remarkably like the original.

Projections

Through the growing number of warehouse and membership stores popular in the 1990s, Quaker offered a larger size of its original brand. The company also offered value-added premiums to the food service-size packages, such as a plastic reclosure device called the Crunch Clip. Such premiums provided product differentiation in the increasingly competitive, yet lucrative, sweetened cereal market. Quaker increasingly relied on promotional packages offered for a limited time to increase its market share.

The basic Cap'n Crunch cereal remained by far the favorite. According to Quaker annual reports, Cap'n Crunch improved its number two position in the expanding presweetened cereal segment in the early 1990s and enjoyed the best overall growth record in its category in the industry.

Further Reading:

"Breakfast Cereals," *Consumer Reports,* October, 1989, p. 280.

"Cereal-Crunching Sleuths Ponder: Where's Cap'n?" *Advertising Age,* September 9, 1985.

"Cereal Namesake Slips into Schools," *Wall Street Journal,* February 14, 1991, p. B-1.

Cleaver, Joanne, "Cereal Picture Stays Sweet," *Advertising Age,* May 3, 1984.

Franz, Julie, "Quaker Oats Finds Cap'n Crunch Loot with Hide-and-Seek," *Advertising Age,* May 26, 1986, p. 53.

"Jay Ward: The Emperor of the Grain Ghetto," p. 12-16.

Hall, Jim, *Mighty Minutes: An Illustrated History of Television's Best Commercials,* New York, Harmony Books, 1984.

"Plastic Clip Keeps Cap'n Crunchy," *Packaging,* March 1992, p. 15.

"Ready to Eat Cereals," *Consumer Reports,* October, 1986, p. 636.

Robinson, William A., "Quaker Puts Wind in Cap'n's Sales," *Advertising Age,* October 10, 1985.

—Frances E. Norton

CARNATION®

Carnation brand evaporated milk—one of the oldest, continuously produced milk products in the country—was first manufactured in 1899 by the Pacific Coast Condensed Milk Company, which was renamed Carnation Milk Products Company in 1916. What once constituted the basis of the company's fortune for many years has long since been eclipsed by a host of instant food products. The Carnation Company, having had yet another name change, was acquired in 1985 by one of the largest food companies in the world, Nestlé S.A. of Vevey, Switzerland, and eventually named the Nestlé Food Company. The Carnation brand, however, continues to be a world leader in the evaporated milk market, and has major shares of dozens of other, nondairy food products.

Brand Origins

When grocer-turned-entrepreneur Elbridge A. Stuart and his partner, Tom Yerxa, established a condensed milk plant outside of Seattle in 1899, his product was nothing new. Gail Borden had begun marketing his Eagle Brand condensed milk in 1853, and in 1866 two Americans started the Anglo-Swiss Condensed Milk Company, later merged with Henri Nestlé's infant formula business. However, unlike other condensed milk that was preserved with sugar, theirs was evaporated by a unique process invented by a Swiss man, John Meyenberg, who had left the Anglo-Swiss Condensed Milk Company to try his fortune in America. Meyenberg brought his "secret" with him, and had it patented in 1884.

Meyenberg's method involved sterilizing milk under intense heat, which afterward required no preservatives or additives. The milk, once canned, could stay "fresh" and whole for many months. It agreed with infants when mother's milk did not, and was safer than most milk in the late nineteenth century, which was often processed in unsanitary conditions, resulting in high bacteria counts and illness for the consumer. Stuart and Yerxa hired Meyenberg, putting him in charge of canned milk production, using his unique formula. Despite having a patent, Meyenberg was so fearful that his formula might be stolen, he even refused to divulge his methods to the partners. Finally, in 1901, Stuart paid him $25,000 to reveal the secret of condensing and evaporating milk.

That same year Yerxa sold his share in the business to Stuart. It had grown steadily, thanks in part to the Alaska gold rush and the huge demand for a product that would keep for months in the wild.

The company had not yet begun to use the Carnation brand name, however.

Early Marketing Strategy

Now in charge of his own company, E. A. Stuart faced the prospect of thousands of red and white labeled cans of evaporated milk piling up in his warehouse without a brand name, in a day and age when brands—like Ivory soap, Uneeda biscuits, Pet Milk, and Red Cross shoes—were increasingly important attention getters. One day in 1901, as he was walking down a Seattle street, his eye caught sight of boxes of cigars with the improbable name of Carnation. In that instant he decided to adopt the name for his own milk product. Carnations would appear on the labels to easily identify the cans, especially for children who might not otherwise remember the brand name.

With a name for his product at last, and new canning facilities installed in his plant, Stuart's product was well launched. However, in the days before national advertising, it was up to Stuart to convince storekeepers to put cans of Carnation on their shelves, often necessitating comparisons between Borden's Eagle Brand and his own. In order to do this, Stuart himself went from grocer to grocer, handing out cans of Carnation from a sample case and also persuading wary housewives that the canned milk contained no additives, just pure, whole milk. While this strategy was laborious and time consuming, it was effective. Once established as a regional success, Stuart traveled to all parts of the country, persuading and demonstrating his samples until they won acceptance. Soon Carnation brand evaporated milk began showing up on grocery shelves on the east coast.

To make Carnation better known, however, an advertising agency had to be engaged. Stuart found one in Chicago in 1906, where a young copywriter by the name of Helen Mar inadvertently suggested a catchy slogan that launched a major campaign for the brand the following year. While listening to Stuart as he was describing the beautiful pastures and healthy cows out West, Mar spontaneously remarked, "Ah, the milk of contented cows!" Stuart, with his innate sense of business, recognized instantly the value of that particular phrase. He adopted the "slogan," and from then on Carnation evaporated milk was sold as "the milk of contented cows." With this combination of business savvy, advertising, and a catchy, easily remembered slogan Carnation evapo-

AT A GLANCE

Carnation brand of evaporated milk founded by grocer turned entrepreneur Elbridge Amos Stuart for the Pacific Coast Condensed Milk Company, in Seattle, WA, 1899; in 1916, company changed its name to the Carnation Milk Products Company and in 1929, to the Carnation Company; 1985, the Carnation Company was acquired by Nestlé, S.A. of Vevey, Switzerland, becoming the Nestlé/Carnation Food Company; 1991, Nestlé USA Inc. formed as a subsidiary of Nestlé S.A. and Nestlé/Carnation Food Company changed its name to Nestlé Food Company.

Advertising: Agency—McCann-Erickson Worldwide, Los Angeles, CA, 1991—. *Major campaign*—None for evaporated milk; (for hot cocoa) "Something magic always happens with Carnation Hot Cocoa."

Major competitor: Pet Milk; Borden's Eagle Brand condensed milk.

Addresses: Parent company—Nestlé Food Company, 100 Manhattanville Rd., Purchase, NY 10577; phone: (914) 251-3000. *Ultimate parent company*—Nestlé USA Inc., 800 N. Brand Blvd., Glendale, CA 91203; phone: (818) 549-6000; fax: (818) 549-6952. *Ultimate ultimate parent company*—Nestlé S.A.

rated milk became the number one condensed milk brand in the country by the outbreak of World War I.

Advertising Innovations

The advertising campaign that introduced Carnation's new slogan in 1907 was limited to such available media as billboards, ads in streetcars, and newspapers. The absence of radio and television made it difficult to reach the product's target market, housewives. Even the majority of newspaper readers were men, who would be little interested in the virtues of canned milk. Therefore, Stuart still felt compelled to travel the country, selling his product to grocers in person.

A 1908 Carnation advertisement in Kansas City emphasized the "purity" of the product. The contrast between fresh milk, straight from the cow, and the sterilized—hence, completely free of germs—canned milk was noted often, and in the era prior to scientific dairy farming, the contrast was probably not exaggerated. In the summer, when exposure to the hot sun caused the bacteria count of fresh milk to skyrocket, "summer sickness" was common. The virtue of drinking sterilized condensed milk was not lost on the consumer.

In 1912, to reach more consumers, the customarily cautious Stuart began advertising in popular glossy household magazines read by millions of women nationwide. Carnation's billboard and streetcar ads also changed. Instead of colorless and informative, they now featured the poignant image of a beautiful young mother and baby gazing out on a picturesque scene of "contented cows" grazing on lush grass, surrounded by mountains. Later, stressing the healthfulness of evaporated milk for babies, Carnation became the first food company in the nation to advertise in *Ebony,* a magazine geared toward African-Americans, which began circulating in the late 1940s.

America's entry into the First World War saw sales of Carnation canned milk skyrocket as it became a staple for the doughboy

in uniform. The Depression of the early 1930s, nonetheless, hit the company hard. The need to advertise was paramount, and radio provided the answer. Nabisco, the cookie and cracker maker, had its own radio program that sent sales soaring, and Carnation decided to do likewise.

In 1931, a half-hour popular music program dubbed "The Carnation Contented Hour" ran west of the Rockies. It proved so successful that it was soon airing nationally. That year, when the American Medical Association approved the safety and wholesomeness of evaporated milk for babies, Carnation lost no time advertising this on its radio program. In addition, Carnation aired news of a company-sponsored slogan contest in 1932, and informed its listeners about improvements to its product. Thus Carnation was able to weather the Depression, until World War II once again sent sales of evaporated milk soaring.

Product Development

For nearly 30 years the Pacific Coast Condensed Milk Company had manufactured only one product—Carnation evaporated milk. E. A. Stuart improved his product significantly when his company became the first in the United States to introduce homogenization. The year was 1905, and Stuart paid a French inventor $2,000 for a machine that could homogenize milk and keep the butter in the milk from separating in the can. This innovative process put Carnation at a distinct advantage over such canned milk products as Pet Milk and Borden's Eagle Brand. Furthermore, the company began adding vitamin D to the evaporated milk in 1934.

The recession that followed the First World War convinced Stuart of the benefits in diversifying his company. In 1926 Carnation entered the ice cream and fresh milk businesses. Several years later the company's product line was further expanded with the acquisition of Albers Bros. Milling Company, which manufactured such diverse items as cold breakfast cereals and pet food, a still relatively new product concept. In the 1930s, on the verge of Carnation's major growth period, Stuart turned the leadership of the company over to his son.

The years after World War II coincided with the population explosion, the rise of suburbia, and the craving for convenience foods. In response to this trend, Carnation underwent some profound changes. In the 1950s and 1960s a barrage of new instant products—the fastest growing and most profitable sector of the company—came out of Carnation's research and development labs. Meanwhile, evaporated milk continued to be a major component in Carnation's product line—several million cases of canned milk are still sold annually—as well as the leading branded canned food in the world, selling better overseas and in Canada, where, despite the sparse population, twice as much evaporated milk was consumed than in the United States.

In 1953 Carnation launched its instant nonfat dry milk, the most important product innovation for Carnation milk in its history. A year later chocolate flavored instant powdered milk debuted, and Carnation instant hot chocolate, the first Carnation product to take advantage of the new television advertising medium, was marketed nationally in 1955. Ten years later Carnation introduced the nondairy coffee creamer, Coffeemate, which eventually garnered the nation's top spot in its market.

In the 1970s and 1980s, Carnation responded to health trends by offering canned milk in three varieties—lowfat, lite, and regular—and targeting its nondairy coffee creamers to the lactose-intolerant consumer. In addition, the company began advertising the fact that Carnation Instant Hot Chocolate is 99% caffeine free.

Meanwhile, with the acquisition of the Carnation Company in 1985 by Nestlé S.A., the world's largest food company, product diversification and sophisticated promotional tactics have accelerated. Coffeemate is now offered in liquid form, as well as in flavors, including amaretto, hazelnut, and Irish creme. Carnation instant cocoa has become the market leader in the United States by targeting youngsters with packaging that features television cartoon characters and games. From frozen foods to baby formulas to pet foods, Carnation became a world leader in product innovation and marketing.

International Growth

A major aspect of Carnation's business was its important foreign markets. The company began its expansion, not in its home country, but in Europe, immediately after the First World War. Carnation and its chief domestic competitor in the evaporated milk market, Pet Milk, agreed to jointly establish the American Milk Products Company in order to funnel their products overseas. Headquartered in Paris, Carnation owned a 65 percent interest and Pet Milk, the remainder. The establishment of high tariff barriers in Europe in the 1920s, prompted the American Milk Products Company to begin manufacturing evaporated milk, first in France and later in Germany.

This important European base expanded continuously, despite keen competition from Great Britain and Holland. Eventually affiliates sprang up in South Africa, Mexico, Peru, and Australia—areas of the world in which canned milk was often much safer to drink than fresh milk. In 1966 Pet Milk sold its share of the company to Carnation, which established an international division that continued its penetration of foreign markets. By the early 1970s, this division had joint ventures worldwide.

The company's acquisition by Nestlé—one of the fastest growing food companies in the world, which weathered the recession of the 1990s with an annual growth rate of five percent—further broadened Carnation's distribution networks, adding channels in virtually every country on earth. Poised to take advantage of Nestlé's inroads in such increasingly important areas as Asia and Eastern Europe, Nestlé's fastest growing market, the Carnation brand will surely benefit from its relationship with the food giant.

Further Reading:

Fucini, J. J. and S. F., *Entrepreneurs; the Men and Women Behind Famous Brand Names and How They Made It*, Boston: Holt & Co., 1985.

Hambleton, Ronald, *The Branding of America*, Dublin, NY: Yankee Books, 1987.

Johnson, Bradley, "Carnation Remixes Advertising Formula," *Advertising Age*, January 7, 1991, p.12.

Marshall, James L., *Elbridge A. Stuart, Founder of Carnation Company*, Los Angeles: Carnation Company, 1970.

Nestlé S.A. Annual Report, Vevey, Switzerland: Nestlé S.A., 1991.

Nestlé USA Inc. Annual Report, Glendale, CA: Nestlé USA Inc., 1991.

Reiff, Rick, "Baby Bottle Battle," *Forbes*, November 28, 1988, p. 222.

Schurman, Jeff, "Carnation Anticipates Growth in the Future," *Leader-Telegram*, March 15, 1992.

Stiling, Marjorie, *Famous Brand Names, Emblems, Trademarks*, Newton Abbot, Vermont: David & Charles, 1980.

Weaver, John D., *Carnation, the First Fifty Years, 1899-1974*, Los Angeles: Carnation Company, 1974.

—Sina Dubovoj

CERTS®

Certs breath mints are the number one selling brand of hard roll breath mints in the nation. When the brand made its debut in 1956, it was the first product of its type—a candy breath mint in tablet form that provided both pleasant taste and breath freshening properties. Before Certs, mint candies and breath fresheners were marketed as separate products. Certs was the first to combine the two types so that consumers could have the sweetness of candy with the extra benefit of having clean breath. Certs users could be sure of protecting their breath, particularly in social situations where people are anxious about bad breath.

From its beginning, Certs has developed through laboratory research, market research, advertising and merchandising techniques, and packaging design. By targeting new flavors and new types of Certs products to different groups of consumers with varying needs and interests, as well as replacing non-performing products with changes or improvements, the brand's owner, the Warner-Lambert Company, has been successful in retaining its market share and leadership since 1970. To ensure consumer awareness and acceptance, each new product entry was accompanied by advertising and promotional efforts, and sometimes even new packaging that helped consumers to identify differences among Certs products.

Brand Origins

Certs was first marketed in 1956 by the American Chicle Company (which later became known as the American Chicle Group). The product grew out of American Chicle's interest in developing a product that had the deodorizing qualities of chlorophyll, but wouldn't stain the tongue green. In the 1940s and 1950s chlorophyll was used in gums, mints, and toothpastes. American Chicle added chlorophyll to its Chiclets brand gum to make Clorets, which were then marketed as breath sweeteners in chewing gum or mint form.

First Candy Breath Mint, Early Marketing Strategy

American Chicle decided to research the properties of chlorophyll in order to determine how it absorbed odors. The result was identification of a substance called Retsyn, a finely homogenized vegetable oil. The droplets of oil are less than ten microns in size and present a wide area for the absorption of oral odors. American Chicle had the product certified for safety by U.S. Testing Laboratories, and in the process gave the product the name of Certs.

Further testing confirmed the breath freshening properties of Retsyn and its staying power in protecting fresh breath, and as of 1993 Certs remained the only mint to contain Retsyn.

Pricing was a key factor in launching Certs. The brand was competing not only with other products made by American Chicle but with brands of other companies. American Chicle couldn't sell Certs for 5 cents like its main competitor, Life Savers, and still afford national advertising. Its own Clorets sold for 15 cents, but it was thought that this price would meet with consumer resistance. The reasoning was that if Certs could be priced at 10 cents, it would be in a strong position when Life Savers raised its price to 10 cents in the future. It was also thought that consumers would be willing to pay for a mint candy that also provided the added benefit of freshening their breath.

Market testing of Certs began along with its introduction. Its initial response from consumers was lackluster in Chicago, the first city in which it was tested. American Chicle decided to change its packaging to gold foil, but consumer response again was poor. The next decision was to introduce new flavors to include peppermint, spearmint, and fruit. Flavors not only give pleasant taste to Certs but help to mask breath odors.

Other marketing changes were enacted: the original 20-count display box was reduced to 12 rolls per box, and various display racks were designed to meet each display need. In addition, several TV commercials were produced and tested on the air to determine which method was most effective in producing sales.

First Commercial Success, Later Product Development

Further testing took place in three cities: Seattle, San Francisco, and Los Angeles. Here, too, advertising and merchandising changes did not have a positive effect on sales. The future of Certs looked dim until a new advertising tactic was developed, one that emphasized the brand's unique characteristics of giving great taste and freshening breath at the same time. The ad campaign "Two Mints in One" was introduced in Los Angeles and achieved the desired results. Sales objectives were realized, and the company decided to launch Certs nationally in the summer of 1960.

By 1970, Certs was available in several different flavors, and still at the same price of 10 cents. The flavors included pep-

AT A GLANCE

Certs brand of breath mints originated in 1956 by the American Chicle Company, a candy and confectionery group begun in 1927 and located in Cambridge, MA, and which later became known as American Chicle Group; American Chicle acquired by the Warner-Lambert Company, 1962.

Performance: *Market share*—29.3% (top share) of hard roll/breath mints. *Sales*—$141 million.

Major competitor: Nabisco Foods Group's Life Savers brand candies.

Advertising: *Agency*—Young & Rubicam, New York, NY, 1979—. *Major campaign*—"Be Certain with Certs," using comedians Bobby Collins, Richard Jeni, and Rita Rudner doing monologues.

Addresses: *Parent company*—Warner-Lambert Company, 201 Tabor Rd., Morris Plains, NJ 07950; phone: 201-540-2000.

permint, spearmint, wintergreen, and four fruit flavors; other flavors included crystal, spring mint, cool spice, and new winter. The target group for the mint was young adults who were concerned about covering up strong food odors, freshening their breath, and keeping it fresh.

In 1982 Sugarfree Certs were introduced. This type of Certs was targeted to health-conscious consumers, particularly women who wanted fewer calories in their breath mints. In 1987 Certs introduced New Sugarfree Certs with NutraSweet, the sugar substitute that was familiar to consumers as an ingredient in many other types of products.

From 1988 to 1991 three new Certs products debuted in order to get the competitive edge on rivals who were introducing candy breath mint products. In 1988 Sugarfree Mini-Mints with NutraSweet were introduced, in peppermint, spearmint, cherry, and assorted fruit flavors. These mini-mints had a different size and shape from other core Certs products, and were marketed in response to Tic Tac producer Ferrero Worldwide, and other candy manufacturers who were selling their mints in small, pellet form.

In 1991 two new Certs products were marketed. Certs Fresh Fruit was targeted to the fruit candy user, and Certs Blizzards Mints were geared toward the older consumer who wanted extra protection against bad breath. In 1993 Extra Flavor Mints were marketed in three varieties: spearmint, peppermint, and wintergreen. These mints are ten percent larger than core Certs.

Innovative Packaging, Advertising

Packaging played a key role in marketing Certs, because as each new product was introduced it was necessary to help consumers differentiate one Certs product from another. For example, Extra Flavor Certs were packaged in gold foil to distinguish from regular Certs in silver foil. In 1988 Mini-Mints were packaged in a clear box to suggest to consumers that this Certs product was a completely new and different type of Certs.

In addition to brandishing distinct packages, each new type of Certs product was introduced with a new marketing theme. The aim was to show consumers how this particular Certs product could bring them benefits and even influence changes in their

lives. From 1960 to 1978 Certs TV commercials used the tagline "Two Mints in One," created by the Bates Advertising Agency. It wasn't until 1989 that the tagline was used again. In the late 1970s and in the 1980s the advertising campaigns focused on romance and how fresh breath could make a person attractive to the opposite sex. Young couples might be kissing or talking, but the tagline would always be, "Be Certain with Certs." The intent was to instill confidence in young consumers that Certs would protect their breath when it was most important to them.

In 1975 the advertising focus shifted to the product's long lasting flavor, and how both the mint itself and its breath freshening qualities lasted. The target group was young, active, social consumers who wouldn't want their breath mints to fade and leave them without protection against bad breath.

In 1978 a similar commercial was aired but with further elaboration on this theme of lasting freshness. New Flavor Formula Certs were introduced as having guaranteed 30-minute breath protection. The flavor crystals were visible specs on the mint that fought strong mouth odor. The target group, however, was the same youthful consumers. The message informed consumers that even though the mint dissolved in 5 minutes, their breath would stay fresh for 30 minutes. And in the 1980s TV commercials became more humorous; a 1980 commercial had a series of couples who were separated by their bad breath. The tagline was "Get Certs. Get Closer."

When Sugarfree Certs were introduced, commercial graphics were used to introduce consumers to the new packaging. A drop of Retsyn was shown hitting the mint and then splashing up into a gold liquid. The new slogan was, "Breath That's Face to Face Fresh." A later print ad depicted a pile of Sugarfree Certs next to a cherry. The small copy beneath the cherry said, "There's more sugar in this cherry than in all these Certs combined." Below was a picture of a pack of Sugarfree Certs along with copy reading, "All that's in it for you is great taste".

From 1982 to 1985 the ad campaign was "The Certs Encounter," which renewed the focus on romance. People were depicted in various face to face encounters that led to romance in such settings as the theater or hiking trips. Some of the commercials depicted the consumer writing to Certs, expressing gratitude to the product for playing its part in creating a positive outcome.

The introduction of New Sugarfree Certs in 1987 also introduced a new type of advertising for the brand: using slow motion and images accompanied by pop music. The commercials showed men and women having fun, and the tagline read, "Everyone Has a Style of Their Own." Pop music was also used in Canadian ads for Certs in 1988. The promotion featured the Canadian rock group Jannetta, as well as Certs Breathless Summer Parties that took place in seven cities across Canada. Radio stations were enlisted to give away tickets to the parties. A sweepstakes prize of $5,000 was also awarded. In addition to radio spots, promotion took place through Sam the Record Man Stores across Canada.

Humor dominated the TV commercials form 1991 to 1992. Comedians Bobby Collins, Richard Jeni, and Rita Rudner talked about funny experiences where bad breath had been a factor. Consumers were able to laugh about the shared anxiety of having bad breath and learn that Certs could relieve that anxiety. Humor was also used in TV and radio commercials for Extra Flavor Mints in 1993. These funny ads stressed the extra value of this Certs product because it was larger than the core Certs.

Performance Appraisal and Future Products

Since 1970, Certs has been the market leader of candy breath mints, a segment of the candy industry that experiences a great deal of activity. In 1991 alone, 53 new mint products were introduced. Moreover, even though it is a candy product, Certs is considered to be breath freshener on a par with other products classified as breath fresheners. In its survey of mouthwashes, *Consumer Reports* included Certs in a category called "other products" that are used to eliminate unpleasant breath odors.

New Certs products can be expected to debut as the company continues to meet its competition and maintain its lead among candy breath mints. The stated policy of the company is to develop new Certs products wherever it sees an opportunity.

Further Reading:

"Best-loved Themes Get Sweet Surprise," *Advertising Age,* September 11, 1989, p. 32.

"Chicle's $100 Million Certs Entry Was Born of 'Certified' Curiosity," *Warner-Lambert World,* May 1986.

Davis, Sue, "Candy Charisma," *Prepared Foods,* mid-April 1992, pp. 69-71.

"Global Gallery: Certs," *Advertising Age,* March 20, 1989, p. 24.

Lazarus, George, "Life Savers Finds a Hole in the Market," *Adweek's Marketing Week,* July 17, 1989, p. 65.

"Mouthwashes," *Consumer Reports,* September 1992, pp. 607-09.

Pellet, Jennifer, "A Surge in New Candy Products," *DM,* September 1990, p. 56-59.

"Rock Band to Beat the Drum for Certs," *Marketing,* April 11, 1988, p. 3.

"Securing A Foothold for Confectionery," *Candy Industry,* July 1992, pp. H2-H10.

Stern, R. J., Tucker Anthony, and R. L. Day, *Company Report of Warner-Lambert,* October 26, 1992.

"Warner-Lambert Certs Historical Television Advertising Highlights," New York: Young & Rubicam.

—Dorothy Kroll

CHEERIOS®

In the often transient world of cold cereals, it is remarkable for a brand to thrive for the length of time that Cheerios has done so. Though never a particularly flashy brand, the "o"-shaped oat cereal has graced breakfast tables since 1941, and the product remains one of the more popular breakfast cereals in America.

The General Mills company had been in business for 13 years when, on May 5, 1941, the U.S. Copyright Office received a new package flat of a cold cereal called "Cheerioats"; the package touted Oneida Community silverware as its first premium. Four months later, a redesigned package, which showed a bowl of the cereal, was registered as a copyright. The cereal remained known as "Cheerioats" until 1945, when the name was shortened to the one it retains today.

Name changes aside, the basic package format has not altered in the past 50 years. What has changed on the package flat is the General Mills logo—in the early years, a trademark millwheel appeared on the box. By 1948 it was replaced by the General Mills flag. In 1956, reflecting the product's heavy presence in television, the logo was encased in a TV screen. In 1961 the design adopted the "Big G," which still appears in the upper left-hand corner.

The bowl of cereal depicted on the package remains constant; the only notable modifications to the cover were the addition of fruit to the serving, the use of a Cheerio to dot the "i" in the name, and the words "toasted oat cereal," first used in 1960. From 1961 to 1974, "floating" Cheerios decorated the box as well.

Brand Development

It's what's inside the box, however, that has attracted consumers for more than five decades. Cheerios was marketed as the first ready-to-eat oat cereal in 1941; back then, the idea of eating oats was still a foreign one to many Americans, who were more familiar with the use of the grain as a source of animal feed. But the National Nutritional Program's blessing of the cereal as an outstanding source of energy helped Cheerios to survive. More than 40 years later, Cheerios would again receive commendation, this time from the WIC (Women, Infants and Children) organization, which lauded the cereal for its high iron and low sugar content. During this year, 1986, Cheerios was the market leader in WIC-approved cold cereal.

The late 1980s and early 1990s produced a new interest in whole grains as a source of dietary fiber. But for those who would equate whole oats with high fiber, *American Health* magazine provided some advice in 1991. Writer David Schardt pointed out that "only about . . . 20% of oat bran is actually fiber (the rest of the bran consists mostly of protein and fat). That's why . . . a cereal such as General Mills Cheerios, which boasts eight grams of oat bran, contains just two grams of fiber." On the other hand, the cereal's claims of low fat are easily substantiated: Schardt singled out Cheerios as a superior source of low-fat iron, adding that even the nuts in Honey Nut Cheerios are "negligible. [That brand] contains only about half an almond per one-ounce serving and actually has less fat than regular Cheerios."

A Cheerio is a distinctive little object, measuring half an inch across and weighing in at about .0025 of an ounce. Some other Cheerios trivia: a one-ounce serving of the cereal contains some 400 individual "o's"; a 15-oz box holds some 6,000 Cheerios; and it would take approximately 3.1 billion Cheerios to circle the globe. The secret to Cheerios' ability to "float" in milk lies in the air pockets formed during a puffing session; the cereal's relative lack of sugar also contributes to buoyancy.

Sometime after the year it was introduced, General Mills changed the cereal's basic formula to a three-grain configuration of oats, corn, and rye. Still billed as "Cheerioats " at that time, the three-grain version was replaced by the original all-oat Cheerios by 1945.

One innovation in Cheerios marketing that helped speed sales first surfaced in 1942, when a slogan reminded consumers that the cereal "makes delicious munching." This was possibly the first time a breakfast cereal had been positioned as a snack food. The idea caught on with at least one segment of society: as many parents will attest, easy-to-handle, easy-to-chew Cheerios are popular as the first "solid" snack for infants to eat.

Premiums and Promotions

The snack promotion was just one in a series of Cheerios marketing efforts, most of which proved successful. As early as 1943, "Cheerioats" were advertised in comic books and adult magazines such as *Saturday Evening Post* and *Look*. In the field of associations and tie-ins, the cereal aligned itself with many issues of the day, both historic and faddish. This trend began in the

AT A GLANCE

Cheerios brand founded in 1941 under the name "Cheerioats"; adopted present name in 1945; produced by General Mills Inc.

Performance: *Market share*—4.7% (1991; highest among national cold-cereal products). *Sales*—$331.7 million.

Major competitor: Kellogg's Corn Flakes; also Kellogg's Frosted Flakes.

Advertising: *Agency*—Saatchi & Saatchi Advertising, New York, NY. *Major campaign*—For adults: "Choose smart. Choose Cheerios"; for children: "You've got a lot to do before lunch."

Addresses: *Parent company*—General Mills, Inc., 1 General Mills Blvd., Minneapolis, MN 55246; phone: (612) 540-2311.

1940s, when Cheerios was packaged in World War II-themed "Yank Packs," and continued into the 1950s, where the company linked the Cheerios brand with 3-D glasses. When Neil Armstrong became the first man to walk on the moon, Cheerios noted the event with a tie-in. Likewise, the space shuttle flights of the early 1980s also produced a premium. Other tie-ins have included associations with the Care Bears cartoon characters and the television series "Star Trek: The Next Generation."

Cheerios also produced a prodigious number of its own promotional items through the decades. From the adult-targeted Oneida Silverware that marked the first batch of the cereal, most other premiums were geared toward the young and young-at-heart cereal-prize collectors. The Lone Ranger provided much inspiration through the 1940s and 1950s, as the company trotted out imitation silver bullets, flashlight pistols and rings, decoder rings, comic books, ID cards, coloring books, and secret badges as Cheerios premiums. Cheerios also associated itself with Walt Disney and comic books. By 1958 such "kid stuff" was being targeted upward with American Bandstand phonograph records. Through the 1960s and 1970s Cheerios offered cartoon-themed breakfast sets and stamp albums. The 1980s brought more diversity to the cereal's premiums. Although the Lone Ranger still made appearances via a "deputy kit," other prizes included Star Wars tumblers, a Space Shuttle kit, stickers celebrating both cartoon characters and BMX racing, sunglasses, boomerangs, magic kits, dollar bills, Cheerios brand tank tops, and personalized tote bags. The cereal acknowledged the late-1980s emphasis on health and nutrition issues with a "Good Fat/Bad Fat" cookbook aimed at young consumers.

Such bonus gifts were available to all consumers of Cheerios. But more exclusive were the consumer contests held during Cheerios' early years, which served as important promotion devices. In 1942 a slogan contest for "Cheerioats" offered a $5,000 grand prize. A tie-in with Walt Disney produced a 1945 contest, with a "wire recorder" as first prize. Between 1950 and 1957 Cheerios ran several other contests. As a sponsor of "The Lone Ranger" television series, Cheerios offered a screen test with the title character, and, in another contest, a chance to win a horse that looked like Silver. There were also competitions to win trips and prizes such as movie cameras and projectors, college scholarships, and bicycles. Contests began to taper off after 1960, a year that featured a Chevrolet Corvair tie-in sweepstakes, wherein adults could win a real Corvair, or kids a model car. General Mills then

halted such contests for Cheerios until 1987, when a "Star Trek" TV walk-on role was awarded, and a 1988 "Kid Power Election" contest offered a trip to Washington, D.C., as grand prize.

Advertising Themes and Variations

Cheerios has used a variety of memorable "spokescharacters" in its half century. During the 1940s, two "mascots" touted the cereal both on the package and in print ads. "Cheeri O'Leary," the Cheerioats girl, was a publicist of sorts, giving out biographical details on the current movie stars. Then there was "Joe Idea," a package mascot who had Cheerios on the brain—in fact, anything circular he saw reminded him of the cereal.

Another pair of animated mascots surfaced in 1953 in television commercials. "Cheerios Kid" and "Sue" were an adventure-themed duo who got into and out of various scrapes for the next 19 years. (They made an encore appearance on television in 1986, capitalizing on the baby-boomer nostalgia craze.) In 1977 the cereal introduced the yodeling "Cheeriodle," a stick-figure animated mascot. He lasted into the early 1980s. Cheerios employed other fictional "stars," including the Muppets, Donald Duck, Mickey Mouse, Mr. Ed, Dick Tracy, and Underdog, to promote the cereal through the years.

Though such kid-oriented spots have proven most successful, Cheerios also targeted adults during the late 1950s and early 1960s with prime-time spots that featured satirist Stan Freberg. Other real-life characters who have associated themselves with Cheerios include an array of actors from decades past—Mischa Auer, William Bendix, Claudette Colbert, Andy Devine, Betty Hutton, Veronica Lake, Fred MacMurray, Dick Powell, and Loretta Young among them. More recent spokespeople include basketball's Harlem Globetrotters and athlete Bo Jackson.

Over the years, Cheerios advertising themes have run the gamut of marketing positions aimed at children and their parents. Slogans during the 1940s and 1950s stressed energy: "He's feeling his Cheerioats!" (1943); "Cheerios gives you GO POWER" (1952); "The power breakfast the whole family loves" (1958)—as well as convenience: "The first ready-to-eat oat cereal" (1945); "The oat cereal that needs no cooking" (1951). By the 1960s, energy attributes were combined with "goodness": "Get that powerful good feeling" (1960); "The Big G stands for Goodness" (1962); and "Go with the goodness of Cheerios" (1964). Beginning in the 1970s and moving into the 1980s and beyond, Cheerios spoke to the health-conscious consumer through campaigns that emphasized that "Nutrition [is] the Cheerios tradition" (1971). Other slogans go into more detail: "Oats, the grain highest in protein" (1971); "We make Cheerios low in sugar, kids make Cheerios number one" (1982); "Lowest sugar of the leading brands" (1988). When the oat-bran craze broke in the late 1980s, the Cheerios package reminded consumers that it had been "For nearly 50 years [an] excellent source of oat bran" and that Cheerios was "Oat bran made simple." For those who believed that only cooked oatmeal could provide the oats they craved, Cheerios reached back to the 1940s for a convenience-themed line, "[The] only leading ready-to-eat cereal made from whole grain oats" (1988). The 1990s brought the idea of adult choice to cereal buying with "Choose smart. Choose Cheerios," the theme of which was interposed with scenes of kayaking, canoeing, and dogsledding. Another version of this theme showed footage of several cereal-box labels, inviting consumers to read all the nutritional content of their cereals before choosing Cheerios. Kids were courted with the energy-driven themeline "You've got a lot to do before lunch."

Music has also played an important role in Cheerios advertising, with such memorable jingles as "He's got Go Power from

A Cheerios cereal box from the 1940s.

Cheerios" and a quintessential 1960s-era tune, "Feelin' groovy, just ate my Cheerios." In more recent years, promotional music

has included "The unsinkable taste of Cheerios" (which stressed that the lack of added sugar kept the o's afloat); and "It's a pow-pow-powerful good-good feelin' with cheer-cheer-Cheerios." Brand variations were introduced utilizing such jingles as "It's a honey of an O . . . Honey Nut Cheerios."

Performance Appraisal

Cheerios is the national leader among ready-to-eat cereals. It garnered a healthy 4.8 percent of the cold-cereal market in 1991, according to *Advertising Age*, and has subsequently held its position, besting such brands as Kellogg's Frosted Flakes and Corn Flakes. In the past several years, General Mills has introduced variations on the original formula. These too have proven successful. Honey Nut Cheerios, launched in 1979, ranks in fifth place among all ready-to-eat cereals, with 3.3 percent of the market share. Apple-Cinnamon Cheerios, which debuted in 1989, also ranks in the top ten; and in 1991 the Multi-Grain Cheerios product was introduced, bringing to four the number of current Cheerios products. Since 1954 the Cheerios brands have reigned as General Mills' top-selling ready-to-eat cereals.

General Mills has diversified Cheerios distribution by producing single-serving boxes aimed at vending machines and cafeteria lines. The company has also benefitted from investment in and expansion of its cereal manufacturing capabilities, highlighted by the opening of a new processing plant in Albuquerque, New Mexico, in July 1992.

Internationally, Cheerios enjoys a strong presence in Canada, though overseas sales were not a major concern at General Mills until 1990, when the company entered into a joint venture with Nestlé, forming the European-based Cereal Partners Worldwide.

Further Reading:

"Cereal: Breakfast Food or Nutritional Supplement?," *Consumer Reports,* October 1989.

Schardt, David, "The Scoop on Breakfast Cereals," *American Health,* December 1991, pp. 58-62.

—Susan Salter

CHEF BOYARDEE®

American Home Food Products Inc.'s Chef Boyardee is the United States' market share leader in canned and microwavable pasta. Its name and trademark picture of a cheerful mustached man in a chef's hat are not the nostalgic creations of a marketing department; they are based on the originator of the product line, Hector Boiardi, an Italian immigrant who truly was a chef. Boiardi's packaged pasta meals have been offering convenient and nutritious food for customers since the 1930s. Chef Boyardee's increasingly extensive product line has remained popular for decades; the unusual shapes of its pasta appeal to children, and the products' ease of preparation appeals to adults.

Early History

Hector Boiardi immigrated to the United States in 1914 at the age of seventeen. A native of northern Italy, Boiardi had already gained six years of experience working in hotels and restaurants when he arrived in the United States. He moved to Manhattan and found a job as a chef at the Plaza, where his brother Richard worked as a waiter. Boiardi became a successful chef, making a name for himself at the Plaza and catering such events as President Woodrow Wilson's wedding reception at the Greenbriar Hotel in West Virginia.

In 1929 Boiardi opened a restaurant in Cleveland, Ohio. Customers, delighted with his Italian tomato-based sauce, began requesting portions to take home. Boiardi accommodatingly bottled his sauce, but received complaints from customers that it did not taste the same at home as it did in the restaurant. He rectified the problem by including with each bottle a package of his special blend of cheese. Later he added a package of uncooked spaghetti and marketed the combination as a complete Italian Spaghetti Dinner.

The Company's Creation

Pleased with the success of his packaged dinner, Boiardi began marketing it and other specialty dishes to neighboring stores. Their popularity resulted in Boiardi spending an increasing amount of time away from his restaurant selling the product. Worried that his restaurant would suffer, Boiardi formed a company with his brothers Richard and Mario and hired a food distributor to handle the sales.

Although the products were popular, customers and even sales representatives had trouble pronouncing the name correctly. As a result, Boiardi reluctantly changed the spelling of the product's name to the phonetically spelled Boy-ar-dee. The company, Chef Boyardee Quality Foods, Inc., began the difficult process of transforming their locally popular products into a nationally known brand.

Chef Boyardee products received a big boost in their distribution when Richard, then maitre d' at the Plaza's Persian Room, served his brother's spaghetti to John Hartford, a cohead of the A & P grocery store chain. History has made no record of his comments, but his opinion can be inferred from the appearance of Chef Boyardee dinners on the shelves of A & P stores a short time later.

In 1938 Boiardi converted the Susquehanna Silk Mill in Milton, Pennsylvania, into the headquarters of his growing business. Chef Boyardee dinners, spaghetti sauces, and canned pastas were soon being distributed over a large area. The brand's growth was interrupted during World War II. Production at the Milton plant was altered to prepare food for troops, making the company a major supplier of rations for the U.S. and Allied Armed Forces.

After the war, American Home Products, also known for such products as Anacin, Dristan, and ChapStick, bought Chef Boyardee Quality Foods from the Boiardi brothers for a reported $6 million. According to *American Home Products,* Hector Boiardi remained a valued advisor until his death at the age of 87 in 1985.

Marketing Toward Children

Chef Boyardee built its reputation on providing good-tasting, nutritious foods that were easy to prepare. Identifying families with children as a prime market for their product, the company addressed parents' concerns by emphasizing the nutrition and convenience of their products. In addition, the company focused much of their efforts on making products that appealed to children. For instance, a typical magazine advertisement, published in 1968 to introduce their new Beef O Getti product, showed a boy in a cowboy outfit helping himself to a portion of the spaghetti rings and beef meat balls. The copy read, "Buckaroos of all ages have it easy spoonin' up Beef O Getti. Nourishing, hearty, delicious."

AT A GLANCE

Chef Boyardee brand of canned pasta created in the 1930s by the chef Hector Boiardi, who sold his specialty foods to customers and local stores from his restaurant in Cleveland, OH; founded Chef Boyardee Quality Foods, Inc., with his brothers Richard and Mario; converted the Susquehana Silk Mill into the company headquarters, 1938; sold company to American Home Products Inc. in 1946.

Performance: *Market share*—62.4 percent (top share) of canned pasta market in 1992. *Sales*—$300 million.

Major competitor: Franco-American SpaghettiOs.

Advertising: *Agency*—Young & Rubicam, New York, NY. *Major campaign*—Imaginary scenes from founder Hector Boiardi's childhood, illustrating what inspired him to create Chef Boyardee.

Addresses: *Parent company*—American Home Food Products Inc., 685 Third Avenue, New York, NY 10017; phone: (212) 878-6300. *Ultimate parent company*—American Home Products Corp., 685 3rd Ave., New York, NY 10017; phone: (212) 878-5000.

Chef Boyardee also attempted to make the products themselves more appealing to children by forming the pasta into unusual shapes children would enjoy. In the early and mid-1980s, American Home introduced such pasta shapes as ABCs, Tic-Tac-Toe, and Dinosaurs. The Campbell Soup Company, maker of SpaghettiOs, fell significantly behind Chef Boyardee in this market. In the mid-1980s, Campbell's attempted to recapture some of the children's market by introducing a product called UFOs. However, American Home countered by bringing out a Chef Boyardee product with pasta shaped like PacMan, and Campbell canceled their entry a short time later.

In the late 1980s Campbell again tried to steal market share from Chef Boyardee's children-centered products by extending their SpaghettiO line with Franco-American TeddyOs, canned pasta shaped like teddy bears, and SportyOs, pasta shaped like roller skates, skateboards, and other sports-related objects. Chef Boyardee was not outdone—in 1990, the company introduced Sharks canned pasta, and in 1991, Teenage Mutant Ninja Turtles canned pasta, which featured larger-sized noodles for a more distinct shape, hit the shelves. The Turtles launching was one of the most successful in the company's history.

Chef Boyardee's Place at American Home

After World War II, American Home sold a range of household products, such as Easy-Off oven cleaner, Black Flag insecticides, and Ekco pots and pans. Their food division grew to include Chef Boyardee, Gulden's mustard, Pam cooking spray, and Jiffy Pop popcorn, among other products. However, over-the-counter medicines and prescription drugs always contributed substantially to the company's profits. By the early 1980s, prescription drugs, medical supplies, and such packaged medicines as Anacin, Dristan, and Dimetapp accounted for 80 percent of American Home's operating profits. Financial analysts urged the company to sell off its less profitable divisions and concentrate on their big moneymakers, as many other large companies involved in pharmaceuticals and medical supplies were doing in the 1980s. Susan Fraker explained in *Fortune* the unlikelihood of American Home's selling off such products as Chef Boyardee: "Historically, . . .

American Home does not walk away from a product. In management's view, the Roach Motel is as important as the cure for diabetes, as long as it's profitable."

Chef Boyardee products have certainly remained profitable. Already entrenched as an American family staple, Chef Boyardee further benefited from the increased popularity of pasta in the 1980s. In just one year, from 1984 to 1985, pasta sales jumped by 6.4 percent. *Advertising Age*'s Pat Gray Thomas, said in 1986, "As pasta marketers increase company size and products, as segmentation expands and waiting markets are tapped, as pasta gains greater recognition for its health benefits, industry experts will continue to predict further growth." In 1992, Chef Boyardee held 62.4 percent of the $569.1 million canned pasta category. Its nearest competitor, The Campbell Soup Company, followed with only 33.8 percent of the market.

Advertising Expenditures

In 1983, *Fortune*'s Susan Fraker described American Home as "one of the nation's most tightly managed companies, renowned for wringing every last cent out of every dollar." Despite this reputation, American Home was the nation's leading advertiser of pasta in 1986. In 1989 their ad budget for canned pasta was $9 million, and the next year their budget for Chef Boyardee pasta was $15.9 million. Despite the addition of several items to their pasta line, Chef Boyardee's advertising budget was scaled back by 32 percent in 1991.

With their dedication to providing foods that are easy to prepare, Chef Boyardee found a natural addition to their product line when they added microwavable prepared pasta dishes. In 1989 American Home Products introduced Chef Boyardee Microwave Meals, a line that grew to 14 pasta and sauce items and soon became the market's leading line of microwavable prepared pastas. In 1991 the company expanded its microwavable products by creating Main Meals, featuring ten pasta varieties in family-sized portions.

In the early 1990s Chef Boyardee also increased the attention they paid to teenage and adult consumers. Reacting to the trend toward more healthful eating, Chef Boyardee developed reduced fat and sodium content formulations for prepared pastas. In addition, they introduced Special Recipe, which American Home Products described in their 1991 annual report as a new line "with a hearty, robust taste that appeals to teenagers and adults."

Chef Boyardee also began a successful new advertising campaign in 1992 that was directed toward an older audience. Produced by Young & Rubicam, the television spots illustrated Hector Boiardi's supposed childhood inspiration to create Chef Boyardee prepared foods. One spot shows little Hector being served an unappetizing gruel by a severe teacher. When he complains, he is expelled from the schoolroom, and an announcer speculates, "If Hector Boiardi had never been seven years old, perhaps he would not have become Chef Boyardee, dedicating himself to hot, wholesome foods that taste the way kids like." Filmed in Italy with Italian actors, the commercials were criticized by some for their unintelligible dialogue, but scored high with consumers.

International Marketing

In the early 1990s, American Home Food Products, the subsidiary of American Home Products Corp. that handles Chef

Boyardee, increased its commitment to raise international sales of its pasta products. By 1991, Chef Boyardee held the leading share of the canned and microwavable pasta market in Canada. The same year, American Home Products licensed certain Chef Boyardee products for marketing in Mexico. In addition, the company hoped that exports of Chef Boyardee to Central America and the Caribbean would increase as a result of their new licensing and distribution agreements.

Chef Boyardee, although ostensibly Italian food, is typically (or perhaps stereotypically) American. It not only is the successful product of an entrepreneurial immigrant, but it also is one of American's first packaged convenience foods. Its effective marketing toward parents and children has kept it the leading national brand in the canned pasta market for years, and perhaps for years to come.

Further Reading:

American Home Products Annual Report, New York: American Home Products Corp., 1991.

American Home Food Products Informational Reports, New York: American Home Products Corp.

"Chef Boy-Ar-Dee Ads to Introduce New Beef O Getti," *Advertising Age,* April 8, 1968, p. 4.

Dagnoll, Judann, "Campbell's SpaghettiOs Gets Saucy New Shapes," *Advertising Age,* July 17, 1989, p. 40.

Fraker, Susan, "American Home Products Battles the Doubters," *Fortune,* July 25, 1983, pp. 59-64.

Fucini, Joseph J. and Suzy Fucini, *Entrepreneurs: The Men and Women Behind Famous Brand Names and How They Made It,* Boston: G. K. Hall, 1985.

Garfield, Bob, "Chef Boyardee Garbles Return to Italian Roots," *Advertising Age,* April 13, 1992, p. 60.

"100 Leading National Advertisers," *Advertising Age,* September 29, 1989, p. 8.

"100 Leading National Advertisers," *Advertising Age,* September 23, 1992, pp. 3-4.

Thomas, Pat Gray, "Pasta Lovers Add Sauce to Food Marketers' Sales," *Advertising Age,* October 13, 1986, pp. S39-S40.

—Susan Windisch Brown

CHEX®

The story of Chex cereals spans from small-time, nineteenth-century origins in homespun philosophy to international distribution and constant change in the fierce world cereal market of the early 1990s. The same Ralston Purina Company that adopted the Chex and company trademark as a symbol of useful simplicity gained valuable market share in the cold cereal category in the late 1980s by marketing such brands as Teenage Mutant Ninja Turtles cereal. Chex reflects these sweeping changes in company identity in the brand's own more subtle shifts from the unchanging staple to the continually new. By 1993 the Chex brand had developed from the one original Wheat Chex to include eight additional cereals, including Bran Chex, Corn Chex, Crispy Mini-Grahams, Double Chex, Graham Chex, Honey Graham Chex, Oat Chex, and Rice Chex. The constant brand innovation and aggressive advertising has drawn controversy to Chex and other major cereal manufacturers in an era marked by relentless television advertising and slippery market share gains and losses. If this aggressive marketing approach has drawn controversy, however, it has also maintained and expanded Chex's U.S. market share while serving as a prelude to the introduction of the brand internationally in the early 1990s. Ralston Purina plans to continue its efforts to emphasize Chex and its other leading brands to accelerate further its growth in sales and profits.

From Straight Square Origins

In his book *Great American Brands,* historian David Powers Cleary recorded the origins of Chex cereal. In 1898 William Danforth, an owner of an animal feed business, saw something in wheat germ that cereal manufacturers of the period had overlooked. Cereal makers of the day removed wheat germ from whole wheat cereals because of perennial problems with the wheat germ quickly growing rancid. A miller from Kansas, however, had discovered a way to keep the wheat germ from going bad. Meanwhile, Danforth believed wheat germ to be a form of nature's own purity and therefore important to sound health. Danforth soon began a collaboration with the Kansas miller to sell a ready-to-eat cereal for people; that collaboration marked the very beginning of what would become Chex cereal.

Since 1894 Danforth had been running a "hand shovel horse and mule feed operation" in St. Louis with two church friends, George Robinson and William Andrews. In 1896 Danforth became president of the company and bought out Andrews' shares, thereby becoming the majority stockholder. When Danforth learned of the advent of new whole wheat with wheat germ in 1898, his company, the Robinson-Danforth Commission Company, began to package this Kansas miller's cracked wheat for grocers in St. Louis. He named the cereal "Purina" after his company's slogan, "where purity is paramount."

At around that time, Danforth grew enamored of the teachings of a charismatic medical doctor, Dr. Albert Webster Edgerly. Writing under the name "Dr. Ralston," Edgerly urged in his book, *Life Building,* that only whole wheat—complete with wheat germ—be utilized, as he believed that form to be more pure.

Cleary reports that Dr. Ralston developed a following of some 800,000 people in health clubs across the nation. Danforth approached Edgerly to discuss joining him in the manufacture and sale of his new Purina cereal. They soon agreed to rename the product Ralston Wheat Cereal and to offer the doctor's endorsement as well. The names Ralston and Purina gained such wide recognition that by 1902, the company name changed to the Ralston Purina Company.

To accompany the new name, Danforth wished to develop a logo that people would remember. He decided on a sharp red and white checkerboard that hearkened back to a memory of his youth and symbolized, to him, his philosophy of healthy living. He drew the trademark from a memory of a family, invariably garbed in identical red and white checkered outfits, who visited his father's general store every Sunday. Neighbors had found this dress habit strange but useful; children could be quickly found and collected when the time came to go home. In his book *Symbols of America,* Hal Morgan describes Danforth's sense that the design would catch on. "If he could remember the red and white checks after all those years, they would make a perfect design theme and trademark for his cereals and grains." The new design met with success and quickly elicited national recognition.

The checkerboard square also represented Danforth's personal philosophy of healthy living. According to Arnold Barach in his book, *Famous American Trademarks,* the four sides of the square symbolized Danforth's four-fold credo: "Think tall, stand tall, smile tall, live tall." Barach also related another meaning that Danforth read into the four sides of his trademark square. Each side of the square represented one of the four aspects of a healthy life, resulting in a balance between the social, mental, physical, and religious sides of life. David Powers Cleary records Danforth's efforts as owner of the company to spread his philosophy among his employees. For about 40 years, Danforth told his employees his thoughts each week in his "Monday Morning Message." Cleary writes also of Danforth's sponsorship of festive activities such as sing-alongs, picnics, skits, and square dances. Naming the company headquarters the "Checkerboard Square," the checkerboard logo on original Chex cereals became Danforth's company-wide logo and philosophical symbol.

Danforth's use of his company to reflect his philosophy earned him a reputation as a strong but somewhat dogmatic leader. He enacted codes of behavior on company premises and rewarded employees whose behavior, throughout the course of their careers, corresponded with his philosophy. He also rewarded employees who attended church regularly and prohibited smoking anywhere on company grounds. Still, as a civic leader in organizations such as the Young Men's Christian Association, the Christmas Carolers Association, and the American Youth Foundation, he commanded respect and admiration from many in the company and in the wider community. Cleary quotes one "incredulous observer," for example, who exclaimed, "He runs that company like a down-home husking bee!" Increasingly then, Chex cereal, with its "pure" whole wheat characteristics and distinctive checkerboard logo, was itself an apt symbol of Danforth's Ralston Purina Company.

By the time of the Great Depression, Ralston Wheat Cereal was losing money for the company, despite the growth of overall company sales to $60 million. The company remedied this lapse in sales by bringing in a famous cowboy, Tom Mix, to lend his name to the cereal. Eventually changing the cereal name to Chex, the company began to diversify the Chex line as well, but at a slow pace when compared to the changes after the television era. *Forbes* reported in 1966, for instance, that until 1965, the Ralston cereal line included only three varieties of Chex cereal—Wheat Chex, Rice Chex, and Corn Chex. From its introduction until 1965, then, Ralston Purina had developed only two Chex varieties beyond the original wheat. In 1965, however, Ralston Purina joined the other major cereal manufacturers in altering their marketing approaches to succeed in the new television-dominated baby-boomer cereal market.

To Non-Linear Success: TV Brands

Forbes reported that between the mid-1950s and the mid-1960s, the number of cereal brands on the market doubled from around 50 to almost 100. The most significant cause for that increase was the new practice of direct marketing to children through television. Previously, a cereal brand would be advertised on a radio show year after year and would draw a reliable, loyal pool of consumers. While children listened to the shows, adults still decided which cereal brands to buy. Companies relied on a small stock of brands to achieve regular sales and profits. With the advent of television, however, these dynamics changed. Based on advertisements they saw on TV, many children assumed a greater role in the decision about which cereals would be purchased. Visual TV ads immersed children's imaginations more thoroughly and more effectively created desire for the featured product. The Kellogg Company benefited most from this trend; creating a host of cartoon characters exclusively to sell one or another brand, it moved from second to first place over the decade and captured over 40 percent of the cold cereal market. Yogi Bear sold Corn Flakes, Tony the Tiger sold Frosted Flakes, and so on. Likewise, General Mills brought out its line-up of animated animals to pitch its products. Ralston Purina was primarily geared for the adult

market, but eventually it too threw itself headlong into the children's market. Even Chex cereal, that symbol of right-angle "purity," was loosened up a bit and pitched in a new variety to children.

Warren Shapleigh, head of Ralston Purina's grocery products division, explained in *Forbes* the reasons for the change. "We found ourselves on a sales plateau." Also, leadership of the company passed in relatively quick succession from William Danforth to Donald Danforth in 1955 and once again to R. Hal Dean in 1963. Under new leadership, Ralston Purina remodeled its Chex marketing approach to profit from the phenomenal growth in the cereal industry. Gone was the adult sales pitch, "Look, Ma! No premiums!" and in came a dancing scarecrow named "Squarecrow" in a television ad campaign created by Ralston Purina's new advertising agency, Foote, Cone and Belding.

By 1971 Ralston Purina introduced another variety of Chex to reach still more effectively the children's market. As all of the new cereals from the mid-1950s to the mid-1960s had been pre-sweetened and half were considered "kid-oriented," Ralston Purina introduced in 1971 a pre-sweetened Chex variety called Sugar Chex. Sugar Chex hit the market in 1971 complete with its own cartoon sales-creature, Casper the Friendly Ghost. The days of simple Chex "purity" had passed; Ralston Purina had begun its new strategy of blending and diversifying the identity of Chex to capitalize on various segments of the broader ready-to-eat cereal market. This strategy would continue to increase sales for Chex in a market that was in a constant state of flux.

The New Chex Changes

Over the next two decades, Ralston Purina continued developing new forms of Chex cereal, each of which targeted a specific market or capitalized on a particular industry trend. In the mid- to late-1970s the dominance of children-targeted cereal in the cold cereal market lessened and products that boasted of nutrition for adults came back in vogue. As a part of this change, bran was utilized with much greater frequency. In 1978 a number of cereal makers introduced bran cereals in concert. The Quaker Oats Company began selling Corn Bran, Nabisco expanded its bran line-up by introducing the new Bran Crunchies alongside its 100% Bran, and General Mills tested its Bran Plus cereal. Ralston Purina, meanwhile, had introduced Bran Chex in the mid-1970s, a cereal that captured one percent of the total cold cereal market. The company further augmented its bran options with the new Honey Bran, a bran cereal pre-sweetened with honey.

While Sugar Chex eventually disappeared from the Chex brand family, Bran Chex remained. Returning to the adult cereal market, Chex had moved full circle back to its marketing origins as a health food, but Ralston Purina continued to diversify the Chex line to keep pace with nutritional trends. Oat Chex became a form of Chex in the mid- to late-1980s, for example, when almost every cereal containing oat bran became a quick sales gainer. That trend ended with the 1980s, however, and while Oat Chex remained on board, Ralston Purina looked for new varieties to keep the Chex brand new. In 1989 Ralston Purina introduced Double Chex, a high-technology creation that combines two grains in one cereal. Double Chex allowed Ralston Purina to market Chex as a nutritional brand utilizing the latest technology, a combination of the traditional and the new. As for the children's cereal market, Ralston Purina developed a series of short-lived brands that were licensed to popular characters or movie figures. Teenage Mutant

Ninja Turtles cereal was one example. Chex targeted the modern adult market through a combination of old health values and new, improved taste, while the licensed brands focused on the children's market. As a result, Ralston Purina was able to augment its total cold cereal market share to 6.1 percent in 1990, up from 5.6 percent in 1987, as reported in *Financial World*. The same article recounted a drop in the first quarter of 1991, however, to only 4.7 percent. While Ralston Purina was able to increase its sales with targeted brand innovations, the cold cereal market remains a mercurial one.

Aggressive Marketing Yields Controversial Success

If the continual re-modeling of the Chex brand name brought with it commercial success in a difficult market, the aggressive advertising associated with recreating the identity of Chex has brought controversy in addition to sales. Ralston Purina has come under fire from federal agencies twice since the early 1970s. The first action was a lawsuit filed in the early 1970s by the Federal Trade Commission (FTC) against all of the major cereal manufacturers, Ralston Purina included but not as a respondent, for unfair methods of competition. The FTC charged that the major cereal manufacturers had proliferated brands needlessly to maintain a shared monopoly and that they had advertised falsely to children. The FTC dropped the case in the early 1980s.

The second run-in with the federal government involved the Food and Drug Administration (FDA) in 1990. The FDA sent letters to Ralston Purina and five other companies warning that these companies should scale back their health claims for their products. The FDA warned Ralston Purina that it would enforce new guidelines if Ralston Purina persisted with its claims that Oat Chex could help reduce cholesterol. The result of this warning has not been reported, but neither of these government actions have significantly changed Ralston Purina's marketing approach concerning Chex.

Strategies for the 1990s

Ralston Purina planned to further develop the Chex brand to continue to increase sales in the early 1990s. In its 1992 *Annual Report,* the company announced its plans to focus less on licensed cereal brands and more on its core brands, including Chex cereal. Two new Chex varieties, Graham Chex and Mini-Grahams, were introduced in early 1993 as a part of this strategy. Ralston Purina also hoped to market Chex internationally. It opened plants in France in 1990 and in Korea in 1992, while construction continued on a third in Mexico. With world cereal leader Kellogg restructuring its organization to focus on international sales, and with second-place General Mills teaming up with Nestlé of Switzerland in a joint-venture to market General Mills cereal worldwide, however, Ralston Purina is sure to find intense international competition. Still, sales of Chex in France doubled in 1992, leading to further investments there by Ralston Purina in 1993. While the cereal market exhibited tight competition worldwide in the early 1990s, Ralston Purina continued to position and re-position Chex cereal for continued success.

Further Reading:

Advertising Age, November 1, 1971, p. 169.

Advertising Age, February 15, 1988, p. 1.

Barach, Arnold B., *Famous American Trademarks,* Washington, DC: Public Affairs Press, 1971.

Biesada, Alexandra, "Life after Oat Bran," *Financial World,* June 11, 1991, pp. 46-9.

Cleary, David Powers, *Great American Brands,* New York: Fairchild Publications, 1981.

"Don't Underestimate the Power of a Kid," *Forbes,* October 15, 1966.

Edwards, Larry, "Cold Cereal Market Shows New Snap," *Advertising Age,* November 27, 1978, p. 1.

"Getting It Both FTC Ways," *Broadcasting,* January 31, 1972, p. 18.

Liesse, Julie, "New Cereals Springing Up," *Advertising Age,* February 22, 1993, p. 13.

Morgan, Hal, *Symbols of America,* New York: Penguin, 1986.

Quimpo, Margie, G., "FDA Questions Health Claims," *Washington Post,* September 15, 1990, p. C1.

Ralston Purina Company, *Annual Report,* St. Louis, MO, 1990, 1992.

—Nicholas Patti

CHIQUITA®

Although there are several premium brand names for bananas, none is as dominant and venerable as Chiquita, the driving force of Chiquita Brands International, Inc.'s $2.4 billion Fresh Foods Group. The history of Chiquita dates back to 1944, but the history of its corporate ancestor dates back to the nineteenth century, when bananas were relatively unknown to the American public. Even though a Spanish friar had introduced bananas to the northern hemisphere in the sixteenth century, the fruit was slow to catch on due to the difficulty in storing and transporting it long distances. All of this changed when Lorenzo Baker sailed into New Jersey with 160 bunches of bananas in 1870 and inaugurated commercial banana trading, which was then, as it is now, a risky commodity business. With the Philadelphia Centennial Exposition of American Independence in 1876, Baker was able to introduce the fruit on a wide scale. There, the American public had its first real taste of bananas, individually wrapped in foil and priced at a nickel apiece. The company Baker founded went through several incarnations from the late 1800s through the early 1900s and, in the 1940s, became the first to put a brand name on fresh fruit when it introduced the Chiquita label. The concept proved so strong a marketing strategy that Chiquita quickly captured the top share of banana sales worldwide, and by 1990 the brand had become such a powerful symbol that the parent company changed its name from United Brands Company to reflect the preeminence of its single greatest brand, Chiquita.

The Early Days

The American banana business began officially in 1885, when fruit importer Baker joined forces with Boston produce agent Andrew Preston, who had enjoyed some success importing bananas from Jamaica, to form the Boston Fruit Company. Fourteen years later Boston Fruit merged with three other produce importers, controlled by Minor C. Keith of Brooklyn, New York, to become the United Fruit Company. By 1903, United Fruit was importing more than 750,000 tons of bananas per year. But the problem of trying successfully to store and ship the fruit had changed little since the time when the Spanish cleric first introduced bananas to North America. Often the fruit arrived bruised and overripe. Around 1905 United Fruit formed what came to be known throughout the world as the Great White Fleet, an armada of fast, new, refrigerated ships capable of transporting bananas and other produce long distances with minimal spoilage.

Marketing Innovation

United's pioneering techniques for growing, handling, and shipping bananas were quickly copied by other fresh fruit firms. What really set the company apart from its competitors were innovations in marketing. In 1944 United Fruit became the first company ever to affix a brand name to a fresh fruit product. The name was Chiquita, which translates into English as "little girl." In September of that year, two young advertising men, lyricist Garth Montgomery and songwriter Len MacKenzie of the Batten, Barton, Durstine & Osborn (BBDO) Agency, wrote a song for the initial Chiquita radio campaign. The first time the jingle was performed, recalled BBDO executive Bob Foreman in *Advertising & Selling,* MacKenzie played the tune on the agency's spinet piano while Montgomery sang "in an unattractive falsetto shaking paper clips in paper cups to give a maraca-like background." For the official presentation to their client, the ad executives refined the act by enlisting the assistance of a secretary to sing the Chiquita song. The version that finally went on the air featured a six-piece band—maracas, jaw-bone, tom-tom, guitar, bass fiddle, and keyboards—backing singer Patti Clayton on the catchy calypso-style tune.

The Chiquita song was an instant hit. It played on the radio almost four hundred times each day, and many popular singers and musicians recorded their own versions of it. Fan mail flooded into the offices of United Fruit. Said a writer for *Time* magazine in mid-1945: "Most spot commercials are either obnoxious or vapid. Chiquita Banana . . . is so different that listeners actually like it. Last week, after more than eight months on the air, it had become the undisputed No. 1 on the jingle-jangle hit parade."

The reasons for the jingle's popularity through the years are many. The music, some point out, is simple, direct, infectious, memorable, and eminently hummable. In addition, the coquettish delivery by "Miss Chiquita" has its own unique appeal. (A group of students at a midwestern university in the 1940s voted Chiquita "the girl they'd most like to get in a refrigerator with.") The song's lyrics, finally, are a story in themselves. Unlike most commercials, the words of the Chiquita song don't urge listeners to buy the sponsor's product. Rather, they tell consumers how to care for bananas. Unlikely as it may seem in the 1990s, in 1944 the American public needed to be educated as to the proper handling of the delicate fruit. Thus, Miss Chiquita sang: "I'm Chiquita Banana, and I've come to say / Bananas have to ripen in a certain

AT A GLANCE

Chiquita brand founded in 1944 in New York by United Fruit Company owners, and Russel G. Patridge, Garth Montgomery, Len Mackenzie, Dik Browne, and Elsa Miranda; brand trademark registered in 1949; United Fruit became United Brands Company, 1970, and was renamed Chiquita Brands International, Inc., 1990.

Performance: *Market share*—40% (top share) of banana category. *Sales*—Majority of Chiquita Brands International's $4.62 billion in sales.

Major competitor: Dole; also Del Monte.

Advertising: *Agency*—W. B. Doner & Company, Southfield, MI. *Major campaign*—Television and print ads lauding bananas as "quite possibly the world's perfect food"; prominent use of soft-sell, soft-focus photography, and emphasis on healthy lifestyles; various point-of-purchase promotions and sticker suggestions ("Unwrap Me Now," "Take Me to School," "Let's Do Lunch") are also used.

Addresses: *Parent company*—Chiquita Brands International, Inc., 250 East 5th St., Cincinnati, OH 45202-5190; phone: (513) 784-8011; fax: (513) 784-8030.

way / When they are flecked with brown and have a golden hue / Bananas taste the best and are the best for you / You can put them in a salad / You can put them in a pie-aye / Any way you want to eat them / It's impossible to beat them / But bananas like the climate / Of the very, very tropical equator / So you should never put bananas / In the refrigerator. No, no, no, no!''

Most consumers at the time did not realize that bananas are not harvested ripe. When allowed to tree-ripen, the fruit develops a very bland flavor; if shipped ripe it would arrive at its destination rotted, mushy, and inedible. Thus, bananas are best harvested and shipped while still green and allowed to ripen under conditions of controlled temperature and humidity. Even if purchased at the stage when they have just turned yellow, bananas are not at their peak flavor. Reportedly, they are best when they have a "golden hue" and have begun to be "flecked with brown." The Chiquita song, therefore, had a message that served the best interests of both the consumer and the company; it informed the public of the best way to handle the product to ensure consumption when the fruit was at its peak of flavor and consistency.

The catchy tune gave Miss Chiquita a voice; now she needed a face. Because of the popularity of the jingle, consumers were eager to buy the Chiquita brand, but at that time there was no way to distinguish the United Fruit product from other bananas. Grocery stores and produce markets invariably removed the fruit from its original shipping container for display, leaving shoppers confronted with a pile of unidentifiable bananas. The solution was to apply a sticker to each bunch of bananas, removing any doubt as to whose product was being offered for sale. Shortly after the Chiquita song's debut, artist Dik Browne was commissioned to design the product's logo. Browne had redesigned the venerable Campbell's Soup kids logo and later became world-famous for his ''Hagar the Horrible'' comic strip. The artist's interpretation of Chiquita featured an animated banana character wearing a Carmen Miranda-style hat and Flamenco-dancer dress. The familiar blue and yellow logo has appeared on billions of bunches of bananas since its introduction in the 1940s. Although the design has been updated through the years (the last restyling took place in 1987,

when Chiquita finally changed from the banana character to a drawing of a real woman), millions of schoolchildren around the world still affix Chiquita stickers to their books, bicycles, and the backs of their friends. Eventually, names of competitors' products such as Dole, Del Monte, and Sunkist were commonly found on a wide variety of fresh produce. However, by the time the competition caught on to this revolutionary idea, Chiquita was firmly entrenched as the world's number one provider of bananas, outselling rival brands three to one.

Modern Expansion

Thus a catchy jingle, a clever logo, and innovative marketing—coupled with ground-breaking agricultural techniques and shipping methods—captured a huge worldwide market for Chiquita. The next step for United Fruit became that of countless other large corporations: diversification. The company had already expanded from bananas into other fresh fruit products and the sugar market, but the 1950s saw the beginning of a major expansion for United Fruit. It became the basis for a giant New York-based conglomerate, acquiring such diverse businesses as A&W Root Beer Company (1966) and Baskin-Robbins (1967). In 1970 the firm was purchased by AMK, a conglomerate that included the Morrell Meat Company and that, when combined with United Fruit's impressive array of holdings, made for a very powerful food empire. Eli Black, a former rabbinical student, was founder and chairman of AMK. He made an effort to improve the company's social consciousness as well as its profits. (He was, for instance, instrumental in improving housing and working conditions for plantation workers in Central America.) Black changed the name of the combined company to United Brands to reflect the broader base of products it now represented.

In the mid-1970s Hurricane Fifi destroyed a huge percentage of the Honduran banana crop, a disaster that had a major impact on the world's top distributor of the fruit. Even clever diversification could not insulate Chiquita from the effects of a natural phenomenon of this magnitude. In 1975 Black hurled himself through the window of his New York City office in the Pan Am building and plunged forty-four floors to his death. It was later discovered that he had been bribing the president of Honduras, paying $1.25 million into a Swiss bank account in exchange for a reduction of the export tax on bananas from $1 per box to 25 cents. Following this disclosure, the government of Honduras fell, and United Brands stock plummeted to its lowest point in history.

During the late 1970s and early 1980s United Brands was run by two brothers, Seymour and Paul Millstein, who had made their name in the New York real estate market. Under their direction, the firm began a move toward consolidation, selling off many of its previous acquisitions, including A&W, Baskin-Robbins, and Foster-Grant. Nonetheless, such streamlining efforts failed to bring the company back to its previous level of fiscal health. In 1982 United Brands showed a loss of $167.3 million on sales of $2.4 billion. Failed management plans, combined with natural disasters, a soft market, and the taint of bribery, had taken their toll.

New Leadership

In the mid-1980s a new leader emerged in the form of Carl H. Lindner, a Cincinnati-based billionaire financier whose American Financial Corporation, a privately held insurance company, owned a significant portion of United Brands' stock. Lindner bought up

87 percent of United Brands' outstanding shares, installed himself as chairman, named his son, Keith E. Lindner, president, moved the company's headquarters to Cincinnati, and began nursing it back to financial health. Under Lindner's direction, United Brands' sales climbed steadily, from $2.3 billion in 1985 to $4.6 billion in 1991. Expenses began dropping immediately when he took over, cash flow doubled in two years, dividends per share of stock went from 2 cents in 1985 to 35 cents in 1990, and the stock's market value rose from $9.25 to $32. Lindner saved money with the move from New York to Cincinnati, and he economized further by disposing of some of the company's least profitable ventures, including international telecommunications, soft drinks, and animal feeds, for a savings of $255 million. At the same time he stepped up efforts in other highly profitable areas, most notably worldwide produce distribution, with the acquisition of a number of international fruit and vegetable concerns, including Frupac in Chile.

Lindner also pushed to ensure Chiquita was the world's number one name in bananas. New marketing strategies touted bananas as a rich source of potassium and capitalized on the concerns of a newly health-conscious consumer market. According to *Adweek's Marketing Week* writer Laura Bird, "Miss Chiquita . . . is no longer the star. The Cincinnati company has made its blue-stickered bananas the main attraction, positioning them as a one-stop-shopping source of vitamins, minerals and energy." A Chiquita spokesperson told Bird: "We're taking advantage of the consumer trend toward fitness. Bananas are one of the most efficient fuels." Television and print ads from the firm's agency, W. B. Doner & Company, promoted bananas as "quite possibly the world's perfect food."

The strategy worked. United Brands not only succeeded in recapturing the lead in worldwide banana sales but proved once again the enormous value of the Chiquita brand. In 1990 the

The original, mid-1940s version of Miss Chiquita.

corporate name changed from United Brands to Chiquita Brands International, Inc. The Chiquita name now appears on such fresh produce products as pineapples, grapefruit, and melons; and the brand is licensed out to other companies, including Beech-Nut, which uses it as a selling point on its baby food jars.

Fresh and Prepared

Chiquita Brands is comprised of two large divisions, Fresh Foods, with 48 percent of the company's total sales, and Prepared Foods, accounting for the remaining 52 percent of total sales. Brands in the Fresh Foods division, in addition to Chiquita, include Consul, Chico, Amigo, Frupac, and Premium. Most of the brands in this division are the result of acquisitions since 1986. Expansion into the world market has resulted in huge gains in this area for the firm. With the removal of trade barriers in 1991, Chiquita became the top exporter of fresh fruit to South Korea. And when the political situation changed dramatically in Eastern Europe, Chiquita quickly set up offices in Russia, Czechoslovakia, Hungary, and Poland. In addition, in recent years the company has entered the Australia and New Zealand markets and increased its sales of fresh fruit in the Middle East.

The Prepared Foods division of Chiquita Brands International accounted for $2.2 billion in net sales in 1991. Prepared Foods brands include Chiquita (fruit juices, banana puree, and other processed fruits and vegetables), Clover, Numar, Club Chef, Ferraro's, Morrell, Nathan's Famous, and Tobin's First Prize. Acquisitions since Lindner's takeover also accounted for great increases in the sales in this division, as did expansion into several new worldwide markets.

Into the Future

Where will Chiquita go from here? Carl Lindner is in his seventies, and industry observers note that there have been a few dark spots on his control of the company. Chiquita attempted to move into the frozen-food market with a line of frozen fruit pops, a failed venture that cost its division an estimated $10 million in 1987. John Morrell, Chiquita's meat-packing flagship, also experienced trouble when it was hit by an ugly year-long labor dispute in 1988. Chiquita made plans to sell the assets of the meat business in 1993. Still, Lindner's status as a financial genius seems to have survived. Furthermore, his son, Keith, has proven his ability as president and chief operating officer over the years. Most importantly, the Chiquita name remains the company's greatest asset. Through several decades, the idea of marketing fresh fruit under a brand name has proven to be a solid advertising strategy—so much so that bananas can be found in supermarkets sporting stickers with logos from Dole, Del Monte, and other competitors. Still, Chiquita Brands has diversified intelligently, and its plans to move constantly into new markets while increasing fruit production, improving shipping methods, and acquiring profitable companies show promise for the future.

The Chiquita name still carries a great deal of weight with consumers, the result, no doubt, of many years of consistent quality and market leadership, but due also to a generation of shoppers having been raised with the Chiquita jingle. Incidentally, in spite of the admonition in the song, "because of modern growing techniques, refrigerated container shipping, and improvements in home refrigerators, it's now okay to put bananas in the refrigerator," according to recent Chiquita literature, "but you don't have to."

Further Reading:

Ahlgren, Priscilla, "Oh, How They've Changed," *Milwaukee Journal*, July 19, 1989, p. 1E.

Barach, Arnold, "Chiquita," *Famous American Trademarks*, Washington, D.C.: Public Affairs Press, 1971, pp. 39-40.

Bird, Laura, "Chiquita's Ad Archive: The Picture of Health," *Adweek's Marketing Week,* January 7, 1991, pp. 32-33.

Chiquita Brands International, Inc., Annual Report, Cincinnati: Chiquita Brands International, Inc., 1989-91.

Dagnoli, Judann, and Laurie Freeman, "P&G Has Thirst for Chiquita Juices," *Advertising Age,* May 7, 1990, p. 16.

Foreman, Bob, "Chiquita Banana and How She Grew," *Advertising & Selling,* September 1945.

Fox, John M., "How Chiquita Helped United Fruit," *Agribusiness Worldwide,* February-March 1980, p. 12.

Hannon, Kerry, "Ripe Banana," *Forbes,* June 13, 1988, p. 86.

Hoover, Gary, "Chiquita Brands International, Inc.," *Hoover's Handbook of American Business 1992,* Austin, TX: Reference Press, 1991, p. 178.

Mejia, John, "Chiquita Testing Appeal with Kiwifruit," *Supermarket News,* June 4, 1990, p. 40.

Morgan, Hal, *Symbols of America,* New York: Viking Penguin, 1986.

Moskowitz, Milton, Robert Levering, and Michael Katz, editors, "Chiquita," *Everybody's Business: A Field Guide to the 400 Leading Companies in America,* New York: Doubleday, 1990, pp. 30-31.

Saxton, Lisa, "Holidays Are Top Banana on Chiquita Logo Stickers," *Supermarket News,* January 21, 1991, p. 37.

Warner, Fara, "Surprise! Chiquita Advises: Eat Bananas," *Adweek's Marketing Week,* April 29, 1991, p. 8.

—*Jay P. Pederson*

COCA-COLA®

The Coca-Cola Company's flagship brand of soft drink is one of the most universally identifiable products. In a recent study of symbols, the Landor organization declared that the Coca-Cola name, in its Spenserian script, is the most widely recognized commercial symbol in the world (and, among all symbols, second only to the cross), and the expression "Coca-Cola" is more widely recognized than any other but "OK."

Brand Origins

According to legend, Dr. John S. Pemberton, a Confederate Army veteran and pharmacist, first developed the syrup for Coca-Cola in May of 1886 when, in an attempt to develop a headache remedy, he boiled down a mixture of sugar, leaves and caffeine-rich herbs in a pot over an open fire in his back yard. Pemberton, inventor of Indian Queen hair dye and Triplex liver pills, took his syrup to top the fountain at Joe Jacob's Pharmacy at Five Points in Atlanta to have it mixed with water. By accident, the soda jerk mixed the syrup with soda water. Pemberton, however, was so impressed by the effervescent solution that he decided to continue mixing the syrup with soda.

Unsure whether to market the refreshing drink as a refreshment or a tonic, Pemberton elected to call it both, "an invigorating beverage, but a valuable brain tonic and a cure for all nervous affections." Pemberton's bookkeeper Frank Robinson suggested the alliterative name "Coca-Cola," as the mixture was derived in part from South American coca leaf and African kola nut extracts. Being something of an expert scribe, Robinson penned the famous script logo, which has survived to this day.

Pemberton began advertising the concoction immediately, distributing the syrup to as many druggists as would accept it. With its exotic ingredients, Coca-Cola caught on slowly with bewildered Atlanta residents. During the first year, Pemberton and a small circle of buyers spent $73.96 on advertising, while taking in only $50 in profit. Meanwhile, Pemberton grew ill and was forced to sell his interest in the business to Asa G. Candler, a successful druggist, for $1,750. Pemberton died in 1888.

Candler was an avid philanthropist who established several endowments and funded numerous projects. He was also a shrewd businessman who lent the Coca-Cola drink a strong image of social responsibility. In 1892, reasonably sure of the drink's commercial potential, Candler bought out Pemberton's partners for $2,300 and, using a horse drawn wagon and hundred-gallon boiling tank, established The Coca-Cola Company as a Georgia Corporation.

Candler gave away coupons for free glasses of Coca-Cola and aggressively promoted the drink with calendars, posters, serving trays, fans, lamps, fountain urns, and clocks. In 1894 Candler opened a syrup manufacturing plant in Dallas and, a year later, plants in Chicago and Los Angeles.

Early Marketing Strategy

By 1895, Coca-Cola was available in every state of the Union, but only at soda fountains. Small Coca-Cola bottlers emerged in Mississippi, Texas, and New England, but in 1899, Benjamin Franklin Thomas and Joseph B. Whitehead secured rights to bottle Coca-Cola in the rest of the country. Thomas and Whitehead later established bottling territories, which they sold to independent bottlers. Candler's Coca-Cola Company, meanwhile, supplied only the syrup. This was the birth of franchised bottling operations which today are prevalent in the soft drink industry. Tied to the soaring sales of Coca-Cola by virtue of the syrup—a feat he could not have achieved without bottlers—Candler offered strong support to the brand by offering durable metal Coca-Cola signs in a variety of designs.

With the campaign against alcoholic beverages, culminating in Prohibition, Coca-Cola was promoted as "The Great National Temperance Beverage." By 1919, with Coca-Cola flowing from more than 70,000 outlets, Candler sold the business to a consortium headed by Ernest Woodruff. Woodruff, a prominent businessman with considerable resources, soon met hardship. Sugar prices increased, and Coca-Cola was locked into fixed prices for the syrup it supplied to bottlers. In addition, the sales force had fallen, and with it went sales.

He turned the business over to his son, who had an immediate impact. As if out to prove something to his father, Robert Woodruff gained respect by constantly asking for opinions and giving generously (and anonymously) to charities. It was his decision to promote more portable bottles of Coca-Cola over fountain sales. Sales of bottled Coca-Cola exceeded fountain sales in 1928.

Fountain service was revolutionized in the 1930s with the introduction of automated dispensers that mixed the syrup and

AT A GLANCE

Coca-Cola brand of soft drink introduced on May 8, 1886 by pharmacist John S. Pemberton as a syrup for mixture with carbonated water; Pemberton's partner, Frank M. Robinson, penned trademark; portions of business sold in late 1880s; Pemberton's remaining interest sold to Asa G. Candler, 1888; Coca-Cola nationally distributed and bottled in 1889; The Coca-Cola Company formed, 1892; Coca-Cola trademark registered, 1893; diet Coke introduced in 1982.

Performance: *Market share*—19.3% of U.S. soft drink market. *Sales*—$15.4 million.

Major competitor: Pepsi-Cola.

Advertising: *Agency*—McCann-Erickson, New York, NY, 1956—. *Major campaigns*—"Always Coca-Cola"; "The Pause that Refreshes"; "It's the Real Thing"; "Things Go Better with Coke"; "Have a Coke and a Smile"; "Coke Is It!"; "Can't Beat the Feeling, Can't Beat the Real Thing."

Addresses: *Parent company*—The Coca-Cola Company, 1 Coca-Cola Plaza, N.W., Atlanta, Georgia 30313; phone: (404) 676-2121.

soda water in perfect proportion straight from the tap. Advertising, however, continued to feature "the bottle."

Packaging

In 1915, seeking a distinctive package for Coca-Cola, Swedish glass blower Alexander Samuelson, working for the Root Glass Company of Terre Haute, developed a highly distinctive curved flute bottle design that could be distinguished even when "felt in the dark." Based on the shape of the kola nut, the 6.5-ounce bottles were standard issue for 40 years, until 1955, when 10, 12, and 26-ounce bottles were introduced. The design was trademarked in 1977.

In 1923, under Robert Woodruff, Coca-Cola introduced a six-bottle carton (the first "six-pack") to encourage home consumption. In 1929 Woodruff pioneered the use of vending coolers and, later, coin-operated dispensing machines. Similar to the bottle, the inverted bell glass was adopted as standard fountain glassware in 1929, and was frequently featured in advertising. Coca-Cola first became available in cans in 1960, and in two-liter polyethylene bottles in 1978.

Advertising

Asa Candler was the first to appreciate the value of advertising Coca-Cola. Because the taste could not be described, he enticed people to simply try Coca-Cola. He also believed (in fact, he proved) that advertising could establish an appeal for the brand based on lifestyles and philosophies—in other words, an image.

Coca-Cola was always featured in real life situations, and always in happy situations. As a result, it gained an enduring reputation for being a happy, sociable drink. Without exception, early ads drove home the message "Delicious and Refreshing." In addition to extolling the virtues of Coca-Cola, advertising implored people to ask for the product by its full name, as "nicknames encourage substitution." Indeed, many had begun to call the product "Coke" and competing bottlers had even begun producing an ersatz cola under the name "Koke." But in 1920 the company won a Supreme Court decision that allowed Coca-Cola

exclusive rights to the name "Coke." This experience later led the company to introduce one of its most famous tag lines, "It's the Real Thing."

The brand received great free publicity in the 1930s, when an American in Cuba added Bacardi rum to his Coca-Cola, and invented the "Cuba Libre." The drink was tremendously popular, particularly after the Andrews Sisters' hit recording of the song *Rum & Coca-Cola*.

Throughout its history, Coca-Cola advertising has strived to convey quality and reinforce the identity by using the script lettering or the name Coke, the bright red and white color scheme and the unique contour of the bottle. These remain the primary references of all Coca-Cola advertising. Coca-Cola's advertising was handled by the St. Louis firm D'Arcy until 1956, when the account was switched to McCann-Erickson. D'Arcy, however, handled some of the company's most memorable ads, including those painted by Norman Rockwell, and the classic Haddon Sundblom Santa Claus. Coca-Cola began broadcast advertising with the advent of commercial radio in 1927, and entered television in the 1950s with sponsorship of Edgar Bergen and Charlie McCarthy.

In order to better reflect the fabric of American society, Coca-Cola became one of the first mainstream brands to feature minorities in its advertising. The company featured African Americans in mass-market media buys as early as the 1950s. McCann-Erickson developed a number of revolutionary ad campaigns for Coca-Cola, including "Things go better with Coke," "Coke is it," and "Can't beat the real thing." Perhaps best remembered is the 1971 television ad that featured a hundred or so people perched atop a hill in Italy, singing "I'd like to teach the world to sing . . ." The ad struck a positive chord during a time of profound social upheaval when, with the Vietnam War raging, at least everyone could agree on Coke.

The company also revived the "Real Thing" theme with great success. No longer associated with imposter colas, the old line sounded hip for the times. Perhaps the most successful ads recently are those for diet Coke, featuring computer-enhanced sequences in which Elton John jams for Humphrey Bogart with Louis Armstrong, and Paula Abdul and Groucho Marx dance for Cary Grant, while singing "Just for the taste of it." This memorable campaign gave way to "Taste it all," and "One awesome calorie," handled by Lintas. Coca-Cola claims that its brand accounts for three-quarters of all soft drink advertising expenditures ever made.

Health Claims

Coca-Cola ceased to be advertised with scurrilous claims, such as "brain tonic," as early as Candler took over the business. From that time, Coca-Cola was promoted only as "Delicious and Refreshing." Despite being promoted as a temperance beverage, Coca-Cola, legend has it, contained minute traces of cocaine, a stimulant and addictive extract of the coca leaf. While the company denies that it had ever added cocaine to the beverage, Candler did, in fact, devise a method to remove cocaine from the syrup, suggesting that a cocaine-like substance may have formed from coca extracts during the production process. Whatever the true story may be, from that time, Coca-Cola contained no stimulant more powerful than simple caffeine.

International Growth

In 1926, soon after becoming president of The Coca-Cola Company, Robert Woodruff established a foreign department in New York City with the mission of making Coca-Cola a global product. To achieve this, he ordered the development of a syrup concentrate that would be cheaper to ship, and a way to manufacture the syrup with beet and other sugars, in light of the worldwide cane sugar shortage.

International growth, particularly in Latin America and Europe, was swift until 1939, when World War II broke out. Woodruff ordered that Coca-Cola be made available wherever there are Americans in uniform. Because Coca-Cola so profoundly raised soldiers' morale, the scheme quickly gained support from the army. General Eisenhower himself ordered ten bottling plants in North Africa. An additional 54 were established throughout the world during the war, laying the pattern for Coca-Cola's postwar international expansion.

Max Keith, the Coca-Cola bottler in Germany who, amazingly, remained in business during the war by selling a variety of fruit flavored drinks, resumed bottling Coca-Cola after the war. His line of flavored drinks, however, had become highly popular in Germany, where they were known as Fanta. Coca-Cola brought Fanta to the United States in 1960 as a separate brand.

Coca-Cola encountered difficulties in France, where the Communist Party simply hated anything American, and in Switzerland,

A 1938 magazine advertisement tells readers to stop and drink Coca-Cola.

where it was seen as a threat to vintners and brewers. Stuck in the middle of the Arab boycott in 1967, the company took criticism from Israel. The company did, however, score tremendous successes with the entry into the Soviet Union and China after President Nixon's rapprochement with those countries in 1971.

Brand Development

After rolling out the Fanta line in 1960, Coca-Cola introduced several new flavors: Sprite (1961), TAB (1963), Fresca (1966) and Mr. PIBB (1972). None of these were extensions of Coca-Cola. In fact, the first true brand extension was diet Coke, which was not introduced until July 8, 1982. While TAB had long been considered the diet version of Coke, its formulation was different. The decision to introduce a diet version of Coke came amid a general trend in the industry to offer low-calorie versions of regular brands. Heavily promoted, diet Coke rode the wave of popularity experienced by diet drinks during the 1980s and is today the world's most popular diet soda (and the third best-selling soft drink overall).

In 1985, threatened by gains from arch-rival Pepsi-Cola Co., Coca-Cola re-examined the popularity of the 99-year old formula in a series of taste tests. These suggested that public overwhelmingly preferred a smoother, sweeter formulation over the original, prompting the company to change the formula for Coke. The public responded with shock and even dismay, and a campaign was begun to return the company to the old formula. Pepsi-Cola, meanwhile, cited the formula change as evidence of people's changing tastes (and supposed preference for Pepsi).

Shocked itself by the failure of its marketing whizzes, Coca-Cola quickly re-introduced the old formula as "Coca-Cola Classic." The "new Coke," as it had become known, was gradually phased out after the company yanked its ads for the unpopular improvement. Refusing to let it die, however, the company put new Coke back on the market in 1992 as "Coke II." In the end, the debacle over the formula proved advantageous for the company. With regular and diet versions of both Cokes on the market, the company added Cherry Coke, a drink invented 80 years earlier by soda jerks, in response to the popularity of fruit sodas among children and certain minority groups. With so many extensions on the market, Coca-Cola actually won back a substantial amount of market share.

The company made a brief foray into merchandising in the 1980s with a nominally popular line of casual wear clothing. This line of shirts and denim pants, made by independent manufacturers, carried the imprint of Coca-Cola. Sales of the products failed to meet expectations, but a strong licensing program for Coca-Cola clothing remained in the early 1990s.

Performance Evaluation

The most successful aspect of Coca-Cola, aside from the appeal of the beverage, is the lifestyle it conveys. It is undeniably the most successful soft drink in the world. Available virtually everywhere, its image as a happy sociable drink plays extremely well in every culture. Having dominated the profitable but saturated American market, the only areas left for growth are foreign countries. To this extent, Coca-Cola is regarded as something supremely, definitively American—more so than Pepsi-Cola, even where that brand has well-established sales. Coca-Cola signifies the rich, free American lifestyle for millions of people; drink a Coke, be an American. With the recent opening of markets in Eastern Europe and the former Soviet Union, Coca-Cola is poised for continued growth.

Further Reading:

Braunstein, Janet, "New Ads Are the Real Thing," *Detroit Free Press,* February 15, 1993, p. 4F.

The Chronicle of Coca-Cola Since 1886, Time Inc., 1950.

Cleary, David Powers, "Coca-Cola," *Great American Brands,* New York: Fairchild Publications, 1981.

"Diet Coke Rings in the New," *Detroit Free Press,* January 4, 1993.

"Diet Coke Taps into the Fountain of Youth," *Detroit Free Press,* February 8, 1993, p. 6F.

"Facts, Figures and Features," Company Document, June, 1992.

Famous American Trademarks, Arnold B. Barach, Public Affairs Press, 1971.

Garfield, Bob, "New Diet Coke Ads Go for a Very Familiar Gusto," *Advertising Age,* January 11, 1993, p. 44.

Konrad, Walecia, and Igor Reichlin, "The Real Thing Is Thundering Eastward," *Business Week,* April 13, 1992, pp. 96, 98.

Morgan, Hal, "Coca-Cola," *Symbols of America,* New York: Viking, 1986.

Winters, Patricia, "Coca-Cola Classic Spring Giveaway Gets Local Accent," *Advertising Age,* March 22, 1993.

Winters, Patricia, "Diet Coke Ads Take an Active Approach," *Advertising Age,* January 4, 1993, p. 33.

Zinn, Laura, "For Coke's Peter Sealey, Hollywood Is It," *Business Week,* March 15, 1993, pp. 84-85.

—John Simley

COORS®

Coors, the original mountain-brewed beer from Colorado, is the flagship brand of Coors Brewing Company, the third largest brewer in the United States. With its Rocky Mountains imagery and the "fresh from the Rockies taste—crisp, fresh, cold, clean and pure" slogan, the Coors brand along with its more popular light version constituted approximately 9 percent of U.S. beer consumption by the early 1990s. Standing as a high quality regional beer brand for a century, Coors was distributed nationally beginning in the late 1970s in response to stiff competition and changing market tastes. In a decade the brand had expanded into all the major markets with its popular low-calorie version, Coors Light. Marketed as the "Silver Bullet," this light brand became the fourth largest selling beer in the United States and only the second light beer in history to exceed the ten million barrel mark. In the late 1980s and early 1990s several more brand extensions, including Coors Extra Gold, Coors Extra Gold Light, Coors Dry, and Coors Cutter were launched, reflecting intensive market segmentation in the industry.

Brand Origins

In 1873 Adolph Herman Joseph Coors traveled to the United States as a stowaway and later started a brewery on the site of an abandoned tannery. Made from quality natural ingredients, Golden Lager, his first brew, turned out a profit in its first year. This success enabled Adolph Coors to buy out his partner, Jacob Schueler, by 1880. Showing a unique flair for marketing, Coors concentrated on devising new ways to distribute his beer. By the end of the century, annual output had increased to 48,000 barrels. During this time, Coors Export Beer and Coors Golden Malt Extract were introduced. Another brew, Golden Select Beer won a prize at Chicago's World Columbian Exposition in 1893.

The advent of Prohibition saw Coors dumping more than 17,000 gallons of beer into Clear Creek in Colorado. (In 1915 environmental awareness was virtually nonexistent and dumping into a creek or river was one way of disposing of waste.) Coors Manna and Coors Hopale, probable ancestors of today's nonalcoholic beverages, were two brews that were introduced during Prohibition. Coors Golden Beer, Coors Golden Export Lager, Coors Bock Beer Special Brew, and Coors Pilsener Beer Extra Dry were among the brands that Coors introduced in the post-Prohibition era. During the late 1930s, the heraldic lion and waterfall were incorporated into the design. The advertising slogan "pure Rocky Mountain spring water" was developed in 1936.

In 1950 Coors Export Lager, a heavier beer preferred by older customers, was discontinued and Coors Banquet became the company's only product. It continued to be the company's only beer for 28 years and inspired a cult following—it became a fad on college campuses; President Ford carried Coors on Air Force One; Henry Kissinger bootlegged it back to Washington from his trips to the West; and actors Paul Newman and Clint Eastwood drank it on movie sets. Relying exclusively on the Coors "mystique" instead of marketing or advertising, the Coors brand—while it was being distributed solely in the West—helped propel the company to among the four largest U.S. brewers by 1969. The company's one-product policy came to an end with the introduction of Coors Light in 1978—a change brought forth by both competitors and the market.

Brewing the Brand

Coors prides itself on avoiding chemicals and additives and using only natural ingredients to prepare its beers. The Rocky Mountain spring water, mentioned in most advertising campaigns, is arguably the most important ingredient of Coors. The natural filtration that the spring water undergoes from its source in the Rockies through miles of rock, gravel, and sand eliminates the need for chemical alterations. Unlike the procedures for most other American beers, the Coors brewing process is entirely natural and requires 68 days, one of the longest brewing processes in the industry. To preserve the brewery-fresh flavor of its beers, Coors does not pasteurize them. In 1959 company scientists and engineers discovered a secret filtration process that exceeded the strictest federal guidelines for purity, thus eliminating the need for pasteurization. Realizing that any beer retains its fresh taste longer if kept cool, Coors uses a refrigerated marketing program and one of the strictest rotation policies to maintain the beer's freshness. Coors Light goes through an extended brewing cycle to reduce calorie count to 105 calories per 12 ounces.

Marketing Strategy

For 100 years, Coors relied on the quality of its beer and lack of competition to sell its brew in the West. The company succeeded brilliantly. William Coors, chairman of the company had bragged in 1975, "We don't need marketing. We make the best beer in the

AT A GLANCE

Coors brand of beer founded in 1873 by Adolph Herman Joseph Coors in Golden, CO; Coors Light introduced in 1978, Coors Extra Gold in 1987, Coors Dry in 1991, Coors Cutter in 1991, and Coors Extra Gold Light in 1993.

Major competitor: Budweiser; also Miller Lite.

Advertising: Agency—(Coors) GSD&M, Austin, TX, 1987-92, Foote, Cone and Belding, San Francisco, CA, 1993--; (Coors Light) Foote, Cone & Belding, Chicago, IL, 1983—. *Major campaign*—"The Right Beer Now."

Addresses: Parent company—Coors Brewing Company, 12th and Ford Sts., Golden, CO 80401-6565; phone: (303) 279-6565; fax: (303) 277-6246.

world." Three years later the tone had changed to, "Our business plan in one word, is survival." During this period Coors lost its hold on western markets to archrivals Anheuser-Busch Companies, Inc. and Philip Morris Companies, Inc.'s Miller because it ignored the marketing of its quality beer. With the lowest advertising dollar investment per barrel in the 1960s, Coors had relied mainly on word of mouth and the Rockies-brewed mystique of its only beer to carry it through what was a very regional industry. In 1973 Anheuser-Busch entered the West by opening up a brewery in California, a market where Coors sold more than all the other brands combined. In 1976 Coors responded with increased marketing expenditures, but by then it was too late. By 1978 Anheuser-Busch had surpassed Coors as the number one brewer in California. In addition, Coors's conservative political positions, trouble with labor unions and Hispanics, and the gradual change of the market toward low-calorie light beers had forced a once cult beer to concentrate on survival.

A study by an independent market research firm showed that Coors had been trampled by the segmentation brought forth by Miller Lite beer. Virtually all the growth in the beer industry was coming from light or super premium beers. Miller's marketing blitz, aimed at displacing Anheuser-Busch from the number one position, capitalized on the changing trends. Soon four out of every ten new light beer drinkers were found to be switching away from Coors. The marketing war that hit the industry had claimed its biggest victim: Coors.

Shaken and stirred, the company regrouped to rectify its marketing mistakes. In 1976 Coors hired J. Walter Thompson to enhance its corporate image. By 1978 the company had rejected its single beer strategy and had introduced Coors Light, its first new product in 20 years. It disbanded its in-house advertising operation, Cadco, and roped in Ted Bates & Co. to advertise the brand. Advertising expenditure, half of the industry average at $9.8 million in 1976, was increased to $66.7 million by 1980.

It was Coors Light, the low calorie version of the original brand, that was the comeback vehicle for the company. Backed by an original advertising campaign, Coors Light became the second largest selling light beer by 1980, just two years after it was launched. By 1985 the brand accounted for nearly 50 percent of the company's volume. Although Coors Light was the fastest-growing national beer on the market, some of that growth came from its parent brand, Coors beer.

The company had decided to take on its competitors on their own turf—the East. The eastern expansion called for doubling total brewery capacity and, more important, building this increased capacity in the East to help the company avoid high transportation costs. The push toward the eastern markets was methodical; only eight more states had been added by 1981. The eastern markets were already saturated by the time Coors arrived. Moreover, Coors found that the most successful beer distributors were already associated with major brands such as Anheuser-Busch, Miller, and Stroh's and unwilling to add Coors. Lack of distribution strength had rendered Coors's advertising largely ineffective.

Coors's cautious approach to expansion was complicated by the fact that it had just one brewery in Colorado—which meant shipping the beer across the country and adding $6 to $7 per barrel. Also, the company did not maintain its western market shares; by 1985, Coors had only 14 percent of the Californian market. Named head of the brewing division in 1985, Peter Coors fundamentally altered the way the company did business. The same year, the company started construction of a brewing and packaging facility in the Shenandoah Valley of Virginia to supply the eastern market and become more competitive with other brewing companies. According to Alan Wolf in *Beverage World,* Peter Coors "transformed his brewery from a strictly manufacturing orientation to one in which the value of solid marketing—on both a regional and now a national level—would never again be overlooked." Distributors saw this as a boon because their network was one of the most important links in Coors's customer chain. Previously they had felt constrained by corporate decisions made in Colorado, but they became partners in the decision-making process.

After decentralizing Coors's marketing approach, Peter Coors negotiated a settlement with organized labor, which, in 1977, had launched a national boycott of the beer. The boycott had hindered Coors's expansion in the heavily unionized New Jersey and New York markets. The company estimated that the 13 million union members had created an anti-Coors group of 54 million people, thus the settlement came as a relief for Coors in the ultra-competitive eastern markets. In 1978 members the of Hispanic community had also boycotted the beer, alleging hiring discrimination. The boycott hit Coors's sales severely in California and Texas—home to the country's largest Hispanic communities and traditionally Coors's largest markets. In 1984 the company signed a trade covenant with six Hispanic groups, agreeing to spend $8.9 million in 1985 on advertising and promotions aimed at Hispanic beer drinkers. Coors brought out Spanish-language campaigns, "Solo Hay Una Coors," for the Coors brand and "La Bala de Plata," for Coors Light.

With the boycotts lifted, Coors sales shot up, stretching the existing breweries to maximum capacity. For the first time in 117 years Coors decided to borrow money, raising $300 million in senior unsecured debt to buy Stroh Brewery Co.'s Memphis brewery in 1990 and build an aluminum rolling mill in San Antonio. By 1992 Coors had also completed a planned expansion of its nationwide distribution network, putting up 27 refrigerated satellite distribution centers with brewery-fresh beer within a day's delivery of each of the distributors. The $35 million investment helped Coors reduce distribution bottlenecks and maintain its high quality standards, ensuring that the customer received the freshest beer possible.

As part of its aggressive advertising campaign to build its sales and image in the 1980s, Coors's marketing department worked to give Coors a dominant position in sports sponsorship. The firm dropped its Coors Light Tennis series in 1980 to focus on motor sports. The company began sponsoring Bill Elliot, one of the hottest drivers on the National Association for Stock Car Auto Racing (NASCAR) circuit. Several years before Coors products were available in the southeast, where stock-car racing is extremely popular, its brand name was already well known. Hundreds of liquor stores carried Elliot's posters promoting Coors beer. Elliot gave Coors national exposure and projected the image of a winner in areas where Coors had not arrived.

Yet Coors did make a few marketing blunders. In 1988 the company rechristened Coors Banquet as Coors Original Draft to take advantage of a perceived market trend toward draft beer. Although the Coors brand, because it was not pasteurized, had been a draft beer all along, the company had never advertised it as such. Consumers were confused, thinking that Coors had changed the beer, and stopped drinking it. In 1989 Coors changed the name to Original Coors beer. New television spots downplayed the draft image, focusing instead on the traditional quality issue. With changing market trends and more focus on new brand extensions, sales of Original Coors began declining steadily. By 1992 it dropped out of the ten largest selling beers list, even though Coors Light continued to be a hot seller.

Advertising and Promotional Activities

Until the beer marketing wars hit the industry in the 1970s, Coors spent approximately $6 million in advertising expenditures annually. According to Chairman William Coors, the company "let the beer sneak in and people find out on their own it's available." Later than most players in the beer market, Coors realized that the Anheuser-Busch/Miller marketing offensive had to be countered by an advertising blitz of its own. After disbanding its in-house advertising operation and signing an outside firm, Ted Bates & Co., Coors increased its advertising budget by nearly six times its previous level in four years.

The early 1980s campaigns were designed to win back lost share in western markets and promote Coors Light. Coors saw early on that sports programming was the best way to reach its target audience of men. But the best sports sponsorship was possible only through network television, where the then-regional Coors did not possess enough clout. Combination buying was seen as the solution; the company teamed up with Stroh's—whose northeastern and northwestern markets complemented Coors markets in the West—and obtained precious network exposure. The Bates agency decided that the brand's "unique selling proposition" would be its position as the only beer brewed in the Rockies. The television theme "taste the high country" put forth an exciting visual image, allowing Coors to have a very distinct look. In addition to network spots during NFL football on CBS and NBC, and ABC's *Wide World of Sports,* Coors also developed syndicated television packages such as Coors's *Western Outdoorsman* that focused on outdoor activities available in Coors marketing areas.

Realizing that Coors's survival in the cutthroat beer industry depended heavily on whether the introduction of Coors Light was a success or not, Peter Coors directed the creation of the Coors Light image. Ted Bates & Co. came out with television commercials that acknowledged that in the minds of the customer, light

beer was an inferior product. The television spots showed a cowboy annoyed at being offered only light beer at the end of a hard day's work. "Have you ever tasted light beer?" he asks disgustedly. But when he sipped the Coors brand he pronounced it "not bad" and added, "I am surprised." This line became a slogan among Coors loyalists. Radio spots were used as secondary means of advertising the Coors Light brand because the creative idea translated easily into radio copy. Conversely, the visual nature of the campaign for Original Coors precluded radio advertising. By the mid-1980s, Foote, Cone & Belding (who began handling the Coors Light account in 1983) discovered that Coors Light drinkers throughout the country had given the brand a nickname—The Silver Bullet. Capitalizing on this catchy nomenclature, the agency began using the tag line, "The Silver Bullet," for Coors Light commercials in 1985.

Actor Mark Harmon served as a spokesman in 40 different Coors spots created by Foote, Coone & Belding in the 1980s. The Coors brand was positioned as a draft beer with the theme, "the American original." The Coors Light campaign theme was, "the right beer now," depicting the energetic, fast-paced lifestyle of the Coors Light beer drinker; in addition a Hispanic campaign entitled, "pura vida," (the good life) was also introduced in an effort to win back the Hispanic market. By the late 1980s, the company had put a lot of advertising muscle toward Coors Extra Gold's "the full-tilt taste" campaign and enlisted the Three Stooges to pitch for Coors, Coors Light, and Coors Extra Gold in a campaign titled, "the original sports nut." By 1992 Foote, Cone & Belding created the first campaign to address the family of Coors brands. It highlighted and reinforced the Rocky Mountain heritage and featured majestic visuals, an original classical composition, and brief printed quotes from company President Peter Coors.

During the 1990s Anheuser-Busch and Coors began a sordid advertising war. Coors fired the first salvo in 1991 with a $5 million, 16-city advertising campaign that pitted Coors Extra Gold against number-one selling Budweiser, whose market share had been dipping. In the spots Coors claimed that 58 percent of Budweiser drinkers preferred Coors Extra Gold—the most direct comparative advertising seen in the beer industry. Coors Extra Gold's "beer is back" campaign also touted the virtue of the beer's deep golden color, comparing it unfavorably with paler brews. Anheuser-Busch struck back at Coors Light's Rocky Mountain imagery through advertisements of tenth-placed Natural Light. The issue was the Virginia water that Coors added to the concentrated brew it shipped East. Anheuser-Busch's campaign attacked Coors for mixing "local water" with the Rocky Mountain spring water, which was central to the Coors mystique. Coors retaliated by filing a suit in Federal District Court in New York City, alleging that the ads were false and misleading and seeking $10 million in damages. Anheuser-Busch filed a countersuit enjoining it from using Rocky Mountain imagery in any of its ads. The court ruled in favor of Anheuser-Busch, lifting a temporary restraining order against it. In an attempt settle the controversy, Peter Coors appeared in a commercial, strolling in the picturesque Shenandoah Valley and convincing the viewers that the Virginia water was comparable to the celebrated water of the Rockies.

In committing itself fully to advertising, Coors also looked beyond traditional means of promotion for the Coors brand. In 1990 Coors brought the "frequent flier" concept to beer marketing, a move designed to explore alternatives to broadcast advertising. Club Coors offered opportunities to earn discounts on hotels, restaurants, and travel. Trying direct marketing as an outgrowth of regional marketing, GSD&M, Coors's marketing agency from Austin, Texas, introduced Club Coors as a way to strengthen brand loyalty.

In an effort to encourage responsible drinking, Coors began broadcasting a series of Coors Light "now, not now" moderation advertisements. This highly successful campaign dramatized that there were many appropriate times to enjoy Coors Light, but also times to limit or refrain from consumption. Motorcycling, hunting, and driving were presented as "not now" times. The campaign was designed to make responsible drinking part of the Coors Light brand identity, thus reinforcing the mainstream campaign, "the right beer now." In 1986 Coors became the first brewer to incorporate an alcohol awareness message in its national product advertising. Titled "gimme the Keys," one spot featured a bartender who would not allow a customer to drive home after he had too much to drink. Consumer response to the moderation commercials was overwhelmingly positive.

Attractive packaging was another aspect of Coors promotion that the brewer emphasized. Always at the forefront of packaging technology, Coors developed the first aluminum can for the beverage industry. In 1983 Coors Packaging Co. was formed to expand Coors's leadership in the packaging area by exploring and marketing new and innovative products, designed to meet the needs of both bottlers and consumers.

Brand Extensions

The full bodied Coors Extra Gold brand was launched in 1987, backed by media blitz, built around the theme, "the full tilt taste." Though it reached a sales peak of one million barrels in 1989, both volume and market share have eroded since. By 1992 sales were down to 0.5 million barrels giving it a 0.3 percent market share in the U.S. beer market. Research indicated, however, that the Coors Extra Gold taste suited European pallets. By 1992 the brand had entered Greece, England, Scotland, and France supported by a strong marketing campaign. Hoping to become a top-five brand in the United Kingdom, Coors Extra Gold was positioned to compete against a range of premium lagers.

1991 saw Coors's first entry into the premium dry category with Coors Dry. Following a successful launch in 14 western states, it was added in four Plains states in 1992. The brand marketed its exclusive "double chilled" brewing method, featuring a unique two-step cooling process, to become the number two dry beer in the western region within four months. In 1991 it won the first place gold medal in the Great American Beer Festival for the best American dry lager. The Coors Dry advertising campaign "feel the chill" used Rocky Mountain imagery to sell the brand in a market that expects double-digit growth annually.

Coors Cutter, a nonalcoholic beverage, was introduced in 1991 to meet growing consumer demand. The nonalcoholic beer market grew by 33 percent in 1991 and by 35 percent in 1992, reflecting changing consumer attitudes about responsible drinking. Helped by an aggressive in-store sampling program and supported by a variety of point-of-sale materials, the Coors Cutter brand gave a strong performance in 1992, selling 280,000 barrels.

International Market

Coors International Marketing Department was formed in 1984 to examine worldwide opportunities for its products. In 1985 it began brewing Coors and Coors Light in Canada under a licensing agreement with Molson Breweries Limited. Subsequently, Coors Light became the number one light beer in Canada. Since April of 1987, Asahi has been brewing the Coors brand in Japan under a licensing agreement with Coors. Planning to have at least 20 markets outside of the United States by 1995, Coors looked at Caribbean markets with its numerous tourists as attractive export opportunities. In 1991 Coors and Coors Light were launched in Puerto Rico through an import representative, V. Suarez & Co. Inc. As part of the ambitious export undertaking, Coors established its first international regional office in Puerto Rico and hired two Puerto-Rican based advertising and promotion agencies.

In 1991 Coors reached an agreement with Jinro Ltd. of the Republic of Korea to build and operate a brewery in South Korea. In 1992 a joint venture named Jinro-Coors Brewing Company broke ground and began construction of that facility, expected to be in operation in early 1994. In addition, in 1993 Coors created UniBev Ltd., a new operating unit of the Coors Import Division, to increase Coors's share of the growing import and specialty beer market.

Coors Extra Gold became the first American beer imported into Greece in 1991. Backed by the largest advertising and promotional campaign for a new premium lager in Great Britain, Coors Extra Gold also found its way into northwest England and Scotland by 1992. Earlier it was chosen as one of only two American beers to be served in the Euro Disney theme park in France.

Future Growth

The brewery's transformation from a reluctant marketer to a highly effective one in 15 years is the main reason that the Coors brand and its Light extension have continued to figure consistently among the top beer brands. Though the sales of the flagship brand Coors have been falling in response to changing demand patterns, Coors Light continues as a dominant player in the light beer segment. The introductions of Coors Cutter and Coors Dry, targeted at new growth segments, have shown that the brand name will continue to be a major force in the beer markets of tomorrow. According to the 1991 Annual Report, "In addition to growing the brands that hold the most potential, our strategy involves introducing quality new brands as the market provides opportunities." The report continued, "We will continue to strengthen our position in the marketplace and aggressively pursue international marketing opportunities to ensure Coors Brewing Company's long-term success in the beer industry."

Further Reading:

"Adolph Coors: Brewing up plans for an invasion of the East Coast," *Business Week,* September 29, 1980, pp. 123-24.

Adolph Coors Company Annual Report, Golden, Colorado: The Adolph Coors Company, 1991.

Adolph Coors Company Corporate Communications Department, "Time in a Bottle," Golden, Colorado: The Adolph Coors Company, 1993.

Adolph Coors Company Corporate Communications Department, "The Adolph Coors Story," Golden, Colorado: The Adolph Coors Company, 1993.

Atchinson, Sandra, and Frons, Marc, "Can Pete and Jeff Coors Brew up a Comeback?" *Business Week,* December 16, 1985, pp. 86-88.

"Coors Beer: What Hit Us?" *Forbes,* October 16, 1978, p. 71.

"Coors' Bitter Brew," *Financial World,* April 30, 1983, pp. 31-32.

Deierlein, Bob, "Coors Changes Distribution System," *Beverage World,* July, 1992, p. 73.

Gardner, Fred, "Coors Battles the Giants," *Marketing & Media Decisions,* June 1981, pp. 64-65, 122-23.

Levandoski, Robert, ''Beer Sales, Optimism Remain Flat,'' *Beverage Industry,* January, 1993.

Poole, Claire, ''Shirtsleeves to Shirtsleeves,'' *Forbes,* March 4, 1991, p. 52.

PR Newswire Association, Inc., ''Coors Brewing Co. Brings Extra Gold to Great Britain,'' *PR Newswire,* August 27, 1992.

Teinowitz, Ira, ''Coors Beer Drops 'Draft,' '' *Advertising Age,* January 23, 1989, p. 3.

Winters, Patricia, ''Coors Shootout; Three Shops Vie in Strategy Shift,'' *Advertising Age,* August 31, 1987, p. 46.

Wolf, Alan, ''Out Here in the Field,'' *Beverage World,* April, 1991, p. 36.

—Ashish Patwardhan

CORONA®

Corona Extra, a mild, golden brand of lager brewed in Mexico, is one of the best-selling imported beers in the United States. Commonly served with a slice of lime wedged in the neck of its clear-glass bottle, the beer has long been popular in Mexico. It was not until 1981, however, that Corona was exported to the U.S. market. Its explosive growth a few years later, which threatened to topple Heineken as the country's best-selling import, was one of the most unexpected developments in the history of the U.S. beer industry.

A Spanish word meaning "crown," Corona is just one of a dozen beers brewed by Grupo Modelo, headquartered in Mexico City. Other Modelo brands exported to the United States include Corona Light, a low-calorie version of the original beer; lagers Modelo Especial and Pacifico; and Negra Modelo, a dark lager.

Historical Background

Mexico has a long history of beer production, beginning with a type of brew made by the area's indigenous people. Many early developers of its beer industry, however, were from foreign lands. The first brewery, or cervecería, in Mexico was set up by the Spanish in the 1500s. Three hundred years later, in the early 19th century, Bernhard Bolgard of Switzerland and Frederick Herzog of Bavaria established breweries in Mexico City. They were soon followed by a wave of German immigrants, who would greatly influence the growing Mexican beer industry. Bolgard, Herzog, and other 19th-century brewers produced ale made from sun-dried barley and brown sugar. When ice machines became readily available in the late 1800s, however, many brewers switched to making lager beers, which were fermented and matured at a considerably cooler temperature.

Grupo Modelo, until 1992 called Cervecería Modelo, was established in Mexico City in 1925 by Pablo Diez, an immigrant from León, Spain. His first beers, including Corona, were made under the supervision of German brewmasters. Over the next half century Modelo experimented with a variety of different beers and, in the process, became the country's largest brewer. Modelo also came to have considerable control over its production. Much of the barley used in its beers, for example, was grown on the company's farms. Modelo owned plants for processing malt, as well as a factory for making glass bottles (the raw material for which was supplied by the company's silica mines). Modelo even made its own cardboard containers. All capital projects, moreover, were undertaken without borrowed money.

By the late 20th century most Mexican beer was made by just three companies—Modelo, Cervecería Cuauhtémoc, and Cervecería Moctezuma—although Cuauhtémoc and Moctezuma were owned by the same holding company, Valores Industriales. Cuauhtémoc, founded in 1891 by St. Louis immigrant Joseph Schnaider, was the country's second largest brewer, making a variety of beers, such as Tacate and Carta Blanca, that competed with Corona in both Mexico and the United States. Moctezuma, producer of competing brands Dos Equis, Superior, and Sol, was established in 1894 under the direction of German brewmaster Wilhelm Hasse.

Early Exports to the United States

In 1981, with a flourishing business in its home market, Modelo began exporting Corona Extra to the United States. It was priced considerably higher than the major domestic beers, though not as high as many European brands. Initially sold just in the Southwest, by the mid-1980s Corona had made extensive inroads into the giant but fiercely competitive U.S. market. By 1987 Corona was available in more than 30 states. By then distribution was being handled by two American companies: Barton Beers Ltd., located in Chicago, for the West and Southwest; and Gambrinus Importing Company Inc. of San Antonio, Texas, for the East and Southeast.

Corona's U.S. exports, just 150,000 cases in 1981, rose steadily along with its increased distribution, although by 1984 its annual sales were still fewer than one million cases. It was the following year that Corona's storied surge began, with U.S. sales in 1985 surpassing five million cases, or nearly 50 percent of all beer exported that year from Mexico. Remarkably the brand took off with only minimal marketing and advertising support. In the United States beer sales tended to be closely tied to expensive television advertisements, often featuring famous sports figures or an unusual mascot, such as a bull terrier. Although Barton and Gambrinus ran print and radio advertisements for Corona, their annual advertising expenditures had reached only about $1 million by the mid-1980s, and it was not until 1988, when some $10 million was spent, that Corona began to be advertised on network television.

Explosive Sales Growth

The five million cases of Corona exported to the United States in 1985 certainly caught the attention of the U.S. beer industry, but the jump to some 22 million cases by 1987 left competing brewers, industry analysts, beer connoisseurs, and even Modelo's management grasping for explanations. In 1986, when 13.5 million cases of the beer were sold, Corona nudged past Molson and Beck's to become the country's second most popular imported beer. By 1987 Corona's gains were clearly reflected in the declining fortunes of other brands, most notably Heineken, whose top share of the imported beer category had dropped from 38 percent in 1982 to a mere 24 percent in 1987. Corona had become the number one import in California, Colorado, and Texas. Although imported beer represented less than five percent of the total U.S. beer market, even such dominant American beer brands as Budweiser, Coors, and Michelob were affected.

Corona's explosive growth caused a production nightmare that other brewers could only dream about. Orders for Corona far outstripped the company's production capacity, but not because its seven plants were incapable of brewing enough beer. Modelo, which manufactured returnable bottles for the Mexican market, instead found itself unable to make enough of the disposable bottles used in the United States. As a result, its recent foray into the eastern United States had to be held back, and promotions were curtailed in order to avoid boosting an already unsatisfied demand. Many of Corona's U.S. sales were to young professionals, or yuppies, in bars and restaurants.

Corona's Appeal

Explanations for Corona's success ranged from glowing testaments of its quality to derogatory opinions of its customers. Part of the appeal, no doubt, was Corona's mild, "light tasting" flavor, which conformed well to U.S. preferences. John N. MacDonough, a vice-president at Anheuser-Busch, explained, "It looks like an imported beer, and it tastes like a domestic. That's the perfect combination." This theory was corroborated by Robert S. Weinberg, a market researcher in St. Louis, who said, "Most people [in the United States] don't like the taste of imports. The beers with character are the ones that aren't very big sellers. Corona is the one that tastes the most like domestic beer."

While Corona gained converts at an almost unbelievable pace, it was received less amicably by some beer experts. Michael Jackson, an internationally known writer on beer, was especially critical of Corona. In his 1988 book *The New World Guide to Beer*, Jackson wrote, "Corona is a beer made as cheaply as possible, so that it can be sold inexpensively to manual workers in Mexico. . . . Corona tastes like a beer made with a very high percentage of corn adjunct [instead of all barley] and a short lagering time. It is thin bodied, with some apple notes." In another context, Jackson was quoted as saying in the *New York Times*, "Yuppies feel macho drinking a Mexican peasant beer . . . I'm not saying Corona is a worse beer than a lot of cheap American beers. I just mark the yuppies for drinking it. They buy a bad beer for a lot of money." Predictably, spokesmen for competing brands echoed these complaints. Leo van Munching, the head of Heineken's import company, derided Corona as "nothing more than Mexican soda pop." The millions of Corona drinkers, many of whom were enthusiastic about the beer's taste, apparently disagreed with such negative judgments. Manuel Alvarez Loyo, a Modelo vice-president, explained simply, "Corona's quality sells itself."

Corona's precipitous climb reached a peak in 1987, and the brand subsequently began a steady slide in U.S. sales. Imports to the United States fell 11.7 percent in 1988, 21.3 percent in 1989, 5.7 percent in 1990, and 15.6 percent in 1991. False rumors, begun in May 1987, that Modelo workers were urinating in the beer likely hurt Corona sales, even after the company began a public relations campaign to inform customers of its strict production controls and clean, modern facilities. These rumors were allegedly started by a competing distributor, Luce & Son of Reno, Nevada, which, as part of an out-of-court settlement, issued a letter of apology. By 1991, however, sales of Corona—further hurt by competing new products, such as dry beer—were barely more than half of the 1987 record. Some industry analysts predicted that Corona would be pushed out of the fickle U.S. market as quickly as it arrived. To help slow this decline Modelo introduced Corona Light, a low-calorie beer, in 1989; its first year's sales of one million cases was a record for an imported beer. Modelo also hoped to increase sales with its new 12-pack containers of both Corona Extra and Corona Light.

Other Foreign Markets

While sales were falling in the United States, the brewery extended its reach to countries in Latin America, Europe, and the Pacific Rim, where Corona was advertised as a premium "beach party" beer. Opening new markets, however, frequently proved difficult. In Spain the Corona name was already trademarked by another company, so the beer was instead sold under the brand name Coronita. A similar problem existed in France and in a number of Latin American countries, but Modelo managed to export Corona to these markets under its original brand name. More serious was the charge in Switzerland, Austria, and Germany that Corona had an unsafe level of nitrosamines, chemical compounds produced naturally in the malting process but suspected of being carcinogenic. Modelo responded by reducing the amount.

By the early 1990s Modelo's efforts to boost its export trade had paid off, as Corona, now with access to more than 55 countries, had become a truly global brand. Corona became the most popular imported beer in Australia, for example, and the second most popular import in Japan. By 1992 Modelo was producing nearly 70 percent of all beer exported from Mexico, as well as half of all beer consumed in its home market. Even in the United States its prospects appeared to be improving. Though still far below its 1987 peak, Corona and other Modelo beers experienced growth in

1992, with a jump of eight percent to 15 million cases (12.8 million cases of Corona Extra). This rebound was partially a result of increasing sales outside of its stronghold in the southwestern states. Reflecting industry confidence in the brand, Anheuser-Busch announced in March 1993 that it was buying 18 percent of Grupo Modelo.

Brand Outlook

By 1992 the success of Corona had transformed Grupo Modelo into the world's 10th largest brewer, with some $1.5 billion in sales. Of its annual production of 2.1 billion liters, almost half were of Corona Extra. Arrangements were being made in 1993 to place Grupo Modelo on Mexican and international stock exchanges. The money raised through public shares were expected to help push Corona into new foreign markets, such as Hungary and Russia.

In the United States, the principal export market, Corona faced not only stiff competition but also a stagnant beer market aggravated by increased excise taxes and an aging population. Contrary to some industry predictions, however, the brand has remained a formidable contender, competing with Molson and Beck's for runner-up in the imported beer category. Instead of a mere trend, Corona has proved to be a durable brand supported by its mainstream taste, foreign cachet, and exotic, beach-party image.

Further Reading:

Adelson, Andrea, "A Workers' Beer Gains Status: Corona Sales Soar in U.S.," *New York Times*, July 11, 1987, pp. 39, 41.

Blair, Ian C., "Imported Beers: The New Order," *Beverage World*, September 1987, pp. 44-45, 48, 111.

Deveny, Kathleen, "Reality of the '90s Hits Yuppie Brands," *Wall Street Journal*, December 20, 1990, pp. B1, B5.

Frees, Jeff, "The Drinking Man: Tall, Thin, and Mysterious," *Esquire*, May 1988, p. 36.

Gibson, Richard, "Anheuser-Busch to Buy 18% Stake in Mexican Brewer [Grupo Modelo]," *Wall Street Journal*, March 23, 1993, p. B4.

Hume, Scott, "Corona Fights Bad-Beer Rumors," *Advertising Age*, August 3, 1987, p. 6.

Jackson, Michael, *The New World Guide to Beer*, Philadelphia: Running Press, 1988, pp. 222-23.

Kuhl, Craig, "Corona Beer: A Head of Its Time," *Beverage World*, February 1987, pp. 50, 55.

Levin, Gary, "Imports Brew New Success," *Advertising Age*, October 5, 1992, p. 38.

Oneal, Michael, "A Mexican Beer Whose Cup Runneth Over," *Business Week*, September 1, 1986, p. 42.

Poole, Claire, "Flat Prediction," *Forbes*, February 6, 1989, p. 10.

Sfiligoj, Eric, "Important Gains," *Beverage World*, February 1993, pp. 52, 54.

Solis, Dianna, "Mexico's Corona Brew Regains the Cachet It Lost in the Late '80s," *Wall Street Journal*, January 19, 1993, pp. B1, B7.

Teinowitz, Ira, "Top-Selling Beers Are Heavy with Lights . . . Corona May Join In," *Advertising Age*, February 20, 1989, p. 34.

Yenne, Bill, *Beers of North America*, New York: Gallery Books, 1986, pp. 84-86, 182-184.

Winters, Patricia, "Heineken Ails as Corona Hops," *Advertising Age*, September 14, 1987, p. 12.

—*Thomas Riggs*

CRACKER JACK®

Cracker Jack, owned by Borden, Inc., is one of the most widely recognized trademarks in the United States and has long reigned as a tremendously popular sweet snack in America. A truly one-of-a-kind American confection, it evokes pleasant images of baseball games, circuses, picnics, and celebrations of all types. In addition, the traditional red, white, and blue package and the cheerful salute of Sailor Jack have long communicated the messages of patriotism, pride, and service.

Another integral element of the Cracker Jack identity is the company's long-standing practice of including a prize within each oblong box. The result of an early marketing gimmick that has now ingrained itself in the minds of faithful consumers, the prize is what makes Cracker Jack unique, as well as a perennial favorite among children. The study and cataloguing of these tiny, custom-made prizes has, with the passage of time, become the serious occupation of collectors and social historians, a development imaginable perhaps only to the product's inventors. The near 100-year history of the Cracker Jack prize represents in effect a rare chronicle of twentieth-century Americana at its best. Cracker Jack's rich past is, of course, intrinsic to its present, and for this reason so many of the marketing slogans have stood the test of time. The candy's producers certainly continue to regard "the snack that's fun to eat" as an appropriate description of Cracker Jack: the popcorn, peanuts, and molasses treat with the toy surprise inside.

Brand Origins

If not for the great Chicago fire of 1871, Cracker Jack might never have been developed. Like the birth of many products and companies, Cracker Jack traces its origins to happenstance. The widespread devastation of the fire created a large demand for rebuilding and, with it, the promise of new opportunities. F.W. Rueckheim , a German immigrant farm laborer, decided to relocate to Chicago to assist with the massive cleanup and to open a popcorn stand with a partner. At the time, he had $200 to his name. Within two years Rueckheim found his small business such a success that he bought out his partner and asked his brother, Louis, to leave Germany and join him. During the next two decades the Rueckheim brothers prospered by adding various candy and marshmallow treats to their line, purchasing more sophisticated equipment, and relocating their business each time demand outgrew production capacity.

Throughout this early period, the precursor of Cracker Jack was an anonymous, fairly ordinary confection sold almost exclusively in bulk and shipped to area retailers in large wooden containers. The only exception was for occasional public events, where the Rueckheims would make and distribute their caramelized peanuts and popcorn on site. In 1893, when Chicago hosted the World's Columbian Exposition, the Rueckheims wisely took advantage of the huge influx of visitors, which numbered some 21 million, and eagerly vended their yet unnamed treat. The reputation of the product, along with demand for it, spread rapidly. The brothers, however, found it a struggle to remedy the popcorn's tendency to stick together in large chunks.

Pivotal Improvements

By 1896 Louis had solved the clumping problem with a formula that still remains a company secret. That same year, Frederick chanced upon the brand name when a salesman tasted the improved mixture and proclaimed, "That's a cracker jack!" Interestingly enough, the earliest documentation for this slang phrase—which means "excellent" or "outstanding"—also dates to this year. Equipped with a dependable product and fashionable brand name, the Rueckheim brothers now turned their attention to packaging changes that would make possible long-distance shipping and preservation of the popcorn. E.G. Eckstein, a packaging expert, was entreated to join the business in 1899; upon his arrival he developed the first wax-sealed carton, a remarkable advance that at once ensured the freshness of Cracker Jack and made nationwide shipments and sales possible. Eckstein later invented a moisture-proof package that further preserved the product's flavor and crispness.

During the beginning of this century Rueckheim Bros. and Eckstein conducted marketing experiments in hopes of besting Cracker Jack's many candy competitors; these experiments often consisted of introducing prizes or premiums within individual packages (a not entirely novel scheme) and met with varying degrees of success. In 1908 more sustained efforts, in the form of in-pack premiums for household items and a small selection of toys, were initiated with Prize Chums, a sister product of Cracker Jack. The intention was to boost impulse purchase sales, but the

AT A GLANCE

Cracker Jack brand founded in 1893 in Chicago, IL, by F.W.
+Rueckheim & Bro. partners Frederick William and Louis
Rueckheim; later developers include E.G. (Henry) Eckstein; in
1902 company was renamed Rueckheim Bros. and Eckstein; in
1922 the company was renamed the Cracker Jack Company;
the Cracker Jack Company was purchased by Borden Co. in
1964; Borden Co. became Borden, Inc., in 1968.

Advertising: Agency—Grey Advertising, Inc., New York, NY,
1975—. *Major campaign*—Traditional symbols of Sailor Jack
and his dog, Bingo.

Addresses: Parent company—Borden, Inc., 277 Park Ave.,
New York, New York 10172-0129; phone: (212) 573-4000;
fax: (212) 371-2659.

results were generally disappointing. Sales would rise and then
fall, an indication that repeat purchases were not taking place.
Eventually, Louis decided that the prize appeal had to be targeted
directly toward children, who were most likely to become repeat
customers. The actual prizes, which promised instant gratification,
would be placed directly inside each package. In 1912, Louis's
idea was implemented with the regular introduction of miniature
whistles, puzzles, spinning tops, yo-yos, and other common toys.
The decision was especially fortuitous, given the proliferation of
movie-houses at that time and, along with it, the sharp increase in
competition from other candies.

Promotions, Promotions, Promotions

Aside from this ingenious marketing strategy, which has continued without interruption for more than 80 years, Cracker Jack
has remained until relatively recent times an unobtrusive advertiser. Instead, it has relied primarily on its reputation, its packaging, and word-of-mouth promotions. By 1902 the candy was
already so widely recognized and sought that an advertisement for
the candy was included in the annual Sears catalogue without
additional description. In 1908 it became forever linked to America's favorite pastime because of Jack Norworth's song, "Take
Me Out to the Ball Game," which included the lyrics "Buy me
some peanuts and Cracker Jack." Such striking examples of early
free advertising contributed greatly to product sales, which
showed such steady increases that by 1923 production of all but
one other Rueckheim treat was curtailed so that the company
could concentrate on fulfilling orders for Cracker Jack.

The battle for dominance in the popcorn-and-peanut field was
won by the Rueckheim company through a focus on promoting
prizes as parts of a series; collectibility, value, and enjoyment were
all natural inducements, they reasoned. As early as 1907, before
Cracker Jack prizes had become a regularity, this concept was in
evidence with such miniatures as the "Cracker Jack Bears," a
series of postcards featuring mascot bears in various venues. The
bears became brand promoters with such rhymed couplets as
"This is the home of 'Cracker Jack'/ Where business never does
grow slack./ We work away from morn till night,/ To make our
sweets and make them right." By 1914 Cracker Jack outdistanced
all other prize promoters with what became a national craze: the
collection of baseball cards, of which Rueckheim Bros. and
Eckstein had printed some 15 million. Soon the company was able
to demand prizes from manufacturers on an exclusive basis,

thereby quelling competition from imitators. Although not all
Cracker Jack prizes either were or are parts of a series, those
having this distinction are the ones most commonly remembered.
Early offerings, in addition to baseball cards, included presidential
coins, train sets, and movie-star cards.

The one advertising campaign that the company employed
during this formative era was originally designed for magazines
and featured a cute young boy dressed in a sailor suit and accompanied by a playful black and white dog. Sailor Jack (modeled
after F.W. Rueckheim's grandson, Robert) and his dog, Bingo,
made their promotional debut in 1916. A red, white, and blue box
was also introduced during this era. Beginning in 1918, Sailor Jack
and Bingo became permanent fixtures on the Cracker Jack box and
served as constant reminders of World War I involvement. The
company cemented this patriotic link through direct assistance to
the troops during World War II, at which time it initiated the firm
policy that all toys utilized by the company would be contracted to
U.S. companies only.

The most notable of all Cracker Jack campaigns ran during the
early 1930s. Titled "The Cracker Jack Mystery Club," the campaign attracted more than 230,000 children to send qualifying
coins and cards to receive club memberships and additional prizes.

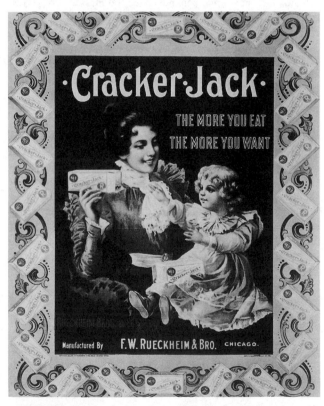

*A Cracker Jack advertisement that appeared in magazines around
1900.*

Specially designed boxes, featuring question marks on the front
label and separate prize compartments within, were created to
heighten interest in the club. The company also experimented
during this period, far less successfully, with new products that
bore the Cracker Jack name. These included Cracker Jack Coconut
Corn Brittle, Coconut Corn Crisp, and Lik-Rish Jack.

Enter Borden

Until Borden 's purchase of Cracker Jack in 1964, there were virtually no changes to the candy itself, only one change to the inner package (the advent of the foil-wrapped package, in 1956), and only a few changes to the product logo (Sailor Jack grew taller, while limiting himself to holding just one box of popcorn, and Bingo, also larger, no longer wrapped his leash around his master's leg). Even the leading marketing phrase—''the more you eat, the more you want''—remained the same. Such consistency was no doubt reassuring to customers, and Borden refrained from tinkering in these areas. However, the new owner did decide to initiate a different form of toy prize, a comparatively complex plastic toy that required assembly by the purchaser. These prizes were so unpopular that production was abandoned within a year. The failed experiment was worthwhile in the sense that it increased attention on the precise appeal of the prizes. The attention culminated in the implementation of a Cracker Jack prize policy that stated that ''the toys must be simple and give immediate playability,'' as well as the introduction of a rigorous market testing process that included independent focus groups. A consulting firm studies how children ages six to 12 react to prizes; expressed preferences help to determine new prizes for Cracker Jack. All toys must appeal equally to both sexes before they are approved for production.

Prizes are subject to size requirements, must contain no small parts, and must have no sharp edges. Metal toys were eliminated, since boxes are scanned carefully for any foreign objects, including metal objects. Prizes are inserted mechanically, with multiple electronic scanners to ensure that every box contains a toy. By 1993, the number of prizes distributed by Cracker Jack numbered more than 17 billion, a stunning testament to the Rueckheim brothers' original marketing wisdom.

The 1980s: The Cracker Jack Decade

With Borden's introduction of a high-speed, continuous-cooking process in 1975, popcorn-popping capacity for Cracker Jack rose to between 18 and 20 tons daily. For over a half-century, Cracker Jack had been the largest user of popcorn in the United States. Now it had the potential to be a major player in the overall sweet snack industry. A flurry of well-planned, large-scale promotions took place during the early 1980s. These included such prize awards as a Mazda station wagon and a Winnebago motor home; the sponsorship of the nationally televised Cracker Jack Old Timer's Baseball Classic; the introduction of snack packs and large plastic tubs for size variety; and the naming of a Cracker Jack collector, Alex Jaramillo, to serve as company spokesperson. Cracker Jack memorabilia began receiving more attention than ever. The end result was the retrieval and cataloguing of the Cracker Jack prizes from the earliest days to the present and the inauguration in 1987 of a permanent display of thousands of rare collectibles at the Center of Science and Industry in Columbus, Ohio. Jaramillo's pictorial history, *Cracker Jack Prizes,* capped the decade and confirmed what many had always believed: the prizes were a vital part of Cracker Jack success.

Future Growth

In recent years Cracker Jack has found itself in an increasingly competitive market environment. In 1992, however, Cracker Jack posted ''sharply higher sales'' due to a mini-baseball-card promotion as well as the introduction of a new flavor, Butter Toffee Cracker Jack. Marketed as ''A *New* Taste Tradition,'' Butter Toffee possesses a more buttery flavor and a more yellowish appearance than the original. The product has attracted a wider range of consumers while still upholding the Cracker Jack tradition of ''a prize in every box.'' In a highly competitive market, Cracker Jack has proven itself through its longevity, if not always its sales.

Further Reading:

''A Funny Thing Happened on the Way to the Final,'' *Advertising Age,* January 7, 1991, p. C33.

''Cracker Jack Adds Variety After 99 Years,'' *Detroit Free Press,* July 30, 1992, p. 1E.

''Cracker Jack Crunches on 1st Line Extension,'' *Advertising Age,* August 3, 1992, p. 23.

The Cracker Jack Story, New York: Borden, Inc., 1989.

The First 100 Years of Cracker Jack, New York, Borden, 1972.

Gershman, Michael, ''Cracker Jack: Prize Package,'' *Getting It Right the Second Time,* Reading, MA: Addison-Wesley Publishing Co., 1990.

Jaramillo, Alex, *Cracker Jack Prizes,* New York: Abbeville Press, 1989.

McGrath, Molly Wade, ''Cracker Jack,'' *Top Sellers, U.S.A.: Success Stories Behind America's Best-Selling Products from Alka-Seltzer to Zippo,* New York: William Morrow and Company, 1983, pp. 44-45.

Morgan, Hal, ''Cracker Jack,'' *Symbols of America,* New York: Penguin, 1986.

Stoddard, Maynard Good, ''Cracker Jack—Full of Surprises,'' *Saturday Evening Post,* March 1981, pp. 82-102.

Ward, Bernie, ''What's in the (Cracker Jack) Box?'' *Sky,* October 1987, pp. 75-82.

—Jay P. Pederson

CREAM OF WHEAT®

Nabisco Foods Group's Cream of Wheat continues to delight families at the breakfast table nearly a century after it was first introduced. The hot cereal with its four varieties has retained a solid position in the hot cereal market. *Business Week* reported that Cream of Wheat has maintained the 15% market share which establishes the cereal as a strong second in its category. Historic advertising campaigns made Cream of Wheat into a household name; brand innovations and reorganizations bringing more efficient production and distribution systems have maintained market share.

Brand Origins and Initial Commercial Success

The Diamond Milling Company in Grand Forks, North Dakota, was barely surviving the depression of 1893. Low prices and reduced demand for flour had depleted the company's operating capital, leaving it in desperate straits. In the meantime Diamond Milling's head miller, Tom Amidon, had been making a breakfast porridge for his family using the middlings, or unused hearts of the wheat grains. According to Hal Morgan in *Symbols of America*, since his family considered the porridge "a special treat," Amidon decided to pitch the idea of selling the food to his employers. Emery Mapes, George Bull, and George Clifford, owners of the Diamond Milling Company, agreed to try it with their New York brokers. Another worker suggested the name "Cream of Wheat" and the company set about packaging it for shipment.

Operating with barely any funds, Amidon cut the cardboard for the cartons, which, with their hand-lettered labels, were crated for shipping in wooden boxes made from waste lumber. Giving no advance notice, Diamond Milling sent ten cases to the New York brokers along with the regular shipment of flour. New York replied with a telegram not more than three hours after receiving the shipment. The telegram read, "Forget the flour. Send us a car of Cream of Wheat."

The mill responded by shifting production entirely from flour to Cream of Wheat. By 1897 the cereal had become so popular, demand had completely outstripped the capacity of the Grand Forks plant. Diamond Milling changed its name to the Cream of Wheat Company and moved operations to a new, larger plant in Minneapolis, offering easy access to necessary raw materials and freight shipping which could reach across the country at relatively inexpensive rates.

Demand continued to rise, and by 1903 it was necessary for the company to relocate yet again. A new and larger factory was built at First Avenue North and Fifth Street in Minneapolis, a location that would become a city landmark. There, the company remained until 1928, when it relocated to the still larger Cream of Wheat factory—now owned by Nabisco —on Stinson Boulevard in Minneapolis, where operations have remained since. Cream of Wheat had proven to be an instant success that grew steadily throughout its first three decades on the market.

Early Advertising

In *The History of Cream of Wheat,* Nabisco reported that the Cream of Wheat company had "no money to spend for a package design" when sending out that first shipment. However, owner Emery Mapes, who had once been a printer, was able to find among his old materials a plate of a black chef slinging a saucepan over his shoulder with one hand and holding a steaming bowl on a plate with the other. Mapes used this to fashion a logo and "brighten up the package." By 1925 the Cream of Wheat Company decided it was time to update the illustration. In *Symbols of America,* Hal Morgan reported that "the more realistic version" was drawn from a photograph that Mapes took of a "handsome waiter" in Kohlsaat's Restaurant in Chicago. Mapes paid the waiter five dollars for the photo, but no record of his name exists.

In his book *The Mirror Makers,* historian Stephen Fox included the Cream of Wheat logo in his list of historical advertising figures that were socially unaware. Fox wrote that "[t]hese ads, created by whites for white audiences, did unfortunately represent blacks as whites imagined them, extending but not inventing typical racial stereotypes." Fox went on to add that "[t]rade characters such as Aunt Jemima, Cream of Wheat's black chef, and the Uneeda slicker boy of themselves made no selling arguments, but by their comfortable familiarity they reminded the public of the product, gently but persistently." The image continues to be used on certain varieties of Cream of Wheat.

The Cream of Wheat Company also aimed to establish its product as a virtual symbol of America itself. Nabisco recalled in its brand history the magazine campaign which the Cream of Wheat Company ran around the turn of the century. The company reportedly bought the efforts of "America's finest illustrators," and soon the campaign had turned into an art collection. The early paintings featured the company's trademark black chef, "sometimes in a subtle, soft-selling guise, other times taking center stage." Nabisco described the paintings as "heavily value-laden," presenting "a romanticized, idyllic view of family life and childhood pleasures" and reflecting "the prevalent attitudes and social climate of America's large, emerging middle class during an era of tremendous growth and social change." The advertising series and art collection eventually became "one of the most successful and longest-running" campaigns in U.S. advertising history. The Cream of Wheat Company made its brand name as familiar in American households as the values it concurrently evoked and purported.

Nabisco and Brand Innovations

In order to invite investment to fund further growth, the founders decided to sell shares of stock in the company, which became the Cream of Wheat Corporation in 1929. The company began expanding, and in 1952 Cream of Wheat (Canada), Ltd. was organized to handle operations at the company's Winnipeg branch. At that point Cream of Wheat's three varieties—regular, enriched quick, and instant—were being sold in a majority of grocery stores on both sides of the border. With 1960 net sales

AT A GLANCE

Cream of Wheat brand of hot cereal developed in 1893 in Grand Forks, ND, by Tom Amidon, head miller of the Diamond Milling Company; the company changed its name to the Cream of Wheat Company in 1897 and again to the Cream of Wheat Corporation in 1929; National Biscuit Company bought Cream of Wheat in 1961 and created the Cream of Wheat division; Nabisco had been the formal abbreviation for the National Biscuit Company since 1941 and was adopted as the official company name in 1971; Nabisco became Nabisco Brands, Inc. when Nabisco and Standard Brands merged in 1981; in 1985, R.J. Reynolds Industries, Inc., acquired Nabisco Brands and became RJR Nabisco, Inc.; in 1992, RJR Nabisco reorganized its domestic food operations into eight divisions answerable to the newly formed subsidiary Nabisco Foods Group; Cream of Wheat is produced by the Specialty Products Division of Nabisco Foods.

Performance: *Market share*—15% of hot cereal category. *Sales*—$98 million.

Major competitor: Quaker Oats Oatmeal.

Advertising: *Agency*—FCB/Leber Katz Partners, New York, NY.

Addresses: *Parent company*—Nabisco Foods Group, 7 Campus Drive, Parsippany, NJ 07054; phone: (201) 682-7131. *Ultimate parent company*—RJR Nabisco, Inc., 1301 Avenue of the Americas, New York, NY 10019; phone: (212) 258-5600.

from U.S. and Canadian operations totalling in excess of $11.5 million, the Cream of Wheat Corporation made an attractive candidate for acquisition by the growing National Biscuit Company, known informally then as Nabisco.

In 1960 Nabisco's board of directors elected Lee S. Bickmore —who strongly believed in the utility of product diversification to further growth—to be company president. The following year Nabisco acquired the Cream of Wheat Corporation for $30 million. Bickmore planned no change of Cream of Wheat organization or distribution—as a division of Nabisco, the Cream of Wheat Corporation would continue to operate as it had.

Cream of Wheat benefitted from Bickmore's dynamic approach to diverse product development. In a 1966 *Forbes* article, Bickmore explained, "Today's consumer keeps wanting something different. That's why the life cycle of food products is shortened and that's why we constantly delete items." None of the varieties of Cream of Wheat were to be deleted, however. Instead, with the strong sales and brand name recognition the cereal had achieved, the Cream of Wheat line was to be expanded. In 1967 Nabisco introduced a new variety, Mix 'n Eat Cream of Wheat, which offered the cereal in individual packets ready to eat after mixing with boiling water. The added convenience of Mix 'n Eat Cream of Wheat established it in the market and would provide impetus for future Cream of Wheat market performance.

In the mid-1980s, the cook-in-bowl segment brought a quick boom to the hot cereal category. Janet Nieman reported in *Advertising Age* that in 1983 alone, the $420 million category grew 3 percent in pound volume and 10 percent in dollar volume. Quaker Oats dominated the category and the instant segment with over 60 percent of the market. The second place entry in the instant segment, however, was Nabisco's Mix 'n Eat Cream of Wheat.

This variety led Nabisco to a 15 to 20 percent market share in the instant hot cereal segment. While Nabisco did not introduce new varieties at the same pace as Quaker Oats, the Mix 'n Eat variety introduced in the late 1960s continued to bring success to the brand.

Recent Innovations and Performance Appraisal

If one segment of the hot cereal market boomed in the mid-1980s, overall growth in the category declined significantly later in the decade and into the early 1990s. Between 1984 and 1989, sales in the category had almost doubled to $743.7 million, but experts doubted that those phenomenal growth rates could be maintained in the 1989-90 sales year. Julie Liesse Erickson of *Advertising Age* reported that advertising spending on new oatmeal hot cereals had reached a plateau; in addition, health conscious hot cereal consumers were abandoning the category for the rash of new healthy ready-to-eat cereal brands. Nabisco failed to join the oatmeal craze until after most of its energy had been expended. In late 1989—after a loss in market share, from 15 percent the prior year, to 13.4 percent—Nabisco augmented its Cream of Wheat line with three varieties of the new Wholesome 'N Hearty oat bran, including apple cinnamon, honey and regular. The introduction of Wholesome 'N Hearty came too late for the product to gain an appreciable share of the market, however, and the cereal was discontinued.

If Cream of Wheat fell slightly from 1988 into 1989, it came back by the end of 1989 to its 15% share. In addition, the brand benefitted from major parent company reorganization in the early 1990s. Nabisco Brands, the producer of Cream of Wheat, was dissolved in favor of the creation of eight divisions in the newly formed company Nabisco Foods Group, a subsidiary of RJR Nabisco, Inc. In *Business Week*, Walecia Konrad described the change as a "sweeping reorganization" of Nabisco's food operations, with the effect of decentralizing marketing, manufacturing and new product-development. "The result," Walecia Konrad wrote, "is cost savings, plus faster new-product introductions and more flexible distribution systems to appeal to consumers' changing shopping habits." In short, Nabisco Foods would no longer be a latecomer to a consumer trend as it had been to oatmeal hot cereal.

Cream of Wheat was to benefit from this greater versatility in a hot cereal market which *Progressive Grocer* reported was continuing to decline in 1992. The previous year General Mills , which had introduced a number of oatmeal hot cereals in the late 1980s, gave up its 8 percent share and dropped out of the declining hot cereal market. In contrast, Nabisco introduced a new flavor at the end of 1992, Cinnamon Toast Instant Cream of Wheat, using a far-reaching newspaper consortium marketing system. *Editor & Publisher* reported that the New York-based newspaper marketing company, National Suburban Marketing, would be delivering free samples of Cinnamon Toast Instant Cream of Wheat to suburban households in the top 50 urban markets, targeting households with children under 14 years of age.

At a time when the hot cereal market has been in an overall decline, and such major competitors as General Mills are giving up, Nabisco Foods is able to draw on the strengths of its newly decentralized organization to introduce a new variety of Cream of Wheat and to target precisely its marketing efforts to its potential consumers. The failure of General Mills to continue in this category may present an opportunity for Cream of Wheat to further expand its market share. Cream of Wheat stands poised to acquire expanded market share in what has recently proven to be a difficult market.

Further Reading:

Advertising Age, June 17, 1991, p. 45.

Cahn, William, *Out of the Cracker Barrel: The Nabisco Story From Animal Crackers to Zuzus,* New York: Simon and Schuster, 1969, pp. 317-18.

Dobrzynski, Judith H., "How Long Can Nabisco Keep Doing More With Less?" *Business Week,* April 23, 1990, pp. 90-95.

Erickson, Julie Liesse, "Hot Cereal Sales May Be Cooling Down," *Advertising Age,* October 2, 1989, pp. 16-17.

Financial World, August 2, 1967, p. 11.

Forbes, January 1, 1966, p. 53.

Fox, Stephen, *The Mirror Makers: A History of American Advertising and Its Creators,* New York: William Morrow and Company, 1984.

Grayson, Melvin J., *42 Million a Day: The Story of Nabisco Brands,* East Hanover, NJ: Nabisco Brands Inc., 1986, pp. 11-12.

The History of Cream of Wheat, Parsippany, NJ: Nabisco Foods Group, 1993.

Kerwin, Ann Marie, "Cereal Company Using FSI Program," *Editor & Publisher,* December 19, 1992, p. 26.

Konrad, Walecia, "RJR Can't Seem to Find a Spot in the Shade," *Business Week,* July 20, 1992, p. 71.

Morgan, Hal, *Symbols of America,* Penguin, 1986.

Nabisco Foods Group Fact Sheet, Parsippany, NJ: Nabisco Foods Group, 1992.

Nieman, Janet, "Hot Cereals' Popularity Steams Nationwide," *Advertising Age,* November 5, 1984, p. 6.

Progressive Grocer, July 1992, p. 64.

Wall Street Journal, August 10, 1961.

—*Nicholas Patti*

CRISCO®

Along with Ivory soap, Crisco has been one of the best-known brands among American homemakers during the twentieth century. With Crisco, The Procter & Gamble Co. showed U.S. businesses how a valuable product could be created in the laboratory and then aggressively promoted until it achieved dominant stature in the marketplace. While other early Procter & Gamble Co. products were lucky to survive a few decades, Crisco remained the most successful shortening in the United States into the late twentieth century.

The Procter & Gamble Co. started out in 1837 as a soap and candle maker. During its early decades, it became acquainted with cottonseed oil—which for decades would serve as the prime ingredient of Crisco—but initially failed to refine it. It succeeded by the 1870s, and began substituting it for elaine oil in soaps when the price of the latter rose too high. At about this time, cottonseed oil was also mixed with lard to create a shortening mixture.

Cottonseed Process

Around 1907, a German chemical engineer, E.C. Kayser, invented a process that could help turn cottonseed oil into a purely vegetable shortening. He soon visited Procter & Gamble laboratories in Cincinnati to show the staff his process, which created a solid white substance from the oil. Procter & Gamble was interested. The possibility of "hardening" a vegetable oil had already tantalized its own researchers, who dreamed of an easy-blending shortening that could be used in the same way as lard. They thought that vegetable shortening would spoil less easily than lard and would taste better.

The company immediately joined in an agreement with the engineer to conduct tests. Their first creation was almost rock solid, obviously unsuited for use as a shortening. The researchers created a softer version of the substance by mixing liquid cottonseed oil with it. Procter & Gamble then sought to secure a plant to house the new process, which employed large amounts of hydrogen. For $1.4 million, it bought the McCaw manufacturing company, located in Macon, Georgia, which was already engaged in shortening production. That plant was transformed into a pilot operation for the process.

The Right Characteristics

The final product had the advantage of being soft and easy to blend. It was also white—a color that many consumers seemed to prefer, given the success of Procter & Gamble's Ivory soap. The company decided to name the product Crisco, which it thought connoted purity and freshness. It had earlier rejected the names Cryst (because of possible religious implications) and Krispo (because of trademark problems)—both nominated as potential names in a contest among Procter & Gamble employees.

The product proved easy to blend in flour and spread on a frying pan. In technical terms, the product was so far ahead of its competitors that the company sought to maintain its advantage by listing animal fat as an ingredient in order to mislead its rivals about its true contents. (In fact, only a tiny amount of animal fat was introduced.) It was hoped that this misleading information would lead other companies to believe that it was a lard-type product.

From its inception, Crisco was sold in "one-pound, airtight tins," according to advertising, although institutions received their supplies in huge barrels emblazoned with the brand name on their tops. Crisco was an early product to include printed recipes inside—they were inserted under the lid. Within a decade, the company was producing Crisco from its first plant located outside the United States, a factory in Hamilton, Ontario. Production there was intended to counter Lever Bros.' growing influence in the Canadian market.

The use of cottonseed oil as a raw material in the production of Crisco presented benefits as well as disadvantages. For one thing, in its hydrogenated form, cottonseed oil had the advantage of a long shelf life, in comparison with lard products. On the other hand, the supply of the oil depended on the vicissitudes of cotton agriculture. For instance, the boll weevil ravaged the crops across the South in 1911, and Procter & Gamble's costs rose alarmingly. The effect on the company was especially great because it also used cottonseed for soap manufacturing, thus making Procter & Gamble the world's biggest user of cottonseed oil. Eventually, the shortages subsided.

Over the long haul, much of Procter & Gamble's success with the new product could be traced back to its marketing and advertising efforts. Crisco's first ad, in the January 1912 *Ladies Home*

Journal, described the product as "a scientific discovery that will affect every kitchen in America." By 1913, Crisco was receiving prominent placement in advertisements for the Procter & Gamble line of products, getting top billing over products such as Lenox soap, Star Naptha and Star soap. The company also used color magazine ads that depicted delicious-looking pastries and provided recipes for such desserts as chocolate fudge.

Aggressive Advertising

Even in the 1920s, Crisco's fortunes were clearly related more to advertising than to price. At about this time, salespeople wanted Procter & Gamble to encourage sales by cutting its price. Richard Deupree, then a top executive at Procter & Gamble, refused. Instead, the company raised prices and put half of the increased revenue into advertising. The gambit worked, and the experience reinforced Procter & Gamble's heavy use of ads to move products.

Another early promotional device was the Procter & Gamble test kitchen and cooking schools. Its goal was to wean the American housewife from the use of lard. Procter & Gamble established a test-bakery to try out the new shortening, and customers were given the opportunity to try it out. The company's bulk-sales department set up shop in a Cincinnati bakery, and had three bakers fry up 4,800 donuts and crullers. The experiment led the company to create a kitchen for testing the shortening and creating recipes.

Soon the show hit the road and proved to be very effective in making homemakers aware of Crisco. The company did similar demonstrations in large cities in cooperation with manufacturers of stoves and cooking equipment as well as suppliers of flour and spices. Procter & Gamble called these exhibitions cooking schools and held them in rented halls. The instructors did not actually "sell" the shortening. It was enough that the can was prominently displayed. Eventually, seven Crisco tours were crisscrossing the country.

Packaging was devised to differentiate it sharply from cooking lard, then Crisco's chief competitor. Instead of a bucket with tapered sides, the way lard was typically stored, the Crisco containers were cylinders with untapered sides. These were not only easier for plant workers to fill, but they were easier to stack in the stores.

Crisco was becoming an indispensable part of the homemaker's arsenal. Procter & Gamble's goal in the early twentieth century was to make and sell products that were designed to make

house work easier. Ad copy contained phrases like "Why have a smoky kitchen?" and "Out of the kitchen by noon." Procter & Gamble products were to have a tremendous appeal as women became more and more emancipated. Soon, they became seen as daily necessities.

Company officials knew they could rely on more or less regular demand for their products. "Consumers buy soaps, Crisco, and so on as they need them," company president William Cooper Procter said around 1919.

Company-to-Store Selling

At the same time, Procter & Gamble began developing a company-to-store selling system for Crisco and other products that bypassed wholesalers and gave the company greater efficiency in its distribution. It was pioneered in the New York area and then extended to the rest of the country. Salespeople traveled by car, horse and buggy, and streetcar. Salespeople would typically introduce themselves with use of the phrase, "I am from the Ivory Soap company," since the Procter & Gamble company did not enjoy such widespread name recognition at the time. Deliveries were made from nearby warehouses. From the start, grocers could earn a discount by buying combinations of Crisco and soap in volume.

Within a decade, Procter & Gamble delivery people became part of the landscape. In remote parts of the country, like the Southwest, salespeople made deliveries in a company car with Procter & Gamble's former moon and stars trademark printed on the side. Typically, the drivers transported samples of Ivory soap, Crisco, Camay soap, and other products.

Ironically, World War I, with its accompanying shortages, provided a singular marketing opportunity. Every sort of meat and dairy product—lard and butter included—was in short supply at this time. Making a patriotic appeal, Procter & Gamble advertising urged consumers to substitute Crisco for other shortening. Since wheat was likewise in short supply, the ads urged housewives to bake with oats and rye, arguing that Crisco "easily blends" with these grains.

By this time, Procter & Gamble had already hit upon recipes as a method to reach housewives across the country, and over the next decades it would resort to this approach again and again. In 1911, Procter & Gamble distributed its first cookbook, "Tested Crisco Recipes." In an ad published around 1917, it offered magazine readers a cookbook entitled "Balanced Daily Diet" for just 10 cents (although its regular value was listed as 25 cents) that presented recipes from the Boston Cooking School and provided many uses for the new shortening.

Radio advertising

In the early 1920s, while radio was in its infancy, Procter & Gamble began advertising Crisco on the airwaves. The first commercials were heard on WEAF in New York, which was experimenting with the new genre of broadcast ads. The demands of marketing had caused Procter & Gamble to focus on radio, and it picked a new advertising agency, the Blackman Company, based in New York, to help with radio ads for Crisco and Ivory soap. That agency had already provided magazine and newspaper advertising, and had, in effect, replaced the Cincinnati printing business that had functioned as Procter & Gamble's agency in the past. Procter & Gamble executives thought the Blackman agency might provide valuable help in the realm of radio advertising. This agency, in a variety of incarnations (first as the Blackman Company and later as Compton Advertising Inc.) held onto the Ivory and Crisco accounts into the 1970s.

The agency's head in the 1920s, J.K. Fraser, turned to a tried and true approach: recipes. One early program was titled *Crisco Cooking Talk,* and its announcers simply read recipes. Crisco was always listed as the shortening ingredient. Others were *Radio Homemaker's Club* and *Sisters of the Skillet,* which also featured Crisco recipes. The first efforts were entire shows, not merely brief advertising spots.

While the programs quickly developed a following, Procter & Gamble executives were not entirely sure that the advertising was as effective as it could be. They had a reason to avoid complacency: At the depth of the recession, the sales of nearly all its products had plummeted. With the help of market researchers, they began looking into their audience's wants and discovered that the most effective shows were entertainment. The previous shows had been too instructional.

Procter & Gamble thus devised a new radio format, the soap opera, which played heavily on emotions to win a radio following. It would prove to be an advertising mainstay for decades. One show during the 1930s was devoted entirely to Crisco. It was *Vic and Sade,* based on a husband and wife comedy team, and it even earned some critical acclaim.

All the company's progress in advertising was not on the radio front. Procter & Gamble also made headway in magazine advertising. They began a series of ads, for both Crisco and the soap products, that dealt with real-life problems. A pie baked with Crisco, for instance, helped a homemaker's husband ingratiate himself with his boss over dinner.

As the nation began slowly emerging from the recession of the 1930s, the advertising seemed more effective than ever—especially for Crisco. Sales of Crisco nearly tripled, while Ivory sales "merely" doubled. People were turning to brand names again, after several years of using off-brands.

Some of the success was due to an evolving brand management system. Under this system, certain executives and teams took responsibility for a particular product line. This was devised to avoid the conflict of interest that inevitably seemed to develop when one group of executives was responsible for the success of two overlapping products, such as Ivory and Camay. In keeping with good brand management, different advertising agencies often specialized in different product lines. By the late 1970s, the company used ten different ad agencies.

In the mid-1930s, however, a different situation was emerging. Longtime competitor Lever Bros. came out with Spry. It was a good shortening and a worthy rival to Crisco. Not to be outdone, Procter & Gamble redoubled efforts to improve Crisco. Procter & Gamble's researchers had continued to undertake research on shortening. It had developed a baker's shortening for institutional use that it called Sweetex—which made it possible to bake lighter, fluffier cakes. But its main new ingredient, monoglyceride, went up in smoke during frying, and thus could not be added to Crisco, since it was used for both frying and baking. But once faced with the threat from Spry, researchers came up with a variant of Crisco that mixed easily with liquids and produced lighter baked goods. Researchers also found that other oils could be used in making

Crisco, and by the late 1940s, soybean oil was Crisco's prime ingredient.

Inventive Packaging

When necessary, the company could prove to be inventive about packaging. When Spry was introduced, Procter & Gamble engineers improved the lid for easier opening and devised a process for keeping the new formula Crisco fresh on the shelves. When the metal for cans became unavailable during World War II, it packed the shortening in glass jars, lined with a paper wrapper to prevent deterioration from exposure to light. Customers, facing shortages, bought up every jar they could. But the company wondered how much customers would buy once the war was over and lard became plentiful again.

The greater availability of lard-type products would not be the only challenge presented by the postwar economy. Crisco marketers were forced to learn to master a new medium, television, the way they had mastered radio. It turned to the soap opera and comedy shows again, with mixed results. One comedy about a young married couple, *The First Hundred Years,* drew a mediocre response, but another, *Search for Tomorrow,* was a success. In addition, Ivory soap and Crisco were among the products that won awards for creative advertising in the early 1950s.

Procter & Gamble managers and researchers, wary of the competition, devised another shortening called Fluffo during the 1950s. It was brownish in color, and ad copy promoted it as "golden" Fluffo. A combination of vegetable oil and lard, it was primarily produced for the West and South. Market research had determined that many customers preferred shortening with this sort of coloring.

One of the reasons the company turned to Fluffo was that lard could be obtained at a good price during this period. The introduction of a new shortening might have been expected to cut into Crisco's sales. Marketers, however, found that creating competition between two products could lead to growth in total shortening sales.

Reorganized Structure

At about the same time, the company was making other improvements. It reorganized its structure and created a food division for the first time. The research staff also came up with an improved formula for Crisco and updated the original Crisco plant in Macon with a new oil processing facility and other improvements.

Over the years, research has continued. Procter & Gamble came out with Puritan Oil, a salad and cooking oil in 1978, and officially brought it under the Crisco banner in 1991, dubbing it Crisco Puritan oil. Crisco Puritan is made from canola oil and has a low level of saturated fats. Over the years, the amount of polyunsaturated fats—far healthier than saturated fats—has increased in Crisco, and palm oil was eventually removed from the recipe because of cardiovascular risks.

Ironically, Crisco would eventually take on an old foe, butter, head-on. In 1983, it introduced Butter Flavor Crisco, which had Crisco's physical properties along with butter's taste and aroma. Procter & Gamble also tested Crisco Sticks, which resembled sticks of butter, and targeted the new product at consumers who bake at home. Many cooks, accustomed to food preparation using sticks of butter, found it easier to measure portions when the shortening was presented in a stick form.

Crisco's packaging was just one sign that it had come a long way. In 1985 the company started using foil-fiber cans—a far cry from its original tin plated steel cans and tubs—and in 1989 it turned to an easy-to-open, peel-top foil lid. Like improvements in its ingredients, Crisco's packaging enhancements suggest that the Procter & Gamble food business depends greatly on innovation. Its history can best be summed up as a series of key improvements in the scientific, marketing, and merchandising realms.

Further Reading:

"Crisco Takes On Butter," *Advertising Age,* December 1992, p. 45.

Liet, Alfred, *It Floats,* New York: Rinehart & Co., 1958.

Schisgall, Oscar, *Eyes on Tomorrow: The Evolution of Procter & Gamble,* Chicago: J. G. Ferguson & Co.

—Gary Hoffman

DANNON®

Dannon yogurt, which has largely defined the U.S. yogurt market since its 1942 debut, maintains a firm hold on its position as the market leader with 30 percent of the $1 billion category. Moreover, Dannon, owned by the Dannon Co. Inc., is also the top-selling brand of yogurt worldwide, marketed under the names Dannon and Danone. Prior to the mid-1940s, yogurt consumption in the United States was limited to small pockets of the population hailing from countries such as Turkey or Greece (where yogurt was considered a staple). However, Dannon carved out a new market for its product based on claims that yogurt delivered health and nutrition benefits in a form both tasty and convenient. Dannon's taste and nutritional appeal have formed the centerpiece of the brand's marketing strategy throughout its 50-year history. Although competition has dramatically increased since the 1970s, Dannon has kept pace with the market, and continues to outsell all other popular brands.

Brand Origins

Although Dannon's official birth date is recognized as 1942, the brand's roots hearken back to 1917, when Isaac Carasso founded the Danone Company in Spain. Mr. Carasso's son, Daniel—after whom the Danone Company was named—began operating a branch of the Danone Co. in France in 1929. During World War II, Daniel Carasso immigrated to the United States. There he put his knowledge of yogurt making to work by founding Dannon Milk Products Inc. in 1942 in the Bronx, New York. Yogurt was a little known and even less understood product when Carasso embarked on his new venture. Nevertheless, he produced and sold 200,000 cups of yogurt that first year, limiting distribution to the local New York market. The following year, Carasso teamed up with Swiss industrialist and amateur biologist, Joe Metzger, and his son, Juan. The three partners moved the company to Long Island City, New York, where they stepped up production.

Six years after he founded Dannon Milk Products Inc., Carasso sold his interest in the fledgling company to the Metzgers and returned to the Danone family business in Europe. Dannon Milk Products continued to grow under Joe Metzger, who, in 1950, moved the company to a new, 30,000-square-foot facility in Long Island City. According to company literature, by 1955, production of Dannon yogurt had increased 200-fold, to 160,000 cups per day. As yogurt gradually gained wider acceptance, Dannon began expanding distribution—first, into Philadelphia, in 1956, and sub-

sequently into the Boston market, in 1959. It was in 1959, after researching the market and determining its growth potential, that Beatrice Foods Inc. acquired Dannon Milk Products from Joe and Juan Metzger. These two men remained with the company as general manager and vice-president of sales and marketing, respectively.

With a new infusion of cash from Beatrice, Dannon was able to increase production even further and also expand its marketing horizons. The company acquired a second manufacturing facility—in Minster, Ohio—and by the late 1970s was producing about one million cups of yogurt per day. By 1979, the Dannon line was launched in California, making it the first perishable dairy product to achieve national distribution. According to a 1981 *Wall Street Journal* article, Beatrice was able to turn Dannon's "early lead in the fast-growing yogurt market into double-digit profit and sales increases by the mid-1970s." However, success had its price. After earnings peaked in 1978, they plunged more than 30 percent in 1979, according to the same *Wall Street Journal* article, which cited distribution problems and intense competition as the culprits. "The difficulties came from trying to expand too fast," the article said, referring to Dannon's decision to enter the California market by shipping products from its Fort Worth, Texas, plant, rather than waiting to build a plant closer to the market. The situation made Dannon a ripe acquisition target. In 1981 Paris-based Groupe BSN (Boussois-Souchon-Neuvesel), one of the world's largest diversified food manufacturers—and by now owner of the Danone brand in Europe—purchased Dannon from Beatrice for $84.3 million—nearly 23 times Dannon's 1980 earnings.

Early Marketing and Advertising Trends

Daniel Carasso and the Metzgers are credited with awakening American consumers' taste buds to yogurt. "Dannon all but created national awareness of yogurt," said a 1986 *Market & Media Decisions* report. From the outset, Dannon was able to build brand identity based almost solely on its product's greatest asset—its health food appeal. There was no serious competitor from which Dannon needed to distinguish itself, no other brand to out-market. Instead, Dannon's greatest challenge was overcoming yogurt's "spoiled milk" image and convincing American consumers to eat the product. Concentrating on one market at a time, beginning with New York, Dannon positioned its product as a delicious

AT A GLANCE

Dannon brand yogurt founded in 1942 by Daniel Carasso, owner of Dannon Milk Products Inc., in Bronx, NY; purchased by the Beatrice Co. in 1959; Boussois-Souchon-Nuevesel (BSN), a French food manufacturer, acquired the brand in 1981, renaming the maker the Dannon Co. Inc.

Performance: *Market share*—30% (top share) of yogurt category. *Sales*—$398 million.

Major competitor: General Mills, Inc.'s Yoplait.

Advertising: *Agency*—Grey Advertising Inc., New York, NY, 1990; *Major campaign*—"Dannon. A very healthy habit. For life."

Addresses: *Parent company*—Dannon Co. Inc., 1111 Westchester Ave., White Plains, NY 10604; phone: (914) 697-9700; fax: (914) 934-2805. *Ultimate parent company:* Groupe BSN, France.

health food snack. Early promotional efforts focused on the health benefits of yogurt; Dannon even distributed pamphlets outlining the medical benefits of eating yogurt. But following the yogurt maker's first major product innovations—yogurt with strawberries on the bottom in 1947 and a low-fat version in the early 1950s—Dannon softened its "Doctor recommended" message to include references to yogurt as "a wonderful snack."

During the 1950s and 1960s, Dannon backed up its marketing efforts with advertising that frequently depicted robust and rosy-cheeked women and children. Typical tag lines included: "Easy to digest, easy to love"; "Of course we feel good. We eat Dannon real yogurt every day"; and "I like Dannon because it helps to keep me young and healthy." Such general messages underscored yogurt's nutritional value, but more specific health claims came under fire in the early 1960s by the Federal Trade Commission (FTC). In 1962 the FTC ordered Dannon to "stop misrepresenting that its yogurt is nature's perfect food, will correct poor eating habits and has intrinsic reducing or antibiotic properties," according to a *Wall Street Journal* report. Research may have since justified some of those early claims, however. By the mid-1980s, the director of science and technology at the National Nutritional Foods Association was quoted by *Advertising Age* as stating that in addition to being a good source of calcium and protein, yogurt "may even have antibiotic and anti-cancer properties." A 50th anniversary brochure published and distributed in 1992 by Dannon reports that yogurt's active live cultures can be digested by lactose-intolerant people and further states: "Recent studies show that yogurt enhances the body's immune system by indirectly increasing T-cell activity, which may offer protection against external environment factors such as viral colds or possibly allergies."

Nevertheless, before such claims were substantiated, Dannon toned down its advertising following the FTC order. In 1964 the yogurt maker's advertising agency launched a radio campaign aimed at selling Dannon purely on taste, rather than nutrition. The tongue-in-cheek campaign poked fun at "overblown advertising claims and so-called miracle-working products," according to a 1964 report in *Printers' Ink*. In one spot, representative of the campaign, a long-distance runner explained that he regularly finished last in races until his coach made him eat Dannon yogurt. "Now I always breeze in first," he said. Asked by the announcer if

Dannon yogurt got him in top condition, the runner replied, "No, I take short cuts." The radio spots—more than 24 of them featuring the same type of humorous twist—were so popular that listeners began sending in suggestions for more.

Expanding Market

Dannon's early marketing strategies proved successful enough to build a solid base of loyal consumers. Nevertheless, for nearly two decades, yogurt remained a "cult product sold mainly by regional dairies," according to *Media & Marketing Decisions* report. Then in the mid-1970s, spurred on by a surge in diet and health-food interest, the market took a sudden and dramatic upward turn. Analysts predicted a potential growth rate of about 15 percent per year. By now, Dannon found itself competing with several regional brands, including Knudsen Corp. and Johnston Food products on the West Coast and Colombo in New England. At about the same time, Dannon was feeling pressure on a broader scale from Yoplait, a relatively new market player. Manufactured in France, Yoplait was introduced to the U.S. market in the mid-1970s, where it built a brand identity on its French pedigree and its rich, creamy taste. Yoplait products were sold in more streamlined, tapered packages—distinctly more elegant than Dannon's standard dairy product shape. To avoid being beat to the punch by the market's newcomer, Dannon rushed its product to national distribution in 1977, making inroads in the health-conscious California market, where Knudsen Corp. and Johnston Food were well entrenched. During that same year General Mills, Inc., eager to jump into the game and able to back its move with plenty of cash, bought the U.S. rights to the Yoplait brand and immediately took Yoplait national.

During this period of rapid market expansion, Dannon deviated little from its marketing strategy: Dannon as a delicious health food. To appeal to the diet-conscious, the yogurt maker launched its "Get a Dannon Body" campaign. It was also during the mid-1970s that Dannon embarked on what probably remains its most memorable advertising scheme. Asked by its client to develop a new TV commercial for Dannon yogurt, Dannon's then-advertising agency, Marsteller Inc., discovered through research that in certain areas of Russia, the people consume enormous quantities of yogurt. Those same people reportedly also lived to be well over 100 years old. That discovery led to a series of TV commercials depicting Russian people in their 90s and 100s picking tobacco or working in the vineyards, chopping wood and riding horses. Believed to be the first U.S. commercials shot in the Soviet Union, the 30-second spots featured copy describing yogurt's health advantages, superimposed over scenes from rural Russia. In one, featuring a 90-year old man eating a cup of Dannon, the camera pans to the man's mother, who is seen beaming as her "little boy" finishes his yogurt. The message was: Eat lots of yogurt, and you, too, can live to be 100. A miracle claim? Maybe . . . or maybe not. Nevertheless, nutrition was once again the focus of Dannon's advertising.

Expanding Product Lines

Although Dannon has always been the market leader in terms of sales, it has occasionally found itself a follower when it comes to product innovation. As more players entered the market, yogurt makers began competing on the basis of new-product introductions. Dannon, which until the late 1970s had relied on a single marketing focus and its long-established reputation as the market's dominant player, entered the 1980s "asleep at the wheel," according to then-director of marketing, Jim Glicker. In 1986, looking back at Dannon's performance a few years earlier, Glicker told *Marketing & Media Decisions* that before BSN acquired Dannon in 1981 Dannon had not been taking seriously changing consumer preferences and competitive moves by other yogurt marketers. As a result, Dannon had become slower to react to the market than some of its competitors. In 1982, Yoplait introduced a custard-style yogurt, followed a year later by a breakfast yogurt containing fruit and nuts. Dannon did not debut its own fruit and nut breakfast yogurt until 1984. The same year it introduced Dannon Extra Smooth, its first attempt to offer a product comparable to the original French-style Yoplait. Meanwhile other competitors were coming out with new products of their own. Kraft's Light n' Lively brand went to market in 1984 with yogurt minipacks aimed at the snack and lunch-box market. Dannon introduced its version of minipacks in 1985.

The unveiling of Dannon Extra Smooth, Dannon's breakfast yogurt, and Dannon minipacks marked just the beginning of Dannon's decade-long phase of product introductions. Some of those products flopped; an early yogurt product for kids and Dan-Up, a yogurt drink, failed to make the grade. Meanwhile, Dannon persevered with products such as Dannon Supreme and in 1988, Dannon Light, a 100-calorie, fat-free, prestirred yogurt, which, according to the company, was the most successful and largest new product launch in either Dannon's or the category's history. In 1989 Dannon introduced its first soft frozen yogurt and in 1990, a six-ounce, nonfat blended yogurt. A year later, Dannon abandoned its hardpacked frozen yogurt products, Danny-on-a-Stick and Danny-in-a Cup. However, in 1992 the yogurt maker began test marketing two new frozen yogurt products, Pure Indulgence and Light hardpacked yogurt, with plans for a full rollout in 1993. Also in 1992, Dannon took a second look at the younger yogurt-eating crowd and debuted a product called Sprinkl'ins, a low-fat yogurt that comes with a packet of rainbow sprinkles for kids to mix in.

The Later Years

Accompanying the new-product onslaught was a dramatic increase in advertising and a temporary shift in Dannon's marketing strategy. By 1985 BSN had almost doubled Dannon's advertising support, raising it to $12 million, according to *Media & Marketing Decisions*. Dannon, which had previously relied on spot TV in yogurt's largest markets—New York, Chicago and Los Angeles—moved toward network television and selected magazines. "Television lets consumers see yogurt, feel yogurt and taste yogurt through the actor's experience, and this is important because in a recent study of foods that people hate, yogurt ranked third after lima beans and liver," an advertising executive told *Advertising Age* in 1986. "With TV, Dannon has been able to entice consumers into desiring the yogurt experience," he added. As Dannon increased its use of television, the yogurt maker also attempted to differentiate itself from the growing number of competitors by shifting its emphasis from yogurt's health properties to Dannon's leadership in the market and its long heritage. "Get a Dannon Body" gave way to "Dannon Is Yogurt"—a slogan devised to inform consumers that "Dannon made the category and that they make a high quality product," another advertising executive told *Marketing & Media Decisions*. Along with this shift in strategy, Dannon redirected its message to a broader audience.

Previously, the yogurt maker had targeted women because they are known to make up the largest percentage of yogurt consumers. However, new "Dannon Is Yogurt" TV spots featured working women, children and businessmen.

The yogurt market achieved its greatest growth during the early 1980s, with sales topping out at $1 billion in 1985. As the number of new players and new products gradually leveled off, Dannon began searching for new ways to increase its share. In 1990 the yogurt maker established a toll-free number connecting consumers to the Dannon Information Center. Designed to provide consumers with product and nutrition information, recipes, and coupons, it is also likely a means of staying in tune with consumer preferences (thereby avoiding another situation in which the market leader is forced to play catch-up in the new-product department). In 1991 Dannon took a new advertising tack designed to create consumer awareness of alternate uses for yogurt. Aware for years that consumers had been substituting yogurt for higher-fat dairy products in cooking, Dannon developed a print ad campaign suggesting consumers substitute yogurt for eggs and oil when baking brownies from a mix. Then, in the fall of 1992, Dannon teamed up with Procter & Gamble Co.'s Duncan Hines brownie mix in an ad campaign produced by Grey Advertising. However, the main thrust of Dannon's advertising had returned in 1992 to the company founder's original theme of yogurt as a healthy snack. Buoyed by research supporting Dannon's claims that yogurt enhances the body's immune system and can help prevent infectious diseases and gastrointestinal infections, Dannon created a new ad campaign with the trademarked tag line: "Dannon. A very healthy habit. For life."

A Conservative Future

The yogurt market has not grown significantly since hitting the $1 billion mark in 1985, despite evidence that about 50 percent of the population has yet to try yogurt. Efforts to tap into that potential market by developing the dessert yogurt niche—with products such as Yoplait's YoCreme and Dannon Supreme—appear to have met with lukewarm success. In 1986 the managing editor of *Dairy Record* told *Marketing & Media Decisions*, "Major marketers are trying to make yogurt follow what happened in ice cream, where there are super-premium ice creams and novelties." Even then, market analysts were skeptical, according to *Marketing & Media Decisions*, which warned "that in the rush to be the latest with the newest, mainly with sweeter and gooier concoctions, marketers will lose what yogurt is noted for, and what leader Dannon is closely identified with—nutrition, tradition, plus low calories." It seems those who do eat yogurt prefer it for reasons of nutrition rather than taste, and the largest percentage of them still prefer the original yogurt, Dannon.

Further Reading:

"Beatrice Foods Acquisition," *Wall Street Journal,* March 10, 1959, p. 11.

"Bureaus: Yogurt Ads," *Wall Street Journal,* July 30, 1962, p. 6.

Carter, Kim, "Growing Yogurt Culture Warms Sales," *Advertising Age,* October 13, 1986, p. S-35.

Cox, Meg, "Beatrice Foods Co. To Sell Dannon Unit For $84.3 Million," *Wall Street Journal,* June 24, 1981, p. 4.

"Dannon: 50th Anniversary," White Plains, N.Y.: The Dannon Co. Inc., 1992.

"Dannon: It Defies Its Own Research," *Printers' Ink,* January 24, 1964, p. 44.

"Dannon Yogurt: Its Cups Overfloweth," *Nation's Business,* March, 1981, p. 89.

Fannin, Rebecca, "Dannon's Culture Coup," *Marketing & Media Decisions,* November, 1986, p. 59.

"Fun Yogurt," *Fortune,* March 9, 1992, p. 69.

Liesse, Julie, "Everything Old Can Be New Again," *Advertising Age,* October 5, 1992, p. 12.

Lubalin, Peter, "To Russia, With Yogurt," *Broadcasting,* January 3, 1977, p. 11.

Pendleton, Jennifer, "Coast Yogurts Attack 'Invaders,' " *Advertising Age,* February 25, 1980, p. 38.

Warner, Fara, "Dannon Tries Frozen Again," *Adweek's Marketing Week,* April 6, 1992, p. 6.

—Katherine J. Paul

DEL MONTE®

For well over a century the red Del Monte shield has appeared on one of the broadest ranges of food products offered by any company worldwide. With sales of $1.43 billion, Del Monte is the leading canner of fruits and vegetables in the United States. The Del Monte label has the distinction of being one of the most recognizable trademarks in the history of American consumer marketing. As Ellen Paris points out in *Forbes,* the company is fond of boasting that "you would be hard pressed to find a household in America without at least one of its products."

Del Monte's history is the history of food processing and packaging on the West Coast. During the gold rush of 1849, thousands of adventurers sought their fortunes in the foothills of California's Sierra Mountains. San Francisco, a military outpost town that was home to just 800 people in 1848, developed into a bustling center of commerce with a population of 35,000 by 1850. Merchants and saloon keepers engaged in battles to see who could separate the most money as quickly as possible from ever increasing numbers of speculators. The constantly rising demand for goods, most of which had to be imported by ship from the East, soon exceeded the supply. Thus was the West Coast made ripe for a number of entrepreneurs, not least of which were a number of pioneering canners, who eventually joined forces and thrived under the Del Monte label.

Del Monte's Ancestry

By the late 1850s, more than $2 billion in gold had been taken from California's mines and streams. Most of the early tent cities had been replaced by more permanent structures. The population of San Francisco had grown to 55,000, and the city vaunted streetcars, sidewalks, gaslit streets, and a sophisticated culture that included more than a dozen theaters and many fine restaurants. Into this cosmopolitan atmosphere came Francis Cutting, a 24-year-old Boston native on his way to British Columbia, where another gold rush was in progress. Cutting saw the opportunities that presented themselves in San Francisco and decided to remain.

Realizing that prospectors heading out of San Francisco for British Columbia would need a supply of easily transportable, preserved food, he purchased a half interest in a bottling operation headquartered in Gold Rush City in late 1858 and began selling pickles to mining camps in the surrounding area. Unfortunately, the largest expense for the fledgling packing company was for the glass jars that had to be brought from the East, either over land or,

more commonly, by ship. Cutting returned to San Francisco the following year to found the first glass factory on the West Coast, thus assuring his packing company a steady supply of containers. For the next forty years, Cutting remained the most innovative West Coast canner. He was the first to manufacture containers locally, the first to use metal containers, and the first to export California produce to the East.

During the 1870s and 1880s, dozens of new canning companies came into existence in northern California. By 1870, many fields and orchards planted by missionaries in prior years were brought under cultivation to produce crops in commercial quantities. Such fruits as grapes, plums, apricots, and peaches, as well as a variety of vegetables, grew in abundance in the favorable climate. An assortment of firms sprouted up as well to preserve these crops by drying or canning. The J.M. Dawson Packing Company (later the San Jose Fruit Packing Company), Griffin & Seegar (later Griffin & Skelley), the Oakland Preserving Company, and a number of others all began operations at this time and ultimately proved to be among the forefathers of Del Monte.

Brand Beginnings

The Del Monte name appeared around 1886, when Tillman & Bendel of Oakland, California, first used it to label a blend of coffee it supplied to the prestigious Hotel Del Monte in nearby Monterey. When Fred Tillman, Jr., left to found the Oakland Preserving Company in 1891, he took with him the Del Monte brand to label his new line of premium-quality canned fruits and vegetables.

In June 1899, eighteen firms (including the Oakland Preserving Company, Sacramento Packing Company, and the Cutting Fruit Packing Company) merged to form the California Fruit Canners Association (CFCA). This consolidation of almost half of the state's canning industry formed the largest canner of fruits and vegetables in the world. Operations would soon range from Los Angeles to Oregon, Washington, Idaho, and Hawaii. Although the CFCA, with such far-flung subsidiaries, was never able to consolidate all of its management functions, its members did agree on the use of the Del Monte label as their prestige brand. The red shield with Old English lettering began appearing on an ever-widening variety of preserved foods, including squash, sweet potatoes, peppers, berries, jams, jellies, cranberry sauce, and olives.

AT A GLANCE

Del Monte brand founded around 1886 in Oakland, CA, by Tillman & Bendel owners, including Frederick Tillman; later developers include California Fruit Canners Association and California Packing Corporation principals; California Packing renamed Del Monte Corporation, 1967; Del Monte Corporation merged into R.J. Reynolds Industries 1979; Del Monte partitioned and sold in 1989; San Francisco operations newly consolidated as Del Monte Corporation (doing business as Del Monte Foods).

Performance: *Market share*—16% (top share) of the canned vegetable category. *Sales*—$1.43 billion.

Advertising: *Agency*—McCann-Erickson, San Francisco, CA. *Major campaign*—Print ads with such slogans as "We Grow Variety" and "The Best Thing Next to Fresh."

Addresses: *Parent company*—Del Monte Corporation; One Market Plaza; P.O. Box 193575; San Francisco, CA 94119-3575; phone: (415) 442-4000; fax: (415) 442-4894.

For several years, the CFCA employed the J.K. Armsby Company, the largest wholesaler on the West Coast, as its exclusive distributor. J.K. and his brother, George Armsby, had long dreamed of consolidating the biggest and best canners in the area, and in 1916 their dream was realized with the formation of the California Packing Corporation (Calpak). This merger brought together such distinguished firms as the CFCA, Central California Canneries, Griffin & Skelley, and Alaska Packers Association. J.K. Armsby was elected president of the new conglomerate and executives from the other constituent firms assumed other executive roles in Calpak. As with the earlier CFCA merger, operations were widely spread and several distinct corporate cultures survived within the new company. The unifying thread was the general agreement that Calpak's premium products—those of uniformly high quality—would bear the Del Monte brand.

Making Advertising History

At the turn of the century, it mattered little to consumers what name appeared on canned products; grocers normally selected and packaged whatever items customers asked for from behind a counter. However, during the 1910s the self-serve grocery store began to catch on and consumers began to realize the benefits of selecting their own items from grocery shelves. Calpak's 1917 Del Monte advertisement signaled the first shift towards placing the responsibility for marketing goods on regional wholesalers. It was the first effort to capitalize on the beginnings of this revolution and to introduce the concept of brand loyalty. When that year's *Saturday Evening Post* carried the first full-page ad for Calpak's premium line, Del Monte made national marketing history by assigning brand name prestige to a line of what were fairly ordinary canned fruits and vegetables.

At the time Calpak began its new marketing plan, World War I was three years old. The only immediate effect of the war was an increase in sales, especially shipments of food to the Allies. The newly opened Panama Canal encouraged foreign sales by making overseas shipments cheaper and easier than ever. When the United States entered the war in 1917, severe rationing measures and export limitations were instituted by the federal government; however, demand for canned goods by the armed forces more than compensated for what Calpak lost in export trade and so the company thrived.

Marketing efforts during wartime took on a patriotic tone. As William Braznell notes in *California's Finest: The History of the Del Monte Corporation and the Del Monte Brand,* ads urged housewives to can their own fruits and vegetables: "Don't blame the grocer if he is temporarily out of your favorite brand," they chided. Another early ad featuring the headline, "Del Monte brand quality . . . not a mere label, but a guarantee," reflected the traditional use of the Del Monte label on premium lines of top-quality products.

With Calpak packaging fruits and vegetables in more than sixty plants spread over several states and two territories, it was a challenge to ensure that high standards of quality were maintained. Consequently, the firm developed incredibly detailed specifications for each stage of production. Standards were clearly established and enforced for size, color, texture, and taste. Processing methods were mandated by the firm's headquarters and regular inspections were performed to verify that each plant carried out procedures exactly. In 1920, to further ensure quality standards, Calpak went into the seed business and supplied growers with seeds produced on its own farms.

Expansion

A major development in the history of the Del Monte brand came in 1925, when Calpak acquired Rochelle Canneries of Rochelle, Illinois. Until this time, Calpak was best known as a fruit processor (an exception being its noteworthy white asparagus, grown in the Sacramento delta). With the purchase of Rochelle Canneries, the firm expanded into Midwest vegetable production, most notably that of corn and peas. While not exactly new products for Del Monte, these were the two most lucrative segments of the vegetable canning industry at the time and Calpak was able to greatly expand production. Within the next few years, the company formed a Midwest Division through the purchase of additional canneries. Calpak acquired a fish-packing plant in the Cannery Row section of Monterey that allowed it to enter the tuna and sardine canning business. In the late 1920s, Del Monte coffee operations were expanded with the start of a coffee-roasting plant in Brooklyn, New York.

The Great Depression brought hard times for Calpak, as it did for nearly every other business both in the United States and abroad. Overproduction had been a problem for fruit packers even in boom years, and the depressed economy after 1929 made the situation worse as consumers lost buying power. Thousands of tons of produce rotted on the ground. In 1932, the company posted the worst losses in its history. To deal with the situation, Calpak initiated an aggressive recovery plan. Excess inventory was liquidated. More than one thousand acres of company-owned fruit trees were destroyed to slow production. Older, obsolete plants were closed; wages and salaries were cut; and expenses were reduced dramatically in all areas except marketing. Calpak began to rebound and within three years it was firmly back in the black. Before the Depression, ads had continually stressed Del Monte's position as a leader in premium quality products, but during the 1930s a subtle shift took place. Ads began to stress value and economy, not an easy task for a premium-priced label. But, as Braznell points out, Calpak marketers convinced consumers that "Del Monte quality was the best and surest bargain," and "only dependable quality pays."

Preparing for War

In 1940, with war again looming on the horizon for U.S. forces, then-Calpak president Alfred W. Eames began preparing his company's contributions to the war effort. Based on the firm's experiences during World War I, Eames felt it prudent to begin greatly increasing production capacity. However, the Calpak board was cautious and hesitated adding new plants when wartime shortages could significantly curtail supplies of available raw materials. Eames won out, however. Calpak opened several new canning lines in the Midwest, renovated a major plant in San Jose, and purchased new glass-packing equipment (a move that paid off when wartime supplies of metal were severely rationed).

Canned food, a staple of all armies since the time of Napoleon, was in great demand during World War II, and Del Monte's position as the premier canner of fruits and vegetables allowed it to keep processing in metal containers to meet the needs of the military. This heavy demand, combined with the increased use of glass containers for civilian sales, helped keep Calpak going through the war years. When the war ended in 1945, more than three-quarters of the Calpak employees who had served in the military chose to return to work for the company. The firm entered the postwar decade in an even stronger position than before due to postwar expansion and the 50 percent rise in per capita consumption of canned goods. People had become accustomed to eating canned produce during the war and packaged fruits and vegetables had now lost much of their negative image as "instant" foods and so consumers made them a regular part of their diet.

Capacity Doubles

The years following World War II saw a $50 million expansion in Calpak's empire, and the firm's capacity more than doubled in four years. In 1950, the company moved into a new, much larger, headquarters in San Francisco, and a short time later Roy G. Lucks was named Calpak's seventh president. During Luck's term of office, Braznell states, "Del Monte moved into the modern era." Lucks felt the firm's potential had scarcely been tapped. During his presidency, which lasted until 1963, Calpak and the Del Monte label moved forward not so much by acquisition of new firms as by improved market research, new technology, new promotions, new products, and consolidation of operating units. Calpak's earnings during the 1950s came from building domestic market share by smarter advertising, capitalizing even more on the Del Monte label, by expanding into overseas markets, and by improving production and distribution methods.

Lucks's successor, Jack Countryman, engineered Calpak's most significant marketing development of the next decade, an innovative and highly efficient warehouse distribution system. With the new system, orders were filled from the one full-line warehouse nearest to the customer, cutting delivery time significantly and, perhaps even more importantly, allowing customers to make smaller, more frequent purchases. This system gave Calpak a serious edge over its competitors, none of whom had the means to follow suit.

New Name, New Direction

From a consumer perspective, Countryman was responsible for an even more significant development. He was concerned about Calpak's position on the stock market. Even though the company's performance put it in the same class as front-runners Polaroid, IBM, and Xerox, he felt its image as a staid, longtime packer of fruits and vegetables made it a less attractive prospect for investors. The task to which Calpak's president set himself was to craft a new corporate image. The first thing Countryman did was change the company name to Del Monte Corporation. Then he had the Del Monte shield, unchanged for decades, streamlined and modernized. Following these outward changes came more substantial changes in the company's product line. Del Monte entered the carbonated beverage and non-carbonated fruit drink markets.

Although the success of these ventures is debatable, it is clear that Countryman was responsible for a whole new way of thinking among Del Monte's upper management, and he opened the door for many unarguably successful ventures, including snack foods, frozen foods, fresh fruit, and real estate. The Countryman years were the best in Del Monte's history. His departure as president coincided with a major recession in the canning industry. Earnings dropped from a record $27 million in 1968 to a low of $14 million in 1970. Del Monte was forced to reorganize domestic operations and decentralize much of the company's decision-making. By 1978, Del Monte had survived several economic crises: the devaluation of the dollar, rising manufacturing costs, and government-instituted price freezes. It emerged from the decade with record sales of $1.56 billion.

Corporate Takeover

In August 1978, then-president Dick Landis returned from his vacation to find that J. Paul Sticht, president of R.J. Reynolds Industries, Inc., was in town and wanted to meet on urgent business. The Reynolds empire included interests in tobacco, transportation, oil and gas exploration, as well as processed foods. Sticht proposed a merger—in substance, an acquisition—between his company and Del Monte. After several weeks of intense negotiation, an agreement was reached in which Reynolds merged all of its food and beverage operations into the new subsidiary, including such high-profile labels as Hawaiian Punch, Chun King, and Patio.

For ten years Del Monte's balance sheet benefited from this association. However, the company also experienced the downside of being part of a mega-conglomerate, most notably undergoing a series of reorganizations and finding itself subject to the whims of a succession of management teams. During the eighties, according to James Walsh, "as Reynolds was merging with Nabisco Brands and setting new standards for executive arrogance and corporate excess, Del Monte became a forgotten asset." Far worse, "the head office in Atlanta kept screwing up profit margins and diluting the Del Monte brand name by linking it with new product lines."

This situation came to a head in 1988 when, in the biggest leveraged buy out in U.S. history, giant Kohlberg Kravis Roberts & Company (KKR) purchased RJR Nabisco for more than $24 billion. To help finance this enormous takeover, KKR auctioned off substantial portions of RJR holdings, including parts of Del Monte, to overseas buyers. Del Monte's fresh fruit operation was purchased by Britain's Polly Peck for $875 million. Kikkoman, the Japanese firm that had been marketing Del Monte products in Japan, bought the U.S. processed foods business as well as all Del Monte rights in Japan. These and a number of other deals resulted in the confusing dissection of a legendary company that had spent more than seventy years striving for unity. Perhaps the most distasteful result was that the long-standing Del Monte label was now owned by several unrelated firms, with vastly differing objectives, commitments, and financial situations.

Salvaging the Future

A Del Monte management team led by marketing vice-president Ewan Macdonald salvaged at least a portion of the company via another leveraged buy out in 1990. Eighty percent of this $1.48 billion deal was financed by outside capital. Despite this, according to Fara Warner in *Adweek's Marketing Week,* San Francisco-based Del Monte has shown itself "one of the success stories to come out of the RJR leveraged buy out, despite the heavy debt load the current owners incurred in buying the brand from RJR. Sales have grown annually by 9% during Macdonald's tenure." Although Del Monte is still ranked as the number one preferred brand in several categories and controls 16 percent of the $3.5 billion canned vegetable market, its future is far from clear, and the company is considered by many analysts to be ripe for yet another takeover. In 1992 it was widely reported that Italian financier Sergio Cragnotti was preparing to offer approximately $800 million in cash and debt-assumption for the Del Monte Corporation. Commenting on the development for the *Wall Street Journal,* George Anders wrote: "If Del Monte's owners aren't able to fetch more money for the food company, they may choose to forgo a sale at present and hold on to the business for another year or two, in hopes of brighter sales prospects later on." In the final analysis, the only thing certain about Del Monte is that it still possesses the strength and power of one of the most recognized and trusted brand names in the history of food packaging.

Further Reading:

Anders, George, "Italian Financier Begins Talks Aimed at Buying Del Monte for $300 Million," *Wall Street Journal,* May 28, 1992, p. A4.

Brand News: A Quarterly Publication for the Employees of Del Monte Foods, March 1991.

Braznell, William, *California's Finest: The History of the Del Monte Corporation,* San Francisco: Del Monte Corporation, 1982.

"Creditors Say Polly Peck Can Offer Shares of Unit," *Wall Street Journal,* October 9, 1991, p. A12.

"Del Monte Names Macdonald CEO," *Advertising Age,* October 22, 1990, p. 46.

"Del Monte Offer Reported Near," *Los Angeles Times,* June 1, 1992, p. D2.

Elliott, Dorinda, "Dole and Del Monte Are Staying Put—No Matter What," *Business Week,* November 18, 1985, pp. 58-59.

Johnson, Bradley, "Vexed over Vegetables: Churlish Children Hawk Del Monte's New Line," *Advertising Age,* January 14, 1991, p. 4.

Loeffelholz, Suzanne, "Thrice Shy: Del Monte and Sansui Are the Jewels in Polly Peck's Crown," *Financial World,* May 29, 1990, pp. 46-48.

Maremont, Mark, "Meet Asil Nadir, the Billion-Dollar Fruit King," *Business Week,* September 18, 1989, p. 32.

"Mexican Investors Agree to Buy a Del Monte Business," *New York Times,* August 13, 1992, p. D6.

Moffett, Matt, "Mexican Group Plans to Buy Fruit Firm from Polly Peck for About $500 Million," *Wall Street Journal,* August 12, 1992, p. A3.

Paris, Ellen, "Swimming Through Syrup," *Forbes,* November 21, 1983, p. 328.

"Refinancing of Debt Related to Buy-Out Is Completed," *Wall Street Journal,* September 13, 1991, p. 2A.

"Royal Foods Agrees to Buy Del Monte Foods International," *Wall Street Journal,* October 19, 1992, p. A11.

"South African Concern Buys a Marketer of Del Monte," *New York Times,* January 8, 1993, p. D3.

Waldman, Peter, "RJR Completes Del Monte Sale for $1.48 Billion," *Wall Street Journal,* January 11, 1990, p. C9.

Walsh, James, "Alone at Last," *California Business,* July/August 1991, pp. 18-21.

Warner, Fara, "What's Happening at Del Monte Foods?" *Adweek's Marketing Week,* November 18, 1991, p. 4.

—Jay P. Pederson

DEWAR'S®

In 1894 President Benjamin Harrison sipped his first glass of Dewar's scotch whisky, and in so doing set the stage for the brand's extraordinary American success story. In 1993, as Dewar's prepared to celebrate its 100th anniversary in the United States, it enjoyed the enviable position of being America's best selling brand of scotch, with 16.3 percent of all scotch whisky sales, and outselling its closest rival by a margin of two to one. This comfortable lead had held strong in spite of sluggish hard liquor sales aggravated by the stock market crash of 1989, the demise of the 1980s' big spenders, a powerful anti-alcohol lobby, and an overall shift in consumer tastes away from hard liquor toward mixed cocktails and non-alcoholic beverages.

According to figures released by the U.S. Distilled Market Import DataBank, $324 million worth of Dewar's was consumed in 1991. The figure was significant in view of the fact that only 17 million Americans were scotch whisky drinkers. Still, Dewar's share of the market was strong enough that even with a premium price of $24 a bottle, the brand ranked a respectable eighth in overall distilled spirit sales, and ran rings around its nearest direct competitors, J&B and Johnnie Walker Black Label.

Also significant was the fact that, although Dewar's was solidly backed by a national ad campaign coordinated by Leo Burnett Co. of Chicago, and financed by $12.5 million annually, its strength in the market remained regional. According to the company's own data, its most loyal customers lived along the Eastern Seaboard, and Dewar's remained comfortably in the number one position thanks to scotch drinkers from Maine to Florida.

New York State, with its large Irish and Scottish population, was the leading market for scotch whisky sales. More than two million cases were sold in the Empire State annually, with Dewar's well ahead of its rivals. New York City also led other large metropolitan areas in scotch whisky consumption with 1.5 million cases annually as compared to Los Angeles, which ran a distant second with just 597,000 cases.

Maybe it had something to do with the fact that a president of the United States helped give Dewar's its early name recognition in this country, but the tiny District of Columbia also ranked among the brand's largest markets. According to statistics released by *Jobson's Liquor Handbook*, residents of the District of Columbia drank an average of 368.1 cases of scotch per 1,000 adults, as compared with New Hampshire with 225.8 cases and New York

with 171.5 cases. Dewar's percentage of those sales remained uniform with figures culled from other parts of the country.

Brand Origins

The origins of the Dewar's brand are much like a Cinderella story. The brand dates back to the 1840s, when John Dewar, a Perthshire, Scotland, farmboy who, at that point, had no experience in the then-fledgling scotch whisky trade, arrived in the town of Perth. He brought with him, however, a vision and commitment that would radically and irrevocably alter the future of the liquor.

The history of scotch whisky did not begin with John Dewar, though it might well have. It was in the 11th century when cloistered monks in England began distilling whisky—a Gaelic word meaning Water of Life—presumably to escape the boredom of their confines. A combination of grains—rye, barley, oats, and wheat among them—blended with malt was used to concoct the brew, which was used largely for personal enjoyment.

At the time, whisky was supposed to be one the best kept secrets in the England, but word eventually leaked out, and by the 16th century, commercial breweries began springing up throughout what was then known as Great Britain, though the greatest concentrations were in Scotland and Ireland. The early distilleries were mostly small operations with few ambitions beyond the modest sales they enjoyed in the specific towns or regions in which they were located. At that point, whisky's popularity was far away from that of such liquors as rum, gin, and brandy—for a long time it remained the drink of choice of only a small clique of devout converts.

John Dewar would change all of that. Curiously, in his early adult life, Dewar was considered a failure. He had been unsuccessful at several occupations, including farming. Finally he moved to Perth and got a job at firm of wine merchants called MacDonalds. It was here that young Dewar's star really began to shine, and it was not long before the firm made him a partner. By 1846, at age 40, Dewar had learned most of the secrets of running a successful liquor business. Armed with this knowledge, he resigned from MacDonalds and set up his own liquor retailing business in a small shop on High Street in Perth.

AT A GLANCE

Dewar's brand of blended scotch whisky founded in 1846 in Perth, Scotland, by John Dewar; after Dewar's death in 1860, leadership of John Dewar & Sons given to sons John Alexander and Thomas Dewar; first exported to England in 1885, then to Australia and South Africa, 1890; in 1894 began exporting to the United States.

Performance: *Market share*—16.3% (top share) of U.S. scotch whisky category. *Sales*—$324 million annually.

Major competitor: The Paddington Corporation's J&B brand; also, Guinness plc's Johnnie Walker Black.

Advertising: *Agency*—Leo Burnett Co., Chicago, IL, 1969—. *Major campaign*—Dewar's Profiles featuring mini interviews with interesting people who drink Dewar's.

Addresses: *Parent company*—John Dewar & Sons Ltd., Dewar House, Haymarket, London SW1Y 4DF, England. *U.S. distributor*—Schieffelin & Somerset, 2 Park Avenue, New York, NY 10016; phone: (212) 251-8200.

Early Marketing Strategy

Dewar garnered his first marketing breakthrough by selling his scotch in labeled bottles. For centuries the only way scotch could be bought was either in kegs or barrels. The convenience of the small glass bottles quickly gained popularity with customers and Dewar was well on his way to becoming a legend.

Dewar soon followed this advance by boldly guaranteeing the quality of the scotch he sold. The guarantee appeared directly on the labels, above Dewar's signature, ensuring quality and fine taste. These innovative moves quickly made Dewar's whisky a big success and it was not long before the brand had outgrown Perth. Not a man to rest on his laurels, Dewar hired a salesman to open up new markets in other parts of Scotland, and before long Dewar had gained a national reputation as a purveyor of fine spirits.

John Dewar died in 1860, and two of his children—John Alexander, 24, and Thomas, 17—began running John Dewar & Sons, Ltd. John Alexander, a shrewd businessman with razor-sharp judgement, is credited with the development of Dewar's first blended whisky. He hired Alexander Cameron, said to be one of the finest blenders of the period, and gave him the responsibility of creating a blend that would be uniquely Dewar's.

Cameron experimented with hundreds of grain and malt blends before developing what he felt was a special mix, well-balanced and full-bodied enough to carry the Dewar name. The final product, enjoyed by millions today, included 40 different malt and grain whiskys, with one of the primary components being Aberfeldy malt whisky, brewed at a custom-made still designed by John Alexander. Other prime ingredients included highly prized spring water from the Scottish Highlands, and waters from some of Scotland's most famous lakes or lochs. Dewar proudly called the blend "White Label." The original design of the Aberfeldy still, built in 1898, remains in use and has never been modified. Dewar also saw to it that the whisky was aged well beyond the government imposed minimum of three years. Dewar's "White Label" spends at least 12 years in its aging casks before it is bottled and sold.

Another key factor in assuring quality and consistency of the blend has been the loyalty of John Dewar & Sons' employees. In the more than 100 years that the scotch has been blended, only five blenders have held the position of master blender. David Howie, Dewar's most recent master blender, has been with the company for more than 40 years.

By the mid-1870s John Alexander was firmly established as the brains behind Dewar's exquisite taste. He then made Thomas, who had a built-in flair for publicity, the brand's marketing and promotion manager. Together the brothers began forging the plans that would make the whisky bearing their family name a household word among alcoholic beverage drinkers around the world.

International Growth

In 1885 the Dewar brothers were ready to expand beyond Scotland. England was their first target, and Thomas was dispatched to London to set up an office there. As one historian noted, "It was like trying to beard the lion in his den." At the time most Londoners were dedicated brandy, rum, and gin drinkers. Nonetheless, the foray into England was immensely successful, and five years later the Dewar brothers were expanding again— this time to Australia and South Africa. By 1892, with the respect and popularity their whisky had garnered, the Dewars were convinced that the world was indeed their oyster. Thomas Dewar embarked on a two-year promotional tour of 26 countries, and by the time he returned home, Dewar's was being represented by 32 new agents worldwide.

The big prize for the brothers, however, was the United States, a market in which scotch whisky had, until then, barely made a dent. A large community of Scottish immigrants had already settled in America, though, and the possibility of a very successful entry into this lucrative market was not lost on the Dewar brothers. In 1894 they established their first U.S. branch on New York City's Bleeker Street, in what is now Greenwich Village. In the years since then, Dewar's has come to be recognized as the leading innovator in its field, with a seemingly endless line of successes, breakthroughs and bold new ideas.

Quality Assurance in Advertising

Today, thanks to its unflagging emphasis on quality, Dewar's is one of the most decorated whiskys in the world. The liquor won its first accolades at the Edinburgh Exhibitions in Scotland in 1886, then again in 1890. Later Dewar's was cited at the Grand Prix of the 1900 Paris Exhibition, and in 1904 the whisky won a Gold Medal at the St. Louis Exhibition.

Crowned heads of Europe have lauded Dewar's scotch since 1893. That was the year Queen Victoria bestowed the first Royal Warrant upon the liquor, and every subsequent British monarch has followed in her footsteps. Dewar's has also been the recipient of royal awards from the Kings of Sweden and Spain. Dewar's received England's Queen's Award for Export Achievement in 1966—the award's inaugural year—and has been its recipient on six occasions since. It is the only distiller in the British Isles to have received this honor so often. The award is a royal recognition of a product's quality, and its contribution to Britain's trade with the rest of the world. Symbols of all of Dewar's awards are displayed on every bottle of "White Label" scotch sold.

Continuing the high profile promotions of the scotch, the Leo Burnett Co. developed an ad campaign featuring "Dewar's Profiles." The ads included short interviews of interesting and intriguing Dewar's drinkers. The campaign was targeted at a younger, upscale demographic group, designed to increase not only Dewar's share, but the market as a whole.

While Dewar's is still bottled in Scotland—as only a *true* scotch whisky is—since the summer of 1992 Dewar's has been imported exclusively into the United States by Schieffelin & Somerset Co. in New York City, which also markets rival brands of scotch whiskys, including Johnnie Walker and Pinch, as well as a wide range of other well-known spirits. Schieffelin & Somerset is a joint venture company with Louis Vuitton Moet Hennessy of France, and the United Kingdom's United Distillers, a division of Guinness plc.

Further Reading:

Bird, Laura, "A Scary Outlook for the Spirit World," *Superbrands 1991* (supplement to *Adweek's Marketing Week*), 1991, p. 61.

Dewar's "White Label" and the American Scotch Whisky Market, New York: Schieffelin & Somerset Co., 1993.

The Dewar's "White Label" Blend, New York: Schieffelin & Somerset Co., 1993.

The History of John Dewar & Sons, New York: Schieffelin & Somerset Co., 1993.

Jobson's Liquor Handbook, 1990, New York: Jobson Publishing, 1990, pp. 69, 71, 77-78, 160, 183.

—*Radcliffe A. Joe*

DI SARONNO® AMARETTO

Di Saronno Amaretto, an almond-flavored liqueur first formulated in 1525 in Saronno, Italy, was the fifth-leading liqueur sold in the United States in 1991. Packaged in a textured, square glass bottle with a square cap and scroll-like logo, Di Saronno Amaretto has been marketed as a premium imported cordial linked with the romance, civilization, and art of the Italian renaissance. Di Saronno Amaretto, like other cordials and liqueurs, emerged from an early history of intimate, small-scale production and relative obscurity, to boom in the United States and internationally in the 1970s and early 1980s. In 1992 Di Saronno Amaretto was the top ranked amaretto in the amaretto subcategory in the United States, claiming a 60 percent market share.

Manufactured in Saronno, Italy, by Illva Saronno S.p.A., Di Saronno Amaretto is imported and distributed by the Paddington Corporation of Fort Lee, New Jersey, a subsidiary of International Distillers and Vintners of Farmington, Connecticut. The Paddington Corporation also imports and markets J&B Rare Scotch, Stubbs Queensland Dry (Australian rum), Malibu (coconut rum), Rumple Minze Peppermint Schnapps, Metaxa brandies, and Knockando Fine Single Malt Scotch Whiskey. International Distillers and Vintners is the largest wine and spirits company in the world.

By 1993, Di Saronno was sold in more than 130 countries including the former Soviet Union, the Far East, and all of Europe. According to *Super-Marketing,* Amaretto di Saronno was the fastest growing liqueur brand in the United Kingdom in the year ending May 1991, up 21 percent from the previous year. These figures were especially striking since liqueur sales in the United Kingdom remained soft during the same period, according to *Super-Marketing.*

Brand Origins

The brand's legend has been closely associated with its marketing. According to the drink's manufacturer, Illva Saronno, Amaretto di Saronno was first formulated during the height of the Italian Renaissance in Saronno, a small village 14 miles northeast of Milan. A painter's model and innkeeper formulated and gave it to Bernardo Luini, a renaissance painter and disciple of Leonardo da Vinci. The model had posed for the fresco of the Madonna in the sanctuary of the chapel of Santa Maria della Grazie, in Saronno, Italy. The cordial, consisting of a distillate of apricot pits steeped in rough brandy, was said to have sparked a passionate romance between Luini and the young model. The original formula was passed down through generations of Italian innkeepers.

According to Illva Saronno, the liqueur was served at pivotal moments in Italy's political and cultural development, during the Risorgimento (the period of Italian political liberation and unification), at the Scala Theater, and during performances of Verdi operas.

Commercial Distribution

Carlo Domenico Reina first patented and commercially sold the liqueur in an apothecary shop in northern Italy in 1800. Reina was part of an aristocratic family in Saronno. In the early 1800s, the Reina family began to market it throughout Italy. It remains the top-selling amaretto in Saronno and Milan. The product did not enter the U.S. market until 1968, when Glenmore Distilleries Company purchased the first importing and marketing rights. Glenmore, well known for its whiskeys and brandies, was rapidly diversifying its holdings when it purchased Di Saronno. It was one of the first brands that Glenmore acquired outside of the whiskey category.

Liqueurs and cordials were booming in the U.S. market when Di Saronno was launched in 1968. According to *Jobson's 1976 Liquor Handbook,* cordials and liqueurs were doubling in volume each decade, with sales tripling every fifteen years. In 1976 liqueurs and cordials together topped the ten-million-case mark for the first time. *Jobson's* attributed the boom in the 1960s and 1970s to the growing youth (18 to 24 year olds) and women's markets. The young were experimenting with new fad liqueurs and mixed drinks. Di Saronno was primarily a women's drink, with women accounting for 60 percent of Di Saronno drinkers. In its first ten years in the United States, Amaretto di Saronno sales rose from 1,500 cases in 1968, to 750,000 cases by 1979. Marketed as an imported premium cordial, Di Saronno often posted gains which were stronger than those of other cordials and premium brands.

Performance Appraisal

The brand had "crested" by the early 1980s, according to *Jobson's 1985 Liquor Handbook,* and was hurt by the large number of "me too" amarettos and the rapid introduction of new fad liqueurs and cordials. Since 1983, when 725,000 cases were sold, the volume of cases has declined incrementally, down to 315,000

AT A GLANCE

Di Saronno brand produced by Illva Saronno S.p.A.; first formulated in 1525 in Saronno, Italy; first patented, produced, and sold in 1800 by Carlo Domenico Reina in Saronno; commercial production initiated in 1943 by the Reina family; first marketed, distributed, and sold in the United States in 1968 by Glenmore Distilleries; in 1986 the Paddington Corporation, a subsidiary of International Distillers and Vintners, took over U.S. marketing and distribution; Amaretto di Saronno renamed Di Saronno Amaretto, 1992.

Major competitor: Hiram Walker's Kahlua brand liqueur.

Performance: Market share—5.5% percent (fifth ranked) of liqueur category.

Advertising: Agency—Saatchi and Saatchi, New York, NY, 1992—. Major campaign—"They Expect Di Saronno. You Serve Them Di Pretendo. Time to Get Real?"; "Moments" campaign, which features the shared moments of intimacy between people that are enhanced by Di Saronno.

Addresses: Parent company—Illva Saronno S.p.A., Via Archimede 311, 21047 Saronno (VA), Italy; phone: (011 39) 39-296-56681. U.S. distributor—Paddington Corp., 1 Parker Plaza, Fort Lee, NJ 07024; phone: (201) 592-5700; fax: (201) 592-0859.

cases in 1991. Preliminary *Jobson's* data for 1992 show a small rise to 325,000 cases in 1992.

The original brand name, Amaretto di Saronno, used in the United States until 1992, may have been a factor in declining consumption in the 1980s; the brand name did not allow Di Saronno to distinguish itself from other amarettos. When people requested amaretto, they may well have gotten other amarettos. *BrandAdvantage* data in 1992 revealed only 13.3 percent loyalty to any amaretto brand. By renaming the brand Di Saronno Amaretto in 1992 and emphasizing brand distinction, Di Saronno hoped to gain a stronger share of the amaretto market. Despite fluctuations in volume sold, however, the cordial has remained highly profitable over the years.

Advertising

Advertising has been critical to Di Saronno Amaretto's success in the United States. In its first ten years, advertising helped to establish the brand and the brand legends. Early advertising campaigns emphasized the story of Luini and the model, the drink as a love potion and a gift, and linked the cordial with Italian high culture and political development. In its first ten years in the United States, Di Saronno was targeted to the growing market of new, young drinkers, the 18-to-24-year-old market. By the mid 1980s, the product was repositioned to appeal to the growing 25-to-44-year-old market. By the early 1980s, Di Saronno was well recognized as a premium imported cordial associated with young, well-educated, affluent people.

Amaretto di Saronno had a legacy as a holiday, after-dinner drink, and gift liqueur. By the mid-1980s, when more than 120 amaretto brands emerged and Di Saronno's sales declined, advertising moved away from the brand legend toward an emphasis on new ways and occasions for consuming it. The brand's positioning has changed every few years since it began to show declining sales in the mid-1980s. The concept of mixability (or splash), intro-

duced in 1985 and 1986, has remained a strong feature of advertising into the 1990s. Di Saronno drink recipes included a spritzer, mimosa, nutty colada, flavored orange juice, coffee and cream. Recipes for Di Saronno cheesecake, brownies, chicken, and baby back ribs have also helped to expand uses.

The in-crowd theme, created by Geer DuBois, was introduced in 1987. The "Amaretto di . . . " campaign used photographs of cutting-edge personalities such as Tama Janowitz, Phoebe Legere, Buster Poindexter, Victoria Jackson, and Carol Alt along with a bottle of Di Saronno, and the caption "Amaretto di *Janowitz.*" According to Debbie Seaman of *Adweek's Marketing Week*, the campaign was an aggressive effort to attract the trendy, 21-to-35-year-old, affluent market, who wanted to be on the move with the in-crowd. Although the campaign attracted considerable media attention, many people neither recognized nor cared about the personalities. The campaign appeared in *People, Playboy, Rolling Stone, Cosmopolitan,* and *Time,* as well as in bus shelters and on billboards. This controversial campaign lasted between 1987 and 1991.

By the early 1990s in the United States, the themes of upward mobility, indulgence and premium products no longer worked effectively. As a result of the economic recession, upward mobility declined; conspicuous consumption was less chic; consumers were saving instead of spending frivolously. Home entertainment declined; stress, exercise, healthy eating and relationships became more important considerations; and people became more interested in less-alcoholic drinks, and low-fat, low-calorie consumption. These changes resulted in Di Saronno's change in emphasis in its advertising to the brand's inherent quality, using it to celebrate genuine times in your life, and in relationships, to reduce the stress in your life, and as a versatile liqueur ideal for year-round consumption.

Brand Development

Although the product's sales appeal has shifted every few years, the formula has remained the same. The unique square bottle, sold in the United States since the product was introduced, was specifically designed for the United States market by a master craftsman in Murano, Italy. Another milestone in the brand's development was renaming it "Di Saronno Amaretto" in 1992. According to the Paddington Corporation, Di Saronno's U.S. parent company, by placing Di Saronno first, the Di Saronno brand is less likely to be confused with other amarettos. An ad campaign in trade publications in 1993 was designed to encourage distributors to serve Di Saronno rather than other imitator brands. These ads complemented others which stressed the superior quality of the Di Saronno brand.

Changes in Ownership and Advertising Agencies

Glenmore Distilleries Company owned Di Saronno's importing and marketing rights between 1968 and 1986. For the first 15 years of ownership, Di Saronno was one of Glenmore's fastest-growing brands. It sold the rights to the Paddington Corporation just three years after Di Saronno's sales had peaked and were beginning to drop. Paddington, who acquired Di Saronno in 1986 and continued to hold the rights in 1993, has been faced with the challenge of expanding Di Saronno's appeal in a climate of decreased alcohol drinking.

By the early 1990s, Di Saronno's advertising agencies had changed frequently, perhaps a measure of the difficulty of devising effective sales strategies in a bad economy. Factors such as changing economics as well as attention to reduced drinking, calories, and fat, mandated new rationales and occasions for buying premium imported liqueurs. As the market shifted, innovative advertising strategies attempted to keep Di Saronno moving. By 1993, Saatchi & Saatchi had been selected and a new "Moments" campaign was launched that featured "the feeling of shared genuine moments between people, focusing on some aspect of friendship or relationships." Despite limited growth in the early 1990s, the brand's sales often performed better than the rest of the liquor industry.

Predictions

By 1993, Di Saronno was a top-selling cordial in the United States. In nearly 500 years, the cordial had been sold as a love potion, an opera-house aperitif, a sophisticated Renaissance liqueur for the young and affluent, and as a healthy relaxant for the stressful 1990s. Despite an economic recession, soft sales of distilled spirits and changing American drinking tastes, by promoting new uses and occasions for the liqueur, sales held steady. As Ray Caro, executive vice-president at Saatchi & Saatchi, Di Saronno's ad agency, concluded in 1993, "Today, people are less formal and don't drink quite the way they used to. Our challenge, therefore, is to contemporize perceptions of when, where and how a liqueur like Di Saronno can and should be enjoyed."

Further Reading:

Ad $ Summary 1991, New York: Leading National Advertisers, 1992.

Amaretto di Saronno Originale: The Original Success, Saronno, Italy: Illva Saronno.

"Cordials and Liqueurs," *1990 Study of Media & Markets,* New York: Simmons Market Research Bureau, 1990.

"Di Saronno Amaretto Enhances Life's Genuine Moments in New Print Campaign by Saatchi," Press Release, Saatchi & Saatchi News Service, February 24, 1992.

"Distilled Spirits and Mixed Drinks," *1990 Study of Media and Markets,* New York: Simmons Research Bureau, 1990.

Elliott, Stuart, "Paddington Selects Saatchi & Saatchi," *New York Times,* November 24, 1992, p. C15.

Jobson's Liquor Handbook 1992, New York: Jobson Publishing, 1992.

1992 Brand Advantage: A Profile of Consumer Brand Usage, Volume 1: *Beverages: Cordials & Liqueurs,* Wilmette, IL: Standard Rate & Data Service, 1992.

"Production of Alcoholic Beverages, 1988-1990: Italy," *Marketing-in-Europe,* January 1992, p.13.

Seaman, Debbie, "On the Road With the In Crowd," *Adweek's Marketing Week,* June 1, 1987, p.30.

"Sector on Ice," *Super-Marketing* (U.K.), August 16, 1991, p.14.

—*Laura Newman*

DOLE® PINEAPPLE

Dole Pineapple, available fresh, canned, or in juice form, is processed by the Dole Food Company, Inc., the world's largest producer and distributer of pineapple. In the early 1990s Dole not only had the largest market share of pineapple in the United States, but on the entire North American continent as well. There are many reasons for the brand's success, but probably chief among them is that the founder of the famous company, James Drummond Dole, was the world's first marketer and distributer of the tasty, spiky fruit.

Brand Origins

Prior to the twentieth century, pineapple had been consumed only by the wealthy, and in popular art and literature, the pineapple was depicted as a status symbol. Christopher Columbus had "discovered" the pineapple in the Caribbean for Europeans, who called it "ananas," a corruption of the Indian word "nana," or aromatic. The English were among the few Europeans who rejected the name "ananas" for "pineapple," in part because the early English settlers and explorers were struck by the similarity between the pineapple and a pine cone; in part, because the flesh of the pineapple was as juicy and munchy as an apple. English colonists in the warmer American colonies of the south adopted the pineapple as a symbol of hospitality. It was a far cry for the pineapple to rise from privileged obscurity to mass production for the domestic market. This development occurred in Hawaii, which until recently produced more pineapples than any area on earth.

Although Dole pineapple is associated with the name of the person who first produced pineapple commercially, such production would not have been possible without the tinkering of an English seaman, Captain John Kidwell. In the 1880s he foresaw the possibility of marketing pineapple, and, after disappointing attempts to tame the wild Hawaiian variety, Kidwell imported a "smooth" strain from Florida, the "smooth Cayenne." This transplantation would revolutionize the future pineapple industry.

Although Kidwell never made a successful business from commercially grown pineapple, the young James Drummond Dole would. Fresh out of Harvard, only twenty-one years old, the dynamic young man arrived in Hawaii in 1899. His cousin, Sanford B. Dole, was a well-connected politician who in a few years would become governor of the newly acquired territory of Hawaii. He would encourage his young cousin's ambition to make a commercial success out of marketing pineapple.

First Commercial Success

By 1901 James Dole had acquired 60 acres of land 18 miles north of Honolulu, in Wahiawa. Groves of smooth Cayenne pineapple were ready to be harvested two years later. The young entrepreneur of the Hawaiian Pineapple Company would not make the mistake of Kidwell, attempting to ship fresh pineapple thousands of miles to market (which in the days before refrigeration took weeks). Rather, he would can it. Nearly two thousand cases of canned pineapple were packaged and marketed in 1903, making Dole the envy of the naysayers and the inspiration to competitors.

Canning was not the only secret of Dole's commercial success, but also his establishment of the cannery on the premises of the pineapple grove. Whereas fresh pineapple can mature for up to one month after harvesting, high-grade pineapple must be harvested when it is mature for the best canning results. Dole's principle of establishing a cannery at or near the groves is today universally applied by all processors.

From approximately 2,000 cases of canned pineapple, the number climbed in two years to 25,000 cases. This success was due to the railroad that was built between Dole's estate in Wahiawa and Honolulu. Dole also decided to transfer his cannery to the city where the annual arrival of thousands of Asian immigrants provided ample labor.

Dole's initial commercial success was also due to low costs; labor was cheap, and when Dole persuaded the American Can Company to manufacture cans in Honolulu, thereby eliminating the expense of importing cans from the mainland, vast quantities of pineapple could be processed quickly and cheaply. However, Dole needed to find new markets for his product before increasing his supply. Except for the populous coast of California, few in the United States had ever seen the savory fruit.

Early Marketing Strategy

Establishing a successful marketing strategy became a high priority for Dole. In 1911 Henry Ginaca, a young engineer and employee of Dole's Hawaiian Pineapple Company, invented a machine that enabled pineapple to be mass produced or processed at the dizzying rate of 100 pineapple cylinders a minute. Coupled with the important cost-saving measures Dole had effected already, the whole United States could be supplied with pine-

AT A GLANCE

Dole brand of pineapple founded in 1901 by James Drummond Dole, owner of the Hawaiian Pineapple Company, in Wahiawa, Oahu, Hawaii; Hawaiian Pineapple became division of Castle & Cooke Company in 1932; name of Castle & Cooke changed to Dole Food Company Inc. in 1991.

Performance: *Market share*—More than 50% of pineapple category.

Major competitor: Del Monte; also Libby.

Advertising: *Agency*—Lord, Dentsu & Partners, Los Angeles, CA, 1991—. *Major campaign*—Four different ads in women's and household magazines featuring recipes requiring Dole pineapple, accompanied by slogan: "How'd You Do Your Dole Today?"

Addresses: *Parent company*—Dole Food Company, Inc., P.O. Box 5132, Westlake Village, CA 91359; phone: (818) 879-6600; fax: (818) 879-6636.

apple. However, the existing market was already saturated with pineapples.

Dole initiated the first national advertising campaign in that prickly fruit's history. Together with other pineapple growers (whom Dole could have easily ruined because of his new pineapple machine; he wisely put it on the market instead), Dole's team financed an advertising blitz in the media of the day: glossy magazines and newspapers. Unusual, exotic names advertised the canned pineapples as well, as "Ukelele" and "Outrigger." The name Dole on canned pineapple was still decades in the future.

The result was a significant increase in demand, and production shot up dramatically with the start of World War I, when food prices inflated sharply. By the last year of the war, 1918, Dole's Hawaiian Pineapple Company was producing one million cases. Advertising directly through the media and indirectly, by virtue of being the biggest processor of pineapples in the world, had paid off.

Advertising Innovations

In response to demand, Dole purchased more land in order to expand his business. In 1922 business expanded further still, with the venerable Castle & Cooke Company becoming the dominant stockholder in Hawaiian Pineapple. By the mid-1920s, another pineapple glut compelled Dole and other pineapple growers to pool their resources and mount an even bigger national advertising campaign than in prewar days. This time, radio was popular and ads could be aired. Catchy slogans in the media such as "It Cuts With A Spoon—Like a Peach," to familiarize consumers with pineapple, and "You Can Thank Jim Dole for Canned Pineapples," were common, although the Dole label did not become affixed to pineapple produced by the Hawaiian Pineapple Company until 1934.

Although sales were brisk and the company was healthy, the Depression severely affected Dole's company. Money for promoting his product was lacking, which triggered his company's misfortunes. His new product, pineapple juice, was intended to lift his company out of the doldrums, but the absence of promotional campaigns thwarted his efforts. In 1932, Dole lost control of the company he started and guided for over thirty years. Castle &

Cooke, the new owners, managed to reverse the Hawiian Pineapple's downward trend. Major advertising campaigns for pineapple juice boosted sales tremendously, putting the company back on a profitable footing by 1936. Sales of juice again increased when Prohibition ended in 1933. Castle & Cooke rushed to advertise the delights of mixing Dole pineapple juice with liquor, especially gin.

Since World War II and the tremendous diversification of Dole products, advertising has been of critical importance. To begin, Castle & Cooke adopted the Dole brand name to intensify the public's awareness of the company's products; by 1950, the Dole brand name dominated the market. Television was the important medium with which to reach the public, and by the 1960s, James Dole's dream of making pineapple as familiar as apples and oranges had been realized.

In the 1970s and 1980s, Dole took advantage of the growing public awareness of healthy food to advertise its products accordingly. Dole is advertised as the healthy choice for health-conscious consumers, especially parents buying for their children. Store promotions of Dole pineapple occur regularly. As a result, sales of Dole pineapple products are still strong. In 1991 Dole Food launched a major advertising campaign in all media, using the slogan "How'd You Do Your Dole Today?" to encourage consumers to eat more vegetables and fruit, including pineapple. Partly because of effective advertising, Dole has the biggest market share of pineapples in North America.

Product Changes

Today Dole Food Company has diversified its pineapple products in ways undreamed of by James Drummond Dole. He had appreciated the need for product diversity and, in the early 1930s, had perfected a means of extracting a flavorful juice from pineapple and canning it. When the Castle & Cooke Company took over Dole's failed Hawaiian Pineapple enterprise in 1932, the new managers capitalized on the juice, ironically affixing it with the name Dole, which both canned pineapple and juice would bear from then on.

With the company out of the doldrums, real incentive for product diversity would not come until the aftermath of World War II. Americans were spending more on food than any nation on earth, and food companies were expanding their markets at dizzying rates. Besides expanding into other fruit products, vegetables, and even real estate, Castle & Cooke expanded its pineapple products as well. From simple pineapple juice there is now an almost bewildering variety of pineapple mixed drinks. Dole pineapple is sold fresh and canned in two sizes; canned Dole pineapple can be had in chunks, sliced, or crushed. It is also possible to buy Dole canned pineapple in a "lite," low calorie "natural juice," for the health-minded consumer. Dole pineapple juice is sold bottled, canned, and frozen.

Byproducts of Dole pineapple juice extraction, such as the enzyme bromelin, are sold to companies manufacturing meat tenderizers and to pharmaceutical companies as an ingredient in digestive aids. Pineapple shells also are used as cattle feed, and the fiber from the fruit is often sold to be woven into mats and bags.

International Growth

Since World War II, expansion into international markets has been an important theme in Dole's history. Not only do Dole pineapple products have the leading market share in Canada and Mexico, but in Japan as well, and it is heading in that direction in Europe. Dole Europe established its headquarters in London in 1989 to take advantage of changes in the European common market. Since 1991, part of Dole's international growth strategy is expanding into Eastern Europe, South Korea, and the Middle East, opening branch offices in those areas. Dole is the world leader in the processing and distribution of fresh fruits, including pineapple, vegetables, and nuts.

Part of the reason for Dole's significant international interests is that Dole has established important manufacturing centers in Thailand and the Philippines, where at present all of Dole pineapple is processed. Other Dole food operations are scattered throughout the world, providing the company with opportunities to expand into those markets.

Future Performance

The history of Dole pineapple has been one of extreme fluctuation, due largely to external economic and political conditions. Pineapple products have always been luxuries rather than necessities. Consumers must constantly be reminded of the benefits of eating a fruit that, while no longer considered a rare delicacy, is nonetheless still far less popular than everyday apples and oranges.

Historically, however, Dole pineapple products have survived many vicissitudes, and Dole is still the most widely recognized brand of pineapple, not only in North America but in the world. Therein lies its strength: international markets. Healthy eating has ceased being merely a trend, instead becoming a necessity. That, too, will assure the continued success of Dole pineapple.

Further Reading:

Annual Report: Dole Food Company, Inc., 1991.

Arnold, Oren, *What's in a Name? Famous Brand Names,* New York: Messner, 1979.

Campbell, Hannah, *Why Did They Name It . . . ?,* New York: Fleet Publ. Corp., 1964.

Cleary, David Powers, *Great American Brands,* New York: Fairchild, 1981.

"Dole Food Co. (Plans to Branch Out to Eastern Europe)," *New York Times,* November 23, 1991, pp. 19, 37.

"Dole Food Posts Lower Profit," *Los Angeles Times,* June 27, 1992, p. D2.

Dole Fresh Fruit Company, Westlake Village, CA: Dole Food Company, Inc., 1992.

"Dole PSA Aimed at Kids' Market," *Supermarket News,* March 23, 1992, p. 37.

Elliott, Stuart, "Public Service Spots Produced by Dole," *New York Times,* March 6, 1992, pp. C5, D5.

Facts On: Dole Fresh Pineapple, Dole Food Company, 1992.

The History of Dole, Dole Food Company, 1992.

Horovitz, Bruce, "L.A. Ad Shops Going After Dole's Account, (Lord, Dentsu and Partners, Inc.)," *Los Angeles Times,* March 9, 1991, p. D2.

Ishikawa, Lisa, "Pining Away (Dole Food Co. Hawaiian Div. Closes Canning Operations)," *Hawaii Business,* August, 1992, p. 35.

Koeppel, Dan, "Dole Wants the Whole Produce Aisle: Branded Fruits and Vegetables Are Turning the Nation's Supermarkets into Dole Country," *Adweek's Marketing Week,* October 22, 1990, p. 20.

Petruno, Tom, "Why Dole Offers More Than Just a Bit of Appeal," *Los Angeles Times,* October 11, 1991, p. D3.

Reinhold, Robert, "After Long Affair, Pineapple Jilts Hawaii for Asian Suitors," *The New York Times,* December 26, 1991, p. A1.

Stiling, Marjorie, *Famous Brand Names, Emblems, Trademarks,* Newton Abbot, Vermont: David & Charles, 1980.

Zwein, Jason, "Pineapples, Anyone? (Dole Food Operations)," *Forbes,* November 27, 1989, p. 286.

—Sina Dubovoj

DOM PÉRIGNON

For years, the "ping" sound of champagne glasses tapped together has provided background music for the celebrations of life's most important occasions. Beginning in the early 1900s, the champagne in those glasses might well have been poured from a bottle of Dom Pérignon (pronounced "perrin-*yon*"), the flagship product of France's leading maker of fine wines, Moët & Chandon, which is owned by LVMH Moët Hennessy Louis Vuitton. The winemaker itself had something to clink glasses over in 1993—its 250th anniversary. For almost 100 years, the name Dom Pérignon has graced bottles of only the finest of Moët & Chandon's sparkling wine. And while not the oldest entry in the company's vintage, Dom Pérignon has a distinguished history.

A Long Vintage

It was in 1743—more than 40 years before the French Revolution—that Claude Moët of France's Champagne region founded a winemaking house that bore his name. The house was—and still is—located in the fertile Marne Valley, just northeast of Paris, near the city of Epernay. The art of vintnery had been a longstanding tradition in the Moët family, but Claude Moët had new ideas for his emerging vineyards. He adopted into practice the research of a monk named Dom Pérignon from the local Abbey of Hautvillers. Dom Pérignon had worked on the premise that by blending the finest grapes from a number of different growths, the result would be a wine superior to the individual tastes of its separate parts. It was also Dom Pérignon who effectively "invented" the double-fermentation process that yields champagne, named for the region of France from which grapes used to make the sparkling wine originate.

With Moët's new potables came new customers, most of them members of France's upper classes. By 1750 Moët champagne was a favorite of Madame du Pompadour, who, legend has it, declared that champagne was the only wine that leaves women still looking beautiful after drinking it. That same year saw the Moët family business expanding into export to Germany, Spain, Eastern Europe, and America.

As the eighteenth century drew to a close, the Moët winery, now in the hands of Claude's grandson Jean-Remy, a confidante of French emperor Napoleon Bonaparte, purchased the Abbey of Hautvillers outright, increasing its winemaking capabilities. With Napoleon's endorsement, Moët champagnes became the toast of the civilized world; Jean-Remy went on to serve as mayor of

Epernay and receive one of France's highest awards, the Officer's Cross of the Legion of Honor. Moët returned the favor by naming a popular vintage, Brut Imperial, in Napoleon's honor.

Jean-Remy's retirement in 1832 left two members of the family in charge—his son Victor Moët and his son-in-law Pierre-Gabriel Chandon de Briailles. This succession of control was marked by a new company name, Moët & Chandon, which would stand for the next century. Under Victor and Pierre's direction, Moët & Chandon enjoyed unprecedented success during the remaining decades of the nineteenth century. The company by then employed nearly 2,000 people to tend the vineyards, crush the grapes, weave baskets, shape bottles, and cut cork.

As Moët & Chandon entered the twentieth century, sales of its wines reached the upper classes on virtually every continent, but fate would soon intervene. When Europe entered World War I, the effects on the French countryside were devastating. German bombs destroyed the original structures, leaving only a few offices that today serve as historical sites; the winemaking, however, continued.

The war's end was a turning point for both Moët & Chandon and oenophiles everywhere. Around 1921 the vintner brought out what connoisseurs would go on to label the finest champagne available—Dom Pérignon. This was the premium brand, the standard-bearer of sparkling wine—but it was not immediately available to the public. Instead, Moët & Chandon reserved this special vintage for important state occasions.

It was not until the mid-1930s, in fact, that then-sales manager Robert-Jean de Vogue was convinced to make Dom Pérignon a commercial product. He brought out a shipment of a 1921 vintage just in time for Christmas of 1936, and then the wine was shipped only to America. As for France, that country was first able to purchase Dom Pérignon in 1949 (the vintage that year was 1943, marking Moët & Chandon's 200th anniversary). The slow introduction to its native country was based on tradition: "In the nineteenth century the French drank only 20 percent of the champagne sold, and in the *belle epoque* before 1914 accounted for only a third of consumption," as an *Economist* article explained.

AT A GLANCE

Dom Pérignon brand of champagne founded c. 1921 by the champagne house of Moët & Chandon for official use; brand first made available to public in 1936; though brand still carries Moët & Chandon label, the company was incorporated as Moët-Hennessy in 1971; merged with Louis Vuitton in 1987 to form LVMH Moët Hennessy Louis Vuitton.

Major competitor: Mumm brand of champagne; also, Perrier-Jouet and Heidsieck Monopole brands.

Advertising: *Agency*—Kirshenbaum & Bond, New York, NY, 1990—. *Major campaign*—Moët & Chandon product line "image" themes include "Moët Makes It Paris," 1986, and "Where Celebration Is Born," 1992.

Addresses: *Parent company*—LVMH Moët Hennessy Louis Vuitton, 30 avenue Hoche, 75008 Paris, France. *U.S. distributor*—Schieffelin & Somerset Co., 2 Park Ave., New York, NY 10016; phone: (212) 251-8200.

Old Traditions and New Technology

Today, Dom Pérignon is a name known worldwide and since 1974 has been the number one selling champagne on the market. But what is not so well known is the painstaking process involved in producing this most sophisticated "bubbly." The rules of production for Dom Pérignon, and indeed all of the Moët line, have been handed down for years. In the case of Dom Pérignon, only two special breeds of grape—white chardonnay and black pinot noir—are harvested from only the oldest and most superior vines. Traditional horizontal presses are still employed to separate the juice from the pulp; though some 4.4 tons of grapes may pass through, only the sweeter juice from the first pressing is suitable for vintage Dom Pérignon. The juice, mixed with yeast and transferred into steel vats, stays at a constant temperature of 66° F and ferments into wine in a matter of weeks.

Champagne is differentiated from regular wine by its effervescence. For years, even the bubbles were the product of manual labor. As an *Economist* writer related: "A hundred feet under the house of Moët & Chandon . . . 80 men spend every day twisting 50,000 champagne bottles each." The reason, as the article explains, is to aid fermentation: "Champagne is bubbly because it is fermented not once but twice—the second time inside the bottle. The bottles are filled with wine already fermented; then yeast and sugar are added. The second fermentation soon follows. It produces fizz, more alcohol and a powdery deposit of dead yeast cells." In order to remove the powder and ensure a clear, sparkling wine, the bottles were placed in a holder called a *pupitre*. Trained craftsmen, called *remueur*, then hand-twisted the holders one quarter turn horizontally and one turn vertically every few days. Eventually, the sediment would collect on the cork, where it was frozen, removed, and replaced with a little more wine and sugar.

It was this process, performed bottle by bottle month after month, that kept hands twisting for a century. But some technology developed later proved itself as effective as hand-turning. In 1978 Moët & Chandon studied a process whereby "technicians drop live yeast into a solution of two chemicals," as Eleanor Tracy noted in *Fortune.* "Each drop dries into a hardened pellet whose chemical coating has holes too small to let out sediment from the yeast but big enough to let in the wine. The wine flows into the pellets, bubbles flow out, and the *remuage* [turning] process is

completed in three days." Best of all, "expert testers in blind tastings have found the flavor up to standard" with this new process. As an added benefit, the bubbles produced by the live-yeast method are smaller and more delicate than those produced in the past—a major goal of champagne makers. Moët & Chandon patented the process in 1981, but it would be another five years before any new-style wine would be made available. "The toughest test for the new technique," according to the *Economist,* "will be to persuade buyers, who have been told for years that the champagne's superiority lies in its method rather than its grapes, that some aspects of the time-honored are dispensable." The article also stated that any new-style Moët wine would be identified as such on the label.

Whether produced in the old-style or new, Dom Pérignon's standards remain at the highest level. If at any point in the production the taste of the wine is deemed unacceptable, the mixture is abandoned. The Dom Pérignon that is finally poured into waiting champagne glasses has been aged at least six years and can be stored in private wine cellars for another ten (the quality of the champagne does not improve after that). The overall packaging of the champagne is typically understated: a large black-tinted bottle—to keep out damaging light—adorned with the dark green label bearing the Moët & Chandon crest. Like all Moët champagnes, Dom Pérignon can be presented in a specially made wicker basket.

Advertising and Promotion

The widely recognized Dom Pérignon name carries such a prestigious reputation that advertising efforts for the brand have been kept low-profile. The champagne does not indulge in any media advertising, preferring to rely on word of mouth. Some campaigns, however, do revolve around the entire Moët & Chandon "image" line. A 1986 television spot, for instance, promoted the idea that "Moët makes it Paris." Later, an image tagline reminded consumers that the fields of Moët are "Where Celebration Is Born." The company marked the end of the Persian Gulf War in 1991 with a special newspaper ad suggesting that this was a good time to break out the champagne.

Sales promotion forms another aspect of Moët's marketing strategy. In 1979 the company debuted a hot-air balloon in the shape of a Moët & Chandon cork. This distinctive sight, dubbed "the Spirit of 1743," has made appearances at the Statue of Liberty, Mt. Fujiyama, and various other points on all five continents. To celebrate its 250th anniversary, the vintner commissioned the creation of books and videos. The Moët & Chandon vineyards are open to historic tours, highlighted by a champagne tasting session.

Mergers and Acquisitions

While the Moët & Chandon designation has stood for its products since the mid-nineteenth century, the business itself has undergone some corporate changes, in name if not in nature. In 1962 the company acquired the rival champagne houses of Ruinart Pere & Fils and Mercier. By 1968 Moët had added Christian Dior perfumes to its roster. And in 1971 the winemaker merged with Hennessy brands, the leading maker of cognac. The joined company was dubbed Moët-Hennessy, and virtually dominated its market. Even flowers got into the act—in 1977 Moët-Hennessy acquired Delbard, a French rose grower, and also bought into America's largest rose nursery, located in California. While these acquisitions made Moët the world's rose leader, the intent was not just to sell flowers, but also to apply rosebush hybrid technology to grape-growing.

In 1987 another merger was forged when Moët-Hennessy joined forces with the fabled luggage maker Louis Vuitton, which then owned Givenchy and Guerlain perfumes. The resulting corporation, LVMH Moët Hennessy Louis Vuitton, created "a new and dashing kind of corporate animal," in the words of *Management Today's* Simon Caulkin, "the first real multinational of world scale in top-of-the-line products." Or, as Moët's chairman, Alain Chevalier, told *Business Week* at the time, "When you say prestige, you'll think of us."

People of wealth and prestige have always favored Dom Pérignon. Microsoft Corporation founder Bill Gates, for instance, is said to keep a refrigerator stocked with the bubbly. Remaining a bestseller, however, takes bulk sales, and as the taste for affluence of the 1980s waned with the onset of the 1990s, a new austerity set in. While pricey—a 1985 vintage of Dom Pérignon fetches $85-$100 per bottle retail—the bubbly had always sold well in the United States, until competition from domestic (California) champagnes, rising prices, an unstable economy, and a move away from alcohol consumption leveled off sales. Conditions were more favorable abroad; *Hotel and Motel Management* reported that Japanese and European demand for Dom Pérignon remains high into the 1990s.

More than just a sparkling wine, Dom Pérignon is a product whose name and image command attention. At least one retailer has used this fact to its advantage, albeit in an unusual way. Miami Subs, a Florida-based fast food chain, made headlines in 1991 when one of its restaurants in the New York area started offering a choice of champagnes, including Dom Pérignon, on the same menu with its decidedly low-end burgers and submarine sandwiches. Though a Miami Subs manager told the *Wall Street Journal* that the promotion was mostly a gimmick, the article added that some executives were warming to the idea—"it is not all that unusual, especially late in the evening, for stretch limos to use the drive-through window for ordering a sub sandwich and Dom Pérignon."

Further Reading:

Caulkin, Simon, "Moët-Vuitton's Joint Vintage," *Management Today,* November 1987, pp. 50-55.

"Champagne: The Bubbly Business," *Economist,* June 21, 1986, p. 76.

Lyke, Rick, "American Champagnes Gain Status," *Hotel and Motel Management,* November 5, 1990, p. A55.

"Moët and Vuitton: The *Dernier Cri* in Chic," *Business Week,* June 15, 1987, p. 49.

"Seaweed in Your Champagne, Sir?," *Economist,* May 28, 1988, p. 86.

"Touché," *Economist,* May 27, 1989.

Tracy, Eleanor Johnson, "A Champagne Maker Finds a New Fizz," *Fortune,* January 6, 1986, p. 65.

"The Trick Is Keeping the Fries Hot While Getting the Bubbly Chilled," *Wall Street Journal,* September 26, 1991, p. B1.

—Susan Salter

DOMINO® SUGAR

Domino sugar has been the most important brand of sugar in the United States for well over a century, although the name "Domino" was not adopted until 1900. Produced by the Domino Sugar Corporation, the world's largest and most important sugar refining company, it is the most widely used brand of sugar in America.

Before the advent of granulated sugar, sweetening of foods had traditionally been done by adding honey or molasses. While refined cane or beet sugar was available, it was too expensive for the average American, and was sold in loaves or hunks that still contained many impurities. Raw sugar was usually boiled in an open vessel, the boiled product strained through blankets and "clarified" with bull's blood and other substances. The Dutch settling on Manhattan island were the first to bring sugar refining to this country, and hence it was in Manhattan that the direct predecessor of Domino Sugar was established.

Brand Origins

In 1807 William Havemeyer, an enterprising young man from London, England, who had been a supervisor in a sugar refining business, established a tiny sugar refinery on land leased from a church in Manhattan. With the help of one assistant, Havemeyer and his brother Frederick, a former sugar boiler, boiled and refined raw sugar, cramped in a 25 by 40 foot room. The business, named W. & F. C. Havemeyer Co., expanded and nine years later the New York refinery was capable of producing nine million pounds of sugar a year. One hundred years later, this amount would be produced in the course of two days. Until refining techniques were improved, a sugar refinery in the early nineteenth century could only produce 50 pounds of refined sugar for every 100 pounds of raw sugar (the rest often turned into molasses or a cruder version of the refined white product). But because the price of sugar was so steep, profits were higher than they would be a century later.

As the business grew, the processing of sugar became more advanced. Instead of boiling raw sugar in an open kettle, a vacuum pan was used; the product no longer was filtered with bull's blood but thoroughly cleaned with a substance known as boneblack, and the end product would be tested scientifically for purity. By the late nineteenth century, a granulating machine had been invented so that sugar could be packaged instead of being sold in unhygienic loaves.

The Havemeyer sugar refining business was handed down from generation to generation and expanded steadily. According to the 1891 obituary for Frederick C. Havemeyer in *The Louisiana Planter and Sugar Manufacturer,* the secret of the Havemeyer family's success in this highly competitive enterprise lay in the fact that they "have always been progressive, quick to adopt all new methods and improvements," thereby putting one sugar refinery after another out of business. In that year, the sugar refinery was renamed the American Sugar Refining Company. The name was appropriate, since by then the company was producing nearly 100 percent of the sugar consumed in the United States.

First Commercial Success

However, times were changing and monopolies of all kinds, including petroleum, tobacco and steel manufacturing, were subject to increasing public criticism and the threat of government prosecution. The specter of future competition from other sugar refiners loomed, especially when Theodore Roosevelt, who would pride himself on being a "trust buster," became president following the assassination of William McKinley in 1901.

It was at that time the American Sugar Refining Company, under president Henry Havemeyer, adopted the brand name Domino. First appearing on granulated sugar cubes resembling dominoes, the name eventually was applied to most of the company's products. With the certainty of future competition, having a trademarked name meant increased awareness of that particular product. This helped to alleviate the concerns surrounding impending rivalry.

The federal government eventually did sue the American Sugar Company for monopolistic practices in 1907. The company managed to weather the storm, however, thanks in large part to the Domino name. The public had come to recognize the brand, and with the company's many years of experience, Domino remained secure.

Marketing Strategy

By the late nineteenth century, a granulator machine had been invented that enabled the processing of sugar in granulated form, allowing it to be packaged. This marked an enormous step in marketing Domino sugar, which could now display its brand name with the product. By World War I, according to a report of the

AT A GLANCE

Domino brand of sugar brand founded in 1807 by William Havemeyer in New York City; company named W. & F. C. Havemeyer Co.; changed its name in 1891 to the American Sugar Refining Co.; became the Amstar Sugar Corporation in 1970; in 1988 company purchased by and became operating subsidiary of Tate & Lyle, changing its name to Domino Sugar Corporation in September of 1991.

Major competitor: C & H; Dixie Crystals.

Advertising: *Agency*—DMB & B, New York, NY; 1991--; *Major campaign*—"Domino Sugar—100% Pure So You Can Be 100% Sure."

Addresses: *Parent company*—Domino Sugar Corporation, 1114 Avenue of the Americas, New York, NY 10036-7783; phone: (212) 789-9700; fax: (212) 789-9747. *Ultimate parent company*—Tate and Lyle, 1409 Foulk Rd., Wilmington, DE 19803; phone: (302) 478-4773; fax: (302) 478-6915.

American Sugar Refining Company, there were more than 100 sweetening alternatives from which a customer could choose, and all of them provided competition for Domino.

As competition became more of an issue, the need for a successful marketing strategy was evident by World War I. The dynamic new president of the American Sugar Refining Company, Earl D. Babst, energetically strove to market Domino sugar. In addition to pursuing the usual marketing avenues in those days, including advertising in household magazines and newspapers, in trolleys, and on billboards, Babst felt it was crucial to the market success of Domino sugar that grocers be persuaded to purchase sugar in packages rather than ladling sugar to the customer from a bulk container. Ladling sugar usually meant giving the customer the benefit of more than the stated price allowed, and kept the customer ignorant of the brand of sugar. While packaged sugar (with the Domino trademark) was more expensive than sugar in bulk, it added up to a savings for the grocer since the customer did not obtain more than the actual purchase price of the product. Sensing grocers' unwillingness to change the decades old method of selling sugar, Babst visited more than 1,000 grocery stores in 1915 to pursue his strategy. In the end he succeeded, making his product better known and more competitive, since packaged sugar that sports a brand name gains greater recognition and demand than a nameless bulk item.

After the First World War had ended, advertising for Domino sugar slowed. Sugar had become a staple item, and people no longer had to be convinced of the need to buy it. In addition, Domino sugar sales received a boost due to the widely held belief, aired in the media of the day, that sugar was very healthful and nutritious. Domino sugar sales climbed to an all-time high in the

year of the stock market crash, 1929. Since that time, however, skepticism about the health benefits of consuming refined sugar has risen, necessitating increased advertising on television, radio, and in the print media. Offers of incentive items have been extensively used to promote purchase, as have newspaper and magazine ads featuring recipes that call for a variety of Domino sugars.

Future Predictions

Domino Sugar does have competition, especially from C & H and Dixie Crystals. There is little doubt, however, that Domino is by far the better known brand. More formidable competition in the future might well come from private label brands and the generic brands of sugar marketed by grocery store chains. Domino may have the advantage in that those alternatives may not provide consumers with the same quality and variety of their sugar products.

Refined sugar will continue to come under attack by health food advocates, no longer on the periphery of public opinion, while weight and heath conscious consumers will opt for noncaloric, artificial sweeteners. Certainly the competition and negative press that sugar receives in the late twentieth century are unparalleled in the history of Domino Sugar. However, sugar is an indispensable item in the American food processing industry, and likely will continue to be. Chances are quite good that Domino sugar will see its way through another century.

Further Reading:

"The American Sugar Bulletin," The American Sugar Refining Company, Special Edition, March 13, 1918, pp. 1-47.

"American Sugar Refining Co.," *Fortune,* February, 1933, pp. 59-65, 115.

"Amstar and Refined Sugars," *Sugar y Azucar,* May, 1991, pp. 25-26.

Bex-White, Janet, and Helen Cohen Smith, "Greenstone Completes Acquisition of Ackerman Advertising," *Business Wire,* February 6, 1992, Sec. 1, p. 1.

"A Century of Sugar Refining in the United States, 1816-1916," The American Sugar Refining Company, 1916.

"Colossal. Mr. Theodore A. Havemeyer's New Sugar Refinery," *Brooklyn Daily Eagle,* July 30, 1883.

Elliott, Stuart, "If All Else Fails, Try Plain English," *New York Times,* August 30, 1991.

Gunderson, Chris G., "Domino Sugar Corporation," Domino Sugar Corp., 1991.

The Louisiana Planter and Sugar Manufacturer, August 8, 1891, p. 17.

"Sugar and Sugar Refining; Havemeyers & Elder, Brooklyn, N.Y.," *Industrial America,* 1876, pp. 457-473.

Tiersten, Sylvia, "Fun and Games," *Incentive,* December, 1989, pp. 58-60.

—Sina Dubovoj

DORITOS®

The success of Doritos brand of tortilla chips serves as a prime example of evolutionary marketing, having developed from a primarily ethnic snack food to the largest-selling snack chip in the United States. For all their success, Doritos are still heavily challenged in the market by potato chips. Doritos also compete with other corn chip brands made by its parent company, Frito-Lay, Inc., including Tostitos.

Brand Origins

During the early 1960s, Frito-Lay experimented with the idea of introducing Mexican-style corn tortilla chips as a snack food and alternative to potato chips. While Frito-Lay already manufactured Lay's and Ruffles brand potato chips and its flagship brand, Fritos, the company saw room for an innovation in the market. The states of Texas, New Mexico, Arizona and California were populated with many people of Mexican or Latin-American extraction. When the company's market researchers discovered that many of these people favored tortilla chips that were larger and more authentic than Fritos brand corn chips, it began design on a new product. The new snack was thinner and lighter than Fritos corn chips and, like traditional Mexican tortilla chips, cut in the shape of a triangle. Also lightly salted, the chip was given the name "Doritos"—roughly, Spanish for "little bit of gold."

Early Marketing Strategy

Doritos were introduced to the southwestern and western United States in 1966, shortly after PepsiCo Inc.. took control of Frito-Lay. Because the product was seen as a novelty, the company felt compelled to instruct those unfamiliar with tortilla chips about when and where to eat Doritos. The new product was specifically positioned as a "unique snack," reinforcing its newness and illustrating its application. In time, Doritos found themselves displacing potato chips in lunch boxes and picnic baskets, on football game snack tables, and in cupboards across America.

To appeal to Mexican-Americans and other Hispanic people, Doritos were introduced to the public specifically as a "Latin snack." Drawing upon this strong ethnic identity, millions of Hispanic customers tried Doritos—and liked them. Propelled by Doritos brand's fantastic popularity in the southwest and California, Frito-Lay introduced the new product throughout the United States. In only four years, Doritos had become a successful national brand.

Early Advertising

Frito-Lay hired Tracy-Locke to handle advertising for Doritos. Drawing upon the company's desired positioning of the product, Tracy-Locke invented the tag line "The new beat in things to eat." In radio and television media, the line was supported with Mexican-style music (carefully avoiding the mariachi style of the Fritos brand's animated sombrero-wearing, trigger-happy Frito Bandito).

Brand Development

Despite Frito-Lay's best efforts to convince consumers to replace mealtime potato chips with Doritos, the tortilla chip continued to be consumed primarily as a snack food. In an effort to increase sales, Frito-Lay planned a brand extension. Just as flavored potato chips had been introduced to strengthen product lines, Frito-Lay rolled out a highly unique variation of Doritos— Taco Flavored Doritos. Flavored with a powdered mixture of chili pepper-related spices, Taco Flavored Doritos helped to increase the brand's annual sales from $10 million in its introductory years to more than $1 billion in 1991.

To replace potato chips as an accompaniment to mealtime sandwiches, however, Doritos needed to establish a newer, more distinct identity. What set Doritos apart from potato chips was their impressive crunch. By contrast, potato chips, being more fragile than Doritos, merely collapsed in the mouth. Seizing upon this quality of Doritos, Tracy-Locke rolled out a new advertising campaign in 1970 featuring goofy-looking comedian Avery Schreiber who was distinguished by his bushy black moustache and mop of hair. After putting a Doritos chip in his mouth, Schreiber bit the chip with such a tremendous crunch that the camera was forced into a shudder and parts of the set fell to the floor. Looking back upon the destruction he had caused, Schreiber exclaimed, "One good crunch deserves another!" Schreiber would continue to wreak havoc by eating successive chips. These memorable television ads not only gave Doritos a strong public identity, they also served to reinforce gains the brand had made after its initial introduction and to sustain growth.

In 1972 Frito-Lay introduced a second line extension, again drawn from the history of tortilla chips. As Taco Flavored Doritos had been uniquely set for Doritos brand, the new line, Nacho Cheese Doritos had a flavor that could not be copied by a potato

AT A GLANCE

Doritos brand of tortilla chips introduced in the southwest and western United States in 1966 by Frito-Lay Inc., a division of PepsiCo Inc.

Performance: *Sales*—$1.2 billion (1992 retail sales).

Major competitor: Potato chip brands; Frito-Lay's Tostitos.

Advertising: *Agency*—Batten, Barton, Durstine & Osborne (BBDO), New York, NY, 1992--; *Major campaign*—Comedian Avery Schreiber, "They taste as good as they crunch"; Comedian Jay Leno, "Crunch all you want, we'll make more."

Addresses: *Parent company*—Frito-Lay, Inc., 7701 Legacy Drive, Plano, TX 75024; phone: (214) 334-7000. *Ultimate parent company*—PepsiCo Inc., 700 Anderson Hill Rd., Purchase, NY 10577; phone: (914) 253-2000; fax: (914) 253-2070.

chip. The addition of a spicy cheese flavor introduced a reassuring "equity" to the brand. Those unaccustomed to tortilla chips and tacos were undoubtedly familiar with cheese flavoring.

Again, Schreiber was featured in advertising, causing minor tremors or sending people reeling from the force of the crunch. Here, however, Schreiber turned to the camera and proclaimed, "They taste as good as they crunch." Despite advertising efforts, sales of Nacho Cheese Doritos sputtered. Aware of Doritos crowded domination of the corn chip market, Frito-Lay paid great attention to the key strategic issue of support allocation between the three brands. From 1973 to 1975, regular, Taco flavored, and Nacho Cheese Doritos were held in careful balance.

In 1975, though, the company decided to concentrate 100 percent of Doritos brand promotional funding on the Nacho Cheese brand. This, it was hoped, would increase sales of the cheese brand while keeping the Doritos brand name fresh in consumers' minds. The decision was risky; Nacho Cheese Doritos had failed to hit sales targets, but tests suggested that consumers were highly willing to give them a second chance. Frito-Lay reintroduced the brand in a larger size bag and created large dump-bin point of purchase displays, making it easy and inviting to grab a bag of the chips. Within a year, the strategy paid off. Nacho Cheese Doritos met initial growth targets and, by 1980, doubled total brand sales.

After 1980, sales growth of all brands of Doritos slowed noticeably. Revenue from the brands continued to rise through aggressive price increases, but annual growth on the basis of poundage levelled off. This stagnation was chiefly attributable to the fact that Doritos brand no longer had the novelty value of being a revolutionary new brand. In addition, the market share was slowly being eroded away by competing tortilla chip brands, store brands and even Frito-Lay's new tortilla chip, Tostitos. This new brand was cut in a large circular shape, but contained no preservatives as did Doritos. Tostitos were made only with corn, oil and salt, and were well appreciated for their simplicity.

The company sought a new Doritos brand position strategy. After considering plans to position Doritos as a premium product "liked by everyone," or return to the ear-blasting crunch and tasty cheese identities, Frito-Lay decided to take an entirely new route. A reliable source of sales growth had long been known to be brand extensions. As Taco Flavored and Nacho Cheese Doritos helped to triple sales, so could additional types of flavored Doritos.

Health Claims

In 1982, Frito-Lay hopped on the light brand bandwagon by rolling out Doritos Crispy Lights. Intended for people worried about fat, and for those who favored a thinner chip with a less severe crunch, Crispy Light appeared perfectly poised as the mealtime replacement for fatty, oily potato chips. Test marketing in West Texas and in Minneapolis indicated success. But in national distribution, the market for health conscious potato chip eaters proved too narrow. Poor packaging and display decisions, coupled with production bottlenecks, contributed to the demise of Crispy Lights.

Product Changes

With stagnant sales growth and the failure of a new product line, Frito-Lay tried again to turn things around. In 1984 the company turned its attention in advertising from the purchaser to the actual consumer. That is, from mothers to the teens for whom they were buying. The campaign, "Definitely Doritos," positioned Doritos as *the* favorite teen snack food. But because of inconsistent funding, the campaign initially showed only mixed results.

The company supplemented the line extension strategy in 1985 by reintroducing Nacho Cheese Doritos. The following year the company rolled out Cool Ranch Doritos, and in 1987 introduced Salsa Rio Doritos. The light Doritos concept returned in 1989, in the form of Doritos Lights. Finally, in 1990, the company rolled out Jumpin' Jack Monterey Jack Cheese Doritos. All advertising of these extensions continued on the teen campaign. But soon demand for Salsa Rio and Doritos Lights began to fall and these brands were discontinued.

Sales of Nacho Cheese, Cool Ranch, and Jumpin' Jack Doritos, however, all remained strong. This may be attributed to the new spokesman Frito-Lay retained. Jay Leno, then a popular comedian known for his lightning wit as a guest on *Late Night with David Letterman* and later as guest host of the *Tonight Show,* became a spokesman for Doritos in 1986. He was a highly recognizable figure and, through his participation in fine tuning the scripts, brought the perfect type of humor to Doritos.

During one appearance on Letterman's show, the host chastised Leno for his commercial endeavor. Leno reached into his pocket, pulled out a bag of Doritos, offered one to Letterman (who refused), and began crunching away, extolling the excellence of the product. Leno was cast in the company's "Challenge" campaign, developed specifically to grab another bit of market share away from potato chips. Due to his broad appeal, Leno transcended the 12 to 34 target audience and even invited the interest of older consumers.

In his commercial spots, the comedian explored people's relationships with Doritos. Leno was seen pasting a note on his mother's refrigerator reading, "Hey Ma, Doritos." Reading a letter from a confused consumer, he reassured the audience, "Crunch all you want. We'll make more." Later Doritos promotions implored teens to "go public" and "break loose" with Doritos. The campaigns succeeded in maintaining a high degree of public awareness of the brand, but were less successful at driving high volumes of sales. If nothing else, they kept teens asking their mothers to purchase Doritos.

Performance Appraisal

After more than 25 years on the market, Doritos have grown from a novelty snack item to a major food product. Doritos now is America's second-largest selling dry food product. Its history has been punctuated with only a few setbacks that have provided valuable lessons in marketing to Frito-Lay brand managers. On the strength of powerful ad campaigns, however, virtually everyone is acquainted with Doritos. Frito-Lay boasts that Doritos has 99 percent recognition among 12- to 17-year-olds. In 1991, when American troops serving in Saudi Arabia requested Doritos by name, the company airlifted a quarter of a million bags.

Future Growth

As competition has evolved in recent years, the most distinguishing factor about Doritos is their variety of flavors. As a result, the brand's greatest competition is likely to be in the form of price competition from increasingly sophisticated discount and store brands. Having lost Leno to the *Tonight Show,* the company is again on the hunt for a cutting-edge spokesperson. The pressure for future campaigns falls on the shoulders of Batten, Barton, Durstine & Osborne, New York, which replaced Tracy-Locke as Doritos' lead advertising agency in 1992.

Faced with the possibility of having saturated the teen market, the company may be expected to draw out baby-boomers who were in their teens when Doritos was first introduced. Additional growth may come from campaigns illustrating circumstances in which Doritos may be consumed as more than just another between-meals snack food.

Further Reading:

Lawrence, Jennifer, ''Crunch Time,'' *Advertising Age,* January 16, 1989, p. 4.

''The Doritos Story'' (company document), Plano, TX: Frito-Lay Company, 1993.

—John Simley

168

DR PEPPER®

For a "misunderstood" soft drink, Dr Pepper, a product of the Dr Pepper/Seven-Up Companies, Inc., has more than made its point in the annals of retailing. The beverage is not just an American soda staple—it is in fact the oldest major soft drink brand in the nation's history. In the 1990s, Dr Pepper was the third-largest selling soft drink in the United States behind Coca-Cola and Pepsi.

Brand Origins

In Wade Morrison's Old Corner Drug Store, in Waco, Texas, in 1885, a young store clerk named Charles C. Alderton mixed phosphorescent water, fruit juices, and sugar to produce a soft drink that was out of the ordinary. To win approval of the formula from his boss, Mr. Morrison, the clerk jokingly called the concoction "Dr. Pepper's drink"—Pepper being the disapproving Virginian father of a woman Morrison had been courting. Morrison apparently got the joke, and enjoyed the drink. So did the citizens of Waco, who helped make the fruity soda a popular attraction at the drug store. In 1887, Morrison approached Robert S. Lazenby with an opportunity to take action on the hot property. A beverage chemist, Lazenby was associated with the Circle A Ginger Ale Company, also in Waco. Morrison gave the chemist a sample of Dr Pepper; Lazenby was impressed enough to agree to refine and manufacture the syrup at his plant. (The young clerk who invented the drink, Charles Alderton, disassociated himself with Dr Pepper, opting instead to turn his talents to the pharmacy trade.)

Dr Pepper—then known as Dr. Pepper's Phos-Ferrates—became a soda fountain choice until 1891, when bottling the beverage led to increased sales. With Lazenby at the helm, Dr Pepper became a top seller in and around Texas. But by 1904, the rest of the world was ready for a taste. Lazenby and his son-in-law, J. B. O'Hara, decided to debut the drink at the 1904 World's Fair in St. Louis, to what they thought would be the widest possible audience. Almost 20 million people reportedly attended the World's Fair, and Lazenby made sure he had plenty of samples of the new beverage on hand. (In this way, Dr Pepper joined the ranks of some other notable St. Louis World's Fair innovations, including hot dogs and hamburgers in a bun, and the ice cream cone.) The success of Dr Pepper at the World's Fair prompted Lazenby and Morrison to found the Artesian Manufacturing and Bottling Company, which would years later become the Dr Pepper Company.

"10-2-4"—Early Marketing Efforts

During the early decades of the twentieth century, Dr Pepper concentrated on building nationwide awareness. This task was helped along around 1910, when the slogan "King of Beverages" began appearing with the logo. Another addition was "Old Doc," a cartoon doctor complete with top hat, monocle and medical bag, who lent humorous appeal to the brand. Around that time, slogans like "Good for Life" and "Liquid Sunshine" also began to show up in promotional efforts. But no early campaign succeeded as effectively as the "10-2-4" theme. Using research that suggested typical people experienced energy slumps at mid-morning, mid-afternoon and late afternoon, Dr Pepper presented the idea that the beverage contained therapeutic qualities that could aid in increasing energy. Advertising of that time urged consumers to "Drink a bite to eat," and recommended taking a Dr Pepper break at 10 a.m., 2 p.m., and 4 p.m. Thousands of Americans took the advice, enabling Dr Pepper to gain headway in the rapidly growing soft-drink market. Even after the campaign had been discontinued, the numbers "10-2-4" continued to appear on Dr Pepper bottles, to the occasional confusion of those who had missed the message the first time.

By the 1950s, the beverage had adopted a new theme—"the friendly Pepper Upper"—which carried the message into the 1960s, when advertising efforts increased with the product's involvement in television in general and in one show in particular. *American Bandstand,* the legendary Philadelphia-based dance show, was a prime target for Dr Pepper. The youthful host, Dick Clark, proved a successful pitchman for the soda. As a result, sales of Dr Pepper climbed, especially among younger consumers. The product line expanded to include Diet Dr Pepper, as well as caffeine-free versions of both regular and diet sodas.

"Be A Pepper"—Later Advertising

By the 1970s, Dr Pepper advertising needed a boost. In order to compete against the reigning giants, Coca-Cola and Pepsi, Dr Pepper needed to position itself as different. With ad agency Young & Rubicam providing the creative strategy, the company debuted a national campaign in 1970 using the "most misunderstood" theme. In several commercials, various "misunderstood" types touted the flavor of Dr Pepper, helping the brand rise to

AT A GLANCE

Dr Pepper brand of soft drink founded in 1885 in Waco, TX, by Charles C. Alderton; distributed through soda fountains until 1891, when partners Wade Morrison and Robert S. Lazenby formed the Artesian Manufacturing & Bottling Company; company later renamed Dr Pepper Company; as a result of a buyout, Dr Pepper Company merged to become Dr Pepper/ Seven-Up Companies, Inc., May 1988.

Performance: *Market share*—Ranked third among all soft drinks (after Coca-Cola and Pepsi); *Sales*—$2.5 billion (1991 figures).

Major competitor: Coca-Cola; also Pepsi.

Advertising: *Agency*—Young & Rubicam, New York, NY, 1970—. *Major campaign*—"10-2-4," c. 1930s; "Be a Pepper," 1970s; "Just what the Dr ordered."

Addresses: *Parent company*—Dr Pepper/Seven-Up Companies, Inc., P.O. Box 655086, Dallas, TX 75265-5086; phone: (214) 360-7000; fax: (214) 360-7980.

fourth among soft drinks. In 1974, the "misunderstood" theme was altered to label Dr Pepper as "the most original soft drink."

Then, in 1978, a new theme took over. A young man sang and danced the praises of his favorite drink, gradually winning over the people around him. The jingle was a simple one, and the chorus—"I'm a Pepper, she's a pepper, he's a pepper, we're a Pepper, wouldn't you like to be a Pepper too?"—burned itself into the American consciousness. The ad became part of the national culture. Even the popular television comedy show *Saturday Night Live* got into the act, with a sketch comparing young, energetic "Peppers" to some sort of cult.

The "Be a Pepper" campaign lasted into 1983. Later advertising themes included "Hold out for the out-of-the-ordinary soft drink" and "Just what the Dr ordered." Diet Dr Pepper had its own campaign as well. Beginning in 1987 with a series of spots called "Personals," the diet drink went on to explore themes such as "Like nothing else," "There's no stopping the taste," and, in 1993, "The taste you've been looking for."

"Dr Pepper commercials have always been wonderfully executed and produced," noted Barbara Lippert in *Adweek's Marketing Week*. "But part of the problem is the drink's back and forth positioning, from outsider oddball to bandwagon mainstream." Lippert reviewed a 1990 spot that re-introduced the all-singing, all-dancing Pepper-pushers. A new, "hipper Pepper," as Lippert put it, was played by actor Terry Gatens, "a pumped-up Huey Lewis look-alike who makes a few Patrick Swayzesque moves." The new lyrics, said Lippert, are clever: "I'm tired of labels and your hipster high tops/no bottled water, no trendy soda pops." What Lippert did not like were the conventional hipper-than-thou images that accompany the music. "As in beer commercials, it's a man's world, where women show up only in short shorts to deliver pizza, or as a comic trio of three big gals shaking in their muumuus on the beach," she reported, adding that in this case, "too much of Doc Rock is prescription hip."

Surviving The Cola Wars

There is no evidence that the "Doc Rock" campaign, or any other, has ever hindered Dr Pepper's progress. During the 1980s the soft drink sidestepped the much-vaunted "cola wars" between market leaders Coca-Cola and Pepsi, and quietly assumed a healthy third-place position in a $46.6 billion-per-year industry. Some of this success can be attributed to the fact that Dr Pepper has no recognized rival. Its fruity flavor is reminiscent of "Cherry Coke," but remains unique. The uniqueness of the flavor may hinder its acceptance in some markets. Dr Pepper's introduction into Great Britain during the 1980s, for example, was unsuccessful.

The Dr Pepper Company was publicly traded on the New York Stock Exchange from 1946 to 1984, when the company was taken private in a leveraged buyout. By 1988, another buyout, this time by Prudential-Bache Interfunding, merged Dr Pepper and another popular soft drink company, Seven-Up, to form the Dallas-based Dr Pepper/Seven-Up Companies, Inc. By early 1993, the stock went public again and was identified on the New Stock Exchange as DPS. Within the company, Dr Pepper and 7UP were the two flagship products. The company's other drinks included Welch's Soda, I.B.C. Root Beer, and Nautilus sport drink. In 1992, Dr Pepper "posted a net loss of $37.5 million, as a result of a debt restructuring charge," according to *Business Week* contributor Stephanie Anderson Forest. Such numbers, she added, "mask the divergent fortunes of Dr Pepper and 7UP.... The company's sales gains last year came mostly from Dr Pepper and from reformulated and repackaged Diet Dr Pepper. The diet soda's volume soared 120 percent, to a 0.9 percent share of the market."

Dr Pepper was mass-marketed using corn syrup, and in a variety of sizes and containers by the 1990s. It was easily identified on supermarket shelves by its bright metallic sheen and large, modern typeface. Regular Dr Pepper sported white type on a red background, while Caffeine-Free Diet Dr Pepper was an eye-catching red-over-gold.

A Tradition Lives On

When Dr Pepper was first marketed it was sold in simple 6-1/2 oz. bottles, and continued to be in one Texas city into the 1990s. In 1990, *Texas Monthly* writer John Morthland tracked down the last Dr Pepper bottler in his state to use both original bottles and real sugar in his product. W. P. "Bill" Kloster, a 71-year-old manager of a 99-year-old Dr Pepper plant in Dublin, Texas, has stuck to the original formula while mass-produced Dr Pepper switched from sugar to less costly corn syrup in 1979. Morthland noted, Kloster even procured old bottles from neighboring plants. "He relies on a 1946 bottle washer and a thirties bottling machine and other Rube Goldberg-type machinery," writes Morthland. "Some equipment is held together with—yes—baling wire."

Such a dedication to tradition reflected Kloster's fondness for the product. As the article noted, Kloster "swears that the drink is smoother and sweeter when it's made with sugar and that it retains more of its original cherry-dominated flavor when it gets warm." While the bottler "is too polite to criticize the status quo," Morthland added, "he longs for the day when sugar prices drop enough so that the entire company can switch back." "I think all Dr Pepper is good," Kloster concluded, "but I think the company would grow much faster if it used sugar."

Further Reading:

Forest, Stephanie Anderson, "A Quick Picker-Upper for Dr Pepper," *Business Week,* April 27, 1992, p. 38.

Lippert, Barbara, "The Doctor's Imitation Blues," *Adweek's Marketing Week,* October 8, 1990, p. 61.

Morthland, John, "Wouldn't You Like to Be a Pepper Too?," *Texas Monthly,* May, 1990, p. 106.

"Pop Rumor," *Forbes,* March 4, 1991, p. 16.

—Susan Salter

DUNCAN HINES®

Cake mixes, ready-to-spread frostings, muffin mixes, brownie mixes, cookies (mixes and ready-to-serve), and microwavable cupcakes, crumbcakes, and brownies are manufactured under the Duncan Hines name by the Cincinnati, Ohio-based conglomerate Procter & Gamble Company (P&G). Since 1956, P&G has owned the exclusive rights to the Duncan Hines name and distinctive logo, a trademark familiar throughout the United States.

Early History

The Kentucky-born restaurant and hotel critic Duncan Hines (1880-1958) gained fame throughout the 1930s and 1940s as an arbiter of good taste in all things related to food and travel. *Adventures in Good Eating, Duncan Hines' Vacation Guide,* and *Adventures in Good Cooking,* his guides to high-class eating and sleeping spots in the United States, Mexico, and Canada, made his name synonymous with excellence.

Motels, hotels, inns, and restaurants that earned his praise were accorded the use of a red-and-white sign bearing Hines's signature and endorsement. Hines, however, retained possession of the emblem, and could remove it should the quality of the establishment become less than what his standards demanded.

Hines-Park Foods, Inc.

In 1948, Duncan Hines was approached by the North Carolinian businessman Roy Park, who at the time had established himself in the upstate-New York city of Ithaca. As Hines described their first discussions in his 1955 *Duncan Hines' Food Odyssey,* "[What] Mr. Park . . . had in mind was seeking out the food packers of the nation who packed and sold the very finest of any one kind of food, and licensing them to pack it under the Duncan Hines brand. Of course, recipes would be formulated that would assure the customer that he would get only a premium-quality product, and there would be a rigid control of quality. . . . In due time we reached an agreement and set up Hines-Park Foods, Inc., with home offices in Ithaca, New York."

In a recent interview, Park said of his first association with Hines, "Duncan was doing guidebooks and giving great speeches. He had a wonderful sense of humor, and was erudite on all matters relating to food. But he wasn't really going anywhere. I thought that by putting his name on lines of top-quality foods, we could reach a larger audience. People would know that the foods were great because of Duncan's endorsement."

Since Hines-Park Foods was centered in Ithaca, the first test market for its products was the upstate-New York region that included Rochester and Albany. A Cincinnati, Ohio radio station survey had revealed that 63 percent of the top income group questioned were familiar with the Duncan Hines name. Armed with this encouraging statistic, the company launched its first nine products—tomatoes, peas, cream-style corn, cut wax beans, kidney beans, pork and beans, tomato juice, grape juice, and coffee.

In the fall of 1949, Hines-Park Food expanded its marketing efforts to a nine-state area through franchising and regional brokers. Strict quality control was still maintained—test kitchens were established in Hines's Bowling Green home and in Ithaca. In 1950, Hines-Park began to distribute products on a nationwide basis with its launch of Duncan Hines ice cream, which was licensed to be manufactured and sold by some 70 producers throughout the country.

With the expansion of the product line, which in 1950 included butter and oleomargarine, a new testing laboratory was established in Indianapolis. "Only the top food products will be given permission to use my name," Hines asserted in a 1950 interview in the *Park City Daily News.* "Periodic checks will be maintained on all Duncan Hines products through the Indianapolis laboratory. Checks will be made at intervals to see that the quality of the product isn't lowered after permission to use the name, Duncan Hines, is given."

Hines-Park expanded its food offerings rapidly and by 1951 there were some 60 canned or processed foods bearing the Duncan Hines logo, with that many more in production. Among the offerings were butter beans, apple slices, canned turkey, wine vinegar, frozen french fries, mushrooms, and such exotic or regional fare as hominy, chutney, chili con carne, and olives. At the same time, Hines continued to travel the country, preaching the benefits of good food and good eating. His thrice-weekly newspaper column, "Adventures in Good Eating at Home," provided readers with a wealth of culinary resources. Hines could be counted on to ferret out even the most obscure recipe from his vast personal library of cook books. He could also provide instructions so that home chefs

AT A GLANCE

Duncan Hines brand founded in 1948 in Ithaca, NY; more than 200 food products marketed under the Duncan Hines name by Hines-Park Foods, Inc., founded by Duncan Hines and Roy Park; purchased by the Procter & Gamble Company, 1956.

Major competitor: General Mills, Inc.'s Betty Crocker; also Pillsbury Co.'s Pillsbury brand.

Advertising: Agency—N.W. Ayre, New York, NY.

Addresses: Parent company—Procter & Gamble Company, One Procter & Gamble Plaza, Cincinnati, OH 45202-3314; phone: (513) 983-1100; fax: (513) 562-4500.

could recreate some of the choicest menus from the nation's most exclusive restaurants.

Catering to those who were willing to spend a few more cents for premium-quality prepared foods was part of Hines-Park's marketing strategy. "We made good food available to those people who had more means," said Park. "Duncan Hines products were sold in grocery stores and in high-class department stores." Park described these products as "carriage foods"—a term which is comparable to today's "gourmet food" moniker. In the early 1950s, Hines also put his name on various food-preparation products like the Duncan Hines coffee pot, manufactured by the Minneapolis, Minnesota-based Jet-o-matic Company.

Duncan Hines Cake Mixes

In 1953, Hines-Park Foods entered into an agreement with the Omaha-based Nebraska Consolidated Mills to produce a line of cake mixes under the Duncan Hines name. Among the first mixes to be introduced were those for chocolate and white cakes, as well as a mix called "three-star," which could be used to produce white, yellow, or spice cakes. The cake mixes, which were among Hines-Park's biggest sellers, required the addition of fresh eggs and water. "Cakes made from mixes calling for the addition of fresh eggs are definitely as good . . . in taste as home made cakes," asserted Hines in an October 1953 interview with the *Milwaukee Journal.* And obviously, many American cooks agreed. "I wouldn't think of using my own recipe when I have a box of your cake mix on hand. . . . I am going to feature your cakes in desserts this summer," asserted Mrs. Roy J. Smith, owner of the Jersey Dell Tea Room (Spirit Lake, Iowa), in a letter to Hines in 1953.

By February of 1953, sales of Hines-Park Food products topped $25 million, and through a combination of sharp marketing techniques and Hines's personality and name recognition, the company continued to prosper. Hines, however, declared that he was not in it for the money, but for his love of food and his desire to ensure that the American people ate as well as they could. When the company was founded, Hines's royalties amounted to about two percent, said Park in a 1950 interview. The percentage was turned over to the Duncan Hines Foundation, Inc. (Ithaca, New York), in which Hines owned no stock. Proceeds were used to improve food products and to assist educated young men and women who wished to make careers of hotel and restaurant management. "My purpose is to improve the health of the nation," Hines asserted in the same interview. Among the beneficiaries of Hines's generosity were Cornell University (Ithaca, New York) and Michigan State University (then Michigan State College, East

Lansing), both of which were endowed with Duncan Hines fellowships.

Prepackaged and partly prepared foods captured the imagination of the American public in the 1950s. "The need to shortcut the homemaker's work stems partly from the fact that 10 million married women are working outside the home. These women comprise more than half of the 19 million American women who have jobs," asserted Hines in the October 12, 1953 issue of the *Milwaukee Journal.* The line of prepared baking products, which Park described in a 1993 interview as "one of our most popular undertakings," grew steadily in the 1950s to match the needs of the busy homemaker and working woman. By 1955, the line included packaged pancake mix and blueberry muffin mix (which included a tin of blueberries to stir into the mix).

Procter & Gamble Takes Over

In 1956, Hines-Park Foods, Inc. and Duncan Hines Institute, Inc. were acquired by the Cincinnati, Ohio-based giant Procter & Gamble. According to an August 1956 article in the *Ithaca Journal,* the newly acquired operations were made subsidiaries of Procter & Gamble, retaining their employees and with Park directing active operations. Hines would continue his involvement in the company as well, concerning himself with quality standards of licensed Duncan Hines products. In the year before control of Hines-Park Foods was in the hands of Procter & Gamble, it had sold more than 100 million packages of products bearing the familiar Duncan Hines logo. Close to 200 different food items were included in the product line.

When Procter & Gamble completed its deal with Hines-Park Foods, it also bought the Duncan Hines prepared mixes and baked foods interest in Nebraska Consolidated Mills. "We bought it with the feeling that we were expanding into a territory with which we already had considerable familiarity," said Procter & Gamble's W. Rowell Chase in 1981. At the time, General Mills and Pillsbury dominated the home baking mix category, but given P&G's expertise in commercial baking, the name recognition of Duncan Hines, and the popularity of the Hines-Park product, Procter & Gamble felt that it had a sure winner.

Coincidentally, Procter & Gamble researchers had been developing a new formula for cake mixes which they believed to be superior to those produced by the competition. In 1958, Duncan Hines Deluxe cake mixes replaced the Duncan Hines layer cake mixes, and the product went national in 1959. The new cake mixes were marketed in a new box especially designed to ensure freshness and protect flavor. In a 1958 article in the *Columbus* (Ohio) *Dispatch,* Procter & Gamble introduced this novel packaging development, in which the mix was sealed in a polyethylene bag and then in a cardboard box which was overwrapped with foil and paper. The box illustration was redesigned to feature the cake on a blue-and-white gingham background. The red-and-white Duncan Hines logo, familiar to those who had frequented establishments endorsed by the gourmet, was displayed in the upper left-hand corner of the box face, where it is to be found on all Duncan Hines products even today.

When Procter & Gamble took over Hines-Park Foods, it also continued to distribute the restaurant and travel guides that bore the Duncan Hines name. *Adventures in Good Eating* was updated and reissued until 1962, when automobile travelers shifted to using the country's ever-expanding system of interstate highways, rather than the back-road meandering made popular by Hines's guide books.

Product Line Extensions

Although the Duncan Hines product line currently offered by Procter & Gamble comes nowhere close to the 200 items marketed by Hines-Park Foods, it does include some 50 dessert items. Among the most popular products are the line of six brownie mixes (including such gourmet flavors as "Gourmet Turtle"); the ever-popular moist deluxe regular layer cake mixes (currently including thirteen varieties ranging from the commonplace white, yellow, and spice to the more exotic banana supreme, dark dutch fudge, and pineapple supreme); and the new microwavable mixes, called Duncan Cups, which comprise six varieties of brownies, cupcakes, and crumbcakes. The line has also recently been extended to include "light" versions of the most popular mixes.

Duncan Hines also offers three varieties of ready-to-serve cookies—chocolate chip, milk chocolate chip, and oatmeal raisin. Capitalizing on the 1990s trend toward home-baked cookie products, the company recently introduced a line of cookie bar mixes. Rivaled by Betty Crocker Supreme cookie-bar mixes, the Duncan Hines product held an 18 percent share of the market in the first six months of 1992, with sales of $2.94 million. In order to attract even more home bakers, Duncan Hines recently began to test market Pantastics, a new cake mix aimed at mothers of young children. Included with the cake mix is a shaped baking pan and a container of tinted frosting.

Further Reading:

Deveny, Kathleen, "Nostalgia Sweetens Sales of Cookie Mixes," *Wall Street Journal,* October 8, 1992, p. B1.

Hines, Duncan, *Duncan Hines' Food Odyssey,* New York: Thomas Y. Crowell Company, 1955.

"Name of Duncan Hines To Be Used on Quality-Controlled Food Products," *Park City Daily News,* June 4, 1950.

"Ohio Company Buys Hines, Park Firms," *Ithaca Journal,* August 17, 1956.

Park, Roy H., interview with Marcia K. Mogelonsky, February 1993.

Rowlands, Clarice, "Variety of Convenience Foods Increasing, Save Time for Millions of Working Wives," *Milwaukee Journal,* October 12, 1953.

Schisgall, Oscar, *Eyes on Tomorrow: The Evolution of Procter & Gamble,* Chicago: J. G. Ferguson Publishing Company, 1981.

Schwartz, David M., "Duncan Hines: He Made Gastronomes out of Motorists," *Smithsonian,* November 1984, pp. 87-97.

—Marcia K. Mogelonsky

EGGO® WAFFLES

When people think of frozen waffles, they most often think of Eggo, the confirmed leader in the frozen waffle category. Sales for the category itself regularly outperform those for most other kinds of frozen foods, and Eggo waffles have reflected this continued growth since the product was launched over 40 years ago. In 1950 the founding company, Eggo Food Products, Inc., was taking advantage of a recent technological breakthrough—the freezer—when they introduced their frozen waffles, which became a quick success. Since then, in response to further advances like the microwave oven, as well as growing concerns about health and nutrition, the Kellogg Company has expanded Eggo's product line to include many different varieties of the brand that remains a clear favorite among consumers today.

Brand Origins and Early Commercial Success

The Eggo frozen waffle was marketed in 1950, but its story began 15 years earlier when the original waffle mix was first developed in the Dorsa family kitchen. In 1935 Frank, Tony, and Sam Dorsa borrowed $35 dollars to buy a waffle iron and began experimenting. Soon they developed a hit waffle batter and began selling it to such area buyers as the kitchens at Stanford University. They made the batter from their kitchen and searched for a name for their new product. Another brother, George Dorsa, came up with the name "Eggo" since the batter had eggs in it. The rest of the year witnessed the beginning of Eggo Food Products, Inc. When a stock broker suggested the brothers incorporate, they sold 37,000 shares of stock at $1 per share, using the money to build a factory in San Jose, California, from which they began selling their canned waffle batter to restaurant outlets.

The company grew quickly in the ensuing years. Eggo Food Products began serving restaurants and even casinos throughout California and in nearby states. The Dorsa brothers began diversifying into other food products, purchasing the Garden City Potato Chip Company, and producing mayonnaise and vegetable oil along with vacuum-canned waffle flour. Eggo Food Products became the largest regional producer of condiments and canned goods to restaurants, at one time selling a total of 2,000 items. In addition, the company supplied the U.S. Army and Navy during World War II.

With the advent of freezers, the Dorsa brothers saw an opportunity to offer consumers even more convenience. Frozen Eggo waffles could be prepared quickly and easily, and might allow children to prepare their breakfast themselves. In 1950 Eggo Food Products gambled and gave up canned waffle flour entirely for the frozen waffle. The food proved so popular that production at their San Jose plant reached a level of 10,000 frozen waffles per hour. Eggo continued to grow as a result of its ongoing commercial success with its new frozen waffle and other products. In 1960 Eggo built a new plant with greater automation. That plant occupied 135,000 square feet, produced mayonnaise at a rate of 1,000 gallons per hour, and produced potato chips in a fully automated process which required people only to feed in potatoes at one end so that the machine could produce bagged potato chips at the other. Two years later Eggo moved all operations, including frozen waffle production, to the new, more efficient plant.

Eggo Food Products employed a variety of advertising techniques early on. In the 1950s the company relied most heavily on direct advertising, hired Bobby Gay to dress in an egg costume and attract the attention of children in stores. The company also used billboard advertising, displaying only the enlarged Eggo name. Newspaper advertising was also used to augment brand name recognition.

Shifting Parent Companies

Eggo remained a small company relative to the size of some of its competitors. While Eggo was well known in the west, it lacked immersion in the national market. However, with the 1966 acquisition of Eggo Food Products by Fearn Foods Inc. of Chicago, which made products that competed with Eggo in the dried soup market, Eggo waffles finally achieved national distribution. In 1968, Fearn merged its new subsidiary, now named Eggo Frozen Products, Inc., with another subsidiary, Mrs. Smith's Frozen Meats.

Just two years later, the Kellogg Company bought Fearn International Inc. and its subsidiaries. Kellogg had begun in 1906 as a manufacturer of corn flakes, diversifying over the following decades into a host of ready-to-eat cereals. After meeting unprecedented sales success with its breakfast cereals, the company diversified still further into related breakfast convenience foods. In 1976 Kellogg bought Mrs. Smith's Pie Company, and in 1977, Pure Packed Foods, a manufacturer of nondairy frozen foods for institutional buyers. With these new subsidiaries came the opportunity to reorganize the production of related brands for greater efficiency. A year after Kellogg acquired Mrs. Smith's, the com-

AT A GLANCE

Eggo brand of frozen waffles founded in San Jose, CA, by Frank, Tony, and Sam Dorsa of Eggo Food Products, Inc., 1950; Fearn Foods Inc. bought Eggo Food Products in 1966; Fearn Foods renamed Fearn International Inc. in 1969 and purchased in 1970 by the Kellogg Company; in 1977, Kellogg transferred the brand from its subsidiary Fearn International to another subsidiary, Mrs. Smith's Frozen Foods Company.

Performance: *Market share*—60.8% (top share) of frozen waffle category. *Sales*—$287 million.

Advertising: *Agency*—Leo Burnett Company, Inc., Chicago, IL, 1970—. *Major campaign*—"L'eggo My Eggo."

Major competitor: Aunt Jemima frozen waffles.

Addresses: *Parent company*—Kellogg Company, One Kellogg Square, Battle Creek, MI 49016-3599; phone: (616) 961-2000.

pany shifted production of Eggo waffles from Fearn International to what would become Mrs. Smith's Frozen Foods Company, where it has remained.

In addition to augmenting sales through a larger variety of products, Kellogg may have diversified in response to rising pressure against much of its cereal business and to a declining U.S. cereal market. Diversification slowed, however, in the early 1980s as the company focused on product development and marketing within its existing industries. Kellogg paid special attention to its ready-to-eat cereals and convenience foods, including Eggo waffles.

Innovating New Eggos

Kellogg began testing new varieties of Eggos in the 1970s, beginning with the blueberry Eggo in 1972. A year later, after blueberry Eggo's national launch, Kellogg reported a 3.3 percent Eggo sales increase as a result. Urged on by this success, Kellogg brought strawberry Eggos through test markets and into national distribution in 1976. Eggo frozen bran waffles also entered Florida test markets in the same year and national U.S. and Canadian markets in the next.

As Eggo sales grew, Kellogg began planning still more varieties, as well as improved packaging equipment and the second phase of a five-year expansion of Mrs. Smith's production and warehouse facilities, which included increasing Eggo production capacity in its Atlanta plant. In 1979 production of all other Eggo products moved to a plant in Milpitas, California, leaving the San Jose Mrs. Smith's plant free to devote all operations to Eggo waffles and other frozen foods. That same year Kellogg introduced frozen waffles in Great Britain under the name Kellogg's Waffles. Equipment to produce the waffles was brought to a plant in Skelmersdale, England, to supply the U.K. and European markets. Attesting to this expansion, when Kellogg president W. E. LaMothe was asked by an *Advertising Age* correspondent in 1978 which products held the most promise, he replied, "Good convenience foods. . . . If we can make products that fit the convenience of the microwave, it should be a broadening opportunity."

Although microwaveable Eggos would not be introduced until late in 1991, Kellogg continued developing new versions of the frozen waffle through the 1980s and early 1990s. After achieving steady gains in market share through the early 1980s, Kellogg introduced the Nutri-Grain Eggo in 1984. More gains in sales and market share followed, and in 1986 Kellogg brought out the Nutri-Grain raisin and bran waffles, the seventh variety. By the end of the year, the popularity of Nutri-Grain and Nutri-Grain with bran and raisins exceeded that of all other Eggo flavors except Homestyle Eggos. The outstanding success of Nutri-Grain Eggos might be attributed to Kellogg's accurate reading of a health conscious market and to Kellogg's major advertising campaign pushing the benefits of nutrition, grains, and fiber in breakfast foods. Kellogg had also introduced three varieties of Nutri-Grain cereals in 1982, and Nutri-Grain Eggos benefitted from the visibility of the Nutri-Grain name across cereal and convenience food categories. Advertising campaigns stressing new, healthier cereals also boosted Nutri-Grain Eggo sales.

Kellogg continued to launch Eggo varieties targeted at consumers who were concerned about health. In 1988 Eggo Common Sense Oat Bran Waffles hit the shelves, with the usual success. In 1990, Kellogg brought consumers the Nutri-Grain MultiBran Waffle, containing brans of corn, wheat, rice, and oats, as well as the new Eggo Nut and Honey Waffles. The next year witnessed Kellogg's introduction of yet another health-oriented frozen waffle, fat-free Kellogg's Special K Waffles. Also in 1991, to capitalize on the consumer craze for miniature food products, Eggo Minis—Homestyle waffles cut and packed in boxes of 48 rather than the standard 8 per box—were unveiled.

That year marked Kellogg's wholesale leap into the microwaveable Eggo with the introduction of Eggo Fruit Top waffles in four flavors—Michigan Blueberry, California Freestone Peach, Vine-Ripened Strawberry, and Rome Apple Seasoned with Cinnamon. These varieties combine the taste of "the fresh flavor of fruit on a crisp waffle" with the added convenience of a preparation time totalling less than two minutes by microwave. The innovation has thus far proved to be a successful one.

Performance Appraisal and Prospects for the Future

By the end of 1991, Kellogg could report that convenience foods accounted for about 20 percent of the company's sales worldwide. The first "primary non-cereal" product line named was Eggo Waffles, followed by Mrs. Smith's frozen pies, Kellogg's Pop-Tarts, and finally Kellogg's Nutri-Grain Bars. While Kellogg had made tentative inroads into international markets with its introduction of frozen waffles in Great Britain, in 1992 Kellogg chairman and CEO Arnold G. Langbo heralded international growth as the major direction for the company through the 1990s and into the next century. Kellogg has been reorganized into four international area divisions to encourage effective international expansion. With a top market share of 60.8 percent, Eggos should stand prepared for still greater success worldwide. Eggo co-founder Frank Dorsa still finds pride in the continuing success of the product he helped invent; he claims that "we have the best frozen waffle in the market, even to this day." Whether that market will expand to truly worldwide scope remains to be seen.

Further Reading:

Crain, Rance, "A Conversation with Kellogg's W. E. LaMothe," *Advertising Age,* October 2, 1978, p. 56.

Hammel, Frank, "Frozen Foods," *Supermarket Business,* September, 1992, pp. 115-6, 160-4.

Kellogg Company Annual Reports, Battle Creek, MI: Kellogg Company, 1973, 1976-79, 1982-88, 1990-91.

"Kellogg Introduced 64 New Products Worldwide in '71," *Advertising Age,* March 20, 1972, p. 52.

Liesse, Julie, "Kellogg Sees Return of 40% Share as Core Brands Rise," *Advertising Age,* June 15, 1992, pp. 1, 54.

Liesse, Julie, "Kellogg Chief to Push Harder for Int'l Growth," *Advertising Age,* August 24, 1992, pp. 4, 26.

Willoughby, Jack, "The Snap, Crackle, Pop Defense," *Forbes,* March 25, 1985, pp. 82, 86.

—Nicholas Patti

ENTENMANN'S®

Entenmann's is the brand name for more than 200 nationally distributed varieties of cakes, cookies, and other pastries produced by Entenmann's, Inc. of Bay Shore, New York. The company stunned the bakery industry in 1990 by introducing the first complete line of sweet baked goods that were both fat-free and cholesterol-free. The innovative product line, which industry magazine *Bakery Production and Marketing* credited in 1991 with creating a new, $500-million a year market for pastries, was heavily promoted to health-conscious Americans. A $10 million television advertising campaign the first year featured a baker telling an eager crowd, "Now you can eat cake."

Entenmann's best-selling products in 1991 were its All-Butter pound cake, chocolate chip cookies, crumb cakes, raspberry Danish twist, and chocolate donuts, all from its traditional line of sweet baked goods. Top sellers among the fat-free product line, which represented about 25 percent of the company's sales, were its Golden Loaf cake and raspberry Danish twist. Entenmann's is a subsidiary of the General Foods Bakery Companies, a holding company of Kraft General Foods, in turn a subsidiary of Philip Morris Companies, Inc.

Company Origins

Entenmann's traces its history to turn-of-the-century Brooklyn, New York, where William Entenmann, a German immigrant, opened a bakery in the fashionable suburb of Flatbush. According to the company, in an innovative turn, Entenmann did what no other baker had done before—rather than wait for his customers to come to his bakery, he delivered fresh bread, cakes and cookies door-to-door from a horse-drawn carriage. A horse and carriage emblem eventually became part of the blue and gold Entenmann's "seal," which is printed on all its packaging. Along with the seal is a message from William Entenmann III, grandson of the founder and former president of the company: "Back in 1898, my grandfather delivered his first baked goods door-to-door by horse drawn carriage. Soon his horse and carriage came to stand for the finest quality in baked goods. Today, the symbol of the horse and carriage continues to stand for quality. . . . It is your guarantee that everything we bake meets the standards that my grandfather held so high."

In 1924 William Entenmann, Jr., took over for his father. Soon afterward, he opened a second bakery in Bay Shore, Long Island. The bakery would eventually grow to more than half a million

square feet and serve the entire northeast. Bay Shore would remain corporate headquarters into the 1990s. William Jr. died in 1951, leaving his wife Martha, who had been a "pastry girl" at the Bay Shore bakery, and three sons, William III, Charles and Robert, to run the family business.

In the 1950s, the rise of supermarkets forced Entenmann's to begin a transition from being a retailer, delivering baked goods door-to-door, to being a wholesaler. During this time, Entenmann's also stopped baking bread to concentrate on cakes and pastries. When William Entenmann, the retired founder, learned of the decision, he reportedly asked his grandson Robert, "Why on earth wouldn't we sell bread?" The apocryphal response was, "Because people want the cakes." That answer, according to company literature, "has echoed through the decades at Entenmann's, where responding to the consumer has always been a driving force."

National Distribution

Despite the changes, however, Entenmann's remained a local brand until the late 1960s, when the company expanded its Bay Shore bakery and began distributing products to the New Jersey and Connecticut markets. In 1975, with many loyal customers from New York having retired to Florida, the Entenmanns opened a 100,000 square foot bakery in Miami that eventually began distributing products as far north as Atlanta. Three years later, Entenmann's was purchased by the Warner Lambert Company, which provided the financial resources for the company to expand again. In 1979 Entenmann's purchased the Burney Bakery in Chicago and began distributing Entenmann's-branded products to major Midwestern cities.

In 1982 Warner Lambert sold Entenmann's to the General Foods Corporation. At the time, chairman and chief executive officer for General Foods Jim Ferguson told the news media, "We think Entenmann's represents an opportunity to expand into a national business, from its present 36 percent [penetration] to at least 60 percent of the U.S. population." The opportunity came two years later when General Foods acquired Oroweat Foods, Inc., a California-based company with a history similar to Entenmann's.

The Dreyers, a family of German immigrants like the Entenmanns, had opened a small bakery in North Hollywood in the early

AT A GLANCE

Entenmann's brand of bakery products founded in 1898 by German immigrant William Entenmann in Brooklyn, NY; Entenmann's, Inc. was moved to Bay Shore, NY, in 1924, and purchased by the Warner Lambert Co. in 1978; in 1982 Warner Lambert sold Entenmann's to the General Foods Corporation, which was purchased by Phillip Morris Companies, Inc., in 1985.

Performance: *Market share*—7% of the bread and cake category. *Sales*—$502 million.

Major competitor: Continental Baking Co's Hostess line.

Advertising: *Agency*—D'Arcy Masius Benton & Bowles, New York, NY. *Major campaign*—(for fat-free, cholesterol-free products) "You can eat cake."

Addresses: *Parent company*—Entenmann's Inc., 55 Paradise Ln., Bay Shore, NY 11706; phone: (516) 273-6000; fax: (516) 273-6000. *Ultimate parent company*—Philip Morris Companies, Inc., 120 Park Ave., New York, NY 10017; phone: (212) 880-5000.

1920s. Their baked goods included a whole wheat bran bread that they called Oroweat. In 1932, Herman Dreyer, son of the family patriarch, and two friends, Ed Nagel and Henry Berkenkamp, formed The Oroweat Foods Company, selling the trademark Oroweat bread and other varieties of wheat, rye and oat-bran breads.

By the mid-1970s, Oroweat had expanded with bakeries located in the Northwest, Denver, and Dallas. When General Foods bought the company in 1984, it had a Western distribution network to link with Entenmann's East Coast and Midwest network. In 1993 Entenmann's products were sold in more than 29,000 stores, reaching more than 75 percent penetration.

Retail Bakery Image

The distinctive, white Entenmann's bakery box with blue lettering and a clear cellophane window was introduced in the 1960s. The package was a major part of the company's efforts to create a retail-bakery image even though its products were sold by supermarkets. Eva Page, vice president of marketing, told a *Bakery Production and Marketing* correspondent in 1991 that Entenmann's "would never change" its package. "The package," she said, "says bakery."

To further strengthen the "bakery experience" for shoppers, Entenmann's encouraged grocers to set up separate displays in high-traffic areas, away from other baked goods on supermarket shelves. In 1987, Entenmann's strengthened its position with supermarkets by releasing the results of a major marketing study that indicated that off-the-shelf display of commercial baked goods also increased the sale of in-store bakery goods.

In addition, Entenmann's emphasized use of high quality, brand-name ingredients, including Kraft cheese, Smucker's jams, Dole pineapple, and Chiquita bananas. The company also produced many of its own flavorings, including vanilla and cocoa, from raw materials. To ensure it's fresh-baked reputation, Entenmann's products were delivered five days a week, with a liberal return policy for cakes and cookies that remain unsold after a short

shelf life. The company operated about 200 "thrift" stores nationwide to sell returned items at discount prices.

Thunder and Lightning

In the fall of 1987, Gregory Murphy, former Midwest general manager for Entenmann's who had recently become president and chief executive officer, met with Kevin Lang, vice-president of operations and technical research, and William Entenmann III, a master baker and former president of the company who was then a consultant. Murphy, concerned with an industry drop-off in the sale of sweet baked goods, presented them with a challenge—to create a line of fat-free, cholesterol-free cookies, cakes and pies that would appeal to health-conscious consumers and still taste good enough to carry the Entenmann's brand name.

"I think Greg had to pick me up off the floor," Lang later told *Bakery Production and Marketing*. "There was a great deal of fear as you looked down the road over where this thing could wind up and how we were going to get there. The thing about a bakery product is that there are so many pieces to it. There're icings, toppings, fillings, dough systems—each with varying fat quantities. And then there was the aspect of taking the fat out of all of those. Then you had to find some formula, some recipe, that would make the product look and taste good."

The task was dubbed Project Lightning, and over the next 18 months, Lang, who had a doctorate in food science from the University of Illinois, researched ways to remove the fat from all the ingredients that went into Entenmann's products. William Entenmann III's role was to decide if the taste, texture and "mouth-feel" of Lang's fat-free creations met Entenmann's standards of quality. As Murphy explained, "What we had done, in effect, was bring art and science together. If the master bakers represent the artists, and the food scientists represent the science, and you bring those two disciplines together, you have a very powerful asset and a highly productive one."

In April of 1989, Lang and Entenmann created a fat-free, cholesterol-free pound cake that tasted close enough to the company's All-Butter pound cake to call it a success. The next step, which was dubbed Project Thunder, was to take Lang's revolutionary new fat-free baking technology and develop recipes for each of the products that Entenmann's planned to introduce. "It was hard," Lang recalled. "I wish I could say that one piece was easier than the other. The streusel was hard. The icings were hard. The fillings were hard. Doughs were incredibly hard. One of the most interesting challenges were pies. How do you make a fat-free pie?"

Entenmann's began test-marketing fat-free products in the Northeast in the fall of 1989. In January 1990, the company officially launched 12 varieties of fat-free loaf cakes, crunch cakes, cookies, coffee cakes, and cheese pastries. By the end of 1991, there were more than 60 products on the company's fat-free menu, including a fat-free apple pie. According to Lang, a conventional Entenmann's apple pie was 70 percent fat. In 1993, the company was still working on fat-free donuts.

Fat-free Success

Sales for Entenmann's fat-free line topped $200 million in 1990, and earned the company numerous accolades, including the 1990 Edison award for New Product Marketer of the Year from the American Marketing Association. In its *Superbrands 1990* supplement, *Adweek's Marketing Week* also called Entenmann's fat-free line of baked goods the best new product for 1990, and in 1991, Entenmann's received the Excellence in Marketing Award for a new product from *Sales & Marketing Management* magazine and was named Wholesale Bakery of the Year by *Bakery Production and Marketing*. However, the greatest accolade may have come from *Consumer Reports,* which reported on a taste test in May 1991 and concluded that the fat-free cakes didn't sacrifice flavor. According to *Superbrands,* 45 percent of Entenmann's early fat-free sales were to customers who previously bought the regular line of products, but 55 percent was new business. The products were sold in the traditional white Entenmann's box with a broad yellow band that proclaimed "Fat Free/Cholesterol Free."

In the early 1990s, Entenmann's was still awaiting patents on its Thunder and Lightning technology and baking processes, and was guarding the secret to its fat-free cakes and cookies zealously. However, in its product announcements, Entenmann's said there were no "secret ingredients" or artificial fat substitutes in its fat-free goodies. Entenmann's said it eliminated fat by eliminating all butter, shortening and tropical oils, and substituting nonfat, skim milk for whole milk. The fat-free recipes also called for egg whites instead of whole eggs, which eliminated much of the cholesterol. Entenmann's fat-free products still contained sugar, which was often the top ingredient. But without the usual fat content, they were significantly lower in calories than traditional baked goods. For example, two "regular" oatmeal cookies contained 120 calories. Two of Entenmann's fat-free Oatmeal Raisin Cookies contained 80 calories. Entenmann's fat-free cakes and cookies also met standards for low sodium products set by the federal Food and Drug Administration (FDA).

Competition

Although Entenmann's was the first line of fat-free sweet baked goods, a few competitors were quick to follow, including supermarket operator Giant Foods, Inc., which began selling fat-free products through its in-store bakeries. Bakery suppliers also followed Entenmann's lead, developing fat-free or reduced-fat cake, cookie, and muffin mixes for retail, in-store, and food-service bakers. However, because fat-free products generally lacked the sweet, rich taste that consumers wanted, other well-known brands were generally "reduced fat" rather than totally "fat-free." Still other competitors appeared to be waiting for Olestra, the fat-substitute developed by Proctor & Gamble, that had yet to be approved by the U.S. Food and Drug Administration (FDA). Proctor & Gamble submitted Olestra to the FDA in 1988; there had been no ruling as of early 1993. In 1991 Entenmann's Murphy told *Bakery Production and Marketing,* "At this point in time, we do not see fat-free products that would meet our quality standards. We do see a number of percentage point fat-removed products in the marketplace, 97 percent fat-free, etc. But I think that's very thin ice." Entenmann's remains the clear leader, then, in the reduced-fat and fat-free segment of the bakery products market.

Further Reading:

"1991 Marketing Achievement Awards," *Sales & Marketing Management,* August 1991, pp. 33-40.

Ahern, Charlotte, "Entenmann's Sales Brisk," *Advertising Age,* May 7, 1990, pp. S4-5.

"Eat Your Cake and Have It, Too?" *Consumer Reports,* May 1991, p. 301.

Garrison, Bob, "Suppliers Fueling Race Toward Fat-free Bakery Market," *Bakery Production and Marketing,* July 1990, pp. 25-26.

Gorman, Tom, "Fat-free Cakes Breakthrough with Entenmann's Expertise," *Bakery Production and Marketing,* January 1990, pp. 58-59.

Grimm, Matthew, "Entenmann's Slims Down," *Adweek,* September 17, 1990, pp. S20-21.

Kimbrell, Wendy, "Entenmann's Inc., Oroweat Find Good News in Bakery DPP Study," *Bakery Production and Marketing,* June 24, 1987, pp. 19-20.

Malovany, Dan and Pacyniak, Bernard, "Projects Lightning & Thunder," *Bakery Production and Marketing,* September 24, 1991.

"Murphy's Law, Generals Rule at GFBC," *Bakery Production and Marketing,* September 24, 1991, pp. 46-52.

Therrien, Loris, "Kraft Is Looking for Fat Growth from Fat-free Foods," *Business Week,* March 26, 1990, pp. 100-101.

Weller, Ed, "Forget What the Consumer Is Saying," *Progressive Grocer,* March 1992, p. 128.

—Dean Boyer

EVIAN®

Evian brand of spring water, owned by Great Brands of Europe, Inc., originates in the soaring Alps, most notably, the Haute Savoie mountains of southeastern France. From its humble beginnings in a flowing spring in the remote peasant village of Evian, its healthfulness was noted first in the late eighteenth century by a passing French aristocrat. From the late 18th to the late 20th century, Evian has become the most exported natural spring water in the world, and one of the most popular national brands in the United States. Ironically, distant France continues to produce the leading national brands of spring water in the United States, with U.S. brands limited at best to regional popularity.

Brand Origins

Evian natural spring water, named after a small village situated on the southern shore of Lake Geneva, is water pure and simple. Hence it is neither processed, manufactured, nor altered in any way. It is, in short, a consumer product that looks and tastes the same now as it did more than 200 years ago. The brand's actual origins are high up in the Haute Savoie, where rain and snow fall and seep down the mountainside through natural rock filters. The water takes approximately fifteen years to travel the short distance from its origins in the recesses of the Alps to the spring waters of the town of Evian, where it arrives rich in calcium, magnesium, and other minerals.

In the summer of 1789, Evian was a sleepy, rustic village, lying just outside of France, as part of the Sardinian state. Evian was remote from the revolution that had just erupted in Paris, whose shock waves were inexorably spreading throughout the countryside. An ailing aristocrat, the Marquis de Lessert, stopped by Evian that year and had a drink of water. In a day and age when city water was not purified or filtered in any way, he was struck by Evian water's clarity and freshness. Sick from kidney stones, soon he was claiming that he was completely cured. That report spread rapidly, even in 1789. When the bloodiest phase of the revolution ended in 1793, and life was back to normal again, Evian was attracting the monied and sophisticated from Paris and other French cities.

The trickle of visitors turned into an unstoppable flow when experts in 1807 determined the mineral content and unvarying temperature of the water. Little was actually known about the link between vitamins, minerals, and health, but common sense dictated that pure, mineral-rich water was wholesome and nutri-tious, especially in that era of bad water. By 1824, the wealthy were bathing in the water and not just drinking it. This marked the beginning of the hydrotherapy treatments that, along with the water, would give the town its fame.

First Commercial Success

In 1826 entrepreneurs in Evian decided to establish a bottling company and market the spring water. The Sardinian Cachat Mineral Water Company was duly established that year. Succeeding years brought unrest and civil disturbance in that French-speaking region of the country, still under foreign (Sardinian) rule. In 1858, with an aggressive new French king on the throne, Louis Napoleon, the Savoy region in which Evian was situated was wrested away from the Sardinian state in Italy, and annexed to France. This affected the bottling establishment in Evian, which changed its name to the Societe Anonyme des Eaux Minerales. The fact that the new king and his wife Eugenie paid regular visits to Evian les Bains was the single best guarantee of Evian water's success.

Indeed, the commercial success of Evian natural spring water was closely linked to the fortunes of the small town. Bottled Evian water sold well regionally because of Evian's reputation as a spa that was visited by royalty. So important was the association between the town as a spa and the popularity and marketability of the water, that the town changed its name in 1864 to Evian les Bains. Several years later, a wealthy banker, M. Girod, invested more money in the bottling plant and determined to market the water more widely.

Early Marketing Strategy

With connections in high places, M. Girod was able to win government (i.e. royal) approval for the company in 1870, followed in 1878, when France was already a republic, by official recognition from the French Academy of Medicine, another government institution, and the French Ministry of Health. This led to a close identification between the water and medicine: one of the earliest advertisements made much of the alleged fact that Voltaire's physician had regularly prescribed Evian water to his patients. Thus the early marketing strategy was to stress the medicinal virtues of Evian water, which in turn was an advertisement to visit the spa waters of Evian itself.

AT A GLANCE

Evian spring water discovered in Evian, a small village in Alps (now part of France), in 1789; in 1826, Evian brand of natural spring water was bottled and marketed by the Sardinian Mineral Water Company; by 1878, the company was called the Mineral Water Society of Evian-les-Bains; in 1970, the French food processing company, Boussois-Souchon Neuvesel (or Groupe BSN SA), Paris, purchased the Mineral Water Society of Evian-les-Bains, which became a subsidiary; Evian Waters of France Inc., owned by Groupe BSN SA, is sole U.S. importer of Evian; Evian Waters of France Inc. changed name to Great Brands of Europe, Inc., 1993.

Performance: *Sales*—$92 million (according to *Superbrands 1992*).

Major competitor: Regional brands of bottled water.

Advertising: *Agency*—TBWA, New York, NY, 1978—. *Major campaign*—Glossy, full page magazine ad featuring all three bottle sizes of clear Evian spring water in stark white background, accompanied by slogan "Some fitness equipment you can't buy at a sporting goods store."

Addresses: *Exclusive American importer*—Great Brands of Europe, Inc., 500 West Putnam Ave., Greenwich, CT 06830; phone:(203) 629-3642; fax: (203) 629-7961. *Parent company*—BSN Groupe, 53 Avenue Victor Hugo, 75116 Paris, France; tel: 33(1) 44 17 32 00; fax: 33(1) 45 01 89 05.

With the rapid evolution of modern medicine in the late 19th century, the medicinal "message" conveyed with and on every bottle of Evian water grew increasingly sophisticated. The company marketing the water (by then calling itself the Mineral Water Society of Evian-les-Bains), engaged researchers to come up with better ways to draw the water from the town spring, and to develop more effective advertisements. In 1902, when Dr. Jules Cottet published his research on the health benefits of drinking large amounts of water to alleviate kidney problems, company ads touted the undisputed wholesomeness of Evian water. This and subsequent medical "discoveries," broadcast throughout France, increased the amount of Evian water sold from two million liters in 1898, to twelve million in 1912. By then, two years before the onset of the First World War, Evian water could be bought throughout Europe.

Advertising Innovations

In 1882 the Mineral Society of Evian-les-Bains approved a budget specifically for advertising, highly unusual for that day and age. Ads placed in major Parisian papers extolled the purity of Evian water. In the late 1890s, advertising became more extensive and bolder—Evian water was advertised along with the spa—for those who were less health-conscious or more concerned with prestige. Ads began appearing in the form of postcards, posters, and a variety of other printed matter. In the early 20th century, one of the most innovative European poster artists of the day, Leonetto Cappiello, illustrated half-clad maidens dancing around a bottle of Evian natural spring water for the glossy magazines. In Evian les Bains itself, the company organized festivals and soirees to market the town's pure water.

After the ravages of World War I, Evian les Bains once more became the resort of the rich and famous. The now famous pink Evian label appeared on all bottles, and while the medicinal

message of Evian water was not lost on the public, the Mineral Water Society sought a broader market. Until World War II, the European advertising theme was focused heavily on infants. Evian was touted as the "water for infants," and welcomed as such, especially when European physicians endorsed it. By the outbreak of the Second World War and for years afterwards, Evian water was still sold only in pharmacies, as a result of its traditional link to medicine and health. The connections to medicine and health were relegated to sidelines, though important ones, after the war.

By 1950, Evian's advertising stressed Evian water as "the water for the whole family," rather than just for infants. Also, in a wine drinking culture such as France, ads stressed that Evian was the ideal complement to wine at a meal and, for gastronomes and gourmands, the water aided digestion. By 1960, the Haute Savoie mountains, the source of Evian water, were featured on the famous pink label, as they are to this day, and Evian made the transition from pharmacies to grocery market shelves.

The big transformation in advertising and marketing occurred when Evian became the sponsor of major international sporting events. This happened in the 1950s when the company sponsored the "Coupe de France" junior soccer championship. In time, Evian would award its own sports trophy to outstanding athletes—regardless of the event—and would become the major sponsor of the 1992 Winter Olympics in France.

Advertising innovations and marketing strategies shifted subtly in the 1970s: a great fitness and health craze swept the United States. At that time, Evian's managers (as of 1970, the Mineral Water Society of Evian-les-Bains was purchased by the French food conglomerate, the Groupe BSN SA) were determined to make it in the United States. Not until 1978 did the first modest foray begin. With western Europe well served by Evian, the United States had the potential of becoming the biggest market for spring water in the world. In the growing environmental consciousness of the 1970s, many Americans were beginning to distrust their tap water.

Evian's American (and Canadian) success story began, as always, with print as the major advertising medium, rather than television. Ads emphasized Evian's link to health, fitness, and sports; from there, the popularity of Evian seemed unstoppable. To keep from growing complacent, Evian's U.S. subsidiary, Evian Waters of France, Inc., also began sponsoring sporting events in the United States to identify itself more closely with fitness. The prewar strategy of emphasizing the healthfulness of Evian water for infants also was revived specifically for the U.S. market. By the late 1980s, Evian was the "yuppie beverage of choice" in the United States, and the best-selling brand of bottled water in the country. Even during the U.S. recession, Evian's sales were strong. By then, the entire bottled water market in the United States was worth nearly four billion dollars. The distant French company had established a national brand in the United States by successful advertising, a feat that eluded purveyors of American and Canadian mineral water. Evian's link with nutrition, wholesomeness, and sports have become traditional advertising themes. Added to these is Evian's newest sponsorship of the World Wildlife Fund.

Product Development

The reasons for Evian's success in Europe and overseas are primarily the water's purity and wholesomeness. Therefore, product development has involved keeping the water that way, a formidable task, considering that several million liters of water are bottled per day. Hence Evian water is tapped by stainless steel pipes at its source and bottled under strict supervision at the plant, where approximately 200 tests are performed daily on the water to ensure its safety and purity. Unlike many purveyors of bottled water, the Mineral Water Society of Evian refuses to add anything to the water to produce flavors or to carbonate it. Hence product innovation has been focused on packaging. Since 1886, when Evian water was first bottled by means of machines, the company has boasted the most modern bottling facility in the world. In 1969, the year Evian began to manufacture its own bottles as well as bottling the water, plastic bottles were used for the first time. Following this major development, Evian was the first bottled water vendor to launch the six pack in 1978. Considering that sales of Evian water in the United States increased tenfold from 1983 to 1988, plastic packaging and a variety of bottle sizes appealed more to the public than changing the appearance or taste of the water.

International Growth

From the late 19th century to the present, Evian's sales and profits have been heavily dependent on the international market. By 1901, Evian was available throughout Europe, with growing demand in the Middle East, Egypt, and Argentina, and in 1905, Evian was exported to the United States for the first time. Currently, Evian water is exported to approximately one hundred countries the world over, which accounts for half of the company's spring water sales. Consequently, the Mineral Water Society of Evian-les-Bains has become the biggest exporter of natural spring water in the world (approximately one billion liters of Evian water is consumed worldwide annually), which makes the

BSN Groupe, which owns the Mineral Water Society, the global leader in bottled water.

Future Predictions

With approximately four hundred vendors of bottled water in the early 1990s, competition in the multi-billion dollar bottled water industry was intense. The vast majority of these purveyors, however, were regional. The health, fitness, and environmental trends of the late 20th century, moreover, seemed destined to exert even stronger influence in the 21st century. Evian has become the world market leader in bottled water. With its effective marketing skills and the crumbling of trade barriers and globalization of bottled water, there are still vast untapped markets in Russia, Asia, and Africa to conquer.

Further Reading:

Annual Report: BSN Groupe, 1991, 1992.

Bellamy, Gail, ''The Bottled Water Wave,'' *Restaurant Hospitality,* April 1992, pp. 140-146.

''Evian Importer Changes Name (Evian Waters of France, Inc. Changes Name to Great Brands of Europe, Inc.),'' *Wall Street Journal,* March 26, 1993, p. A6(W).

Fahey, Alison, ''Ad Spigot Flowing Like Water,'' *Brandweek,* November 16, 1992, p. 4.

Grimm, Matthew, ''Reebok, Evian and Warner Team to Put More Power in Walking,'' *Brandweek,* September 14, 1992, p. 73 (2).

The Source, Societe des Eaux Minerales d'Evian, 1989.

Wolfensberger, Beth, ''Water, Water, Everywhere,'' *New England Business,* October 1990, pp. 24-32.

—Sina Dubovoj

FIG NEWTONS®

For the past one hundred years, Fig Newtons have been among the most popular cookies in the United States. Since 1891 the cookie has remained unchanged in appearance and taste. Produced by the Nabisco Biscuit Company (one of seven operating companies of the Nabisco Foods Group, a subsidiary of RJR Nabisco, Inc.), Fig Newtons are the third best selling brand of cookie in the country. Over one billion are sold annually.

Brand Origins

Fig Newtons were first produced in 1891, when baker James Henry Mitchell invented a machine that would allow a cake-like cookie, filled with fig jam, to be made. The machine was actually a funnel within a funnel, so handy and effective that the Kennedy Biscuit Works snatched it up and started to produce the famous cookie, which became an immediate success. The name of the cookie originally was "Newtons," taken from the town of Newton, a suburb of Boston.

The Kennedy Biscuit Works later became part of the National Biscuit Company (N.B.C.). The company, which was established in 1898 by Chicago attorney Adolphus W. Green, was a consolidation of dozens of bakeries eager to tap a growing consumer market desiring quality, attractively packaged, and sanitary food products. The National Biscuit Company stood on the brink of revolutionizing food manufacturing. Prior to that time, food "available at a popular price was not only poor in quality but totally lacking in consistency," noted Melvin J. Grayson in *42 Million a Day: The Story of Nabisco Brands*. "The food processing industry had two additional problems that were more or less unique: spoilage and contamination," continued Grayson. "Virtually all food was sold uncovered and in bulk, open to the elements as well as to whatever health hazard happened to be around."

Green and his united bakeries, determined to eliminate the faults in food production and distribution at that time, endeavored to "enhance the quality of their merchandise, improve consistency, extend the shelf life and go a long way toward putting an end to contamination," noted Grayson. One of the first products to roll out of the company's bakeries, Uneeda biscuits, was a simple cracker neatly packaged in waxed paper within a cardboard box. The uniqueness of this new "In-er-Seal" packaging created a sensation, and sales skyrocketed.

Between 1902 and 1912 a whole series of cookie products, many of them still on the market in the 1990s, were produced by the bakeries of the National Biscuit Company, including Fig Newtons Cakes (renamed in 1898 to identify the filling); Fig Newtons were marketed nationally for the first time a dozen years after being invented in the local bakery of the Kennedy Biscuit Works.

Importance of a Name, a Symbol

Neither the taste, shape, or size of Fig Newtons has been changed in over one hundred years. The importance of the name in the early success of the cookie is attested to in the lawsuit that Nabisco waged against Apple Computer Inc. In 1992 the computer company insisted on endowing a brand of new computer devices with the hallowed name of Newton, a moniker Nabisco insists still is indispensable to the success, one hundred years later, of Fig Newtons cookies.

Besides placing great importance on the names of its products from the beginning, the National Biscuit Company, as part of its marketing strategy, was sure to identify its brands with a company symbol or trademark. Corporate chairman Green searched for an emblem that would most ideally symbolize the company. One night while thumbing through a book that contained medieval Italian printers' marks, Green was captivated by one mark in particular. "It was an oval surmounted by a cross with two horizontal lines instead of one," Grayson described. "It was said to represent the triumph of the moral and spiritual over the evil and worldly." The symbol came to encompass various names and products affiliated with N.B.C., and soon found its way onto the Fig Newtons package. With this symbol on all of its cookie packages, N.B.C. products were instantly identifiable to the public as early as 1900.

Advertising Innovations

In its early days, the National Biscuit Company was distinct from other companies in that it expended large sums of money on advertising and, before Fig Newtons even came on the market, advertised nationally. In pre-World War I days, advertising could be carried on in the printed media, usually newspapers and household magazines, but even more effectively in trolley cars by means of ads mounted within the cars. Adolphus Green was a dedicated believer in advertising, hiring a company advertising manager as well as an outside advertising firm.

AT A GLANCE

Fig Newtons brand of cookie (name originally "Newtons") founded in 1891 by baker James Henry Mitchell; brand later produced by Kennedy Biscuit Works, which became part of the National Biscuit Company, founded in 1898; company changed name to Nabisco, Inc., 1971, and merged with Standard Brands Incorporated to form Nabisco Brands, Inc., 1981; Nabisco Brands (which later became Nabisco Foods Group) merged in 1985 with R. J. Reynolds Industries, Inc., which changed its name in 1986 to RJR Nabisco, Inc.

Major competitor: Keebler brand of cookies; also Pepperidge Farm brand of cookies.

Advertising: Agency—FCB/Leber Katz Partners, New York, NY. *Major campaign*—Ads for Fat Free Fig Newtons stating, "Fat Free Newtons are more than a cookie—They're fruit and cake!"

Addresses: Parent company—Nabisco Foods Group, 7 Campus Drive, Parsippany, NJ 07054; phone: (201) 682-5000. *Ultimate parent company*—RJR Nabisco, Inc., 1301 Avenue of the Americas, New York, NY 10019; phone: (212) 258-5600.

Radio soon became an important advertising medium in the 1920s, when one out of three Americans owned a radio. In 1934 the National Biscuit Company sponsored a highly popular three-hour Saturday night dance music program, which gave Fig Newtons ample opportunity to be advertised over the air. Later, Arthur Godfrey would be broadcasting on radio stations from coast to coast, advertising Fig Newtons and other Nabisco cookies and crackers to tens of millions.

In the days before television, companies advertised their products in motion picture theaters, and the Fig Newtons brand would not fail to be seen on the screen. In 1952, further advertising strategies included placement of the company's official trademark—which was now embedded in a triangular, red seal—on the corner of every package of N.B.C. cookies and crackers. In advertising it was referred to as "the famous Red Seal," a guarantee of quality. And after World War II, N.B.C. stepped up its advertising budget to include television appearances. Eventually, the company's name changed to Nabisco (a name resulting from a combination of the words National Biscuit Company), as many TV viewers and radio listeners reportedly were confusing N.B.C. with the TV and radio stations NBC.

New Marketing Strategies

With the merger of Nabisco and R. J. Reynolds in the mid-1980s, more funds were available for advertising purposes; by 1991, RJR Nabisco reportedly was spending nearly $400 million dollars annually on advertising.

Another outcome of the merger between Nabisco and R. J. Reynolds was a new emphasis on special promotions, evidenced in the one hundred year "anniversary" tin of Fig Newtons, a container resembling one of the first Fig Newtons packages. Special occasion and "holiday cookies" are part of Nabisco's advertising goal to introduce new cookie products at "strategic" times. Thus far, the concept seems to have worked well.

"Strategic" advertising by Nabisco is also evident during major sporting events, especially golf and tennis matches. In the 1980s a "Team Nabisco" of current and former professional

athletes advertised Fig Newtons and other Nabisco cookie products on television during major sporting events. And in the following decade, according to Judann Dagnoli in a 1992 *Advertising Age* article, Nabisco has attempted to promote cookies at video store outlets with considerable success, a concept that Nabisco reportedly planned to expand (for instance, timing Fig Newton cookie ads with new video releases). Innovative advertising and the large costs that go with it have paid off, as Fig Newtons have maintained their high selling status despite the fierce competition among such leading cookie companies as Keebler and Pepperidge Farm.

Product Development

While the basic recipe for Fig Newtons has not been changed in over one hundred years, they have not gone undeveloped. First, there was the name alteration: from Newtons in the 1890s to Fig Newtons Cakes, when the National Biscuit Company first marketed them, to Fig Newtons Fruit Chewy Cookies. Besides fig-filled Fig Newtons, there are several other flavor choices, such as Raspberry Newtons and Apple Newtons. Nabisco has busily marketed recipes that call for Fig Newtons in pies and cakes. Perhaps the most significant product extension was the 1992 introduction of the highly successful Fat Free Newtons. Research and development are an intrinsic part of a large company like Nabisco, and this new product took almost one and a half years to develop. According to *Business Journal of New Jersey,* Fat Free Fig Newtons (as well as Fat Free Apple Newtons) have become one of Nabisco's most popular cookies and fastest-selling products.

International Aspects and Future Predictions

Fig Newtons are the third most popular cookie in the country. So many of them are eaten in the United States that figs have to be imported to make up for the shortfall of domestic figs, almost all of which come from California. International links are therefore extremely important to Nabisco. Fig Newtons are but one of dozens of cookie and cracker brands produced by the Nabisco Biscuit Company, a subsidiary of RJR Nabisco. Nabisco cookie products, including Fig Newtons, are doing extremely well in international markets, and the future of Nabisco probably will be determined there. Latin America constitutes by far the biggest market for Nabisco cookies, especially in recent years as democracies have stabilized, resulting in greater economic prosperity. Future markets opening in eastern Europe and Russia promise to be very profitable arenas for the Fig Newton cookie business well into the next century.

Further Reading:

Aragon, Lawrence, "Is It a Cookie or a Computer? Battle Looms Over 'Newton,' " *Business Journal* (San Jose, CA), June 29, 1992, sec. 1, p. 1.

Berry, Jon, "Inside Nabisco's Cookie Machine," *Adweek's Marketing Week,* March 18, 1991, pp. 22-23.

"The Business of the Baby Boom," *Business Journal of New Jersey,* February 1992, sec. 1, p. 30.

Cahn, William, *Out of the Cracker Barrel: The Nabisco Story, from Animal Crackers to Zuzus,* New York: Simon & Shuster, 1969.

Campbell, Hannah, *Why Did They Name It . . . ?,* New York: Fleet Publishing, 1964.

Fact Sheet, Parsippany, NJ: Nabisco Foods Group, 1992.

Grayson, Melvin J., *42 Million A Day: The Story of Nabisco Brands,* East Hanover, NJ: Nabisco Brands, Inc. (Corporate Affairs), 1986.

Hwang, Suein, "Healthy Eating, Premium Private Labels Take a Bite out of Nabisco's Cookie Sales," *Wall Street Journal,* July 13, 1992, p. B1.

McElgunn, Jim, "Colorful Cookie Campaign," *Marketing,* June 18, 1990, p. 1.

Miller, Cyndee, "Nabisco Turns 200, Still Has Room for Marketing Growth," *Marketing News,* March 16, 1992.

Nabisco Announces 100 Year Anniversary for Fig Newtons (news release), Nabisco Brands, Inc., May 1991.

Nabisco Biscuit Company's Fig Newtons Tin Reveals Past (news release), Nabisco Brands, Inc., August 2, 1991.

Nabisco Introduces Fat Free Newtons (news release), Nabisco Brands, Inc., January 24, 1992.

RJR Nabisco, Inc.: Annual Report, New York: RJR Nabisco, Inc., 1991.

Stiling, Marjorie, *Famous Brand Names, Emblems, Trademarks,* Newton Abbot, VT: David & Charles, 1980.

Zbytniewski, Jo-Ann, "A Snack Food Free-for-All," *Progressive Grocer,* September 1992, pp. 121-22.

—*Sina Dubovoj*

FLEISCHMANN'S®

The Fleischmann's brand of margarine, a product of the Nabisco Foods Group, is one of the best-selling margarines in the United States. In packages displaying the eye-catching Fleischmann's name and the words "made from 100% corn oil" emblazoned and outlined in red inside a single white drop of corn oil, the Fleischmann's brand has been offering zero cholesterol, low saturated fat, and 100 percent pure corn oil margarine to health-conscious consumers since 1958.

Brand Origins

The Fleischmann's brand dates back to 1863 when Charles Fleischmann moved to the United States from Austria, where he managed a distillery. He was appalled by what he had considered to be the inferior taste of American bread. After returning to Austria to gather samples of the yeast used in the baking of Viennese bread, Fleischmann came back to the United States, accompanied by his brother Maximilian. The Fleischmann brothers took their yeast and their ideas to James M. Gaff, a well-known Cincinnati distiller, and the three partners went into the yeast-making business as Gaff, Fleischmann & Company. In 1868, the United States' first standardized yeast appeared and revolutionized American baking. Later opening a subsidiary called the Fleischmann Distilling Company, the partners began producing America's first distilled gin.

Both the gin and bread quickly captured a large market, and at the Great Centennial Fair in Philadelphia in 1876, the Fleischmann brothers proudly exhibited their yeast in a special "Vienna Bakery" display. So impressed were visitors with the warm, fresh bread that demand for the yeast skyrocketed. The partners made plans to build a fourth production facility in Peekskill, New York. Five years later, after the death of James Gaff, the firm's name was changed to Fleischmann and Company, and in 1905 it became the Fleischmann Company. Innovation continued when, in the Bronx, New York, in the early 1920s, the Fleischmann Company built a research center where scientists could investigate the role of fermentation in yeast production and conduct other yeast-related experiments.

On June 28, 1929, the Fleischmann Company, the Royal Baking Powder Company, and Chase & Sanborn consolidated to form Standard Brands Inc. in New York City. Fleischmann, now a division of Standard Brands, was deprived of its market for gin during 1920s Prohibition and concentrated on yeast production.

Armed with testimonials from medical authorities, the division launched a "Yeast for Health" advertising campaign. Nationwide sales subsequently rose from less than $1 million in the early 1920s to nearly $10 million by 1937.

Following the repeal of the Eighteenth Amendment of the U.S. Constitution prohibiting the sale of alcohol, the Fleischmann Division returned to making gin at its Peekskill distillery. Yeast production continued, and during World War II, Fleischmann shipped dry yeast to military men and women; at home, Fleischmann's yeast accounted for approximately 90 percent of the yeast purchased on the West Coast. In 1942 Standard Brands acquired the Standard Margarine Company of Indianapolis and added margarine—named Blue Bonnet after the Texas state flower—to the product line bearing the Fleischmann's brand name.

Adapted to a Health-Conscious Market

In the postwar years, the Fleischmann's brand remained popular. With the passage of the Margarine Act of 1950, which permitted the sale of yellow precolored margarine and repealed the margarine tax, margarine consumption increased dramatically. Yellow-colored margarine soon became predominant. With increased store availability for the product, new margarine manufacturers capitalized on the opportunity to expand their markets by establishing plants or acquiring existing facilities. The Standard Margarine Company, one such margarine manufacturer, was bought by Standard Brands.

Also during the 1950s, scientific studies linking diet with heart disease and other ailments began to surface, with evidence indicating that substituting polyunsaturated fatty acids for some of the more saturated fatty acids might prove beneficial in lowering the incidence of heart and vascular diseases. Ever alert for new product possibilities and mindful of medical theories on cholesterol and health, Standard Brands opened the Fleischmann Research Center in Stamford, Connecticut, in 1956.

Two years after the research center opened, Standard Brands developed the first margarine made entirely from corn oil. Fleischmann's 100% Corn Oil Margarine, in both the traditional foil-wrapped sticks and the soft variety in plastic tubs and bowls, was unconventional and innovative and the first margarine designed specifically for healthy living. Ideal for low-cholesterol and modified-fat diets, it marked a radical departure from its tropical

AT A GLANCE

Fleischmann's brand of margarine founded in 1958 by Standard Brands, Inc.; several different varieties of Fleischmann's margarine introduced in the 1960s; Standard Brands merged with Nabisco, Inc., to form Nabisco Brands, Inc., 1981; Nabisco Brands merged with R. J. Reynolds Industries, Inc., in 1986 to form RJR Nabisco, Inc., which holds Nabisco Foods Group, including Fleischmann's Division; later additions to the Fleischmann's line include Regular, Light Corn Oil Spread, Diet, Soft, Soft Sweet Unsalted, Sweet Unsalted, Squeeze, and Move Over Butter.

Performance: *Market share*—(Fleischmann's) 9.1% of margarine category; (Fleischmann's Light) 4.1% of margarine category. *Sales*—(Fleischmann's) $137.5 million; (Fleischmann's Light) $61.5 million.

Major competitor: Van den Bergh Foods' Shedd's Spread, Promise, and I Can't Believe It's Not Butter.

Advertising: *Agency*—FCB/Leber Katz Partners, New York, NY. *Major campaign*—"Fleischmann's margarines help you take control of cholesterol."

Addresses: *Parent company*—Nabisco Foods Group, 7 Campus Drive, Parsippany, NJ 07054; phone: (201) 682-5000. *Ultimate parent company*—RJR Nabisco, Inc., 1301 Avenue of the Americas, New York, NY 10019; phone: (212) 258-5600.

coconut or palm oil-based predecessors. Physicians and nutritionists immediately hailed Fleischmann's as a polyunsaturated weapon against excessive serum cholesterol. Midwestern farmers, who had at last found a market for the oil obtained from corn kernels, were also pleased.

Developed More Margarine Varieties

Over the years, as margarine received more attention and yeast diminished in popularity, Standard Brands decided to divest the Fleischmann Division of its yeast operation. As more and more government and privately funded studies linking eating with health appeared, Americans were paying increased attention to the composition of the foods they consumed. So, in the 1960s, Standard Brands took steps to make available foods that were lower in fat, salt, and artificial flavors and colors and higher in protein, vitamins, and beneficial minerals.

In keeping with the company's philosophy, more varieties of the famous Fleischmann's brand debuted in the 1960s, all sold in one-pound packages: Sweet Unsalted Fleischmann's Corn Oil Spread, in the distinctive emerald-green paraffined box, and its soft version in the plastic twin-tubbed, emerald-green cardboard sleeve, both boasting 68 percent corn oil and no salt, cholesterol, or milk, for modified-fat and sodium- and milk-free diets; Fleischmann's Light Corn Oil Spread, in quarters and in tubs, composed of 60 percent corn oil and containing 25 percent less fat, salt, and calories than margarine; Fleischmann's Extra-Light Corn Oil (in sticks and in tubs) with 50 percent less fat, salt, and calories than regular margarine; Diet Fleischmann's; and Squeeze Fleischmann's.

Because Fleischmann's was developing new varieties of margarines, sales became incremental, that is, they didn't represent merely sales stolen from other brands. And, since the Fleischmann's sales representative could offer the retailer a wider array of products than his competitors, he carried more weight with the retailer, and the retailer could, consequently, give him more time and Fleischmann's products more shelf space.

Health Issues in the 1980s and 1990s

In the 1980s Fleischmann's—which after several mergers came under the ownership of the Nabisco Foods Group, held by RJR Nabisco, Inc.—continued to thrive. It was once again confronted with public concerns about the benefits of margarine, however. Reports published in 1986 indicated that certain margarines were contaminated with trace levels of n-nitrosomorpholine (NMOR), a volatile nitrosamine that the National Toxicology Program had classified as a potential human carcinogen. What remained unclear, however, was whether NMOR occurred as a result of the testing protocol or by some commercial production technique. Canadian studies confirmed the presence of the chemical in several margarines and also identified its source as being the paper wrappers, which contained between 5 to 73 nanograms of NMOR. According to a 1986 report in the *Journal of Food and Science,* even though the core of a stick of margarine evidenced no NMOR, the outer 1 centimeter could be contaminated by as much as 14 parts per billion NMOR. Fleischmann's weathered these findings by pointing out that its margarine quarters were wrapped in foil.

In 1987 emphasis on low cholesterol and health added new interest to the margarine category. Lever Brothers' touting of Promise Margarine as being "heart smart" the previous year had triggered Fleischmann's advertising blitz. In its campaign, Fleischmann's said that its premium brand could help reduce the level of cholesterol in the body. RJR Nabisco then spent $12.7 million on its new product entries in the margarine category, with the bulk of the money directed toward the six items in its premium Fleischmann's line.

Further health issues arose in 1990, when a report by Dutch nutritionists Ronald P. Mensink and Martijn B. Katan appeared in the *New England Journal of Medicine* and drew sudden public attention to transfatty acids. Created during hydrogenation—the process of hardening liquid vegetable oils to margarine—transfatty acids were shown to have raised the blood cholesterol of healthy adults. In addition, the substances lowered HDL cholesterol, a cholesterol believed to protect the body against heart and vascular diseases. In the United States, many margarines were found to contain more transfatty acids than saturated ones. A 1985 review of the possible health effects of transfatty acids had concluded that the compounds posed no significant hazard to health, but further research was recommended.

Dutch scientists Mensink and Katan took up the challenge. Their study in the *New England Journal of Medicine* indicated that a diet high in saturated fats produced the biggest rise—18 milligrams (per deciliter)—in LDL cholesterol, the "bad" cholesterol that increased the risk of coronary disease. The diet replacing saturated fats with transfatty acids, however, caused only a 14-milligram elevation in LDL. But the researchers were surprised when they turned their focus to HDL, the "good" cholesterol; the high-trans diet had actually reduced HDL an average of 7 milligrams, a decline of 12 percent from the baseline diet. Fleischmann's countered by asserting that the Dutch studies had not accurately depicted the typical American diet, that transfatty acids in butter produced the same effect on HDL cholesterol and that margarine remained superior to butter because it contained no cholesterol at all and had a lower overall percentage of cholesterol-elevating saturated fat. Fleischmann's went on to recommend that consumers who were concerned about transfatty acids should choose a tub-type variety of Fleischmann's with liquid—not partially hydrogenated—corn oil.

Marketing Strategy

Fleischmann's has always targeted its advertising toward *all* consumers concerned with healthful eating—from young children to senior citizens. All margarines have been developed with a view to providing consumer satisfaction and promoting good dietary habits. Fleischmann's margarines' ingredients are categorized in terms of intended use, nutritional value, and health content. In addition, the manufacturers have sought to keep abreast of scientific developments in the field of nutrition and to make modifications in their products when the bulk of scientific evidence warranted them and when the alterations were permitted by governmental regulations. Believing that people have a right to know what they are eating, Fleischmann's product developers have provided nutritional and other helpful label information on the packages.

The bulk of Fleischmann's advertising has appeared with coupons in the print media, especially in color supplements to the Sunday newspapers. In addition, Fleischmann's has consistently used its marketing budget to become a force in special promotions. In 1993 it sponsored the American Medical Association's Fat/Cholesterol Education Program. Aside from the billions of impressions of the Fleischmann's name registered through television, radio, and news and magazine coverage, Fleischmann's was afforded the opportunity to engage in aggressive advertising and promotions tied in with the events.

Fleischmann's Focus for the Future

Despite its sales volume and market growth, Fleischmann's continued to search for ways to introduce new products and improve existing ones. In 1992, executives reorganized the three basic U.S. business units in the Nabisco Foods Group into six, more focused units in an attempt to define priorities. The Fleischmann's Division, one of the six new units, showcased various refrigerated products, including Egg Beaters. As physicians and scientists continued to learn about the human body and how to keep it healthy, Fleischmann's margarines planned to focus on developing innovative margarines to reflect the company's mandate of adapting to changing times and consumer priorities.

Further Reading:

Austin, Beth, "Lever Is Spreading Margarine Battles," *Advertising Age,* August 10, 1987, p. 12.

"Brand Scorecard," *Advertising Age,* January 18, 1993, p. 18.

"Butter and Margarine," *Consumer Reports,* December 1989, p. 249.

"Butter and Margarine," *Consumer Reports,* December 1990, p. 281.

"The Butter-Margarine Maze: Weighing Up Fats, Calories, Cholesterol," *Chatelaine,* September 1990, p. 145.

"Butter vs. Margarine," *Consumer Reports,* September 1989, p. 551.

Cahn, William, *Out of the Cracker Barrel: The Nabisco Story, From Animal Crackers to ZuZus,* New York: Simon & Schuster, 1969.

Callahan, Maureen, "How Butters, Margarines, and Spreads Stack Up," *Better Homes and Gardens,* April 1991, p. 49.

Clark, Paul, "The Marketing of Margarine," *European Journal of Marketing,* July 1986, p. 52.

Davis, Riccardo A., "New Spread Formation: Nabisco, Unilever Set to Roll Butter Substitutes," *Advertising Age,* August 3, 1992, p. 5.

Grayson, Melvin J., *42 Million a Day: The Story of Nabisco Brands,* East Hanover, NJ: Nabisco Brands, Inc., 1986.

Johnston, Mike, "Crisis in the Eye of the Beholder," *Marketing,* November 14, 1991, p. 15.

Laurence, Jennifer, Judann Dagnoli, Julie Liesse Erickson, and Steven W. Colford, "States Have Sights on Margarine Ads," *Advertising Age,* September 1, 1989, p. 2.

Leblang, Bonnie Tandy, "Spread Yourself Thin: The Straight Skinny on Butter, Margarine, and Cooking Oils," *American Health: Fitness of Body and Mind,* September 1991, p. 45.

"Margarine: Melting Down Distinctions Among Brands," *Mayo Clinic Nutrition Letter,* May 1990, p. 1.

"Margarine Still Comes out on Top," *Southern Living,* June 1991, p. 123.

"Nitrosamines and Margarines," *Science News,* March 1, 1986, p. 137.

Riepma, Siert F., *The Story of Margarine,* Washington, DC: The Public Affairs Press, 1970.

The RJR Nabisco 1991 Annual Report to Shareholders, Book One RJR Nabisco, Inc., 1992.

The RJR Nabisco 1991 Annual Report to Shareholders, Book Two, RJR Nabisco, Inc., 1992.

"Say It Ain't So, Oleo! Even Margarine May Be Bad for the Heart," *Time,* August 27, 1990.

"Study Spreads Concern: Does Margarine Raise Cholesterol?," *Mayo Clinic Nutrition Letter,* November 1990, p. 7.

Thomas, R. L., "Lab of the Year Promotes Creative and Efficient R & D," *Research and Development,* May 1986, p. 74.

Webb, Denise, "More Fat Facts: Butter vs. Margarine—Which Is the Better Choice?," *Weight Watchers Magazine,* February 1991, p. 19.

Williams, Mina, "Shoppers Ignore Margarine Study So Far," *Supermarket News,* August 27, 1990.

—Virginia Barnstorff

FOLGERS®

Folgers is the single largest coffee brand in the United States. Its initial product line centered on mainstream ground coffee. As coffee consumption began declining in the United States in the 1960s and 1970s and consumer tastes shifted, Folgers introduced gourmet coffees, decaffeinated coffee, and instant coffee. The Folgers product line is backed by the marketing muscle of parent company Procter & Gamble (P&G), which manufactures consumer products ranging from Ivory soap to Crest toothpaste.

Brand Origin

The Folgers brand was created in 1850 by James A. Folger, who started selling roasted and ground coffee beans to miners during the California Gold Rush. In 1859 he became a partner in a coffee and spice mill, and when it went bankrupt during the recession of 1865, Folger bought out his partner. He persuaded the firm's creditors to allow him to continue operating the business and changed the firm's name to J.A. Folger & Company.

Unlike other coffee roasters Folgers did not own any coffee plantations. Instead, it bought its coffee beans all over the world. As the brand grew in popularity, two headquarters were set up, one in San Francisco and one in Kansas City, each marketing to a different geographic area and acting like a separate company. The two companies were merged at the end of 1960. One of Folgers' highest profile commercials when it was an independent company resulted from its sponsorship of San Francisco Giants baseball games, where the announcer often said, "When I say coffee, I mean Folgers."

The Folgers brand slowly expanded eastward. In 1959, for example, it was introduced to Chicago, touching off a promotion battle with rival brands. Within six months, Folgers was the third leading brand, with 10 to 15 percent of the market, behind Hills Brothers and Maxwell House. The Chicago push, with its $500,000 ad campaign, was the largest local advertising and promotion campaign by a coffee company to that time. *Advertising Age* estimated Folgers 1959 sales to be $110 million. In early 1963 the expansion was continued into Wisconsin. Later in the year the product began coming in "the coffee can of the future," a container opened with a can opener and resealed with a plastic cover, which was promoted on television and in newspapers.

By the early 1960s Folgers was the largest independent coffee company and second-largest nonretail seller of coffee in the United States. It was the fourth-largest seller of instant coffee, and the largest seller of ground coffee west of the Rockies. Folgers was a leading brand in the South and Midwest as well. It had five plants, and 15.1 percent of total regular coffee sales in the U.S. grocery market. Folgers had 15 percent of sales of regular ground coffee and seven percent of the decaf market. Sales were about $160 million a year. Top management had decided that the family-owned company, which had grown into one of the largest independent coffee wholesalers in the United States, had reached a point where it should either go public or be sold. After a year of working out details, Folgers was sold to consumer marketing giant Procter & Gamble on November 30, 1963, for $130 million in P&G stock. It became a subsidiary of P&G, operated initially by the same management.

Purchase by Procter & Gamble

Procter & Gamble was one of the United States' largest manufacturers of detergents and soaps—its best known being Ivory soap—and was pushing into food marketing. It already produced Duncan Hines baking mixes, Jif and Big Top peanut butter, and Crisco and Fluffo vegetable oils. The purchase of Folgers attracted the attention of the U.S. Federal Trade Commission (FTC), however, which initially threatened to force P&G to sell the coffee brand. The FTC contended that P&G's size gave it unfair advantages in promoting its products, including the ability to win discounts of 30 percent or higher in its purchases of network television advertisements. In February of 1967, the FTC voted three to two to allow P&G to keep Folgers, after P&G agreed not to move into any other grocery store products through mergers for seven years, and not to buy any other coffee companies for ten years. P&G also agreed to restrictions on its promotions of Folgers, saying that it would not accept Folgers advertising discounts for five years if the discount was linked to advertisements of other P&G products. The firm also agreed to not promote Folgers in conjunction with any of its other products for five years.

P&G considered the restriction on discounts of little significance because Folgers was able to earn maximum advertising discounts through its own spending. The two dissenting commissioners felt that the consumer products giant should have been forced to divest Folgers because accepting the purchase would accelerate a trend toward domination of the coffee market by large conglomerates. The FTC noted that in the five years ending in

AT A GLANCE

Folgers brand coffee founded in 1850 in San Francisco by James A. Folger; brand bought by Proctor & Gamble in 1963.

Performance: *Market share*—22.7% (top share) of regular ground coffee market. *Sales*—$1.13 billion.

Major competitor: General Foods Inc.'s Maxwell House.

Advertising: *Agency*—N. W. Ayer, New York, NY. *Major campaign*—"The best part of wakin' up is Folger's in your cup."

Addresses: *Parent company*—Proctor & Gamble Company, One Proctor & Gamble Plaza, Cincinnati, OH 45202-3314; phone: (513) 983-1100; fax: (513) 562-4500.

1962, the combined share of the top five nonretailer coffee companies climbed to 62.9 percent from 48.1 percent. They also worried that competition would be injured because P&G would have advantages in buying green coffee and getting financing for Folgers.

Market Expansion

Procter & Gamble began pushing Folgers east of the Mississippi, where it still had limited presence. The firm rejuvenated Folgers advertising, switching to the New York advertising agency Cunningham and Walsh, which had formerly been in charge of the brand's advertising east of the Rockies. The campaign featured the fictional Mrs. Olson, who was soon to be inextricably associated with Folgers by many consumers. Played by actress Virginia Christine, Mrs. Olson offered testimonials about Folgers qualities, delivering them as if speaking to members of her own family.

Folgers' perennial rival was Maxwell House, owned by General Foods. In 1972 the two coffees faced off in Cleveland when Folgers was introduced there. In 1973 Folgers was introduced to Philadelphia with a 23-week campaign that included television ads, coupons, and door-to-door samples of six-ounce jars. Folgers had 20.4 percent of the U.S. market compared with 24.3 percent for Maxwell House in the regular coffee market, while Folgers had 6.8 percent of the instant market, down from 7.3 percent in 1971.

Coffee itself was becoming less popular as consumers turned to cold sweet beverages such as soft drinks. In 1974, 32.8 percent of U.S. consumers drank coffee, down from 75 percent in 1962. With declining overall coffee consumption in the background, the price of coffee began a period of fluctuation in the mid-1970s, largely because of poor harvests in Brazil, the world's largest coffee grower. In 1975 Brazil's coffee crop was severely damaged by frost, while civil war in Angola interfered with that country's coffee crop. The price of unroasted beans soared from 70 cents a pound in July 1975 to $3.33 a pound in April 1977. Things got so bad by the end of the decade that Folgers raised prices four times in the first three months of 1979. After the fourth raise, of 25 cents, the list price of Folgers coffee was a record $4.43 a pound, up $1.35 in three months. While prices subsequently dropped, the price surge drove many consumers away from coffee. Folgers followed rival Maxwell House in introducing a "high-yield" coffee in a 13-ounce can as one way of holding onto price-conscious customers.

The price rises came at a bad time for Folgers, right in the midst of its push into the eastern markets, and it was forced to delay an all-out push. As a result of the 1977 price rise, Folgers lost $55 million. But when the price of beans finally fell, Folgers retail price followed at a slower rate, and the resulting profits helped Folgers finance its push into the East. In 1978 Folgers began a major battle with chief rival Maxwell House. P&G had years of experience in promoting brands and moving them into new markets, and it used its usual arsenal of heavy television advertising and consumer discounts to push Folgers. Folgers gained throughout the East, with the exception of New York City, where coffee drinkers preferred stronger blends of coffee. Folgers was promoted heavily, using discounts and a huge coupon mailing, but captured only eight percent of the New York market. In Boston, Baltimore, Atlanta, Jacksonville, Florida, and other large markets, Folgers captured more than ten percent of the market. The *New York Times* reported that Folgers was spending $1.5 million a month on advertising throughout its eastern expansion area, and increased its share of the $3 billion U.S. ground coffee market to 27 percent by 1979. These gains were often at the expense of small local coffee-roasting companies.

General Foods, maker of Maxwell House, fought hard against the Folgers expansion, countering the brand's discounts and coupons with its own. In Wilkes-Barre, Pennsylvania, General Foods introduced a brand called Horizon that was packaged in a can the FTC thought looked suspiciously like a Folgers can.

Decaffeinated Coffee

The decaffeinated coffee market grew rapidly in the late 1970s and early 1980s as consumers worried about the effects of caffeine. Folgers was lagging behind in this volatile market, particularly in the market for instant decaffeinated coffee, and sought to make up ground in 1984 when it launched Folgers decaffeinated instant without any of the usual test marketing. P&G was generally moving to introduce products faster and had released other products with little or no test marketing. General Foods and Nestlé had introduced decaffeinated instants in 1983—General Foods with decaffeinated versions of Maxwell House and Yuban, and Nestle with a decaffeinated Nescafe.

The ads for Folgers decaf pushed taste rather than the lifestyle theme that had been used in many commercials for decaffeinated coffee. The ads emphasized that the new decaffeinated coffee had all the taste of regular Folgers, lacking only the caffeine. The decaf line was introduced with a national television and coupon newspaper ad campaign handled by the advertising firm Cunningham and Walsh and costing between $15 and $20 million.

P&G further revamped Folgers by switching to a new package and dropping the twenty-year-old ad campaign featuring Mrs. Olson. The new campaign used a slice-of-life approach centering on a ranching family, rather than a spokesperson. The new package featured a larger "mountain-grown" label and copy about Folgers' aroma and flavor. Folgers performance had been mediocre, with its share of the ground roast market slipping from 27.3 percent in 1979 to 24.9 percent in 1983. Some analysts felt that the elderly Mrs. Olson was not the most effective way to reach younger consumers, the age bracket least interested in coffee but most important for future sales. The Cunningham and Walsh advertisement, called "Wakin' up," began with a shot of a horse in a field on a sunny morning, and moved to a picture of the repackaged Folgers.

Product Changes

In the mid-1980s a bad harvest in Brazil again caused coffee prices to rise. This time Folgers rolled out a new product to fight price rises. Folgers Special Roast flaked coffee used a new fast-roasting technology to get more coffee from less bean. Special Roast came in a 11.5-ounce can that was said to produce as much brewed coffee as a one-pound can, but cost a dollar less. Over the next two years other manufacturers, unable to match Folgers' prices, also switched to 13-ounce cans of fast roast coffee. Some industry observers felt the scheme would hurt the coffee industry in the long run, asserting that high-yield coffees do not taste as good as regular coffee.

Such criticism did not slow Folgers. A coupon campaign was run that reached 55 percent of U.S. households. The coupons offered 40 cents off Folgers and 35 cents off a low-calorie sweetener P&G had just acquired. P&G spent heavily on Folgers advertising, putting in $31.3 million for the nine months before March 1986, compared with $20.2 million for the same nine-month period a year earlier. Many other coffee brands also spent heavily on coupons to keep consumers buying.

In April of 1987 Folgers entered the premium-coffee market, the fastest growing segment of the coffee industry, along with decaffeinated. Archrival General Foods had already built a presence in the premium-coffee market with Yuban and Maxwell House Private Collection. Industry observers felt that Folgers Colombian Supreme was geared to compete with Yuban, which had a three percent national share and an 18 percent share on the West Coast. Advertising for the new line was handled by the New York-based Wells, Rich, Greene, and *Advertising Age* reported that about $1 million was spent on producing the initial television commercials.

A total of $298 million was spent on Folgers advertising between 1977 and 1987, including $151 million on network television, $141 million on local television, $3.6 million on radio, and $1.1 million on magazines. This figure was second among P&G brands to Crest toothpaste's $318 million. Folgers advertising came to $38.8 million for 1986 alone.

Wholesale coffee prices were erratic throughout the mid-1980s, reaching five dollars a pound in 1986, then falling to less than two dollars a pound in early 1987. When U.S. import quotas were reestablished later that year prices reached $2.87 a pound. In the meantime, consumers continued to move from coffee toward soft drinks, with the total coffee market falling by nearly 19 percent in 1987. These factors hurt the profitability of Maxwell House, and ad spending on that brand was slashed. P&G decided to take advantage by pushing Folgers hard, spending $33 million on advertising in 1987, using the New York firm N. W. Ayer, the successor to Cunningham & Walsh. By 1989 the market share of regular Maxwell House had fallen to 16 percent, versus 23 percent for regular Folgers. Decaffeinated Folgers held a 4.2 percent share and Folgers flakes had 5.0 percent. Per capita coffee consumption in the United States continued to decline, but a growing emphasis on premium coffees increased overall sales of coffee four percent, to $2.7 billion.

In late 1989, Folgers introduced another premium blend, Folgers Gourmet Supreme, a mixture of Arabica and Colombian beans. The total cost of the introductory television and print campaign was put at $10 to $15 million and was handled by N.W. Ayer. The product was seen as a response to Maxwell House, which dominated the gourmet coffee market, which stood at $600 million in 1988, or about eight percent of the $6.3 billion coffee market. Gourmet Supreme was packaged in black cans with gold lettering and was sold in 16 varieties. It came in three can sizes for both regular and decaffeinated as well as a brick pack.

In 1990 Folgers was hit by a boycott over its use of beans from civil-war-ravaged El Salvador. P&G said that only two percent of its beans came from El Salvador, but created still more controversy when it pulled ads of all P&G products from a Boston television station that aired a commercial by the boycott sponsors, Neighbor to Neighbor. Also in 1990, Maxwell House renewed the ten-year market-share battle with Folgers, introducing new products including pre-made coffee in refrigerator cartons. Advertising for all General Food's coffees was increased to $100 million a year, and Folgers increased spending to keep pace. The war between Folgers and General Foods had cost both of them money, as prices were constantly cut and coupons constantly issued. Meanwhile, consumers were calling for better coffee, and Folgers was reformulated to include a higher percentage of better beans.

P&G also moved on another front, offering Folgers in a teabag-like package that made individual cups of coffee. Folgers Singles, which came in regular and decaffeinated versions, had been introduced in Boston in 1988, but were not offered widely until late 1990. Folgers became the first major coffee brand to be sold in a coffee bag in the United States. Analysts believed the bag allowed Folgers to become less of a commodity and more of a convenience product, allowing premium prices to be charged for it, and differentiating it from the competition.

Further Reading:

Dagnoli, Judann, "Fast Roast Turns into Weighty Issue," *Advertising Age,* October 3, 1988, p. S3.

"Folger Buy Puts P&G into Coffee Marketing," *Advertising Age,* September 3, 1963, p. 1.

"Folgers Solidifies Gains in Chicago Invasion," *Advertising Age,* August 10, 1959, p. 3.

"FTC Pact Lets P&G Keep Folger," *Advertising Age,* February 27, 1967, p. 1.

Jervey, Gay, "Folgers Perks Minus Mrs. Olson," *Advertising Age,* September 27, 1984, p. 2.

Jervey, Gay, "P&G Rushes Folgers to Perky Decaf Field," *Advertising Age,* August 23, 1984, p. 2.

Lawrence, Jennifer, "Folgers Puts Coffee in the Bag," *Advertising Age,* January 21, 1991, p. 3.

Luxenberg, Stan, "Folgers Scores in the Coffee Wars," *New York Times,* January 28, 1979, p. Fl.

"Proctor & Gamble Adds Coffee Line," *New York Times,* August 23, 1963, p. 1.

Proctor & Gamble: The House that Ivory Built, Chicago: NTC Business Books, 1988.

Saporito, Bill, "Can Anyone Win the Coffee War?" *Forbes,* May 21, 1990, p. 99.

Winters, Patricia, "New High-Yield Folgers Battles Coffee Price Rise," *Advertising Age,* March 17, 1986, p. 1.

—*Scott M. Lewis*

FRENCH'S®

Guided by the unusual notion in 1904 that "mustard must be mild," French brothers Francis and George discovered in their novel mild and creamy "yellow" mustard a product that caught on like wildfire. That product, French's mustard, has remained the best-selling mustard in America to this day. Over the years, the line of mustards offered under the brand name has expanded, the product has been presented in a variety of advertising campaigns, the parent company has been sold and merged and then resold once again, and competition has recently grown fierce. Still, the allure of the original mild, bright yellow mustard has kept customers buying and has brought to all of French's mustards a brand loyalty that has positioned the line as the clear leader in overall mustard sales. Today, French's Mustard—owned by Durkee-French Foods, a division of Reckitt & Colman PLC—is also available in additional flavors, including Sweet Onion, Horseradish, Bold'n Spicy, Dijon, and Creamy Spread.

Brand Origins and First Commercial Success

The R. T. French Company had not begun by selling prepared mustard. The company was created in 1880 in Ithaca, New York, when Robert Timothy French ceased working as a salesman for a New York City wholesaler of coffee, tea, and spices and began his own company. Robert Timothy French's two sons, George and Francis, joined him and the company moved in 1883 to Rochester, New York, where it produced a variety of products ranging from spices to bird seed.

When the French brothers brought out their new kind of mustard in 1904, it represented an innovation in mustard packaging and dramatically shifted the way Americans thought about mustard. In their book, *Entrepreneurs: The Men and Women behind Famous Brand Names and How They Made It,* Joseph J. and Suzy Fucini recount that Americans thought of mustard as a spice that was typically "hotter-than-fire." Francis French noticed in 1904 that mustards were used only sparingly and that "people did not like them." He and his brother then decided to design a mustard that people would enjoy. They prepared a bright yellow, lighter and creamier mustard called "French's Cream Salad Mustard" and made it available for 10 cents per nine-ounce jar. They introduced it with the hot dog at the St. Louis World's Fair in 1904 and met with instant commercial success. By 1912, the French Company built a new plant in Rochester, New York, devoted to mustard production and a second one ten years later to keep up with growing consumer demand.

The French brothers combined their mild mustard product with an innovation in mustard packaging—a ready-to-eat mustard pre-prepared in a jar. Before then, the most convenient form available was a powder that would then need to be mixed with vinegar or water to obtain the final product. This method was pioneered by Mrs. Clements early in the eighteenth century, when she invented mustard powder in Durham, England. When she died, however, she took her recipe for Durham mustard with her to the grave. Not until the early nineteenth century had someone else begun to make mustard powder. In Norwich, England, Jeremiah Colman began

blending into a powder the finest quality yellow and black mustard seeds after hulling and milling them in substantial quantities. He then exported his mustard powder around the world. It was not until the turn of the twentieth century that a still more convenient form of mustard was introduced by the French brothers, featuring as well their more broadly popular mild mustard taste.

Marketing Strategies

The French Company promoted its mustard in the ensuing decades by three primary tacks. It strove to convince Americans of the high quality and pleasing taste of its product, to teach Americans the many possible uses for mustard, and to achieve brand name recognition and loyalty. In short, the French Company strove to create desire for its mustard brand.

Distinct packaging brought French's Mustard brand name recognition from its introduction in 1904. By providing their mustard already prepared in a jar, the French Company participated early in what social historian Daniel J. Boorstin calls "the packaging revolution" in his book *The Americans: The Democratic Experience.* "As late as 1920," Boorstin wrote, "few of the housewife's purchases were packaged." Brand names generally accompanied packaged goods and not unpackaged ones. Then with the rapid proliferation of prepackaged goods with brand names over the next few decades came the rise of the self-serve grocery store and unprecedented national advertising campaigns for its products. The package connected the product to its brand name and the corresponding advertising campaign. The French Company introduced its mustard in 1904 packaged in a jar complete with its brand name; in 1915, the company adopted the French's Pennant as its official logo—a move that differentiated the product on the shelves through a visual symbol as well as a brand name. Finally in 1921, the company invested in its first official advertising campaign. The product on the shelf could now be identified—through its packaging, brand name, and logo—with its own advertising campaign.

The French Company had used other means of advertising earlier, however, and would continue to do so even after beginning official advertising campaigns. For instance, the company made use of any official recognitions of its product's quality. According to the French Company's timeline, the company "formulated the national standards of purity and labeling of spices in interstate commerce upon the signing of the Pure Food and Drug Act" in 1906. In his book *Revolution at the Table: The Transformation of the American Diet,* Harvey A. Levenstein describes the impact of the 1906 Pure Food and Drug Act on the U.S. consumer and food industry. The government stamp of approval arising from the new regulations mitigated widespread concerns over the safety of canned and bottled products and made it more difficult for smaller, more local manufacturers to gain market share by cutting costs through the use of dangerous preserving chemicals or inferior food ingredients. The implications for French's mustard follow from Levenstein's industry-wide observations and explain how the company stood to benefit from higher standards and more detailed

AT A GLANCE

French's brand mustard developed in 1904 in Rochester, NY, by Francis and George French of the R. T. French Company; bought in 1926 by Reckitt & Colman Ltd., now Reckitt & Colman PLC; merged in the late 1980s with Durkee Famous Foods, creating the Durkee-French Foods division of Reckitt & Colman; split from a number of Durkee-French Foods brands when the Durkee trademark and some French's spices—but not French's Mustard—were sold to Burns, Philp & Company Limited in 1992.

Performance: *Market share*—33% (top share) of mustard category. *Sales*—$70.88 million.

Major competitor: Nabisco Foods Group's Grey Poupon brand.

Advertising: *Agency*—Ketchum Advertising, New York, NY. *Major campaign*—Talking sandwiches express their preference for French's, "America's favorite mustard."

Addresses: *Parent company*—Durkee-French Foods, P.O. Box 942, Wayen, NJ, 07470; phone: (201) 633-6800; fax: (201) 633-3633. *Ultimate parent company*—Reckitt & Colman PLC, One Burlington Lane, London W4 2RW, United Kingdom; phone: (01) 994-6464.

labeling. French's mustard assured greater brand name loyalty by placing the government seal of approval directly on its bottles and thus could solidify its initial mastery of the new mustard market against any potential competitors. Displaying that government seal would connect the French brand name and mustard product with the national news of higher standards; French's mustard bottles instilled trust in the quality of the mustard within. Even in 1964, after another French Company landmark advertising campaign, the company still aimed at garnering brand name recognition, trust, and loyalty through official recognitions of the quality of its mustard. In 1964, the French Company returned to the World Fair, this time held in New York, to make a "guest appearance" as "the official mustard," according to the French Company's timeline.

Throughout the years, the French Company combined major advertising campaigns to foster brand name recognition with efforts to increase the number of ways consumers would think to use their mustard. When the French Company introduced its mustard on a hotdog at the St. Louis World's Fair in 1904 it coupled the two products together indefinitely. In 1924, French's launched a major effort to suggest new uses. It established the Housewives' Service Department, headed by a succession of home economists, for the sole purpose of suggesting new uses of mustard and other French Company products. When combined with major advertising campaigns, these uses would connect to the brand name as well as to mustard generally. The company continued to accompany direct marketing efforts with major advertising campaigns. The most notable campaign was the promotion in 1939 of "Hot Dog Dan the Mustard Man" to "something of a folk hero's status in his time," according to the French Company's timeline. A whimsical character first imagined by French's advertising manager, Hot Dog Dan formed the centerpiece of the company's advertising and promotions at the time. An advertising campaign launched in 1989 stressed both brand name recognition and one possible use of the mustard. The French Company collaborated with J & J Snack Foods to promote their pretzels and mustard

together. This advertising campaign drew once again on French's historic marketing strategy—to combine drives for brand name recognition with specific product uses.

Shifting Parent Companies

Ironically, the French Company, which had invented the mass production and distribution of bottled mustard as opposed to mustard powder, was bought by the British company that had been producing mustard powder. The J & J Colman Company began producing powdered mustard in 1814 and expanded in 1903 with the purchase of Keen, Robinson and Company, a food company that had been in existence since 1742. In 1938, J & J Colman merged with Reckitt & Sons to form Reckitt & Colman Ltd. as the culmination of many years of efforts at collaboration. Part of those earlier efforts included acting together in all of their overseas business. As a result of those earlier collaborations before they merged, the company that would become Reckitt & Colman bought the French Company in 1926 for $3.8 million.

In 1986, Reckitt & Colman bought the U.S. food producer Durkee Famous Foods and subsequently merged French and Durkee into one division, Durkee-French Foods. Similar to the French Company, Durkee Spices and Famous Sauce was an upstate New York company that premiered probably the world's first commercially packaged salad dressing, Durkee's Famous Sauce. Today, Durkee-French Foods produces spices, mustards, sauces, and gravy.

In July, 1989, Reckitt & Colman began a major restructuring to prepare for the European Community market unification. They intended to discontinue a number of lesser brands to seek a more unified identity throughout Europe. Perhaps as a part of this restructuring, they withdrew from the U.S. spice business, selling that part of Durkee-French Foods to Burns, Philp & Company Limited of Australia, for $86 million in early 1992. Burns Philp bought the Durkee name but granted the license to Reckitt & Colman to continue using the Durkee name on some products. Likewise, Reckitt & Colman retained ownership of the French's trademark, but granted Burns Philp the license to use the brand name on some of French's spices, which had been sold to Burns Philp. French's mustard, therefore, has been separated from most of the herbs, spices, and sauces previously produced from the Durkee-French Foods division.

The implications of this reorganization on the future performance of French's Mustard are as yet unclear. As a result of this withdrawal from the U.S. spice business, Reckitt & Colman assumed a 9.1 million pound trading loss, according to a September 1992 company report. Information about any changes for French's mustard at Reckitt & Colman have not yet been released.

Recent Product Development and Future Growth

Reckitt & Colman focused development efforts on French's mustard in order to increase its sales, marketability, and market share. In the 1970s and early 1980s, Reckitt & Colman enacted a planned program of expansion that included the streamlining of the company and the development of innovative products. French's mustard was one of those products. In 1971, the French Company introduced their new Sweet Onion mustard. Over the next two decades, four more kinds of mustard were developed and introduced: in 1973, French's Horseradish mustard; in 1982, French's Bold'n Spicy; in 1983, French's Dijon; and in 1990,

French's Creamy Spread mustard, an all natural, no cholesterol, low fat mustard.

This product development has contributed to French's ongoing success in an industry that has grown more competitive as it has grown larger. French's mustard was a commercial success from the start and has remained in a clear leadership position in the U.S. mustard market. Production leaped ahead in the first few decades after its 1904 introduction and grew through major advertising campaigns and product development. In 1980, when the French Company celebrated its centennial, it sold 500,000 jars of mustard each day. In February, 1992, *Advertising Age* reported French's as the clear leader of the $214.8 million mustard category with a 33 percent market share, followed by Nabisco Food Group's Grey Poupon with 17.9 percent and American Home Food Products' Gulden's with 9 percent.

Competition has grown fierce, however, and although French's leads the overall category, it has failed to gain significant headway in some of the subdivisions. In the specialty mustards segment, which accounts for $87.9 million of the mustard category, French's has failed to gain a significant percentage. In this segment, Grey Poupon leads with a 43 percent share, whereas French's creamy mustard line, launched in 1991, has gained no more than 5 percent. French's might benefit from new Food and Drug Administration proposals requiring nutritional labeling on condiments, but the labeling has so far failed to shift consumer tastes drastically. Competition in this specialty mustards segment grew more sharply in 1992, when CPC International began a foray into the segment with its well-known brands Hellmann's and Best Foods. The CPC International mustard was called Dijonnaise and targeted Grey Poupon as its major opponent. This increased competition will render capturing a segment of the specialty mustard segment more difficult for French's.

French's Mustard prepares itself for the challenge of heightened competition in the 1990s. A 1990 advertising campaign designed by Ketchum Advertising in New York emphasized the broad and ongoing popularity of French's Mustard—"America's favorite mustard"—while shedding a fresh light on the product. The ad featured the memorable image of talking sandwiches asking for French's Mustard for seasoning. With strong advertising campaigns focusing on French's current sales leadership, French's may maintain its lead. However, the effect of the reorganization within Reckitt & Colman on the brand's future performance is yet unknown.

Further Reading:

Blair, B., and others, in Bell Lawrie White & Co., Ltd., "Reckitt & Colman—Company Report," Infotrac General Business File: Thomson Financial Networks Inc., September 9, 1992.

Boorstin, Daniel J., *The Americans: The Democratic Experience,* New York: Random House, 1973, p. 443.

Burns, Philp & Company, Ltd., *Annual Report,* June 30, 1992, p. 39.

"French (RT) and J & J Snack Foods Co-launching Cross-promotion for Pretzels/Mustard," *U.S. Distribution Journal Buyers Guide,* February, 1989, p. 53.

"French's Creamy Spread Mustard Is All Natural, No Cholesterol, Low Fat," *Lookout* (Foods Edition), June 25, 1991, p. 095F9.

Fucini, Joseph J. and Suzy, *Entrepreneurs: The Men and Women behind Famous Brand Names and How They Made It,* Boston: G.K. Hall & Co., 1985, p. 196.

"Hold the Mayo, CPC Has Mustard," *Advertising Age,* February 3, 1992, p. 34.

"In the Beginning . . . There Was Mustard: An Anecdotal History and Historic Timeline," Wayne, NJ: Reckitt & Colman Inc., 1993.

Levenstein, Harvey A., *Revolution at the Table: The Transformation of the American Diet,* New York: Oxford University Press, 1988, pp. 38-41.

New York Times, January 25, 1992, p. 39(L).

Papazian, Ruth, "Condiments: Are Healthy Times Ahead?," *Supermarket Business,* December 1990, pp. 73-74, 78.

Roux, G., in McIntosh & Company, "Burns Philp—Company Report," Infotrac General Business File: Thomson Financial Networks Inc., September 10, 1992.

Wall Street Journal, November 30, 1992, p. C13(E).

—Nicholas Patti

FRISKIES®

Friskies

The Carnation Company, often associated with evaporated milk and instant hot chocolate, had the distinction of being the first company in the world to manufacture a food specifically for cats. While dog food was obtainable as early as the First World War, food especially for cats was unavailable until Carnation introduced the simple dry cat food in the late 1950s. So popular was the product that other companies quickly jumped on the cat food bandwagon, and Carnation eventually became the second largest pet food manufacturer in the world. Since its introduction, cat food has steadily outstripped dog food in sales, and is available in a multitude of varieties. With more than a billion dollars in cat food sales at stake, nothing is too good for the furry felines. Friskies, meanwhile, is no longer marketed by Carnation, which was acquired by Nestlé S.A. in 1985 and dissolved six years later, but by the Friskies PetCare Company, successor to the former Carnation pet food division.

Brand Origins

By the time the first Friskies cat food came on the market in 1958, Carnation had been in business for nearly 60 years. The manufacture of cat food was really an outgrowth of Carnation's successful dog food processing enterprise, in which it had been a pioneer in the 1930s. Carnation's first experience with animal feed coincided with the acquisition of its first subsidiary in 1929. The Albers Bros. Milling Company had been in the grain business, especially feed grains. The company had the reputation of being a product innovator and a pioneer in the processing of nutritional feed for animals.

As a subsidiary of Carnation, the Albers company proceeded to develop the first nationally marketed dry dog food, dubbed Friskies, in 1936. At the end of the Second World War the time seemed propitious for the introduction of the world's first cat food. Felines were outstripping the number of dogs in the country, the belt tightening days of the Depression and the war—when canned dog food was taken off the market because of metal shortages—were over, and the popularity of convenience foods of all kinds had set in with a vengeance by the 1950s. In the early part of that decade, as an outgrowth of product development, Carnation's research and development specialists turned out a special pet food that could be fed to small dogs, puppies, and finally, cats.

It was soon discovered that cats disliked the new "puppy food," and therefore the product continued to cater to the canine population. Nevertheless, when a sales manager at Carnation suggested that the company develop a special food for cats, he was regarded as eccentric. He persisted, however, claiming he had "talked to too many ladies with cats," until he finally obtained grudging approval for a modest venture into the cat food business—the world's first.

After coming to an agreement with a fish canning firm in Newport Beach, California, the first Friskies dry cat food was in the works. The food consisted of the fresh mackerel byproducts provided by the fish plant, along with cereals, some vegetables, and vitamins. A trial sale was conducted in the western states in 1956, and Carnation executives were astounded at its success, given that overall pet food sales in the mid-1950s were flat. Other flavors soon followed, as well as new cat food ideas.

Early Marketing Strategy

The concept of "test marketing" Friskies cat food was central to Carnation's early marketing strategy. When the food was introduced in 1956, it was marketed first in the western states, perhaps because it was most cost effective—Carnation's world headquarters were located in Los Angeles—and because marketing executives at the company were convinced that westerners were most amenable to new product ideas.

The Carnation Company had been a seasoned, sophisticated user of advertising for many decades by the time the world's first cat food came on the scene. Friskies cat food was first marketed when television could be used as an advertising medium, as was radio. Product surveys were also conducted, mainly of housewives—as the result of one such survey, "Little Friskies for Cats" came on the market. For many years the bright smiling face of a cartoon cat graced every box and can of Friskies as an easily identifiable logo. Sunday newspaper supplements were apt to contain full page ads featuring a plump cat, always licking its chops, with a paw protectively holding down a can of Friskies.

Not content with mere TV and radio advertising, in 1955 Carnation established a public relations department in an effort to intensify its publicity of pet food products. The high profile department published a well regarded *Friskies Research Digest* for professional veterinarians and animal breeders, which discreetly advertised continuing and new products. In addition, the paperback books *The Dog You Care For* and *The Cat You Care For,*

AT A GLANCE

Friskies brand of cat food was first manufactured by the Carnation Company in the mid-1950s; in 1985, Carnation was acquired by Nestlé S.A. of Vevey, Switzerland, and became Nestlé/Carnation Food Company; 1991, Nestlé USA formed as a wholly owned subsidiary of Nestlé S.A.; 1992, Friskies pet food division established separately as Nestlé USA subsidiary Friskies PetCare Company, Inc.

Performance: *Market share*—13% (Friskies dry cat food). *Sales*—$114.9 million (Friskies dry cat food).

Advertising: *Agency*—A number of agencies for different Friskies products, including McCann-Erickson Worldwide, Los Angeles, CA since 1992. *Major campaign*—(For canned cat food) "Good Taste Is Easy to Recognize!"

Major competitor: Kal Kan brand pet food; also Ralston Purina and Heinz.

Adresses: *Parent company*—Friskies PetCare Company, Inc., 800 North Brand Boulevard, Glendale, CA 91203; phone: (818) 549-6000; fax: (818) 549-6952. *Ultimate parent company*—Nestlé USA Inc. (address same as above). *Ultimate ultimate parent company*—Nestlé S.A.

were made available to the general public. This did more to raise the prestige of Friskies' products than mass media advertising.

Initially there was trepidation concerning the East Coast's receptivity to cat food, especially New York's. When canned cat "treats" were first test marketed in 1958, they sold well in the West but failed dismally in the East. However, when this product was reformulated as an all meat cat food called "Buffet," it was test marketed first in New York. Expecting at most a modest demand for the new pet food, only 45,000 cases of Buffet were shipped. In a short time this consignment had to be tripled. Buffet's success was phenomenal, setting the stage for the national distribution of Friskies Buffet canned cat food.

Product Development

Carnation was acquired by Nestlé S.A., a huge Swiss food producer, in 1985, later becoming part of Nestlé's wholly owned subsidiary, Nestlé USA, formed in 1991. The consolidation of pet foods into a separate company, Friskies PetCare Company, Inc., took place in 1992. Currently the second largest manufacturer of pet foods in the United States, the company has worked to constantly formulate new products and establish overseas markets in order to achieve and maintain that status.

With the phenomenal success of its initial cat food product, the Carnation Company focused research and development efforts on studying the dietary habits of cats. Unlike dogs, cats have an uncanny ability to distinguish a multitude of flavors. Cats also proved unreceptive to sweets, which dogs loved. These factors led to the development of a series of new cat food products that captured the nuances of taste that cats loved.

The highly successful Friskies Buffet was introduced in the 1960s, at a time when the cat population was exploding and cat food was reaping greater sales than dog food. The selection of the name was critical to the identity of the product, indicating that the canned cat food was not only flavorful but also of high quality. It became the number one seller in cat food on the market.

Product development in the 1970s reflected the overall trend in the pet food industry, to which Carnation was no exception. Dog and cat foods increasingly catered to the emotional and psychological needs of the pet owner, rather than to the basic dietary needs of pets. Such highly popular cat food products as Friskies Bright Eyes—the first in the line of "gourmet" cat foods—introduced in the early 1970s, reflected this trend.

Chef's Blend, launched in the late 1970s, was touted as a multi-flavored dry cat food, and was soon followed by Fancy Feast canned cat food. In 1988 Friskies dry kitten formula was introduced, the first cat food specifically for kittens, made more attractive by unique packaging. Predictably, this was followed a year later by Friskies canned kitten formula. Fresh Catch canned cat food, marketed in the early 1990s, was the only "all fish" cat food on the market.

Convenient packaging, a multitude of flavors, and above all, a wide range of choices enabled Carnation—and later, Friskies Pet-Care Company—to be a major player in the fiercely competitive world of pet foods. There were more households in the United States with pets than with children, and four times more pet food is sold in supermarkets than baby food. The importance of this lucrative market cannot be understated.

International Markets and Future Growth

By the time Friskies cat food was developed, Carnation already had an international distribution network for its chiefly dairy food products. In 1966, however, Carnation International was formed to market the company's pet foods. Canada and Australia, which had an especially high pet population and few pet food alternatives, became Friskies' most important international markets. With the rise in the standard of living and the increasing number of pet owners in Japan, that country, too, has become an important market for Friskies cat and dog food products. In the 1970s strenuous efforts were made to promote Friskies products in France and England, with considerable success. Spain and Italy also register large market shares for Friskies pet foods.

During the early 1990s, with more than 400 varieties of pet food, the domestic pet food market reached a virtual saturation point. Competition among the half dozen giant pet food manufacturers, which produce over 80 percent of today's pet food, has become increasingly intense, causing a steady growth in the importance of international markets. The manufacture of pet food is almost entirely an American industry, and while competition may be fierce at home, there are not, as for so many other products, foreign competitors, signalling great possibilities overseas. As a subsidiary of Nestlé, S.A., Friskies PetCare has the advantage of distribution networks in virtually every country on earth.

Long term political stability and a steady increase in economic prosperity are the chief ingredients for a pet food's success. Fifty years ago cat food would have struck most Japanese as bizarre. Nowadays, Japan is an increasingly important pet food market. A decade ago, pets were banned in China. Ten years from now, Friskies may be feeding a billion Chinese cats and kittens.

Further Reading:

Advertising Age, September 6, 1991, p. 43.

Bird, Laura. "Iams and Hill's Wage a High Fibre, Low-Cal War against Ralston Purina and Carnation," *AdWeek's Marketing Week,* October 1, 1990, p. 20.

''The Friskiest Cat in America Contest: Carnation Company,'' *AdWeek's Marketing Week,* November 14, 1988, p. 20.

Fucini, J.J. & S.F., *Entrepreneurs; the Men and Women behind Famous Brand Names and How They Made It,* Boston: Holt & Co., 1985.

Hackett, R., *The Pet Food Industry, an Economic, Marketing and Financial Investigation,* New York: Morton Research, 1977.

Hambleton, Ronald, *The Branding of America,* Dublin, NY: Yankee Books, 1987.

Kroll, Dorothy, *The Pet Industry,* Norwalk, CT, 1989.

Nestlé S.A. Annual Report, Vevey, Switzerland: Nestlé, S.A., 1991.

Nestlé USA, Inc. Annual Report, Glendale, CA: Nestlé USA, Inc., 1991.

Rothein, P., *The Pet Industry, New Developments in Food & Health Products,* Stamford, CT, 1985.

Schifrin, Matthew, ''Mom's Cooking Was Never Like This (Superpremium Pet Foods),'' *Forbes,* August 19, 1991.

Weaver, John D., *Carnation, the First Fifty Years, 1899-1974,* Los Angeles, 1974.

—Sina Dubovoj

FRITOS®

Fritos brand corn chips represent one of the cornerstones that helped build Frito-Lay, Inc., into a multi-billion-dollar empire that produces an ever-increasing variety of a corn-based salty snacks as well as many varieties of potato chips. The story of Fritos brand corn chips begins in 1932 when a Texan named Elmer Doolin bought a corn-chip recipe and a seven-store delivery route from a local Mexican-American in San Antonio for $100 and began preparing the chips in his mother's kitchen. At that time, "fritos" were already well-known in the Southwest as a fried corn meal snack (the word "frito" means fried in Spanish). Cooks would cut flattened corn dough into ribbons, and then season and fry them.

Around 1933, Doolin moved his company to Dallas, and soon hired a sales force to make regular deliveries to stores; in addition, under licensed agreements, he handled the products of potato chip manufacturers. Doolin's enterprise prospered, and, by the 1940s, he was buying color advertisements in magazines like *Ladies Home Journal* and *Better Homes & Gardens,* and selling Fritos brand franchises. In the 1950s he stepped up his national advertising, bringing out the "Munch a Bunch of Fritos" campaign.

In 1961, two years after Doolin's death, H. W. Lay & Company, a potato chip manufacturer owned by Herman Lay, and the Frito Company merged—a move that would improve Fritos' already-rising fortunes. Lay had been a Fritos franchise holder, and his company had become famous for its ability to carefully develop and utilize sales routes. His salespeople were among the first to stock the merchandise for the store owner and set up point-of-purchase displays. He relied on careful training for both salespeople and their managers.

After the merger, the Lay company began to dominate within the organization's ranks, and its finely tuned store-door delivery system was put into effect for Fritos corn chips and other products. A long-time Lay consultant, Colin Warwick, told *Advertising Age* in a 1979 interview that the merger could best be seen as "Lay Co. manpower marrying the Frito Co. money."

An Improved Delivery System

The "store-door" delivery system was a tool for increasing revenues, and its effectiveness seems to have been related to the system's ability to "work" a particular sales territory intensely. In Washington, D.C., at about the time of the merger, the Lay company found that it could increase revenues simply by adding 5 trucks to an area normally covered by 15. The move did not dilute the amount of business per truck.

This delivery system, as part of the Frito-Lay arsenal, would be the bane of competitors for decades. "No question, 88 percent of the secret of Frito-Lay's magic is its store-door marketing," business consultant and author Thomas J. Peters told *Fortune* magazine in 1982. In 1965, when the Pepsi-Cola Company bought Frito-Lay to form PepsiCo, Inc., the company—with its unique delivery system and heavy advertising—had already become a formidable marketing-distribution presence. According to Warwick, advertising was highly effective because the route salesperson could follow through with proper displays and product arrangement inside the store. By fall of 1968, Frito-Lay was well into a new advertising campaign for its flagship brand: the "Frito Bandito" series. It was the first big campaign since the PepsiCo merger and it was deemed highly effective.

Effective Advertising

Part of the reason for Fritos' success was that Fritos corn chips were easier to promote than potato chips. Unlike potato chips, the corn-chip snack was unique. While a massive ad campaign would boost consumption of all potato chips, an expenditure on Fritos would largely boost consumption of only that snack, and not other products. Fritos corn chips thus represented a nearly ideal product to advertise.

Frito-Lay gave the new campaign's creative concept high marks for effectiveness. It featured a Mexican bandit, complete with his six-gun blazing, a long mustache, and sombrero. The cartoon character spoke in a heavy accent and liked Fritos corn chips enough to rob or connive to get them. The New York agency Foote, Cone and Belding began the concept as a radio and television campaign, and in 1969 expanded it into print. The Frito Bandito ads made their first magazine appearance in the January, 1969, issue of the *Ladies' Home Journal,* promoting a Fritos sweepstakes. Ads also appeared in *Life* and *Better Homes & Gardens.*

One of the most memorable commercials had a "space" theme. In 1969, as NASA prepared for the first lunar landing, the agency produced a spot showing the Bandito already on the moon before the first astronauts arrived, standing next to a parking meter. The Frito Bandito greeted the astronauts by saying, "I am

AT A GLANCE

Fritos brand corn chips created by Elmer Doolin when he purchased a small-scale fried corn meal product and its delivery route, 1932, in San Antonio, TX; Doolin's Frito Company relocated to Dallas, c. 1933, and was merged with the Nashville-based potato chip manufacturer H. W. Lay & Company, 1961, to become Frito-Lay, Inc.; company merged with the Pepsi-Cola Company to form PepsiCo, Inc., 1965.

Performance: *Sales*—$320 million.

Major competitor: Anheuser-Busch, Inc.'s Eagle brand snacks.

Advertising: *Agency*—DDB Needham /Chicago, Chicago, IL, 1988—. *Major campaign*—"I Know What I Like and I *Like* Fritos."

Addresses: *Parent company*—Frito-Lay, Inc., 7701 Legacy Dr., Plano, TX 75024; phone: (214) 334-7000; fax: (214) 334-2019. *Ultimate parent company*—PepsiCo, Inc., Purchase, NY; phone: (914) 253-2000; fax: (914) 253-2070.

the moon parking attendant. Now if you will kindly deposit one bag of crunchy Fritos corn chips for the first hour." The ad agency created a mock-up of the lunar module and used large amounts of silicate to create moonlike conditions for the shooting.

Criticism over "Frito Bandito"

The ads, however, generated criticism. Objections arose both to the violence and the ethnic portrayal in the commercials. Frito-Lay soon felt compelled to eliminate the use of guns from the spots. But it stuck with its Frito Bandito character for two more years despite criticism from Mexican-American groups about alleged ethnic prejudice. One early critic, an organization called Mexican Americans in Gainful Endeavor, had told the company: "This organization is opposed to your 'Frito Bandito' television commercials, as we feel that they perpetuate the stereotyped Mexican image, which is false and is an injustice to the person of Mexican descent."

Other companies had used a comic Mexican character in ads, and they also drew criticism from Mexican-American organizations. An Arrid deodorant commercial featured a sweaty bandit-type as the ultimate test for its effectiveness. Nick Reyes, the Mexican-American group's executive director, described it as "a Mexican bandit spraying his underarms, saying that if it will work for him, it will work for you."

Though Frito-Lay stayed with its Frito-Bandito campaign, the company did clean up the Bandito's unsavory appearance. Throughout the campaign, the company described him as "a cute lovable character." It also noted that the company's sales staff, including many Mexican Americans, liked the Bandito. A survey undertaken about this time in Los Angeles and San Jose showed 85 percent of Mexican Americans had no problem with the character, and only 8 percent opposed it.

Yet the ethnic issue remained a sore spot. During the summer of 1969, a Mexican-American group petitioned three San Antonio stations for free air time to respond to the ads, citing the FCC's fairness doctrine. The stations refused. Later, Mexican-American leaders began talking about a boycott of Fritos corn chips. One argument was that the ads caused Mexican-American youth to lose self-esteem. Bill R. Jones, then national advertising manager for

Frito-Lay, told *Broadcasting* magazine that "the facts indicate that we are not offending a large group. We continue to survey, and any time we find we're offending a substantial group of Mexican Americans, we'll be the first to take the Frito Bandito off the air." He described the ads' opponents as a "vocal minority trying to impose its views on the majority of the people."

Bandito Banned

The protests soon had an effect. After months of complaints from its Mexican-American community, especially the Mexican-American Anti-Defamation Committee, radio station KNBC in Los Angeles pulled the commercial off the air. Jay Rodriguez, a spokesman for the station, said, "The day is past when you put a Negro on TV with a watermelon. But the Mexican-American is being shown as a crumby, sloppy bandit type." Other stations started following suit. Within weeks, two more stations, KPIX and KRON in San Francisco, announced they were banning the ads. In 1970 the company ended the campaign.

During this period, Fritos corn chips were a highly successful national product, and their success did not go unnoticed by a regional competitor. As reported in a February, 1968, *Advertising Age* article, when a Chicago-based company, Jays Foods, Inc., operating exclusively in the Midwest, started selling a product it also called "fritos," Frito-Lay announced it would sue anyone who infringed on its trademark. Jays countered by charging Frito-Lay with monopolistic practices.

Federal anti-trust regulators closely watched Frito-Lay, zeroing in on the Pepsi-Frito-Lay combination. In September of 1968, as reported in an *Advertising Age* article at that time, just as the new Fritos advertising campaign was gaining momentum, the Federal Trade Commission ruled that PepsiCo could not create tie-ins between Frito-Lay products and Pepsi-Cola in most of its advertising. The ruling allowed PepsiCo to keep Frito-Lay, but it could not acquire any snack or soft-drink producer for ten years.

Spin-off Products

In the early 1970s Frito-Lay was responding to new trends: consumer desires for healthy snacks and varied products. With freshness in mind, the company instituted a policy of stamping corn chip and potato chip packages with expiration dates and pulling them off the shelves when that date expired. The company also became deeply involved in new product research, and, ironically, a Mexican theme proved to be promising in the Frito-Lay test kitchens. The company introduced regular Doritos brand tortilla chips, eventually spinning off taco- and nacho-flavored Doritos. Products with names like Ruffles, Munchos, Funyuns, and Chee-tos, each with multiple varieties, began filling grocery store shelves.

Fritos corn chips, though, were still king at Frito-Lay. Though new management units were created at about this time to handle the new products (and each product had its own brand manager), the Fritos brand unit remained at the top of the pecking order. In his book *The Other Guy Blinked: How Pepsi Won the Cola Wars*, Roger Enrico, who would one day head PepsiCo's beverage operations as well as Frito-Lay, recalled taking his first position in the company as an associate brand manager on Funyuns, then a new onion-flavored snack. His supervisor ran the Chee-tos brand name, and the supervisor on the highest level managed the Fritos brand.

Doritos tortilla chips eventually topped the Frito brand as the biggest revenue-producing corn-based product, generating a whopping $550 million in annual sales by the early 1980s and becoming one of the snack-food success stories of the century. Yet after a decade of new products, the Fritos brand held its own. During the 1970s it was bringing in several hundred million dollars in annual revenues, and during the early 1980s it remained one of six key products that brought in at least $150 million a year in annual retail sales. The brand also began to take on new flavors, including Fritos' Wild N' Wild Ranch and Non-Stop Nacho varieties.

The Basic Corn Chip

Fritos continued to own the original corn-chip market. Potential competitors such as Anheuser-Busch, Inc.'s Eagle brand seemed to realize that success would only come to them if they devised unique products, so their products did not exactly duplicate Fritos. By the same token, Frito-Lay had learned to respect and protect the basic Fritos recipe.

One story, told by Enrico, bears this out: when he arrived at Frito-Lay in the early 1970s, he learned that someone once changed the Frito formula, unbeknownst to the management. The change caused sales to plummet, and the company was forced to hire consultants to investigate the decline. They discovered the change in the ingredients. Management, upon learning about the change, immediately ordered a return to the old recipe. According to Enrico, the moral of the story is simple: "When you have a gold standard, a product so well-loved that when people think of your company, it's the first thing that comes to mind—for God's sake, cherish it."

Future Opportunities and Challenges

Fritos, once the company's biggest non-potato product, was one of many Frito-Lay brand names in the 1990s. But it still had untapped potential for the company as an export. It was one of three products—the others were Chee-tos and Ruffles—that the company chose to export to Poland. At the time, the company was also busy investigating exports to the rest of Eastern Europe. New

York-based Young & Rubicam handled advertising for the product in Gdansk and Warsaw, Poland. The ads were to appear on billboards, buses, and shelters—which were described as the best media for target-marketing in Eastern Europe. Frito-Lay turned the distribution over through its international division, PepsiCo Foods International.

Over the years, Frito-Lay created more varieties of snacks to meet changing consumer tastes and market conditions. A company fact sheet in 1993 listed six Fritos varieties: Original Corn Chips, Bar-B-Q Flavored Corn Chips, Chili Cheese Flavored Corn Chips, Crisp N' Thin Corn Chips, Dip Size Corn Chips, and Wild N' Wild Ranch. Yet, industry-wide, corn chip consumption slumped in the early 1990s. The company responded by refocusing the product more carefully. Acknowledging that Fritos' prime market was aging, and snacking less often, Frito-Lay altered the Fritos marketing strategy, giving the product more new varieties and a brighter package designed to appeal to the youth market.

Further Reading:

Enrico, Roger and Jesse Kornbluth, *The Other Guy Blinked: How Pepsi Won the Cola Wars,* New York: Bantam, 1986, pp. 8-9, 36-41.

"Frito Bandito Is First to Moon," *Advertising Age,* March 31, 1969, p. 102.

"Frito-Lay Plans Legal Moves to Protect Name, *Advertising Age,* February 12, 1968.

Kaplan, Elisa, "Frito-Lay: Still King of the Snack Food Hill," *Advertising Age,* April 30, 1979, pp. S2-S48.

"KNBC Rules Frito Bandito off Air Waves," *Advertising Age,* December 1, 1969, p. 1.

"Mexican American Group to Ask Equal Time vs. Bandito," *Advertising Age,* December 15, 1969, p. 2.

Morrison, Ann M., "Cookies Are Frito-Lay's New Bag," *Fortune,* August 9, 1982, pp. 64-68.

"PepsiCo Accepts FTC Pact Barring Frito-Lay Tie-ins," *Advertising Age,* September 16, 1968.

"Time to Answer Frito Bandito?," *Broadcasting,* December 15, 1969, pp. 40-41.

—Gary Hoffman

GALLO®

Diversity is the key to the dominance of Ernest and Julio Gallo's wines in the United States wine market. Producing one out of every three bottles of wine made in the United States by 1991, the E. & J. Gallo Winery made wines for the dessert, table, "pop," cooler, and varietal markets. Gallo's sixteen brands accounted for 26 percent of the 1993 U.S. wine market, and seven were among the top 20 sellers, according to the *New York Times*. Gallo's success is legendary in the wine industry. In fact, according to the *Los Angeles Times*, within the wine industry it is said "that it is hard to make a bad wine at Gallo considering the superb grape availability, scientific know-how and limitless funds for experimentation." Gallo's most popular brands have included Thunderbird, Boone's Farm, Hearty Burgundy, Andre sparkling wine, and Bartles and Jaymes wine coolers.

Birth of a Winery

According to the legend of the Gallo empire, after the repeal of Prohibition in 1933 Ernest and Julio Gallo originated what would be the largest wine company in the world equipped with only $5,900.23 and two library pamphlets on wine making. Wine critic Colman Andrews recounted in the *Los Angeles Times* that in the early days of their partnership Julio said, "I will make all the wine you can sell," and Ernest declared, "I will sell all the wine you can make." Clearing $34,000 their first year, the brothers reinvested their profits to spur growth. Buying inexpensive, sweet grapes like Thompson seedless, Tokay, and Muscatel from California's Central Valley, they made table wines, selling them to Eastern distributors that bottled and sold the wine under different labels. Taking more control over their wine in 1940, the brothers were the first in the industry to purchase their own bottlers and recruit a zealous sales force to ensure their Gallo brand wine optimal shelf space. With the capacity to mass-produce and effectively sell its wine, the company continued to grow, acquiring distribution facilities, its own bottle-making plant, an aluminum cap-making plant, prime Sonoma Valley growing land, and a state-of-the-art research lab. Their Ph.D.-staffed research lab developed many technological innovations, which included computerized wine blending, stainless steel fermenting tanks to inhibit the growth of foul-tasting bacteria that flourished in traditional wooden tanks, and ultraviolet-ray-blocking green tinted bottles. Throughout the entire history of the company, up to the time of Julio's death in 1993, Ernest and Julio kept control over company operations firmly in their own hands. Into his eighties, Julio oversaw wine production, tasting each batch before it was released. Ernest continued to rule the winery after Julio's death, commanding marketing and advertising, and opening new markets for Gallo's premium wines. *New York Times* wine critic Frank J. Prial said, "The Gallos' influence has been enormous—and far more positive and benevolent than most people think."

Establishing the Gallo Name

Gallo's early image was tied to low-end wines. *Impact,* an industry newsletter quoted in the *Los Angeles Times,* credited Gallo's success to its recognition "early on that the majority of Americans were unfamiliar with wine and did not much care about corks or barrel aging." The company's 1957 introduction of Thunderbird, a lemony fortified wine, resulted in sales of 2.5 million bottles that year. Radio spots triggered mass appeal for Thunderbird with the jingle, "What's the word? Thunderbird. How's it sold? Good and cold. What's the jive? Bird's alive. What's the price? Thirty twice." Gallo capitalized on the public's thirst for inexpensive, drinkable wines by adding another brand called Night Train Express to its line of dessert wines, which also included Gallo brand sherry, port, Tokay, and muscatel. By 1967 Thunderbird was the largest selling dessert wine and its sales contributed significantly to Gallo's profits into the early 1970s.

The popularity of dessert wines began to decline in 1967, as table wines grew ever more popular. At this time, "the winery entered what employees have called Gallo's most creative and exciting period, both in product development and marketing," a former employee told Ellen Hawkes in *Blood and Wine: The Unauthorized Story of the Gallo Wine Empire*. Even though Gallo's jug wines were outselling competitors and the Gallo Vin Rose made history in the table wine market by shipping one million cases in a year, the company continued to introduce new wines. Boone's Farm wine, a lower-alcohol, soda-like wine that sold in concord grape, loganberry, blackberry, and apple-flavored varieties, opened a wine category known as "pop" wine because of its sugary effervescence. Boone's Farm was the best-selling kind of wine in the United States by 1970, noted Hawkes, adding that Boone's Farm and Ripple, another bubbly fruit-flavored wine with a higher alcohol content, helped convert "a new segment of consumers to table wines," namely college students. *Time* reported that six of Gallo's brands accounted for 90 percent of the 60 million gallons of pop wine sold in 1971.

Gallo had grown into the world's largest wine company by adapting to changes in consumers' tastes. As more customers bought premium varietals (wines named after their dominant grape), Gallo was prompted to produce more expensive, better brands. Gallo's image upgrading developed out of its Hearty Burgundy decanter wine, which was a blend of Petite Sirah and Zinfandel grapes and Gallo's standard supply of lower-quality grapes from the Central Valley. Gallo's first varietals were Chablis Blanc, a blend of Colombard and Chenin Blanc grapes, and Pink Chablis, a sweeter, bubbly blend of Grenache Rose and Muscatel. A large advertising campaign introduced Pink Chablis, and "it was called America's favorite table wine" in 1970, noted Hawkes. To further refine Gallo's brand image, the Gallo name was removed from many of its jug wines and replaced with the Carlo Rossi brand name.

Knowing that good wine starts with good grapes, Julio experimented with grapes to find the varieties that would make the best wines. Former Gallo executive George Frank told *Fortune* that Julio "works with grapes as if he's pursuing the Holy Grail." Julio persuaded Gallo's suppliers in California's San Joaquin, Stanislaus, Merced, and Fresno counties to grow higher quality varietal grapes like French Colombard, Chenin Blanc, Zinfandel,

AT A GLANCE

Gallo brand of wine founded in 1933 in Modesto, California by brothers Ernest and Julio Gallo. It continued to be solely owned by the Gallo family into the 1990s. E. & J. Gallo wines are sold under the Gallo, Carlo Rossi, Livingston Vineyards, G and Q, Thunderbird, Ripple, Boone's Farm, Andre sparkling wine, Tott's, and Bartles and Jaymes wine coolers labels.

Performance: *Market share*—27% (top share) of the U.S. wine market. *Sales*—Over $1 billion.

Major competitor: Heublein Inc.'s brands of wine, including Almaden and Inglenook.

Advertising: *Major campaign*—"It's time to change the way you think about Gallo." The majority of Gallo's advertising focuses on its varietals.

Addresses: *Parent company*—E. & J. Gallo Winery, Modesto, California 95353; phone: 209-579-3111.

Cabernet Sauvignon, and Petite Sirah in 1967 by offering them fifteen-year contracts. In addition, Gallo continued to offer growers support through its growers' relations department, which offered a wealth of information on viticulture techniques. Thus, the growers were given the security of long-term business and a base price of $75 per ton, and the Gallos secured a steady supply of good grapes.

Re-establishing the Gallo Name

In the late 1970s and early 1980s Gallo introduced a few varietals that were praised by critics but inhibited in sales because of the Gallo name on the label. Gallo's name was bound to the poor reputation of its Thunderbird brand wine and the low price of its jug wines. To increase the company image it slowly introduced varietals of ever-increasing quality. It started with blush varietals, White Zinfandel and White Grenache. "Although blush varietals may not be the wine snob's idea of a premium varietal wine, in terms of getting a foot in the door, they have worked very well for Gallo," noted Larry Walker in the *San Francisco Chronicle*. Gallo began marketing upscale wines in the early 1980s. Under the label the Wine Cellars of Ernest and Julio Gallo, the company introduced a chardonnay in 1981 and a limited-release cabernet sauvignon in 1982. The cabernet was considered a "better effort" by Terry Robards in the *New York Times*, who also felt the wine would "be compared favorably with many Cabernets that sell for considerably more."

By 1988, Gallo produced the majority of the industry's varietals—they were 40% larger than the nearest varietal competitor—and began to be perceived as a producer of some fine quality wines. It refined the look of its Hearty Burgundy, switching it from an aluminum screw-top jug to a corked 750 milliliter bottle. Gallo also began to put vintage dates on its wines, a practice it had shunned for many years in order to blend wines from different years to achieve a "consistent style and quality," according to the *New York Times*. In another effort to increase quality, Gallo built an underground cellar, where it aged its Chardonnay in 650 Yugoslavian oak tanks. Furthermore, Gallo prepared its vineyard land in the Dry Creek Valley of Sonoma County to grow varietal grapes. Gallo continued to increase its share of the varietal market, and, according to the *San Francisco Chronicle*, by 1991 its share had grown from "virtually zero" in the early 1980s to about 20

percent. Wine consultant Ed Everett told the *San Francisco Chronicle* that Gallo's success in improving its image was due to consumers of a new generation that had "skipped jugs, so they don't have that image problem with Gallo."

As consumer tastes continued to move toward premium wines in the 1990s, Gallo began to phase out the use of its name on its inexpensive brands, replacing it with Livingston Vineyards where the labels did not already read Carlo Rossi. Gallo's dessert wines, including Port and White Port, will be sold under the "G and Q" brand name. In keeping with upscale market trends, in 1993 Gallo began to market its White Zinfandel, White Grenache, Sauvignon Blanc, Chardonnay, and Cabernet Sauvignon in 187 milliliter bottles that were available individually or in packs of four.

Bartles and Jaymes: A Notable Achievement

In 1985, with the table wine market stagnant, Gallo entered the newly formed wine cooler market. Wine coolers were made with low-quality, cheap grapes, which were mixed with fruit juices and water, a product that *Fortune* noted was initially "far more profitable than straight wine." Gallo's financial strength allowed it to storm the dense 100-brand cooler market, hurling its Bartles and Jaymes wine cooler into the top-selling position within eight months of its introduction. To gain its market position, Gallo spent millions on its advertising campaign, which featured two candid farmers with dry senses of humor who ended each commercial with the line, "Thank you for your support." The 100-plus Bartles and Jaymes ads created a cult-like following for the wine coolers. One television spot recorded the fictitious beginning of the Bartles and Jaymes wine cooler company. Ed, the ad says, remortgaged his house and "wrote to Harvard for an MBA" to help them start their business. At the end of the ad Frank asks the viewer to buy Bartles and Jaymes "as a personal favor to Ed, who has a balloon payment coming up." To keep Frank and Ed "fresh," *Marketing and Media Decisions* reported that Gallo limited their appearances only to television commercials, although the 50,000-member Bartles and Jaymes fan club did receive signed pictures of the two. Gallo used its marketing savvy to guarantee shelf space by granting supermarkets and large liquor chains discounts. The stores bought the coolers in large quantities to obtain the product at a discount and then gladly put up prominent in-store displays to advertise them. In addition, Gallo bottled its coolers in smooth-necked clear bottles that looked like white wine bottles, thus differentiating its product from competitors like California wine coolers and Sun Country, whose green bottles appealed to beer drinkers.

By 1988, however, wine coolers were beginning to look like a flash in the pan. The market's growth of 500 percent and 300 percent in 1984 and 1985, respectively, had slowed to just 6 percent in 1987, according to *Impact* as quoted in the *Los Angeles Times*. The product appealed mostly to women and people who wanted a lower-alcohol alternative to beer. A wine industry consultant told the *Los Angeles Times* that "maybe for some people it was a fad, but we believe there are hard-core wine cooler drinkers out there who will continue to drink these products." Acting on this idea helped Gallo survive the decline of the cooler market. Actually, Lewis Perdue, writing in the *San Francisco Chronicle*, regarded Gallo's handling of the Bartles and Jaymes wine coolers as the company's most notable achievement. He remarked that Gallo's ability to "almost single handedly create the wine cooler market" and then "cut its losses" by "de-emphasizing the product" when the market met its saturation point was quite shrewd, because Gallo's competitors lost profits by reacting too slowly. Gallo eased off on its wine cooler advertising, discontinuing the contracts with farmers in 1992, but continued to supply its established customer base with wine coolers.

Selling the Wine

New York Times contributor Terry Robards ascribed Gallo's considerable success in the wine industry to "marketing expertise that is the envy of the other producers." Ernest Gallo controls every aspect of Gallo marketing. Ernest spread Gallo wines across the country by recruiting distributors who would "open doors for him," noted *Fortune,* adding that Ernest's "distributors deal with the stores like no others. They build floor displays, lift cases, and dust bottles on the shelves." Ernest monitored his distributors by spontaneously touring stores in a region to make sure Gallo wines were displayed properly. "Ernest doesn't want you to take him on a tour," one distributor told *Fortune,* "If he sees you turning left, he'll tell you to turn right."

The aggressiveness and zeal of Gallo salespeople is the result of Ernest's vigorous sales training programs. All Gallo trainees must memorize the "Big Red Book," a 300-page training manual that details even the smallest aspects of a salesperson's day. *Fortune* noted an example of the book's meticulous explanations—the ten-point strategy necessary to fulfill Gallo shelving requirements. The seventh point is: "Wherever there is a decided price advantage in buying a larger size, the larger size should be placed to the right of the smaller size." Moreover, Ernest advised the salespeople on the six types of retailers and how to sell to each one, and on the importance of involving themselves in politics. "Sales managers were instructed to . . . contribute heavily to politicians' campaigns" to influence legislation and win over dry regions, a former employee told Hawkes. With this specific instruction and Ernest's iron-fisted command, Gallo increased or maintained its profits in a declining market into the 1990s.

Ernest Gallo's control extended beyond his own salespeople. His quest for perfection proved difficult for advertising agencies to satisfy. Young and Rubicam was Gallo's advertising agency of record for more than 18 years, but Gallo is also noted for having worked with fifteen agencies in a twenty-five year period. One former creative director told the *New York Times* that Ernest "would pound you until you broke." And Leonard Matthews, a former advertising executive who once wooed the Gallos, recalled in the *New York Times* that "you'd wait up to three hours in the parking lot because there was no reception room in the building," and once into the meeting Ernest would want "things that would drive creative people up the wall, like, 'Could you combine the first half of this commercial to the second half of that one?'" Another advertising executive told the *New York Times* that he remembered Ernest firing his company after they toiled for two months. Ernest simply said, "I don't see anything here. I guess the relationship is over."

Gallo's advertising focused on television spots in the late 1980s and into the 1990s; it did not run any print or radio advertisements and does not "believe in" sponsoring events, sporting or otherwise, Gallo spokesperson Daniel Solomon told *Marketing and Media Decisions.* The man who finally won Ernest's confidence was Ogilvy & Mather's creative director Hal Riney. He created an upscale television spot for Gallo varietals that combined romantic music by academy-award winning Vangelis and pictures of sunny vineyards and weddings with the closing line:

"All the best from Ernest and Julio Gallo." After creating the Bartles and Jaymes advertisements, Hal Riney formed his own advertising agency and took the Gallo accounts with him. He continued to work with Gallo until 1989 when he abruptly resigned the Gallo account as cooler sales declined. Since Hal Riney's seven-year relationship with Gallo ended, Gallo has not had another advertising agency "of record," but it has paid several agencies to create commercials for it.

Another Look at Gallo's History

Ernest Gallo's unflagging managerial control over the Gallo winery has not been viewed by all observers as an indication of his benevolent entrepreneurial spirit. In 1986 Ernest and Julio brought a lawsuit against their younger brother, Joseph Gallo, Jr., who wanted to name his dairy business "Joseph Gallo Cheese." Ernest and Julio did not want the brand name of their company to be associated with Joseph's business. During the trial that ensued, Joseph's attorneys accused Ernest and Julio of defrauding Joseph of his share in the $100,000 estate of their father, which included a winery. But the courts upheld Ernest and Julio's charge of trademark infringement and found no basis in the counterclaim that Joseph had been deprived of an inheritance.

In 1993 Ellen Hawkes published *Blood and Wine,* a sensational account of the Gallo winery's origins, which received mixed reviews. Challenging the legend that Ernest and Julio started their empire with only $5,900 and a couple of pamphlets, Hawkes claims that the brothers inherited a modestly substantial sum from their father, who had made his money as a bootlegger during Prohibition. Joseph, Sr., was, in Hawkes's description, a brutal man operating inside and outside the law, who inflicted harsh beatings on Ernest, Julio, and their mother until his death in an apparent murder-suicide in which he shot his wife and then himself. Ernest and Julio's childhoods are characterized in Hawkes's book by beatings and overwork in the vineyards. Joan O'C. Hamilton summarized in *Business Week:* "This hellish history indelibly marked the sons. Ernest vowed early to succeed at all costs, and, as an adult, Hawkes writes, he rules by humiliation and fear." After interviewing many people—anonymously and on the record—who were associated with the winery, Hawkes put together a story of cut-throat competitiveness at Gallo, in which the company's salespeople carried out such practices as going into stores and puncturing bottle caps on competitors' wines so that they would spoil, and spraying oil on rival wine bottles so they would collect dust and appear to have lingered, unwanted, on store shelves.

Hawkes claimed that because the Gallos wield so much power that many of her sources were afraid to be identified, some of her allegations could not be readily verified. A Gallo spokesperson dismissed Hawkes's unauthorized account as "so obviously contemptible and despicable as not to merit any comment." *People* magazine contributors Larry Writer and Johnny Dodd noted that while Hawkes's "book has been well reviewed, critics have found fault with her use of anonymous sources." Hamilton, on the other hand, praised Hawkes's research, saying she "bolsters her account with 53 pages of detailed notes on her sources, which include a remarkable number of on-the-record interviews."

Forecasting the Future

In the early 1990s, Gallo remains solidly the at the top of the U.S. wine industry. Its Andre sparkling wine, White Zinfandel, and Sauvignon Blanc ranked number one in 1992; its Cabernet Sauvignon ranked fourth; and its Chardonnay ranked ninth. The company is now poised to enter the super-premium wine market. "The Gallos have always maintained that with their resources, they could produce wines as good or better than anyone else's," the *New York Times Magazine* reported. With their superior resources, they expect to produce a $60 cabernet sauvignon and a $30 chardonnay under the brand name Ernest and Julio Gallo. However, it is unclear how the company will make the transition to a new generation of leadership. When Julio died in a car accident in May, 1993, there was no apparent heir to take over control of Gallo's wine production, although his son Robert and son-in-law James Coleman had worked closely in the vineyards with him for years. Ernest, at age 84, continued to work full time, showing no signs of retiring or even slowing down.

Further Reading:

"American Wine Comes of Age," *Time,* November 27, 1972, pp. 76-84.

Chroman, Nathan, "Gallo Expands Line of Varietals: Zinfandel, Cabernet Sauvignon and Others Are Fine Value Wines," *Los Angeles Times,* August 21, 1986, p. 24.

Ellis-Simons, Pamela, "There's Gold in Them Thar Hicks: Marketing of Bartles & Jaymes Wine Cooler," *Marketing and Media Decisions,* March, 1987, p. 69.

Fierman, Jaclyn, "How Gallo Crushes the Competition," *Fortune,* September 1, 1986, pp. 24-31.

Hamilton, Joan O'C., "Days of Wine and Neurosis," *Business Week,* May 3, 1993, pp. 12-17.

Hawkes, Ellen, *Blood and Wine: The Unauthorized Story of the Gallo Wine Empire,* New York: Simon & Schuster, 1993.

Kowsky, Kim, "Winemaker Julio Gallo Dies in Car Crash," *Los Angeles Times,* May 3, 1993, sec. A, pp. 1, 19.

Pace, Eric, "Julio Gallo, 83, Wine Industrialist, Dies," *New York Times,* May 4, 1993.

Perdue, Lewis, "The Power Brokers: The 10 Most Influential People in the Wine Business," *San Francisco Chronicle,* January 13, 1993, food section, p. 1.

Prial, Frank J., "Passing the Jug," *New York Times Magazine,* November 15, 1992, p. 48.

Robards, Terry, "Wine Talk," *New York Times,* September 8, 1982, sec. C, p. 15.

Rothenberg, Randall, "The Media Business: The Client Whom Ad Agencies Hate to Love," *New York Times,* May 2, 1988, sec. D, p. 10.

Walker, Larry, "Gallo Just Keeps on Growing: World's Top Vintner Making Big Push into Premium Wines," *San Francisco Chronicle,* November 28, 1991, p. B1.

Wollenberg, Skip, "Growth Slowed Markedly Last Year: Cooler Makers Hope to See Hotter Sales This Summer," *Los Angeles Times,* July 2, 1988, sec. 4, p. 6.

Writer, Larry, and Johnny Dodd, "Grapes of Wrath," *People,* June 14, 1993, pp. 121-124.

—Sara Pendergast

GATORADE®

Gatorade Thirst Quencher is a non-carbonated drink that replaces essential bodily fluids lost during strenuous exercise. Introduced in 1967, the beverage—made of water, glucose, inorganic salts, citric acid, and lemon-lime flavoring—is absorbed by the body twelve times faster than water. Since The Quaker Oats Company acquired the brand—along with Stokely–Van Camp—in 1983, Gatorade has enjoyed a 90- to 95-percent market share of the sports drinks category it created.

Brand Development

At the University of Florida in 1965, James Robert Cade, a physiologist and renal specialist, studied the metabolism of members of the football team in response to the coach's request. A research team led by Dr. Cade developed a formula designed to prevent dehydration and replace fluids and blood sugars lost during strenuous exercise.

The University of Florida football team, the Florida Gators, tested the first designated "sports drink" during the 1966 season. The Gators noticeably outplayed other teams during the second half of games and went on to win the Orange Bowl on New Year's Day, 1967. The coach attributed their increased endurance to the beverage named, appropriately, "Gatorade."

Combating fluid and mineral loss during exercise, especially in hot southern climates, had become a serious pursuit. When Robert Cade sought University support in marketing the drink, his offer was declined, so he and fellow developers formed the Gatorade Trust and sold the rights to Gatorade to Stokely–Van Camp in 1967. Under the royalty agreement the trust received three cents per gallon sold and $25,000 a year. In 1969 university officials claimed that Gatorade, the result of a research project, belonged to the University of Florida, and all royalties were theirs. Two-and-a-half years later, the University of Florida was granted a royalty payment of one cent per gallon of Gatorade sold, and the Gatorade Trust, four cents per gallon. Within twenty years, the Gatorade Trust was earning approximately $12 million in royalties per year; Dr. Cade's portion was $1.2 million.

No sooner was one suit settled than another began. In 1971 the state department of Health, Education & Welfare jumped into the fray as well. They charged that Gatorade, invented at the University of Florida with funding from the U.S. government, was created with federal grants—which outline that all inventions by recipients of such grants are the property of the government. The government's suit failed; according to one Justice official quoted in the August 16, 1971, *Advertising Age*, "thousand of things [had been] invented under government sponsorship" and approved for marketing with no legal fuss.

Early Marketing

Within its first two years of ownership, Stokely–Van Camp distributed Gatorade to professional teams and, through schools, to amateur athletes. Stokely issued Royal Crown Cola a license to distribute carbonated Gatorade.

By February 1970 the first batch of competitors surfaced: Canada Dry's Viva; Pillsbury's Superade; Becton, Dickinson, and Company's Sportade; the Pittsburgh Brewing Company's Hop'n Gator; and Bud Adams' QuicKick. Canada Dry used an Olympic ski champion to represent Viva, while Adams, owner of the Houston Oilers, had his team officially endorse QuicKick, which presented the most serious threat to Gatorade.

Investigating new markets, Stokely used mobile catering trucks in Atlanta near factories to see if workers went for Gatorade. The company and its licensee Royal Crown also planned to stock vending machines in sports arenas. At the same time market tests were initiated with different sized bottles and cans, as well as a new choice of flavors.

In the early 1970s cyclamate, the noncaloric sweetener used in Gatorade, was banned as a carcinogen, and a resulting recall of Gatorade cost Stokely $1.4 million. In August 1970 the firm sued the Pittsburgh Brewing Company, charging that the product Hop'n Gator violated Stokely's trademark rights.

Advertising Choices

In 1970 Stokely spent nearly $3.5 million via the advertising agency Lennen & Newell to market Gatorade in measured media. While the Gatorade Trust tussled over ownership rights with the University of Florida and the Department of Health, Education & Welfare, Stokely executives waited uncomfortably. Gatorade had yet to prove profitable.

In 1972 Stokely moved advertising from the financially troubled Lennen & Newell to Chicago-based Clinton E. Frank, Inc. The following year a new carbonated version of Gatorade was

AT A GLANCE

Gatorade brand created in 1965 at the University of Florida by a research team led by Dr. James Robert Cade; name inspired by the university football team, the Gators, who tested the drink; Stokely–Van Camp bought the rights to market Gatorade in 1967; in 1983 The Quaker Oats Company acquired Stokely–Van Camp.

Performance: *Market Share*—90% of sports drink market; number two in juice-drink category behind Ocean Spray. *Sales*—$685 million.

Major competitor: Ocean Spray juice drinks.

Advertising: *Agency*—Bayer Bess Vanderwarker, Chicago, IL; *Major Campaign*—"Be Like Mike": Michael Jordan of the Chicago Bulls is spokesman; viewers invited to "be like Mike."

Addresses: *Parent company*—The Quaker Oats Company, P.O. Box 9001, 321 North Clark Street, Chicago, IL 60610; phone: (312) 222-7111; fax: (312) 222-8323.

introduced through independent bottlers in five states. Continuing its research into athletic performance, in 1981 Stokely brought out Gatorlode, designed to quickly increase an athlete's carbohydrate count.

The Gatorade Splash

To maintain its lead over new isotonic products, Stokely contacted the National Football League athletic trainers in an effort to get Gatorade out to NFL teams. The company could thereby reach a large number of ready consumers—both the players and those watching the game, live or from their living rooms. Stokely obtained a licensing agreement from the NFL, and soon Gatorade was visible along the sidelines of NFL games. Gatorade and athletics went hand in hand. A familiar sight for sports fans over the years has been the dousing of the coach with a tub of Gatorade after an important victory.

By 1981 Gatorade sales accounted for 14 percent of Stokely's total sales, and the company felt that it was time to move the product overseas. Licensees in Japan, England, France, West Germany, Nigeria, and Venezuela began to produce and market Gatorade.

Quaker Takes Over

In August 1983 Quaker Oats bought Stokely–Van Camp for $230 million, topping an offer from Pillsbury by fifteen dollars a share. Most analysts thought the offer too high, but Quaker had plans to re-enter food operations after some time spent in diversified consumer products.

Quaker Oats decided to devote consistent advertising and promotional support to the Gatorade brand, which was, according to a Gatorade spokesperson, "underdeveloped at that time." While NFL coverage gave the product high visibility, there was room to grow both internationally and with the weekend athlete market.

Continuing with high profile sports marketing, Quaker chose Foote, Cone & Belding for advertising but quickly switched to Chicago's Bayer, Bess, Vanderwarker in 1984. Sidelines visibility was still the major game plan, and Gatorade became the official sports drink for a number of professional leagues: joining the NFL were the lucrative markets of the National Basketball Association

(NBA) and Major League Baseball. Gatorade also became the sponsor for Olympic events and obtained contracts to sponsor and supply Gatorade for nearly every professional and major college sports association in the United States.

Competition Surfaces

In the mid-1980s the sports drink market experienced another growth spurt, and many companies tried to get a piece of the growing sports drink market. The Suntory Water Group persuaded the New Orleans Saints football team to make Suntory's sports drink 10-K its official beverage. However, Suntory was prevented from displaying 10-K in coolers on the sidelines because Gatorade's contract with the NFL specified that all teams have Gatorade coolers on the sidelines during games. Another competitor was launched in 1986 when trainers advised the San Francisco 49ers football team to drink more fluids to reduce injuries, but the team refused to drink Gatorade. Owner Edward J. DeBartolo decided to develop another drink, and three years and five million dollars later, PowerBurst was launched. Designed by Vitafort International of Mill Valley, California, and produced by PowerBurst Corporation of Fresno, California, PowerBurst was represented by quarterback Joe Montana and running back Roger Craig.

Coca-Cola Company introduced PowerAde, a fountain sports drink, in March 1990. Soft drink giants like Coca-Cola could afford to bide their time, waiting until the sports drink market opened up before jumping in. Coke wisely used its loyal fountain-account business to distribute its new product, thereby assuming less risk than if it confronted Gatorade head-on in the bottled and canned beverage market.

The Pepsi-Cola Company—having test-marketed its sports drink contender, Mountain Dew Sport, in 1989—introduced the drink on a larger scale in April 1990. In keeping with high-profile sports associated with Gatorade and PowerBurst, Pepsi chose Bo Jackson—a well-known football and baseball star—as their endorser. By September 1991 All Sport replaced Mountain Dew Sport as the Pepsi contender; the product had less carbonation and was available in four flavors.

The Science of Sports Drinks

Mountain Dew Sport, PowerAde, Powerburst, and 10-K were just a few of dozens of sports drinks entering the market to challenge Gatorade in the late 1980s. What distinguished one from the other? Pepsi claimed that test markets chose carbonated Mountain Dew Sport 2-to-1 over Gatorade for taste. Quaker Oats' John Breuer, as quoted in the *Philadelphia Business Journal,* April 23, 1990, countered: "You can't test Gatorade sitting around. It doesn't taste good. You've got to try it during or after physical exercise." In addition, Mr. Breuer, vice-president of marketing for the grocery specialty division, stated that Quaker Oats' market research showed that consumers prefer a non-carbonated drink after vigorous exercise.

Of chief importance, however, was the science behind the sports drinks. Through the Gatorade Sports Science Institute, grants are given to universities pursuing sports science research. In 1985 the Gatorade Exercise Physiology Laboratory was established in Barrington, Illinois, to conduct research in exercise and sports nutrition. Typical testing performed at the lab analyzes functions of the human body such as dehydration, exercise performance, circulation, respiration, gastric emptying, and body composition. Through lab research Quaker Oats established criteria for the optimal sports drink components, which should make the drink taste good, promote rapid fluid absorption, provide energy to working muscles, and maintain physiological balance.

PowerBurst had its own scientific ax to wield, claiming that PowerBurst contained minerals Gatorade didn't—magnesium, pantothenic acid, and biotin. PowerBurst had vitamins; Gatorade had none. PowerBurst had one-fourth the sodium and twice the potassium of Gatorade. Finally, added Richard D. Strayer, Power-Burst's CEO, as quoted in the October 16, 1989, *Los Angeles Times,* Powerburst's "energy source" was fructose, which "has a longer absorption time so it stays in the body longer." Gatorade countered—with facts backed up by a bevy of scientists—that fructose had been shown to cause gastrointestinal problems and impair performance because it is absorbed more slowly in the small intestine than glucose.

Big League Moves

Quaker's next move was to sign Chicago Bulls basketball player Michael Jordan—who already represented Coke, Nike, McDonald's, and General Mills' Wheaties—as a Gatorade endorser. In mid-June, 1991, the firm offered Jordan a ten-year, $18 million contract. The headline of the *Adweek Marketing Week* story for June 24, 1991, read: "Gatorade Tries to Steal Jordan from Coke." Some accused Quaker of being quick to the trigger. As Timothy Ramey, analyst at County NatWest Securities USA commented in the March 26, 1990, *Crain's Chicago Business:* "Now that seemingly everyone is coming after them, Quaker's reacting—or overreacting—like they did when General Mills came after them in oatmeal."

But with a market that grew 18 percent in 1990 to $635 million, why wouldn't Quaker defend its territory? Nearly 80 sports drinks were introduced from 1986 through 1992. Minding the home store, in mid-1991 the company introduced a new tropical fruit–flavored Gatorade, and new packaging: a 23.5-ounce aluminum can called The Slammer, and the Gator Gallon.

When Jordan signed with Gatorade, Coke and Quaker went head-to-head. Quaker launched the "Be Like Mike" campaign in 1991, expanding on it the following year with ads displayed on retail shelves and broadcasts from the Barcelona Olympics. The firm hoped to sponsor both the 1992 NBA playoffs (Jordan's Chicago Bulls won) and the Summer Olympics (Jordan played, the United States won). Coke won the latter contract, paying $35 million; still Quaker showed up, official sponsor of the U.S. team. Interestingly, in January 1992 Quaker and Coke considered teaming up, with Coca-Cola Enterprises, a bottling division, to expand distribution of Gatorade. No agreement was reached.

International Outlook

Gatorade's overall growth slowed in the early 1990s, while competition intensified. Target markets changed; Quaker offered Gatorade Light for those who preferred a lower-calorie drink. The company introduced a grape-flavored Gatorade, and with Freestyle, a better-tasting isotonic, Quaker hoped to defeat soft-drink style rivals. The new message about Gatorade for consumers was: It wouldn't be there if it didn't work.

Poor Gatorade sales in first quarter 1992 was the first drop since Quaker bought the brand in 1983. Gatorade brought in nearly a quarter of Quaker's corporate profits; the company counted on the 20 percent annual sales its leading brand had been enjoying for seven straight years. *Financial World's* July 7, 1992, issue stated that "the company's 'Be Like Mike' ads flopped as badly as Quaker stock, which has fallen 27 percent since the beginning of the year."

In April 1992 Quaker formed a separate division, The Gatorade Company, to oversee national growth and international expansion. Like many American companies, Quaker looked to expand overseas as its U.S. market matured. To gain recognition, Quaker hired European and international celebrities for its overseas ads. Gatorade is now marketed in Canada, Mexico, Venezuela, Brazil, Argentina, Puerto Rico, Italy, Germany, England, Spain, Belgium, and Korea.

Further Reading:

"Battle Bubbles over Gatorade Profits," *Business Week,* September 6, 1969, p. 33.

Crown, Judith, "Selling Brands Abroad," *Crain's Chicago Business,* February 24, 1992, p. 13.

Davis, Riccardo A., "Philadelphia Is Battleground for Sports Drink War," *Philadelphia Business Journal,* April 23, 1990, p. 17.

Dubashi, Jagannath, "Quaker Oats: The Gatorade Effect Wears Off," *Financial World,* July 7, 1992, p. 12.

Fahey, Allison, "Power Boost for PowerAde," *Advertising Age,* April 27, 1992, p. 2.

"Gatorade Company Sues Citrus-Flavor Beer Maker," *Wall Street Journal,* August 26, 1970, p. 17.

"Gatorade Exercises Several Options," *Beverage World,* June, 1991, p. 14.

"Gatorade Performance Series," The Quaker Oats Company: Chicago, Illinois, 1992. "Gatorade's Sales Rise from 5% to 14% of Total Sales," *Beverage World,* February, 1982, p. 25.

Grimm, Matthew, "Gatorade Sets up Michael Jordan for a Summer Blitz," *Adweek's Marketing Week,* March 30, 1992, p. 4.

——, "Gatorade Tries to Steal Jordan from Coke," *Adweek's Marketing Week,* June 24, 1991, p. 5.

La Ganga, Maria L., "Dueling Drinks: Rivals Go After No. 1 Gatorade in Sports Beverage Industry," *Los Angeles Times,* October 16, 1989, p. 5.

Liesse, Julie, "Gatorade is Cornerstone to Quaker's Growth," *Advertising Age,* May 18, 1992, p. 12.

——, "Gatorade: Peter Vitulli," *Advertising Age,* July 6, 1992, p. S1.

——, "New Quaker Sports Drink in Test Markets," *Crain's Chicago Business,* June 4, 1990, p. 45.

——, and Winters, Patricia, "Quaker Set to Pour on Support for Gatorade as Rivals Debut," *Crain's Chicago Business,* March 26, 1990, p. 37.

Manges, Michele, "Sports Drink Makers Out to Tackle Gatorade," *Wall Street Journal,* August 10, 1989, p. B1.

McCarthy, Michael J., "Coke Fields a Sports Drink to Challenge Gatorade's Hold," *Wall Street Journal,* March 6, 1990, p. B1.

McCormick, Jay, "Quaker Shifts Strategy with Stokely Buy," *Advertising Age,* August 1, 1983, pp. 4, 30.

Meller, Paul, "Beware Yanks Bearing Drinks," *Marketing,* March 5, 1992, pp. 23-4.

"No Profits on Gatorade, Stokely's McVey Says," *Advertising Age,* August 16, 1971, pp. 1, 59.

Prince, Greg, "Isotonic Tenacity," *Beverage World,* September, 1991, p. 52.

"Quaker Oats to Introduce Light Version of Gatorade," *Wall Street Journal,* February 20, 1990, p. B6.

Scott, Jeffry, "Coca-Cola May Help Quaker Go Worldwide with Gatorade," *Atlanta Constitution,* January 24, 1992, p. 8.

"Stokely's Carbonated Gatorade," *Wall Street Journal,* April 3, 1973, p. 44.

"Stokely Taps Frank for Bulk of Ads," *Advertising Age,* April 3, 1972, p. 3.

"Stokely–Van Camp to Market Gatorade," *Sales Management,* January 1, 1968, p. 51.

"Stokely–Van Camp to Offer Companion to Gatorade Drink," *Wall Street Journal,* May 27, 1981.

"Stokely–Van Camp Uncaps Special Drink for Athletes," *Wall Street Journal,* August 24, 1967, p. 7.

"Wrestling with Gatorade: Everyone's Out to Refresh the Sweat Set," *Sales Management,* February 15, 1970, pp. 84-86.

—Frances E. Norton

GERBER®

Gerber®

Gerber brand baby food, with more than 250 products, is by far the domestic category leader. Gerber has been offering increased convenience and quality nutrition to parents of young children since 1928. Since its introduction with the first commercially successful baby food, the Gerber baby logo has gained worldwide recognition as a symbol of quality and trust. Although baby food has been the Gerber Products Company's core business, the company has leveraged the Gerber brand to diversify into other baby product categories, such as clothing and baby care items. Gerber's continuing success can be attributed to its reputation, effective marketing efforts, and dominant presence in the product's primary distribution channel, supermarkets.

Brand Origins

Gerber baby food was conceived out of a mother's frustration in 1927. Prior to Gerber, mothers were destined to the drudgery of cooking and straining meals for their infants as soon as they were ready to begin digesting solid foods. However, Dorothy Gerber, the mother of a seven-month-old daughter, was just the person to demonstrate the tediousness of this task and the need for a better solution. The Gerber family owned the Fremont Canning Company in rural Fremont, Michigan. Dorothy knew the task could be done at the plant and convinced her husband, Daniel F. Gerber, to pursue the matter. With the approval of his father, Frank, Dan arranged for the plant's first baby food samples. After passing the muster of baby taste testers, pediatricians, and nutritionists, Gerber was ready for the commercial launch that would forever change the way American mothers feed their babies.

Early Marketing Strategy

Once Dan Gerber had obtained initial favorable feedback, he was faced with tough questions in trying to formulate an appropriate marketing strategy. Unfortunately, some unfavorable product history had already been established. Gerber was not the first baby food to be marketed commercially. Another food processor had attempted to market prepared baby food, but had failed in its attempts to distribute it in grocery stores, and had been relegated to a small niche drugstore market serving babies with sensitive stomachs.

In order to find solutions to potential problems, Gerber went to the mothers directly and questioned them regarding their willingness to buy commercial baby food—where they would like to buy it and what they were willing to pay for it. Their answers indicated that Gerber baby food could be positioned at local grocers as a premium priced, highly nutritious alternative to home cooking.

The high price could be commanded, surprisingly not because of increased convenience, but because of the nutritional benefits the canning process afforded the product. Mothers couldn't efficiently capture all the vitamins and minerals in the home cooking process. Many dissolved in the water and evaporated in the steam. In addition, Gerber was able to obtain fresher produce than was generally available. The added nutritional value of commercially prepared baby food was the factor that allowed Gerber to obtain the margin necessary to cover the start-up costs of the new product.

At first Gerber had difficulty convincing middlemen to push the product through the distribution channels necessary to reach the grocers' shelves. Gerber again relied on the mothers and believed that they could solve the problem by drawing the product up into the marketplace. To attempt to do so, Gerber decided to run an advertising campaign with coupons offering samples of the baby food in exchange for a small fee and information about the household's shopping habits. If a sufficient response ensued, the coupons would serve as evidence of the product's potential demand for the reluctant distributors.

In order to most effectively draw attention to the coupons, Gerber decided to include a baby's picture. Artist Dorothy Hope Smith submitted an unfinished sketch of a neighbor's baby, indicating it would be finished if Gerber approved of the rough form. The sketch was accepted in its original state and has remained as the world recognized Gerber trademark.

The advertising strategy worked, and within six months of the campaign's launch, Gerber was successful in placing its original five varieties of baby food on grocers' shelves in most major markets.

Commercial Success

Gerber's initial success attracted the attention of more than fifty competitors. The heightened competition helped to further crystalize Gerber's long-term strategy. Gerber decided that to effectively compete against the major food producers, the company should understand babies, not just baby food. Gerber en-

AT A GLANCE

Gerber brand baby foods introduced commercially by Fremont Canning Company in 1928; developed by Daniel F. Gerber, Sr.; Fremont Canning Company renamed Gerber Products Company in 1941.

Performance: *Market share*—71% (top share) of U.S. baby food market. *Sales*—$771.1 million (for consolidated food segment).

Major competitor: Heinz baby food; also Ralston Purina's Beech-Nut baby foods.

Advertising: *Agency*—Grey Advertising, New York, NY, 1991—. *Major campaign*—"Gerber. Because you only want the best for your baby."

Addresses: *Parent company*—Gerber Products Company, 445 State St., Fremont, MI 49413; phone: (616) 928-2000.

hanced its relationship with the medical and dietetic community. The focus soon led to a continuing tradition of producing baby care publications which has helped to further promote and legitimize the brand.

By 1941 the Fremont Canning Company's primary product was Gerber baby food—at volumes that continued to dominate the market. Its name was appropriately changed to the Gerber Products Company. Within two years, Gerber could claim, "Babies are our business—our only business"—a slogan adopted in October, 1948.

Advertising and Marketing

Gerber has found that direct mail works most effectively in reaching new customers. New customers are identified almost immediately by Gerber through the use of birth record lists, which are effective in reaching approximately 80 percent of newborn babies. Gerber uses the information to send a series of mailings, including coupons that are timed to the stage of the child's development.

This highly effective marketing technique has been very successful overall. Gerber, however, has found that its market share varies widely between regions in the U.S. market. In order to increase its market share in lagging locations, Gerber has developed region-specific advertising programs, as well as products focused on specific market segments.

Gerber has realized that increasing regional volume will not have a great impact on its overall sales potential, so its marketing strategy has also included efforts to expand the length of time infants and toddlers consume its food products, increase its international presence, and widen the breadth of product category offerings for infants, toddlers, and children.

Product Development

For over 50 years Gerber has operated Gerber's Research Center, the largest private industrial center in the world devoted exclusively to infant nutrition and care. The center's research is disseminated to parents and the medical community and used for new product development. In 1989, for example, a Gerber research team produced a document called "Dietary Guidelines for Infants" of which more than one million copies were distributed.

"Dietary Guidelines" was well received by doctors. The facility has developed its new products through this kind of research. The line of Gerber 1st Foods, 2nd Foods, and 3rd Foods divides different kinds of baby food products by the nutritional needs of babies at various stages of development. Product labels then make it easier for parents to choose among the appropriate foods to satisfy the baby's individual preferences while ensuring his or her nutritional needs.

Gerber also researched ways to expand its product viability into the toddler years. Research in this area extends not only to nutritional needs, but also to child development. In 1991 and 1992, researchers conducted sensory studies on toddlers for 75 Gerber products, testing for flavor, aftertaste, aroma, and texture. Consumer research indicated that many adult foods do not adequately satisfy the needs of toddlers, so Gerber Graduates toddler foods were created for children ready for tabletop foods—from ages one through three. The line of 23 products—including main dishes, snacks, fruits and vegetables, cereals, bakery items like cookies and pretzels, and calcium enriched juices—was introduced nationally in 1992.

In an effort to further enhance market share, Gerber has attempted to be sensitive to the tastes of prevalent U.S. ethnic markets, which have traditionally purchased more than average quantities of baby food. The Tropical line was launched in 1991 specifically to appeal to the Hispanic market, which accounts for large population percentages in areas where Gerber had historically held less market share.

International Market

Gerber has ventured into the global arena through exports as well as by opening overseas production facilities in Costa Rica, Mexico, Poland, and Venezuela. In all, the Gerber brand is available to more than 70 countries in 12 different languages.

The diversity in worldwide tastes has been a challenge for Gerber. The company established an international nutrition service team to ensure that the introduction of new products in foreign countries would be acceptable, given established infant feeding and care norms. The basic strategy has been to add nutritional supplements to foods prevalent in the region's diet. This strategy has resulted in diverse offerings: minnows, lamb brains, mung beans, and seaweed, to name a few.

Glass Scares

Within a two-year period, Gerber experienced two separate waves of reported incidents involving glass fragments found in its baby food. The first wave occurred in 1984 when two New England consumers reported glass pieces found in Gerber juices. Even though investigations failed to identify any operations-related cause, Gerber recalled 550,000 bottles of juice. The publicity generated by the recall prompted a temporary drop in baby food sales.

The second wave occurred in 1986 with 645 nationwide unsubstantiated reports of glass fragments. This time Gerber was not willing to recall the products in question, especially when government investigations failed to produce any evidence of a common cause or link to Gerber's operations. Several of the incidents resulted from accidents or intentional tampering initiated by the consumers themselves. Several parents were eventually arrested for filing false claims. Despite Gerber's willingness to stand its ground and defend its product, the ensuing publicity once again resulted in lost sales, this time estimated at $10 million. Gerber's presence in the market plummeted to the decade's low of 61.9 percent. Within nine months Gerber recovered its market share, and in 1993 the company held nearly 72 percent of the U.S. market.

The Competition

Over the years Gerber has not only survived challenges from 73 competitors, but has dominated the U.S. baby food market. In 1992, the domestic market was shared with only two other major rivals, Beech-Nut Nutrition Corporation and the H. J. Heinz Company, holding 13 percent and 14 percent of the market respectively.

Beech-Nut has identified a niche by advertising the absence of sugar in selected baby food fruits, and by utilizing high-quality branded supply sources, a marketing approach known as double branding. Beech-Nut also introduced and heavily promoted a concept in the U.S. market borrowed from its success in Europe—the Stages line, introduced in 1984. The concept entails introducing babies gradually to new tastes and textures based on the baby's age. Beech-Nut's Stages line, like the Gerber line of 1st, 2nd, and 3rd foods, is clearly labeled to help take the guesswork out of buying baby food, especially for first-time parents.

Heinz has positioned itself as an inexpensive brand in the baby food business with two-tier strategy to combat Gerber's well-developed line. Heinz offers the least costly traditional jarred baby food and also offers a dry instant alternative. The instant alternative, introduced nationally in 1984, was also a concept borrowed from European operations where it is popular. The conceptual advantage is that parents can mix only the amount of baby food needed—eliminating waste and leftover jars in the refrigerator. Gerber also tested a similar instant product with Heinz in 1982, but because only about five percent of the market appeared interested in purchasing it Gerber ceased developing the line.

Legendary Independence

In 1984 Paul Brown noted in *Forbes* that Gerber had been noticeably absent from the plethora of food business takeovers occurring at the time. The company, long recognized for its conservatism, was determined to remain independent. In 1977 Anderson, Clayton & Co. had offered a 50 percent premium over the purchase price of the stock on a tender offer. In response, Gerber filed court action as a delay tactic. Faced with a drawn out legal battle, Anderson, Clayton withdrew. Although it was generally acknowledged that Gerber was undervalued during the takeover spree, it remained untouched largely because of its legendary desire to remain independent.

Performance Appraisal

In the fiscal 1992 operating year (ending March 31, 1992), Gerber realized an 11.1 percent sales increase in its worldwide food category over 1991 to $771 million. This sales volume represented a 71 percent share of the $900 million U.S. baby food market. The 11.1 percent growth was largely due to a four percent increase in food prices, implemented in two tiers, and a four percent volume increase in the U.S. and Canadian markets.

The domestic market for baby food is influenced mainly by two factors: new births and quantity consumed per baby. Although Gerber has little influence over the birth rate, which has flattened at about four million per year, it has had some influence over consumption patterns. Partially as a result of expanding its product line, Gerber raised the amount of food it sold per baby from a low of 553 jars per baby in 1982, to 637 jars by 1992.

Gerber's attention to distribution has also afforded considerable advantage. Its sales force of approximately 600 has a distinct competitive advantage, being the only direct force in the industry. This asset has been effective in maintaining Gerber's overwhelming presence in the grocery aisles. In 1992 the average number of Gerber varieties carried by account was 147—an increase of more than six percent from the year before. Attention to distribution has also enabled Gerber to widen its distribution net to include mass merchants, who had traditionally carried nonfood items. The concept of including baby food with other Gerber branded products in a one-stop shopping concept has appealed to mass merchandise stores and increased Gerber sales.

Gerber has also increased brand awareness by increasing the breadth of products marketed under the Gerber label. Gerber's ability to leverage its brand recognition has led to many new and successful products in addition to increasing baby food sales through increased cross-promotional opportunities. The company has used the "Superbrand" concept to successfully market a baby

Dorothy Hope Smith's unfinished sketch of a neighbor's child became the well-known Gerber Baby.

formula in joint effort with Bristol Myers. Other products marketed under the "Superbrand" umbrella include toys, nursers, clothing and safety devices.

Future Predictions

Gerber believes its greatest opportunity for expansion lies in the international market, especially given the fact that the United States accounts for only 2 percent of the world's births, yet 90 percent of Gerber's sales are made to this 2 percent. In 1991 Gerber began exporting to Europe, a market formerly controlled by its licensee, CPC International. The CPC agreement was initiated in the late 1960s, but over the years, instead of flourishing under the licensee, Gerber found its share contracting. In reacquiring its brand, Gerber plans to completely reenter the European market—the second largest existing baby food market in the world next to the United States. In serving its newly developing European market, Gerber intends to utilize its investment in its production plant in Poland to establish a regional supply source. In 1991, in anticipation of its increased international efforts, Gerber switched most of its worldwide advertising account to Grey Advertising due to their international network. In 1992 Gerber's international sales goal was to reach $500 million by 1996. Achievement of this goal would more than double its international market presence.

Through Gerber's ongoing plans to increase domestic market dominance by prolonging the product life cycle, being attentive to sagging regional areas, and expanding brand awareness and distribution through the ''Superbrand'' concept, the domestic internal goal of 75 percent market share may be reached within the next few years. A quote from Gerber's 1992 annual report encapsulates its past success and future potential: ''Our heritage of earning and maintaining trust with all constituencies is both the foundation of our growth, and the reason we can continue to grow, into a truly global company.''

Further Reading:

Brown, Paul B., ''Unloved but Not Unworthy,'' *Forbes,* November 19, 1984, p. 286.

Cleary, David Powers, *Great American Brands,* New York: Fairchild, 1981, pp. 112-119.

Coupe, Kevin, ''Baby Needs,'' *Supermarket Business,* September, 1986, p. 106.

Fannin, Rebecca, ''High Stakes at the High Chair,'' *Marketing & Media Decisions,* October, 1986, pp. 62-72.

''Gerber Goes with Grey,'' *Wall Street Journal,* February 28, 1991, p. B3.

Gerber Products Company Annual Reports, Fremont: Gerber Products Company, 1991-1992.

Gershman, Michael, *Getting It Right the Second Time,* Reading: Addison-Wesley, 1990, pp. 119-123.

Hanes, Phillis, ''Baby Food Goes Multicultural,'' *Christian Science Monitor,* June 18, 1992, p. 14.

Kanner, Bernice, ''Into the Mouths of Babes,'' *New York,* November 17, 1986, pp. 27-31.

Larson, E. J., *Gerber Products Company—Company Report,* The First Boston Corporation, November 4, 1991.

Loewy, B. A., *Food Conference Summary Notes—Industry Report,* S. G. Warburg & Co. Inc., April 10, 1992.

Maki, Dee Ann, ''A Fuller Platter to Choose From,'' *Advertising Age,* October 3, 1988, p. S-2.

McCarthy, Michael, and Cathy Taylor, ''Gerber's Global Growth Will Free Grey Advertising,'' *Adweek,* October 28, 1991, p. 3.

McGill, Douglas C., ''Making Mashed Peas Pay Off,'' *New York Times,* April 9, 1989, p. F4.

McHugh, B. D., *Gerber Products Company—Company Report,* William Blair & Company, October 22, 1991.

Mitchell, Russell and Judith H. Dobrzynski, ''Why Gerber Is Standing Its Ground,'' *Business Week,* March 17, 1986, pp. 50-51.

''Open Wide,'' *Fortune,* March 13, 1989, p. 140.

Pick, Grant, ''Gerber's Baby Under Stress,'' *Across the Board,* July-August, 1986, pp. 9-13.

Shapiro, Eben, ''Looking for More Mouths to Feed,'' *New York Times,* June 11, 1992, p. D1.

Spencer, R., *Gerber Products Company—Company Report,* Paine Webber Inc., March 19, 1992.

Strnad, Patricia, ''Gerber Seeks 'Superbrand' Role,'' *Advertising Age,* April 9, 1990, p. 26; ''New Gerber Account Whets Shops' Hunger,'' *Advertising Age,* April 30, 1990, p. 54; ''Gerber to Grow in Europe,'' *Advertising Age,* March 18, 1991, p. 17.

—Louise L. Groden

GLEN ELLEN®

Glen Ellen Winery, located in the wine-producing region of Sonoma County, California, is a family-owned business that has achieved remarkable success only a few short years after its inception. The brand quickly became known nationally as a high-quality yet reasonably priced line of wines. Glen Ellen has pioneered the so-called "fighting varietal," a wine made from a single type of grape—such as chardonnay or zinfandel—and priced under $10 for a standard-sized 750-milliliter bottle. By 1991, Glen Ellen wines had achieved a strong market share in the category of domestically produced wines sold in the United States. The company's labels enjoy a wide distribution and brand awareness in major markets throughout the United States. Glen Ellen also sells its wines in 28 other countries, with exports accounting for around six percent of annual production. The United Kingdom is the most enthusiastic overseas consumer of the Glen Ellen brand.

Product Lines

Each year the Glen Ellen Winery produces more than ten varieties of wine and four varietals—cabernet, merlot, chardonnay, and white zinfandel. Glen Ellen also sells cabernet, sauvignon bland, white zinfandel, and chardonnay under the M.G. Vallejo label. In the $4-7 range, the Glen Ellen "Proprietor's Reserve" and M.G. Vallejo lines usually account for around 85 percent of annual sales. The Benziger Estate label, a premium line, features several vintages, including cabernet sauvignon, red zinfandel, and pinot blanc. Priced around $15 per bottle, these are the company's serious entry into the boutique wine category. While accounting for less than 15 percent of yearly sales, these premium vintages are important. Vintners carefully cultivate and produce these labels, considering them "showcase" products and often entering them into competition against European vintages. Another premium line, Imagery, is sometimes used for introducing experimental products to the market and features unique artist-commissioned labels.

Company Origins

The Glen Ellen Winery was founded in Glen Ellen, California, in 1981. Its founders were the Benziger family, residents of White Plains, New York. Father Bruno Benziger had been co-owner of Park-Benziger, a New York-based wine and liquor import firm. His son Michael Benziger had worked both in the northern California wine business and with Park-Benziger after graduating from college. In the late 1970s, he convinced his father to sell his interest in Park-Benziger and use the capital to finance a family-owned winery in Sonoma County, California. The 85 acres of land Mike Benziger found near Glen Ellen had previously been owned by an eccentric doctor who used only some of it for vineyards. The rest of the Benziger family, including mother Helen and siblings Patsy, Joe, and Chris, soon moved to California to assist in the new business.

Until the early 1980s, the American wine industry had been dominated by large-scale companies such as E & J Gallo and Almaden Vineyards, purveyors of reasonably priced jug wines. Their products were made from mixtures of grapes and were generally packaged in large 1.5 liter containers that retail for approximately $3 per bottle. Their only competitors in the domestic wine market were premium wines priced at $8 a bottle and up. The Benziger family's original plan was to join the ranks of the upscale wineries by creating a brand that would be produced from a carefully cultivated stock of grapes, available only in limited amounts, and targeted toward the upscale wine consumer.

The Benziger family's first attempt at wine production took place when their facilities were not yet complete. They toiled late into the night to produce the first bottles of Glen Ellen chardonnay and sauvignon blanc. Hampered by a lack of electricity, they nonetheless persevered by using car headlights for lights and storing the wine in a rented milk truck. This inventiveness paid off as both wines won the top prizes in the 1981 Sonoma County Harvest Fair, giving the fledgling winery some favorable free publicity.

Factors in the domestic wine market provided the company with a unique opportunity. The first was a shift in overall wine consumption among U.S. consumers. Demographics showed that while people were generally drinking less wine, the average buyer was both younger and spending more per bottle. At the same time, the California wine industry, long overshadowed by the centuries-old European winemakers, was maturing and gaining respect from wine connoisseurs. There was also a shift in the grape market—the specific varieties had generally increased in quality over the years but wine sales had dropped off, creating a surplus of grapes.

It was here that Bruno Benziger saw an opportunity for a medium-priced wine for the domestic market. Glen Ellen would

AT A GLANCE

Glen Ellen brand of wines founded in 1981 in Glen Ellen, CA, by the Benziger family.

Performance: *Market share*—3.5 percent of the domestic wine category. *Sales*—$161.3 million.

Major competitor: Sutter Home; also E & J Gallo Winery's White Grenache.

Advertising: *Agency*—In-house, 1981—. *Major campaign*— Glen Ellen stresses in its advertising that it "puts quality in, takes intimidation out" in choosing a wine.

Addresses: *Parent company*—Glen Ellen Winery, 1883 London Ranch Road, Glen Ellen, CA 95442; phone: (707) 935-3000; fax: (707) 935-3016.

purchase the surplus grapes in bulk from the other vintners and growers, and then blend, bottle, and sell the wine for $4-7. He originally saw this as a sort of cash-flow wine whose quick profits would finance the Glen Ellen's premium wines. These first affordable wines, packaged in 750-milliliter bottles, were simply labeled red or white similar to the jug wines. According to strict industry standards, however, the grape content was specific enough for the bottles to be directly labeled as to their content. At the suggestion of a wholesaler, the Benzigers decided to promote the new wines in this way. Soon bottles of Glen Ellen chardonnays and sauvignon blancs appeared on shelves with a "Proprietor's Reserve" label, adding an upscale image to the product while it remained reasonably priced. This practice aroused the ire of well-established vintners, but they soon followed Glen Ellen into the medium-priced field. Thus, a new niche in the domestic wine market, the fighting varietal, was created.

Early Marketing Strategy

Bruno Benziger took advantage of his extensive distributor contacts (from his Park-Benziger days) to make the Glen Ellen brand quickly available across the United States. The winery produced 35,000 cases in its second year of operation, and by 1985 was bottling 600,000 cases annually. In 1984, as rivals flooded shelves with varietals similar to Glen Ellen's, the company introduced its second label, M.G. Vallejo. (This new line was named after the first Spanish governor of California.) By 1988, six years after its start-up, Glen Ellen's production reached 2.38 million cases. Its competitors in the field of fighting varietals included Fetzer Vineyards, Robert Mondavi, and Sutter Home. Even Gallo attempted to join the mid-priced category in the late 1980s with the introduction of a white grenache whose accompanying ad campaign targeted price-conscious but educated wine drinkers.

Brand Development

A reason for Glen Ellen's success is that it strives to remain essentially a family operation. The winery feels that by en-franchising its 350-plus employees as "family members," a quality product can be assured through each individual's high level of commitment. The Benziger family asserts that its forte is making and marketing wine, not cultivating vineyards. Most wineries own large tracts of grape-growing land to produce the company's yield, and then blend and bottle their wines on the premises. Conversely, Glen Ellen farms out much of the actual winemaking to subcontractors. With the exception of the Benziger Estate wines, Glen

Ellen's vintages are produced from grapes purchased from more than 200 California growers. This gives the company more flexibility to react to market fluctuations. For instance, Glen Ellen works with growers throughout California. When adverse weather affects a crops in certain areas, it does not greatly affect the year's total output.

Resulting reductions in overhead have allowed Glen Ellen to spend more capital in effective marketing strategies. Yet one disadvantage to this system is that the company is more affected by shifts in the market price of grapes. Because so many companies began to produce mid-range varietals, the demand for these grapes skyrocketed and reduced Glen Ellen's profit margins. Any attempt to increase point-of-purchase prices caused a sharp decline in sales. Some industry analysts criticized Glen Ellen for relying on subcontractor growers, asserting that a winery needs total control over every aspect of the winemaking process to insure a uniform quality of its product.

Glen Ellen Expands

The year 1989 brought several changes to both the Benziger family and Glen Ellen Wines. The family suffered the loss of its founder and leader, Bruno, who died in July. Mike Benziger, who had formerly concentrated on the winemaking process, became chief executive officer. His brother Joe replaced him in the production area of the winery while brother-in-law Tim Wallace headed up Glen Ellen's marketing division. Also in 1989 Mike Benziger bought back his father's interest in Park-Benziger. Val du Mont, a varietal produced by the Skalli winery in Sete, France, joined the family of wines produced in conjunction with the Glen Ellen winery and distributed by Park-Benziger. Meanwhile, the Glen Ellen and M.G. Vallejo lines continued to do well in the moderately-priced category, which grew in overall popularity among consumers. Glen Ellen's final figures for 1989 showed a 13 percent increase in sales from the previous year.

In the late 1980s Glen Ellen finally introduced the premium wine it had originally planned on producing, Benziger Estate. This wine entered a much more competitive niche of the market, where bottles priced $12 and upward are generally purchased by a more demanding wine consumer. At the time of its introduction, the Benziger label of such wines as cabernet sauvignon and red zinfandel were competing in a high-end category that had recently seen flattened sales. The popularity of the mid-priced varietals had contributed to this drop. Mike Benziger asserted in a November 1989 *Beverage World* article, however, that "the purpose of the Benziger [Estate label] program is not to move quantity and move boxes, but to build image and status for the winery by first being the very best wine."

Advertising Strategy

Nearly five percent of Glen Ellen's annual production is comprised of wines produced for consumption on domestic and international airline flights. This has successfully introduced both Glen Ellen's flagship label as well as more experimental lines to a captive audience, who might otherwise hesitate to try a new product. It serves a dual purpose as a test market and a vehicle to increase brand awareness of Glen Ellen.

One theme that Glen Ellen stresses in its promotions can be best paraphrased as "Glen Ellen puts quality in, takes intimidation out." Glen Ellen spends less on advertising than its competitors and concentrates on print ads in beverage trade magazines and off-site display materials. Radio advertising is also done in selected markets, usually in conjunction with special promotions. Outside agencies are sometimes hired to create marketing concepts, but generally most of the work is created in-house.

Packaging

Wines under the Glen Ellen brand can be found in shouldered 750-milliliter bottles, which can be purchased individually or by the 9-liter case. The Glen Ellen Proprietor's Reserve carries a square label that is yellow for the white wines and pink for the rosés. M.G. Vallejo labels are larger and a bit flashier, with white and gold lettering on a black background. Benziger Estate labels feature gold lettering, on a marbleized green field. Since 1991 Glen Ellen has also bottled selected wines in small 187-milliliter bottles. This has been successful in inducing consumers to try both the company's standard chardonnays or cabernets as well as newer varietals. To communicate to the buyer that the wine remains of the same quality, the smaller bottles are miniature versions of Glen Ellen's usual packaging design. They are also convenient for distribution to the airline sales segment.

Glen Ellen is known for taking some chances occasionally in its packaging. Glen Ellen became the first among California vintners to try out a risky proposition—a metal screw top instead of a cork. Screw tops were generally found only in the lower-end jug wines. The cork, grown mainly in Portugal, has long been *de rigueur* among wine connoisseurs and the general public. Corks conveyed old-world cachet, yet their practical reason for existence was to let a certain amount of air evolve a wine. However, in the last few years cork quality has sharply declined, with the result that dry corks ruined otherwise decent bottles of wine. By 1991 wine industry experts estimated that nearly five percent of wine produced was spoiled due to poor-quality corks.

In 1990 Glen Ellen produced a new varietal from Italian dolcetto grapes. Introduced under the winery's Imagery label, the light rosé was new to the American market, and Glen Ellen feared that consumers would store it instead of drinking it right away. This wine was similar to the French Beaujolais Nouveau, in that should be enjoyed as close to the harvest of its grapes as possible and not stored for any length of time. The solution was to put a screw cap on, with the exhortation "unscrew the cap tonight" prominently displayed on a neck tag. The dolcetto tested favorably in its markets, but Glen Ellen was not entirely willing to be the first in the field to completely reject the cork. Although industry sentiment runs high in favor of the innovation, Rusty Eddy, director of public relations at Glen Ellen, noted that consumers do not seem ready to make the adjustment in terms of perceived quality.

Performance Appraisal

Glen Ellen's sales have increased by several percentage points each year since the brand's inception. By the 1990s, Glen Ellen

Wines had achieved sales figures of $161.3 million dollars. This translated into tenth place in the domestic wine category and a 3.5 percent market share. The following year, Glen Ellen rose a notch to ninth place. Beverage industry experts attribute Glen Ellen's success to several factors, including effective marketing strategies that competitors have been quick to emulate. Glen Ellen's apparent eagerness to experiment—whether successful or not—has also helped the label gain such an impressive market share in so short a span of time. Being a family-owned company may have helped it weather both some of the repercussions of a sluggish economy of the late 1980s and early 1990s as well as profound changes within the alcoholic beverage market itself. Glen Ellen Wines have created a niche in the domestically-produced wine category of the mid-priced varietal, but undoubtedly competition from more established and successful wineries continually threatens Glen Ellen's position.

Future Growth

Since much of Glen Ellen's sales come from their mid-priced Glen Ellen and M.G. Vallejo lines, it seems likely that Glen Ellen will strive to assure that this segment remains profitable. The boutique wines such as Benziger Estate and Imagery have achieved only a nominal degree of success in this highly competitive category (but it was not expected that these would achieve the same degree of success so quickly). In all likelihood, Glen Ellen will continue to produce a quality wine at a reasonable price and rely heavily on this segment of the market to weather any future storms. Glen Ellen seems willing and able to experiment. Since much of the company's initial success and growth came from pioneering the fighting varietal, the winery has been inclined to introduce innovations in the areas of marketing, new products, and packaging. Small experimental lines such as Imagery can easily absorb a failed product launch without much financial distress. It is likely that Glen Ellen could someday again hit upon yet another undiscovered niche in the market.

Further Reading:

Galvin, Andrew, "The Impossible Dream," *Beverage World,* November, 1989, pp. 22-83.

"Glen Ellen Puts on a New Face," *Beverage World,* May, 1990, p. 14.

Goldberg, Howard G., "A Drink of Premium Wine Is a Twist of the Wrist Away," *New York Times,* January 8, 1992, p. C3.

Sheeline, William E., "Fighting Varietals," *Fortune,* September 12, 1988, pp. 11-14.

"Superbrands 1992: America's Top 2000 Brands (supplement)," *Adweek's Brandweek.*

"Superbrands 1991: America's Top 2000 Brands (supplement)," *Adweek's Marketing Week.*

Weisman, Kathleen, "Mike Benziger's Fighting Varietals," *Forbes,* February 19, 1990, pp. 134-137.

—Carol Brennan

GOLD MEDAL®

Washburn, Crosby & Co. had three grades of flour entered in the 1880 Millers' International Exhibition in Cincinnati. Each grade of flour entered won an award, the gold, silver, and bronze medals, beating competitors from around the world. The company gave to their top grade flour the name it had earned: Gold Medal. Gold Medal flour, a cornerstone product when Washburn, Crosby & Co. reformed as General Mills, Inc. in the 1920s, has set the standard for the highest quality flour for more than a century. Generations of families have baked with the assurance that Gold Medal is the "superlative" flour, keeping it the number one seller in the flour industry and a leader in General Mills' product lines.

Hard-Kerneled Wheat

The making of flour dates back to the earliest civilizations and to humankind's need to feed itself. The first attempts at milling were very crude: wild grain was crushed between stones. This grinding did produce a flour meal, but unwanted particles had to be picked out by hand. It was millenniums before millers learned to produce palatable flour efficiently. One miller who experimented with innovations that improved flour quality and ultimately changed the standards of the American milling industry was Cadwallader Colden Washburn, whose great prestige guaranteed the innovations a fair trial.

Born in 1818, Washburn borrowed enough money when he was 21 to leave his native Maine. He wandered the Mississippi Valley, where he taught school, clerked, surveyed land, and, at Mineral Point in Wisconsin Territory, set up a law office. In 1844 he began to establish a fortune as a Wisconsin land agent, buying up the land grants given to veterans of the Mexican War and selling them as valuable timber and mineral properties.

Washburn's personality and abilities won him wide repute. He was elected in 1854 to the United States Congress, in which two of his brothers also sat as representatives from Maine and Illinois. Washburn also served as governor of Wisconsin. His public service extended to the military during the Civil War. He raised a regiment of cavalry and was major-general in the Mississippi campaigns, including the fighting around Vicksburg.

Washburn started down yet another vocational path when he purchased a failing Minneapolis mill in 1856, located on a prime site beside the Falls of St. Anthony on the Mississippi River. He erected his first flour mill in 1866. As it turned out, he was at the right place at the right time. The Minnesota wheat crop grew from two thousand bushels in 1850 to fifteen million by 1869. Minneapolis millers became important merchants of the state's most valuable crop.

Many changes contributed to the transformation of the flour industry from a very localized one to one with far-flung markets. Small local mills produced most of America's flour until the middle of the nineteenth century, with sales usually confined to the immediate area of the mill. There was no national marketing of flour and very little branding. If branded at all, flour carried the mill's name or the name of the wheat grower. George Washington registered his name as a trademark for flour in 1772.

The newly settled farms on the western prairies upset the closed pattern of milling in the 1830s as they began to ship grain and flour east. By the 1860s, Minnesota and the Dakotas had become a major source of grain for the rest of the country. But the wheat planted by farmers in the northern plains states sold for less than the wheat raised in the East. The problem was the hard-kerneled wheat they had to plant in the spring because of the harsh winters. The shells (bran) of the spring wheat shattered and mixed with the flour in normal milling creating a coarse, dark meal instead of the white flour milled from the soft-kerneled winter wheat of the East.

Washburn was one of the first flour makers to solve the problem. With his partners, George H. Smith, an expert miller, and George H. Christian, a Southerner who had come north after the Civil War to become a flour broker, he hired a Canadian engineer named Edmund La Croix to build a device known as a middlings purifier. The device used air currents and sieves to separate the flour from the bran. In 1871, the Washburn B mill led the way in the large-scale application of this system, known as "New-Process" milling. The process turned Minnesota flour from a second-rate product into a premium grade. It also contributed to the further expansion of wheat farming in the region. More mills sprang up, and in the decade of the 1870s the value of northwestern flour grew from $7.5 million to more than $41 million.

Patent Flour

Washburn, however, wanted to make further improvements. American mills had relied on stone grinding wheels for centuries, even though the use of water power and steam engines had

AT A GLANCE

Gold Medal brand of flour founded in 1880 in Minneapolis, MN, by Washburn, Crosby & Co.; earned its name by winning the gold medal at the 1880 Millers' International Exhibition in Cincinnati, OH; became leading product of General Mills, Inc., a network of regional mills organized under the guidance of James Ford Bell, of Washburn Crosby & Co. in 1928.

Performance: *Market share*—Top share of family flour category.

Major competitor: Pillsbury Flour; also Chelsea Milling Co.'s pouch packaged mixes and Martha White Foods, Inc. flour.

Advertising: *Agency*—DDB Needham, Chicago, IL, 1989—.

Addresses: *Parent company*—General Mills, Inc., One General Mills Blvd., P.O. Box 1113, Minneapolis, MN 55440; phone: (612) 540-2311.

increased their capacity. Meanwhile, the Europeans had developed a method that passed wheat slowly through a series of chilled rollers to produce a fine white flour.

After forming a partnership with John Crosby in 1877 to create Washburn, Crosby & Co., Washburn hired William de la Barre, an Austrian-born engineer, and sent him to Europe to find out about the advanced roller technique used in mills there. De la Barre was gone nearly five months. In Germany, Switzerland, and Austria, he found the doors shut to him. He took a workman's position in Budapest for ten nights so he could enter a mill and study the technology. When he returned to Minneapolis he completed plans for a section of a Washburn mill, incorporating some of the stolen technology and adding improvements. The most notable change was the replacement of porcelain rollers with steel. The technique soon spread beyond the Washburn mill, and the claims of "roller process" or "patent" flour showed up on the labels of many competing brands. Patent flour is a high-grade wheat flour that consists solely of the nutrient-rich endosperm.

A catastrophe set the stage for implementation of the experimental roller process. A little after seven o'clock on the evening of May 2, 1878, the Washburn "A" New-Process mill blew up because of dust, a very flammable and hazardous byproduct of the milling process. A small initiating explosion shook accumulated dust from walls and ceiling. The next blast razed the solid walls, six feet thick at the base, and led to the destruction of five other mills. Eighteen people died in the blast, fourteen inside the mill.

Foundations were being laid at the time for an addition to a Washburn mill. After the accident, Washburn paced off extra feet for the foundation. The result was an oversized building, with 18 feet of vacant space. An advisor, W. D. Gray, suggested putting in a small experimental roller. A man named Oscar Oexle came to Minneapolis with Wegmann porcelain rollers, gravity purifiers, reels, and ideas for the project. Additionally, the mill used belts to drive half the roller assemblies. The method proved so superior it became a standard for American mills. The experimental mill had a low capacity, but the flour quality was high and the yield satisfactory. Originally designed to make six grades of flour, the number was reduced to three, the largest number for which there was a market in America. These three grades were the three that won the top awards at the 1880 exhibition in Cincinnati.

Advertising to Consumers

Washburn Crosby & Co. was one of the first millers to advertise. Previously millers limited themselves to calendars and other occasional advertisements. The first Washburn, Crosby & Co. periodical advertisement intended for the trade appeared in 1884 in the *Northwestern Miller*. The company's successor firm, the Washburn Crosby Co., was the first to initiate national consumer advertising of its flour by purchasing a one-inch space for a single insertion in the September, 1893 issue of the *Ladies Home Journal*. The ad told readers that two bakers at the Chicago World's Fair used Gold Medal flour exclusively, and invited them to send for a free souvenir booklet.

As the growth of a national market took shape, Washburn Crosby & Co. decided in 1899 to concentrate on a single top-brand flour: Gold Medal. Before, different brands sold in different parts of the country. The circular design adopted as a stencil for barrel heads has carried through with little change as a design for consumer-sized bags of flour. The current logo consists of the words *Baking Success Since 1880* in dark blue capital letters arched over the Gold Medal medallion and two orange wheat stalks arched underneath. Within the orange medallion, the words *Gold Medal* are in dark blue letters outlined in white. Dark blue "stitching" separates the words and the perimeter of the medallion. Gold Medal packages also bear the words "A Symbol of Quality." By the time the *Ladies Home Journal* ad appeared, flour was sold for home use in smaller than full-size 196-pound barrels. In 1905, Gold Medal was sold in large, hand sewn fabric bags. When fabric became scare during World War I, the company developed a new paper sack tied with twine.

Advertising manager Benjamin Bull thought up Gold Medal's most famous slogan, first used in 1907. According to one story, he was given a wordy advertisement for approval. Each paragraph began with "Eventually" and went on at length to describe the merits of Gold Medal flour. Bull, an argumentative man, crossed out all but the first "Eventually" and scrawled in the margin, "Why not now?" Among the other slogans that have been used for Gold Medal flour are "Good for everything you bake and everything you bake with it is good," and, in the 1950s, "White thumb of success."

Betty Crocker

An early promotion for Gold Medal led to the creation of one of America's most widely known characters, the "Helpful Home Economist" Betty Crocker, "America's First Lady of Food." In 1921, Washburn Crosby & Co. offered consumers a pincushion resembling a flour sack if they correctly completed a jigsaw puzzle of a milling scene. More than 30,000 people sent in the completed puzzle, plus a flood of questions about baking.

The advertising staff tapped the collective wisdom of laboratory personnel, home economists, and office personnel and their wives to answer the questions and come up with recipes. Advertising manager Sam Gale believed a woman would be an appropriate spokesperson to personally reply to each letter. The spokeswoman's surname was chosen to honor a popular, recently retired director of the company, William G. Crocker. Betty was chosen because it was a friendly, familiar-sounding name. The company invited women employees to submit sample Betty Crocker signatures. The one judged most distinctive is still in use as correspondents answer Betty Crocker's mail and home economists operate her kitchens to test products and create new recipes.

Through the years Betty Crocker's image has changed. A Betty Crocker face appeared in some print ads in the 1920s, but the first ''official'' Betty Crocker portrait appeared in print ads for Gold Medal flour soon after it was painted in 1936. Washburn Crosby Co. sponsored radio programs when other companies thought housewives were too busy to listen. When the company saved a local station from bankruptcy, it started the *Betty Crocker Cooking School of the Air*. The program expanded to thirteen regional stations, each with its own Betty Crocker voice reading the scripts written by staff in Minneapolis. The program moved to the fledgling NBC network in 1927, where it continued for 24 years.

Growing Flour Markets

What the steel roller mill did for the grinding of wheat, James Ford Bell did for the milling industry. When his father, James S. Bell, came to the presidency of the Washburn Crosby Co. in 1889, a large part of the milling capacity of Minneapolis was in the hands of a few individually owned companies. Nationwide trafficking of flour was causing the decline of community milling. Large producers, manufacturing under more favorable circumstances and in great volume at lowered unit costs, had an economic advantage even though they were at a distance from the end market. In 1904, by starting a new mill in Buffalo, the Washburn Crosby Co. initiated the migration of Minneapolis millers eastward. The millers of the Northwest, who had already won almost worldwide acceptance for their flour, realized they must make adaptations in the way they did business if they were to keep their status.

While many other industries had merged to pool resources, plants, and marketing facilities, small mills still struggled with problems as lone operators. James Ford Bell, who succeeded his father as president of Washburn Crosby Co., was an acknowledged leader in operational, marketing, and management developments. Bell studied the situation. Besides the unpredictability of wheat crops, he saw glaring inconsistencies among millers in their pricing, shipping and marketing practices which became apparent at the consumer level and proved a detriment to the entire industry. In 1928 he presented to the Washburn Crosby Co. board of directors his idea for a solution: a merger of reputable millers located in strategic wheat-growing and wheat-consuming areas across the country into a single organization.

Birth of General Mills

Bell's proposed organization was a careful assembly of units strategically located with reference to new wheat fields, shifting population, changing rates, and altered consumption, and it was the first attempt to give all these factors due weight in shaping a comprehensive plan for serving the whole people of the continental area. By 1929, the design was complete, with twenty-seven operating companies integrated into the Washburn Crosby Co. to become the largest miller in the world, General Mills, Inc.

Many of the ideas and names American consumers take for granted, including Bisquick, the nation's first prepared baking mix, Gold Medal flour, Betty Crocker, Wheaties, and Brown 'N Serve Rolls, came from the companies absorbed in the General Mills organization and from the vast program of research and development made possible by the merger. With more than 110,000 employees, General Mills is a leader in packaged foods and restaurants, ranking number one in flour, cake mixes, and frozen fish. The 1950s brought an expansion of General Mills into

foreign countries. In 1992, the company had operations in Canada, minority ownership in flour milling joint ventures in Latin America, and export and technology activities.

Quality Assurance and Consumer Service

General Mills declares that it works hard to carry on the Gold Medal tradition of superlative quality and innovation. That tradition dates back to 1893, when Washburn, Crosby & Co. was the first American miller to set up a testing room. In 1898, James F. Bell, still a student at the University of Minnesota, persuaded the company to rent two rooms over a saloon in which to study the moisture and ash content of flour and the extraction of oil from wheat germ. In 1921, the company expanded its commitment to consumer service and product quality by sponsoring cooking schools across the country and employing a trained home economist to carefully test its gold-medal winning flour. Consumer service and satisfaction remain a priority for General Mills. One example is General Mills' response when its flour products were found to be tainted with a harmful insecticide. The company set up several toll-free telephone numbers and gave out refunds.

The company has also responded to concerns about the nutritional value of flour. In the 1930s, it became apparent that health essentials were being eliminated from flour. General Mills used a number of thiamin-laden streams to make an excellent vitamin flour; however, the flour failed in the marketplace because it was darker than usual patent flours. After chemists learned how to produce enough vitamins to effectively add them to flour, practically the entire American milling and baking industry embarked on an enrichment program in 1940, adding thiamin, niacin, riboflavin, and iron. In more recent years, General Mills added calcium to Gold Medal flour, helping at the same time to enrich its lead over Pillsbury Flour.

Brand Improvements and Outlook

Several products other than flour have carried the Gold Medal brand name. In 1923, Washburn Crosby Co. expanded its product line from just flour to packaged foods under the name Gold Medal Products. The company introduced one of the first of those products in 1924. It was a flaked cereal derived from the whole kernel of wheat, as tasty as it was nourishing. An employee's wife named it ''Wheaties.''

When General Mills bought the Robin Hood brand from Multi-Foods Corporation, the deal included a line of packaged mixes. While the company retained the Robin Hood name in established markets, it reformulated, repackaged, and expanded distribution of pouch mixes to certain areas under the Gold Medal brand name. The brand is on Golden Corn Muffin Mix, Pizza Crust Mix, Blueberry Muffin Mix, Biscuit Mix, Buttermilk Pancake Mix, and Fudge Brownie Mix packaged mixes. Chief competitors are Jiffy mixes made by Chelsea Milling Co. and Martha White mixes made by Martha White Foods, Inc. The sales volume for the Robin Hood and Gold Medal pouch mixes grew more than 70 percent in 1992, driven by improvements to established products, expansion into new markets, and introduction of a new cake line. General Mills' Foodservice Division also distributes Gold Medal Low Fat Variety Muffin Mix. The principal brand product, Gold Medal flour, even without an advertising campaign, maintained its number one share position in the $440 million family flour market in 1992.

General Mills is a corporate giant, but the profitability and popularity of its cornerstone product—Gold Medal flour—causes its management to worry about the same problems 19th century millers battled: the appeal of the flour meal and fluctuations in the price of flour based on the success or failure of the wheat crop. However, because of General Mills' commitment to quality, a regular schedule of brand improvement, and consumer service, Gold Medal will probably continue to be a winner on the grocer's shelf.

Further Reading:

Byrne, Harlan S., "General Mills: Paced by Gains in Cereals' Market Share, It Exceeds Growth Targets," *Barron's,* April 20, 1992, pp. 47-48.

Campbell, Hannah, *Why Did They Name It . . . ?,* New York: Fleet Publishing, 1964, pp. 16-20.

Fox, Stephen, *The Mirror Makers: A History of American Advertising and Its Creators,* New York: Vintage, 1985, p. 159.

General Mills Annual Report, Minneapolis: General Mills, Inc., 1992.

General Mills: Historical Highlights, Minneapolis: General Mills, Inc., November, 1989.

Groner, Alex, and editors of American Heritage and Business Week, *The American Heritage History of American Business & Industry,* New York: American Heritage, 1972, p. 170.

Moskowitz, Milton, Robert Levering and Michael Katz, editors, *Everybody's Business. A Field Guide to the 400 Leading Companies in America,* New York: Doubleday, 1990, pp. 13-15.

Sellers, Patricia, "A Boring Brand Can Be Beautiful," *Fortune,* June 5, 1989, p. 173.

Sharp, Harold S., *Advertising Slogans of America,* Metuchen, NJ: Scarecrow Press, 1984, p. 186.

Storck, John, and Walter Dorwin Teague, *Flour for Man's Bread: A History of Milling,* Minneapolis: University of Minnesota Press, 1952.

The Story of Betty Crocker, Minneapolis: General Mills, Inc., July, 1992.

Zeitz, Baila and Lorraine Dusky, *The Best Companies for Women,* New York: Simon and Schuster, 1988, p. 141.

—Doris Morris Maxfield

GORDON'S®

"Four bottles [of Gordon's London Dry Gin] are consumed every second of the day and night," boasted P. J. Tanqueray, director of Tanqueray Gordon & Company in 1989. Working out the math of that statement produces a consumption rate of 345,600 bottles per day, or over 126 million per year. Those figures made Gordon's the world's best-selling gin, and the second best-selling brand in the United States. It is sold in over 140 countries and, worldwide, is the fifth-largest-selling brand of spirits. In the early 1990s in the United States, Gordon's gin was manufactured and distributed by United Distillers Glenmore, a subsidiary of Guiness PLC.

The Gordon's formula of gin is a trade secret, but like most other gins, Gordon's is made from nearly pure, distilled grain alcohol, which is then diluted with water and flavorings known as botanicals. Gordon's botanicals include the juniper berry, coriander, angelica root, cassia bark, cinnamon bark, lemon peel, orange peel, and licorice. The water, alcohol, and botanical mix is then distilled a second time to produce a clear liquor, as is done with vodka.

Early Days

In 1769 Alexander Gordon celebrated his wedding by founding Gordon & Company, with the idea of producing a quality gin. Although Gordon's father had been a gin distiller, the company founded in 1769 was not a simple continuation of the family business. The older Gordon's gin production coincided with an act of Parliament in 1690 that allowed, and even encouraged, the free production of distilled spirits. Most of the gin of that era was poor quality home brew, made with polluted water and little or no flavoring. When public intoxication became rampant and could not be stopped, Parliament tried to tax gin out of existence in 1736, but the trade persisted, and the tax was repealed in 1742.

Alexander Gordon's idea was to produce a quality, consistent liquor with an established name. He found an unpolluted water source near London at Clerkenwell and his business prospered. Part of his success came from England's new transportation system. A series of canals developed across England, making it possible for London-distilled gin to be shipped cheaply throughout Great Britain. Gordon's was only one of several London gins to thrive during this period. The largest distiller in Alexander's day was Sheriff Booth, and Booth's gin continued to be the number one brand well into the nineteenth century.

The gin trade was becoming increasingly respectable. In 1792 Alexander was made a member of the Worshipful Company of Distillers, which was much like a lodge. In 1810, he served as the group's upper warden, placing him among the social elite of London distillers.

Originally, gin was sold to taverns in casks, and the tavern keepers sometimes diluted the gin with water or refilled kegs with cheaper gins. Alexander was conscious of the need to preserve his brand's integrity, and he once complained that he had not been able to sell his gin in bottles. Alexander died in 1823, but the company's leadership remained in the family's hands until 1888, when his grandson, Charles, retired to devote his full time to inventing. By then, the gin was bottled and carried the Boar's Head trademark that came from the Gordon family's coat-of-arms.

Gordon's in the Nineteenth Century

The Gordon's formula has remained consistent since 1769, but the distilling process has changed. In 1831, the invention of a new still permitted the creation of a purer alcohol. The resulting "London dry" style of gin was less harsh than gin distilled in the old way. Dutch gin brands continue to offer the old type of gin.

During the nineteenth century, two major events increased gin sales dramatically. In 1850, Parliament removed the excise tax on exported gin, making it profitable to sell London gin around the world. Then, during the 1890s, came the *phylloxera* plague that destroyed most of the world's vineyards. Wine and brandy became prohibitively expensive for many people, and sales of Scotch whisky and London gin climbed to new heights.

The changing business climate offered opportunity for new marketing techniques. In 1898 Gordon's merged with another distiller, Tanqueray, to form the Tanqueray-Gordon Company. Gordon's, by this time, had become the major gin in the mass market, while Tanqueray sold to a higher class of customer. Together, the two brands formed an unprecedented marketing power in the gin business.

Gordon's in America

Although Gordon's was known in America before Prohibition, the story of Gordon's success in the United States began with the repeal of the 18th Amendment to the Constitution, the Prohibition Act, and the resumption of legal alcohol beverage distribution

AT A GLANCE

Gordon's brand of gin founded in 1769 in London, England, by Alexander Gordon for his firm Gordon & Co.; renamed Gordon's London Dry Gin after introduction of new distilling process; in 1898, merged with Tanqueray to form the Tanqueray-Gordon Company; in 1935, the first American distillery opened in Linden, New Jersey, allowing Gordon's to sell gin in the United States at domestic prices; in 1947, American distribution was taken over by the Renfield Corporation; Renfield's operation was bought in 1986 by Schenley Industries Inc. of Dallas, Texas; in 1985, the British Gordon's brand was bought by Guinness PLC who consolidated spirits under the United Distillers subsidiary; in 1987, United Distillers bought Schenley Industries, gaining control of the distribution of Gordon's in the United States; in 1991, Glenmore Distilleries of Louisville, Kentucky, was acquired by, and later merged with, United Distillers to form United Distillers Glenmore; in 1992, Schenley was closed, placing Gordon's under United Distillers Glenmore.

Performance: *Market share*—13.17% of gin category.

Major competitor: Seagram's; Tanqueray; Gilbey's; Beefeater.

Advertising: *Agency*—Grey Advertising, New York, NY, 1960—. *Major campaign*—"Good Times & Gordon's Gin."

Addresses: *Parent company*—United Distillers Glenmore, 6 Landmark Square, Stamford, CT 06901; phone: (203) 359-7100; fax: (203) 359-7199. *Ultimate parent company:* Guinness PLC, 39 Portman Square, London W1H 9HB, England; phone: 44 71 486 0288; fax: 44 71 486 4968.

throughout most of the country. With the end of Prohibition, several British gin makers, including Gordon's, quickly opened distilleries in the United States.

Gordon's distillery opened in Linden, New Jersey, in 1935. Later, a distillery opened in Illinois. The operation was an immediate success as Americans switched from drinking imported gin to the much less-expensive domestic bottles. In 1934, the United States imported 139,000 proof gallons of gin, but the next year, with the rise of American gin distillers, imports collapsed to 59,000 proof gallons. Gordon's has been distilled in the United States ever since, except for a brief hiatus during World War II. Between October 8, 1942, and August 31, 1945, America's distilleries were devoted to wartime manufacturing needs and no gin was made.

Packaging

One American innovation was Gordon's clear bottle, which shows off its clear contents. The style has since been imitated by manufacturers of both gin and vodka, and is now used by Gordon's throughout the world except in England. There, Gordon's gin is bottled in its original dark green color. The British bottle also uses the original label, white with black lettering. The American label, designed in the 1930s, is yellow with red lettering. The label prominently displays the 1769 date of its origins, includes Alexander Gordon's signature, and bears a statement about how the recipe has remained the same over the centuries. Both the British and American labels display the Boar's head.

U.S. Advertising

Gordon's has been promoted in the United States as a traditional English gin available at domestic prices. The approach has given Gordon's a strong cross-niche market. As a popularly priced gin, its chief rival is Seagram's gin, and as a traditional London dry, its major rival is Beefeater's. A 1992 survey by *Beverage Dynamics* found that the average sales price for both Seagram's and Gordon's gin was nearly identical, $8.12 for Gordon's and $8.03 for Seagram's. This price gave both of those gins a heavy advantage over imported Beefeater's $14.80 average cost.

Price is only one consideration in buying gin, however. The others are prestige and image. Although Gordon's is proud of its traditional flavoring, most experts doubt that drinkers can distinguish between gins, especially when the gin is mixed with vermouth or tonic and served chilled. During the 1960s, *Consumer Reports* conducted two studies of gin and found both times that experts tended to contradict themselves when tasting gin. To justify paying nearly twice as much for a bottle of gin whose contents are indistinguishable from a cheaper brand, advertisers have to sell the brand name. As John Pennachio, who marketed Tanqueray gin, bluntly told *Beverage Dynamics* in 1992, "This is an image-driven category." Gordon's, thus, has always pushed its traditional image.

The result is a strong appeal to both price- and image-conscious customers. Buyers who are chiefly motivated by price may be willing to pay a few pennies extra to get an image-brand like Gordon's. Meanwhile, buyers who are concerned with image may still be willing to save themselves many dollars by buying a less expensive brand like Gordon's that, despite its price, carries prestige. This positioning has made Gordon's second only to Seagram's in the American market.

Gordon's has been marketed by Grey Advertising since 1960. A 1985 ad campaign used the slogan, "I could go for something Gordon's . . . the possibilities are endless." The campaign had intended to equate the Gordon's brand with quality and class and was used to promote both Gordon's gin and Gordon's vodka. Many Gordon's campaigns also emphasized tradition and British origin. A typical ad campaign for promoting Gordon's image was one introduced in 1987 as a two-page spread in magazines. On page one was a photograph of something classically British, such as the ruins of Stonehenge. The picture had the lighthearted caption, "England. Known for its famous rock groups." Page two offered a photograph of a Gordon's gin bottle, captioned, "And its gin." At the bottom of the page appeared the slogan, "The gin of England. And the world! Gordon's."

By the early 1990s, Gordon's marketing shifted away from associations to the classically English. As *Beverage World* reported in 1991, in its place Gordon's new approach "appealed to the 'social, contemporary and discriminating' gin drinker." Gordon's began the "Good Times & Gordon's Gin" campaign to appeal to this market. The campaign was successful—Gordon's attracted a more upscale clientele, one closer to Beefeater customers than Seagram's. *BrandAdvantage* reported that Gordon's drew 41 percent of its customers from households earning over $50,000, bringing the brand into more direct competition with Beefeater, which attracted 49 percent of the demographic group and left Seagram's with 28 percent. By contrast, households earning less than $20,000 only account for 15.5 percent of Gordon's customers, while Seagram's drew 38.6 percent from that group.

Changes in Ownership

During the 1980's, as part of the worldwide restructuring of brands, Gordon's went through many rapid changes. The Gordon's operation in America had been handled by the Renfield Corporation since 1947. In 1986, a Dallas-based liquor distributor, Schenley Industries Inc., bought Renfield.

In 1987, Schenley was bought by United Distillers, a subsidiary of Guinness PLC, the giant beverage firm built on the Irish drink Guinness stout. Guinness had already purchased the British end of the Gordon's operation, Tanqueray Gordon, as well as Glenmore Distilleries, which it merged with United Distillers to form United Distillers Glenmore. In 1992, United Distillers Glenmore closed the Schenley unit, taking over the direction of Gordon's.

This tangled financial history had little or no impact on the Gordon's brand itself. Gordon's advertising continued to be handled by Grey, and its image continued to be that of a quality gin. The label was altered slightly, but the Gordon's formula remained the same.

Hard Times

More serious changes were reflected in long-term trends that had nothing to do with the financial wizardry of the 1980's. The final quarter of the twentieth century was a difficult time for gin producers. The sale of distilled spirits declined drastically in the United States from its peak in 1971 when 3.06 gallons per U.S. adult were consumed. By 1991, it had fallen to 1.97 gallons.

While the drop may have reflected changing lifestyles and the growing emphasis on health and fitness, it also reflected a change in people's alcohol tastes. In 1964 the Gallup Poll reported that 63 percent of adult Americans drank alcohol, and in 1991 the same polling organization found that 64 percent of adult Americans drank. Statistically, these numbers indicate no change in drinkers; however, what people drank had changed seriously. According to *Jobson's Liquor Handbook,* in 1964, American alcoholic consumption was evenly distributed between spirits and beer. Wine sales were just a sliver of expenditures. By 1991 the scene had changed. Beer still held onto half the expenditures, but spirits had slipped to almost one third, with wine making up the rest. These trends seriously damaged gin sales. In 1975, gin sales accounted for 9.8 percent of spirit beverages; in 1991, that market share had dropped to 8.6 percent as vodka sales continued to press the gin market. Likewise, in 1977, gin sales in America amounted to 18.2 million 9-liter cases. By 1991, that number had fallen to 12.7 million cases, a decline of about one third. *Jobson's* predicted that by 1996 sales would be down to 10.5 million.

Facts like these bred fierce competition. By the early 1990s, Seagram's was outselling Gordon's, and, even more important, it was expanding its sales at a time when the total amount of gin sold in America was declining. That meant that Gordon's had to fight just to keep sales as they had been. *Jobson's* revealed an added difficulty for Gordon's. Gin drinkers in the 1990s were the least brand-loyal of all spirit-consumers. Despite Gordon's troubles in the American market, its strong sales and reputation in over 140 countries gave it good resiliency to compete for its share in the American market in the twenty-first century.

Further Reading:

BrandAdvantage: A Profile of Consumer Brand Usage, Volume 1, Beverages, Wilmette, IL: Standard Rate & Data Service, 1992.

Dagnol, Judann and John P. Cortez, ''Summer's Gin Game,'' *Advertising Age,* May 6, 1991, p. 20.

''Distilled Spirits & Mixed Drinks,'' *1990 Study of Media & Markets,* New York: Simmons Market Research Bureau, 1990.

Dougherty, Philip H., ''Advertising: 'Ambitious' Campaign Set for Gordon's Dry Gin,'' *New York Times,* June 3, 1981, p. D20.

Doxat, John, *The Gin Book,* London, England: Quiller Press, 1989.

''Gin, The Original Dutch Courage,'' *Consumer Reports,* July 1967.

''Glenmore and United Distillers (USA) Merge,'' *PRNewswire,* July 11, 1991.

''Guinness Reports Results for Year Ended Dec. 31, 1989,'' *PRNewswire,* March 22, 1990.

Hood, Donne Jean, ''A Splash of Gin,'' *Beverage Dynamics,* July/August 1992, pp. 55-58.

Hu, Tun Yuan, *The Liquor Tax in the United States, 1791-1947: A History of the Internal Revenue Taxes Imposed on Distilled Spirits by the Federal Government,* New York: Columbia University, 1950.

Jobson's Liquor Handbook 1992, New York: Jobson Publishing Corp., 1992.

Liquor Industry Marketing 1986, New York: Jobson Publishing Corp., 1986.

''Makings For A Martini,'' *Consumer Reports,* November 1960, pp. 591-5.

Meller, Paul, ''From Liquor to Liqueur: United Distillers Extends World's Biggest Whisky Johnnie Walker into Liqueur,'' *Marketing,* July 16, 1992, p. 2.

''Retail Guide to Gin, Vodka, Rum, Tequila,'' *Beverage Dynamics,* June 1992, pp. 27-35.

''United Distilers Reorganizes Its North American Operations,'' *PRNewswire,* February 3, 1992.

Vivant, Don, ''The Cultural History of Gin,'' *Forbes* (supplement), September 28, 1992, pp. 110-12.

Winters, Patricia, ''Gordon's Gin Gets Punny'' *Advertising Age,* September 21, 1987, p. 26.

—Laura Newman

GRAND MARNIER®

Grand Marnier Liqueur

Grand Marnier, a distinctive orange-flavored liqueur, historically has been the top-selling imported French liqueur in the United States and the most profitable for retailers and wholesalers on a per-bottle basis. Since 1946, Carillon Importers Ltd. of New York has imported and distributed Grand Marnier and considered it one of the firm's super-premium labels. Grand Marnier has been called the quintessential French after-dinner drink and was often used for gourmet cooking. For the French, the liqueur conjured up a history of unique flavor. Its bitter orange taste came from blending green curacao oranges from the Caribbean that were hand-peeled, sun-dried, then macerated and distilled in a cognac base. Grand Marnier, since its inception in the mid-1800s, has been considered one of the finest curacao liqueurs by cordial connoisseurs world-wide. Eighty-proof Grand Marnier Cordon Rouge became available in 1.75 liters, 750 milliliters, and miniatures in the United States.

Brand Origins

Grand Marnier was created in France in the nineteenth century by Louis Alexandre Marnier-Lapostolle at his father-in-law's distillery outside of Paris. The firm's founder, Jean-Baptiste Lapostolle, was highly respected for the fine liqueurs his family produced. His son Eugene built upon this success by expanding the business to include the production of cognac from the Charente region. Marnier-Lapostolle created history of his own by using his brother-in-law's cognac as a base for Grand Marnier.

Grand Marnier's production did not change in its 100-year history. Once blended, the mixture was aged in oak vats and carefully filtered to eliminate impurities. The rich, amber-colored liqueur was then bottled in its uniquely shaped bottle with the red ribbon and wax seal. According to *Grossman's Guide to Wines, Beers, and Spirits,* Grand Marnier belonged to a long line of world-famous specialty cordials that were produced under heavily guarded formulas and marketed under registered trademarks. Most of these liqueurs originated from one house or monastery, with centuries of tradition behind them.

Liqueurs were prepared by mixing or redistilling various spirits, like brandy, rum, gin, and whisky, with certain flavors: fruit, flowers, seeds, herbs, barks, roots, peels, and berries. To be considered a liqueur or cordial, terms often used interchangeably, the alcoholic mixture had to be at least 2.5 percent sugar by weight. Some liqueurs were labeled dry if they did not contain enough sweetening agent.

Grand Marnier gained prominence in French high society. Marnier-Lapostolle was a bon vivant and popular in the Paris grand hotel and haute cuisine scene of his time. He befriended and helped support Cesar Ritz, of the Ritz hotel fame, and was credited with financing the opening of Paris's Ritz Hotel at the end of the nineteenth century. It was no surprise that Grand Marnier became a staple of the Ritz wine list and a mandatory ingredient in the best kitchens of Paris. The liqueur was marketed as an ''elixir of style, good living and hospitality'' and became France's leading liqueur export, according to company officials.

During the 1920s and 1930s, known as France's La Grande Cuisine era, famous chefs like Escoffier developed recipes using Grand Marnier, including Grand Marnier Souffle, Crepes Suzette, Canard a l'Orange, and other creations, with much encouragement and sponsorship from the Marnier family. French chefs were responsible for expanding Grand Marnier's use as a key cooking ingredient and topping in desserts and other drinks.

Influence of Carillon Importers Ltd.

Carillon has been a subsidiary of London-based Grand Metropolitan, one of Britain's five largest corporations, specializing in real estate, food, distilled spirits, and retail eye care concerns, since 1980. As part of Grand Metropolitan PLC's IDV group (International Distillers and Vintners), Carillon has been credited with helping spearhead the conglomerate's leadership in distilled spirit sales.

Carillon drew on Grand Marnier's success and made the liqueur appealing to American tastes. The U.S. market eventually grew to represent one-third of total worldwide sales. Founded immediately after Prohibition, Carillon Importers marketed products as diverse as Mumm Champagne and W.C. Fields Bourbon. Continuing the traditional association of Grand Marnier with fine dining, in the 1970s Carillon created what company officials termed their most successful marketing tool—the Grand Marnier Chefs Ski Race series, which attracted nearly 1,500 food professionals across the country.

The Grand Marnier Chefs Ski Race served as a major fundraiser for Carillon's charities, with $500,000 in donations going to

AT A GLANCE

Grand Marnier brand of liqueur founded by Louis Alexandre Marnier-Lapostolle, who blended bitter curacao orange with fine cognac more than 100 years ago; the liqueur has been imported and distributed in the United States by Carillon Importers since 1946.

Performance: *Market share*—6.1% of cordial and liqueur market in the United States. *Sales*—399,000 cases in 1989 (fifth best selling cordial and liqueur brand).

Major competitor: Kahlua; also, Southern Comfort, Bailey's Irish Cream, and Amareto di Saronno.

Advertising: *Agency*—TBWA, New York, NY, 1980—. *Major campaign*—A series of surrealistic images of the Grand Marnier bottle by Dutch painter Bralt Bralds.

Addresses: *Parent company*—Carillon Importers Ltd., 500 Frank W. Burr Blvd., Teaneck, NJ 07666; phone: (201) 836-7799. *Ultimate parent company*—Grand Metropolitan PLC, 20 St. James Square, London SW1Y 4RR; phone: 071 321 6000; fax: 071 321 6001.

fight hunger alone. In 1985, Carillon established the Grand Marnier Foundation, which sponsored the restoration and rededication of several neglected New York landmarks, including the Joan of Arc Monument in Manhattan's Riverside Park, the Bronx World War I Monument, and the Lafayette Monument in Manhattan's Union Square. The Foundation also supported Futures for Children, the Wilkes-Barre, Pennsylvania, Ballet Theatre, Citymeals-on-Wheels, and the Sky Ranch for Boys.

Carillon President and Chief Executive Officer Michel Roux was cited as the power behind its brand marketing. Roux started out as the company's first salesman in 1970 and became president 12 years later. By maintaining control of Carillon brands among a small team of upper-level executives, Roux facilitated quick decision-making and created distinctive ad campaigns. His "tightly knit" staff included a senior vice president of marketing and sales; a senior vice president of administration and finance; a vice president of marketing services; and a public relations director. As Roux explained in the company's public relations materials, "There are no brand managers and no 'little caesars.' You don't have to go through layers of fat to implement ideas."

Roux also credited Carillon's long relationship with advertising agency TBWA and public relations firm David S. Wachsman Associates as a key to the company's success. In *Advertising Age,* Cara S. Trager praised Carillon and TBWA's open relationship for "smashing stereotypes," noting that "The client encourages the agency's input in marketing, market research, merchandising, new product development and packaging decisions."

Advertising Innovations

Since 1980, TBWA has continually emphasized Carillon's long-standing association with the arts, and often created innovative and "whimsical" advertising campaigns for the entire product line, which included Absolut vodka, Bombay gin, Fernet Branca and Punt e Mes aperitifs, and Laurent Perrier champagnes.

For example, Carillon commissioned artist Andy Warhol in 1985 to paint his famous rendition of the Absolut vodka bottle. Surreal art also inspired print advertisements for Grand Marnier.

Spanish surrealist Gervasio Gallardo created a series of award-winning paintings featuring Grand Marnier in evocative settings. La Grande Passion became familiar to magazine readers as portrayed in drawings and paintings by French artist Sempe. Creme de Grand Marnier ads were often set in romantic settings. Marvin Shanken, editor and publisher of *Impact* and *Market Watch,* told *Advertising Age* the ads were not only a departure from traditional advertising, but "gutsy." Shanken referred to the Grand Marnier ads as "one of the great campaigns in our business." Each advertising campaign was pretested to determine its eye-tracking and stopping power, the magazine reported.

Carillon used tissue overlays in individual brand ads to distinguish its products from some 60 to 80 competing cordial liqueur products. Competitors often criticized Carillon for not being particularly innovative and questioned whether such ads would stir up sales. But Carillon officials responded by telling *Advertising Age* that "Above luck, it's unique products, backed with research, breakthrough advertising and an entrepreneurial spirit" that helped make its brands successful.

Product Changes

Grand Marnier's product line expanded in 1983 with the addition of Creme de Grand Marnier, Carillon's first entry in the cream liqueur category. Considered "the second generation of cream liqueurs," Creme de Grand Marnier was a complex blend of Grand Marnier and fresh cream from France's Normandy region. In 1984, the firm launched La Grande Passion, a blend of Armagnac and tropical passion fruit. In addition to Grand Marnier, the house of Marnier-Lapostolle created several other Marnier brands using fruit flavors and cognac, including Cherry Marnier, made from Dalmatian cherries.

Over the years, the product was released in many variations and special editions. Some notable product introductions include: Grand Marnier Cuvee du Centenaire, created in 1927 and packaged in limited collection of distinctive black and gold bottles to celebrate the centennial of the Marnier-Lapostolle Company; Grand Marnier Cuvee Cent-Cinquantenaire limited edition, a special blend of aged cognac and curacao to celebrate the firm's 150th anniversary; Cognac Marnier, aged three years before being released to market; Cognac Marnier V.S.O.P. Fine Champagne, distilled by the Charentaise method and aged five years before market; Cognac Marnier X.O. Grande Fine Champagne, produced from very old cognac; Armagnac Lapostolle X.O., distilled from three grape regions; and Chateau de Sancerre, derived from the Sauvignon grape and bottled at vineyards on the banks of the Loire River.

Performance Appraisal

Carillon was the only distilled spirits importer to have experienced gains for all its major labels since 1983, according to Roux. Absolut vodka and Bombay gin were the firm's fastest growing brands, and Grand Marnier remained the top-selling imported French liqueur in the United States. *Advertising Age* called Carillon "possibly the best of the new breed of liquor marketers and certainly the most successful," and noted the firm was "certainly one of the strongest in terms of growth."

The overall downturn in the distilled spirit market since the 1980s did not affect the cordial and liqueur industry, although sales volume for some brands began leveling off. According to the Wine and Spirits Wholesalers Association, as reported in a May

1992 issue of *Beverage World,* increased federal excise taxes and a new pricing structure were to blame for declining volumes in the early 1990s. Other industry information sources blamed the national recession and the Persian Gulf War, coupled with a continued moderation movement, for a 4 to 4.5 percent drop in 1991 sales.

The Distilled Spirits Council of the United States also reported that spirit sales fell as much as 12 percent through the first half of 1991, marking the year as the industry's worst since World War II. Carillon officials said that Grand Marnier experienced a 3 percent growth in sales in the last quarter of 1992 and attributed it to the brand's strength in the gourmet cooking market.

Further Reading:

Bird, Laura, "A Scary Outlook for the Spirit World," *AdWeek Western Advertising News,* September 23, 1991, p. S61.

Carillon Importers Ltd., public relations materials, David S. Wachsman Associates, 1993.

"Distilled Spirit Sales Slide 4%," *Beverage Industry,* June 1992.

Espey, James, "The Big Four: An Examination of the International Drinks Industry," *European Journal of Marketing,* September 1989, p. 47.

Grossman, Harold J., *Grossman's Guide to Wines, Beers, and Spirits,* New York: Scribner's, 1983.

Hochstein, Mort, "Cognac Dusts Off Image, Aims for Broader Appeal," *Nation's Restaurant News,* November 16, 1992, p. 19.

Jobson's Liquor Handbook, A.C. Nielsen and Jobson Publishing, 1992.

Sfiligoj, Eric, "The Beverage Market Index for 1992," *Beverage World,* May 1992, p. 30.

Trager, Cara S., "Carillon and TBWA Smashing Stereotypes," *Advertising Age,* July 26, 1984, p. 48.

—Evelyn Dorman

GREEN GIANT®

The world's leading processor of branded vegetables, Green Giant is the top-selling U.S. brand in the fresh-frozen line, and the second largest brand, behind Del Monte Corp., in its canned vegetable segment. Since its inception, Green Giant has been synonymous with freshness, quality, wholesomeness, and value. As part of the Pillsbury Brands division of Grand Metropolitan PLC, the familiar yet always innovative Green Giant vegetable line owes its strong and continued success not only to these tangibles but to a series of national marketing campaigns, which for more than a half-century have refined and perfected the unique legend of the Green Giant.

Brand Origins

The Green Giant symbol arose in 1925, one year after The Minnesota Valley Canning Company, located in the agriculturally rich river valley area surrounding Le Sueur, Minnesota, had begun to seriously stress product individuality with its bold marketing of a rigorously tested and researched Del Maiz brand of cream style corn. The move was considered particularly ambitious at the time because Del Maiz was a golden sweet corn, rather than a white, which was then the most widely preferred American variety. However, at least three important reasons underlying this decision—the product's superior sweetness, its increased tenderness, and the ease with which it could be produced—validated the marketing plan, which eventually revolutionized corn-eating habits in the United States. This same farsightedness applied to the production and development of peas, a commodity which Minnesota Valley had begun packing in 1907 and the first such to carry the Green Giant brand.

Tiny, fancy peas, called "Early Junes," were the longstanding staple of grocers and consumers until the 1920s. This changed following the market lead of company board member and general manager Ward Cosgrove, who upon his return from a trip to Europe in 1921 declared that he had found a new, giant variety of pea, the "Prince of Wales." Impressed not only by the pea's size, but its tenderness and sweetness as well, Cosgrove immediately began overseeing the lengthy process of hybrid research that would result in a large, marketable crop. By 1924 the regional company was able to market a limited quantity of these new peas with the words "Green Giant" on the label. However, corporate attorney Warwick Keegin soon found that these words alone were merely descriptive and, consequently, unpatentable under the current trademark laws. He suggested the addition of an actual giant to the label, to function as the legitimate symbol for the brand. Local artist and writer Jack Baker was commissioned to produce the original sketches.

Borrowing from the giant in *Grimm's Fairy Tales* as well as depictions of an Indian Spirit from Hiawatha-land, Baker produced a flesh-colored, disagreeable-looking figure wearing a bearskin, who appeared more gnomish than gigantic; in fact, the monstrous peapod he carried dwarfed him in size. Yet, this unbecoming Green Giant did not deter sales and by 1928 the first magazine ad campaigns were launched. Two years later, by which time Keegin had convinced Cosgrove to strengthen the trademark by coloring the giant green, the company's first national ads began appearing in *Ladies' Home Journal*.

Early Marketing Strategy

However ugly he was, the original Green Giant nevertheless blended beautifully with Cosgrove's overall marketing strategy, which was to focus on the unique size of his peas. Typical ad copy from this era described his product as "Great Big Tender Peas" that "have a size, shape and flavor all their own. Many are fully one-half inch in diameter yet you will find them as delicate, fresh and full-flavored as the smallest early garden midget." Ironically, this pronounced emphasis on advertising, unusual for a primarily regional cannery, would likely not have taken place had private-label, chain-store grocers willingly stocked the peas when first introduced. Instead, these grocers predicted little or no demand for the product and uniformly refused to place their labels on it. Following his own instincts, Cosgrove marketed directly to consumers. Grocers soon had no choice but to stock Green Giant peas to meet the rising demand.

Cosgrove also recognized that the Green Giant symbol need not be restricted to peas only. Del Maiz corn, which eventually became Niblets, also began featuring the eye-catching giant. Cosgrove's vision for growth, his business acumen, his determination to develop, test, and promote distinctive products—all contributed greatly to the success of his company, over which he presided until 1953. Yet, without the arrival in 1931 of a young Chicago copywriter, the evolution of the Green Giant symbol, and thus the future of the company, would have been vastly different.

Advertising, Production, and Packaging Firsts

Early in his career, Leo Burnett, founder of one of the world's largest advertising agencies, found himself in the awkward situation of substituting on short notice for his senior colleague, a notorious philanderer who was scheduled to meet with Green Giant brand owners. Burnett's diligence and willingness to make two long train trips from Chicago to Le Sueur to compensate for his colleague's oversights won the admiration of Cosgrove, who from then on requested that the Erwin Wasey agency send Burnett. When he broke away from this agency in 1935 to form his own, Minnesota Valley became Burnett's first client.

By this time, Cosgrove's company had made numerous strides in manufacturing. These included the construction of the world's largest single corn and pea cannery, the introduction of vacuum-packed canned vegetables, and the perfection of an original, systematically timed planting and harvesting schedule, called the "Heat Unit" method, that ensured the freshest produce in the quickest amount of time. This last innovation, which necessitated that harvest and pack crews work round the clock, had initiated Jack Baker's slogan "Picked at the fleeting moment of perfect flavor." Burnett capitalized on all of these aspects of Minnesota Valley with his first ads, but he focused primarily on the logo itself, unchanged since the time the giant was colored green.

AT A GLANCE

Green Giant brand of canned and frozen vegetables originated in 1925 in Le Sueur, MN, by The Minnesota Valley Canning Company general manager Edward (Ward) B. Cosgrove; The Minnesota Valley Canning Company renamed Green Giant Co. in 1950; Green Giant merged with the Pillsbury Company in 1979; Grand Metropolitan PLC acquired the Pillsbury Company in 1988.

Performance: *Market share*—14.1% (top share) of frozen vegetables category; 12% of canned vegetable category. *Sales*—Over $500 million.

Major competitors: Del Monte, Libby's (canned), Bird's Eye (frozen).

Advertising: *Agency*—Leo Burnett Co., Chicago, IL. *Major campaign*—"HO HO HO Green Giant."

Addresses: *Parent company*—Pillsbury Company, 200 S. 6th St., Pillsbury Center, Minneapolis, MN 55402; phone: (612) 330-4966; fax: (612) 330-4937. *Ultimate parent company*—Grand Metropolitan PLC, 20 Saint James Square, London, SWI 4RR England.

Although the giant's metamorphosis would continue throughout the 1940s and 1950s, Burnett's first efforts during the mid-1930s to create a tall, handsome, and smiling figure clad in leaves essentially guided all later developments. His last-minute addition of the word "jolly" to the proof of a *Ladies' Home Journal* ad became the final flourish to what is one of the most recognized and successful characters in advertising history. Not surprisingly, the numerous campaigns that followed, directed by Burnett, shared with the canning company a tendency toward further important innovations.

The 1950s marked a new era for Minnesota Valley, beginning with the company's new name, Green Giant Co., a testament to the centrality of the brand that reshaped it into a nationally recognized, consumer-oriented business. By the company's 50-year anniversary, several new vegetables had been added to the product line, and canneries operated in eight states as well as in Canada. Sales in 1952 had reached an all-time record of $46.8 million; in the company's first year of operations in 1903, sales totaled a mere $18,400. Undoubtedly the most important corporate decision of this decade was for the Green Giant to be advertised via television. This newer medium promised to supersede radio, of which the company had already taken full advantage with ads featured on the popular Fred Waring Show.

In his television debut in 1959, the Green Giant appeared in the guise of a rubber-skinned puppet. This awkward puppet, according to a *Brandnews* retrospective, had "a leering grin" and "lurched to a 'Fee-Fi-Fo-Fum' music track." Following this inauspicious beginning, the Burnett agency redoubled its efforts to create a more visually and musically appealing commercial spot. The result, due largely to the teamwork of account manager Bob Noel and art director Cleo Hovel, was the "Valley Campaign," in which the Green Giant took the form of a real actor dressed in leaves and green body makeup. Through a pioneering combination of stop-motion, live action, and animation, the Giant was convincingly placed in a miniature farming valley with cartoon characters who told a product story; to this scene Noel added a song, "Good Things from the Garden," and gave the Giant the jolly, resounding words "Ho-Ho-Ho." Noel's conviction that the Giant should play a relatively silent and predominantly off-camera role of mysterious overseer helped to turn the spot, in the opinion of Roger E. Bengston, into "one of the most successful and long-lived advertising campaigns in business history."

International Growth, Mergers, and the Little Green Sprout

This novel commercial format proved particularly successful when it was used in 1961 to announce the company's daring entry into the frozen food market with a completely new product: flavortight, boil-in-the bag cooking pouches. In these spots the Giant wore a red muffler to emphasize the packaging move, which was targeted directly at frozen-food leader Birds Eye, whom the company hoped to overcome not only through its new packaging but also through its emphasis on quality and an expanded vegetable line. That same year, Green Giant began marketing its products overseas. In 1966 the company went public and was listed on the New York Stock Exchange. Like a number of flourishing corporations at the time, Green Giant sought to diversify itself and thus increase its revenues. Typical ventures included the opening of the first Jolly Green Giant restaurant in 1969 and a Green Giant Home & Garden Center the following year. However, by the mid-1970s the company had lost much of its focus and momentum and an outside manager, Thomas Wyman, was brought in to redirect the company.

Meanwhile, at least one successful strategy continued. This was the reliance on the Little Green Sprout character, since his introduction in 1973, in the valley commercials and ads. The Sprout's function was that of an innocent foil to the omnipresent but quiet giant. It was his responsibility to pose the same questions

The Green Giant as he appeared on a label in the late 1920s.

that a consumer might, questions which would elicit authoritative responses from the Giant while serving the dual purpose of establishing the Sprout as the Giant's chief, and charming, apprentice. It is this highly versatile and appealing campaign that has continued with few changes for some two decades.

By 1979 Green Giant was again lean and profitable, as well as ripe for acquisition. The Pillsbury Company, one of America's oldest and best-recognized names in the food industry, was the logical buyer, for it was centered in Minneapolis and shared many of Green Giant's goals and values. At the time of the mid-year merger, projected sales for Green Giant were $548 million on net earnings of $15.6 million. In addition, Green Giant stood as the one national vegetable producer that specialized in both frozen and canned packaging.

When British-based Grand Metropolitan acquired Pillsbury in 1988 it naturally kept Green Giant, which had risen to the top, individually if not overall, with such new frozen vegetable products as "Corn-on-the-Cob." Green Giant's reputation as a leader in research, development, and quality assurance was also important to Grand Met, which through the merger became one of the ten largest and most distinguished food companies in the world.

Appraisal and Predictions for the Future

Although several changes have taken place within Pillsbury since the merger, Green Giant has managed to retain its individuality while benefiting from the added financial backing of Grand Met. The "Brands Are Our Business" company has been and will most likely remain hesitant to alter the character of the equally prized Green Giant label. Consequently, Green Giant has been free to do what it has always done: continue its strong advertising campaigns while emphasizing product differentiation and value.

Among Green Giant's most promising forays under Grand Metropolitan are its introduction of American Mixtures, frozen vegetable combinations, and Green Giant Fresh, an extended line of high quality, fresh fruits and vegetables marketed under the Green Giant label. Regional test marketing for the Fresh line began in 1990 and national production is expected once rapid distribution processes—to accommodate the farmer's market-fresh, branded produce—have been perfected.

Over the course of its long and rich history, the Green Giant logo has appeared on over 40 separate products and is now a prominent trademark in 55 countries. Always a leader in its own right, in 1991 Green Giant was finally able to overtake longtime competitor Birds Eye for the top share of the overall frozen market, thus proving that traditional, value-laden advertising can still generate success in a fast-paced industry marked by some of the most contemporary and enticing campaigns. It is no wonder that when former Green Giant Group president Gary Klingl was asked by *Giant Line*, "Why is Green Giant better than the competition?" he responded, "First and foremost, our brand makes us better. There's something really wonderful about it and it's helped us become the number one vegetable processor in the world."

Further Reading:

Bengston, Roger E., *A History of the Green Giant Company, 1903-1979* (Ph.D. thesis), Minneapolis: University of Minnesota, 1991.

"Ho! Ho! Ho!" and "A Sprout Is Born," *Brandnews* (Pillsbury/Grand Met), March 1991, pp. 2-3.

Erlich, Reese, "Plants in Mexico Draw Criticism: Some Say Free Trade Would Cost More U.S. Jobs," *The Christian Science Monitor*, October 4, 1991, p. 8.

Feyder, Susan, "Pillsbury Turns to Wyman for Consumer Foods Blend," *Minneapolis Star*, September 14, 1979.

Gershman, Michael, "Green Giant: Pea Nuts," *Getting It Right the Second Time*, Reading: Addison-Wesley, 1990, pp. 56-7.

"Up from the Valley," *Giant* (Green Giant Company), October 1974, pp. 5-8.

Grand Metropolitan PLC Annual Reports, London, England: Grand Metropolitan PLC, 1988-1992.

Liesse, Julie, "Green Giant's Growth Ho-Ho-Hopes," *Advertising Age*, May 28, 1990, p. 20.

"Green Giant Heats Up in Freezer Case," *Advertising Age*, November 11, 1991, p. 25.

"Green Giant Revives Vegetable Entree Line," *Advertising Age*, July 6, 1992, p. 31.

McGrath, Molly Wade, "Jolly Green Giant," *Top Sellers, U.S.A.: Success Stories Behind America's Best-Selling Products from Alka-Seltzer to Zippo*, New York: William Morrow and Company, 1983, pp. 116-17.

Minnesota Valley Canning Company/Green Giant Company Annual Reports, Le Sueur and Minneapolis, 1929-1978.

Morgan, Hal, *Symbols of America*, New York: Penguin, 1986.

Pillsbury Company Annual Reports, Minneapolis: Pillsbury Company, 1979-1988.

Powell, William J., *Pillsbury's Best: A Company History from 1869*, Minneapolis: The Pillsbury Company, 1985.

Superbrands 1991 (supplement to *Adweek's Marketing Week*), 1991.

"The View from the Top about the 'Bottom'," *GiantLine* (Pillsbury/Grand Met), Spring 1992, p. 6.

Wickland, John A. "50 Years of Sales Keep Green Giant's Smile Jolly," *Minneapolis Tribune*, May 24, 1953.

World's Greatest Brands, New York: John Wiley & Sons, 1992.

—*Jay P. Pederson*

GREY POUPON®

The best-selling brand of "specialty" mustard in the United States today, Grey Poupon was one of the first gourmet mustards to be introduced to the American consumer. Imported Grey Poupon mustard was originally sold in distinctive earthenware containers; Nabisco Foods Group today markets the product in eight-ounce glass jars imprinted with the familiar antique-style lettering of the original. Capitalizing on two trends of the mid-1980s—Americans' interest in gourmet and international cuisine, and their quest for low-calorie, low-fat food products—Grey Poupon found a profitable niche in the rapidly expanding upmarket food trade. Commanding a 78 percent market share among the Dijon segment in 1992, Grey Poupon is for many Americans the mustard of choice to go with everything from the lowly hot dog to the fanciest charcuterie plate.

Brand Origins

Developed in the city of Dijon, France in 1777, Grey Poupon mustard is a blend of brown or black mustard seeds, white wine, and herbs. The mustard was the brainchild of Monsieur Grey, a British inventor who perfected the recipe, and Monsieur Poupon, a French businessman who provided the financial support to produce it. Grey also developed a steam-operated machine that automated the mustard-making process. The original Grey Poupon mustard shop still exists in Dijon, but all the Grey Poupon mustard sold in America since 1977 has been manufactured in Oxnard, California. In 1946 the Farmington, Connecticut based food company Heublein, Inc. purchased the secret Grey Poupon recipe. By 1977 all domestic Grey Poupon mustard was being produced exclusively in Heublein's Oxnard plant. Heublein was acquired by R. J. Reynolds in 1983, at which point the Grey Poupon brand was assigned to Del Monte, another Reynolds subsidiary. In a further takeover, the Oxnard plant became part of Nabisco in 1986, and it is under the specialty products division of the Nabisco Foods Group that Grey Poupon is sold today.

Product Line Extensions

In 1982 Grey Poupon Dijon mustard was joined by Grey Poupon Country Dijon mustard, a coarser-textured Dijon mustard product created by the inclusion of whole mustard seeds instead of ground ones. Country Dijon, sold in the same eight-ounce jars, but with the relief-printed typeface in brown instead of blue, was only the second Grey Poupon product to be introduced in the more than

200-year history of the mustard. As Americans began to experiment with European-style foods and eating habits, mustard sales flourished, and Grey Poupon Dijon and Country Dijon cornered the Dijon segment.

In the early 1980s, the mustard category was divided into three segments: yellow, spicy brown, and Dijon. In 1989 Nabisco launched Grey Poupon Parisian mustard, a special blend of premium brown and yellow mustard seeds, white wine, spices, and a European-style blend of fine herbs. According to the Nabisco press release introducing the new line, the mustard—developed especially for sandwiches—was "inspired by the mustards used in the cafes of Paris." By creating a non-Dijon product with the well-respected Grey Poupon name, Nabisco was able to move quickly into the spicy brown mustard segment.

By the late 1980s and early 1990s, a new mustard segment—flavored mustard—was gaining in popularity with the American public. Supermarket sales of flavored mustards, such as honey mustard, accounted for nearly $22 million of the $232 million prepared mustard category in 1992. Many of the flavored mustards were manufactured by smaller producers, but by 1992, Grey Poupon became the first mainstream brand to aggressively support an entry into the segment. The three new Grey Poupon products, flavored with honey, horseradish, and peppercorns, were packaged in the distinctive eight-ounce Grey Poupon jar. Market research demonstrated that in 1992, honey and horseradish mustards accounted for 79 percent of the flavored mustard segment. By introducing flavored mustards under the Grey Poupon name, the company took advantage of brand recognition to move into that lucrative area.

Advertising Strategy

A classic case of using advertising to enhance the image of an everyday product, the most famous Grey Poupon television and print ad campaign transformed a lowly condiment into an exclusive, high-class food "accessory." To understand the success of the campaign and the evolution of mustard from blue-collar condiment to a gourmet food, the atmosphere of the 1980s must be considered. By mid-decade, the economic mood of the country lent itself to opulence and grand displays of wealth. The booming stock market and thriving economy allowed adventuresome, young entrepreneurs and arbitragers to amass large fortunes. Suddenly, Americans' attitudes towards all aspects of style—

AT A GLANCE

Grey Poupon brand of Dijon mustard founded in 1777 in Dijon, France, by the British Mr. Grey and the French Monsieur Poupon; product brought to United States by Heublein, Inc., which was acquired by R.J. Reynolds in 1983, at which point the brand was assigned to its Del Monte subsidiary. The product again changed hands in 1986, when R.J. Reynolds merged with Nabisco Brands, and is now with Nabisco Foods Group.

Performance: Market share—78 percent (top share) of Dijon mustard segment.

Major competitor: Durkee-French Foods's Vive la Dijon; CPC International Inc.'s Dijonnaise.

Advertising: Agency—Lowe & Partners, New York, NY, 1964—. *Major campaign*—Print and television spots showing opulent situations; voice-over asking, "Pardon me. Do you have any Grey Poupon?"

Addresses: Parent company—Nabisco Foods Group, 7 Campus Drive, Parsippany, NJ 07054; phone: (201) 682-7131. *Ultimate parent company*—RJR Nabisco, Inc., 1301 Avenue of the Americas, New York, NY 10019; phone: (212) 258-5600.

clothes, furnishings, art, interior design, and food—were changing. In the realm of cooking, nouvelle cuisine, a new French food style that veered away from rich sauces and heavy cream, became the rage. Mustard, particularly Dijon, became a more visible flavor, being recommended as a condiment as well as an ingredient in glazes, sauces, and marinades.

The New York-based Lowe Marschalk advertising agency had been running Grey Poupon's advertising campaign since 1964, placing small ads for the product in targeted magazines. In 1981, however, Lowe Marschalk noted the increased interest in mustard, and changed its strategy. In a 1986 interview in *New York* magazine, Andrew Langer, then president of Lowe Marschalk, remarked, "A country that was changing in terms of business style, even politics, was changing in terms of palates. If we were going to grow, we couldn't remain in the low-volume gourmet section—there's dust on everything. But we also didn't want to drive away the gourmets when they realized that Grey Poupon was in their neighbor's fridge. We were on a tightrope: Could we talk to the rest of the world and not lose those people and that class attitude?"

To appeal to both groups, Lowe Marschalk San Francisco developed the popular ad campaign in which Grey Poupon is depicted as an affordable luxury. In the first television spot, two Rolls Royces pull alongside of each other, and the occupant of one

vehicle asks his counterpart, "Pardon me. Do you have any Grey Poupon?" "Certainly," the other driver replies. The ad was tested in Seattle in 1981 and yielded a 100 percent increase in sales. The ads that followed depicted such equally luxurious situations as an exchange between the captains of two yachts, and one in French between travelers on the Orient Express. In each case, the dialogue was the same; the now-famous tag line "Pardon me, do you have any Grey Poupon?" made the product a household name.

By 1992 the ad agency, now called Lowe & Partners, New York, decided to add a note of whimsy to its successful decade-long campaign. The new Grey Poupon television spots show the automobiles jockeying for position so that the mustard handoff can be made. When the cars are close enough, the Grey Poupon is passed between the cars, but as the camera cuts away, the sound of breaking glass can be heard. The spot ends with a voice-over saying, "Oh dear." Print ads have followed the same general format, depicting luxurious settings and high-class mustard eaters. On the day of President Bill Clinton's 1992 inauguration, a Grey Poupon ad appeared in newspapers, depicting two American-made limousines involved in a mustard handoff outside of the White House.

Future Predictions

Lines of mustard products continue to grow. The Englewood Cliffs, New Jersey food giant CPC International Inc. introduced Dijonnaise, a dijon-mustard blend with a creamy texture. The mustard giant Durkee-French Foods also markets a dijon style mustard, called Vive la Dijon. With Grey Poupon's venture into the flavored mustard category, it is likely that the other multinationals will follow suit. The recent marketing strategies for mustard have touched on two of Americans' recent food obsessions—low fat / low calorie products, and those which have a certain cachet. Grey Poupon has securely held first place in the Dijon mustard category for a number of years. With its line extensions, successful marketing strategies, and name recognition, it will undoubtedly remain the product leader.

Further Reading:

Fee, Caroline, "Grey Poupon Family Adds New Member," Nabisco Foods Group Press Release, September 21, 1989.

Kanner, Bernice, "When You're Haute, You're Hot," *New York*, January 27, 1986, pp. 14-19.

"Rolls-Royces Block Road for Grey Poupon," *Advertising Age*, March 18, 1991, p. 42.

Smith, Ann, "Grey Poupon is Cutting the Mustard Three New Ways," Nabisco Foods Group Press Release, November 18, 1992.

—Marcia K. Mogelonsky

GUINNESS® STOUT

Guinness, a dark, almost black beer, is the best-selling stout in the world. Founded in Dublin in 1759, the Guinness brand has long dominated the Irish beer market and by the late 20th century was sold in around 130 countries. In the United States, where stout is not a popular drink, Guinness represented just a small share of the imported beer category, but it maintained a loyal following among the country's most demanding beer connoisseurs.

Like other Irish stouts, Guinness has a dry, roasted, slightly bitter flavor, complemented, however, by other more subtle tastes and aromas. Poured into a glass, the beer is crowned by a long-lasting, creamy head. While it is a fine accompaniment to a wide variety of foods, the combination of Guinness stout and oysters has been particularly famous. In the 19th century, British prime minister and novelist Benjamin Disraeli enjoyed such a meal on what he termed "the most remarkable day hitherto of my life."

Guinness Brewing Worldwide, the brand's parent company, was in the early 1990s the world's eighth-largest brewer by volume but the third most successful by operating profit. In addition to Guinness stout, it brewed more than 30 other beer brands, including Harp lager, Smithwick's ale, Kilkenny Export ale, Macardles ale, Premier Export lager, and Kaliber lager (non alcoholic). Guinness PLC, parent company of Guinness Brewing Worldwide, also owned the world's largest spirits company, United Distillers, and gained about three-fourths of its profits from spirits production. The Guinness name was also widely known from the famous fact book, *The Guinness Book of Records*, first published in 1955 as a source for settling trivia questions in pubs.

Brand Origins

Stout, a dark, roasted brew most popular in Ireland, has its origins in another beer type, porter, which was developed in London probably during the early 1700s. Although by the end of the century it became the dominant beer style in Britain, few of its original characteristics are known with certainty. Like stout, porter was a virtually black beer, and like both stout and ale, it was fermented with yeast that floated on the top of the fermenting vessel. The early porter was likely a blend of beers mixed at the brewery. It became known as the drink of the common man and especially of London's market porters, from which it derived its name. Porter remained popular in the 1800s, but the style virtually disappeared by World War II. When porter regained some fashion in the late 20th century, the term was being applied to a number of quite dissimilar dark beers.

The term stout was initially used to describe a strong porter, or one with a high level of alcohol. A strong porter, thus, was a stout porter. It was later abbreviated to just stout. The term had already gained currency by the first half of the 18th century when English writer Jonathan Swift wrote: "Should but the Muse descending drop/ A slice of bread and mutton chop/ Or kindly when his credit's out/ Surprise him with a pint of stout."

Ireland, where Swift lived much of his life, began brewing porter and stout much later than England did, although many in Ireland were certainly aware of this dark brew by the mid-1700s. It was during this period that Arthur Guinness, the founder of the Guinness brand, entered the field of brewing. In 1756, at the age of 31, he leased a brewery in Leixlip, a town just west of Dublin. Because Ireland had export restrictions and tariffs on beer, Guinness then considered moving to Wales, but his search there for an existing brewery was unsuccessful. Guinness turned his sights on Dublin, where he found a small ale brewery at St. James's Gate, an outer defensive point to the old walled city. This location had been the site of a brewing operation at least as far back as the mid-1600s, but the brewery had been closed in 1750 after its owner, John Paul Espinasse, was killed in a fall from a horse.

From the new owner, Mark Rainsford III, Guinness was able to lease the brewery under unusual, though exceptionally favorable, terms. Signed on December 31, 1759, the lease provided him with "a dwelling-house, a brewhouse, two malt houses, and stables" and specified a 45-pounds sterling annual rent that was to be honored for 9,000 years. This document was still in force more than two centuries later.

Early Development

An experienced brewer, Guinness was able to begin operations quickly, and by 1763 the brewery was producing a significant amount of ale, which was sold in the pubs of Dublin and surrounding towns. The brewery's first export, a mere six-and-one-half barrels, was shipped to England in 1769.

The brewery's early development was threatened by an increasingly bitter feud with the city over water rights. The lease had granted Guinness the right to draw water "free of tax or pipe

AT A GLANCE

Guinness brand founded in 1759 in Dublin by Arthur Guinness; brewery incorporated in 1886 as Arthur Guinness Son and Co. Ltd.; became public limited company, Arthur Guinness & Sons Ltd., in 1982; renamed Guinness PLC in 1986.

Performance: *Market share*—Guinness brand commands 2.3% of imported beer category in the United States.

Major U.S competitor: Heineken; also Modelo Brewing Group's Corona Extra, Beck's, Molson Golden, and other imported beers.

Advertising: *Agency (U.S.)*—Weiss, Whitten, Carroll, Stagliano Inc., New York, NY. *Major 1993 campaign*—"Almost as satisfying as a pint of Guinness," print advertisements featuring black-and-white photographs of people indulging in unusual, humorous pleasures.

Addresses: *Parent company*—Guinness Brewing Worldwide Ltd., Park Royal Brewery, London, NW10 7RR; phone: 081 965 7700; fax: 081 965 1882. *Ultimate parent company*—Guinness PLC, 39 Portman Square, London, W1H 9HB; phone: 071 486 0288; fax: 071 486 4968.

money," a condition, however, that was not recognized by the municipal corporation. In 1775, after more than a decade of impasse, the corporation decided to fill in the channel from which Guinness received his brewing water. A group of workers, led by a corporation committee, was then sent to the brewery to carry out the order. Confronted by the group, Guinness warned that he would use force to protect his right to the water, but the committee responded by calling for the sheriff. When the sheriff arrived, Guinness reportedly grabbed a pickaxe from one of the workers and, using much "improper language," persuaded the group to leave. Not until nine years later, in 1784, was the issue finally resolved.

For nearly two decades Guinness produced only ale, although he took great interest in the porter that English brewers were beginning to export to Dublin. In 1778, after experimenting with this darker, stronger brew, Guinness introduced his own porter, and by the late 1780s his Guinness Extra Strong porter was being exported to London. So successful was Guinness's new beer that in 1799 the brewery stopped producing ale entirely, turning its full attention instead to a variety of Guinness porters.

Under the leadership of Arthur Guinness, who ran the brewery until his death in 1803, the company developed a profitable, though mostly local, business. Ale and porter had been exported to England, and Guinness's West Indies porter, a hoppy, high-quality beer, was being shipped to the Caribbean islands. Even so, these sales represented just a small share of the brewery's production. It was the founder's son, Arthur Guinness II, who oversaw the first great expansion in export trade, a development that helped the company become the largest brewery in Ireland by 1830. During his 52-year tenure, marked by a more than 50-percent growth in Guinness production, sales were increasingly directed toward the English market, where porter was the dominant beer style. Guinness porter also began to be shipped to Africa by the 1820s and, following a wave of Irish emigration, to the United States as well. By 1855, when his son Benjamin Lee Guinness took control of the company, Guinness had become the top-selling brand in England.

During this period of expanding production and exports, the company brewed a number of different porters, including Guinness's Extra Superior porter, which began to dominate the brewery's sales. Later renamed Guinness Stout, it was just 4 percent of sales in 1821, but twenty years later its share had increased to more than 80 percent. Like other porters, as well as ales, Guinness stout was brewed with malted barley, hops, and top-fermenting yeasts, but the brew mash also included a quantity of roasted unmalted barley, giving the beer a roasted flavor. Appearing virtually black in normal settings, it was a deep, ruby red when held to a bright light. Sales benefited from its reputation for promoting strength, good health, and virility. The medical community, in fact, helped establish this reputation. In the mid-1800s, for example, a prestigious medical journal in Britain proclaimed that Guinness stout was "one of the best cordials not included in the pharmacopoeia."

Benjamin Guinness, born in 1798, had extensive brewing experience before taking over operations in 1855, and he used his great knowledge and exceptional organizational skills to capitalize on his father's gains. Under his leadership Guinness exports and production grew rapidly, creating a windfall of profits that likely made him the richest person in Ireland. It was also during this time that the traditional Irish harp became the Guinness trademark. First used in 1862, the symbol was prominently placed in the center of the bottle's label.

When Benjamin Guinness died in 1868, the brewery was passed down to his two sons, Edward and Arthur. This partnership lasted only eight years, and in 1876 Edward took complete control of the company. In 1886, when the brewery was incorporated as Arthur Guinness Son and Co. Ltd., Edward continued as chairman. The millions of pounds raised through public shares of the new corporation were directed partially toward expanding and upgrading the St. James's Gate brewery, which by this time was the largest in the world.

Early 20th-Century Production and Advertising

By the turn of the century, Guinness stout had become a truly international beer, sold in Europe, North America, Africa, and Asia. The prominence of Guinness in its home market, where it competed against other stout brands, such as Murphy's and Beamish, was reflected in the country's literature. James Joyce, who referred to Guinness stout as "the wine of the country," wrote in *Finnegans Wake,* "Let us find that pint of porter place . . . Benjamin's Lea . . . and see the foamous homely brew, bebattled by bottle—then put a James's Gate in my hand." Guinness could also be found in the works of English writers, such as Graham Greene, as well as those of A. J. Cronin, the noted Scottish novelist. Samuel Beckett, who first tasted Guinness in the 1920s while attending Trinity College, Dublin, was reportedly a lifelong admirer of Guinness stout.

In the 1920s production of Guinness surpassed 3 million barrels per year. To handle the growing demand, a second Guinness brewery, located at Park Royal in London, was opened in 1936. Not taking success for granted, in 1929 the company began its first advertising campaign, "Guinness is good for you," which played on the beer's long-standing reputation for promoting strength and good health. Advertisements claimed that Guinness could enrich blood, calm nerves, and build strong muscles. One advertisement, with a picture of Santa Claus carrying a giant tree with one hand, reminded customers, "Christmas is coming . . . Guinness for strength." In another "Guinness for strength" poster, a man was shown holding up a car with one hand and using a tool with the other. A bottle of Guinness was suspended just above his outstretched left foot. Other early print campaigns included "My Goodness—My Guinness," featuring a zookeeper who found the animals enjoying his stout. In one such advertisement, a polar bear was sitting in a shallow pool and holding a bottle of Guinness between his two front paws. Tilting his head back slightly and smiling, the bear appeared ready to quaff the brew. Meanwhile, the uniformed zookeeper, shown suspended in the air behind the bear's pool, had his arms and legs outstretched in obvious shock. Such quirky, humorous advertisements continued to be an effective sales tool throughout the century.

Product Innovations

As long as stout remained the dominant beer style at home and provided strong exports abroad, Arthur Guinness Son and Co. Ltd., chaired by successive generations of the Guinness family, was content to focus on its core brand. In the 1950s, however, light-colored lagers—the style of beer most popular on the European continent and in the United States—became increasingly popular in England and Ireland. The company responded in 1960 by introducing its own lager, Harp, which took its name from the Guinness trademark. Harp soon became one of the top-selling lagers in Britain, and its success spurred the company into brewing other "blond" beers. By the early 1990s the brewery was producing more than a dozen non-stout brands, including such ales as Kilkenny, Macardles, and Smithwick's, as well as Premier Export lager. Its 1990 purchase of Spanish brewer La Cruz del Campo S.A. brought the lager Cruzcampo under its control. Kaliber, a lager introduced by the company in 1986, was a non-alcoholic beer.

Guinness stout was also offered in new forms. In 1959, for example, the company introduced its new Draught Guinness for the pub market. Slightly less bitter than the bottled stout, this product was known for its especially creamy, surging head, which was created by pressurizing the metal kegs with a mixture of carbon dioxide and nitrogen. Some thirty years later, in 1989, the company introduced Draught Guinness in cans. The can—a result of $8 million in research—was also pressurized by a mixture of carbon dioxide and nitrogen, and functioned as a miniature keg. Its secret was a patented piece of plastic called the widget ("smoothifier" in the United States), which was placed in the bottom of the can. When the can was opened, a small amount of beer trapped in the smoothifier was forced through a tiny hole, causing a stream of little bubbles that made the frothy head. In 1992 the product was introduced in the United States as Pub Draught Guinness.

The same patented in-can system was used in another new product, Guinness Draught Bitter, a dry, copper-colored ale introduced nationally in Britain in 1992. The company's decision to use the Guinness name on a non-stout brand in the United Kingdom came as a surprise to many in the industry, but its marketing goal was clear. In Britain, bitter represented half of all beer bought in pubs but only 30 percent of the take-home trade. Guinness Draught Bitter, by mimicking the appearance and taste of real draught beer, was aimed at customers dissatisfied with the existing canned bitters. The new Guinness product was not sold in the United States, where bitter was an exceptionally specialized product produced only by microbreweries.

Brand Outlook

In 1982 Guinness became a public limited company, Arthur Guinness & Sons Ltd., and in 1983 Guinness Brewing Worldwide was formed as a subsidiary; three years later Arthur Guinness & Sons Ltd. changed its name to Guinness PLC. Such changes appeared superficial compared to the company's 1986 purchase of Distillers Company, one of the world's largest producers of spirits and owner of such popular brands as Johnnie Walker, Gordon's, Dewar's, and Tanqueray. As a result of this purchase, in the early 1990s about 59 percent of the company's sales were in spirits, 40 percent in brewing, and less than 1 percent in other concerns. Moreover, about 75 percent of its profits came from liquor distilling.

Despite the new emphasis on spirits, Guinness stout remained one of the company's most important products, accounting for about 40 percent of its beer sales and an even higher percentage of its brewing profits. Moreover, in an increasingly global economy, marked in the brewing industry by joint ventures and special licensing agreements, Guinness stout had a number of unique advantages. For example, it did not directly compete with the world's major lager brands, making it easier for Guinness to enter into foreign partnerships. One such joint venture existed in Malaysia and Singapore, where Guinness stout and Heineken lager were being produced by Asia-Pacific Breweries. In Ireland, Guinness brewed under license both Budweiser and Carlsberg, two of the world's best-selling lagers.

Guinness was also placing greater emphasis on the giant U.S. market, where 25 percent of all beer was consumed. The multimillion dollar advertising campaign launched in the early 1990s for the company's Harp lager reflected this focus. A new push, however, was also planned for the venerable Guinness stout, which in 1992 sold about two million cases in the United States (excluding pub receipts), representing a little more than two percent of the country's imported beer category. In 1993 Guinness Import Company, the brand's U.S. distributor, introduced a new advertising campaign, "Almost as satisfying as a pint of Guinness," which featured black-and-white photographs of people indulging in unusual pastimes. In one photograph, a man, standing on two large blocks of ice, was shown being towed by a car. The goal of the campaign was to loosen up Guinness stout's serious image. Such advertisements were expected to increase the brand's visibility, but significantly higher U.S. sales were likely to come only with a general shift in consumer preference from pale, mild tasting lagers to darker, more flavorful, high-quality beers.

Further Reading:

Bidlake, Suzanne, "Guinness Bitter in the Can Echoes Rival Brands," *Marketing,* April 4, 1991, p. 8.

Bryant, Adam, "The Beer Industry Is Moving to Capitalize on Consumers' Desire for More Hefty Brews," *New York Times,* February 5, 1993, p. C15.

Guinness Brewing Worldwide: Committed to Being the World's Foremost Brewer, London: Public Affairs Department, Guinness Brewing Worldwide Ltd., 1992.

Guinness PLC Report and Accounts 1992, London: Guinness PLC, 1993.

Hollreiser, Eric, "Keg in a Can," *Adweek's Marketing Week,* January 20, 1992, p. 41.

Jackson, Michael, *The New World Guide to Beer,* Philadelphia: Running Press, 1988, pp. 157-59, 179-81, 220.

Marcom, John Jr., "The House of Guinness," *Forbes,* June 12, 1989, pp. 85-91.

Palmer, Jay, "Stout Fellow: A New Head Man Brews Up a Recovery at Guinness," *Barron's,* March 4, 1991, pp. 12-13.

Prokesch, Steven, "Guinness to Buy Largest Brewer in Spain," *New York Times,* November 22, 1990, p. D1-2.

Winters, Patricia, "Guinness Views Gold in New Lager," *Advertising Age,* July 4, 1989, p. 36.

—Thomas Riggs

HÄAGEN-DAZS®

The Häagen-Dazs brand of superpremium ice cream leads the market with a 58.4 percent share of the estimated $250 million category. Introduced in small containers bearing an ersatz Danish name and a map of Scandinavia, Häagen-Dazs Company Inc.'s flagship brand recast the ice cream market more than 30 years ago by offering consumers their first taste of super-rich, expensive ice cream. Since 1961, consumers have demonstrated a willingness to indulge themselves in the pricey "Häagen-Dazs experience" in return for the brand's quality and consistency. Häagen-Dazs was the first ice cream to offer products containing no artificial ingredients or flavors. While the list of Häagen-Dazs flavors has blossomed from the original three to about 20, the basic recipe remains unchanged. And despite trends toward healthier, low-fat snacks and desserts, the rich, calorie-laden concoctions of Häagen-Dazs remain popular. The Bronx-born ice cream stands as America's most popular superpremium ice cream despite an impressive cast of competitors. More than 250 Häagen-Dazs retail franchise outlets exist in the United States, and Häagen-Dazs products are also sold in Europe, Asia, and Australia.

Humble Beginnings

The Häagen-Dazs brand exists today because Polish immigrant Reuben Mattus was determined to make a living, and ice cream was the only business he knew. As a child, he moved to Brooklyn with his widowed mother and grew up in a family of ice cream marketers. During the post-World War I era when the Mattus family business was established, the ice cream market in New York was characterized by "dozens of little ice cream companies, most of them run by immigrants," according to Calvin Trillin in the *New Yorker*. The Mattus family sold lemon ice, popsicles, and ice cream sandwiches before entering into bulk ice cream production with a brand called Ciro's Ice Cream. Ciro's was first supplied to candy stores, then grocery stores, and eventually supermarkets.

The 1940s brought breakthroughs in refrigeration, revolutionizing ice cream marketing and threatening many small, independent ice cream makers. Large companies could now mass produce and distribute their frozen confections through grocery stores which the companies themselves supplied with "refrigerated cabinets." Although small companies tried to display their products in the same cabinets, the large corporations persuaded state lawmakers to rule the practice illegal. The situation worsened in the 1950s, according to Trillin, who wrote that "as supermar-

kets spread across the country and American housewives seemed to be judging foodstuffs purely on their cost and convenience, the entire ice cream industry was competing to produce the cheapest possible ice cream in the largest possible containers. It was a competition that small, independent ice cream companies were unlikely to survive." Trillin noted that "after years of being knocked about in the unruly procession of ice cream makers, Reuben Mattus just turned around and marched smartly in the opposite direction." In 1961 Mattus, an innovator determined to survive, invented Häagen-Dazs—the best, most expensive, ice cream in the U.S. market. In doing so he wagered—long before consumers displayed any interest in gourmet or natural foods—that people would pay more for a superior product.

Marketing Magic

Whether it was merely a lucky gamble by a desperate, small-time businessman, or pure niche-marketing genius, Mattus succeeded by creating a product unique to the U.S. market and cloaking it in an exotic image. While most ice cream makers were pumping 50 percent air—the legal limit—into their products, Mattus added very little air to Häagen-Dazs. His ice cream had 16 percent butterfat compared with 12 to 14 percent in other brands. Mattus used no artificial ingredients or flavors. (This became a common strategy in the 1990s, but it was highly unusual in the early 1960s.) He ignored the trend of using gallon and half-gallon cartons and instead packaged his product in pint-sized containers. The combination of ingredients and manufacturing process made Häagen-Dazs only slightly more expensive to produce. By charging 50 percent more than his competitors charged for regular ice cream, however, Mattus established Häagen-Dazs as the market's first high-priced, high-profit ice cream.

To complete his brand's image, the Häagen-Dazs name was added. Mattus told Trillin that while searching for a European name to add some "continental cachet" to his new brand, he thought of Denmark because it was dairy country and was the home of Premier Is, a Copenhagen-based ice cream brand recognized for quality and consistency. According to Trillin, Mattus also "figured that the strangeness of the phrase would be an advantage: slowing up shoppers for the split second required to register the words might be enough to cause some of them to take another look."

AT A GLANCE

Häagen-Dazs brand of ice cream founded in 1961 in the Bronx, NY, by independent ice cream maker Reuben Mattus; brand acquired in 1983 by the Pillsbury Co.; Pillsbury Co. acquired by Grand Metropolitan PLC in 1989.

Performance: *Market share*—58.4 percent (top share) of the superpremium ice cream segment. *Sales*—$147 million.

Major competitor: Ben & Jerry's Homemade Ice Cream.

Advertising: *Agency*—BBDO, New York, NY 1990—. *Major campaign*—Häagen-Dazs ranks with "other good pleasures such as satin sheets without pajamas, Nathan's hot dogs, that first fishing pole, Le Montrachet, Cole Porter and breakfast in bed"; a proper diet can not be maintained without the "four basic food groups: caviar, brioche, artichokes, and Häagen-Dazs."

Addresses: *Parent company*—Häagen-Dazs Company Inc., Glenpointe Centre E., Teaneck, NJ 07666; phone: (201) 692-0900; fax: (201) 907-6700. *Ultimate parent company*—Pillsbury Co., Pillsbury Center, 200-T South 6th St., Minneapolis, MN 55402; phone: (612) 330-4966; fax: (612) 330-7355. *Ultimate ultimate parent company*—Grand Metropolitan PLC, 20 St. James Square, London SW11 Y4RR, England.

Conservative Growth

Before consumers could look or buy, Mattus had to convince distributors that a market existed for expensive ice cream. Initially, distribution was limited to New York gourmet shops. Throughout the 1960s, distribution expanded quietly and conservatively, first to urban centers and college towns in the Northeast. The slow-and-steady growth strategy was considered a factor in the brand's ability to escape notice by larger companies that could have easily used their vast resources to either launch their own gourmet products or simply snuff out the tiny Häagen-Dazs brand. Häagen-Dazs took more than a decade to build a solid base of consumers and establish a national network of distributors. By 1976 the brand was marketed in more than 25 states. The first Häagen-Dazs "dipping store" was opened in New York, and Mattus had discontinued marketing all Ciro's products to focus exclusively on the Häagen-Dazs brand.

Growing Competition

Trillin quoted Mattus as saying, "All my life, people copied me. I would start something; they would copy it and undermine me." Surprisingly, it took nearly two decades before competitors picked up on the Häagen-Dazs gold mine. Competition surfaced first at the regional level, with companies that copied the product and its image. Products such as Alpen Zauber and Frusen Gladje appeared alongside Häagen-Dazs in grocer's freezers. Mattus was particularly irked by these newcomers because both were manufactured by old competitors of Ciro's; one of the original owners of Frusen Gladje was Mattus's cousin. Mattus tried to protect the Häagen-Dazs "unique Scandinavian marketing theme" by taking Frusen Gladje to court and charging its manufacturers with trademark infringement. He lost the case. Then, in 1981, Häagen-Dazs sent a letter to its distributors about a new policy that prohibited them from marketing competing brands. "If a distributor in the exercise of his best judgment elects to handle one of these other brands, it is our intention . . . not to supply him with Häagen-Dazs ice cream," the letter stated, according to Trillin.

With its distribution in place, Häagen-Dazs had no trouble maintaining a comfortable lead among the growing number of superpremium ice cream brands. By the early 1980s, sales had climbed to $115 million (excluding sales from the 244 Häagen-Dazs franchise stores). Impressed by the brand's national success and staying power, the Pillsbury Co. acquired Häagen-Dazs in 1983. Mattus stayed on and kept the brand's marketing strategy intact. Meanwhile, another superpremium ice cream was quietly making headway in the New England market. Ben & Jerry's ice cream boasted the same high standard of quality as Häagen-Dazs, but evoked a more down-to-earth image. Initially a regional brand found only in Vermont, Ben & Jerry's soon attracted an almost cult-like following. But when the brand's owners decided to expand, they ran into problems with distributors who informed them of the Häagen-Dazs policy of no competing brands.

Ben & Jerry's had not planned to challenge Häagen-Dazs; in fact its unconventional owners were somewhat embarrassed by the success of the venture they had intended to be a simple means of making a modest living. When tested, however, their marketing instincts proved as keen as those of the creators of Häagen-Dazs. Ben & Jerry's sued Häagen-Dazs over its exclusive distribution policy. Predicting public sentiment would be on their side—a case of the corporate giant pushing the little guy around—Ben & Jerry's launched a massive publicity campaign with the slogan "What's the Doughboy afraid of?" (referring to the Pillsbury's recognizable animated spokescreature). This phrase also appeared on packages of Ben & Jerry's along with a toll-free number that customers could call to receive packets containing bumper stickers and form letters to sign and mail to Pillsbury's chairman. Co-owner Jerry Greenfield even personally picketed Pillsbury's Minneapolis headquarters to generate publicity and support for his Vermont ice cream.

Ben & Jerry's won a temporary victory in the Boston market when the feuding ice cream makers agreed to an out-of-court settlement allowing distributors to handle both Ben & Jerry's and Häagen-Dazs for two years. Because of this, Ben & Jerry's gained a national presence and became the number two superpremium brand in the United States in the 1990s. "If Häagen-Dazs had not agreed to the out-of-court settlement, we would have potentially lost distribution in Boston," Ben & Jerry's general manager told *Advertising Age* in 1986. "And if we had not penetrated Boston, we would not have been able to move into New York and other markets nationwide."

The out-of-court settlement with Ben & Jerry's did little to alter the distribution strategy of Häagen-Dazs elsewhere. According to a 1986 *Advertising Age* report, Häagen-Dazs subsequently "filed a bevy of lawsuits against competitors and distributors" in several markets, accusing them of interfering with the brand's distribution system. In effect, Häagen-Dazs tried to freeze out its small, independent competitors in much the same way the large ice cream makers had tried to freeze out Mattus's own Ciro's brand in the 1940s. Other brands tried to fight the strategy, including Double Rainbow Gourmet Ice Cream and Perche No!, both from San Francisco. Double Rainbow told *Dun's Business Month* that Häagen-Dazs had hampered his firm's growth, "because some distributors are afraid to lose Häagen-Dazs business if they carry my product." Häagen-Dazs scored a marketing victory when a federal judge in San Francisco ruled that "Häagen-Dazs Co. acted properly in severing ties with distributors who also sell a competing brand of ice cream," according to a 1988 *Wall Street Journal* report.

Advertising

During more than two decades of growth, Häagen-Dazs defied conventional marketing wisdom by shunning media promotions in favor of word-of-mouth advertising. With the exceptions of a single print ad campaign to launch Häagen-Dazs in the Los Angeles market in 1973 and promotional efforts handled by Mattus on a New York radio station serving the Jewish community, Häagen-Dazs did not advertise until 1986. Mattus told *Advertising Age* in 1977 of his conviction that consumers would gladly pay more for quality and that large-scale ad campaigns for a quality product would only "arouse suspicion." For its first print campaign in the Los Angeles market, Häagen-Dazs sold itself on its image of sophistication and indulgence by telling consumers that Häagen-Dazs ranked right up there with "other good pleasures such as satin sheets without pajamas, Nathan's hot dogs, that first fishing pole, Le Montrachet, Cole Porter and breakfast in bed."

In 1986, no longer under control of the Mattus family, Häagen-Dazs embarked on its first national print campaign by appearing in *People* and *Life* magazines and several national food publications. Mark Stevens, then president of the Häagen-Dazs unit, told *Marketing & Media Decisions* the brand had turned to advertising to create a "unified image that word-of-mouth can't give." He added, "We also realize that one-third of ice cream eaters have never heard of Häagen-Dazs. While the awareness is high in New York, this is a national problem." The first ads were aimed at "a very select" group of consumers, the company said, with the long-range goal of enhancing the brand on a "very, very careful scale." Using a blend of sophisticated snob-appeal and humor, the first ads conveyed the message that a proper diet could not be maintained without the four basic food groups: caviar, brioche, artichokes, and Häagen-Dazs. The company used a non-packaged goods approach to further emphasize that its ice cream was not just a product, but an indulgence "like a Mercedes or jewelry," one executive told *Marketing & Media Decisions*.

The Häagen-Dazs brand was 30 years old before it made its television advertising debut in 1991. Before introducing Häagen-Dazs frozen yogurt, Häagen-Dazs unveiled a print and television campaign designed "to communicate the Häagen-Dazs experience," an executive told *Advertising Age*. Six months later, Häagen-Dazs print ads were making news. Objections were raised by audiences at home and abroad to ads featuring a couple, in various stages of undress, sharing a tub of Häagen-Dazs. The copy accompanying one such picture read: "Throughout the 1960s and 1970s the sales of Häagen-Dazs mounted steadily, relying purely on word of mouth." Whether the ads sold ice cream or not, they unquestionably provoked response. A British reporter told *Fortune* magazine that the ad displayed "the most blatant and inappropriate use of sex as a sales aid yet." By the following year, Häagen-Dazs had revised the ads, using more humor and "more real, less perfect" models this time, the company told *Marketing* magazine. But the goal of attracting attention to the brand and creating an image had been achieved.

International Growth

While advertising has played a secondary role in Häagen-Dazs's brand development, other marketing strategies have figured prominently in the brand's promotion, both in the United States and abroad. Before Pillsbury Co. acquired Häagen-Dazs, the brand had entered the Canadian market via an exclusive distribution agreement with a Canadian firm. After the acquisition, Pillsbury took the brand to Japan. Then London-based Grand Metropolitan PLC swallowed up Pillsbury—and with it Häagen-Dazs—which became one of Grand Met's prime global brand candidates. In keeping with the brand's anti-advertising strategy, Grand Met approached the European market first through gourmet shops and quality hotels and restaurants to build name recognition and establish an image. Next, as was done in the United States, the company established upscale ice cream parlors in high-traffic areas where consumers could "sample the product in the best possible setting," a Grand Met executive told *Marketing* magazine in 1990. Finally, Häagen-Dazs products were distributed to supermarkets.

Using this successful strategy, Grand Met has been able to push the Häagen-Dazs brand into such international markets as Singapore, Hong Kong, Japan, France, the United Kingdom, Italy, Germany, Spain, and Australia. The company has stated that the Häagen-Dazs mission is "to be the leading worldwide marketer of luxury frozen desserts and snack products."

Product Development

Thirty years after Reuben Mattus mixed up his first batch of Häagen-Dazs, the brand maintains the strict standard of quality that defines the superpremium category. Company literature boasts that a simple flavor such as Häagen-Dazs strawberry required six years of testing before it was ready for public consumption. By 1992, there were approximately 20 Häagen-Dazs flavors, most packaged in pint containers. In 1990 the company offered four flavors in quart-size cartons. Beyond new flavors, the Häagen-Dazs product line remained fairly stagnant until 1986, when the company introduced an ice-cream bar line and its Sorbet & Cream line—a fruit sorbet and ice cream combination containing about one-third fewer calories than regular Häagen-Dazs. In 1991 Häagen-Dazs entered the frozen yogurt market with five yogurt flavors containing all-natural ingredients and no preservatives.

The superpremium ice cream category experienced its greatest growth spurt during the 1980s. But as the market became more crowded and the 1990s recession loomed larger than ever, growth slowed, provoking a "blizzard of new flavors" in the hope of spurring sales, according to a 1992 *New York Times* report. Häagen-Dazs responded with flavors such as carrot cake passion (containing actual chunks of carrot cake) and triple brownie overload, with pecans and chunks of fudge. The flavors were part of a new line, Häagen-Dazs Extraas, introduced in 1992. Häagen-Dazs told the *New York Times* that the Extraas line was targeted at college-age adults and adolescents, rather than the 25 to 45-year-old crowd responsible for the bulk of Häagen-Dazs sales.

Despite trends toward healthier, low-fat snacks and foods, the superpremium ice cream category is here to stay, according to analysts. Häagen-Dazs is banking on that fact that consumers are not likely to abandon their favorite indulgence, and the company seeks to expand the brand worldwide. "We will continue to provide a luxurious indulgence to people around the world," the company said.

Further Reading:

Alter, Jennifer and Jervey, Gay, "Pillsbury Gets into Ice Cream," *Advertising Age*, June 13, 1983, p.1.

Austin, Beth, "Ice Cream War Hot at High End," *Advertising Age*, September 7, 1987, p. 41.

"Ben & Jerry Try Putting the Doughboy on Ice," *Advertising Age,* March 11, 1985, p. 70.

Bidlake, Suzanne, "Häagen-Dazs Goes for More Playful Angle," *Marketing,* June 25, 1992, p. 5.

Blyskal, Jeff, "Calories Do Count," *Forbes,* August 13, 1984, p. 54.

Brit, Bill, "Häagen-Dazs Pushes Cold Front across the World," *Marketing,* October 4, 1990, pp. 30-31.

Brit, Bill, "Häagen-Dazs Samples Ice Cream Push," *Marketing,* January 4, 1991, p. 30.

Brown, Paul B., "Pricey Ice Cream is Scooping the Market," *Business Week,* June 30, 1986, p. 60.

Cox, Meg, "Pillsbury Agrees to Buy Häagen-Dazs, Private Ice-Cream Maker, and Franchisor," *Wall Street Journal,* June 7, 1983, p. 3.

Cuneo, Alice Z., "Häagen-Dazs Makes Freezer Case," *Advertising Age,* August 4, 1986, p. 4.

Fannin, Rebecca, "Who's Taking a Licking?" *Marketing & Media Decisions,* June 1989, pp. 38-46.

"Häagen-Dazs' Cold War with Rivals," *Dun's Business Month,* September, 1986, pp. 21-22.

"Häagen-Dazs May Demand Exclusivity, Judge Rules," *Wall Street Journal,* June 30, 1988, p. 4.

"Häagen-Dazs Takes Ad for Calif. Debut," *Advertising Age,* August 13, 1973, p. 10.

Hammonds, Keith H., "Is Häagen-Dazs Trying to Freeze Out Ben & Jerry's?" *Business Week,* December 7, 1987, p. 65.

Hogan, Karen, "Häagen-Dazs Plays It Cool on Sexy Ads," *Marketing,* August 15, 1991, p. 7.

Ingrassia, Lawrence, "Ice Cream Makers' Rivalry Heating Up," *Wall Street Journal,* December 21, 1988, p. B1.

Janis, Pam, "The 100% Pure Ice Cream—No Additives and No Ads," *Advertising Age,* September 5, 1977, p. 10.

Liesse, Julie, "Häagen-Dazs Dips into TV Ads," *Advertising Age,* February 11, 1991, p. 16.

Lil, Jane H., "In the Cut-throat World of Ice Cream, Flavormania!" *New York Times,* August 2, 1992, p. F8.

Maremont, Mark, "They're All Screaming for Häagen-Dazs," *Business Week,* October 14, 1991, p. 121.

"Mushy Marketing Practices Produce Soft Growth for the Ice Cream Market," *Marketing News,* August 31, 1984, p. 12.

"Pillsbury's Häagen-Dazs Forms Venture in Japan," *Wall Street Journal,* September 18, 1984, p.18.

Rapoport, Carla, "No Sexy Sales Ads, Please—We're Brits and Swedes," *Fortune,* October 21, 1991, p. 13.

"The Scoop on Ice Cream Sales," *Business Week,* September 20, 1982, p. 73.

Trillin, Calvin, "Competitors," *American Stories,* Boston, Houghton Mifflin Company, 1991, pp. 137-154.

Wentz, Laurel, "Häagen-Dazs Strategy Shows Grand Met Brand Development," *Advertising Age,* April 27, 1992, p. 114.

—Katherine J. Paul

HAWAIIAN PUNCH®

Hawaiian Punch is the second best-selling brand, behind Hi-C, in the $9 billion fruit beverage market and one of the top 25 grocery brands in the United States. Although a perennial favorite among children and one of the most widely recognized brand names among all American consumers, Hawaiian Punch has nonetheless suffered due to underexposure during the 1980s, when it was subject to the financially and managerially troubled Del Monte Corporation and RJR Nabisco corporate merger. Since 1990, the year in which The Procter & Gamble Company (P&G) purchased the powerful yet lagging brand, Hawaiian Punch has attempted to stage a comeback. "Punchy," the brand's ubiquitous cartoon spokesperson, is perhaps the single greatest reason for hope that the brand will chart a new course of success equal to that of decades past. First created in 1961, Punchy has been revamped to appeal to contemporary, pre-adolescent tastes in fashion and music and has showed signs of enduring, despite at least one report that the brand itself may be an "endangered species" on the marketing scene.

Brand Origins

According to "The History of Hawaiian Punch" and "Hawaiian Punch Brand History," the fruit drink traces its origins to 1934, when the Pacific Citrus Products Company, based in southern California, began marketing a punch concentrate to area restaurants, soda fountains, and ice cream manufacturers. An "exotic blend of juices, yellow/amber in color," the concentrate was invented, according to separate sources, by A. W. Leo and Ralph E. Harrison. A treasurer at Pacific Citrus, Reuben P. Hughes, bought the company with the aid of other investors for around $200,000 in 1946, eventually renaming it the Pacific Hawaiian Products Company. "Leo's Hawaiian Punch," as the company's rising brand was then known, had yet to be marketed directly to consumers or converted into a ready-to-drink format. Hughes undertook the first of these tasks almost immediately by introducing quart bottles of Hawaiian Punch concentrate for sale to retail grocery outlets in the western United States. In 1949, Hughes developed "Rosy Red" Hawaiian Punch concentrate and saw his company's annual sales increase to $3 million. The following year, he created the direct predecessor of Fruit Juicy Red and the modern Hawaiian Punch line, a ready-to-serve red Hawaiian Punch which was unveiled in a 46-ounce can and distributed nationally.

Rolling with the Punches: Ad Campaigns and New Owners

During the 1950s skyrocketing sales for the Hawaiian Punch brand, as well as for other company fruit juice products, catapulted Pacific Hawaiian well into the middle ranks of U.S. food and beverage corporations. Thus the stage was set, in 1962, for one of the most successful and long-running advertising campaigns in TV history. Launched by the Atherton-Privett agency, the campaign's goal was to capitalize on the fun image evoked by the Hawaiian Punch brand. Punchy, a buoyant cartoon character with a winning smile, became the personification of this goal; his

gimmick—the delivery and follow through to the line "How 'bout a nice Hawaiian Punch?"—became an instant classic and ensured Punchy's creators an award from the Character Advertising Association in July. This same year, Pacific Hawaiian went public with a listing on the New York Stock Exchange. In February 1963, on the heels of Punchy's debut, R. J. Reynolds Tobacco Company (RJR), now RJR Nabisco, Inc., acquired Pacific Hawaiian for approximately $40 million, nearly double the beverage company's sales for the nine months ended in September. The purchase was especially significant for RJR in that it represented the billion-dollar company's first foray into non-tobacco products. Hughes accepted a seat on the Reynolds board of directors and retained the position until he retired in 1976.

Meanwhile, the development of the Punchy campaign and the Hawaiian Punch line was accelerated under the newly created RJR Foods division. Primarily targeted at children, the ads from this period stressed the brand's "seven kinds of fruit" and "one of a kind fruit taste." In 1978, singers Donny and Marie Osmond were used to help sell the brand. Shortly thereafter, Del Monte merged with RJR and assumed management of Hawaiian Punch and several other RJR Foods properties. In 1982, the target market for the juice drink was broadened under the "Sail Away" campaign to include young adults, who were featured in sun-and-surf settings filmed near Maui. However, for much of the 1980s, Del Monte largely restricted promotion of the brand to inexpensive point-of-sale and packaging strategies. In 1984, the annual advertising budget of Hawaiian Punch was $10.6 million, but by 1989 it had been drastically cut to just $45,200.

Punchy: Down for the Count or Going the Distance?

Despite this ostensible brand neglect prior to the purchase of Hawaiian Punch by Procter & Gamble, Zachary Schiller reported in a March 1990 *Business Week* article that: "A recent survey of 1,000 people found that the drink's name recognition and image among consumers rank below only six other P&G brands—and above such powerhouses as Pampers and Head & Shoulders," and that "a third of consumers think they saw the [Punchy] ad on TV in the past three months, even though it hasn't run in more than three years." Schiller found several analysts willing to venture an opinion on the brand's enduring power. One considered the ad "both a visual and sound mnemonic, reminding viewers of the name with both the line and the blow that accompanied it." Another perceived it as "the pretty, comfortable gag America looked at and liked, innocently delivered." Yet another succinctly remarked, "They [RJR] did it long enough, and it stuck."

With $130 million in annual sales and an eminently recognizable name, Hawaiian Punch represented obvious superbrand potential for Procter & Gamble as well as a chance to pit itself more successfully against juice-market rival Hi-C, owned by Coca-Cola. According to Alecia Swasy in the *Wall Street Journal*, because Procter & Gamble's Citrus Hill orange juice brand had been suffering in competition with Coca-Cola's Minute Maid and Seagram's Tropicana, the company had plans to "build the fruit-

AT A GLANCE

Hawaiian Punch brand of fruit drink founded in Fullerton, CA, by Pacific Citrus Products Company owners, including Ralph E. Harrison and A. W. Leo; later developers include Reuben P. Hughes and the Atherton-Privett Agency; Pacific Citrus renamed Pacific Hawaiian Products Company, 1950; Pacific Hawaiian purchased by R. J. Reynolds, 1963, and renamed Pacific Hawaiian Products Company, Inc. (a Delaware subsidiary of Reynolds); Hawaiian Punch brand managed by Del Monte after Del Monte merged in 1979 with R. J. Reynolds Industries, which became RJR Nabisco, Inc.; Del Monte Corporation (doing business as Del Monte Foods) created via leveraged buy-out, 1989; Hawaiian Punch brand sold to The Procter & Gamble Company, 1990.

Performance: *Market share*—2.3% (second-highest) share of fruit beverage category. *Sales*—$209 million (estimate).

Major competitor: Coca-Cola's Hi-C.

Advertising: *Agency*—N W Ayer, New York, NY, 1991—. *Major campaign*—"It's Not Just Red Anymore": combination of live action and animation in which rap music and street dancing by Punchy and younger actors support the brand as a high-energy youth drink, available in seven fruit juice flavors.

Addresses: *Parent company*—The Procter & Gamble Company, 1 Procter & Gamble Plaza, Cincinnati, OH, 45202-3315, phone: (513) 983-1100.

beverage end of the market through acquisitions." Toward this end, P&G purchased Sundor Group Inc., makers of Sunny Delight, in 1989 and rolled out a new line of SunSip Punchline Coolers the following summer. "Clearly, however," wrote Laurie Freeman in *Advertising Age,* "Hawaiian Punch is P&G's juice-drink jewel. P&G intends to double the brand's $130 million in annual sales within two to three years, industry sources say, adding that the goal seems reachable."

In June 1990, Punchy returned to TV in a 60-second ad created by the New York agency N W Ayer. Capitalizing on the trend toward nostalgia in marketing, Ayer produced "Punchy's Greatest Hits," a collection of vintage Hawaiian Punch commercials spanning the years 1962 through 1975. The following year, Ayer and P&G followed up with a Northeast test campaign entitled "It's Not Just Red Anymore," which continued to evolve after national introduction in 1992. Designed in support of several new Fruit Juicy colors and flavors of Hawaiian Punch, Ayer's spots feature a combination of live action and animation and are notable for their upbeat music, setting, contemporized Punchy character, and tagline "Nothing else has the punch." The new product introduction helped boost initial sales by 40 percent. A clever presidential promotion campaign targeted at children ages 6 to 13, with Punchy as the favored candidate ("No one else has the punch"), also appeared in 1992, replete with an essay contest which ran in the September issue of *Learning 92.*

This renewed emphasis on advertising notwithstanding, Hawaiian Punch was placed on *Adweek's* list of "Endangered Species" in 1991. In a cover story entitled "Dinosaur Brands" (declaring the impending extinction of a number of products, including Ovaltine, Tang, and Royal Crown Cola), *Adweek's* editors wrote: "The growing ranks of dinosaur brands will place new pressures on marketers. Companies like P&G will have to justify the existence of two standards of profit—high performers like Cover Girl and Oil of Olay, dinosaurs like Folgers and Crisco—under the same corporate roof. Those same companies will face the difficulties of structuring career tracks for two separate classes of brand managers—the innovators and the dinosaur keepers." Hawaiian Punch ranked in the list tellingly subheaded, "While not exactly dinosaurs yet, the following brands are considered endangered if something isn't done to turn them around."

Given rising birth rates and Procter & Gamble's strong commitment, as one of the largest advertisers in the world, to expand the brand both nationally and internationally, Hawaiian Punch's demise appears an unlikely scenario. As one consultant remarked in an August 1992 *Advertising Age* article: "Punchy is like the Kool-Aid pitcher man. He keeps coming back and seems to work for the brand."

Further Reading:

"Dinosaur Brands (Inset: 'Endangered Species')," *Adweek's Marketing Week,* June 17, 1991, p. 19.

Elliott, Stuart, "Pugilistic Pitchman Still Packs a Wallop," *USA Today,* June 26, 1990, p. B1.

Freeman, Laurie, "P&G Muscle Backs Punch," *Advertising Age,* February 5, 1990, p. 43.

Freeman, Laurie, "P&G Shifts Strategy in Juices: New, Diverse Products May Make It More Effective Player," *Advertising Age,* June 18, 1990, p. 33.

"Hawaiian Punch Brand History" and "The History of Hawaiian Punch," Cincinnati, Ohio: Procter & Gamble.

Hill, Gladwin, "Reynolds Buys Pacific Hawaiian," *New York Times,* February 9, 1963, p. 5.

Lawrence, Jennifer, "Insider Taste Test: AA Kids Brush up on Crest Flavors," *Advertising Age,* April 8, 1991, p. 20.

Lawrence, Jennifer, "Truly Punchy Candidate: Hawaiian Punch Character Throws Straw Hat in Ring," *Advertising Age,* August 10, 1992, p. 40.

Lev, Michael, "Reuben P. Hughes, 79; President of the Maker of Hawaiian Punch," *New York Times,* January 6, 1991, p. 22.

"Punch of Color," *Advertising Age,* October 14, 1991, p. 6.

"Ralph E. Harrison: Hawaiian Punch Inventor," *Washington Post,* August 14, 1990, p. B6.

"Reuben P. Hughes: Hawaiian Punch Maker," *Washington Post,* January 7, 1991, p. B6.

Schiller, Zachary, "The Punch P&G Will Put Behind Hawaiian Punch," *Business Week,* March 26, 1990, p. 42.

Swasy, Alecia, "P&G Agrees to Buy Hawaiian Punch from Del Monte," *Wall Street Journal,* January 29, 1990, p. B10.

—Jay P. Pederson

HEALTHY CHOICE®

Inspiration can strike at any time. The trauma of a heart attack inspired Charles Michael ("Mike") Harper to create the Healthy Choice brand of prepared foods. In its first four years of existence, Healthy Choice foods reaped millions of dollars for ConAgra Inc., an Omaha-based food manufacturer. Harper, the chief executive officer of ConAgra with manufacturing and acquisitions expertise, spent years using his savvy to boost the profits of the company whose food products—including the Banquet frozen food line—were well known to shoppers. Under Harper's guidance, ConAgra total sales rose "from $600 million in 1974 to an estimated $23 billion [during the 1991] fiscal year," according to *Advertising Age.*

By 1985 Harper was well established as ConAgra's leader but, at the same time, he was headed for trouble. In many ways a typical consumer, Harper had built up a lifetime of bad habits. Then a two-pack-a-day smoker and high-volume coffee drinker, Harper also shared the poor eating habits displayed by many Americans. His weaknesses were roast beef sandwiches and hot fudge sundaes but, as he told Trish Hall in a *New York Times* interview, "I ate anything I could get my hands on. . . . Greasy pork chops. Anything. This is a terrible thing to say, but I was too busy [to eat properly]." That year, however, Harper's unhealthy lifestyle caught up with him, and a heart attack landed him in intensive care for a week.

Recovering at home, Harper invited a ConAgra colleague, vice-president of marketing L. James Kennedy, over for lunch. The main course was turkey chili concocted by Harper's wife, Josie. The low-fat chili was both spicy (so spicy, in fact, it made Kennedy's bald spot sweat, according to the *Times*) and satisfying. "More importantly," Hall continued, Kennedy and Harper "had the same realization at the same moment: 'It dawned on both of us that foods that are good for you can taste good.' " And so Healthy Choice was conceived.

A Brand Is Born

Getting Healthy Choice products ready for manufacture took about four years. By late 1989 the first such offerings made their debut at a lavish celebration at New York's Plaza Hotel. The initial ten frozen dinners contained various multi-course meals. For example, the Salisbury Steak dinner featured a portion of low-fat beef in mushroom sauce, potatoes in butter sauce, a side of green beans, and apple chunks in cinnamon-raisin sauce. As generous as

this meal appears, its weight is less than 12 ounces, it contains just 300 calories, and is low in fat, sodium, and cholesterol.

All Healthy Choice meals conform to a strict set of standards, according to the *New York Times.* "The dinners must have no more than 25 percent of the daily recommended amounts of salt and cholesterol. None of the products gets more than 30 percent of their calories from fat, the limit recommended by the federal government. On average, however, Healthy Choice products get 18 percent of their calories from fat."

Convincing supermarket managers to stock this totally new concept in frozen dinners proved challenging. "ConAgra [at first] had to pay retailers to carry the fledgling brand," *Business Week* reporter Lois Therrien noted. "But soon they were clamoring for it." As it turned out, the time was right for a well-presented frozen-meal alternative. Though such prepared items as Stouffer's Lean Cuisine and Weight Watchers frozen foods had been available for some time, the "healthy"—as opposed to "dieting"—aspect of Healthy Choice sparked the interest of consumers.

As Pamela Ellis-Simons related in *Marketing and Media Decisions,* the concern with good nutrition was burgeoning in the United States. Ellis-Simons, citing ConAgra figures, wrote that at the time of Healthy Choice's debut "29% of the population couldn't care less about what they eat. But 20% of Americans are restricted dieters and a surprising 30% are so-called 'health-conscious.' " Still, Ellis-Simons noted, "it was a gutsy move to introduce a 'health' product in the largely male frozen-food dinner market. Most low-cal entrants have fared tepidly in this stagnant and price-competitive part of the freezer section." In the case of Healthy Choice, Ellis-Simons continued, the meals are "targeted at men and women 25 years and older, although it skews 45 and older. But its plain 'home' cooking and non-exotic fare . . . was most popular with males."

The People's Choice

Once it became clear that people were ready to embrace this new line of food, Healthy Choice began rapidly expanding its product line. Within a few years, the distinctive green label was showing up on virtually any kind of prepared food a shopper could want. A health-watching consumer might begin with breakfast—anything from Healthy Choice's own muffins, to omelets (Western-style or turkey sausage) to a breakfast sandwich (which Harper

AT A GLANCE

Healthy Choice brand of prepared foods conceived in 1985 by Charles Michael Harper, chief executive officer of ConAgra Inc.; first appeared as a line of frozen dinners in 1989, has expanded to include more than 150 different prepared foods.

Performance: Market share—ranks third with 18.8 percent share of frozen-dinner market (1992); ranks sixth with a 4.4 percent share of frozen-entree market (1992). *Sales*—$178 million (dinners); $150 million (entrees)

Major competitor: Stouffer's Lean Cuisine; also Budget Gourmet Light & Healthy.

Advertising: Agency—Campbell-Mithuen-Esty, Minneapolis, MN, 1989—. *Major campaign*—"Listen to your heart. Make a Healthy Choice"; "The balance of taste and nutrition."

Addresses: Parent company—ConAgra. Inc., One ConAgra Drive, Omaha, NE 68102; phone: (402) 595-6000.

vows he eats every weekday morning). Lunch might be a sandwich prepared with a vast choice of branded low-fat cold cuts, perhaps complemented by one of at least ten Healthy Choice soups. For dinner, the choices grow exponentially. There are dozens of full-course dinners and large-portion single entrees—chicken, fish, pasta, beef, and any number of Italian, Mexican, or Chinese specialties—plus, of course, the low-fat chili that began it all. Even dessert-lovers can enjoy guiltless pleasure. Healthy Choice markets its own frozen dairy products, with flavors such as Butter Pecan, Mint Chocolate Chip, Coffee Toffee, and Rocky Road. In all, the Healthy Choice product line had topped 150 different items by 1992.

Of course, ConAgra's rivals were not about to give up without a fight. With Healthy Choice sales climbing, a "cornucopia of copycat products and claims from such competitors as Stouffer's Le Menu and Weight Watchers" became the norm, according to Steve Weiner of *Forbes*. Weight Watchers practically acknowledged ConAgra's success when they ran ads touting the fact that its line "uses no butter, tropical oil, chicken fat or cream," and adds, " 'maybe we should have called them Health Watchers.' " In addition, Stouffer's, makers of the faltering Lean Cuisine, "hurriedly launched Right Course, a line of 11 controlled-content entries that, with almost medical precision, lists its cholesterol, sodium and fat content right on the front of the box."

Advertising Themes

Despite the efforts of rival prepared food makers, Healthy Choice continued to widen its lead in market share. Just one year after the line was introduced, "Healthy Choice chalked up sales of $300 million and became the No. 1 premium frozen diner," according to an *Advertising Age* report. Advertising for the brand first appeared in 1989—and the star of the premiere Healthy Choice commercial was none other than Mike Harper. Harper at first resisted going the route of Chrysler's Lee Iacocca and Wendy's Dave Thomas. "The last thing that a dying ad agency does is put the CEO on TV," he told *Advertising Age*. But ConAgra's agency, Campbell-Mithuen-Esty of Minneapolis, persisted. The result was a spot that *Adweek's Marketing Week*'s David Kiley called "a heartfelt pitch" showing Harper discussing his heart attack and subsequent change of lifestyle. "He quips that his wife is after his job or, demonstrating his vitality, flies off in a

bi-plane." Ellis-Simons added, "In another commercial, *Family Ties*' Michael Gross joked that he likes to be able to pronounce everything he reads in the labels, which is why he eats Healthy Choice." The tag line for the commercials: "Listen to your heart. Make a Healthy Choice."

Print ads, as well, touted both mature consumers and younger, upscale types demonstrating their vigor. The diversity in spokespeople underlined the marketing strategy to position Healthy Choice as a low-fat premium meal, rather than a Pritikin-like recovery food for heart patients. Yet, the premium aspect of Healthy Choice has worked both to the line's advantage and its disadvantage. "The company is not offering mounds of rice with vegetables on top," as Trish Hall's noted; instead, Healthy Choice refuses to compromise its standard of fare. Harper told Hall, "The American consumer, and I would include myself, will not sacrifice the pleasure of eating for good nutrition." But the large portions and diversity of product has also made Healthy Choice among the most expensive of frozen dinners, even in the "premium" category. And despite the high volume sold, by February of 1992 the line was "not yet profitable," according to Hall, "because the money is being spent on expansion."

Growing Pains

By early 1993, it became clear that something was amiss with Healthy Choice. From its initial first-place position, "in frozen dinners, the brand's foundation, sales slid 25 percent, or some $57 million" in 1992, noted Richard Gibson of the *Wall Street Journal*. "While frozen-entree sales are up, they trail archrival Lean Cuisine. . . . Indeed, Healthy Choice is an also-ran in nearly every category it entered." The brand retaliated by cutting prices on its higher-volume entries—but "even with the discounts, some supermarkets are dropping parts of the line for poor performance. Finally, the brand's cheeses have been plagued by an embarrassing product recall." According to Gibson, Healthy Choice "appears to have fallen victim to two classic miscues." First, ConAgra "tried to do too much too fast, sometimes sacrificing quality and endangering the brand's image as it has sought to outrace the competition down supermarket aisles."

Gibson suggested that early enthusiasm over Healthy Choice led to a "megabrand" mentality. "Execution is critical in building a megabrand, and few companies have done it right," he continued. The rapid expansion of the Healthy Choice line frustrated many in the supermarket industry. Gibson quoted a retailer as saying, "They [ConAgra] absolutely kill us with all the variety." Healthy choice also made miscues in promotion. "ConAgra first sold the fish in January 1992, the off-season, and didn't heavily promote the product during the following Lent," noted Gibson. As for Healthy Choice hamburger, "the extra-lean meat was wrapped in a plastic tube, so some butchers put it in with frozen breakfast sausage. 'Who buys frozen hamburger?' "

Gibson also noted that the company may have been driven "more by a desire to please its revered chairman than to satisfy consumer palates." Indeed, Healthy Choice, referred to as "Mike's brand," has always reflected the passions of Harper. "There's no question that Healthy Choice wouldn't exist today had it not been for Mike's leadership," a former ConAgra executive told Gibson. "He stimulated the general managers in cheese and red meat to come along with products that would fit. It was his drive, his imagination and his persistence that made it go." On the other hand, Harper's infectious attitude may have stimulated poor decisions where cooler heads may otherwise have prevailed. (To add to the company's woes, a 1993 study widely reported in newspapers suggests that Americans' attention to health issues is not as pressing as it was in the 1980s.)

For his part, Harper, who retired in autumn of 1992, acknowledges in Gibson's piece that ConAgra, which had enjoyed growth up until the introduction of Healthy Choice, "could have made a lot more money in the short term" without the brand, "but he expresses confidence that [ConAgra] will become a 'money machine' in three to five years." Succeeding CEO Philip Fletcher is confident in Healthy Choice's future. "There's great strength in being first," he insisted.

Whatever the future holds for Healthy Choice, Mike Harper has still made his name frozen-food history for introducing a new way to think of nutrition. In the *Forbes* profile, Harper looks back on the "old Mike"—the retailer who thought, "If people want to eat a salty and greasy whatever, then we'll make a salty and greasy whatever." Following his brush with death, the "new Mike"

reflects: "We in the food industry didn't believe bad eating was our fault, because we didn't believe there was a market for healthy foods. Well, we were wrong."

Further Reading:

Ellis-Simons, Pamela, "One from the Heart," *Marketing & Media Decisions,* March 1990, pp. 32-36.

Gibson, Richard, "Chairman's Brand: 'Healthy Choice' Foods of ConAgra Flounder after Healthy Start," *Wall Street Journal,*

Hall, Trish, "How a Heart Attack Changed a Company," *New York Times,* February 26, 1992.

Kiley, David, "Amid 'Healthy' Foods' Frozen Wasteland, ConAgra Sleds Ahead," *Adweek's Marketing Week,* April 9, 1990, p. 4.

Liesse, Julie, "Harper: ConAgra's Healthy Choice," *Advertising Age,* January 7, 1991.

Therrien, Lois, "ConAgra Turns up the Heat in the Kitchen," *Business Week,* September 2, 1991, pp. 58-60.

Weiner, Steve, "How Josie's Chili Won the Day," *Forbes,* February 5, 1990, p. 57.

—Susan Salter

HEINEKEN®

Heineken, a golden lager brewed in The Netherlands, is the most widely exported beer in the world. Distributed throughout Europe, Africa, Asia, and North and South America, it is the best-selling imported beer in countries including Japan, Canada, and Australia. In the United States Heineken has been the top-selling import since 1933.

Heineken's parent company is Heineken N.V., headquartered in Amsterdam. Heineken N.V. is the largest beer producer in Europe and the second largest in the world, trailing only the American giant Anheuser-Busch. Despite its tremendous size, the Heineken brewery has remained family controlled and widely known for its strict loyalty to quality brewing. In addition to its flagship brand, Heineken Lager Beer, the company produces brands including Heineken Special Dark, Amstel, Amstel Light, Buckler (nonalcoholic), Murphy (an Irish stout), Dreher, '33', and Mützig.

Brand Origins

Beer has been brewed in what is now The Netherlands for more than a thousand years. A concoction of barley, yeast, and salty water was made by early farmers, and by the 10th century commercial brewing was an important part of the area's economy. Most existing Dutch breweries are at least 250 years old.

In this long history of beer production, Heineken is a relatively new brewing company. The idea of Heineken beer was born in the 1860s, when a young man, Gerard Adriaan Heineken, was seeking to develop a successful business venture in Amsterdam. With little money of his own, he looked to his mother for financing and tried to propose a business idea that would appeal to her. He knew his mother was disgusted by the gangs of men, still drunk from late-night binging on hard liquor and home-brewed alcohol, who roamed the streets of Amsterdam each Sunday morning. In a letter to his mother, the young Heineken suggested that drunkenness would decrease if the men were drinking a less powerful brew.

In 1864, with his mother's financing, Heineken bought one of Amsterdam's largest breweries, De Hooiberg (the Haystack), which was built in 1592. An exceptional brewer and businessman, Heineken saw the sales of his new beer grow quickly, and by 1868 he closed De Hooiberg to establish an even larger brewery just outside Amsterdam. Further growth allowed Heineken to build a brewery in 1874 in the Dutch town of Rotterdam.

Technical Developments

Like other brewers of his time, Heineken was initially able to make beer only during the cool months when ice was available. Beer production was begun by malting and crushing barley and steeping it in hot water. The resulting liquid, called wort, was boiled with hops and then cooled with ice and fermented with yeast. For his lager beer, the fermented liquid was allowed to mature at a temperature slightly above freezing. (The term lager—a German word meaning storehouse—refers to this stage of cold storage.) As a result of a new cooling system invented by Carl von Linde, Heineken was able to brew year-round beginning in 1873, a change that greatly expanded the company's production capacity.

Heineken also took advantage of advances in biological research. In 1879 he hired Dr. Elion, a pupil of noted scientist Louis Pasteur, to breed a type of yeast especially suitable for making beer. Dr. Elion's research eventually led to the Heineken A-yeast, which since 1888 has been a major determinant in the flavor of Heineken beer. The success of the new yeast was quickly evident. At the 1889 World's Fair, Heineken beer was given the Grand Prix Paris, an award still mentioned on Heineken labels.

Early Exports

As Heineken beer developed a loyal following within the small market of The Netherlands, the brewery started to look beyond its national borders to expand sales. Exports to France began in 1876, just 12 years after Gerard Heineken bought De Hooiberg, and soon the brewery was sending its beer to the Dutch colonies and to other countries in Europe. By 1900 Heineken beer was sold as far away as Asia.

When Gerard Heineken retired in 1914, his son, Dr. Henri Pierre Heineken, took over the company's brewing operations. Over the next half century Henri Heineken played an important role in keeping Heineken not only a top-selling brand but also a high-quality beer. Under his leadership, production techniques and product consistency were greatly improved, thus enhancing the company's reputation for exceptional brewing standards.

It was Henri Heineken who made the critical decision to start exporting beer to the United States. In 1914, in order to see for himself the possibilities of this vast new market, he sailed to New York on the Dutch ship Nieuw Amsterdam. Before he arrived, however, he met the ship's Dutch bartender, Leo van Munching,

AT A GLANCE

Heineken brand founded in 1864 in Amsterdam, The Netherlands, by Gerard Adriaan Heineken; control of Heineken's Beer Brewery Company passed down in 1914 to his son, Dr. Henri Pierre Heineken, and later to his grandson, Alfred Henry Heineken; company renamed Heineken N.V. in 1968.

Performance (all Heineken brands): *Market share*—53% (top share) of beer category in The Netherlands; 28% (top share) of imported beer category in the United States. *Sales (Heineken N.V., all beers)*—Dfl 7.3 billion ($3.8 billion)

Major U.S. competitor: Modelo Brewing Group's Corona Extra; also Beck's, Molson Golden, and other imported beers.

Advertising: *Agency (U.S.)*—Warwick, Baker & Fiore, New York, NY. *Major campaign*—"Just being the best is good enough."

Addresses: *Parent company*—Heineken N.V., 2e Weteringplantsoen 21, 1017 ZD, PO Box 28, 1000 AA Amsterdam, The Netherlands; phone: 011-31-206-70-91-11.

who impressed Heineken with his extraordinary knowledge of beer. Van Munching was hired on the spot to become Heineken's U.S. importer. For the next several years Van Munching was successful in distributing Heineken beer to many of New York's fine restaurants, bars, and hotels, but Prohibition temporarily closed his import business in 1920.

When consumption of alcoholic beverages was again made legal in 1933, Heineken was the first foreign beer to reach the country's shores. On April 14, 1933, the *New York Times* printed this announcement: "The first legal shipment of imported beer in thirteen years arrived in Hoboken, N.J.; it was about 100 gallons from the Heineken brewery in Rotterdam, and was brought here on the S.S. Statendam as a test shipment." Though limited to Van Munching's distribution in the New York area, Heineken became the top-selling imported beer in the United States in 1933, and sales continued to rise until World War II, when Van Munching entered the U.S. Navy. After the war ended in 1945, Van Munching started a new business, Van Munching & Co., which served as a nationwide distribution service for Heineken beer.

Product Development and Advertising

Since World War II Heineken has greatly expanded its operations, developed and acquired new brands, enhanced its quality control, and begun an international marketing strategy. These advances came about under the management of Henri Heineken's son, Alfred H. Heineken, who rose to prominence during this period.

Alfred Heineken significantly influenced the marketing strategy and advertising of Heineken beer. In the late 1940s he was sent by his father to New York, where he worked closely with Van Munching's sales staff and took advertising and business classes at night. He was also able to observe American consumer habits, such as the purchase of beer in supermarkets for home consumption. In The Netherlands and other European markets, beer was still consumed largely in pubs, which often had special licensing agreements to sell the beer of a single brewery. When Alfred Heineken returned to Holland in 1948, he began a new marketing campaign to sell Heineken beer in Dutch grocery stores, and to

boost these sales, he began the company's first radio advertisements.

The adoption of American marketing techniques in The Netherlands was the beginning of the brewery's attempt to develop a common international strategy for selling its beer. For much of its history, Heineken beer has been marketed quite differently in each country. Since the 1960s an important part of the company's international marketing strategy has been product diversification. In 1968 Heineken bought Amstel, Holland's second-largest brewery, and in 1971 purchased the Bokma distillery, placing one of The Netherlands's most popular gins under Heineken's control. In 1983 it bought Murphy, an Irish brewery producing stout. As a result of further acquisitions and joint ventures, by the early 1990s Heineken was selling more than 20 different beer brands, as well as various soft drinks, spirits, and wine, in more than 150 countries. It also controlled 90 breweries outside The Netherlands. Even with diversification into other beverage types, beer still made up more than 80 percent of Heineken's sales.

In the early 1980s the company began a new international advertising campaign under the slogan, "When you make a great beer, you don't have to make a great fuss." There were "no catchy jingles . . . no beach volleyball games" in Heineken advertisements, the campaign claimed; for Heineken "just being the best is enough." With these advertisements Heineken was differentiating itself from cheaper beers, whose commercials often featured young people socializing, playing sports, or engaged in other activities not intrinsically related to beer.

In the late 1980s Heineken began an advertising campaign in the United States featuring its two leading brands, Heineken lager and Amstel Light. In one television commercial a man extolled Heineken as the country's number one import, while another man praised Amstel Light as the best-selling imported low-calorie beer. This advertisement was successful in using Heineken's established presence in the U.S. market to increase public awareness and sales of Amstel Light.

Heineken's reputation as a high-quality, fashionable beer has greatly helped the company's profit margin. Although Heineken has remained a moderately priced beer in The Netherlands, in the United States it has been typically sold at a price 50 percent higher than Budweiser, the top-selling U.S. brand. The price difference reportedly far exceeded the cost difference in production and shipping. According to analysts at Lehman Brothers in London, in 1991, although less than 3 percent of Heineken's beer sales were in the United States, these sales provided the company with about 23 percent of its pretax profits.

Brand Outlook

Because Heineken is an international beer, changes in the global economic market could have a major impact on its sales. Especially important to Heineken have been plans for the economic union of western Europe, where in the early 1990s it had a nine-percent market share, the largest of any European beer company. As goods and people were beginning to cross national borders with growing regularity, there was expected to be an even greater uniformity in the company's European advertising.

With a small home market, Heineken's sales strategy will continue to focus on exports. In 1993 Heineken began for the first time to export its beer to Germany—the country with the highest per capita beer consumption—where the market has been dominated by hundreds of small German breweries. Heineken was also considering the purchase of additional breweries and brands, including some in eastern Europe. With a new joint venture company called Vietnam Brewery Limited, established in 1991 with Food Company 2 of Ho Chi Minh City, Heineken continued to find new markets for its beer across the globe. Even so, with falling international trade barriers expected worldwide, Heineken was preparing for fiercer competition from other European beer brands, such as Kronenbourg and Carlsberg, as well as by such low-cost American brands as Budweiser.

In the United States Heineken gained greater control over distribution with its 1991 purchase of Van Munching & Co., the only U.S. importer of Heineken beer. Although sales to the United States have surpassed 70 million gallons per year, the company has shown no intention of having Heineken beer brewed within the borders of this lucrative market. Any thoughts about such a move were likely dashed by the experience of Löwenbräu, a German beer that threatened Heineken's U.S. market share in the 1980s. U.S. sales of Löwenbräu dropped quickly after it began to be brewed in Texas. The Netherlands has continued to be the origin of all Heineken beer sold in the United States, with much of it brewed at a facility in 's-Hertogenbosch, which has been set up to handle the differing labeling requirements adopted by the U.S. states.

Further Reading:

Fromson, Brett Duval, "Cheers to Heineken," *Fortune,* November 19, 1990, p. 172.

Fuhrman, Peter, "Making Haste Slowly," *Forbes,* November 9, 1992, pp. 44-45.

Heineken Factsheet 1991, Amsterdam: Heineken N.V., 1991.

"Heineken Looks at Brewers," *Wall Street Journal,* April 7, 1992, p. A13D.

Heineken N.V. Annual Report 1991, Amsterdam: Heineken N.V., 1991.

"Heineken Three Ways," *Beverage World,* May 1992, p. 16.

"Heineken Sets '93 to Enter Germany," *New York Times,* April 3, 1992, p. D3.

"Heineken to Buy U.S. Distributor," *New York Times,* December 8, 1990, p. 35.

Jackson, Michael, *The New World Guide to Beer,* Philadelphia: Running Press, 1988, pp. 20, 135-37.

Levin, Gary, "Imports Brew New Success," *Advertising Age,* October 5, 1992, p. 38.

"Sibling Beers Get Own Ads," *New York Times,* September 16, 1991, p. D9.

Van Dijk, Nico, "Dutch Beer: The World's Safest Drink?" *Europe,* September 1992, pp. 22-23.

Winters, Patricia, "Import Fight Looms: Sales Drop Leads to Share War," *Advertising Age,* May 29, 1989, pp. 3, 50.

The World of Heineken, Amsterdam: Heineken Internationaal Beheer, 1992.

—*Thomas Riggs*

HEINZ® KETCHUP

Heinz brand of tomato ketchup, in a clear-glass bottle with the familiar keystone-shaped label, was touted as "America's thickest, best-tasting ketchup" and became the world's best-selling brand of ketchup. This condiment, manufactured continuously by the H. J. Heinz Company since its introduction in 1876, has graced kitchen tables, grocer's shelves, and the finest hotel tablecloths. In the late 1980s, after more than 100 years in production, Heinz brand of ketchup was stocked in 47 million U.S. households—or one out of every two. Seemingly as American as apple pie, tomato ketchup was not, however, invented in the United States.

The Development of Ketchup

In the late 1600s, English sailors visiting Malaysia and Singapore tasted a tangy sauce unavailable in their country. The Chinese had been the first to produce this sauce—pronounced "ketsiap"—made from the brine of pickled fish or shellfish. When they returned home, the English seamen tried to recreate the sauce with herbs, spices, and fish brine, later adding mushrooms, walnuts, and cucumbers. Soon New England ship captains travelled to the Far East, where they tasted subtle sauces, and to Mexico and the Spanish West Indies, where tomatoes were grown and used in a number of ways. Maine families began planting tomatoes and, like the English, attempted to create a flavorful sauce to eat with fish cakes, meat, and beans.

The first references to "ketchup" were in the *English House keeper's Pocketbook* of 1848 and the *Book of Household Management,* published in 1861; both books lauded the condiment's widespread uses in the kitchen. But making ketchup, like any preserving, was a bit of a chore— families boiled tomatoes all day and night over a hot, heavy kettle, constantly stirring to prevent the sauce from burning. When this popular sauce was first commercially bottled and sold in 1876 by the F. & J. Heinz Company in Pittsburgh, it was a welcome relief to many.

The Young Henry Heinz

Henry J. Heinz got his start in his mother's garden, helping her tend the produce and selling the surplus from a hand-held basket when he was eight years old. As he learned more about gardening, Heinz's mother let him try out various methods of cultivation and hotbeds. Eventually she gave a plot of land to produce solely for commercial profit. With a wheelbarrow Heinz could sell to more neighbors in Sharpsburg, Pennsylvania. By age sixteen he was driving a horse-drawn wagon and delivering three times a week to Pittsburgh grocers. Heinz woke at two or three a.m. in order to make the morning delivery to the city. Always on the lookout for more efficient ways of doing business, he convinced the Pittsburgh grocers to accept late evening deliveries of his produce, stored carefully to withstand the trip and overnight shelving. Heinz thereafter avoided working odd hours that cut into his next day's productivity.

In 1869 Heinz formed a partnership in Sharpsburg with his friend L. C. Noble to sell grated horseradish fresh from Heinz's garden. The firm moved to Pittsburgh, doing well until a sudden bankruptcy in 1875. Heinz paid all related debts before launching the 1876 start-up of F. & J. Heinz with his cousin Frederick and brother John. In its first year the company produced pickles, horseradish, and what would become a world-renowned product—bottled ketchup. By 1888 Heinz gained financial control of the company as well, changing the name to H. J. Heinz.

Early Packaging

In the late 1800s packaging was done solely for utilitarian purposes. Heinz decided to put his ketchup in a narrow-necked bottle for two reasons: to make it easier to pour, and to reduce the amount of contact with air (which darkened the sauce). The first bottles of ketchup were closed with corks hand-dipped in a special wax for an airtight seal. Contamination was avoided by the use of the wax-dipped corks, which were then covered with foil imprinted with the Heinz keystone logo. A strip of paper was banded around the neck of the bottle to cover the uneven bottoms of the hand-cut foil.

With the keystone-embossed foil and the paper neckbands, the H. J. Heinz Company cleverly used routine food-packing necessities to its advantage. As a result of these packaging choices, Heinz established a unique presence in the market. In 1895 a 17-ounce "Imperial Bottle" of Heinz was introduced, with a delicately-embossed symmetrical shape designed to appeal to higher-end hotels, restaurants, and upper-income families. Other packaging variations developed at this time included a less-ornate 12-ounce octagon-shaped bottle that became a trademark style and an 8-ounce bottle that contained a new product—Tomato Catsup made a bit spicier and with choice tomatoes. This brand was also packed in stone jugs and glass and wooden barrels. The turn of the century brought the time-saving innovation of screw-top lids.

AT A GLANCE

Heinz brand of ketchup founded in 1876 by Henry J. Heinz of F. & J. Heinz company in Pittsburgh, PA; in 1888 the firm was reorganized as the H. J. Heinz Company, and was incorporated in 1905 with Henry J. Heinz as president; company became famous for its keystone label, complete with a pickle insignia, and the slogan "57 Varieties" coined by president and founder Henry J. Heinz in 1896.

Performance: *Market share*—53% (top share) of the grocery ketchup market; 86% of food-service ketchup market.

Major competitor: Hunt-Wesson Inc.'s Hunt's.

Advertising: *Agency*—Leo Burnett, Chicago, Illinois. *Major campaign*—"The taste is the test"; "Anticipation."

Addresses: *Parent company*—H. J. Heinz Company, P.O. Box 57, Pittsburgh, PA 15230; phone: (412) 456-5700.

While the original reason for the well-known "neckband" was no longer necessary with screw-top lids, Heinz continued to keep them on the top of his ketchup bottles as a trademark. Another key decision Heinz made very early on was to bottle his product in clear glass, a novel practice at the time. A glass bottle both preserved the flavor of the tomato and proudly displayed the freshness and high quality ingredients contained in Heinz ketchup.

The Advertising of Genius

Around 1880 Heinz decided to decorate a horse-drawn wagon with drawings of the keystone label, and a little girl holding Heinz products in her arms. (The image of the sweet girl remained, with later variations showing the girl in a sunbonnet leaning over a bench upon which sat a basket of Heinz products with the caption, "Mama's Favorites." The circulating wagon made Heinz products obvious to any passerby. Thus, for a minor investment of decorating a produce-carrying vehicle that had to be driven anyway, Heinz gained visibility.

In an effort to make his product known to the national market, Henry J. Heinz attended the 1893 World's Fair in Chicago. Because his stand in the food-products area was a bit out of the way, the young company scattered brass disks around the grounds, imprinted with a promise of a souvenir from the Heinz exhibit. All who queried were given bright green pickle pins made of plaster with the words "Heinz Keystone" written across them. With this stunt, Heinz created his image as an advertiser beyond compare. For bringing so many people to the area, Heinz was given an honorary banquet by other food vendors at the fair. Over the years, the Heinz Pittsburgh plants continued to distribute millions of the pickles pins, although they were later made of plastic.

Within three years Heinz created a slogan that would remain with the company for decades. While travelling on New York City's elevated train in 1896, Heinz saw a shoe store sign advertising "21 Styles." He thought the phrase was catchy, and came up with the slogan "57 Varieties" to describe what his company had to offer. In fact, the H. J. Heinz Company already produced more than 57 varieties. Heinz adhered to the phrase simply because he liked the sound of the number 57; "58 Varieties, or 59 Varieties, did not appeal at all to me," Heinz stated some years later. Heinz then drew a street-car ad to be distributed all over the United States. The public latched onto the slogan, which is still displayed on the Heinz label.

By 1900, with his advertising reputation well-known, H. J. Heinz ensured his fame by erecting the first giant electric sign. Located in New York City at Fifth Avenue and 23rd Street, the sign featured a 40-foot long pickle illuminated with twelve hundred bulbs. This display cost $90 a day to run. Capitalizing on his recent success, in 1910 Heinz printed a small dark-green pickle on the bottom of the keystone label, for further product recognition. The pickle remains a key element of the Heinz label. These efforts paid off; the H. J. Heinz Company became the largest producer of ketchup, pickles, and vinegar in the nation. By 1905 Heinz was manufacturing in England as well.

The Federal Food and Drug Act

In the late 1800s, assuring that a product was made fresh and stayed fresh was no minor boast. At that time, both commercial and home canners relied on strong chemical preservatives. At a local grocery store, a tin called "Canning Powders" was available to homemakers. Retailers used the same combination of chemicals, including benzoate of soda, borax salicylic acid, benzoic, and formaldehyde. While these substances provided near-perfect preservation of food, they could be harmful when ingested in high quantities. Opposition to their use grew over the years.

The battle was heating up when Henry Heinz put his effort and reputation into the fight for the Pure Food Laws. Heinz's son Howard went to Washington to campaign for the issue. Because only a handful of manufacturers had managed to store food without the use of harsh chemicals, the lobbying was fierce. Heinz had nothing to lose because he already complied with the pure food standards—his ketchup, comprised of natural ingredients, was preserved by natural means. By 1906, with the aid of Dr. Harvey Wiley, chief chemist for the U.S. Department of Agriculture, the first Pure Food Laws were passed. Dr. Wiley joined the H. J. Heinz Company as bacteriologist in 1912. In 1940 a "Standard of Identity" was issued for ketchup by the United States government, to assure consumers that the product was made from tomatoes.

Factory Innovations

In 1905 H. J. Heinz became the first food manufacturer to establish a research department. With bacteriologists on site at the Pittsburgh plants, Heinz sought to apply scientific principles to back up the traditional methods already in use in food manufacturing. Laboratory specialists, for example, could pinpoint the exact temperature to cook tomatoes to remove not only bacteria—destroyed at the boiling point of water—but also bacterial spores, that require higher temperatures to be eliminated.

The secrets in food processing, however, were guarded by those high-ranking employees who were privy to them. When Dr. Riley first arrived at Heinz he wasn't quite sure how to be of use in such an environment. In the March 27, 1956 issue of the *Christian Science Monitor*, Riley commented, "Every operation was a secret. For instance, pickles. It seemed that only men with certain God-given knowledge could successfully salt cucumbers into pickles." Within six years of Riley's arrival, however, Heinz initiated a quality control department to establish specific scientific controls for products. H. J. Heinz II, when interviewed for the same *Christian Science Monitor* article, commented, "We think we may have been the first in American industry to use that phrase, but if we were not, we at least created it for ourselves out of our own experience."

That same experience was based on founder Heinz's conviction that improvement of the quality of commercial food starts with the seed of the tomato plant, and the dirt in which it is grown. He also believed that if foods could be preserved naturally in the kitchen, they could be preserved naturally in industry. These two concepts were emphasized not only in the daily operation of the Heinz plants from year to year, but also in the flow of advertising from decade to decade.

Modern Advertising Elements

Due to the increased awareness of pure food processing, in 1910 a new ''shoulder'' label was added to Heinz ketchup bottles, proclaiming the product to be ''free from benzoate of soda artificial preservatives or color.'' The label continued to appear on Heinz ketchup bottles until 1938, when most companies complied with government regulations. The tactic of advertising a product's purity was advanced, a tribute to Heinz's foresight in matters of consumer consciousness.

To strengthen the reputation of Heinz ketchup as a wholesome, fresh-tasting product, advertisements relayed the process of ketchup-making in short descriptive phrases. For example, in *Ladies Home Journal* of April 1926 an add touted the ''Heinz pedigreed tomato seed. Heinz greenhouses, gardens, farms. . . . Tomatoes slowly cooked—water boiled out—goodness left in.'' More unusual—but fitting, for Henry Heinz—was the opening claim of the ad: ''Fifty-seven years' experience.'' Heinz Ketchup was first introduced in 1876, 50 years earlier, but Heinz decided to conveniently include the experience with his first partnership to add up to his magic number, 57.

Another notable element in the 1926 ad was the final line, ''The taste is the test.'' This became another well-known Heinz slogan. An ad which came out the following year used the same phrase. With the all-caps headline ''WHY YOU LIKE IT,'' the ad went on the say, ''The first and main reason why you like Heinz Ketchup so much is that it tastes good. The taste is the test.'' The ad included an offer for a free recipe book, available upon request. In a separate heading, the ad stated that Heinz's product is ''the largest selling ketchup.''

In 1932, with the Great Depression underway in the United States, Heinz decided that taste wasn't the only test. Now ''the largest selling ketchup in the world,'' the ad emphasized how Heinz Ketchup ''gives plain cooking [a] Chef's touch.'' The entrance of ''makes plain foods taste like more,'' evolved into a later catch-phrase, ''makes good foods taste better.'' By the end of the 1940s, Heinz and Ketchup went together naturally. As stated in a 1949 issue of the *Saturday Evening Post,* ''Heinz Ketchup, although not the first commercial tomato ketchup, has led the American market for so long that it has determined the shape of almost all ketchup bottles because the public just naturally recognizes that shape as ketchup.'' No ketchup producer could hope for a higher compliment.

Continued Marketing Efforts

In 1956 Heinz tested a wide-mouthed ketchup bottle in Pittsburgh and Detroit for three months. Results confirmed, however, that the original narrow-mouthed 14-ounce size was still America's favorite. The company could not hold on to its lead in the marketplace, and by the early 1960s the Heinz's market share dipped to 24 percent behind Hunt Foods. In 1964 R. Burt Gookin, executive vice-president of finance who joined Heinz as an ac-

countant in 1945, was asked to produce a financial analysis of the firm to pinpoint its weaknesses. Because marketing was the problem area, older staff took early retirement and were replaced by younger staff. The new big guns—led by Heinz's Louis Collier and Paul D. Townsend from Procter & Gamble—offered different sized ketchup bottles to gain more shelf space and launched an aggressive advertising campaign in 1966, dubbing Heinz ''the slowest ketchup in the West.'' Heinz's market share climbed each year for five consecutive years, reaching 34 percent. Continuing with the slow-pour theme, Heinz scored another success with its ''Anticipation'' campaign in 1974. By 1978, Heinz's lead in the retail ketchup market rose to 40 percent; its share in food service was 60 percent. Heinz broke its own advertising records that year, spending close to $7.5 million on its staple product, ketchup. Interest in healthier food alternatives led Heinz to introduce onion and low-salt ketchups in the 1980s. An ad campaign that focused on children gave Heinz a boost, as sales increased to a record $280 million by 1986.

Competition Tightens

In the 1990s the company addressed the public's environmental concerns by introducing a recyclable plastic ketchup bottle. An earlier version, a squeezable bottle launched in 1983, was made of an opaque plastic that was not easily recycled. The new clear-plastic container, consistent with Heinz's time-honored clear glass bottle, could also be recycled into high-value items such as carpeting and egg cartons. Competitors were still packaging products in the same, less costly material that Heinz had used for previous bottle. Del Monte insisted, according to a 1991 *Wall Street Journal* article, that its bottles were ''nearly as recyclable,'' and that Heinz was prematurely claiming success.

Tough competition surfaced in another guise as salsa, a new American favorite, outsold ketchup by $79 million in 1991. With more than a century of experience, Heinz relied on its perspective and premium image to meet the challenges. As Daniel Best summarized in *Prepared Foods,* ''Historically, the company's greatest successes have hinged upon combining rigid quality control with packaging innovations.''

International Outlook

The H. J. Heinz Company began producing ketchup in the United States beginning in 1876 and expanded to Great Britain in 1905, and to Canada in 1909. Upon H. J. Heinz's death in 1919, the company was run by his son Howard, who established a Heinz branch in Australia in 1935. In 1941 Howard died and son Henry John Heinz took over, expanding the company to the Netherlands, Venezuela, and Italy. Acquisitions in the early 1960s included Star-Kist and Ore-Ida Foods. R. Burt Gookin, named chief executive officer in 1969, was the first non-family member appointed to the position. He expanded the company's interests beyond its traditional product line, a process that continued through the 1990s. Under Anthony O'Reilly, appointed chief executive officer in 1979, expansion to continental Europe, the Pacific Rim, and Africa proved that Heinz Ketchup—as the 1932 ad proclaimed—was indeed ''the largest selling ketchup in the world.''

Further Reading:

Alberts, Robert C., *The Good Provider,* Boston: Houghton Mifflin, 1973.
All About Ketchup, Pittsburgh: H. J. Heinz Company, 1991.
Ballen, Kate, ''Barbara L. Behrman,'' *Fortune,* July 20, 1987, p. 92.

Baum, Arthur W., "In Grandpa's Shoes—Young Mr. Heinz of Pittsburgh," *Saturday Evening Post,* June 25, 1949, p. 32.

Best, Daniel, "Heinz Hitched to Ketchup Quality," *Prepared Foods,* September, 1990, p. 66.

Fletcher, Noel, "China Anticipates Ketchup's Arrival," *Journal of Commerce and Commercial,* September 8, 1986, p. 8A.

"Getting Carpet out of Ketchup," *Environment,* May 1990, p. 21.

"The Good Steward," *Forbes,* March 1, 1971, p. 24.

"Hall of Fame," *Fortune,* January 30, 1978, p. 93.

Hannon, Kerry, "The King of Ketchup," *Forbes,* March 21, 1988, p. 58.

Heinz, H. J. II, "H. J. Heinz Company Story," *Christian Science Monitor,* March 26-28, 1956.

"H. J. Heinz Company," *Advertising Age,* September 9, 1979, p. 108.

Hirsch, James, "Heinz to Unveil Recyclable Bottle for its Ketchup," *Wall Street Journal,* April 9, 1990, p. B6.

Ingham, John, "Henry John Heinz," *Biographical Dictionary of American Business Leaders,* London: Greenwood Press, 1983, p. 567.

"Ketchup Bottle Become Recyclable," *Design News,* June 11, 1990, p. 48.

Michels, Antony J., "Hot Sales for Mexican Sauces," *Fortune,* October 7, 1991, p. 14.

Morgan, Hal, *Symbols of America,* New York: Penguin, 1986.

Pierson, John, "Ketchup Bottles Produce Dollop of Controversy," *Wall Street Journal,* June 25, 1991, p. B1.

Pritchett, Kevin, "You Know Washington's Involved When It Ends Up in a Bottleneck, *Wall Street Journal,* February 11, 1992, p. B1.

Schwartz, Judith D., "Heinz Keeps Ketchup in the Thick of It," *Adweek's Marketing Week,* August 26, 1991, p. 18.

Swank, Edith, *The Story of Food Preservation,* Pittsburgh: H. J. Company, 1943.

Tomato Ketchup, Pittsburgh: H. J. Heinz Company, 1988.

"World of 57 Heinz," *Newsweek,* October 20, 1958.

—Frances E. Norton

HELLMANN'S®

Mayonnaise was created in France in the mid-1700s. Its origins are traced to two different sources. In the first, a chef in Bayonne, France, mixed a sauce called "bayonnaise." According to a more credible story, the chef of the Duc de Richelieu made a batch in 1756 to celebrate the Duc's victory over the British on the Mediterranean island of Minorca. The menu called for a cream sauce, but when cream was not available the chef substituted cooking oil, eggs, and seasonings, creating what came to be known as mayonnaise.

According to the U.S. Federal Standard of Identity, mayonnaise must contain at least 65 percent vegetable oil by weight, at least 2.5 percent vinegar, lemon juice, or both, and some egg or egg yolks. A preservative may be added, but not artificial coloring or flavoring. Mayonnaise may contain standard natural seasonings with the exception of saffron or turmeric, whose yellow colors might suggest added egg yolk.

Brand Origins

The man who introduced mayonnaise to the United States, Richard Hellmann, was born in Vetschau, Germany, in either 1876 or 1880. Hellmann entered the food business in Germany then worked for Crosse & Blackwell, a British grocery firm, travelling as far as Australia while on the job. In 1903 Hellmann immigrated to the United States and worked in the wholesale grocery business. Two years later he opened a delicatessen on Columbus Avenue in New York City. His wife made several versions of mayonnaise to serve with sandwiches and salads sold in their delicatessen. From customer surveys Richard Hellmann discovered that the "blue ribbon" formula was more popular and he began to produce that version only. The recipe has remained the same over the years. Prominently displayed on the counter with a blue ribbon wrapped around the jar, the Hellmann family's mayonnaise rapidly became known. Hellmann offered ten cent portions, ladled into wooden boats, for customer purchases.

His wife's spread was selling so well that by 1912 Hellmann was packaging it in jars with the label, "Richard Hellmann's Blue Ribbon Mayonnaise." The label also described the product as "the home made salad dressing made of eggs, oil, and vinegar, spices, sugar and salt." Below the circular white background, at the top, was a large blue ribbon tied in a bow; and below, on a semi-circular black border, was the caption, "this true mayonnaise is perishable / keep cool but do not freeze."

Soon Hellmann began delivering his mayonnaise via truck. By 1913 the shopowner realized he did not have enough space in the back of his deli to produce the quantity of mayonnaise needed. Plans for commercial production were drawn up and in 1915 Hellmann built a manufacturing facility in the Astoria area of Queens. The business was incorporated the following year as Richard Hellmann's Inc. Sometime during these early years Hellmann found time to sell his successful deli in order to take a vacation through Europe. Upon his return to America, Hellmann bought the store back. By 1920 a second mayonnaise manufacturing plant was needed; the new, larger structure was built in Long Island City, New York. Within six years Hellmann was manufacturing his product in Chicago, San Francisco, Atlanta, Dallas, and Tampa.

Mergers

In 1927, Hellmann merged his company with the Postum Company, which began large-scale acquisitions in the mid-1920s. Later renamed the General Foods Corporation,, the company had the breadth to sell Hellmann's mayonnaise in a variety of markets. Colby M. Chester joined Edward F. Hutton in expanding the company and redesigning the sales approach. "We acquired other products not by buying patents or starting new factories," Chester offered in the September 14, 1929, *Business Week,* "but by buying factories and corporations which owned products . . . All were well-known products which we wanted, and easy to sell."

After the 1927 merger, Richard Hellmann remained on the board of directors of the parent company. Hellmann also went on to other business ventures, as president of Scarsdale's Richell, Inc., and director of Brooklyn's Fulton Savings Bank. Hellmann died at the age of 94 in a Greenwich, Connecticut, nursing home on February 3, 1971.

In 1932 Best Foods, which had been producing its own mayonnaise since 1922, acquired the Hellmann's brand. The company marketed the condiment west of the Rocky Mountains as Best Foods mayonnaise, deciding to retain that name to build on a franchise it had established on the West Coast. East of the Rockies the name remained Hellmann's real mayonnaise; the product in both regions, however, was the same, based on Mrs. Hellmann's "blue ribbon" recipe. Within two years production was expanded; a Bayonne, New Jersey, facility began manufacturing the product.

AT A GLANCE

Hellmann's brand of mayonnaise founded in 1905 by Richard Hellmann and first sold in his New York City delicatessen; commercial production began in 1912; Hellmann consolidated his company with the Postum Company, later renamed General Foods Corporation, 1927; Best Foods acquired Hellmann's label, 1932; CPC International acquired Best Foods, 1958; product sold internationally under Hellmann's, Best Foods, Lady's Choice, and Fruco labels.

Major competitor: Kraft mayonnaise; also Kraft Miracle Whip salad dressing.

Advertising: *Agency*—BBDO, New York, NY. *Major campaign*—"Bring Out the Best."

Addresses: *Parent company*—CPC International Inc., P.O. Box 8000, International Plaza, Englewood Cliffs, NJ 07632; phone: (201)894-4000.

In 1937 Mrs. Paul Price, the wife of one of Hellmann's sales distributors, created a cake using mayonnaise as a main ingredient. Mayonnaise, replacing the shortening or butter usually used, made the cake moist and rich. Chocolate mayonnaise cake became a favorite; Best Foods continued distributing the recipe over the next fifty years.

Sales of Hellmann's mayonnaise grew steadily through the 1940s under the new company's guidance. Hellmann's mayonnaise eventually became Best Foods' most profitable product. Best Foods, with experience overseeing a variety of grocery items, marketed Hellmann's mayonnaise with another popular brand, Skippy peanut butter, and displayed the two together on supermarket shelves. In the early 1960s print ads were scheduled for the two brands in many magazines, including: *Good Housekeeping, Ladies' Home Journal, Sunset Magazine,* and regional editions of *American Home, Better Homes & Gardens, Family Circle, McCall's, Redbook,* and *Woman's Day.*

Enter CPC International

In 1958 CPC International, then going by the name Corn Products Company, acquired Best Foods, which had grown to be a $118 million business. Corn Products' William T. Brady decided in the mid-1950s that the firm should concentrate its efforts in consumer products, a market which had high profit margins and was comparatively stable. The changeover affected Hellmann's for the better. While the recently acquired Best Foods division was experienced in the sales and marketing of consumer products, the Corn Products Company had an international presence.

That presence was based on representatives knowing basic details about the product. Paul Fischer, head of Best Foods' Switzerland office for Knorr soup, tried it twice daily and tested all new flavors personally. Fischer looked forward to the possibilities of selling Hellmann's mayonnaise in Europe. He planned to market it, as quoted in the March 1962 *Fortune,* as "a 'miracle spread' . . . where you can have people slapping it on bread, crackers, everything." Corn Products hoped Best Foods could capitalize on its various markets, eventually interchanging all products from one country, and one whole region of the world, to another. By 1963 Hellmann's mayonnaise was selling well in Mexico and the company was preparing a product introduction in France.

The ultimate owner of the Hellmann's brand, the Corn Products Company, changed its name to the sleeker CPC International Inc. in the mid-1960s. After one brief return to the old name (initiated in 1975), the company remained CPC International Inc., thus underlining its new streamlined and global emphasis.

While many multinational companies saw their overseas businesses merely as extensions of their domestic operations, Corn Products, according to James Cook in the March 3, 1980, *Forbes,* "had always viewed its overseas businesses as rooted primarily in local needs." Subsidiaries were managed, staffed, and supplied by local residents, and intended to be very familiar with local markets. Each was expected to be self-sufficient, and generally succeeded in this endeavor.

Thus products were tailored to suit the tastes of the market they were sold in. Over the years, chefs working for Corn Products' Best Foods division lived in the localities where products were to be sold. When necessary, they would reformulate brands accordingly. Hellmann's mayonnaise changed just slightly depending on where it was sold. According to the *Forbes* article, the mayonnaise "took on a lemony overtone in Colombia, became more mustardy in Europe, more vinegary in Britain and Ireland, but retained its original subtlety and blandness in Japan."

Product Line Extensions

As food products companies grew increasingly larger and global through the 1960s and 1970s, competition tightened everywhere. While brand recognition was always key to maintaining sales, line extensions were one way to try and corner new markets. A number of advertising agencies were working with Best Foods during the early 1960s on a commission system. The system allowed the advertisers to decide which team would work on a given account, and to make related budget decisions. Some of these agencies included Dancer-Fitzgerald-Sample; Foote, Cone & Belding; Lennen & Newell; and Sullivan, Stauffer, Colwell, & Bayles.

In 1966 Best Foods allocated over $30 million to advertise a range of products over a six-month period. The 21 new items to be introduced in regional areas or through test markets represented the company's largest effort ever. In the mayonnaise arena, a line extension was in order. For some reason, Hellmann's sold much better on either coast, and in northern and southern regions, than it did in the midwest, where salad dressings were more popular. In response to this regional preference, and to try and break salad dressing's near three-to-one edge over mayonnaise in the midwest, Best Foods had created Hellmann's Spin Blend several years earlier. By 1966 the product was expanded from Kansas City and Cleveland to Wisconsin, Minnesota, and South Dakota. The product Spin Blend kept the Hellmann's name because, according to the Best Foods philosophy quoted in the May 16, 1966, *Advertising Age:* "People get old, not products."

The company apparently knew what it was talking about; Hellmann's Spin Blend salad dressing continued to sell in the midwest over the next decade. By 1975 Best Foods moved the product into the Chicago market. The advertising agency Dancer-Fitzgerald-Sample handled the campaign, emphasizing a pointed message. On television and in print the ad stated that Hellmann's Spin Blend had "one-third less oil than the leading salad dressing"—which was Kraft's Miracle Whip.

By 1978 Hellmann's and Best Foods brand mayonnaise had enjoyed twenty years of steady volume increases, and ten years of profit growth. This growth occurred in spite of Kraft's imitation mayonnaise contender and Hunt-Wesson's version, which had been introduced in the previous decade. Best Foods watched the competition's campaigns unfold, while considering a variety of possible advertising responses. The company decided to forgo dramatic alternatives, choosing instead to emphasize the quality of Hellmann's mayonnaise. Both competitors withdrew their products, leaving Hellmann's to dominate a $360 million retail market.

In the late 1970s Best Foods worked on new advertising, and in 1980 a nationwide program was launched. Emphasizing network and spot television ads, the slogan created ran, "It wouldn't be home without Hellmann's (Best Foods)." Hellmann's was introduced in Portugal, and test marketing was conducted in Spain.

A 1912 jar of Hellmann's mayonnaise.

Sales of a Hellmann's sandwich spread began in Ireland, building on a well-established mayonnaise market. Hellmann's sold especially well in Brazil and Argentina, and in Colombia under the Fruco label; in all three countries it was the leading brand.

To better address consumer concern for safety in packaging, Hellmann's, always sold in jars, was given a tamper-evident seal in 1985. Within two years Best Foods introduced portion-control packets of Hellmann's, to be distributed in restaurants and other food-service establishments.

75th Anniversary

Best Foods geared up for an anniversary celebration of its strong and popular brand in 1987. The company commissioned the Peter Kump New York Cooking School to bake, appropriately, a chocolate mayonnaise 75th birthday cake. Best Foods also sponsored the first "New York City Deli Challenge." Seven of New York's most popular delis made their best sandwich to present to a panel of "deli-food aficionados," well-known magazine and newspaper editors. Best Foods' goal was to take participants back in time to the days when immigrants like Richard Hellmann opened America's first delicatessens.

A single event devoted to a variety of Best Foods brands was also scheduled for 1987, slated for January and February, since the first two months of a year were generally lower sales months than any others. The theme was "Brands Across America," promoted in conjunction with Hands Across America, a non-profit organization which aids the homeless and hungry throughout the United States. The goal was to generate sales of a variety of Best Foods products; for each refund certificate a customer mailed in, the company contributed one dollar to the Hands Across America fund. Some brands generated sales increases of 20 percent over the previous year.

Health Concerns

By the 1980s it was clear that business as usual wouldn't work in the mayonnaise category. The product was still selling well, but consumer interest shifted to healthier, low-fat foods. While the United States did have a strict Standard of Identity for the ratio of ingredients used to make mayonnaise, that standard, according to *Consumer Reports,* had nothing to do with the actual taste of mayonnaise: "There's plenty of room for taste differences among products called mayonnaise, and even more among the mayonnaise look-alikes—salad dressings and imitation products."

Flavor, while important, was only one factor mayonnaise consumers were considering. If a company could make a low-fat, low-cholesterol, low-sodium mayonnaise, that producer could corner a new market. By 1984 there were at least 38 mayonnaise products or derivatives—salad dressings and imitation mayonnaises—available in the United States. The imitation mayos were often marketed as diet foods: less oil, and the product was a reduced-calorie one; no egg, and it was cholesterol-free. *Consumer Reports* came up with its own classic mayonnaise recipe, then used a taste-testing panel to measure all 38 mayonnaise products against the original. The only conclusion as far as Hellmann's was concerned was that the brand, along with its competitor, Kraft Miracle Whip, were in the middle of the range of prices for mayonnaise. Where calories were counted, the more real the mayonnaise, the higher the calories. The vegetable oil content, 65 percent by weight according to the federal standard, was the cause of this.

CPC International's Best Foods division introduced Hellmann's Light in early 1987. Every effort was made to assure that Hellmann's Light mayonnaise was as close to the original product in taste and texture as possible. In print advertising Best Foods described the Hellmann's product as the "best tasting" light mayonnaise. In television ads, the campaign also emphasized the brand's tried-and-true theme, "Bring out the best." Although Kraft already had a product out, within two years Hellmann's Light mayonnaise was outselling the Kraft version by a two-to-one margin. Not only did Hellmann's Light make a sizable profit its first year on the market—it added profits, seven percent in volume, and three market share points to the brand as a whole.

Once the light mayo market was established, CPC was ready to launch Hellmann's cholesterol-free version. While it was thought that sales of the new mayo could cannibalize the excellent sales of

Hellmann's Light, the higher profile that the mayonnaise category in general might obtain would offset that factor. One irony regarding cholesterol-free mayonnaise was that the cholesterol in mayo comes from egg yolk called for in the recipe. The amount of cholesterol in a single serving is quite small; at an average of seven milligrams per tablespoon, the amount is negligible. There was a demand for the product, however—what the market wanted, it would get.

The advent of Hellmann's Light and cholesterol-free versions spurred Kraft to more heavily advertise its Miracle Whip as lower in fat and calories, and more tangy in flavor, than regular mayonnaise. Kraft was a serious threat to Hellmann's—Kraft's Miracle Whip already had a 91 percent share in the salad dressing market, and its mayonnaise garnered 20 percent of total mayonnaise sales. By 1989 CPC was allocating $345 million—close to 7 percent of sales—to advertise the new Hellmann's products, nearly doubling what it spent the previous year.

Contemporary Issues

CPC International's goal was to represent its products as more healthful, yet still good-tasting. The company withdrew a fat-free version of mayonnaise because, though it was similar to a competing Kraft product, it did not represent the "real" Hellmann's flavor. In 1992, the company combined no-fat mustard and soybean oil with standard mayonnaise ingredients (excluding egg yolks) to create Hellmann's Dijonnaise. The label described the product as "a uniquely delicious, creamy blend of Dijon mustard, spices, and a touch of white wine."

The point was to differentiate the new products from the standard, while not pushing the consumer to reject either brand for reasons pertaining to health or flavor. Hellmann's maintained its dominant market share of 50 percent, bringing Best Foods an estimated 40 percent of the company's total profits. Since its development in the early 1900s, nearly four billion pounds of Hellmann's real mayonnaise have been sold.

Further Reading:

"Ad Week: 2 Paths to Market Goals," *Advertising Age,* September 4, 1978.

Cook, James, "Handsome Is as Handsome Does," *Fortune,* March 3, 1980, p. 43.

"Corn Products Finds Other Fields Green," *Business Week,* July 5, 1958, p. 76.

CPC International Inc. Annual Reports, Englewood Cliffs, New Jersey: CPC International, 1980-1991.

Crain, Rance, "At Best Foods It's New Wares, Old Names," *Advertising Age,* May 16, 1966, p. 3.

"Food Mergers," *Business Week,* September 14, 1929, p. 32.

Hwang, Suein L., "Its Big Brands Long Taunted as Fatty, CPC Tries a More 'Wholesome' Approach," *Wall Street Journal,* April 20, 1992, p. B1.

Lazarus, George, "Spread Out: CPC to Unveil Cholesterol-free Mayo," *Adweek's Marketing Week,* March 13, 1989, p. 61.

"Mayonnaise & Its Look-alikes," *Consumer Reports,* September, 1984, p. 535.

"Mayonnaise, An American Favorite," "Bringing Out the Best for 75 Years," Englewood Cliffs, N.J.: Best Foods, CPC International, 1987.

"New Whispering Sweepstakes to Push Skippy Peanut Butter," *Advertising Age,* May 27, 1963, p. 10.

"Richard Hellmann Dies at 94; Founded Mayonnaise Company," *New York Times,* February 4, 1971, p. 38.

Therrien, Lois, "How CPC Is Getting Fat on Muffins and Mayonnaise," *Business Week,* April 16, 1990, p. 46.

"Uncommon Market," *Fortune,* March, 1962, p. 98.

—Frances E. Norton

HERSHEY'S®

More than any other single product, Hershey's brand of milk chocolate bar has come to symbolize America's ongoing love affair with sweetened milk chocolate. The popular confection, packaged in its trademark wrapper with bold silver lettering, is an American institution and the first success story in the history of affordable chocolate candy. Consumers have shown great loyalty to Hershey's milk chocolate bar, with and without almonds. Since its first mass production in 1900, the product has ranked among the top 20 most popular American candy bars year after year. Nicknamed "the Great American Chocolate Bar" in its advertising campaigns, Hershey's milk chocolate, manufactured by Hershey Chocolate U.S.A., is just that—a symbol of simplicity and consistent quality that has endured throughout the 20th century.

In *The Ledger,* a reporter for the Federal Reserve Bank of Boston notes that the Hershey's name has come to represent "good, old-fashioned, mass-produced American candy made from high-quality ingredients and sold at prices that most people can afford." Indeed, today's Hershey's milk chocolate is remarkably similar in taste and relative price to its turn-of-the-century prototype. Recent studies indicating that a moderate consumption of chocolate candy does not promote tooth decay, acne, or heart disease have helped to keep candy bar sales brisk even in the era of the health-conscious consumer. *Forbes* contributor Janet Novack concludes "chocolate candy is a growth area for Hershey," adding: "Fears that a nation obsessed with thinness might sour on sweets proved unfounded."

Brand Origins

Chocolate is derived from cocoa beans, which grew in the Americas exclusively until Columbus arrived. Native Americans in tropical climates where cocoa grew used the beans for consumption and trade, believing them to be gifts from the gods. Columbus brought cocoa beans back with him to Spain on his fourth voyage to America, and the passion for sweetened chocolate bloomed among the European aristocracy. For centuries, chocolate remained far too expensive for all but the wealthiest individuals, who generally drank it in beverage form, like coffee. The industrial revolution brought innovations to the manufacture and use of cocoa—a chocolate factory opened in New England in 1765, and "eating chocolate," the earliest form of modern day chocolate candy, was developed about a century later, in 1847.

Ten years after "eating chocolate" made its debut, Milton Snavely Hershey was born in a farmhouse near Derry Church, Pennsylvania. Hershey was a Mennonite, a descendent of German immigrants who had settled central Pennsylvania in the 1700s. His family was extremely poor, and he was only allowed to attend school through the fourth grade. Then his father put him to work as an apprentice to a printer in Gap, Pennsylvania.

Printing did not appeal to Hershey. While still in his teens he moved to Lancaster, Pennsylvania and apprenticed himself to a candy maker. In 1876, at the age of eighteen, Hershey opened his own candy shop in Philadelphia. He made confections at night and sold them all day, almost ruining his health in the process. The business failed after six years, and Hershey followed his father on a silver-prospecting expedition to Colorado. The pair did not find any silver, but Hershey added to his knowledge of candy production by working in Denver for a manufacturer of caramels.

One of the things Hershey learned in Denver was that superior results could be achieved when fresh milk was used to make caramels. He attempted to put this secret to work for himself in candy-making ventures in Chicago, New Orleans, and New York City. In each case he failed to make a profit consistently and was often on the brink of financial ruin. In 1886 he returned to Lancaster, took a loan from his aunt, and began making caramels with fresh milk from the local farms. He was almost thirty and still found himself making the rounds with his candy in a basket under his arm.

Success came to Hershey seemingly overnight. Quite by chance, an English importer sampled some of his fresh milk caramels and placed a sizeable order for them. The demand for the unique-tasting candies led to rapid expansion, and within a few years Hershey was presiding over a large factory he had built, the Lancaster Caramel Company.

In *Great American Brands: The Success Formulas that Made Them Famous,* David P. Cleary writes: "Inevitably, the magic of fresh milk in candy would turn Milton Hershey's attention, more and more, from caramel to milk chocolate." The Swiss had developed a palatable milk chocolate in 1876, and by 1893 a German company had devised machinery for its manufacture. Hershey bought the machinery at the Chicago International Exposition of 1893 and transported it back to Lancaster, where he began to experiment with it. His first product was chocolate-covered

AT A GLANCE

Hershey's brand of chocolate bar founded in 1900 in Lancaster, PA, by Milton Snavely Hershey as a product of the Lancaster Caramel Company; Hershey sold the Lancaster Caramel Company in 1900 and opened the Hershey Chocolate Company in Derry Church, PA, in 1905; company renamed Hershey Chocolate Corporation in 1927; name changed to Hershey Foods Corporation in 1968; product later manufactured by Hershey Chocolate U.S.A., a division of Hershey Foods.

Performance: *Market share*—36% (top share) of candy category (includes other Hershey-owned candies). *Sales*—$2.9 billion (includes other candies and food items, domestic and international).

Major competitor: Mars, Inc.'s M&Ms & Snickers

Advertising: *Agency*—DDB Needham, New York, NY, and Ogilvy & Mather, New York, NY. *Major campaign*—"The Great American Chocolate Bar."

Addresses: *Parent company*—Hershey Chocolate U.S.A., P.O. Box 815, Hershey, PA 17033-0815; phone 800-468-1714. *Ultimate parent company*—Hershey Foods Corporation, 100 Crystal A Drive, P.O. Box 810, Hershey, PA 17033-0810; phone: (717) 534-7631; fax: (717) 534-7896.

caramels, but by 1900 he had developed the Hershey's milk chocolate bar.

The Right Place, The Right Concept

Hershey sold his caramel factory in 1900 and plowed the profits into a new venture—an affordable milk chocolate candy, available on the mass market. His goal was to produce a "wrapped, milk chocolate bar which would be purchased with the nickel in a man's pocket." Hershey bought some land near his hometown of Derry Church and built a huge factory for the manufacture of his new candy. The location was ideal for its proximity to the rich dairy farms of central Pennsylvania and the big cities along the Eastern Seaboard.

Chocolate candy was not a novelty in 1905, but it was still expensive and was generally sold in large blocks or packaged in boxes. Hershey pioneered the idea of a single serving of milk chocolate, packaged individually to preserve freshness and cleanliness. He also formulated his own specific milk chocolate and strove to maintain consistency in the product. By 1905, Hershey's product was being mass produced and distributed nationally.

Hershey recruited a massive sales force and instructed his workers to "put Hershey's milk chocolate bars on every counter, shelf, stand, and rack in every retail establishment in the United States—food store, restaurant, drug store, ice cream parlor, and soda fountain." As Hershey predicted, the candy bars sold as fast as they came off the production line. The success of the Hershey's milk chocolate bar was so phenomenal that in 1906, just a year after its national introduction, the town fathers of Derry Church decided to rename the hamlet Hershey, Pennsylvania.

Cleary notes: "The bold combination of mass production, mass distribution, and point-of-sale display was highly effective." As the years passed, the taste of Hershey's milk chocolate remained consistent, and the packaging settled into its current format. The candy sold itself so well that the Hershey Chocolate

Company, later Hershey Chocolate Corporation, did not advertise at all in the media for a staggering 68 years. Competition from other candy bars came full force in the 1920s, but by that time Hershey was a giant in the industry with its Hershey's milk chocolate bar, Hershey's milk chocolate with almonds bar, Hershey's Kisses chocolates (1907), and Mr. Goodbar chocolate bar (1925). All of the products—even the tiny Kisses—bore the Hershey's name, prominently displayed.

Recognizing that it had created an American icon in Hershey's milk chocolate bars, the corporation and the town of Hershey promoted the product in a unique way: in the 1960s the doors to the factory were opened to the public for tours, and the town installed large aluminum Kisses-shaped street lights. Hershey, Pennsylvania became popular enough as a tourist mecca that a separate company, now called Hershey Entertainment & Resort Company (HERCO), developed Hersheypark amusement complex as well as the Hotel Hershey and Zoo America. Hershey's Chocolate World, the official visitors center of Hershey Foods Corporation, contains a ride-through display and many other attractions involving the candy bar manufacturing process. The factory itself discontinued public tours in 1973, when Chocolate World opened.

Product Changes

Very few changes have been wrought in Hershey's milk chocolate over the years. The recipe is virtually the same as the one Milton Hershey formulated himself, and the wrapper style dates to before the Second World War. The only significant changes in the product have been variations on the size: bite-sized Hershey's Miniatures were introduced in 1939, and larger bars, such as the four-serving seven-ounce bar and the 2.2 ounce Big Block, have remained popular through the 1990s. Other Hershey products, such as baking cocoa, ready-to-eat pudding, and chocolate milk, have capitalized on the instant recognition of the Hershey's milk chocolate bar packaging, using the same chocolate-colored background and silver lettering. *Forbes* correspondent Rita Koselka maintains that at the end of World War II, "Hershey had as much international brand recognition as did Coca-Cola."

This popularity was achieved without any media advertising, saving the company millions and millions of dollars in its first 60 years of existence. Hershey Chocolate Corporation was able to remain the nation's biggest chocolate manufacturer well into the 1960s, with net profits increasing every year. One pivotal acquisition was the H. B. Reese Candy Company in 1963, giving Hershey the rights to Reese's peanut butter cups.

Consumer awareness of snack foods as a health risk has never dented the sale of Hershey's milk chocolate or other Hershey's candies. For decades, chocolate bars were thought to cause hyperactivity in children, promote tooth decay, provoke attacks of acne pimples, and lead to heart disease. Most of these assertions have been disproved by scientific research. A regular-sized Hershey's milk chocolate bar contains less than half the cholesterol and only a fraction of the sodium found in a one-ounce piece of whole milk cheddar cheese. Hershey's milk chocolate bars also contain less caffeine than a cup of decaffeinated coffee. Recent studies suggest that chocolate candy—despite its high sugar content—poses less risk to teeth than do raisins, crackers, or granola bars. Chocolate candy is high in saturated fat, but the major fatty acid in chocolate is stearic acid, which has been shown in recent studies not to raise blood cholesterol levels. Since chocolate is high in fat and calories, however, moderate consumption, as an occasional treat within a balanced diet, is recommended.

Meeting Market Challenges

The Hershey Chocolate Corporation changed its name to Hershey Foods Corporation in 1968. At roughly the same time, the company began to lose its dominance of the confections market to rival Mars Inc., the maker of M&Ms and Snickers bars. This loss of share led Hershey to use media advertisement for the first time in the mid-1960s, and executives soon developed the "Great American Chocolate Bar" slogan for the flagship product. Rapid inflation of cocoa and sugar prices in the 1970s caused all candy makers to raise prices, but the major companies fought the inflation by diversifying into other food products, creating new candies, and buying other confectionery operations. In Hershey's case, the company moved into the pasta industry and also acquired Y&S Candies in 1977 (licorice) and Peter Paul/Cadbury in 1988.

Hershey Foods and Mars Inc. battle continually for top market share in the $8.7 billion American candy industry. In the early 1990s, Hershey maintained a slender lead, posting $220 million in profits in 1991. Rita Koselka contends that Hershey's conservative marketing practices and reluctance to advertise denied it a lucrative international market for its Hershey Bars after World War II, but in recent years the company has moved into Canada, Germany, and the Far East both with the standard Hershey products and with the acquisition of foreign candy makers. Koselka concludes: "With skill and some luck, Hershey may yet make up for lost time in the overseas market."

Investment analysts paint a bright picture for Hershey Foods. The corporation is insulated from takeover by the fact that fully 42 percent of its stock and 77 percent of the voting rights are held by a trust set up by Milton Hershey that supports a school for disadvantaged children. The Trust is required to act in the best interest of the school, and any action it takes is subject to review by the Pennsylvania Attorney General to ensure that it is acting in the best interests of the students at Milton Hershey School. This state of affairs has created a climate of security for Hershey executives and personnel. Although a relatively small company within the food and beverage business, Hershey remains the largest American manufacturer of chocolate goods, with ten major facilities in the United States and others in Canada, Mexico, and Germany.

"You can almost get a cavity by breathing the air near the plant on East Chocolate Avenue," writes Andrew Kupfer in *Fortune*. The main facility in Hershey, Pennsylvania is the world's largest chocolate factory. In 1991 and 1992, Hershey Chocolate U.S.A. won the Equitrend Outstanding Quality Award for its Hershey's milk chocolate bar, which ranked number one in consumer name recognition. With such a proven track record, the "Hershey Bar" is likely to remain an industry standard well into the future. As for the company that manufactures it, Janet Novack concluded that Hershey Foods "is still squeezing most of its profits from the sweetest end of its business"—the end that Milton Hershey made possible with the famous Hershey's milk chocolate bar.

Further Reading:

"Candy Is Dandy: Some Facts about America's Sweetest Industry," *MetroKids* (Philadelphia), October 1992, pp. 5-6.

Cleary, David Powers, *Great American Brands: The Success Formulas that Made Them Famous*, Fairchild Publications, 1981, pp. 166-171.

Federal Reserve Bank of Boston, "How Sweet It Is!," *The Ledger: Economic Education Newsletter*, June 1988, pp. 1-2.

Hershey Foods Corporation 1991 Annual Report, Hershey, PA: The Hershey Foods Corporation, 1992.

Koselka, Rita, "Candy Wars," *Forbes*, August 17, 1992, pp. 76-77.

Kupfer, Andrew, "The Sweet Smell of Success," *Fortune*, April 24, 1989, pp. 31-32.

Lawrence, Steve, "Bar Wars: Hershey Bites Mars," *Fortune*, July 8, 1985, pp. 52-57.

Novack, Janet, "The High-Profit Candy Habit," *Forbes*, June 29, 1987, p. 76.

A Profile of Hershey Foods Corporation, Hershey, PA: Hershey Foods Corporation, 1992.

—Anne Janette Johnson

HI-C®

Hi-C Fruit Drinks have been a favorite among children for decades and have consistently ranked among the top in the fruit drink category. As part of the Coca-Cola Company's Coca-Cola Foods, they have played an important role in the division's success. The foods division is the largest segment of Coke's non-soft drink business and also includes Minute Maid, the country's largest producer of orange juice, Five Alive citrus beverages, and Bacardi tropical fruit mixers. The brand benefits from Coca-Cola's global presence and strong network of national and international marketing systems. Hi-C is the leading fruit drink in the children's market and in the aseptic drink box category. Packaging innovations and response to consumer interest in nutritional beverages have helped Hi-C remain a strong brand.

Brand Origins

Originally an orange concentrate used to make orange soda for Woolworths, Hi-C was formulated in 1947 by Clinton Foods. Later, the milk man distributed it in a small area of upstate New York and suggested it be used not only as a beverage, but also as a flavoring agent. Hi-C approached its present form when Dick Brown developed a ready-to-serve product in a 46-ounce can. Having created a convenient form for the drink, Clinton Foods ensured that the product's taste would be preserved by lining the can with enamel. Hi-C's name was derived from the fact that it contained 10 percent fruit juice and had a full day's supply of vitamin C as recommended by the U.S. Department of Agriculture.

In 1948 Hi-C was introduced with in-store demonstrations in Tampa, Florida, and its success there led to expansion throughout the Southeast. Grape and fruit punch Hi-C were introduced in the 1950s, and their popularity added to the brand's momentum. By 1951, Hi-C could be bought in stores across the nation.

Hi-C's early advertising expenditures were modest; promotions included skywriting, in-store demonstrations, and promotional ties with the circus. Hi-Cecil the Giraffe, the product line's mascot, dates to this period. Advertising emphasized Hi-C's convenience and quality. Its wholesomeness, due to its fruit juice and vitamin C content, was an important selling point. An early slogan pits Hi-C against nutritionally bankrupt sodas: "You're being a good mother because you're not serving a carbonated soft drink."

Hi-C's ultimate owner changed several times—first, when Clinton Foods was bought by Minute Maid Company, and again when Minute Maid was acquired by the Coca-Cola Company. The acquisition was part of a major initiative by Coke to enter the juice market and maintain the dominance of the beverage industry it had enjoyed since its founding. Upon entering the juice market, Coke's initial strategy was to position juice as a soft drink and encourage its consumption throughout the day, rather than only at breakfast. Hi-C fit in well with this strategy. To convince the public, Coke more than doubled Minute Maid's advertising budget and applied its own highly successful advertising and marketing techniques to the new line of beverages. Today, Hi-C is still promoted as a drink for "breakfast or any other time of the day." The Hi-C logo has changed little, continuing to feature the prominent letters "Hi-C" and bold fruit graphics.

Early Advertising Strategies

Coca-Cola's earliest marketing and advertising strategies indicate that Hi-C's target market was children. Coca-Cola touted the beverage as the first noncarbonated fruit drink. Its special cans featured the "Mom-Top" detachable pull-ring and were sold in six-packs of 12-ounce cans. Hi-C's popularity with children and their parents can be at least partially attributed to the fact that, without carbonation, the cans could be packed in lunches and carried all morning without threatening to explode when eventually opened.

Satisfying mothers of young children proved to be a wise strategy for Hi-C. During the product's lifetime, more women entered the work force than at any previous time in history. As these women left the traditional roles of full-time wife and mother, they required products that appealed to their children, were easy to prepare, and provided nutritional benefits as well. The 1960s and 1970s saw the development of such products as children's TV dinners and frozen foods, all designed for preparation by a busy mother after a long day of work outside the home. Hi-C could be easily used by children, either at school or at home by themselves after school, and, unlike soda, was not perceived as containing only sugar.

In addition, Hi-C was born at a time when more Americans were beginning to give serious thought to the contents of the foods they ate. People began reading labels and questioning the use of preservatives and other chemical ingredients. Although Hi-C was not a "100 percent natural" product, it was among the better alternatives, in terms of nutrition and convenience, available at the time.

Growth and Expansion

In 1978 the company introduced a powdered, presweetened variety of the product in 6 flavors, hoping to compete in what was then a growing segment of the fruit drink category dominated by Kool-Aid. By 1979 there were 30 Hi-C beverage products, including 11 flavors of the ready-to-serve and 8 flavors of the powdered variety. The late 1970s and early 1980s were prosperous years for Coca-Cola Foods. The Foods division was the largest segment of their non-soft drink business by 1980, and in 1981 Hi-C held the number one spot in its category, despite an overall category decline. Throughout the 1980s Hi-C continued to enjoy double-digit volume growth.

By 1986, Hi-C held a 30 percent market share. The company added new flavors steadily and in 1986 introduced Hi-C 100, a blend of 100 percent fruit juices "enhanced with natural flavors." Although this new product extension was meant to appeal to children, it was also intended to satisfy parents' nutritional concerns.

Hi-C has also piggybacked on parent company Coca-Cola's aggressive pursuit of foreign markets. Coke, already well positioned in the Japanese market, took advantage of the country's overproduction of tangerines in 1973 to introduce orange Hi-C into the Japanese market, a wise entry into a growing Japanese fruit drink market. In 1991 Hi-C introduced an isotonic sports drink aimed at Japanese children.

Hi-C will undoubtedly continue to benefit from Coca-Cola's dominance of foreign markets. The company's 1992 annual report saw East Central Europe, the former Soviet Union, Indonesia, India, Africa, and China as its biggest potential markets. Factors like youthful populations, undeveloped soft drink industries, movement to market economies, and preference for western brands were all viewed as positive indicators of success for Coca-Cola's beverage lines.

Packaging Innovations

In 1981 Hi-C was test marketed in aseptic packaging. This revolutionary new process required that a sterilized container be filled with separately sterilized liquid and then given an air-tight seal. This unique packaging resulted in a shelf life of six months and required no refrigeration or preservatives. After test marketing

proved successful, the product was introduced nationally in January of 1983. With this introduction, Coca-Cola became the first company in the United States to nationally market a product in aseptic packaging. The "juice boxes," as this type of packaging came to be known, were an "immediate success" according to the company's 1983 annual report, and Hi-C's volume jumped by 21 percent.

Hi-C was also one of the first fruit drinks available in plastic bottles. The August 19, 1991, edition of *Supermarket News* noted the potential of what was then an innovative package and recognized Hi-C as one of the first to switch from glass to plastic. The article quoted a grocery buyer as saying "Hi-C is now in 64-ounce [plastic] bottles—and it looks so good. Sales have really responded well." Shatterproof plastic bottles for children's drinks were a natural choice for concerned parents.

As of 1993, Hi-C was available in aseptic nine- and three-packs, single-serve cans, 64-ounce bottles, 46-ounce cans, and one-gallon plastic bottles with handles.

The Children's Market

Although originally conceived as a product for adults, Hi-C quickly evolved into a drink primarily for children. With the introduction of aseptic packaging and the "juice box," its categorization as a children's product was further solidified. In fact, Coca-Cola's early entry into aseptic packaging and the popularity of the juice box among children were among the main factors contributing to Hi-C's success. By 1987 Hi-C held 28 percent of aseptic drink sales. Aseptic packaging had grown to a $360 million business in the United States by the mid-1980s. Coke had demonstrated tremendous foresight and had invested more than $20 million in aseptic packaging equipment since 1981.

Marketing to children, however, presents unique opportunities and challenges. Colors, textures, and flavors that seem bizarre or unpalatable to adults are often exactly what excites children. Hi-C has capitalized on some of these opportunities with fun flavor names like Stompin' Banana Berry, Boppin' Berry, Jammin' Apple, and Ecto Cooler. The Ecto Cooler flavor, added in 1990 to tie-in with the release of the film *Ghostbusters II,* is green and refers to the slime produced by the ghosts in the film, a reference that has helped make it one of the brand's most popular flavors.

In 1992 Hi-C teamed up with the Walt Disney Company for the product's first promotional tie-in with characters from a prime-time network program, "Dinosaurs." During the same year, Hi-C beverages were included in Sara Lee Meat Group's "Lunch 'n Munch Lunch Snacks." In recent years Hi-C has been tied with such television shows and movies as *Beverly Hills 90210* and *Duck Tales,* which are popular with children and preteens.

Performance Appraisal

Hi-C's fortuitous entry into the fruit drink market coincided with growing consumer concern with nutrition, and Coca-Cola's early use of aseptic packaging gave the product a strong push; both of these factors contributed to Hi-C's strong performance in the 1970s and 1980s. In addition, Coca-Cola Foods has been quick to capitalize on subsequent industry trends such as plastic bottling and value packaging. Consistent introduction of new flavors and promotional tie-ins have also helped the brand's sales. However, although Hi-C held the number one spot in the juice drink category for many years during the 1980s, an influx of competitive brands contributed to a decline in Hi-C's market share.

In addition to an increasingly crowded field, Hi-C seems to also have suffered from a lack of attention from Coca-Cola Foods, which has focused most of its energy on Minute Maid juices. Ironically, major competitor Procter & Gamble seemed to have the opposite strategy: the company sold its Citrus Hill orange juice brand to shift its focus to its juice drink brands, Sunny Delight and Hawaiian Punch.

Future Performance

According to *Beverage World, the Beverage Marketing Annual Industry Survey,* in 1991 the fruit beverage industry grew by 6.6 percent, passing traditional leaders such as soft drinks and bottled waters. Fruit drinks have held a certain advantage over fruit juices in recent years because of fluctuations in fruit prices. Hellen Berry, Beverage Marketing's vice president of market research, told *Beverage World,* "The Florida crop freeze of December 1989 limited the availability of fresh fruit for orange juice, pushing up the price to extremely high levels. These price increases on orange juice made the lower-priced fruit drink segment much more enticing for consumers. That growth carried over into 1991, helped by the recession."

Industries in Transition reported in December of 1992 that although the cola market growth has decreased to approximately 1.5 percent per year, so-called alternative beverages, a category that includes bottled iced teas and coffees, mineral waters, sparkling waters, fruit-flavored water, juices, and sports drinks, grew at a rate of about 10 percent for 1991.

Part of the reason for Hi-C's market share decline is the tremendous influx of competitors, produced by both large food companies and smaller, emerging companies. Hi-C's main competitor, Hawaiian Punch, has been part of Procter & Gamble since the company bought Del Monte in 1990. Hawaiian Punch and Kool-Aid have aggressively pursued the children's niche of the

fruit drink market and in recent years have offered more variety in flavors, colors, and packaging. In March of 1993, Procter & Gamble announced that it would test market a new, calcium-fortified version of Hawaiian Punch that will include "all the calcium of milk with a full-day supply of vitamin C." Kool-Aid's new "Kool Bursts" and General Mills' "Squeezit" both come in miniature plastic versions of traditional soft drink bottles and have been a big hit with kids. According to *Advertising Age,* "Their success has dented sales of the old standby, Coca-Cola Foods' Hi-C." Kool-Aid has also been creative with product names, recently adding Grape Bluedini to flavors like Pink Swimmingo, and Mean Green Puncher. Upstart company Juice Bowl Products has capitalized on a growing environmental awareness among children by introducing the only all-natural juice drink in recyclable juice boxes targeted to children. Libby's Juicey Juice recently introduced a 100 percent juice blend and in their advertising directly compared the brand's 100 percent to Hi-C's 10 percent.

The growth of the juice blend drinks segment may have a negative impact on drinks like Hi-C. Many of the blends contain no added sugar, and *Supermarket News* reports that they are becoming increasingly popular with parents. The article also indicates that some grocery chains report "blends are taking sales away from packaged fruit drinks like Hi-C and Hawaiian Punch."

Further Reading:

Alaimo, Dan, "Blendin In," *Supermarket News,* February 3, 1992, p. 13.
Beverage World, July 1992.
The Coca-Cola Company Annual Reports, Atlanta: The Coca-Cola Company, 1960-92.
Klepacki, Laura, "Plastic Bottles Get Juiced," *Supermarket News,* August 19, 1991, p. 23.
Lazarus, George, "Kids' Drinks Fruitful for 'Two Generals,' " *Chicago Tribune,* December 3, 1992, p. 4.
Louis, J. C., and Harvey Z. Yazijian, *The Cola Wars,* New York: Everest House, 1980.

—Kate Sheehan

HIRES®

Hires Root Beer is the oldest continuously marketed soft drink in the United States. As the first nationally marketed root beer, Hires at one time made the claim that its founder Charles Hires invented the drink. In fact, root beer and hundreds of other herbal brews have been in existence for hundreds of years. Similar beverages were made in Europe and South America.

Some of the earliest root beers were made in colonial America from molasses, water, yeast, and a variety of herbs, including sarsaparilla, vanilla, licorice, cinnamon, and bruised birch and sassafras bark. Hires' great contribution was that he discovered an especially good recipe and successfully commercialized it.

Brand Origins

In 1860 Charles Elmer Hires, an apothecary pharmacist, left his $1-a-week job in Millville, New Jersey, and moved to Philadelphia. While there, he attended classes at the Philadelphia College of Pharmacy and the Jefferson Medical School. In 1869 he rented a small store front at the corner of Spruce and Sixth Streets and established a drug store. With $400 in savings and a $3000 loan, he equipped the store with all the necessary furnishings. He did not, however, have sufficient funds to procure supplies.

Burdened by his debt, Hires one day noticed that a nearby excavation yielded tons of fuller's earth, a useful clay that could be used for filtration, for removing oil, or as a catalyst. He convinced the construction workers to dump the clay behind his store three blocks down the street, rather than truck it three miles away to a landfill. He processed the clay into small disks, which he sold by the barrel to drug wholesalers in Philadelphia in exchange for much-needed pharmacological and medical supplies. In all, the processed clay netted the entrepreneur $6000.

Shortly afterward, Hires got married and took his honeymoon at a rural farmhouse in Morristown, New Jersey. While there, his hostess served an herbal drink made of 16 wild roots and berries, including juniper, pipsissewa, spikenard, wintergreen, sarsaparilla, and hops. Greatly impressed by the taste of the drink, although dismayed by its powerful laxative effect, Hires asked his hostess for the recipe. She obliged and even took Hires out into the woods and fields to identify the wild plants she used to make the drink.

Back in Philadelphia, Hires recreated the drink and spent several years working to lessen the laxative punch of the drink by altering the formula. Having perfected the concoction, he offered a sample to Dr. Russell Conwell, founder of Temple University, who also marvelled at the taste.

Early Marketing Strategy

Hires said he planned to call the drink Root Tea, at which point Conwell suggested that a name like Root Beer would have more widespread appeal and give the product a greater natural presence in taverns. The drink was, after all, brewed rather than steeped (some root beer recipes, allowing enough fermentation, were capable of producing powerful elixirs with as much as 10 percent alcohol content).

While Hires' recipe was quite tame, the temperance movement was gathering strength. Everywhere the campaign had a deleterious effect on sales of beverage alcohol. Pennsylvania coal miners, Conwell reasoned, were hard drinkers. Give men a temperance drink called "beer," he said, and they will buy it.

Hires put a sign out in front of his pharmacy reading, "Hires Root Beer 5¢." Soon Hires was unable to keep up with the demand for his product and was persuaded to begin marketing packets of the herbal ingredients used to make the root beer. Customers could thus boil the mixture with four pounds of sugar, five gallons of water, and half a cake of yeast to yield five gallons of home-made root beer for 25 cents.

Perhaps the greatest stunt in the brand's history occurred in 1876, when Hires featured his root beer at the Centennial Exposition in Philadelphia. Serving free glasses of the finished product, Hires hawked his brewing kits for 25 cents each. In addition to selling a lot of kits, he gained extremely favorable and enduring exposure. The following year, Hires sold enough kits to produce nearly 12,000 glasses of home-brewed root beer. Within five years, this number increased to 1.5 million.

Brand Development

In 1884 Hires decided that he could sell greater quantities of his root beer if he could save people the trouble of brewing it. With his laboratory acumen—which also yielded another invention, condensed milk—Hires developed a syrup extract suitable for

AT A GLANCE

Hires brand root beer was founded by Charles E. Hires and introduced in 1876 at the U.S. Centennial Exposition in Philadelphia, Pennsylvania; acquired in 1958 by Continental Foods; sold to Crush International in 1962; Crush and its holdings (including Hires) acquired by Proctor & Gamble in 1980; Crush was sold to Cadbury Schweppes in 1989.

Performance: *Market share—5.4 %.*

Major competitor: A&W Root Beer; also Barq's.

Addresses: *Parent company*—Cadbury Beverages, Inc., 6 High Ridge Park, Stamford, CT 06905; Phone: (203) 329-0911. *Ultimate parent company*—Cadbury Schweppes plc, 25 Berkeley Square, London W1X 6HT England.

mixing directly with "charged," or carbonated, water. This enabled fountain operators to serve Hires Root Beer on demand.

The creation of a syrup extract allowed bottlers to get into the act. Rather than serve the mixture, they bottled the liquid in glass bottles with cork or rubber and ceramic stoppers. The root beer could be continuously bottled or prepared in production runs with other soft drinks, and could be stored for long periods before shipping or serving.

The bottled product first became available in 1893. Initially, Hires encountered great opposition from grocers for allowing bottlers into the act. Sales of bottled root beer, they complained, would cut into their sales of the extract. Hires held off for several years. Cognizant of Coca-Cola's growing success in bottling, however, Hires began producing syrup in large quantities in 1905 at his own expense. This enabled him to establish a large bottling network throughout New England, the South, and the Pacific Coast.

While the name Root Beer proved successful in making the product popular, it also created difficulties for the company, which ran afoul of the Women's Christian Temperance Union, formed in 1874. The group claimed that, despite Hires' claims to the contrary, any sweet fermented beverage is alcoholic, and that root beer was no less sinful than any other beer. Worse yet, the Union organized a national boycott of Hires.

The "Root Beer War" raged for three years from 1895 to 1898, and was fought mostly in newspapers. For Hires, this was an unfortunate venue in which to fight righteous Christian women. Sales plummeted and, at one point, Charles Hires considered dropping the business to concentrate on producing condensed milk.

Unexpectedly, a chemical laboratory that was intrigued by the Root Beer War decided to test the beverage to determine its actual alcoholic content. In its conclusion, the lab disclosed that Hires Root Beer contained half the alcohol of homemade bread. Hires immediately published these findings nationwide in full-page advertisements. The laboratory's conclusions forced the Women's Christian Temperance Union to concede the poor grounding of its charges and admit it was wrong.

Packaging

The first Hires package wasn't for root beer, but for the herbs used to make root beer. In the earliest stages of the brand, before

bottling and syrup production, Hires was strictly a home brew kit. Named Hires Household Extract, the bright yellow package was highly distinctive for its time.

The first bottles of Hires Root Beer appeared in 1893. Most of these first bottles were 14-ounce Hutchinson-stoppered bottles that featured a paper label. About 1897, however, Hires began using the metallic crowns that are common today. The transition took several years to accomplish, as bottlers were required to refit their operations. Still, Hires was one of the first brands to feature crown seals, which did not become common until after 1900.

Advertising

Hires discovered the power of advertising at an early stage of his business. In 1877 he was accosted in a cable car by George W. Childs, publisher of the *Philadelphia Public Ledger* newspaper. Childs advised Hires to advertise his root beer. When Hires replied that he had no money for advertising, Childs said that he would instruct his bookkeeper not to send any bills to Hires until asked for them. Hires took out a one column-inch ad in Childs' newspaper and, gradually, sales began to climb. Some weeks later, Hires sent for his bill. Hires was astounded at the amount due: $700—a hefty amount for that time.

While expensive, the exercise demonstrated to Hires the effect advertising could have on sales. For the next ten years, he diverted nearly every penny of profit into advertising. In fact, Hires pioneered the use of broad column ads, including full-page spreads, that editors had previously rejected as too brash.

Another popular advertising medium of the day was the stock card, a small cardboard sheet with a color print and tag line. These cards, supplied to Hires by the Errickson Card Works in New York, introduced Hires' earliest messages, including such innocent questions as "Why don't you drink Hires Root Beer?"

In 1888 Hires began using the first point-of-purchase advertising, sales displays. These displays were usually placards that carried the brand's name, a beautiful picture, and various tag lines. Hires introduced its first character on these media in 1891, when the cherubic "Hires Boy" was featured for the first time. The plump, rosy-cheeked mascot was intended to instill a health equity that competing soft drinks, particularly Coca-Cola, used to great effect.

Hires was promoted as "a temperance drink," targeted specifically toward housewives. While this campaign failed to convince the Women's Christian Temperance Union, Hires countered their call for a boycott with the previously mentioned national advertisements trumpeting laboratory testing that disproved claims that root beer was intoxicating. These ads were perhaps the first use of scientific testing, including clinical endorsements, in advertising.

In 1895 the Hires Boy gave way to the unnamed "boy in a straw hat." This figure, a classic quasi-Huck Finn figure, was less successful than the bulb-headed Hires Boy—perhaps because he appeared unruly and hickish—and was utilized for only a few years.

The December 1897 issue of the *National Bottlers Gazette* remarked that, "Mr. Hires is a business phenomenon and his success is due entirely to a liberal use of printer's ink." Indeed, that year Hires took out a full-page color ad in *Ladies' Home Journal*, a bold promotion that had not been attempted before.

Having witnessed the great rise in popularity of Coca-Cola, Hires began to imitate that brand's promotional activities. Unable to match Coke in spending, Hires took note of the hundreds of accessories Coca-Cola gave away to fountain operators, including trays, mirrors, lights, and a variety of other soda bar equipment. Hires imitated Coca-Cola, offering his own accessories embossed with the Hires name and frequently including illustrations from the stock cards. These did not forestall Coke from overtaking Hires in sales, but did serve to keep Hires in the game.

Hires' three sons—Harrison, Charles Jr., and John Edgar—who entered the business in 1910, failed to convince their father to drop the Hires Boy from advertising. They did, however, succeed in introducing a new character in 1915, a bug-eyed soda jerk named Josh Slinger. Josh was featured on trays and other accessories, but was phased out after the Hires Boy reappeared in a dinner jacket. Use of the Hires Boy finally ceased after 35 years, in 1926.

Health Claims

Although he could not deny the stimulating effect of his root beer, Hires initially avoided scurrilous health claims. Competing soft drinks such as Moxie and Coca-Cola, however, succeeded in garnering strong public interest with bogus claims that their products served as healthful "brain tonics" and general remedies.

By the time Hires began advertising with stock cards, he felt it necessary to play up his root beer's unproven health benefits. When the competition became more fierce, Hires made grander, more overt claims, such as "For good health, for pure blood" and "Just what the doctor ordered." In 1897 Hires elevated his claims, claiming that his root beer was, "Soothing to the nerves, vitalizing to the blood, refreshing to the brain, beneficial in every way." At the same time, however, Hires resisted pressure to add caffeine to his root beer, as Coca-Cola had done. In addition, Hires refused to substitute cheaper ingredients for those in his recipe. "I'd rather make less money than use any questionable or unproven ingredient," he once said.

Because of its own grand health claims, Coca-Cola was slapped with taxation as a proprietary medicine under the Pure Food and Drug Act of 1906, a development that put a quick end to soft drink health claims. Hires Root Beer, on the other hand, was not affected by the Act.

International Growth

Hires appeared only sporadically outside the United States, primarily in Canada and Cuba. Bottlers in these countries placed orders for Hires syrup, but their production was negligible when compared with the volumes that were produced in the United States. The lack of emphasis on foreign markets, which has persisted to today, stemmed from Hires' decision to concentrate on the American market and competitors such as Coca-Cola and Pepsi. In addition, the temperance equity that proved so effective in the United States did not translate to foreign countries, where consumption of alcohol presented less of a social stigma.

Performance Evaluation

Hires survived difficult economic conditions during the early 1900s and World War I, when sugar prices skyrocketed and plummeted, by reducing production, securing exclusive sugar supply contracts, and passing price increases along to bottlers.

Unlike many competitors that were ground up by these difficulties, Hires remained in business simply by scaling back. When the economy recovered, Hires found itself in a somewhat less crowded market because of the failure of other brands. Hires was distributed by a solid network of bottlers that had few other root beer brands to choose from. In fact, Hires was the only nationally marketed brand of root beer. This afforded bottlers access to a trusted, consumer-tested brand with proven sales attributes.

Hires remained popular as an alternative to colas and fruit-flavored soft drinks. Heavy promotion by Coca-Cola and a variety of other competitors succeeded in elevating the popularity of other drinks, largely at the expense of Hires. Still respected for its purity and organic formulation, Hires nonetheless gradually lost market share.

By World War II, though, having survived the Great Depression, Hires remained the nation's top brand of root beer. Under difficult economic conditions, the homemade extract product surged in popularity because it was cheap. When the war ended, demand for the bottled product returned. The brand's ability to retain customers by converting them to home brew helped Hires to remain in the public consciousness.

This was especially important, as hundreds of brands were forced off the market entirely during the war. When they returned, the battle for market share was a whole new ball game given the added competition from well-promoted upstarts.

Hires continued to be manufactured in large quantities, both as home brew extract and in bottles, during the 1950s. By 1960, however, sales of the extract began to fall steadily. Promotion of the product ceased entirely, and all advertising centered on the bottled root beer.

Peter W. Hires, grandson of the founder, became president of the company in 1955. Hires shifted the company's promotional strategy from the older themes to one emphasizing youth. This helped to bring in younger drinkers and retain aging ones.

The Hires company, meanwhile, was acquired in 1958 by Continental Foods. In 1962 Continental sold the company to Crush International, which maintained the brand alongside its flagship orange soda.

The soft drink market gradually became segmented during the 1960s. As a result, brand loyalties grew stronger and cola drinkers became less likely to buy other types of soft drinks. This cleared the way for root beer brands to compete with each other in what became a better defined market. Hires was brought into direct competition with other root beer brands, including Barq's, Dad's, store brands, and regional lines such as Canfield's and Graf's. While the soft drink market grew by 35 percent between 1966 and 1970, the root beer segment grew by 100 percent. Hires outsold its nearest competitor nearly three-to-one.

The best-known root beer, however, was not available in bottles. A&W Root Beer could only be purchased from that company's nearly ubiquitous root beer stands. Hires eventually lost its leading position in the root beer market to A&W after that brand became available in bottles and cans in 1971.

Reacting to the public demand for sugar-free drinks, Hires introduced a sugar-free version of its root beer in 1973. The formulation was changed in 1985 using aspartame, replacing an earlier sweetener that some claimed was carcinogenic. Two years later the extension's name was changed to Diet Hires.

In 1980 Procter & Gamble acquired Crush and the Hires brand along with it. After nine years, Procter & Gamble sold Crush to Cadbury Schweppes plc, which continues to produce Hires Root Beer. Despite the frequent changes in ownership and pressures to cut production costs, Hires is still manufactured with genuine flavorings.

Future Predictions

While Hires lost its number one position in the root beer market to A&W in the mid-1980s, it remains that brand's strongest competitor. Hires is most often found in grocery stores and is "bottled" primarily in cans and two-liter bottles. A premium brand, Hires is available to 92 percent of the U.S. population, and has established itself as the second-ranked root beer in the nation. Promotion is regional, with a focus on its primary markets.

Further Reading:

Corrigan, Patricia, "The Roots of Root Beer," *Pittsburgh Press,* January 8, 1989.

"Extracting the Secrets of Root Beer," *Encounters,* July/August, 1991.

Gershman, Michael, "Hires Root Beer," *Getting It Right the Second Time,* Reading, MA: Addison-Wesley, 1990.

"Hires' Root Beer," *The Antiques Journal,* January 1977.

Morgan, Hal, "Hires Root Beer," *Symbols of America,* New York: Penguin, 1986.

"The New Century: Hires' Root Beer," *The Antiques Journal,* February 1977.

—John Simley

INGLENOOK®

Inglenook, one of the top ten selling wine brands in the United States, has been known as a trailblazer and creator of first-rate wines, chiefly Cabernet Sauvignon. The glory days of Inglenook wine began in the 1880s and continued through the late 1930s, when the firm became the premier California winery to limit its production to varietals. For over 100 years the standard Inglenook label, depicting a classic filigree style with founder Gustave Niebaum's interwoven initials, emphasized that each bottle held bona fide wine. The Inglenook name rarely turned a profit for its original owners. The 1960s spurred an increase in production of jug wines under the Inglenook Navalle line at the expense of quality. In the early 1980s parent company Heublein, Inc., producing other wine brands such as Beaulieu Vineyard Wines, Charles Lefranc Cellar, Le Domaine, Rutherford Estate, Almaden, and Christian Brothers, initiated an image enhancement program, stressing once again the excellence of bottling. Besides wines, Heublein distributes brandies, wine-based apéritifs, and liquors, such as Arrow Five Star brandy, Lejon vermouth, Black Velvet Canadian whiskey, Jose Cuervo tequila, Irish Mist liquor, Don Q rum, and Smirnoff vodka. In 1987 Grand Metropolitan PLC of London purchased Heublein, but Heublein continued direct management of Inglenook. With the 1990s showing an overall consumer apathy towards generic wines, tilting instead towards medium-priced, premium wines, Inglenook's strategy is to return to its vintage-labeled traditions and maintain the brand's top ten status.

Brand Origins

One of the veterans of the California wine dynasty, Inglenook was founded in 1897 by retired Finnish sea captain Gustave Niebaum. Having secured his fortune in the Alaskan fur trade at age 26, Niebaum decided to adopt a rural lifestyle and pursue his dream of making fine wines that could compete with Europe's. He found the ideal spot in the small town of Rutherford, in the heart of California's Napa Valley. He purchased a vineyard formerly owned by Scotsman G. B. Watson called Inglenook, loosely translated as a hearth side seat in Scottish.

An extraordinary man who could converse in seven languages, Niebaum quickly set to work planting new vineyards with vines imported from Europe. He constructed a prodigious three-story stone winery, resembling a chateau. Niebaum inspected the winery daily with white gloves, allowing the name of Inglenook to appear on only the best wines. Never a courtier of publicity, he remained a solitary figure, hiring others to deal with the less salient aspects of the wine business: wine dealers and reporters. According to James Conaway's book *NAPA*, Gustave Niebaum lived an honorable life, anchored by these words: "A business is but the lengthened shadow of a man."

In 1882 Inglenook produced 80,000 gallons of wine. Seven years later, the brand won a special prize for superiority and quality at the Paris Exposition. When Niebaum died in 1908, Inglenook had achieved an international reputation.

Early Operations

Prohibition shut down the Inglenook winery from 1920 through 1933. Niebaum's widow restated Inglenook at repeal and assigned wine maker Carl Bundschu (of Gundlach-Bundschu) as the winery's chief rehabilitator. Bundschu, along with Gustave Niebaum's grandnephew, John Daniel, Jr., who later became general manager of the winery in 1937, reestablished Inglenook's eminence as a producer of consistently pure wines.

John Daniel, Jr., was totally devoted to the success of Inglenook. He represented Inglenook at professional meetings and encouraged Californians to invest in the winery. Like Niebaum before him, Daniel obtained counsel from oenologists and other wine experts on a regular basis. Bundschu wrote ornate promotional letters and organized wine tastings, as well as other publicity events, at Inglenook. Bundschu's frequent alcoholic binges led Daniel to replace him in 1937 with another German wine master, George Deuer, who had worked previously at competitors Christian Brothers and Beringer.

Unlike Bundschu, Deuer had no interest in customers or promotional gimmicks—wine making was all that mattered to him. Daniel learned much from Deuer, who created vintages with the same antiquated equipment used in Niebaum's day. According to Conaway in *NAPA*, premium varieties of grapes were employed, including "not just Cabernet, Pinot Noir but also Johannisberg Riesling, Semillon, a bit of Chardonnay, Gamay Beaujolais, Charbono."

In 1941 Daniel became a board member of the Wine Institute, an organization of California wine producers devoted to preventing inferior wines from reaching the market. He was always

AT A GLANCE

Inglenook brand of wine founded in 1879 in Rutherford, CA, by retired Finnish fur-trader and seaman Captain Gustave Niebaum; Carl Bundschu (of Gundlach-Bundschu) and John Daniel, Jr., a great-nephew of Captain Niebaum's wife, reopened the winery at Repeal, 1933; John Daniel, Jr., became general manager, 1937; United Vintners, a cooperative of Allied Grape Growers devoted to bulk and jug wines, bought Inglenook, 1964; brand sold to liquor conglomerate Heublein Corporation (later called Heublein, Inc.), 1969; Heublein in turn became owned by the London-based firm Grand Metropolitan PLC, 1987.

Performance: *Market share*—Ranked fifth in wine category. *Sales*—6.51 million 9-liter cases sold annually.

Major competitor: Robert Mondavi (in the upper tier wine category); Sebastiani and Gallo (in the middle tier wine category); and Taylor California Cellars, Paul Masson, and Gallo (in the bottom tier wine category).

Advertising: *Agency*—Goodby, Berlin & Silverstein, San Francisco, CA, 1990—. *Major campaign*—"Inglenook. Lasting Impressions. Since 1879."

Addresses: *Parent company*—Heublein, Inc., 16 Munson Road, Farmington, CT 06034; phone: (203) 240-5000; fax: (203) 674-9082. *Ultimate parent company*—Grand Metropolitan PLC, 20 St. James's Square, London SW1Y 4RR; phone: 071 321 6000; fax: 071 321 6001.

concerned with maintaining and upgrading the reputation of Inglenook and California wines. Once he told a wine critic visiting Inglenook that "Wines are like children. No matter how much love and attention you give each of them, some always turn out better than others. We've always followed a policy of gentle guidance rather than rigid regimentation in making our wines." It was this ideology that drove Daniel to eccentric measures of quality control, utilizing only superior casks at wine tastings, sometimes sampling 100 of them at one time. He often abolished all but a quarter of the casks, selling them under a different label. According to Conaway's *NAPA*, the " 'cask wines' that emerged from the process were not only fine but also wildly under priced."

Inglenook steadfastly maintained its reputation of producing consistently good wines, but sacrificed profit. Daniel hired Joe Sousa to oversee the vineyards and also took on promoter Jimmy Blumen to execute more showy public relations strategies. Inglenook wines began to be seen in restaurants of the elite on both the east and west coasts. Inglenook's finest wines won medals for quality while the remainder were merchandised off in bulk, often undersold for under 20 cents a gallon. Even though the winery was losing money, Daniel zealously prohibited sticking the Inglenook label on any wine beneath his expectations.

Prior to World War II, Daniel had to plead with the public to purchase his vintages. During the war, however, importation of European vintages was prevented so California wines, especially Cabernet Sauvignon, rose from $2.00 to $3.50 a bottle. Inglenook's obsolete equipment impeded increased production to satisfy the need. Only so many grapes could be pulped with the single crusher in the whole winery. Daniel unwillingly earmarked the winery's vintage selections. The greatness of Inglenook was quality assurance, not commercial success in terms of volume production and marketing.

In the 1940s and 1950s Inglenook achieved increasing levels of popularity. During this period Daniel instituted several changes, impacting the California wine industry for years to come. The first innovation was the vintage dating of wines, facilitating the choices made by consumers. To award a wine a vintage date, 95 percent of the grapes for a particular wine must have been harvested in the said calendar year. The second key move was the initiation of "Napa Valley" as the name of origin, or appellation. The third major influence Inglenook had on other brands was its emphasis on varietal selections. A varietal is defined as a wine christened after the predominant grape type in its contents. Inglenook was also one of the pioneers to drive forward "estate bottling," formerly applied by producers for vintages made from vineyards they owned and could view from the winery itself.

Change of Ownership and Strategy

The mid-1960s were a time of change for Inglenook. John Daniel, Jr., was approaching retirement without any heirs. The winery was getting further and further into debt. Other wineries, such as Almaden and Beringer, were outdistancing Inglenook in production. Deuer, his chief wine maker, was retiring. Renovations of the winery, necessary for future growth, were costly; returns on investments would not reach fruition for several years down the line.

As a result, Daniel sold the winery to United Vintners, a subsidiary of Allied Grape Growers, in 1964 for $1.2 million. Under United Vintners, which had also bought out the familiar wine brands of Italian Swiss Colony and Petri, Inglenook was entirely updated. Production was moved from the winery to a plant in Oakville, California, whereas the Rutherford estate was used as a repository and to create a favorable impression on tourists. Wine production rocketed skyward but the quality of Inglenook's vintages tumbled. Larry Solari, chairman of United Vintners, added a line of inexpensive generic wines that appalled the wine critics, and threatened Inglenook's enduring reputation. Navalle, a rosé, was one of the largest sellers and a way for Daniel—when he owned Inglenook—to use up extra Gamay Beaujolais grapes. Navalle was named after the stream traversing the estate. United Vintners produced gallons of the sweet, pink wine from Central Valley grapes, blurring the distinction between Navalle and Inglenook in the eyes of the consumer. Daniel was dismayed by these actions of the cooperative and retired after two years as a consultant.

Brand Development

In 1969 United Vintners was bought out by the giant liquor conglomerate, Heublein. Heublein continued to increase Inglenook's production throughout the 1970s. Inglenook was expanded to include three lines of wines: "Napa Valley" varietals, the major group; a long list of varietals and generics combined together under the "Inglenook Vintage" label; and finally, a line of jug wines labeled "Inglenook Navalle," carried over from the days of United Vintners. Navalle rocketed upwards in production from 5,000 cases to eight million cases under Heublein.

Heublein organized Inglenook into two distinct divisions: Inglenook-Napa Valley and Inglenook-Navalle. Inglenook-Napa Valley produced higher quality estate and reserve bottled wines, while Inglenook-Navalle made large quantities of jug wines in a separate plant in Madera, California. Inglenook-Napa Valley stressed seven varietals: Cabernet Sauvignon, Merlot, and Sauvignon Blanc—created from Bordeaux grapes grown at Inglenook's original Rutherford estate—and Chardonnay and Pinot Noir—fermented from Burgundy grapes cultivated at the established Oak Knoll and Carneros vineyards; Zinfandel and Charbono rounded out the list of varietals. Charbono, produced by fewer than ten wineries in California, became a specialty at Inglenook-Napa Valley.

As the image of Inglenook continued to decline, Heublein's wine division initiated a major revitalization program in 1979. The original stone winery was revamped, the estate vineyard was replanted, and the quality of bottled wines improved significantly. Dennis Fife and John Richburg were brought on board as general manager and wine maker respectively to improve the brand's vintage varietals. New labeling emphasized Inglenook-Napa Valley and deliberately separated it from Inglenook-Navalle. The line of seven varietals was trimmed to six. Cabernet Sauvignon, Merlot, Chardonnay, and Sauvignon became part of Inglenook's Reserve product line, putting the emphasis on their long-standing reputation as brand originals. In 1983 a new product line called "Reunion" was added, consisting primarily of Cabernet Sauvignon grown at the original estate vineyards. Reunion was created from the original vineyards tilled by John Daniel, Jr., to produce Inglenook's renowned vintages. In 1985 Inglenook debuted "Niebaum Reserve Claret," a limited-production, red Bordeaux blend. "Gravion," another Bordeaux, was a proprietary blend of oak-aged Semillon and Sauvignon Blanc.

Heublein also initiated changes in the Navalle line. The beginning of the 1990s saw the introduction of "Navalle Selections," the primary label for a lower-priced line of varietals. Bottled in 750-ml and 1.5-liter containers, the wines of strictly California origin were comprised of Chardonnay, Sauvignon Blanc, Cabernet Sauvignon, and White Zinfandel. The headquarters of "Navalle Selections" remained in Madera. Inglenook has continued to use the Inglenook-Navalle name for generics in magnum, or 1.5-liter bottles, and for a line of generics and varietals marketed in 18-liter bag-in-the-box containers. The 18-liter packaging was purchased primarily by major institutions, such as hospitals and the military. The idea of a plastic bag enclosed within a cardboard box was started by Scholle, an Australian firm. As the wine is drawn from the box by an outside spigot, the bag collapses, preventing air from getting to the wine and spoiling it.

In the early 1990s Inglenook produced 150,000 cases of wine annually from its 72 acres in Rutherford and the Carneros, including the rented 270 acres in the Napa Valley. Almost 50,000 cases were Cabernet Sauvignon. By the end of 1991 the Navalle line sold 2.5 million cases.

Later Marketing Efforts

The mid-1980s introduced a major advertising campaign by Inglenook. According to *Advertising Age,* advertising for the brand became more individualized: "The theme, 'The wine that celebrates you,' is an evolution of its earlier 'Wine that celebrates food' message, with a more emotional, personal tone." Wine was promoted for more social, less high society occasions. To further market their wines to the general public, Inglenook from 1986 to 1987 offered rebates of $1.00 or more on already discounted 1.5-liter "Party Size" bottles and carafes. Part of the Navalle line, varieties included Navalle Chablis, Navalle California Blush (a new blend of white and red varietal wines, and Inglenook's first attempt nationally into the blush wine market), Burgundy, Vin

Rose, and Chenin Blanc. This promotion, targeted at price-conscious purchasers, was inaugurated with in-store displays. For Inglenook's Navalle California Blush in particular, purchasers were encouraged to mail in the proof of purchase and front label from the 1.5-liter to earn an even higher $1.50 refund.

Inglenook Navalle Wines changed their look in 1989, "leaning toward a romantic, 'California-style' image," reported *Beverage World.* "A redesigned labeling system" was instituted for its White Barbara—a blush varietal—Chablis, Burgundy, and Vin Rose wines that made up the bulk of Inglenook's 18-product line. "The new labels, created by Mittleman/Robinson Design Association in New York use a California chateau illustration, a departure from the traditional black and gold gothic manor house used on the previous design." Each grape variety was matched to a specific label color, which aided consumer identification.

1989 was a time of growth for Inglenook and other brands into the premium wine category. As number three in the "sub-premium" varietal segment, Inglenook added a line into the premium vein and, according to *Marketing & Media Decision,* "contemporized its packaging by adding more color so it would 'jump off the shelf.'" At a time of intensive price competition among brands, Inglenook offered an alternative merchandising gimmick: value-added promotions, "so consumers got something instead of the usual refund," according to Joan White, marketing director for Heublein wines. Calendars and date books highlighted one or two wines each month, along with an explanation of each vintage's nuances. National print advertising hit the college educated buyers in such publications as *People, Bon Appetit, Newsweek, Money,* and *Food & Wine.* In 1989 Inglenook was rated as number nine in most advertised table wines, having expended $984,000 in marketing promotions.

In 1991 Inglenook-Napa Valley teamed up with Kikkoman, a manufacturer of oriental condiments. Napa Valley wines were paired with favorite summertime barbecue recipes. Recipes suggested by both companies were hung from bottles of Inglenook Chardonnay, Sauvignon Blanc, Zinfandel, and Cabernet Sauvignon, linking premium wines to informal social gatherings. A chart that matched wines and seasonings to barbecued meats was also part of this joint merchandising effort.

Performance Appraisal

Inglenook came a long way, growing from 80,000 gallons of wine produced by founder Gustave Niebaum in 1882, to 8 million in case sales more than 100 years later. In 1987 Inglenook was the sixth-largest brand of table wine in the nation.

In the 1980s Inglenook grappled with the increasing popularity of varietals over generics. Due to a health and fitness boom, consumers were not only drinking less, but they were drinking better wines. Although the public continued to buy inexpensive, jug wines everyday, they stressed premium-priced varietals on special occasions. According to Charles Traynor, vice president of wines and marketing at Heublein, Inc., as reported in *Market Watch,* "Our on-premise generic wine business is getting hurt by varietal wines." The Inglenook-Navalle line was faced with the crisis of "increasingly sophisticated consumers in markets where generic wines once reigned virtually unchallenged," continued *Market Watch.*

Despite the threat to the generic wine market, Inglenook held the number five spot of best-selling U.S. wine brands in 1990, garnering $155 million in sales. In 1991 Inglenook dropped to number ten, carrying $160.7 million in sales, but, according to *Superbrands 1992,* recaptured the number five position in 1992. Red wine sales increased in 1992 due to the "60-Minutes" feature on the French Paradox (a theory that credits French people's high red wine consumption for their lower incidence of heart disease than people in the United States, even though the French eat foods higher in fat and smoke more). According to *Market Watch,* "red wine volume in U.S. supermarkets was up 46 percent over the same period in the previous year." Inglenook-Navalle showed "double-digit growth," reported Mike Jacobson, marketing director for Heublein Wines Division, in *Market Watch.*

Future Outlook

Throughout changes in ownership, Inglenook has clung to its original name, steeped in quality and tradition. Its reputation, especially for Cabernet Sauvignon, has been legendary. "Inglenook makes good wines," reported esteemed wine critic Jack J. Prial in his May 13, 1992, column "Wine Talk" in the *New York Times.* "Its most important label, Reserve Cask Cabernet, is consistently excellent." According to Prial, however, while the image of Beaulieu (another Napa Valley winery under Heublein ownership) "remained uncompromised," the Navalle line unfortunately tainted the image and long-standing reputation of Inglenook.

According to Victor Gallegos, marketing manager of the Inglenook brand, the distinct Inglenook-Napa Valley and Inglenook-Navalle lines will be modified in 1993 into a three-tiered structure of the brand Inglenook: Inglenook Vineyards will consist primarily of generics; Estate Sellers will be composed of mid-priced varietals; and Inglenook-Napa Valley will include the esteemed Gustave Niebaum Collection. The merger of Inglenook-Napa Valley with Inglenook-Navalle, another division of Heublein specializing in less expensive jug wines, has caused some reorganizational shake-ups. Both divisions are now a single entity and operate as part of Heublein's Fine Wine Group.

The 1990s have appeared to be an era of reputation building for Inglenook. With citizens imbibing less across the board due to health concerns and an increasing sophistication in wine choices, "workhouse 'generics' such as Carlo Rossi, Gallo, Almaden, and Inglenook are fast becoming relics," reported *Superbrands 1991.* "A new generation of Superbrands, all of them premium-and mid-priced, is climbing the charts and redefining wine marketing." It appears that Inglenook's new three-tiered line structure, emphasizing premium and estate bottled wines, will keep its name in the eyes of consumers for years to come.

Further Reading:

Bagot, Brian, "Brand Report No. 161—Domestic Wine: Wine Tastings," *Marketing & Media Decisions,* May 1989, pp. 100, 102, 104.

Barrett, Jean T., " '60-Minutes' Broadcast Boosts Red Wine Sales," *Market Watch,* November 1992, p. 33.

Bird, Laura, "Losing Ground, Vintners Till New Soil," *Superbrands 1991* (supplement to *Adweek's Marketing Week*), p. 60.

Conaway, James, *Napa,* New York: Avon Books, 1990, pp. 42-43, 48-51, 54-55, 62-63, 66-67, 68-81, 93, 132-133, 181, 499.

Fahey, Alison, "Just Say Slow," *Superbrands 1992* (supplement to *Adweek's Marketing Week*), p. 50.

"Heublein Offers Blush Wine," *Food & Beverage Marketing,* March 1987, p. 32.

"Inglenook-Kikkoman Team for Recipe Promo," *Nation's Restaurant News,* September 2, 1991, p. 34.

"The Inglenook Look," *Beverage World,* May 1989, p. 12.

"New Product Shorts," *Food & Beverage Marketing*, April 1987, p. 52.

"Party Time," *Beverage World,* February 1987, p. 22.

Prial, Frank, with Rosemary George & Michael Edwards, *The Companion to Wine,* Prentice Hall General Reference: Mirabel Books Ltd., 1992.

Prial, Frank J., "Inglenook Wines Rise above Their Airline Image," *New York Times,* May 13, 1992, sec. C, p. 8.

Roby, Norman S. and Olken, Charles E., *The New Connoisseurs' Handbook of California Wines,* New York: Alfred A. Knopf, 1992.

Ross, David L., "The Varietal Boom!," *Market Watch,* July/August 1988, pp. 26, 33, 37.

Stroud, Ruth, "Flat Sales Force Winery Changes," *Advertising Age,* March 12, 1984, p. 66.

"Top Wine Executive Resigns from Heublein," *Market Watch,* November 1992, p. 82.

—Kim Tudahl

J&B®

J&B Rare Scotch whisky has adhered to distilling processes developed in the 17th century while adapting to ever-changing trends in the liquor industry. Out of roughly 2,000 commercial blends from 110 individual distilleries, J&B has remained a world leader. By the early 1990s, it ranked second in the Scotch whisky category, led by Dewar's Blended Scotch whisky (marketed by Schenley Industries). Produced by Justerini & Brooks, Ltd., the distinguished wine merchant founded in 1747 and holding offices in both London and Edinburgh, the brand is owned by International Distiller's and Vintners (IDV), a subsidiary of the British conglomerate Grand Metropolitan PLC. The Paddington Corporation, based in Fort Lee, New Jersey, is the sole distributor and marketer in the United States, Scotch whisky's greatest market. Beginning in the 1980s, an overall decline in alcoholic beverage consumption was met by increased advertising spending and new marketing strategies. By the 1990s, the company had achieved unusually creative and successful ad campaigns and increased market share for J&B Scotch.

Origins

The roots of J&B Scotch date back to 1749, when a poor Italian distiller named Giacomo Justerini arrived in London and formed a wine and spirits business with British investor George Johnson. Almost a century later, the profitable business was bought by Aldred Brooks and renamed Justerini and Brooks. The initials of the new firm were thereafter used for the label of their most famous Scotch whisky, J&B. The brand, and Scotch whisky in general, had skyrocketed in popularity by the late 1930s. In Britain of 1938-39, whisky accounted for 70 percent of liquor sales, according to a 1961 article in the *Economist*. During World War II, shortages of the drink brought a rise in gin consumption, which slowly lost ground to resurgent whisky by the 1950s. In addition, Americans had developed a taste for imported whisky, and from the 1950s onward the United States represented the largest market for Scotch. In 1961 alone, Scotch exports to the United States were 23 percent higher than the year before.

The success of Justerini and Brooks prompted the 1952 formation of a public company under the name United Wine Traders. Meanwhile, two brothers, Walter and Alfred Gilbey, were building a wine merchant business in London. They had set up their first distillery in Camden, producing Gilbey's London Dry gin. In 1910 they moved into the port market, and Smirnoff vodka was added to their portfolio in 1953. In 1962 they teamed up with United Wine Traders to form International Distillers & Vintners, which annually sold over 60 million cases of spirits, of which 1.38 million cases were J&B Rare Scotch in 1988. In 1990, the chairman of IDV, George Bull, paid tribute to this history by opening a historical gallery at the firm's head office at York Gate, Regent's Park, London. The display contained artifacts, documents, and photographs, including a bottle of J&B Scotch bearing a royal warrant from the uncrowned Edward VIII.

Scotch in the United States

In the 1950s, the rise of Scotch in the United States was largely driven by a demand for a whisky that would taste lighter than its American counterparts, which tended to be distilled and stored in a way that produced a dark whiskey with a strong taste (American whiskey is spelled with an "ey" to set it apart from its British relative). First in line were Cutty Sark (blended by Berry Bros. & Rudd) and J&B Rare, blended for clients who wanted Scotches lighter than those blended by the Scots themselves. Paddington Corp., a controlled subsidiary of the Ligget Group, Inc., became the exclusive distributor of J&B Rare Scotch whisky in the United States. Paddington bought the J&B Rare from Justerini and Brooks, Ltd., abroad and then sold the Scotch to its own customers, primarily wholesalers in the United States. By 1968, J&B Rare ranked second after Cutty Sark, whose slogan, the "No. 1 Selling Scotch," would not remain true for long. Other competitors included Johnnie Walker Red, Dewar's, Ballantine's, Black & White, and Teacher's. Even lighter Canadian whiskies included Hiram Walker's Canadian Club and Seagram's VO, both bottled in Canada, and bulk-imported brands like Brown-Forman's Canadian Mist.

In order to save their slipping market share, U.S. whiskey producers began their own production of light whiskey in 1972. Such production had been illegal until 1969, when the Internal Revenue Service's Alcohol, Tobacco & Firearms Division outlined new regulations that would permit light whiskey to be taken out of storage in 1972 and legally sold. Traditionally, American whiskeys were either straights (bourbon or rye) or blends of straights and neutral spirits. They had to be distilled at under 160 proof (80 percent alcohol), and aged in new, charred-oak barrels, yielding a heavier body than foreign-made whiskies. Light whiskey, on the other hand, could be taken off the still at

AT A GLANCE

J&B Rare Scotch whisky dates back to 1749, when Giacomo Justerini and his partner, George Johnson, started a London wine and spirits business; in the mid-19th century the business was bought by Aldred Brooks and renamed Justerini and Brooks, Ltd.; in 1952 it was reorganized as a public company under the name United Wine Traders, which merged with the producers of Gilbey's Dry gin in 1962 to form International Distillers & Vintners (IDV); the Paddington Corporation became the sole marketer and distributor of J&B Rare Scotch whisky in the U.S.; in 1972, IDV was acquired by the British conglomerate Grand Metropolitan, PLC.

Performance: *Market share*—10.1% (1990) of Scotch whisky category. *Sales*—1.38 million cases (1989).

Advertising: *Agency*—Saatchi & Saatchi Advertising, NY, and Lowe & Partners, NY. *Major campaign*—White letters on a bright green background with "ingle ells, ingle ells. . . . The holidays aren't the same without J&B." (Ad produced by Grace & Rothschild, NY, holding the J&B account until February, 1993).

Major competitor: Dewar's Scotch whisky (Schenley Industries).

Addresses: Parent company—International Distillers and Vintners Group (IDV). *Ultimate parent company*—Grand Metropolitan PLC., 20 St. James's Square, London SW1Y 4RR; phone: (071) 321 6000. *U.S. distributor*—Paddington Corporation, 1 Parker Plz. 19th Floor, Fort Lee, NJ, 07024; phone: (201) 592-5700; fax: (201) 592-0859.

between 160 and 190 proof (80 percent to 95 percent alcohol) and stored in used barrels, producing a drink relatively low in flavoring agents. The new regulations were timely, as Canadian whiskey's market share had climbed from 5.4 percent to 9.6 percent from 1962 to 1972; and Scotch's market share had risen from 9.1 percent to 13.8 percent over the same period, according to a July 15, 1972, *Forbes* article. Though the new product presented American distillers with considerable risk, it also cut into an open and growing market for import brands like J&B Rare.

New Temperance and New Marketing

In addition to the increased competition of light whiskies, J&B Rare had to contend with an overall decline in alcohol consumption in the 1980s. Volume of spirits consumption decreased about 3 percent annually in the late 1980s, according to a November 4, 1991, article in *Fortune*. In 1991, overall liquor consumption in the United States declined by about 6.5 percent, double the rate of the previous years, according to *Impact,* an industry source. Scotch consumption matched that trend, decreasing from 13.9 percent of total U.S. liquor consumption in 1979 to 9.3 percent in 1988 and 9.0 percent in 1989, according to a June 25, 1990, *Business Week* report. Yet industry earnings did not necessarily suffer. "Even with worldwide consumption in decline," wrote Bill Saporito in a November 4, 1991, *Fortune* article, "the industry projects a decade of solid earning growth ahead, as new markets develop and old ones are harvested like so many cognac grapes." New marketing strategies and increased advertising support contributed greatly to such growth.

J&B Rare, like its main competitors, focused on the process of trading up—industry lingo for convincing consumers who may

drink less, to drink better. The Justerini & Brooks heritage itself reinforced an image of quality and tradition. A 1982 *New York Times* travel feature on Edinburgh, for example, playfully described the J&B home office as "the kind of establishment where there is a tacit understanding that the sales assistant is in every way your social superior." And a 1984 *Washington Post* article, describing the traditional tenor of St. James Street in London, focused on the J&B house there: "They do an upscale business and even help customers build individual 'cellars' by storing wine for them and making judicious additions each year." J&B Rare marketing aimed for similar discrimination, though in a more popular arena.

In other promotional areas, in 1981 J&B Scotch assumed majority sponsorship of the $200,000 LPGA pro-am tournament, one of the richest tournaments in the LPGA. The event, known as the 200,000 J&B Scotch Pro-Am, drew 80 of the best women golfers in the world to the famous Desert Inn and Las Vegas golf courses. In 1983, continuing its sponsorship of women's professional sports, J&B selected Martina Navratilova and Mary Decker as recipients of the J&B Scotch/WSF Professional and Amateur Sportswomen of the Year Awards. In 1992 golf sponsorship traveled to Africa, where more than 12 African countries were represented in the inaugural Justerini and Brooks Golf Classic at the Windsor Golf and Country Club, Nairobi.

In January 1987, Paddington Corp. moved its estimated $11 million J&B Scotch account from Backer & Spielvogel to Grace & Rothschild, both in New York. J&B represented the largest account that the $25 million G&R agency had contracted since its 1986 formation. The shift initiated a generation of ads that would project a new J&B image well into the 1990s.

Rejuvenated Image

Paddington set an example for other Scotch marketers by revamping its advertising with a contemporary edge directed at younger drinkers. In a June 5, 1989, article in *Advertising Age,* David Margolis, brand manager for J&B Scotch, explained that "When someone goes into a bar they want their friends to see them buying the hot, stylish brand. It's image that matters." Accordingly, a G&R ad campaign begun in 1987 positioned the Scotch as "the high-quality, stylish and sophisticated Scotch," and reinforced this image with abstract and humorous ads. "J&B on the rocks," for example, showed the letters J and B written on pebbles. "J&B among friends" showed the J, the ampersand and the B equally distributed among the letters f-r-i-e-n-d-s. Moving away from emphasis on product, taste, or tradition, the new generation of ads focused instead on humor and visual technique to self-consciously draw attention to themselves and, by extension, the product. In 1988 J&B Rare ranked second in liquor ad spending, at $7.6 million, according to a September 28, 1988, *Advertising Age* article.

In April 1987, the campaign landed J&B Rare in *Spy* magazine, where Paddington Corp. sponsored three special inserts at a cost of roughly $100,000, according to *New York Times.* The first insert, appearing in the May issue, had the simple title, "The J&B Scotch Handbook: New York on the Spur of the Moment: Night Life." At the top of all eight pages, where the tag, "Advertisement," would customarily appear, was the running title, "A J&B supplement designed to look like a real story in *Spy.*" The inserts were created by Drental Doyle Partners, the ad agency and design firm for *Spy.*

Numerous other campaigns reflected growing emphasis on advertising and promotion support to compensate for rising competition and declining consumption. In the spring of 1989, Paddington sponsored "urban rock climbing" in financial districts across the United States. Business professionals were invited to scale a 30-foot, 20,000-pound polymer mountain festooned with the J&B logo. A similarly extreme strategy was employed in a promotional campaign developed by Einson-Freeman from 1985-87 for New York. A single proof-of-purchase seal redeemed prizes worth more than the required purchase of one bottle of J&B Scotch—a VCR movie valued at $49.95; a miniature FM radio worth $29.95; and a watch with a retail value of $19.95. By 1987, a 10-year decline in the New York market was halted and case sales increased.

Gimmicks and wordplay also figured into J&B marketing of the 1980s. One ad showed a pile of dates (the fruit) with the headline "J&B on a date." Print ads for the 1991 Christmas season featured white letters on a bright green background that read, "ingle ells, ingle ells," followed by the observation that "The holidays aren't the same without J&B." Extending such punning to the visual realm, G&R designed a Californian billboard with the words, "J&B With a Twist" and a structural twist in the actual sign to reinforce the message. On the other coast, J&B Rare Scotch sponsored a 1988 holiday-season contest for the "bravest and fanciest gift wrapper in New York." In order to address a larger audience, in October 1992 Paddington Corp. contracted with Gannettwork for an eight-month media program valued at $2.6 million. J&B ads appeared in both USA Today and out-of-home media to augment 11 key markets.

In February 1993 the Paddington Corp. announced that it had consolidated its premium spirits-brands accounts at two New York-based agencies: Saatchi & Saatchi Advertising and Lowe & Partners. The accounts, with combined billings estimated at $28 million to $30 million, had been previously divided among Saatchi, Grace & Rothschild, and Geer, Dubois. The change, which news sources attributed to a change in management at Paddington, suggested new directions for 1990s advertising.

International Market

From its early years, J&B Scotch catered to an international market. By the late 19th century, Scotch distillers like J&B increasingly explored overseas markets, particularly in the British dominions and colonies—India and Ceylon, Australia and New Zealand, Canada and South Africa. After World War II the company's tradition of overseas trade continued, with the United States becoming the principal importer. J&B was honored with the Queen's Award for Export Achievement in 1972, 1973, 1978, 1985, and 1989.

With the diminished alcohol consumption of the 1980s, leading companies began stressing the development of global brands. Not only did Grand Metropolitan craft a global image and market position for J&B, but it systematically acquired scores of distribution companies—like Paddington in the United States—to sell the brand in diverse markets both to wholesalers and directly to retailers. In Southern Europe, for example, trade barriers that kept whiskey out of Spain fell when that country became part of the European Community. Spaniards quickly began abandoning their native brandies for Highland malts. By 1989 whiskey accounted for 22 percent of the Spanish spirits market, up from 9 percent in 1985, and Spain became the single biggest European market for

J&B. Similarly, lifting of trade restrictions in Eastern Europe prompted the 1991 establishment of a Hungarian trading company to sell brands such as J&B Scotch, Smirnoff vodka, and others. IDV Hungaria Ltd. made a distribution agreement with Hungarovin, which handled 70 percent Hungary's wine exports.

The 1990s marked J&B expansion into Asian markets. In December 1992 IDV's Justerini and Brooks launched a new deluxe blended Scotch whisky in Pacific duty free stores. Marketed as J&B Jet, it was a blend of 40 different whiskies, all of which are at least 15 years old and mostly distilled in the Speyside region. Packed in a black glass bottle and gift carton with gold and red lettering, the whisky was sold at almost twice the cost of J&B Rare. In February 1992 IDV agreed to acquire Ekpac Food & Wine, Ltd., in Hong Kong and Food & Beverage, Ltd., in Singapore, which had distribution facilities in Singapore, Malaysia, and Indonesia. IDV also agreed to a joint venture and distribution arrangement with Masterbrands Co., Ltd., in Thailand. In January 1993 J&B Rare moved into Japan, when IDV established a joint venture with Nikka Whisky Distilling Co. to directly sell J&B.

Performance Appraisal

J&B Rare had consistently held a top place among blended Scotches in the United States. In 1968 it was second in its category, following closely behind Cutty Sark. By 1981 it was second again, while first place had been assumed by Dewar's. That year, J&B ranked 14th in the category of liquor brands, with sales of 2.18 million cases. By 1989, still ranking second in its category behind Dewar's, J&B had risen to 6th place in the distilled liquor category. In 1992, IDV's trading profits rose 18.1 percent to 235 million stg, powering half-year group pre-tax profits to end-March up 6.9 percent to 402 million. Lehman Brothers analyst John Wakely, saying that IDV had the right products in the right places, used the Spanish success of J&B as an example.

Despite its tenure as one of the leading whiskies, J&B continued to feel the pressures of higher liquor taxes, the health lobby, a growing temperance movement, and declining markets in the United States and Northern Europe. Nevertheless, in a November 4, 1991, *Fortune* article, Mr. Wakely insisted that the liquor industry had devised a no-lose strategy. "Everything you think of as bad for this industry is good for it," he said. "Tax increases on alcohol may hurt volume, but they encourage consumers to trade up, thus reducing price competition. If advertising is prohibited, the money targeted for it will drop straight to the bottom line. And every new attack on booze does more to ensure that no new competitor would even think of joining the fray. . . . " Whether or not J&B Rare Scotch proves as bullet-proof as Wakely implied, it has maintained a strong hold on the U.S. Scotch market for well over 30 years and has taken bold strides in global leadership. Its ability to walk a straight line in the future depends on its continued status as a dependable, not easily subdued, drinking partner.

Further Reading:

"Back to Scotch," *Economist,* December 23, 1961, p. 1236.

Balzer, Robert Lawrence, "Spirits; Single-Malt Scotches; An Informal Tasting Finds Distinctive Flavors, Bouquets and Colors," *Los Angeles Times,* November 12, 1989, Magazine, p. 34.

Barnard, Alfred, *The Whisky Distilleries of the United Kingdom.* New York: Augustus M. Kelley, Publ., 1969.

"Distillers Get Ready to Serve Light Whiskey," *Business Week,* February 22, 1969, p. 58.

Dougherty, Philip H., "J&B Scotch Focusing On a Younger Market," *New York Times,* April 15, 1987, p. D20.

Dougherty, Philip H., "Scotch Account Given to Grace," *New York Times,* July 30, 1987, p. D18.

Elliott, Stuart, "Paddington Merges Accounts," *New York Times,* February 11, 1993, p. D22.

Elliott, Stuart, "Visions of Sugarplums and Puns," *New York Times,* December 13, 1991, p. D15.

"Fifth Export Award Goes to Grand Metropolitan's J and B," *Reuter Grocer,* December 2, 1989.

Horovitz, Bruce, "Going Abroad Can Save Advertisers a Bundle," *Los Angeles Times,* June 14, 1988, Business, p. 6.

"IDV Opens New Gallery at York Gate Tracing Company's History," *Reuter Off-License News,* September 20, 1990.

"J and B De Luxe Jets Into Duty Free," *Reuter Off-License News,* December 10, 1992.

"J and B Wraps Up the Year," *PR Newswire,* December 12, 1988.

Jones, David, "GrandMet Profits Driven Higher by Drink," *Reuters,* May 14, 1992, BC Cycle.

"Light Whiskies," *Forbes,* July 15, 1972, p. 40.

Meller, Paul, "IDV UK Shapes Spirits Shake-Up," *Haymarket Publications Ltd. (UK),* May 14, 1992, p. 4.

Meyer, Stephen, "Spin the Bottle," *Advertising Age,* June 5, 1989, p. 17.

"J&B Scotch Golf Tournament," *PR Newswire,* November 18, 1981.

"Paddington/J&B Scotch Has Contracted with GANNETTWORK for Eight-Month Media Program," *Business Wire,* October 22, 1992.

Prokesch, Steven, "Britain's Evolving Beverage Industry," *New York Times,* March 29, 1992, Section 3, p. 15.

Saporito, Bill, "Liquor Profits Runneth Over," *Fortune,* November 4, 1991, p. 172.

Nihon Keizai Shimbun, "Foreign Realignments Spell Liquor Dealership Overhaul," *Nikkei Weekly,* February 1, 1993, p. 10.

Wiltz, Teresa Y., "It's Enough to Drive the Distillers to Drink," *Business Week,* June 25, 1990, p. 98.

Winters, Patricia, "Scotch Ads Take Livelier Twist," *Advertising Age,* May 2, 1988, p. 88.

—Kerstan Cohen

JACK DANIEL'S®

Jack Daniel's whiskey, in its most popular black label form, ranks third in total retail sales of all distilled spirits in the United States, stands as a market leader among all whiskey varieties, and is regarded as a top brand in the premium liquors category. This last distinction is most significant, for it is that quality image that most contributes to the whiskey's enviable profit margins and unique reputation among consumers. Packaged in old-time, square bottles, Jack Daniel's Tennessee Whiskey is the embodiment of its founder and namesake, a pre-Prohibition entrepreneur who strongly believed in combining the best ingredients with sour-mash fermentation and a charcoal-mellowing process unique to his own state. This laborious process is believed to produce one of the smoothest, purest whiskeys in the world. Because of this, as well as an effective, long-running, nostalgia-driven advertising campaign, the brand has become a singular presence in the liquor industry; few other comparable products approach Jack Daniel's historic success in both earnings and brand recognition.

Brand Origins

Jack Daniel was born within five miles of the hollow in Lynchburg where his distillery, founded in 1866, still stands. This area, nestled among the Cumberland Mountains and ideal for whiskey-making, fostered a number of small backwoods operations during the nineteenth century, many of which managed to turn a modest profit by selling their unaged moonshine to local bar owners. Daniel, the youngest and most neglected child of a large family, learned the whiskey trade at an early age after he left home and went to work for a part-time distiller, preacher, and jack-of-all-trades named Dan Call. Within three years Call made Daniel a full partner, imparting the secrets of sour-mash fermentation to him. Shortly before the Civil War, Call was forced by his church to sell his moonshine business; thus Daniel, at the age of 13, became the sole owner.

Daniel then made his "discovery" of Cave Spring, a reliable water source situated close to hardwood sugar maples and rich agricultural land; quality water, wood, and grain, Daniel knew, were the three essentials for making fine whiskey. Although Cave Spring had been used by a number of small distillers before Daniel, he was the first to capitalize on its large-scale potential. It was his intention to relocate his operations from the Call farm to the Cave Spring site near Lynchburg, which had the additional advantage of a newly built railroad line for long-distance transpor-

tation. Unfortunately, the Civil War intervened. Daniel, undeterred, proceeded during the next several years to spread his name and wares beyond the remote confines of Lincoln County (later renamed Moore County); this he accomplished through clandestine, dangerous trips with a friend to Huntsville, Alabama, where both Confederate sympathizers and Union troops welcomed his Tennessee sour mash.

Following the war, Daniel leased and eventually purchased the Cave Spring hollow, as well as 500 acres surrounding it. He then became the first whiskey-maker to register his business with the federal government, which had implemented a system for regulating and taxing the spirit industry. Thus, Jack Daniel's Old Time Distillery, the name visible on each clay jug of Daniel's sour mash at the time, also became Distillery No. 1, "The Oldest Registered Distillery in the United States."

Personalized Touches

The next three decades saw Jack Daniel and his Tennessee whiskey become institutions in the region. As his distillery began to thrive, Daniel adopted a striking, ornate form of attire, replete with tie, vest, gold watch, long frock coat, and wide-brimmed planter's hat. This he wore with uncompromising regularity, whether in his office, in the plant itself, or on the road. He also became known for the often-voiced pledge to his product and customers: " 'Y God, every day we make it, we're going to make it the best we can." By 1887 he was labeling his whiskey Jack Daniel's Old No. 7; most likely he chose the number solely as a symbol of good fortune. When his distillery modernized and began packaging with glass, Daniel left his final legacy, the square bottle. After all, as the legend has it, he was known as a "square shooter."

Tennessee Whiskey: More Than a Bourbon

Underlying these and numerous other portraits and anecdotes is the product itself. The most obvious "secret" of Jack Daniel's Tennessee Whiskey is Cave Spring, which issues a steady stream of pure limestone water at a constant temperature of 56 degrees. The iron-free nature of the water is vital to the integrity of the product. Sour-mash fermentation, while not essential, helps ensure flavor consistency from batch to batch. This process, also called "yeasting back," involves the recovery, storage, and reintroduction of old mash during each new fermentation process, similar to

AT A GLANCE

Jack Daniel's brand was founded in 1866 in Lynchburg, TN, by Jasper (Jack) Newton Daniel; later developers include Lem Motlow and Reagor Motlow, successive presidents of Jack Daniel Distillery; Jack Daniel Distillery became a wholly owned subsidiary of Brown-Forman Distillery Corp. in 1956, which was renamed Brown-Forman Inc. in 1984 and Brown-Forman Corporation in 1987; Jack Daniel's currently part of Brown-Forman Beverage Company, a division of Brown-Forman Corp.

Performance: *Market share*—2.2% of total liquor category. *Sales*—$502.7 million.

Major competitor: Jim Beam (Jim Beam Brands Co.).

Advertising: *Agency*—Simmons, Durham & Associates, St. Louis, MO.

Addresses: *Parent company*—Brown-Forman Beverage Company, P.O. Box 1080, Louisville, Kentucky 40210-1091; phone: (502) 585-1100. *Ultimate parent company*—Brown-Forman Corporation, 850 Dixie Hwy., Louisville, Kentucky 40210-1091; phone: (502) 585-1100; fax: (502) 774-7833.

what is done in sourdough bread-making. High standards for selecting the corn, rye, and barley malt for each batch also help to ensure this same consistency. What ultimately defines Jack Daniel's, however, is the charcoal-filtration process it undergoes. Without it, it would be classified as a bourbon: a whiskey made with not less than 51 percent corn and aged in charred oak barrels for not less than two years.

Called the "Old Lincoln County Process," charcoal-mellowing, as perfected by Jack Daniel, consists of burning large ricks of cut maple in the open air; grinding the new charcoal to a fine uniformity; and then packing it into ten-foot deep vats, where, over the course of ten days, the distilled whiskey is allowed to drip slowly through. In addition to lending a faint smokiness to the alcohol, the mellowing, or leaching, removes any lingering traces of corn taste and other impurities. The guiding principle is that a far cleaner whiskey than average can then be placed into barrels to color and age (a period of time that, for the Jack Daniel's brand, lasts anywhere from four to six years). The Jack Daniel's brand has remained unique among whiskeys for its dependence on this process, which no other distiller utilizes to the same degree or in the same manner.

During his lifetime, Daniel twice earned international acclaim for his product, winning gold medals in 1904 at the World's Fair in St. Louis and in 1905 at Liege, Belgium. Later medals were received at Ghent, Belgium, in 1913; the Anglo-American Exposition at London, in 1914; London again in 1915 (Certificate of the Institute of Hygiene); Brussels in 1954 (Star of Excellence); and Amsterdam in 1981.

Lem Motlow, Proprietor

In 1906, near the end of his life, Daniel deeded ownership of the distillery to his nephew Lem Motlow, yet remained active in the business until his death five years later. In 1907 Motlow introduced the slogan "All Goods Worth Price Charged" on bottles and jugs of Jack Daniel's, thereby emphasizing the value of the branded and meticulously processed whiskey. Like his uncle, Motlow possessed a flair for business and a strong appreciation for

tradition. Were it not for his cunning and persistence in the face of a series of unfavorable events, the Jack Daniel Distillery would likely have floundered. In a 1990 *New Yorker* article, Motlow's latter-day counterpart, marketing head Roger Brashears, offered a succinct account of this pivotal company figure: "Old Lem was snakebit with trouble. First, Moore County went dry, then Prohibition come along, then, after Repeal, there was the Depression, then come World War II. But when he died, in 1947, he was rich."

Motlow acquired his initial wealth during the Prohibition years not through underground manufacture of whiskey but through mule-trading. When he returned after this long enforced absence to the distillery business, he not only had the necessary capital for plant renovation and expansion, he also had the resources of Lynchburg, which had become something of a center in the South for mule-trading, largely because of his own efforts. Following World War II, Motlow willed ownership of the business to his four sons. Reagor Motlow presided over operations until the Brown-Forman Corporation—a Kentucky-based manufacturer of such liquors as Early Times, Canadian Mist, and Southern Comfort—purchased the distillery in 1956.

The Lynchburg Campaign

Two years before the Brown-Forman purchase, the Lynchburg advertising campaign was launched. A corporate announcement dated January 10, 1955, summarized the anti-Madison Avenue marketing plan: "We'll use pictures that make our advertising

Jack Daniel's whiskey was once stored in crocks brandishing the words "All Goods Worth Price Charged," a slogan created by Jack Daniel's nephew, Lem Motlow.

look like it sounds. The subject matter of Jack Daniel's photography shall center around those things inherent to how and where it is made . . . the burning ricks, the Hollow, the old crocks and bottles, the ducks . . . for these symbols are the heart of the difference that makes Jack Daniel's unique." Central to the plan throughout its unusually long history has been the town of Lynchburg, hailed as "a tiny little town where things never change much." In an example of reality mimicking advertising, the town and the distillery have settled on an officially designated population of 361, no matter the rate of births, deaths, and incoming or outgoing population. True to its original intent, the ad campaign thrives with the special labors of Ted Simmons, the president of the Simmons, Durham & Associates advertising agency. Simmons makes an annual pilgrimage to Lynchburg to discover offbeat photo opportunities that recall and reaffirm the past. The continually updated pairs of black-and-white photos and nostalgic vignettes, though featured in dozens of well-known national magazines, never appear twice in the same publication during a calendar year.

In 1972 Lynchburg was placed on the National Register of Historic Places. Brown-Forman has since wisely capitalized on this fact through mention of the designation in ads as well as through warm appeals to the public to "drop us a line" or "visit us here in Lynchburg." The constituency of Jack Daniel's customers has grown accordingly, along with the Lynchburg area tourist business and such related promotions as Jack Daniel's memorabilia, anniversary decanters, and performances by Mr. Jack Daniel's Silver Cornet Band (originally formed in 1892 and recreated in 1978).

Present and Future

Until the early 1980s the Jack Daniel's brand experienced strong growth of 11 percent annually. Following a few years of declining sales, which the company attributed to changing drinking habits among U.S. consumers, Jack Daniel's renewed its solid sales track and began emphasizing marketing and sales overseas, eventually becoming one of the hottest liquor brands in the international marketplace, where it is available in more than 100 countries. In 1988 the distillery introduced its first new brand, Gentleman Jack Rare Tennessee Whiskey. Before that time, the three Lynchburg products, all made from the same process, were Jack Daniel's, in both 86 and 90 proof, and Lem Motlow's 90 proof, a one-year-old version of Jack Daniel's. Gentleman Jack was completely new in that it was the first and only whiskey to be charcoal-mellowed twice before aging. Production of this premium brand remains extremely limited. Other spinoff products, in the form of low-alcohol, ready-to-serve beverages, followed. Such

drinks as Lynchburg Lemonade and Tennessee Mud were successfully test-marketed in fiscal 1992 and then launched nationally with the advertisement: "There's a little Jack Daniel's and a lot of great taste in Jack Daniel's Country Cocktails."

Of course, the original Jack Daniel's Tennessee Whiskey remains the mainstay of the Lynchburg distillery and of Brown-Forman, for it is the conglomerate's most profitable brand, with annual worldwide sales of four million cases and a 20 percent lead over the nearest competitor in the premium category, according to company literature. In a company-sponsored consumer research study, Jack Daniel's ranked first in the three all-important categories of "top-of-mind awareness," "unaided brand awareness," and "total brand awareness." Jack Daniel's rising appeal among young consumers as well as women of all ages is just one of several promising indications that the "Smooth Sippin' Tennessee Whiskey" will continue to enjoy its prominent position among premium brand liquors for years to come.

Further Reading:

Bigger, Jeanne Ridgway, "Jack Daniel Distillery and Lynchburg: A Visit to Moore County, Tennessee," *Tennessee Historical Quarterly*, Spring 1972.

Brown-Forman Corporation Annual Reports, Louisville: Brown-Forman Corporation, 1956-1992.

Carlson, Eugene, "Jack Daniel's Hopes the Other Guy's Liquor Is Quicker," *Wall Street Journal*, May 18, 1990, p. B2 (E).

Fucini, Joseph J., and Suzy Fucini, "Jack Newton Daniel," *Entrepreneurs: The Men and Women Behind Famous Brand Names and How They Made It*, Boston: G. K. Hall & Co., 1985, pp. 8-10.

Jackson, Michael, "Tennessee," *The World Guide to Whiskey*, Topsfield, MA: Salem House Publishers, 1987, pp. 183-91.

Morgan, Hal, *Symbols of America*, New York: Penguin, 1986, p. 97.

"Squire," *New Yorker*, August 13, 1990, p. 24.

"Jack Daniel's Strategy Is Turning 35," *New York Times*, July 20, 1989, p. D19 (L).

"A Scary Outlook for the Spirit World," *Superbrands 1991*, p. 61.

—Jay Pederson

JELL-O®

JELL·O®

Jell-O brand gelatin is the nation's oldest and best-selling gelatin dessert. Owned by Kraft General Foods, Inc., a subsidiary of Philip Morris Companies Inc., Jell-O gelatin enjoys an extraordinarily high name recognition among American households. Jell-O gelatin sales peaked in 1968, almost 70 years after its introduction, with a typical household buying an average of 15.6 packages a year. Although the gelatin dessert market shrank considerably from 1970 to 1990, Jell-O has consistently maintained a market share of nearly 85 percent due largely to its award-winning advertising, marketing, and product development campaigns.

Brand Origins

The first U.S. patent for gelatin, a form of pure protein derived from beef and veal bones, cartilage, tendons, and other tissues, was given in 1845 to Peter Cooper, inventor of the famous "Tom Thumb" locomotives. Cooper described his new dessert in a rather uninspired manner as "a transparent, concentrated substance containing all the ingredients for table use in a portable form and requiring only addition of hot water to dissolve it so it may be poured into molds and when cold will be fit for use."

Cooper never manufactured his new product, and in 1897 it was adapted by Pearl B. Wait, a cough syrup manufacturer in Le Roy, New York. Wait's wife, May, coined the name Jell-O, and Wait attempted to sell fruit-flavored versions of Cooper's invention door-to-door. After two unsuccessful years, Wait sold the product and name to his neighbor Orator Francis Woodward for $450.

According to *Spinning Wheel,* Woodward was a man with a tremendous amount of energy and a strong marketing savvy. He had quit school at age 12 to enter into business for himself. By 1897 his Genessee Pure Food Company was already doing quite well selling Grain-O, a caffeine-free coffee substitute, coast to coast. Jell-O, however, was a complete failure; Americans at that time preferred rich cakes and pies and were simply uninterested in a colorful, fruit-flavored transparent dessert. Legend has it that sales were so low within the first two years that Woodward offered to sell the entire Jell-O business to his plant superintendent, A. S. Nico, for $35. Nico refused the offer.

First Commercial Success

Woodward then began an advertising campaign that sent Jell-O gelatin sales soaring. He took out a three-inch, $336 ad in the nationally distributed *Ladies Home Journal* featuring fashionably coiffed ladies wearing clean white aprons and triumphant smiles, heralding the hither-to unknown Jell-O as "America's most famous dessert." This campaign was quickly followed by a massive postal distribution of free samples of Jell-O accompanied by brightly illustrated booklets proclaiming the many delicious and easy ways to prepare Jell-O in strawberry, raspberry, orange, or lemon flavors. Aware of the large number of immigrants to the United States at that time, Woodward had the booklets translated into French, German, Swedish, Spanish, and Hebrew.

Woodward was also a strong believer in a personal approach to selling. The company employed snappy salespeople to appear at local fairs, church banquets, parties, and socials and demonstrate the simplicity of Jell-O gelatin. Many homemakers left carrying free samples and fancy molds inscribed with the Jell-O trademark. Store owners received the same charming sales pitch, and in 1902 sales jumped from almost nothing to $250,000. Four years later, sales nearly topped the $1 million mark. In 1909, not long after Jell-O sales took off, the Genessee Pure Foods Company discontinued sales of Grain-O, and Woodward devoted all of his energy to the million dollar product that at one time he almost could not give away.

By the 1920s Jell-O's earnings were well into the millions of dollars. In 1925 Genessee Pure Foods, changing its name to the Jell-O Company, transferred stock to its former Grain-O rival, the Postum Cereal Company, Inc. Postum then embarked on a buying spree, snatching up such well-known brands as Log Cabin Products and Hellmann's Blue Ribbon Mayonnaise. In March of 1927 Postum Cereal Company changed its name to Postum Company, Inc. to reflect its ever-widening range of products. Two years later the Postum Company, buying all the assets of Clarence Birdseye's General Foods Company, adopted the name General Foods Corporation. In 1979 Philip Morris Companies united General Foods with Kraft Inc. to create Kraft General Foods, Inc., the largest food company in the United States.

AT A GLANCE

Jell-O brand of gelatin introduced in 1897 by Pearl B. Wait; brand sold in 1899 to Orator Francis Woodward, founder of the Genessee Pure Food Company; Genessee Pure Food Company became Jell-O Company and was acquired by Postum Cereal Company, Inc., 1925; Postum Cereal Company renamed Postum Company, Inc., in 1927, then General Foods Corporation in 1929; Philip Morris Companies Inc. combined Kraft Inc. and General Foods Corporation in 1989 to form Kraft General Foods, Inc., parent company of the Jell-O brand.

Performance: *Market share*—Top share of gelatin desserts category; Jell-O Frozen Pudding Pops hold 4.8% of ice cream, frozen novelty, and sherbet market.

Advertising: *Agency*—Young & Rubicam, New York, NY. *Major campaign*—Bill Cosby as spokesperson for various spin-off products.

Addresses: *Parent company*—Kraft General Foods, Inc., 250 North Street, White Plains, NY, 10625; phone: (914) 335-2500. *Ultimate parent company*—Philip Morris Companies Inc., 120 Park Avenue, New York, NY 10017; phone: (212) 880-5000.

Early Advertisements

The simple Jell-O package, with its large, red block letters has seen few design modifications since 1897. However, much more attention was given to the elaborate Jell-O recipe booklets that contained drawings by such famous American artists as Maxfield Parrish, Linn Ball, and Norman Rockwell. Much of the early child-like charm of Jell-O gelatin can be attributed to Rose O'Neill, who drew most of the Jell-O illustrations appearing in national advertisements from 1908 to 1917.

Brightly illustrated recipe booklets for Jell-O gelatin were so successful that they formed the cornerstone of the product's marketing and advertising efforts for more than 70 years. The company received an estimated quarter of a billion requests for booklets in the first half of the twentieth century, and expended great effort to create new recipes. In 1950 it was credited with "fostering the wide growth of home-economics test kitchens in the industry," according to *Modern Packaging.*

Equally important in solidifying Jell-O gelatin's early image was the "Jell-O Girl." The Jell-O Girl was actually Elizabeth King, the four-year-old daughter of Franklin King, an advertising executive who was commissioned to create a trademark that would establish the notion that Jell-O pleases children and is easy to prepare. Elizabeth was photographed playing with Jell-O boxes in her nursery, and in 1908 Rose O'Neill created a more modern drawing of the child. The Jell-O Girl's waif-like image continued to adorn advertisements, china dishes, spoons, boxes, and recipe books until 1950.

Radio Advertising

In 1928 General Foods became a pioneer in radio advertising when it joined with Borden Co. and others to sponsor the Radio Household Institute. By 1933 Jell-O was sole sponsor of *The Wizard of Oz,* for which it paid $51,214. Jell-O gelatin's biggest radio advertising success, however, came with its sponsorship of the Jack Benny Show, one of the most famous associations in radio advertising history.

From 1934 to 1944, listeners who tuned in Sunday evening could hear the famous "Jell-O again! This is Jack Benny," followed by Benny and Don Wilson's witty banter about the six delicious flavors—strawberry, raspberry, cherry, orange, lemon and lime—and ending with the happy jingle "J-E-L-L-O!" Benny and Jell-O were so closely linked in the public mind that when Benny switched to another sponsor in 1944, many people commented that "it just didn't seem right" to hear Benny begin his show without saying "Jell-O Again!" Sales of packaged desserts doubled from 1941 to 1950, and in 1950 Jell-O out-sold all other brands of packaged desserts combined.

Jell-O remained virtually untouched by competition for almost another 20 years. But by 1970, Jell-O sales had peaked and its age was beginning to show. Sales volume began slipping two to four percent annually. The decline was attributed in part to the arrival of ready-to-eat snack puddings and the growing number of women in the work force. Although Jell-O gelatin was once considered simple and convenient, more and more women no longer had the time to prepare the dessert that required four hours to set. Instead, they opted for ready-to-eat desserts, especially frozen ones.

In 1979 General Foods attempted to boost slipping sales by creating an advertising campaign that presented Jell-O in a new light. General Foods increased its advertising expenditures by 25 percent to $10 million dollars. Young & Rubicam, who had developed the product's advertising campaigns since 1929, used a market-research approach, interviewing hundreds of customers

A drawing of a Jell-O box and a young girl are part of a Jell-O advertisement that appeared in magazines in 1919.

about how they felt towards Jell-O. The ad agency found that, in general, Jell-O reminded people of pleasant family gatherings. It dropped the Jell-O gelatin ad campaign of the time, a weak version of the product's by now over-used recipe campaign: "To make exciting desserts on a budget, start with Jell-O gelatin." Replacing it was a jazzed-up television spot that hit upon Jell-O gelatin's emotional appeal that featured fast-paced shots of people of all ages giggling as they shook plates of the brightly colored dessert. The jingle sung in the commercial was, "Watch that wobble, see that wiggle, taste that giggle."

Ten years later, Jell-O saw its sales jump by seven percent—the biggest gain since Jell-O was at its peak in 1968—thanks to Jell-O Jigglers, a promotion scheme that was a variation of the old product-use advertising methods. Aware of the continuous decline in the dessert market, Kraft General Foods was seeking to reposition Jell-O as a snack rather than a dessert. Jigglers, which could be cut into shapes and eaten by hand, fit the bill. More important for Jell-O sales was the fact that Jigglers required four parts Jell-O to one part water. Kraft General Foods threw its support behind the promotion with television and print ads run in both Spanish and English, recipes printed on the backs of boxes, and a free Jiggler mold offered in exchange for proof-of-purchases. The campaign increased Jell-O gelatin sales by nearly 15 percent and won *Adweek*'s promotion of the year award in 1990.

Jell-O Pudding and Pie Fillings

Perhaps the biggest spin-off of the Jell-O brand is Jell-O pudding and pie fillings. Capitalizing on high name recognition, Kraft General Foods introduced the banana, chocolate, and vanilla pudding desserts in 1932 and an instant version in 1953. Packages were printed with the same red block letters, and box colors corresponded to the various flavors. In 1973, to combat competition from Hunt's Snack Pack pudding, Jell-O hired Bill Cosby as its pudding spokesperson. Cosby so delighted television viewers with his stories about "pudding experts" that in 1988 Young & Rubicam even decided to rerun some of the classic Cosby commercials.

Jell-O Pudding Pops

Cosby also became pitchman for the Jell-O brand's most lucrative product spin-off: Jell-O Pudding Pops. General Foods had experimented with a form of frozen pudding back in the 1960s, but the product was never test marketed because it was considered "hard as a rock." In the 1970s, however, the idea came to mind to work with the same emulsifying product used to keep General Food's Birds Eye Cool Whip soft. The notion of a frozen pudding evolved to frozen pudding on a stick in chocolate, vanilla, and banana flavors, and the new Jell-O Pudding Pops were test marketed in 1979. They were then introduced nationally through a $25 million advertising campaign targeted at children and young mothers. The television spot featured Cosby telling kids, "Mom won't throw you into the old dungeon because she knows Pudding Pops are made with real pudding!"

Kraft General Foods beat competition in the frozen novelties market through heavy advertising that also capitalized on the fact that Pudding Pops contained less calories and fat than other ice cream products. Sales for Pudding Pops topped the $100 million mark within a year of the product's introduction.

Brand Development

Few changes have been made to the original Jell-O gelatin recipe outside of improving its "richer, locked-in" taste, although flavors have varied considerably since the introduction of the

original strawberry, raspberry, orange, and lemon. By 1905 cherry and chocolate flavors were added, and in 1911 peach was introduced. Following the dictates of consumer preference, peach and chocolate were discontinued in the 1920s. In 1930 lime was added to create the famous "six delicious flavors" touted by Jack Benny on his radio show. The six flavors formed the Jell-O line until 1955 when apple was introduced in response to the growing popularity of Jell-O as a salad ingredient. By 1961 the number of flavors reached an even dozen with the addition of black raspberry, black cherry, grape, orange pineapple, and blackberry. In 1992 a blue-colored raspberry/blueberry flavor was added to the line, just in time for consumers to make red-white-and-blue desserts for the Fourth of July.

General Foods took some rather small steps in the early 1970s to combat the onslaught of ready-to-eat snacks that were encroaching on the Jell-O market share. Jell-O 1-2-3, a "self-layering dessert" with gelatin on the bottom, fruit-flavored chiffon in the middle, and cream on top, was first introduced into regional markets in 1969. Although sales were expanded into the national market in 1970, results were not quite stellar. It was ultimately discontinued in 1973 then reintroduced nationally in 1989.

In response to diet-conscious eating habits, Jell-O brand sugar-free gelatin was introduced nationally in 1984. A year after sugar-free gelatin hit the markets, sugar-free instant pudding was introduced. Jell-O no-bake fruit-topped cheesecake was put on the national market in 1991.

Performance Appraisal and Future Predictions

Jell-O remains among Kraft General Food's top five products, primarily because of strong and consistent advertising campaigns. Over the years, the shiny, colorful desert has also wiggled its way into becoming a symbol of American culture. In 1992 the *Wall Street Journal* printed a front-page article about a resurgence of interest in Jell-O, inspired not by a heavily funded advertising campaign, but by a sort of nostalgia for a simpler way of life. The Smithsonian Institution has sponsored symposiums on the product's history and its cultural significance, and in the early 1990s a successful restaurant selling only dishes made from Jell-O opened in Greenville, Massachusetts.

Jell-O has enjoyed little direct competition in the gelatin market since its introduction in 1897. At that time, many Americans regularly ate formal desserts, and Jell-O was considered a convenient and tasty alternative to more complicated pies and cakes. As the eating habits of Americans changed, however, people ate formal desserts less frequently and instead opted for handy ready-to-eat snacks. Jell-O continued to hold the largest share of the market, but the product now appealed primarily to senior citizens rather than to children and families.

The success of Jell-O products has always been due to consistently strong marketing efforts based on developing new recipes and uses. Over the years, the General Foods Kitchen has developed 1,773 different ways to prepare Jell-O. In 1990 Kraft General Foods began positioning Jell-O as a snack food, using a highly successful recipe campaign for its Jigglers. The Jigglers recipe required four boxes of Jell-O to one part water and could be eaten by hand, a far cry from the elaborate recipes of the 1930s and 1940s.

"Recipes really do help sell products," Stephanie Williams, associate director of techno-culinary services at Kraft General

Foods told the *New York Times* in 1989. As if to prove her point, Kraft General Foods declared in its 1991 annual report, "Our Jell-O brand remained strong, aided by the Jell-O gelatin Alphabet and Holiday Jigglers promotions."

Further Reading:

Abrams, Bill, "Jell-O's Revival Shows Sales Can Grow With Older Products," *Wall Street Journal,* September 11, 1980, p. 1.

Gershman, Michael, "Jell-O: The Big Shake-Up," *Getting It Right the Second Time,* Addison Wesley, 1990, pp.42-47.

Giges, Nancy, "GF Fights Incursions on Jell-O," *Advertising Age,* August 30, 1971, p. 1.

Guyon, Janet, "General Foods Gets a Winner With Its Jell-O Pudding Pops," *Wall Street Journal,* March 10, 1983, p. 33.

"Jell-O," *Modern Packaging,* December 1950, p. 88.

"Jell-O . . . " *General Foods Family Album,* White Plains, NY: General Foods Corporation, 1948, pp. 6-7.

"Jell-O Used to Be a Side-Line," *General Foods Salesgram,* White Plains, NY: General Foods Corporation, January 1937, p.3.

Kiley, David, "Jell-O Jiggles a New Snack Positioning, and Sales Jump," *Adweek's Marketing Week,* June 16, 1990, p. 10.

Kraft General Foods, Inc., Annual Report, 1991.

"Promotion of the Year," *Adweek's Marketing Week,* December 10, 1990, p. 36.

Salmans, Sandra, "Big Hopes for Pudding Pops," *New York Times,* July 14, 1981, p.D1.

Spiller, Dr. Burton, "The Jell-O Story," *Spinning Wheel,* March 1972.

Additional information was provided by the Kraft General Foods Archives Department and the Le Roy Historical Society.

—Maura Troester

JIF®

Jif peanut butter was introduced by Procter & Gamble Company, one of the oldest companies in the nation, in 1958. Since then, Jif has skyrocketed to the number one spot in the highly competitive peanut butter market, outdoing even its toughest competitors, Skippy and Peter Pan. With a one-third share of a category in which Americans spend $1 billion annually, Jif is truly a brand success story. There were many factors contributing to this success, notably Procter & Gamble's well established reputation, marketing skills, and Jif's unique rich flavor.

Brand Origins

While only about ten percent of the world's peanuts are produced in North America, Canadian and U.S. residents consume more peanut butter than any people on earth. Peanut butter itself did not appear until the turn of the century, although peanuts were being grown in the South long before that time, mainly as food for slaves, children, and hogs. It was the work of two men, however, that endowed the peanut with dignity and importance. The distinguished scientist George Washington Carver had begun to experiment with peanuts, and by the early twentieth century he had devised more than 300 uses for the nut. In the meantime an anonymous St. Louis doctor was inspired in 1890 to crush some peanuts in a food grinder, hoping that the peanut "butter" would be an easily digestible, nutritious food for his patients. This turned out to be so popular that the idea caught on, and soon peanut butter was being manufactured nationwide.

It wasn't until the 1920s that peanut butter began to closely resemble the product now sold in stores. Previously, peanut butter consisted simply of crushed peanuts with a little salt added. Unfortunately it stuck to the roof of the mouth, and when the jar sat unused, oil would rise to the top. To resolve these problems, research was conducted in factory labs, and the proper combination of stabilizers and emulsifiers, as well as sugar, was developed. By the 1950s the Food and Drug Administration (FDA) ruled that a product labeled "peanut butter" had to contain at least 92 percent peanuts and be free of all preservatives and colorings.

Peanut butter, with its long shelf life, was used by the armed forces throughout World War II, and included in all postwar food relief shipments to the devastated countries of Europe, two factors that served to drive up demand for the spread. This, in addition to the fact that more money was spent on groceries in the United States than in any other country, was not lost on the executives at

Procter & Gamble who became convinced to enter the peanut butter business. Although the company had little experience in the industry, Procter & Gamble had the resources and a mastery of the advertising media that almost guaranteed a successful entry into the market.

In 1955, while Procter & Gamble researchers were hard at work formulating a unique recipe for the company's new peanut butter, executives decided to purchase an already flourishing peanut butter firm, allowing them to learn the business from experts. With the acquisition of the W. T. Young Company, manufacturer of Big Top Peanut Butter, Procter & Gamble had the technology and experience necessary to launch their product—all that was lacking was a name. Executives eventually chose Jif mainly as a marketing tool—the name was easy to spell, pronounce, and remember. First test marketed in grocery stores in 1956, Jif peanut butter was introduced nationally two years later. It was an immediate success, capturing a 15 percent share of the market in large part because of the rich peanut butter taste and the company's well honed marketing techniques.

Early Marketing Strategy

Jif arrived on the market just as the television medium was gaining momentum. TV provided the perfect opportunity for Procter & Gamble—thus far known primarily as the maker of Ivory soap and other detergent products—to change their image, as well as advertise their peanut butter. According to a 1950 article in *Broadcast Television* magazine, no other company ever mastered the medium like Procter & Gamble. By the time Jif was launched nationwide, Procter & Gamble already sponsored numerous TV shows and soap operas. As early as 1949, the company had formed Procter & Gamble Productions, Inc. to actually produce radio shows and TV and motion picture films that would tout their products. Early advertising of Jif was also conducted in newspapers and household magazines, in which Jif was introduced as "The New Peanut Butter that Melts in your mouth."

Sales of Jif, though high, remained flat into the mid-1960s. To boost profitability, Procter & Gamble launched a new advertising campaign that singled out mothers, the buyers of peanut butter. Television ads emphasizing that "choosy mothers choose Jif" were highly effective in boosting sales. Jif garnered the second highest share of the market, behind Skippy brand and followed by Peter Pan, to which it hung on until well into the 1970s.

AT A GLANCE

Jif brand of peanut butter introduced nationally in 1958 by Procter & Gamble Company.

Performance: *Market share*—33% (top share).

Major competitor: CPC International's Skippy; also ConAgra, Inc.'s Peter Pan.

Advertising: *Agency*—Grey Advertising Agency, New York, NY. *Major campaign*—"Choosy mothers choose Jif."

Addresses: *Parent company*—Procter & Gamble Company, 1 Procter & Gamble Plaza, Cincinnati, OH 45202; phone: (513) 983-1100.

Advertising Innovations

The 1974 recession caused many peanut butter lovers to begin purchasing store brand and generic spreads. To counter this decline in sales, Procter & Gamble skillfully advertised the uniqueness of Jif compared to other brands of peanut butter. In a successful mid-1970s commercial entitled "Candid Choice," mothers at the grocery store were given samples of different peanut butters, including Jif, and asked to choose the one they preferred. After choosing Jif brand, the women enumerated the reasons for their preference. The ad caused a noticeable boost in sales—so much so that Jif was the only peanut butter brand during the recession to actually improve its business, though it still remained number two.

In 1979 when drought hit the south and the peanut crop failed, fear spread among industry producers that people would stop buying peanut butter for the duration, and learn to do without, even after the drought ended and peanuts were abundant once more. Moreover, kids at a certain age form peanut butter tastes that remain decisive for the rest of their lives; without peanut butter for a year or two, this could fail to happen. Hence, in order to keep from straining demand, Procter & Gamble's marketing strategy was to decrease its amount of advertising. Jif, on the other hand, remained available for purchase, although the supply was rationed to all retailers. For the first time in the company's peanut butter history, Procter & Gamble had to go abroad to China to buy peanuts. The strategy worked, chiefly because loyal Peter Pan and Skippy fans bought Jif when their own brands were unavailable, and stuck with Jif thereafter. Not only did Jif survive this industry setback, the brand emerged with the top share of the market, a position the peanut butter has continued to hold.

Peanut butter use has shot up in the late twentieth century, but so has the competition, with more than 100 companies competing for their share of the huge market. More recent advertising has been targeted at the rapidly growing Hispanic population in the United States, a largely untapped market for peanut butter. Television ads run in areas with large populations of Hispanic Americans, and feature people being irresistibly drawn to Jif. Meanwhile Procter & Gamble decided to lower the price of Jif—reducing the usual price allowances to retailers—and aggressively advertising this move in newspapers and grocery store promotional campaigns. According to an article by Dick Rawe in the *Cincinnati Post*, despite their lower price allowances, some grocers could be persuaded to see an advantage in the company's new advertising stratagem "because it lets retailers know where prices are going to be," and in the process, simplifies accounting costs. Some of the biggest retail grocers, including Bigg's and Kroger, saw this as a

pioneering way to attract customers. It also puts Jif at a major advantage over other peanut butter brands, helping to insulate Jif from increasing competition.

Product Changes

When Jif first appeared on the market, it was not called peanut butter—it contained less than the FDA's mandatory 92 percent peanuts—but "peanut spread," a name the company was willing to accept because Jif was considerably easier to spread than other leading brands. Because of Jif's success with the public, Procter & Gamble decided to stop manufacturing Big Top Peanut Butter. By 1960 Jif could be called "peanut butter" after researchers discovered a way of retaining the spreadability and adding more peanuts. Market research revealed that kids who had grown up on Jif preferred a more complex taste as adults, and in 1972, Procter & Gamble was ready with a "crunchy" version of Jif. This proved so popular that Procter & Gamble experimented with "extra crunchy," which was produced by adding chopped roasted peanuts to the creamy version in the last stage—after homogenization—of peanut butter processing. Also in 1972, Procter & Gamble hit on the idea of improving the rich flavor of Jif by sweetening the peanut butter with molasses—which continues to be used— rather than honey.

The 1980s marked an increase in environmental awareness and concern, and, appropriately, Procter & Gamble began using recyclable plastic containers, rather than glass. An aluminum foil "Freshness Seal," guaranteed the product's quality. In 1989 all peanut butter manufacturers changed their ingredient statements from "Grade #1 Peanuts" to "Selected U.S. Fresh Roasted Peanuts" for the sake of accuracy. The 1980s also produced growing public consciousness of cholesterol, a factor that produced yet another change in the ingredient statement in August of 1991, which from then on would list the type of vegetable oil contained in Jif. In 1992 the company began specifying whether the oil was fully or partially hydrogenated.

Growing health consciousness, coupled with recessionary times inspired Procter & Gamble to come out with its highly successful Simply Jif. The peanut butter, a low salt, low sugar version of regular Jif, was available in 18 and 40 ounce jars. Later, the big five pound Valu-Pack plastic containers were marketed, although they sold mainly in warehouse type stores. Producing different sizes of Jif noticeably chipped away at Skippy and Peter Pan's sales.

The product changes also reflected Procter & Gamble's sensitivity to consumer needs and timely responsiveness to them—part of the secret of Jif's enormous popularity—and the growing profitability, despite recessionary times, of Procter & Gamble's food division. These factors, together with market indications that peanut butter consumption will continue to rise, seem to assure Jif peanut butter's future growth.

Further Reading:

Asher, Sandra Fenichel, *The Great American Peanut Book*, New York: Tempo Books, 1977.

Deutschman, Alan, "Nutty Economics," *Fortune*, April 23, 1990, p. 324.

Freeman, Laurie, "P&G Unit Back in the Black," *Advertising Age*, September 17, 1990, p. 16.

History of Procter & Gamble Peanut Butter Products, Cincinnati: Procter & Gamble Company, 1992.

"Homemakers Use of and Opinions about Peanuts and Tree Nuts," *Market Research Report No. 203,* Washington, DC: U.S. Dept. of Agriculture, 1957.

Koeppel, Dan, "Skippy Launches Three-Pronged Bid to Catch Jif," *AdWeek's Marketing Week,* July 31, 1989, p. 32.

Lief, Alfred, *"IT FLOATS"; The Story of Procter & Gamble,* New York: Rinehart & Company, 1958.

Procter & Gamble Company Annual Report, Cincinnati: Procter & Gamble Company, 1991.

Procter & Gamble, the House That Ivory Built, Lincolnwood, IL: NTC Business Books, 1988.

Rawe, Dick, "Festivas Here: P&G Extends Test Market for Corn Chips Snack," *Cincinnati Post,* March 19, 1992.

Rawe, Dick, "P&G Move Cuts Prices on Consumer Products," *Cincinnati Post,* January 4, 1992.

Schisgall, Oscar, *Eyes on Tomorrow; The Evolution of Procter & Gamble,* Chicago: J.G. Ferguson, 1981.

Speech of Carol Talbot, Procter & Gamble, Before the Joint Council of Economic Educators, Cincinnati: Procter & Gamble Educational Services Dept., October 10, 1991.

Stiling, Marjorie, *Famous Brand Names, Emblems, Trademarks,* Newton Abbot, VT: David & Charles, 1980.

Van Tuyl, Laura, "Peanut Butter's Popularity Spread; Old Time Company Finds Niche Growing," *The Christian Science Monitor,* June 14, 1989, p. D2.

—Sina Dubovoj

JIM BEAM®

Jim Beam brand bourbon is the number one bourbon in America, leading all others in sales, both in the United States and abroad. Its history stretches back almost 200 years, and its parent company, Jim Beam Brands Co., is one of the oldest family-run businesses in the nation. Jim Beam bourbon is a truly American product, yet it is also consumed throughout Europe and Asia, where it enjoys the status of a sophisticated drink. Jim Beam's image in America has changed with the times, enabling it to remain a top-selling brand since the repeal of Prohibition. Seen as a strong, manly drink in the 1950s, Jim Beam recast itself as a light, mixable whiskey in the 1980s. In the 1990s Jim Beam stressed its classic good taste, contrasting itself with "fad" drinks that come and go.

Though Jim Beam is a moderately priced spirit, fine packaging has helped it hold its own against imported whiskeys with classier auras. The Jim Beam Brands Co. also markets several higher priced bourbons such as Beam's Choice, Bonded Beam, and Booker's. In addition, Jim Beam's line of specialty decanters, ranging from glass cocktail shakers and bowling pins to fine china figurines of Kentucky mountain men, Maori tribesmen, opera characters, wildlife, and classic cars, has attracted enthusiastic collectors worldwide.

Brand Origins

Jim Beam bourbon is a type of whiskey made from a mix of fermented corn, rye and barley malt. The name "bourbon" derives from Bourbon County, Kentucky, where American pioneers first began making this distinctive spirit. Bourbon differs from Scotch and Irish whiskeys in the high percentage of corn in its grain mash. The first Kentucky bourbon makers devised this particular grain mix in an effort to find an economical way to store the corn they grew. Corn was difficult to store and expensive to transport in its grain form, but distilled corn liquor would keep forever and was easy to ship. Bourbon was used almost like cash among Kentucky's early settlers: Abraham Lincoln's father is said to have sold his Kentucky farm for $20 and 400 gallons of bourbon.

Bourbon had a central place in the Kentucky pioneer economy. So when Jacob Beam headed west with his family to settle near what became Clermont, Kentucky, he brought an old copper still with him. Jacob Beam settled in Kentucky in 1788, where he was primarily engaged in farming until 1795, when he began to make whiskey from a grist mill. In 1795 he sold his first barrel of bourbon, and from then on he worked as a commercial distiller.

This was well before the era when brand name foods and beverages became standard in American households, and Jacob Beam's bourbon probably had no name as such or fancy packaging. But today's Jim Beam follows Jacob's early recipe. The liquor is aged four years in new charred white oak barrels. It is cooked at a lower temperature than other bourbons, and distilled at a lower proof as well, to give it a fuller flavor. The strain of yeast used to ferment the grain mash has also been passed down as successive generations of Beams took up the family business.

Jacob's son David M. Beam, born in 1832, was the next Beam to run the distillery. But it was his son, James Beauregard Beam, who eventually gave his name to his bourbon. Jim Beam joined the family business in 1880, at age 16. The distillery operated uneventfully until 1920, when Prohibition made the manufacture, transportation, and sale of liquor illegal. Jim Beam shut down the distillery. But as soon as Prohibition was repealed in 1933, Beam began bottling bourbon again, now under the rather unremarkable name of Old Tub. In 1942 the bourbon was renamed Jim Beam and was made available in the square, white-labelled bottles in which it is still sold. Beam sold the family business to Harry Blum of Chicago in 1945, though Beam family members continued to work in the distillery. Jim Beam himself died in 1947 at the age of 83.

Some of the legendary Jim Beam's business practices were recalled by his grandson, Booker Noe, who worked in the distillery from 1951 to 1992. Noe remembered his grandfather efforts to create the special strain of yeast used in the family bourbon recipe upstairs in his attic at home. This yeast culture was so precious that Jim Beam brought portions of it home with him on weekends in case some disaster struck the plant.

Marketing

But no matter how special the yeast, how ancient the recipe, these factors alone could not guarantee bourbon sales. Hampered by the interruptions in sales caused by Prohibition and then World War II, Jim Beam bourbon nonetheless enjoyed strong customer bases in the South and West, where bourbon was seen as a hearty, manly drink. In 1952 Jim Beam rapidly increased its sales, as the company attracted a wider market by virtue of a national advertis-

AT A GLANCE

Bourbon from the Beam family distillery first produced in 1795 by Jacob Beam in Clermont, KY; the distillery operated continuously until 1920, when it shut down for Prohibition; reopening in 1933 to sell "Old Tub " brand bourbon, renamed "Jim Beam" in 1942; company sold to Harry Blum of Chicago in 1945, and incorporated as James B. Beam Distilling Co. in 1947; company bought by American Brands Co. in 1967, remains a wholly owned subsidiary.

Performance: *Market share*—2.3% (sixth largest) of distilled spirits category. *Sales*—$334 million.

Major competitor: Jack Daniel's Black.

Advertising: *Agency*—Fallon McElligott, Minneapolis, MN. *Major campaign*—"You always come back to the basics."

Addresses: *Parent company*—Jim Beam Brands Co., 510 Lake Cook Road, Deerfield, IL 60015; phone: (708) 948-8888. *Ultimate parent company*—American Brands Co., 1700 E. Putnam Ave., Old Greenwich, CT 06870; phone: (203) 698-5000.

ing campaign. Magazine ads stressed the brand's long history and tradition, and innovative packaging projected a new image of Jim Beam as a status drink.

The Beam company had been selling Jim Beam in special "Pin Bottles," shaped like bowling pins, since 1941. These charming decanters were made of glass, with a wooden top. Expanding on the success of the Pin Bottles, Beam's marketing committee decided in 1952 to design a special holiday decanter in an effort to grab a bigger share of the next year's Christmas whiskey sales. Accordingly, in 1953 the company launched a fancy cocktail shaker Jim Beam decanter. The cut glass bottle featured a gold-plated vacuum closure, projecting an image of luxury. Profits for the targeted holiday period soared 22 percent. This success encouraged the Beam company to continue to issue specialty bottles and to aim for a tonier image overall.

The following year's decanter came in the form of a glass coffee carafe made for Beam by the Corning Glass Company. Through marketing surveys, Beam found that sales of the fancy carafe not only definitely enhanced the image of the entire Beam line, but also seemed to spur increased sales for Jim Beam in the regular square bottle. For the Beam distillery's 160th anniversary, the company marketed $160 cases of 160-year-old whiskey and named it, unsurprisingly, Beam's 160. Overall Jim Beam sales jumped 32 percent. Beam sales continued to rise, from approximately $17 million in 1952 to more than $82 million in 1962. Reviewing this ten-year climb in profits, Beam Vice-President William Carroll explained in an April 1962 article in *Advertising Age* that people had come to identify Beam as "the distillery with the beautiful bottles."

The specialty Jim Beam bottles soon took on something of a life of their own. As they became increasingly elaborate and creative, a collector's club sprang up to buy and trade them. Though the early decanters generally had the appearance of liquid containers, later decanters increasingly resembled statuettes and figurines, with no obvious caps or pouring lips. Wildlife, military and sports heroes, cars, telephones, trolleys, footballs, even Beam computer terminals, were replicated in china as Jim Beam decanters. Additional decanters were cast to commemorate special events such as Hawaiian statehood, the 25th anniversary of the

Corvette sports car, or the release of the 1976 Paramount motion picture *King Kong.* Some bottles embedded special features such as calendars, thermometers, or music boxes. The variety and ingenuity of these bottles was so immense that the collectors club numbered between 15,000 and 20,000 members by 1979.

This interest continues today. "The Beamer," a newsletter for Beam bottle collectors, is published in Australia and New Zealand, Beam bottle conventions have met since 1971, and an illustrated guide to the collection has been published annually since 1967. Though the Beam company does advertise its new decanters, the activities of the collectors club and its publications operate independently of the distillery, driven by the enthusiasm of Beam bottle fans. Some of the rarer bottles fetch prices in the hundreds of dollars.

Print advertising in the 1950s and 1960s also aimed to portray the elegant tone denoted by the early decanters. The Beam company placed colorful ads in relatively up-scale magazines such as the *New Yorker, Harper's, The Atlantic, Playbill, Town & Country,* and *Saturday Review,* as well as in such men's magazines as *Playboy* and *Sports Illustrated,* and in daily newspapers nationwide. A 1959 campaign stressed the Jim Beam brand's venerable history by showing fifth- and sixth-generation members of the Beam family gathered around the well where Jacob Beam drew water for his 1795 brew. The series of full color ads told the story of the Beam family and their long practice in the art of distilling. The four Beam men were pictured dressed in suits and ties and projected the air of successful businessmen. An ad campaign for Beam's Choice, a premium brand, that ran concurrently, was also aimed at a well-to-do clientele. These ads featured drawings of historical figures such as Archimedes, Galileo, and others, under the title "Genius," and ran primarily in the *Wall Street Journal.* These two campaigns indicated that Jim Beam bourbon was not just a drink for rugged types, but could appeal as well to people of culture, higher education, and professional income.

Bourbon grew in popularity in America during these two decades, and Jim Beam sales rose year by year. In 1964 Jim Beam was the second most popular bourbon in the United States, behind the National Distillers Products Co.'s Old Crow brand. A 1965 advertising drive aimed to vault Jim Beam into first place, again by portraying Jim Beam as a status brand. Magazine ads in *Ebony, Esquire, House Beautiful, Life, Look, Newsweek,* and others repeated the theme "Since when do you drink bourbon?," answered by "Since I tasted Jim Beam." Photo illustrations showed a couple at a ski lodge, billiard players clad in tuxedos, and various other holiday and leisure scenes. That year brought record sales of almost $90 million. In 1967 Beam's sales were so good the company could afford to tell people to drink less. Ads for Beam's Choice, the company's premium brand, declared that the bourbon was too good "to waste on people who overindulge." The advertisement continued in that vein, noting that the bourbon "was meant to be sipped and savored. Not wolfed down." By 1970 Jim Beam had passed Old Crow to become the nation's top-selling bourbon.

International Markets

While bourbon grew in popularity in the United States, overseas markets also expanded. Though bourbon was a rare sight abroad in 1950, by 1965 it was a status drink in Europe, and Jim Beam had garnered distributors in 75 countries. In addition, Jim Beam was bottled abroad at nine foreign plants. Exporting by the barrel saved the company money in foreign tariffs, but even so, a bottle of Jim Beam in Europe cost consumers several dollars more than comparable Scotch whiskey. Jim Beam's management complained about unfair tariffs in France, Japan, Mexico, and elsewhere, yet the high price of bourbon was in some ways an asset. Jim Beam's European ads featured men in tuxedos in yet another campaign designed to showcase their product as an upper-crust drink. These ads may have seemed more accurate than their counterparts in the United States, where Jim Beam had always been moderately priced. By 1973 Jim Beam was the number one bourbon both in U.S. and foreign sales.

Bourbon sales began to slip in the late 1970s, both at home and abroad. Consumers increasingly turned to rum and vodka. Health-conscious consumers also turned away from bourbon toward lighter whiskeys from Scotland and Ireland, and toward lighter drinks in general. In 1985, however, Jim Beam found itself in a boom market again, as Japanese drinkers became fascinated with this American classic. Jim Beam became an extremely popular drink at trendy Tokyo bars.

Brand Development

The sudden mid-1980s boom in interest in bourbon in Japan spurred sales of Jim Beam there, but the rest of the world continued its turn away from bourbon. In 1969 bourbon had been the most popular drink in America, with Jim Beam a top seller; by 1974, bourbon sales were falling, and in 1980 the trend away from so-called "brown goods" was clear. But though overall bourbon consumption fell, Jim Beam's sales continued to increase. In 1983, for example, though bourbon sales overall fell six percent, the Jim Beam brand managed to post a modest 2.5 percent growth. Nevertheless, Beam's management acted to capitalize on the American market's growing taste for lighter, more moderate liquors. New advertising displayed Jim Beam as a mixer by picturing the bourbon bottle surrounded by cocktail ingredients such as orange juice and tonic water. Other ads showed young drinkers socializing. Lane Barnett, vice president of marketing for Jim Beam, remarked in a 1985 interview in *Advertising Age*, "We target those old, infamous yuppies. It hurts my teeth to use that word, but yuppies are willing to buy premium products." The Beam ads were in strong contrast to the more traditional imagery of its competitors, who stuck with outdoorsy themes of rural landscapes and flocks of wild birds. Beam's marketers, however, were determined to attract a younger consumer base.

After featuring Jim Beam as a mixable liquor, the next step was to sell it in cocktail form. In 1985, after successful test marketing in Australia, the Beam company introduced Jim Beam and cola in a can, under the name Zzzingers. Lemon-lime, ginger ale, and lemonade flavors soon followed. Sales were initially quite good, with 750,000 cases sold in the new product's first six months.

Meanwhile, Jim Beam's parent company experimented with a variety of other cocktail mixtures and new specialty liquors using some of its lesser-known brands. The Beam company marketed the "Danish Merry," a pre-mixed cocktail of Bloody Mary mix and Aalborg brand Akvavit. Another concoction pushed briefly by the company was a yogurt and cognac liqueur called Tresnais. The Beam company also sold a decaffeinated coffee liqueur, Kamora, and a line of flavored schnapps, a mid-1980s "hot" drink.

All this experimentation took an about-face in the 1990s. Taking to heart a marketing forecast that said the 1990s would be a time when people would become disenchanted with the perceived materialism of the previous decade, Beam management agreed on a new "Back to Basics" campaign. Instead of pushing Jim Beam as a new, light, mixable, status drink, the latest campaign implied that Jim Beam bourbon was a product that survived all fads. Accompanying the slogan "You always come back to the basics," the ads followed changes in haircuts, dance steps, and lipstick colors through several decades, depicting the "basic" crew cut, two-step, or simple red color as both the earliest and latest styles. Thus the "basic" look was projected as both old-fashioned and newly in style. Of course, Jim Beam fit this pattern as well. This campaign allowed Jim Beam to appeal to younger consumers, while at the same time assuring older drinkers that their taste for bourbon had always been on target.

Performance Appraisal

Jim Beam brand's total retail sales were close to $350 million in 1990. Jim Beam has remained the top-selling bourbon brand since 1968, and in 1991 it was ranked number six in the United States in distilled spirit sales. Jim Beam maintained its place as a leading brand despite declining interest in bourbon worldwide, and actually increased sales in years when the total liquor market shrank. Though Jim Beam has always been a moderately priced bourbon, skillful advertising lent the brand snob appeal, and this marketing strategy may have contributed to its success.

In 1986, American Brands Co., Jim Beam's ultimate parent company, purchased the liquor business of the National Distillers & Chemical Corps. This made the Beam company America's third largest liquor business, up from ninth place. In 1991 seven popular liquor brands from the Joseph E. Seagram & Son's Co. came under the Beam company's management. This deal gave the Jim Beam Brands Co. the number one spot in the distilled spirits market. The company's increasing clout in the liquor market may also have contributed to the Jim Beam brand's continued rise in sales. But the "back to basics" campaign seems to say the most about Jim Beam's success. Jim Beam is a classic brand from an old recipe, yet it has avoided potentially harmful "old-fashioned" labels. The attraction of bourbon has endured from generation to generation, and the durability of Jim Beam as a leading brand seems quite likely.

Further Reading:

"A Scary Outlook for the Spirit World," *Superbrands*, 1991, p. 61.

Avery, Constance, and Al Cembura, *A Guide to Jim Beam Bottles*, 13th ed., El Cerrito, CA: Cerrito Printing, 1988.

"Beam Account is Back at Weiss," *Advertising Age*, September 21, 1970, p. 3.

"Beam Boosts Bourbon, Family History, Too, In Fall Campaign," *Advertising Age*, September 14, 1959, p. 181.

"Beam's Choice Too Good for Souses, New Campaign Says," *Advertising Age*, October 23, 1967, p. 3.

"Beam to Integrate Holiday Ads with Current Campaign," *Advertising Age*, October 19, 1964, p. 50.

Borders, William, "Uncertain Future for Scotch," *New York Times*, September 19, 1980, p. D1.

"Bourbon and the Balance of Payments," *Forbes*, May 15, 1973, pp. 103-106.

"Carroll Calls Packaging Vital Factor in Beam's 10-Year Climb in Sales, Profits," *Advertising Age*, April 23, 1962, pp. 34-35.

"Distillers Must Cope with a Sobering Future," *Business Week*, May 2, 1983, pp. 110-112.

"For Scotch, Sales Flow Faster," *Business Week*, March 2, 1968, pp. 69-70.

Gooding, Kenneth, "Never Mind the Taste—Feel the Effects," *Financial Times,* March 20, 1974, pp. 28-29.

Jervey, Gay, "Liquor Makers are Mixin' It up With Cocktails," *Advertising Age,* August 26, 1985, p. 1.

"Jim Beam Sets Magazine Drive," *Advertising Age,* Jan. 25, 1965, p. 50.

King, Resa, "American Brands Is Breaking Its Cigarette Habit," *Business Week,* September 14, 1987, pp. 86-94.

"Liquor Sales Drop 4% in '91," *Advertising Age,* March 30, 1992, p. 46.

Marshall, Christy, "Decanters Get National Splash," *Advertising Age,* March 19, 1979, p. 50.

Maxwell, John C. Jr., "Guide to Tippling," *Barron's,* January 11, 1971, pp. 11, 24-25.

McGeehan, Pat, "Beam Expects Success From Its Mixed Results," *Advertising Age,* March 3, 1986, p. 67.

Norris, Eileen, "James Beam Not Resting on Its Bourbon," *Advertising Age,* July 18, 1985, pp. 31-32.

Prestbo, John A., "Bottling Plants Abroad Help Bourbon Makers Boost Foreign Sales," *Wall Street Journal,* January 12, 1965, p. 1.

"Pricing Impairs Liquor Sales," *Advertising Age,* March 19, 1979, pp. 43-44.

Snyder, David, "Beam to Pop Top on Schnapps Cooler Market," *Crain's Chicago Business,* March 10, 1986, p. 8.

"Spirited Gains in Store for James Beam Distilling," *Barron's,* March 15, 1965, p. 31.

Underwood, Elaine, "Back to Bourbon," *Adweek's Marketing Week,* October 14, 1991, p. 12.

—*A. Woodward*

JOHNNIE WALKER®

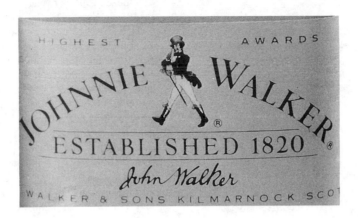

Johnnie Walker blended Scotch whisky is a leading brand in the United States and the best-selling blended Scotch whisky in the world. It is packaged in a rectangular bottle bearing the image of a striding man and is sold in at least five varieties: Red Label, which is a minimum of three years old; Black Label, which is 12 years old; and the increasingly aged Oldest, Premier, Gold Label, and Blue Label. It first gained worldwide prominence following World War II when Scotch became the drink of the rich. During the 1970s, it suffered the effects of a glut or "whisky loch." In the 1980s and early 1990s it regained profit levels when its owner, Guinness PLC, exploited Scotch's cachet as a drink of the rich.

Brand Origins

In 1820, the original John Walker opened a grocery store on King Street in Kilmarnock, in the Ayrshire district of Scotland. Like others of its type, Walker's grocery provided a method by which a woman could obtain spirits without being seen coming out of a bar. Walker traded locally at first but he began to engage in the English trade after 1843 when a railway running from Glasgow via Kilmarnock to the south opened. Over the following decade, that trade grew despite a disastrous flood that almost ruined his business in 1852.

In 1856 Walker's Glasgow-educated son Alexander joined the firm and began to move it into the wholesale whisky business. He sold the product to ships and introduced whisky, whose meaning in Gaelic is "water of life," to English merchants who were in Kilmarnock to buy carpets and tweeds.

Up to the mid-1850s, the Walkers were selling single malt whiskys, each of which was distilled by an independent maker. Soon after Alexander joined the firm, the family instituted the recently invented "vatting" process in which as many as 40 single malt whiskys were blended with neutral grain whiskys to produce a milder product with a more standardized taste. This blended variety became a product of choice and by the mid-1860s the Walkers were producing 100,000 gallons a year. In Scotland it was called Walker's Kilmarnock Whisky; for export it was labeled Old Highland.

Marketing in the Late 1800s

To get Old Highland to foreign ports such as New York or Boston, Alexander joined other Scottish manufacturers who consigned their wares to merchant vessels. The captains of these vessels sailed to various ports and sold the goods at the best prices obtainable and, after retaining a fixed percentage to cover freight and services, remitted the balance to Scottish firms.

For the English market, Alexander opened an office at 3 Crosby Square in London. In the early 1880s, the English were abandoning French brandy and warming up to blended whisky, which they found more palatable since vatting. Alexander took advantage of this new interest and made a grand show of his presence in the capital. He made his sales calls in a specially built carriage drawn by two superb ponies. The pomp of his presence attracted attention and increased the orders he desired.

Changing of the Guard

In 1889 Alexander Walker died and his third son Alexander became head of John Walker and Sons. The younger Alexander had studied law and had learned the whisky trade under the Glasgow distillers and blenders, Robertson and Baxter. In 1890, he hired a local boy named James Stevenson, who soon emerged as an administrative genius and would play a major part in strengthening and expanding Scotch sales. Under Alexander Walker and James Stevenson, the Walker firm continued to grow. They bought independent distilleries to assure supplies, they opened a branch in Birmingham, England in 1897, and in 1907 they moved the London offices to Dunster House, Park Lane.

In 1908, the "Johnnie Walker" brand name came into use. It was created to accompany a poster painted by artist Tom Brown. Brown's poster depicted a striding man who held a cane and wore a top hat, morning coat, and white trousers. That image, along with the slogan "Born 1820, still going strong," still graces Johnnie Walker bottles and has become one of the most successful advertising devices in history. Simultaneous with the advertising campaign, the firm created Johnnie Walker Red Label and Johnnie Walker Black Label, both of which became instant hits.

Between 1908 and the outbreak of World War I, the Johnnie Walker brand expanded very quickly. But while sales boomed, Johnnie Walker and the four other great whisky concerns, Dewar's, Buchanans, Haigs, and Mackies, began to worry about the increasing power of Distillers Company Limited (DCL), which was gradually taking control of Scotland's independent distilleries. In response to the DCL threat, the Big Five, as they were

AT A GLANCE

Johnnie Walker brand of Scotch whisky founded in 1820 in Kilmarnock, Scotland, by John Walker; ownership remained in the Walker family until 1923 when John Walker & Sons, Ltd. went public as a prelude to being acquired by Distillers Company Plc. in 1925; distillers acquired by Guinness plc in 1986.

Performance: Market share—8.29% (third share) for Red, 3.67% for black. *Sales*—$7.6 million.

Advertising: Agency—Smith/Greenland, New York, NY (Johnnie Walker Black); Avrett, Free & Ginsberg, New York, NY (Johnnie Walker Red). *Major campaigns*—Print ads proclaiming, "The richness of Red," and other ads with the tag line, "And he drinks Johnnie Walker."

Addresses: Parent company—Guinness PLC, 39 Portman Square, London, W1H 9HB; phone: 071 486 0288; fax: 071 486 4968.

called, considered amalgamation. Talks began in 1909 but broke down in June of the following year.

War and Aging

At the outbreak of World War I in 1914, Johnnie Walker had become the largest blender and bottler of Scotch whisky in the world. The war itself ended the threat of overproduction since wartime shortages forced the firm to stop all sales of bulk in England and to restrict the sales of certain qualities of bottled whisky.

During the war, Stevenson, who had been tapped for the Ministry of Munitions, convinced British Prime Minister Lloyd George that an excess of cheap whisky was causing an outbreak of public drunkenness. In response, George enacted the Immature Spirits Act, which compelled distillers to keep all whisky in bond for three years. Since this caused shortages, the effect of the act was to triple the price of whisky and make it very profitable.

DCL Takes Over

The war increased the demand for spirits. At the same time it caused heavy losses to independent distilleries which, one by one, sold out to DCL. After the war, low whisky stocks kept barrel sales down and made the bottle the dominant way of selling. In the United States, Prohibition was the means by which Scotch whisky achieved its dominant position of prestige. Scotch was thought by some to have medicinal properties and was thereby, to some extent, an exception to the "Great Experiment." One indication of Americans' increasing taste for the drink was the Scotch-makers' ballooning exports to Canada, the British West Indies, and the Bahamas from which, it is speculated, the whisky was smuggled into the United States.

DCL continued to grow after World War I. Like other whisky executives, Alexander Walker and James Stevenson felt a growing pressure to join the expanding amalgamation. As a prelude to this in 1923, they floated John Walker & Sons Ltd. as a public company. Then in 1925 they joined the other four members of the "big five," a subsidiary of Distillers Company Limited.

Restrictions and Postwar Boom

Johnnie Walker prospered during the remainder of the 1920s and 1930s. With the outbreak of World War II in 1939, however, pressure began to build to curtail distilling. In 1941 the British government prohibited patent-still distilling and the following year it prohibited all distilling. This condition did not end with the war. It was not until 1949 that the government allowed full-scale distilling and not until 1953 that it ceased rationing supplies of grain to the distillers. In fact, by the time John Walker & Sons was able to resume full scale production, the United States was in the midst of a postwar economic boom in which Scotch whisky was embraced as a sign of success. In this climate Johnnie Walker Black Label emerged as a personal favorite among those who appreciated premium quality products. Back in Scotland, the booming export business necessitated the expansion of John Walker's Hill Street premises at Kilmarnock where, in 1955, the company completed a new integrated blending, bottling, warehousing, and cooperage complex.

By the early 1960s Scotch whisky had become the paramount force on global whisky markets and Johnnie Walker had become first in world-wide whisky sales. But while Scotch's cachet and Johnnie Walker's quality had brought it to the top of the distilled beverages market, Distillers was doing little to coordinate the promotion of the product. According to *Forbes,* the company "largely left marketing to hundreds of importers around the world."

While sales continued to grow, by 1963 Johnnie Walker faced stiff competition both from brands such as Cutty Sark and J&B, who benefited from the trend toward "lighter" whiskys, and from low price importers such as Inver House and Highland who shipped their product in bulk and had it bottled in the United States.

Despite competitors, in the late 1960s Distillers was confident enough of Johnnie Walker's future to build a new blending plant on a 32-acre site at Barleith, which is near Kilmarnock. The facility's vats were the largest of their type in the world. The company kept bottling and transportation at Hill Street but upgraded it so that bottles of many different sizes could be mechanically filled, corked, and labeled with different labels for different markets.

By this time, 85 percent of all Johnnie Walker Scotch was being exported. Much of it went to the United States where Canada Dry and then Somerset Importers Ltd. distributed it. In the mid- and late 1960s, these distributors supported the brand with campaigns such as "the luck of the Scotch" for Red Label and "Put your friends on 'Black' list" and "A small way of paying yourself back for all the years of struggle it took to get where you are," for Black Label.

The "Whisky Loch"

Distillers and the other Scotch makers had banked on regular increases of Scotch consumption in the United States. What they did not bank on was a marketing onslaught from American whisky and what *Forbes* called "the demise of country club America's Scotch habits." Faced with this strong home-grown challenge, Scotch's share of the American market slumped in the mid-1970s. To make matters worse, excess capacity produced a glut that insiders called the "whisky loch."

To keep profits up, Distillers sold its surplus through cut price, private-label brands. This practice undermined the price of all

Scotch whiskys (the real price of Scotch halved in the United States between 1970 and 1980) and endangered its status as the most elegant—and profitable—of liquors aside from cognac.

Nor was the United States the only place where Scotch (and therefore Johnnie Walker) was in trouble. Distillers had maintained much higher prices for distributors that exported to Europe than it had for those who sold in the United Kingdom. In 1978, when the European Community found this practice against the rules of the Common Market, Distillers threatened to pull the brand from U.K. shelves in order to maintain Red Label's estimated 75 percent share of the European market.

While Black Label remained profitable and, according to a March, 1978 article in *Business Week,* Red Label continued to account for perhaps 15 percent of the 70 million cases of Scotch sold worldwide, Distillers and Johnnie Walker seemed to be in decline. Between 1980 and 1984, Red Label lost 2.2 percent in world market share despite campaigns such as Somerset Importers Ltd.'s "Turn to Red."

Recalling the era in 1990, Robert Heller of *Management Today,* wrote, "At Distillers, the cardinal sins were, first, complacent failure to react to competition: second, unsound decisions when the competitive inroads became so severe as to force belated reaction: third, innovative inertia which missed opportunity after opportunity: and finally, lack of cohesion that redoubled the impact of these defects. Distillers became a classic example of reverse synergy—the process which makes the whole worth less than its parts."

Guinness Takes Over

Given this situation, the company did not seem capable of reviving the brand. In 1986, that job was handed to Guinness PLC, the conglomerate that produces the famous stout and the *Guinness Book of World Records.* That year, Guinness acquired Distillers in a $4.1 billion stock swap. Subsequently Guinness head Ernest Saunders was charged with manipulating Guinness' stock price to increase the value of the bid. In the wake of the scandal, Saunders left and in 1987 was replaced by veteran marketer Anthony Tennant, who had previously headed the liquor section of Grand Metropolitan PLC, which owned Smirnoff Vodka and J&B Scotch.

Tennant moved swiftly to revive the fortunes of Distillers' stable of brands. He moved order-taking to a central office in Glasgow and took control of distribution. With Anthony Greener, the Guinness group managing director, he raised the price of Johnnie Walker Black Label in a general move toward emphasizing the luxury value of premium brands. "People are drinking less by volume and more by value, and that will go on," Greener told *Forbes* in 1989. "What we're doing is much more akin to selling perfume than selling fast-moving consumer goods."

In the United States, a $25 million advertising campaign that featured women saying things like "He thinks it's fine for me to make more than he does. And he drinks Johnnie Walker," helped boost Red Label into the third position and Black Label into the ninth position in the Scotch race.

In the Far East the company played to status-conscious businesses and introduced three pricey new varieties, Johnnie Walker Gold Label at $70 a bottle, Johnnie Walker Premier at $85 a bottle, and Johnnie Walker's Oldest (Blue Label in the United States), which included single malt whiskys that had been aged up to 60 years, at $140 a bottle in duty-free shops.

The Future

Having turned to an approach akin to the perfume business in which the method is to sell status, the marketers of Johnnie Walker seem to have found a way to increase profits in a shrinking market. As Anthony Greener told *Financial World,* "We can say we are pleased to have turned the corner."

Further Reading:

Brander, Michael, *The Original Scotch,* New York: Clarkson N. Potter, Inc., 1975.

Cavanagh, John and Frederick F. Clairmonte, *Alcoholic Beverages: Dimensions of Corporate Power,* New York, St. Martin's Press, 1985.

Daiches, David, *Scotch Whisky: Its Past and Present,* New York: MacMillan Company, 1969.

"Distillers Co. Fights Back," *Fortune,* October, 1963.

"Distillers Co.: Price Problems Make Johnnie Walker Red Leave Home," *Business Week,* March 13, 1978.

Forget, James, "Scotch: Fashioned for Happier Times," *Advertising Age,* July 27, 1981.

"Guilty, in the Guinness Trial," *Economist,* September 1, 1990.

Heller, Robert, "Hard Core Reform," *Management Today,* November, 1990.

Jobson's Liquor Hand-Book, 1992.

Lockhart, Sir Robert Bruce, *Scotch: The Whisky of Scotland in Fact and Story,* London: Putnam & Company, 1981.

Marcom, John Jr., "The House of Guinness," *Forbes,* June 12, 1989.

Maremont, Mark, "Ernest Saunders Markets His Innocence," *Business Week,* August 14, 1989.

McDowall, R. J. S., *The Whiskies of Scotland,* New York: New Amsterdam, 1986.

Prokesch, Steven, "Guinness Takes a Luxury Tack," *New York Times,* May 10, 1992.

Reir, Sharon, "Getting Scotch Off the Rocks," *Financial World,* August 6, 1991.

Stead, Deborah, "Jury in Guinness Case Is Told about a Scheme," *New York Times,* February 19, 1990.

—Jordan Wankoff

JOSE CUERVO®

The origins of Tequila Cuervo, the top-selling tequila in the United States, can be traced back to Mexico's first millennium A.D., when Aztec Indians made beverages from cactus-like plants for their ritual ceremonies. Tequila is named after a town near Guadalajara, settled by a tribe of local Indians that settled the village in 1656 and have since vanished. Though the drink has evolved enormously over the centuries, it has retained much of the mystique of its ancient Mexican origins.

The drink's mooring in Mexico's local history has not hindered its widespread growth and progressive change. A steady export of tequila into the United States began after World War II. This trade had flourished by the 1990s, as the United States, the world leader in tequila consumption, imported 85 percent of Mexico's production. In 1964, Heublein Inc., became the sole U.S. distributor for Grupo Cuervo, S.A., and Cuervo has remained the market leader ever since, accounting for 45 percent of category sales in 1991. From 1979 to 1989, tequila sales doubled in the United States, spawning new markets that range from Mexican food accompaniments to mixers. In addition to standard "silver" tequila—most popular for drink mixes—Cuervo introduced two premium labels of variations of the drink: Cuervo Especial (Gold), and 1800, an optimally aged sipping tequila. In 1992, Cuervo also introduced various value-added drinks, including Jose Cuervo Margaritas. The drink that was once commonly referred to as "cactus juice" became a highly marketed and sophisticated spirit with growing sales, despite a decline in the alcoholic beverages industry at large.

Early History

Tequila can be traced as far back as the first millennium A.D., when the Aztecs processed a cactus-like plant (later called the maguey by conquering Spaniards). From the maguey—which furnished sweeteners, textiles, paper, needles, and building materials—the Aztecs also extracted juice, which they fermented into pulque, a milky beverage used in religious ceremonies. The Spaniards distilled the indigenous drink in their stills to create a brandy-like spirit that they called mezcal. Mezcal is made not from maguey, but from blue agave, a different plant genus, but tequila is still considered its direct relative.

These precursors did not disappear when tequila was finally developed. In Mexico City, pulquerias still thrive, dispensing pulque that, like beer, is fermented but not distilled. Mezcal is also a common drink, particularly in Oaxaca state. It resembles tequila, though it is considerably harsher in character, as attested by British author Malcolm Lowry's description of mezcal as "ten yards of barbed wire." And mezcal can be distinguished from its later relative by the much mystified, though generally innocuous, agave caterpillar that is often transplanted from its maguey habitat to the confines of a mezcal bottle.

The Cuervos, the "first family" of tequila, developed the drink in the mid-18th century. On November 2, 1758, Jose Antonio de Cuervo was awarded land by the king of Spain for his management of the church in the parish of Tequila, which is in the Mexican state of Jalisco. The property included a small mezcal wine refinery, "La Martinena," and a stand of blue agave. By the end of the 18th century, the drink was popular with local miners and other members of the working class, gaining added popularity with a surge in tequila taverns in the region. During several periods of government prohibition of distilled spirits, the industry went underground, but in the late 1790s, after 11 years of official prohibition, repeal was granted with government regulation. In 1795, Don Jose Maria Guadalupe de Cuervo was granted the first legal permission to make mezcal wine in the District of Tequila, continuing the tradition started by his family a generation earlier. Not until the late 19th century did this type of mezcal wine become commonly called tequila, referring to the dry, acidic, silicate-based soil near and around the town of Tequila, the optimal growing spot for the blue agave used to make the drink. In fact, in the mid-19th century, the official drink was called *vino mezcal de Guadalajara,* mainly because the largest producer, Tequila Cuervo, S.A., was based in that city.

Tequila Manufacture

Despite shifts in name, there has been little change in the process of producing tequila. The first step is harvesting the blue agave, an ornamental plant of the lily family, *genus amaryllis.* The plant is best described as a bulbous heart radiating a corona of sword-like leaves edged with needle-sharp thorns. Agaves may grow as tall as six feet, with a similar diameter. The root structure, however, seldom reaches deeper than a foot beneath the surface of the silicate soils in which it grows. After a relatively long maturation of eight to ten years, the agave's heart, or *piña,* sprouts a single rapid-growing stalk called a *quixote,* which, if permitted to grow, will flower after several months, dispense pollen, and signal the impending death of the plant. For tequila production, the heart

AT A GLANCE

Jose Cuervo brand of tequila officially founded on November 2, 1758, when the king of Spain awarded Jose Antonio de Cuervo land in Tequila, a village in the Mexican state of Jalisco; property included a small mezcal wine factory and a substantial stand of blue agave, the plant distilled to make the drink; in 1795, Jose Maria Guadalupe de Cuervo was granted the first exclusive permit from the government of New Galicia to produce *vino mezcal de Tequila*—mezcal wine from the town of Tequila; in 1964, Heublein Inc., began U.S. distribution of tequila for Tequila Cuervo, S.A., one of the leading Mexican producers.

Performance: *Market share*—46.77% (top share) of tequila category. *Sales*—2,080,000 cases.

Major competitor: Tequila Sauza.

Advertising: *Agency*—Grybauskas & Partners, New York, NY.

Addresses: *U.S. Distributor*—Heublein Inc., P.O. Box 388, Munson Road, Farmington, CT 06032; phone: (203) 231-5000; fax: (203) 674-8428. *Ultimate parent company*—Grand Metropolitan PLC, 20 St. James's Square, London SW1Y 4RR England; phone: 071 321 6000; fax: 071 321 6001.

of the agave must be cut out and processed just before the quixote sprouts, before the plant's sap is consumed by the flowery shoot. Field workers, called *mescaleros,* slash away the spiked *pencas* (leaves) with machetes and then rely on long-handled tools to detach the roots. The dislodged piñas, weighing up to 200 pounds, are then transported to processing plants.

Steam-cooking is the first step in processing the agave hearts. In the past, distillers excavated special holes in which the *piñas* were buried with coals and wet earth, left partially open for ventilation. Such cooking holes were eventually replaced with large brick steam ovens, where the *piñas* are heated for 48 hours, followed by 8 hours of cooling. They are then conveyed to a hydraulic crushing mill, where the sugars are separated from the fibers, producing *aguamiel*, or honey water. In fermentation vats, yeast is added to the aguamiel to produce a must in which the yeast converts sugar to alcohol over the course of several days. The resultant mash is then piped into copper retorts, called *ollas*, where it is distilled twice to produce water-clear, 150-proof "white" tequila, which is diluted with demineralized water to 80-proof and exported as standard silver tequila. Some reserves are aged for two to six months in redwood tanks to produce "gold" tequila—called a *reposado*—like Cuervo Especial. Premium varieties are aged in oak whiskey barrels for a stay between one and three years. Cuervo 1800 is one such *añejo* tequila.

Tequila in the United States

The arrival of the railroad to Guadalajara around the beginning of the 20th century also marked the transformation of tequila from a local beverage to a major export commodity. From the outset, the United States was the thirstiest customer. During World War II, the U.S. market surged to unprecedented levels: tequila exports, at 6,000 gallons in 1940, rose to 1.2 million by 1945.

But consistent growth did not continue without careful planning and new marketing strategies. At the war's end, tequila exports plummeted until, by 1948, shipments reached an all-time low of 2,500 gallons. In response, the first tequila producers'

association, Camara Regional de la Industria Tequilera, was established in 1949 in Guadalajara. It passed the first modern laws governing the industry. In 1964 Heublein Inc. of Hartford, Connecticut, made an exclusive agreement with Grupo Cuervo, S.A., to market Jose Cuervo brand tequila in the United States. By 1986, according to Camara statistics, Mexico produced approximately 47 million liters (13 million gallons) of tequila, of which 68 percent was exported to over 70 countries. The United States alone consumed 90 percent of Mexico's exported tequila. In 1988, John C. Maxwell, Jr., of Wheat First Securities reported to *Advertising Age* that Jose Cuervo tequila had a 14.9 percent increase to 1.59 million cases that year. And in 1990, Heublein sources recorded a 1.5 percent rise in total U.S. tequila consumption—to 4 million cases—despite a general malaise in spirit sales.

Tequila Control

Increases in production and export business also increased the need for regulation and control. In May of 1973 the Republic of Mexico officially laid claim to the name "tequila." And in 1978, the government established a decree controlling production of all tequila. Using its standards laboratory and border inspectors, the Tequila Chamber was to assure that all tequila leaving the country had met its specific requirements. These included four main stipulations: 1) that only sugars from the agave tequilana Weber, blue variety, be used; 2) that agaves for tequila must be harvested primarily in the state of Jalisco (and in parts of the states of Michoacan and Nayarit, in west-central Mexico, and in the state of Tamaulipas); 3) that aguamiel must be distilled twice; and 4) that the final product must be produced from no less than 51 percent reducing sugars obtained from the cooking of the agave. These regulations helped maintain consistency in a growing export market.

But while tequila had taken up residence north of the border, matters did not look as bright in the Mexico of the 1980s. By 1982, domestic consumption declined in tandem with the Mexican recession. According to a 1991 report of the American Chamber of Commerce of Mexico, agave growers suffered from the artificially low market prices and lack of financing that racked the whole agricultural industry. Consequently, many agave fields were abandoned and several producers went out of business. Domestic consumption decreased to 13 million liters by 1986, according to Luna Zamora, author of a 1992 study *The History of Tequila.* Despite productive efforts at increasing exports and a particularly aggressive marketing campaign in the United States, the industry had still not fully recovered by the early 1990s. Agave prices, for example, increased from 12.50 pesos per kilo in 1984 to 740 pesos per kilo in 1991, figures that were further complicated by price controls of the government's anti-inflation pact. Brewers' profits fell dramatically.

Like many other tequila companies, the three biggest producers, Tequila Cuervo, Tequila Orendain de Jalisco, and Tequila Sauza, offered financing to farmers to revitalize the fields. Prohibited by Mexican law to directly invest in the countryside, the companies expanded on already existent plans, such as providing property owners with seeds and helping them clear land for new cultivation, according to Tequila Chamber president Jorge Berrueta. By the 1990s, domestic demand had rebounded, and exports sustained growth at 15 percent a year, Christine MacDonald reported in *Business Mexico.*

Critics of company financing programs, however, argued that the agave supply could be artificially raised to force down market prices. Luna Zamora noted that brewers controlled about 70 percent of the agave harvest, a situation that threatened to throw farmers out of the market all over again. Nestor Arana Garcia, president of the Regional Tequila Growers Union, accused brewers of trying to control market price by controlling agave production. And disgruntled growers accused tequila makers of sidestepping the rule minimizing agave content to 51 percent a bottle.

New Tequila Image

Over the years, big companies have launched aggressive marketing campaigns in order to spur export demand for tequila. One of the earliest initiatives was to change the long-standing image of tequila as firewater suited only to rough cowboys and Mexican bandits. The agave itself fell prey to this image, as it was named after the Greek goddess Agave, who tore her son to pieces during a fit of inebriation. Strictures of the 1940 Tequila Chamber helped foster an image of a refined drink with stringently controlled qualities of color, flavor, chemical composition, scent, and gradation. Subsequently, every batch passed a test by a panel of *tequileros,* discriminating masters of the drink. Though tequila had gained prestige by the 1990s, it still lagged behind other premium spirits. "The prestige isn't like cognac or champagne, but it should be," said Jorge Camacho Ornelas, president of the Tequila Industry Regional Chamber. And Guillermo Romo de la Pena, president of Tequila Herradura, suggested in a 1993 issue of *Mexico's Expansion* magazine that "the agave should be as dignified as the grape." Agreeing with these principles, Cuervo introduced and heavily marketed a new line of so-called *añejo,* or aged, sipping tequila called Cuervo 1800, in addition to the *joven abocado,* a medium-dry variation called Cuervo Gold.

Marketing Strategies

For companies like Cuervo, introducing premium tequilas was just one of many broader marketing strategies used to show their wares. In addition to promoting tequila in general, Cuervo had to distinguish its particular blend, especially against a surge of smaller Mexican distillers exporting bulk tequila, often of inferior quality, with obscure labels and low prices. Cuervo stressed strict quality controls, imposed by tequileros with refined organoleptic, or sense-tuned, tastes. Cuervo also priced itself strategically, above cheaper grades of tequila, but below competing spirits; a fifth of top tequila generally cost less than $15, while a comparable Scotch often costs more than $30. Grand Metropolitan PLC's 1988 acquisition of Heublein Inc. through its wine and spirits arm, International Distiller & Vintners (IDV), added additional financial support to Cuervo. By the end of that year, promotional spending on Cuervo Especial rose 80 percent to $4.1 million, and Jose Cuervo spending rose 14 percent to $4.2 million, according to a September 1988 *Advertising Age* report. In March of 1991, Heublein/IDV's Mexican affiliate, Lanceros S.A. de CV, took a minority stake in Jose Cuervo, S.A., thereby strengthening "the long-standing relationship between IDV Heublein and Cuervo," according to George J. Bull, chair of IDV. Bull also said it would allow IDV to expand distribution of Jose Cuervo tequilas in selected markets.

Cuervo also depended on lifestyle marketing and cross-merchandising to support its brand. By the 1970s, unsolicited publicity had already done some of the work: the Rolling Stones and the

Eagles sang about Tequila Sunrises. Other references included Jimmy Buffet's "Margaritaville," Bobby Bare's "Pour Me Another Tequila, Sheila," and Shelly West's "Jose Cuervo, You Are a Friend of Mine." In addition, Mexican food was a rising fad. With its Cuervo line in an advantageous position, Heublein ventured outside of liquor to cross-merchandise in food. In 1990, it teamed up with Tio Sancho in a California program called Fiesta de Mexico, expanding to other local food suppliers during the year. Cuervo also ran a series of in-store promotions tied to Mexican holidays like Cinco de Mayo as well as some American feast days, and it advertised on billboards and in magazines like *Details* and *Rolling Stone.* The company sponsored both amateur and professional volleyball tournaments on beaches nationwide. In 1990 Cuervo Gold Crown awarded $450,000 in prize money at three events in Boulder, Colorado, Santa Cruz, California, and Clearwater Beach, Florida. A Cuervo-sponsored amateur volleyball tournament held at 14 locations nationwide culminated in a $20,000 championship at Lauderdale-by-the-Sea, Florida. Cuervo brought various competitions to the 1991 ski slopes of the Northeast, organizing snow volleyball, margarita lime tosses, and other activities. In Carson City, Nevada, Cuervo promoted "The World's Sixth Annual International Whistle Off," featuring virtuoso whistler Francisco Hernandes of Tequila, Mexico, who twittered at the annual event from 1978 to 1983.

Margarita Mania

Perhaps the greatest selling point for Cuervo was the craze for margaritas, drinks made with lime juice, orange liqueur, tequila, and optional crushed ice. Virtually unknown in the 1970s, the margarita became the third most popular drink served in bars and restaurants by 1989, and the first, along with gin and tonic, by 1991. Michael J. McDermott remarked in a *Food and Beverage Marketing* article that "tequila is more associated with margarita-slurping yuppies than with bikers and cowboys." Capitalizing on this wave of margarita drinkers and margarita machine buyers, Heublein introduced Jose Cuervo Margarita Mix to bring the drink into the home. In May of 1992, Heublein signed a licensing agreement with TGI Friday's Inc., an international chain of popular theme restaurants, introducing a new line of TGI Friday's Authentic Frozen Drinks. Gold Margarita, along with other restaurant specialties, was made available for home consumption. To cap off its drink campaign, Heublein also began restaurant and bar distribution of "The Cuervo Chronicles," a guide to premium tequila-based drinks available on premises. Examples included the tequila sunrise, bloody Maria, cactus flower, Jose Cuervo spike, and others.

Performance Assessment

Cuervo tequila managed to grow appreciably in a liquor industry otherwise troubled by the health and social concerns of the 1980s and 1990s, such as the stringent new laws against driving under the influence of alcohol, strong anti-alcohol lobbying groups such as Mothers Against Drunk Drivers (MADD), and increased so-called sin taxes on alcohol. The Distilled Spirits Council of the United States (DISCUS) estimated in 1991 that sales had been declining at a rate of about 2 percent for a decade. Yet Jose Cuervo tequila managed to grow 3 to 4 percent a year. This growth engendered a strong outlook for the future. And such an outlook, in turn, prompted Dave Thatcher, branch manager of a Quality Beverage outlet in San Antonio, Texas, to remark that "tequila is still in its infancy." Although this infant is at least

1,200 years old, if not older, it promises to be around a good deal longer.

Further Reading:

Balzer, Robert Lawrence, "Entertaining: Spirit of the Southwest," *Los Angeles Times,* July 10, 1988, p. 48.

Delson, Jennifer, "Distillers Duck Barroom Brawl," *Calgary Herald,* February 12, 1993, p. E8.

Elliott, Stuart, "Grybauskas Receives Heublein's Cuervo," *New York Times,* November 30, 1992, p. D9.

"Grand Met Unit to Take Stake in Mexican Drink Firm," *Reuters,* March 1, 1991.

"Heublein Acquires Marketing Rights to TGI Friday's Authentic Frozen Drinks," *PR Newswire,* May 1, 1992.

"Heublein International Whistle Off," PR Newswire, September 23, 1983.

"Jose Cuervo Tequila," press kit, Hartford: Heublein Inc., 1993.

MacDonald, Christine, "Exports and New Financing Schemes Keep Tequila Flowing," *Business Mexico,* July, 1991.

McDermott, Michael J. "Jose Cuervo vs. the World," *Food and Beverage Marketing,* June, 1991, p. 12.

Moore, Paula, "Tequila Craze Gives City a Shot in Arm," *San Antonio Business Journal,* V. 5, No. 5, p. 1.

"Tequila-makers Seek to Distill Prestige," *Chicago Tribune,* February 21, 1993, p. W12.

Zamora, Luna R., *The History of Tequila: Its Region and Its Men,* México, D.F.: Consejo Nacional para la Cultura y las Artes, Direccion General de Publicaciones, 1991.

—Kerstan Cohen

KAHLUA®

Kahlua coffee liqueur is the best-selling imported liqueur in the United States, holding a 36 percent share of the market. Produced by Kahlua S.A. in the northern Mexican town of Ramos Arizpe and distributed in the United States and Canada by Hiram Walker & Sons, Inc. (a division of Hiram Walker-Allied Vintners), this coffee-flavored liqueur has been consistently marketed not just as a drink in and of itself, but as an ingredient in after-dinner cordials and many desserts.

It is difficult to pinpoint a date when Kahlua liqueur was first bottled. We do, however, know the origin of the oldest bottle known. Believed to have been produced around 1937, this particular bottle was discovered in 1988 in the wine cellar of a food and spirit establishment in Pasadena, California. The liqueur was distilled and bottled by Jose de Miguel Vincent in Mexico, and imported by Hulse Importers in San Francisco. However, at that time the majority of Kahlua was imported through Los Angeles wholesaler Alfred Hart.

Although several importers distributed Kahlua in the United States during the 1930s and 1940s, it was not a widely known or sampled liqueur until the early 1950s when Jules Berman, an entrepreneur well known to many in Southern California industry circles, came across Kahlua on a trip to Mexico. He became so enamored with Kahlua's unusual taste that in 1951 he bought the rights to bottle and import the liqueur from the Schenley Co., a distributor of distilled spirits in Dallas, Texas. Under Berman, U.S. sales of Kahlua rose from 1,200 to 60,000 cases annually. In 1965, Berman sold the brand to Hiram Walker and Sons, who began marketing Kahlua through its subsidiary Maidstone Wine and Spirits. Hiram Walker was purchased by Allied-Lyons in 1986, and its name was changed to Hiram Walker-Allied Vintners.

Production and Manufacturing

The coffee beans in Kahlua come from the state of Veracruz along the Gulf of Mexico. In the production of Kahlua, the beans are first roasted and then ground before they are poured into a large drum. The drum rotates while gas jets below heat its contents, gradually turning the once green beans a rich brown color. The newly roasted beans are then transferred to another large container where they are mixed and cooled while being sprayed by cool water. The beans are then ground twice before they reach the desired consistency for brewing.

At this point, a sample of the bean is taken to the lab for brewing and further quality control tests. If the beans are found acceptable, approximately 480 kilos are transferred into a pressure cooker above a large stainless steel tank, in which a coffee concentrate is formed by letting the water in the lower tank percolate upwards. The concentrate is then placed in another tank for cooling. Once cooled, it is poured into another container where alcohol (distilled from sugar cane), flavorings, and a portion of syrup are added.

After passing through a filtration system, the mixture is left to settle, and then is checked for clarity, density, proof, and color. The mixture is then loaded into tanker-trucks that have been inspected for sanitary purposes and, when needed, steam cleaned. Once loaded, samples are extracted from each shipment and sent to laboratories in Livonia, Michigan. Upon passing the final tests, the mixture is sent to Fort Smith, Arkansas, where the final portion of syrup is added and the liqueur is bottled for the U.S. and Canadian markets.

Kahlua S.A.

From the moment a visitor steps inside the Kahlua production plant in Ramos Arizpe, the flavor of the region is evident. The lobby is tastefully trimmed with Mexican ornaments and artifacts. In the lunchroom is more of the same: fringed tablecloths and hand-painted ceramic dishes. A mariachi band composed of Kahlua employees sometimes plays for other workers during breaks. According to a Kahlua spokesperson, the atmosphere at Kahlua S.A. is like one big happy family; the employees are able to do their work but are also able to enjoy themselves.

Early Marketing

In the early 1950s Kahlua was averaging sales of only about 1,200 cases per year until Berman bought the rights to bottle and import the liqueur for $50,000 from the Schenley Co. He began the first real promotional campaign for Kahlua, touting it as more than just a liqueur. He marketed it as a highly mixable product, pushing recipe ideas such as Kahlua over ice cream and Kahlua and coffee. Berman also invented the Black Russian, a combination of vodka and Kahlua that grew to become a standard at bars. In just over 10 years, annual sales of Kahlua reached 60,000 cases.

AT A GLANCE

Kahlua brand of liqueur founded by Kahlua S.A., in the northern Mexican town of Ramos Arizpe, and distributed in the U.S. and Canada by Hiram Walker & Sons, Inc. (a division of Hiram Walker-Allied Vintners); rights to bottle and import Kahlua purchased by Jules Berman in the 1950s, then by Maidstone Wine & Spirits, a subsidiary of Hiram Walker and Sons, in 1965; Hiram Walker purchased by Allied-Lyons in 1986.

Performance: *Market share*—36% of Imported Cordials/Liquors Competitive Case Sales (largest share of market). *Sales*—1.76 million 9-ml. cases.

Advertising: *Agency*—Eisaman, Johns, and Laws, Inc., Chicago, IL. *Major campaign*—"Do Something Delicious" series of full-page magazine advertisements promoting Kahlua as a mixer to make many drinks like Kahlua and coffee, Kahlua and cream, and the Kahlua White Russian.

Addresses: *Parent company*—Kahlua S.A., Ramos Arizpe, Mexico. *U.S. distributor*—Hiram Walker & Sons, Inc., P.O. Box 33006, Detroit, MI 48232-33006; phone: (313) 965-6611. *Ultimate parent company*—Hiram Walker-Allied Vintners, Kilver Street, Shepton Mallet, Somerset, BA4 5ND, England.

Berman had strong interest in Latin American culture and, by the time he purchased Kahlua, he had assembled an impressive collection of terra cotta statues from the pre-Columbian era. Recognizing the allure of these figures and the "south-of-the-border" mystique they created, Berman began incorporating them into magazine ads and tabletop tents. Soon, the "Kahlua statues" became almost as well known as the liqueur. Berman's collection toured the United States and was shown at such prestigious museums as the Art Institute of Chicago, the Metropolitan Museum of Art, and the Los Angeles County Museum.

In the early 1970s, a little over five years after Hiram Walker bought Kahlua from Berman and began distributing it through its Maidstone Wine and Spirits unit, Kahlua's marketing program went into full gear. Maidstone hired Los Angeles ad agency Eisaman, Johns, and Laws, Inc.. While advertisers of Kahlua go to great lengths to ensure that consumers have as many uses for the liqueur as possible, they also aim to provide the public with a consistent and conspicuous product identity. Very little of Kahlua's image has changed over the years. Even the pre-Columbian statues from Berman's collection continue to appear in magazine ads.

The 1937 bottle found in the basement in Pasadena is almost identical to bottles found on store shelves in the 1990s. One interesting difference is that the older bottle depicts a turbaned man sitting below a Moorish archway. ("Kahlua" is slang in Arabic for coffee, and some people speculate that the liqueur was introduced to Mexico by Turks or Moroccans.) At some point, the turbaned man on the label was replaced by a man with a sombrero, the Moorish town in the background was modified slightly to resemble a Mexican town, and a second label bearing the inscription, "Imported from sunny Mexico" appeared just below the bottle neck.

Continuing the advertising tradition started by Berman, Eisaman, Johns, and Laws began creating ads promoting the standard Black Russian and Kahlua and coffee as well as newer drinks such as Kahlua and cream and the White Russian, a mixture of Kahlua,

cream, and vodka. "Our notion was really to take advantage of the brand's mixability," said agency president Dean Laws in 1990. "We've always been careful to present its uses as opposed to the brand itself."

The agency's marketing approach has consistently been to expand on this concept. The company began promoting Kahlua as a culinary ingredient in the early 1970s and developed a recipe book that included Kahlua in recipes for such diverse foods as Cornish game hens, chile, and banana cake. Magazine ads with tags like, "Do something delicious," or "Everything it touches turns delicious," promoted well-known combinations such as Kahlua and coffee or Kahlua and cream. Copy at the bottom of the advertisement provided an address where one could write to obtain a free recipe booklet. In a 20-year period, numerous booklets and over 200 drink recipes using Kahlua have been published.

Performance Appraisal

Overall sales of alcohol dropped 22 percent during the 1980s as consumer attitudes towards alcohol consumption grew more conservative. During that time, however, Kahlua's sales grew 17 percent to 1.7 million cases a year, and by 1984 Kahlua led the imported cordial category with a 9 percent market share. Industry analysts credited the decision to market Kahlua as a dessert ingredient and not simply as an alcoholic beverage as the primary factor

The oldest known bottle of Kahlua is said to date back to 1937.

in its success. Another reason for its success, said Laws in a 1986 *Marketing & Media Decisions* article, is Kahlua's coffee flavor, a taste, he said, Americans are "virtually weaned on." Cordial and liqueur consumption peaked in 1986, with 18.9 million 9-liter cases sold. Kahlua continuously led the market, with sales hovering around 1.7 million cases.

In 1989, with sales of 1.4 million cases, Kahlua held a 41 percent share of the imported cordial and liqueur market. Kahlua far outsold the number two imported cordial, Bailey's Irish Cream, which held a 24 percent market share. The following year, Kahlua sales rose 9 percent. However, in 1991, as overall sales of imported cordials and liqueurs dropped 21 percent, sales of Kahlua also declined.

Also that year, a direct competitor to Kahlua was introduced. Hoping to benefit from the trend toward physical fitness that hit the United States in the 1980s, Spirits International introduced Sweet 'N Low Coffee Liqueur, a beverage with a taste similar to Kahlua, but with 50 percent less calories. After obtaining the Sweet 'N Low license from the Cumberland Packing Corporation of Brooklyn, Spirits International introduced the product in regional markets in September of 1991. A 750-milliliter bottle with a small recipe booklet hanging from its neck asserted its position on liquor store shelves. The booklet contained recipes for such drinks as the "Skinny Black Russian." A print campaign by Georgopoulis/L.A. with the slogan "Lighten up your spirits" further enticed the health-conscious consumer. The new liqueur was offered at a price $2 to $3 lower than the price of Kahlua per bottle, providing an even stronger selling platform for the new drink.

Although Kahlua sales grew 5 percent in 1992 to capture 36 percent of the market, its share was being threatened by both "look-alike" brands and the growing popularity of imported cordials such as Bailey's Irish Cream and Grand Marnier. Bailey's Irish Cream held the number two position with a 23 percent market share. That same year, sales of Grand Marnier grew 97 percent, propelling it into the number three position with an 11 percent market share. Kahlua did maintain the lead market share in 1992, but its sales of 1.4 million cases were significantly below 1984 sales of 1.7 million cases, due to the strong performances of other players in the imported liqueur market and to declining consumption of alcohol and other economic factors.

Since the 1950s Kahlua has benefited from a unique and consistent product image. Its market position has rarely been challenged. However, Kahlua might be facing some unexpected battles in the 1990s as similar products emerge in the marketplace and overall consumption of alcohol—and liqueurs in particular—declines.

Further Reading:

"Brand Reports 129: Brandies, Cordials, Liqueurs," *Marketing & Media Decisions,* January 1986, Vol. 21, No. 1. p. 102.

Darling, Juanita, "For 28 Years, Woman Has Been the Cream in Kahlua's Coffee," *Los Angeles Times,* July, 22, 1990, p. D1.

"Hiram Walker & Sons Absorbs Maidstone Wine & Spirits," *Impact,* June 1, 1991, p. 26.

Jobeson's Liquor Handbook, 1991, p. 129.

Jobeson's Wine & Spirits Industry Marketing, 1991, p. 126.

"Kahlua Pours It On," *Advertising Age,* October 10, 1988, p. 24.

"Kahlua Toasts Labeler—Productivity Up 33%," *Packaging,* February 1988, Vol. 33, No. 2, p. 72.

"The Story of Kahlua," *Catering Toady,* April, 1988, pp. 16-17.

Zaklan, Nicholas, "Kahlua's Secret of Sweet Success," *Daily News,* March 5, 1990, Sec. 6.

—Maura Troester

KAL KAN®

Kal Kan brand of dog foods encompasses a number of canned and dry dog food products designed to appeal to canines of various ages, physical conditions, and social standings. In 1990, Kal Kan Foods Inc., a wholly owned subsidiary of Mars, Inc., brought out 40 new varieties of dog food under the product name Pedigree (a brand name used by Kal Kan since 1987), which became the best-selling brand in its category. In 1991, Kal Kan launched Expert, a superpremium brand of dry and canned dog food, to compete directly with the "specialty" dog foods Hill's Science Diet and Iams Company's Iams, which are exclusively available in specialty pet shops and veterinarians' offices. With estimated overall sales in 1991 of about $4 billion (including cat food), Kal Kan still lags behind Ralston Purina, the industry leader, although it has made considerable gains in its market category.

Kal Kan's Pedigree Dog Food

Like other pet products, dog food used to be merely another item pet owners would pick up during a weekly grocery trip. Brand loyalty may have played a secondary role to value pricing, and many dog owners were not particularly concerned if Spike and Fido ate a variety of brands, depending on their price and availability.

However, during the 1980s—a thriving decade in the industry with many new designer products and gourmet foods—dog food found a new market. Suddenly a significant number of pet owners became concerned with the taste, texture, and nutritional value of dog foods. "Yuppie puppies" were fed such recherche selections as special senior foods ("for their later years"), health food ("available only through your veterinarian"), and even doggie ice cream.

In a 1991 interview, Kal Kan's vice president of marketing and sales explained the evolution of Kal Kan dog foods from cereal-based meat substitutes to meaty, palatable products. "In the U.S.," John Murray pointed out, "the pet food business grew out of the grain-based livestock feed business. The result was dry food lacking in palatability to sharp-toothed carnivores like dogs and cats. Canned foods were often based on meat substitutes like textured vegetable and soy proteins. These too lacked palatability. And products made of meat by-products often had an odor and high fat content unappealing to pet owners as well as the pet."

In order to improve the situation, Kal Kan began to upgrade product quality. Rather than competing with the products of industry leaders, the company introduced new foods based on meat, rather than vegetable proteins. Animals seemed to find the menu offerings more palatable, owners were pleased with the appearance and smell of the new products, and Kal Kan managed to increase its sales from less than $200 million in mid-1987 to more than $500 million in 1991. Pedigree became the best-selling canned dog food in 1990, with a 23.76 percent market share, just ahead of Grand Met USA's Alpo and Carnation's Mighty Dog.

In 1990, the first major spin-off of the Pedigree line was launched. In order to compete with Purina Puppy Chow and Alpo Puppy, Kal Kan extended its product line to include Pedigree Puppy (canned and dried) in 1990. At that time, Purina held about 65 percent of the puppy food segment, while the other third was controlled mainly by Alpo and Quaker Oats' Cycle.

Pedigree Expert—A Superpremium Product Line Extension

One of the biggest threats to supermarket pet food manufacturers was the introduction in the mid-1980s of superpremium dog and cat foods. Usually available only through specialty pet shops and veterinarians' offices, these products professed to provide pets with a healthy alternative to store brands. In 1991, specialty outlets had captured some $1 billion of the $6.7 billion pet food market. The leader in the specialty segment, Colgate-Palmolive's Hill's Pet Products, cornered some 40 percent of that niche, followed by Iams Company's Iams (35 percent), and other smaller labels. The three leading manufacturers decided to fight back by making superpremium brands available in the supermarket.

Industry leader Ralston Purina, with a 26.4 percent market share, expanded its Purina O.N.E. line; Quaker, with 10.1 percent share, revamped its Cycle line; and Kal Kan, with a 12.4 percent market share, launched Expert, a 36-product extension to Pedigree. The line includes low-calorie, high-energy, and senior versions, all in dry and canned varieties. Also included are dog treats for healthful snacking.

Kal Kan decided to place its Expert line squarely in the supermarket pet food aisle instead of launching a two-pronged attack on specialty sales. This tactic was the preferred strategy of Purina and Carnation, both of whom market upscale brands distributed both inside and outside of the grocery store. According to company vice president John Murray, "Kal Kan is focusing on big brand names rather than creating different lines for different distribution channels." Murray contends that this way of marketing Kal Kan products "may result in some lost sales opportunities in the short run." He feels, however, that overall it will cause fewer trade conflicts and less fragmentation of brands.

Other pet food manufacturers have joined in the superpremium race. In December of 1991 and January of 1992, Alpo extended its line to include "life stages" varieties. Other brands have launched "lean" pet food products to coincide with pet owners' quest for low-calorie offerings.

Based on the idea that pet owners often have very strong interpersonal relationships with their dogs and cats, pet food manufacturers have begun to employ the "if it's good for me, it's good for my dog" strategy. Providing "scientifically formulated" healthy offerings with advertisements and package labeling that often mimic the health-oriented promotions used to sell "light" and "healthy" people-food, the companies have had great success in selling diet dog food to diet-conscious dog owners. Even Milk

AT A GLANCE

Kal Kan brand of dog food founded in 1950; became known as Pedigree brand dog food in 1987; more than 40 different varieties of dog food are marketed under the product name of Pedigree. Kal Kan Foods Inc. is a wholly owned subsidiary of Mars, Inc.

Performance: *Market share*—12.4% of total pet food market (1991). *Sales*—$4 billion (1991).

Advertising: *Agency*—Backer Spielvogel Bates. *Major campaign*—Establishment of Pedigree Expert "boutiques" with interactive computers.

Major competitor: Ralston Purina's O.N.E.; also Quaker Oats Company's Cycle; Grand Met USA's Alpo; and Carnation's Mighty Dog.

Addresses: *Parent company*—Kal Kan Foods Inc., Box 58553, Vernon, CA 90058; phone: (213) 587-2727. *Ultimate parent company*—M&M/Mars Inc., 6885 Elm St., McLean, VA 22101; phone: (703) 821-4900. *Ultimate ultimate parent company*—Mars, Inc.

Bone repackaged its long-standing favorite dog treats in a box with more nutrition information on the label.

Advertising and Marketing Strategies

The move to high nutrition specialty dog food products, like Kal Kan's Pedigree Expert and its rivals Quaker's Cycle and Purina O.N.E., has caused a space shortage in the already overcrowded supermarket pet food aisle. In order to promote the benefits of these high performance pet food products, manufacturers are depending more and more on point-of-purchase promotions and displays.

Kal Kan's $50 million launch of Expert in 1991, orchestrated by the New York ad agency Backer Spielvogel Bates, included a $20 million network and spot TV and print campaign touting the nutritional benefits of the line. The rest of the first-year budget was spent in the creation of free-standing inserts, trade allowances, public relations, and other promotions. Since the 36-product line is so extensive, Kal Kan requested four feet of shelf space in which to set up Expert "boutiques." These point-of-sale zones include interactive computers, as well as free leaflets and brochures extolling the virtues of healthy food for dogs.

Such eye-catching displays as the Expert boutique are one of the best ways to attract the attention of busy shoppers, and dog food manufacturers have been cashing in on the profits that point-of-purchase materials yield. According to a 1992 article in the *Wall Street Journal*, dog food displays prompted an increase of 64 percent in units sold over a 13-week period. A problem Kal Kan Expert Centers may face is the possibility of finding themselves occupying the four feet of shelf space immediately beside the four-foot Purina O.N.E. Pet Nutrition Center. At that point, value pricing and brand loyalty will be the influencing factors that govern shoppers' choices.

Future Prospects

The recession has certainly taken its toll on the pet food industry. According to *Progressive Grocer*'s 1992 Supermarket Sales Manual, pet foods, which accounted for 1.89 percent of store sales, had a 1991 volume of $5,303.64 million. This represented a change of −0.33 percent from the previous year. For the five years between 1986 and 1991, the average growth rate of the category was 3.41 percent. Dog food totals slipped six-tenths of a percent, to $2.9 million, according to the *Wall Street Journal*. At the same time, the number of dogs residing in American homes has increased, suggesting that owners are shopping carefully for less expensive dog food.

Some supermarket analysts point out that pet owners may be reluctant to spend big dollars on superpremium pet foods when they can't afford anything but generic labels for themselves. On the other hand, those people who did not feel the pinch have been shunning supermarket pet foods, buying their dogs superpremium offerings from specialty shops. As *Progressive Grocer* points out, in both 1990 and 1991 nongrocery pet food sales increased about 20 percent. Both trends bode ill for supermarket pet food manufacturers.

In order to regain control of the dog food industry—or at least to maintain a hold on the portion they still possess—supermarket pet food manufacturers have had to join the long list of other food industry giants who are engaged in EDLP (everyday low pricing) strategies. Price reductions have been adopted by all the major pet food manufacturers. A 1992 *Wall Street Journal* study indicated that recession-weary pet owners are shying away from premium-priced superpremium lines, and companies have moved quickly by lowering the price of these products.

Other marketing tactics pet food companies have had to employ include product consolidation. Kal Kan decided in 1992 to unite the marketing of Expert with the regular line of Pedigree dog food, selling both lines in the same advertisements.

In general, many analysts feel that the only area with major growth potential is dry dog food, an area in which Kal Kan already has a number of strong products. According to the *Wall Street Journal*, in 1992 some 53 percent of the dog food category was dry food, 28 percent was canned, 3 percent was soft-moist, and 15 percent snacks. Traditionally cheaper per pound than canned foods, the dry products are also easier to serve and less messy to clean up. Many pet owners also feel that dry food is healthier for dogs than canned food.

Small increases are being seen in the "doggy treat" category as well. Rewarding one's dog for good performance with a dog snack is still a popular behavior among pet owners, and in this segment, Kal Kan is well positioned, with snacks marketed under the Pedigree Expert brand.

Although the overall market was flat in the early 1990s, pet foods remained a colossal industry both in the United States and worldwide. Mars, the international leader in the pet food market, distributed its products to more than 30 countries. The Pedigree division garnered 60 percent shares by value and volume in the United Kingdom's pet food market. In 1987, in response to a suggestion from Kal Kan's Japanese product manager, the company began slicing the meat in Pedigree dog food in chunks, facilitating the Japanese use of chop sticks in feeding their dogs. Pedigree quickly became Japan's best-selling dog food. With the domestic pet food market reaching a saturation point, Kal Kan has continued its efforts to enlarge its market, both by focusing on international sales and by consistent product innovation.

Further Reading:

Deveny, Kathleen, "Displays Pay Off for Grocery Marketers," *Wall Street Journal,* October 15, 1992, p. B1.

Gibson, Rachel, "Pet-Food Shoppers Watch Their Pennies," *Wall Street Journal,* October 22, 1992, p. B1.

Hammel, Frank, " 'Only the Best' for Our Reigning Cats and Dogs," *Supermarket Business,* February, 1992, pp. 87-90.

Johnson, Bradley, "Kal Kan Sets $15M for Push," *Advertising Age,* February 26, 1990.

"Kal Kan Goes Upscale," *Advertising Age,* September 24, 1990, p. 3.

"Kal Kan: Adding Quality, Value to the U.S. Supermarket Shelf" (advertisement), *Supermarket Business,* June, 1991.

Liesse, Julie and Bradley Johnson, "New Pet Food Scrap in Supermarkets," *Advertising Age,* January 26, 1991, p. 3A.

O'Shaughnessy, Maryellen, "Kal Kan Scraps for Big Share of Dog-Eat-Dog Pet Industry," *Business First of Greater Columbus,* August 12, 1991.

"Pet Foods—1992 Supermarket Sales Manual," *Progressive Grocer,* July, 1992, p. 84.

—Marcia K. Mogelonsky

KEEBLER®

The Keebler Company, the Elmhurst, Illinois-based subsidiary of Britain's United Biscuits Holdings PLC, has been an aggressive competitor in both the cookies-and-crackers and the salty-snacks markets in the United States. The popularity of the Keebler elves, who are among the most well-known advertising characters in the nation, has enabled the brand to garner a second place spot in the cookies-and-crackers market, and hold onto the number four position in the salty snacks category. In the early 1990s, the top Keebler products included Zesta, Wheatables, and Town House crackers, O'Boisies and Ripplin's potato snack chips, and an extensive line of Keebler brand cookies.

The Keebler name traces its origins to Godfrey Keebler, a baker who opened a shop in Philadelphia in 1853 and earned a local reputation for cookies and crackers. In 1927, as the advent of cars and trucks was enabling local and regional bakers to deliver their goods to a much larger area, several of these bakeries, including Keebler's, joined together to create the United Biscuit Company. The bakers could then take advantage of the new distribution methods, while splitting the costs incurred. By 1944, 16 bakeries had joined the United Biscuit network, which marketed cookies and crackers under a variety of brand names in 45 states. In 1966, the company decided to reorganize under a single brand name. United Biscuit Company became Keebler Company when that name was chosen over the others to represent all of the company's products. United Biscuits Holdings PLC, one of the largest food manufacturers in the United Kingdom, acquired the Keebler Company in 1974. Keebler operated as a division of UB Foods U.S., a holding company created in 1986.

The Keebler Elves

Since 1968, the name Keebler has been associated more with elves than with a Philadelphia baker. That was the year Leo Burnett Co., a Chicago-based advertising agency, created the Keebler Elves to represent the company. Over the years, store displays and animated TV commercials have created an entire elfin community, with the fun-loving Keebler Elves creating "uncommonly good" products at the Hollow Tree Bakery. The Hollow Tree was a central element of the Keebler logo and corporate headquarters were at One Hollow Tree Lane in Elmhurst, Illinois.

New elves were often introduced to promote new products. For example, in 1991, Fryer Tuck, a pudgy elf modeled on Friar Tuck of Robin Hood fame, was introduced to help sell Munch'ems, and two teen-age elves, Zoot and J.J., were introduced to help sell Pizzarias. However, the head elf was squeaky-voiced Ernie Keebler, who had been Keebler's chief spokesman for more than 20 years. Keebler Elves became so popular that in 1990 the company created the Keebler Elf Fun Club. Children who joined the club received an Ernie T-shirt and poster.

Crackers

One of Keebler's best-selling products was also the company's oldest, Zesta Saltines. In the 1920s, the Streitmann Biscuit Company, which later became one of the United Biscuit group of companies, created Prize soda crackers. While the crackers were successful, the name was confused with another company's brand, so in 1925 the bakery ran a contest to rename the crackers. The name "Zesta " was chosen from more than 10,000 entries. Keebler also marketed a large variety of other crackers, including Town House, Club, and Stone Creek.

Keebler entered the snack-cracker market in 1988 with the introduction of Wheatables, which the company promoted as "oven toasted for an unbelievable crunch." Three years later the company followed up with Munch'ems, which had the texture of a cracker and the taste of a chip, placing them in the new "chippers" snack category. Munch'ems had $85 million in first-year sales. Keebler also paired two of its popular cracker brands, Town House and Club, with cheddar cheese to create sandwich snacks.

Despite the popularity of Wheatables and Munch'ems, the snack crackers created a controversy because of Keebler's advertising claims. In a typically light-hearted Keebler Elves commercial, Ernie Keebler explains to Fryer Tuck that he was not consulted on the new crackers because they are "baked, not fried." The original "baked, not fried" claim appeared on packaging for both Wheatables and Munch'ems. However, the Frito-Lay Co. said the claim gave the impression that Keebler's crackers were lower in fat than other snack crackers, when in fact Wheatables and Munch'ems were sprayed with vegetable oil after baking, making their fat content comparable to fried products. The National Advertising Division, a unit of the Council of Better Business Bureaus, agreed with the charges, and Keebler eventually discontinued the "baked, not fried" advertising.

AT A GLANCE

Keebler brand of snacks founded in 1853 by Godfrey Keebler, a Philadelphia baker; in 1927 Keebler Bakery became part of a federation of companies in the United Biscuit Company; company adopted Keebler as single corporate brand name and became Keebler Company, 1966; Keebler purchased by United Biscuits Holdings PLC in 1974.

Performance: *Market share*—17% of cookie and cracker category; 5.1% of salty snack category. *Sales*—$1.5 billion.

Major competitor: Nabisco Foods Group's brands of snacks.

Advertising: *Agency*—Leo Burnett Co., Chicago, IL, 1968—. *Major campaign*—Animated Keebler Elves baking "uncommonly good" products at the Hollow Tree Bakery.

Addresses: *Parent company*—Keebler Company, One Hollow Tree Lane, Elmhurst, IL 60126-1581; phone: (708) 833-2900; fax: (708) 530-8773. *Ultimate parent company*—United Biscuits Holdings PLC, Church Road, West Drayton, Middlesex, England UB7 7PR; phone: 0895 432100; fax: 0895 448848.

Cookies

In 1992, Keebler was the second largest maker of cookies in the United States, behind Nabisco. There were more than 40 different cookies bearing the Keebler brand name, including such popular varieties as the venerable Pecan Sandies, Chips Deluxe, and E.L. Fudge, a fudge-coated shortbread cookie in the shape of Ernie, the head Keebler Elf.

Several of Keebler's most popular cookie brands are coated in fudge, including Deluxe Grahams, Fudge Stripes, Fudge Sticks, and Grasshopper, a fudge mint cookie. In 1992 Keebler introduced Toffee Toppers, a shortbread cookie covered in fudge and topped with dribbles of toffee. The company also repackaged its other fudge covered cookies under the name "Fudge Shoppe."

Keebler tip-toed to the edges of the confectionery business in 1992 with the introduction of its Sweet Spots, a cookie with a chocolatey drop in the center. The company hoped the new cookie would appeal to candy lovers. Raisin' Ruckus, an oatmeal cookie with chocolate-covered raisins, was introduced the following year.

One of Keebler's cookie varieties, Soft Batch, involved the company in a lengthy and expensive patent-infringement battle with Procter & Gamble, which claimed that Keebler, Nabisco, and Frito-Lay had stolen the recipe for its Duncan Hines brand of ready-to-eat cookies, which were crispy on the outside and soft on the inside. All three companies launched dual-texture cookie brands in 1984, just ahead of Procter & Gamble's national rollout. The suit was settled out of court in 1989, with Keebler and Nabisco each agreeing to pay Procter & Gamble about $53 million. Frito-Lay agreed to pay about $19 million. When the settlement was announced, Keebler spokesman Stuart Greenblatt made it clear in an *Advertising Age* article that the Soft Batch cookies Keebler was then marketing did not infringe on Procter & Gambles's patent. Since then, the once-hot soft cookie market has dwindled in size.

Salty Snacks

Keebler entered the highly competitive salty-snack market with a fundamental product, pretzels. Then in 1985, the company combined baking and frying to create Tato Skins, a potato snack

chip that looked like the popular restaurant appetizer. The chips were brownish on one side, like a baked-potato skin, and white on the other. In 1992 Tom Garvin, who was president and CEO of Keebler at the time, declared in *Adweek's Marketing Week,* "We've heard from our competitors and they still can't figure out how in blazes we did that."

O'Boisies potato snack chips were introduced in 1988, and quickly became Keebler's bestselling salty-snack brand. According to the *Journal of Business Strategy,* O'Boisies were a serendipitous discovery. Keebler was experimenting with different prototypes when it "inadvertently created a chip with bubbles, which is normally not a desirable attribute. However, the 'crackly texture' intrigued the marketing department, as well as the consumer. The new proprietary manufacturing process virtually insulated O'Boisies from imitation and provided Keebler with a fortuitous technical advantage."

Made from dried potatoes rather than fresh potatoes, O'Boisies, Tato Skins, and Ripplin's, a thick, rippled chip introduced in 1989, were advertised as "potato snack chips" not "potato chips." This avoided a controversy that had plagued the

Ernie Keebler has been a Keebler spokesperson for more than 20 years.

potato chip industry since General Mills introduced Chipos, the first chips made from dehydrated potatoes, in the late 1960s. When Chipos were introduced, the Potato Chip Institute International, later to become the Snack Food Association, filed suit in federal court seeking to stop General Mills from calling its product "potato chips." The court eventually ruled that Chipos and later products—including Procter & Gamble's Pringle's—could be called potato chips only if the words "made from dried potatoes" also appeared on the package. In 1975 the Food and Drug Administration ruled that the disclaimer had to appear in type at least half the size of the largest type that used the words "potato chips."

Keebler further filled out its salty-snack line in 1990 with the introduction of its first corn chip, the ring-shaped Hooplas! , and Pop Deluxe, a ready-to-eat brand of popcorn in White Cheddar and Honey Caramel Glazed flavors. The following year Keebler introduced Pizzarias, the first national-brand snack chip made from real pizza dough. Adam Burck, new product development manager, stated in *Adweek's Marketing Week* that Keebler researched pizza dough recipes "all the way back to the Renaissance" before selecting a process for Pizzarias. The chips, shaped like small slices of pizza, came in three varieties, cheese, pepperoni and supreme. Despite a market history of failed pizza-flavored snacks, Pizzarias were an instant success with more than $75 million in sales the first year, helping to earn Keebler the American Marketing Association's New Product Marketer of the Year award.

Keebler ran into problems, however, when it introduced Quangles in 1992. Designed for the health conscious, multi-grain chip market, the round chips were promoted as "a new angle on snacking." *Crain's Chicago Business* reported that production and distribution delays prompted the company to cancel the advertising program that was to accompany the product launch, leading to poor consumer response. Efforts were stepped up for the introduction of Chacho's, launched in 1993. The first nationally distributed, restaurant-style flour tortilla chip, the snacks came in three flavors, including a cinnamon and sugar "dessert" variety.

Miniatures

In 1987 Nabisco created a marketing craze with the introduction of Ritz Bitz, a bite-sized version of Ritz crackers. Keebler responded with miniature versions of its popular Pecan Sandies, Magic Middles, and Chips Deluxe cookies and the introduction of Elfkins, a bite-sized fudge-filled cookie in the shape of Keebler Elves.

The company also introduced a mini version of its Town House Cheddar crackers. Town House Cheddar Jrs. were an immediate success: the company's 1987 annual report to employees said Town House Cheddar Jrs. had achieved a "remarkable 13 percent share of the cheese cracker segment in just four months." But reflecting the unpredictable nature of the snack industry, Cheddar Jrs. had been discontinued by 1990.

Changes Ahead

In 1968, the year that the Keebler Elves magically appeared, Tom Garvin also went to work for Keebler. Ten years later, Garvin, a Chicago native and graduate of Loyola University, became president and chief executive officer, overseeing the introduction of many of Keebler's most successful brands. But after an average annual growth of 21 percent between 1985 and 1991, Keebler's profits fell by 50 percent in 1991. In January 1993, *Crain's Chicago Business* reported, "After years of turning dough into dollars, Keebler Co.'s earnings are crumbling." The "bumbled" introduction of two new products, including Quangles, was cited as the reason for much of Keebler's financial woes, as was the inability to keep stores supplied with its new Sweet Spots. A week later, Garvin was forced to resign by the parent company, United Biscuit Holdings PLC.

Meanwhile Keebler was looking at the growing market for less expensive, private-label products that would appeal to recession-weary consumers. Two weeks before Garvin was forced out, United Biscuits acquired Bake-Line Products, Inc., and announced that Keebler would operate the Des Plaines, Illinois, maker of private-label cookies. Rather than produce lower-priced private-label versions of its own brands, speculation was that Keebler would produce look-alikes to its competitors most popular cookies and crackers. Executives hoped this strategy, along with plans for a new salty snack, would once again put Keebler's sales on the rise.

Further Reading:

Berry, Jon, "The Big Brawl In Snack Food," *Adweek's Marketing Week*, September 23, 1991, p. 4.

Berry, Jon, "Frito, Keebler Roll Out the Big Guns," *Adweek's Marketing Week*, April 1, 1991, p. 8.

Berry, Jon, "Keebler Elfkins Take On Nabisco's Mini Bear," *Adweek's Marketing Week*, February 4, 1991, p. 7.

Berry, Jon, "Keebler Springs to Life," *Adweek's Marketing Week*, January 6, 1992, p. 18.

"Clubbing Tots," *Fortune*, February 26, 1990, p. 11.

"The cookie war and how it crumbled," *U.S. News & World Report*, September 25, 1989, p. 18.

Crown, Judith, "After a stale year, Keebler fights back," *Crain's Chicago Business*, January 11, 1993, p. 3.

Freeman, Laurie, "P&G wins lawsuit, loses market," *Advertising Age*, September 18, 1989, p. 72.

Hodock, Calvin L., "Strategies Behind the Winners and Losers," *The Journal of Business Strategy*, September/October 1990, pp. 4-7.

Jensen, Jeff, "NAD crunches Keebler's 'Baked not fried' ad claim," *Advertising Age*, October 19, 1992, p. 12.

Klepacki, Laura, "A Display of Mite: Miniature cookies and crackers are making a big impact in snacks," *Supermarket News*, December 9, 1991, p. 13.

Liesse, Julie, "Keebler bites on new products," *Advertising Age*, March 30, 1992, p. 56.

Schnorbus, Paula, "Nibble, Nibble," *Marketing & Media Decisions*, June 1988, pp. 123-138

Warner, Fara, "It's a Chip! It's A Cracker! It's Chippers!," *Adweek's Marketing Week*, July 29, 1991, p. 6.

—Dean Boyer

KELLOGG'S CORN FLAKES®

The dry cereal industry has undergone periodic bursts of proliferation and specialization over the last forty years, but Kellogg's Corn Flakes remains a beacon of tradition and simplicity—and a best-selling one at that. For decades the most popular dry cereal in the United States, Corn Flakes has wilted a bit in recent years and yielded market share to rivals—a natural development, considering just how many rivals it has today—but it remains one of the top three brands in a business in which competition seems to become more vigorous with every passing year. Originally developed in the late 19th century as a healthy alternative to high-fat meat-and-eggs breakfasts, dry cereals are now a staple of the American breakfast table. Corn Flakes is produced by the Kellogg Company of Battle Creek, Michigan, the world's leading manufacturer of dry cereals and also the producer of Eggo frozen waffles, Pop Tarts breakfast pastries, and Whitney's yogurt.

Brand Origins

To call Kellogg's Corn Flakes one of the first American health foods is neither an exaggeration of its place in gastronomical history nor a distortion of the intention of its inventors. The idea of making dry cereal from toasted corn mush was originally developed by W. K. Kellogg while he was working at the Battle Creek, Michigan, sanitarium run by his brother, Dr. John Harvey Kellogg. Dr. Kellogg devoted his entire professional life to exploring the connection between diet and health; patients who came to the Battle Creek Sanitarium were required to give up meat, caffeinated beverages, alcohol, and tobacco in exchange for the promise of better health (himself a vegetarian, like the Seventh Day Adventists who founded the sanitarium, Dr. Kellogg remarked in his ninety-first year that he had "done pretty well for a grass eater"). Shortly after he became superintendent in 1876, he began to experiment with various combinations of grains, seeking to produce tastier and more digestible grain products. Shortly thereafter, he developed the combination of wheat, cornmeal, and oatmeal that is still known today as granola.

Dr. Kellogg's experiments were successful by almost every conceivable standard. The food products that he had developed for therapeutic purposes proved so popular that many of his former patients kept buying them by mail after they left Battle Creek Sanitarium. Within fifteen years of taking the reins of the institute, Dr. Kellogg had set up a company, Sanitas Food, with his younger brother W. K. as manager, to handle the thriving mail order business. In 1894 the Kellogg brothers developed a flaked cereal by running boiled wheat mush through metal rollers that had been used to grind granola, then letting it cool and dry. Four years later, W. K. Kellogg experimented by replacing the wheat mush with corn mush, and the concept of Corn Flakes was born.

Early Marketing Strategies

Corn Flakes quickly became Sanitas Food's best-selling item, and it did not take long for W. K. Kellogg to see its marketing potential. But Dr. Kellogg, lacking his brother's shrewdness, refused to expand the company's marketing beyond the limited mail order operations in which they were already engaged. In 1895 former Battle Creek Sanitarium patient C. W. Post crept up on the Kelloggs by developing a cereal-based coffee (Postum) and a dry cereal (Grape Nuts) based on products that they had developed for institutional use. It irked W. K. Kellogg that his company stood idly by as imitators capitalized on ideas that he had helped originate. In 1903 he and his longtime associate Arch Shaw expanded Sanitas Food's marketing efforts by launching the first major ad campaign for Corn Flakes, spearheaded by a slogan that emphasized the cereal's tastiness rather than its healthful qualities: "A Breakfast Treat—That Makes You Eat."

Dr. Kellogg remained adamantly opposed to the mass-marketing of Sanitas products, however, concerned about possible conflicts between business interests and medical ethics. So in 1906, W. K. Kellogg broke with his brother and went into business on his own, founding the Battle Creek Toasted Corn Flake Company (the company adopted its current name in 1922). He quickly changed the name of his sole product from Sanitas Corn Flakes to Kellogg Toasted Corn Flakes, having realized that the former was for more likely to kill appetites than excite them (" . . . the word 'Sanitas' partakes too much of a disinfectant," he wrote at the time). Kellogg designed another appeal to the taste buds when he altered the recipe for Corn Flakes by adding malt flavoring to the corn mush. He also created a longtime trademark for the brand at this time: his signature. In 1903, wary of copycat companies that were popping up like mushrooms around Battle Creek, he had begun to stamp his signature on Sanitas products, accompanied by the warning: "Beware of imitators. None genuine without this signature." Shortly after branching out on his own, Kellogg extended this trademark to Corn Flakes. Kellogg's red-inked signature on boxes of Corn Flakes became so distinctive that it inspired

AT A GLANCE

Kellogg's Corn Flakes developed in 1898 in Battle Creek, MI, by W. K. Kellogg; first widespread commercial distribution in 1903 by Sanitas Food, which was run by Kellogg and his brother, dietician Dr. John Harvey Kellogg; from 1906 marketed by Battle Creek Toasted Corn Flake Company, which was renamed Kellogg Company in 1922.

Performance: *Market share*—3.2% (dollar volume) of dry cereal category. *Sales*—$204 million.

Major competitor: Frosted Flakes and Rice Krispies, also by Kellogg; General Mills' Cheerios.

Advertising: *Agency*—Leo Burnett, Chicago, IL.

Addresses: *Parent company*—Kellogg Company, One Kellogg Square, Battle Creek, MI 49016-3599; phone: (616) 961-2000; fax: (616) 961-6596.

a 1936 Rea Irvin cartoon in the *New Yorker;* the drawing shows a weary Kellogg at his desk with pen in hand, being hailed by several smiling men in suits as workers moving lots of Corn Flakes boxes scurry about. The caption reads: ''HISTORIC MOMENTS IN THE ANNALS OF AMERICAN INDUSTRY / An efficiency engineer discovers that printing will save Mr. Kellogg from having to sign his name on each of the Corn Flakes boxes.''

Corn Flakes received another of its enduring trademarks in 1907, when ''The Sweetheart of the Corn,'' an attractive country lass holding a shock of corn, first appeared on the box. One legend has it that the original model for the Sweetheart was a company employee. But W. K. Kellogg's biographer, Horace Powell, states that she was the creation of a Philadelphia printing establishment that had created her as a trademark for a farm implement company; when the original client turned it down, the printers substituted corn for the armful of wheat that she had originally held, and sold the concept to the Kellogg company. The Sweetheart, of course, assumed different forms through the years, always updated to suit the times; and the use of her likeness to sell Corn Flakes was more periodic than constant. But the company nonetheless considered her an important part of marketing its leading brand. A Kellogg executive said in the mid-1950s, ''At the present time the Sweetheart figure is probably printed over one hundred million times a year. How much is the Sweetheart worth to us? . . . Our Sweetheart is not for sale.''

These two ad campaigns proved so successful that they became virtual trademarks for the brand, but they were by no means the only marketing ventures that the Kellogg company made on behalf of Corn Flakes. In 1906, when his fledgling company was still struggling, W. K. Kellogg staked much of his working capital on a full-page ad in the *Ladies Home Journal.* Another one of the very first campaigns to promote Corn Flakes was a newspaper insert in Dayton, Ohio, that was supplemented by a ''walking ad''—a man walking around in a costume that consisted of an eight-foot tall papier-mache ear of corn. The Kellogg company launched another remarkable advertisement on behalf of Corn Flakes in 1912 when it commissioned a moving electric sign that was mounted atop a building in downtown Chicago. The sign first showed a crying child accompanied by the legend, ''I want Kellogg's,'' which then metamorphosed into a smiling child and the caption, ''I got Kellogg's.''

First Commercial Success and International Expansion

Kellogg was one of the first American producers of consumer goods to use advertising on such a large scale, and it worked. Sales grew from 33 cases per day to 2900 cases per day within Corn Flakes' first few years on the market. In 1909 annual sales surpassed one million cases. International expansion quickly followed this initial success. Corn Flakes made its debut in Canada in 1914, and spread to Australia in 1924 when the company built a manufacturing plant in Sydney. The Kellogg Company built its first British factory in Manchester in 1938, and began producing Corn Flakes in Mexico in 1951, when it built a plant some 300 miles north of Mexico City, in the heart of the Mexican corn belt.

Corn Flakes in the Age of Television

The recipe for Corn Flakes has remained unchanged since W. K. Kellogg transformed the product from a private-label health food to a mass-marketed breakfast staple. The Kellogg Company has fiddled with Corn Flakes only twice. It did so for the first time in 1952, when it created a pre-sweetened version of the cereal aimed at the first of the Baby Boom generation. This sugar-coated version was named Frosted Flakes and became a smashing success, and it has always been marketed separately from Corn Flakes. Thirteen years later, Kellogg tinkered with its best-seller again, but with considerably less success. Possessed with the idea of adding freeze-dried bananas to Corn Flakes, it went to great expense to launch the new product, buying the rights to the pop standard ''Yes, We Have No Bananas'' and hiring comedian Jimmy Durante to sing an altered version (''Yes, We Now Have Bananas'') in a television commercial. The Corn Flakes-and-freeze-dried bananas combo was marketed as a convenience food: Simply add milk, and *voila!*—a bowl of cereal with all the desired extras already added in. This new version was a flop, however, and disappeared from the shelves within a year.

What has changed about Corn Flakes over the years is the way in which it is marketed, and in this, the brand has intersected with American popular culture many times since the 1950s. The dry cereal business changed dramatically early in that decade for two basic reasons: the Baby Boom and the advent of television. The former created a vast new market for breakfast cereals, the latter a new and effective way of reaching that market with advertising. Cereal companies (among which Kellogg was still top dog) created pre-sweetened cereals designed to appeal to juvenile palates and sold them through television commercials aimed at children. As one industry executive told *Forbes* in 1966, ''With television, we began to sell children our product before they could talk.'' Suddenly, Corn Flakes had to compete against a vast array of sticky-sweet rivals for market share, including its own sugar-coated alter-ego.

Kellogg, however, refused to concede the field to pre-sweetened cereals and defended its longtime mainstay. In the late 1950s, it began working closely with animators at Hanna-Barbera Studios, sponsoring a number of television cartoon shows that featured brand-new characters, among them immortals Yogi Bear and Huckleberry Hound. In turn, these characters were featured in commercials hawking Kellogg cereals. Each character was associated with a particular cereal, and Corn Flakes was fortunate enough to draw none other than Yogi himself, the wise-cracking denizen of Jellystone Park, friend of Boo-Boo and scourge of Ranger Smith.

Another innovation in the marketing of Corn Flakes that dates from this time is one that can still be seen on every box of the cereal. Recognizing that some sort of graphic icon was needed more than catchy slogans in an age in which children and television were the two most important factors in cereal advertising, Kellogg introduced the now-ubiquitous red-and-green rooster logo in 1958. Named Cornelius Rooster, this logo was featured in an animated television commercial in 1990, which showed him unable to cock-a-doodle-doo until he had his morning bowl of Corn Flakes.

Recently, Kellogg has turned to the use of celebrities to plug Corn Flakes. A television campaign from the mid-1980s did not feature direct celebrity endorsements, but showed people in a library reading a book listing personages from the sports and entertainment worlds who eat Corn Flakes. "The surprise is the people who eat them," was the theme. Kellogg has also issued limited-edition boxes of Corn Flakes featuring photos of successful American Olympians. In the Olympic year of 1992, for example, one edition bore the likeness of speed-skater Bonnie Blair. Another featured basketball Olympians Larry Bird, Karl Malone, Chris Mullin, David Robinson, and John Stockton; one version showed the five of them wearing their gold medals, while another showed them dribbling in formation, looking up into the camera.

Performance Appraisal

Given its phenomenal early success and W. K. Kellogg's enduring shrewdness as a marketer and businessman, it is no surprise that Corn Flakes remained the best-selling cereal in America throughout the first half of this century. What is surprising is that it has managed to defend that position so well in the years since then. For one thing, there are so many more challengers now than in W. K. Kellogg's time. Between the early 1950s and the mid-1960s alone, the number of dry cereal brands on the market nearly doubled, from about 50 to almost 100; later, the market saw a boom in high-fiber cereals that emerged as a response to the fitness craze in the late 1980s. Making matters even more difficult for Kellogg, the company has always dominated the dry cereal market (except for a blip in the mid-1950s, when it fell behind General Foods), holding at least 40 percent of the market since the mid-1960s; it is therefore the first target that comes to mind when a rival wants to expand its own market share.

Corn Flakes was the best-selling cereal by tonnage in the United States throughout the 1970s, rivalled only by Kellogg brethren Frosted Flakes and Rice Krispies and General Mills' Cheerios. All through the decade, Corn Flakes maintained a 7 to 8 percent share of the market. Kellogg slumped periodically in the 1980s, however, hurt by its general inability to make significant inroads in the burgeoning high-fiber cereal market, and major rival General Mills began to steal market share. In the early 1990s, however, Kellogg began to fight back by refocusing its advertising efforts on core brands like Corn Flakes. In June 1992 *Advertising Age* reported that Corn Flakes held 3.5 percent of the cereal market by dollar sales. Since it has always been a simple and relatively inexpensive product, Corn Flakes' market share by dollar sales has always been lower than its share by tonnage sold; based on historical data, that 3.5 percent dollar market share would equal approximately 5 to 6 percent of tonnage sold. Frosted Flakes and Cheerios have occasionally been described as America's most popular breakfast cereal in recent times, but it is clear that Corn Flakes still holds a very significant portion of the cereal market.

Prospects for Future Growth

How well Corn Flakes will sell in the future will no doubt depend on Kellogg's continuing business savvy and marketing prowess and its ability to withstand assaults on its dominant position by General Mills and other rivals. Corn Flakes is a low-tech, old-fashioned cereal in an industry that has figured out how to design specialized new products as specific responses to demographic shifts. In the 1950s pre-sweetened sugar cereals for kids were all the rage, and in the 1980s high-fiber recipes proliferated, tailored to adults worried about their health and regularity. But somehow, Corn Flakes has managed to survive with its position as an industry leader more or less intact. In a world full of specialized, high-tech alternatives, its simplicity and wholesomeness seem like refreshing virtues. In 1985 a 92-year-old Corn Flakes loyalist wrote to Kellogg: "I am in good health, my vision is good, I have all my permanent teeth. I give credit to Corn Flakes. . . . I could use a little more hair on the top of my head. However, I am sure Kellogg's Corn Flakes will provide."

Further Reading:

"Don't Underestimate the Power of a Kid," *Forbes,* October 15, 1966, pp. 65-68.

"Kellogg: Still the Cereal People," *Business Week,* November 26, 1979, pp. 80-93.

Liesse, Julie, "Kellogg Sees Return of 40% Share as Core Brands Rise," *Advertising Age,* June 15, 1992, p. 1.

McManus, Kevin, "Corn Flakes, a Breakfast Original," *Advertising Age,* January 6, 1986, pp. 34-35.

Powell, Horace B., *The Original Has This Signature—W. K. Kellogg,* Englewood Cliffs: Prentice-Hall, 1956.

—Douglas Sun

KELLOGG'S FROSTED FLAKES®

Almost from the moment that the Kellogg Company placed it on the market, Kellogg's Frosted Flakes has been the most popular pre-sweetened dry cereal in the world and one of the most popular of all breakfast cereals. Despite some stiff competition in recent years, it has demonstrated a durable appeal to the Baby Boomers for which it was created, as the members of that celebrated demographic group have passed from sugar-happy childhood into relatively sober adulthood. Frosted Flakes is produced by the Kellogg Company of Battle Creek, Michigan, the world's leading manufacturer of dry cereals and also the producer of Eggo frozen waffles, Pop Tarts breakfast pastries, and Whitney's yogurt.

Brand Origins

Frosted Flakes made its debut in 1952 under the name Kellogg's Sugar Frosted Flakes. Kellogg had been the world's leading manufacturer of dry cereal virtually from the founding of the company in 1906. Its continued success, however, was due almost entirely to Kellogg's Corn Flakes. Corn Flakes was a long-running hit with children and adults alike, but Kellogg sensed the need for some innovation and expansion of its product line as the 1950s rolled around. The Baby Boom had begun, and it seemed only logical to respond to this demographic development by creating pre-sweetened cereals targeted especially toward children. Frosted Flakes was preceded by Corn Pops in 1950 and followed by Honey Smacks in 1953.

The recipe for Frosted Flakes has always been very simple, consisting essentially of Corn Flakes covered by a sugar frosting. Corn Flakes is made from heated corn mush with malt added for flavoring; the semi-liquid batter is baked and dried under heat, then extruded through rollers so that it is flattened and broken into flakes. The flakes are then toasted to make them crisp. The formula for Corn Flakes is one of the dry cereal industry's primordial concoctions, having been developed by W. K. Kellogg himself in 1898 while he was working for the dietary sanitarium run by his brother, Dr. John Harvey Kellogg, in Battle Creek, Michigan. In order to become Frosted Flakes, the plain corn flakes are sprayed with a sweetened coating to give them their frosted appearance and sugary taste.

Marketing Strategy

Throughout its history Frosted Flakes has had a boisterous anthropomorphized tiger named Tony as its spokesman. Tony the Tiger has graced every box of Frosted Flakes, and his animated form has made at least a cameo appearance in every television commercial for the brand, accompanied by his signature roar, "They're gr-r-r-eat!" He is arguably the most famous cereal mascot in the world (possibly rivaled by the Kellogg's Rice Krispies trio of Snap, Crackle, and Pop).

Though the years have not dimmed Tony's appeal, his appearance has changed in subtle ways since his debut. At first, he was depicted as having a long, lean body that tapered toward the hindquarters, and narrow eyes that turned down slightly to conform to his longish face. From about 1960 through the 1970s, however, Tony was given a more vigorous appearance, with a fuller chest and a broader face, shaped rather like an oval laid on its side and the ends sharpened to points. A logo from 1960 shows him with angular, sharply drawn features and a perfectly triangular bib tied beneath his perpetual grin. Finally, in the 1980s, Tony's angles were softened into more naturalistic curves and his chest and arms became fully developed, vaguely suggestive of a bodybuilder's upper torso. His most recent remodelling seems appropriate for a time when public concern over health and physical fitness has inspired a significant change in the dry cereal industry. In the mid-1970s, Kellogg introduced a pint-sized version of Tony named Tony Jr.—complete with chubbier cheeks and a schoolboy cap—to advertise Frosted Rice, a product that proved much less successful than Frosted Flakes.

Tony and the Age of Television

Tony the Tiger was born and came of age in a time when cereal companies were just discovering that they had a whole new demographic group to which they had to appeal—children—and an effective new medium through which they could reach them—television. As one industry executive told *Forbes* in 1966, television suddenly allowed the companies "to sell children our product before they could [even] talk." Besides Tony, such perennial spokesmen (spokescreatures?) for pre-sweetened cereals as Captain Crunch and Lucky Charms' Lucky the Leprechaun made their debuts in animated television commercials during the 1950s and early 1960s. Kellogg even went so far as to sponsor the development of some of Hanna Barbera's classic animated characters—Yogi Bear, Huckleberry Hound, and Quick-Draw McGraw, to name a few—using them to plug Kellogg cereals in between their on-screen escapades.

AT A GLANCE

Kellogg's Frosted Flakes brand cereal developed in 1952 in Battle Creek, MI, by the Kellogg Company, based on the recipe for Kellogg's Corn Flakes that company founder W. K. Kellogg had invented 54 years earlier.

Performance: *Market share*—5.1% of cold cereal category. *Sales*—$336 million.

Major competitor: Corn Flakes and Rice Krispies, by Kellogg's; also General Mills' Cheerios.

Advertising: *Agency*—Leo Burnett, Chicago, IL. *Major campaign*—Tony the Tiger, an animated anthropomorphized tiger who appears on the box and in every commercial for Frosted Flakes, always declaring, "They're gr-r-r-eat!"

Addresses: *Parent company*—Kellogg Company, One Kellogg Square, Battle Creek, MI, 49016-3599; phone: (616) 961-2000; fax: (616) 961-6596.

Tony's tremendous appeal helped make Frosted Flakes the most popular of the fledgling pre-sweetened cereals. Conversely, however, it also made him and his corporate bosses a target for those who were concerned about the mixture of entertainment and advertising in children's television. During the 1970s, cereal companies came under increasing fire from consumer groups who felt that television advertising targeted at children manipulated a vulnerable sector of the population. As the activist group Action for Children's Television put it, "The advertiser . . . uses all the wiles of trick photography, fantasy, animation and promises of 'free gifts' and 'surprises' to sell his cereal to children. Of course, the sell is easy; children still believe what they are told. . . . " Consumer activists also charged that pre-sweetened breakfast cereals were no more nutritious than candy.

Kellogg responded by altering its advertising content, and enlisted Tony the Tiger to help with the new campaign. Where previous commercials for Frosted Flakes and other pre-sweetened cereals had emphasized "gr-r-r-eat" taste, Kellogg now stressed the nutritional value of its products aimed at children. Tony and other Kellogg mascots were shown pitching their products as just one part of a breakfast that would include milk, fruit, and other wholesome foods. The phrase "part of a complete breakfast" became a familiar refrain.

Later Marketing Developments

The controversy over commercials for pre-sweetened cereal was just one part of the larger debate over what constituted proper content for children's programming—and soon enough, changing demographics would mute it anyway. As the 1970s yielded to the 1980s, the Baby Boomers for whom Frosted Flakes had been created and who had grown up with Tony the Tiger were reaching adulthood and outgrowing sugary breakfast cereals. The brand came under increasing pressure, especially from General Mills' unsweetened Cheerios, to maintain its market share and position of eminence.

Kellogg fought back with characteristic energy and savvy. In the mid-1980s the company launched an ad campaign that pitched Frosted Flakes to adults. The new commercials featured characters, their faces hidden by shadow, confessing that they continue to eat Frosted Flakes even as adults. The premise of these spots was

that adult consumption of and affection for Frosted Flakes was a phenomenon more common than generally acknowledged; therefore, the product had transcended its origins as a children's cereal. Its catchphrase was, "the taste adults have grown to love." Tony the Tiger's role in this campaign was a supporting one; he simply appeared at the end of each commercial to proclaim that Frosted Flakes were not just for kids anymore and, of course, to utter his trademark cry.

The increasing importance of health and physical fitness in the 1980s spawned an array of high-fiber cereals targeted at adults, and put even more pressure on pre-sweetened cereals as the decade wore on. In 1986 Kellogg switched from its emphasis on adults in advertising for Frosted Flakes to target children once more, but with an emphasis on sports and fitness. The new campaign used a combination of animation and live action to show Tony helping children engaged in various forms of athletic activity, and featured the slogan, "Kellogg's Frosted Flakes bring out the tiger in you."

In the early 1990s, Kellogg used the popularity of professional sports to supplement Tony the Tiger's appeal. In 1991 the company issued a limited edition of boxes featuring the World Series champion Minnesota Twins. Kellogg followed up the next year with limited edition featuring the National Hockey League's 1991-92 Stanley Cup champions, the Pittsburgh Penguins. Kellogg also signed a sponsorship agreement with Major League Baseball and began a national promotion in which Tony would grace the box cover wearing the uniform of one of the twenty-four major league teams, depending upon the region of the country to which the box was being shipped. Boxes of Frosted Flakes being sold in the Los Angeles area, for example, would feature Tony dressed in the colors of either the Los Angeles Dodgers or the California Angels.

Performance Appraisal

It is an interesting aspect of Kellogg's success that the company has had to innovate so infrequently. For half a century, it held a firm grip on the dry cereal market mainly on the strength of its original product, Corn Flakes (although Rice Krispies, introduced in 1928, has also proven an enduring success). Even in 1979, *Business Week* pointed out that four out of the five best-selling dry cereals in America were Kellogg products that were at least twenty-five years old. One of those four, of course, was Frosted Flakes. Shortly after it made its debut, Frosted Flakes became the best-selling pre-sweetened cereal and one of the most popular of all dry cereals. Throughout the 1970s, it held a 6 percent share of the total dry cereal market by tonnage sold. Even in the mid-1980s, as Kellogg grappled with marketing in the post–Baby Boom era, Frosted Flakes remained the company's second-best seller (behind Corn Flakes) by units sold, and the best-seller industry-wide in terms of dollar sales.

Prospects for Further Growth

In 1989 Frosted Flakes yielded its position as dollar-volume best-seller to Cheerios, but it bounced back in the early 1990s as Kellogg, faced with a serious overall challenge from General Mills, refocused its marketing efforts on its core brands. In fact, the late 1980s and early 1990s saw Kellogg and General Mills engaged in a bitter struggle over not just the domestic market, but over markets in Europe and Asia, which are far from saturated and where potential for growth is tremendous. Whether or not Kellogg can continue to dominate the cereal industry with aging products like Frosted Flakes is not entirely clear. It is clear, however, that Frosted Flakes has shown enviable staying power in an increasingly competitive business (the number of dry cereal brands nearly doubled in Frosted Flakes' first twenty years on the market). Frosted Flakes has shown a strong and consistent ability to appeal to the public palate, and there seems to be plenty of life left in the old tiger yet.

Further Reading:

"Don't Underestimate the Power of a Kid," *Forbes,* October 15, 1966, pp. 65-68.

Franz, Julie, "Kellogg's Market Share Starting to Flake," *Advertising Age,* January 27, 1986, p. 63.

"Kellogg: Still the Cereal People," *Business Week,* November 26, 1979, pp. 80-93.

Liesse, Julie, "Kellogg Sees Return of 40% Share as Core Brands Rise," *Advertising Age,* June 15, 1992, p. 1.

—Douglas Sun

KELLOGG'S POP-TARTS®

The Kellogg Company turned the toaster pastry into a hot-selling favorite among U.S. and Canadian consumers with its phenomenally successful brand, Pop-Tarts. Writing in *Adweek's Marketing Week* in August of 1991, Fara Warner reported that "the mix of gooey fruit, not-so-flaky pastry and frosting just keeps rockin' to double-digit growth." The brand virtually owned the category with a 75 percent market share. Its closest rival was still at a meager six percent in 1990. Since 1964 sales have continued to grow through innovative product development and marketing strategies covering domestic and international markets. What started as an early foray away from breakfast cereals in the 1960s has become a high-power seller in its own right. Kellogg promoted Pop-Tarts in its 1992 "Second Quarter Report" as a "delicious breakfast or snack alternative."

Brand Origins

Kellogg had begun in 1906 as the Battle Creek Toasted Corn Flake Company. It had diversified from corn flakes to three other cereals by 1922, including Krumbles in 1913, All-Bran in 1916, and 40 Percent Bran Flakes in 1923. In 1952, 85 percent of Kellogg's sales still derived from ten of their breakfast cereals. In the 1950s Kellogg took advantage of the opportunities presented in the postwar baby boom and the advent of television by bringing out a line of pre-sweetened, "kid-oriented" cereals and advertising them with cartoon characters on Saturday-morning television. New products included Sugar Frosted Flakes, Sugar Smacks, Sugar Corn Pops, Sugar All-Stars, and Cocoa Krispies. Kellogg invented Tony the Tiger and also used such cartoon salescreatures as Yogi Bear, Huckleberry Hound, and Quick Draw McGraw to sell its new brands to children.

With the barrage of television advertising, buying habits changed, and, instead of perennial brand loyalty, families began to stock several types of products. The number of brands on the market doubled from 50 to 100 from the mid-1950s to the mid-1960s. Soon pre-sweetened products accounted for almost 25 percent of all cereal sales. Kellogg benefited most from these changes. With its host of new cereal brands complete with brand-specialized cartoon characters and a $46 million advertising budget in 1965, Kellogg "knocked General Foods out of first place, and soon had more than 40% of all the cereal business," *Forbes* reported in 1966.

After gaining market share and sales in cereal, Kellogg searched for related breakfast items that could both draw on and complement the recent success in breakfast cereals. The company settled on a food of taste and convenience, the toaster pastry. "Toaster pastries joined the breakfast line-up in 1964 as Kellogg's Pop-Tarts," according to a company pamphlet. Pop-Tarts represented both a diversification from cereal and an expansion of the cereal line into a breakfast line.

Marketing Strategy

When Kellogg's Pop-Tarts were introduced, ads highlighted the item's convenience and often featured "Milton the Toaster." Advertisements also consisted of the full brand name and the slogan "drop 'em into the toaster—or eat 'em just as they are" printed across the side of the toaster with Pop-Tarts popped up. Pop-Tarts were marketed then and now as a food of convenience and a snack of nutrition. In a 1991 article in *Adweek's Marketing Week,* Fara Warner criticized Kellogg's claims of the nutritional value of Pop-Tarts by writing, "Pop-Tarts. Nutrition. Right." Yet Kellogg nutritionist Donna Thede affirmed the nutritional claim within the context of other snack foods, stating that each Pop-Tart has only 210 calories and 6 grams of fat. Sugar content is relatively high in the product with varieties such as "Brown Sugar Cinnamon" or "S'mores." Pop-Tarts are fortified with six vitamins and minerals, but only marginally so in comparison with some of Kellogg's more nutritious cereals.

Kellogg's marketing strategy of claiming nutrition for Pop-Tarts is a part of the larger, historic strategy to market Pop-Tarts to adults as well as children. Hoping to appeal to grown-up baby boomers as well as to today's children and adolescents, Kellogg continues to direct marketing schemes for pre-sweetened cereals and Pop-Tarts to all age groups. For example, in a 1984 *Advertising Age* article, a Kellogg spokesman described Frosted Flakes as "a nutritious cereal that adults like" and added, "It's a good tasting cereal—all we're trying to do is make people less hesitant about eating it." Advertisements for Pop-Tarts function similarly by attempting to make adults feel less conspicuous about eating Pop-Tarts and more comfortable giving Pop-Tarts to their children. Kellogg boasted in its 1988 *Annual Report* that it has "built a loyal franchise with teenage consumers" in its "so hot they're

AT A GLANCE

Kellogg's Pop-Tarts brand of toaster pastries introduced in 1964 in Battle Creek, MI, as one of the Kellogg Company's early diversifications from and complements of ready-to-eat cereal.

Performance: *Market share*—75 percent (top share) of toaster pastry category. *Sales*—$285 million.

Major competitor: RJR Nabisco Inc.'s Toastettes tarts.

Advertising: *Agency*—Leo Burnett & Company, Chicago, IL, 1964—. *Major campaign*—"So hot they're cool"; children chastising their parents for skipping breakfast and offering Pop-Tarts as a quick and tasty meal.

Addresses: *Parent company*—Kellogg Company, One Kellogg Square, P.O. Box 3599, Battle Creek, MI 49016-3599; phone: (616) 961-2000; fax: (616) 961-2871.

cool'' campaign. In the early 1990s, Kellogg ran commercials that featured children chastising their parents for skipping breakfast and offering Pop-Tarts as a quick and tasty meal.

Product Innovations

While Kellogg has devoted attention to advertising and marketing Pop-Tarts, the company has also worked to develop new flavors and varieties and has raised the brand's overall quality. In 1978, for example, Kellogg's expanded the basic Pop-Tarts line with the addition of chocolate chip and cherry chip varieties. The success of these two new varieties furthered market share for Pop-Tarts. While sales continued growing in the early 1980s, Kellogg reformulated the packaging and ingredients of the brand. Kellogg added nutritional value comparisons with granola bars on boxes. In 1983 Kellogg switched exclusively to Smucker's fruit preserves as the fruit filling in Pop-Tarts. This shift to a higher-quality ingredient once again boosted sales and helped Kellogg maintain its lead in the toaster pastry category. In 1986 Kellogg introduced "Peanut Butter and Jelly" Pop-Tarts; in 1990 "Milk Chocolate"; and in 1992 "S'mores." Kellogg reformulated the "Dutch Apple" flavor to "Apple Cinnamon" in 1991 and improved the blueberry variety in 1992. In the early 1990s, Kellogg produced Pop-Tarts in 15 flavors.

Prospects for Growth

Pop-Tarts Have been a commercial success since their introduction in the 1960s. In a 1978 interview in *Advertising Age*, Kellogg President W. E. LaMothe labeled convenience foods as the products holding the greatest promise for the company. In the early 1990s, Kellogg developed a strategy for international growth to increase Pop-Tarts sales. In 1992 Kellogg streamlined North American operations by merging Kellogg USA (formerly Kellogg's U.S. Food Products Division) with Kellogg Canada to form Kellogg North America. Other divisions include Kellogg Europe, Kellogg Asia Pacific, and Kellogg Latin America. With distribution facilities in 150 countries worldwide, Kellogg will continue to expand all of its brands worldwide. Kellogg Europe introduced Pop-Tarts in Great Britain and Ireland in 1992.

Pop-Tarts entered the 1990s with clear sales leadership in the U.S. toaster pastry category. Sales in the U.S. and Canada continued to meet high growth rates into the 1990s while the brand was available for the first time in mid-1992 in Great Britain and Ireland. The Kellogg Company plans to develop markets and sales around the world, and Pop-Tarts is one brand that stands to benefit tremendously from this international expansion. In the 1991 *Annual Report*, Kellogg described the high position that Pop-Tarts continues to maintain in the company today: "Although ready-to-eat cereal will remain Kellogg Company's number one product line, continued leadership and growth in convenience foods represents a substantial opportunity and high priority for the 1990s."

Further Reading:

Crain, Rance, "A Conversation with Kellogg's W. E. LaMothe," *Advertising Age*, October 2, 1978, p. 56.

"Don't Underestimate the Power of a Kid," *Forbes*, October 15, 1966, pp. 65-68.

The History of Kellogg Company, Battle Creek, Michigan: Kellogg Company, 1986.

"Kellogg Appealing to Adults," *Advertising Age*, September 27, 1984, p. 31.

Kellogg Company, *Annual Report*, Battle Creek, Michigan: Kellogg Company, 1978-1991.

"Kellogg Company," *International Directory of Company Histories*, v. II, Chicago: St. James Press, 1990, pp. 523-526.

Liesse, Julie, "Kellogg Chief to Push Harder for Int'l Growth," *Advertising Age*, August 24, 1992, pp. 4, 26.

Warner, Fara, "Pop-Tarts Keep On Toastin'," *Adweek's Marketing Week*, August 12, 1991, p. 8.

—Nicholas Patti

KELLOGG'S RAISIN BRAN®

Since Kellogg's Raisin Bran was introduced in 1942, it has been one of the "stars" of the Kellogg's family of cereals. A health-conscious public with an ever-increasing interest in grain products and, in particular, bran, has kept Kellogg's Raisin Bran an industry leader and one of the perennial favorites at the American breakfast table. Kellogg's Raisin Bran Flakes is produced by the Kellogg Company of Battle Creek, Michigan, the world's leading manufacturer of dry cereals and the producer of Eggo frozen waffles, Pop Tarts breakfast pastries, Mrs. Smith's pies, and Whitney's yogurt.

Brand Origins

In the meat 'n' potatoes era of the late nineteenth century, W.K. Kellogg was a dietary anomaly. He believed in a vegetarian diet that especially emphasized grains, and these beliefs helped change the eating habits—and especially the breakfast habits—of the American public for generations to come. In 1898 he introduced the product that eventually became the leading dry cereal in the industry, Kellogg's Corn Flakes. Kellogg had already created a wheat flake cereal and he kept experimenting to improve these products, as well as to create new ones. In 1916 he introduced Kellogg's Bran Flakes, capitalizing on the popularity of bran. In 1942 raisins were added to the flakes, a combination that proved to be immensely popular. Two decades later, Kellogg's tried to duplicate his success with another fruit/grain wedding, adding freeze-dried bananas to Corn Flakes. It was an unhappy marriage and was withdrawn from the market. Despite stiff competition in the marketplace, however, the serendipitous blend of raisins and bran, aided by a strong marketing policy, has kept Kellogg's Raisin Bran a top breakfast favorite through the years.

Marketing Strategy

Early in his business endeavors, it was clear that W.K. Kellogg was cognizant of the importance of marketing. He had quickly touted Kellogg's "toasted" Corn Flakes when that product was unveiled, spending one-third of the first year's profits on print and radio ads and door-to-door sample giveaways. Surging sales encouraged him to do the same with future products. In 1916 he introduced Kellogg's Bran Flakes to the public and promoted it with widespread ads aimed at health-conscious consumers. In 1942, when he presented Kellogg's Raisin Bran Flakes to the public, ads stressed that the cereal was "fortified" with vitamins.

With the nation at war and the public concerned about maintaining an adequate diet because of meat rationing and other changes in dietary circumstances, it was a wise advertising ploy. Kellogg's Raisin Bran quickly rose to a leading position among Kellogg's growing stable of cereals.

In the 1950s Kellogg entered the classroom to talk about proper nutrition. Young baby boomers learned about Kellogg's cereals and took the information home. Even more important, perhaps, was Kellogg's entrance into the realm of television advertising. On Saturday mornings, Kellogg's Raisin Bran and other Kellogg cereals were touted on the new media via shows such as "The Howdy Doody Show." Sales and profits doubled over a decade, which prompted W.K. Kellogg to pour additional money into advertising.

Kellogg's heavy advertising schedule drew fire in the early 1970s when the Federal Trade Commission accused the company and its leading rivals, General Mills and General Foods, of using massive advertising (12 percent of sales revenue), brand proliferation, and shelf space allocation stipulations to keep out competitors and thus maintain high prices and profit margins. There was no disputing the profit margins, but the companies argued that advertising and product proliferation were the result of competition, not monopoly. The cereal companies prevailed following a lengthy hearing.

The disagreements with the FTC ultimately did little to discourage advertising. When the company's market share began to sag in the late 1970s, Kellogg's responded by increasing its advertising budget. The company has always used its cereal boxes as a means of advertising.

In recent times, Kellogg's Raisin Bran has been caught up in what industry insiders call "The Raisin War." Kellogg has challenged its rivals with a heavy advertising campaign that features the jingle/song "Two Scoops of Raisins In Every Box!" in print and TV ads. The company also devised an advertising campaign centered around a music-loving group of animated raisins that proved to be enormously popular.

Indeed, Kellogg has never been a timid company in the area of advertising expenditures. To regain U.S. market share in the late 1980s, the company heavily increased its marketing expenditures,

AT A GLANCE

Kellogg's Raisin Bran brand cereal introduced in 1942, a combination of Kellogg's Bran Flakes (introduced in 1916) and raisins; brand originated by W.K. Kellogg.

Performance: *Market share*—3.7% of cold cereal market.

Major competitor: General Mills Inc.'s brands of cereal.

Addresses: *Parent company*—Kellogg Company, One Kellogg Square, Battle Creek, MI 49016-3599; phone: (616) 961-2000; fax: (616) 961-6596.

exceeding the previous year's figures by as much as $100 million a quarter. In 1991, though media spending in general dropped, Kellogg further increased its advertising budget on core brands such as Raisin Bran. Media spending on Raisin Bran was increased a whopping 57 percent to $23.8 million. The tactic paid off in an apparent slowdown in private-label cereal sales, most of which directly target core cereal brands such as Raisin Bran. For the first five months of 1992, private-label products claimed an 8.1 percent share of the market, down slightly from the previous year. By the third quarter of 1992, Kellogg's outsized media outlay made the company the fifth–largest advertiser in the country. It's nearest competitor in the breakfast cereal arena, General Mills, was the 15th–largest advertiser.

Will Kellogg's continue its costly ad promotions? In November 1992, as reported in *The Wall Street Journal,* Kellogg's CEO Arnold G. Langbo called for an end to the promotional spending war among the cereal giants. Analysts applauded Langbo's call. Noted Joanna Scharf Rosien of S. G. Warburg, "The biggest negative on Kellogg has been the huge increases in spending, and if they plan to moderate that, it's a strong fundamental positive." However, some analysts are doubtful that Kellogg will cut back. While pushing for a more traditional ratio of promotion to sales, Mr. Langbo did not miss the opportunity to serve notice on General Mills that Kellogg would do whatever is necessary to maintain its huge market share leads in Europe.

A Look at Global Markets

With shrewd business acumen and a eye to ever-expanding markets, W.K. Kellogg introduced its cereals to the British Isles—whose inhabitants were known to be prodigious cereal consumers—in the early 1920s. At the same time, he opened a plant in Sydney, Australia. Over the years, Kellogg has opened plants in South Africa, Mexico, Ireland, Sweden, the Netherlands, Den-

mark, New Zealand, Norway, Venezuela, Colombia, Brazil, Switzerland, and Finland.

The plants have put Kellogg's core brands—including Raisin Bran—in cereal bowls in more than 150 countries. In the early 1990s, for the first time, Kellogg's overseas sales volume exceeded its U.S. sales—53 percent to 47 percent. Industry analysts expect that, at least in the immediate future, Kellogg will continue its dominance of the world cereal market.

Prospects for Future Growth

After three consecutive years of market share decline, Kellogg's had a good year domestically, securing a 37.4 percent share of the $8 billion ready-to-eat cereal market in 1991. In August 1992 *Advertising Age* reported that the company is poised to refocus on global expansion. "We didn't do any geographic expansion in the 1980s," Langbo noted. "But now we're going to do lots of that." Kellogg is building a 100-percent company-owned cereal plant in Latvia, scheduled to open in 1994. It's already distributing products in Poland, Hungary, and Czechoslovakia. A plant in India is also targeted, as well as entry into the vast market of China. Langbo hopes to make core brands such as Raisin Bran a global presence, but he acknowledges it may be uphill work. In the markets of Eastern Europe, cereal for breakfast is a totally new concept. Langbo compared the situation to that in Germany and France in the early 1950s, where cereal consumption has always been low—1.8 pounds per person in France, for example, as compared to 10.1 pounds in the United States.

The battle for cereal primacy in Europe is apt to be fiercely contested, as Nestlé and General Mills have joined forces as Cereal Partners Worldwide. Nestlé, as the world's largest food company, may have a tactical advantage over Kellogg with its access to markets and powerful distribution system. Kellogg responded to news of the agreement by increasing advertising spending in Europe by 19 percent to an estimated $160 million, as compared with an estimated $35 to $50 million push from Cereal Partners, who in the early 1990s remained a relatively small presence with only 5.9 percent of the industry's market share.

Further Reading:

Gibson, Richard, "Kellogg Co.'s Chairman Seeks to End Cereal Firms' Promotion Spending War," *The Wall Street Journal,* November 2, 1992.

Knowlton, Christopher, "Europe Cooks Up A Cereal Brawl," *Fortune,* June 3, 1991.

Liese, Julie, "Kellogg Chief to Push Harder for Int'l Growth," *Advertising Age,* August 24, 1992.

—Joy Darlington

KELLOGG'S RICE KRISPIES®

Since 1926 Kellogg's Rice Krispies has been "talking" to consumers. The cereal's "Snap, Crackle and Pop" was created through a unique process in which oven-toasted rice is filled with tiny air bubbles. The consumer does the rest by adding milk, which is unevenly absorbed and causes an irregular swelling of the starch. As the remaining starch structures break down, they produce their famous sound. Kellogg's Rice Krispies is owned by the Kellogg Company of Battle Creek, Michigan, the world's leading manufacturer of dry cereals and also the producer of Eggo frozen waffles, Pop Tarts breakfast pastries, Mrs. Smith's pies, and Whitney's yogurt.

Brand Origins

Enthusiastic about all grains, W. K. Kellogg had already developed corn, wheat, and bran into popular cereals when he turned his attention to rice. Rice flakes had been on the menu at his brother's sanitarium in Battle Creek, but W. K. Kellogg wanted to create a totally new cereal. He began to experiment with rice puffs, and the result was exactly what he had hoped for—a totally different cereal he named Kellogg's Rice Krispies. Its crunchy taste and, in particular, its unique sound set it apart from other cereals and gave it a lively personality. Cartoonists loved to poke fun at it, and their attention probably boosted sales. One newspaper cartoon showed a cereal manufacturer presenting a bowl of cereal to his board. "It's the greatest thing since Snap, Crackle and Pop," he claims. "It says grace!"

Since Rice Krispies was introduced to the public, there have been five extensions of the cereal: Cocoa Krispies, Fruity Marshmallow Krispies, Frosty Marshmallow Krispies, and the 1993 addition Rice Krispies Treats cereal, which the Kellogg Company based on the recipe featured on Rice Krispies boxes for more than 50 years. The marshmallowy, buttery taste of the recipe has been duplicated in the cereal but, to appeal to a fat-conscious generation, it has only one gram of fat per serving. The immensely popular Rice Krispies Treats cereal was so in demand shortly following its introduction that the Kellogg Company had to take out ads explaining to consumers that it is trying to keep store shelves stocked.

The cereal will have to continue to do well to emulate its parent. Since the day it was created, Rice Krispies has been a star in Kellogg's cereal lineup. As reported in *Advertising Age,* the market's fifth-largest brand outperformed the category with a 9 percent sales increase for the year ending May 1992. This increase slightly boosted Rice Krispies' market share to 3.2 percent.

Early Marketing Savvy

Three strange little characters named Snap, Crackle and Pop, made their debut with Rice Krispies in 1928, bringing to life the sound the cereal made when flooded with milk. Snap and Pop wear tall Baker's hats; Crackle, the middle one, is outfitted with a long dunce cap. Elflike, with jumbo-sized ears and long, pointy noses, the trio has been hard at work since they were created, singing, dancing, and frolicking on cereal boxes and in advertisements. The trio are three of what *Forbes* called Kellogg's "super pitchmen": cartoon characters that were expensive to create but, because they have captured the attention of the young audience at which they were aimed, were worth every penny of what they cost. The added advantage of using cartoon pitchmen is that children who can't read—and even those who can't talk—can recognize the pitchmen and let their parents know this is the cereal they want.

In the 1950s Kellogg entered the new medium of television with gusto. It used its trio of Rice Krispies pitchmen on carefully selected programs that would appeal to the young, including the *Howdy Doody Show.* Later television advertising has appeared during PBS's *Reading Rainbow,* CBS's *Schoolbreak Specials,* and ABC's *Afterschool Specials.*

The first big threat to Rice Krispies' continued growth came in the 1950s with the introduction of presweetened cereal, which baby boomers loved. However, presweetened cereals eventually came under heavy attack from consumer advocates, who charged that these cereals were no more nutritious than candy. Rice Krispies held its own as a nonsweetened cereal that was still "fun to eat."

Perhaps a bigger threat to Rice Krispie's continued growth was the aging of the baby boomers. In the 1970s the generation passed from the under-25 age group, which consumes an average of 11 pounds of cereal a year, to the 25-30 age group, which eats less than half as much cereal. Cereal market growth dropped and Kellogg's market share fell from 43 percent in 1972 to 37 percent in 1983.

AT A GLANCE

Kellogg's Rice Krispies brand of cereal founded in 1926 by W. K. Kellogg, president of the Kellogg Company; brand extensions include Cocoa Krispies, Fruity Marshmallow Krispies, Frosty Marshmallow Krispies, and Rice Krispies Treats.

Performance: Market share—3.2% of the cereal category. Sales—$227.8 million.

Major competitor: General Mills' Triples.

Advertising: Agency—Leo Burnett Company, Chicago, IL, 1949— . Major campaign—Familiar animated characters Snap, Crackle and Pop featured in television and print ads and on cereal boxes.

Addresses: Parent company—Kellogg Company, One Kellogg Square, Battle Creek, MI 40016-3599; phone: (616) 961-2000; fax: (616) 961-6596.

Kellogg's response to sagging sales was to invest in more advertising, and it continued to rely on consumer recognition of its Rice Krispies pitchmen. The trio's features softened through the years and their ears are a size or so smaller, but their noses are still on a par with Pinnochio's. Kellogg's still counted on Snap, Crackle and Pop to market Rice Krispies successfully. By 1985 with the continued aging of the baby boomers and a new generation to pitch to, Kellogg had regained much of its market share of approximately 40 percent.

Marketing in Later Years

As presweetened cereals continued to draw criticism from consumer groups, the younger generation of the early 1990s seemed to be listening again to Snap, Crackle and Pop's noisy chatter. According to Nielson Marketing Research figures for the year ending May 1992, Rice Krispies outperformed the category with a 9 percent sales increase—compared to the category's overall 6.6 percent rise—and saw its market share slightly boosted to 3.2 percent.

Nostalgia was perhaps another reason for Rice Krispies' climbing sales. Most parents can remember Rice Krispies holding a place in their family cupboard. It was certainly more nutritious than the presweetened brands, and it was fun. The 1990s, according to some analysts, is a retro-minded era. Kellogg's is successfully pitching its core brands as cereals to go back to and to introduce to your children—and grandchildren.

Prospects for Future Growth

By the end of 1992 an economic slump was being blamed for slow growth in several key markets, including Germany and Australia. Sluggish sales were also reported in Brazil and Mexico—key markets for Rice Krispies. Kellogg was hopeful that an upturn in world economies, plus its own persistent marketing skills and promotions, would boost its core products' sales.

Two major changes in Europe promised to elevate sales. One was the proliferation of the continent's supermarkets, which will serve as prime arenas to display Kellogg's products. Second, commercial TV stations—more forums for Kellogg to display its wares—were also expanding. Kellogg hoped to influence European homemakers, who prefer traditional breakfasts of bread, cheese, eggs, and meat, to switch to quicker, convenient, and cheaper cereal breakfasts. If more Europeans accepted this pitch, the market, according to *Fortune,* could quadruple by the year 2000, making cereal the fastest growing food category.

As the population grew and Kellogg's entry into new global markets in Europe and Asia increased in the early 1990s, Rice Krispies, a perennial favorite, hoped to garner a larger market share. Children in Eastern Europe and Asia alike may be delighting to the peculiar noises in their cereal bowls.

Further Reading:

"Don't Underestimate the Power of a Kid," *Forbes,* October 15, 1966, pp.65-68.

Knowlton, Christopher, "Europe Cooks Up A Cereal Brawl," *Fortune,* June 3, 1991.

"Less Snap, Crackle & Pop," *Detroit Free Press,* March 26, 1993.

Liese, Julie, "Kellogg Chief to Push Harder for International Growth," *Advertising Age,* August 24, 1992; "From Cereal to Snack to Cereal," *Advertising Age,* January 11, 1993, p. 20.

—*Joy Darlington*

KOOL®

Kool, like its major competitors Salem and Newport, has always been available only as a menthol brand. While other brands have established menthol versions of their regular cigarette, none of these dominates the market like the menthol brands. Kool is the oldest nationally distributed menthol brand in the United States, and is second only to Salem in sales volume among menthols. It has, however, suffered some weakness in its sales precisely because it has been around so long. Having originally established itself as a major brand with a broad demographic customer mix during the postwar era, Kool has subsequently witnessed the narrowing of its market to certain sectors of the population. Lower- and middle-income people and African Americans have emerged as its largest customer groups in the 1980s and the 1990s.

Brand Origins

During the 1920s, cigarette makers began to experiment with flavorings in their tobacco mixes in an effort to broaden the market for cigarettes. While chocolate, lemon, and vanilla extracts were (and continue to be) tried, by far the most successful was menthol. Menthol, a complex white crystalline substance extracted from peppermint, was most commonly sprayed over tobacco leaves during the manufacturing process. When the cigarette was burned, the substance emitted its cool minty flavor into the smoke, giving smokers a blast of coolness from an otherwise common cigarette.

While many manufacturers offered menthol brands, none were nationally distributed or advertised. As a result, sales of menthols never exceeded more than a fraction of a percent of the total market. However, in the early 1930s Brown & Williamson, one of the larger tobacco companies of the day, began laying plans to introduce a new 70-millimeter menthol brand for national distribution. Drawing from the qualities of menthol, the company named the brand "Kool"—using a "K" because the name "Cool" could not be trademarked.

Early Marketing Strategy

Introduced to test markets in February of 1933, Kool tested well with consumers. In preparation for a national roll-out, the company devised a cartoon mascot, Willie the Penguin, who was to be featured in print ads skating around a pond in a tuxedo with a Kool cigarette in his beak. Further promotion came in the form of B&W coupons when the brand went into national distribution in August of that year. Coupons were common as cigarette premiums

and were redeemable as discounts or could be used to purchase a variety of products at special rates. Kool maintained fair growth in the market, mostly because of its uniqueness as a menthol cigarette and its muscle as a national brand from a major company.

In 1936, to broaden its public profile, Brown & Williamson began using Kool in conjunction with its Raleigh brand to sponsor network radio programs. By 1937 the brand sold more than four billion units, accounting for 2.5 percent of the total cigarette market. While this seems a small portion of the market, 2.5 percent growth was fairly phenomenal in a market with extremely strong brand loyalty.

Much of this growth may be attributed to the fact that Kool rarely replaced any smoker's regular brand, but was consumed along with that regular brand. For some smokers, nonmenthol cigarettes frequently caused irritation of the throat and a dry cough. These smokers soon discovered that Kool did not produce as much of a burning sensation in their throats as their regular brands. This benefit was later featured in Kool's advertising, in one instance depicting two office workers discussing the irritation of smoking all day. One of the workers offers his friend a Kool, imploring him to take a break from his regular brand. Reveling in his discovery, the friend asks, "Do you take a break with Kools?" "Sure," the worker replies. "In fact, some people like Kools so much, they smoke them all the time." Unfortunately, this campaign did little to propel Kool beyond this special-use niche.

In fact, sales declined from 1938 to 1941, despite the addition of bonus coupons and new advertising. As other brands advanced, Kool's market share fell even faster than its sales. In 1940, Brown & Williamson dropped Kool from the radio, cut the brand's price, and reduced the number of coupons—all signals of a strong retreat. Then, in 1941, Brown & Williamson made one last attempt to bolster Kool's sales, presumably before abandoning the brand. New ads featured an updated version of Willie the smoking penguin and extolled the virtues of menthol. Rather unexpectedly, Kool's market share stabilized and, in a growing market, sales began to increase. This trend continued for several years, despite the materials shortages that occurred during World War II.

Brown & Williamson pulled its coupons from Kool in 1943, but maintained its successful advertising campaign throughout and after the war. Kool returned to radio in 1947 with spot ads. This helped to stimulate consumer interest in menthol cigarettes and to retain many smokers who experimented with Kool.

Packaging

One of the cigarette industry's greatest challenges was perfecting a package that would preserve the freshness of the tobacco. For years, cigarettes were wrapped in foil and paper labels and sealed with a band (adapted from cigar bands). But because this package was not air tight, cigarettes—particularly fragrant menthol brands—continued to have short shelf lives.

While many manufacturers began to wrap the entire package in cellophane, Brown & Williamson tried something special for Kool. The company borrowed Reynolds' Metal Plyseal Pack, a heat-sealed foil pack that did not require cellophane. But test marketing of the package in Wisconsin and Minnesota where, presumably, shelf lives were longest, proved unsuccessful. In addition, the added cost of the unconventional package cut the profit margin on Kool. Plyseal was discontinued entirely in 1952.

The company has tested and introduced more than a dozen variations of Kool, including light and ultra-light brands, and a separate line of lights featuring an unusual white filter. In each instance, the company has featured Kool in a variation of the established label, a green rectangle on a white package, featuring the Kool name with interlocked O's.

Advertising

In 1951 Brown & Williamson began advertising Kool in the new medium of television, gradually increasing TV ads until there were as many as radio ads. By 1953 Kool sales were double what they were in 1946, and market share climbed to 2.9 percent. Television proved an especially effective means of advertising for Kool. In fact, sales of the brand began to slide shortly after broadcast advertising of cigarettes was discontinued in 1971.

Brown & Williamson has used a variety of advertising agencies, including, but not limited to, Campbell-Mithun-Esty, Ted Bates Advertising, and Cunningham & Walsh of New York, for the bulk of its advertising for many years. The agencies developed such memorable themes as "Come all the way up to Kool" and "Lady be cool" and helped to define Kool as a high-quality menthol cigarette.

In 1975, as other cigarette brands turned to sponsorship of auto racing and tennis matches, Brown & Williamson began using Kool to sponsor popular jazz festivals. The sponsorship programs were so successful that they were later extended to folk and country music shows. While the sponsorships have kept the Kool name in the public consciousness, the company and its agency began to encounter difficulty maintaining a unique Kool image, particularly during the 1970s when the brand was subjected to an onslaught from dozens of new menthol brands. Brown & Williamson, however, has never abandoned the central themes of Kool advertising: high quality and full menthol flavor.

Health Claims

Kool has never been promoted as a low tar and nicotine brand but rather as a full flavor menthol cigarette, but there have been a few notable changes in the product in regard to health concerns over the years. In 1956, in response to a competitor's entry into the market with a filter-tipped menthol brand, Brown & Williamson added a cork and cellulose acetate filter to its king size brand. In 1972, in response to growing demand among smokers for lower tar and nicotine cigarettes, Kool introduced a low tar and nicotine extension, Kool Milds. Although never directly positioned as the health-conscious smoker's brand, Kool Milds succeeded in stemming market share losses to competing low-tar menthol brands.

International Growth

Kool is one of the few American brands that is available overseas. While nonmenthol competitor Marlboro dominates the American cigarette export market, fewer than a dozen of America's 176 brands are exported. The low number of export brands results from strict import laws enacted by foreign governments to protect their domestic tobacco industries. In addition, it is most economical for a company to enter a foreign market with only a single brand, rather than a family of brands, to capitalize on the reputation of that brand and concentrate promotional funds.

As a result, Brown & Williamson began exporting Kool to major (urban) markets in the Far East and South America during the early 1970s. Kool proved popular in these warm-weather markets, where a menthol brand was not only unusual, but perhaps more refreshing.

Brand Development

Brown & Williamson, noting the popularity of longer cigarettes, began test-marketing an 85-millimeter Kool in 1953, taking the king size version to the national market in March of 1954. Heavy promotion of the longer size helped to increase the brand's market share to 3.4 percent that year.

In 1956 Kool faced its most serious challenge to date: a direct competitor. R. J. Reynolds, which manufactured Camel and Winston, noted the increasing popularity of menthol brands and introduced its own, Salem, that year. Backed by the Reynolds reputation and an advertising blitz, Salem succeeded in winning away a number of Kool smokers, and attracted a significant number of nonmenthol smokers as well. In response, Brown & Williamson reintroduced its king size version with a colored, and therefore immediately identifiable, filter. This helped to stem losses to Salem which, driven by heavy promotion, continued to rack up market share.

To meet the advertising challenge, Brown & Williamson updated its campaigns, and in 1958 added the tag line, "Snow-fresh Kool, America's most refreshing cigarette." In 1960, the company redesigned the Kool package and, in advertising, dropped Willie the Penguin and strongly promoted Kool's menthol reputation. The ads helped Kool remain strong until late in 1961, when overexposure and a lack of variety in the commercials caused sales to retreat slightly.

Brown & Williamson increased the menthol content of Kool in 1962 and ran a different style of advertisement, laying the claim that Kool had more menthol than other brands. Using a "problem/solution" approach, the ads proved extremely effective, boosting Kool sales to more than 14.5 billion units, and to 19 billion in 1964. By 1965, Kool led menthol brands Salem and Belair with nearly 5 percent of the market. That year, however, no fewer than 10 new menthol brands hit the market. Promoting only the king size and a new 99-millimeter Kool, Brown & Williamson managed to push Kool sales over 28 million in 1967, representing nearly 40 percent of the menthol market and more than 6 percent of the total market.

Having discovered that nearly 80 percent of the extra-length menthol market was comprised of women, Brown & Williamson began special promotions of Kool Filter Longs on daytime television in 1969, using the tag line, "Stylishly Long, Refreshingly Cool. Lady Be Cool."

On the strength of king size Kool and strong growth of Kool Longs, Kool sales climbed to more than 44 billion units in 1971, representing 8.2 percent of the market. But at the end of 1970, the tobacco industry voluntarily terminated all broadcast advertising in order to avoid government intervention in cigarette advertising. With the elimination of the broadcast mediums that built Kool's strong position, Brown & Williamson was forced to revamp the brand's ad campaigns for print, outdoor, and transit media. Unfortunately, the themes did not translate well. In addition, rumors ran rampant that Brown & Williamson planned to remove Kool from the market. Kool sales began a steady slide.

In 1971 the company tried new media, especially ads aimed at diffusing the rumor of the brand's demise, and initiated a campaign in which Kool smokers could purchase an 11-foot Sea Snark sailboat (fitted with a Kool logo sail) for $88. Brown & Williamson received more than 18,000 orders for the sailboats.

Sales having rebounded, Brown & Williamson introduced another extension, low-tar Kool Milds. This 84-millimeter light brand was created specifically to capitalize on the emerging demand for lower tar and nicotine cigarettes, as well as to ease past a special tar and nicotine tax in New York City. Kool Milds were positioned differently from the regular brands. Print ads were very similar to Salem ads, depicting rural scenes during springtime and carrying tag lines like "Enjoy a cooler kind of mild." During its second year, Kool Milds emerged as the largest-selling light menthol brand on the market.

Kool finished 1972 as the nation's fourth best-selling brand, behind Marlboro, Winston, and Pall Mall, with 9 percent of the total market. Also that year, with more than 35 percent of the market, Kool became the top-selling menthol, leading Newport, Salem, and Alpine. In 1974 the company offered the king size brand in a flip-top box. Strong growth in the line helped Kool reach nearly 40 percent of the menthol market, with more than 61

billion units sold annually. However, sales of the original 70-millimeter straight brand continued to fall to nearly one billion.

Having begun sponsoring jazz and soul music festivals in 1975, Kool's sales demographics began to change. Increasingly, with the loss of many female smokers to Virginia Slims and Benson & Hedges, and the virtual evaporation of the 1940s' middle-class segment, Kools were consumed in greater proportion by lower-income and black Americans.

Emphasizing broader demographics in its advertising through an "Americana" campaign, Kool sponsored a variety of sweepstakes, giving away everything from lighters to yachts and a Rolls-Royce. These gimmicks failed to sustain Kool's growth, however, and by 1978 sales had retreated to just over 59 billion units. In an attempt to shore up lagging sales in a shrinking market, Kool added 100-millimeter Milds in 1979, high-filtration 85- and 100-millimeter Light and Ultra Light extensions in 1981, and a Milds box in 1986. While these helped stem some losses, sales of the "industrial strength" menthol lines began to decline.

Performance Appraisal

In 1991, after five lackluster years of falling sales, Brown & Williamson concluded that Kool was viewed as too old-fashioned by key consumers. Having witnessed the strong turnaround that the cartoon Cool Joe brought to the older Camel brand, Brown & Williamson decided to resurrect the penguin mascot. The new spokesbird, said to be a cousin of Willie, made his debut that year, cast as a Ray Ban-wearing hipster uttering irreverent quips like "So I'm a penguin, get used to it." The campaign, designed to appeal to younger, wealthier whites and all females, ran with the re-introduction of Kings, Milds, Lights, and Ultra Lights.

Critics of the campaign said it lacked originality, had a flip approach to the identity, and might be attractive to youth. Despite criticism, however, the penguin succeeded in significantly raising public awareness of the new Kool line and did, in fact, stimulate sales among the target audience. And it took none of the heat that Reynolds incurred for Cool Joe's alleged appeal to children.

For all the attempts to "fix" Kool, it remains a declining brand with a narrow and aging customer base. Its strong position in the market, however, will afford Brown & Williamson many opportunities to revive its flagship brand.

Future Predictions

Menthol brands have grown in popularity since Kool invented the market in 1933. While total cigarette consumption has levelled off in recent years, menthol brands have grown to more than 26 percent of that market. Kool, which has held in excess of 6 percent of that market, fell to less than 5 percent in 1991, marking an alarming decline.

Kool is confined in its market by upscale Benson & Hedges, feminine Virginia Slims, low-tar Carlton and Now, and the equally powerful menthols, Salem and Newport. This leaves Kool little room for expansion or innovation. As other brands have added white filter lines, slim lights, and 120-millimeter extensions, Brown & Williamson may be forced to consider a remake of its brand. However, in 1992 Kool remained the company's flagship brand as the sixth leading cigarette in the United States. Kool, Salem, and Newport continue to command the menthol market, a trend that began in the 1980s.

Further Reading:

"For Cigarettes, a Grim Slide Picks Up Speed," *Adweek's Marketing Week,* Superbrands 1991.

"Kool Brand History," Louisville, KY: Brown & Williamson Tobacco Corporation.

"Kool Tries to Update Image," *Advertising Age,* September 30, 1991.

"This Penguin and Ads Are Far from Kool, Folks," *Advertising Age,* October 21, 1992.

"Three Faces of Kool," *Advertising Age,* October 14, 1991.

—John Simley

KOOL-AID®

The image is almost a cliché—a group of youngsters cluster around a homemade stand, selling Kool-Aid for a nickel a glass on a hot summer day. Kool-Aid, the brightly-colored, artificially-flavored brand of powdered beverage mix, has been a fixture of childhood since the Great Depression. It has survived the onslaught of bottled juice drinks and disposable juice boxes and is the top performer among all powdered drink mixes. The enduring popularity of Kool-Aid can be traced to its cost per serving, which is lower than the average juice or soda beverage, as well as its ease of purchase and preparation. The makers of Kool-Aid, General Foods USA, have bolstered their product with a series of aggressive advertising campaigns, some of which appeal to the nostalgia of parents, and some of which cater to the whims of children.

Little Store on the Prairie

Kool-Aid was developed in Hastings, Nebraska, in 1927 by E. E. Perkins, the owner of the Perkins Products Company. Perkins had worked a variety of jobs—printer, mail order salesman, and postmaster—before opening his own company in 1914. Originally, Perkins Products sold a number of mail-order items. The outfit offered 125 household articles, including toothpaste, spices, and perfumes, primarily to rural folk who could not find well-stocked general stores nearby.

By the mid-1920s, Perkins discovered that one of his most popular mail-order items was "Fruit Smack," a small bottle of flavored syrup that could be diluted in water to make large quantities of fruit-flavored beverage. The only problem with "Fruit Smack" was its packaging. Glass bottles were expensive to ship and could break with rough handling. Perkins developed a method to take the remaining water out of the product and then package it in a paper pouch. The process was complete by 1927, and the enterprising Perkins called his invention Kool-Aid. The name was an acknowledgement that the fruit drink sold better in the summertime.

The first home of Kool-Aid was a small clapboard building on a windswept prairie. Demand for the product soon exceeded availability, and Perkins expanded his operation several times. Within a few years he phased out all of the other products in his mail-order business to concentrate on Kool-Aid. He moved the manufacturing plant to Chicago in 1931. There too the dual processes—production of the powder and creation of the paper packets—expanded to meet demands, especially after World War II when sugar became more readily available again.

In 1953 Perkins decided to retire. Concerned about heavy estate taxes that might force the sale of his company after his death, he approached General Foods with an offer to sell Perkins Products. One of the first food conglomerates, General Foods already had numerous best-selling products under its umbrella, including Birds Eye frozen foods, Jell-O, Log Cabin Syrup, Minute Rice, and Gaines dog food. Still, the acquisition of Kool-Aid was a milestone for General Foods, because it was the company's first powdered beverage and was a proven performer with a streamlined, efficient manufacturing process already in place. It was also the first established business General Foods bought in the postwar era. In a company magazine, *GF News,* published in June of 1953, a reporter commented, "Kool-Aid, the soft drink in powdered form that's known in almost every home where there are children, comes in ready-made with a history of increasing sales and profits over the past 25 years."

A Fat, Smiling Pitcher

The benefits of the General Foods sale for Kool-Aid were the wealth of advertising and marketing savvy that its new owner could offer. The Foote, Cone & Belding advertising agency was awarded the Kool-Aid account in 1954. The company's art director, Marvin Potts, mused for some time about how to promote Kool-Aid's strong points—its appeal as a thirst-quencher and its affordability. One cold winter day, Potts watched his son trace drawings on a frosty window pane. Soon the idea gelled in Potts's mind: he would create a big, round, frosty pitcher to convey, in one image, the idea of generous quantity for the price and cool relief for thirst.

During the summer of 1954 the frosty pitcher began to appear in Kool-Aid advertising. Different spots featured the pitcher with a "5 cents" drawn into the frost, a heart and arrow drawn on the pitcher, or a minimalist smiling face drawn on the pitcher. The smiling-face pitcher quickly proved to be the favorite and was trademarked by 1956. Kool-Aid advertising still features the smiling pitcher in both animated and choreographed spots. Its recent incarnation is "Kool-Aid Man," a life-sized puppet usually surrounded by dancing children.

Ingredients and Nutritional Value

The main ingredients in a prepared glass of Kool-Aid are water and sugar. Kool-Aid can be bought unsweetened or with the sugar already added, but in either case, sugar remains the principal substance in the beverage. The same qualities that made Kool-Aid popular in the Great Depression years still held in the 1990s. The small packages are easy to carry home from the grocery store and are colorful and appealing to youngsters. The beverage is easy to prepare—even a pre-schooler can learn the proper proportions of sugar and water to mix (although adult supervision is recommended if glass pitchers are used). For years the makers of Kool-Aid have stressed the fact that the product is both cheaper and lower in sugar content than carbonated soft drinks. This advertising strategy is still used in commercials geared toward parents.

Artificial flavors are a Kool-Aid staple, but Kraft General Foods offers no specifics about their uses in the product. The process of developing artificial flavors has been known to chemists since the nineteenth century. Natural flavors were broken down to their chemical compounds, and the compounds were produced synthetically. In *It's All on the Label: Understanding Food, Additives, and Nutrition,* Zenas Block wrote, "There are over *seven hundred* synthetic flavors permitted as food additives that are not GRAS ('generally regarded as safe' by the Food and Drug Administration). There are twenty-four synthetic flavors that are GRAS. The consumer has no way of telling which is in the food: the GRAS product or the non-GRAS additive." Block added, "There is an enormous amount of ignorance on the subject of flavors. One theory presented is that *all* additives and especially artificial flavors cause hyperactivity in children, but nobody has been able to duplicate the work reported. On the other hand, nobody has ever claimed that highly colored, artificially flavored foods are good for you." Specifically addressing artificial flavor in beverages, Block noted, "If you are nervous about the safety of artificially flavored drinks, you should also be nervous about the safety of naturally flavored drinks. There are some natural flavors that have been found to be dangerous. . . . But, there is absolutely no evidence of any kind that indicates danger from either source [natural or artificial] of flavorings now permitted for use."

A federal Food Additives Amendment of 1958 disallowed the use of any food-coloring ingredient that produced cancer—in any amount—in laboratory animals. Numerous food colors were tested, and seven are approved for use in food and beverages. Kool-Aid uses these seven in varying amounts to produce a rainbow of colors for its different mixes. "Black Cherry" flavor, for instance, includes Red 40 and Blue 1. The other components of powdered Kool-Aid are all generally regarded as safe by the Food and Drug Administration. Kool-Aid contains citric acid for tartness, calcium phosphate to retard caking or clumping when the powder gets damp, and ascorbic acid (Vitamin C). An eight-ounce glass of Kool-Aid with sugar provides 100 calories and ten percent of a daily requirement of Vitamin C. It has no other nutritive value, but it contains no fat or sodium. Kraft General Foods emphasizes that prepared Kool-Aid has 25 percent less sugar than the leading sugar-sweetened colas.

For a brief period during the mid-1960s, Kool-Aid marketed a sugar-free, artificially sweetened mix. The mix did not sell well, primarily because parents were concerned about the safety of artificial sweeteners—particularly for children. In the 1980s Kool-Aid introduced a new sugar-free mix made with NutraSweet.

Modern Marketing Strategies

Keeping pace with market demands in recent years, Kool-Aid can now be found in disposable juice boxes and in frozen desserts called Kool Pops. Sagging sales on traditional Kool-Aid in the late 1980s sparked a new promotion—the "Wacky Warehouse Club." Television commercials encourage children to save proof-of-purchase stamps from Kool-Aid packages and then mail them in for toys or other merchandise. The mail-in campaign gives Kraft General Foods a database of young consumers' names and addresses. *Direct-Marketing* magazine reports that the Wacky Warehouse campaign has helped boost Kool-Aid's preference rating past even Coca-Cola and Pepsi-Cola among children under the age of twelve. Kraft General Foods has also employed the expensive "claymation" technique in a series of commercials for parents. Animated clay figures—adult mother bears—discuss the fact that Kool-Aid has less sugar and is less expensive than soft drinks.

Six to twelve-year-old children remain the primary target of Kool-Aid advertising, both on television and in supermarket aisles. For decades the hand-sized Kool-Aid packages have been decorated with bright colors and stylish cartoons. During the 1990s, various flavor packets depicted "Kool-Aid Man" skateboarding, surfing, playing beach volleyball, and singing in a rock band. Flavor names are chosen to appeal to younger children: a consumer can choose "Surfin' Berry Punch," "Great Bluedini," "Rock-a-dile Red" or "Sharkleberry Fin" as well as standard flavors such as "Black Cherry," "Lemonade," "Grape," and "Strawberry."

The sophisticated advertising campaigns have managed to keep Kool-Aid in style among youngsters and reluctantly accepted by parents. It does not seem to matter that the principal thirst-quencher in Kool-Aid is mere water. The product is hip, tasty, and inexpensive—a combination that has spelled success for Kool-Aid.

Further Reading:

Bernarde, Melvin A., *The Food Additives Dictionary: The Essential Handbook for Learning What's in the Food You Eat,* New York: Simon & Schuster, 1981, p. 28.

Block, Zenas, *It's All on the Label: Understanding Food, Additives, and Nutrition,* Boston: Little, Brown, 1981, pp. 71-72; 222.

"GF Welcomes Kool-Aid," *GF News,* June 1953, pp. 3-7.

"How to Come Smiling Through," *GF News,* July 1963, pp. 18-19.

"Kool-Aid Pours It On," *Adweek's Marketing Week,* April 27, 1992, p. 5.

"Kool-Aid vs. Colas," *Advertising Age,* April 27, 1992, p. 2.

"Kraft General Foods Leads the Way in Food Data Bases," *Advertising Age,* October 21, 1991, p. 22.

Morgan, Hal, *Symbols of America,* New York: Penguin, 1986, p. 115.

Moskowitz, Milton, Robert Levering, and Michael Katz, editors, *Everybody's Business: A Field Guide to the 400 Leading Companies in America,* New York: Doubleday, 1990, pp. 3-6.

"Not Just for the Little Guys," *Direct-Marketing,* May 1991, p. 20.

"Roving Warehouse," *Food-and-Beverage Marketing,* July 1992, p. 22.

"When Does a Bonus Start Being a Plug?," *Wall Street Journal,* September 20, 1991, p. B1.

—Anne Janette Johnson

KRAFT® CHEESE

Kraft, a brand name owned by Kraft USA, is the leading brand of cheese in the United States. For nearly a century, cheese bearing the Kraft name has been praised for its high quality, flavor, and texture by consumers, retailers, and food processors using it as an ingredient in a variety of prepared products. Kraft cheese was the first to appear in many different forms and packages, some of which actually revolutionized the way cheese was marketed and used by consumers. Throughout the years, Kraft has made innovations to ensure that its cheese stays fresh during storage and to enhance convenience for consumers.

Kraft process cheese was one of the first and most successful of its kind, developed as a means of extending shelf life and preserving flavor. Made partly from natural cheese, the process cheese maintained the same nutritional integrity of natural cheese made from milk. Kraft cheese was also the first to appear in individually wrapped slices. (Prior to that, cheese had to be sliced by a retailer, and the consumer could not be certain of a cheese's brand name.) Later developments were individually wrapped slices of some process and natural cheeses and hard cheeses in blocks, shredded, and strings.

Another first for Kraft was the development of nonfat cheese. With the media reporting that fat can pose health risks and that dairy products have high fat content, consumers were demanding reduced fat products. Strong consumer response to the first nonfat cheese led Kraft to introduce further nonfat varieties.

Brand Origins

In 1903 James L. Kraft established a wholesale cheese business in Chicago. For the next few years, he sold standard varieties of cheese using a horse and wagon each day to pick up cheeses in the wholesale warehouse district and then distribute them to retail stores. By 1914 nearly 30 varieties of cheese were packaged under the brand names of Kraft and Elkhorn, and distribution was expanded nationally. Around this time, the company started to make its own cheeses, and within a couple of years, Kraft would develop a completely new type of cheese.

In 1915, after many years of experiments, Kraft successfully developed and the following year patented a method of producing process cheese that would have an extended shelf life, be of uniform flavor, and be sold in a convenient package. The idea came about because Kraft believed the flavor and perishability of

cheese could be improved. At that time, American cheddar cheese was the most widely sold in the country, and it either got moldy or dried quickly. Also, the flavor could be strong or bitter.

Process cheese requires grinding and blending one or more varieties of natural cheese and then pasteurizing them. "Lots" from natural cheeses are selected, then cut into small pieces and transferred to a cooker. A small amount of emulsifying salts is added, color may be added, and the blended, pasteurized melted cheese then flows through a filling machine for packaging. Next, it is chilled and shipped to retailers. The procedure takes place without any waste, and the cheese has a uniform quality.

Natural Cheese Developments

Natural cheese is produced directly from milk or whey and is made by coagulating or curdling milk, stirring and heating the curd, draining off the whey, and gathering or pressing the curd. Curing, or holding it for a specific time at a certain temperature and humidity, will give the cheese a desirable flavor and texture. Shortly after Kraft introduced process cheese in 1915, several natural varieties were added, including Edam, Gouda, and Roquefort cheese. Natural cheese products put on the market in the following years included Cheddar, Colby, Swiss, Muenster, Provolone, and Mozzarella.

Kraft markets natural cheese in various forms. Long slices of Swiss and Muenster cheese are separated by paper and packaged in a plastic bag that hangs on a hook in a store's refrigerator case. Swiss, Muenster, Provolone, and Light Sharp Cheddar can be packaged in a small bundle of slices ready for sandwiches.

Blocks or chunks of cheese, requiring consumers to slice the cheeses themselves, were marketed in many varieties under the Cracker Barrel label. These cheeses include many forms of cheddar, such as Light Sharp Cheddar, Natural Cheddar, Sharp Cheddar, Extra Sharp Cheddar, Medium Cheddar, Sharp White Cheddar, and Extra Sharp White Cheddar. Other types of block cheese are Baby Swiss and California Pepper Jack.

Maintaining the tradition of bringing consumers a high level of convenience, Kraft also marketed some natural cheese varieties in shredded form, including Swiss, Sharp Cheddar, Mozzarella, Light Naturals Low Moisture Part Skim Mozzarella, and Natural Low Moisture Part Skim Mozzarella. These ready-to-use shredded cheeses are marketed under the Kraft or Polly-O label and are typically used by consumers as a pizza or taco topping.

Individually wrapped Mozzarella string cheese was another form intended to make cheese consumption easier, particularly for use as snacks in or outside the home. Kraft marketed string cheese under the Polly-O brand, which was acquired in 1986 when Kraft USA bought Pollio Dairy Products Corp. of Mineola, New York, a cheese company established in 1899 and known for Polly-O mozzarella cheese.

First Cheese in Slices

In 1949 Kraft introduced into limited markets (with national rollout the following year) an innovation that changed the way that cheese was used by consumers. Kraft Deluxe Process Cheese packaged as slices was the first commercial item of its type. By 1950 other process and natural cheeses were in national distribution, including American, Old English, Swiss, Pimento, and Brick. Each package contained 8 slices. Consumers were receptive to the new slices because they didn't stick together, were easy to separate, and stayed fresher. Each slice was of the same size and quality and was ideal for a sandwich. The idea also appealed to retailers who preferred the pre-sliced cheese to having customers wait for a clerk to slice cheese. Kraft was also pleased because sliced cheese could now be identified by the Kraft brand.

The first package of slices was a carton of two three-pound packages, with each three-pound package containing three one-pound stacks of sixteen slices. Eventually, all process and natural varieties were packaged as slices. Different varieties had specific weights and thicknesses, such as Kraft Sharp Old English in thick,

one-ounce slices, and Kraft Deluxe in three-quarter-ounce slices. In 1965 another innovation appeared in the form of individually wrapped slices so that consumers could more easily remove one or more slices from the package. Kraft Deluxe American and Light N' Lively American were among the first varieties with this packaging.

Quality Assurance in Packaging

Throughout the years, packaging for Kraft cheeses underwent several changes as the company sought to give cheese greater protection while being stored by retailers and consumers, and greater ease of use to consumers. Process cheese was originally packaged in tins of two sizes—three-and-a-half ounces and seven-and-three-quarters ounces. Since the cheese could safely be shipped over long distances, the U.S. government ordered more than 6 million pounds in tins to feed soldiers overseas in 1917 during World War I.

In 1921 the tins were replaced by five-pound, foil-wrapped cheese loaves of American, Pimento, Swiss, Brick, and Old English varieties packaged in wooden boxes, which could then be used as storage containers. One month after this packaging innovation was introduced to consumers, 15,000 units per day were being sold. Yet, the Kraft company was less pleased with this packaging because when the cheese was sliced by a grocer, the product lost its brand identity. The solution was to introduce a half-pound package in 1925 and a two-pound package in 1932. By 1942 the United States was involved in another war, and the government once again asked Kraft for tinned cheese for its armed forces.

Natural cheeses, too, have appeared in different types of packages. Fold-tight bags were used for shredded cheeses, and reclosable zipper bags for slices. Both products were later packaged in resealable zipper bags to ensure total freshness during storage.

First Nonfat Process Cheese

With consumers becoming more health- and weight-conscious and concerned about fat and cholesterol intake, dairy products, with their high fat content, were a prime target for losing market share. Kraft was the first to introduce a nonfat cheese product so that consumers could still enjoy cheese while reducing their consumption of fat.

In 1990 Kraft Free Singles began being test marketed, and by 1992 the process cheese product was available in the eastern half of the United States. Free Singles contained approximately 45 calories per one-ounce serving compared to 90 calories for a regular serving, which is equal to one-and-one-third slices. Each serving contained less than half a gram of fat. Priced slightly higher than the regular version, the cheese was available in 12- and 7.5-ounce packages. According to Diane Rand, a Kraft General Foods spokesperson, "A large portion of consumers buying the fat-free cheese are either new customers or returning to the category."

More reduced fat cheeses followed Free Singles. Kraft Cracker Barrel Light, a sharp cheddar cheese, contains 90 calories and 5 grams of fat per ounce. Kraft Light Naturals, a sharp cheddar, contains 80 calories and 5 grams of fat per ounce. Kraft Golden Image Cheddar style contains 100 calories and 9 grams of fat per ounce. The Monterey Jack variety and Kraft Light Naturals with Peppers contain 80 calories and 5 grams of fat per ounce. The

Swiss cheese contains 90 calories and 5 grams of fat per ounce. And, the mozzarella selection contains 80 calories and 4 grams of fat per ounce.

Advertising and Marketing

From its earliest days, the Kraft company used advertising as a means of acquainting consumers with its products and building brand identity. In 1911 advertising for Kraft cheese first appeared on elevated trains, outdoor billboards, and circulars that were mailed to retail grocers. Later, consumer magazines and journals ran color ads. Radio was used as early as 1933, when the company sponsored a two-hour musical and variety show called *Kraft Musical Revue.* The show later developed into a one-hour format and became the weekly *Kraft Music Hall,* which featured leading show business personalities.

Kraft was also an early television advertiser, sponsoring the first commercial network program, *Kraft Television Theater.* The highly acclaimed program debuted in 1947 on WNET-TV in New York and was broadcast on nearly 8,000 local TV sets. The show ran until 1958, after setting audience and studio production records. In 1958 the radio show *Kraft Music Hall* moved to television and was hosted first by Milton Berle, and then by Perry Como, Andy Williams, and John Davidson.

In addition to building brand awareness through advertising, Kraft has used test marketing to introduce new products to consumers and gauge their acceptance. Establishing brand awareness is of utmost importance since consumers first look for the type of cheese desired, such as sliced or shredded, and then look for a brand name. A selection of a particular size package is then made within a brand.

International Expansion

From its beginning, the Kraft company was interested in expanding its cheese business to other countries. The methods used included acquiring foreign cheese companies, opening up sales offices or manufacturing plants, and marketing U.S. brands overseas. As far back as 1912, J.L. Kraft & Bros. Co. established a New York City office to develop an international cheese business. In the ensuing years, cheese companies were purchased in Canada, Australia, Germany, and Belgium; sales offices were opened in London and Germany; manufacturing plants were established in England and Mexico; and U.S. brands were marketed in England, Canada, Australia, and Spain.

Future Products

In the early 1990s, more nonfat and low-fat cheeses were expected to be introduced as Kraft General Foods expands its Healthy Favorites label for health-minded consumers. Many of Kraft's major competitors have expanded their reduced–fat cheese lines. In 1992 Kraft estimated that light cheeses accounted for 10 percent of the total cheese market but were growing at an annual rate of 30 percent. The sales of Kraft's first nonfat cheese, Kraft Free Singles, reached Kraft's targets for a successful new product in less than one year of national distribution.

In addition, cheese is a popular ingredient in new products developed by various types of food processors. Some processed items containing cheese are baked goods, baking ingredients, snacks, sauces, toppings, fillings, condiments, desserts, entrees, fruits, vegetables, pet food, processed meat, side dishes, and soup. Kraft USA uses cheese as an ingredient in some of its own processed foods, such as Kraft Macaroni & Cheese, Kraft Deluxe Dinners, and Kraft Side Dishes. Food processors like the versatility of cheese as an ingredient because it can be melted, poured, powdered, shredded, fried, microwaved, sprayed, and baked into products.

Further Reading:

"American Cheese and 'Cheeses,' " *Consumer Reports,* November 1990, pp. 728-731.

"Building Profits With Cheese," *Progressive Grocer,* July 1990, pp. 14-15.

Burros, Marian, "If Butterfat Is Cut, Cheese Doesn't Cut It," *New York Times,* June 3, 1992, p. C 1.

"Cheese," *Supermarket Business,* April 1991, p. 10.

"Cheese in Slices," *Kraftsman,* January 1953.

"Cheese Makes Progress in New Product Conquest," *Prepared Foods,* May 1991, p. 129.

"A Chronological History of Kraft General Foods," Kraft General Foods Archives Department, August 1992.

Dexheimer, Ellen, "Retail Dairy Through a Crystal Ball," *Dairy Foods,* June 1990, p. 18.

Dryer, Jerry, "Convenience: More Than Just a Fact of Life," *Dairy Foods,* July 1992, p. 25.

"James Lewis Kraft," Kraft Archives.

"Kraft USA Rolls Out Fat-Free Cheese Slices," *Supermarket News,* January 13, 1992, p. 38.

Liesse, Julie,"ConAgra, Kraft Start Cheese War," *Advertising Age,* July 6, 1992, p. 3.

Liesse, Julie, "KGF Eyes ConAgra Counter," *Advertising Age,* June 10, 1991, p. 1.

"The 1992 Supermarket Sales Manual," *Progressive Grocer,* July 1992, pp. 80-81.

"Now . . . Cheese in Slices," *Kraftsman,* February 1950.

"100 Leading National Advertisers," *Advertising Age,* September 23, 1992, pp. 52-53.

Lenius, Pat M., "Shredded Cheese Sales on March," *Supermarket News,* August 19, 1991, p. 47.

Philip Morris Companies Inc., Annual Report, 1991.

—Dorothy Kroll

LAND O LAKES®

Not many creations come into the world picture-perfect. One of the exceptions may be the Indian Maiden trademark used by Land O'Lakes Inc., a Minnesota-based food and agricultural cooperative that has steadily added both products and members since its 1921 beginnings. First painted in 1924 to publicize the first American butter made with pure sweet cream, the maiden soon came to represent a successful quest for strict standards of hygiene in dairy-industry processing and packaging. Later her job description changed; she became a reassuring symbol of quality to brand-loyal shoppers trying new Land O'Lakes products like margarine-butter blends, low-fat spreads, and cholesterol-lean cheese. Still the mark of an industry leader, the trademark appears these days on a 600-item list of food products.

The maiden was three years in the future when the Minnesota Creameries Association was born. A 350-member-strong statewide cooperative, the organization was formed as a troubleshooter to face off against a tough market caused by intense competition and rivalry between too many small cooperatives.

Setting the Stage

Finding a market niche was no easy feat. American butter quality was unreliable, because primitive cooling and separating techniques made it easier for some farmers to send sour cream to the butter manufacturer than to meet the strict deadlines necessary for sweet cream. Also at fault were the manufacturers, many of whom tried to cut the cream's sour taste with soda before bulk-packing their decidedly second-rate product in the big, unsanitary tubs commonly used by grocers.

The Association faced the fact that market penetration would have to wait until their members could offer a uniformly excellent butter that would not deteriorate in transit. They tackled the challenges methodically. Taking on the question of packaging first, they decided to discourage the sale of bulk butter, working instead towards standardized, hygienic one-pound packages as an industry staple. Next, to ensure that their members produced the best butter possible for their cooperative, they decreed that nothing but sweet cream was ever to be used as a base. Underlining this resolution, they then drew up a point system covering composition, salt content, and flavor. Their criterion was unwavering: a maximum score of 100, with a minimum of 93 for any butter sold through the cooperative. This move brought applause from state and federal inspectors, who willingly allowed the cooperative to put a government-endorsed certificate of quality inside each package.

It took the Association about a year to hurdle these obstacles and move on to formulating a marketing plan for all members. Its rules were simple: each creamery had to consign its butter to the cooperative for a period of two years. The Association then graded, branded, and sold the product at the best possible price, after which the creamery received its share of net profits, minus expenses. The reward for all this diligence was swift—within a month of its May 1922 opening, the Minnesota cooperative's New York sales office was receiving 80 shipments of sweet cream butter per week.

Enter the Indian Maiden

The butter was off to a rousing start, and the Assocation attacked the task of reaching potential consumers with zest. Opting for an attention-getting splash, they held a widely advertised name-the-butter contest in February, 1924. The competition's kickoff triggered a flurry of advance orders from Minnesota grocery stores anxious to keep pace with demand; its close brought the suggestion of "Land O'Lakes" from two unrelated contestants. This name pleased the cooperative, who were confident that the link with pure Minnesota waters would be a permanent selling point for their butter. A 430,000-pound order from the U.S. Navy put an extra burnish on the campaign's success, which was given even more luster when the state governor sent packs of Land O'Lakes butter to President Coolidge as a Christmas greeting.

The power of advertising had impressed the Association. Determined to fulfill their product's considerable marketing potential, they now decided that a trademark would make it instantly identifiable. And what better trade character for the legendary home of Hiawatha and Minnehaha than an Indian maiden?

Until the end of the decade Land O'Lakes butter wrappers showed a landscape of trees and sky. In the foreground, painted by her forgotten creator, the Indian Maiden knelt by a lake, the legend "Sweet Cream Butter" just above her head. The trademark made an eye-catching picture on billboards, attracting so much attention that the cooperative changed their own name in 1926 to Land O'Lakes Creameries, Inc. As Land O'Lakes, they sold 12.5 million one-pound packs of butter in 1927. By 1929 the total soared to 28.5 million packs—almost half of the American butter sold that year.

Marketing Magic

The cooperative held the top market share throughout the bleak Depression years, thanks to national and regional marketing strategy set in 1928. The first shot at national advertising, set for September and October 1930, was aimed at *Good Housekeeping,* a magazine long regarded by readers as a bastion of wholesome domesticity. Regional advertising, budgeted by a thrifty 1928 decision to share costs with distributors, appeared in such prominent eastern markets as Washington, D.C., and Boston. In both regional and national ads the Indian Maiden shared space with Uncle Sam, prominently displayed to emphasize government approval of the cooperative's grading standards. By 1933, advertising was firmly entrenched as a Land O'Lakes priority large enough to warrant the services of a professional agency. Minnesota-based Campbell-Mithun Inc. was chosen and has been handling the Land O'Lakes account ever since.

Sophisticated marketing techniques went into effect immediately. Aware that Depression-era shoppers would expect more for their scarce food dollars, the agency concentrated on premium

AT A GLANCE

Land O Lakes brand butter originally produced by the Minnesota Cooperative Creameries Association, founded on July 8, 1921; sold under the trade name Land O'Lakes (later Land O Lakes, without apostrophe), the butter became so well known that the association changed its name to Land O'Lakes Creameries, Inc., in 1926, and later to simply Land O'Lakes, Inc..

Performance: *Market share*—32% (top share) of butter category. *Sales*—$2.6 billion.

Major competitor: Regional brands of butter; also margarine brands.

Advertising: *Agency*—CME-KHBB Advertising, Minneapolis, MN.

Addresses: *Parent company*—Land O'Lakes, Inc., P.O. Box 116, Minneapolis, MN 55440; phone: (612) 481-2222; fax: (612) 481-2000.

selling. Their first promotion, "Hiawatha" pattern silverware offered at a reduced price for product labels, helped to sell 85 million pounds of butter in 1934. Between 1936 and 1938 a recipe book was shown in *Ladies Home Journal,* proving to be an irresistible bargain to 200,000 readers at the nominal price of 10 cents with a coupon. All ads bore the image of the Indian Maiden, updated courtesy of a painting presented to Land O'Lakes in 1928; sharing her place of honor was a seal from the American Medical Association, which had endorsed the butter in 1931.

In 1938 the advertising agency stopped Land O'Lakes' magazine advertising, choosing instead to step up the radio sponsorship that had started in 1927. In contrast with the first programs, which had consisted of agricultural and cookery news aimed at members of the cooperative, the new coverage brought publicity through the use of celebrities in all fields. Well known though she was, the Indian Maiden could not be used over the air, but was always present in the extensive newspaper and regional advertising that formed the backbone of the Land O'Lakes marketing strategy.

World War II

World War II brought considerable change. Military needs and material shortages made butter expensive to produce and difficult to obtain; consumption dropped 57 percent between 1940 and 1946, plummeting from more than 17 annual pounds per person in 1940 to about 10.5 pounds by 1946. Campbell-Mithun vetoed vigorous marketing slants for Land O'Lakes butter, opting instead to keep their client's name before the public by using it in humorous cartoons.

Nevertheless, Land O'Lakes held on to its peak position all through these years, partly by setting up an export division to cater to hungry export markets. In a second move, the cooperative introduced a new product called nonfat dry milk powder. It was made from the milk solids remaining after cream had been churned, and had previously been used as pig-food. The dry milk proved to have a long shelf life as well as the high-protein power deemed necessary for feeding the troops and relieving the ravages of starvation in concentration camp survivors.

Marching in step with the wartime drums, the two innovations proved profitable. By 1946, the cooperative's 25th anniversary

year, there were twenty foreign outlets, which had helped to sell almost a billion pounds of dairy foods.

The 1950s: More Is More

By 1950, member creameries of the cooperative covered 22 districts in Wisconsin, Minnesota, and the Dakotas. Each district had an elected representative on the Land O'Lakes Board of Directors. To cope with the ongoing concerns of this large enterprise, the board was subdivided into committees dealing with such questions as finance, advertising, and credit.

It was also the board's responsibility to incorporate the methods of a new era in American business. Streamlined supermarkets were replacing the familiar little grocery store, and franchising was bringing opportunities to both established companies and small entrepeneurs. Both developments merited the board's concentrated attention.

Land O'Lakes met the supermarket challenge by directing regional sales offices to target sales that were fewer in number but larger in volume. In 1952 they entered the franchiser ranks by buying Bridgeman Creameries, an ice cream manufacturer with 15 stores dotted around Minnesota and South Dakota. Mindful of both the fine Bridgeman reputation and their own, the board kept the name on some varieties of ice cream; others bore the famous Indian Maiden trademark, which was presently found also on the cottage cheese, flavored yogurt, and ice cream novelties that came with Bridgeman's 1966 purchase of Yegen Dairy of North Dakota.

Along with these innovations came butter's first serious competitor—margarine. Margarine was now big business, its former reputation as a wartime butter substitute notwithstanding. Known as "oleomargarine," it was manufactured and sold in all but 15 states, in both uncolored and yellow versions. Of the two, the yellow variety was much preferred by America's 33,000 margarine suppliers. Simple economics supported their choice: margarine could be dyed yellow at a nominal cost, whereas white had to be kept fresh in specially tailored, expensive plastic packaging. However, both varieties being cheaper than butter, they were eagerly snatched up by cost-conscious food-shoppers.

By 1951 butter sales had sagged by 17 percent. To change this downturn into a growth opportunity, the Indian Maiden came to America's attention once again, faithfully proffering her butter pack in the Sunday advertising sections of the ten largest eastern newspapers, as Campbell-Mithun launched their first four-color ad campaign since 1934. (This time, though, there was a difference. The butter wrapper had been streamlined in 1939 by graphic artist Jess Betlach, who had placed the maiden against a simple yellow background to represent butter.) Carried simultaneously in black and white by other newspapers, the ads first emphasized the flavor of sweet cream butter, then moved on to stress the product's freshness. In 1957, in another four-color spread underlining image, freshness, and mood, Land O'Lakes used a half-gallon copper can as a subtle reminder of the half-gallon of sweet cream that went into every pound of butter. Despite Land O'Lakes' best efforts, however, by 1957 margarine overtook butter sales. By 1960 the lead was widening, though advertising and marketing had upped butter sales by 13 percent. Still, in 1959, combined sales stood at $178.5 billion.

In 1960 Land O'Lakes revived the idea of premiums, buttressing their copper can with offers of copper butter dishes and jam jars for a price plus a Land O'Lakes label. Using the time-honored marketing idea of cooperation with other companies, they also joined the Pillsbury Grand National Bakeoff, offering 16-page books of winning recipes in national magazines like *McCalls*. Recipes were also well to the fore on butter packs, in supermarket dairy cases, and in newspapers.

Butter Hits the Big Time

These valiant efforts did not hide the need for a new department focused entirely on merchandising. Added in 1963, the merchandisers immediately budgeted 60 percent of their available advertising dollars for magazine publicity and 30 percent for newspapers. Streamlined strategy brought swift results: a 1964 advertising budget of $1.6 million sent sales figures soaring to $243.8 billion, a 6.5 percent rise in just one year. In a second coup, Land O'Lakes made its first appearance on the Fortune 500 list, in place number 254. Despite these triumphs, Land O'Lakes did not rest on its laurels; one 1964 campaign urged shoppers to buy confectionery baked with butter, while a second showed how an everyday hamburger could be sparked up when mixed with chopped herbs.

The 1970s began with a merger. Iowa-based Farmers Regional Cooperative (Felco), an agricultural supplies concern whose sales would reach $90 million by 1970, joined Land O'Lakes in 1970, bringing soybean processing, feeds, and fertilizer into the Land O'Lakes lineup. Although only some of the new agricultural products carried the tradename Land O Lakes (the apostrophe was eliminated in 1972), the acquisition allowed the company to bring a circular service line to farmers, supplying them with their agricultural needs and then selling their crops. In deference to the new lines, the cooperative also dropped the word "Creameries" from their name, which became simply "Land O'Lakes, Inc."

Margarine Joins the Lineup

In 1967 the world's first successful heart transplant spun the word "cholesterol" into the consumer's vocabulary. Although this new awareness would not begin to affect butter sales for some years, the timing seemed right for Land O'Lakes to start producing margarine. Extensive testing of formulas based on both soybean and corn oils began in 1972, and test marketing began the following year.

The Indian Maiden looked most dramatic on the copper-colored wrapper of the corn oil margarine. Against the golden sunburst of the soybean-oil-based product, she looked as fresh and wholesome as the product she was representing. Both packs were so effective that Land O'Lakes executives agonized lest margerine sales overrun butter. For this reason, margarine ads were tested with the bold crossplug, "Margarine from America's No. 1 Butter Maker, Land O'Lakes."

The executives need not have worried; their butter was still so popular by 1976 that they were able to introduce But-R-Cups—pat-size servings in foil-topped containers for restaurants and other foodservice areas. By 1981, a backward look confirmed that, although the butter market was generally flat (per capita consumption having fallen from 5.1 pounds in 1971 annually to 4.3 pounds), the Land O'Lakes share had increased at a steady 1 to 2 percent for the past three years.

The Lean Lifestyle

Still, success did not lull the cooperative into ignoring the public's quest for a healthier lifestyle. Since 1971, marketing executives had been gauging the numbers of their retail butter customers by offering sweepstakes that dangled tempting prizes. These figures showed that consumers had changed. They no longer wanted the gourmet food the cooperative's recipes had always stressed; now they needed leaner methods for everyday meals. Following their new principle of lifestyle demographics, Land O'Lakes now began to produce leaner versions of longtime staples. In 1984 they rolled out their Country Morning Blend, a mix of 60 percent butter and 40 percent corn oil margerine, following up with a light version (52 percent vegetable oil) in a meadow-green and yellow pack that displayed the Indian Maiden trademark to perfection. Both versions proved to be winners, as did Lean Cream Sour Cream (later renamed Light Sour Cream), introduced with television advertising in 1987 and joined by No-Fat Sour Cream in 1992. Land O'Lakes introduced their Light Butter in 1993. Made primarily of butter, the product relies on the addition of water, skim milk, stabilizers, preservatives, and nutritional additives for its lightness.

Following marketing methods that had been proved sturdiest, Land O'Lakes introduced their "Reward Yourself" campaign in the 1990s. Designed to let the cooperative see where its best customers are, it offers a catalog of brandname goods, such as light appliances, at 65 percent discounts. In exchange, shoppers send proof-of-purchase seals from salted, unsalted, whipped, blended, or light butter—all of which are instantly recognizable by the Indian Maiden trademark on the wrapper.

Further Reading:

"Dairy Group's Push Boosts Baked Goods Made with Butter," *Advertising Age,* March 23, 1964.

Franz, Julie, "Land O'Lakes Spreads Name into Bread Market," *Advertising Age,* March 25, 1985.

"Land O'Lakes Adds Light Touch," *Chicago Tribune,* March 10, 1992.

Land O'Lakes Annual Reports, Minneapolis: Land O'Lakes, 1991.

"Land O'Lakes' But-R-Cups for Foodservice Features Extended Shelf Life," *Food Engineering,* June 1976.

"Land O'Lakes Put $1,600,00 in Ads, Stockholders Told," *Advertising Age,* March 22, 1965, p. 4.

"Land O'Lakes Sets New Corporate Course with Nationally Marketed Consumer Foods," *Marketing News,* December 23, 1983.

"Marketing Briefs: Bonus for Frequent Butter Buyers," *Dairy Foods,* March 1990, p. 50.

"Marketing Front: Land O'Lakes," *Food & Beverage Marketing,* December 23, 1987, p. 6.

Neiman, Janet, "Marketing Flows at Land O'Lakes," *Advertising Age,* February 23, 1981, pp. 4, 80.

"Oleo Freedom," *Business Week,* July 1, 1950, pp. 50-52.

Ourusoff, Alexandra, et al, "What's in a Name?" *Financial World,* September 1, 1992.

"Premium Light Dessert," *Dairy Foods,* October 1990, p. 55.

Ruble, Kenneth D., *Farmers Make It Happen,* Minneapolis: Land O'Lakes, 1973.

Ruble, Kenneth D., *Men to Remember,* Minneapolis: Land O'Lakes, 1947.

U.S. Dept. of Agriculture, *Dairy: Situation and Outlook Yearbook,* Washington D.C., August 1992, p. 21.

We've Got the Combination, Minneapolis: Land O'Lakes.

"What's New Portfolio," *Adweek,* March 25, 1991.

—*Gillian Wolf*

LAY'S®

In a market with fierce regional loyalties, more Lay's brand potato chips are sold than any other potato chip in the world. For more than half a century the Lay's brand has been presented to consumers as a traditional, straightforward product—thinly sliced potatoes that are fried in oil and salted. Although such Lay's flavored varieties as barbecue and sour cream and onion possess their fair share of the potato chip market, Lay's original recipe is by far the most popular variety. The brand's familiar slogan, "Betcha Can't Eat Just One," updated after 50 years to "Too Good to Eat Just One," helped raise Lay's from the ranks of the regional potato chips to its position as the leading national brand.

Brand Origins

Herman W. Lay founded H. W. Lay and Company in 1938 in Atlanta, Georgia, with Lay's potato chips as its flagship product. Lay's success contributed to the decision by the Frito Company to merge with H. W. Lay and Company in 1961. With headquarters in Plano, Texas, Frito-Lay, Inc., increased distribution of Lay's potato chips to cover more territory. In 1963 the company created for Lay's the slogan "Betcha Can't Eat Just One," around which it centered its advertising. For years, television and print ads showed people foolishly betting that they could eat just one chip and losing.

In 1965 Frito-Lay merged with the Pepsi-Cola Company, forming PepsiCo, Inc. With the ample resources of PepsiCo behind them, Frito-Lay set out to make Lay's potato chips the leading brand in the nation. By the end of the decade, as one of 400 companies producing potato chips in the United States, Frito-Lay had made Lay's one of the three best-selling brands. Its two largest competitors were American Brands (formerly American Tobacco Co.), which sold potato chips under different brand names in different parts of the country, including Humpty-Dumpty brand, and the food division of Borden, Inc., which sold Wise potato chips.

The Fabricated Chip

In 1969 Lay's position as a leading national brand was challenged not only by other rising regional brands but by a new type of potato chip. Procter & Gamble Company and General Mills, Inc., two companies with powerful advertising and distribution capacities, introduced Pringles and Chipos respectively. Both brands were made from mashed or dehydrated potatoes molded into a uniform shape, which allowed them to be stacked in a can, as Pringles were, or packaged in a foil-lined box, as were Chipos. These changes in processing and packaging solved the traditional potato chip's biggest problems: fragility, bulky packaging, and short shelf life. Consequently, Procter & Gamble and General Mills could make their potato chips in one location and ship them nationwide, while traditional potato chips, Lay's brand included, had to be made in regional factories.

Existing potato chip manufacturers felt threatened by the new products and the substantial resources their manufacturers could use to advertise and distribute them. The Potato Chip Institute filed suit against General Mills for false advertising, claiming General Mills's description of its product as a potato chip was misleading. Harvey Noss, executive vice president of the Potato Chip Institute International, the potato chip industry's trade association, explained to *Business Week*, "A potato chip is a thin raw slice of potato fried in deep fat. Period. The industry has spent millions establishing this." The suit, however, had little ground since the Food and Drug Administration had already ruled that Procter & Gamble was allowed to use the potato chip label on Pringles as long as they specified on the packaging that the product was made from dried potatoes or potato flakes.

Lay's Reaches Number One

Despite Pringles' manufacturing and distributing advantages, traditional potato chips remained more popular—and Lay's brand became the most popular of all. Lay's market share peaked in the late 1970s, having proven that a potato chip brand could break through the regional limits of potato chip distribution to become a national favorite. By 1982, Lay's potato chips contributed significantly to Frito-Lay's 40 percent share of the salty snack industry and required a major portion of the production capacity of the company's 43 plants.

In the early 1980s Frito-Lay continued to combat regional loyalty by investing $50 million a year in advertising its brands, an amount that accounted for 80 percent of the total advertising done in the industry. Lay's success could not be attributed solely to advertising, however. Frito-Lay had created an immense, efficient store-door delivery system, which allowed the company to keep tight control over Lay's quality.

AT A GLANCE

Lay's brand potato chips introduced in 1938 in Atlanta, GA, by Herman W. Lay, owner of H. W. Lay & Company; company merged with the Frito Company to form Frito-Lay, Inc, 1961; company merged with the Pepsi-Cola Company to form PepsiCo, Inc., 1965.

Peformance: *Market share*—Top share of potato chip category. *Sales*—$966 million.

Major competitor: Regional brands of potato chips.

Advertising: *Agency*—BBDO Worldwide, New York, NY, 1991—. *Major campaign*—Basketball stars Larry Bird and Kareem Abdul-Jabbar betting that Lay's are "Too Good to Eat Just One."

Addresses: *Parent company*—Frito-Lay, Inc., 7701 Legacy Drive, Plano, TX 75024; phone: (214) 334-7000; fax: (914) 334-2019. *Ultimate parent company*—PepsiCo, Inc., Purchase, NY; phone: (914) 253-2000; fax: (914) 253-2070.

The National Competition

Hoping to reproduce Lay's success, other companies increased their efforts to expand nationally. Borden's Wise Snack Division, at that time the second-biggest producer in the nation, acquired several popular regional chip companies, enlarging its potato chip production by 70 percent in three years. Procter & Gamble marketed three "improved" varieties of Pringles, and Anheuser-Busch, Inc., introduced Eagle Snacks. Anheuser-Busch used their contacts with beer wholesalers to distribute their new products into such markets as bars, taverns, and airports. John H. Pumell, Anheuser-Busch's planning vice-president, told *Business Week,* "We're not charging up the hill into Frito's fortress. But we feel they are vulnerable [outside the supermarket]."

Lay's expansion slowed in the 1980s. The salty-snack industry was booming, but most of that growth was in non-potato chip products. The industry's tonnage doubled from 3 percent in 1979 to 6 percent in 1981. Most of that growth was in the corn chip market, which grew 16 percent in both 1980 and 1981, and in the tortilla chip market, which grew 25 percent in that same time period. Industry potato chip sales, however, were flat. Frito-Lay followed the general industry pattern, growing 20 percent a year from 1976 to 1981, but achieving that growth in salty snacks other than potato chips.

Frito-Lay's largest concern in the early 1980s was not increased competition from national marketers, but changes in consumer attitudes toward snack foods. A trend was developing toward more healthful eating, and, increasingly, consumers were looking at potato chips as a food to restrict or eliminate from their diets. In response, Frito-Lay launched a new advertising campaign that focused on nutrition, including print ads that compared their products' calorie levels to that of whole milk and their salt levels to that of bread. In 1981 the company began including nutritional information on their packaging. Former Frito-Lay president D. Wayne Calloway explained to *Business Week:* "As the industry leader, we felt it was time for someone to refute the idea that these products are not wholesome food."

The trend toward more healthful eating did not affect the salty snack market as expected; in fact, it continued to boom. Americans spent $3.3 billion on deep-fried chips in 1986, up 75 percent from 1980.

Resurgence of the Regional Chip

Never completely overwhelmed by the national brands, regional varieties grew in popularity in the late 1980s, as did increasingly unusual varieties of potato chips—thick or thin sliced, made from white or sweet potatoes, seasoned with Cajun, barbecue, or Italian spices, vinegar, cheese, jalapeno peppers, or sour cream with onion or chives, to name a few of the variations. Old-fashioned kettle-cooked chips also made a comeback. Unlike most factory processes for cooking chips, which can produce 2,500 pounds in an hour, the kettle method produces only 500 pounds an hour, and the resulting chip is harder and crunchier.

Although the national potato chip producers easily introduced unusually flavored chips of their own, they had a more difficult time fighting consumers' returning regional loyalties. Some major national producers responded by buying regional potato chip companies and continuing to produce their products without advertising the change in ownership. For instance, according to Mimi Sheraton in *Time,* "Wise now offers New York Deli chips along the Eastern Seaboard and as far west as Dallas, packed in a passionate purple bag that bears no hint of Borden or Wise," and "similarly, New Englanders who cherish the lingeringly greasy Cape Cod chips, old-fashioned and hand cooked in Hyannis, will find no clue on the package that the company now belongs to Anheuser-Busch."

Lay's Brand Loses Some Ground

Lay's market share suffered with the resurgence of regional potato chip brands and consumers' desire for new chip formulas and flavors. Frito-Lay experimented with new flavors and their own kettle-cooked chip, but their expanded product line was not designed to return consumers to the old standby Lay's potato chips. However, even though the Lay's brand lost some of its lead in the market, it still remained ahead of the pack.

Frito-Lay's general success in the 1980s led to problems in the early 1990s. According to Wendy Zellner in *Business Week,* Frito-Lay "grew fat on all its success. . . . It boosted prices faster than inflation. And it allowed lapses in quality, such as too many broken chips in each bag." As a consequence, consumers increasingly bought rival products. Anheuser-Busch's Eagle Snacks won more of the market primarily by producing high-quality products at prices up to 20 percent lower than those of Frito-Lay.

Company and Product Changes

In 1991 Roger A. Enrico, formerly president and CEO of PepsiCo Worldwide Beverages, took over as chairman of Frito-Lay. With the experience he gained in the cola war between Pepsi and Coca-Cola, Enrico set out to trim the excesses from Frito-Lay's administration and revitalize the image of its staple products. He eliminated 1,800, or 60 percent, of Frito-Lay's management and administrative jobs, closed 4 of its 40 U.S. plants, and reduced the company's product line by almost 100 package sizes and flavors. Enrico used the savings from this harsh paring, an estimated $100 million annually, to offset the cost of new products, lower prices, and better marketing.

As part of the company's overhaul, Frito-Lay shifted its attention from creating new products and flavors to revitalizing its principal brands—Doritos, Ruffles, and, of course, Lay's. Steve Liguori, former vice president of marketing for Frito-Lay, explained to *Advertising Age* reporter Jennifer Lawrence: "During the eighties, we didn't do a whole lot of feeding and caring for our existing brands. We almost had an attitude if it was an old brand, it was a tired brand and it wasn't exciting and we wouldn't put a lot of effort against it. We've radically changed that frame of mind."

Frito-Lay's strategy for renewing consumer interest in Lay's included the first formula change for the chips in their history. To enhance the flavor of the chip, the company developed a new frying process and switched from frying in soybean oil to frying in cottonseed oil. In addition, the salt content was lowered 12 percent to accommodate consumers' increasing preference for less salty snacks. Liguori explained in a press release what the company thought they had achieved with their changes: "We combined Frito-Lay's patented potatoes with a revolutionary way to make and package Lay's and Ruffles so they taste even more like the original potato and stay crisper and crunchier. We also developed a quality control process to ensure only the best-looking chips go into the finished bags."

New Advertising

To go along with the new taste, Frito-Lay hired the advertising agency BBDO Worldwide in New York City to update the image of Lay's potato chips. BBDO redesigned the packaging and came up with a new twist on Lay's potato chips' well-known slogan, "Betcha Can't Eat Just One." The new version emphasized the improved taste and quality while maintaining the familiarity of the old version: "Too Good to Eat Just One." The new ad campaign featured the first television advertisements for Lay's in a decade. The ads co-starred basketball players Larry Bird and Kareem Abdul-Jabbar. Bird, unable to eat just one Lay's potato chip, loses a bet with Abdul-Jabbar and must shave his head. BBDO took advantage of the spokesmen's unusual size by placing in stores life-size cutouts of Larry Bird, who is six feet, nine inches tall, and Kareem Abdul-Jabbar, who stands seven feet, two inches tall.

Although the new campaign relied on big-name endorsers and high-profile television ads, Frito-Lay did not ignore its regional competitors. The company introduced the "Lay's Challenge," a chip-to-chip comparison against regional brands that asks consumers which potato chip they prefer. The campaign helped increase Lay's market share in regions with strong local potato chip brands. For instance, Lay's doubled its market share in the Baltimore-Washington area, where Utz potato chips hold approxi-

mately one third of the market. Liguori told *Business Week* why Frito-Lay had mistakenly not pursued competitors on a regional level in the last decade: "We were too big and too stodgy to worry about going after these local opportunities."

Frito-Lay, according to Zellner in *Business Week,* may have given their national potato chip competitors their biggest blow by discounting some of its key brands. Eagle Snacks, which established its reputation on low prices, has maintained its market share but, according to analysts, might have lost $15 million to $30 million in 1992. Borden attributed its 33 percent drop in snack food operating profits in the second quarter of 1992 to a potato chip price war.

Lay's was the first potato chip brand to achieve national prominence, and once it held the lead market share, it did not let go. Still, although it has maintained the lead share for decades, it has gradually lost ground to other national brands, to re-interest in regional brands, and to the simple proliferation of varieties of salty snacks. With their attention refocused on Lay's brand potato chips, Frito-Lay hopes to regain some of those lost market share points. Liguori told *Advertising Age*'s Lawrence, "We are a big company with big resources, and we're going to marshal our resources behind these fewer, more focused activities to do big things."

Further Reading:

"Frito-Lay Changes Taste of Its Chips to Boost Share," *Wall Street Journal,* May 8, 1992, p. B5.

"Frito-Lay Changing Lay's, Ruffles Taste," *Vending Times,* May 1992, p. 3.

"Frito-Lay May Find Itself in a Competition Crunch," *Business Week,* July 19, 1982, p. 186.

"Frito-Lay Re-Invents Its Lay's and Ruffles Potato Chips," *Frito-Lay News Release,* May 7, 1992.

Lawrence, Jennifer, "Enrico Makes His Mark on Frito-Lay," *Advertising Age,* May 18, 1992, p. 26.

"Party Gets Rough for Potato Chippers," *Business Week,* November 8, 1969, p. 36.

Sheraton, Mimi, "One Potato, Two Potato . . . ," *Time,* March 30, 1987, p. 77.

"Who Makes the Best Potato Chip?," *Consumer Reports,* June 1991, pp. 379-83.

Zellner, Wendy, "Frito-Lay Is Munching on the Competition," *Business Week,* August 24, 1992, pp. 52-53.

—Susan Windisch Brown

LEA & PERRINS®

The original Worcestershire (pronounced Wuh-stuh-shuh, or Wuh-ster-sheer), Lea & Perrins brand sauce is consumed in more than a hundred countries and ranks as the leading condiment of its type in the United States, New Zealand, and elsewhere. Its 40 percent share of the domestic Worcestershire market is approximately twice that of its closest competitor, Heinz. One of the oldest and most esteemed grocery products, Lea & Perrins traces its origin back to the early 1800s, when an Englishman brought a recipe from India to the English county of Worcester. A sauce that was likely similar to it, *garum,* dates back to ancient Roman times.

Beginning in the late 1830s, Lea & Perrins was regularly exported to Manhattan, and production in the United States began by the turn of the century. Descendants of the original owners of the English and American Lea & Perrins businesses retained the business until 1967, when the Imperial Group gained control. From the mid-1970s until the mid-1980s, Lea & Perrins experienced a dramatic decline in market share, due to changing eating habits and poor brand management. In 1986 another British conglomerate, Hanson PLC, took over Imperial but within two years divested Lea & Perrins, which had begun to rebound, for a premium price. The new owner, BSN Groupe (the largest food company in France and one of the largest in all of Europe), has demonstrated a far greater commitment to marketing and development than the two previous owners and has, according to *Forbes,* effected double-digit increases in sales for the sauce since 1989.

The Legend of a Legend

According to popular legend, in 1835, Marcus, Lord Sandys retired his post as the Governor of Bengal and returned to his native county of Worcester with an Indian sauce recipe. He delivered it to two druggists in the small market town of Worcester and asked if they could duplicate it. The druggists, John Wheeley Lea and William Perrins, had been in business together as Lea & Perrins since 1823. In the course of their partnership, they had developed a catalogue of some three hundred items, from food products to trusses. In Michael Kenyon's words, ''The concoction put together from his lordship's recipe—several gallons of the stuff in stone jars—proved so foul that it was consigned to a cellar and forgotten. Not until two years later, when clearing out the cellar, did the partners take a second sniff and then, warily, a taste, and discover that the matured brew was all right. Better than all right. Apart from minor modifications, and the crucial maturing,

the recipe for today's Worcestershire sauce is the one brought back from India by Lord Sandys.''

Although perhaps not wholly accurate, the above anecdotal account has stood the test of time and serves to point out one of the sauce's greatest claims to uniqueness in quality and taste: that it is *aged* for a full two years. Lord Sandys's only form of remuneration, apparently, is the obscure acknowledgement on the label, which states: ''from a recipe of a nobleman in the county.'' In any event, Lea and Perrins prospered as pharmacists (they were the first Englishmen to open a chain of drugstores) as well as sauce purveyors. Lea & Perrins sauce grew into an international phenomenon through early efforts by the two partners to place cases of it aboard passenger liners, for use at mealtimes while at sea. A 1919 advertisement alluded not only to changing methods of travel but to the unvarying preeminence of the already classic sauce: ''Steam takes the place of sail but no sauce has superseded Lea & Perrins, the Original and Genuine Worcestershire. A wonderful liquid tonic that makes your hair grow beautiful.''

Despite a host of competitors, Lea & Perrins alone proved befitting of royalty, to whom it has been served since 1904, and worthy of the stamp ''By Appointment to Her Majesty the Queen.'' As a further distinction, Lea & Perrins won the exclusive, legally protected right, in 1906, to employ the phrase ''the original and genuine'' Worcestershire sauce in its labeling and advertising.

The Secret Isn't Only in the Sauce

Many of the ingredients, if not the proportions, in the sauce's ''unique secret recipe'' are known and include tamarinds, garlic, anchovies, shallots, chilies, sugar, cloves, molasses, vinegar, and salt. The fish and vegetables in particular are carefully selected from around the world and allowed to mature before mixing in large, 6,000-gallon fir vats with the other ingredients. After mixing, the dark, pungent mass of liquids and solids is transferred to other tanks for aeration; eventually, the solids are pressed, strained, and discarded while the remaining liquid is tested for salt level and viscosity, diluted, pasteurized, and bottled.

Notwithstanding its unique recipe, Lea & Perrins' ''*real* secret ingredient,'' says Ransom Duncan—heir of the American Lea & Perrins, headquartered in Fair Lawn, New Jersey—''is time.'' John Buckland, factory chief at the Worcester plant, concurs:

AT A GLANCE

Lea & Perrins brand of Worcestershire sauce founded in 1835 in Worcester, England, by Marcus, Lord Sandys, and Lea & Perrins owners John Lea and William Perrins; brand sold to Imperial Group, 1967; Imperial Group sold to Hanson PLC, 1986; Hanson PLC sold to HP Foods Ltd. (English) and Lea & Perrins, Inc. (American) sold to BSN Groupe, 1988.

Performance: *Market share*—40% (top share) of Worcestershire category. *Sales*—$50 million (estimate).

Major competitor: Heinz Worcestershire sauce; also Durkee/French Foods Steak Sauce and Nabisco Brands' A-1 Steak Sauce.

Advertising: *Agency*—HDM, New York, NY, 1989—. *Major campaign*—"That's better": various humorous TV spots emphasizing the proper way to enhance the flavor of meat.

Addresses: *Parent company*—Lea & Perrins, Inc., 15-01 Pollitt Drive, Fair Lawn, NJ 07410-2795; phone: (201) 791-1600; fax: (201) 791-8945. *Ultimate parent company*—BSN Groupe, 7, rue de Teheran, 75008, Paris, France; phone: 33(1) 44 35 20 20; fax: 33(1) 42 25 67 16.

"The secret is time, and the balancing of ingredients. We test every ingredient before we buy it. There are variations from year to year, but these balance out during the long maturation" (*Gourmet*). The only noticeable difference between the American and English sauces is in the packaging; the American bottle has for over a hundred years carried a paper wrapper, while the English never has. After Imperial Group purchased Lea & Perrins in 1967, two other countries, Canada and Australia, were added to the list of its manufacturers.

Worst Years for the Worcestershire Giant

From 1974 until 1983, Lea & Perrins saw its market share steadily decline for the first time in its history, from 42.1 to 33.3 percent. Although by no means a fatal drop, the decline was serious in that it meant a virtual reversal for the number one and number two brands. Wrote Michael Kaplan, "Ironically, the competition [French's] had gained its lead by going to market with a cheaper, lower-quality sauce. Lea & Perrins's loss of share was further exacerbated by a change in American eating habits: Worcestershire sauce is applied primarily to beef, and health-conscious Americans had begun to shun red meat in favor of increasing amounts of fish and poultry." Then Steve Silk was hired as marketing director at the Fair Lawn headquarters. Kaplan wrote: "Working with Creative Food Services, a culinary-consulting firm in nearby New Rochelle, New York, Silk came up with the idea for a white wine Worcestershire sauce, which would be lighter in flavor and color and specifically balanced for chicken and fish recipes." The sauce was distributed nationally in October 1986—along with a comprehensive advertising program devised by McCann-Erickson advertising agency—and helped boost the company's market share nearly back to its former level, thus regaining the number one position.

In August 1988, a month after BSN's purchase of Lea & Perrins, Silk remained optimistic of the revived brand's future, stating "We want a broader array that will let us fulfill our company vision of being the leading marketer of premium enhancers in the United States." A growing trend toward regional and ethnic cuisine, with an emphasis on sauces, gave further

support to such plans. Yet, that same year, Lea & Perrins senior product manager Wade Souza noted in *Supermarket Business* that white wine Worcestershire sales were "not quite up to our expectations"; Martin Levine, author of the article, found that the sauce had "encountered more competition than the company envisioned from other major suppliers, including A-1 and Durkee Famous Foods."

"BSN's Big Four"

BSN has the reputation of being a lean, well-managed, marketing-oriented company devoted to maintaining a commanding presence in the European food business. Its 1988 purchase of Lea & Perrins and HP Foods for a combined 53 million francs ($90.9 million) represented the first step in accomplishing another of its major goals: successfully competing on a large scale in both the British and American markets. The mastermind of BSN's growth from a small, family-owned glass manufacturer into a diversified corporation whose 1991 revenues totaled $12.3 billion is Antoine Riboud. According to Rita Koselka, "Riboud presses the presidents of BSN's 80 operating companies to bring down costs—but never at the cost of developing new products and building their brand names." Riboud's acquisition chief, Henri Giscard-D'Estaing (son of the former French president), operates by the same philosophy.

When Lea & Perrins president Dennis Newnham met with Giscard-D'Estaing, according to Kouselka in *Forbes*, "the Frenchman astounded him by complaining that Lea & Perrins' earnings were so high that Newnham couldn't possibly be reinvesting enough in the business. He was right. Lea & Perrins' previous owner, Britain's Hanson Trust, Plc., had been draining cash from the company and neglecting advertising and new product development. BSN ordered Newnham to cut L & P's profit objective in half, and to reinvest the other half in the business." By the fall of 1988, Lea & Perrins had hired a new ad agency to handle its $6 million account; the resulting "That's better" campaign, designed to rekindle interest in Worcestershire as a cooking ingredient, was underway by mid-1989.

Despite positioning in a comparatively lackluster market, the Lea & Perrins line of sauces—which may be expected to grow in the coming years—is, according to Koselka, part of BSN's "big four," along with Dannon, Kronenbourg beer, and Evian bottled water. In such elite company, and backed by the deep pockets of BSN, the sauce will almost certainly maintain its past glories, if not surpass them.

Tradition and Versatility: The Final Secret

The original Worcestershire sauce has remained just that: original, and closely tied to national traditions. From Belgian steak tartare to Chinese *dim sum* to British shepherd's pie to American barbecued beef to the universal Bloody Mary, Lea & Perrins has long held its niche. Hence, it is still touted as "the world's most versatile sauce." Flavoring, marinade, browning agent, aphrodisiac, or hangover cure—the concoction of John Lea and William Perrins has, like its accompanying legend, stood the valuable test of time.

Further Reading:

"BSN Acquires HP Foods, Lea & Perrins from Hanson," *Wall Street Journal*, July 7, 1988, p. 18.

"BSN Acquires 2 Hanson Units," *New York Times*, July 7, 1988, p. D4.

Clayton, Dawn Maria, "When Ransom Duncan Hits the Sauce, You Can Bet It's His Family's Famous Worcestershire," *People Weekly,* October 4, 1982, pp. 53-4.

Dagnoli, Judann, "Saucy Campaigns: Perrins, Heinz Try to Spice up Market," *Advertising Age,* June 5, 1989.

Kaplan, Michael, "Lea & Perrins' Steve Silk," *Adweek's Marketing Week,* August 1, 1988, special report pp. 34-6.

Kenyon, Michael, "Worcestershire Sauce," *Gourmet,* October 1989, pp. 122, 234-241.

Koselka, Rita, "A Tight Ship," *Forbes,* July 20, 1992, pp. 141, 144.

Levine, Martin, "Consumer Expenditures Study: Condiments," *Supermarket Business,* September 1988, pp. 136-37.

—*Jay P. Pederson*

LIFE SAVERS®

Life Savers, the hard candy with the hole in the middle, has held a major part of the U.S. hard candy market since World War I. Its trademark shape—a miniature life preserver—made Life Savers stand out from its competition since the candy was initially produced in 1912. The first Life Savers were peppermints, and a variety of other mint flavors followed. Fruit drops were introduced in 1924, and the classic Five Flavor tube was put on the market in 1935.

Today there is a wide range of Life Saver flavors, but the shape of the candy remains the same. Expanding population growth, especially the Baby Boom following World War II, meant a steady broadening of the Life Savers market. To keep abreast of its competitors, Life Savers, a product of Nabisco Foods Group, has branched out into associated products such as sugar-free breath mints, Gummi Savers, a soft, chewy version of the candy with the hole, chewing gum, bubble gum, and mini mints. The classic Life Savers roll candy, however, has proven itself not a fad, but a perennial candy favorite.

Brand Origins

During the hot Cleveland summer of 1912, chocolate maker Clarence A. Crane, hoping to boost his lax warm-weather sales, decided to manufacture a hard mint that would not melt. Crane wanted to make a mint that would be noticably different from the square Austrian and German imported mints that dominated the market at that time. He came up with a ring shape and had a pharmaceutical pill manufacturer press them out for him. He packaged his new Pep-O-Mint Life Savers in small cardboard tubes marked with the slogan "For that stormy breath!" and packed them along with his regular orders to all his distributors. Despite the new mint's novelty appeal, there is no evidence that Life Savers sold particularly well, and the story might have ended there if an enterprising advertising man had not entered the scene.

Edward John Noble was a New Yorker employed by the Ward & Gow Company as a streetcar advertising salesperson. Having a knack for being in the right place at the right time, Noble had landed in San Francisco on a business trip on the very day of the great 1906 earthquake and fire. Lodged in a hotel ten stories up, the young man nevertheless came to no harm. Later in his life he would serve as Under Secretary of Commerce in the Franklin D. Roosevelt administration and bring his business expertise to the New Deal.

Noble met Clarence Crane while on a selling trip to Cleveland. After sampling a Life Savers mint, Noble became excited by the product's future. Noble was sure Life Savers could be a hit, but chocolatier Crane was not interested in promoting his mints; to him they were just a seasonal sideline of his career. So Crane offered to sell his existing stock and the rights to the candy to the young Noble for $5,000. Noble went back to New York City and conferred with his childhood friend, J. Roy Allen, who was interested in the deal and borrowed $1,500 from his mother. The two men together came up with $3,800 and talked the Cleveland manufacturer's price down to $2,900, leaving them $900 in start-up capital. Noble and Allen incorporated in 1913 as Mint Products Co., rented loft space in New York, and hired six young women to package the candies, which were delivered in bulk from Cleveland.

The young company, however, was soon in terrible trouble. Though Crane had managed to distribute his new candy far and wide through his established distribution network, Allen and Noble were able to swing only a single repeat order. Candy and drug stores wanted no more of the little mints: the cardboard packaging had quickly absorbed the peppermint flavor from the candy and imparted an odor of glue to its contents. Moreover, the package was difficult to open, often tearing customers' fingernails and after it was opened, tended to spill the candy everywhere. Though Noble had devised a new foil package that had none of these problems, he could only convince a few of his old customers to sell them. To win their business, he was forced to exchange his fresh mints for the stores' old stock, an expensive maneuver. Noble had to pay his six workers out of money he was still earning as a streetcar advertising salesman.

Nevertheless, the two business partners persevered. Roy Allen searched for new outlets for Life Savers, trying to find places that had not seen the old, messy cardboard tubes. He hit on the unconventional strategy of marketing the candy in saloons, which at the time traditionally set out a free dish of cloves for their customers to chew in order to take the alcohol off their breath. Allen reasoned that Life Savers could serve the same purpose, though customers would be charged a nickel. Sales were slow at first but began to pick up.

Another improvement Allen and Noble brought to Life Savers was the design of a carton that could be set up in stores as a miniature display case. The case sat out by the cash register, and customers with a nickel in change could be easily swayed to spend it on mints. In this way, the candy practically sold itself. But Allen and Noble still had a hard time finding enough willing retailers to keep their new business afloat.

Without enough money to pay for heavy advertising or to hire salaried salesmen, the two partners recruited young people as Life Savers peddlers operating as independent contractors. With no capital or fixed place of business, the salespeople went door-to-door to retailers all across the country. The peddlers were so young—some even fresh out of high school—that Roy Allen had to have them endorsed by their parents. But the strategy was successful; sales rose from 940,000 tubes in 1914 to 6,725,000 in 1915.

The war in Europe also helped boost sales by cutting off imports mints produced by Life Savers' competitors. In fact, sales grew astoundingly, rising to more than 22 million tubes in 1916, then to over 53 million the following year. In 1916, though, the government imposed severe sugar rationing measures, and Life Savers' sales suffered. The company had to raise the price of a roll from 5 to 6 cents, ration its distributors, and drop its West Coast business. In spite of these difficulties, partners Noble and Allen

AT A GLANCE

Life Savers brand of candy founded in 1912 in Pep-O-Mint flavor by Clarence A. Crane; further developed by Edward John Noble and J. Roy Allen, owners of Mint Products Co., incorporated in 1913; Wint-O-Green flavor introduced in 1920; Five Flavor tube introduced in 1935. Mint Products Co. incorporated in New York City as Life Savers, Inc.; company absorbed by Drug Inc., 1929; Drug Inc. dissolved in 1933, leaving Life Savers Corporation, which merged with Beech-Nut to become Beech-Nut Life Savers, Inc.; Beech-Nut Life Savers, Inc., merged with E.R. Squibb & Sons, Inc., to form Squibb Beech-Nut, Inc.; Life Savers, Inc., a division of Squibb, purchased by Nabisco Brands, Inc., 1981; Life Savers and Planters Nuts divisions consolidated in 1987 into Planters Life Savers Company, which was dissolved; in the early 1990s, Life Savers became a product of the LifeSavers Division of Nabisco Foods Group, which is held by RJR Nabisco, Inc.; brand extensions of Life Savers include Breath Savers, Life Savers Holes, and Gummi Savers.

Performance: *Market share*—(Life Savers) 27.1%; (Breath Savers) 12.9%; (Life Savers Holes) 4.9%; (Life Savers Fruit Juicers) 2% of hard roll/breath mint category.

Major competitor: Warner-Lambert Co.'s Certs; also, Ferrero's Tic Tacs.

Advertising: *Agency*—FCB/Leber Katz Partners, New York, NY.

Addresses: *Parent company*—Nabisco Foods Group, 1100 Reynolds Blvd., Winston-Salem, NC 27102-0064; phone: (919) 741-2000; fax: (919) 741-6602. *Ultimate parent company*—RJR Nabisco, Inc., 1301 Avenue of the Americas, New York, NY 10019-6013; phone: (212) 258-5600.

went ahead and built a large new factory in Port Chester, New York. People were eager to buy Life Savers, and sales began to grow again in the 1920s. The partners opened a Life Savers subsidiary in Australia in 1920 and sold it a year later for a phenomenal profit, earning $500,000 off an initial investment of $30,000. In 1925 the company netted its first million dollars in sales and sold 170 million packages of Life Savers. That same year, the company incorporated in New York City as Life Savers, Inc., and partner Roy Allen sold out his shares and retired a millionaire three times over.

In 1929 the company was bought out by a holding company called Drug Inc. The management of Life Savers, Inc., however, was not altered by the new owners, and in 1933, when Drug Inc. dissolved, E. J. Noble was still in charge of his company. The only difference was that the Life Savers now had two subsidiaries of its own, Pine Bros. of Philadelphia, makers of Pine Bros. cough drops, and Beech-Nut of Canada, Ltd., a chewing gum manufacturer. The new, larger company continued to thrive, netting approximately 90 percent of the American nickel mint business by 1938.

Early Marketing Strategy

The initial success of Life Savers was due to several factors. For one, as E. J. Noble had quickly realized in 1912, the product was unique. No one was marketing little ring-shaped mints before Clarence Crane came up with Life Savers. Another factor that helped spread the candy's popularity was Noble and Allen's dedicated search for new retail outlets for their product. With the

advantage of the Life Savers portable display case, the mints could be sold in a variety of locations, not just in candy and drug stores. Life Savers sold well in saloons and later became a standard item at the large chain of United Cigar stores. Through the persistence of Noble, Allen, and their army of peddlers, Life Savers became available at theaters, barbershops, and shoe-shine and news stands throughout the country.

None of the retail locations chosen by Allen and Noble catered particularly to children, the traditional consumers of sweets. Even the pricing of Life Savers at five cents a roll at first set it apart from most other candies. When Life Savers first appeared, only Hershey's chocolate bars and packs of Wrigley's gum sold for a nickel, while most other candy was sold to children by the piece or in larger, more expensive packages for the adult market. But the Life Savers market was essentially the same as the cigarette market: young, urban, white-collar adults. Life Savers management was quite explicit in aiming the candy at an upscale adult market, explaining in a 1938 article in *Fortune* magazine, "You would offer the president of the U.S. a Life Saver, but you wouldn't offer him a piece of chewing gum." Life Savers candy was touted as a gentleman's habit, not a child's sticky treat.

Besides placing the product in the kind of businesses young men frequented, Life Savers, Inc., carried out some more direct advertising. One 1930s campaign involved hiring attractive young women to hand out free samples of Life Savers in cities across the country. The instructions given to the district sales managers who were in charge of hiring the young women stressed that the women should be of "fair pulchritude" and "ladies in every sense of the word." The ladies, the instructions read, had to be able to put up with men who would kid them and "to take it with grace and dignity and without any attempt at return wisecracking." Moreover, she had to be able to fit gracefully into the red, white, and blue Life Savers uniform, which meant essentially that she was five feet four inches tall, with a 34-inch bust, 26-inch waist and 36-inch hips. The young women handed out their samples on street corners, and in stores and office buildings, while reciting the slogan "Life Savers are always good taste." The campaign was clearly designed to attract the attention of a young male market.

Life Savers, Inc., also used men as walking advertisements. Sometimes encased in eight-foot-high tin Life Savers packages, the men walked along in these giant tubes, barely able to see out of a screen cut in the front. One squadron of five or six tube men in New York City fell victim to rowdy Columbia University students who shoved the helpless fellows onto their sides and rolled them down a hill.

A similar gimmick was the purchase of cars that were made to look like giant Life Savers tubes on wheels. The early model tube car was found to be a menace to traffic, since the drivers could see and maneuver little better than the men who had been rolled down the hill at Columbia. A later model had the driver perched in front of the tube, and in 1938 at least 130 of the cars were in use as display and delivery vehicles.

Other advertisements played on the name Life Savers, utilizing news clippings about lifesaving, and passing out sample Life Savers on beaches. An early display ad showed a man in a boat tossing a Pep-O-Mint candy on a rope to a lovely, drowning young woman. Playing on the shape of the product, Life Savers developed a tradition of sending a free box of the candies to any golfer who made a hole-in-one. The names of the early flavors also played on the hole in the candy: Pep-O-Mint, Vi-O-Let, Lic-O-Rice, etc.

Company Reorganizations

Candy consumption boomed in the United States at the end of World War II, when millions of servicemen supplemented their rations with sugar products. The population growth following the war meant an expanding consumer base, and the rise in disposable income led to a steady increase in candy sales. Life Savers continued as one of the most popular candy brands in the country.

In 1956 Life Savers, Inc., which had owned the Canadian subsidiary of Beech-Nut since 1933, merged with American Beech-Nut to become Beech-Nut Life Savers, Inc. Beech-Nut had established gum brands and also made baby food and other food and beverage products. The new, larger company did well; with the fastest growing segment of the population being children, candy and gum were gaining adherents. In addition, an August 17, 1964, *Barron's* report noted that increasing fears about smoking were leading people to candy and gum as cigarette substitutes. Life Savers had long been positioned in the traditional cigarette market, selling to urban young men, so it is not surprising that sales grew comfortably in the 1950s and 1960s, reaching $12.8 million a year by 1964.

The company was reorganized again in 1967. A large pharmaceutical manufacturer, E.R. Squibb & Sons, Inc., merged with Beech-Nut Life Savers to form Squibb Beech-Nut, Inc. This was not the first time the Life Savers brand had come under the control of a drug company, having been part of Drug Inc. for a short time in the 1930s. The new company also imitated the structure of several other large, profitable drug and food companies, such as Bristol Meyers and Warner-Lambert Co. Squibb's management was excited by having a combined sales force with expertise in drugs, food, tobacco, and confections. The new company did well on the whole, and the new management of the Life Savers brand embarked on several product changes as well as introducing new related products.

Brand Development

By the time Life Savers came under the control of Squibb Beech-Nut, the brand had a somewhat classic status that precluded major changes. Yet to keep abreast of increasingly competitive markets, the company experimented with various Life Saver spin-offs, including gum, a soft drink, and breath mints; some were successful, some not. The Life Savers fruit-flavored soft drink, for example, was to have debuted in 1970, but it quickly floundered. Supermarkets in the Southern California test market area complained that Squibb Beech-Nut had set the price too high. The stores wanted to set their own prices, and as a result, Squibb Beech-Nut postponed its test market plans indefinitely and cancelled a scheduled television advertising campaign.

The next year, a Life Savers stick chewing gum came on the market, selling for the standard price of ten cents for an eight-stick pack. Gum had been a sore point with Beech-Nut when it first merged with Squibb. Squibb's management had noted that Beech-Nut's gum earnings had fallen off since the 1960s, as competition ate into Beech-Nut's share of the market. Of the big three gum makers, the Wrigley Co. had about half of all U.S. sales, followed by Warner-Lambert's American Chicle division, with roughly 25 percent of the market, and Beech-Nut with about 20 percent. These three companies were highly competitive, as the gum mar-

ket blossomed in the 1970s from roughly $650 to $700 million a year to $1 billion a year by 1978.

In an effort to increase its share of this market, Squibb Beech-Nut launched two more gums after the Life Savers sticks: Life Savers Care*Free, a sugarless gum, and Bubble Yum bubble gum. Care*Free was in direct competition with Trident, made by Warner-Lambert Co. Ads for Care*Free emphasized that each stick of Care*Free contained 32 percent more gum than Trident. Care*Free sales grew quickly, and by 1979 the new product had pulled almost even with Trident as the United States' best-selling sugarless gum.

Introduced in 1975 to capitalize on the fast-growing bubble gum market, Bubble Yum also enjoyed success. Its competition included Wrigley's Whammo and Warner-Lambert's Bubblicious. Bubble Yum proved instantly popular, selling out so quickly in test markets that advertising had to be suspended in order to minimize out-of-stock problems. Squibb had to build a $6 million addition to its manufacturing plant in order to accommodate its new bubble gum business. By 1978 Bubble Yum was close to the top position in the American bubble gum market and was also being marketed overseas in Germany and England. Bubble Yum held the top market share for several years, before slipping off in the early 1980s.

Another brand innovation in the late 1970s was a sugarless breath mint that had been in development from 1971 to 1977. Finally introduced in 1979 as Breath Savers, the candy was pitted against analogous Warner-Lambert Co. products, namely Certs, and Ferrero's Tic Tacs.

Life Savers candy itself changed little. In 1971, the size of the famous hole shrank, and the amount of candy around the hole grew by 10 percent. The classic five-cent roll had been retailing for six, seven, and eight cents in different parts of the country, and Squibb Beech-Nut used the size increase as an excuse to promote a new unified price of ten cents a roll. The ad campaign accompanying this change used a protest letter signed by approximately 200 members of the "Help Preserve the Life Saver Committee."

The letter's signatories were actually employees of Beech-Nut or of the advertising agency that wrote the ad. The letter complained that altering the size of Life Savers was a shocking jolt to tradition. The copy read in part: "Through prohibition, drought, floods, earthquakes, depression, inflation, war and other unpleasant happenings, a person could feel that there was something in this world that never changed—Life Savers." In fact, the shrinking of the hole with the addition of more candy left the roll itself exactly the same size as it had always been. The paper outer wrapping was replaced with foil, but these were hardly earth-shaking changes. The price rose again in 1974, from 10 to 15 cents and has risen several times since, retailing in the 1990s at approximately 50 cents a roll.

Life Savers advertising continued to emphasize the enduring nature of the brand. A 1979 television ad campaign, for example, featured actor Henry Fonda reminiscing about his childhood, when his grandfather would pass out Life Savers treats to all the little Fondas. The actor remarked that what was good back then was still good today. Indeed, though flavors were added, dropped, or improved throughout the brand's history, no significant change altered either the candy or its success.

Performance Appraisal

In 1981 Squibb Beech-Nut sold its Life Savers division to the giant food company Nabisco Brands, Inc., for $250 million. In that year, Squibb had reported a decline in sales and profits for its Life Savers division, even though Life Savers, Bubble Yum, and Care*Free were all three still at the top of their respective markets. Squibb's rationale for the sale was that the company wanted to shed its food lines and concentrate on pharmaceuticals. In 1985 Nabisco consolidated Life Savers with its Planters Nuts division, to create a new subsidiary called Planters LifeSavers Company. The company remained stable in spite of ongoing changes in its parent organization; Nabisco merged with tobacco giant R.J. Reynolds in 1988 to form RJR Nabisco, Inc. In the early 1990s the LifeSavers portion of Planters LifeSavers was named a division of the Nabisco Foods Group of RJR Nabisco.

By 1989, Life Savers had seen an increase in sales from the year it joined Planters, and the total share for Life Savers candy and all its line extensions was estimated at more than 40 percent of the overall hard rolled mint candy market. But Life Savers did not see spectacular growth in these years, and marketers continued to tinker with line extensions. Life Savers Holes, which were mini mints designed to compete with other successful small candies like Certs Mini Mints and Tic Tacs, were test-marketed in 1989, launched officially in 1990, then repackaged and relaunched in 1991.

While the Life Savers brand of the early 1990s was not experiencing the rapid growth of the brand's early years, it is a testament to the candy's endurance in the market place that some of the very first flavors made were still being sold. Five Flavor, Cryst-O-Mint, and the original Pep-O-Mint could be purchased at drug stores, corner newsstands, supermarkets, and from vending machines throughout the United States.

Overall, the worst years for Life Savers were the brand's first few, during which Clarence Crane's ineffectual packaging sabotaged the chances for repeat business that new owners Roy Allen and Edward Noble expected. But the two entrepreneurs worked hard to find the right packaging and presentation for their unique candy. Once Life Savers caught on, they did not ever fall significantly out of favor with the candy-consuming public. Though competition among candy brands became more intense in the latter decades of the twentieth century, leading to the multiplication of line extensions and new fad candies in the confection industry, Life Savers' continuing place in the market still seemed assured.

Further Reading:

"Ads Cancelled as Life Savers Drink Hits Price Hassle," *Advertising Age,* August 3, 1970, p. 1.

"From Pop to Boom," *Forbes,* September 18, 1978, p. 16.

Gershman, Michael, *Getting It Right the Second Time,* Reading, MA: Addison-Wesley Publishing Company, Inc., 1990, pp. 100-104.

Hammer, Alexander A., "Squibb and Beech-Nut Merging," *New York Times,* July 28, 1967, p. 39.

Harper, Sam, "Life Savers, Chicle Ready for Candy Roll Market Clash," *Advertising Age,* December 3, 1979, p. 1.

Haugh, Louis J., "Bubble Yum Latest Entry in Growing Gum Market," *Advertising Age,* December 15, 1975, p. 2.

"Hole in One," *Fortune,* February 1938, pp. 87-94.

James, Frank, "Nabisco Brands to Buy Squibb's Life Savers Unit," *Wall Street Journal,* November 13, 1981, p. 10.

Jervey, Gay, "Bubble Yum to Stick at DFS," *Advertising Age,* June 7, 1982, p.4.

Lazarus, George, "Life Savers Finds a Hole in the Market," *Adweek's Marketing Week,* July 17, 1989, p. 65.

"Life Savers Develops a Candy That's Dandy," *Sales and Marketing Management,* March 17, 1980, pp. 81-82.

MacGregor, Donald, "E.J. Noble—A Real Business Man in the Commerce Department," *American Business,* June 1989, pp. 16-19.

McGrath, Molly Wade, *Top Sellers, U.S.A.,* New York: William Morrow and Company, Inc., 1983, pp. 112-113.

"Nabisco Promotes Several Executives in Consolidation," *Wall Street Journal,* January 17, 1985, p. 40.

O'Connor, John J., "Life Savers' Famous Hole—It Gets Diminishing Diameter," *Advertising Age,* January 18, 1971, p. 49; "Care*Free on Trident's Heels," *Advertising Age,* January 15, 1979, p. 2; "Breath Savers Chews on Certs," *Advertising Age,* January 29, 1979, p. 6.

"Perfect Couple," *Forbes,* April 15, 1968, p. 40.

Pluenneke, Geraldine, "Reach for a Sweet," *Barron's,* September 14, 1970, pp. 11-14.

Sherrid, Pamela, "Cookies, Peanuts . . . and Life Savers?" *Forbes,* December 7, 1971, pp. 103-104.

"Sweet Inflation," *Time,* February 8, 1971, p. 79.

Willatt, Norris, "Candy Is Dandy," *Barron's,* August 17, 1964, pp. 11-14; "How Sweet It Is," *Barron's,* August 28, 1967, pp. 5-18.

—A. Woodward

LIPTON®

The Lipton name has reigned supreme in the U.S. tea market since its founder, Thomas J. Lipton, first introduced the brand in 1890. However, as the market has splintered over the years and other tea marketers have crowded in, Lipton has had to struggle to remain the leader in certain segments of the market, which remains relatively small in the United States—about $1 billion overall. Lipton is perhaps most recognized for being the first tea successfully marketed in bags, rather than in loose tea form. The brand owes much of its success to its founder, Sir Thomas J. Lipton, whose picture is featured on every red and yellow box of Lipton tea bags. Throughout its history, the Thomas J. Lipton Co. has focused on perfecting the tea bag that it first introduced in the early 1900s. In 1952, the tea marketer debuted its patented Flo-Thru Tea Bag. And as late as 1993, the Lipton brand was still trading on its reputation for tea bag innovation with television commercials stating, simply: "Lipton: A better tea bag. A perfect cup of tea." As tea drinkers' tastes have evolved, Lipton has acted quickly to fulfill tea drinkers' demands—with varieties of tea including instant, flavored, herbal, and ready-to-drink. While the Thomas J. Lipton Company is part of the Unilever Group conglomerate, the Lipton name continues to evoke, first and foremost, the image of a steaming cup of tea.

Brand Origins

Lipton tea was founded by Sir Thomas J. Lipton, a self-made millionaire who by the age of 40 had parlayed his family's modest grocery business into a chain of hundreds of shops throughout the British Isles. As his grocery business expanded, the enterprising and flamboyant Lipton traveled the world in search of suppliers who could meet his growing demands for the many food products he sold at retail. His travels eventually took him to places like Ceylon and Sri Lanka, where he sought better sources of tea.

There he discovered that a coffee blight had wiped out most of the crops, and desperate plantation owners had begun growing tea instead. Lipton bought several plantations and began managing the tea estates with the same zeal and innovative spirit that had turned his family grocery store into a thriving chain. He is also credited with revolutionizing tea production methods. Originally in Ceylon, tea was grown high on hillsides, then picked and carried down treacherous paths to factories below. Dissatisfied with what seemed an inefficient, dangerous system, Lipton devised his own system of aerial wires linking the fields and facto-

ries. He had the tea placed in sturdy sacks and attached to overhead cables, which allowed the sacks to glide effortlessly down the mountain to the factory door. Once in the factory, the tea was mechanically processed, to ensure cleanliness and quality.

Early Marketing Strategies

Though Lipton's production improvements undoubtedly contributed to the Lipton success story, it was his blend of tea and marketing genius that made the Lipton name synonymous with tea—first in Britain, and later in the United States. According to company records, Lipton first introduced his own blend of tea in Scotland in late 1888 or 1889. Lipton Tea was an immediate success in the British Isles for several reasons, the first of which was quality—Lipton set high standards for his blend, particularly with regard to taste and consistency. Lipton also broke with tradition by selling his tea in pound, half-pound, and quarter-pound packets. Before this time, tea typically was sold from open chests or drawers, leading to more rapid deterioration of the tea and customer distrust as to the exact weight and quality of what they were buying. Lipton tea packets helped preserve the freshness and flavor of the unique blend. And because they were clearly marked as to weight, price, and quality, they inspired consumer confidence.

Despite the quality blend and improved packaging, Lipton sold his tea for 60 percent less than other grocers due to yet another marketing innovation. Tea was typically purchased at auctions by tea buyers, who in turn sold the product to retailers. Lipton's own plantations supplied some of his product, but they could not meet the full demand. So Lipton employed his own staff of tea buyers, eliminating the need to rely on professional buyers who charged high prices. According to *The Lipton Magazine,* this elimination of the middleman allowed Lipton to sell his special blend " . . . at the equivalent of 30 cents a pound while the shopkeeper down the street was selling tea of similar quality at 50 cents."

U.S. Invasion

A little more than one hundred years after the Boston Tea Party, tea drinking was reborn in the United States in part through Lipton's ambitious marketing efforts. On the lookout for new markets, Lipton set his sights on the United States in 1890, after having discovered that the tea trade, which he had revolutionized in less than two years in Britain, was virtually nonexistent stateside. In 1890, what little tea was available in American retail stores was of relatively poor quality. And in the restaurant and hotel trade, tea was unheard of—a fact Lipton learned when waiters in Chicago responded to his request for a cup of tea by bringing him coffee instead. They didn't stock tea, Lipton was told. Inquiries at other hotels and restaurants produced the same response.

Sensing great potential, Lipton began by setting up headquarters in Chicago and dispersing a chain of agents to sell Lipton-brand tea first to hotels and restaurants and later to grocery stores. Lipton's reintroduction of tea into the U.S. market exceeded even his expectations, leading him to quickly send for more inventory from London and Ceylon. Before long, he added offices in New York to distribute his tea, which was still being packed in London. Then in 1909, Lipton established his first U.S. packaging plant, in New York City, under the name Thomas J. Lipton Inc. In response to the growing demand, Lipton opened a combination headquarters and tea packaging plant in Hoboken, New Jersey, in 1919. In 1937, six years after Lipton had died, the Thomas J. Lipton company was acquired by Unilever Group. The company remained in Hoboken until 1963, when a new headquarters was built in Englewood Cliffs, New Jersey.

Product Innovation and Evolution

Early growth of the Lipton brand came easily. The market was wide open, and Lipton had been the first to identify and penetrate it. However, to sustain that growth, Lipton relied on innovation and sensitivity to changing consumer preferences, and, although Lipton was the first tea sold in packets, it was not the first to be packaged in tea bags. Its founder was, however, the first to capitalize on the marketability of tea bags. Lipton first distributed tea in small, hand-tied bags to hotels and restaurants. Later, he adapted the bags for home use. According to *The Lipton Magazine,* "Lipton continually worked to build a better tea bag, changing from surgical gauze to a specially developed filter paper which imparted none of its own taste to the tea inside." In 1952, the Thomas J. Lipton Company began marketing tea in its patented Flo-Thru Tea Bags, four-sided bags designed to improve flavor by exposing more of the tea to the hot water.

Although the company devoted more than 40 years to improving the original tea bag, ironically, most future product innova-

tions evolved out of consumer demand for non-bagged tea products. In 1960, Lipton launched its first instant tea aimed at iced tea drinkers who preferred the convenience of being able to make iced tea without first going to the trouble of brewing hot tea. A few years later, Lipton improved on its instant tea by marketing a presweetened iced tea mix. By 1965, iced tea consumption had surpassed that of hot tea, although some iced tea drinkers continued to use bagged tea, rather than mixes. According to the Tea Association of the U.S.A Inc., by 1992, between 75 and 85 percent of the tea consumed in the United States was consumed in an iced version. Although Lipton remains the No. 1 tea marketer overall, with a strong lead in the bagged tea market, Nestle's Nestea is a formidable challenger in the instant tea category.

Throughout the past several decades, the tea market has continued to splinter. In some cases, Lipton has been the innovator, while in others, it has followed the lead of competitors. In 1972, Lipton introduced Iced Tea-in-a-Can. The product was produced through agreements with local bottlers who made the product, according to Lipton specifications, and distributed it to retailers. In 1977, Lipton test marketed a line of flavored tea bags, which it began distributing nationwide the following year. According to *The Lipton Magazine,* "Flavored teas were designed to provide a change of pace for traditional tea drinkers and to attract new, younger consumers to our tea products." The flavored teas were followed in 1981 by a line of caffeine-free herbal teas. In the early 1980s, Lipton debuted several market firsts. A full line of iced tea mixes with NutraSweet was introduced in 1982 and went national in 1983. Also in 1983, Lipton became the first major tea marketer to offer decaffeinated tea bags. Prior to this time, decaffeinated tea was limited to the specialty tea markets. Lipton's 97 percent caffeine-free product did not go national until 1986. One year later it commanded eight percent of the bagged tea segment. In 1988 Lipton became the first brand to market naturally decaffeinated tea bags, using a process that combined pure, sparkling water and natural effervescence.

The Herbal Tea Segment

In 1970, a small company by the name of Celestial Seasonings began marketing herbal teas. The Celestial Seasonings brand, packaged in artful boxes decorated with snippets of philosophy, captured the marketing essence of herbal tea with its whimsical flavors such as "Sleepy Time" and "Morning Thunder." After a decade of unchallenged growth, Celestial Seasonings suddenly found itself side-by-side on grocers' shelves with Lipton, which entered the herbal tea market in 1981. In 1984 Kraft Foods acquired the Celestial Seasonings brand for about $40 million. Backed by Kraft's marketing clout, Celestial Seasonings set out to hold Lipton at bay and retain its position as the major marketer of herbal teas. At one point, the two tea marketers took their rivalry to consumers in advertisements. While Lipton boasted that it had six of the top ten herbal tea brands, including the number one flavor, "Cinnamon Apple," Celestial Seasonings retaliated by revealing in an advertisement it had racked up 47.4 percent of herbal tea sales in 1986 — and that Lipton could claim only 34.2 percent.

By 1987, the herbal tea market had become a $100-million annual playing field. But in January of that year, Kraft, on the verge of being acquired by Philip Morris, decided to exit the market. After turning down an offer by Celestial Seasonings' management to buy the brand, Kraft agreed to sell Celestial Seasonings to Lipton. The deal, which would have given Lipton more than 80 percent of the market, was formally announced and seemed a sure thing until R.C. Bigelow, a small herbal tea producer best known for its Constant Comment label, challenged it. Bigelow, with a mere 13 percent of the market at the time, went to court in an attempt to bar Kraft from selling Celestial Seasonings

A historical advertisement for Lipton brand teas.

to Lipton, claiming the deal violated anti-trust laws. Bigelow intended to convince the court that Kraft and Lipton were threatening smaller brand names, such as their Constant Comment. Claiming that many supermarkets allowed major brands to choose the best shelf space, Bigelow argued that Lipton's purchase of Celestial Seasonings would enable it to dominate the second and third shelves, overshadowing the smaller players. After seven months of court arguments, Kraft abandoned the deal and sold the Celestial Seasonings brand to its managers after all.

Team Effort

In early 1992, Lipton teamed up with PepsiCo to create a new ready-to-drink tea known as "Lipton Original." The drink augmented, rather than replaced the brand's already existing ready-to-drink tea in cans. Bottled, rather than canned, the tea was introduced in three varieties: sweetened with lemon, sweetened without lemon, and unsweetened without lemon. At the time, Lipton commanded nearly half of the $400 million dollar ready-to-drink iced tea market, followed by number two, Snapple. However, new competition was coming from all directions: in the same year, Coca-Cola joined forces with Nestle to introduce ready-to-drink Nestea; Perrier allied with Celestial Seasonings to market a line of ready-to-drink herbal iced teas; and A&W had plans with Tetley Tea to market an entire line of "real brewed" ready-to-drink iced teas in exotic flavors. In fact, the ready-to-drink segment was responsible for driving growth in the tea market in 1992, accord-

ing to Joseph Simrany, Executive Director of the Tea Association of the U.S.A. Following almost a decade during which the tea market remained flat, Mr. Simrany said 1992 saw a two percent increase in pounds of tea sold, largely due to the ready-to-drink market.

Advertising Strategies

In the days when Thomas J. Lipton was just beginning to market Lipton Tea, he used advertising to its fullest advantage. His first ad slogan—"Direct from the tea gardens to the tea pot"—capitalized on his method of eliminating outside tea buyers, which allowed him better control over quality while keeping his prices lower than competitors'. The use of a picture of a Tamil native, sipping Lipton Tea, gave the brand an exotic image. Lipton launched his first campaign with more than the usual flair—a procession of men in Oriental dress carried 80 tons of tea from the Glasgow, Scotland, docks to Lipton's stores, according to *The Lipton Magazine.* Advertising also played a big role in Lipton's foray into the U.S. market in 1890. Again, according to *The Lipton Magazine,* Lipton embarked on a six-figure coast-to-coast advertising campaign to ensure that the Lipton name dominated the new U.S. tea market.

Despite the fact that the bagged tea market is the slowest growth category, Lipton has fairly consistently focused its advertising efforts on brand name awareness. Only occasionally has it directed advertising to a particular segment. The brand's marketers have argued that by directing attention to the Lipton name, they can effectively advertise for iced tea and hot tea in the same basic sales message. Several exceptions to this strategy occurred in 1983, when Lipton came out with a big campaign for its Iced Tea Mix with NutraSweet, featuring then-tennis star Chris Evert-Lloyd, and also introduced a campaign for its new decaffeinated tea bags, "the newest way to be a Lipton Tea lover." However, for the most part, Lipton advertising has tried to boost sales across the board by focusing on its core product. Slogans have included, "When Lipton blows the whistle, you're gonna have some great iced tea," "This is Lipton Tea time," (featuring people relaxing and happily drinking tea), and "Lipton: A better tea bag. A perfect cup of tea."

Future Directions

Following years of steady growth, then a burst of activity in the ready-to-drink market, Lipton finds itself still the market leader because of its early positioning and strong brand-name awareness. The overall market remains small—about $1 billion, according to the Tea Association of the U.S.A. Joseph Simrany, Executive Director of the association, predicts the next growth segment will be the specialty tea market, similar to the development of the gourmet coffee market. Simrany also said he expects the market will see some further growth overall as health-conscious consumers turn from coffee and soft drinks to the natural goodness of tea. "On the horizon, I think you're going to see tea marketers place an increasing emphasis on the link between tea and good health," Simrany said. "We have yet to see any negative effects from drinking tea—I think they're going to position tea as a healthy drink."

Further Reading:

Dagnoli, Judann, "Lipton Plans Ad Push to Get Things Brewing," *Advertising Age,* November 26, 1990, p. 3.

Dagnoli, Judann, and Julie Liesse Erickson, "Lipton Expands Tea Lead with Celestial Seasonings," *Advertising Age,* December 14, 1987, p. 12.

Fahey, Alison, "Looks Like Hot Summer for Iced Tea, *Advertising Age,* May 4, 1992, p. 4.

Friedman, Martin, "Tea Market Quietly Simmers," *Adweek,* September 28, 1987, p. 55.

Hume, Scott, "NutraSweet Ads Boost Lipton," *Advertising Age,* July 25, 1983, p. 4.

Jacobs, Sanford L., "Herbal Tea Makers Fight in Courtroom About Shelf Space," *Wall Street Journal,* June 10, 1988, p. 28.

Jacobs, Sanford L., "R.C. Bigelow Wins Ruling Barring Sale of Tea Maker, *Wall Street Journal,* June 22, 1988, p. 32.

Jervey, Ray, "Lipton Jumps into Fray with Decaffeinated Tea," *Advertising Age,* May 2, 1983, p. 1.

"Kraft Agrees to Sell Celestial Seasonings to Unilever Tea Unit," *Wall Street Journal,* December 9, 1987, p. 4.

Lafayette, Jon, and Judann Dagnoli "Lipton Near Sending JWT More Tea Biz," *Advertising Age,* February 17, 1992, p.1.

"Lipton Goes on the Offensive," *Business Week,* September 5, 1983, p. 102.

The Lipton Magazine, Englewood Cliffs, N.J.: The Thomas J. Lipton Company, 1989.

Mangelsdorf, Martha E., "The Brave New World of Antitrust," *Inc.,* December 1988, p. 19.

O'Connor, John J., "Nestle, Lipton Iced Tea War Heats up Again," *Advertising Age,* May 22, 1972, p. 1.

"Pepsi, Coke in Tea Tete-a-Tete; Short-term Break for Barq's?" *Beverage World,* December 31, 1991, p. 8.

Rowland, Mary, "Change Is Brewing in Tea," *Working Woman,* April, 1989, p. 85.

—Katherine J. Paul

LITTLE DEBBIE®

Little Debbie is the runaway domestic leader in snack cakes sold annually. In 1992 the Little Debbie snack line helped account for 52 percent of all snack cakes sold in the United States by its parent, McKee Foods Corporation, the largest private company of its kind in the country. By comparison, McKee's closest competitor, Continental Baking's Hostess Twinkies, posted only an 18 percent market share. Family-owned and operated, McKee Foods Corporation is the David to such Goliaths as Nabisco Brands, Continental Baking, and Interstate Bakeries. McKee's battles with these and other food giants is in the niche of snack cakes, the driving force behind the company's 400 percent growth in sales since 1982. This figure is all the more remarkable when one considers the company's extremely low profile, lack of full-scale national distribution, and cautious approach to expansion. McKee's success is fundamentally that of Little Debbie, a versatile line first launched in 1960 that now includes more than thirty regular and seasonal snacks under such names as Nutty Bars, Figaroos, Oatmeal Creme Pies, Caravellas, Golden Cremes, Devil Cremes, and Swiss Rolls. Granola bars, granola cereals, and other bakery products under the Sunbelt label are also graced with the popular Little Debbie insignia, unchanged since its inception.

Humble Origins

The company that gave birth to Little Debbie was born during the heart of the Great Depression. A young North Carolina couple, O.D. and Ruth McKee, lost their savings after a bank failure and moved from their home in Hendersonville to Chattanooga, Tennessee, in 1933. O.D. found work as a bakery salesman, selling Virginia Dare Cakes from Becker's Bakery, a local establishment, for five cents each. By 1934 O.D. had purchased his own delivery truck, but soon found that Jack's Cookie Company, another Chattanooga bakery, was up for sale. O.D. cashed in his truck, and he and Ruth became owners and operators of their first business. According to McKee's publication, "The Story Behind Little Debbie Snack Cakes," the two "were ideal business partners because her cautious, conservative nature was the perfect complement to his risk-taking, adventuresome spirit."

In 1935 O.D. moved the business to a new location and began making soft cookies and cakes. A year later they transferred the business to Ruth's father, Symon D. King, and returned to North Carolina to launch a new bakery. Located in Charlotte and named Jack's Cookie Company (like its predecessor), the business was

highly successful. In 1946 the innovative O.D. built a new, state-of-the-art plant. During this period he also invented a soft oatmeal creme pie, "the company's oldest continuous product," according to *Milling and Baking News*.

Bigger Plans

The McKees sold their Charlotte business in the early 1950s and considered retiring. However, they decided instead to return to Chattanooga and manage the original Jack's, which was now called King's Bakery and was owned by Ruth's brother, Cecil King. In 1954 O.D. and Ruth purchased the company stock and the foundation for the McKee Baking Company was born. O.D. assumed the familiar roles of salesman, inventor, and production manager, while Ruth operated as purchaser, personnel manager, and office manager. The acquisition of a new plant in nearby Collegedale three years later signified the actual launch of the McKee Company. It was at this location that the company established its headquarters and grew into a major private corporation. The original Collegedale plant was expanded more than a dozen times before a sister plant was added. In 1982 the McKee family launched a third plant in Gentry, Arkansas; a fourth followed eight years later in Stuarts Draft, Virginia. By this time Ruth had passed away and O. D. had handed management of the operation over to his sons, Ellsworth and Jack.

Little Debbie Debuts

In 1960 the company made history in two ways. First, after having led the industry in mass production of small snack cakes, it conceived the "family" pack of twelve individually wrapped cakes sold as one multipack unit. Second, it began affixing the Little Debbie brand, named after Ellsworth's daughter Debra, to its products. Both Little Debbie and the family pack remain the company's most significant generators of sales. A proliferation of snack cake varieties since that time—including the introduction of the Sunbelt line in 1981—has fueled the momentum generated by these two landmark events.

In 1982 McKee Baking, with $130 million in sales, ranked 22nd in the industry, behind such billion-dollar giants as Continental and Interstate. Sales at the time were concentrated principally in the Midwest, Southwest, and West. By 1987, however, the company was able to boast annual sales growth of 10 to 15 percent. This success was primarily due to the popularity of the

AT A GLANCE

Little Debbie brand of snack cakes founded in 1960 in Collegedale, TN, by McKee Baking Company owners O.D. and Ruth McKee; McKee Baking renamed McKee Foods Corporation in 1991.

Performance: *Market share*—52% (top share) of snack cake category (all McKee products).

Major Competitor: Continental Baking Company's Hostess Twinkies; Interstate's Dolly Madison snacks.

Advertising: *Agency*—Luckie Advertising Agency.

Addresses: *Parent company*—McKee Foods Corporation, P.O. Box 750, Collegedale, TN 37315-0750; phone: (615) 238-7111; fax: (615) 238-7127.

Little Debbie snacks, a product line that by that time had expanded to 32 varieties available in 41 states (the number of varieties has since grown to 38). McKee succeeded in outperforming Continental's Hostess, Interstate's Dolly Madison, and other major national brands through its low pricing. According to *Forbes* writer William Stern, the feisty competitor sells its products through supermarkets for 50 to 70 percent less than other comparable items. Surprisingly, the company's net margins, even given their low prices, are approximately six percent, while the average for the industry is 5.5 percent. "What's to stop McKee's giant competitors from matching its low prices?" queries Stern. "Common sense. Most of them are unionized and can't match McKee's low costs. They are giant corporations with giant overhead, while McKee is a family business. And even with lower prices, it would take them years to get the economies of scale McKee gets from its overwhelming market share." McKee maintains its low overhead by employing an independent distribution system and by expanding production only to keep pace with demand. Another advantage it has over the competition is the long shelf life of its naturally preserved products; indeed, its products' shelf life is some three to four times that of Hostess Twinkies.

Private Profits, Public Commitment

Since 1980, McKee has enhanced its market share by selling to convenience stores as well as supermarkets and by periodically rolling out national television campaigns, the most memorable of which was a series launched in 1985 that featured Rich Little in a variety of humorous impersonations. New products, including Little Debbie Fancy Cakes and the Little Debbie Snack Favorite line, also serve as powerful inducements to buyers, at least half of which are age 15 and under. Now named the McKee Foods Corporation, the company markets to 44 states and has achieved sales of at least $525 million. Under CEO Ellsworth McKee, the Tennessee bakery has preserved its highly private identity and strong family management (many third generation McKees, including Debra, hold high positions within the company). Although investment houses and bakery competitors, especially Continental, have hoped for the family to sell, the McKees have shown no inclination to do so. Given its present, enormously profitable status, as well as rising consumer demand and snack cake share, it would make little sense to entertain such thoughts. Moreover, there seems a palpable feeling at McKee foods that to sell the company would be to sell an integral part of the family—Little Debbie, an overachiever that's made the whole clan proud.

Further Reading:

"The Bakery Top 40," *Bakery Production*, June 1983, pp. 74-5.
"Family Clout Backs Philosophy of Independence in Era of Mergers," *Milling & Baking News*, November 11, 1988, p. 45.
"McKee Baking Will Build a $25 Million Cookie and Snack Cake Plant," *Milling & Baking News*, February 10, 1987, pp. 1, 13.
"McKee Baking Sets July Start for Production at New Virginia Plant," *Milling & Baking News*, May 8, 1990, p. 11.
"McKee Plans 'Little Debbie' Plant in Virginia," *Bakery Production*, May 1987, p. 20.
"McKee's New Snack Plant Begins Production," *Bakery Production*, August 1990, p. 28.
Stern, William, "Mom and Dad Knew Every Name," *Forbes*, December 7, 1992.

—Jay P. Pederson

LOG CABIN®

Log Cabin syrup, a product of Kraft General Foods, was one of the earliest maple syrup blends to be manufactured in response to the rising cost of pure maple syrup in the late 1800s. The Log Cabin brand was created by Patrick J. Towle, a Chicago grocer, who combined syrup made from sugar cane with enough maple syrup to give "Towle's Log Cabin Maple Syrup" the sought-after taste of maple. In 1887 Towle sold his grocery in Chicago and moved to St. Paul, Minnesota, where he established the Towle Maple Syrup Company. Towle and his descendents ran the company until 1927, when it was purchased by the Postum Company, which later became General Foods Corporation. In time, Log Cabin would become the biggest-selling breakfast syrup in the United States.

In 1993 Log Cabin is represented by the original Log Cabin syrup as well as four brand extensions: budget-priced Log Cabin Country Kitchen, introduced in 1956; Log Cabin Lite, introduced in 1989; Country Kitchen Lite, first presented in 1990; and Country Kitchen Butter, introduced in 1991. Three other brand extensions introduced over the years are no longer on the market.

There is no record of how much maple syrup Towle used in his original blend, but the formula has changed over the years, particularly as the cost of maple syrup increased as supplies dwindled. By the 1980s, Log Cabin contained just two percent maple syrup and was made primarily from corn syrup with maple flavoring. None of the brand extensions contained maple syrup. There were a few pure maple syrups, or blends with at least 15 percent maple syrup, available in the United States. But they were primarily local brands, relatively expensive, and often marketed to the tourist trade. Maple syrup, in liquid or powdered form, also was available by mail order. But many of the popular maple-flavored syrups, including several of Log Cabin's biggest competitors such as Aunt Jemima and Mrs. Butterworth's, contain little or no maple syrup.

The Discovery of Maple Syrup

Maple trees grow throughout the northern temperate regions of the world, but the sugar maple, or hard maple, which is prized by furniture makers and produces the sugary sap that is boiled down into maple syrup, is native only to the eastern half of North America, from Newfoundland to the Great Lakes. Vermont is the leading maple-syrup producing state in the United States, followed by New York, New Hampshire, Connecticut, and Massachusetts, but most maple syrup today comes from the Canadian province of Quebec.

The American colonists learned how to make maple syrup from the Indians, who had long enjoyed the sweetness of "sinizi-buckwud," the Algonquin name for both maple sugar and maple syrup. Maple sugar was a staple of the Indians' diet and the maple tree was a central figure in their religious and cultural celebrations. Native legend tells of an Indian chief who angrily threw his tomahawk into a maple tree. The next morning the chief pulled out his tomahawk and sap began oozing from the gash. It collected, quite by accident, in a cooking pot at the base of the tree. That evening, the chief's wife, believing the pot to be filled with water, began boiling the day's dinner. As the sap continued to boil, it slowly turned to maple syrup, and when the unhappy chief tasted the sweet, sticky maple syrup for the first time, his anger and bitterness disappeared.

Despite the long, arduous process of turning sap into syrup—it takes about 35 gallons of sap to make one gallon of syrup—American colonists readily embraced maple sugar as a home-grown substitute for expensive cane sugar, which had to be imported. Maple sugar was an important food in the American diet throughout the 1700s. By the late 1800s, however, maple sugar and maple syrup were becoming expensive luxuries, especially outside the New England states. Many people who preferred the taste of maple syrup had to make do with less expensive corn syrup or molasses. It was this need for an affordable, maple-flavored syrup that led Patrick J. Towle to create Log Cabin syrup in 1887. Towle reportedly named his syrup "Log Cabin" in honor of his boyhood hero, Abraham Lincoln. He registered the log cabin as a trademark in 1897.

The Log Cabin Tin

In 1897 Towle began to sell his syrup in small cabin-shaped tins manufactured in St. Paul by the Horn & Danz Company, a forerunner to the American Can Company, which continued to make the tins into the 1950s. The handmade cabin design was patented by James William Fuller of St. Paul on April 20, 1897. The packaging was an enormous success and helped popularize Towle's Log Cabin Maple Syrup. The tins came in various sizes, from half pints that were small enough to be used at the kitchen table to half gallons. When the syrup was gone, the empty containers became sought-after toys for more than 50 years and remain highly desirable collectibles today.

AT A GLANCE

Log Cabin brand syrup created in the 1880s by Patrick J. Towle; originally called "Towles Log Cabin Maple Syrup," brand was marketed by the Towle Maple Syrup Company, later known as the Log Cabin Products Company until 1927, when the company was purchased by the Postum Company; in 1929 the Postum Company became General Foods Corporation; in 1985 General Foods was acquired by Philip Morris Companies Inc., which also acquired Kraft, Inc. in 1988; in 1989 Kraft and General Foods were merged to form Kraft General Foods, Inc.

Major competitor: The Quaker Oats Company's Aunt Jemima; also Lever Bros. Company, Inc.'s Mrs. Buttersworth.

Advertising: Agency—Ogilvy & Mather, New York, NY, 1985—. Major campaign—"Rich maple flavor. And mornings to remember"; television campaign recalling "Mom's pancakes" and "family breakfasts."

Addresses: Parent company—Kraft General Foods, Inc., 250 North St., White Plains, NY 10625; phone: (914) 335-2500. Ultimate parent company—Philip Morris Companies Inc., 120 Park Avenue, New York, NY 10017; phone: (212) 880-5000.

A brief history published by the General Foods Corporation says, "The tin became as much of a tradition at Sunday breakfast as pancakes, waffles or French toast." In 1981 the Tin Collectors Association published an article in its newsletter, *Tin Type*, in which Norman Reed, a collector of Log Cabin tins, wrote: "Kids in those years gone by would build Log Cabin 'towns' composed of the many designs and sizes of these little tins, and would spend many a quiet summer afternoon driving their tin and cast-iron cars and trucks up and down the streets of the little cities built of Log Cabin Syrup tins."

Collectors have identified several distinct generations of the Log Cabin tins. The earliest cabin-shaped tins had colorful paper labels showing an outdoor scene and a "certificate of purity" that offered a $500 reward for evidence of impurity. In 1909 a border was added to the paper labels that gave the tins the appearance of a log cabin. Around 1919 the company, known as both the Towle Maple Products Co. and The Log Cabin Products Co., began using tins with labels printed directly on the metal using lithography. Later Log Cabin tins carried a variety of labels, including one that depicted a series of cartoon characters praising the syrup inside (1933-1942) and a Frontier Village series in the early 1950s that showed ten different pioneer buildings, including a jail, doctor's office, and blacksmith's shop. One series of Log Cabin tins in the late 1930s was equipped with wheels so that the container could be used as a pull-toy when the syrup was gone.

During World War II, tin shortages forced General Foods to begin selling Log Cabin syrup in glass containers. The June 1942 issue of *GF News Letter* reported that "[Japanese] gains in Malaya were reflected in the . . . tin can order of February 11. This affected our packaging. Fortunately the company had experience and machinery for packaging both Log Cabin Syrup and Maxwell House Coffee in glass." The syrup itself almost disappeared from grocers' shelves during World War II because of sugar rationing, and was in limited supply until late 1947. In November of that year, *GF News Letter* reported that "Log Cabin Is Back," and said ". . . newspapers, magazines, and radio are celebrating its return in the largest campaign in the history of Log Cabin." The company newspaper added that the plant in Hoboken, New Jersey,

where General Foods had moved the syrup-making operation in 1929 to be closer to its suppliers, "is now working full blast on a schedule that calls for more Log Cabin in the last six months of 1947 than for any previous 12 month period in its history."

The cabin-shaped tin can made a brief reappearance after the war, including the Frontier Village series, but was soon replaced by an antique-design glass bottle that came to symbolize Log Cabin Syrup for the Baby Boom generation. In his article on Log Cabin tins published in *Tin Type*, collector Norman Reed wrote: "By 1949, it was suspected that the whimsical cabin-shaped tins with which Log Cabin had been identified for so many years may have outlived their usefulness as a sales tool." General Foods stopped buying tins for syrup in 1955. However, in 1972, the company issued a tin cabin-shaped coin-bank that was a replica of the Frontier Village home scene, and in 1979 it issued another bank that was a replica of a pre-World War II Log Cabin syrup tin. In 1987, to celebrate its centennial, Log Cabin issued another tin. Like the tins, the Log Cabin glass bottles were designed to be used after the syrup was gone, either as a vase or decorative decanter. However, they never became as popular as the tins. The glass containers were replaced by plastic in the 1980s.

Towle's and Log Cabin products

Although the Log Cabin brand name has been associated exclusively with syrup for most of its history, Towle's Log Cabin Products Co. marketed several related products in the early 1900s, including Towle's Log Cabin Maple Butter and Towle's Log Cabin Ready Spread, which the label said could be used for "Frosting and Filling Layer-Cakes, Cookies, etc., in making Puddings, Sauces, etc., and to be used on Griddle Cakes, Bread, Biscuits, etc, instead of Syrup and is better and much cheaper than butter." The "Towle" name was also carried on other products, including Towle's Circus Syrup and Towle's Bucket Syrup, which was made in St. Paul by the Pioneer Maple Products Co., which the Towle family apparently started after selling the Log Cabin Products to the Postum Company.

Advertising

Like many products at the turn of the century, Towle's Log Cabin Maple Syrup was promoted with a variety of novelty items. In addition to the cabin-shaped tins, five silver-plated "advertising spoons" with cut-out versions of the Log Cabin trademark on the handles were made available. The spoons were first sold in 1905 by mail order for 10 cents in stamps. Other Log Cabin memorabilia included cabin-shaped jugs, coin banks, trading cards, ink blotters, embossed bottles, bottle openers, spatulas, potholders, recipe books, and pottery syrup-dispensers in the shape of a tree trunk.

In the early 1900s, Log Cabin syrup was marketed primarily to women, the homemakers of the era, as a way to please their husbands. For example, a magazine advertisement for Towle's Log Cabin Syrup in 1926 was headlined "How to be happy though married" and promised housewives "a little gem of breakfast wisdom." The text of the ad read that "A husband has a disposition . . . [a]nd usually it's about as good as his breakfast. . . . That's why millions of women today always use Log Cabin Syrup."

In 1993 Kraft General Foods launched a major television advertising campaign that hoped to tap into consumer nostalgia for simpler times. The commercial showed a drawing of a snow-covered log cabin in a rustic setting. As smoke rose from the chimney through animation, an unseen announcer urged viewers to remember their childhood and family breakfasts: "Remember waking up to the hiss of mom's pancakes hitting the griddle, and looking forward to drowning them in rich, mapley Log Cabin syrup?"

Further Reading:

"GF Product Roll Call," *GF News Letter*, November 1947, pp. 1-3.

Goodrum, Charles, and Helen Dalrymple, *Advertising in America: The First 200 Years,* New York: Harry N. Abrams, Inc., 1990.

Hake, Ted, *Hake's Guide to Advertising Collectibles*, Radnor, PA: Wallace-Homestead Book Company, 1992, p. 151.

"Pancake Syrups: How Far from the Tree?," *Consumer Reports,* January 1992, pp. 60-64.

Reed, Norman, "The Log Cabin Syrup Tin—A History," *Tin Type*, Tin Container Collectors Association, 1981.

Seligmann, Jean, "Where Has All the Syrup Gone," *Newsweek,* May 8, 1989.

The Story of Log Cabin Syrup, White Plains, NY: General Foods Corporation.

—Dean Boyer

LOUIS RICH®

Louis Rich, a U.S. leader in processed turkey, has changed dramatically since its founder, Louis H. Rich, started a beef distribution company in Rock Island, Illinois, in 1921. Market changes brought product changes, and Mr. Rich's company focused primarily on chickens by the 1930s, turkeys by the 1950s and 1960s, and processed turkey foods from the late 1970s through the 1990s. The rise of health consciousness in the 1970s focused attention on the low-fat, high-protein qualities of turkey and contributed to the growing success of Louis Rich products. In 1979 the brand was acquired by the Oscar Mayer Foods Corporation, the category leader in processed luncheon meats. With the technical, financial, and management resources of such a large partner, Louis Rich expanded its product line in the early 1990s. Though the rate of growth of processed turkey slowed in the early 1990s, causing strategic replanning at Oscar Mayer, the market promised to continue growth alongside trends in healthier, lighter foods.

Brand Origins

In 1921 Louis H. Rich borrowed $600 from his brother-in-law, Morris Fox, to buy a used truck and start a business buying calves from local farmers, then having them slaughtered and dressed, and selling them to meat markets. The meat business was not new to the young entrepreneur. His father, Wolf Rich, had operated a kosher butcher shop in Rock Island, where he raised his family after moving from Bilarutka, Russia at the turn of the century. Louis Rich's initiative expanded quickly. Realizing that poultry and eggs were a largely untapped resource on the farms he frequented in Iowa and Illinois, he added them to his inventory. After two years, chickens and eggs proved so profitable that he discontinued calves altogether. In 1923 he founded the Rock Island Produce Company and began to hire staff. By 1926, he had expanded beyond local markets, focusing instead on the metropolitan centers of Chicago, Philadelphia, and New York. The company invested in storage coops at railway stations and in regularized shipping arrangements. At that time, chickens were transported in specialized railway cars with built-in coops and a chicken attendant, a "car man," to feed and supervise the birds.

In 1931 the Rock Island Produce Company was incorporated. In the early 1930s, as many as ten cars of live chickens were transported daily. By the middle of the decade, however, advancements in refrigeration and poultry processing enabled the company to slaughter and dress the birds in the Rock Island plant, and ship them fresh to various markets. The advent of mechanical plucking—replacing the laborious process of picking feathers by hand—also helped efficiency. Mr. Rich introduced the so-called "New York dressed poultry" line that accounted for 90 percent of company sales.

Early Marketing

In the late 1930s, the dressed chickens of the Rock Island Produce Co. were given names, of sorts: Louis Rich introduced the Silver Eagle and Three Star brands. This new brand identity was enhanced by a motto, "Clean as a Whistle," emphasizing the hygienically sound environment in which the birds were raised and processed. It also emphasized the effortless, featherless, and unmessy process of preparing dressed poultry, which continued to rise in popularity.

World War II served as another marketing impetus, opening up the international market and stimulating higher production in the face of higher demand. By 1939, the Rock Island Produce Company was supplying Britain with eggs individually stamped "Product of the United States." With U.S. involvement in 1941, the company began supplying chickens and eggs to the armed services. To meet increased demand, a new plant was operated in Galesburg, Illinois, from 1940 to 1945. In 1944, the company rented a temporary buying station in West Liberty, Iowa. And in 1946, a tomato-canning factory there was refurbished to process poultry.

Changing Market

In the early 1950s, Rock Island Produce Co. faced market changes that would require adaptation. Lower land and labor costs, among other influences, shifted chicken farming to the Southeastern states, at the expense of Iowa, the former leader and a stronghold for Louis Rich's operations. With diminished chicken supply, the company expanded to turkeys, remodeling its West Liberty plant in the mid-1950s to accommodate the bigger birds. Though the Rock Island plant continued to process chickens, by 1960 supply was so low that it closed altogether. The company had shifted exclusively to turkey.

Also in 1960, the company reorganized. Louis Rich went into semi-retirement for health reasons and passed operations over to his children. While Louis remained chairman, his daughter

AT A GLANCE

Louis Rich brand of meat introduced by Louis H. Rich in 1921 in Rock Island, IL, as part of a local beef distribution business; 1923, Rich named the business the Rock Island Produce Company; company was incorporated in 1931; 1960, the founder's children assumed control and changed the name to Louis Rich Foods, Inc.; in 1974 the company was restructured, creating Louis Rich, Inc., Holding Company; in December of 1979 the company was acquired by Oscar Mayer Foods Corp. and renamed Louis Rich Company; in 1981, Oscar Mayer was acquired by General Foods Corporation which was purchased by Philip Morris Companies, Inc. in 1985; General Foods Corporation merged with Kraft, Inc., another subsidiary, to form Kraft General Foods, Inc. in 1989.

Performance: *Sales*—$277 million (*Superbrands 1991* [supplement to *Adweek's Marketing Week*], 1991, p. 91.).

Major competitor: Mr. Turkey.

Advertising: *Agency*—Foote, Cone & Belding, Chicago, IL, 1992—. *Major campaign*—"Switch to Rich."

Addresses: *Parent company*—Oscar Mayer Foods Corporation, P.O. Box 7188, Madison, WI 53707; phone: (608) 241-3311. *Ultimate parent company*—Kraft General Foods, Inc., Three Lakes Drive, Northfield, IL 60093; phone: (708) 646-2000. *Ultimate ultimate parent company*—Philip Morris Companies, Inc.

Roselyn served as director, son Martin oversaw operations and production, and Norman directed sales and marketing. In deference to its founder, the company was renamed Louis Rich Foods, Inc.

One of the first objectives of the siblings was to energize business by widening the market for turkey. Due to the bird's seasonal demand, operations had been running only part-time since the company had turned exclusively to turkeys. From July through December business prepared for the holiday season. The rest of the year fell dormant. In 1964 the Riches tried an innovative strategy that not only revitalized business, but changed the turkey industry in general by deciding to cut whole turkeys into parts and market them separately to the food service industry. No longer would large birds be suitable only for large feasts; smaller parts could be prepared for any occasion. The sum of the parts quickly proved more profitable than the whole turkeys as conventionally sold.

Different parts found different markets. A Boston company contracted to buy and can the white breast meat. For the remaining dark meat, the Riches quickly discovered an exceedingly hungry European market. By the late 1960s, Louis Rich was the leading brand of turkey in Europe, which accounted for 25 percent of Louis Rich sales. Germany and the Netherlands imported especially large quantities of thighs and drumsticks. European demand for dark meat became so great that the company, facing an oversupply of white meat, sought new markets to keep production in equilibrium. They found producers in Philadelphia who processed turkey rolls by binding oven-roasted turkey breasts with gelatin. In 1968, Louis Rich developed its own ready-to-serve, pre-cooked turkey-breast product. In addition to unusually high quality standards, the product gained attention by its shape. Unlike the cylindrically-shaped competition, Louis Rich's product was molded into the shape of an actual turkey breast. It became the

best-selling oven-roasted turkey product in the United States. It also foreshadowed the company's future success in processed turkey foods.

The Age of Turkey Processing

The early 1970s marked a period of rapid change at Louis Rich. On November 14, 1970, Louis Rich died, followed by his wife, Ida Fox Rich, on July 23, 1971. In addition to such personal loss, the company faced a significant decline in sales to Europe, which had developed competitive markets of its own. In order to consolidate sales and maintain the delicate balance between white and dark meat sales, the company developed a series of pre-cooked, ready-to-serve processed meats. Turkey ham, made from surplus thigh meat, was introduced in 1970. It was followed by other turkey cold-cuts, including salami, bologna, pastrami, and frankfurters. These new products caused some controversy in an industry dominated by pork and beef. Louis Rich counteracted by emphazing its honesty and the quality of its ingredients. 1970 sales reached $17 million, up from $3 million in 1960. Louis Rich became the largest processor of turkey in the United States.

Such growth entailed greater facilities and a wider market. The company expanded its market to both coasts by acquiring new plants—one in Newberrry, South Carolina, in 1972, and another in Modesto, California, in 1974. Also in 1974, the Louis Rich, Inc., Holding Company was created. Such growth permitted introduction of processed turkey, formerly sold only wholesale, into the retail market. For the first time, grocery store consumers had access to packaged turkey parts as well as a variety of sliced turkey products in consumer-sized packages.

Marketing Innovation

To secure its turkey empire, Louis Rich depended on a wide range of marketing strategies. Ideas were culled from all ranks of the company. The Riches, following the accessible management style of their father, typically held so-called "Quality Assurance Lunches." They lunched with a different group of employees each week to eat and critique the products of each respective group. These lunches, combined with more formal planning, resulted in such innovations as vacuum-sealed, convenience-sized packages for retail. And even before laws mandated comprehensive product information, Louis Rich responded to the health-consciousness of the 1970s by providing detailed nutritional information on many of its labels. The company also extolled the healthfulness of turkey in numerous advertising campaigns throughout the 1970s. Sales grew favorably, to $164.7 million in 1979.

Sales were so favorable, in fact, that the company attracted the attention of Oscar Mayer Foods Corporation, the U.S. leader in processed meats, which acquired the company in December of 1979. Though 1980 sales reached $200 million, they were lower than anticipated. In a *PR Newswire* report in November of 1980, Oscar Mayer president and chief executive officer, Jerry M. Hiegel, voiced disappointment with a drop in income for the year, partly attributable to low prices for pork products that cut the margins on Louis Rich Turkey. Yet the outlook remained positive.

Brand Development

A positive outlook proved justified, as Louis Rich sales rose to $450 million in 1985, and the brand continued to diversify. Reflecting the company's growth, several additional plants were acquired, in addition to the construction of the first new Louis Rich plant, located in Tulare, California. Ground was also broken for a facility in Sedalia, Missouri, projected to be the largest Louis Rich plant ever. New products were also introduced. In 1991 the company introduced Louis Rich Turkey Bacon, a product with half the fat of its pork cousin. The product was supported with network TV and radio spots by D'Arcy Masius Benton & Bowles, as well as coupon inserts. At the 15th International Food Products Exhibition held in Paris, France, in 1992, Louis Rich Turkey Bacon was one of seven U.S. products recognized as the most outstanding. In the May, 1992, volume of *Progressive Grocer,* Everette Fortner, brand manager for Louis Rich Breakfast Meats, noted that the product would create incremental sales, especially for "lapsed users," or people who had given up bacon for health reasons, but missed the taste and supported a healthier bacon product.

The company also introduced Louis Rich Turkey Sausage Links in 1991, adding to a line that already included Oven Roasted Turkey Breast, Fresh Ground Turkey, Honey Roasted Breast of

A billboard advertises turkey packed by the Rock Island Produce Company, the original name of Louis H. Rich's company.

Turkey, Turkey Smoked Sausage, Hickory Smoked Turkey Breast, Fresh Turkey Breast Slices, and Bun-Length Turkey Franks. In a May, 1987 article in *Forbes,* Ruth Simon suggested that such products reflected a "throw the bird in the grinder and let's see what comes out attitude." Yet sales figures indicated that consumers were less critical: volume of Louis Rich products was up 10.0 percent in 1988 and 13.7 percent in 1989, according to *PR Newswire* reports.

Health Concerns

Capitalizing on the health-consciousness that set turkey on its market ascent in the 1970s, Louis Rich and its competitors continued to emphasize health benefits well into the 1990s. Early in the decade, however, some claims began to backfire, as many consumers and health experts criticized misleading labels on products that weren't as healthy as their labels seemed to indicate. Food producers came under pressure to change those labels that might make buyers believe they were purchasing healthy items. In a July 15, 1991, *Time Magazine* article, Christine Gorman identified the worst culprits as those products claiming to be 80 percent, 90

percent or even 99 percent fat free. Though technically correct, the labels tended to mislead consumers by basing their calculations not on the composition of calories, but on weight, including water content. Louis Rich Turkey Bologna, for example, accurately claimed to be "82 percent fat free, 18 percent fat" on the label. However, while the recommended average daily intake of calories from fat is 30 percent, actually 75 percent of the calories in the meat were derived from fat. Likewise, in 1989 Louis Rich Turkey Ham proclaimed itself 95 percent fat-free, even though 51 percent of the calories in the meat came from fat.

Along with physiological health issues, the 1990s media focused increasingly on environmental health. Louis Rich responded by investigating packaging alternatives and by conserving where possible. In 1990, Subway, the sandwich franchise supplied by Oscar Mayer/Louis Rich products, combined efforts with their suppliers to design reusable shipping containers. The result was shipping boxes that, once unloaded, could be converted to takeout containers. In a May, 1990 article in *Prepared Foods,* Fred DeLuca, Subway president, said that "it was time we made our contribution to a safer environment and recycling efforts."

Performance Appraisal

Louis Rich grew and evolved from a local beef business, to a poultry operation, to a part-time turkey purveyor, to a full-time turkey processor, culminating in big company support after its 1979 acquisition by Oscar Mayer. The 1980s marked a period of diversification in processed turkey products, with an eye on projected growth in a health-conscious market seeking alternatives to pork and beef products. Turkey met such criteria. In 1991, Americans gobbled twice as much turkey as they did in 1970. Yet by the early 1990s, the industry saw a leveling-off of demand for turkey-based products. The growth rate of Louis Rich turkey products declined to 3 to 4 percent, from 10 to 12 percent in the late 1980s. "When your history in the 1980s was in the double-digits, 3 percent to 4 percent is a shortfall," said John Bowlin, president of Oscar Mayer Foods, in a July 1992 *Prepared Foods* article. In order to adapt, the company increased efficiency and closed several plants. In May of 1992 Louis Rich cut back 1,440 jobs by closing the processing plant in Tulare, California—a facility that had been completed in 1989 to accommodate anticipated growth. Mr. Bowlin stressed the importance of keeping business operations as lean as their new lines of "healthy" products.

Despite reduced rates of growth in the early 1990s, Louis Rich products could count on vigorous growth strategies under the parentage of Kraft General Foods's Oscar Mayer. Aggressive marketing was reflected in a new generation of ads, including an offbeat roadshow, featuring former NFL all-star and ABC sports announcer Lynn Swann, traveling the country to display the perfect turkey sandwich, among other things. In 1992, Louis Rich also revamped its packaging, introducing a high profile red-diamond logo and resealable packages. Steve Shanesy, the turkey's marketing manager, claimed that consumers associated the color with appetite appeal. The design change was supported with a 3-month, $5 million ad campaign, focusing on magazines. A TV ad campaign displayed the packaging with the theme, "Taste the Difference Slow Roasting Makes." And in October of 1992, the company shifted the estimated $14 million Louis Rich advertising account from DMB & B to Foote, Cone & Belding, Chicago. Understanding that turkey could not fly on its own, Louis Rich/ Oscar Mayer in the early 1990s was eager to lend it a hand.

Further Reading:

Gorman, Christine, "The Fight Over Food Labels," *Time Magazine,* July 15, 1991, p. 52.

Kleinfield, N. R., "General Foods Waits for the Payoff," *The New York Times,* September 15, 1985, Sect. 3, p. 1.

Littman, Margaret, and Ann Meyer, "Bowlin Preaches (and Practices) a Lean Future for Oscar Mayer," *Prepared Foods,* July, 1992, p. 30.

The Louis Rich Company, Madison, WI: Oscar Mayer Foods Corp., 1991, 26 p.

Scott, Jeffry, "Ad News," *The Atlanta Journal and Constitution,* September 1, 1992, p. F2.

Simon, Ruth, "Will the Turkey Fly this Time?" *Forbes,* May 18, 1987, p. 210.

Snow, Jane, "Don't Let 'Low-Fat' Labels on Luncheon Meats Fool You; Some are Really Loaded," *Chicago Tribune,* October 19, 1989, p. C7.

Strauss, Gary, and Linda Dono Reeves, "A Fine Line Becomes Finer; More Ads Meld with Entertainment," *USA Today,* September 8, 1992, p. 6B.

"Subway, Oscar Mayer/Louis Rich Combine in Packaging Reuse Effort," *Prepared Foods,* May, 1990, p. 228.

Superbrands 1991 (supplement to *Adweek's Marketing Week*), 1991, p. 91.

"The World Food Industry Gathers at Paris to Show Off Its Best," *Progressive Grocer,* May, 1992, Vol. 71, No. 5, p. 113.

—Kerstan Cohen

LUCKY STRIKE®

The name Lucky Strike has been an American mainstay for over 100 years. Originally a brand of chewing tobacco, the brand name was revived and reused on a new cigarette that was introduced in 1916 by the American Tobacco Company. The new Lucky Strike cigarette was a brand that integrated domestic tobacco with Turkish tobacco. Introduced in response to competition from R. J. Reynolds's Camel brand, Lucky Strike overtook the competition and helped build the American Tobacco Company into one of the largest tobacco companies in the world. Lucky Strike was a mainstay in the standard cigarette market until the 1960s. At that point, due to increasing health concerns, the move toward filtered, lighter brands, and further product differentiation through advertising, Lucky's market share began to plummet, despite increased expenditures on advertising. Though Luckies now come in a filtered brand, total market share remains relatively low. Today Lucky Strike is largely a nostalgic name, remaining popular with the shrinking market of die-hard smokers.

Brand Origin

The name Lucky Strike was originally associated with a brand of cut plug chewing tobacco in the late 1850s. Tobacco at that time was pressed into tight lumps or plugs so as to distribute its moisture content; thus, it would not spoil in humid weather. After the Civil War, brand names became an important competitive weapon in the plug market. James Thomas, of Richmond, Virginia, began using Western dark burley leaf in his plug. The rush of people out west opened up new markets for tobacco products and, with the California gold rush in full swing, "Lucky Strike" was a natural name for the times. Thomas's nephew R. A. Patterson manufactured the Lucky Strike plug.

Plug was the main tobacco product for quite some time, until it was gradually replaced in popularity by smoking tobacco in the late 19th century. The smoking tobacco surge that took place around the turn of the century also included Lucky Strike, which was manufactured as a pipe tobacco in 1900. Of course, the name Lucky Strike would become most well-known as a cigarette brand introduced by the American Tobacco Company in 1916.

The beginnings of Lucky Strike cigarettes are a prime example of a company competing by learning how to make the same product as its competitors but doing it better. This was the case when Lucky Strike was introduced into battle with Camels. The American Tobacco Company, and its leader, George Washington Hill, had been locked in a fierce competitive battle with the R. J. Reynolds company in the early part of the 20th century. Reynolds had introduced Camel cigarettes with the phrase "the Camels are coming." This new cigarette combined the very popular Turkish blend tobacco with some type of domestic blend that swept out the competition. American Tobacco could not compete with this new taste in cigarettes. Nor could American compete with the new low price of ten cents for a pack of twenty cigarettes.

George Washington Hill bought himself a pack of Camels, set about trying to determine what was contained in the tobacco blend, and then marketed his own brand of blended cigarette under the name Lucky Strike. As Hill put it, the competition "forced us to put out Lucky Strike." Hill had the Camels analyzed, and it was discovered that Reynolds used burley tobacco in its cigarettes. Hill then turned to his vice president in charge of manufacturing plug tobacco, Charley Penn, giving him the task, though he had no experience with the product, of blending a cigarette better than Camels. Penn got the burley blend used earlier in plug chewing tobaccos and other smoking tobaccos. The burley was wrung out, dried, then blended into the mixture, before being dried again. Within five years of its introduction, Lucky Strike passed the seven billion mark in annual sales, growing by more than 20 percent per year from 1923 to 1925.

Marketing Strategy

At the time of Lucky Strike's appearance on the market, competition in the industry was largely based on cost-cutting as opposed to product differentiation. Because quality was largely the same, firms with lower costs could undercut their competitors. This is precisely what Camel did prior to the introduction of Luckies.

G. W. Hill's strategy, however, was also to market Lucky Strike to a broader market. After World War I, cigarette smoking, once relatively limited and stylish, became commonplace. Camel was often referred to as the "truck driver's cigarette." But Hill marketed Luckies with flamboyant campaigns such as "Reach for a Lucky instead of a Sweet," as well as appealing to bizarre expert advice such as, "With men who know tobacco best, it's Luckies two to one" and many more peculiar slogans. Coupled with the showmanship of the chant of the tobacco auctioneer and the popularity of the "Lucky Strike Hit Parade" shows on radio and television, Hill was assured a prominent place in marketing history and moved Lucky Strike into the top market share spot in 1929.

This move to the front of the cigarette market was also pushed by production innovations in the handling and packing of tobacco leaf. One innovation particularly important in the war for market share that was going on in the mid-1920s between the American Tobacco Company and R. J. Reynolds was the Arenco packer. The Arenco packing machine was especially helpful, providing increased speed by combining the packing and stamping processes in a small sized machine. Although Reynolds was the first to introduce the Arenco packer, by early 1927 the Arenco packer in American's mid-town Manhattan factory was turning out Lucky Strikes at a rate of 97,000 per hour. The adoption of this technique by American enabled it to be in the position to cut prices: On April 21, 1928 the price of Lucky Strikes were reduced from $6.45 to $6.00 (per thousand cigarettes), matching the decrease that Reynolds announced for Camels on the same day.

The new brand needed a name and Hill went through old brands of American Tobacco, happening upon Lucky Strike. Once Hill had chosen the Lucky Strike name, he decided the prior brand's Elizabethan packaging, with its scrolls and curlicues,

AT A GLANCE

Lucky Strike brand of cigarette founded in 1916 by George Washington Hill of the American Tobacco Company (name originally used for plug chewing tobacco and pipe tobacco).

Performance: *Market share*—0.4% of cigarette category. *Sales*—$2.04 billion.

Major competitor: Philip Morris Corporation's Marlboro; R. J. Reynolds Tobacco Co.'s Winston.

Addresses: *Parent company*—The American Tobacco Company, P.O. Box 10380, Stamford, CT 06904; phone: (203) 352-8000. *Ultimate parent company*—American Brands Inc., P.O. Box 811, Old Greenwich, CT 06870; phone: (203) 698-5000.

didn't match the cigarettes. He devised the well-recognized red circle with its bold "Lucky Strike" lettering surrounded by gold trim.

Lucky Strike was one of the first brands in 1940, along with the brands of P. Lorillard and Liggett and Myers, to come wrapped in cellophane with a "zipper opener," a red tear strip for ease in opening the cellophane wrapper. This zipper design was criticized by the competition which claimed that the zipper destroyed the effectiveness of cellophane as a moisture-proof package.

Advertising

The early advertisements for Lucky Strike focused on the generous portion of burley leaf, which was combined with Maryland tobacco to make the Lucky Strike blend. The ads also called attention to the "toasting" process, which, contrary to the advertising, did not distinguish Luckies. All cigarette brands used this process, which was merely a way of drying the tobacco.

G. W. Hill employed several very effective ad campaigns from the early 1920s through the post-World War II period. These campaigns catapulted Lucky Strike sales from 13.7 billion in 1925 to 43.2 billion in 1930. The very first ads were billboards that showed a piece of toast on a fork; in 1923 Hill did some dramatic sky writing of the brand's name in white smoke over 122 cities. To reach out to women smokers, Hill used such women heroes as Amelia Earhart, Gertrude Lawrence, and Billie Burke in his "Reach for a Lucky instead of a Sweet" campaign. By 1928 Lucky Strike led all brands in market share.

With the onset of the Great Depression markets slumped for all brands and American Tobacco took a defensive stance as consumers bought less tobacco and rolled their own. With the passing of the economic crisis, Hill began some ad campaigns designed to demonstrate his product's quality—"Luckies Use Only the Center Leaves" and "Cream of the Crop" caught the eye of many consumers and the brand shot back into first place in market share by 1941. Hill supplemented the print advertising with radio spots, the most famous of which was his "Hit Parade" program, lasting 25 years. His radio spots also appealed to nationalistic sentiment; one spot used the expression, "Sold American!" All the while, Hill managed to spend less on advertising than his competitors.

The advertising battles continued on through the 1940s and Hill's last two advertising campaigns were his most successful. The first, appealing to patriotic fervor surrounding the U.S. en-

trance into World War II, was a 1942 campaign consisting of the slogan "Lucky Strike Has Gone to War." The slogan referred to the fact that the ink bases used for some of the colors in Lucky's package were in short supply. With the new slogan, Lucky's sales increased by 38 percent in just six weeks from the beginning of the ad campaign.

Hill's last campaign ran in newspapers and included James Chapin's painting of a tobacco farmer holding a golden leaf. The ad appeared in 50,000 newspapers between 1943 and 1946, and was accompanied by the slogan "Lucky Strike Means Fine Tobacco," with the gold color returned to the label. "George's Genie," as the farmer in the painting became known, pushed Lucky Strike to the top of the cigarette market in 1946. G. W. Hill died that same year.

International Growth

Since the link between smoking and cancer was made public in 1952, and the U.S. Surgeon General's report was released in the late 1960s, domestic consumption has declined steadily. The U.S. tobacco industry has pushed open export markets to make up for the sagging domestic consumption. But the industry in general has taken an international perspective throughout the post-World War II period. In fact, export markets were opened immediately after World War II; for example, U.S. postwar development assistance included tobacco exports to the Third World under the Food for Peace Program, also known as P.C. 480, the "Agricultural Trade Development and Food Assistance Act," which created markets in many other countries, including Thailand, the Philippines, and Taiwan. So, despite intense opposition to the cigarette, both from consumers and government, the industry has managed to keep sales afloat with its export markets.

For the industry as a whole, international expansion continues into the 1990s. According to *Multinational Monitor,* for the past decade, operating under the authority of Section 301 of the 1974 Trade Act, the U.S. Trade Representative has threatened to impose severe trade sanctions against countries which deny U.S. tobacco companies market access. In addition, the opening up of the Eastern European market is pointing toward new ventures in the infant capitalist societies.

As cigarettes continue to drop in popularity, Lucky Strike's meager market share shrinks still further. Smokers, seeing Lucky Strikes mainly as nostalgic, have either switched cigarette brands or quit smoking altogether. However, it was Lucky Strike that gave competitive momentum to the American Tobacco Company, generating huge profits that gave the company room (and the funds) necessary to move quickly into other growing markets.

Further Reading:

The American Tobacco Story, Stamford, CT: American Tobacco Company, 1964.

Cleary, David Powers, *Great American Brands,* Fairchild Publications, New York, 1981.

Tilley, Nannie M., *The R.J. Reynolds Tobacco Company,* University of North Carolina Press, Chapel Hill, 1985.

"Tobacco Buster," *Multinational Monitor,* January/February, 1992, pp. 27-30.

"Tobacco Lords," *Multinational Monitor,* January/February, 1992.

Maxwell Report (quarterly), Wheatfirst Securities, Inc., 1992 issues.

—*John A. Sarich*

M&M'S®

M&M's brand of plain chocolate candies celebrated its 50th anniversary in 1990 and is going strong as one of the nation's top-selling confections. It remains an extremely popular brand, applying its successful formula to meet consumer demands. Although marketing and product plans are closely held by M&M/Mars, the secret of the brand's popularity is a small chocolate or chocolate-coated center, covered with a crunchy, colorful candy coating, and adorned with an "m" or other design. This "formula" has been only slightly modified in recent years to alter color assortments and designs, appealing to diverse tastes and seasonal preferences. By preserving the essential qualities of M&M's candy, M&M/Mars has made an enduring and endearing symbol of America's sweet tooth.

Brand Origin and Founder

The Mars company originated in 1911 when Frank C. Mars made a variety of butter cream candy in his Tacoma, Washington home. Quality and value were the foundations of the first candy factory, which employed 125 people. In 1920 Frank Mars relocated to larger quarters in Minneapolis where the Snickers and Milky Way bars were created. The firm was originally named the Mar-O-Mar Company, but was renamed Mars Candies in 1926.

With the rapid growth of the company, larger quarters were sought and a new plant was built in 1928 in a suburb of Chicago. Sales actually quadrupled during the lean years of the Depression and new products were introduced, including Mars Almond bar, Snickers bar, and 3 Musketeers.

Frank Mars hired his son Forrest to work in the candy operation after his graduation from Yale. In the early 1930s, Frank gave Forrest some money, the foreign rights to manufacturer Milky Way, and instructed him to start his own business abroad. In 1940, Forrest returned to the United States and founded what would become M&M Candies in Newark, New Jersey. Here M&M's plain chocolate candies were introduced, followed by M&M's peanut chocolate candies in 1954. The name "M&M's" was derived from the initials of Mr. Mars and an associate at that time, Bruce Murrie.

Because of the need for a larger facility, a new plant was constructed in Hackettstown, New Jersey in 1958. Since that time, manufacturing facilities have been established across the United States and abroad. In 1964, Forrest merged his business with the Mars Company owned by his father. M&M/Mars is now headed by Forrest's children, Forrest Jr., John, and Jacqueline.

Early Marketing Strategy

According to company literature, when plain M&M's were created in 1940, they were promoted as a "neat, convenient treat that would be easy to eat in almost any climate." Many stores discontinued or reduced stock of chocolate during the summer months because it had a tendency to melt in the heat. This feature of M&M's convenience inspired the 1954 advertising slogan "the milk chocolate melts in your mouth, not in your hand."

American soldiers in World War II were able to enjoy M&M's because, when packed in the troops' provisions, the candy-coated chocolates withstood heat better than solid chocolate. At that time, M&M's were slightly larger than they are now and were packaged in small paper tubes. They also came in a violet color, which was later replaced by tan that appears in the current assortment of plain M&M's. When peanut M&M's were introduced in 1954, they came only in brown.

M&M's were advertised in the mid-1950s on television by two animated characters named Plain and Peanut, who dove into a swimming pool filled with liquid chocolate. Then the two characters took showers in a stream of colorful liquid candy, thus completing the "process" of becoming M&M candies. The Plain and Peanut characters endure today in the form of candy dispensers and a variety of other associated items, as well as in some of the company's advertising.

Product Basics

Initially, Hershey's chocolate was used for the center of the M&M's candy. As the M&M formula was improved, M&M/Mars stopped doing business with Hershey and made their own chocolate centers.

The ellipsoid chocolate centers of plain M&M's are made by machine. Seams or rough edges resulting from the mechanical process are eliminated by "tumbling" the centers in other machines. The centers of peanut and almond M&M's are formed by coating the nuts with chocolate. For peanut butter M&M's, a peanut butter center is formed and surrounded by chocolate. All the centers are then subjected to a process known as "panning." During this process, the centers are color-coated in a revolving

AT A GLANCE

M&M's brand of chocolate candies founded in 1940 in Newark, New Jersey, by Forrest E. Mars, Sr.; merged with Mars, Inc. (founded by Forrest's father, Frank C. Mars), in 1964; currently M&M/Mars national headquarters located in Hackettstown, NJ.

Performance: *Market share*—M&M Peanut Chocolate Candies ranks third with an estimated 7.3% of chocolate brand category; M&M Plain Chocolate Candies ranks fourth with an estimated 6.0% of chocolate brand category. *Sales*—$1 billion (combined estimate; top confectionery sales in manufacturer's dollars).

Major competitor: Hershey's Reese's Peanut Butter Cups; also Brach's candies.

Advertising: *Agency*—Backer Spielvogel Bates, New York, NY. *Major campaign*—"Melts in your mouth not in your hand."

Addresses: *Parent company*—M&M/Mars, High St., Hackettstown, NJ 07840; phone: (908) 852-1000. *Ultimate parent company*—Mars, Inc., 6885 Elm St., McLean, VA 22101; Phone: (703) 821-4900.

pan, while sugar and corn syrup are added. The "m" or a seasonal decoration is placed on the candy with a process similar to offset printing. The specially designed machines are calibrated so that they do not crack the thin sugar shell.

Brand's Success

M&M's come in an assortment of colors, some of which have received a lot of public attention through the years. The ratios are determined by consumer preference tests, which indicate the assortment of colors that pleases most people and creates the most attractive presentation. Plain and mint flavored M&M's contain, on average, 30 percent browns, 20 percent each of yellows and reds, and 10 percent each of oranges, greens, and tans. Peanut, peanut butter, and almond M&M's contain colors in the ratio of 20 percent each of browns, yellows, greens, oranges, and reds, with no tan colored pieces. The company notes that the ratio may vary somewhat especially in the smaller bags because the colors are combined in large quantities, and the bags are filled on high-speed packaging machines by weight, not by count.

M&M's color is important enough to the company that M&M/Mars has issued a "Colors" brochure that includes a question about the possible special qualities of green M&M's. The brochure explains that no extraordinary powers have been attributed to this color candy "either medically or scientifically."

Product Innovation and Pricing

M&M/Mars' strategy for the continued success of the line in recent years has been to introduce product extensions of the popular M&M's. These extensions include Holidays M&M's, which were first introduced for the 1985 Christmas season and are now available four times a year in festive, seasonal colors. These include a Valentine's Day blend, which is 50 percent red and 50 percent cream; an Easter blend, which is 20 percent each of pastels yellow, blue, green, pink, and purple; an Autumn blend, which is 20 percent each of brown, rust, pumpkin orange, yellow, and red; and the original Christmas blend, which is 50 percent red and 50

percent green. The brand is also available in plain, peanut, almond, and mint chocolate flavors.

Almond M&M's were first introduced in 1988, and mint followed in 1989. Both are now available for sales year-round in certain areas of the country. According to *Advertising Age*, the company introduced Peanut Butter M&M's in fall of 1990. M&M/Mars was cautious about rolling out the peanut butter variety in order to be sure that the peanut butter candies didn't merely reduce sales of chocolate and peanut M&M's.

A competitive pricing strategy also contributes to the brand's profitability. In 1992, M&M/Mars ran a promotion for several brands, including M&M's, in which consumers received a five cent refund for every single and king-size wrapper they returned. While there was no limit to the promotion, consumers had to turn in at least 20 wrappers at a time. In addition, Mars reduced the wholesale list price on larger sizes of M&M's candies in 1992 an average of 9.4 percent. According to the *Wall Street Journal*, industry analysts said the cut, which returned prices to 1987 levels, was a response to increased competition for shelf space and to the difficulties experienced by retailers in promoting the larger bags at higher prices.

Controversies

Red M&M's were discontinued from 1976 to 1987 because of public concern surrounding the red dye #2 food coloring. M&M/Mars did not use that particular dye in the production of red M&M's, but in the company's own words, it "wanted to avoid consumer confusion or misplaced concern." In 1985, however, the company introduced Holidays chocolates in red and green as Christmas approached. And due to popular demand, red M&M's chocolate candies returned to market in 1987, deriving their color from red dye #40.

The press frequently reported on the apparent promotional "mistake" made by Mars, when the company refused to permit M&M's to appear in the hit movie *ET: The ExtraTerrestrial*. Hershey gained much valuable exposure with the notable appearance of Reese's Pieces in the movie. But M&M's remained the favorite with the American public, outdistancing Reese's in growth during the period.

International Status

M&M's/Mars international strategy is to position the M&M's brand the same in all countries, like McDonald's and Coca-Cola, according to M&M's product manager at the Mars unit in Belgium. The company does not necessarily require similar positioning for other international brands. Examples cited in *Advertising Age* indicate that what is known as the Milky Way candy bar in the United States is one of Europe's best-sellers under the name Mars bar. Europe's Milky Way bar is in fact called 3 Musketeers in the United States.

M&M/Mars has been relaunching M&Ms all over Europe since 1983, replacing two local brands, Treets and Bonitos. In 1987, M&M/Mars formally introduced M&M's in the United Kingdom. The promotional campaign was the largest campaign for a confectionery product in the country, entailing TV commercials, posters, and a special M&M's road show featuring a simulated roller coaster ride. Rowntree, an English candy company, responded to the launch by increasing advertising and promotion of its Smarties, a brand of candies similar to M&Ms.

Performance, Competition, and the Future

As with other pertinent data related to its product, M&M/Mars is very guarded about market share information on M&M's brand. According to *Confectioner's* ranking of the 1991 Confectionery Elite, M&M's chocolate candies rank the highest at one billion dollars in annual sales in manufacturers' dollars. M&M's far outrank sales of other confections, with Snickers bar and Brach's candy following at $600 million and Reese's at $500 million.

Also among the Top 10 Chocolate Brands in 1991, M&M's peanut chocolate candies rank third with a 7.3 percent share of the chocolate market, and M&M's plain chocolate candies rank fourth with a 6.0 percent share of the market. In fact, M&M/Mars manufactures four of the top ten chocolate brands and occupies the number one slot with Snickers brand at 9.5 percent.

According to the *New York Times,* the candy industry is a highly concentrated, $8.7 billion business. And an industry analyst projects that the market is growing at a rate of 2.5 percent per year. Hershey and M&M/Mars have competed for the top position for decades. They remain close to even in the candy market as a whole.

There has been a trend in the candy industry toward bite-size varieties, which should benefit a brand like M&M's. Smaller portions appeal to dieters and people seeking to their limit sugar intake. In response to this trend, M&M/Mars recently introduced Milky Way miniatures. Also, candies with nuts have increased greatly in popularity because of their protein content and perceived wholesomeness. M&M/Mars has met this consumer demand by introducing almond and peanut butter M&M's.

Further Reading:

Abelson, Reed, "Uncovering Mars' Unknown Empire," *Fortune*, September 26, 1988, pp. 98-104.

A Little Illustrated Encyclopedia of M&M/Mars, M&M/Mars, Hackettstown, NJ.

Brenner, Joel Glenn, "Melts in Your Mouth, Not in Your Hand," *Washington Post,* January 7, 1991, p. 3.

Colors, M&M/Mars, Hackettstown, NJ, 1991.

"Confectionery Elite," *Confectioner,* March/April, 1992.

Fisher, Christy, "Milky Way Cuts Calories," *Advertising Age,* January 20, 1992, p. 3.

Fucini, Joseph J. and Suzy, Fucini, *Entrepreneurs: The Men and Women Behind Famous Brand Names and How They Made It,* Boston: G.K. Hall and Company, 1985.

Gaby, Robin, "M&M's Celebrate Golden Year," *News Journal,* February 23, 1990.

Hwang, Suein L., "M&M/Mars Sweetens Prices with Refund," *Wall Street Journal,* April 7, 1992, p. B1.

Kitt, Janette, "Securing a Foothold for Confectionery," *Candy Industry,* July, 1992, p. H2-H10.

McGrath, Molly Wade, *Top Sellers U.S.A.,* New York: William Morrow and Company, Inc., 1983.

Meier, Barry, "Dubious Theory: Chocolate as Cavity Fighter," *New York Times,* April 15, 1992, p. A1.

Meyers, Janet, "M&M/Mars' Strategy: Candy Line Extensions," *Advertising Age,* June 12, 1989, p. 4.

Meyers, Janet, "M&M's Go Peanut Butter," *Advertising Age,* July 23, 1990, p. 17.

Meyers, Janet, "Mars Opens Umbrella for Candy Bar Pitch," *Advertising Age,* March 26, 1990, p. 3.

Our Most Important Ingredient Is Quality, M&M/Mars, Hackettstown, NJ, 1980.

Owen, David, "Seeing Red: The Mysterious Moves of a Nationally Prominent Candy Manufacturer," *Atlantic,* October, 1988, pp. 34-37.

Pegnam, Peter, "Sticky Situation: DeConcini Warns Fake M&M Maker," *Tucson Citizen,* June 9, 1987.

Rutherford, Andrea C., "Candy Firms Roll Out 'Healthy' Sweets, but Snackers May Sour on Products," *Wall Street Journal,* August 10, 1992, p. B1.

Steinhauer, Jennifer, "America's Chocoholics: A Built-in Market for Confectioners," *New York Times,* July 14, 1991, sec. 3, p. F10.

Wentz, Laurel, "M&M's Continues Global Roll," *Advertising Age,* September 14, 1987, p. 90.

—Janet Reinhart Hall

MARLBORO®

Philip Morris Companies, Inc.'s Marlboro brand is the most widely consumed brand of cigarette in the world. Packaged in variations of the familiar crested red-and-white package, Marlboro also is the most recognized brand in the world. Originally established as a brand for women, Marlboro overcame this unsuccessful incarnation and was reintroduced primarily as a men's cigarette. Ensuing advertising developments, especially the creation of the famous "Marlboro Man" cowboy, established the brand as the choice for the free, rugged individualist, adventure-seeking, self-secure consumer.

Brand Origins

In 1924, after the long women's suffrage movement succeeded in gaining greater independence and political rights for women, the Philip Morris tobacco company introduced a brand of cigarette aimed specifically at women. The brand, called Marlboro, came in two versions featuring either a red or ivory hollow "beauty tip," that allowed women to draw from the cigarette without having their lips touch the paper. Attempting to appeal to a women's sense of vanity, Marlboro carried the tag line, "A cherry tip for your ruby lips." Marlboro was slightly longer than other cigarettes and priced as a premium brand. Despite its clever appeal, Marlboro remained unpopular, never gaining more than a quarter percent of the market.

Throughout the 1940s, doctors were featured in advertisements recommending certain cigarette brands for their supposed health-enhancing virtues. Yet, with an increase in health problems attributed to smoking, these same spokesmen actually began prescribing filtered brands—such as Benson & Hedges—which were thought to be less harmful. In the early 1950s several filtered cigarette brands entered the market, including Winston, Parliament, Kent, Viceroy, Tareyton, Parliament, and L&M. They were widely criticized because their filters softened the "bite" of the tobacco and because their English names carried an effeminate image.

Philip Morris retained researcher Elmo Roper to determine whether filtered brands stood to grow in popularity. The company suggested that Roper run market tests with the anemic Marlboro brand, realizing that its popularity could scarcely drop any lower. Roper concluded that filtered brands were destined to gain market share because of the growing awareness of smoking-related health problems. In addition, the population was growing, and more women were beginning to smoke. The filtered Marlboro brand exhibited great potential under these circumstances. In 1954 Philip Morris decided to reintroduce Marlboro as a filtered brand. The company acquired Benson & Hedges, and put its president, Joseph Cullman III, in charge of resurrecting Marlboro.

Packaging

The new Marlboro was packaged in a flip-top box whose design was licensed exclusively from the Molins Manufacturing Company in England. The red-and-white striped, crush-resistant box was very popular with test subjects. Marlboro was test mar-

keted in Dallas and Fort Worth, Texas, in May of 1954. Sales, however, were barely measurable; the brand was a flop. The product was redesigned once more. The tobacco was enriched, and the red-and-white striped package—which had given Marlboro the appearance of candy or chewing tobacco—gave way to a solid red design. The variations of the package were tested, including one without the familiar crest. Marketing analysts Cheskin & Associates determined that the crested design was preferred by 71 percent of consumers, who felt that it indicated greater quality.

Advertising

Because the initial brand introduction failed so miserably, Philip Morris fired Cecil & Presbrey, the advertising agency in charge of Marlboro, and transferred the account to Leo Burnett & Company. Burnett's first task was to give the brand broader appeal and break its reputation as a feminine brand. To position Marlboro as a he-man's cigarette that women also liked, Burnett looked for masculine symbols to match with the brand. Testing ads in November of 1954 (again in Dallas and Fort Worth), Burnett featured sailors, aviators, hunters, and cowboys. Eventually, the cowboy emerged as the most popular Marlboro symbol in Texas—as might be expected—as well as in New York and 25 other markets. Under the slogan "flavor, filter, fliptop box," Marlboro became the fourth most popular filter cigarette in the United States in less than a year. Sales rose from $18 million in 1954 to more than $5 billion in 1955. The cowboy, known as the "Marlboro Man," was further modified in 1955 when Leo Burnett added a macho anchor tattoo to the cowboy's arm. While reinforcing the masculinity of the product, the tattoo suggested that discerning men of the world chose Marlboro.

Marlboro was cleverly marketed. In 1956, at a time when the game was growing in popularity, Marlboro became the first major brand of any product to sponsor professional football. As other brands sponsored radio and television shows, Marlboro sponsored a college newspaper column by humorist Max Schulman. A new strategy became necessary when, in 1958, *Reader's Digest* featured a story on the effects of nicotine, declaring that only Kent's "micronite" filter was effective. Growth in sales of the Marlboro brand fell flat for two years. Burnett attempted to jump start sales with an ad featuring the lusty sexpot of the day, Julie London, singing, "Where there's a man, there's a Marlboro." People quickly forgot the health claims, and began to regard smoking as daring and exciting. As might be expected, all brands experienced a boost from this sexual representation of smoking. Marlboro stood as the third most popular brand in the United States, and by the 1970s had jumped to the number-one spot.

Brand Development

In 1962 Leo Burnett & Company purchased the publication rights to the Elmer Bernstein score, *The Magnificent Seven*. The theme was played over television and radio ads for Marlboro, featuring the now familiar Marlboro Man. Through incessant repetition, the "Marlboro Country" campaign established the

AT A GLANCE

Marlboro brand of cigarettes introduced in 1924 by Philip Morris Companies, Inc.

Performance: *Market share*—26 percent (top share) of cigarette category. *Sales*—$9.0 billion.

Major competitor: RJR Nabisco Inc.'s Camel and Winston.

Advertising: *Agency*—Leo Burnett & Company, Chicago, IL. *Major campaign*—The Marlboro Man/Marlboro Country.

Addresses: *Parent company*—Philip Morris Companies, Inc., 120 Park Avenue,New York, NY 10017; phone: (212) 878-2165.

theme so thoroughly with the brand that, even 20 years after it ceased, people still identify the theme with Marlboro. Television advertising, which by the 1960s had become the most powerful advertising medium, was used to feature the Marlboro Man and his companion horse in artful panoramas of cattle-driving country. As the music played, the Marlboro Man was seen looking out over the land, or relaxing around a campfire, like a scene from the immensely popular show *Gunsmoke* (some people actually confused the two and their themes). Imagery now was more important than mere words in advertising. In fact, the Marlboro Man never uttered a word.

Despite the Surgeon General's declaration that smoking was detrimental to the health, Marlboro continued to grow in popularity. Sales grew by ten percent annually, well into the 1970s. In 1971, cigarette advertising was banned from broadcast media. The imagery of the Marlboro Man, however, was so firmly established that it translated easily to billboard and print advertising. In fact, other advertisers were precluded from using cowboys because they were so closely associated with the Marlboro Man. In addition, opportunities to promote cigarettes continued to diminish. Beginning with the broadcast advertising bans, cigarette ads were no longer welcome on many billboards or in certain magazines, nor were the brands welcome as sponsors of many sporting events. As these avenues to public attention continued to dwindle, well-established brand identities such as Marlboro grow in value.

International Growth

Through aggressive advertising to maintain sales growth, Marlboro became the most recognized American brand in the world. According to a *Business Week* article, in 1993 Marlboro had a 25 percent market share in Argentina and the European Community and boasts a 30 percent share in Mexico. Even among nations with strong anti-American sentiment, Marlboro became extremely popular. This is, perhaps, because the Marlboro Man was regarded as an individual, and not necessarily the agent of American policy. In other countries, the appeal was fairly obvious. The Marlboro Man represented freedom and self determination, and all other things American. Among those unable to gain American citizenship, Marlboro represented a taste of the American lifestyle.

While continuing to downplay the detrimental health effects of smoking, tobacco companies generally are faced with a saturated domestic market in which cigarette consumption is falling. In order to continue growth, companies such as Philip Morris have engaged in ambitious efforts to develop foreign demand, hoping to tap such potentially lucrative markets as Europe, Asia and South America. The companies have met opposition from two fronts. Health authorities in these markets, as well as in the United States, decry the companies' efforts to "export death" in the name of corporate profit. Additionally, foreign imports of popular American brands such as Marlboro threaten to weaken these countries' balance of trade with the United States, and damage their domestic tobacco industries.

Performance Appraisal

When Marlboro was reintroduced in 1954, Philip Morris was the smallest of America's six leading tobacco companies. Because of Marlboro, it now is the largest. Marlboro capitalized on the popularity of filtered cigarettes and, in the process, caused "straight" brands such as Camel and Lucky Strike to offer filtered variations, merely to stay in the game. Cigarette consumption began to fall in the 1980s, by as much as two percent annually, but Marlboro continued to rack up annual growth of three percent or more. Faced with saturated markets, Philip Morris began brand "extension," marketing variations of the original product. In 1958 the company introduced a soft-pack version of the product. A menthol variation was added in 1966, a 100-millimeter brand in 1967, and Marlboro Lights in 1972. A 25-count package was introduced in 1985, and in 1992, a medium strength variety joined the line.

With restricted opportunities for advertising, Marlboro has had the luxury of relying on brand recognition for sales. In a 1987 *Forbes* article, a writer noted, "The brand does not try to compete on price, and the tobacco in it, though high quality, is no more expensive than its competitors." Yet, during the early 1990s, the introduction of cheaper, generic brands of cigarettes—even by the brand's parent company—has threatened the dominance of Marlboro. According to a *Business Week* article, in April of 1993, Philip Morris announced "that it would slash prices on its premium brand and boost promotion spending—forfeiting as much as $2 billion in profits." In 1993 Philip Morris launched the "Marlboro Adventure Team" campaign. Based on the amount of Marlboro cigarettes purchased, customers could send for outdoor gear with the Marlboro logo and be entered in drawings for adventure trips sponsored by the company.

The American cigarette market is populated with more than 175 brands and their variations. Marlboro, however, dominates the market with a 26 percent share of sales, and demand in foreign countries for highly visible American products is high. Marlboro's growth in these markets, while dependent on trade restrictions, is virtually assured.

Further Reading:

Carey, John, and Mark Landler, "Even Philip Morris Feels the Pull of Gravity," *Business Week,* February 15, 1993, pp. 60-62.

Gershman, Michael, *Getting it Right the Second Time,* Reading: Addison Wesley, 1990, p. 3.

Gershman, Michael, "Here's One Tough Cowboy," *Forbes,* February 9, 1987, p. 108.

"Gridlock on Tobacco Road," *Business Week,* April 26, 1993.

Hoover's Handbook, New York: Philip Morris Companies, 1991.

"A New Trail Boss for Marlboro," *Business Week,* May 3, 1993.

"Secondhand Smoke at RJR Nabisco," *Business Week,* May 3, 1993.

—John Simley

358

MAXWELL HOUSE®

Maxwell House coffee is produced by General Foods USA, an operating arm of one of the largest food manufacturers in the world, Kraft General Foods Inc. Despite intense competition in the coffee industry (coffee is the most heavily marketed beverage in grocery stores) and declining consumption of coffee over the years, Maxwell House is the second best-selling coffee with a 16.5 percent share of the market. The story of its success has been a combination of entrepreneurship, sheer luck, and creative marketing techniques that began with its turn of the century slogan, "Good to the last drop!"

Brand Origins

Coffee lovers can be grateful for the tenacity and entrepreneurial spirit of Joel O. Cheek, who developed a brand of coffee far superior to any other available at the time in the late nineteenth century, forcing competitors to improve the quality of their coffee. In a day and age when there were few beverage alternatives, coffee was a beloved drink; except for the aroma, it would scarcely be recognized by today's consumer. Absent from groceries were instant coffee, gourmet, and decaffeinated varieties. Coffee beans were scooped out of a barrel, ground at home (the right blending of coffee beans is an art at which few excelled), and simply boiled in a pot on a stove.

The inconvenience of this method was brought home during the Civil War. Both Union and Confederate troops realized that coffee was a necessity, but transporting beans and coffee grinders was out of the question. Hence, coffee was ground into a pulp that hardened and could be sliced into bricks, which were distributed to each soldier, who broke off what he needed and placed it in boiling water. The state of coffee by the time Joel Cheek began selling it wholesale from burlap bags in the 1870s had not improved.

In 1873 the founder of the famous Maxwell House brand was a poor, but ambitious, traveling salesman for a wholesale grocery firm in Kentucky. Riding on horseback from grocer to grocer throughout the Cumberland River valley, the 21-year-old Cheek sold a variety of food products, but none interested him more than coffee. With the instinct of a true coffee lover, he realized that the person who could improve the taste of coffee by coming up with just the right blend would have a huge and unchallenged market, since Americans consumed more coffee than any nation on earth. Constant travel, however, kept him from experimenting with cof-

fee beans, until his firm promoted him to a full partner, which meant settling permanently in the bustling city of Nashville. Cheek spent all of his free time coming up with the perfect blend, a task that took him nearly twenty years.

Early Marketing Strategy

Less ambitious men would have given up, but Cheek had the dogged persistence of a true entrepreneur. The year was 1892, and Cheek, using his persuasive powers, convinced the manager of Nashville's most renowned hotel, the Maxwell House, to serve his blend of coffee on a trial basis. Not surprisingly, the coffee created a sensation, and the hotel manager was quick to see the potential of Cheek's coffee for his restaurant. From then on, no other coffee was served in its distinguished dining room.

It was then that Cheek decided to call his nameless blend "Maxwell House," not only out of gratitude for the opportunity he received, but also because of his business savvy—the Maxwell House hotel was synonymous with high quality and famous throughout the south. To capitalize on his new brand's success, Cheek went into business with John W. Neal, and established a coffee plant in Nashville that was soon producing the most popular brand of coffee in the southern states.

First Commercial Success

At the turn of the century Maxwell House coffee, manufactured in Nashville and in a new coffee plant in Houston, was still only regionally known. The potential for national recognition was there, but the right marketing strategy had not yet been determined. Joel Cheek, however, had an accidental bit of good luck. The extremely popular Teddy Roosevelt, the youngest president in U.S. history, paid homage to the late President Andrew Jackson with a visit to the Jackson mansion, the Hermitage, outside of Nashville. Because of the Maxwell House hotel's renown as a stopping place for hungry dignitaries, it was natural that Roosevelt would dine there. Cheek, by then one of the city's first citizens, happened to be present when he overheard the President exclaim over his delicious cup of coffee, "It's good to the last drop!"

While less clever men might have been merely pleased by the compliment, to Cheek the statement was the inspiration he needed to transform his coffee into a nationally known brand, with the

AT A GLANCE

Maxwell House brand of coffee founded in 1892 in Nashville, TN, by Joel O. Cheek, a partner in the Cheek, Norton & Neal grocery firm formed with partners John J. Norton and John W. Neal; 1901, Cheek and Neal form the Nashville Coffee and Manufacturing Company; 1903, name is changed to the Cheek & Neal Coffee Company and incorporated in 1905 as the Cheek-Neal Coffee Company; Cheek-Neal Coffee Company bought out by Postum Cereal Company, becoming the Maxwell House Products Company in 1928; the following year Postum Cereal Company changed its name to the General Foods Corporation; 1985, General Foods Corporation bought by Philip Morris, Inc., and later merged with Kraft Inc. to form Kraft General Foods Inc.

Performance: *Market share*—16.5% of coffee category (*Advertising Age*, May 4, 1992, p. 46). *Sales*—$1.0 billion (*Superbrands 1991* [supplement to *Adweek's Marketing Week*], 1991, p. 64).

Major competitor: Procter & Gamble Company's Folger's.

Advertising: *Agency*—D'Arcy Masius Benton & Bowles (some sources say Ogilvy & Mather), New York, NY, 1989—. *Major campaign*—"Good to the Last Drop"; (for Cappio) "The thrill is the chill."

Addresses: *Parent company*—General Foods USA, 250 North St., White Plains, NY, 10625; phone: (914) 335-2500. *Ultimate parent company*—Kraft General Foods Inc., 3 Lakes Dr., Northfield, IL 60093; phone: (708) 998-2000. *Ultimate ultimate parent company*—Philip Morris Companies, Inc.

help of a few words from a famous and well-liked personage. It did not take long for the slogan—and the brand—to become well known throughout the country. This occasioned a heated debate in academic circles as to the grammar of "*to* the last drop." Finally, a Columbia University English professor pronounced the phrase correct, ending the controversy. Arcane and uninteresting to the public as the debate may have been, it focused even more of the nation's attention on the increasingly popular Maxwell House. After a Maxwell House coffee plant opened its doors in Brooklyn in 1921, the brand quickly superseded all other coffee brands in the New York metropolitan area.

Advertising Strategy

Less than a dozen years after Teddy Roosevelt uttered his famous words, Maxwell House coffee became the most popular brand in the country. However, the advertising slogan and logo—an inverted cup with the last drops of coffee dripping out—which have remained unchanged since their use began, would not be enough for Maxwell House to maintain its leadership position. In the face of increasing competition and the volatility of the market—the U.S. coffee industry is entirely dependent on foreign coffee beans—Maxwell House needed to rethink its advertising.

Fortunately for Cheek, his growing coffee business coincided with the rapid advances in communications. Just as he had pioneered the production of fine blended coffee, so too did his company achieve other firsts. Maxwell House was the first in the 1920s to advertise aggressively and imaginatively on the radio, then later in that decade, "coffee concert programs" were offered on several radio stations. In 1932 the company began sponsoring its own show, the "Maxwell House Showboat" radio program.

Maxwell House was also the first coffee in the 1950s to advertise on TV and later, on color television. TV advertising has won Maxwell House several plaudits, including the coveted Effie Award for best commercial advertising in 1983. The "Good to the Last Drop" slogan was featured prominently in TV commercials in the mid-1980s, interwoven with a particular emotional situation. Using computer technology to conduct market research into the most effective advertising themes led Maxwell House to a successful ad campaign for the 1990s. The spots reflected the back-to-basics attitude of the nation with ads that were full of nostalgia for the "good old days" and featured commemorative Maxwell House cans with the original, turn-of-the-century design.

Product Innovations

Maxwell House's popularity was based on its unique blend of coffee, which was specially roasted, blended, and ground at the plant before it ended up packaged and ready for the market. Ground coffee, even when carefully packed, quickly grows stale, hence packaging was all important. Maxwell House beat out its competitors by being the first to develop packaging that would ensure a long shelf life. In the late 1920s Maxwell House developed and patented the revolutionary process of vacuum packing, an innovation the company was quick to advertise. This was followed in 1931 by the invention of very high vacuum packaging that Maxwell House called Vita Fresh.

In the years after World War II, the packaging of Maxwell House changed often. From cans to special commemorative canisters, to carafes, to "cans of coffee in a percolator," as described in one company publication, Maxwell House strove to make the containers interesting and appealing, especially when advertised on color TV. The year 1963 saw the introduction of an important innovation—the "keyless can" that could be resealed after opening with a plastic lid that came with the can. More recently, in 1983, the company developed the "Vac Bag," yet another means to preserve freshness with, in this case, a four ply sealed vacuum bag.

That same year Maxwell House became the first brand of coffee in the United States to switch from soldered to welded seals on all of its coffee cans. Two years later, the company began using Fresh Lock in each can and bag of regular Maxwell House, Maxwell House Master Blend, and Maxwell House decaffeinated coffees. A small packet containing freshness preserving minerals, Fresh Lock removed what air and moisture still remained, even in a high vacuum packed can. In 1987 Fresh Lock won *Packaging* magazine's annual competition for what the publication deemed "the most innovative retail packaging development."

Brand Development

With competition for his coffee becoming increasingly intense, Cheek set about developing new products. Realizing that there were almost as many people who drank tea as coffee in this country, the company started the Maxwell House Tea operation in 1917. The tea's popularity could never compare with that of the coffee, and the last Maxwell House Tea was produced in 1953. By then Maxwell House was involved in marketing its "soluble" or instant coffee.

Cheek sold his thriving business in 1928 for $40 million to the food producer, the Postum Company. The previous year Postum—which became General Foods Corporation in 1929 in order to reflect the company's variety of products—had bought the rights to manufacture Sanka, the decaffeinated coffee first produced in 1907 by the German chemist, Dr. Roselius. At that point research efforts were bent on not only improving Maxwell House's packaging, but developing an instant coffee as well. Maxwell House turned out to be the first brand to produce a soluble coffee—at first only an odorless powder—just in time for it to be "taste tested" by the troops in World War II. After the war Maxwell House began national distribution of its instant coffee, which was later improved upon with the addition of a coffee aroma and "flavor buds" to enhance the taste.

The 1950s were boom years for the coffee industry—at no time in American history had coffee consumption reached such a peak. To satisfy the insatiable demand and more sophisticated coffee palates, new products were developed. Besides improvements in the taste and smell of instant coffee, the first "freeze dried" coffee, Maxim, was introduced to test markets in 1964. Two years later Maxwell House introduced a coffee specifically for use in the popular electric percolator. In 1976 Maxwell House became the first brand to offer a coffee especially suited for the increasingly popular drip method of brewing.

The 1970s proved to be a difficult period for the coffee industry, due not only to a deadly frost that decimated over half of Brazil's coffee crop in 1975—forcing Maxwell House to raise its coffee prices 500 percent—but also to a gradual decline in coffee consumption. In response to such factors, coffee producers began taking advantage of advanced technology and became more creative with their brands' offerings. Brim decaffeinated, both ground and freeze dried, came out in that decade, as did General Foods International Coffees, and Mellow Roast coffee. Maxwell House Master Blend, the first increased-yield coffee, was introduced in 1981.

Philip Morris, Inc. acquired General Foods Corporation in 1985. Thereafter, new products appeared in rapid succession. To reduce the time it took to prepare the morning coffee, Maxwell House came out in 1989 with Maxwell House Filter Packs, in which the ground coffee came premeasured in filters. In response to the growing national fondness for gourmet coffee, Maxwell House Private Collection of Fine Coffees and Maxwell House Rich French Roast ground coffee came on the market. Other gourmet products joined the Maxwell House brand, including "easy to make" Maxwell House Cappuccino, as well as Maxwell House Cappio, or iced cappuccino. When Maxwell House researchers discovered that many coffee consumers were already mixing decaffeinated and regular at home, Maxwell House Lite, a blend of both regular and decaffeinated, was introduced.

Future Growth

The coffee market depends heavily on the often unpredictable supply of coffee beans which is, in turn, dictated by weather conditions. Precisely for this reason, Maxwell House has had to be adaptable, and adaptability is the key to success in the coffee industry. As a result, when the industry suffered during the Great Depression, Maxwell House did very well, going on to weather the difficulties of the 1970s. Heavy investment in marketing and new product lines paid off. The key to Maxwell House's future growth will depend increasingly on international markets, many of which, including southeast Asia and China, are still largely untapped and extremely lucrative.

A large part of Maxwell House's success has derived from its strong international standing—overseas sales of the brand have risen continuously over the years. Maxwell House is the number one selling brand of coffee in Canada, while Kraft General Foods International is the clear leader in the heavily competitive coffee market in Europe—where coffee products have been changing to reflect popular tastes—generating a 1991 profit of $16 billion. A case in point, Germany's largest selling brand is Jacobs Kroenung, a Maxwell House product that also offers a "lite" version. With the fall of communism in Eastern Europe, American products have become enormously popular. Taking advantage of this sentiment, Maxwell House has begun to make new and profitable inroads into Poland, Czechoslovakia, and Hungary.

Maxwell House coffee is also Kraft General Foods International's fastest growing product in Asia and the Pacific Rim. The number one selling coffee in Japan is Maxwell House's freeze dried, microwaveable Maxim. South Korea, where Maxim is also among the most popular brands, is becoming an increasingly lucrative market. China continues to be a growing coffee market and the sale of Maxwell House coffees is constantly on the rise. The Australian market for Maxwell House is strong, while Indonesia and Thailand are growing markets where Maxwell House is also making profitable headway.

Imaginative marketing and product diversity are traditional Maxwell House strengths, now paying off in Europe and Asia. With new product lines constantly being tested and marketed, Maxwell House has been able to maintain its leading edge in the fiercely competitive coffee industry, and offer the public an attractive and interesting array of delicious coffees.

Further Reading:

Advertising Age, May 4, 1992, p. 46.

Agnew, Joe, "Regular Coffee Grinding Down as Gourmet Brands Percolate," *Marketing News,* Oct. 23, 1987, p. 6.

Arnold, Oren, *What's in a Name? Famous Brand Names,* New York: Messner, 1979.

Bird, Laura, "Thirst's Many Flavors," *Superbrands* (supplement to *Adweek's Marketing Week*), September 1991, p. 64.

Campbell, Hannah, *Why Did They Name It . . . ?* New York: Fleet Publications Corp., 1964.

Cleary, David Powers, *Great American Brands,* New York: Fairchild, 1981.

Dagnoli, Judann, "G.F. Brings Back Slow Roast Coffee," *Advertising Age,* June 18, 1990, p. 20.

Dunkin, Amy, "Maxwell House Serves Up a Yuppie Brew," *Business Week,* March 2, 1987, p. 62.

Fucini, J. J. and S. F., *Entrepreneurs: The Men and Women Behind Famous Brand Names and How They Made It,* Boston: Holt & Co., 1985.

Hambleton, Ronald, *The Branding of America,* Dublin, NY: Yankee Books, 1987.

Hoggan, Karen, "Going for the Grind," *Marketing Date,* August 29, 1991, pp. 12-13.

Horak, Kathy, "Manager Brews Growth Strategy for Coffee," *Business Journal-Jacksonville,* February 7, 1992, p. 8, Sec. 1.

Jacob, Heinrich Eduard, *Coffee: the Epic of a Commodity,* New York: Viking Press, 1935.

Maxwell House Coffee: A Chronological History, Northfield, IL: Kraft General Foods Archives Dept., 1992.

Maxwell House Messenger, Northfield, IL: Kraft General Foods, Summer 1980.

Miller, Cyndee, "Nostalgia Makes Boomers Buy," *Marketing News,* November 26, 1990, pp. 1-2.

Philip Morris Companies, Inc. Annual Report, New York: Philip Morris Companies, Inc., 1991.

Sapporito, Bill, ''Can Anyone Win the Coffee War?'' *Fortune,* May 21, 1990, pp. 97, 100.

Sivetz, Michael, *Coffee Technology,* Westport, CT: AVI Publishing Co., 1979.

Stiling, Marjorie, *Famous Brand Names, Emblems, Trademarks,* Newton Abbot, VT: David & Charles, 1980.

—Sina Dubovoj

MAZOLA®

Mazola®

Mazola 100 percent corn oil is the leading corn oil in the United States and Germany, and the number two product in the United Kingdom. The product is manufactured and sold in a number of Latin American countries as well, successfully introduced through its parent, CPC International Inc., a dominant food company noted not for being the largest in the industry, but among the most tightly run.

Mazola corn oil dates back to 1911, when it was produced as a sideline product of the Corn Products Refining Company based in Argo, Illinois, with corporate offices in New York City. Mazola was first packaged in a can, with a drawing of a corn cob forming the body of an Indian maiden, presumably the original harvester of the plant.

Parent Company Origins

The Corn Products Company was formed in 1906 by E. T. Bedford, a director of Standard Oil; the company was responsible for 90 percent of corn refining in the United States, making it an effective monopoly. Following a 1916 antitrust judgment the company remained, as reported in the March 1962 *Fortune,* in corn refining—"transforming the kernel into various products with a strong emphasis on sales to industry." Some of those products were corn oil, corn syrup, and corn starch.

Bedford extended the company overseas beginning in 1919, expanding into manufacturing plants and investments. Through the 1920s and 1930s Corn Products set up large facilities in Argentina, Brazil, and Mexico. Affiliates were carefully established in Czechoslovakia, England, France, Germany, Holland, Italy, Switzerland, and Yugoslavia. All of the former were either 100 percent or majority owned by Corn Products, though the company preferred its subsidiaries be staffed and operated by local persons. Such an attitude gave Corn Products a universally strong position in its various foreign locations, paving the way for smooth introduction of products to those markets.

After the Second World War, Corn Products found its reliance on a single commodity made it extremely sensitive to the ups and downs of both the commodity market and the business cycle. Following the war, profits fell in four out of ten years. As reported in the March 1962 *Fortune,* "total Corn Products sales in 1953 were slightly below sales in 1947 and showed relatively little expansion in the decade."

It was clear that the company had to widen its vision. William Brady, who joined Corn Products in 1919, the year founder E. T. Bedford began the company's European expansion, was named chief executive in 1956. It was fitting that Brady initiated an expansion effort which catapulted the company into the league of American food company giants.

Mazola, a Core Product

Mazola corn oil, tied directly to the company's core business, sold steadily through the 1930s and 1940s. Since consumer products were just a sideline of the Corn Products Company during these years, the brand was not forcefully marketed until the late 1950s, when Brady changed his company's emphasis. When Corn Products acquired Best Foods in 1958, a true marriage was formed, for Best Foods had a line of already well-known brand names such as Hellmann's mayonnaise, Skippy peanut butter, and Rit dyes. Best Foods brought its skills in grocery marketing to Corn Products, giving Mazola corn oil the expertise it needed to become an internationally recognized brand.

Under Best Foods' guidance, Mazola was quickly redesigned. As described in *Business Week*'s July 5, 1958, issue, the corn oil was packaged "in a bottle with an eye-catching label, instead of the old, dowdy can." Though Mazola still lagged behind Wesson oil, the redesign combined with renewed marketing energy increased sales by 50 percent over the previous two-year period.

Best Foods combined its experience producing Nucoa margarine with Corn Products' Mazola corn oil to manufacture a new product, Mazola margarine. At this time Best Foods pointed out the health benefits of Mazola corn oil and its derivatives in a high-profile advertising campaign. Corn oil's naturally high ratio of polyunsaturated fats to hardened fats could sometimes result in a reduction of cholesterol in the bloodstream. This fact was emphasized in a new format, continuing a theme Corn Products had formerly used with the slogan, "Listen to your heart." The health claims stemmed from research uncovered in the late 1950s. Mazola was the first to use such information in advertisements.

By 1962 the publicity surrounding Mazola margarine's debut increased recognition of the benefits of corn oil in general. Mazola corn oil sales increased by 45 percent over 1958 figures. By 1967 CPC considered the nutrition-based advertising for Mazola so

AT A GLANCE

Mazola brand of corn oil founded in 1911 by Corn Products Refining Company, which was formed in 1906 by E. T. Bedford; Corn Products merged with Best Foods Company in an exchange of stock, 1958; changed name to CPC International, mid 1960s; original Mazola product symbol was corn-bodied Indian maiden; figure evolved to use of Native American woman as commercial spokesperson promoting the goodness of maize.

Major competitor: Hunt-Wesson/ConAgra's Wesson oil; also Proctor & Gamble's Crisco oil.

Advertising: *Agency*—BSB, New York, NY. *Major campaign*—Stressing health benefits of corn oil, which is low in saturated fat.

Addresses: *Parent company*—CPC International Inc., P.O. Box 8000, International Plaza, Englewood Cliffs, NJ 07632; phone: (201)894-4000.

effective it used the approach to promote a number of Best Foods' brands.

New Advertising Tactics

Best Foods was working with a number of advertising agencies by the mid-1960s, on a commission system. This allowed the various advertisers to choose whichever team they deemed best to work on a product. The four agencies Best was using were Dancer-Fitzgerald-Sample; Foote, Cone & Belding; Lennen & Newell; and Sullivan, Stauffer, Colwell & Bayles.

Copy for Mazola continued the theme that corn oil was a healthful product. John M. Volkhardt, vice president and national marketing director for Best Foods, summed up the new ads in the May 16, 1966, *Advertising Age* by stating that Mazola corn oil was healthful "no matter what your age." Print ads showed a Mazola bottle with a straw in it and another Mazola bottle with a baby-bottle nipple on the top. The ad went on to say that new babies don't need Mazola 100 percent corn oil, because they are born with a proper balance of polyunsaturated and saturated fats. But the balance changes, the ad pointed out, as the child grows. The Mazola ads sought to persuade mothers to get a jump on the natural declining balance by giving their babies polyunsaturated corn oil early on. The copy stated, "This is why a number of pediatricians are insisting that highly polyunsaturated oils, such as Mazola, be included in infant diets."

Advertisements aimed for the newly-married woman as well, in contrast to the married mother targeted in the previous ad. In June issues of *Life* and *Look*, a bottle of Mazola corn oil was pictured next to a bridal flower bouquet with the caption: "What every bride should know about new Mazola 100% corn oil." Copy stated that Mazola corn oil "will help balance the kind of fats your lord-and-master eats." The ad appealed to the romance—and humor—of the newlywed.

Best Foods budgeted a total of $30 million to advertise its products in 1966. Introductions included Diet Mazola margarine, which was test-marketed in Jacksonville, Florida. Of 21 products introduced, only four had new brand names. Mazola was more than 50 years old by 1966, but the brand still had plenty of

leveraging power. According to Best Foods' philosophy: "People get old, not products."

A Change in Emphasis

The ultimate owner of the Mazola brand, the Corn Products Company, changed its name to CPC International Inc. in the mid-1960s. After one brief return to the old name (initiated in 1975), the company remained CPC International Inc. During the 1970s, a slight shift was made in the marketing of Mazola corn oil. CPC went directly at its competition, Wesson and Crisco oils. Many who used salad oils considered corn oil beneficial, according to senior product manager John Link; yet those consumers didn't know that of the three leading sellers, Mazola was the only national brand containing pure corn oil. This was the new emphasis, distinguishing Mazola from the others. The ads continued to maintain that Mazola was higher in polyunsaturated fats than its competitors, and added that foods fried in Mazola corn oil came out lighter and easier to digest.

Best Foods budgeted $5 million to advertise Mazola in 1974; the account was handled by De Garmo Inc. Run in selected markets early in the year, then expanded to most markets in the United States, advertisements were placed both on television and in a variety of magazines, such as *Family Health, Good Housekeeping, National Geographic,* and *Reader's Digest.* A follow-up campaign further reinforced the health benefits of Mazola oil. A spokesman pointed out that a dietary program to reduce serum cholesterol included skim milk, lean meat, fewer eggs, and Mazola corn oil. The source of the diet was an article Best Foods discovered in a medical journal. The company was not allowed to name the university or the doctors who conducted the study. Interestingly, a competitor of Mazola margarine used the same study in its ads. Fleischmann's margarine cited a clinical study which included its margarine—along with skim milk, fewer eggs, and other reduced fats—which comprised a healthy diet and lowered serum cholesterol levels an average of 17 percent.

Competing Health Claims

By 1976 Mazola was no longer the only vegetable oil making health claims in its commercial advertising. In December Best Foods charged that Proctor & Gamble's ads for Puritan oil did not comply with the National Association of Broadcasters' code authority guidelines. The category of margarines, oils, and related products was one of only four segments requiring pre-screening and code board clearance. P&G's ads stated that sunflower-based oil could lower cholesterol and contained more polyunsaturated oil. "It even looks lighter," the copy read, according to the December 31, 1976, *Advertising Age.*

Best Foods' complaint—backed up by other margarine and vegetable oil marketers—was that the Puritan ads were not specific about which cholesterol the product ostensibly lowered: serum cholesterol made by the body, or dietary cholesterol introduced into the body through foods. Another important element of the dispute was the status of self-regulatory guidelines in the advertising and broadcasting industry. Peers worried that if P&G did disregard regulations, it was "leaving the door open for more government interventions," as reported in *Advertising Age.* Procter & Gamble countered that the issue was not significant, and that it had submitted its commercials to the code authority for review. The commercials continued to air as the discussion continued.

Not only was Mazola hit by Procter & Gamble's low-cholesterol product, Puritan oil; Wesson came out with its own healthier version of oil called Sunlite. Best Foods managed to maintain its 16 percent share of the vegetable oil market with Mazola. In addition to its straight-ahead advertising, Best Foods focused on other, more entertaining promotions. The company had been sponsoring television celebrity concerts in 25 markets. Ten of these "concert specials" by Rhodes Productions were bought for 1977 syndication to promote Mazola corn oil, among a number of company products.

In mid-1977 the ad agency Dancer-Fitzgerald-Sample created a memorable commercial using an Apache woman as spokesperson for Mazola margarine. The effort was to find a new means of differentiating Mazola from its competition. Once again, the distinguishing characteristic of Mazola—whether the subject was margarine or oil—was that it was made from pure corn oil. As expressed by agency management supervisor George Dean in the April 16, 1979, *Advertising Age,* "We looked for a vehicle which would not simply generate brand awareness, it had to be relevant to the subject, corn, to do the job we wanted to do." Since the native Americans introduced the first settlers to the goodness of corn, the agency decided an American Indian spokesperson could best represent the product and distinguish Mazola from its competitors. The commercial inspired a significant amount of positive reactions from consumers and native Americans alike, generating just the kind of response and recognition Best Foods hoped for.

International Developments

The challenge with respect to Mazola was twofold at this time. Best Foods was continuously demonstrating to Americans that corn oil was good and good for them; in addition, the grocery marketer had to find ways to use its parent company's international presence to sell Mazola in more foreign locations. During the 1960s, the presence of CPC's international office in Zurich was a definite plus for Mazola sales. The office supplied technical and marketing services on an as-needed basis in the company's various foreign markets, paving the way for product introductions.

Mazola oil was introduced in Germany and Latin America under William Brady's tenure at the old Corn Products Company. CPC reached 18 foreign countries in 1958; just over twenty years later the company operated in 45 countries all over the globe. As reported in the March 3, 1980, *Forbes,* "By the 1970s CPC's international operations had come to dominate the company, providing 63% of [1979] sales, vs. 50% in 1970, and 36% in 1960." By 1980 Mazola was one of CPC's leading international food brands in Europe. The company was producing the brand in Uruguay by 1985. Mazola was the number one corn oil brand in Germany in 1991, and number two in the United Kingdom. Mazola was sold, as well, in Italy and in seven Latin American countries.

Contemporary Brand Development

According to CPC International's 1980 annual report, "In North America television is the most widely used advertising medium." In May 1983 a new product manager for Mazola created a commercial so controversial that the networks could not accept it. The new campaign was based on recent research which the product manager used to claim that Mazola could help lower blood pressure. The networks' criticism was that the evidence was

too recent; they preferred at least ten years of research substantiation.

While those facts were sorted out, one outstanding commercial showed a father advising his son to eat right in order to stay young at heart. The ad tied in with themes used for Mazola in the past, that healthy eating should start early in life. The company "put all our weight behind that one commercial," the product manager stated in the May 1983 *Marketing & Media Decisions.* "We find that male presenters work well against women." Since the target market for Mazola oil was women 25 and older, the strategy made sense.

Also at this time, advertising for Mazola was placed in more selective areas—television spots were concentrated in large urban areas, print ads were clustered in magazines with the highest circulations, and greater newspaper exposure was planned for a successful, lengthy, educational print ad created by a former marketing director. Continuing some Mazola advertising traditions, the brand was advertised in eight medical publications and at sports medicine conventions. The company also participated in a number of health and fitness-related promotions, sponsoring cholesterol-testing centers, a YMCA race in New York City, and the U.S. Olympic teams. Mazola was also one of the products involved in sponsoring Best Foods' "Brands Across America" campaign, in conjunction with Hands Across America, a nonprofit organization dedicated to help the homeless and hungry.

Projections

By 1985, of the $190 million CPC International Inc. devoted to advertising worldwide, only $6.4 million was designated for Mazola corn oil, a drop of 31 percent from 1984. As reported in the April 15, 1985, *Advertising Age,* CPC was "considered by retailers to be giving Mazola lukewarm support." In the same article a brand manager responded, "We feel we do provide Mazola corn oil with enough ad support for long-term growth."

Most important was Best Foods' reaction to the number of competing "healthy" types of vegetable oils, such as olive, canola, sunflower, and safflower. The April 20, 1992, *Wall Street Journal* reported that "sales of Mazola—have nose-dived, as consumers defect to cheaper and self-proclaimed 'healthier' alternatives." In response, CPC introduced Mazola RightBlend, with 51 percent corn and 49 percent canola oil, which had only one gram of saturated fat per tablespoon, compared to two grams in the original Mazola corn oil.

An industry shake-up was predicted by some analysts in May 1993, when all food producers were required to comply with the Food and Drug Administration's 1990 Nutrition Labeling and Education Act. The FDA challenged CPC and its competitors to substantiate their pure vegetable oil and no cholesterol claims, or to change their product labels. If history is a test, Mazola corn oil—with more than eighty years' experience in the market—stands to hold its position as a popular and trusted consumer brand.

Further Reading:

Bird, Laura, "Washington Cracks Another Whip Against Misleading Claims," *Adweek's Marketing Week,* May 20, 1991, p. 7.
Cook, James, "Handsome Is as Handsome Does," *Fortune,* March 3, 1980, p. 43.
"Corn Products Finds Other Fields Green," *Business Week,* July 5, 1958, p.76.
"Corn Products in 14 Countries," *Fortune,* September 1938, p. 58.

CPC *International Inc. Annual Reports,* Englewood Cliffs, New Jersey: CPC International Inc., 1980-1991.

Crain, Rance, "At Best Foods It's New Wares, Old Names," *Advertising Age,* May 16, 1966, p. 3.

Dean, George, "Mazola Indian Represents Product Benefits of Corn," *Advertising Age,* April 16, 1979, p. S-26.

"Did Not Violate NAB Code by Airing Ads for Puritan: P&G," *Advertising Age,* January 3, 1977, p. 1.

Fannin, Rebecca, "Mazola Bets on Health," *Marketing & Media Decisions,* May 1983, p. 66.

Franz, Julie and Ruth Stroud, "Wesson Looks for Mazola Corn Oil to Slip," *Advertising Age,* April 15, 1985, p. 6.

Giges, Nancy, "P&G Bristles at Best Foods Gripe on Puritan Ads," *Advertising Age,* December 31, 1976, p. 1.

Hwang, Suein L., "Its Big Brands Long Taunted as Fatty, CPC Tries a More 'Wholesome' Approach," *Wall Street Journal,* April 20, 1992, p. B1.

"Mazola Ads Push Benefits of Corn Oil," *Advertising Age,* April 8, 1974, p. 40.

"Mazola Ads Tie in With Lower Cholesterol Diets," *Advertising Age,* May 26, 1975, p. 2.

"100 Leading Advertisers," *Advertising Age,* September 26, 1985, p. 61.

Telzer, Ronnie, "Single Event Is Better Way for Best," *Advertising Age,* November 16, 1987, p. S-11.

Therrien, Lois, "How CPC Is Getting Fat on Muffins and Mayonnaise," *Business Week,* April 16, 1990, p. 46.

"Uncommon Market," *Fortune,* March, 1962, p. 98.

—Frances E. Norton

MIGHTY DOG®

Mighty Dog was the first canned dog food that consisted entirely of real meat, with no byproducts and no cereals. It was developed and manufactured by the Carnation Company, a leader in the evaporated milk and instant hot chocolate industries. By the 1970s, the Carnation Company had also become the second largest producer of pet food in the world, and upon its introduction in 1973 Mighty Dog sales soared; it became the leading dog food in the United States. While the Carnation Company was sold to Nestle S.A. of Vevey, Switzerland in 1985 and has since been dissolved, Friskies PetCare Company, Inc. (part of Nestlé USA, the wholly owned subsidiary of Nestlé S.A.) continues to manufacture Mighty Dog in a wide variety of flavors.

Brand Origins

By the time Mighty Dog came on the market in 1973, Carnation had been in business for nearly sixty years, and the manufacture of this first all-meat canned dog food represented the evolution of Carnation's successful venture in the processing of dog food, which began in 1929. The company had developed the first dry dog food in 1936, called Friskies, which was extremely successful (until that time the only dog foods on the market were a brand of canned horse meat and dog biscuits). Dog food became a separate division of Carnation, which introduced Friskies canned dog food in 1948.

First Commercial Success

In the decade of the 1960s, the nation's dog and cat population had grown three times faster than that of humans. By the early 1970s, the pet food industry was tallying over two billion dollars in sales, and twenty years later, sales of pet food would total over seven billion dollars. In response to the rapidly growing market Carnation introduced nine new Friskies products nationally during the 1960s.

Convenient packaging soon became a goal of Carnation's Friskies canned dog food, which sought to appeal to many dog owners who used only half of the large can of dog food daily. The remainder of the food would be refrigerated, becoming congealed and creating an odor in the refrigerator. Designs for a single serving can were soon generated. To be advertised as a dog food with ''no leftovers!,'' the new product would provide relief for the dog owner and a daily fresh meal for the pet.

By the time the single serving can was ready for market testing, the product had also changed—to a pure beef dog food. This was the first pure beef canned dog food in the United States. Although Carnation's competitor Alpo had already marketed an ''all meat'' dog food, Alpo's product consisted of meat byproducts. Carnation's latest product would be real beef, with no byproducts. The product was tested successfully, particularly with smaller dogs, and was named ''Mighty Dog.''

The commercial success of Mighty Dog in 1973 was rapid. Dogs loved it, proving that it was the most palatable dog food on the market, while owners found the single serve can an added convenience. Of all Friskies products, none had prompted such enthusiasm among consumers.

Early Marketing Strategy

Emphasizing the benefits of a single serving can and an all-meat content, marketers of Mighty Dog ensured that their product would be the most popular brand of dog food available in the early 1970s. Clearly the early marketing strategy reflected a trend in the pet food industry; dog and cat foods increasingly catered to the psychological and domestic needs of the pet owner, rather than to the basic dietary needs of pets. Mighty Dog was no exception. By studying closely the personal needs of the dog owner rather than the dog, Carnation ended up developing their most successful dog food product.

Advertising Innovations

The Carnation Company had been a seasoned, sophisticated user of advertising for many decades by the time Mighty Dog came on the scene. Having established a public relations department in 1955, the company discreetly advertised its traditional and new products in its own publications such as the highly regarded *Friskies Research Digest* for professional veterinarians and animal breeders, and the paperback books *The Dog You Care For* and *The Cat You Care For,* sold to the general public.

In addition to being featured in Carnation's publications, Mighty Dog took advantage of both television and radio advertising. For many years the friendly face of a small, grey poodle graced the label of every can of Mighty Dog, becoming an easily identifiable logo. Although the dog food was tested on small dogs and featured a small dog on its label, Mighty Dog was never

AT A GLANCE

Mighty Dog brand of dog food introduced by the Carnation Company in 1973; Carnation Co. acquired by Nestlé, S.A. of Vevey, Switzerland, in 1985; company named changed to Nestlé/Carnation Food Company, 1985; Friskies pet food division (manufacturer of Mighty Dog) established separately as Friskies PetCare Company, Inc., in Glendale, CA, in November, 1992.

Performance: *Market share*—9% of dog food category.

Major competitor: Mars Inc.'s Kal Kan; also Alpo.

Advertising: *Agency*—Dailey & Associates, Los Angeles, CA, 1992—. *Major campaign*—"It Makes Your Dog a Mighty Dog!"

Addresses: *Parent company*—Friskies PetCare Company, Inc., 800 North Brand Boulevard, Glendale, CA 91203; phone: (818) 549-6000. *Ultimate parent company*—Nestlé USA Inc., 800 North Brand Boulevard, Glendale, CA 91203; phone: (818) 549-6000. *Ultimate parent company*—Nestlé SA.

advertised as strictly "small dog" chow. Furthermore it carried the subtitle of "Pure Beef No By Products" and the "no leftovers" promise, as well as widely available discount coupons, all of which added to its popularity.

Although advertising declined in the 1980s, the company's reorganization in late 1992 led to a dramatic change in advertising. Colorful, imaginative TV ads extolling the nutritional value of Mighty Dog and its variety of flavors and textures once again are instructing and entertaining dog owners.

Product Development

Mighty Dog is but one of a dozen Friskies dog food brands that make the Friskies PetCare Company the second largest manufacturer of pet foods in the United States. Since its introduction in 1973, Mighty Dog has acquired ten different flavors. While it has not become the "health food" for dogs of many superpremium brands, Mighty Dog continues to command a healthy nine percent of the competitive dog food market.

International Growth

By the time Mighty Dog had been developed in the 1970s, Carnation had an international distribution network for its many food products. During that time, strenuous efforts were made to promote Mighty Dog in France and England, with considerable success. Currently Spain and Italy register the biggest market shares for Friskies pet foods, including Mighty Dog.

As a subsidiary of Nestlé, S.A., Friskies PetCare has the advantage of distribution networks in virtually every country worldwide. Long term political stability and a steady increase in economic prosperity are the chief ingredients for a pet food's success.

Future Predictions

The pet food market has been declining over the past few years. With over four hundred varieties of pet food on the market, the domestic market seemingly has reached the saturation point. Competition among the half dozen giant pet food manufacturers, who produce over 80 percent of today's pet food, is more intense than ever.

The forecast, however, is far from dismal. To begin with, pet food manufacture is almost an entirely American industry. While competition is fierce at home, there are not, as for so many other products, foreign competitors. The household pet population also keeps growing steadily. In addition, there are further possibilities for Mighty Dog overseas, as other countries begin to recognize a need for healthy diet alternatives for their pets.

Further Reading:

Annual Report: Nestle, S.A., 1991.

Annual Report: Nestle USA, Inc., 1991.

Bird, Laura, "Iams and Hill's Wage a High Fibre, Low-Cal War against Ralston Purina and Carnation," *AdWeek's Marketing Week,* October 1, 1990, p.20.

Fucini, J. J. & S. F., *Entrepreneurs; the Men and Women behind Famous Brand Names and How They Made It,* Boston: Holt & Co., 1985.

Hackett, R., *The Pet Food Industry, an Economic, Marketing and Financial Investigation,* New York: Morton Research, 1977.

Hambleton, Ronald, *The Branding of America,* Dublin, NY: Yankee Books, 1987.

Kroll, Dorothy, *The Pet Industry,* Norwalk, CT, 1989.

Rothein, P., *The Pet Industry, New Developments in Food & Health Products,* Stamford, CT, 1985.

Schifrin, Matthew, "Mom's Cooking Was Never Like This (Superpremium Pet Foods)," *Forbes,* August 19, 1991.

Weaver, John D., *Carnation, the First Fifty Years, 1899-1974,* Los Angeles, 1974.

—Sina Dubovoj

MILK-BONE®

Milk-Bone brand of dog biscuits, a long-time leader in the dog snacks category, was acquired by the National Biscuit Company (a predecessor of Nabisco) in 1931. Just one of numerous expansion and diversification efforts the company undertook, the bone-shaped meat, cereal, milk, and mineral product with high nutritional—and even some breath-freshening—properties soon became a top-seller. Today Nabisco Foods Group, a subsidiary of RJR Nabisco, Inc., produces and successfully markets a complete line of Milk-Bone dog treats.

Brand Origins

The origins of Milk Bone dog biscuits date back to the early 1900s, when the unusual bone-shaped snacks first became popular with dogs and their owners. F. H. Bennett, a baker on the lower east side of New York, originally developed the biscuits in a corner of his bakery. The F. H. Bennett Biscuit Company, which was incorporated in 1917, was later named Wheatsworth, Inc. A manufacturer of cracker, cake, cereal, and flour varieties, this company gained a national reputation with its Wheatsworth trademark.

When the National Biscuit Company first acquired Wheatsworth in 1931, the Milk-Bone operation was considered of little value in comparison to the other products Wheatsworth generated. However, Milk-Bone would flourish over the years, even helping to increase company sales during the Depression, while other Wheatsworth products did not always fare as well. Throughout World War II, the Milk-Bone bakery produced biscuits for the Army and Marine Corps' war dogs. By the 1960s more than three billion Milk-Bone brand biscuits were enjoyed by millions of dogs, and many dog owners were showing strong brand loyalty. In fact, according to *42 Million a Day, the Story of Nabisco Brands,* Nabisco began receiving letters praising Milk-Bone that were signed with dog names. When a local labor dispute shut down some California supermarkets, one man wrote, "I can manage all right with whatever's already in my refrigerator, but my dog needs his Milk-Bone Dog Biscuits. Please send me a box to tide him over, and bill me."

Brand Development

While Milk-Bone biscuits were originally popular as a treat or dessert for dogs, in the 1940s advertisements began to focus on their nutritional benefits. Milk-Bones were described as "an additional food for the dog, helping to keep his teeth clean, giving him something to chew on, helping cleanse his breath." The hard and crunchy biscuits provided an important alternative to soft dog foods. Latter-day ads called Milk-Bone "the crunch food" and "the better teeth cleaner for your dog."

By 1955 consumer demand for Milk-Bones was so high that the bakery in New York that had produced the biscuits could not keep up with it. Consequently, Nabisco's Buffalo bakery was converted to accommodate Milk-Bone production, with new methods that allowed for faster and more efficient output. Stricter sanitary and quality control procedures were incorporated, as with other Nabisco products.

Wide band ovens—some as long as football fields—were used. These ovens allowed mass production to proceed on a straight-line basis and ensured consistent quality while economizing operations. Dough of controlled thickness was rolled onto sheets that were fed into cutting machines. Biscuits were stamped out and entered the oven on a moving steel band. Burners on the top and bottom of the ovens worked in tandem with the band speed to produce consistent baking.

New Products

Milk-Bone Flavor Snacks were introduced in the 1960s. They consisted of six individual flavors and colors. Milk-Bone Butcher Bones, made with real meat chips, followed. By 1989 Nabisco, the leader in the then $430 million dog-food-snacks market segment, introduced Milk-Bone T.C. (tartar control) biscuits and rawhide strips. Nabisco invested $15 million in the initial distribution of the five product line. T.C. was developed in response to the rapidly growing canine dental industry, which, with 75 percent of all dogs purportedly suffering from periodontal problems, had a huge potential customer base. Caroline Fee, a spokesperson for Milk-Bone, told *Advertising Age* that the texture of Milk-Bone T.C was "specially formulated to control tartar and plaque buildup." The product, however, had no medicinal ingredients, such as fluoride. Milk-Bone also came out with breath-freshening Milk-Bone Mint-Flavored dog biscuits in the late 1980s.

In early October 1992, Milk-Bone Butcher's Choice dog biscuits were offered in small, medium, and large varieties. They were flavored with meat juices and came in beef, chicken, liver, and bacon flavors. The new biscuits were promoted with full-page advertisements. For the 1992 Christmas season Nabisco offered bell, stocking, and Christmas tree-shaped Milk-Bone Flavor Snacks dog biscuits. Boxes featured three different holiday scenes: one depicting three dogs tugging at stockings hanging on a fireplace; another showing two dogs dreaming about the biscuits; and the third featuring a dog looking under the tree, waiting for its snack biscuits. The biscuits were offered in seven assorted flavors.

Marketing Strategies

By 1990 Nabisco was losing some of its market share to competitors. Purina introduced Purina Biscuits in 1989, launching its new product with a $12 million promotional campaign. By 1990, according to Julie Liesse and Judann Dagnoli in *Advertising Age,* Purina Biscuits ranked fifth in the overall dog snacks market, with an 8 percent share. An advertising war between the major brands of dog snacks began. Purina ran a TV ad in which a cartoon dog quips, "If it isn't Purina, bury it in the yard." Heinz also went after Milk-Bone with an ad stating that "a nationwide taste test says dogs prefer Meaty Bone two to one over Milk-Bone dog biscuits." The Heinz product was number two at the time, with a 13 percent share of the market.

AT A GLANCE

Milk-Bone brand of dog biscuits founded in 1908 in New York, NY, by F. H. Bennett; F. H. Bennett Biscuit Company (incorporated in 1917) renamed Wheatsworth, Inc.; acquired by National Biscuit Company in 1931. National Biscuit Company founded in 1898; changed name to Nabisco, Inc., 1971; merger of Nabisco, Inc. and Standard Brands Incorporated to form Nabisco Brands, Inc., 1981; Nabisco Brands merged with R. J. Reynolds Industries, Inc. in 1985, which changed its name in 1986 to RJR Nabisco, Inc.; Specialty Products Division is one of seven operating companies of Nabisco Foods Group, a subsidiary of RJR Nabisco, Inc.

Performance: Market share—40% (top share) of biscuit segment of dog snacks category. *Sales*—$167.7 million (1989 estimate).

Major competitor: Ralston Purina's Purina Biscuits; also H. J. Heinz Company's Meaty Bone.

Advertising: Agency—FCB/Leber Katz Partners, New York, NY, 1986—. *Major campaign*—Underscores teeth-cleaning and breath-sweetening properties; tag line: "Twice a day, everyday, all it takes is a Milk-Bone."

Addresses: Parent Company—Nabisco Foods Group, 7 Campus Drive, Parsippany, NJ 07054; phone: (201) 682-7100. *Ultimate parent company:* RJR Nabisco, Inc., 1301 Avenue of the Americas, New York, NY 10019; phone: (212) 258-5600.

Nabisco saw Purina's marketing strategy as being based on selling its biscuits for lower prices. That was not consistent with Nabisco's image of Milk-Bone, nor with the company's financial goals. To counter, beyond offering its new tartar control biscuits, Nabisco introduced a network television commercial that hit the airwaves in early September of 1991. The ad featured a dog asking his off-camera master why he was being given those "new biscuits," adding "Don't you love me anymore?" The spot pointed out that Milk-Bone contained half the fat of Purina and ended with, "Please give me back my Milk-Bone."

While all this competition was going on, the *Wall Street Journal* published a short article in 1990 stating that Nabisco Brands was planning to sell its pet-snacks division. A senior vice president described the division as "very profitable"—annual sales had reached about $150 million—and was quoted as saying that Nabisco's pet-snacks division "didn't meet our strategic fit." He added that talks with potential buyers had not started. Apparently they never did. Milk-Bone's competitors were eager to take over the industry leader, which at the time held 40 percent of the dog biscuit market, but the business was taken off the block later that year. In RJR Nabisco's 1991 annual report, the president of Nabisco Foods Group said, "Our Milk-Bone business is one good example of where we successfully withstood a massive attack by other companies."

Also in 1992, Milk-Bone came up with an innovative marketing approach. Tucked into 10 million boxes of Milk-Bones, T. C. biscuits and rawhide strips, and Flavor Snacks, were trading cards portraying U. S. Customs Drug Detecting Dogs. The cards, which clearly appealed more to dog owners and their kids than to dogs, featured such heroes as Snag, a Labrador Retriever who has sniffed out more than $780 million worth of drugs. With these unusual trading cards Milk-Bone maintained a unique focus on dogs that its customers—dog lovers—could appreciate, and at the

same time was clearly seeking both to do some good in the community and to create an image for itself. Milk-Bone gave 100,000 sets of the cards, which include a message to children about the dangers involved in drug-use, to the U. S. Customs drug Outreach program.

Future Growth

Market analysts have frequently questioned the desirability to consumers of the time-honored standard dog treat, the grain-based biscuit. The market in the 1980s and early 1990s seemed to be heavily leaning toward treats that appeal more to humans and their trends, such as gourmet and health food products for dogs. Robert E. Linneman and John L. Stanton, Jr., wrote in a 1992 article in *Business Horizons* that many dog owners were simply not buying

A Bennett's Milk-Bone Dog Food box, circa the 1920s.

snacks like Milk-Bones: "This type of treat usually occupied a couple of shelf facings in the supermarket, but a good percentage of dog owners didn't buy them. . . . They wanted treats for their dogs—and grain did not seem a very tasty treat. This makes sense. After all, when was the last time you saw your dog attacking a wheat field? Finally, when more expensive dog snacks, such as jerky or beef, were put on the market, the non-users flocked to buy them. Interestingly, at a time when dog ownership is going down, revenue from premium snacks is going up."

All-natural, gourmet, designer pet products mirrored human consumer trends during the 1980s. Small manufacturers came up with such new products as Popcorn for Pets, Whole Wheat Cookies for Dogs, Pasta for Pets, and a dental kit, which were exhibited at industry trade shows. In addition, deli products for pets took on a new dimension as did frozen hot meals for pampered pets. Other food products were available only through veterinarian offices, specialty pet stores, and feed stores. This sort of product upgrading was projected by market analysts to keep the pet food category growing by about 22 percent throughout ensuing years—up to $7.4 billion in sales by 1995. *Adweek* contributor Robert McMath commented in 1990 that "all natural, gourmet, value-added, and designer pet products are rocketing to widespread usage."

While pet food sales have remained fairly stagnant during the early 1990s, pet snacks have shown a small increase. Milk-Bone, with both its solid array of products—such as Tartar Control biscuits and rawhide strips, Butcher's Choice, and Flavor Snacks—and its solid place as a market leader with a known and trusted product, is well positioned to weather the uncertainties of economic recession and passing trends in consumer behavior.

Further Reading:

Cahn, William, *Out of the Cracker Barrel: The Nabisco Story from Animal Crackers to Zuzus,* New York: Simon & Schuster, 1969.

Cornfeld, Betty, and Owen Edwards, *Quintessence: The Quality of Having It,* New York: Crown Publishing Group, 1993.

Dagnoli, Judann, "Toothcare for Terriers," *Advertising Age,* November 20, 1989, p. 8.

"Doggie Dearest," *Detroit Free Press,* May 18, 1992.

Donahue, Christine, "At RJR Nabisco, New Owner KKR Is Already Wielding the Knife," *Adweek's Marketing Week,* August 21, 1989, p. 4.

Fact Sheet, New York: RJR Nabisco, Inc.

Grayson, Melvin J., *42 Million a Day: The Story of Nabisco Brands,* East Hanover, NJ: Nabisco Brands, Inc., 1986.

Kirk, Jim, "Barking Up the Right Tree," *Prepared Foods,* July 15, 1990, p. 146.

Liesse, Julie, and Judann Dagnoli, "Gnawing Milk-Bone: Purina, Heinz Nip at Leader's Share," *Advertising Age,* April 2, 1990, p. 40.

Linneman, Robert & Stanton, John L. Jr., "Mining for Niches," *Business Horizons,* May-June 1992, p. 43.

McMath, Robert, "Packaging Trends 1990," *Adweek Eastern Edition,* September 17, 1990, p. S192.

"Milk-Bone Bites Purina," *Advertising Age,* September 16, 1991, p. 14.

"Nabisco Brands, Inc.," *International Directory of Company Histories,* Detroit: St. James Press, pp. 542-544.

"Nabisco's Blitz Advertising," *Business Week,* September 27, 1976, pp. 95, 98.

RJR Nabisco 1991 Annual Report to Shareholders, Books One & Two, New York: RJR Nabisco, Inc., 1992.

"RJR Says It Plans to Sell Nabisco's Pet-Snacks Line," *Wall Street Journal,* April 16, 1990, p. B2.

—Anne C. Hughes

MILLER®

While not the "king of beers," Miller Lite is the strongest contender to the throne long held by Budweiser and its parent, Anheuser-Busch, Inc. Miller Brewing Company, which reigns as the number two brewery in the United States, holds an overall 22.3 percent share of the premium malt beverage market and boasts three Miller brands among the top 10 in terms of millions of barrels shipped. Tellingly, the original Miller superbrand, Miller High Life, is now struggling at number ten to remain in the elite pack. Far prior to 1986, when annual advertising for High Life peaked at $87 million, the "champagne of beers" showed signs of fizzling. The problem of Miller's shrinking sales was originally identified during the 1970s, by former Miller president John A. Murphy, as one of poor target marketing. However, once this problem was largely corrected through aggressive, pin-point advertising, new signs of deterioration during the 1980s could best be explained as a "cannibalizing" phenomenon, with Lite as the culprit.

Miller Lite, conceived in 1973 and rolled out nationally in 1975, was the first successful low-calorie beer and, for that matter, the first "light" product of any kind to take hold in the public consciousness. By 1978, no less than 18 imitations in the beer industry had risen to challenge it. A true Cinderella story, Lite is now the number two beer overall and still accounts for approximately half of Miller's revenue, which in 1992 totaled nearly $4 billion. However, its success has shown signs of fading during the early 1990s in what has become a flat-growth industry further and further segmented by new product introductions. Miller Genuine Draft, Miller Genuine Draft Light, Miller Reserve, Miller Reserve Light, Miller Lite Ultra, and Miller Clear have all emerged to fill new market needs; whether they can attain superbrand status, as High Life and Lite have done, is largely up to the whims and tastes of consumers. Although brand founder Frederic Miller's simplistic 19th-century slogan "Quality, Uncompromising and Unchanging" still holds for the company that bears his name, the large line of Miller beers now in production discloses, in contrast, a modern theme of complex market tracking, multimillion dollar advertising budgets, vicious beer wars, and continuing financial uncertainty.

Brand Origins

Born in 1824 to a prominent German family, Frederic Edward John Miller received a classical education in France. Upon gradua-

tion he spent his early adult years in Nancy, in northeastern France, learning the brewing trade from his uncle. He supplemented his knowledge with trips to several beer-producing regions of his homeland and eventually leased the royal Hohenzollern brewery in Sigmaringen, Germany, where he produced beer "by gracious permission of his highness." In 1854 Miller and his family immigrated to the United States to escape rising economic and political turmoil in Germany. According to the "Miller History" and an anniversary article in the *Milwaukee Sentinel,* "after spending a year based in New York City and inspecting various parts of the country by river and lake steamer," Miller settled in Milwaukee and was believed to have remarked, "A town with a magnificent harbor like that has a great future in store."

Miller had in mind not just commerce in general but the continuation of the promising career he had launched overseas. In 1855 he acquired a failed five-year-old brewery for $8,000. Named the Plank-Road Brewery, the business was located west of the city, in the Menomonee River Valley, on a site noted for its water source and rich agricultural surroundings. During that first year, Miller sold 300 barrels of his eponymous beer at around $5 per barrel. He soon gained a reputation as "a resourceful businessman, establishing a beautiful beer garden that attracted weekend crowds for bowling, dancing, fine lunches and old-fashioned 'gemuetlichkeit.' "

In 1873 the brewery was renamed Frederic Miller's Menomonee Valley Brewery; by 1888, the year he died, Miller's business had become the Frederic Miller Brewing Company. Miller's children by his second wife, Lisette Gross, inherited ownership and management of the brewery, which remained primarily a family-dominated, regional concern until well into the twentieth century.

The Girl in the Moon

Miller High Life was born in 1903 through the efforts of Fred and Ernst Miller (sons of the founder) and their nephew Carl Miller. Carl, who managed the brewery at the time, took his young daughter Loretta there for a tour. While perched atop a bar in the company dining room, she apparently struck a pose that inspired her father to conceive the "Girl in the Moon" symbol that would soon grace bottles of Miller beer. The event occurred at a time when the brewery was searching for an appropriate name for a

AT A GLANCE

Miller High Life brand of beer founded December 30, 1903, in Milwaukee, WI, by Miller Brewing Company owners, including Carl, Ernst, and Fred Miller; Miller Lite founded in 1973 by Miller executives John Murphy and Larry Williams and graphic designer Walter Landor; later developers include McCann-Erickson creative director Bob Lenz and advertising executives at Backer & Spielvogel; Miller Brewing Company acquired by W. R. Grace & Co., 1966; Miller became subsidiary of Philip Morris, Inc. (later Philip Morris Companies, Inc.), 1969.

Performance: *Sales*—$3.97 billion (overall). *Market share*—Overall domestic premium beer category: 22.3% (number 2 brewer); Miller Lite: 9.7% (number 2 slot); Miller Genuine Draft: 3.3% (number 6 slot); Miller High Life: 2.8% (number 10 slot).

Major competitor: Anheuser-Busch, Inc.'s Budweiser and Bud Light brands; also Coors Light.

Advertising: *Agency (for Miller Lite)*—Leo Burnett Company, Inc., Chicago, IL, 1991—. *Major campaign (for Miller Lite)*—Evolving series featuring lyrics "C'mon, let me show you where it's at"; Miller Lite also sponsors "major sports and entertainment properties." *Agency (for Miller Genuine Draft)*—Backer Spielvogel Bates, Inc., New York, NY. *Major campaign (for Miller Genuine Draft)*—"Get Out of The Old. Get into the Cold"; exclusive malt-beverage sponsor of the National Basketball Association. *Agency (for Miller Clear)*—Cliff Freeman and Partners, New York, NY, 1993—. *Major campaign (for Miller Clear)*—Humorous commercial in which Miller laboratory experts unveil Miller Clear to astounded executives from marketing.

Addresses: *Parent company*—Miller Brewing Company, 3939 West Highland Blvd., P.O. Box 482, Milwaukee, WI 53201-0482; phone: (414) 931-2000; fax: (414) 931-6312. *Ultimate parent company*—Philip Morris Companies, Inc., 120 Park Ave., New York, NY 10017; phone: (212) 880-5000; fax: (212) 878-2167.

new premium pilsner that it planned to sell. Ernst was enlisted to travel the country to fulfill this need; after unsuccessful stops in Kansas City and Omaha, he entered New Orleans and headed to the loading docks. There he discovered a large cigar factory bearing the name High Life Cigars. The image evoked by the words "High Life" seemed particularly fitting, and the brewery promptly acquired the factory and rights to the brand name for $25,000. Meanwhile, Fred Miller, known for his artistic talent, was assigned to sketch the High Life girl, which according to the most reliable sources was indeed modeled after Loretta.

However, the original brand emblem—a strikingly attired woman brandishing a whip and boldly standing atop a case of beer—bears only superficial resemblances to the one introduced on bottles in 1936, in which the Miller girl is gracefully perched on a crescent moon. This emblem was further refined in 1944, when it was placed at the centerpoint of a "soft cross" Miller High Life label; in this version, the woman, her whip gone, sports an updated hair style, a simplified costume, and a more natural pose in which she is face-forward and smiling. The "Girl in the Moon," though no longer part of the distinctive gold Miller cross, is still used for promotional purposes and has regularly appeared on collectibles dating as far back as 1907.

The Champagne of Beers

Miller High Life acquired its sobriquet, "The Champagne of Bottled Beer," in 1906 when a contest was held by the brewery to create a winning slogan. From that time until the 1950s, Miller prospered as a company devoted to promoting its high-quality, premium, light-colored beer. Following World War II, Miller was still largely removed from the heady competition among the nation's top brewers. In 1947 Schlitz was indisputably "the beer that made Milwaukee famous." At the turn of the century, this brand had been number three, behind Pabst and Budweiser. Now it was the frontrunner. (A decade later, Budweiser would take that honor, and hold it.) Miller, although respected, was a dark horse at the time and had yet to break into the ranks of the top ten.

In the same year that Schlitz assumed the lead, Frederick C. Miller (a grandson of the founder), then 41, assumed control of his family's brewery and launched a sweeping, three-pronged program of plant expansion, improved distribution, and national advertising. He succeeded in quadrupling the company's sales within a six-year period, though a crippling 77-day strike in 1953 caused sales to plummet by 30 percent. Then suddenly, in 1954, a private plane crash at General Mitchell Field in Milwaukee left both Miller and his twenty-year-old son, Frederick, Jr., dead. No doubt this tragedy, coupled with the aftermath of the strike, seriously affected the near-term future of the company, but by the mid-1960s Miller was again on the move and had acquired a reputation as one of the country's fastest-growing breweries. The company president during this pivotal era—when controlling interest in the company was purchased first by New York conglomerate W. R. Grace & Company for $36 million and then three years later by tobacco giant Philip Morris for $130 million—was Charles W. Miller (no relation to the founder). Under his guidance, the company's flagship brand moved from number eleven to eight, while sales increases from 1965 to 1969 outpaced the industry average by nearly four-to-one.

Quality control and sound brand management in the face of potential obstacles were among the key contributors to this growth. According to a 1969 *Forbes* article, "even though Miller High Life was a national brand like Budweiser, Schlitz and Pabst, for years the company had only one brewery. So it had to ship long distances. This required top quality control to prevent the beer from spoiling, and today Miller beer has perhaps the longest shelf life of any major beer." Although the company successfully developed a beer concentrate during the early 1960s to help reduce shipping costs, it ultimately decided to shelve the project after a government ruling demanded explicit labeling of the substance. As *Forbes* quoted Miller, "This was the kiss of death . . . so we didn't do it. But working with this concentrate taught us how to brew our beer exactly the same way in other locations. Our competitors can't do this; their beer tastes different from brewery to brewery. Once we were able to do this, we were able to expand with new breweries in Texas and in California."

Marlboro Meets Miller

According to a May 1976 *Forbes* article with a different slant, "Miller was a sickly company run by an aging management group when Philip Morris acquired it from W. R. Grace in 1969. Its High Life beer was one of the three truly national premium-priced brands, along with Budweiser and Schlitz, yet several regional brewers outsold it in the U.S. market." Philip Morris's purchase of Miller, as it turned out, proved the final key to Miller's meteoric rise both as a brand and as a brewery. Philip Morris president

George Weissman waited until late 1971 before installing his own management team of tobacco executives at Miller. Either indifferent to, nonplussed, or bemused by Weissman's move, most beer executives and industry experts were unprepared for the full-scale assault Miller was poised to launch to quickly overcome competitors and become a dominant player in the market.

To this end, Weissman's new man at the helm, John Murphy, made a conscious decision to employ the same marketing techniques that spurred the Marlboro Man to fame during the 1960s. For Miller High Life, a venerable but underperforming brand, the problem was one of poorly positioned advertising: the latest campaign was a model of refinement featuring jazz trumpeter Al Hirt. "Sold for years as the champagne of beers, High Life was," according to a 1976 *Business Week* article, "attracting a disproportionate share of women and upper-income consumers who were not big beer drinkers." "A lot of people drank the beer, but none of them in quantity," stated Murphy.

The solution seemed as simple as selling cigarettes to the heavy cigarette-user through a strong brand association. Instead of being held back by the "champagne" crowd, High Life would now be targeted at blue-collar workers, younger drinkers, and males in general, who together comprised the bulk of beer drinkers measured in terms of consumption. "Under Murphy, advertisements for High Life began featuring young people riding in dune buggies and oil drillers sipping on a cool one after squelching an oil blowout." This association strategy also carried with it an added element of "reason-to-buy" promotion.

Simple yet effective, "Now Comes Miller Time," developed by the McCann-Erickson agency, carried the High Life brand through an enormously profitable decade. The introduction in 1972 of the 7-ounce pony bottle also contributed to a rise in sales and was an early indication of the company's intention to unite segmented buyers under an umbrella of Miller products appealing to differing consumer preferences. In 1975 Miller Brewing posted sales of $658 million and became the fourth-highest beer-seller in the country. Two years later Miller High Life overtook Schlitz's number two position on the charts. With the financial clout and marketing savvy of Philip Morris backing it, the Miller brand name had by this time truly come into its own.

Let There Be Lite

By 1980, Miller was the second largest brewer in the United States. The company attained this enviable ranking with the help of the High Life brand; however, another, newer product would be responsible for sustaining the feat. This product was Miller Lite. As early as 1978, William Flanagan, writing for *Esquire,* decreed the now legendary product "by any measure, the most successful in the history of the beer industry." Much later, in 1991, brand and marketing authority David A. Aaker conferred even greater status on Lite, lauding it as "one of the most successful new products ever introduced" (in the history of advertising). Why was the product so successful? Some might argue that it was inherently unique. Others would say that its introduction was well-timed. Still others might contend that it benefited from highly effective advertising. All would probably be correct to some degree.

Miller Lite originated the low-calorie beer category on a national basis, and the category is now responsible for one-third of all domestic beer sold. The first light beer was marketed by the Piels Brewing Company under the name Trommer's Red Letter in 1964, but was taken off the market within weeks of its introduction; the beer had been expressly promoted to women drinkers. Then, in 1967, came a beer by Rheingold named Gablinger's; marketed to men who had a desire for staying slim, Gablinger's also failed. This same year, Peter Hand Brewing of Chicago, makers of Meister Brau, began similarly promoting Meister Brau Lite. The brand survived for five years but was largely unsuccessful. In June of 1972 Miller acquired the Chicago brewer and the Lite trademark, along with several others. Existing market research for Meister Brau Lite, according to Flanagan, "showed a lot more consumer interest in a low-calorie beer than sales had reflected, even among heavy drinkers."

Miller chief Murphy and marketing head Larry Williams decided to refurbish the brand and then take a page from the High Life campaign to re-target and promote it. With the fitness craze fully underway, they reasoned that the time was ripe as well. After brewmasters modified the original recipe and graphic designer Walter Landor—who had made his reputation with several designs for Philip Morris cigarettes—completed his work, Miller Lite was prepared for test-marketing in four cities in mid-1973. The results were so favorable that a national rollout was planned for January of 1975, supported by an advertising budget of $12 million.

Bob Lenz, creative director at McCann-Erickson, was handed the task of devising a television campaign that would promote the brand to the largest segment of the beer-drinking population while avoiding the potentially negative connotations of the phrases "low-calorie" or "diet" beer. According to Michael Gershman in *Getting It Right the Second Time,* when "Lenz saw an ad featuring New York Jets star Matt Snell on a New York bus [he] put 'beer' and 'athletes' together in his mind." The first Lite commercial, starring Snell, was taped in July of 1973. Little did anyone realize at that time that the spot would lead to dozens more over a nearly 20-year period, and that its highly touted product would be the catalyst for a proliferation of all types of light foods as well as light beverages.

The "Tastes Great/Less Filling" commercials, which over the years featured the likes of Bob Uecker, Bubba Smith, Dick Butkus, Wilt Chamberlain, John Madden, Mickey Mantle, Joe Frazier, and non-sports figures Rodney Dangerfield and Mickey Spillane, were resoundingly successful not only because of their celebrity casts, but also because of the wisecracks and comfortable settings (first bars exclusively, then a number of other sites later). The tag line "everything you always wanted in a beer—and less" and the phrase "less filling" were also successful as clever inducements that did not deter from the macho, or at least "regular guy," image the ads were attempting to promote. When Anheuser-Busch unveiled its Natural Light beer, it seemed to borrow heavily from the Lite commercials, and even employed former Lite spokespersons. Lite countered with what were considered even funnier sketches, which revolved around debates of "Tastes Great/Less Filling" and starred Tommy Heinsohn and referee Mendy Rudolph.

It is said that a good product, good timing, and classic commercials all coalesced in Lite's introductory year to achieve sales for the brand of $100 million and a production of 12.6 million barrels, or approximately 20 percent of Miller's total output. In 1979 Lite surpassed Schlitz in the premium beer rankings; four years later, Lite settled into the number two position behind Budweiser, where it has since remained.

The only initial negative news for the brand was that its very existence spawned a host of competitors, all of which were permitted—despite Miller's best legal efforts—to use the word "light" for their own brand-name, low-calorie beers. Aside from its impact on the low-cal beer market, which was enormous and continued throughout the 1980s, Lite's greatest influence was on the skyrocketing size of advertising budgets for the big brewers, which in turn was, and continues to be, tied to new product introductions.

High Life Revisited

High Life's reign as the number two beer, which had begun in 1977, was almost over before it started. Production for the aging superbrand had already peaked by 1979. By 1985, this number was nearly halved, though High Life had managed to hold the number three slot after being edged aside by its "lighter" counterpart. This same year, the company reacted to stem the tide by spending $60 million with a new ad agency, J. Walter Thompson, to launch the "Made the American Way" campaign. By 1986,

Logo for Miller's top-selling Lite, the first successful low-calorie beer.

such dire prognostications as Matthew Heller's in *Forbes* were becoming common: "High Life each day looks more like a dying label. And [Thompson's campaign] failed to resuscitate it."

Many observers saw High Life's misfortune as simply the necessary balance to Lite's dramatic rise in prominence. Statistical evidence would seem to support this view. According to Aaker, "As sales of Miller Lite went from 9.5% share of the U.S. beer market in 1978 to 19% in 1986, the Miller High Life brand declined from 21% to 12% in the same period."

However, to assume that the success of Lite was the only factor in High Life's rapid slide would be an oversimplification. Perhaps at least as important were the peaks and valleys of domestic beer consumption in general. During the 1970s baby boomers were in their prime beer-drinking years; because of this, as well as strong brands and effective advertising, Miller's beer volume rose 640 percent over a ten-year span. Yet, in accord with changing demographics, this increase was abruptly halted after 1981, when Miller reached an all-time shipment high of 40.3 million barrels (a record 43.6 million barrels was shipped in 1991, but that figure included significant growth in exports).

In 1991 *Adweek's Marketing Week* bestowed the unwelcome distinction of "dinosaur brand" on Miller High Life and a number of other well-known but fading products; wrote the editor, "Like the brontosaurus and triceratops of old, these brands have failed the Darwinian selection process, and have probably matured beyond the point where they can ever grow or change again with the times." Of Miller High Life, Matthew Grimm provided one further elucidation of the central problem: "Company marketers seem busier launching other brands—super-premium Miller Reserve, Miller Genuine Draft Light and Miller Lite Ultra—than tending to the flagship. High Life's demise was not pre-ordained. Anheuser-Busch, for example, spawned an equal number of share-building extensions. Yet its flagship, Budweiser, remains No. 1 in the country. Venerable High Life is like a parent of ungrateful children, fading fast on its way to the poorhouse."

The Miller Children

Miller Genuine Draft, brewed through a cold-filtered process developed by Japan's Sapporo Breweries, was introduced in 1985 and rolled out nationally in 1986. Since that time, it has earned a reputation as the fastest-growing premium beer in the nation. In the words of Patricia Sellers in *Fortune,* Genuine Draft is "the industry's most successful new product since Bud Light came out in 1981"; by the end of 1992 it ranked as the sixth best-selling domestic beer. Its appeal is primarily to "young, upscale drinkers," a segment that the "Tastes Great" Lite ads had seemed to unconsciously eschew and the High Life ads appeared to lose during the 1980s.

The introductions of Genuine Draft and its cohorts (Miller Reserve and Reserve Light in 1990, and Lite Ultra and Genuine Draft Light in 1991) have proven prescient moves, for in 1991 Miller Lite reported its first sales decline ever. Since then, several analysts have been speculating that Lite's reign as the number two beer may be near an end. Both Bud Light and Coors Light have been mentioned as possible replacements.

Advertising Shuffles

In Lite's favor, however, are concurrent predictions that the low-calorie beer segment will constitute 50 percent of the market by the year 2000. With present control of around 40 percent of the low-cal premium market, Lite can ill afford to follow in the footsteps of High Life. Consequently, Miller Brewing continues to treat it as the company's flagship brand, paying special attention to updating its advertising. In 1991 Miller retired the "Tastes Great" campaign and the Backer agency—which now manages the growing Genuine Draft account—in favor of Leo Burnett. Burnett's "It's it. And that's that" TV spots—allegedly designed as an assault on Budweiser by establishing Lite as *the* beer to drink, light or otherwise—were largely unsuccessful, though. The campaign has since evolved into a number of sketches, one featuring dancing aliens, with the Chris Kenner lyrics "C'mon, let me show you where it's at" as a nostalgic musical backdrop.

Burnett's possession of the valuable Lite account, estimated at $100 million, is considered tenuous by many. In December of 1992 the agency lost the High Life account, estimated at just $5 million, to Young & Rubicam, adding yet another creative contender to the ongoing fight for Miller's most lucrative accounts. As the decade unfolds, a shuffling of creative talent is certain to continue.

"Clear" Future?

In early 1993 Miller Brewing began test-marketing Miller Clear in four major metropolitan regions. Clear, which arrived on the heels of another colorless beverage introduction, that of Crystal Pepsi, was preceded in the beer industry by Zima Clear Malt, launched in 1992 by the Coors Brewing Company. The fate of the product is anything but certain, unless the first Clear commercial, produced by Cliff Freeman and Partners, has anything to say about the brand's success. According to Laura Bird in *Adweek's Marketing Week,* "With cartoonish sound effects and a cast of caricatures, the spot recalls the popular ad campaigns of decades past, such as Federal Express's 'fast talker' and Wendy's 'Where's the Beef,' starring people who were more laughable than enviable." The spot concludes after "the white-coats pull a paper bag off the new product, and the suits go bug-eyed when they get the crystal-clear view; one double-chinned marketer's hair instantly turns a fearful white." While the success of Miller Clear remains to be seen, it seems certain that the Miller name, in one form or another, will endure.

Further Reading:

Aaker, David A., *Managing Brand Equity: Capitalizing on the Value of a Brand Name,* New York: The Free Press, 1991.

"Acquisitions: A Deal Between Grandchildren," *Time,* September 30, 1966, p. 108.

"America's Nightmare," *Beverage World,* December 1992, p. 16.

"Anheuser's Plan to Flatten Miller's Head," *Business Week,* April 21, 1980, pp. 171, 174.

Bird, Laura, "Miller Ads Address Teen Drinking," *Adweek's Marketing Week,* March 25, 1991, p. 5.

Fahey, Alison, "This Is War," *Brandweek,* July 13, 1992, pp. 24-29, 32.

Fahey, and Jim Kirk, "As A-B and Coors Spar, Miller's Set to Make Beer War Frothier," *Brandweek,* November 23, 1992, p. 8.

Fahey, "Beer Markets Feel the Cold Draft of 1992," *Brandweek,* January 11, 1993, p. 9.

Flanagan, William, "The Charge of the Lite Brigade," *Esquire,* July 18, 1978, pp. 73-76, 78, 81-83.

Garfield, Bob, "Party Aliens See the Lite, Even if Miller Doesn't," *Advertising Age,* June 22, 1992, p. 39.

Gershman, Michael, "Lite Beer: Athletic Supporters," *Getting It Right the Second Time,* Addison-Wesley, 1990, pp. 63-68.

Goldman, Kevin, "Y & R Appears to Be Sneaking up on Leo Burnett's Millers Account," *Wall Street Journal,* December 9, 1992, p. B10.

Goldman, "New Miller Lite Spots," *Wall Street Journal,* January 15, 1993, p. B5.

Grimm, Matthew, "Introducing Miller Daft," *Adweek's Marketing Week,* March 20, 1989, p. 4.

Grimm, "Dinosaur Brands: Miller High Life," *Adweek's Marketing Week,* June 17, 1991, p. 19.

Heller, Matthew, "Draft, Or Daft?," *Forbes,* June 30, 1986, pp. 112-13.

"High Life Execs Quit at Miller," *Advertising Age,* July 23, 1984, pp. 1, 86.

"Hitting the Right Spot in *Lite Reading* Promo," *Publishers Weekly,* November 25, 1983, p. 44.

"How Miller Won a Market Slot for Lite Beer," *Business Week,* October 13, 1975, pp. 116, 118.

Hume, Scott, "Miller under Pressure," *Advertising Age,* January 18, 1988, pp. 3, 93.

Hume, "What MacDonough Will Bring to Miller from A-B," *Advertising Age,* September 28, 1992, pp. 3, 52.

Jabbonsky, Larry, "Wall St.: Happy Brew Year?," *Beverage World,* February 1993, pp. 32-35.

Kennedy, Tony, "Nothing Wrong with This Pitcher: It's Simply Filled with Miller Clear," *Star Tribune,* March 31, 1993, p. 1D.

Kirk, Jim, "Clear Beer for Miller," *Adweek* (Midwest Edition), January 18, 1993, pp. 1, 6.

Landler, Mark, and Julia Flynn, "Three Shops with Plenty to Sweat About," *Business Week,* July 20, 1992, pp. 74-75.

Lazarus, George, "The Lite Years: How Miller's Move Started It All," *Adweek's Marketing Week,* August 15, 1988, p. 9.

Levin, Gary, "Big Ads Back on Super Bowl," *Advertising Age,* January 18, 1993, pp. 1, 52.

"The Light Beer Game," *Forbes,* January 15, 1976, pp. 30-31.

Maier, Frank, "The Battle of the Beers," *Newsweek,* March 9, 1981, pp. 68-69.

"Make Way for Miller," *Forbes,* May 15, 1976, pp. 45-47.

Merwin, John, "A Billion in Blunders: Hubris," *Forbes,* December 1, 1986, p. 104.

"Milestones: Frederick C. Miller, 48," *Time,* December 27, 1954, p. 59.

"Miller Time, Part II," *Fortune,* December 10, 1984, p. 10.

Morgan, Hal, *Symbols of America,* New York: Penguin, 1986.

Philip Morris Companies Inc. Annual Report 1991 and *Philip Morris Companies Inc. Third Quarter Report 1992,* New York: Philip Morris Companies, Inc.

Prince, Greg, "Budweiser Still King, But Genuine Draft Shuffling Deck from the Bottom," *Beverage World,* March 1991, p. 28.

Prince, and Eric Sfiligoj, "Miller and Molson Likely to Lend Each Other a Helping Hand," *Beverage World,* February 28, 1993, p. 3.

Sellers, Patricia, "Busch Fights to Have It All," *Fortune,* January 15, 1990, pp. 81, 84, 88.

Shapiro, Eben, "Philip Morris's Miller Brewing Unit Is Buying 20% of Canada's Molson," *Wall Street Journal,* January 15, 1993, p. A3.

Teinowitz, Ira, "Miller Calls Out Barley Reserve," *Advertising Age,* May 14, 1990, pp. 3, 66.

Teinowitz, "Big Brewers Join Ranks of Clear-Minded," *Advertising Age,* January 25, 1993, p. 42.

"Turmoil among the Brewers: Miller's Fast Growth Upsets the Industry," *Business Week,* November 8, 1976, pp. 58-62, 67.

"Worth Fighting Over," *Forbes,* December 15, 1969, pp. 20-21.

—Jay P. Pederson

MINUTE MAID®

Minute Maid

Minute Maid brand of orange juice is the category brand leader in the United States with a well-differentiated line of frozen concentrate and chilled varieties. Minute Maid has been offering consumers the convenience and quality of its frozen concentrated orange juice since 1946. The Minute Maid brand umbrella has since grown to include other fruit juices, punches, and -ades, as well as the Minute Maid brand orange soda, which contains 8 percent Minute Maid orange juice. Although Minute Maid has at times struggled to maintain a market share leadership position against its orange juice competitors, it has continually demonstrated its ability to pull ahead. In addition to prevailing against the competition, the brand has survived a series of corporate changes. The latest change merged the Minute Maid Corporation with the Coca-Cola Company in 1960, which ultimately placed the management of the Minute Maid brand within the Coca-Cola Foods Division. Coca-Cola Foods leads the competition in marketing fruit juices and drinks domestically with Minute Maid orange juice as its core product. Other brands marketed by Coca-Cola Foods include Hi-C, Five Alive, Bright and Early, and Bacardi tropical fruit mixers.

Brand Origins & Early Marketing

Minute Maid was the first orange juice brand developed as a frozen concentrate. In 1946 John M. Fox, the brand founder, initially marketed the concentrate through door-to-door salesmen in Massachusetts. Fox founded Florida Foods, Inc., in 1945. Within a year, the company name was changed to the Vacuum Foods Corporation. Vacuum Foods was affiliated with the National Research Corporation which had developed a high-vacuum evaporation process that eliminated 80 percent of the water to reduce orange juice to a concentrate while retaining the full flavor. Ultimately, the concentrate was frozen and successfully marketed as a convenient product available year round. Minute Maid frozen concentrate achieved a strong grocery store presence, and by the early eighties, had become the biggest seller in the frozen food aisle.

Early marketing stressed the superior taste of Minute Maid's frozen concentrate as opposed to canned orange juice, as well as its convenience compared to squeezing fresh oranges. Minute Maid's name had been created to focus customers' attention on how quickly the product could be transformed into orange juice.

Early advertising emphasized Minute Maid's time savings, claiming the product saved a full five minutes in preparation time.

The 1948 launch of the Bing Crosby radio campaign boosted early sales dramatically. During his daily radio show, Crosby personally endorsed the brand, leading consumers to believe that Minute Maid was his orange juice of choice. Some also mistakenly believed that he owned the company. Given Crosby's immense popularity at the time, the impact on sales was tremendous.

Innovative Packaging

Minute Maid instituted a major packaging change in order to more effectively combat competitors' products that had imitated Minute Maid's original white, orange, and green color scheme. In order to differentiate Minute Maid and catch consumers' attention, a label with a black background was adopted in 1964. At the time it was extremely uncommon to associate the color black with food products, since Western culture has often ascribed negative connotations to the color. Minute Maid, however, associated the color black with class and quality. The new product package enabled the Minute Maid brand to strongly contrast with competitors' packaging and to protect its valuable customer loyalty.

Notable Advertising

Minute Maid's advertising has made an effort to associate the quality of the product with the promotional vehicle. Bing Crosby's radio advertising in the late 1940s and early 1950s, and his prime time television spots from 1968 through 1977, were a successful effort to associate Minute Maid with one of the era's most popular celebrities. Another notable promotional tool was Minute Maid's long-term association with the New Year's Day Tournament of Roses Parade—a wide-reaching, televised event to which Minute Maid has entered floats or provided sponsorship over the years.

Minute Maid has been associated with the United States Olympic Team since 1978. For Minute Maid, the Olympics tie-in symbolizes the best in America. The marketing program for the 1992 Olympics began in October of 1990 with a two-year, $120 million marketing program, designed to raise $10 million of support for the U.S. Olympic teams and to guarantee at least $1.5 million worth of contributions to the U.S. Olympic Hopeful Training Fund. Minute Maid marketed the tie-in with television commercials, a sweepstakes for Olympic trips and tickets, comparative packaging, as well as coupons and displays.

Product Development

Minute Maid's long-term product development emphasis has been on enhancing the quality of the product by retaining the full orange flavor in the production process and through packaging efforts to prevent the flavor from being altered due to oxygen penetration. As the orange juice market has matured however, the product has become less of a commodity and the market has responded to increasing differentiation. This product evolution process has demanded Minute Maid's constant attention to maintaining its market share leadership.

In July of 1987, Minute Maid launched its calcium fortified orange juice nationally. Unfortunately, Minute Maid was not the only entrant to this market. Citrus Hill, the most recent national competitor, had entered the market a month earlier with a strong promotional budget. Minute Maid introduced the product in response to the national concern over the calcium intake of women and children that had spurred a calcium-added product trend. Minute Maid's new product was ounce for ounce equivalent to milk in calcium content and was priced the same as its regular juice varieties. The promotional pitch highlighted the product's increased nutritional value rather than the specific medical study health claims utilized by Citrus Hill. Minute Maid's introductory advertising was pitched to the entire family with the generally appealing campaign of "Minute Maid—now orange juice is even more nutritious."

In 1988 Minute Maid found itself responding to another marketing trend. Since 1986, sales of ready-to-serve chilled juices had out-paced the sales of frozen concentrate due to a continuing consumer trend toward more convenient products. Minute Maid ready-to-serve varieties were all from concentrate which meant that the orange juice's water content was removed and added back later. Tropicana, the industry's number two competitor, had seen its Pure Premium product clobber other chilled orange juice competitors. Pure Premium differed from the other products because it was not produced from concentrate. The orange juice was the result of squeezing and pasteurizing. Minute Maid found itself losing chilled juice market share to its competitor mainly because of Tropicana's not-from-concentrate entry. In May of 1988, Min-

ute Maid introduced Premium Choice with the brand's largest product introductory advertising campaign ever in order to strengthen its share of the chilled orange juice market. The introductory theme was "Minute Maid—the gourmet O.J." Like Pure Premium, Minute Maid Premium Choice is made from 100 percent Florida oranges, which are squeezed and the juice then pasteurized.

In 1989, Minute Maid regained the product introduction lead with the first "pulp-free" orange juice introduced in the United States. The product was first introduced in Canada, through Cola-Cola Foods, where it had achieved a 5 percent share of the entire orange juice market in two years. The product was the result of research that had indicated children tend to dislike pulp, and families tend to buy what satisfies children.

Advertising Woes

In 1982, Coca-Cola Foods won a case against Tropicana for an advertisement for its Pure Premium juice. The commercial depicted oranges being squeezed directly into the carton. The ruling prohibited marketers from describing orange juice as "juice as it comes from the orange" when it is in fact pasteurized and processed.

In 1988, Tropicana sued Coca-Cola to force the company to stop making similar claims about its Minute Maid Premium Choice orange juice. The slogan used to describe the Minute Maid product on the carton as well as in some advertising stated the juice was "100 percent pure Florida orange juice straight from the orange." Ultimately, Coca-Cola removed the advertising rather than contest the law suit.

The Citrus Hill Fresh Choice entry found itself the subject of an FDA clamp-down on its package labeling in 1991. The FDA objected to the use of terms such as "fresh" and "pure" when its chilled product was made from concentrate. The FDA action helped to ensure that not-from-concentrate entries such as Minute Maid Premium Choice could continue to differentiate their products effectively.

The Competition

In 1992 Minute Maid shared the market with two other national brands; Tropicana, acquired by the Seagram Company in 1988, and Citrus Hill, introduced by Procter & Gamble in 1981. In addition to the two national branded competitors, Minute Maid competes with a multitude of private labels (mostly supermarket branded products) which compete almost exclusively on price.

Although as of April 1992, Minute Maid led in the overall orange juice category, Tropicana led in the chilled orange juice segment with 29.1 percent of the market compared with Minute Maid's 20.5 percent. Tropicana has long differentiated its product by marketing a not-from-concentrate squeezed pasteurized juice and commanding a price premium. Because of the faster spoilage of pasteurized juices, Tropicana could not nationally market its products until the late 1980s when packaging technology further increased shelf life. Citrus Hill was the most recent category entrant. Procter & Gamble hoped the brand would gain a significant market share in the lucrative $3 billion orange juice market through extensive advertising efforts and differentiated products. The brand, however, experienced a relatively short life, and Procter & Gamble uncharacteristically announced in September of 1992 that it was discontinuing the brand. In the months prior to the announcement, Citrus Hill had incurred a 16 percent decline in its frozen share and a 13 percent decline in its chilled share compared to prior year sales.

Performance

The first year of recorded sales of Minute Maid juices in 1946 amounted to $374.5 thousand, and by 1951, they had grown to $29.5 million—a tremendous five-year increase. Continuing efforts to build Minute Maid's market share through increased brand awareness and product development has continued to spur rapid growth. For the 52 week period ending April 17, 1992, Minute Maid held 26.2 percent of the frozen orange juice segment and 20.5 percent of the chilled segment. According to the October 5th issue of *Advertising Age,* Minute Maid exceeded $500 million in sales for the year ending July 11, 1992.

In the 1991 calendar year, 47.5 percent of the Coca-Cola Foods division's juice volume was Minute Maid orange juice, amounting to 271 million gallons of the 1.1 billion gallon orange juice market. 1991 marked a 16.8 percent increase in orange juice volume for Coca-Cola Foods. In the chilled segment, in which Coca-Cola Foods had been intensely competing with Tropicana for market share, Minute Maid Premium Choice contributed a 38 percent volume gain.

Market Trends

Of the available fruit juice flavors, orange is by far the favorite in the United States. In 1991 orange was more than triple the volume of the next favorite flavor—apple. In 1991 the growth rate of the fruit beverage industry was greater than any other beverage category. Michael Bellas, president of Beverage Marketing, explained this phenomenon in *Beverage World:* "Consumers' continued concern for healthy, nutritional beverages and all-natural products has further spurred the [fruit beverage] industry's growth." Although the orange juice market is mature, Minute Maid will likely benefit from further increases in health-conscious consumer spending.

However, fruit drinks, as opposed to fruit juices, have obtained the lion's share of the fruit beverage category growth so far. Fruit drinks are being chosen by consumers due to their wider array of flavors at more stable prices. Minute Maid orange juice prices were highly susceptible to the Florida citrus crop freezes of the 1980s, particularly its Premium Choice product which is marketed as being made from 100 percent Florida oranges. The brand's most competitive market entry in terms of pricing is its frozen concentrate. For this product Minute Maid supplements its Florida crop with orange suppliers from around the world, thus allowing for more leverage in pricing.

Future Opportunities

The Coca-Cola Company has been actively narrowing its interests in recent years by selling off several diverse beverage holdings as well as other lines of businesses not linked to its core soft-drink business. In 1991 Anthony Ramirez reported in the *New York Times:* "Only a slightly profitable food subsidiary, the maker of Minute Maid orange juice, is left of what once was a range of diversified interests, and analysts are clamoring for Coke to sell that vestige." In 1991 the Coca-Cola Foods division, of which Minute Maid is a large part, contributed 14 percent to total Coca-Cola Company operating revenues, and only 4 percent to operating income. For a time, Coca-Cola displayed some reluctance to invest in Minute Maid's future. However, according to a Coca-Cola Foods spokesperson, as the 1990s progress, both food analysts and Coca-Cola corporate management have adopted a highly favorable outlook for Minute Maid, and Coca-Cola has indicated that it has no intention of divesting this brand.

The international market remains an area of vast possibility for Minute Maid. While the brand already enjoys a global presence through distribution at worldwide McDonald's locations, the retail market in Europe provides a fertile market opportunity. By the year 2000, the European orange juice market is expected to reach one billion gallons, and analysts have noted strong opportunities for quality products such as Minute Maid Premium Choice and Tropicana Pure Premium.

Wherever Minute Maid's future opportunities will lead, whether through expanded product lines or distribution, its long heritage of experience as a top consumer brand will provide the basis for continuing strength and evolution.

Further Reading:

"Ad Notes," *Wall Street Journal,* October 18, 1990, p. B6.

"Ad Spending of '100' Edges Upward," *Advertising Age,* September 28, 1988, p. 4.

Arble, Meade, "Big-3 Orange Juice Firms Eyeing Europe for Growth; Tropicana, Minute Maid and Citrus Hill," *Supermarket News,* June 1, 1992, p. 44.

"The Beverage Market Index for 1992," *Beverage World,* May 1992, p. 30.

"The Big Squeeze," *Fortune,* May 23, 1988, p. 12.

"Brand Scorecard," *Advertising Age,* October 5, 1992, p. 16.

Buchan, James, "Marketing and Advertising; Putting the Squeeze on the Juice Sector," *Financial Times,* February 23, 1989, p. 28.

Burros, Marion and Denise Webb, "Eating Well," *New York Times,* August 5, 1992, p. C4.

"The Coca-Cola Company Annual Report," Atlanta: The Coca-Cola Company, 1991.

"Coca-Cola Launches New Juice Aimed at Tropicana," *Reuter Business Report,* May 19, 1988.

"Coca-Cola Sued Over Its Claim of 'Pure' Juice," *Los Angeles Times,* July 6, 1988, sec. 4, p. 2.

Dagnoli, Judann, and Jennifer Lawrence, "P&G Squeezed," *Advertising Age,* January 30, 1989, p. 6.

Fahey, Alison, "Beverages," *Ad Week Supplement,* October 12, 1992, p. 56.

Fahey, Alison, and Jennifer Lawrence, "The People Behind Today's Marketing Success," *Advertising Age,* July 6, 1992, p. S-10.

"FDA Puts Squeeze on P&G Over Citrus Hill Labeling," *Wall Street Journal,* April 25, 1991, p. B1.

Freeman, Laurie, and Jennifer Lawrence, "Brand Building Gets New Life," *Advertising Age,* September 4, 1989, p. 3.

Garfield, Bob, "Minute Maid Serves Its Juice Family-Style," *Advertising Age,* May 15, 1989, p. 74.

Jabbonsky, Larry, "The Answer Man," *Beverage World,* March 1992, p. 25.

Lawrence, Jennifer, articles in *Advertising Age:* "Minute Maid Pours $50M into New Blitz," May 15, 1989, p. 3; "Minute Maid Adds Pulpless O.J.," September 25, 1989, p. 44; "Coca-Cola to Shake Tropicana," May 23, 1988, p. 3; "Big Squeeze; Minute Maid Adds Calcium," July 27, 1987, p. 3; "Minute Maid Teams with '92 Games," July 23, 1990.

Lawrence, Jennifer, and Judann Dagnoli, "Minute Maid Claims O.J. Lead," *Advertising Age,* March 26, 1990, p. 12.

Lazarus, George, "Competitors Eye Citrus Hill Stake," *Chicago Tribune,* October 19, 1992, p. C4.

Lipton, Amy, ''Consumer Expenditures Study; Refrigerated Foods,'' *Supermarket Business,* September 1988, p. 182.

''Message Clear for 1987 Advertising,'' *PR Newswire,* February 26, 1987.

''Minute Maid Goes for the Gold with Olympic Tie-in and Bush PSA,'' *Beverage World Periscope Edition,* November 30, 1990, p. 7.

''Minute Maid Says Abundant Orange Juice Supply Should Be Viewed As an Opportunity to Increase Consumption,'' *Business Wire,* October 8, 1992.

Munkelt, Albert G., ''The Heritage of the Minute Maid Brand,'' Coca-Cola Foods, 1984.

PR Newswire, Coca-Cola Foods, May 19, 1988.

Ramirez, Anthony, ''It's Only Soft Drinks at Coca-Cola,'' *New York Times,* May 21, 1990, p. D1.

Rothenberg, Randall, ''The Media Business; Tropicana Suit Challenges Ads for Minute Maid Juice,'' *New York Times,* July 6, 1988, p. D16.

Schiller, Zachary and Gail DeGeorge, ''What's For Breakfast? Juice Wars,'' *Business Week,* October 5, 1987, p. 110.

Sfiligoj, Eric, articles in *Beverage World:* ''Healthy Growth,'' May 1992, p. 48; ''The Beverage Market Index for 1992,'' May 1992, p. 30.

Stacy, John D., ''The Future of Fruit Drinks,'' *Beverage World,* August 1987, p. 26.

Sugarman, Carole, ''Orange Juice in a Squeeze,'' *Washington Post,* January 23, 1991, p. E1.

''A Tough Battle in Orange Juice,'' *New York Times,* March 14, 1988, p. D11.

Winston, Arthur, ''Damages Vis-a-Vis Direct Marketing,'' *DM News,* January 15, 1990, p. 22.

—Louise L. Groden

MIRACLE WHIP®

Miracle Whip

Miracle Whip, with its "tangy zip" flavor, is by far the best-selling spoonable salad dressing in the United States. Introduced as a less expensive alternative to mayonnaise in the 1930s, Miracle Whip, with its distinctive flavor—the result of a secret mixture of spices—has garnered widespread popularity. Initially used mainly in such dishes as potato salad and macaroni salad, effective advertising promoted Miracle Whip as a spread for sandwiches as well. In addition, consumer concerns about health and nutrition prompted the brand's parent company, Kraft General Foods, Inc., to launch reduced-fat and non-fat versions of the dressing.

Brand Origins

The Kraft Cheese Company, founded in Chicago, introduced its first successful mayonnaise in 1927. Made from a base of vegetable oil, Kraft mayonnaise became a fierce competitor with the industry-leading Hellmann's mayonnaise, a brand rivalry that would continue throughout the century. Beginning in the late 1920s Kraft underwent numerous structural changes. In 1928 it merged with Phenix Cheese Corporation, headquartered in Chicago, to become Kraft-Phenix Cheese Corporation. Just two years later, in 1930, Kraft-Phenix was purchased by the National Dairy Products Corporation of New York. Daily operations, however, changed little from the purchase by NDPC, which acted mainly as a holding company. The Kraft-Phenix name, moreover, remained on the company's products.

In the 1930s both the Depression and changing dietary habits brought pressure for product innovation. The economic downturn left customers with less money to spend and, as a result, they began to demand low-cost alternatives to basic products. Partially for reasons of health, Americans were also beginning to eat more salads, on which cold mayonnaise and boiled dressing—a thick, creamy, sweet sauce often containing eggs, milk or cream, starch, and a variety of such spices as mustard, sugar, salt, and paprika—were common toppings. Capitalizing on both trends, in 1933 Kraft-Phenix created a new, lower-cost salad dressing called Miracle Whip. The product, similar in color and consistency to mayonnaise, was first introduced at a spectacular, optimistic setting—Chicago's Century of Progress World's Fair. At the company's booth, fairgoers were able to try Miracle Whip, but before long the rest of the country also learned of the new salad dressing.

Confident of the prospects of Miracle Whip salad dressing, Kraft-Phenix began a massive, national advertising campaign stressing, in print and on the radio, the product's high-quality ingredients, lower cost, and unique flavor. One advertisement, printed in a 1934 issue of *The American Weekly,* featured a picture of "famous Philadelphia hostess" Mrs. Benjamin Strawbridge with the caption, "I like it better than mayonnaise," and the added tag line, "Yet it costs less!" The advertisements were successful in spreading the word about Miracle Whip, and the public responded with apparent enthusiasm. Just a little more than two years after its introduction, Miracle Whip was the best-selling salad dressing in the United States.

Although similar in ingredients to mayonnaise, Miracle Whip was less expensive because it contained less oil. Starch, a thickener commonly used in boiled dressing, was added to provide a similar texture to mayonnaise. The lower cost of Miracle Whip did not make it an inferior product. High-quality ingredients were used for both Miracle Whip and Kraft mayonnaise, and many people actually preferred the sweeter, tangier taste of Miracle Whip. The spice formula of Miracle Whip, a highly guarded trade secret, has, in fact, produced one of the most distinctive and successful food products in the United States. No other spoonable salad dressing has been able to mimic the unique tast of Miracle Whip salad dressing.

Advertising

Throughout the 1930s Miracle Whip continued to be advertised as a high-quality product with a unique flavor, and quality was attributed to both the ingredients and the process. A 1937 advertisement claimed that "it contains far more of the costly ingredients that make the difference between fine and ordinary salad dressings. And these choice ingredients are blended more completely, whipped to velvet-smooth creaminess, in the exclusive Miracle Whip beater." As a measure of the product's success, the advertisement also boasted that Miracle Whip outsold "the next twenty leading salad dressings combined!" By 1939 the product was advertised as great for sandwiches as well.

During World War II, the renamed Kraft Cheese Company became a large supplier of food for the U.S. military, and its connection to the war effort was emphasized in its marketing for Miracle Whip. "Salads help build strong Americans!" led one 1942 advertisement illustrating a variety of fresh, shiny vegetables and fruits. Just above the illustration was a drawing of Uncle Sam

AT A GLANCE

Miracle Whip brand of salad dressing introduced in 1933 by Kraft-Phenix Cheese Corporation; Kraft-Phenix changed name to Kraft Cheese Company, 1940, then to Kraft Foods Company, 1945; National Dairy Products Corporation renamed Kraftco Corporation, 1969; Kraftco Corporation became Kraft Inc., 1976; Kraft Inc. purchased by Philip Morris Companies Inc., 1988; Kraft Inc. merged with General Foods Corporation, another Philip Morris subsidiary, to form Kraft General Foods Corporation, 1989.

Performance: *Market share*—90% (top share) of spoonable dressing category (*Advertising Age*, January 21, 1991, p. 55).

Major competitor: Hellmann's mayonnaise; Best Foods mayonnaise.

Advertising: *Agency*—J. Walter Thompson, Chicago, IL, 1991—. *Major campaign*—"Get cooking with Miracle Whip."

Addresses: *Parent company*—Kraft General Foods, Inc., Kraft Ct., Glenview, IL, 60025; phone: (708) 998-2000. *Ultimate parent company*—Philip Morris Companies, Inc., 120 Park Ave., New York, NY 10017; phone: (212) 880-5000.

standing arm-in-arm with an American father and son, and below it was the "U.S. Official Food Guide," which stressed the importance of eating "leafy greens, fruits and vegetables." Other wartime advertisements encouraged people to grow their own vegetables in "victory" gardens, because "in wartime, it's a patriotic duty to plan nutritious meals . . . Salads are Mighty Nutritious . . . With *Miracle Whip*, they are Mighty Good." To help alleviate problems resulting from wartime food rationing and shortages, the Kraft Kitchens, a division of the company established in 1924, developed new recipes for salads, dishes prepared from leftovers, and even an exceptionally popular Miracle Whip chocolate cake. In a 1944 Miracle Whip advertisement, Kraft apologized that its product was "being made only in limited amounts, because of government restrictions."

After the war the country experienced an economic boom, boosting the sales of Miracle Whip and other Kraft products. The company itself changed its name to Kraft Foods Company in 1945. Miracle Whip soon became the dominant salad dressing not only in the United States, but in Canada, as well. In addition, other foreign markets around the globe opened up to Miracle Whip. It was introduced in Venezuela and the Philippines in 1965, Australia in 1966, England in 1967, and Belgium in 1968.

Changes in American eating habits continued to affect the way Miracle Whip was both used and advertised. Growing nutritional concerns beginning in the 1960s led to the use of Miracle Whip as a base for vegetable dips, for example. Customers also began to use Miracle Whip more and more on sandwiches. Reflecting this trend, a 1983 advertisement featured an almost empty Miracle Whip jar turned upside down on a thick slice of white bread. The caption read, "A sandwich just isn't a sandwich without the tangy zip of Miracle Whip salad dressing from Kraft." Miracle Whip had become "The Bread Spread."

Brand Development and Outlook

Although Miracle Whip was initially developed with less oil in order to make it cheaper than mayonnaise, it had the side benefit of also having considerably less fat and fewer calories. However, as consumers became more conscious of health and nutrition concerns, new products were developed. In addition to the regular Miracle Whip salad dressing, Miracle Whip Light was introduced in 1984, and Miracle Whip Free, the first non-fat spoonable salad dressing, was launched in 1991.

Although Miracle Whip has dominated the spoonable salad dressing category, Kraft has not been complacent with its success. Kraft has firmly reacted to another food trend; with increasingly busy lives, customers were making fewer meals, including salads and sandwiches, the main uses of Miracle Whip. As a result, the company introduced a new advertising campaign, "Get cooking

An advertisement for Miracle Whip from the late 1930s.

with Miracle Whip," featuring recipes for interesting, quickly prepared dishes that required salad dressing. Recipes were advertised in *McCall's, Ladies' Home Journal,* and other magazines, as well as on the back of Miracle Whip jars. Customers were also offered a free recipe book.

Additional Miracle Whip products, or changes to the existing ones, were possible with advances in food processing or the development of new food ingredients. For example, according to an *Advertising Age* interview with Roger Deromedi, vice president of marketing for the grocery division of Kraft USA, the company has considered using Simplesse, a fat substitute produced by NutraSweet, in its Miracle Whip and mayonnaise brands. All product innovations, however, were likely to complement, not replace, Miracle Whip salad dressing's secret "tangy zip" flavor.

Further Reading:

"Fifty Years of Miracles," *Kraft Ink,* vol. 7, no. 2, 1983, pp. 15-17.

"Kraft Fat-Free Mayonnaise," *New York Times,* January 21, 1991, p. 33.

Liesse, Julie, "Kraft Mayo, Miracle Whip Shed Fat," *Advertising Age,* January 21, 1991, p. 55.

—*Thomas Riggs*

MOLSON®

MOLSON
Beer & Ale

Molson, established in 1786 near Montreal, is the oldest continuously operating brewery in North America. The brewery produces over 40 Molson brands, each targeted to a different consumer group, including Molson Golden, Molson Light, Molson Special Dry, Molson Export, Molson Canadian, Molson Excel, and Molson Canadian ICE. The brewery also produces other Canadian beers, including O'Keefe and OV. The ownership of the brewery is divided between The Molson Companies Limited (40%), Foster's Brewing Group (40%), and the Miller Brewing Company (20%).

In the United States, Molson is the most widely recognized brand of Canadian beer. Through mergers, acquisitions, cost-cutting measures, and innovative advertising, Molson Breweries has become the top-selling beer company in Canada and the largest beer exporter to the United States. Molson Golden, a full-bodied, smooth ale, is its flagship brand in the United States.

Brand Origins

Molson, the second-oldest company in Canada, has been in existence longer than the country itself. Its founder, John Molson, immigrated from Lincolnshire, England, to Montreal, Quebec, in 1782 at the age of 18. The British had defeated French troops for control of Quebec just two decades earlier, and when John Molson arrived, he found the area a North American center for French culture and tastes. As in France, wine was the most popular alcoholic beverage. The area had no operating breweries, and imported beer was quite expensive. British control, however, brought profound changes to the region. By the 1780s there was a growing number of settlers from Britain, as well as from the recently formed United States, where thousands of people loyal to the British crown were looking for a new home. These immigrants brought with them a thirst for inexpensive, high-quality beer.

Thomas Loyd, a former neighbor in Lincolnshire, helped the young Molson find a home when he first arrived. At the time Loyd was building a malting house and other brewing operations near the St. Lawrence River just downstream from the city's crumbling fortified walls. The location was ideal for providing a steady flow of brewing supplies. By the autumn of 1782 Loyd had sold 50 hogshead of ale, and in January 1783, convinced of the brewery's prospects, Molson decided to become a partner in the business.

Although it is not known with certainty why the partnership dissolved, in 1785 Molson acquired complete ownership over the business. Molson then had plans to expand the brewery, and in June 1785 he sailed back to England to settle his estate. There he bought new brewing equipment and, equally important, studied John Richardson's *Theoretic Hints on an Improved Practice of Brewing Malt-Liquors*. This book, published in 1777, was one of the first scientific treatises on brewing and helped Molson, a novice in beer production, to design his brewing practice. The treatise continued to be an important reference for generations of Molson brewmasters.

Molson returned to Montreal in 1786. With the help of his future wife, Sarah Insley Vaughan, he reopened the brewery on July 23, and by the end of the year the brewery had produced 80 hogshead of Molson's new ale. This output, equivalent to more than 4,300 gallons, would be enough to fill about 50,000 modern beer bottles.

Early Commercial Success

The Molson brewery was a success from the beginning. In 1787 he said, "My beer has been almost universally well liked beyond my most sanguine expectations." As the owner of Quebec's only brewery, Molson had no local competition, and Montreal, a burgeoning fur-trading town, seemed to hold promise of increasing sales. Molson's success, however, was not merely the result of good timing. He had created a high-quality product at a low cost. Molson did this in part by using locally grown barley and hops—along with water, the main ingredients in beer—which were both fresh and inexpensive. To farmers who agreed to grow his barley, he even provided the seeds without cost. Believing that sales would come from such care, Molson proclaimed, "An honest brew makes its own friends."

Brewing in the late 18th century was done without the convenience of modern machinery. Because beer had to be fermented at a cool temperature, refrigeration was a major challenge for Molson and other brewers of his time. The solution—controlled use of ice from the St. Lawrence River—limited his brewing season to the city's 20 weeks of winter temperatures.

Brand Development

Expanded brewing operations, advances in bottling and packaging, and the growth of Quebec's population brought rising sales for Molson beers. In 1796, just a decade after its founding, the

AT A GLANCE

Molson founded in 1786 near Montreal, Quebec, by English immigrant John Molson; in 1911 it became a joint share company called Molson's Brewery Ltd.; in 1973 brewing operations were renamed Molson Breweries of Canada Ltd., while the parent company became The Molson Companies Limited; as a result of joint venture agreements in 1989 and 1993, ownership of Molson Breweries divided between The Molson Companies Limited (40%), Foster's Brewing Group (40%), and the Miller Brewing Company (20%).

Performance: (all Molson brands): *Market share*—50% (top share) of beer category in Canada; 19% (second share) of imported beer category in the United States. *Sales*—C$1.18 billion (U.S.$950 million).

Major competitor: Labatt Breweries' brands of beer.

Advertising: *Agency*—Lintas, New York, NY. *Major campaign*—"Take Care," stressing beer consumption in moderation.

Addresses: *Parent companies*—The Molson Companies Limited, Scotia Plaza, 40 King St. W., Suite 3600, Toronto, Ontario, Canada M5H 3Z5; phone: (416) 360-1786; fax: (416) 360-4345. Foster's Brewing Group, Area 1, 1 Garden St., South Yarra, VIC 3141, Australia; phone: 011-613-828-2424; fax: 011-613-828-2556. Miller Brewing Company, 3939 West Highland Blvd., Milwaukee, WI, United States 53201-0428; phone: (414) 931-2454; fax: (414) 931-6312.

Molson brewery produced more than 40,000 gallons of beer, a figure that would reach some 750,000 by 1866.

The growing sales also came about through the company's introduction of new brands. Since 1786 the Molson brewery has produced scores of different ales and lagers under a variety of names. Among ales, for example, the brewery has produced XX Mild ale, Molson's "Extra" Mild ale, Molson's India Pale ale, Molson's Export ale, and Molson Stock ale. Molson's first lager, introduced in 1955, was sold under the brand name Crown and Anchor.

For much of the company's history, product innovations were introduced by the various members of the Molson family who ran the brewery. The first descendants of John Molson to enter the business were sons John Jr., William, and Thomas, who signed a partnership agreement with their father in 1816. After the elder John Molson retired in 1828, the brewery took on a number of different names reflecting the family members in charge. In the mid-19th century the brewery was called Thos. & Wm. Molson & Company, but when Thomas retired in 1861, it became John H. R. Molson & Bros., named after Thomas's son. When the brewery was reorganized as a joint share company in 1911, the company name was changed to Molson's Brewery Ltd.

20th-Century Expansion

In 1920, two years after the end of World War I, the production of Molson brands stood at about three million gallons, despite the fact that every Canadian province except Quebec had prohibition laws forbidding the consumption of beer. While some of Molson's competitors in other areas of Canada were forced to close down, Molson, located in Montreal, was able to continue to produce and sell beer. In 1930, when prohibition had been lifted in all provinces except Prince Edward Island, Molson's sales had shot up to

15 million gallons, and by 1949 the brewery had reached a production level of 25 million gallons.

Since 1950 the sale of Molson brands has been affected by the company's expansion of facilities, acquisitions of smaller breweries, joint ventures, and exports to foreign markets, especially the United States. Beginning with its second brewing plant, opened in Toronto in 1955, Molson eventually expanded brewing operations to every Canadian province. It bought its first smaller brewery, Sick's, in 1958 and soon afterward purchased two more. By the early 1960s production had jumped to more than 100 million gallons, and in 1971 Molson established Martlet Importing Company in Great Neck, New Jersey, to export its beer to the United States.

Molson embarked on a diversification program in the late 1960s that would eventually make it an international corporation. In 1968 it purchased Anthes Imperial Ltd., based in Ontario, which specialized in office supplies, construction equipment, and steel materials. Disappointed with the results, Molson sold most of its interest in Anthes within a short time of the purchase, but over the next two decades it either bought or entered into joint ventures with a number of other corporations. In 1972 it acquired Beaver Lumber, a large Canadian firm, and in the next few years it bought numerous other hardware and lumber operations, a network that was transformed into a chain of home improvement stores. Molson then entered the field of chemical products manufacturing with its purchase of two American companies—the Diversey Corporation, in 1978, and the BASF Wyandotte Corporation, in 1980. To reflect its new diversity, the parent company changed its name in 1973 to The Molson Companies Limited.

In 1989 Elders IXL, an Australian company that later became Foster's Brewing Group, merged its North American brewing operations with Molson. Elders IXL, the producer of one of the world's best-selling beers, Foster's lager, was also the owner of Canada's third-largest brewery, Carling O'Keefe Breweries of Canada Limited. The resulting joint venture company, equally owned by Elders IXL and The Molson Companies Limited, was called Molson Breweries. The additional brands from the Carling O'Keefe Breweries increased Molson's share of the Canadian beer market from 33 to 53 percent, making it the largest Canadian beer company. Labatt, the previous Canadian leader, was left with a 42 percent market share. In the United States the merger took the form of a separate corporation, Molson Breweries USA, which distributed many of the brands of the new joint venture.

Ownership of the brewery fragmented again in 1993, when the Miller Brewing Company bought 20 percent of Molson Breweries, leaving the Foster's Brewing Group and The Molson Companies Limited each with a 40 percent interest. Miller also bought 100 percent of Molson Breweries USA, giving the U.S. brewery exclusive rights to distribute Molson beer in the United States.

Molson Brands in the U.S.

By the early 1990s there was a wide range of Molson brands, although some were marketed to only limited areas in Canada. Of those with the Molson name, just six—Molson Golden, Molson Light, Molson Special Dry, Molson Export, Molson Canadian, and Molson Exel—were sold in the United States.

Molson's largest selling U.S. import, Molson Golden, is a clean, full-bodied ale. Marketed to young, active consumers, Molson Golden was in the early 1990s not only the top-selling Canadian beer in the United States but also the second-best-selling U.S. import, topped only by Heineken (Holland). Competing brands from Canada included Labatt's Blue and Moosehead. First brewed in the early 1950s and initially exported to the U.S. market in 1971, Molson Golden has played a central role in the brewery's attempt to expand its U.S. market share.

Molson Light, the second-best-selling imported light beer in the United States, has been advertised as a "crisp hearty, light beer with a hoppy aroma and a full body texture." Introduced in the U.S. market in 1978, its sales in the early 1990s were the fastest growing of any imported light beer.

Molson Special Dry has competed against such beers as Labatt's and Bud Dry. Advertised as being "smooth" and "clean" with "no lingering aftertaste," it was first brewed for the Canadian market in 1989 and began to be sold in the United States in 1990.

Although it has been the top-selling ale in Canada, Molson Export has had only limited success in the U.S market. Introduced in the United States in 1971, this amber-colored, "spicy" ale has been marketed as having a "fine hop aroma and flavor, hearty robust taste and notable ale yeast character." Molson Export was first brewed in 1903 but reformulated to make it lighter in the early 1950s.

Molson Canadian, a premium lager, has been the best-selling brand in Canada. Even so, like Molson Export, its sales have been small in the United States. Molson Canadian has a more distinct hop taste than, for example, Molson Golden and is advertised as "mainstream, crisp, clean, smooth." It entered the U.S. market in 1971.

Molson Excel, produced for the Canadian market in 1991, was the brewery's first nonalcoholic beer and quickly gained the top share of Canada's nonalcoholic beer market. Sales in the United States began in 1992.

Molson Breweries has also produced and exported to the United States a number of brands without the Molson name, including OV, O'Keefe, Calgary, Arctic Bay, and Cinci (sold only in the state of Michigan). Under special licensing agreements, it has been the distributor in Canada for a variety of U.S. brands, such as Miller Genuine Draft, Coors, and Coors Light.

Advertising and Public Relations

Despite John Molson's pronouncement that "An honest brew makes its own friends," the Molson brewery has not neglected marketing and advertising. Labels, first used in the 1840s, were an important part of the company's early marketing strategy. Initially printed in England, labels were glued to the bottles by hand until the early 20th century, when the brewery acquired a mechanical labeling system. Molson placed its first newspaper advertisements in Montreal in 1859.

In the early 20th century Molson also began to advertise with promotional items, including colorful playing cards and a series of calendars featuring the "wholesome girl next door." Both the cards and the calendars reminded customers that Molson was "the ale your great grandfather drank." In the 1920s and 1930s the brewery introduced a number of promotional timepieces for taverns, hotels, and restaurants, including a striking red and black neon clock.

Advertising has often focused on the Molson name rather than the individual brands. This has been done through newspaper, radio, and television advertisements and the sponsorship of special events and programs, such as concerts. The Montreal Canadiens hockey team, bought by Molson in 1957, has helped make Molson a household name among hockey fans. Other sporting events sponsored by Molson include minor league baseball, college football, pro-beach volleyball, tennis, skiing, golfing, bicycling, sailing, and motor racing.

Some Molson advertisements have highlighted Canada's vast wilderness areas and its clean, mountain rivers. Although Molson beer is brewed primarily in the country's large cities, such as Montreal and Toronto, a small percentage is produced in Canada's sparsely populated provinces. In the late 1980s a television campaign featuring scenic areas of Canada suggested that Molson was "a breeze going down."

The Molson name has also been connected to a number of humanitarian and environmental causes. Through the Molson Companies Donation Fund, a percentage of the parent company's profits has been given to charitable organizations such as the United Way. The brewery has also publicized its efforts to use returnable bottles and recyclable materials. In 1991 Molson began a multimillion dollar "Take Care" campaign in the United States, stressing moderation in alcohol consumption. This campaign marked the first time that a beer company discussed on television the problems associated with pregnant women drinking alcoholic beverages.

Brand Outlook

In the early 1990s, the future of the Molson brands was expected to increasingly depend on their success in the giant U.S. market. Molson Breweries USA had already made significant sales gains. In 1992, for example, when foreign beer brands overall lost market share in the United States, Molson increased its U.S. sales by more than 2 percent. With this gain, Molson had captured 19 percent of the U.S. imported beer market, up from about 10 percent in the late 1980s. With the expected fall of international trade barriers, Molson Breweries hoped to continue increasing its U.S. market share and to make the Molson name synonymous with Canadian beer.

Further Reading:

Banks, Brian, "Continental Draft: Molson Brews Up a Strategy to Export its Canadian Success to the Mighty US," *CA Magazine,* December 1991, pp. 28-31.

Belserene, Paul, *Cheers for 200 Years!: Molson Breweries 1786-1986,* Montreal: The Molson Companies Limited, 1986.

Came, Barry, "In Search of a Bigger Gulp: A New Brewing Giant Looks South," *Maclean's,* January 30, 1989, p. 36.

DeMont, John, "A Global Brew: Canada's Two Beer Giants Confront Flat Sales at Home and New Threats from Abroad," *Maclean's,* July 24, 1989, pp. 28-29.

Fucini, Joseph and Suzy, *Entrepreneurs,* Boston: Hall, 1985, p. 223.

Galvin, A., "Molson Gets New Packaging, Advertising, as Momentum Builds," *Beverage World Periscope Edition,* July 31, 1989, p. 3.

Harrison, Michael, "Brewing Beer Wars: The Challenges Grow for a Protected Industry," *Maclean's,* July 16, 1990, pp. 34-36.

Jackson, Michael, *The New World Guide to Beer,* Philadelphia: Running Press, 1988, pp. 198-201.

Maher, Tani, "Molson-Elders: A Case of Deja Vu," *Financial World,* March 7, 1989, p. 20.

Molson Breweries USA, Reston, Va.: Molson Breweries USA, n.d.

The Molson Companies 1992 Annual Report 206th Year, Montreal: The Molson Companies Limited, 1992.

''Molson Revives Canadian Wildlife Ads,'' *Modern Brewery Age,* May 6, 1991, p. 2.

Symonds, William C., ''There's More Than Beer in Molson's Mug,'' *Business Week,* February 10, 1992, pp. 108-109.

Yenne, Bill, *Beers of North America,* New York: Gallery Books, 1986, pp. 14-16, 124-137, 176-181.

Woods Jr., Shirley E., *The Molson Saga 1763-1983,* Toronto: Doubleday Canada Limited, 1983.

—Thomas Riggs

MORTON® SALT

Morton salt, produced by Morton International, Inc. in Chicago, is the leading producer of salt in North America, a leadership position that never has been seriously challenged. This success is unique because it is not rooted in the taste of the salt, which basically has remained the same throughout history, nor in the appearance of the actual salt; rather, Morton Salt's huge success originated in its unique packaging, its patented spout, and even more so, in the endearing "umbrella girl" logo that has graced Morton salt since 1914. Few products in this country bear an image or a symbol that is recognized from coast to coast. Creating the celebrated umbrella girl and catchy slogan, "When it rains, it pours," was part inspiration and part sheer good luck.

Brand Origins

Present-day Morton Salt can trace its origins to 1848. In that year Richmond & Company, a small firm marketing salt produced in Syracuse, New York, opened for business in Chicago. The Midwest was the "Wild West" in those days, untamed but developing rapidly, and salt could be shipped to the bustling region via the Erie Canal. Cumbersome and expensive as this was, from the moment the sales agency opened its doors in the "Windy City," it was doing a brisk business. Salt was not only indispensable in human consumption but in animal fodder as well, and with the exploding population of the region, it was a godsend for midwestern merchants to be able to place their salt orders with the Chicago firm.

Even better was the discovery of salt mines in nearby Saginaw, Michigan, in the 1850s. Although the Syracuse salt industry declined as a result, the Chicago sales agency flourished as it switched to marketing midwestern instead of eastern salt. By 1881, the enormously profitable business had changed hands several times. In that year a young store clerk, Joy Morton, bought his partner's share of the business. He renamed it the Joy Morton Company and directed it until his death in 1934.

Early Marketing Strategy

The secret of Joy Morton's success in the salt business was his sound business instinct. For several years after he had taken over the business he concentrated his energies on cutting the expense of transporting salt, a bulky commodity. Hence, from a marketer of salt, Joy Morton saw the wisdom of becoming a salt producer. He acquired salt producing sites that lay on rivers, so that the product

could be easily and cheaply transported, helping reduce the time it took to fill a customer's order.

So successful was Joy Morton in this strategy that by 1890 his business had expanded into a virtual salt empire, with his company controlling the manufacture and sale of salt from the beginning stage of processing to shipping the finished product. In those days it mattered little what salt looked like; there was no uniformity in packaging or appearance. Typically salt was shipped to store merchants in barrels, and the homemaker would scoop out of the barrel as much of the grainy, brinish-looking substance as she needed. On a damp, rainy day salt would cake, making it difficult to use and even less attractive to look at.

With the foundation of his business secure, and already the biggest salt merchant in the Midwest, Joy Morton turned his strategy to resolving the problem of his product's quality and appearance. His attempts were not always successful. Store merchants were unhappy with Morton's idea to "bag" salt in standard three-to-five-pound packages instead of an entire barrel. Nevertheless, Morton continued to experiment with better packaging, sensing that with the public's increasing awareness of hygiene, open barrels of food in stores would soon be unacceptable. By 1912, Morton's Table Salt in the familiar blue canister with its patented pouring spout appeared. Morton also sensed that by placing his own name on the label, the customer could trust that the salt was the best quality on the market.

By then a team of researchers working for the company had developed a purified salt that, for the first time in history, flowed freely in damp weather. The year was 1914. Joy Morton left it up to his son Sterling to devise an effective marketing strategy that would introduce the new table salt, purified, pouring freely, and sold in attractive blue canisters with a unique aluminum pouring spout.

First Commercial Success

By then, Joy Morton & Company had changed its name (in 1910) to the Morton Salt Company. The company had never advertised, let alone on a national scale. But times were changing. Ivory Soap was a nationally recognized product because of that company's advertising campaign featuring the catchy slogan "Ivory soap—it floats." So for the first time in Morton salt's history, the company turned to an advertising agency for a logo

AT A GLANCE

Morton brand of salt founded in 1848 by Richmond & Company, a small, midwestern salt sales company, in Chicago, IL; incorporated as the Morton Salt Company in 1910 by owners Joy Morton and son Sterling Morton; renamed Morton International, Inc. in 1965; company combined with Norwich company in 1969, to form Morton-Norwich Products, Inc.; in 1982 Morton-Norwich Products, Inc., merged with Thiokol Corporation to form Morton Thiokol, Inc.; Morton International, Inc., separated from Thiokol in 1989, once again becoming an independent company.

Performance: *Market share*—More than 50% of salt category. *Sales*—$466 million.

Major competitor: None.

Advertising: *Agency*—DDB Needham Advertising Worldwide, Chicago, IL. *Major campaign*—"When it rains, it pours," featuring little girl holding umbrella and open container of Morton Salt.

Addresses: *Parent company*—Morton International, Inc., 100 North Riverside Plaza, Chicago, IL 60606-1596; phone: (312) 807-2000.

that could be placed on the blue canisters and in an advertisement that would be placed in the leading national magazine for homemakers, *Good Housekeeping*. The ad agency submitted for Sterling Morton's scrutiny a dozen sample ads, and, if none pleased him, they had three other ads "in reserve."

Those first dozen did not appeal to Sterling Morton, but his attention was caught by one of the substitute ads. Being the father of a little daughter, he was struck by the drawing of a cute girl, holding an umbrella in pouring rain, with a canister of salt in her arm, tilted backward, spout open, with salt pouring freely out of the can. To him, that one picture said it all: salt pouring freely in rainy, damp weather, with the attractive new canister and spout prominently displayed as well. At a meeting it was decided that the image lacked a catchy slogan. Mention was made of the proverb, "It never rains but it pours," which Joy Morton rejected as too negative. In moments the proverb was restated, coming out as "When it rains, it pours." With the umbrella girl image and irresistible legend attached, the ad was launched for the next twelve months in *Good Housekeeping*. Its success was astounding. From a respectable salt maker, Morton Salt became the best-known salt in the United States, the only one that flowed freely in damp weather.

Advertising and Product Changes

Since 1914, when the umbrella girl first appeared on Morton Salt products, down to the present day, there have been no major advertising innovations. Rather, the image and slogan in time became deeply imbedded in the national consciousness, and its timelessness added to the appeal of the ad. The winsome umbrella girl with the upside down can of salt appears at present on all Morton Salt products, packaging, and company stationery, having undergone few alterations. The umbrella girl has been updated to conform to current fashion, but even these minor changes have occurred at long intervals: 1921, 1933, 1941, 1956, and, most recently, 1968.

In 1924 the Morton Salt Company began producing iodized table salt as a preventive against the then common disease of goiter. The product change boosted sales and contributed to the marketing of the product. In the late twentieth century the trace element iodine is contained in many foods that were less abundant in the twenties, and consequently Morton Salt produces both iodized and non-iodized table salt.

Even before Joy Morton bought out his partner's share in the Chicago salt company in 1881, salt came in more than one form: salt for human consumption and salt for animal fodder. Nowadays salt comes in a myriad of forms for thousands of uses, all of which Morton produces; in fact, Morton is still the world's leading producer and marketer of salt largely because of the company's ability to diversify its product lines. Even table salt is no longer "ordinary": there are, as examples, Morton Garlic Salt, Morton Nature's Seasons Seasoning Blend, even a "no salt" substitute and a low sodium "lite salt" seasoning.

The fastest selling salt product, water conditioning salt, is sold as Morton Pellets, Morton Super Pellets, and Morton System Saver Formula Pellets; agricultural salt contains trace-mineralized salt developed in the research labs of Morton International, Inc., in Woodstock, IL. Morton produces and markets salt for the essential food processing industry, as Morton Star Flake Dendritic salt and Morton Culinox 999 salt. In the 1950s came the highway boom and the demand in winter for highway salt. Currently there are five basic salt industries within the Salt Division of Morton International, Inc.: highway salt production, salt for food processing, "table salt," water conditioning salt, and agricultural salt. In addition to the Salt Division's five main product areas, salt has thousands of uses in a highly developed industrial economy: in medicines, in the manufacture of cars, soap, clothing and shoe apparel, and paper, to name a few. In recognition of its leadership status and global interests, the Morton Salt Company changed its name in 1965 to Morton International, Inc. Currently, Morton Salt constitutes a single division within Morton International.

Performance Appraisal

Throughout its history, Morton salt has been in the enviable position of having no national competitor on the North American continent. Although Morton salt is by no means the only brand of salt in the United States, no other salt producer dates back as far, nor does any other have a nationally identifiable ad image or logo. That being the case, sales of table salt and other salt products have been solid, although "unspectacular," according to Jordon Goodman in a 1992 *Money* magazine article. The fortunes of table salt in particular have been uneven. In recent years medical research proving a link between hypertension and salt intake led to a steady decline in table salt sales. However, the company's research and development into substitute and "lite" salt products in the eighties helped to reverse the decline in sales by the end of the decade. Meanwhile, other Morton Salt products, especially water conditioning pellets and highway salt, continually turn out high profits. In the early 1990s, despite a severe recession, salt manufacture and sales made up 20 percent of Morton International's business, and in 1991, the worst year of the recession, salt *sales* produced record returns. Salt *earnings* had increased 26 percent over the previous year, the worst year of economic slowdown. Much of this profitability stemmed from the high demand in ice-bound Canada for highway salt. According to Marc Reisch in *Chemical and Engineering News,* salt sales in 1991 resulted in Morton International's "highest return on sales."

International Growth

In 1954 the Morton Salt Company , as it still was called then, expanded outside of the boundaries of the United States for the first time. In that year Morton Salt acquired the Canadian Salt Company Ltd. in Windsor, Ontario, and the West India Chemicals, Inc. on the Bahamian island of Inagua. The Canadian subsidiary has since proved to be highly profitable, despite the fact that Morton table salt, called "Windsor Salt," lacks the appealing umbrella girl and catchy legend that in part explains the huge success of Morton table salt in the United States over the years. The purchase of a salt mine in the Magdalen Islands in Canada has enabled Morton Salt's Canadian subsidiary to maintain a leading position in that country; indeed, there is not a single major competitor of salt in Canada.

Over two million tons of solar evaporated salt are produced at the Morton salt subsidiary, West India Chemicals, in the Bahamas. The majority of this salt is exported to the eastern coast of the United States, where it is used in water softening.

Morton Salt's 26-ounce cans of table salt and its water softening pellets are major export items, particularly to Mexico (Morton Salt's most important foreign market), South America, the Caribbean basin, the Pacific Rim (Australia and New Zealand), and the Middle East.

Outlook

Morton salt's history is the best indicator of where the future may be taking it. Although the eventual end of the recession may see stronger or more numerous competitors, Morton Salt continues to lead the salt industry in the United States. This leadership position, which Morton Salt products have maintained for well over a century, will be hard to match, let alone overtake. Diversity in product uses has been the key to growth in sales for Morton Salt. In addition, should Mexico, Canada, and the United States ratify the North American Free Trade Agreement, sales of Morton Salt products to Mexico are expected to increase significantly. Due to these factors and abundant salt deposits, Morton salt's growth in coming years appears to be assured.

Further Reading:

Arnold, Oren, *What's in a Name? Famous Brand Names,* New York: Messner, 1979.

Campbell, Hannah, *Why Did They Name It . . . ?,* New York: Fleet Publ. Corp., 1964, pp. 42-47.

Eskew, Garnett L., *Salt, the Fifth Element: The True Story of a Basic American Industry,* Chicago: Ferguson & Assocs., 1948.

Fucini, J. J. and S. F., *Entrepreneurs: The Men and Women Behind Famous Brand Names and How They Made It,* Boston: Holt & Co., 1985.

Goodman, Jordan E., "Morton Is Worth More Than Its Salt," *Money,* January 1992, pp. 64-65.

Hambleton, Ronald, *The Branding of America,* Dublin, NY: Yankee Books, 1987.

Morton International Fact Book, Chicago: Morton International, Inc., 1991.

Morton International, Inc. 1991 Annual Report, Chicago: Morton International, Inc.

Salt, Today and Yesterday, Chicago: Morton Thiokol Inc.

Stiling, Marjorie, *Famous Brand Names, Emblems, Trademarks,* Newton Abbot, VT: David & Charles, 1980.

—Sina Dubovoj

MOUNTAIN DEW®

In an era that has been termed the "cola cool-down," Mountain Dew brand soft drink stands out among the competition as a particularly popular and uniquely appealing soft drink product. The citrus-flavored soda scored an estimated 4.3 percent market share in 1992 and ranks as the number six soft drink brand overall, directly behind Dr Pepper and ahead of Sprite and 7UP. Most importantly, according to *Beverage Industry*'s Annual Soft Drink Report, published in March of 1993, Mountain Dew demonstrated "the best statistical performance of any Top 10 brand," with increases in volume and market share of 7.2 and 5 percent, respectively. Mountain Dew has been managed since 1964 by Pepsi-Cola Company, the world's number two soft drink manufacturer. Until recently, Pepsi has allowed the Mountain Dew brand to grow steadily and comparatively unattended—at least, in relationship to flagship brands Pepsi and diet Pepsi—from its humble origins as a rural soda-pop, to a niche teen beverage, to its near superbrand soft drink status.

The low-key Mountain Dew marketing approach changed markedly in 1992, when Pepsi doubled its advertising spending for the brand to $20 million and launched high-profile campaigns for both Mountain Dew and Diet Mountain Dew. The trend continued in 1993, with an additional increase in spending of 44 percent. Driving this heightened emphasis on Mountain Dew are a number of factors, not least of which is brand Pepsi's five-year consecutive decline in market share. The primary reason, however, is the still skyrocketing appeal of the Mountain Dew name among teens and young adults and PepsiCo's realization that specially targeted brand promotion as well as line extension (e.g., caffeine-free versions of Mountain Dew and Diet Mountain Dew) might potentially propel the soft drink into the elite company of the industry leaders.

Brand Origins

Mountain Dew was launched by the Hartman Beverage Company in Knoxville, Tennessee, during the late 1940s. The original drink had a lemon-lime syrup base and a hillbilly brand image. In 1958 The Tip Corporation of America, a regional bottler of Pepsi, purchased Mountain Dew. The new owners retained the brand image but altered the soft drink recipe by adding orange flavoring and reducing the carbonation, thus achieving a unique, citrus taste. In September of 1964, Pepsi-Cola purchased The Tip Corporation and Mountain Dew, which had grown into a highly successful regional brand with the help of a modest television and radio campaign. Featuring the slogan, "It'll Tickle Yore Innards," the campaign revolved around an animated character named Willy the Hillbilly.

Pepsi executives decided to retain Willy as the brand spokesperson and proceeded to rapidly expand distribution, achieving production and sales through some 130 franchises by the end of the first year. According to the company's 1964 Annual Report, Mountain Dew's "sharply rising sales are becoming the excitement of the industry. In plant after plant, in only a few short weeks, with minimum effort, it soared with startling rapidity. Its popularity proved wide and immediate, even in larger urban markets." Within two years under Pepsi, Mountain Dew saw case sales rise from 9.4 million to 39.3 million and distribution extend to 92 percent of the United States. Although Willy would eventually be released from his duties, he took center stage in 1966 in the "Yahoo Mountain Dew" ads, among them a television commercial classic entitled "Beautiful Sal."

Mountain Dew entered the 1970s on the heels of another memorable campaign entitled "Get That Barefoot Feeling," but its prospects for rapid and sustained expansion already appeared cloudy. Following five years of flat sales for the brand, Pepsi began repositioning it in 1973 to appeal more strongly to active youth, a niche consumer group who were likely to adopt the high-energy soft drink (Mountain Dew contains approximately 50 percent more caffeine and 10 percent more sugar than most colas) if successfully targeted. "Hello Sunshine, Hello Mountain Dew" became the new theme for the reinvigorated brand in 1974, and sales over the next several years soared. By 1978, well over 100 million cases were being sold annually, and Mountain Dew had acquired "for its third year" a reputation "as the fastest growing major soft drink in the United States," according to Pepsi's 1978 Annual Report.

Successes and Failures

Four successive campaigns—"Reach for the Sun, Reach for Mountain Dew," "Give Me a Dew," "Dew It To It," and "Dew It Country Cool"—carried the brand through the 1980s, during which time Mountain Dew nearly doubled in volume and overtook Slice to become Pepsi-Cola Company's third-largest brand. Three beverage spinoffs highlighted the decade and signaled continually rising brand awareness and growth potential for Mountain Dew.

AT A GLANCE

Mountain Dew brand soft drink founded in the late 1940s in Knoxville, TN, by the Hartman Beverage Company ; The Tip Corporation of America purchased Mountain Dew brand, 1958; Tip Corporation acquired by Pepsi-Cola Company, 1964; Pepsi-Cola Company became subsidiary of PepsiCo, Inc., 1965.

Performance: *Market share*—4.3% (number six position) of soft drink category. *Sales*—$2.3 billion.

Major competitor: Coca-Cola Classic; also other brands of soft drinks, including diet Coke, Dr Pepper, Sprite, and 7UP.

Advertising: *Agency*—BBDO Worldwide, New York, NY, 1964—. *Major campaign*—"Get Vertical," featuring R&B guitarist Bo Diddley and a variety of high-intensity displays of athleticism by professional stuntmen.

Addresses: *Parent company*—Pepsi-Cola Company, 1 Pepsi Way, Somers, NY 10589-2201; phone: (914) 767-6000. *Ultimate parent company*—PepsiCo, Inc., Purchase, NY 10577; phone: (914) 253-2000.

During 1985, Diet Mountain Dew (at 24 calories per 12-ounce serving) was test-marketed successfully and then rolled out nationally three years later, since which time case sales have grown from 30 million to 52 million. Commenting on Diet Dew's introduction, the *Atlantic Constitution*'s Jeffry Scott wrote: "As baby-boom teens move into their 20s and 30s—and even middle-age—they've also begun switching to lower calorie and diet brands. To keep them in the fold and maintain its brand presence on the shelves, Mountain Dew needed a competitive diet version. Mountain Dew just now seems to be coming of age, and the timing of the new diet version probably couldn't be better."

Mountain Dew Red and Mountain Dew Sport, predictably perhaps, failed to follow in Diet Dew's footsteps. In 1988 Pepsi had plans to test market Red as a fun-image beverage with teenage appeal in what then appeared to be a ripe market: cherry soft drinks. Cherry Coke and Cherry 7UP had already garnered market share, and Pepsi wanted in. Mountain Dew Red, however, never got off the ground and neither, for that matter, did the cherry-flavored market (Cherry Coke and Cherry 7UP are still being sold, but their market shares have dwindled to 0.6 and 0.2, respectively).

Mountain Dew Sport, unveiled for test-marketing in 1989/1990, appeared a more promising extension, especially after being supported by a commercial starring multi-talented athlete Bo Jackson. An electrolyte beverage with Vitamin C, Sport was created to compete head-to-head with the long-reigning sports beverage champ, Gatorade. Despite Pepsi's marketing clout, Sport proved no match for the Quaker Oats-owned drink (which, as of early 1993, continued to control approximately 90 percent of its market category) and was quickly withdrawn.

Although not the determining factor in Sport's demise, the commercial, which pitted Jackson against an alligator in a number of athletic tests, was certainly no help according to Barbara Lippert. "The strategy was to 'jump start' the new brand by attaching it—and proving its superiority—to its better-known rival. But the jump start backfires. The name 'Mountain Dew Sport' is so unmemorable, and the live alligator is such an unforgettable visual device that the whole spot becomes one long, if

subtle, Gatorade reminder (the gator even walks past a Gatorade logo at one point)." With the recent introduction of All Sport, Pepsi has served notice that it intends to renew its fight with Gatorade while this time preserving the Mountain Dew and Diet Mountain Dew brands for focused promotion as "core four" products, along with Pepsi and diet Pepsi.

Vertical Future?

Considering that Coca-Cola's Mello Yello, with a distant 0.7 market share, is Mountain Dew's only major contender in flavor and that colas are likely waning in popularity, the future for the number six brand appears bright indeed. Thanks to a number of "high-octane" TV spots created by BBDO (the same agency that produced the flawed Jackson commercial), the brand experienced impressive growth in 1992. Diet Mountain Dew, tied for the first time in prime network advertising with its namesake, led the entire Pepsi line with an 18.4 percent increase in volume. The spots, entitled "Get Vertical" and "Do Diet Dew," debuted on the 1992 Grammy Awards presentation, a longtime venue for the flagship Pepsi brand. Three of the four minutes purchased by Pepsi were devoted to Mountain Dew as part of a concerted effort, in the words of marketing executive David Novak, "to catapult Mountain Dew to the big brand status it deserves."

According to Cara Appelbaum in *Adweek's Marketing Week*, "The numbers speak volumes. Cola sales took a dip last year for the first time in more than a decade. So it is little wonder that on this year's Grammy Awards, Pepsi-Cola Co. is plugging its Mountain Dew citrus soda over brand Pepsi." Since their debut, the spots (featuring the music of Bo Diddley and such death-defying sports as bungee jumping, cliff-kayaking, and boogie-board waterfall diving) have been continually updated and were prominently featured during a 14-minute media blitz of college basketball's 1993 "March Madness." According to a company press release, the recent Dew ads are targeted at "active 'twentysomething' men" because "Dew's image—its bravado and connection to exotic adventure—plays to their quest for newness and adventure."

The only negative news for the Mountain Dew brand is that diet soft drink sales decreased for the first time ever in 1992; however, Diet Dew seems not to have noticed. It remains, in the words of *Beverage Industry*'s Robert C. Levandoski, a "brand worth watching" and may well crack the top 10 in years to come. Pepsi also has reason for cautious optimism regarding two new rollouts, caffeine-free versions of Mountain Dew and Diet Mountain Dew. Two caffeine-free soft drinks, caffeine-free diet Coke and diet Pepsi, have edged into the top ten but have shown either declining or flat growth. Whether the market has soured on this subcategory or simply colas in general remains to be seen. What remains certain is that Mountain Dew and its health-conscious cousin have come into their own as prized brands in Pepsi's portfolio. As consumers continue to search for alternatives to colas, Dew and Diet Dew may well be expected to outpace the industry and soar to ever higher heights.

Further Reading:

Appelbaum, Cara, "As Cola Sales Dip, Pepsi Turns on Mountain Dew," *Adweek's Marketing Week,* February 24, 1992, p. 6.

De Lisser, Eleena, "PepsiCo Posts 11% Profit Rise Before Charges," *Wall Street Journal,* April 28, 1993, p. B5.

Grimm, Matthew, "Quaker's Gatorade, Coke and Pepsi Will Find, Is No Pushover," *Adweek's Marketing Week,* March 12, 1990, p. 4.

Lenius, Pat Natschke, "New Sports Drinks Heating Up Competition," *Supermarket News,* October 1, 1990, pp. 18, 20.

Levandoski, Robert C., "Are Colas Losing Their Market Clout?," *Beverage Industry Supplement,* March 1993, pp. 14-15.

Levandoski, " 'Beverage Business' Is Busy, Busy, Busy," *Beverage Industry Supplement,* March 1993, p. 22.

Levandoski, "Big Three Continue Hold in *Beverage Industry*'s Top 10," *Beverage Industry Supplement,* March 1993, pp. 8-9.

Levandoski, " 'Diet Decade' Spurs Industry to New Heights," *Beverage Industry Supplement,* March 1993, pp. 10-11.

Levandoski, "Franchise Companies Keep Sales Bubbling in Tough Times," *Beverage Industry Supplement,* March 1993, pp. 18-19.

Levandoski, "Modest 1.5% Growth Seen in 1992; Improvement Likely in '93," *Beverage Industry Supplement,* March 1993, pp. 4-7.

Lippert, Barbara, "Bo's a Sport, but Not for Mountain Dew," *Adweek's Marketing Week,* June 25, 1990, p. 77.

Mountain Dew Brand History and *Mountain Dew: Major Advertising Campaigns,* Somers, NY: PepsiCo, Inc., 1992.

Mountain Dew/Diet Dew Debut on Grammys; Mountain Dew Asserts Big Brand Status (press release dated February 18, 1992), Somers, NY: PepsiCo, Inc.

"NAD Upholds Mello Yello Ads," *Advertising Age,* October 16, 1989, p. 74.

PepsiCo, Inc. Annual Reports, Somers, NY: PepsiCo, Inc., 1964, 1965, 1978, 1989-91.

"Pepsi Unveils New Ads," *Wall Street Journal,* March 18, 1993, p. B7.

Scott, Jeffry, "Finally, Pepsi Pops Diet Mountain Dew," *Adweek's Marketing Week,* March 21, 1988, p. 57.

Willman, Michelle L., "New Sports Drink Challengers Step into the Ring with Champ," *Beverage Industry Supplement,* March 1993, pp. 42, 44-45.

Winters, Patricia, "Mountain Dew Gets Ready for Red," *Advertising Age,* April 4, 1988, p. 74.

Winters, "Mello Yello Slams Leader," *Advertising Age,* June 20, 1988, p. 4.

Winters, "Mountain Dew Sports New Rival to Gatorade," *Advertising Age,* October 9, 1989, p. 2.

—Jay P. Pederson

NABISCO® SHREDDED WHEAT

Nabisco Shredded Wheat, one of the oldest and best-known cereals in the United States, had barely finished its 1992 centennial celebration when Kraft General Foods acquired the brand for $45 million. The price tag reflected the value of a product that helped launch America's ready-to-eat cereal industry. More than a hundred years after its birth, Shredded Wheat still consisted of one simple ingredient—100 percent whole wheat—despite an increasingly complicated cereal industry marked by intense competition and worldwide brands. Competition between the six major players—Kellogg Co.; General Mills, Inc.; RJR Nabisco, Inc.; Quaker Oats Co.; Ralston Purina Co.; and the Post unit of Kraft General Foods, Inc.—compounded by pressures from private label cereals, was termed the "cereal wars" by the media during the 1990s. The Shredded Wheat product line, consisting of Original Nabisco Shredded Wheat, Spoon Size Shredded Wheat, Shredded Wheat 'N Bran, and Nabisco Frosted Wheat Squares, endured its share of casualties, losing 2.8 percent of its market share in 1991, even as overall cereal consumption continued to grow. Despite such erosion, Shredded Wheat's brand equity and no-frills, high-fiber appeal lent it the grit to reinforce Kraft's arsenal.

Brand Origins

Shredded Wheat was invented in 1892 by Henry Perky, a Denver lawyer and entrepreneur allegedly seeking a remedy for his chronic indigestion. He found that cooked whole wheat could be eaten as a soft, very digestible cereal. He developed a machine to press wheat into small shred-like strips and, with his brother, John, launched the Cereal Machine Company to manufacture small shredding machines for home use. Few consumers had tasted boiled, shredded wheat, and fewer had a use for the machines. The project stagnated, prompting Perky innovate further.

He discovered that baking his boiled, shredded strips turned them into easy-to-distribute, dry biscuits. In 1893 Perky set up shop above a Denver grocery store and peddled his product locally. The success of this business resulted in subsequent growth and relocation: he moved to Boston and established a plant on Ruggels Street; the following year he built another plant with 11 shredding machines in Roxbury, Massachusetts; and in 1895 he established a bakery in Worcester, Massachusetts, which was still unable to keep up with retail orders from around the country. In 1901 Perky moved to Niagara Falls, New York, where he opened a plant that would become a landmark and a showcase for the American food industry and established the Shredded Wheat Company. Called "The World's Finest Food Factory" and "The Palace of Light," the plant was air-conditioned and included a large auditorium for employee dances and assemblies. The 10-acre site spread from the factory to the Niagara River and was land-scaped with lawns, flower-bordered walks, playgrounds, and tennis courts that were open to both visitors and employees.

Production involved machines with thinly grooved wheels shredding water-softened red and white wheatberries into fine porous strands resembling thin spaghetti. As the shreds of wheat

from one shredder moved down a conveyer belt, they were covered with shreds from the other shredders, until the desired weight and thickness were achieved. The slogan "It's all in the shreds" referred to this process, and to the 14 layers of wheat to each Big Biscuit, and the 12 layers constituting the Spoon Size, Wheat 'N Bran, and Frosted Wheat Squares varieties. A cutting and slitting process then folded the filaments into little biscuits, which were baked in massive ovens (with an average length of 100 yards in the 1990 plants). Perky's Niagara Falls Shredded Wheat Company was acquired by Nabisco in 1928 and renamed the Natural Food Company. Change continued, as the company title became The National Biscuit Company in 1930 and Nabisco in the 1950s. Despite such change, the cereal remained very much the same, with continued production in Naperville, Illinois; Toronto, Ontario; and Niagara Falls, Ontario (the New York Niagara plant was retained by Nabisco after the Kraft deal to produce Triscuit snack crackers). The unchanged nature of Shredded Wheat characterized marketing efforts which, in the 1990s, increasingly capitalized on the back-to-basics absence of sugar, salt, or artificial flavors. "With Shredded Wheat," explained Patrick O'Mally, manager of the Naperville plant, "people can customize their own breakfast."

Early Marketing

The earliest and most integral marketing effort was Perky's 1901 establishment of the Niagara Falls plant, which served not only as a model production facility, but as a major promotional locus, drawing roughly 100,000 visitors each year and perpetuating the product's identity as "the original Niagara Falls cereal." As late as the 1950s, Shredded Wheat containers typically depicted the famous cataracts, skirted by the flag-turreted factory. In addition to attracting tourists, the falls, a natural wonder themselves, helped reinforce the cereal's image of natural healthfulness. Ads for the cereal included a 1905 trolley car advertisement which suggested, "Shredded Wheat Biscuit . . . with peaches and cream." A 1907 magazine advertisement promoted timelessness by depicting a sequence of female faces, from childhood to old age, each radiating the best humors of their stations, and the heading, "For Every Age in Every Season." The copy began, "The joy of childhood, the strength of girlhood, the support of motherhood, the comforting solace of old age." The hot cereal alternative was recommended in a 1927 ad, marked by a Norman Rockwell painting of a young woman holding a steaming bowl: "Two Shredded Wheat biscuits, heated in the oven, poured over with hot, rich milk. . . . "

Advertising Innovation

Despite its long-term appeal, the Shredded Wheat brand began to lose significant stakes in a ready-to-eat cereal market characterized by fierce competition. Market share steadily declined the late 1980s, from a 5.2 percent pound share in 1988 to 3.3 percent for the 1992 year ending October 5, according to Nielsen Marketing. Research analysts linked the decline to several factors. Breakfast Bears cereal, based on Nabisco's Teddy Grahams cookies, did not hold up well in milk. Additionally, Fruit Wheats, featuring fruit encased in wheat shreds, never caught on with consumers. Shredded Wheat With Oat Bran, introduced during the bran fad in 1988, faded with the fad by 1991. Lower sales were also attributed to lower ad spending. In 1989, the company spent $22 million on its cereals; that figure decreased to $8 million by 1992, according to an LNA/Arbitron Multi-Media Service report. Finally, RJR Nabisco was the target of the biggest leveraged buyout ever, won by Kohlberg Kravis Roberts & Co. in October 1988. Analysts linked the shakeup to additional strain on Nabisco's cereal line. In short, sales and brand support both declined in the late 1980s, prompting efforts at revival.

The first step to revival was increased spending in advertising and promotion. In July 1990 Nabisco broke a network TV campaign for Shredded Wheat, stressing the brand's history and continuity. The theme was that "Food fads come and go, but not Nabisco Shredded Wheat." A similar theme, and further spending, marked strategies for the cereal's centennial birthday. A network TV spot showed Dick Clark, the host of *American Bandstand*, celebrating the "birthday for a living legend," which he said "is not me, although you probably think I've been around forever." A consumer promotion stashed certificates worth $100 each in 10,000 boxes of cereal. Other incentives included full-page ads with 35-cent coupons, and a mail-in certificate for a free night at a bed and breakfast. Other appeals have capitalized on social issues and current concerns. The box was made from recycled fiber and was labeled as such. A 1987 television ad presented new roles and images for women while proclaiming the cereal's nutritional superiority.

Health Claims and Kellogg

Since its inception in 1892, Shredded Wheat was marketed as a health food; but not until the late 1970s, when nutritional science and labeling laws focused consumer health concerns, were its salt, sugar, fiber, bran, cholesterol, vitamins, and fat content monitored with exactitude. Market competition helped turn such measurements, which reflected well on the cereal, into dangerous tags. In 1990 Kellogg , the world's largest maker of breakfast cereal, test marketed a new shredded wheat with extra fiber and vitamins. Kellogg called it "the most nutritious shredded wheat you can buy," and asked in promotional ads, "With this kind of nutrition, why would you pick anything else?" A legal quarrel began, with lawyers from Nabisco demanding that Kellogg stop making "false claims of nutritional superiority" or face a lawsuit. Kellogg responded with a lawsuit of its own asking a federal judge to declare that the company was not making false claims and to bar Nabisco from suing Kellogg. Finally, the dispute was "amicably resolved to both parties' satisfaction," according to a Kellogg spokesman. Kellogg subsequently eliminated its package reference to "the most nutritious shredded wheat."

Though this particular conflict between Nabisco and Kellogg was resolved, it highlighted the ongoing friction within the increasingly tight cereal market. At stake in the Kalamazoo suit was a $500 million market for shredded wheat cereal, of which Nabisco held about 60 percent in 1989, while Kellogg held about 40 percent, according to Ronald Strauss, an analyst with William Bair & Company. For the $6.5 billion ready-to-eat cereal market as a

A Shredded Wheat store display card as it appeared in 1915.

whole, however, the figures were quite different: according to Nielsen Marketing Research, for the 52 weeks ended August 8, 1992, Kellogg had a 36.9 percent share of the market; General

Mills was second, with a 29.1 percent share; Kraft General Foods' Post unit followed at 11.3 percent; Quaker Oats Co. held 7 percent; Ralston Purina Co. had 5.2 percent; and Nabisco was sixth at 3.1 percent. To ensure its leading share, Kellogg acted aggressively on the shredded wheat front because it "has had a shortage of new products or the right products," according to Mr. Strauss. Shredded wheat would make a good "new product" precisely because it was such an old one.

International Market

Shredded Wheat was also a strategically valuable brand in the rapidly growing, international ready-to-eat cereal market. In 1992 Shredded Wheat was delivered to 30 foreign destinations, while the £580 million British market alone grew by more than 90 percent, according to Marketing Publications, Ltd., an English information service. Nabisco 's overseas role, however, has changed rapidly since the 1980s. In November 1988, Ranks Hovis McDougall acquired Nabisco's British cereals arm, comprising Shredded Wheat, Shreddies, and Team Wheatflakes. The £80 million sale gave RHM just over a fifth of the British market, behind Kellogg, which dominated the market with a 49 percent share, followed by Weetabix. Only months later, RHM launched a new, nut-filled, version of its staple cereal called Shredded Wheat Gold. With a £1.5 million television campaign, the company targeted "young style-conscious adults" in order to compete against Kellogg's successful rival brands, Raisin Splitz and Toppas. By 1990, however, RHM's share of cereal sales declined from 20 percent in 1988 to 8 percent, according to Marketing Publications. Despite its Nabisco acquisition, RHM was losing market ground. In 1990 General Mills began operations of its Cereal Partners Worldwide (CPW) joint-venture with Nestlé, S.A., and in 1991 CPW acquired RHM and, hence, the European Shredded Wheat brand. This brought an immediate 14 percent share of the crucial European market and represented yet another strategic move against the world leader, Kellogg.

New Parent Company

In September 1992 General Mills made the headlines in the ongoing cereal wars. It announced plans to purchase the North American ready-to-eat cereal business of RJR Nabisco for $450 million in cash. This would have reunited Nabisco's worldwide Shredded Wheat product and would have boosted Big G cereals by 3 percentage points, putting it within 3 points of Kellogg. But the Canadian Bureau of Competition and the Federal Trade Commission reviewed the proposal unfavorably and it did not proceed. The FTC is the primary U.S. federal agency responsible for reviewing antitrust issues in proposed mergers. Instead, Kraft General Food, Inc. followed through with the same deal, in November, and passed FTC guidelines after brief review. Kraft incorporated the Nabisco lines into its Post line of breakfast cereals, boosting the company's share of the market to 14.5 percent of cereal sold, from 11.5 percent, analysts said. The

proven record of Shredded Wheat made it an appealing investment. "Introducing new products is risky, so this is a good way to acquire more share," said First Boston analyst Rebecca Barfield.

Predictions

Kraft's acquisition of the Shredded Wheat brands was strategically significant. "The ready-to-eat cereal category has great potential for expanded growth and operating income. We plan to revitalize the acquired brands by putting Kraft General Foods' marketing and promotional resources behind them," said Richard P. Mayer, chairman and chief executive of Kraft General Foods North America. But the competition is sure to retaliate. As Mary Guthrie, staff writer for the *Los Angeles Times,* warned on January 2, 1993, "Breakfast cereal lovers: sharpen your coupon clippers! A new wave of coupon and promotional wars is coming soon. . . . " If Henry Perky had lived into the 1990s, the cereal wars might have aggravated his indigestion, but with its simple, healthy, natural appeal, Shredded Wheat could easily survive for another hundred years.

Further Reading:

Burrough, Bryan, and John Helyar, *Barbarians at the Gate: The Fall of RJR Nabisco,* New York: Harper & Row, 1990.

Dagnoli, Judann, "Nabisco Acts to Stop Cereal Share Slide," *Advertising Age,* Feb. 3, 1992, p. 1.

Hawkins, Chuck, "Wanna Sue RJR Nabisco? Get in Line," *Business Week,* Aug. 26, 1991, p. 27.

Guthrie, Mary, "Shredded Wheat Sale Expected to Ignite Mayhem," *Los Angeles Times,* Jan. 2, 1993.

Hume, Scott, "Big G to Get Nabisco Cereals; Who Gets Ads?" *Advertising Age,* Sept. 7, 1992, p. 33.

James, Tom, "Falls Plant Shifts to Triscuits Only as Shredded Wheat Line Is Sold," *Business First-Buffalo,* Vol. 8, No. 47, Sec. 1, p. 2.

Johnson, Mike, "RHM Brand Turns to Gold; Ranks Hovis McDougall PLC Introduces Shredded Wheat Gold," *Marketing Publications, Ltd. (England),* p. 4.

Kalish, David, "Who's That Girl," *Marketing & Media Decisions,* Oct. 1987, pp. 20-21.

Lampert, Hope, *True Greed: What Really Happened in the Battle for RJR Nabisco,* New York: New American Library, 1990.

Liesse, Julie, and Judann Dagnoli, "Kellogg, Nabisco Fight for Shreds," *Advertising Age,* Aug. 20, 1990, p. 6.

Ramirez, Anthony, "2 Cereal Giants Fight Over Shredded Wheat," *New York Times,* Sect. 1, p. 37.

Rankine, Kate, "Shredded Wheat to RHM in £80m Deal," *Daily Telegraph,* p. 17.

Rector, Peggy, "Naperville Toasts Shredded Wheat," *Chicago Tribune,* May, 22, 1992, p. D3.

Reuters Information Service, "Nabisco to Sell Cold Cereal Business to Philip Morris," *Los Angeles Times,* November 17, 1992, p. D3.

Ryan, Nancy, "Kraft Parent Has Taste for Shredded Wheat," *Chicago Tribune,* November 17, 1992, p. C1.

—Kerstan Cohen

NESCAFÉ®

Nescafé is the world's leading brand of instant coffee. Though its success has been limited in the United States, in much of the world its name is synonymous with instant coffee. With coffee consumption losing ground to cold, sweet beverages, parent company Nestlé began a push to attract consumers to a new, liquid form of Nescafé beginning in the 1990s. Nestlé, one of the largest food companies in the world, has specialized in instant beverages from milk to coffee, and also owns the Taster's Choice and Hills Bros. coffee brands.

Brand Origin

Nescafé became the world's first instant coffee when it was introduced in 1938 in Switzerland at the Nestlé Company, which specialized in milk-related products. Other attempts had been made to create an instant coffee, but consumers had found their taste and aroma lacking. Nescafé brand had its genesis in the early 1930s due to a unique situation: Brazil had a coffee surplus so large that it threatened to deflate world coffee prices. The Brazilian Coffee Institute contacted Nestlé, wanting it to produce "coffee cubes" that would be instantly soluble in hot water. The Institute believed that such a product, backed by Nestlé's marketing arm, would increase the demand for coffee and use up the surplus.

Nestlé technicians spent years on the problem, and finally found a solution in 1937. Nescafé was created by spray-drying brewed coffee and adding carbohydrates to seal in the coffee flavor. The product was a powder rather than a cube so consumers could more easily regulate the coffee's strength. Production of Nescafé began in Switzerland in 1938, and in France, Britain, and the United States the following year. It was virtually unadvertised in Europe, since production was limited at first and the food laws in many countries had to be changed to accommodate this revolutionary product. World War II disrupted coffee supplies, as well, temporarily preventing Nestlé from completing factories in Europe or conducting an introductory advertising campaign.

Nescafé was introduced in the United States in September 1939 in the New York and Philadelphia markets. A plant was built in Sunbury, Ohio, that year to manufacture the product. Nescafé's first U.S. sales campaign began in July 1940, and the product became an immediate hit, with annual production reaching one million cases by 1944. One impetus was the war: Nescafé, along with evaporated milk and powdered milk, was used extensively by the U.S. armed forces, which brought it all over the world and made instant coffee a staple beverage. The armed services introduced Nescafé to the civilian populations of Europe and Asia as the war progressed, and it soon reached Latin America as well.

Product Reintroduction

But the war also caused patent protection to be relaxed in the United States, so Nescafé imitators sprang up. Raw materials could not reach Europe, and even those factories that had not been destroyed did not have materials to make Nescafé. Even in the United States, most Nescafé production went to the military and the initial advertising campaign was not as extensive as the product warranted. In 1946 a price war broke out as several brands of instant coffee fought for consumer attention. To rekindle excitement, Nestlé reintroduced Nescafé with a broad advertising campaign and quickly built new factories throughout the world to keep up with consumer demand, which boomed after going unsatisfied during the war. A plant was built in Freehold, New Jersey, for example, to manufacture Nescafé for the U.S. market.

Nescafé had about 30 percent of the U.S. instant coffee market by the early 1950s. But then General Foods introduced its instant coffees—led by Sanka—and vigorously promoted them. By the mid-1960s Nescafé's U.S. market share had eroded to around 12 percent, while General Foods had 40 percent. Dissatisfied with this decrease in market share, in 1962 Nestlé moved the $4 million Nescafé ad account from William Esty Company to McCann-Erickson, which already handled the ads for other Nestlé products. About 75 percent of Nescafé's ad budget was spent on television, but General Foods spent even more on its Maxwell House Instant and Yuban brands, and also used an intensive campaign of promotions and special packaging. Nestlé tried promotions, like packaging two two-ounce jars of Nescafé as a salt-and-pepper set and giving away coffee trees, as well as airing television and print ads, but could not increase its market share.

Brand Expansion

In 1966 a new, natural flavor Nescafé was introduced, which Nestlé said could be made as strong as desired without bitterness. It was supported by an intense network and spot television ad campaign by Leo Burnett. The freeze-dried Nescafé Gold Blend was also introduced, but in the meantime Nestlé had created another freeze-dried coffee brand, Taster's Choice, and put more effort and money into promoting it. Taster's Choice proved more

AT A GLANCE

Nescafé brand of instant coffee founded in 1938 in Switzerland by Nestlé S.A.; Nescafé briefly was produced by the Nestlé/Hills Bros. Coffee Company, which became part of the Nestlé Beverage Company in 1991.

Performance: *Market share* 9.7% of the U.S. instant coffee category.

Major competitor: Kraft General Foods' Maxwell House Instant and Sanka.

Advertising: *Agency*—McCann-Erickson Worldwide, New York, NY, 1962—. *Major campaign*—"Make a fresh start."

Addresses: *Parent company*—Nestlé Beverage Company, 345 Spear St., San Francisco, CA 94105, phone: (415) 546-4600. *Ultimate parent company*—Nestlé USA Inc., 800 N. Brand Blvd., Glendale, CA 91203; phone: (818) 549-6000; fax: (818) 549-6952. *Ultimate ultimate parent company*—Nestlé S.A.

successful than Nescafé, and a decaffeinated version was soon introduced.

Trying to follow up on the success of Taster's Choice decaf, Nestlé introduced Nescafé Decaffeinated in 1975. It was initially introduced to the eastern United States, using an ad campaign that emphasized value and quality. Both Nescafés were also repackaged in clear glass jars to show their granulation. Regular Nescafé got a new red label with the legend "largest-selling instant coffee in the world" under a yellow globe. The advertising campaign, handled by Leo Burnett, featured prime-time television spots and print support including coupons.

In the early 1980s coffee consumption continued to decline, especially in the United States, although a greater percentage of coffee drinkers were drinking instant. Nescafé Regular's share of the U.S. instant market declined from 8.7 percent in 1978 to 7 percent in 1982, while Nescafé Decaffeinated sank from 2.5 percent share in 1978 to 2.1 percent in 1982.

In the fall of 1983 Nestlé attempted to revitalize the Nescafé line by launching Nescafé Custom Blended Instant, which included three flavors and a decaffeinated version. The ad campaign, themed "Nescafé . . . taste your way," featured print and television ads by McCann-Erickson, as well as a large number of coupons. The flavors were Brava, which Nestlé described as "bold and dark"; Silka, a much milder blend; Classic, with a more traditional American-roast flavor; and Decaf, a decaffeinated version of Classic. The Custom Blended line had been developed in a year, demonstrating an aggressiveness Nestlé had not previously manifested.

In the mid-1980s a bad harvest in Brazil again caused coffee prices to rise. Nestlé management viewed the price rise as an opportunity because they felt instant coffee offered a better price-value relationship than ground coffee. At the same time, rival General Foods announced a new process that it claimed better captured the flavor and aroma of coffee in its instant coffees, and the two again fought for market share.

In 1986 Nescafé Mountain Blend regular and decaffeinated coffees were introduced. They combined select mountain-grown coffee beans and New Orleans style chicory flavor. The decaffeination was done naturally using water and coffee bean oil. The

same year, parent Nestlé Foods moved to a new headquarters in Purchase, New York. By 1989, Nescafé Regular had a 7.3 percent share of the U.S. instant coffee market, while Nescafé Decaffeinated had 2.7 percent, a gain of less than one percent since 1982.

To reinvigorate its U.S. presence, Nestlé combined its coffee operations into the Nestlé/Hills Bros. Coffee Company in 1990. The Nescafé, Taster's Choice, Hills Bros., MJB, and Chase & Sanborn brands were all put under the auspices of the San Francisco-based company. Later in the year Nestlé/Hills Bros. itself was reorganized to form the Nestlé Beverage Company, which became one of six divisions of Nestlé USA Inc. in 1991. The $7 billion Nestlé USA bought all of Nestlé's U.S. advertising, and therefore Nescafé's as well.

The Asian Market

But if Nescafé was having trouble in the United States, it was still doing well in the rest of the world, where it remained the leading brand of instant coffee. In the United Kingdom, Nestlé's coffee brands did so well, supplying 48 percent of instant coffee sold in 1989, that the Monopolies and Mergers Commission examined Nestlé's business practices. However, it concluded that Nestlé's success resulted from greater efficiency and marketing success than its rivals, not unfair business practices.

In Japan Nestlé had a 70 percent market share, with Nescafé being its leading brand. Nescafé had been popular since the postwar occupation, when it became a valued black market item. It had staved off an attempt by General Foods to penetrate the market. By the early 1990s, however, the Japanese were turning increasingly to drip coffeemakers and beverages other than coffee. In response, Nescafé's advertising was repositioned to stress the appeal of coffee itself rather than just touting Nescafé as the best instant. In September 1991, Nescafé was introduced in Korea, where it quickly became a leading brand.

One lesson Nescafé learned in Japan was that consumers liked iced coffee. Iced coffee, usually sold in cans, became a $3.7 billion market in Japan between 1975 and 1990. Nescafé Mocha Cooler was introduced in five U.S. cities in 1990. The product was sold in a package like a milk carton and stocked in the dairy case. It was supported by ads themed "The cooler for an uncool world," which appeared on outdoor signs, radio, and television. Iced coffee was expected to attract younger consumers who preferred cold, sweet beverages. Nescafé Mocha Cooler was described as tasting like a coffee milkshake. The ads were by McCann-Erickson Worldwide, as were the ads for a 1991 joint venture between Nestlé and Coca-Cola. Coca-Cola Nestlé Refreshments Co. was designed to capitalize on Coke's distribution expertise and Nestlé's ready-to-drink coffees, like Nescafé Mocha Cooler.

The venture first went to work in Korea, where Coca-Cola Nestlé introduced two flavors of Nescafé liquid canned coffee, "rich" and "regular." The two firms put up $100 million and installed 2,700 vending machines. The coffees cost about half the price of a cup of coffee in a Korean restaurant and were advertised on television. The television ad used traditional Korean music, and showed a man and woman meeting in front of a coffee machine on a busy street.

Future Growth

A series of ads by McCann-Erickson Worldwide for regular Nescafé, renamed Nescafé Classic, began in 1991. The ads were atmospheric, pushing the theme of "Make a fresh start," rather than copy touting the product's qualities. Several of the ads showed middle-aged singles having their first date in years.

In mid-1992 Nescafé was reformulated and called Nescafé Coffee Crystals. Nestlé said that it spent over 20,000 man-hours developing the new product. Nescafé Coffee Crystals were packaged in bold new graphics with a metallic finish, partly to attract consumers' attention and partly to indicate that the product had been reformulated. The product was promoted with the Nescafé World Mug, a globe-shaped glass coffee mug consumers could get by mailing in Nescafé inner seals.

Through its many changes and local adaptations over the years, Nescafé has continually dominated the international instant coffee market and demonstrated successful brand management. Its consistent advertising and innovative packaging have led to name recognition among 90 percent of instant coffee consumers. With its aggressive moves into new formulations and new types of coffee, like iced coffee, Nescafé is positioned for continued success in the face of ever-changing consumer coffee habits.

Further Reading:

"Arm Breaking in Japan," *Forbes,* October 1, 1990.

Dagnoli, Judann, "Iced Coffee Next for Coke, Nestlé," *Advertising Age,* May 21, 1990.

Darlin, Damon, "Coke, Nestlé Launch First Coffee Drink," *Wall Street Journal,* October 1, 1991, p. B1.

Heer, Jean, *World Events 1866-1966, The First Hundred Years of Nestlé,* Chateau de Glerolles, Rivaz, Switzerland, 1966.

"Instant Nescafé Shifts to McCann from Esty Shop," *Advertising Age,* April 16, 1962, p.3.

Lipman, Joanne, "Account for Coke-Nestlé Venture Is Awarded to McCann-Erickson," *Wall Street Journal,* March 21, 1991.

O'Connor, John J., "Nestlé Ready to Introduce a Decaffeinated Nescafé Entry," *Advertising Age,* January 20, 1975, p. 1.

—Scott M. Lewis

NESTEA®

Nestea is the number two-selling brand of instant tea in the United States, capturing over 28 percent of the soluble tea market in 1992. Developed by Nestlé S.A., a multinational food manufacturer headquartered in Switzerland, Nestea was one of the first instant teas on the U.S. market. Nestlé, originally known for its milk-related products, also produces Taster's Choice instant coffee and Nestlé Quik chocolate drink mix. The general consumer trend away from coffee and toward cold, sweet beverages in the 1980s and 1990s has placed Nestea in an ideal position for continued growth. With an extensive product line, which includes tea bags and a variety of instant teas packaged in powdered and ready-to-drink forms, Nestea is positioned to compete in both the hot and cold and the regular and decaffeinated segments of the tea industry. A strategic alliance formed with Coca-Cola Company in 1990, named the Coca-Cola Nestlé Refreshments Company, resulted in the production and distribution of bottled Nestlé products and a substantial increase in sales of Nestea.

Brand Origin

The Nestea brand name has been well known by consumers for over 40 years. Nestea was introduced in 1948 by Nestlé, whose tremendous success with Nescafé, the first instant coffee, inspired the company to develop a similar instant tea product. The original Nestea, which was dissolvable only in hot water, was not as well received as Nescafé had been a decade earlier. Nestlé continued to work on refining Nestea, however, and eight years later produced the first 100 percent instant tea mix that was soluble in both hot and cold water. Nestea's sales slowly increased in the mid- and late 1950s as iced tea became a more popular beverage. In 1959 Nestea became the first 100 percent tea mix on the market. Capitalizing on this new feature, Nestlé created an advertising campaign that emphasized the 100 percent pure tea advantage to Nestea with the slogan ''Nestea is total instant tea.''

Brand Expansion

In the early 1960s iced tea sales gained momentum, particularly in the Midwest, and the battle for market share began. Nestlé led the industry with Nestea, which held a 40 percent share of the instant tea market, with Lipton and Tetley following in second and third place. In 1963 Salada Foods beat its competitors to the national market with the first iced tea mix—a premixed, sugar-sweetened tea that contained lemon flavoring. Nestlé, Lipton, and several other tea makers soon followed suit, all introducing their own brands of instant tea mix. Nestea's premixed brand, which was also flavored with sugar and lemon, was placed on the market in 1965 along with a low-calorie instant mix.

With the influx of new tea products, instant tea sales soared in 1964, rising 39 percent and earning between 15 and 20 percent of the total tea market. Sales again rose approximately 40 percent in 1965, and Nestlé and Lipton continued to vie for the largest share of the instant market. Nestea retained its position as the top-selling instant tea maker and further expanded its product line in 1967 with the introduction of an unsweetened version of its lemon-flavored iced tea mix. Many other companies introduced product line extensions as well, and the instant tea wars continued throughout the late 1960s and early 1970s. By 1972, sales of Nestea and Lipton accounted for approximately 85 percent of the market for instant and iced tea, which was estimated to be almost $160 million. Nestea attained a 50 percent share of the instant tea category, leading Lipton by 20 percentage points. However, in the iced tea mix segment of the market, Lipton edged out Nestlé, earning a 40 percent share to Nestea's 35 percent. Nestea had attained the top-selling position in iced tea mix sales as well, but forfeited the number one spot to Lipton after Nestlé pulled its low-calorie instant off the market.

In the 1960s and 1970s instant and iced tea sales varied greatly depending upon geographic location. Popular in the Midwest, instant tea was rejected by East-coast and Southern consumers, who preferred the more traditional method of making iced tea by brewing loose tea or tea bags. This preference gave Lipton a distinct advantage in these markets since it promoted iced tea drinking primarily through its Flo-Thru tea bag advertisements. To expand Nestea's instant tea sales in New England, in 1972 Nestlé launched the largest-to-date regional campaign of any of its products. The new Nestea ads, which were handled by Leo Burnett USA of Chicago, demonstrated to consumers how much easier and more convenient it was to prepare Nestea than iced tea made with tea bags. The ads also portrayed drinking Nestea as a refreshing experience. The refreshing-taste concept soon evolved into what became Nestea's most famous advertising slogan, ''Take the Nestea Plunge.'' New national ads featured an individual drinking a glass of Nestea and then falling into a swimming pool with the glass still in hand. The commercials were extremely successful, and Nestlé continued the promotion for several years.

AT A GLANCE

Nestea brand of instant tea introduced in 1948 by Nestlé S.A.; placed under the management of Nestlé Beverage Company, a subsidiary of Nestlé USA Inc., in 1990; in 1992, Nestlé formed a partnership with Coca-Cola Company called the Coca-Cola Nestlé Refreshments Company to market and distribute ready-to-drink coffee, tea, and chocolate beverages, including ready-to-drink bottles of Nestea.

Performance: *Market share*—28.2% (number two) of the soluble tea market.

Major competitor: Lipton tea.

Advertising: *Agency*—McCann-Erickson Worldwide, New York, NY, 1989—. *Major campaign*—"The Nestea Plunge."

Addresses: *Parent company*—Nestlé Beverage Company, 345 Spear Street, San Francisco, CA 94105, phone: (415) 546-4600. *Ultimate parent company*—Nestlé USA Inc., 800 N. Brand Blvd., Glendale, CA 91203; phone: (818) 549-6000; fax: (818) 549-6952. *Ultimate ultimate parent company*—Nestlé S.A.

Sales of both instant tea and tea bags steadily increased in the 1980s. Nestlé and Lipton prevailed as the dominant tea companies, controlling the majority of industry market share, though competitors such as Proctor & Gamble and Tetley and a host of other smaller brands continued to seek out new markets. Lipton outsold Nestea in the mix category and Nestea topped Lipton in the instant tea segment. To further penetrate existing tea markets, Nestlé introduced its own brand of tea bags, which it test marketed in Wichita, Kansas, in 1982. Packaged with the familiar green and yellow Nestea label, Nestea hot tea bags were later offered nationally in 24, 48, and 100-bag boxes.

Product Reintroduction

A general trend in the more health-conscious public of the 1980s was to view instant and processed products as somehow inferior and unnatural. To combat this perception, Nestlé technicians came out with a reformulated version of Nestea in 1982, which improved the flavor and clarity of the tea. In conjunction with the reintroduction of Nestea, Nestlé discontinued the "Take the Nestea Plunge" campaign, believing that consumers had come to associate the slogan more with the general concept of iced and instant tea than with the Nestea brand name. Nestlé also switched advertising agencies from Leo Burnett USA to J. Walter Thompson, whose strategy was to reposition Nestea as a natural product that was "as clear and fresh as the outdoors." The new advertising campaign featured commercials and print ads with television star Dan Haggerty, who was well known for his role as backwoodsman Grizzly Adams in the television series of the same name. The commercials were set outdoors in the mountains and showed Haggerty drinking Nestea and proclaiming, "There is nothing like it under the sun." The campaign was a push to compete with Lipton's latest commercials, which utilized another well-known spokesperson, Don Meredith. The new Nestea campaign was not as successful as Nestlé had anticipated, and the company thereafter returned to its familiar and still popular "Take the Nestea Plunge" concept.

In the 1980s many consumers expressed concern with the possible negative effects of caffeine and thus turned to decaffeinated beverages. Soft drink sales had risen dramatically during the

1970s, and with the introduction of caffeine-free colas, soft drink industry sales skyrocketed. Sales of decaffeinated teas rose substantially as well, nearly doubling between 1984 and 1986. Lipton responded to the rising demand for caffeine-free beverages by introducing a 97 percent decaffeinated instant tea in 1983.

Nestlé did not immediately respond to this trend, however, instead introducing a sugar-free version of Nestea in 1985 that was sweetened with NutraSweet. Nestea Sugarfree was the first low-calorie tea mix Nestlé had produced since the 1960s. The following year, Nestlé began marketing Nestea Iced Teasers, fruit-flavored tea mixes that were low in calories and came in a variety of flavors, including lemon, wild cherry, and orange. Nestlé was not alone in its newest venture—Lipton and General Foods were also developing powdered fruit tea mixes. Finally, in 1988 Nestlé joined the decaffeinated market with two products: Nestea Decaffeinated 100 percent tea mix and Decaffeinated Sugarfree Nestea iced tea mix, both of which were well received.

Brand Revitalization

In an effort to streamline production, Nestea and all other Nestlé beverage products were consolidated and placed under the newly formed Nestlé Beverage Company of San Francisco, California, in 1990. The Nestea brand product line was thereafter positioned to begin yet another push to gain market share in the tea industry.

By the early 1990s, an estimated 127 million people—half the population of the United States—consumed tea in the United States on a daily basis. Approximately 80 percent of industry sales were in the iced tea category. Leading soft drink companies recognized the tremendous potential for growth in the instant and iced tea markets and sought to enter the industry. In 1990 Nestlé announced plans to join forces with Coca-Cola Company, the world's largest soft drink manufacturer, to market ready-to-drink coffee, tea, and chocolate beverages. Under the agreement, the beverages were marketed with the Nestea, Nestlé, and Nescafé brand names and were distributed by Coca-Cola bottling. This new alliance, the Coca-Cola Nestlé Refreshments Company (CCNR), commenced operations in 1991. CCNR began producing and distributing ready-to-drink Nestea in bottles in the United States and Taiwan in 1992. CCNR announced plans to eventually expand distribution of Nestlé beverage products in international markets with the exception of Japan, where Nestlé and Coca-Cola remained competitors.

Fresh-brewed bottled tea had been popularized beginning in 1988 by the New York-based company Snapple, which had captured the public's interest with its variety of bottled teas. Sales of Nestlé and Lipton canned ready-to-drink teas were mediocre and both companies sought alternative methods of packaging and marketing their ready-to-drink teas. Cold-packed ready-to-drink teas, which had to rely on preservatives, had not fared well on the market because of a metallic aftertaste caused by the preservatives. In 1992 Coca-Cola Nestlé Refreshments introduced Nestea's first bottled tea, which was available in wide-mouthed, 16-ounce bottles. The tea was hot-packed, which eliminated the need for preservatives and resulted in a superior flavor. The roll-out of Nestea's newest product line extension was accompanied by an elaborate ad campaign featuring the tag line, "The way iced tea was supposed to taste but never did . . . till now. Taste the plunge." Advertising agency McCann-Erickson of New York handled the new promotions.

Up until Nestlé's joint venture with Coca-Cola, Lipton's canned tea had been distributed by Coca-Cola bottling. Thereafter, Lipton formed a partnership with Pepsi-Cola called the Pepsi Lipton Tea Partnership to distribute its new ready-to-drink bottled tea, Lipton Original Iced Tea, and the latest battle in the iced tea wars began. In 1992 Snapple earned the top share of the ready-to-drink bottled tea market, with $21.6 million in sales. Lipton, while earning the number two spot with sales of $18.6 million, experienced a 20.1 percent decrease in sales from 1991. Nestea, which finished third in 1992 with $12 million in sales, registered a spectacular 182 percent increase in its bottled tea sales. A 1992 market study revealed that Nestea was the only major brand of instant tea and tea bags to gain both volume and market share.

For over four decades Nestea has been a leader in the instant tea industry. Nestlé's aggressive tactics for capturing the tea industry sales have resulted in strong, continued growth for the Nestea product line and a positive future in the market.

Further Reading:

Heer, Jean, *Nestlé: 125 Years, 1866-1991,* Vevey, Switzerland: Nestlé S.A., 1991.

Jabbonsky, L. and A. E. Wolf, "Ready to Go," *Beverage World,* September, 1991, p. 58.

Jervey, Gay, "New Nestea Pitch a Natural," *Advertising Age,* April 5, 1982.

Jervey, Gay, "Nestea Dips in Bags as Market Heats Up," *Advertising Age,* May 16, 1983, pp. 2, 72.

Kanner, Bernice, "The Big Chill," *New York,* June 8, 1992, pp. 20-22.

Moore, M. H., "Boston Tea Party," *Mediaweek,* October 12, 1992, pp. 14-18.

"Tea for Two, but Make It Decaf," *Forbes,* July 14, 1986, p. 89.

—Shannon Young

NESTLÉ® CHOCOLATE

Nestlé chocolate encompasses dozens of varieties and is the sixth most popular brand of chocolate in the world. Among Nestlé-owned brands are such American classics as Baby Ruth, Butterfingers, Oh Henry!, and Raisinets. Chocolate confections and beverages, however, are only some of the thousands of products manufactured by the monolithic Swiss holding company Nestlé S.A., the world's biggest food enterprise. Its largest subsidiary, Nestlé USA, produces not only chocolate but Carnation evaporated milk, coffee, pet food, and an array of frozen foods. Chocolate, however, is the product most commonly associated with the name Nestlé. The principal reasons for Nestlé brand chocolate's success are undoubtedly related to the land of its origins, Switzerland, where chocolate-making reached the pinnacle of perfection.

Brand Origins

Henri Nestlé was a storekeeper and amateur chemist in the small town of Vevey, Switzerland, who liked experimenting with food. Because of the incredibly high infant mortality rate in Switzerland in the mid-1800s, with one out of five babies dying because of an inability to digest mothers' milk, Nestlé was determined to come up with an infant formula that would be more digestible than breast milk, and just as wholesome. In 1867, after a dramatic incident in which he saved the life of an infant with his new baby formula, Nestlé invested his capital in the world's first infant formula factory, the Farine Lactee Henri Nestlé. In 1875 Nestlé retired and sold his company to Swiss investors, who retained the name Nestlé. By then, his factory was producing condensed milk as well as baby formula. The fact that a chocolate factory was located next door to Nestlé's plant was to have fateful consequences, however.

The owner of the chocolate factory, Daniel Peter, was experimenting with chocolate bars, trying to improve their grainy coarseness. For eight years Peter's experiments dragged on. One day in 1875, Peter added some of Nestlé's condensed sweet milk to chocolate, giving birth to the world's first milk chocolate bar. With the addition of Rudolph Lindt's newly discovered cocoa butter, the Swiss chocolate industry took off. "Peter's Chocolate" became the first commercially successful chocolate bar. Without Nestlé's condensed milk, the invention of the milk chocolate bar may never have occurred in Switzerland.

In 1905 the Farine Lactee Henri Nestlé merged with its arch rival, the Anglo-Swiss Condensed Milk Company, to form the Nestlé and Anglo-Swiss Condensed Milk Company. In so doing, Nestlé took advantage of its former competitor's well-established branches abroad, especially in England and the United States. Later that year, the Swiss General Chocolate Company, makers of Peter's Chocolate, contracted with the newly merged company to market its chocolate brands overseas through Nestlé's well-established distribution network. In return, the chocolate brands would bear the name Nestlé. In this way, Nestlé chocolate came to be known throughout Great Britain, Canada, and the United States. In 1929 Nestlé absorbed the Swiss General Chocolate Company and began to enter the chocolate-making business in earnest. Because of the high tariff barriers erected by most national governments after the First World War, the Swiss were among the first to realize that to stay in business, chocolate would have to be manufactured in the countries that formerly imported Swiss chocolate. The first Nestlé factories opened in the United States in the 1920s, and soon this became the biggest overseas market for Nestlé chocolate.

Product Development

In the late nineteenth and early twentieth centuries, chocolate was considered a nutritious food, and during World War I, precious cargo space was set aside in shipping vessels for cocoa beans to be turned into chocolate bars for the soldiers. The gains in sales as a result of the war were maintained afterwards with the advent of radio, allowing for more effective advertising than ever before. The Second World War, while it strained Nestlé's capacity to produce chocolate as a result of blockades and trade embargoes, nonetheless enormously expanded the chocolate business. Right after the war, television advertising helped promote Nestlé to make it the number one selling brand of chocolate in the world.

By the 1930s, when the new Nestlé Crunch bar and Toll House chocolates were introduced, Nestlé had established a worldwide distribution network that would stand the company in good stead as it came out with new products. One of Nestlé's main strengths continues to be the presence of over 400 Nestlé factories in sixty-three foreign countries. Nestlé Crunch was an instant success, and remains available virtually unchanged from its first appearance in 1938. In the following year, because of the onset of war, Nestlé International moved its headquarters to the United States, beginning Nestlé's large scale penetration of the U.S. market. Ten years later, the biggest Nestlé chocolate factories were located in the United States.

AT A GLANCE

Nestlé brand of chocolate originated in 1875 in Vevey, Switzerland, when Daniel Peter added condensed milk from the Farine Lactee Henri Nestlé Company to chocolate from his Swiss General Chocolate Company to make the world's first sweet milk chocolate; 1905, the Farine Lactee Henri Nestlé and the Anglo-Swiss Condensed Milk companies merged to form the Nestlé and Anglo-Swiss Condensed Milk Company; 1929, the Nestlé and Anglo-Swiss Condensed Milk Company merged with the Swiss General Chocolate Company and renamed its chocolate products Nestlé; 1947, company renamed Nestlé Alimentana S.A.; 1977, company renamed Nestlé, S.A.

Performance: *Market share*—10% of U.S. candy bar category.

Major competitor: Hershey Foods Corp.'s brands of chocolate.

Advertising: *Agency*—McCann-Erickson Worldwide, Los Angeles, CA, 1991—. *Major campaign*—Chocolate chip recipe with slogan, "Make Your House a Toll House."

Addresses: *Parent company*—Nestlé USA, Inc., Corporate Offices, 800 North Brand Boulevard, Glendale, CA 91203; phone: (818) 549-6000. *Ultimate parent company*—Nestlé S.A.

Nestlé expanded its chocolate brands through acquisition of successful products from other manufacturers as well as development of new products. Perhaps earlier than most food companies, Nestle's research and development arm was of prime importance, beginning with baby food and canned milk products. After World War II, Nestlé introduced the world's all-time favorite chocolate drink additive, Nestlé Quik, and gradually added other non-chocolate flavors. In 1973 the Nestlé Quik Bunny was introduced on television to the delight of child audiences, making the chocolate drink additive a major seller.

While the 1970s coincided with a growing interest in healthy eating, market analysts noted that candy consumption, especially chocolate, did not decline. Nestlé continued to expand its brand by introducing semi-sweet chocolate morsels in 1982. Another non-confection chocolate, Nestlé baking cocoa, was introduced in 1987. By 1990, one major American chocolate brand after another was acquired by Nestlé, including Butterfingers, Baby Ruth, Oh Henry! , Raisinets, and Goobers. Nestlé's Sweet Success, a diet meal replacement "for chocolate lovers," was developed in 1993. The list of new products was long and varied in different countries, but for the most part Nestlé continued to expand its brand of chocolate candy to include ever more colorful (for example, children's favorites Yummy Mummies, Nerds, and Pixy Stix) and sophisticated (for example, the elegant Peruginas) products.

International Growth

Over the years, virtually all of Nestlé's sales have been made outside of its native Switzerland. Half of Nestlé's sales derived from eastern Europe, in part because of the fall of communism, the historically sophisticated chocolate palates of eastern Europeans, and the still insatiable desire for western goods. In 1991 Nestlé bought the principal chocolate manufacturing firms in Hungary and in the Czech republic. Meanwhile Nestlé began constructing new factories in southeast Asia and making inroads in the historically unreceptive Indian market. Another Nestlé confectionery establishment was developed in China.

In 1991 Nestlé USA, Inc. was formed as a parent company for the six Nestlé food divisions in the United States, in large part to promote savings by consolidating advertising expenditures. Although Nestlé USA became Nestlé S.A.'s largest operating division, the company has also focused its attention on western Europe, where American competitors have tried to enter Nestlé's historical backyard. In late 1990 Philip Morris, Inc. acquired the chocolate and coffee enterprise Jacobs-Suchard, giving it access to major European markets, including the emerging markets of Asia. Jolted by the emergence of a major foreign competitor in the chocolate and coffee markets, Nestlé increased its investment in U.S. companies, raised its media expenditures by over 10 percent, and streamlined its operations. The result is a company that shows strong future growth potential.

Further Reading:

Annual Report: Nestlé, S.A., 1991.

Chocologie, Union of Swiss Chocolate Manufacturers, 1992.

Johnson, Bradley, "Nestlé Unifies Image (Corporate Ad Campaign)," *Advertising Age,* October 26, 1992.

Nestlé in Profile, Nestlé Alimentana Co., 1964.

"Nestlé to Double in Size by the Year 2000," *AdWeek's Marketing Week,* March 30, 1992.

Nestlé USA, Inc., 1991.

Palmer, Jay, "The Chocolate Juggernaut: Nestlé Mounts an Aggressive Push around the Globe," *Barron's,* July 8, 1991.

"The Story of Chocolate," The Chocolate Manufacturers Association of the USA, 1992.

Wolflisberg, Hans J., *A Century of Global Operations; The Flavorful World of Nestlé,* New York: Newcomen Society, 1966.

—Sina Dubovoj

NEWPORT®

Newport is the flagship brand of Lorillard Tobacco Company, the tobacco subsidiary of the Loews Corporation, a major conglomerate. In a market populated with 176 brands, Newport is one of the few cigarette names to maintain an immediately discernable identity, due mainly to a well-supported regime of advertising and promotion. As a result, Newport has grown to become the nation's most popular menthol brand and the third best-selling cigarette overall.

While Newport competes within the same general market as Salem, Kool, Virginia Slims, and Benson & Hedges menthol brands, it retains a unique formulation and taste that sets it apart from other cigarettes. Newport is a full-flavor menthol cigarette that has a delicate balance between tobacco taste and menthol flavor, positioned between Kool—which has a heavy menthol taste—and Salem—which is sweeter and more minty.

Brand Origins

Smoking had become an extremely popular habit in the years after World War II. As the cigarette market gradually became saturated, a number of manufacturers began testing off-shoots of such well-established brands as Camel, Lucky Strike, and Chesterfield. This experimentation produced such successful entries as Marlboro, Winston, and Benson & Hedges. The lone menthol brand, Kool, a sleeper since its introduction in 1933, began to pick up sales during this period, indicating to other manufacturers that the public had at long last accepted a flavored cigarette.

Lorillard, a company built on its Old Gold and, later, Kent and True brands, watched the growth of the menthol category closely. When competitor R.J. Reynolds burst into this market in 1956 with Salem, its menthol counterpart to Winston, the entire industry stepped up plans for their own entries.

Lorillard formulated a new brand specifically blended to unite the qualities of a straight tobacco brand like Chesterfield and the new minty menthols. Because Lorillard wished to establish product differentiation, the menthol brand did not provide the same potent menthol blast as Salem. Newport was intended to occupy the middle ground between the two menthol brands, offering a balance of tobacco and menthol taste. The brand was named Newport, after the Rhode Island summer vacation home of the Lorillard family. Advertising for the Newport brand initially em-

ployed a seaport image, drawing images of open skies, fresh ocean air, and the refreshing splash of salt water on the face.

Lorillard introduced Newport in May of 1957. Although a nationally marketed product, it came to sell best on the East and West coasts of the United States, where Newport chipped away at the bold leads established by Kool and its slightly sweeter competitor, Salem. Newport's intermediate place in the market was clearly defined by the tagline "a hint of mint."

Packaging

As Salem had been given a bold green package to evoke an association with mint leaves, Newport adopted an equally identifiable color scheme. The Newport package was designed with a grayish turquoise blue tone, in order to establish its own identity. The Newport name appeared in simple sans serif type, as opposed to Salem's gothic script. To finish it off, the Newport package was given a highly distinctive logo. Unlike the ornate coat-of-arms on Marlboro and Pall Mall, though, the Newport logo was a simple, boomerang-shaped white crescent, inspired by the spinnaker of a sail boat.

Newport packages were immediately identifiable on cigarette displays. While Marlboro and Winston were in bright red packages, and Salem in green, Newport was the sole brand in slate turquoise. Unlike the older brands, each of these could be easily identified by consumers, even from a great distance.

In 1967 Lorillard updated the Newport package. The single slab blue color scheme was replaced by an alternating series of horizontal blue and green lines, chosen to reinforce the mint and menthol identities of the brand. The top quarter of the package was a single white band with the name Newport written across it. The spinnaker design was reduced in size slightly and placed in the lower right-hand corner. Completing the design change was a conversion of the cigarette itself to a "printed" filter. Previously white, like Salem, Newport now had a cork filter similar to that of Marlboro and Winston. Colored filters were a holdover from early cork filters from the 1940s. When pressed fabric filters became common during the 1950s, manufacturers began printing the image of a cork on the filter. The new, more modern design attracted a number of consumers away from competing brands, such as Kool.

Advertising

In 1957 Lorillard's Newport and Kent advertising accounts were picked up by Lennin and Newell, which created Newport's first tagline, "A hint of mint makes the difference." This statement helped distinguish Newport from other menthol brands whose tobacco flavor was quashed by their heavy menthol content.

Lorillard moved its Newport account to Grey Advertising in 1968. The new agency created the line "Newport makes your world taste good," which was used during the early 1970s. The new agency and look for Newport, however, failed to sustain sales growth. By 1972 Newport sales were less than half what they were seven years earlier. That year the Newport account was given to the Will Graham Company, which later became the Ally & Gargano firm. Graham elevated the Grey creation "Alive with pleasure" from minor copy to a bold headline and added a new subline, "After all, if smoking isn't a pleasure, why bother?"

Print and billboard advertising—the primary media open to cigarette advertising after 1971—emphasized couples or small groups having highly pleasurable experiences depicted against a bright kelly green background with the Newport name in dayglow orange. These colors were used in magazines beginning in 1984, when the pigments became available in that medium.

Meeting Consumers' Demands

No brand of cigarette in modern times has ever claimed to be beneficial to consumers' health. In fact, after the U.S. Surgeon General reported that smoking could cause cancer and other illnesses, consumers began to switch from straight brands to filtered brands such as Marlboro, Winston, Kent, and Benson & Hedges. As consumer tastes continued to evolve toward lighter cigarettes, a number of manufacturers began to introduce lowered tar and nicotine formulations of their regular brands. Lorillard followed this trend in the industry in 1977 with the introduction of Newport Lights, mainly a defensive action against Salem Lights and Kool Milds, which were introduced earlier in the 1970s.

Newport Lights, containing approximately 30 percent less tar and nicotine than regular Newport, retained the printed filter. The package design closely followed that of the original Newport, but substituted a white background for the turquoise used on the parent brand's package. Newport Lights were offered as an alternative for smokers who desired lower tar and nicotine but favored Newport's light menthol flavor. The brand's introductory ad copy featured the line, "Lighten up with Newport Lights."

Brand Development

When it was first introduced, Newport was available only in an 85-millimeter length. During the 1960s the company added a 100-millimeter size, after Kool introduced its own longer version. "100s" were popular with women, who were attracted by the slimmer appearance and economy of a longer cigarette. Newport experienced impressive growth at this time. While the brand trailed Kool, Salem, and Belair, it sold 8.7 billion units in 1965, a year in which ten new menthols hit the market.

Lorillard introduced an 80-millimeter box version in 1967, after its design change. The flip-top box, European in origin, had been in growing use by a number of brands since 1955 and enabled packages to resist crushing in purses and shirt pockets.

Sales of Newport declined steadily from about 1968 to 1972, when only 4.1 billion units were sold. At that time Lorillard undertook an exhaustive analysis of the brand's market, the first the company had ever performed for its Newport brand. The study revealed that Newport was most popular in urban areas of the northeastern United States, and within that demographic segment, among young black males, even though advertising had never specifically targeted this group.

In an effort to broaden Newport's appeal, Lorillard extended its advertising muscle outside the northeastern strongholds to the Southeast and West Coast. Within existing urban markets, billboard ads were placed to boost sales within specific neighborhoods. The effort paid off slowly as sales began to climb and the demographics of the franchise began to diversify. In 1980, three years after Newport Lights were put on the market, Lorillard introduced the 80-millimeter size of its light cigarette in a box package, followed by a 100-millimeter soft pack a year later. Both the regular and light 100s were introduced in a box in 1984, further broadening the appeal of Newport to consumers with highly specific demands.

The original Newport became available in packages of 25 in 1985, after Marlboro and a handful of others introduced similar value packs. The larger package was introduced to more closely approximate consumers' average daily consumption. But the proliferation of generics and other lower-priced brands resulted in the higher-priced 25-pack being used primarily as a promotional pack.

Brand Extensions

In order to tap into the burgeoning "women's brands" market, Lorillard developed a full-circumference, light 100-millimeter filter cigarette, which was white with a distinctive tricolor pastel band around the filter. The new brand, available in full menthol and nonmenthol versions and named Newport Stripes, was packaged in a flip top box with a completely new design: all white with vertical pastel stripes, which emphasized length and created the illusion of a skinnier box.

The Newport Stripes advertising campaigns made strong use of fuchsia backgrounds. But despite heavy use of female-oriented fun, Newport Stripes failed to achieve its sales goals. Lorillard introduced another extension, Newport Slim Lights, in 1992. The new, slim-circumference, 100-millimeter Newport brand was as distinctively slim as its intended competitors, Virginia Slims and Salem Slim Lights. Featuring a white filter, Newport Slim Lights' package was a white box with vertical teal stripes concentrated at the side of the package to create the impression of a yet slimmer package. Formulated as a full-menthol light, Newport Slim Lights were promoted specifically to women and use the same "pleasure" theme.

Performance Appraisal

Lorillard's effort to broaden the demographic and geographic appeal of Newport has been a great success. The brand and its extensions garnered 4.8 percent of the American cigarette market in 1992, posting sales of 25 billion units. Much of this success may be attributed to the creation and targeted marketing of a very strong brand image. Newport's tremendously popular image, as portrayed in its long-running "Alive with pleasure" advertising campaign and through its promotions, is what has driven the brand and its line extensions to the number one menthol cigarette position. Particularly in a market where dozens of minor brands often copy the product and promotional formulas of larger brands, Newport has managed to carve out a specific and enduring identity among consumers.

Future Predictions

Newport's ventures into producing cigarettes of varied lengths and strengths and into developing specifically targeted extensions have proven the brand's ability to cover all bases in the cigarette market. As manufacturers continue to experiment with 120-millimeter lengths, skinnier cigarettes, fancier packages, more sophisticated imagery, and even new flavorings, Newport has positioned itself to cover a broader middle ground. The brand remains essentially what it was when it was introduced, a light menthol, and its extension into fringe markets is likely to proceed only where the value of the Newport name will propel sales, hopefully without diluting the unique image that has been so carefully assembled around it.

Further Reading:

"Lorillard: Soaring Skyward on a Filter Tip," *Business Week,* November 2, 1957, pp. 158-160.

Newport brand history, New York, NY: Lorillard Tobacco Company.

—John Simley

9-LIVES®

Heinz Pet Products' 9-Lives brand of cat food, in its canned, semi-moist, and dry varieties, has become well known over the years through the popularity of its brand spokescat, Morris, an orange tabby whose face graces all its packaging. The 9-Lives brand has consistently held a first- or second-place market share in the canned cat food category in its thirty-plus years of existence, and has remained a strong contender in the dry, moist, and cat treat segments as well.

Beginnings

The brand was rather quietly introduced in 1954 by Star-Kist Foods, Inc., a producer of tuna and other fish products in addition to its cat food line. Within two years of the 9-Lives introduction, StarKist reintroduced the brand as a gourmet canned cat food, thus launching the gourmet category in the feline food business. From 1958 through 1968 more than 25 cat food brands entered the gourmet category, a sign that the market held real profit potential.

By the early 1960s, StarKist, a privately-held company, had annual sales of approximately $70 million. Pittsburgh-based H. J. Heinz Company, a major player in the food processing industry, expressed interest in acquiring StarKist in early 1963. Heinz president Frank Armour, Jr., planned to make the company a division of Heinz, while maintaining the administration, processing, and sales and marketing departments of the new subsidiary. Joseph J. Bogdanovich remained as head of operations. Star-Kist properties at that time included two plants—the company headquarters, at Terminal Island, California, and one based in Puerto Rico—as well as processing installations in Peru, West Africa, and Samoa. With the purchase of Star-Kist, Heinz entered the cat food business and the canned tuna industry.

Pet Food Boom

Heinz was apparently well informed of the burgeoning pet food industry when it acquired Star-Kist; combined sales of cat and dog food were above $500 million in 1964, and were expected to rise to $700 million by 1968. Heinz spent close to $1 million on 9-Lives advertising in 1963 alone, while rivals Quaker Oats with Puss 'n Boots Cat Food, Ralston Purina with Purina Cat Chow, and Carnation with Friskies Pet Food were spending anywhere from $1.5 to $2.7 million on cat food advertising.

The category growth trend continued throughout the 1960s, making pet foods one of the most explosive growth products in the supermarket industry. At the 10th annual convention of the Pet Food Institute in 1964, food products consultant Lawrence Spiegel stated that "pets are occupying a family role which is best described as 'humanization.' " It would be in the direction of this "humanization," an *Advertising Age* article went on to state, that new pet foods would be developed and the merchandising energies to sell them would be expended. Morris the Cat, the 9-Lives representative who entered the scene not two years after the pet-humanization phenomenon was recognized, epitomized such a focus. No amount of exposure proved too much for Morris, provided Heinz and its advertising agency Leo Burnett did all the work to set up various promotions, commercials, fan clubs, and newsletters.

The Unflappable Morris

Morris the Cat had humble beginnings. He was found in an animal shelter in Lombard, Illinois, by animal trainer Bob Martwick, who was immediately impressed by the cat's spunk. The fifteen-pound orange tabby seemed thoroughly disinterested in the shelter and its daily indignities. In 1969, Morris became 9-Lives first and foremost spokescat. The dignified, collected, almost haughty qualities Martwick observed when Morris still lived in the shelter stayed with the cat when he made his screen debut. Morris, as described by Jim Hall in *Mighty Minutes: An Illustrated History of Television's Best Commercials,* "was to prove just as 'cool' in the pressure cooker of motion-picture production."

Morris arrived on the national scene with perfect timing. In *Advertising Age,* Edwin H. Vick, chairman of the annual Pet Food Institute convention and president of Strongheart Products of Kansas City, predicted that cats (and dogs, too) were "gaining new status. The 1970s will see pets coming into the spotlight as a major hobby in the U.S." Vick extended his statement to say that pets, "formerly incidental bystanders on the American scene," would be "figuring much more importantly as companions, as a form of recreation, and as an aid in mental health programs."

Morris may not have qualified for the latter duty, since one of his biggest thrills came from outwitting his television master's intentions at every turn. As summarized in *Mighty Minutes,* "Morris exemplified the independence that cat owners cherish in their pets." He condescended to his master, a doting, silly woman

AT A GLANCE

9-Lives brand of canned cat food founded in 1954 by Star-Kist Foods, Inc.; 9-Lives gourmet canned cat food first offered in 1956; acquired by H. J. Heinz Company, 1963; Morris the Cat is first "spokescat" in market, 1969; Heinz established separate divisions, the Heinz Pet Products Company and the StarKist Seafood Company, 1988; Heinz combined the two companies, 1992.

Performance: *Market share*—26% (top share) of canned cat food category; 17.7% of wet cat food category; 15.5% of moist cat food category; 5.6% of dry cat food category. *Sales*—$250 million.

Major competitor: Ralston Purina's Purina Cat Chow.

Advertising: *Agency*—Leo Burnett USA, Chicago, IL. *Major campaign*—Morris the cat, a finicky eater with a sarcastic sense of humor, will only eat 9-Lives.

Addresses: *Parent company*—Heinz Pet Products, 1 Riverfront Place, Newport, KY 41071; phone: (606) 655-5700. *Ultimate parent company*—H. J. Heinz Company, Box 57, Pittsburgh, PA 15230-0057; phone: (412) 456-5700; fax: (412) 456-6128.

with a high-pitched voice. "Playing with yarn is stupid," Morris confided to television viewers in his deep, relaxed voice, "but cat owners expect it." In another commercial, perhaps hearkening back to his animal-shelter days, Morris and his owner visited a kennel. As Morris indifferently observed the scene, his owner squealed, "Oh, look, Morris. Puppies! Aren't they cute?" Morris responded in typical fashion: "Silly, stupid, sloppy, maybe," the big orange cat sniffed, " but not cute. Cats are cute." In another prime example, Morris and his "owner" spent a day at the beach. The woman single-handedly constructed walls, castles and towers. "Look, Morris, I made you a sand castle!," his owner bubbled over with excitement. "Good," the unflappable Morris replied. "Reserve the dungeon for yourself."

9-Lives Products

Morris, like many cats, demonstrated a qualified love for his master, tolerating her as long as he was fed his favorite food, 9-Lives. As Morris explained in one commercial, "A cat who doesn't act finicky loses the respect of its master"—at which point Morris would magnanimously yield and eat his 9-Lives dinner.

Cat food producers were up against an odd fact specific to pet owners. As one industry executive noted in *Printers' Ink*, "Pet owners are notorious brand switchers. We know that the owner looks at the pet and thinks it needs variety. It doesn't." But practical facts do not necessarily have a bearing on consumer buying habits. And this is why the promotion of Morris the Cat was so ingenious. Morris was popular not only because he represented feline independence so staunchly and comically, but also because his finicky habits mirrored those of his master. It was the choosy, brand-switching pet owner that the 9-Lives commercials were intended to sway by showing that Morris would only eat 9-Lives.

Heinz Pet Products rode the crest of the pet craze in general, and Morris' popularity, in particular. In November, 1969, the *Progressive Grocer* reported that pet food manufacturers "were literally flooding the marketplace with new items." Within a year

of Morris' entry on the national scene, Heinz worked on a number of new product introductions. In 1970 the company offered the first formed canned cat food, another gourmet item called "9-Lives burgers," and finally, 9-Lives dry cat food.

The dry cat food market—representing only 5 percent of total industry sales through the 1950s—grew rapidly through the 1960s, and 9-Lives wanted to take advantage of the trend. By 1964, dry cat food accounted for 30 percent of sales. Since Ralston Purina had already cornered well over half of that 30 percent market share, 9-Lives had some catching up to do in the dry food category.

Variety, then, became important to support brand names. In 1972, Heinz introduced 9-Lives morsels, and within three years a diced form of food was offered. Neither of these achieved great market success. In 1975, however, a popular soft-moist food was launched under the name 9-Lives Square Meals. After experiencing several name changes, 9-Lives decided on the name Tender Meals as its moist food contender.

Industry Trends

While supermarket and convenience store operators appreciated the growth in pet food sales, they didn't have enough shelf space for the proliferation of brands. They criticized the manufacturers tendency to introduce an item with heavy advertising, then let the brand die. In the meantime, the grocers were stuck with the products on their shelves. Many supermarket owners would then drop the items at their own discretion, a process they thought the manufacturers should take responsibility for.

One of the most important elements in the industry, given the proliferation of established and new brands, was packaging. Typical complaints of grocers were that if paper bags and cellophane wrappers were not torn or penetrated by various parasites in transit to the merchandisers, the pet food packages risked other forms of breakdown on the store shelves. Heinz, along with its competitors, strove to repackage its cat food to meet merchant and consumer needs. Attention to packaging stood to benefit Heinz 9-Lives in the long run; the more easily 9-Lives was recognized on the shelf, the more likely it would be chosen.

By 1973, 9-Lives was the market leader in cat food with an estimated 18 percent to 20 percent of industry sales. Sales of cat food, according to the Heinz Star-Kist subsidiary, had doubled during the previous three-year span. Accordingly, Heinz announced plans for an $8 million expansion of its Muscatine, Iowa plant. The addition would increase the company's total cat food production capacity by 25 percent. The Iowa expansion brought 9-Lives production closer to major markets and large suppliers of cat food ingredients than existing plants.

Advertising Changes

To spice up its 9-Lives dry cat food, which held less than 3 percent of the total market, in 1978 Star-Kist enlisted the services of Sylvester the Cat, a Warner Bros. cartoon character. The campaign featured Sylvester, whose face would dominate packaging and advertising. Leo Burnett USA used animated television commercials, similar to the Morris series, with the cartoon cat Sylvester.

Retailers in the East and parts of the Midwest considered the Sylvester launch merely a repackaging, since they already stocked 9-Lives dry cat food with a Morris on the box. In the West and

Southwest, however, the redesigned cat food was viewed as a new product introduction, intended to compete with new offerings like Good Mews by Ralston Purina and Crave by Kal Kan Foods. In ad spending, Star-Kist was competing with more established brands like Carnation Company's Chefs Blend and Ralston Purina's Meow Mix. To fulfill its claim, printed in *Advertising Age,* that it would spend "50 percent more dollars than used to introduce Meow Mix," Star-Kist had to budget $9 million for its new dry blend.

The original Morris the Cat died in 1978 to the dismay of many fans. He was seventeen years old. The 9-Lives campaign was among the 1979 *Advertising Age* annual award-winners. Running in its tenth year at that time, 9-Lives was the oldest promotion to receive the honor. Advertiser Leo Burnett's promotion of Morris succeeded to such a degree, in fact, that most respondents in the *Advertising Age* roster recognized the name Morris far more frequently than the name 9-Lives, and did not always associate the two as representing the same product. While Morris was gone, his personality lived on: a Morris look-alike who understudied the original was recruited to continue as the new star of the successful and long-running campaign.

The 9-Lives brand became the first cat food to establish a partnership with the American Humane Association in 1973. The brand published an annual cat calendar the following year. Soon

Morris, 9-Lives' "spokescat" since 1969.

after, Morris had the honor to serve as Spokescat for the National Adopt-A-Cat Month and National Cat Health Month promotions.

In 1988, Morris ran for President of the United States. By making Morris an independent presidential contender, Leo Burnett USA hoped the cat's social and political consciousness would be better demonstrated to the public. As reported in *Marketing News,* "Parodying an actual presidential bid, the ad campaign will include press conferences, a series of policy statements, 30- and 15-second TV spots, and bumper stickers." More than 24 reporters and 10 TV camera crews attended Morris' first press conference at the National Press Club, "when he announced his intention to claw his way into the White House."

The theme of the comical campaign was stressed in the slogan "9-Lives in every bowl and a satisfied cat in every kitchen." Most importantly, 9-Lives manufacturers wanted people to show their support for Morris by electing 9-Lives as their favorite cat food brand. Whether or not Morris' presidential bid was responsible, by May 1988 9-Lives enjoyed the top share in canned cat food with a commanding 27 percent of the market.

Another popular forum for Morris lovers was the Morris Report, a 52-page full-color quarterly conceived in 1986 by 9-Lives and publisher Alan Weston Communications of Burbank, California. The quarterly was designed to reach the one-third of all households which own a cat. After the initial free offering to veterinarians and persons already on the 9-Lives mailing list, the Morris Report reached a circulation of 35,000. Consumer mail generated by the quarterly resulted in thousands of letters, photos, and cartoons received monthly at 9-Lives offices.

Uniformity in Packaging

Taking advantage of the surge in Morris' popularity, Star-Kist commissioned an outside designer to refashion the 9-Lives labels on all canned, boxed, canistered, and bagged products. Redesigned labels highlighted Morris in a dignified, unruffled expression on every package, with color bands indicating different flavors. The new logo emphasized brand uniformity, part of Star-Kist's effort to increase its share in the dry and moist cat food categories.

9-Lives brand experienced some growing pains in the 1980s, but it was all for the best. Sylvester the Cat was dumped in favor of the ever-popular Morris character in 1986. 9-lives dry food was renamed 9-Lives Crunchy Meals. The following year, Cat Treats were introduced, making 9-Lives the first brand to offer a complete line of canned, moist, dry and snack food in the attempt to meet all consumer needs. In 1989 the company added 9-Lives Kitten Dinners to the roster.

Parent-company Heinz established two separate divisions, Heinz Pet Products and the Starkist Seafood Company, in 1988. While Heinz Pet Products continued to concentrate on the dry and moist cat food categories, its first priority was to further establish leadership in the canned segment. The company acquired several regional and private-label brands, increasing its share by 6 percent. Prior to the Heinz acquisitions, Ralston Purina led the $2.1 billion market in 1987 with a 31 percent market share; Carnation came in second at 21 percent, with Heinz at 19.1 percent. As stated in an *Advertising Age* article, Heinz officials claimed acquisitions moved it past Carnation to a 29 percent share of the total market. Heinz maintained its advertising relationship with Leo Burnett USA, Chicago, allocating $15 million to introduce a new size of 9-Lives canned.

Maintaining Market Share

In 1992, Heinz combined StarKist Seafood Company and Heinz Pet Products Company into one operating unit once again. Responding to environmental concerns, 9-Lives was the first cat food to provide both dolphin-safe tuna and steel recycling logos on its cans. The company concentrated on specialty markets for growth. 9-lives Lean Entrees, introduced in 1990, was a gourmet item 95 percent fat-free and 15 percent to 30 percent lower in calories than competing brands. Though a specialty item, 9-Lives Lean Entrees were distributed only in supermarkets. Sales materials for the low-calorie contender stated that "most adults concerned about their own fat intake would also like to limit their pet's fat consumption."

In the attempt to enter the specialty market full-scale, Heinz Pet Products bought partial ownership of Veterinary Centers of America (VCA), the largest chain of vets' offices in the U.S. in January 1993. Heinz also entered a joint venture with the VCA to develop, manufacture and market new pet products and services. This new link was crucial for Heinz's continued leadership in pet food sales. By 1993, supermarkets accounted for 70 percent of total sales, while veterinary offices, pet shops, warehouse clubs, and mass merchandisers like Wal-Mart and Kmart were steadily increasing their percentage of sales.

Though sales increased, the company kept costs under control to secure future growth. As testimony to the strength of 9-Lives canned, the consistent leader over 9-Lives dry and moist versions, the category jumped 10.8 percent in sales from 1992 to 1993, a $189.7 million increase. Heinz was the only company to enjoy such a rise in its sales. To reduce costs, however, Heinz limited production at its Terminal Island, California plant in 1992 to one shift per day; the company simultaneously reported a 15 percent increase in productivity. With the world's largest pet food facility operating in Bloomsburg, Pennsylvania, and international food products company H.J. Heinz as a corporate parent, the 9-Lives brand will continue as a dominant player in the pet food industry.

Further Reading:

9-Lives Product Information, Heinz Pet Products, 1993.

Dagnoli, Judann, "9-Lives Goes on a Diet," *Advertising Age,* August 6, 1990, p. 13.

Edwards, Larry, "Star-Kist Hires Sylvester for Rerun of 9-Lives Dry," *Advertising Age,* December 13, 1978, p. 2.

Folse, Lynn, " 'Morris Report' Database Delivers Direct Dividends," *Advertising Age,* May 16, 1988, p. S-1.

Hall, Jim, *Mighty Minutes: An Illustrated History of Television's Best Commercials,* New York: Harmony Books, 1984.

"Heinz Seeks to Acquire Star-Kist Foods, Inc.," *Wall Street Journal,* January 25, 1963, p. 8.

"H. J. Heinz Agrees to Buy for Stock 90 Percent of Star-Kist," *Wall Street Journal,* February 26, 1963, p. 8.

H. J. Heinz Company Annual Report, Pittsburgh, Pennsylvannia: H. J. Heinz Company, 1992.

"H. J. Heinz Unit to Expand Cat Food Operation by 25 Percent," *Wall Street Journal,* October 12, 1973, p. 9.

Liesse Erickson, Julie, and Marcy Magiera, "Cats' New Popularity Makes Marketers Purr," *Advertising Age,* December 26, 1988, p. 2.

Liesse, Julie, "Pet Foods Lose Bite in Supermarket," *Advertising Age,* March 15, 1993, p. 18.

McGrath, Robert, "Food for Felines Is the Cat's Meow," *Adweek's Marketing Week,* December 19, 1988, p. 17.

"Morris the Cat Gets Canned," *Design News,* January 6, 1984, p. 41.

"Nine Lives (Leo Burnett)," *Advertising Age,* April 16, 1979, p. 50.

O'Farrell, Larrie, "Pet Foods: The Continuing Boom," *Printers' Ink,* October 16, 1964, p. 27.

"Pet Food," *Progressive Grocer,* November, 1969, p. 48.

"Pet Foods of Future to Be More 'Human,' Spiegel Tells Institute," *Advertising Age,* September 11, 1967, p. 75.

"Pets Gain New Psychological Status, Strongheart's Vick Advises Institute," *Advertising Age,* September 8, 1969, p. 6.

Schniedman, Diane, "9-Lives Tosses Its Spokescat's Hat into the Ring," *Marketing News,* September 11, 1987, p. 14.

—Frances E. Norton

NUTRASWEET®

NutraSweet brand of sweetener, produced by The NutraSweet Company, a subsidiary of Monsanto Company, is the best-selling sweetener in the world. The low-calorie, high-intensity sweetener has been hailed as the miracle ingredient of the 1980s because it ushered in a whole new category of sugar-free foods and beverages. NutraSweet does contain some calories, but as a result of its high intensity—it is 180 times sweeter than sugar—only a tiny amount is needed, and very few calories are added to a product.

The introduction of NutraSweet in 1981 enabled food and beverage processors around the world to purchase the first industrial ingredient that could replace sugar and satisfy health- and weight-conscious consumers at the same time. Before NutraSweet, the only available low-calorie sweeteners were saccharin and cyclamates, both of which had taste and safety problems.

By the time NutraSweet's patent on aspartame, the sweetener's generic name, expired in the United States on December 14, 1992, NutraSweet had been approved for use in 90 countries around the world and could be found in some 5,000 products. Its familiar red and white swirl logo appeared on product labels of such items as soft drinks, dairy products, candies, diet foods, and even over-the-counter drug products.

As a reward for undertaking the time and expense of discovering aspartame, NutraSweet was the only manufacturer of the sweetener for 11 years, until its U.S. patent expired in 1992. The market for other aspartame producers was thus opened. Although its patent in Europe had expired in 1986 and it was competitive with other sweeteners, 90 percent of the brand's sales were in the United States.

During the 1980s The NutraSweet Company was preparing for the patent expiration and loss of sales to competitors by developing new products. The company hoped in the early 1990s that a new sweetener 50 times sweeter than the current NutraSweet product would be ready to put on the market by the year 2000.

Brand Origins

NutraSweet was discovered by accident in 1965. James Schlatter, a scientist at G.D. Searle & Co., a pharmaceutical company, was working with various proteins for an ulcer drug. He happened to lick his finger and noticed a sweet taste. After years of testing and waiting for approval from the U.S. Food and Drug Adminis-

tration (FDA), NutraSweet was sanctioned for use in the United States in 1981. It had been approved before then for use in several other nations. In the ensuing years, there were some periodic questions about NutraSweet's safety, but the FDA always upheld its approval in light of overwhelming evidence confirming its safety.

NutraSweet is a protein-based sweetener possessing a clean, sweet flavor and, unlike other popular sweeteners, has no aftertaste. NutraSweet is not a carbohydrate and is not metabolized like one. Endorsed by regulatory agencies in 90 countries, the World Health Organization, and the American Dietetic Association, it is a product that can be used by everyone in the population, including diabetics. From the beginning, food and beverage manufacturers have embraced NutraSweet, since the taste and quality of their products could be maintained. The first product to contain the sweetener was a gum ball. Shortly after, different types of dairy products containing NutraSweet—including yogurt, frozen dairy desserts, frozen novelties, toppings, flavored milks, cocoa and shake mixes—were put on the market. Some manufacturers found that by replacing sugar with NutraSweet, the caloric content of certain dairy products could be lowered by as much as 50 percent.

First Commercial Success

Beginning in 1983 it was the soft drink industry that gave NutraSweet its widest usage. At first, most of the soft drinks used NutraSweet blended with saccharin, which necessitated that a warning appear on the products' labels about the alleged dangers of saccharin. The first product to carry 100 percent NutraSweet was Coca-Cola's Diet Sprite, followed by the other soft drink giant, Diet Pepsi. Many lesser known brands followed, and by the time NutraSweet's patent expired, diet soft drinks accounted for 30 percent of the total soft drink market. The NutraSweet Company developed a heat-stable version of its sweetener that was approved by the FDA in the early 1990s and could be used in baked, canned, and roasted foods.

Early Marketing Strategy

Early marketing techniques employed by The NutraSweet Company included a requirement that food and beverage manufacturers display the company's swirling logo and the implementation of high prices in order to recover the great expense of the nearly decade-long FDA approval process. Both strategies would

AT A GLANCE

NutraSweet brand of sweetener discovered in 1965 by James Schlatter, a scientist at G.D. Searle & Co. The NutraSweet Company formed in 1985 as a subsidiary of Monsanto Company, which acquired G.D. Searle & Co. NutraSweet approved for consumption by U.S. Food and Drug Administration (FDA), 1981; introduced in packet form as Equal, 1982; first appeared in a major soft drink, Coca-Cola's Diet Sprite, 1983; introduced as a spooned sweetener, NutraSweet Spoonful, 1992; U.S. patent expiration, 1992.

Performance: *Market share*—75% (top share) of aspartame category. *Sales*—(United States) $700 million; (worldwide) $954 million.

Major competitor: Holland Sweetener Company, a joint venture of DSM of the Netherlands and Tosoh Corp. of Japan.

Advertising: *Agency*—Chiat/Day/Mojo Inc., Venice, CA, 1990—. *Major campaign*—"Spoons," TV and print ads launching NutraSweet Spoonful.

Addresses: *Parent company*—The NutraSweet Company, P.O. Box 730, 1751 Lake Cook Road, Deerfield, IL 60015-5239; phone: (708) 940-9800. *Ultimate parent company*—Monsanto Company, 800 North Lindbergh Blvd., St. Louis, MO 63167; phone: (314) 694-1000.

later be bones of contention with manufacturers, many of whom were looking forward to patent expiration so they could purchase aspartame perhaps less expensively from other companies.

Since NutraSweet was an ingredient rather than a product to be sold directly to consumers, the company had to develop a special type of marketing strategy. Initially the focus was on products, but later it was on image-building. The brand was launched by mailing gum balls sweetened with NutraSweet to three million Americans. The company then shifted to image advertising for the ingredient so that consumers would associate it with the overall quality and purity of a particular product containing the sweetener. Art Massa, public relations director for NutraSweet, explained to Fara Warner in *Adweek's Marketing Week,* "We had to pre-sell the consumer on NutraSweet."

The NutraSweet Company spent approximately $20 million a year advertising its logo and contributed money to the advertising campaigns of manufacturers that displayed it. In 1983 the company began an ad campaign to educate consumers about what the sweetener lacked—calories and a bitter taste. The commercials further directed consumers to look for the logo on the labels of their favorite products. Brand awareness was fostered through the prominent display of the NutraSweet logo on many top-selling products, such as Diet Coke and Diet Pepsi.

The requirement of using the NutraSweet brand logo was also meant to gain the loyalty of manufacturers. Consumers caught on to the idea of looking for products with the NutraSweet logo because it came to represent a safe, reliable ingredient. In this way, the logo has actually expanded the healthy food and beverage marketplace for manufacturers. According to John Lewis, Nutra-Sweet's vice president of marketing, "We have taken a high intensity sweetener that nobody had heard of before 1980 and turned it into a trusted household name in the 1990s."

While The NutraSweet Company made an effort to protect its market share after patent expiration, many manufacturers viewed it as arrogance typical of a monopoly. One unnamed executive was quoted in *Beverage World* as saying that companies using NutraSweet in their products were treated "more like hostages than customers." The NutraSweet Company reported plans to drop the logo requirement by 1994.

The high prices that made NutraSweet the most expensive ingredient in soft drinks were to be lowered at patent expiration. Until then, manufacturers in the United States paid approximately $50 to $70 per pound, compared to $35 to $40 per pound in Europe and Canada, where patents had already expired. While the price of NutraSweet in Europe was still lower than in the United States, it could have been even lower minus the markup from anti-dumping duties, which were imposed on the company by the European Economic Community (EEC) in 1990 following complaints of anti-competitive pricing by NutraSweet's major competitor, the Holland Sweetener Company. The penalties imposed were as high as $33.20 per pound on imported NutraSweet in 1992.

Advertising Innovations

Market research shows that 98 to 99 percent of consumers recognize the NutraSweet logo. The red and white logo colors were selected because red was thought to connote high quality and, when put together with white, suggests something sweet. John Lewis stated that consumer trust in the logo "clearly gives [NutraSweet] a terrific competitive advantage."

For the celebration of NutraSweet's 10th anniversary in 1991, TV and print ads focused on the first product to use the sweetener, the gum ball. A sweepstakes was run and consumers were invited to look for products with the logo and then try to win a prize; they were told to dial a toll-free number and punch in the Universal Product Code (UPC) to learn if they were instant winners. A total of 18,001 prizes—including a trip to any of the 50 countries where NutraSweet was used in products—were distributed.

Print ads and TV commercials for diet soft drinks and other products advertised the use of NutraSweet in the product. Soft drink commercials included the tagline "with 100 percent Nutra-Sweet." As patent expiration neared, however, the sweetener came to be referred to as "the secret ingredient." Diet Pepsi commercials used the phrase "with 100 percent Uh-Huh," and the NutraSweet logo appeared without any voiceover. In order to retain consumers' high awareness level, brand identification ads on network and cable television began about five months before patent expiration.

Product Changes

As an industrial ingredient, NutraSweet needed to be easy to use and handle by food and beverage processors. The NutraSweet Company approached several major customers and asked them how the sweetener could be improved. Some companies reported that the powdered form of the sweetener was too dusty and did not flow well; in addition, they found the 25-kilogram drums containing NutraSweet too costly. In response, the company introduced in 1989 a granular form that was shipped in packages 16 times larger than the drums, making NutraSweet more cost-efficient for large customers. The smaller drum size continued to be available to customers who preferred it. The granular form—comprised of particles ten times as large as those in the powder—was expected to replace the powder form in soft drinks because it was better suited to liquids. The granules provided better flowability and dispersion and greater density.

International Market

International marketing had always been an important strategy for NutraSweet brand development, but in the early 1990s, with the approaching patent expiration, there were plans for more global expansion. In 1991 ground was broken for a new plant to manufacture NutraSweet in Gravelines, France, with production due to go on line in 1993. The plant was a joint venture with Ajinomoto Co. Inc., a Japanese food ingredient company and long-time partner of The NutraSweet Company. The French plant was intended to improve service to European customers and increase NutraSweet sales throughout the continent, considered to be the fastest-growing market in the world for the sweetener. By 1998 the company planned to have manufacturing plants on three continents—North America, Europe, and South America.

The international market, however, already had lower priced competitors, and some of NutraSweet's major customers buy from them. Holland Sweetener Company, which is expected to be NutraSweet's major competitor in the United States, sells aspartame to Coca-Cola for its European manufacturing operations. The international market is also comprised of more products that are blends of aspartame with other, less expensive sweeteners and thus have lower prices. While The NutraSweet Company discourages the use of NutraSweet in combination with other sweeteners, its patent on blends of aspartame and saccharin expired in 1991, paving the way for domestic processors to produce blends. In addition, several companies in Japan, Brazil, and the United Kingdom are developing new types of high-intensity sweeteners that will compete with NutraSweet in the international marketplace.

Performance Appraisal and Future Predictions

The NutraSweet Company does not break down sales for aspartame used as an industrial ingredient, but it reported worldwide sales of aspartame in 1991 at $954 million, representing a 2.3 percent rate of growth over the previous year. The worldwide market for all types of sweeteners was estimated at $1.2 billion in 1991. The United States accounted for NutraSweet's largest market: $700 million in sales was reported for 1991.

The NutraSweet Company stated publicly that it expected to lose about $200 to $250 million in sales in the United States, or 20 percent of its market, during its first year of competition to generic look-alikes of aspartame. To compete with lower priced sweeteners sure to enter the market, the company sought to decrease manufacturing costs and charge lower prices to processors. Robert E. Flynn, chairman and chief executive officer of the company, said, "We have invested nearly $400 million to become the world's low-cost producer of aspartame." Smaller food and beverage makers would be able to afford NutraSweet and use it to develop new types of products. These smaller companies hoped that prices would drop between 25 and 50 percent as they had when patents expired in some foreign countries. Anticipating government sanctioning of NutraSweet in more foods and beverages, the company almost doubled its production capacity from 1989 to 1992. And, in 1993 the government did approve new uses for aspartame; consumers would soon see the NutraSweet swirl on cake mixes, candy, and low- and non-alcoholic beer

But the company also wanted to retain its two largest customers, soft drink makers Coke and Pepsi, which together bought 65 percent of all aspartame made worldwide. In April of 1992 the two beverage makers signed long-term contracts for domestic and foreign use at a price of $30 per pound. At the time, a NutraSweet Company spokesman reported that four of the company's top ten customers had extended their agreements beyond patent expiration.

Another strategy was to develop new products, not only because generics would be marketed but also because new types of artificial sweeteners would be available. One new product was termed the next-generation sweetener for use as an industrial ingredient. Called Sweetener 2000, it is 10,000 times sweeter than sugar, has no calories, and will cost fractions of a penny per pound. The sweetener was not expected to make its debut until near the turn of the century.

A third strategy was to enter the consumer market, which is the second-largest market for sweeteners. The NutraSweet Company had been marketing aspartame in tabletop form since its introduction of Equal in 1982. Equal, packaged in packet form, was intended mainly for use in restaurants and other eating places to compete with Sweet N' Low, a sweetener made with saccharin. In 1992 two other tabletop sweeteners were introduced, SweetMate and NutraSweet Spoonful. SweetMate was 60 percent cheaper than Equal and had a stronger, sweeter taste than NutraSweet. NutraSweet Spoonful, aimed at Sweet N' Low users who prefer the more intense taste of saccharin, is a granulated sugar alternative packaged in a glass jar. Containing only two calories per teaspoon compared with sugar's sixteen, it is as sweet as sugar and designed to be used as a spooned sweetener for home use.

Further Reading:

"Granular NutraSweet Available in U.S. Soon," *Beverage Industry*, June 1989, p. 29.

Jabbonsky, Larry, "Swirling Dervish," *Beverage World*, April 1992, pp. 44-45.

Monsanto Company Annual Report, 1991, pp. 15-17.

Naude, Alice, "Sweet Dreams," *Chemical Marketing Reporter*, June 15, 1992, p. 8.

"NutraSweet, Pfizer Debut New Items," *Chemical Marketing Reporter*, June 15, 1992, p. 7.

"100 Leading National Advertisers," *Advertising Age*, September 23, 1992, p. 48.

"Pepsi and Coke Set NutraSweet," *New York Times*, April 22, 1992, sec. D, p. 6.

Petersen, Laurie, "NutraSweet Uses Promo to Boost Ad Message," *Adweek's Marketing Week*, July 8, 1991, p. 22.

Shapiro, Eben, "Europe Venture Plans NutraSweet Challenge," *New York Times*, January 28, 1992, sec. D, p. 4; "NutraSweet's Race With the Calendar," *New York Times*, April 8, 1992, sec. D, p. 4.

"Soft Drink Ingredients, A Consumer's Guide," National Soft Drink Association, January 1985, p. 5.

Therrien, Lois, "How Sweet It Isn't at Nutrasweet," *Business Week*, December 14, 1992, p. 42.

Warner, Fara, "NutraSweet Launches New Ads," *Adweek's Marketing Week*, May 20, 1992, p. 6.

Warner, Fara, "NutraSweet Previews Ads for New Substitute," *Adweek's Marketing Week*, June 8, 1992, p. 9.

—*Dorothy Kroll*

OCEAN SPRAY®

The Ocean Spray brand name, tied since inception to the cranberry, is the single most potent force behind its corporate parent's rise to prominence as the largest domestic seller of canned and bottled juice drinks. Through a series of pioneering marketing strategies begun in the early 1960s, the tart red berry, once served only as a sauce at special holidays, has demonstrated such enormous versatility that its product line of fresh fruits, juices, and value-added products continues to unfold as new flavor and food combinations are discovered. Ocean Spray Cranberries, Inc., parent company of the Ocean Spray brand, harvests, processes, packages, promotes, distributes, and sells almost all the cranberries grown in the United States and Canada. Ocean Spray's trademark blue and white logo can be found on supermarket shelves in many countries worldwide; since 1976, it has graced a number of non-cranberry products, including fresh grapefruit and grapefruit juice. By continuing to emphasize quality products that appeal to consumers looking for healthy, low-calorie alternatives to soft drinks, Ocean Spray has maintained its leadership in the still-expanding packaged juice industry.

A Cranberry Primer

Cranberries and blueberries are the only fruits indigenous to America's unique wetlands environment. There are over one hundred different cranberry varieties, many hybridized over the past hundred years from wild vines native to low-lying bog areas. Cranberries once provided the North American Indians with a rich source of Vitamin C and were a main ingredient in *pemmican,* a high-energy cake of crushed cranberries, dried venison, and melted fat. Indians also used the red berries to make dyes and poultices. Gifts of the fruit were made to the pilgrims as a sign of peace, and the red berries were very likely on the menu during the first Thanksgiving feast in 1621. Early colonists named the unusual fruit "crane-berry" because of the resemblance of the cranberry bush's flower to the head of a crane.

The fruit became popular and was exported by New England colonists to Europe in the eighteenth century. Whaling ships often carried barrels of cranberries in their holds to supplement the crew's diet; the fruit's high Vitamin C content helped ward off the scurvy that plagued sailors during long months at sea. However, it wasn't until 1810 that they were cultivated on a large scale. Captain Henry Hall of East Dennis, Massachusetts, noticed that wild cranberries growing near his home flourished after the wind blew a covering of sand from the nearby dunes over young spring growth. The sand covering caused the new shoots to root and the vines to spread more rapidly. Hall experimented by transplanting some of the vines and covering them with sand. The process worked, and wholesale cranberry cultivation began soon after.

Cranberries are a perennial crop, and cranberry vines will survive indefinitely. In fact, certain vines growing in Cape Cod's ideal conditions have been yielding fruit for over one hundred and fifty years. The unique requirements of the cranberry vine—acidity, peat soil, moist conditions, and a long growing season extending from April to November—considerably limit cultivation. The "bogs" in which cranberries take root are the result of glacial deposits and, in their commercialized state, consist of low beds lined with clay and constructed of peat and gravel, sandwiched between layers of sand. Consequently, cranberry production continues to be limited to selected regions in Massachusetts, New Jersey, Oregon, Washington, and Wisconsin, as well as parts of Canada (particularly British Columbia). Of the 26,000 acres currently under cultivation, 12,500 are in Massachusetts. Because of this, it was natural that the New England coastline would one day be the "cranberry capital of the world."

Brand Origins

In the early 1900s, a Boston lawyer named Marcus L. Urann developed a recipe for cranberry sauce that could be preserved in tins. Urann began marketing his creation in the Boston area in 1912 under the catchy name "Ocean Spray." Limiting his product line to either whole or jellied cranberry sauce, he acquired a reputation as an expert promoter and producer, and he soon became known as the "Cranberry King." A shrewd businessman, Urann foresaw the benefits of joining with other cranberry growers to market and sell cranberry products to the general public. In May 1930 he approached John C. Makepeace, owner of the Makepeace Preserving Company of nearby Wareham, as well as another competitor in the cranberry market, Elizabeth F. Lee, director of the Enoch F. Bills Company of New Egypt, New Jersey, with a monumental proposal. Urann told the other cranberry growers that competition between the three was hurting each business and suggested that they form a partnership. The incorporation papers were filed the following month, but a point of contention soon arose between Urann and Makepeace that almost destroyed the efforts of the three business owners. Makepeace was concerned

AT A GLANCE

Ocean Spray brand cranberry products were founded in 1912 in South Hanson, MA, by Ocean Spray Preserving Co. owner Marcus L. Urann; later developers include Hal Thorkilsen; Ocean Spray merged with Makepeace Preserving Co. and Enoch F. Bills Co. to form Cranberry Canners, Inc., 1930, which was renamed National Cranberry Association, 1946, and became Ocean Spray Cranberries, Inc., 1959.

Performance: *Market share*—21% (top share) of shelf-stable juice category. *Sales*—$974 million.

Major competitor: Tropicana Products, Inc.

Advertising: *Agency*—R.L.I. *Major campaign*—Conservatively dressed actor claiming: "It's amazing what a little cran can do!"

Addresses: *Parent company*—Ocean Spray Cranberries, Inc., 1 Ocean Spray Dr., Lakeville-Middleboro, MA 02349-0001; phone: (508) 946-7704; fax: (508) 946-7704.

over Urann's delay in transferring ownership of the widely recognized Ocean Spray name and trademark. Fortunately the matter was resolved with the transfer of the Ocean Spray name on August 14, 1930, and Cranberry Canners, Inc. was born.

Although the newly formed grower cooperative was able to combine resources to everyone's advantage, the cranberry business remained a seasonal operation that ended when the tinned sauce arrived on grocery store shelves in time for Thanksgiving and Christmas dinners. Urann was quick to see that opportunities for growth could be found in developing new uses for the fruit. Enthusiastic over the future of the young cooperative, he composed an encouraging letter to Massachusetts cranberry growers. "Work as you must, worry as you will," he wrote, "kill bugs and flow for frost, still your profit depends upon the supply and demand for cranberries. . . . Let us Cape Codders throw out our chest, take pride and every day boost and blow for Ocean Spray Brand Cranberry Sauce. Ten million people will visit Cape Cod this year and they shall not pass without seeing, feeling, hearing and tasting cranberries."

Early Marketing Strategy

In 1933 Ocean Spray Cranberry Juice Cocktail first appeared. Its advertising proclaimed it "A pleasant, smooth drink with delicious flavor and sure relief from faintness, exhaustion, and thirst. A glass when retiring promotes sleep and a clean mouth in the morning—even to the smoker." Although its claims of healthfulness and smoothness were perhaps a bit exaggerated, Cranberry Juice Cocktail proved a reasonably successful forerunner of its sweeter contemporary. Six years later the company introduced Ocean Spray Cran, a more agreeable tasting cranberry syrup intended as a mixer with alcoholic beverages. Urann saw his market for cranberry products broaden and the profits of his cooperative continue to grow.

Throughout the 1940s, as the benefits of membership in Cranberry Canners became apparent, growers from other states joined the collective. By 1941, the cooperative stretched westward from the bogs of Cape Cod to the wetlands of Oregon and Washington. Growers could now benefit from the exchange of regional cultivation techniques as well as the pooling of advertising and processing expenses. Cranberry Canners had fifteen processing plants

nationwide by 1943, thereby keeping pace with yearly harvests. During this decade, Ocean Spray Cranberry Juice Cocktail was improved by the addition of corn syrup sweetener to appeal to consumer tastes. The company's creativity helped it during World War II, when shortages of sugar and the tin used to can cranberry sauce became rationed. The November 1943 cranberry harvest was dehydrated, packaged, and sent to the troops overseas. The company marketed Ocean Spray Cranberry-Orange Marmalade for domestic consumption until the war was over and sugar was again available. Because of its willingness to supply the war effort, Cranberry Canners received the Achievement "A" award from the War Food Administration. Following the war, the company returned to normal production with a fresh perspective. As an outward demonstration of its newfound spirit, the company changed its name to National Cranberry Association (NCA) in 1946, reflecting a growing national profile.

In addition to changes to the collective's name, its advertising, and its product line, the years following World War II marked the start of the company's international operations. In 1950 Canadian growers joined the collective; this step would open the door to new markets for Ocean Spray. By 1980 the company had opened its fourth foreign packaging operation in Melbourne, Australia, and its continued investment in the growing international market has helped transform it into a sophisticated global organization.

Necessity Is the Mother of Invention

The 1950s saw many changes for the NCA. Of greatest impact were the retirements of Marcus Urann as president and general manager at the age of 81, and Makepeace as secretary-treasurer at age 84. The collective found itself with new leadership for the first time since its inception. Meanwhile, the NCA continued its trend toward product innovation. Ocean Spray Fresh Cranberries made their way onto store shelves several weeks before Thanksgiving in 1946. By 1951 the product line also included Ocean Spray Cape Cod Cranberry Sundae Topping, as well as a line of dietetic cranberry products, each bearing the Ocean Spray brand. In 1957 the company took its first step into the frozen foods market with the introduction of Ocean Spray Frozen Cranberries and Ocean Spray Frozen Cranberry-Orange Relish. Near the close of 1959, Ocean Spray had posted sales of $25 million.

The cooperative underwent yet another name change, this time to Ocean Spray Cranberries, Inc., to more closely identify itself with the popular brand name devised by Urann. Sales for the holiday season were promising, but two weeks before Thanksgiving the U.S. Department of Health announced that the herbicide aminotriazole, used by some growers to kill poison ivy in cranberry bogs, caused cancer in laboratory rats. Grocers swiftly pulled "cancerberries"—as they were dubbed by consumers—off store shelves, and sales for that years's crop plummeted.

The start of 1960 dawned for Ocean Spray with the realization that it was too dependent on a single product line and needed to diversify. Although the U.S. government granted a subsidy to growers for fruit not treated with aminotriazole, the supply of cranberries far outpaced the demand from still-cautious consumers. Ocean Spray set out on the road to recovery as the result of an idea by Hal Thorkilsen, an MIT chemical engineer and executive at Philip Morris, to turn excess cranberries into a line of juice drinks. The advice of Thorkilsen, who would later become the company's CEO, paved the way for the introduction of Ocean Spray Cranapple, Grapeberry, and Crangrape bottled juices.

Ocean Spray based each of its new juices on its core product, Cranberry Juice Cocktail. The combination of new products, an aggressive marketing program, an overhaul of production facilities, and a renewed commitment to quality control set the cooperative back on its feet. After 1968, the supply of cranberries from growers once again equaled the demand of the marketplace; by 1971, cranberry harvests topped 100 barrels per acre for the first time in the history of the collective.

Drenching the Competition

In the years that followed, increasingly health-conscious Americans started looking for replacements for soda pop. Ocean Spray had the answer, and marketed its juice line with the slogan "It's good for you, America!" In 1976, responding to America's still-growing concern over healthy diets and the company's desire to diversify its product line, Ocean Spray joined with citrus growers in Florida's Indian River to market the first shelf-stable citrus beverage, Ocean Spray Grapefruit Juice, in glass bottles.

As the company moved into the 1980s it continued to develop and market new products. Crantastic, its first multijuice drink, appeared on supermarket shelves in 1981. Two years later Ocean Spray introduced its popular Mauna-La'i, a concoction of exotic guava juice blended with the tartness of lemon. In 1985 Ocean Spray introduced a liquid concentrate version of its best-selling Cranberry Juice Cocktail, another innovation designed to compete with the frozen juice market. 1991 saw the introduction of Ocean Spray Ruby Red Grapefruit Juice, promoted as a low-acid, "not too sweet" cousin to the company's other popular grapefruit juice products.

In addition to mixing cranberry juice with other flavors, the company also made an addition to its food product line by introducing Ocean Spray Cran-Fruit Sauces—crushed strawberries, raspberries, apples, and oranges which added sweetness to the tart cranberry. Packaged in convenient plastic tubs, the new products were an outgrowth of the desire to keep sales up during normally slow periods between holidays. 1989 saw the introduction of Craisins, the second non-drink product to bear the Ocean Spray brand label. These dried cranberries, lightly sugared to diminish their naturally tart flavor, were sold as a snack food, as well as an ingredient in processed foods for such companies as Pepperidge Farm, Campbell Soup, Lender's, Tyson, and Kellogg.

Ocean Spray Refreshers burst onto store shelves in 1990 as an "escape from sugary sweet." In flavors such as citrus cranberry, orange cranberry, and citrus peach, Refreshers was directly aimed at the lucrative Baby Boomer market, who at 37 percent of the population was then the target of only 19 percent of juice industry advertising.

Advertising Innovations

The first few years after World War II found the company putting renewed energy into advertising and publicity for its broadening product line. The 1948 Massachusetts Cranberry Festival was enlivened by a humorous skit depicting the "marriage" of cranberries and chicken. According to a company publication entitled "The History of Ocean Spray," "In a colorful ceremony that brought to a close the cranberry festival . . . the Little White Hen and the Little Red Cranberry became flavor-mates forever and vowed always to appear on the dinner tables of the nation. The wedding climaxed a year-long romance between chicken and cranberry sauce—a romance fostered by NCA in an effort to make

chicken and cranberry sauce as inseparable as lamb and mint jelly, pork and applesauce.''

The 1950s were the Golden Age of television and the Ocean Spray product line was one of many to take advantage of the new medium: a commercial promoting the chicken/cranberry sauce combination ran in key cities twice a week beginning in 1952. By the early 1980s, surveys showed that the Ocean Spray brand was perceived by consumers as an emblem for health-conscious and "natural" products, and sales of Ocean Spray Cranberry Sauce, which hadn't been advertised since 1970, were down by two-thirds, encroached on by private label products. Echoing its earlier ad campaign, the company boosted its cranberry sauce with the slogan, "It goes with a lot more than just turkey." Eighty-five percent of the advertising budget was sunk into TV spots, while packaging innovations such as "paper bottles" added to the company's health-conscious image and made its "take-along" juices appeal to a more active consumer. The company's most memorable TV ad was the 1989-91 campaign positioning popular jazz musician Bobby McFerrin dancing against a colorful Caribbean background of beach, surf, and sun, and singing "So tangy, so crisp, so cool . . . Ocean Spray . . . It's music to your mouth!" The ads accentuated the "full, quirky cranberry-osity of the drinks," according to Barbara Lippert of *Adweek's Marketing Week,* and their slant was unusual—a challenge to customers to break from the mundane. By such innovations Ocean Spray became the biggest seller of canned and bottled juice drinks in the United States.

More recent advertising strategies have found Ocean Spray wrestling prized shelf space away from other brands at the local supermarket. In 1988 it became the sponsor of the national tour of the Ringling Brothers Barnum & Bailey Circus. Discount tickets were offered through visible store displays that attracted consumers due to joint advertising on television and radio and in print media. The venture proved successful as sales of Ocean Spray products rose during the promotional period. In another promotional effort, the Refreshers juice line was marketed through summer concert and festival sponsorships. In 1991, in the company's home state, Ocean Spray Refreshers became the "official juice drink of the 95th Boston Marathon''; over 40,000 free samples of the beverage were given away to spectators.

Environmental Concerns

By 1987 Ocean Spray was faced with a favorable yet troubling consequence of its successful marketing and advertising program: supply couldn't keep pace with the increasing demand for the cranberry. Strict environmental controls were limiting bog expansion in the company's home state, and the concerns of local environmentalists proved valid the following year when the company pleaded guilty to illegally dumping cranberry peelings and other acidic waste into a Massachusetts river and sewer system. Ocean Spray accepted responsibility, paid the fine, and donated water treatment equipment to the town of Middleboro.

Although cranberry production involves many acres of endangered wetlands, the land includes 85 to 90 percent more land than is actually used in production. These fields, forests, streams, ponds, and reservoirs supporting the actual cranberry bogs provide a refuge for many species of plants and animals, including bald eagles, blue herons, osprey, Canadian geese, coyotes, bog rushes, and cotton grasses. One of Ocean Spray's major marketing battles has been to align itself with rather than against environmentalists over wetlands-related issues. Growers see their role in preserving a substantial portion of this endangered area as actually aiding environmental causes.

Looking to the Future

"Ocean Spray Cranberries Inc. has managed to take the homely, tart-tasting little cranberry beyond the familiar sauce of the holiday season to a range of products like sherbet and yogurt, cookies and muffins, and even bagels," proclaimed the *New York Times* in late 1992. "It's amazing what a little cran can do" carried Ocean Spray into the 1990s, and the company's forward-looking marketing strategies would seem to bear this out. Looking well beyond the traditional supermarket venue, Ocean Spray has begun packaging juice products specifically for the food service market, which account for one-third of total juice sales. The company continues to discuss ways that cranberries can be integrated into new products conceived by other major food corporations.

The cooperative's primary focus has always been to create an image of quality for its brand name, and to aggressively develop new markets. "As Ocean Spray enters its seventh decade, our business is sound and the future is full of promise," corporate leaders stated to shareholders in the 1991 Annual Report. A vending agreement between Ocean Spray and beverage giant PepsiCo that was signed the following year seems to have made good on that promise. The gain from Pepsi's expert marketing of single-serving cans through vending machines, convenience stores, and other traditional avenues will result in rising sales for Ocean Spray, and the juice manufacturer's health-conscious image will be an asset for the carbonated beverage manufacturer in a time when healthy products are held in high regard. Due to this unique venture, Ocean Spray predicts that single-serving juice sales will account for one-third of the company's revenue by the year 2000.

Where else will the company look for ideas? " 'You always see people at parties mixing Cranberry Juice Cocktail and sparkling mineral water,' " remarked a beverage consultant for a 1992 issue of *Adweek's Marketing Week.* The joint venture between PepsiCo and Ocean Spray has the potential for far more than shared shelf-space in the corner vending machine. The only limita-

tion directly facing the company as it approaches the next century is the shortage of fresh fruit due to limited wetlands. However, with the ingenuity, creativity, and energy characteristic of this New England corporation, no problem seems insurmountable.

Further Reading:

Appelbaum, Cara, "Ocean Spray Swaps Juice for Japanese Iced Coffee," *Adweek's Marketing Week,* October 28, 1991, p. 6.

Berry, Jon, "Ocean Spray Joins the Pepsi Generation," *Adweek's Marketing Week,* March 9, 1992, pp. 18-21.

Bird, Laura, "Ocean Spray Goes for Grownups," *Adweek's Marketing Week,* June 3, 1991, p. 7.

Buell, Barbara, "How Ocean Spray Keeps Reinventing the Cranberry," *Business Week,* December 2, 1985, p. 142.

Dagnoli, Judann, "Frozen Novelties Catch a Chill," *Adweek's Marketing Week,* March 27, 1989, pp. 25, 65.

Dagnoli, Judann, "Ocean Spray Pours 'Diet' Line Extension," *Advertising Age,* December 4, 1989, p. 24.

Dagnoli, Judann, "Ocean Spray Splash: $30M Campaign Will Support Refreshers Juice", *Advertising Age,* June 17, 1991, p. 50.

Donahue, Christine, "Can Ocean Spray Sell Cranberry Sauce Off-Season?" *Adweek's Marketing Week,* June 26, 1989, p. 25.

Elliott, Stuart, "Ocean Spray and Napier Try to Tinker with Success," *The New York Times,* September 11, 1991, p. D16.

Garcia, Shelly, "Ocean Spray's Three-Ring Circus," *Adweek's Marketing Week,* September 5, 1988, pp. S8-S9.

"The History of Ocean Spray Cranberries, Inc.," Lakeville-Middleboro, Massachusetts, Ocean Spray, 1981.

"How Ocean Spray Gave Cranberries Some Sparkle," *The New York Times,* November 26, 1992, pp. D1-2.

"Juice Vending Growth Jumped off the Chart," *Beverage Industry,* May 1990, p. 24.

Lippert, Barbara, "McFerrin Puts a Happy Spin on Ocean Spray's Cran-coctions," *Adweek's Marketing Week,* April 24, 1989, p. 63.

Moskowitz, Milton, Robert Levering, and Michael Katz, eds., "Ocean Spray," *Everybody's Business: A Field Guide to the 400 Leading Companies in America,* New York, Doubleday, 1990, pp. 49-51.

"Not Crazy about Craisins," *Time,* June 26, 1989, p. 59.

Ocean Spray Cranberries, Inc. Annual Report, Lakeville-Middleboro, Ocean Spray, 1991.

Skolnik, Rayna, "Ocean Spray's Canny Marketing," *Sales & Marketing Management,* August 18, 1980, pp. 31-35.

—Jay P. Pederson

OLD MILWAUKEE®

Old Milwaukee, the eighth-largest selling beer in the United States, also became the Stroh Brewery Company's best-selling brand. Owned by Stroh since its 1982 acquisition of Joseph Schlitz Brewing Company, Old Milwaukee grew to be the fifth most popular brand and has been instrumental in Stroh's continued strong presence in a beer market characterized by flat sales. Sold in the popular-price category and targeted toward the 21-34 age group, Old Milwaukee was the second-largest selling brand in that low price popular beer segment. Popular beer, which is the second-largest category after premium brands, accounts for approximately 22 percent of beer sales. Old Milwaukee's established brand name and good-quality image allowed Stroh to introduce brand extensions like Old Milwaukee NA (to take advantage of the burgeoning non-alcoholic beer segment), Old Milwaukee Genuine Draft, and Old Milwaukee Genuine Draft Light in 1991.

Brand Origins

Old Milwaukee's special recipe was created in 1849 by August Krug, founder of the Joseph Schlitz Brewing Company. The brand name was introduced during the Prohibition era in the form of Old Milwaukee Brew, a non-alcoholic beer. Named after the one-time beer capital in the Wisconsin city, it began to have a presence in U.S. markets around 1934. "The original popular-priced beer," as Stroh described it, Old Milwaukee was just a popular regional beer for decades thereafter. Schlitz Brewing kept perfecting the formula for a popular-priced beer; upon arriving at a satisfactory one by the 1960s, it began a concerted marketing effort. In the meanwhile, Schlitz Brewing had grown to be the biggest name in American beer after Anheuser-Busch, and it decided to expand distribution of Old Milwaukee to a national basis in 1975. Historically targeted at blue-collar workers, it grew to be the top brand in the popular-priced segment.

The seventies were a period of consolidation for the beer industry; the number of breweries declined from 80 to 50 and became increasingly competitive. Anheuser-Busch, Miller Brewing Company, Schlitz, Pabst, and Coors Brewing Company sold almost 70 percent of all the beer in the United States. Miller revolutionized the industry's marketing practices by introducing market segmentation, and poured millions of dollars into expanding capacity. Schlitz Brewing suffered from high costs and low operating rates. To cut costs, it adopted a production process with a considerably reduced fermentation time. It proved to be a disas-

trous mistake. The new process did succeed in lessening cost but at the expense of its image. Though the company never announced the change, drinkers noticed the difference. Schlitz became known for making "green beer" and lost its customers. Its rival, Anheuser-Busch, announced that it would not compromise quality to cut costs; Schlitz's image problem worsened and profits plunged.

Marketing Strategy

With the big two in the beer business, Anheuser-Busch and Miller Brewing, trying to dominate the market, Stroh went into debt to acquire F&M Schaefer Corporation in 1981 and Joseph Schlitz Brewing Company in 1982, making it the third-biggest beer brewing company. Stroh was going national on a big scale and consequently had strong ambitions for Old Milwaukee. In the fiercely competitive business, Stroh wanted to have a brand competing in each segment of the beer market. Key changes were made in Old Milwaukee's advertising and marketing strategies. Stroh invested heavily in the popular-priced brand on a national basis. For the first time in six years, national television, as opposed to spot, was used with the aim of impressing upon consumers and the trade Old Milwaukee's high quality image. The strategy clicked and Old Milwaukee recorded the highest volume increase of any top brand in 1983, netting it the number seven position among 1983's top-selling beer brands. Strong marketing support and changing consumer perceptions of popular-priced beer had transformed Old Milwaukee from a small-time regional beer into a nationally successful brand.

Old Milwaukee's "It doesn't get any better than this" advertising campaign had each commercial building upon the previous one showing 21-34 year olds in a variety of activities and drinking the brand. Stroh launched a new commercial for Old Milwaukee every spring on network television, cable, and print to address the high demand during summer; the brand name was even used to sponsor a NASCAR racing team, run a sweepstakes contest, and a variety of other promotional activities. This marketing blitz helped in making Old Milwaukee a national brand name and the fifth-largest selling beer in 1985. But by then, other brands from Anheuser-Busch, Miller Brewing, and Coors had intensified efforts to regain market share, and in 1986 Old Milwaukee was back to 18 percent of the popular-priced segment, a return to 1981 levels.

AT A GLANCE

Old Milwaukee brand of beer founded in 1848 by August Krug, president of Joseph Schlitz Brewing Company, which was acquired in 1982 by Stroh Brewery Company.

Performance: *Market share*—3.4% of domestic beer category (1991). *Sales*—6.6 million barrels.

Major competitor: Busch; also, Keystone and Anheuser-Busch, Inc.'s Natural Light.

Advertising: *Agency*—Hal Riney & Partners, San Francisco, CA, 1990—. *Major campaign*—"It doesn't get any better than this."

Addresses: *Parent company*—Stroh Brewery Company, 100 River Place, Detroit, MI 48207-4291, phone: (313) 446-2000; fax (313) 446-2206.

Flat industry sales and a crippling increase in excise tax meant that Stroh found itself in bad financial shape with neither the money nor the marketing wherewithal to tackle the biggest beer companies, which by the nineties were joined by Coors. Coors, in an aggressive effort to become large enough to compete with Anheuser-Busch and Miller Brewing, tried to acquire the Stroh Brewing Company in 1991. The deal did not go through, but by then Stroh had lost its focus on the market and, as a result, a lot of market share. Meanwhile the market had shown clear indications of shifting toward the light and non-alcoholic brands and the growth in the market, if any, came from these areas. Stroh, in keeping with the philosophy of competing in every segment of the beer market, launched three new brands, Old Milwaukee NA, Old Milwaukee Genuine Draft, and Old Milwaukee Genuine Draft Light, thereby extending the Old Milwaukee brand family to keep it contemporary. Once financially crippled, Stroh came back in the spring of 1991 with new advertisements and promotions, reflecting a 50 percent increase in advertisement spending on its bread-and-butter brand, Old Milwaukee. By the end of the year, this renewed marketing vigor had made Old Milwaukee the eighth-largest selling brand in the United States.

Advertising and Other Promotional Activities

Until 1981, when Old Milwaukee was included in the Stroh beer portfolio, it was predominantly a regional brand. Before Schlitz Brewing went national in the 1970s, the Old Milwaukee brand was advertised and promoted on a regional basis. For example, it was advertised at the Great Circus Parade in Wisconsin—a parade sponsored by the Schlitz Brewing Company from 1963 to 1973 and part of the Old Milwaukee Days Celebration on the Fourth of July. It was around 1973 that the advertising campaign which declared "It doesn't get any better than this" was introduced; twenty years later the tag line was still being used, even though the brand had undergone changes in both its parent company and advertising agency.

It was only in 1982, when Stroh acquired Joseph Schlitz Brewing, that the ambitious plans of its parent company began to show in energetic advertising and promotional campaigns for Old Milwaukee. Its advertising budget was beefed up by 30 percent to $20 million, and for the first time in six years commercials began to air on national television. One Old Milwaukee commercial showed several contented-looking men and women, all casually dressed, gathered around a campfire at twilight enjoying the beer. It ended with the tag line, "It doesn't get any better than this."

The television ads were run on all three networks, both in prime-time and late-night slots, mainly during sports events. The network ads were supplemented by co-op spots on televised college and professional football games. Spots were also added on cable because of the sports programming and more economical rates. For the first time in its history, Old Milwaukee began using national print ads to reach those sub-audiences who rarely watched television, such as hunting and fishing enthusiasts and car buffs. In order to get retail trade attention, it began to advertise in trade publications. There the ad headlines proclaimed "it doesn't sell any better than this," or "another bestseller comes to national television." Gaining precious shelf space by communicating to the retailer that Old Milwaukee had become a national brand with a very strong sales track record was critical in selling the beer.

Changing consumer perceptions were reflected in the increasing significance of market research. Most of it was focused on getting to understand the Old Milwaukee drinker in general and what the Bud and Miller drinkers thought of Old Milwaukee. Promotions aimed at wholesalers, retailers, and consumers also began to be an important aspect of the marketing strategy. Sweepstakes, giveaways, and discounting helped focus the trade's attention on Old Milwaukee. Women were targeted for incentives such as refunds and product discounts, because while a lot of beer was consumed by men, it was actually bought by women. Annual contests like the "Good as Gold" Contest, which featured a six-pack's weight in gold as the prize, and "Trucks and Bucks" sweepstakes, awarding pickup trucks and $1,000 prizes to winners, were a regular feature of Old Milwaukee's advertising mix. Sponsorship of off-beat events like a series of nationwide chili-cooking contests on one hand, and of a NASCAR racing team that competed in a 31-race national circuit on the other, showed how Old Milwaukee tried to become a big brand name in the country.

Old Milwaukee's customary "It doesn't get any better than this" ad campaign had been on the air since 1973; but in 1991, one element of this long-running campaign, the Swedish Bikini Team ad, sparked an unsavory controversy. In what the company meant as a spoof on the "sexploitative" commercials brewers were known for, Stroh's ad agency Hal Riney and Partners created the Swedish Bikini Team to promote the Old Milwaukee brand. The commercial featured five bikini-clad women descending on an all-male camping trip. Five female Stroh employees stated publicly that the ad was representative of the company's attitude toward sexual harassment. Then the Bikini Team appeared on the cover of *Playboy,* creating even more controversy. Overall sales, however, especially to the younger consumers at whom the ads were aimed, took off. For the 1992 spring season, however, Old Milwaukee steered clear of bikini-clad women and featured Jack and Andy, two longtime friends from Altoona, Pennsylvania, who had gone their separate ways, but who reunited for an outdoor adventure. The ad agency insisted that the new ads were not a replacement for the Bikini Team, but only the next element in the long-running campaign.

Through 20 years, the brand was handled by various advertising agencies. In 1986, BBDO resigned the $20 million Old Milwaukee account because of its planned merger with Doyle Dane Bernbach & Needham Harper Worldwide, which handled a $100 million account with Stroh rival Anheuser-Busch. The account went to Grey Advertising, but by 1990 had moved to San Francisco's Hal Riney and Partners. Stroh was looking for advertising and promotional activities that would create niches instead of always going head to head with Anheuser-Busch and Miller Brewing. Consistency was the hallmark of the Old Milwaukee advertising campaign. Over time, it executed a campaign that provided a uniform image to consumers, retailers, and wholesalers.

Product Line Extensions

With the advent of health- and fitness-consciousness in the seventies, beer drinkers began to favor light beers. Originally developed for women, with the rationale that it would be a way to increase the number of beer drinkers, it soon became clear that male drinkers too were interested. In July 1980, Joseph Schlitz Brewing Company, which owned the Old Milwaukee brand then, introduced Old Milwaukee Light as a "separately brewed, full-flavored product that will build on the excellent taste and growing consumer franchise of Old Milwaukee beer." Television and newspaper advertising claimed, "We got the taste of light right." Packaging resembled the parent brand Old Milwaukee, while it featured the word 'light.' The acceptance of light beer among male beer fans increased through the eighties, with the light beer category showing a better than ten percent compounded annual growth rate. Taking advantage of this growth and the image of its parent brand, Old Milwaukee Light ranked as the sixth-largest selling beer in the United States by 1990.

Stroh Brewery entered the fast-expanding draft beer market with Old Milwaukee Genuine Draft and Old Milwaukee Genuine Draft Light. These were two of the three new products that Stroh introduced in 1991 with the goal of recapturing market share in a flat beer market. These packaged draft products captured the popular flavor of Old Milwaukee in a cold-filtered, non-pasteurized beer. Drier in taste than their parent brand and priced at the popular-brand level, the Genuine Draft and Genuine Draft Light extensions were brewed using new filtering equipment to offer the fresh taste of real draft beer.

Bottled draft beer was targeted primarily at young male drinkers, in an attempt to shore up the weak premium beer segment. Bottling draft beer effectively took a popular product traditionally associated with drinking establishments and brought it into the home. Draft beer sales showed considerable variability: they grew dramatically between 1979 and 1983, then plunged into a downward spiral that did not end until 1990. The introduction of the bottled and canned draft beer made use of the name of the parent brand, riding the goodwill of the Old Milwaukee image. Extending Old Milwaukee's popular name into the packaged draft segment made sense for the cash-starved Stroh Brewing Company. The Old Milwaukee name saved money on advertising and marketing that would have been necessary to introduce a new brand name. Old Milwaukee Genuine Draft was priced below the market leaders in that segment, so as not to compete directly with them.

Hal Riney and Partners used humor to publicize the new brands. In one commercial, a spectator at a ball game asked a vendor for draft beer. The vendor promptly sent a whole keg down the aisle, much to the annoyance of the fans in the row. "Everyone's always loved fresh draft beer," intoned the announcer. "Unfortunately it's only come in one size." This joke formed the core of three TV commercials aimed at the growing market for packaged draft beers with the tag line, "Real draft beer without the keg."

In an otherwise flat market, the only other segment that offered real growth opportunities was the non-alcoholic one. In response to this growing demand, Stroh introduced the third Old Milwaukee brand extension of 1991: Old Milwaukee NA (NA stood for non-alcoholic). Introduced in select markets in 1991 and launched nationally in 1992, Old Milwaukee NA rose to among the top four domestic non-alcoholic brews within a year.

Central to the production of Old Milwaukee NA was Alfa-Laval's Centritherm technology, which converted the regular Old Milwaukee into the NA version through its alcohol removal process. Using the Centritherm evaporator, the evaporation took place more rapidly at a relatively low temperature (100 degrees Fahrenheit), which contributed to flavor enhancement; hence Old Milwaukee NA contained the same integrity and taste as its parent brand. Non-alcoholic beers had 0.5 percent alcohol compared to 4 to 5 percent for traditional beers.

Jack and Andy, familiar characters in Old Milwaukee's upbeat commercials, also found their way into Old Milwaukee NA spots. In these ads, the two outdoorsmen took a wild ride through the Florida Everglades while drinking the non-alcoholic brew. Radio and print ads featured prominently in Old Milwaukee's NA advertising mix.

Like its famous parent brand, Old Milwaukee NA competed in the popular-price segment, where there were no other non-alcoholic beers with national impact. Miller Brewing Company's Sharp's, the top-selling non-alcoholic beer, and Anheuser-Busch's O'Doul's both sold at premium prices. Since the Old Milwaukee presence was stronger "off-premise" than in taverns and restaurants, Stroh Brewing hoped that the same would be true of the NA version, so it would turn out to be a major player in the non-alcoholic market.

The market for non-alcoholic brews was expected to grow in the future with increasing concerns about social responsibility and driving safety. Consumer attitudes toward drinking were also changing, and the beer market expected non-alcoholic beverages to step in place of alcoholic beers. Non-alcoholic beer sales volume increased about 33 percent in 1991, ending up with one percent of the beer market.

International Presence

In 1986, Stroh International was established to expand Old Milwaukee and other Stroh products into world markets. It exported beer to more than 80 countries, including Canada, Panama, England, Hong Kong, and Australia. Stroh's international presence dated back to the 1950s; it also sold a wide range of products to U.S. military and diplomatic personnel stationed outside the continental United States.

In 1989 Old Milwaukee was accused by Canadian brewers of dumping beer in Canada, charges that Stroh vehemently denied. The company maintained that consumers were drinking Old Milwaukee because of its high quality and good value. Canadian brewers could not produce beer as cheaply because they were not as large as their American counterparts, who had greater economies of scale. Canadian provincial laws required production of beer in the province where it was sold. Hence politically powerful Canadian brewers were able to lobby successfully to have beer exempted from the free trade agreement between the United States and Canada which took effect January 1, 1989.

American beer exports gave a strong showing in 1991 with an estimated 9.3 percent climb to 4.6 million barrels. Stroh Brewing seemed well poised to take advantage of this growth. The company saw international sales as one of its greatest areas of growth because of its production efficiency, which allowed it to respond quickly to fulfill international orders. This was a crucial aspect of international business, since beer was considered perishable.

The Future

Since the 1960s Old Milwaukee has been positioned as a popular/sub-premium brand; this positioning could be the main reason that the brand continued to be among the top ten beers in an intensively competitive industry with very limited growth. The January 1, 1991, doubling of the excise tax on beer, combined with the U.S. recession and manufacturer price increases, caused the beer market to go flat in 1991-92. Consumers felt the pinch and shifted down from the premium brands to the popular or light segments, in which Old Milwaukee continued to be a major player. Formerly strapped for financial resources, Stroh Brewing pumped massive amounts of marketing dollars into the Old Milwaukee brand family to keep it competitive.

Increasingly beer lovers looked for non-alcoholic beverages because they did not want to mix drinking and driving. Light and packaged draft beers also continued to drive growth in the beer market. "We believe that the next step is into the lower calorie light products, which may incidentally be lower in alcohol content," said Stroh Brewing Company President Bill Henry in *Modern Brewery Age*. By quickly introducing the non-alcoholic and draft extensions of the Old Milwaukee name, the company showed that it was alert to changing industry trends and willing to strategically compete in those market segments which it traditionally dominated, instead of competing with the major brewers head-on. The company clearly stated that it wanted to reclaim its number three position in the beer industry. Old Milwaukee and all its brand extensions acted as the vehicles for this growth; and with the company willing to provide plenty of marketing support, the Old Milwaukee name could continue to have a major presence in the popular beer category.

Further Reading:

Aaker, David, "Guarding the Power of a Brand Name," *New York Times,* December 1, 1991, p. F13.

"About the Company," Corporate Communications Department, The Stroh Brewery Company.

"Battling Back; Stroh Brewery Company's President Bill Henry Reveals Company's Plans," *Modern Brewery Age,* September 9, 1991, p. S10.

"Beer Sales Respond to Aggressive Marketing," *Beverage Industry/Annual Manual 91/92,* pp. 36-40.

Cooper, Michael, "What Calls Itself 'Old,' Is Growing Rapidly, and Has a New, Caring Parent? Old Milwaukee," *Marketing and Media Decisions,* March 22, 1984, pp. 53-56.

Cortez, John, and Ira Teinowitz, "More Trouble Brews for Stroh Bikini Team," *Advertising Age,* December 9, 1991, p. 45.

Cortez, John, and Ira Teinowitz, "Stroh's Back: New Products Set for 1991," *Crain's Detroit Business,* March 25, 1991, sec. 1, p. 3.

David, A., "Buddies Beat Out Babes in Newest Stroh Spots," *Detroit News,* June 5, 1992, sec. E, p. 1.

Markiewicz, David, "Old Milwaukee Rolls Out Ads to Draft Fans for New Beers" *Detroit News,* August 22, 1991, sec. E, p. 1.

von Koschembahr, John, "The Beer Wars: It's No Picnic," *Financial World,* September 15, 1978, pp. 34-37.

—*Ashish Patwardhan*

ORE-IDA®

Ore-Ida frozen potatoes have dominated their retail food segment as few other products have, and have helped Ore-Ida Foods, Inc. grow to about $800 million in sales and 4,500 employees. The company is a diversified frozen food company and a division of the H. J. Heinz Company.

Ore-Ida had its beginnings in the fresh produce and food-processing operations of two brothers in Ontario, Oregon: F. Nephi Grigg and Golden T. Grigg. In the 1920s, the two sold the produce of their own vegetable farm and soon began adding the produce of other farmers. The first big product for the pair was sweet corn, which they delivered to nearby cities. In the beginning, they kept it cool by picking it at night and by packing it with ice. This foreshadowed the role that advanced frozen-food processing techniques would play in the company's operations.

About 20 years later, after World War II, the company turned to freezing to keep produce fresh. Corn was originally processed in a local plant owned by a struggling out-of-state firm, the Bridgford Company of California. In the late 1940s and early 1950s, the brothers increased their corn acreage, and along with some new partners, organized a new company, the Oregon Frozen Foods Company. After Bridgford closed due to its financial difficulties, the Griggs' company made arrangements to lease the frozen food plant, and they eventually bought it.

Diversification into Potatoes

One purpose of the new plant was to process frozen potatoes, but this idea did not immediately inspire confidence. Bankers were skeptical about it; they thought the potatoes would turn black if they were frozen. By putting up raw potatoes, receivables, and the frozen potatoes themselves as collateral, they were able to get the loans they needed to start up their own potato processing operation. The potato subsidiary was called Ore-Ida Potato Products and it joined Oregon Frozen Foods as yet another subsidiary of the parent company, then known as Oregon Industries Company.

By 1960, Ore-Ida employed 1,300 workers and produced about 25 percent of the nation's processed potatoes—product weighing 350 million pounds—and had expanded nationwide. Such Ore-Ida products as french fries and Tater Tots—a hash brown product Ore-Ida invented in 1953—were made at the new facility. Another product made available about this time was instant flake potatoes. As the company moved into a high-growth period, it designed new

quality control techniques. Field supervisors patrolled the fields armed with two-way FM radios, constantly informing the headquarters about what fields were ready for harvest.

In 1961, the company went public as Ore-Ida Foods, Inc. It was then recognized as a power in the frozen potato business. The 1962 Seattle World's Fair named it as its official supplier of instant flake potatoes. To meet growing demand, Ore-Ida had to acquire a major fleet of trucks and trailers to transport potatoes and other products across the country. By 1961, it had 27 truck and trailer units and by 1963, that number expanded to 30. At about this time, it also expanded its product line to include onion rings and chopped onions, and in 1963, it had a new plant to process onions.

Expansion into the Midwest

Fueled by sales of more than $31 million in 1963, the company expanded rapidly. It bought a plant in Burley, Idaho, that was next-door to its first processing factory. Each was capable of processing more than a million pounds of potatoes every day. And, to bolster its presence near important Midwestern markets, it built another plant in Greenville, Michigan, in the midst of a large potato-growing area. This plant became operational in 1965. That extra capacity helped fuel a startling rise in Ore-Ida's frozen potato output, from 69 million pounds to more than 206 million pounds during a six-year period.

Ore-Ida's successes attracted attention. Late in 1965, the H.J. Heinz Company bought the Oregon-based firm to bolster its position in the expanding frozen food business, and subsequently ran it as a subsidiary. The former Ore-Ida management found their places at the reins of the new subsidiary, along with some key Heinz officers. Backed by Heinz, Ore-Ida would accelerate its expansions, with sales rising from $100 million in 1965 to $350 million in 1984. A raft of new brand-name potato products emerged, including Golden Crinkles, Pixie Crinkles, and Natural Fries.

Under Heinz, the company was reconfigured. In the late 1960s and early 1970s, it consolidated activities in Boise, Idaho, relocating its headquarters from Ontario, Oregon, and its sales and marketing function from San Francisco. At the same time, it overhauled manufacturing facilities and put more emphasis on marketing to strengthen the company's market position. Ore-Ida was helping to create—and was profiting from—a huge expansion in the frozen potato market during this period. Per capita potato consumption annually was 2.7 pounds in 1960, 11.7 pounds in 1970, and 16.9 pounds in 1980.

Competition with Bird's Eye

During the mid-1970s, Ore-Ida went head-to-head against its biggest competitor, Bird's Eye. Ore-Ida was the most popular frozen potato producer in the Midwest and West. But Bird's Eye was dominant in the important Northeast market, which had a high per-capita consumption of french fries. The company made inroads in the Northeast by promoting Tater Tots, hash browns, and dinner fries, all products that Bird's Eye did not have.

At about this time, Ore-Ida was marshaling its marketing clout. It started by making regional television commercial buys for the first time in 1974, and went to national advertising in 1975 with Doyle, Dane, and Bernbach's "All Righta" campaign. Two different versions of the tag line were used: "Ore-Ida is All Righta" and "When It's Ore-Ida, It's All Righta." The advertising increased "unaided awareness" of the Ore-Ida campaign from 35 percent to 65 percent, according to the ad agency. Sales climbed 12 percent a year during the mid-1970s. The only wrinkle during this period was a shortage of potatoes in 1974, which cut down on shipments. One vehicle for advertising during this period was *Reader's Digest.*

For one reason or another, competitor after competitor pulled out of the retail frozen potato race. In 1977, Boise, Idaho-based Simplot Corporation, the country's biggest potato processor, withdrew. It had earlier made its name as the main potato supplier to McDonald's. But the most notable retreat was that of Lynden Farms. This Carnation subsidiary arrived on the scene during the 1970s after becoming a player in the food service industry. The rationale for the retail foray was Carnation's conviction that convenient processed foods could lure fast-food customers back to the family kitchen.

From Ore-Ida's standpoint, the new competition cut too close for comfort. One product's name was Tater Pops, which Ore-Ida thought was too close to its Tater Tots product. Ore-Ida sued and

won. Carnation eventually changed the name and the packaging for its potato products, but pulled out of the retail frozen potato market in 1981.

Retail Predominance

After these withdrawals, the main competitors to Ore-Ida's potatoes remained private-label, B-grade, and generic products. The private labels are its toughest competitor, and they gain strength when an oversupply of potatoes enable them to slash prices. In the late 1980s, the private, B-grade and generic labels together represented about 40 percent of the market, while the rest of the market virtually belonged to Ore-Ida.

As it prospered, a series of new Heinz purchases were placed under Ore-Ida's direction. They helped make the company the nation's largest diversified frozen foods company in total sales and in retail tonnage. The new members of the Ore-Ida family would eventually include Wethersfield, Connecticut Weight Watchers Foods, and Torrance, California-based Bavarian Specialty Foods. In the early 1980s, Ore-Ida president Paul Corddry, buoyed by the expansions, said: "Ore-Ida has continued to develop better procedures and equipment, new product ideas, and stronger marketing strategies."

In 1983, Ore-Ida was among the top ten best-selling food brand names in the country. In 1986, the company held more than half the retail frozen potato market in the United States, and it even held more than 10 percent of the food service market—which includes such giants as McDonald's (which produced an estimated 650 million pounds of frozen fried potatoes each year during the 1980s). Ore-Ida's own research in the 1980s, according to *Advertising Age,* showed that french fries were featured in 23 percent of all restaurant meals. Roy Rogers, Hardee's, and Burger King predominated as Ore-Ida's customers, and by the early 1980s, their business was nearly as important to Ore-Ida as the retail market.

As the market softened in the recessionary early 1980s, Ore-Ida closely monitored its potatoes' quality and visual appeal as it competed for the food-service industry. And, to meet consumers' ever-changing tastes, it brought out new shapes and sizes.

Product Development

After undertaking extensive consumer research, Ore-Ida brought out five products during the early 1980s: Home Style, Crispy Whips! , Cheddar Browns, Crispy Crowns, and Golden Patties. In addition, paying heed to Americans' growing health consciousness, Ore-Ida began merchandising Lites, a 100-calorie per serving potato product. The strategy was to exploit new uses of potatoes and to penetrate sections of the market that did not customarily use home potato products.

In 1987, frozen potato sales were falling, and *Advertising Age* then attributed the decline to the still-expanding fast-food industry, and low prices for fresh potatoes. Ore-Ida made its first major departure from the "Ore-Ida is All Righta" theme. The campaign included "soft-sell" commercials showing children chatting about Ore-Ida potatoes. The ads' main thrust was that caring mothers serve their kids Ore-Ida potatoes, and one commercial depicted a little girl sidelined during a basketball game because she was too short. Her mother made it up to her by serving her an "extra-big breakfast" of Ore-Ida hash browns.

As Ore-Ida became a major company, research played a prominent role. Back in the 1950s, Ore-Ida established its first research laboratory. It pioneered desert farming under its newly created Skyline Farms sub-unit (which was sold in 1973), and created an agricultural research center. It later set up agricultural tours so that farmers from different regions could share their expertise. As late as the 1970s and 1980s, it experimented with solar energy and with methane gas production from potato waste.

Some advances have focused on new environmental technologies. In the early 1980s, it established a new plant in Plover, Wisconsin, that its manager described as the most efficient and technologically advanced in the industry. Likewise, in the early 1990s, the Ore-Ida plant in Pocatello, Idaho, made headlines in the trade journals when it began freezing its Weight Watchers Enchiladas with a state-of-the-art spiral ammonia refrigerant, with cost and sanitary advantages over the former cryogenic spiral refrigerant.

The consumer and product research has proven useful as Ore-Ida has moved to expand internationally, especially in Japan. Products were also developed for use in toaster ovens, common in that country's kitchens. During the early 1980s, it commissioned a McKinsey & Company study on the Japanese market for products popularized by American fast food. Among the first products that Ore-Ida sold in Japan were french fries made in Ontario, Oregon, and distributed through Kentucky Fried Chicken restaurants there. (KFC had decided that the Japanese consumer wanted potatoes fried, not mashed.)

Other advances focused on new foods for the American consumer. In 1987, Ore-Ida sold a total of 39 products. In the early 1990s, the company (along with some competitors such as Edgewater Foods International LP and Cafe Quick Enterprises, Inc.) came out with french fries that were cooked from scratch in vending machines. The idea was to come up with fries that tasted as fresh and crispy as those the fast-food restaurants produced.

By the 1990s, new competition was rearing its head, and the company was too slow in reacting to consumers' needs, according to one Ore-Ida executive. "We had too long a cycle of new product development and capital investment," Pat Kinney, Ore-Ida's vice president of sales told the *Wall Street Journal* in January of 1993. Simplot was back in the retail market with MicroMagic microwaveable fries, and Milwaukee-based Universal Foods Corporation was offering curly and batter-dipped fries. Not to be outdone, Ore-Ida came up with its own versions, and then responded with frozen mashed potatoes and fast-food-style french fries known as Fast Fries.

The fries were aimed at customers who had tried similar home-use products and found them wanting. To meet demands for healthy foods, the fries have half the fat found in fast food fries. The mashed potatoes, complete with small lumps, cater to those who yearn for home-style cooking, and the ads showed a grandmother type microwaving the package. Those and other innovations were intended to keep the company a major power in the frozen food industry.

Further Reading:

Honomichl, Jack J., "Spuds on Ice," *Advertising Age,* November 15, 1985, p. 3.

"Latest in Vending Machines: One That Cooks for You," *New York Times,* April 13, 1988, p. D6.

"The Meat and Potatoes," *Forbes,* July 30, 1984, p. 102.

"New on the Laser Menu: Potato Skins, Well Done," *New York Times,* January 22, 1992, p. D5.

Stern, Gabriella, "Ore-Ida Dishes up New Potato Products," *Wall Street Journal,* January 14, 1993, p. B1.

—Gary Hoffman

OREO®

For the majority of its eighty-year existence, the Oreo cookie has been the most popular commercially made cookie brand in the United States. Oreo cookies are produced by the Nabisco Biscuit Company, one of seven operating companies of the Nabisco Foods Group, a subsidiary of RJR Nabisco, Inc. According to Melvin J. Grayson in *42 Million a Day: The Story of Nabisco Brands,* Oreo cookies outsell every other cookie product in the world.

Brand Origins

Making its debut in 1913, the Oreo cookie was created by the National Biscuit Company (N.B.C.). The company, which was established in 1898 by Chicago attorney Adolphus W. Green, was a consolidation of dozens of bakeries eager to tap a growing consumer market desiring quality, attractively packaged, and sanitary food products. Prior to that time, food "available at a popular price was not only poor in quality but totally lacking in consistency," noted Grayson in *42 Million a Day.* "The food processing industry had two additional problems that were more or less unique: spoilage and contamination," continued Grayson. "Virtually all food was sold uncovered and in bulk, open to the elements as well as to whatever health hazard happened to be around."

Green and his united bakeries, determined to eliminate the faults in food production and distribution at that time, endeavored to "enhance the quality of their merchandise, improve consistency, extend the shelf life and go a long way toward putting an end to contamination," noted Grayson. One of the first products to roll out of the company's bakeries, Uneeda biscuits, was a simple cracker neatly packaged in waxed paper within a cardboard box. The uniqueness of this new "In-er-Seal" packaging created a sensation, and sales skyrocketed.

Despite the enormous success of Uneeda biscuits, the company was ever on the alert for new product ideas. Among the cookie and cracker products to follow Uneeda were Oysterettes Crackers, Zuzu Ginger Snaps, Premium Saltines, and Barnum's Animals Crackers, which were introduced in 1902. It wasn't until ten years later that the National Biscuit Company would concoct what was to become the world's most beloved cookie. A 1912 company memo listed several new upcoming cookie products, among them Oreo, which the memo, according to Grayson, described as "two beautifully embossed, chocolate-flavored wafers with rich cream filling."

Why Did They Name It "Oreo"?

The origin of the peculiar name "Oreo" remains shrouded in mystery. But the success of the product was related to the easily pronounced, appealing name. The name may have derived from the French word for gold, *or,* because the color predominately used on the original packaging of the cookies was gold, and "oreo" would have sounded more melodic.

Another version of the name's origins states that because the original test shape of the cookie was a small hill, N.B.C. Chairman Green, who was a classics lover, named it "or," the Greek word

for hill (and "or," then, came out sounding better as "oreo"). Whatever the true origin, the name "oreo" stuck, and forever after became instantly identified with the chocolate sandwich cookie filled with vanilla icing.

Early Marketing Strategy

While the taste and shape of the Oreo cookie (the hill test shape was rejected in favor of flat, round wafers) remained unchanged, the size and design of the cookie altered slightly over the years to appeal to changing public taste. In addition, great care went into the appearance of the cookie, and stamped on each decorated Oreo was the easily identifiable company trademark.

The N.B.C. symbol played an important part in the success of the company's early marketing strategy. Planning to place the company trademark on all N.B.C. products, Green searched for an emblem that would symbolize the company itself. One night while thumbing through a book that contained medieval Italian printers' marks, Green was captivated by one mark in particular. "It was an oval surmounted by a cross with two horizontal lines instead of one," Grayson described. "It was said to represent the triumph of the moral and spiritual over the evil and worldly." The symbol came to encompass various names and products affiliated with N.B.C.; eventually enveloping the Oreo name, the symbol is stamped within the wreath-like design found on each Oreo cookie.

Embossed with the ancient symbol and christened with the melodious "Oreo" name, the new cookie was instantly identifiable and well launched by 1913. It was marketed as the "Oreo biscuit," and in 1921 the name was altered to "Oreo sandwich," to emphasize that the cookie could "come apart" and be eaten, if desired, icing first.

Advertising Innovations

In its early days, the National Biscuit Company was distinct from other companies in that it expended large sums of money on advertising and, long before Oreo cookies came on the market, advertised nationally. In pre-World War I days, advertising could be carried on in the printed media, usually newspapers and household magazines, but even more effectively in trolley cars by means of ads mounted within the cars. Adolphus Green, a dedicated believer in advertising, hired a company advertising manager as well as an outside advertising firm.

Radio soon became an important advertising medium in the 1920s, when one out of three Americans owned a radio. In 1934 the National Biscuit Company sponsored a highly popular three-hour Saturday night dance music program, which gave Oreo ample opportunity to be advertised over the air. Later, Arthur Godfrey would be broadcasting on radio stations from coast to coast, advertising Oreo and other Nabisco cookies and crackers to tens of millions.

In the days before television, companies advertised their products in motion picture theaters, and the Oreo brand would not fail to be seen on the screen. In 1952, further advertising strategies

AT A GLANCE

Oreo brand of cookies first marketed in 1913 by the National Biscuit Company; company changed name to Nabisco, Inc., 1971; merger of Nabisco, Inc., and Standard Brands Incorporated to form Nabisco Brands, Inc., 1981; Nabisco Brands, Inc. (which later was renamed Nabisco Foods Group) merged in 1985 with R. J. Reynolds Industries, Inc., which changed its name in 1986 to RJR Nabisco, Inc.

Performance: *Sales*—$303 million.

Major competitor: Keebler brand of cookies; also Pepperidge Farm brand of cookies.

Advertising: *Agency*—FCB/Leber Katz Partners, New York, NY. *Major campaign*—"Unlock the magic" slogan.

Addresses: *Parent company*—Nabisco Foods Group, 7 Campus Drive, Parsippany, NJ 07054; phone: (201) 682-5000. *Ultimate parent company*—RJR Nabisco, Inc., 1301 Avenue of the Americas, New York, NY 10019; phone: (212) 258-5600.

included placement of the company's official trademark—which was now embedded in a triangular, red seal—on the corner of every package of N.B.C. cookies and crackers. In advertising it was referred to as "the famous Red Seal," a guarantee of quality. And after World War II, N.B.C. stepped up its advertising budget to include television appearances. Eventually, the company's name changed to Nabisco (a name resulting from a combination of the words National Biscuit Company), as many TV viewers and radio listeners reportedly were confusing N.B.C. with the TV and radio stations NBC.

Marketing under RJR Nabisco

With the merger of Nabisco and R. J. Reynolds in the mid-1980s, more funds were available for advertising purposes; by 1991, RJR Nabisco reportedly was spending nearly $400 million dollars annually on advertising.

Another outcome of the merger between Nabisco and R. J. Reynolds was a new emphasis on special promotions. During the Christmas season of 1990, 40 million of the special Oreo White Fudge Covered cookies sold out in six weeks. Coinciding with the launch of White Fudge Covered Oreo cookies were decorative holiday tins, which contained not only Chocolate Fudge Oreo cookies but Christmas stories for children. The special "holiday cookies" were part of Nabisco's advertising goal to introduce new cookie products at "strategic" times. Thus far, the concept has reportedly worked well.

The concept of strategic advertising was also evident during major sporting events, especially golf and tennis matches. In the 1980s a "Team Nabisco" of current and former professional athletes advertised Oreo cookies and other Nabisco cookie products on television during major sporting events. And, according to Judann Dagnoli in a 1992 *Advertising Age* article, Nabisco went on to promote Oreo cookies at video store outlets with considerable success, an innovative concept that Nabisco planned to expand (for instance, timing Oreo cookie ads with new video releases). Innovative advertising has seemingly paid off, as Oreo has maintained its number one selling status despite the fierce competition among such leading cookie companies as Keebler and Pepperidge Farm.

Product Development

In 1974 the regular Oreo cookie adopted its formal name, the Oreo Chocolate Sandwich Cookie; the product tastes exactly as it did in 1913 but is somewhat smaller than the original. The elaborate floral design stamped on each regular Oreo is a change from the original wreath (but as in 1913, the flower design on each cookie surrounds the name "Oreo" encompassed in the identifiable Nabisco trademark symbol).

In deference to growing environmental concerns, Oreo cookies are packed in recyclable material. Despite fierce "cookie wars" among leading cookie manufacturers and the pressure to produce tasty low-fat and low-sugar cookies, Oreo cookies have held their own since 1913. In fact, by the 1990s, the number of Oreo cookie products has grown to include six variations, including the Oreo cookies covered in white and chocolate fudge, and the Oreo Double Stuf, with double the icing of regular Oreo cookies.

Aside from these variations, there are the very popular "Mini Oreo" cookies, a brand rated by *Business Week* as one of the best new consumer products introduced in 1991. The Nabisco Biscuit Company was careful to ensure that the miniature cookies,

Mini Oreos, a popular bite sized version of the Oreo cookie, were introduced in 1991.

like their full-size predecessors, could be twisted apart; in the 1990s, as in pre-World War I days, part of the appeal of the Oreo lies in the consumer's ability to eat the cookie any way he or she likes—sometimes filling first. Besides creating various incarnations of the Oreo cookie, Nabisco has used Oreo cookies to produce such products as Oreo Cookies 'n Cream Ice Cream in three different flavors, as well as Oreo Cookies 'n Cream On-A-Stick and Oreo Cookies 'n Cream Sandwich.

Oreo products continue to reflect the major advertising thrust of the Nabisco Biscuit Company and the Nabisco Foods Group: to build on its core products and to introduce strategic new ones, a strategy that has enabled Oreo to maintain its national and worldwide stature.

Future Predictions

Oreo is but one of dozens of cookies and crackers produced by RJR Nabisco's subsidiary Nabisco Biscuit Company. While Oreo is among the company's best-selling products, market analyst Suein Hwang reported in a 1992 *Wall Street Journal* article that "the surge in health conscious, older consumers and 'empty nesters' with no children to feed means that Nabisco can't just rely on its . . . Oreos . . . for future growth." Perhaps not in the United States, but the Oreo brand has done extremely well in international markets, and the future of Nabisco will probably be determined there. Thus far, traditional international markets, and the new markets opening in eastern Europe and Russia, promise to continue being very profitable arenas for the Oreo cookie business well into the next century.

Further Reading:

Berry, Jon, "Inside Nabisco's Cookie Machine," *AdWeek's Marketing Week,* March 18, 1991, pp. 22-23.

Cahn, William, *Out of the Cracker Barrel: The Nabisco Story, from Animal Crackers to Zuzus,* New York: Simon & Shuster, 1969.

Campbell, Hannah, *Why Did They Name It . . . ?,* New York: Fleet Publishing, 1964.

Dagnoli, Judann, "Oreo Gets Mini-Mized: Nabisco Shrinks No. 1 Cookie in Sixth Line Extension," *Advertising Age,* July 1, 1991, p. 10.

Dagnoli, Judann, "Nabisco Plots Strategy to Sell Oreos with Videos," *Advertising Age,* May 4, 1992, p. 3.

Fact Sheet, Parsippany, NJ: Nabisco Foods Group, 1992.

Grayson, Melvin J., *42 Million A Day: The Story of Nabisco Brands,* East Hanover, NJ: Nabisco Brands, Inc. (Corporate Affairs), 1986.

The History of Oreo Chocolate Sandwich Cookies, Nabisco Brands, Inc., 1992.

Hwang, Suein, "Healthy Eating, Premium Private Labels Take a Bite Out of Nabisco's Cookie Sales," *Wall Street Journal,* July 13, 1992, p. B1.

McElgunn, Jim, "Colorful Cookie Campaign," *Marketing,* June 18, 1990, p. 1.

Miller, Cyndee, "Nabisco Turns 200, Still Has Room for Marketing Growth," *Marketing News,* March 16, 1992.

News Release, Parsippany, NJ: Nabisco Foods Group, March 15, 1992; October 21, 1991.

RJR Nabisco, Inc.: Annual Report, New York: RJR Nabisco, Inc., 1991.

Stiling, Marjorie, *Famous Brand Names, Emblems, Trademarks,* Newton Abbot, VT: David & Charles, 1980.

Superbrands 1992: America's Top 2,000 Brands (supplement to *Adweek* magazines), 1992, p. 87.

—Sina Dubovoj

ORVILLE REDENBACHER'S®

Orville Redenbacher's Gourmet Popping Corn is the leading national brand of supermarket popcorn. With sales of $244.3 million, the brand commands 38.5 percent of the microwave popcorn market and 19 percent of the nonmicrowave unpopped popcorn segment. Owned by Hunt-Wesson Inc., Orville Redenbacher's was positioned from the start as a superior brand of popcorn worthy of its higher price tag. The brand is closely identified with its founder, Orville Redenbacher (his real name), whose smiling, spectacled face, poised atop his trademark bow tie, graces every package of his popcorn.

Until the late 1950s, Americans ate most of their popcorn away from home, often at movie theaters. However, as television made its way into the home, so did home-popped popcorn. Only supermarket brands were available to consumers until Redenbacher introduced his name brand in the mid-1960s, claiming that his superior hybrid popped lighter and fluffier than any popcorn available in the market. In the mid-1980s, the popcorn market heated up as several other popcorn makers followed Orville Redenbacher's lead into a new niche—the microwave popcorn market. Popcorn, which is naturally low in fat and high in fiber, is frequently referred to as the healthiest member of the snack-food family. Orville Redenbacher's strategy of linking a wholesome product with an equally wholesome and highly visible spokesman has enabled the brand to fend off would-be competitors in a market it created. Today, Orville Redenbacher's trademarked name appears on a host of popcorn products, including Original Gourmet Popping Corn; Gourmet Hot Air Popping Corn; Gourmet White Popping Corn; Gourmet Popping and Topping Buttery Flavor Oil; Gourmet Microwave Popping Corn in Butter, Natural, Cheddar Cheese, and Caramel flavors, with Salt-Free and Light varieties of the Butter and Natural flavors; and Smart-Pop in Butter flavor.

Brand Origins

By the time Orville Redenbacher's Gourmet Popping Corn was ready to market in 1965, the man behind the product had devoted nearly 25 years to pursuing the perfect strain of popcorn seed. In fact, his interest in popcorn is said to have originated as far back as the early 1920s, when, as a teen, he grew popcorn as a sideline on the family's Indiana farm. After finishing high school, he attended Purdue University, graduating in 1928 with a degree in agronomy. Jobs as a high school teacher and later as a county agricultural agent followed his graduation. In 1940, Redenbacher went to work managing what was then Indiana's largest farming enterprise, the 12,000-acre Princeton Farms. Here, Redenbacher began raising hybrid corn seed. It was during this time that he met Charlie Bowman, manager of a seed program at Purdue. By 1941 Redenbacher, convinced he could develop a much-improved popcorn seed, had built a processing plant at Princeton Farms and had begun drying popcorn seed.

In 1951, after a decade of working together on hybridization projects, Redenbacher and Bowman formed a partnership and bought George F. Chester & Son Inc., a small firm in Valparaiso, Indiana, that raised and sold seed for corn used as animal feed. They renamed the company Chester Inc. and began experimenting with various popcorn seeds. As the firm grew and diversified— into the manufacture of liquid fertilizer and other agricultural chemicals—Redenbacher and Bowman, with the assistance of an Iowa State graduate student, continued to work on developing an improved strain of popcorn. Finally, in 1965, the years of research paid off. Though yet to be officially named, Orville Redenbacher's Gourmet Popping Corn was ready to pop. Unfortunately, however, the market wasn't. During the next four years, farmers and processors dismissed the product, claiming it was just too expensive to produce and that no one would pay that much extra for popcorn, even if the claims of "lighter and fluffier" were true.

Undaunted, Redenbacher packed up his popcorn and went door to door peddling his product to grocery store owners across the country—but with little success. In 1970 he sought help from a Chicago advertising agency. The agency, which no longer exists, devised a marketing strategy that not only worked, but eventually became the mainstay of the brand's strategy. Redenbacher and Bowman told the admen they wanted to name the product "Red Bow." However, impressed with Redenbacher's somewhat eccentric pursuit of the perfect popcorn, the agency advised them instead to name their product after the 63-year old Redenbacher and to put his face on the product's label. Furthermore, they recommended charging a premium for the popcorn and selling it on quality, not price. Following the agency's advice, Bowman and Redenbacher continued knocking on distributors' doors. Later that year, a company by the name of Blue Plate Foods, then a New Orleans-based subsidiary of Hunt-Wesson Inc., took an interest in the new product and volunteered to market it. During the next two

AT A GLANCE

Orville Redenbacher's brand of popcorn founded in 1965 by Orville Redenbacher and Charlie Bowman, partners in Chester Inc., a diversified agricultural company in Valparaiso, IN; brand marketed by Blue Plate Foods, a subsidiary of Hunt-Wesson Inc., beginning in 1971; in 1976 brand sold to Hunt-Wesson Inc., then a subsidiary of Beatrice Foods; Hunt-Wesson later acquired by ConAgra Inc.

Performance: *Market share*—38.5% (top share) of the microwave popcorn category; 19% (top share) of regular popcorn category. *Sales*—$244.3 million.

Major competitor: Betty Crocker Pop Secret (microwave); also American Pop Corn Company's Jolly Time (regular).

Advertising: *Agency*—Ketchum Advertising, San Francisco, CA, 1975—. *Major campaign*—"Do one thing, and do it better than anyone."

Addresses: *Parent company*—Hunt-Wesson Inc., 1645 W. Valencia Dr., Fullerton, CA 92633-3899; phone: (714) 680-1000. *Ultimate parent company*—ConAgra Inc., One ConAgra Dr., Omaha, NE 68102; phone: (402) 595-4000.

years, Blue Plate worked at developing the brand and marketing it to grocery customers, primarily in the South and Southeast.

In 1972 Hunt-Wesson, recognizing the product's potential, stepped in and launched a campaign to take Orville Redenbacher's Gourmet Popping Corn national. Redenbacher, who continued to figure prominently in the brand's marketing strategy, embarked on a national tour, appearing on radio and TV programs to promote his Gourmet Popping Corn. Radio and TV appearances were a snap for Redenbacher, who back in his days as a county agricultural agent had been the first to broadcast his radio shows direct from the corn fields. The public bought the image—and the popcorn. Sales soared and in 1976 Hunt-Wesson (then owned by Norton Simon, Inc., but eventually sold to ConAgra Inc.) bought Orville Redenbacher's Gourmet Popping Corn from Chester Inc. for about $8 million, according to a 1979 report in *Money* magazine. Although $8 million might seem a tidy sum, according to *Money* magazine, Redenbacher and Bowman each got about $350,000 out of the deal—the rest went to assets that had not yet been paid off. Hunt-Wesson continued to pay Redenbacher for the use of his name and for public appearances. In the early 1990s Redenbacher, in his eighties, continued to promote Orville Redenbacher's popcorn through TV commercials.

A Mind for Marketing

"I was determined I could succeed in marketing my popping corn based on its high quality rather than low price," Redenbacher told *Marketing News* in 1988. Though not an instant success, Orville Redenbacher's Gourmet Popping Corn over time built a consistent image as a premium product. As the first such product in the market, the brand could create an identity based solely on its unique appeal. "The popcorn is really different," *Money* magazine said in 1979. "When popped, it has hardly any husk. It is particularly tasty. And since each popped piece is bigger than with other popcorn varieties and since almost all the kernels pop, 2 1/2 ounces of Redenbacher's produces about the same volume as four ounces of regular popcorn." Of course all those advantages did not come cheap. In the 1970s, production costs were higher than any existing supermarket popcorns. First, Orville Redenbacher's

required more acreage to grow and more expensive harvesting machines to cultivate. Secondly, it had to be dried longer—first while it was still on the ear, then after being removed. Finally, the packaging was more expensive: traditional popcorn was packed in ordinary plastic bags or cardboard boxes, whereas Orville Redenbacher's was packed in glass jars to prevent the kernels from drying out beyond the optimum popping point. The result was that consumers were being asked to pay almost three times more for Orville Redenbacher's brand than for any other variety available at the time. In fact, before the brand was sold to Hunt-Wesson, Orville Redenbacher's sported a label proclaiming "World's Most Expensive Popping Corn."

Having established a brand identity based on quality at a premium price, the challenge remained to convince consumers that Orville Redenbacher's was truly worth shelling out the extra change for at the grocery counter. Banking on Redenbacher's personal passion for popcorn and the strong link between the product and the personality, Hunt-Wesson relied on Redenbacher to sell his story and his product to the growing number of at-home popcorn eaters long after he had sold the rights to the brand. In 1975, Ketchum Advertising took over the Orville Redenbacher's account at a time when there was virtually no competition in the gourmet segment. Annual sales of the brand were a mere $2 million. Advertising dramatized product superiority, according to a case history furnished by Ketchum. "Perhaps more importantly, it gave America a wry, homespun, highly credible spokesperson who was just off-beat enough that you'd really believe he spent his life making the best popcorn possible," the case history stated. As sales grew and competitors popped onto the scene, Orville Redenbacher's took its place at the top of the category, where it has remained ever since.

Competitive Pressures

As Redenbacher's fame grew, so did the popularity of the product he represented. By the early 80s, American consumers' taste for popcorn had been thoroughly whetted, in part by the recognition of popcorn as a low-calorie, high-fiber snack food. The American Cancer Society, the National Cancer Institute, and the American Dietetic Association were all singing the praises of popcorn as an alternative to snacks high in fat, salt, sugar, and preservatives. And not only was it healthier, popcorn—even premium-priced popcorn—was less expensive than most other snack foods.

Not surprisingly, products similar to Orville Redenbacher's began cropping up with hopes of grabbing a share of the gourmet popcorn market. Among them were Borden's Cracker Jack Extra Fresh Popping Corn, American Pop Corn Co.'s Jolly Time popcorn and Pillsbury's Hungry Jack Microwave Popcorn, sold in the freezer case. Then the market really steamed up as Orville Redenbacher's rolled out its first line of shelf-stable microwave popcorn and General Mills debuted its microwavable Betty Crocker Pop Secret. Before long, the microwave category began to segment into butter and nonbutter varieties, as well as salt-free and cheese flavored. Sales of microwave popcorn soon surpassed those of the nonmicrowave segment, fueled in part by the popularity of home videos. In 1989 Orville Redenbacher's created still another niche with its introduction of Orville Redenbacher's Gourmet Light Microwave Popcorn. The product contained less salt and a lower fat content, and was offered in both butter and nonbutter flavors.

Betty Crocker Pop Secret followed suit. In 1992 Orville Redenbacher's debuted Smart Pop, a substantially lower fat version than its Light microwave popping corn. During the same year, Hunt-Wesson also began testing the first Orville Redenbacher's ready-to-eat popcorn line. Test markets included Milwaukee, Phoenix, and St. Louis. The bagged popcorn was initially available in natural, white cheddar cheese, and caramel flavors, in addition to a natural light variety.

A Consistent Advertising Strategy

Throughout the explosion of sales and competitive pressure, Ketchum's case history said, advertising has remained consistent with the initial creative solution: "Trust the product superiority and, even more, trust in the power of the real Orville, the popcorn expert, to touch people and sell his product." Adhering to that philosophy, Ketchum has not once in its two decade association with Orville Redenbacher's aired a television campaign that has not focused on Redenbacher himself as the spokesperson. Typical vignettes feature Redenbacher expounding on the qualities that set the brand apart from its competitors. In one campaign, Redenbacher talked without a script about his personal success. In another, he elaborated on the many aspects of growing and packaging superior popcorn. One of the brand's most recognizable tag lines sums up not just the product, but Redenbacher's life as well: "Do one thing and do it better than anyone." In more recent years, Redenbacher's grandson Gary has begun appearing in commercials with his grandfather. Public relations efforts have also played heavily off Redenbacher's popularity. He has appeared at grand openings, county fairs, and on TV talk shows. When he celebrated his 80th birthday in 1987, Edelman Public Relations, which handled the account, orchestrated a nationwide celebration. "Specially decorated Amtrak lounge cars on cross-country trains featured samples of the corn and Orville Redenbacher T-shirts," according to a 1988 report in *Public Relations Journal.* The "world's largest birthday card" was circulated in major cities and Redenbacher was recognized in *USA Weekend* and on the *Today* show.

In 1989 Orville Redenbacher's capitalized on the age-old association between popcorn and movies via a print ad campaign featuring headlines that played off popular movies, such as "The Light Stuff," "Pop Gun," and "Romancing the Corn." Redenbacher and his grandson Gary appeared, appropriately costumed, in the black and white ads that appeared in such general audience publications as *Family Circle, People,* and *TV Guide.* "We're just playing on a picture that's already in people's heads," a Ketchum adman told *Advertising Age.*

Although the clever print ads were popular, a later series of TV and radio ads for Orville Redenbacher's Light Microwave Popcorn were not so popular—at least not with the National Advertising Division of the Council of Better Business (NAD). The

council decided the brand had exaggerated its claims about the product's low fat and calorie levels. Although Hunt-Wesson disputed the fat and calorie analysis done by General Mills, maker of Betty Crocker Pop Secret Light Microwave Popcorn, asserting that the methodology was inconsistent, NAD did not find Hunt-Wesson's explanation convincing. Several ads, which claimed the "Light" product contained fewer calories and less fat than other leading brands, were subsequently modified or discontinued.

International Inroads

Today, the Indiana popcorn farmer with the funny name appears on microwave popcorn packages in about ten countries. Hunt-Wesson first took the brand international in 1986, when it launched Orville Redenbacher's microwave butter and nonbutter versions in Japan. The product continues to be sold in Japan, though success in that market has been somewhat limited. The brand was launched in several Scandinavian countries in 1988 and introduced to Mexico in 1989. Other international launches included the United Kingdom in 1990 and Denmark and Brazil in 1992. Plans call for Orville Redenbacher's to be sold in Germany by 1994. Packages destined for overseas markets contain bilingual labeling and, of course, the brand's single most identifiable trademark—the "Popcorn King" himself, whose image transcends any language barriers.

Further Reading:

"After a Rough Beginning, Gourmet Corn Goes National, *Advertising Age,* February 26, 1973, p. 130.

Brown, George Hay, "Four Personal Views Give Insight to Marketing," *Marketing News,* February 29, 1988, p. 2.

"Buttering Up," *Public Relations Journal,* June 1988, p. 23.

Case History: "Orville Redenbacher," San Francisco: Ketchum Advertising.

Cortez, John P., "Redenbacher's Tests New Popcorn in Bags," *Advertising Age,* March 30, 1992, p. 13.

Fabricant, Florence, "The Din of Popcorn Fills the Land," *New York Times,* March 28, 1990, p. C1.

Johnson, Bradley, and Erickson, Julie Liesse, "Popcorn Leaders Make Light Moves," *Advertising Age,* July 24, 1989, p. 2.

Kelly, Janice, "NAD Pops Rendenbacher 'Light' Ads," *Advertising Age,* April 1, 1991, p. 32.

Leon, Hortense, "Gourmet Popcorn Business Popping," *Advertising Age,* May 3, 1984, p. M52.

Neiman, Janet, "Popcorn Market Segments, Adds Brands," *Advertising Age,* July 5, 1982, p. 18.

Runde, Robert, "A Popcorn King Who's in the Chips," *Money,* November, 1979, p. 106.

—Katherine J. Paul

OSCAR MAYER®

Despite the fact that various products in the Oscar Mayer line of processed meats have preservatives and fats—two things that American consumers say they do not want in their food—Oscar Mayer tops the list of food superbrands. With 1992 annual sales of $2.1 billion, the Oscar Mayer brand, which is owned by the Oscar Mayer Foods Corp., stretches across a variety of products from sliced bacon to pre-packaged lunch combinations. Its success is in large part due to the company's ability to package beef, pork, and poultry products into new products that continually meet consumer demands. For over a century, different products have come and gone, yet the Oscar Mayer name remains, creating a sense of brand continuity and giving new products a high level of brand recognition.

Oscar F. Mayer's business grew from a neighborhood meat market to a regional sausage maker, to a national sausage specialist, and finally to an international food processing conglomeration. Sales of $59 on the first day of business grew to more than $2 billion annually by 1988, and Oscar Mayer territory expanded to include the United States and Canada, Venezuela, and regions of Asia.

Early History

Young Oscar F. Mayer's apprenticeship in the meat industry began at an early age when, in 1873, he moved from Bavaria to Detroit, Michigan, with the John Schroll family. The 14-year-old immigrant soon found work as a "butcher boy" in a neighborhood meat market. In 1876 he and the Schroll family moved to Chicago, Illinois. Chicago was fast becoming the primary receiving center for the vast herds of cattle and pigs raised on Western ranches. As meat packing became the city's main industry, it spawned a number of related industries and inspired the saying that, in Chicago, "everything of the pig was used except the squeal." Mayer soon found a job working in the bustling Chicago stockyards for (future rival) Armour & Co.

With his stockyard and market experience, young Mayer was well positioned to benefit from his experience in the booming meat industry. In 1883 Oscar, 24, and his brother Gottfried, 21, signed a lease for the Kolling Meat Market, a failing business on Chicago's North Side. Besides offering traditional meat cuts, the brothers' specialties included Westphalian hams and "Old World" style sausages. Within five years, the brothers developed the ailing store into a thriving business, so good in fact that the Kolling family refused to renew their lease in 1888. Rumor was that the owners hoped to continue the meat market on their own, capitalizing on the strong reputation the Mayer brothers had established.

Undaunted, the Mayers, now joined by a third brother, Max, borrowed $10,000 and built their own meat market with upstairs living quarters for the family a few blocks away on Sedgwick Avenue. First day sales totaled $59, a respectable figure for 1888. The new market was immediately successful.

Soon Oscar Mayer's reputation for quality meat products at reasonable prices spread, and Oscar Mayer salesmen were delivering bacon, pork sausages, and lard throughout Chicago and its suburbs. By 1913, company sales totaled $2.69 million. Five years later, sales totaled $11 million, one-third of which were to the U.S. military to feed troops serving in World War I. In 1919 the company bought a bankrupt farmers' cooperative so it would have its own supply of raw materials; the Madison, Wisconsin, location grew into a production plant over the years, and in 1955 the firm's corporate office was moved from Chicago to Madison.

Sales expanded to the eastern states during the 1930s and 40s and, with the purchase of a processing plant in Los Angeles, spread to California and the western states during the 1950s. By 1961, Oscar Mayer products were distributed virtually all across the United States, and the company was expanding into foreign markets.

Early Marketing

During Oscar Mayer's early years, brand names were uncommon among butchers. Most foods were sold without labels or packaging, and the brothers relied primarily on word-of-mouth to carry the reputation of Oscar Mayer meats. The only other means of drawing attention to Oscar Mayer products was a neatly painted, glass-paneled delivery wagon pulled by a well groomed horse named Strawberry.

Because most meats and sausages look very much like each other, establishing any form of brand identification was next to impossible. In 1904 the three brothers broke from tradition and adopted the brand name "Edelweiss." According to a company-published history, "there was little point in making a better product if shoppers in meat markets couldn't tell one brand from

AT A GLANCE

Oscar Mayer brand meats introduced in 1883 in a Chicago, IL, meat market called Oscar F. Mayer & Bro., owned by Oscar F. Mayer and his brothers Max and Gottfried; the brothers adopted the brand name "Edelweiss " for bacon, lard, and pork sausage, and the brand name "Moose " for heavier bacons and baker's lard, 1904; in 1917 the company trademark was changed to "Approved," with the tag line "Meats of Good Taste" added in the early 1920s; corporate name officially became Oscar Mayer & Co., 1919; "Yellow Band" trademark with the name Oscar Mayer introduced, 1936; company acquired by General Foods Corporation, and the meat firm's name changed to Oscar Mayer Foods Corp., 1981; in 1985 General Foods acquired by Philip Morris Companies, Inc., which acquired Kraft, Inc., 1988; Oscar Mayer Foods became part of the newly formed Kraft General Foods, Inc., 1989.

Performance: *Sales*—$2.1 billion.

Major competitor: Sara Lee Corp.'s brands of meats; also ConAgra Inc.'s brands of meats.

Advertising: *Agency*—J. Walter Thompson, Chicago, IL, 1959—. *Major campaign*—Series of television commercials capitalizing on good will created by earlier Oscar Mayer ads; tags lines: "Remember when you wished you were an Oscar Mayer wiener?" and, "Remember when your bologna had a first name?"

Addresses: *Parent company*—Oscar Mayer Foods Corp., P.O. Box 7188, Madison, WI, 53707; phone: (608) 241-3311; fax: (608) 242-6108. *Ultimate parent company*—Kraft General Foods, Inc., Three Lakes Dr., Northfield, IL 60093-2753; phone: (708) 646-2000. *Ultimate ultimate parent company*—Philip Morris Companies, Inc., 120 Park Ave., New York, NY 10017; phone: (212) 880-5000; fax: (212) 878-2167.

another.'' The name was chosen for somewhat sentimental reasons—Edelweiss is the name of an Alpine flower indigenous to Bavaria—but the flower also symbolized freshness and purity. More importantly, it brought growing brand recognition at a time when competition in the meat business was heating up.

The new brand name appeared on rinds of Oscar Mayer bacon slabs, boxes of pork sausage, pails of lard, and on Oscar Mayer delivery wagons. Another trademark, "Moose," was coined for heavier bacons and baker's lard. Near the end of World War I, a new trademark, "Approved," replaced the earlier two. The tag line "Meats of Good Taste" was added during the 1920s.

Oscar Mayer's most innovative marketing strategy occurred in 1929 when it began placing yellow paper bands with the Oscar Mayer name around every fourth wiener. Previously all brands of hot dogs hung in the butcher's case with no means of identifying them. This innovation proved successful, and Oscar Mayer continued to develop ways to package and identify many more of its products.

Advertising

At the turn of the century, clear identification of the Oscar Mayer brand went far to distinguish it from competitors in the meat case. It also allowed the company to start spending money on advertising its brand name, something rarely done in the meat industry at that time. In 1915 Oscar Mayer budgeted $2,000 for advertising expenditures, primarily for tinted photos of hams and sausages to be displayed in store windows. Shortly after, advertising expanded to include print ads for its new brand name "Oscar Mayer's Approved Meat Products."

Several ads capitalized on Oscar Mayer's sales to the U.S. military during World War I. One specific ad touted Oscar Mayer's 93 different meat products as "endorsed by the four great meat authorities: the food scientist, the dealer, the American housewife and the U.S. government." The ad also employed the theme of conservation and value, closing with the line, "These are meats for war-time economy."

Over the years Oscar Mayer employed several gimmicks such as toy rings, inflatable hot dogs, and miniature "wiener whistles" in order to catch the interest of children and thus the attention of their mothers. Perhaps the most successful attraction was the midget chef "Little Oscar" and his Wienermobile, introduced in 1936. Little Oscar immediately captured the public's fancy, as he conducted cooking demonstrations and appeared in parades, store openings, and later in television commercials. He was so well known by 1963 that an advertising executive is said to have exclaimed, "There's no point in doing a survey on Little Oscar's popularity—*everyone* knows him!"

The Wienermobile, a vehicle in the shape of a giant hot dog, was just as popular as Little Oscar. It was driven everywhere Little Oscar went and toured the United States in the 1950s and 60s. In the mid-1970s Little Oscar and his Wienermobile were retired in favor of other promotions and more television commercials, which could reach a wider audience in a shorter amount of time.

Television advertising began as early as 1950, when Oscar Mayer sponsored a local program in Philadelphia, Pennsylvania. Sponsorship of local children's shows and daytime dramas continued until 1965, the year Oscar Mayer began buying national network advertising. Three years later Oscar Mayer began prime-time television advertising with sponsorship of the *Gentle Ben* show.

Oscar Mayer's well known "Wiener Jingle," written in 1963, aired on almost all Oscar Mayer ads. The catchy jingle, "Oh, I wish I were an Oscar Mayer wiener, that is what I'd truly like to be. Cause if I were an Oscar Mayer Wiener, everyone would be in love with me!," was interwoven into each ad and became one of the longest-running commercial songs in the United States.

In 1977 the company launched a series of newspaper and magazines ads that became part of an overall marketing scheme that featured in-store displays, coupon programs, premium offers, and joint efforts with manufacturers of complimentary products such as beverages, cheese, and snack foods. But in 1990 the company's advertising agency, J. Walter Thompson, launched a television campaign designed to capitalize on the nostalgia people might have felt for older Oscar Mayer commercials. One 30-second advertising spot shows the Wienermobile arriving in town, followed by the tag line, "Remember when you wished you were an Oscar Mayer wiener?"

Another spot capitalizes on the high regard consumers had for the jingle, "My bologna has a first name, it's O-s-c-a-r. My bologna has a second name, it's M-a-y-e-r. Oh, I love to eat it every day, and if you ask me why I'll say, 'Cause Oscar Mayer has a way with b-o-l-o-g-n-a." The jingle was first used in a 1973 TV commercial called "Fisherman." The new 1989 commercial, called "Mrs. Von Lehmden," featured an elderly woman making bologna sandwiches for some neighborhood children playing baseball, and ends with the tag, "Remember when your bologna had a first name?"

Oscar Mayer even ordered a new fleet of Wienermobiles, and in 1988 hired teams of recent college graduates to drive across the country to appear at social functions, just as Little Oscar did 40 years earlier. The new Wienermobiles seated six passengers and came equipped with a sunroof, microwave, refrigerator, cellular phone, and a stereo system that could play the Wiener Jingle in 21 musical styles. Drivers were required to have a perfect driving record and a taste for hot dog puns. The program, at a cost of over $1 million per year, "is more efficient than media buying," said vice president and general manager Richard Searer in a 1992 *Wall Street Journal* article.

Packaging Innovations

By the middle of the 1940s, marketing and science had come to bear on how meats were sold and packaged. "To merchandise our product through to the ultimate customer is, in brief, the chief formula for success," stated a company report around 1943. The report correctly forecasted an era that would demand convenient packaging and self-service marketing of meat products. Oscar Mayer prepared itself to meet the demands of a new era. On one end of Oscar Mayer's new merchandising structure was advertising, on the other was packaging.

By 1944 Oscar Mayer had embarked on an extensive research program into the manufacturing and packaging of its products.

An Oscar Mayer window display from the 1930s.

The first innovation born of this research was the "Kartridg-Pak," a means of banding hot dog strings together in a compact packet resembling a cartridge belt. This process proved so successful that Oscar Mayer incorporated a separate business to manufacture and sell the Kartridg-Pak machines to its competitors. Other packaging/marketing innovations followed. 1946 saw the development of the "Sack-O-Sauce," which offered a convenient and

separate package of sauce to accompany Oscar Mayer's canned meats. In 1949 saran tubes called "Chub" packages were developed to package liverwurst and other sandwich spreads, and "set new standards of freshness, convenience and self-service eye-appeal." 1950 saw the introduction of the familiar "Slice-Pak" line of lunch meats in vacuum-sealed clear plastic packs with metal bases.

Most of these packaging innovations were designed to keep air, "the arch enemy of meat freshness," away from products. Later innovations were designed more with an eye towards consumer convenience and included the "Seal N' Serve" resealable lunch meat packages, bacon packages with a "back window" to view representative slices, and easy-open hot dog packages, which evolved into resealable zipper packages in 1990.

Product Development

When Oscar F. Mayer & Bro. opened its doors in 1883, sausages were made according to age-old traditions passed down from master to apprentice through the centuries. Gottfried Mayer, chief sausage maker during the first part of the company's history, learned the art of sausage making from the German "wurstmachers" before coming to the United States. Like other sausage makers at that time, he kept his recipes carefully guarded in a little black book, which he consulted from time to time to dig up forgotten specialties.

In 1883 Oscar Mayer's original line included German specialty sausages from Gottfried's book as well as loose pork sausage, pork sausage in natural casings, blood sausage, souse, head cheese, bologna, hot dogs, and liver sausage. By 1929, the company had 25 different varieties of sausages on the market. By Oscar Mayer's 75th anniversary in 1958, the company could boast that "Oscar Mayer people make over 200 types of sausages, luncheon meats, (and) smoked and canned meat products."

The conveniently packaged Oscar Mayer product line of the late 20th century is a far cry from the recipes found in Gottfried Mayer's little black book. As consumer preferences changed, old favorites such as souse and head cheese were eventually replaced by Bacon Bits, Ham Steaks, Cheese Smokie Links, Sub Sandwich Variety Packs, and the Healthy Favorites line of lunch meats low in fat, sodium, and cholesterol.

For nearly three decades, Oscar Mayer sales continued to grow at a steady pace, even when industry cycles turned unfavorable. By 1988, however, sales were slumping, following a series of unsuccessful new product introductions. The company entered into an extensive study of its past product developments and responded with a joint packaging/marketing effort called Lunchables Lunch Combinations. Lunchables, a prepackaged lunch combination featuring cheese, lunch meats, and crackers, was introduced in 1989 and was heralded by industry analysts as the most promising product from the company in 15 years.

Oscar Mayer Lunchables won a "Sial d'Or" medal for outstanding new product, awarded annually by trade press editors worldwide. Lunchables created a new convenience lunch market that was quickly copied by rivals Sara Lee Corp., Bryan Packing, and StarKist Seafood Company. By September 1992, the convenience lunch market had grown to $181.1 million.

Performance Appraisal and Future Growth

For over a century Oscar Mayer has demonstrated an ability to remain profitable even when industry cycles turned unfavorable. In 1969 Oscar Mayer held the meat industry's largest profit margin; 22 years later in 1991, it still held strong, racking up $2.5 billion in sales.

Oscar Mayer's history of innovative packaging designs and marketing savvy have kept it at the forefront of the meat business. The firm's introduction of Lunchables in 1990, as well as the addition of products lower in fat, salt, and cholesterol, have done much to improve the brand's sales and helped it meet changes in consumer eating habits. Meanwhile, though, competitors have intensified their efforts to edge Oscar Mayer out of its number one position, and the company's $2.5 billion sales total fell short of its projected 1991 goals. Still lower sales in 1992 reflected lower raw material costs and lower finished product prices, the sale of its small seafood subsidiary, and the elimination of some lower-volume, lower-margin products in the Oscar Mayer line. The firm also closed some manufacturing plants as it increased production efficiencies and found itself with excess production capacity.

Meat processing is traditionally a slow-growing industry. The prepared meat market is also very mature and provides Oscar Mayer with a challenge for additional growth. Over the years the brand has been able to overcome the odds and remain profitable. Continued success depends on the company's ability to remain at the forefront of innovation through new packaging, product development, and marketing programs.

Further Reading:

Berry, Jon, "The Tug of War for America's Tastebuds," *Superbrands 1991* (supplement to *Adweek's Marketing Week*), 1991.

"Brands: Out to Launch," *Adweek—Eastern Edition,* November 11, 1991, p. 24.

Dolan, Carrie, "If You Really Cut the Mustard, You Will Relish This Job," *Wall Street Journal,* July 7, 1992, p. 1A.

Ginsberg, Stanley, "The Wurst Is Yet to Come," *Forbes,* March 2, 1981, p. 40.

"Goliath KGF Loses Steam after Merger," *Advertising Age,* January 27, 1992, p. 16.

Link: Employee Publication of Oscar Mayer & Co., Madison, WI: Oscar Mayer & Co., September, October 1963.

Links with the Past: A History of Oscar Mayer & Co., Madison: Oscar Mayer & Co., 1979.

Mayer, Oscar G., Jr., *Oscar Mayer & Co.: From Corner Store to National Processor,* The Newcomen Society in North America, 1970.

Meyers, Harold B., "For the Old Meatpackers, Things Are Tough All Over," *Fortune,* February 1969, p. 89.

"Nothing If Not Resourceful," *Forbes,* April 14, 1980, p. 77.

"Oscar Mayer Ads Ask Adults, 'Remember When?'," *USA Today,* February 28, 1990, p. B10.

Scuderi, John, "Scoring with Combinations," *Supermarket News,* January 6, 1992, p. 29.

A Tradition and a Company: 75th Anniversary, Madison: Oscar Mayer & Co., 1958.

"U.S. Companies Win International Acclaim," *Food-Engineering,* October 1990, p. 19.

—Maura Troester

PARKAY®

Parkay brand of margarine, known for its smooth texture and buttery taste, is one of the oldest and best-selling margarines in the United States. Introduced in 1937 as a low-cost and good-tasting butter substitute, it has since been advertised for its health advantages. Parkay, like other margarines, contains no cholesterol and a relatively small amount of saturated fat.

Kraft General Foods, Inc., the parent company of Parkay, has produced a wide variety of foods, such as hot dogs, cheese, coffee, and mayonnaise. Its line of Parkay products includes not only Parkay margarine, but also Parkay whipped margarine, Parkay soft margarine, Parkay light spread, and Parkay Squeeze spread. One of Kraft's most successful brands, Parkay has greatly benefited from innovative advertising, as well as from years of research and development in food flavorings and food processing.

Brand Origins

For thousands of years people have been eating butter—a solid, yellowish food composed largely of fat, water, and air—which is made by churning cream or milk. Rich and highly caloric, butter has traditionally been used as both a spread and a cooking oil. Although highly prized throughout history, butter was often in short supply. Rancid butter, sometimes resulting from improper storage, was also a common problem, although the Romans actually preferred its flavor to that of fresh butter.

The first margarine, or butter substitute, was developed in the late 1860s by Hippolyte Megè-Mouriès, a French chemist. At the time, France was suffering from a butter shortage, and his new product, made principally of churned beef fat and milk, won a butter-substitution contest sponsored by French emperor Napoleon III. In 1873 the product was patented in the United States. Later margarines replaced animal fat with vegetable oil, which was both cheap and abundant. In the United States opposition to the product by the dairy industry led to both federal and state laws restricting the sale of such butter substitutes. Margarine, in fact, was initially classified as a harmful drug.

Despite organized opposition to margarine, by the 1930s its production in the United States had surpassed 300 million pounds per year. Margarine was cheaper than butter—a fact especially important during the Depression—and the quality of margarine had been substantially improved. Much of this margarine, or Oleomargarine, as it was commonly called, was made from coconut, cottonseed, or soybean oil. The Kraft-Phenix Cheese Corporation, a producer of not only cheese but also salad dressing, mayonnaise, and other food products, decided to enter this growing market by introducing a new product, Parkay Oleomargarine, which it began to sell and advertise in selected regions in 1937. By 1940 the product was distributed nationally.

Product Development and Advertising

The major appeal of Parkay and other margarines was their low cost. Although a substitute for butter, margarine did not taste exactly like it, nor, because of various laws, did it look like butter. Many states banned the sale of yellow-colored margarine, and in those states where the practice was legal, colored margarine was subjected to a 10-cent federal tax. As a result, Parkay margarine was sold white, and customers who wanted their margarine to look like butter had to blend food coloring into it.

Even so, Kraft was able to advertise other qualities of margarine that were similar to butter. In one of its first advertisements, published in a 1937 issue of *California Retail Grocers Advocate,* Parkay was billed as being a "3-Value Food"—that is, a good source of both vitamin A and vitamin D, as well as a "wonderful *energy food.*" These vitamins, found naturally in butter, were added to Parkay, but the advertised energy value came from its inherently high number of calories. In fact, Parkay margarine, based in vegetable oil, had about the same number of calories as butter (100 per tablespoon).

Soon shoppers were told about uses particularly suited for Parkay. In the February 1940 issue of *Ladies' Home Journal,* customers were given three reasons to use the Kraft product. "It *tastes* swell spread on biscuits and bread!" said a well-dressed young boy in the advertisement. His mother claimed, "It's a wonderful *flavor* shortening for baking!" while his father, shown eating breakfast in a brown suit, stated, "It sure makes fried foods *taste* better." Health claims were also featured. The advertisement pointed out that one pound of Parkay had 8,000 U.S.P. units of vitamin A, "the growth vitamin so vital to perfect health—especially important to children." Further, Parkay, "made by Kraft in a brand new plant," was produced from "wholesome, carefully selected and skillfully blended farm products."

The following year, just prior to the United States' entry into World War II, Kraft was advertising a "Parkay Margarine Con-

AT A GLANCE

Parkay brand of margarine introduced in 1937 by Kraft-Phenix Cheese Corporation; as a result of mergers and other concerns, parent company renamed several times; in 1988 Kraft, Inc., purchased by Philip Morris Companies, Inc.; in 1989 Kraft merged with General Foods Corporation, another Philip Morris subsidiary, to become Kraft General Foods, Inc.

Performance: *Market share*—14% (second share) of table spread category. *Sales*—$301 million.

Major competitor: Nabisco's Blue Bonnet margarine; also Van Den Bergh Foods Co.'s I Can't Believe It's Not Butter and Shedd's Country Crock margarine and spread; Mazola margarine; Land O'Lakes margarine.

Advertising: *Agency*—Leo Burnett, Chicago, IL, 1991—. *Major campaign*—"For better buttery taste, just say Parkay"; a television commercial featuring a group of talking containers of Parkay margarine.

Addresses: *Parent company*—Kraft General Foods, Inc., Kraft Ct., Glenview, IL 60025; phone: (708) 998-2000. *Ultimate parent company*—Philip Morris Companies, Inc., 120 Park Ave., New York, NY 10017; phone: (212) 878-2165.

test.'' Customers were encouraged to submit a sentence, 25 words or less, beginning with the words ''I like Parkay Margarine because,'' which would be ''judged on the basis of originality, sincerity and aptness of thought.'' The winner received coupons worth $600.00—the average annual food bill in the early 1940s for an American family of four—which could be used at any store carrying Parkay margarine.

After the war, Kraft, still hindered by state and federal laws, continued to make its margarine white. One advertisement in 1946 apologized to customers for the inconvenience: ''Please understand that these taxes and laws now prevent us from relieving homemakers of this chore of coloring Parkay Margarine at home.'' As a consolation, customers were instructed on the best way to color the product: ''Unwrap the Parkay and place it in a large bowl. Soften to room temperature . . . Tear open the wafer of certified coloring enclosed in the package and sprinkle contents over Parkay in the bowl. Blend yellow coloring in gradually, using a large spoon or a blending fork.''

By 1948, however, Kraft had developed its ''COLOR-KWIK'' package, which reduced mixing time to about a minute and a half. The new feature was a small ''yellow color-bubble'' placed on the margarine's transparent inner packaging. The customer took the packaging out of the Parkay box, pinched the bubble that released the yellow food coloring, kneaded the packaging until the margarine was evenly yellow, and then reshaped it with the help of the box. Along with this improvement, the new Parkay also featured a much higher level of vitamin A—15,000 U.S.P. units per pound. In 1948, however, Kraft also finally came out with a precolored product, Yellow Parkay Oleomargarine, which was sold in quarter-pound sticks at a price per pound 10 cents higher than its noncolored margarine to cover the federal tax.

In the late 1950s Kraft introduced the ''new sweet chilled'' Parkay. This process was said to keep the product's ''delightful flavor uniform in quality over many weeks'' and to allow it to be spread ''smoothly even when ice cold.'' In a 1958 advertisement run in both *Sunset* and *Western Family*, customers were offered a

pair of ''glamorous Powers Model Nylons absolutely free'' in exchange for 10 proof-of-purchase coupons from boxes of Parkay.

Kraft continued researching ways to improve the flavor and texture of its margarine. Because Parkay was supposed to taste as much like butter as possible, researchers tried to define butter's distinct blend of flavor components and then devise a similar blend for Parkay. Moreover, attempts were made to have the flavor of Parkay ''release'' more quickly to the body's senses. After years of research, Kraft came out with its new ''country fresh flavor'' Parkay margarine in 1970.

Parkay's country fresh flavor was also used in other Parkay products, such as Soft Parkay and Squeeze Parkay. Squeeze Parkay, successfully introduced in 1969, is thought to be the first liquid spread to be sold in the United States. It was especially popular for use on pancakes, corn-on-the-cob, popcorn, and vegetables.

The Talking Package

In the early 1970s, with sales of more than 200 million pounds per year, Parkay was the second-best-selling brand of margarine in the United States. Competition, moreover, was fierce. Only five

A newspaper ad from Parkay's past, introducing both yellow margarine and quarter-pound sticks.

brands had more than a five percent share of the national margarine market, and some 500 margarine brands existed.

Despite the introduction of country fresh flavor, market studies indicated that Kraft advertising had not been successful in equating Parkay Margarine with an especially buttery flavor. Thus, a new television advertising campaign, ''Flavor Says Butter,'' was started in 1973. Featuring a talking container of Parkay Margarine, the advertisement was so successful that within a year Parkay had become the country's number one margarine.

The campaign eventually featured dozens of different commercials, although in each the star was a talking cup or stick of Parkay. Cast for the supporting role were a variety of ordinary people, celebrities, and even Santa Claus. The person, for example, would be sitting next to a container of margarine and say "Parkay," but the container would immediately retort "butter." After a short argument in which the container's only reply would be "butter," the person would open the container, taste the margarine, and then concur by also saying "butter." The container, however, playfully responded "Parkay." In 1979 a "Flavor Says Butter" commercial featuring a little girl spelling out the name Parkay won the prestigious Cleo award for the best dairy product advertisement.

These commercials, developed by Needham, Harper and Steers advertising agency, were not accepted by the television networks until Kraft could prove that Parkay actually tasted like butter. Blind taste tests conducted in 1972 and 1975 indeed confirmed that most people could not taste the difference between Parkay and the leading national butter.

Health Claims

Vegetable oil, the main ingredient in Parkay, has been at the focal point of margarine's success. Readily available and inexpensive, it has provided an affordable base for a butter substitute. The low cost was one of the most important reasons for the early success of margarine, but, decades later, customers learned of a possible health benefit of vegetable oil, which is considerably less saturated than butterfat and thus believed by many to be better for the heart. The combination of low prices and less saturated fat, along with improvements in flavor and texture, has allowed Parkay and other margarines and table spreads to overtake butter in sales. In 1900 per capita butter consumption was 20 pounds per year in the United States, while at the same time per capita margarine consumption was less than two pounds. By the late 1980s the average American ate each year more than 10 pounds of margarine or other table spread and less than five pounds of butter.

Parkay Products

By the early 1990s there were a variety of Parkay products, including Parkay margarine, Parkay whipped margarine, Parkay soft margarine, Parkay light spread, and Parkay Squeeze spread. Together they represented about 14 percent, or the second largest share, of the table spread category. All contained soybean oil as the first ingredient. Among Parkay's competitors were Blue Bonnet, I Can't Believe It's Not Butter, and Mazola, although scores of other brands existed. Land O'Lakes, the largest butter producer in the United States, also sold a margarine that competed with Parkay. Shedd's, made of soybean oil, was the leader of the table spread category.

In the United States all margarine, including Parkay margarine, was required to be at least 80 percent fat, or about the same percentage as butter. As a result, both butter and Parkay margarine had about the same number of calories, 100 per tablespoon. The source of fat in Parkay margarine— partially hydrogenated and liquid soybean oil was the product's first ingredient, followed by water, salt, whey, sodium benzoate (a preservative), lecithin (an emulsifier), artificial flavor, vitamin A palmitate, and beta carotene (a pigment added to make the margarine yellow). Its package boasted that Parkay margarine had "70% less saturated fat than butter." Parkay whipped margarine, similar in ingredients to regular Parkay margarine, contained more air and thus had only 60 calories per tablespoon. By weight, however, the two Parkay brands had about the same number of calories.

Parkay soft margarine, introduced in 1965, differed from regular Parkay margarine mostly by the addition of another type of fat, mono- and diglycerides, which helped create a smoother, softer texture. Like regular Parkay margarine, Parkay Soft had 100 calories per tablespoon and just two grams of saturated fat.

Parkay Light, with only 40 percent oil, by law could not be called a margarine. Instead, it was labeled a spread, which was a more general term. Its first ingredient was partially hydrogenated soybean oil and, like Parkay Soft, it contained mono-and diglycerides. Because of its lower fat content, Parkay Light had just 70 calories per tablespoon. It was first sold nationally in 1978.

Parkay Squeeze spread, a liquid containing 64 percent oil, was also labeled as a spread. Each tablespoon had 90 calories. Like other Parkay products, its first ingredient was soybean oil (not hydrogenated), but Parkay Squeeze also contained a small amount of hydrogenated cottonseed oil. National distribution of the product began in 1973.

Brand Outlook

Although margarine and other table spreads have overtaken butter in sales, by the early 1990s the outlook for these butter substitutes was uncertain. Overall sales for spreads were declining, as were the sales of Parkay, from $359 million in 1988 to $301 million in 1992. The product's improvements in taste and texture, however, have placed Parkay margarine in a strongly competitive position against other brands. Indicative of its success, in 1989 a panel of taste experts hired by *Consumer Reports* rated Parkay margarine among the best-tasting spreads in the United States.

Further Reading:

Burros, Marian, "Now What? U.S. Study Says Margarine May Be Harmful," *New York Times,* October 7, 1992, p. A1.

"Butter vs. Margarine," *Consumer Reports,* September 1989, pp. 551-556.

"A Dietary Shield Against Lung Cancer [margarine]?" *Science News,* October 12, 1991, p. 237.

"Let's Hear It (Again) for Parkay," *Kraftsman,* March 1971, pp. 4-7.

"Please Do Squeeze the Parkay," *Kraftsman,* summer 1973, pp. 4-5.

"Say It Ain't So, Oleo!" *Time,* August 27, 1990, p. 53.

"Talking Our Way into No. 1: Parkay Margarine Commercials Say Just Enough to Butter Up Consumers' Interest and Kraft Sales," *Kraft Ink,* no. 3, 1979, pp. 20-22.

"The Trouble with Margarine: Is It Any Better Than Butter for Your Health," *Consumer Reports,* March 1991, pp. 196-197.

—Thomas Riggs

PEPPERIDGE FARM®

Pepperidge Farm, Inc.'s distinctive baked goods, cookies, crackers, and frozen products pioneered the marketing of upscale foods. Although the brand holds only a small portion of the markets it is in, it leads premium-product segments. Born of a mother's concern for her family's health, the brand and its products have come to represent a variety of food themes, from wholesome goodness to sheer indulgence. Brands under the Pepperidge Farm label include American Collection cookies, Distinctive cookies, Wholesome Choice cookies, Goldfish crackers, and Hearty Slices and Light Style breads.

Brand Origins

Margaret Rudkin, founder of Pepperidge Farm, was born in New York City and learned to cook from her Irish grandmother. Rudkin unknowingly started her career in commercial food when she prepared a preservative-free loaf of whole wheat bread for her son, who was allergic to the artificial ingredients in commercial breads.

Rudkin's bread was based on cookbook recipes, but she experimented with the tried-and-true by adding honey and molasses, and using stone-ground wheat flour. When Rudkin's doctor scoffed that bread made with stone-ground flour alone would be too coarse, she offered him a loaf. As the story goes, he "immediately" ordered more for himself and his patients. She named the bread after her family's Connecticut farm, which was dotted with Tupelo, or Pepperidge trees.

Early Marketing Strategy

Rudkin had developed a thriving mail-order business through health professionals and their patients by 1937. Operating out of her own kitchen, she soon progressed to dealing with local grocers, and was finally compelled to move her bread making to a large outbuilding on the farm and hire an assistant. When the number of customers in New York City grew too large for mail order, Rudkin contracted with a commercial grocer to sell her bread. Rudkin's husband delivered those early shipments during his daily commute by train to work.

Sensing a demand for high-quality white bread, Rudkin made her first move to diversify Pepperidge Farm's offerings by creating a recipe for all-natural bread made from unbleached white flour in 1937. By 1940 her branded breads sold 20,000 loaves each week, despite its cost, which was three times the normal price for a loaf of bread.

Although World War II rationing slowed production, Pepperidge Farm planned for expansion in the postwar years. The company opened its first modern, large-scale bakery in the neighboring community of Norwalk, Connecticut, in 1947 and began to expand the scope of the brand to include dinner rolls and more varieties of breads. The brand grew so popular that just two years later a second plant was opened in Downingtown, Pennsylvania.

In the 1950s Rudkin explored the possibilities of branching out into the cookie business, but was determined that Pepperidge Farm would not produce ordinary cookies. Rudkin traveled to Belgium, where she found a recipe worthy of Pepperidge Farm's upscale clientele. She reached an agreement with the Delacre Company in Brussels, which allowed Pepperidge Farm to produce "biscuits," as cookies are known in the trade. The company's pursuit of excellence compelled it to import a 46-meter-long oven and bring Delacre employees to train Pepperidge Farm's new cookie bakers. Biscuits would eventually constitute 50 percent of Pepperidge Farm's sales.

From Regional to National Brand

In 1956 advertising giant David Ogilvy adapted a character from Fred Allen's radio show to represent the old-fashioned quality of Pepperidge Farm goods. Ogilvy put "Titus L. Moody" on a haystack, wearing a string tie and overalls, extolling the health bread that was "a-bustin' with vitamins" for Pepperidge Farm's first television advertisement.

Pepperidge Farm became affiliated with Campbell Soup Company on January 1, 1961, and Margaret Rudkin was named chair of the board in 1962. She died in 1967 after garnering awards from *Fortune* magazine, lecturing at the Harvard Business School, and being recognized as a leading American businesswoman.

Gordon McGovern took over Pepperidge Farm in 1968 and led the company in just over a decade from its status as a regional bakery with $100 million annual sales to a national company selling $400 million. Under McGovern's leadership, Pepperidge Farm pioneered the mass marketing of upscale food products. The brand's marketers set their products apart from the Wonder Bread, saltines, and vanilla wafers in supermarkets through high shelf

AT A GLANCE

Pepperidge Farm brand of fresh and frozen baked goods founded in 1937 by Margaret Rudkin at her farm near Norwalk, CT; her company, Pepperidge Farm, Inc., became a subsidiary of Campbell Soup Company in 1961; company has four major business units: bakery (breads, rolls, croutons, and stuffing), biscuit (cookies, crackers, and snacks), frozen foods, and foodservice.

Performance: *Sales*—$597 million.

Major competitor: Entenmann's Inc.'s brand of baked goods.

Advertising: *Agency*—Ogilvy & Mather, New York, NY, since the 1950s. *Major campaign*—Elderly character, originally "Titus L. Moody," subsequently "The Country Gentleman," declaring, "Pepperidge Farm remembers."

Addresses: *Parent company*—Pepperidge Farm, Inc., P.O. Box 5500, 595 Westport Avenue, Norwalk, CT 06856; phone: (203) 846-7000, fax: (203) 846-7369. *Ultimate parent company*—Campell Soup Company, Campbell Place, Camden, NJ 08103; phone: (609) 342-4800.

placement, premium prices, and an emphasis on the products' high quality and all-natural ingredients.

In the early 1980s, Pepperidge Farm held 5 percent of the cookie market, and was the fastest growing segment of the Campbell Company. At that time, fruit cookies and snack bars were added to the brand's lineup, and Pepperidge Farm sought to expand its product line into other arenas.

Product Experiments

In 1980 Pepperidge Farm offered its first main-meal product, "Deli's." The nonmicrowaveable vegetable- and meat-filled pastry was created to fill a need for small, convenient meals among single people, working women, and other Americans who tended to eat several small meals per day. Marketers at Pepperidge Farm hoped that Deli's would expand sales and reduce the company's dependence on frozen sweet goods, a product whose market had declined in the late 1970s.

Unfortunately, Deli's became the first in a string of product failures under the label. In 1982 Lucasfilm, the company that produced a string of hit movies in the 1980s, including *ET* and the *Star Wars* trilogy, approached Pepperidge Farm with a proposal to license cookies based on characters from *Star Wars*. The agreement, which would give Lucasfilm a percentage of sales, but no up-front licensing fee, seemed relatively risk-free for Pepperidge Farm. The introduction of the cookies was coordinated with the May 1983 release of the third *Star Wars* movie, *Return of the Jedi*. Freestanding displays were the only promotional tool, and the cookies had strong sales at the start. However, about nine weeks into the promotion, sales lagged. When Pepperidge Farm was ready to move the cookies to the regular shelves, supermarket owners wouldn't cooperate. They would not risk using valuable shelf space for a product with a falling sales record.

Pepperidge Farm Apple Juice, the third product failure in the early 1980s, was introduced in 1982 in the Northeastern United States. The "premium blend of five kinds of apple juice" was expected to fill a vacuum in the apple juice segment, where no single brand dominated. However, other juice makers cut their prices by up to 40 percent to push Pepperidge Farm out of the market.

Although many different factors condemned these products to failure, all of the cases have one element in common: the three products flew in the face of one of Margaret Rudkin's founding principles, that of quality first and foremost. Deli's started out a high-quality product, but when their value deteriorated, sales followed suit. The *Star Wars* cookies were perceived as too expensive to give to children on a regular basis. Worse, they were cheaply made, had a short shelf life, and did not really fit in with the upscale image of the Pepperidge Farm brand. The apple juice was simply not the high-quality product that Pepperidge Farm customers had come to expect, but was released anyway.

The company's financial losses from the misguided products topped $7 million, and may have influenced drops in Pepperidge Farm's market shares of other goods. The silver lining to this cloud of failures was that Pepperidge Farm avoided the "cookie wars" that started with the 1983 introduction of Frito-Lay, Inc.'s "Grandma's Cookies." The "crunchy-chewy" cookies were very popular, and Procter & Gamble joined the battle later in the year with its Duncan Hines cookies. By the time RJR Nabisco and the Keebler entered the fray, the competition had gotten expensive: within two years the four companies spent almost $100 million on advertising. As Bill Saporito observed in a 1986 *Fortune* article, that spending pace was "unprecedented and unsustainable."

Refocus on Quality and Cookies

Richard Shea became Pepperidge Farm's fourth president in five years in 1984, and worked to restore the brand's image. Shea took charge and eliminated a great many products, including the infamous Deli's and *Star Wars* cookies. Shea also brought Pepperidge Farm back on the quality track by bringing many outdated bakeries up to modern-day standards. Computerized delivery systems helped get the company's products to commercial outlets faster than industry standards: cookies arrived less than five days after coming out of the oven, whereas other brands averaged five to ten days, and breads were shelved in three days, whereas the industry averaged five days. "Project Freshness" revitalized Pepperidge Farm's emphasis on basic quality—a key feature of the brand's image.

Shea didn't shun all new products, however. A renewed partnership with Belgium's Delacre Company, also a Campbell affiliate, resulted in a line of butter cookies with molded chocolate tops, the "Distinctive Chocolatier" line.

Despite the industry-wide "cookie wars," in 1985 Pepperidge Farm still dominated the premium cookie segment of the retail cookie market. Cookies contributed 50 percent of the company's income, and Pepperidge Farm decided to try to increase that figure. In 1986 the brand introduced its "American Collection" of "lumpy-bumpy" cookies, chock-full of nuts, raisins, and chocolate. The new product helped raise the brand's share of the packaged cookie market a full point, from 3.5 to 4.5 percent.

The American Collection cookies soon became Pepperidge Farm's most popular, fastest-growing product. Whereas sales of "crunchy-chewy" cookies were cut in half by 1985, Pepperidge Farm couldn't keep up with demand for the American Collection. By 1989 Pepperidge Farm had garnered 6 percent of the $2.5 billion packaged cookie business, its highest share in history.

Further Line Expansion

In July of 1988 Pepperidge Farm added a line of single-serve desserts to the American Collection. Advertising for the rich desserts featured Ogilvy & Mather's old-fashioned Country Gentleman. The company raised its advertising budget for the brand from $12 million in 1986 to $18 million in 1987. Competition in this segment included such national brands as Keebler Company and the Kitchens of Sara Lee, as well as regional competitors like Baby Watson cheesecake.

By 1989 the American Collection desserts had earned second place in the single-serve frozen sweet goods market with a 33 percent share, second only to Weight Watchers. But a recession began to cut into sales, lowering all segments of Pepperidge Farm's business in 1990 and 1991: cookie sales in supermarkets were down 9 percent, cracker sales fell 8 percent, and frozen sweetgoods dropped 9 percent. In order to salvage profits, Pepperidge Farm's parent, Campbell Soup Company, slashed the subsidiary's advertising budget by 55.5 percent for fiscal year 1991-1992.

When a primary competitor, Entenmann's, offered its fat-free, shelf-stable cakes in 1989, Pepperidge Farm hesitated. It took two years for the company to roll out a 98 percent fat-free pound cake and a new line of low-fat cookies and crackers dubbed "Wholesome Choice." In 1992 the line was expanded to include frozen muffins. That year, Pepperidge Farm began nutritional labeling of all the brand's products and introduced several new items, including "Soft Baked" and "Family Request" cookies and new varieties of "Hearty Slices" bread. Pepperidge Farm was rewarded for its efforts that year when *Bakery Production and Marketing* magazine named it the "Wholesale Bakery of the Year."

Some of the marketing budget was restored in 1992 to promote these new products, bringing the resources up to $12 million. Pepperidge Farm officials were banking on the growing demand for "healthy" cookies, which they expected to grow from $39 million to as much as $500 million by 1995.

Promotion for the newest products stuck with the Country Gentleman and his "geezer chic," as Barbara Lippert in *Adweek's Marketing Week* dubbed the early 1990s preoccupation with endearing and often reassuring senior citizens. This time, the character was joined by a weight-conscious female friend to emphasize the healthy aspects of the products as well as their old-fashioned goodness.

In 1991 Pepperidge Farm introduced its cookies and crackers to Ontario, Montreal, and western Canada. Pepperidge Farm breads were added to the Canadian selections the following year. Bilingual packaging for the French-Canadian products was produced in United States plants, which numbered ten in 1993. The brand's export system extended to 22 countries worldwide.

Outlook

Campbell Soup Company, the ultimate parent of Pepperidge Farm, renewed its commitment to growth on the strength of its major brands in the early 1990s. The company increased its overall advertising expenditures for 1992 by 11 percent, and worked to capitalize on the reputation earned by Pepperidge Farm over its 55-year history. As long as the brand established by Margaret Rudkin can maintain her standards of quality and nutrition, it will continue to dominate upscale markets. And as nutritional concerns continue to shape consumer buying habits, Pepperidge Farm can only stand to benefit.

Further Reading:

Berry, Jon, "And Now, a 'Healthy' Chocolate-chip Cookie," *AdWeek's Marketing Week,* July 29, 1991, p. 6.

Cohen, Jeffrey, "Marketing All Stars: Tom Healy," *AdWeek's Marketing Week* (supplement), November 27, 1989, p. MRC34.

Dagnoli, Judann, "Just Desserts," *Advertising Age,* December 7, 1987, p. 73.

Felgner, Brent H., "Consumer Expenditures Study: Baked Goods," *Supermarket Business,* September 1990, pp. 137-39.

Giges, Nancy, "Pepperidge Farm's Fallow Ground," *Advertising Age,* February 21, 1985, pp. 2-3.

Lippert, Barbara, "Ol' Titus Moody: On the Cutting Edge of 'Geezer Chic'," *AdWeek's Marketing Week,* December 14, 1987, p. 19.

Machan, Dyan, "Pepperidge Farm's Doughboy," *Forbes,* March 20, 1989, pp. 198-99.

"Pepperidge Cookin'," *Advertising Age,* August 26, 1991, pp. 3, 38.

"Pepperidge Farm Turns into a Tough cookie," *Sales & Marketing Management,* January 17, 1983, p. 24.

Rudkin, Margaret, *The Margaret Rudkin Pepperidge Farm Cookbook,* New York: Atheneum, 1963.

Saporito, Bill, "A Smart Cookie at Pepperidge," *Fortune,* December 22, 1986, pp. 67, 70, 74.

"Slumping Pepperidge Farm Turns Up the Heat on O&M," *Advertising Age,* June 24, 1991, pp. 1, 60.

"Sour Juice and Crumbled Cookies at Pepperidge Farm," *Business Week,* June 4, 1984, pp. 31-32.

—April S. Dougal

PEPSI-COLA®

For much of its existence, Pepsi-Cola has lived in the shadow of its larger arch-rival, Coca-Cola. No longer regarded as "the other cola," Pepsi brands dominate the soft drink category with a market share in excess of 30 percent.

Pepsi employs many of the same ingredients of other colas, but is differently formulated to be bracer, and perhaps a bit lighter to the taste. Chemical analysts suggest that Pepsi's taste differs from Coke's because Pepsi's citrus acids are derived from lemons, while Coke's come from oranges. But because the recipes are closely guarded secrets, and because both companies spend millions each year reinforcing differentiation, the actual difference may never be known. Through vigorous advertising and product personality development, Pepsi has developed a reputation as the cola for more discriminating palates.

Brand Origins

Pepsi-Cola was invented in 1893 by Caleb Bradham, a 31-year old pharmacist in New Bern, North Carolina. In an attempt to develop a popular product that would keep people returning to his drug store's fountain, making it a more popular and profitable gathering place, Bradham concocted a syrup out of kola nut extract, vanilla, pepsin, sugar, and rare oils, and mixed it with carbonated water. Only one of several drinks he had developed, this one proved especially popular. It became known locally as "Brad's drink," and achieved Bradham's aim of keeping the fountain packed with customers.

Five years later, on August 28, 1898, Bradham renamed the drink "Pepsi-Cola," after the ingredient pepsin, a fluid that aids in digestion. By 1902 Bradham had developed his soft drink into a business independent of the pharmacy. He established the Pepsi-Cola Company and registered the name with the United States Patent Office. The trademark was awarded on June 16 of the following year.

Bradham began bottling the drink at a rented warehouse and ran advertisements for the drink in small North Carolina newspapers. In 1903 he produced 7,968 gallons of Pepsi syrup and proved the viability of a bottling operation. Bradham moved the facility in 1904 to the larger Bishop factory in New Bern. That year he turned out 19,848 gallons of syrup—enough to begin independent bottling franchises. The first of these were established at Charlotte and Durham in 1905. Two years later Pepsi was bottled by 40 franchises, and more than 100,000 gallons of syrup was produced.

Early Marketing Strategy

Bradham considered Pepsi in bottles to be more marketable because it was more portable. In all promotion and business development, he concentrated on the development of bottling operations over fountain sales. With the introduction of motor vehicles and, spurred by demand for the bottled product, Bradham retired his horse-drawn syrup deliveries and began trucking the concentrate to bottlers. In 1908 the bottling network grew to 250 franchisees in 24 states.

At the dawn of World War I, Bradham controlled one of the country's most successful and profitable enterprises, but the war caused several changes in the dynamics of production that Bradham was ill-prepared to handle. Price controls during the war held the price of sugar to 5.5 cents per pound. When the war—and the price controls—ended in 1919, the price of sugar skyrocketed.

When sugar climbed to 26 cents per pound in 1920, Bradham bet that the price would continue to rise. He purchased massive quantities of sugar and options for more. By the end of the year, however, sugar producers entered the market with millions of tons of product, forcing the price of sugar to drop to two cents per pound. Bradham attempted to salvage his position by borrowing cash, selling assets, and offering additional share issues. By 1922, however, his business collapsed, with only two plants remaining in operation. After a failed reorganization, Bradham returned to his pharmacy and put the Pepsi-Cola business up for sale.

In 1923 he sold the business to the Craven Holding Corporation for $30,000. Craven sold Pepsi-Cola to Roy Megargel that same year. But Megargel failed to revive the brand and was forced into bankruptcy in 1931. The Pepsi brand was discovered later that year by Charles C. Guth, president of Loft Industries, a candy and fountain store chain. Guth purchased an 80 percent interest in the business from Megargel and reincorporated the company.

Brand Development

Guth's impact was immediate and profound. Installing himself as general manager of the Pepsi-Cola Company, Guth declared Bradham's original formula for the drink unsatisfactory. He ordered Loft's chief chemist, Richard J. Ritchie, to "fix it," and

AT A GLANCE

Pepsi introduced as "Brad's Drink" by New Bern, NC, pharmacist Caleb Bradham in 1893; reformulated in 1931; diet Pepsi introduced in 1964.

Performance: *Market share*—16.1% of soft drink category. *Sales*—$12 billion.

Major competitor: Coca-Cola.

Advertising: *Agency*—BBDO, New York, NY, 1962–; *Major campaigns*—"Pepsi Cola Hits the Spot," "Pepsi: The Choice of a New Generation," and "You Got the Right One Baby."

Addresses: *Parent company*—Pepsi-Cola Company, 1 Pepsi Way, Somers, NY 10589-2201; phone: (914) 767-6000; fax: (914) 767-7762. *Ultimate parent company*—PepsiCo, Inc., Purchase, NY 10577; phone: (914) 253-2000; fax: (914) 253-2070.

removed pepsin as an ingredient. Satisfied with the result, Guth cancelled Loft's contract with Coca-Cola, which he deeply despised, and replaced their syrup with Pepsi.

Still, Guth didn't have enough capital to outpromote Coke, and his distribution network was poor. Then, in 1934, as the first signs of economic recovery from the Great Depression occurred, Guth attempted a bold move. He noted that brewers failed to recycle their two-cent return bottles, and he enlisted Pepsi bottlers to re-use them at a fraction of the cost of new bottles by pasting a Pepsi label over the brewers'.

Beer bottles, however, held 12 ounces—double the size of soda bottles. He saw this as a great gimmick, offering twice as much Pepsi for five cents, the same price as other sodas. Initial market tests in Baltimore confirmed the value appeal to Depression-weary consumers, and the new size was rolled out nationwide.

Pepsi-Cola became immensely popular, eclipsing its earlier national profile on the strength of an innovative ad campaign. Guth moved the Pepsi-Cola company to Long Island in 1935 and, because of strong interest by bottlers, set up a new franchise system based on territories.

Guth's strong personal interest in Pepsi-Cola put him at odds with Loft management, which sued him in 1933 for misappropriating company funds to purchase Pepsi. After three years of litigation, Guth lost, but was retained as a consultant on the business.

Coca-Cola, meanwhile, sued Pepsi for infringement on the name "cola." Walter Mack, who had unseated Guth, discovered that in an earlier suit against Cleo Cola, Coca-Cola had paid the company to lose its case. Mack located the cancelled check and horrified Coca-Cola lawyers by exposing the fraud in court. Reeling from embarrassment, Coke struck a deal with Pepsi that ended all infringement claims.

By 1941 Loft's Pepsi subsidiary had become bigger than its regular lines of business. Loft absorbed its subsidiary, changed its name to the Pepsi-Cola Company, and gained a listing on the New York Stock Exchange.

The company's business was disrupted again during World War II. This time, however, the price of sugar wasn't as much of a

problem as the availability of sugar. To ensure ready supplies, the company purchased its own sugar plantation in Cuba. Sales during wartime held steady. But after the war, despite government price controls and the Cuban sugar plantation, Pepsi was forced to raise its prices first to six, and then to seven cents a bottle. This caused Pepsi's market share to drop from 23 to 16 percent, while Coke's rose from 77 to 84 percent.

In 1949 Pepsi hired Alfred N. Steele, a disgruntled middle manager at Coca-Cola, as its new president. Steele and the 15 managers he brought with him held intimate knowledge of Coca-Cola and its weaknesses. To rejuvenate Pepsi, he invested $38 million in new plant and equipment, bolstered the franchise agreements, and began an aggressive grocery store sales effort. He also standardized the taste of Pepsi with less sugar, giving the drink a lighter, crisper taste. Coke, relative to Pepsi, was now an older drink with a heavier taste.

Extensions

The first extension of Pepsi-Cola came in 1964, when the company introduced diet Pepsi. The industry's first diet drink, diet Pepsi was aimed primarily at fashion-conscious women who were concerned with the consequences of drinking a beverage high in sugar. This image was reinforced by the company's "Girl Watchers" ad campaign. Although cautiously promoted at first, Diet Pepsi soon inspired numerous imitators.

The next product variation occurred in 1975 when Pepsi, seeking an alternative diet cola, introduced Pepsi Light, a diet version of Pepsi with a blast of lemon. However, the new brand failed to meet its sales projections, and after only a few years promotion was halted.

As public preference for caffeine-free drinks began to emerge in 1982, the company introduced Pepsi Free, a caffeine-free version of Pepsi, in both regular and diet formulations.

In 1992 Pepsi introduced Crystal Pepsi and Diet Crystal Pepsi—clear, naturally flavored, lighter, and less sweet colas. These new drinks, caffeine- and preservative-free, are aimed at the upscale health drink market. In labeling Crystal Pepsi with the Pepsi name, Pepsi-Cola demonstrates that soft drink manufacturers are battling for every tenth of a percent of market share. Pepsi expects the brand to garner two percent of the $49 billion soft drink market, which translates to nearly $1 billion in sales.

Packaging

The first variations in the appearance of Pepsi were confined to logotypes. The first Pepsi logo, in 1898, was an ornate script. This was refined several times over the years until 1950, when the script was featured on the blue and red yin-yang swirl bottlecap. The script gave way to block capital letters in 1962. In 1987 the logo consisted of block letters bisecting the bottlecap swirl, enclosed by red and blue bars on either side. This square logo was replaced in 1991 by italic block letters over a thick line, with the bottlecap swirl in the lower right corner of the emblem.

The first packaging variation for Pepsi-Cola came in 1948, when Pepsi was sold for the first time in cans. Until that time, Pepsi was only available at soda fountains or in a smooth glass bottle. Recognizing the success of Coca-Cola's distinctive (and trademarked) fluted bottle, Pepsi introduced its own unique bottle in 1958. The new design contained several parallel indentations that swirled down the bottle at a slight diagonal pitch from top to bottom. In time, the "swirl bottle," became every bit as distinctive as Coca-Cola's.

In 1963 Pepsi increased the size of the bottle to 16 ounces. Ten years later, the company introduced a two-liter party mixer size bottle. Packaged in the industry's first recyclable metric bottle, it was intended for America's imminent changeover to the metric system. But while this conversion never materialized, several of Pepsi's competitors soon followed with their own two-liter bottles. Today, soft drinks are the only major products (with the possible exception of cigarettes) that are measured metrically. Later, the company introduced four-packs of clear 16-ounce plastic bottles. These resealable, lighter, shatterproof packages are cheaper and more easily recyclable than either glass or aluminum.

Advertising

One of the first ads for Pepsi-Cola, appearing in 1909, featured the race car driver Barney Oldfield, who endorsed Pepsi as "A bully drink . . . refreshing, invigorating, a fine bracer before a race."

In 1934, when Pepsi began selling its cola in 12-ounce bottles, Guth personally developed the tagline, "Pepsi, the nickel drink, worth a dime." Continuing on this theme in 1939, the company

The Pepsi logo as it appeared in 1898.

began an immensely successful ad campaign with new lyrics for a plucky old English hunting song, D'Ye Ken John Peel. The jingle, "Pepsi-Cola hits the spot, 12 full ounces that's a lot, twice as much for a nickel too, Pepsi-Cola is the drink for you," became one of the most widely recognized tunes of the day, and even made its way into sheet music and juke boxes.

With this success came numerous failures, including Mack's expensive and unsuccessful campaign to replace spinach with Pepsi as the rejuvenator of Popeye. After World War II, price increases forced Pepsi to abandon its popular nickel jingle.

Perhaps the most profound change in Pepsi's image came after Steele was named president of Pepsi-Cola in 1950. Steele's wife, the actress Joan Crawford, took an active role in her husband's business. Crawford took every opportunity to plug Pepsi and, in the process, helped change Pepsi's image from one of value to one

of sophistication and exclusivity. With Pepsi being promoted as a statement and an experience, the Pepsi theme became "Be sociable, have a Pepsi," and "The light refreshment."

When Steele died in 1959, Crawford assumed his seat on the company's board. Her contributions in this capacity were controversial, as the movie star imposed her formidable personality on the other members, forcing the company into several unsuccessful endeavors.

Later that year, Pepsi was featured at the American exhibition of the Moscow Fair, where the company won a tremendous publicity windfall when Donald Kendall orchestrated a photograph of Soviet Premier Nikita Krushchev and Vice-President Richard Nixon sharing a Pepsi. Five years later, the company repeated this success when a company promotions man slipped bottles of Pepsi into the naive hands of the Beatles and snapped their picture.

During the 1960s, Pepsi turned its focus to youth, discovering the purchasing power of the postwar "baby boom" generation. The company changed its advertising theme to "Now it's Pepsi, for those who think young." This gave way in 1963 to its celebrated "Pepsi Generation" campaign, with contemporary images serving as the basis for several other themes during the next ten years. The first of these was, "Taste that beats the others cold, Pepsi pours it on," in 1967. Two years later, this was succeeded by, "You've got a lot to live, Pepsi's got a lot to give." In 1973 Pepsi introduced the "Join the Pepsi people, feelin' free" campaign. Somewhat less memorable campaigns of the 1970s included "Have a Pepsi Day!" in 1976, "Catch that Pepsi Spirit," in 1979 and "Pepsi's got your taste for life," in 1981.

Pepsi's most notable campaign in recent years featured the singer Michael Jackson in a series of flashy ads, followed by Pepsi sponsorship of the performer's reunion tour with his brothers. This 1984 campaign was overshadowed, to a great extent, by a mishap during filming of one of the spots in which an incendiary device exploded prematurely, setting fire to Jackson's hair.

In 1986, Jackson joined Lionel Ritchie and Michael J. Fox as part of the company's "Entertainment Marketing" strategy. In 1990 Fred Savage and Billy Crystal were added, and a new diet Pepsi campaign starring Ray Charles was introduced. Based on "Uh-Huh," the universal grunt of approval, the campaign featured the venerable blues singer proclaiming "You got the right one, baby," as a Supremes-like trio sang "Uh-Huh." This popular and memorable theme was repeated in several different ads, built around Pepsi's light, crisp taste.

Health Claims

When formulating Pepsi-Cola, Bradham's choice of kola extract added some caffeine to the mix. Unlike many of his competitors, he did add stimulants. The brand's main rival in later years, Coca-Cola, contained a more generous shot of caffeine to boost its marketability as a headache remedy and "brain tonic." It also contained some addictive coca leaf extract which, some have maintained, was intended to make people dependant on the drink. Unlike Coke, which also was invented by a pharmacist, Pepsi was never promoted with any claims of medicinal utility.

International Growth

Pepsi-Cola's first international expansion came in 1934, when a Canadian subsidiary was formed. By 1938 Pepsi had 85 Canadian bottlers operating under franchise agreements. Pepsi established another subsidiary in Cuba in 1935. An English subsidiary was opened in London in 1936, and a year later the company registered its trademark in the Soviet Union. Pepsi's position was strengthened considerably in 1940, when William B. Forsythe was placed in charge of the brand's international growth. By 1956, under Forsythe's direction, Pepsi-Cola was produced by 149 bottlers in 61 foreign countries.

As Pepsi and Coca-Cola battled for exclusive domination in large foreign markets (Coke moved boldly into China), Pepsi sealed its first production agreement with the Soviet Union in 1972, becoming the first western consumer product to be introduced into the USSR. Two years later, the company opened its first Soviet bottling plant. Not willing to cede the billion-strong Chinese market to arch-rival Coke, Pepsi concluded a bottling agreement with the People's Republic in 1981, and began production in 1982. Today, Pepsi's overseas sales are strongest in Latin American and Middle Eastern markets.

Performance Evaluation

Pepsi outsold Coca-Cola in store sales for the first time in 1976. Thereafter, in 1983, Pepsi replaced Coke at Burger King outlets when Pepsi purchased the burger chain. In response to Pepsi's success, Coke reformulated its product in 1985 to better compete with Pepsi. Coca-Cola was forced to return to the old formula by an unexpectedly negative reaction by consumers, bordering on outrage, and the incident gave Pepsi several opportunities to declare Cola War victory and lambaste its competitor for losing favor with the public. To the chagrin of Pepsi, however, Coke's mistake led to the creation of several brand extensions that ultimately increased that company's market share.

Future Predictions

The battle for market share in the soft drink market has shifted from allied brands (Pepsi also controls Mountain Dew and Slice) to extensions of the flagship brand. As a result, it is likely that additional attempts, such as a lemon, orange, or chocolate variation, will be introduced under the Pepsi name.

Through excellent placement and advertising, Pepsi has gained a solid reputation for quality and unique flavor, building Pepsi into an extremely valuable name with a distinct personality. Although business writers have suggested for years that Pepsi lives firmly in the shadow of Coca-Cola, Pepsi has a strong and loyal following that could not be achieved if it were merely an inferior imitator. The loyalty of Pepsi drinkers is likely to remain Pepsi's strongest asset for many years.

Further Reading:

Gershman, Michael, "Pepsi-Cola," *Getting It Right the Second Time,* Reading, MA, Addison-Wesley Publishing Company, Inc., 1990, p. 150-57.

"Pepsi-Cola," *The World's Greatest Brands,* New York, John Wiley & Sons, Inc., 1992, p. 33.

Pepsi-Cola Company Milestones, Somers, NY, Pepsi-Cola Company.

"Pepsi-Cola Company Unveils New Company Logo," Pepsi News Release, September 23, 1991.

The Pepsi-Cola Story, Somers, NY, Pepsi-Cola Company.

"Sparkling Rollout for Crystal Pepsi," *Ad Age,* December 14, 1992, p. 46.

Winters, Patricia, "Pepsi Customizes Promo," *Ad Age,* January 11, 1993, p. 38.

Zinn, Laura, "Pepsi's Future Becomes Clearer," *Business Week,* February 1, 1993, p. 74-75.

—John Simley

PERDUE®

An old agricultural expression used to claim, "Pigs is pigs," and by extension, the phrase could just as easily have said that chicken is chicken. But such wisdom would never have gone down well in the world of marketing, and Perdue chicken is a perfect example of this fact. Since 1968 broilers and chicken parts sold under the Perdue name have been a hit with consumers, especially along the Eastern Seaboard. An earned reputation for quality accounts for much of Perdue chicken's popularity, but fortunate marketing has been no less important. Perdue chicken is produced by Perdue Farms Inc. and owes much of its success to the charisma of the company's longtime CEO, Frank Perdue, who began pitching his own products several years after Perdue Farms began processing and selling under its own brand name in 1968. In the process, Frank Perdue turned his company into the fourth-largest producer of raw chicken in the United States and himself into a regional pop culture icon.

Brand Origins

Perdue Farms began as a modest family business. The company was founded in 1920 by Frank Perdue's father, Arthur W. Perdue, who bought $5 worth of laying hens and went into business selling eggs in Salisbury, Maryland. For its first two decades, the company remained a tiny, family-run organization, in large part because of Arthur Perdue's unwillingness to go into debt to finance expansion. Frank Perdue went to work for his father in 1939. Shortly thereafter, the Perdues realized that maintaining their sole focus on eggs limited their profit potential. During the 1940s they shifted their emphasis away from egg production and began turning out broiling chickens for resale to processors like Armour and Swift & Company. By 1952, when Frank Perdue succeeded his father as president of the company, Perdue Farms was racking up annual sales of $6 million on a volume of 2.6 million birds.

Over the next 15 years, Frank Perdue pursued his vision of turning the family business into a fully integrated breeding operation. By 1967 the company could boast of one of the largest grain storage and poultry feed milling operations on the East Coast, soybean processing plants, mulch plants, a hatchery, and some 600 farmers raising birds under the Perdue name. Perdue Farms was also boasting annual sales of over $35 million.

At about this time, however, the company faced a serious threat as processors began to buy chickens directly from farmers, cutting out middlemen like Perdue Farms. Processors were thus able to expand their profit margins and squeeze their outside suppliers by driving harder bargains with them. Perdue Farms responded to this challenge by becoming a processor itself, adding its own processing operations and going retail, delivering the processed birds to market on its own, and under its own name. The Perdue brand name made its debut in retail meat counters in 1968. The company chose New York City as its first target market because of the city's high concentration of people with above-average incomes and its reputation for having consumers who are hard to impress, figuring that if Perdue chickens would sell there, they would sell anywhere.

Frank Perdue had his doubts about whether or not this move into retailing would succeed, but he would soon find himself pleasantly surprised. For one thing, Perdue Farms held a significant advantage over its major competitors—easy access to the major urban markets of the Eastern Seaboard. Salisbury is only a several-hour truck ride away from New York, Philadelphia, and Washington, D.C., and only an overnight drive away from Boston and Hartford. Perdue Farms could beat its competition to the most lucrative markets with fresher products. In addition, the company's redoubled efforts to produce high-quality chickens paid off: to ensure that he could grow birds that were more tender than the rest, Perdue had hired two professors from North Carolina State University to write a computer program that would supervise the feeding of his chickens, establishing formulae that would keep the birds as healthy as possible at each stage of their growth.

Marketing Strategy

But most importantly of all, advertising generated consumer awareness of the Perdue brand name beyond the company's fondest expectations. In 1972 the company hired Scali McCabe Sloves, a small New York agency, to handle its advertising; Scali McCabe Sloves in turn made perhaps the most fateful decision in the history of Perdue Farms—the decision to put Frank Perdue himself on the air. In print, on radio, and on television, the voice and visage of Frank Perdue became a known presence in the Northeastern United States almost from the very start. *Inc.* described him as a most unlikely corporate spokesman—"slender, laconic, whiny-voiced, balding, droopy-lidded, long-nosed"—but Perdue's earnest appeals based on the quality of his product carried him through. *Business Week* once wrote that he possessed "all the fervor and sincerity of a Southern preacher" in his television commercials.

Catchy slogans also helped. One print advertisement that ran in the early 1970s showed a stern-visaged Perdue with his arms folded, and above him the words: "Everybody's chickens are approved by the government. But my chickens are also approved by me." In a lighter vein, another ad told wives, "If your husband is a breast or leg man, ask for my chicken parts." Humor could effectively balance the cumulative effect of Perdue's natural intensity. An early print ad featured a drawing of three chickens sitting at a dinner table with napkins tied around their necks and was captioned, "My chickens eat better than you do," a slogan that he also pronounced in broadcast spots. Perdue may have uttered the most immortal of all his slogans, however, when he informed his audience that, "It takes a tough man to make a tender chicken." His success as a front man for his own company in major media markets during the 1970s and 1980s inspired advertising agencies to make pitchmen out of other CEOs, such as Eastern Airlines' Frank Borman and Chrysler's Lee Iacocca. It also drew the attention of New York City Mayor Edward Koch, himself something of a Frank Perdue look-alike and no stranger to the value of publicity, who once called Perdue, "an upper-echelon chicken guy."

AT A GLANCE

Perdue brand chicken first appeared in grocery stores under the Perdue brand name, 1968; brand owned by Perdue Farms, a company founded in 1920 by Arthur W. Perdue and later taken over by his son Frank, who is largely responsible for the popularity of the Perdue brand.

Major competitor: Tyson and Holly Farms brands of chicken.

Advertising: *Agency*—Scali McCabe Sloves, New York, NY. *Major Campaign*—Frank Perdue, Perdue Farms' peppery longtime CEO, pronouncing witticisms about his company's broilers, e.g., "It takes a tough man to make a tender chicken."

Addresses: *Parent company*—Perdue Farms Inc., P.O. Box 1537, Salisbury, MD 21802; phone: (410) 543-3000; fax: (410) 543-3292.

But this transformation of a Maryland chicken farmer into a media icon would have meant nothing if it had not inspired more people to buy Perdue chickens. Between 1972 and 1984, Perdue Farms' sales doubled every two years. By the end of that period, the company was selling 260 million birds per year and generating revenues of over $500 million.

Later Marketing Developments

"We sell perfect chicken parts, not parts of the perfect chicken," Frank Perdue claimed in one of his later broadcast spots, but Perdue Farms was not content with bringing broilers and raw chicken parts to the peak of their natural goodness. During the 1980s the company branched out, developing variations on the theme of perfect chicken. In 1983 it introduced chicken franks— hot dogs stuffed with chicken instead of pork or beef—by hiring a fleet of pushcarts and fanning them throughout New York City. In 1985 rival Holly Farms responded to the growing popularity of prepared food products by selling fillets and bite-sized chicken nuggets; Perdue Farms fought back by launching a line of prepared chicken products under the name Perdue Done It!, which included breaded and pre-cooked nuggets and cutlets. Holly Farms had watched Perdue Farms' success in marketing under its own brand name and began doing so itself in 1971, mounting a deliberate challenge to Perdue in 1980s. The two went nose-to-nose during the decade, but neither could quite out-do the other. Both succeeded well enough, though, so that in 1985 the two companies together accounted for one-fourth of all the fresh chicken sold in the United States.

In 1990 Perdue Farms introduced ground dark meat flavored with rosemary. The product was designed as a low-fat alternative to other ground meats. And in 1991 the company began marketing roasted chickens under the Perdue Done It! label.

Frank Perdue resigned as CEO in 1988 at the age of 67, but remained his company's chairman and sole advertising spokesman. A tireless promoter, he had once served his father as salesman, ranging up and down the Eastern Seaboard to meet with buyers. Even once he became president, Perdue still made a habit of attending supermarket openings to keep his company's profile as high as possible. He told *Inc.* why he put so much energy into publicity: "My father wouldn't do it, but I'll do anything it takes for this business because I consider it more my baby than it was his. I was totally into it without any letup for 20 to 30 years. I've been the principal force in its growth."

Performance Appraisal, Future Growth

The figures bear out Frank Perdue's statement. When he stepped down as CEO, he and his family held 90 percent of the company's stock, and his personal fortune was estimated to be at least $350 million. Perdue Farms was also one of the 50 largest privately held companies in the United States. Sales grew 525 percent between 1968 and 1984, and an estimated 22 percent of the American population had seen Perdue's visage on television by the mid-1980s.

Frank Perdue was ultimately succeeded at the helm of Perdue Farms by his son, James, who graduated from University of Washington with a Ph.D. in marine biology in 1983 before joining the family business. Low-key by nature, James Perdue has announced no plans to appear in television commercials. He has, however, inherited something of a challenge from his father. Perdue Farms' revenue growth has leveled off in recent years, as the U.S. poultry industry as a whole saw its 20-year sales boom come to an end. Chicken sales grew at a rate of four to five percent per year during the 1970s and 1980s, but early in the 1990s per capita consumption of the bird declined while production continued to increase. For Perdue Farms, sales leveled off at $1.2 billion in 1991 and 1992.

Catchy slogans and appealing broadcast spots notwithstanding, it seems that how well the company does is tied to the overall popularity of chicken with the American consumer. The continuing success of Perdue Farms depends a great deal on whether the taste of chicken and concerns over the relative healthfulness of white versus red meat can sustain growth in the poultry industry as a whole. But it is certain that Perdue Farms has come down to its third generation of Perdues as a noteworthy success story, from which a significant portion of the American public learned that it takes a tough man to make a tender chicken.

Further Reading:

Barmash, Isadore, "The Quieter Style of the New Generation at Perdue," *New York Times,* July 16, 1992, p. F7.

Giges, Nancy, "Holly Farms, Perdue Face Off in Chickie Run," *Advertising Age,* September 16, 1985, p. 4.

Mamis, Robert A., "Frank Perdue," *Inc.,* February 1984, pp. 21-23.

"Perdue Chicken Spreads Its Wings," *Business Week,* September 16, 1972, pp. 113-16.

—Douglas Sun

PERRIER®

During most of the late 1970s and 1980s, Perrier, owned by Perrier Group of America, Inc., accounted for 14 percent of total U.S. sparkling water sales. The story of the Perrier brand of imported sparkling water was one of such astounding success in that period that many in the industry credited the brand with actually creating bottled water as a distinct market segment within the beverage industry. The drama of Perrier's sky-rocketing success, however, was matched by a subsequent downslide. With rather modest beginnings, Perrier rose to a dominant position in the marketplace only to be struck down by difficult circumstances which, in the early 1990s, it still strives to overcome.

Brand Origins

Perrier, the upscale market's favorite imported mineral water for more than a decade, is named for Dr. Louis Perrier, a French physician and entrepreneur. In 1903, Perrier and the English aristocrat St. John Harnsworth pooled their resources and talents to make the spring they purchased in Vergèze, France, into a prosperous business venture. No doubt the patriotic Perrier and his partner were heeding the decree of the Emperor Napoleon III, who in 1863 ordered that the spring waters of Vergèze be bottled "for the good of France."

Early Marketing Strategy

In 1907, soon after the business was founded, the sparkling water in the now-familiar green-tinted bottles was already a high-priced item—"the champagne of bottled waters"—selling at nearly $1.00 and available only in gourmet and specialty-food shops throughout the United States. In the mid-1970s, however, the French parent company—Source Perrier, S.A.—established Great Waters of France, an American subsidiary, and began to import and market the product much more widely, distributing smaller bottles in addition to the original 23-ounce bottles, at a dramatically lower price. The first step was to distribute it to bars and restaurants, where Perrier served as a substitute for alcoholic beverages. Next it was moved onto the shelves of the country's mainstream food stores and supermarkets and marketed to consumers as a healthful alternative to soft drinks that still maintained some of its original cachet as a specialty item.

To that end, advertisers drew on the legendary past of the Perrier source, which presumably dates back to the first century, when the spring was the site of Roman baths used by the builders of the great Roman aqueduct and the nearby Temple of Diana. In 218 B.C., the legend goes, it was reputedly the resting place for Hannibal. Promoters also banked on the appeal of natural carbonation "from the center of the earth" as well as the mystique conveyed by the notion of delicate gases trapped in a "spring that was formed over 140 million years ago in the volcanic eruptions of the Cretaceous Era." Within a short period, Perrier, the only bottled water whose marketing and distribution were national in scope, became the leading brand.

The bottled water industry has traditionally been regional in nature, mainly consisting of small, local companies. The market for bottled water—both still and sparkling—has much of its base in the health-conscious consumer, the person seeking pure drinking water and a natural life-style in keeping with the health-and-fitness trends of the late 1970s and throughout the 1990s. Great Waters of France thus set out to conquer the relatively affluent, sophisticated consumer who saw sparkling water as a healthy substitute for alcoholic beverages and high-calorie soft drinks. In the marketing campaign that Perrier began in the mid-to-late 1970s, the dollar amounts invested in advertising and promotion were unprecedented in the bottled water industry.

Perrier's Profits Skyrocket

Along with the entire bottled water industry, but at a faster pace, Perrier's rate of growth was phenomenal, moving from about $500,000 in wholesale sales in 1976 to $12 million in 1977, to about $35 million in 1978. In 1978, Perrier had captured 14.3 percent of the entire bottled water market, topped by only two domestic brands—Sparkletts (Foremost McKesson) and Arrowhead Puritas (Northwest Industries). By 1979, it dominated the sparkling and still mineral water market with sales of $65 million, representing approximately 20 percent of that market (which included Poland Spring, Montclair, and many other brands). Seeing an opportunity to expand beyond its importing activities, in 1979 Perrier established a second subsidiary through which it acquired and marketed nearly ten domestic spring and purified water brands in the following decade.

From 1980 to 1989, the bottled water industry as a whole, and the Perrier brand in particular, enjoyed annual double-digit growth—from an $80 million industry to one worth some $2.5 billion—even emerging relatively unscathed by a fairly strong recession at the beginning of the decade. Analysts attribute the remarkable, sustained growth of the trade to a number of fortuitous circumstances, including equally remarkable growth in disposable income of the target market, as well as the persistent and pervasive emphasis on the importance of health and fitness. During this period, Perrier maintained its place among the top ten bottled waters, with virtually no competition among imports of either sparkling or still water. It led all others in media/advertising expenditures, appealing to its ever-growing market with such tag lines as "Perrier. Earth's first soft drink." The company virtually dominated the restaurant and hotel business, where other brands could barely gain a foothold, and in 1985 began to market lemon-, lime-, and orange- flavored Perrier. By the end of the decade, U.S. sales accounted for some $100 million, representing about 13 percent of the U.S. sparkling water market and nearly 25 percent of Perrier's market worldwide.

The Bubble Bursts

But in the first week of February 1990, the Perrier brand suffered a serious setback that resulted in "one of the most celebrated consumer goods recalls in the history of these United States," according to *Beverage World*. A group of scientists working in a laboratory at the Mecklenberg County Environmental

AT A GLANCE

Perrier brand of mineral water founded in 1903 by Dr. Louis Perrier, a French physician and entrepreneur, and St. John Harnsworth, an English aristocrat, who purchased source of mineral water, a spring in Vergèze, France; in mid-1970s Source Perrier, S.A. (Paris, France) established an American subsidiary, Great Waters of France, for U.S. import and marketing; later called Perrier Group of America, Inc.; Perrier Group of America purchased by Nestlé Source International of Paris, France.

Performance: *Market share*—6% of bottled sparkling water category. *Sales*—$50 million.

Advertising: *Agency*—Publicis FCB, New York, NY, November, 1992—. *Major campaign*—Spotlighting Perrier's lightness and effervescence; prior campaign (with agency Waring & LaRosa) used the tag line, "Perrier. Part of the local color."

Major competitor: Evian (not a sparkling water).

Addresses: *Parent company (U.S.)*—Perrier Group of America, Inc., 777 West Putnam Avenue, Greenwich, CT 06830; phone: (203) 531-4100. *Ultimate parent company:* Nestlé Sources International, Paris, France.

Protection Department in North Carolina was using a small supply of Perrier as a testing control for other substances being tested for hazardous chemicals and other impurities. These scientists discovered traces of benzene—an industrial solvent and suspected carcinogen—in the Perrier itself. Within days Perrier Group of America, the (PGA) announced a recall from the entire North American market—a total of some 72 million bottles.

The company initially speculated that the presence of the benzene was a residue from the solvent used to clean the bottles. Several days later, however, immediately preceding a historic worldwide recall totaling some 160 million bottles, officials announced that the problem was in the filter system, and not, as originally suspected, in the bottle-cleaning process. Explaining that benzene is a naturally occurring substance found in the gases at the spring itself, officials acknowledged that the charcoal filters used to keep out contaminants—most notably, hydrogen sulfide—were being changed less often than usual, thus permitting some traces of the substance to sneak through.

Although the recall was executed on the basis of a very small sample—four to 19 parts per billion of benzene in about 13 bottles—and although no harm occurred because of it, the company was nevertheless faced with a daunting public relations and advertising challenge. The task was to demonstrate to consumers that PGA acted forthrightly and deliberately in its efforts to identify and rectify the problem; to maintain consumer awareness of Perrier during its ten-to-fourteen-week absence from store shelves, restaurants, and hotels; and, once restored to the marketplace, to assure buyers that the product was safe. Soon after the recall, the company announced that it would spend $25 million in an ambitious campaign to achieve these goals. The public relations firm of Burson Marsteller was called upon to implement the PGA strategy, with the ultimate goal of restoring the company to its premier position as the number one bottled water import. The hope was that what enabled the Perrier label to make its mark on the American marketplace in the first place—namely, the best advertising money could buy—would do the job one more time. However, another popular bottled water imported from France, Evian,

had in the meantime quickly and quietly taken Perrier's place, aggressively laying claim to shelf space; likewise, Perrier's absence from the hotel/restaurant market opened the floodgates for other brands—most notably San Pellegrino and Saratoga Spring—to penetrate that particular market. In dollar terms, company spokespeople claimed losses amounting to some $78 million (40 percent of U.S. sales), a figure that included post-recall expenses.

The Advertising and PR Gurus Go to Work

The advertising and public relations dilemma was dealt with in three stages. Initially, after the recall, the company acknowledged that it had identified the problem and fixed it. In the second phase, a series of humorous ads was launched to deal with the fact that there was no Perrier on the shelves. The ads included radio news flashes of UFO-type "sightings" of the product and print ads with the tag line, "Perrier. Worth waiting for". Finally, the Waring & LaRosa agency created light, airy ads with the theme "Perrier's back" to coincide with the product's reappearance on the store shelves in April and May of 1990.

Although company representatives claimed that Perrier regained some two-thirds of its original market share soon thereafter, at the end of 1992 the brand had plummeted to eighth place in the bottled water category in supermarket sales and its market share had dropped to 3.4 percent. In its first new image-building campaign since the recall, in April of 1992 the company began a print-only advertising campaign, still with the Waring & LaRosa agency, with the tag line, "Perrier. Part of the local color," in an effort to position the product as a normal part of everyday life. By the end of the year, PGA had once again changed agencies, this time engaging the New York City-based Publicis FCB.

Perrier's Performance a Sign of the Times

But just as the success of this product was marked by a fortuitous set of circumstances that fostered its meteoric rise to the top of the charts, equally unpropitious conditions, such as economic recession, new competition, and the recall, were responsible for the company's inability to stage a complete comeback to its pre-recall status in the marketplace. For example, the protracted and deep recession that coincidentally began around the time of the benzene debacle, hitting especially hard in the heart of "Perrier country"—the northeast and the west coast—resulted in a profound drop in disposable income, and was accompanied by a change in the national psyche. Not only had the class of young, upwardly-mobile consumers of the 1980s virtually dropped out of sight, but political, social, and economic conditions—both at home and abroad—created a more sober, if not cynical, climate less in keeping with the notion that drinking bottled water of questionable purity was the answer to promoting a longer, healthier life. And drinking bottled water as a status symbol lost much of its cachet.

Illustrative of this new-found sobriety was the seriousness with which the Perrier fiasco was treated, not only by consumers, a growing number of whom began to demand standards for the industry as a whole, but by government agencies and lawmakers, public interest organizations, and even the industry's own trade group, the International Bottled Water Association (IBWA). Although the Food and Drug Administration (FDA) regulates bottled water as a food, mineral water is excluded from that category, and the FDA neither provides definitions for various types of bottled water nor does it require companies to include the source of water on labels or to test their water for certain chemicals. But after the benzene crisis, which, of course, drew the FDA's attention, the company's practices were closely scrutinized and regulated. For example, the FDA would not permit Perrier to re-enter the market using labels that read "naturally sparkling," citing the company's own assertion that it extracts the water and carbon dioxide from the spring *separately*. In addition, PGA had to remove the words "calorie free" from its labels, a misleading claim according to the FDA. On the other hand, the words "Nouvelle Production" were placed on the label at the company's own initiative and were meant to reassure consumers that the water was bottled post recall and was subject to stringent quality control testing, including double filtration of the gases plus increased monitoring of gas systems.

Along with the FDA, state health officials and others were prompted to take a closer look both at the Perrier brand and at the industry as a whole. The public health bureaucracy in New York State (Perrier's largest market), for example, was particularly rigorous in its demands—on the eve of the Perrier relaunch, the company was asked to provide samples to the New York State Health Commission, which questioned the purity of the product and barred the company from characterizing it as "sodium free." This objection came soon after the agency ordered Perrier, as a condition of state re-certification, to submit samples weekly for contaminant testing, at least until October of 1990. Furthermore, an agreement was made that the company would run ads throughout the state urging consumers to make sure that the Perrier they were buying had the "Nouvelle Production" label on it, as an added protection against the possibility that some pre-recall bottles may not have been removed from every shelf. And, finally, the company was ordered to print the following message on its label by October 1990: "The carbonation of Perrier mineral water comes from a naturally occurring source deep beneath the spring."

The Industry Asks for Regulations and Standards

The IBWA, which is on record as petitioning for federal standards for the industry for over 12 years, has established a code for bottled water regulations, which lists more than 200 contaminants that should be subjected to testing, defines various types of bottled water, and provides additional guidelines for product quality. By 1990, 11 states had regulations based on the IBWA code. At present, the IBWA requires its members (more than 300 companies) to test products for some 52 contaminants. The standards for bottled water are typically the same as those established or proposed for public drinking water supplies, but can be stricter, particularly in regard to certain elements, such as lead, and adherence to FDA good manufacturing practices. For information about a particular water, a consumer can ask the producer if it has been inspected by the IBWA, and companies that produce inspected water can provide consumers with copies of their latest chemical analysis. While these kinds of self-imposed regulations and industry standards are probably good public relations, they may also serve to protect the public from purchasing products under false assumptions, and from possible impurities in bottled water. Friends of the Earth, a Washington, D.C. environmental group, conducted a study in 1989 that showed that public water systems were the source for more than one-third of bottled water sold in the United States. Although some question the notion that bottled water is healthier, the conclusion of this study was that bottled water was safe.

Fortunately, the Center for Disease Control reports that no one has been known to fall ill as a result of drinking bottled water. And some states, like New York, California, New Jersey, and Connecticut, have set up stricter safety rules than the federal government's. There has been some movement in Congress to enact regulatory legislation for the bottled water industry. Senator Patrick Moynihan of New York and Texas's representative John Bryant both introduced bills, but each bill died in committee. Among other provisions, the proposed legislation would have automatically subjected bottlers to the Environmental Protection Agency's national primary drinking water regulations and would require source labeling. Bottled water has always been regulated as a drinking water by the EPA, and as a food by the FDA, and has had to meet drinking water standards, FDA packaging processing codes, and sanitation standards. On January 5, 1993, the FDA proposed regulations that would require the rigorous standards and establish the uniform definitions for bottled water for which the industry had been lobbying.

Perrier Brand—A Viable Product or a Relic-in-the-Making?

Despite the continued optimism expressed by its spokespeople, the jury is still out on whether Perrier sparkling water will ever fully regain its place as the number one import of the American bottled water industry or whether, like the Coke bottle in the film *The Gods Must Be Crazy* that literally fell from the skies and landed in the middle of a pre-industrial African tribe, the green, pear-shaped Perrier bottle will eventually come to be seen as an artifact symbolic of a mysterious custom from another era. Its fate probably lies somewhere between the two, and will depend largely on the direction of the American economy. The powerful advertising aimed at a health-and-fitness, status-conscious consumer that links Perrier to a specific lifestyle—the very factor responsible for Perrier's unprecedented success—loses its impact in a time of prolonged economic downturn, when its target market all but disappears from view. But Perrier remains confident in its product and its image. Its marketing goal in the early 1990s is to reaffirm the unique light and effervescent qualities of its original product.

Further Reading:

"A Takeauver?" *The Economist*, November 30, 1991, p. 68.

Barton, Laurence, "A Case Study in Crisis Management: The Perrier Recall, *Industrial Management & Data Systems*," 1991, pp. 6-8.

"Best Sellers," *Beverage World Sourcebook, 1991-1992*, pp.19-27.

"Beverage Market Index for 1991," *Beverage World Sourcebook, 1991-1992*, p. 6.

Bird, Laura, "A Nation Thirsty for Change, *Adweek's Marketing Week*, September 17, 1990, p. S104.

Bird, Laura, "Perrier, $30 million the Poorer, Plans Spring Relaunch," *Adweek's Marketing Week*, March 12, 1990, p. 4.

Bird, Laura, "Will Perrier's Recall Cast a Pall on Other Water Brands?" *Adweek's Marketing Week*, February 19, 1990, p. 3.

Bird, Laura, "Perrier Imports New Image from France," *Adweek's Marketing Week*, June 10, 1991, p. 9.

" 'Bloom off the Rose' as Water Market Matures," *Beverage Industry Annual Manual, 1980-81*, pp. 62-67.

"Bottled Water, *Beverage World 1992-1993 Databank*, p. 16.

"Bottled Water Explosion: Market to Double by '83," *Beverage Industry Annual Manual, 1979-1980*, pp. 43-51.

"Bottled Water Popularity Should Double by 1990," *Beverage Industry Annual Manual, 1984*, pp. 89-90.

"Bottled-water Sales Begin to Sparkle," *Business Week*, November 7, 1970, p. 44.

"Bottled Water Trends: Volume Up 13.5% in '85," *Beverage Industry Annual Manual, 1987*, pp.45-46.

Brookes, Warren T., "The Wasteful Pursuit of Zero Risk," *Forbes*, April 30, 1990, pp 160-172.

"Bubble, Bubble, Toil and Trouble," *The Economist*, January 25, 1992, p. 68.

"Chairman of Perrier Leaves; Post Goes to Vice Chairman," *New York Times*, June 30, 1990, sec. 1, p. 31.

"Company News: Nestle-Perrier Link Is Studied," *New York Times*, March 26, 1992, p. 3.

"Company News; Perrier Regains Ground in Sales," *New York Times*, July 12, 1990, p. 4.

"Company News: Perrier Sales Back," *New York Times*, June 28, 1991, sec. D, p. 4 "Company News; Perrier to Revise Its Label," *New York Times*, August 31, 1990, p. 3.

"Corporate Error—and Arrogance (Editorial), *New York Times*, February 14, 1990, p. 24.

Crumley, Bruce, "Fizzzz Went the Crisis," *International Management*, April 1990, pp. 52-53.

Crumley, Bruce and Elena Bowes, "Perrier Moves to Publicis; $60M Worldwide Account Consolidated by Nestlé," *Advertising Age*, November 30, 1992, p. 1.

Davis, Lisa, "Perrier Hit with Class Action Suit by Seltzer Sisters, *San Francisco Business Times*, May 14, 1990, p. 9.

Davis, Tim, "Forum Focuses on Forces Driving Beverage Change," *Beverage World Periscope Edition*, April 30, 1992, pp. 10-12.

de Bono, Edward, "Taking Creativity More Seriously," *Executive Excellence*, August 1991, pp. 12-13.

Dolliver, Mark, "French Perrier Spot May Offend Eco-aware Americans," *Adweek Eastern Edition*, June 17, 1991, p. 17.

Dowd, Maureen, "No Perrier? A Status Bubble Bursts," *New York Times*, February 11, 1990, p. 34.

Duff, Mike, "Consumer Expenditures Study: Soft Drinks," *Supermarket Business*, September 1990, p. 187.

Epstein, Jacques and Sylvie Deparis-Maze, "French Takeovers: Perrier, C'est Fou!" *International Financial Law Review*, April 1992, pp. 25-26.

Fahey, Alison and Steven W. Colford, "H2O Marketers Mop Damage," *Advertising Age*, April 15, 1991, p. 1.

Fahey, Alison, "Perrier Ads Sell Common Appeal," *Advertising Age*, April 6, 1992, p. 38.

"Fragile Glory," *Economist*, March 7, 1992, pp. 85-86.

Giges, Nancy, "Europeans Buy Outside Goods, but Like Local Ads," *Advertising Age*, April 27, 1992, p. I-1.

Hall, Jonathan O., "Bottled Water Bastion: Import Brands Face a Tidal Wave of Domestic Competitors in the '90s," *Beverage World*, p. 98.

Hall, Jonathan O., "Bottled Water: The New Reality," *Beverage World*, October 1991, p. 66.

Hochstein, Mort, "New Brands Rush to Battle Perrier in Water Market," *Nation's Restaurant News*, February 11, 1991, p. 33.

Kiley, David, "Perrier Tries to Woo Back Frightened Water Lovers," *Adweek's Marketing Week*, April 9, 1990, p. 46.

Kochilas, Diane, "Water, Water, Everywhere," *Restaurant Business*, November 20, 1991, pp. 189-190.

Kurzbard, Gary and George J. Siomkos, George J., "Crafting a Damage Control Plan: Lessons from Perrier," *Journal of Business Strategy*, March-April 1992, p. 39.

Landler, Mark and Lisa Driscoll, "You Can Lead a Restaurateur to Perrier, but . . . ," *Business Week (Industrial/Technology Edition)*, June 25, 1990, pp. 25-26.

"Leading Bottled Water Brands—Estimated Wholesaler Sales 1987-1991," *Jobson's Liquor Handbook*, 1992, p. 235.

Lever, Robert, "Nestlé Makes Splash in Perrier Acquisition," *Europe*, May 1992, p. 33.

Lippert, Barbara, "Perrier Is Reformulated for a New Era," *Adweek's Marketing Week*, May 7, 1990, p. 69.

Magiera, Marcy, "Bottled Waters Spring Up: National Marketers Plunge Into Market, *Advertising Age*, September 21, 1987, p. 24.

"Management Brief: When the Bubble Bursts," *The Economist*, August 3, 1991, pp. 67-68.

Mandese, Joe, "Print Bucks Stop Here," *Marketing & Media Decisions*, November 1990, pp. 28-29.

Mayer, Martin, *Whatever Happened to Madison Avenue? Advertising in the 90's*, New York: Little, Brown, 1991.

McDonald, B., "Bottled Water Industry Considers Capitol Hearings a Signal of Coming Regulations," *Beverage World Periscope Edition*, May 31, 1991, p. 1.

Meier, Barry, "Company News; Perrier to Bow to F.D.A. and Change Label," *New York Times*, April 19, 1990, p. 6.

"Perrier Production Halted Worldwide," *New York Times*, February 11, 1990, p. 34.

"What to Drink, If Not Perrier?" *New York Times*, February 14, 1990, p. 1.

Meyer, Ann, "Bridge over Troubled Perrier Waters," *Prepared Foods*, June 1990, p. 41.

"Newsmakers 1990," *Advertising Age*, December 24, 1990 p. 1.

"Only Water, Soft Drinks Show a Per Capita Increase," *Beverage Industry Annual Manual, 1984*, pp.11-12.

O'Neill, Molly, "The Return of Perrier Is Noted, Sort Of," *New York Times*, May 16, 1990, p.11.

O'Neill, Molly, "With a Spurt and a Gurgle, Perrier Is Back on the Shelves," *New York Times*, April 28, 1990, p. 27.

"Perrier Says Employees Failed to Change Filters," *New York Times*, February 15, 1990, p. 12.

"Perrier's Launch Stalled—Again—Over Health Concerns, *Adweek's Marketing Week*, April 30, 1990, p. 5.

"Perrier Woes Began with Blip on Carolina Screen," *New York Times*, February 12, 1990, sec. A, p. 18.

"Perrier: Bottled," *The Economist*, March 7, 1992, p. 84.

"Perrier Hopes to Bubble Its Way into America's Goblets," *Advertising Age*, July 25, 1977, p. 1.

"Perrier: Heavy Users Came Back," *Advertising Age*, October 21, 1991, p. 36.

Pfaff, Fred, "The Search for Perrier's Single Source," *Marketing & Media Decisions*, July 1990, pp. 28-29.

Prince, Greg, "A Call to Economic Arms?" *Beverage World*, March 1992, pp. 86-92.

"Perrier's Image Suffers Benzene Headache," *Beverage World, Periscope Edition*, March 31, 1990, p. 1.

"Perrier Takeover Bid Taken Better than Packaging Suit Delivered by Nora," *Beverage World Periscope Edition*, December 31, 1991, p. 4.

"Publicis Exec Aids Nestlé's Perrier Bid: Future of Water Accounts Unclear," *Advertising Age*, November 30, 1992, p. 38.

"Take Two: President Ron Davis and Sales & Marketing VP Kim Jeffery Explore the Long Road Back as Perrier Seeks to Regain Its Shelf Status," *Beverage World*, May 1990, p. 38.

"The Perrier Group Quartet Sings the Highest Corporate Share Tune," *Beverage World*, March 1991, p. 30.

Ramirez, Anthony, "Perrier Recall: How Damaging Is It?" *New York Times*, February 13, 1990, sec. D, p. 1.

"Perrier to Return to U.S. Early Next Month, *New York Times*, March 7, 1990, sec. D, p. 1.

"Retail Sales and Share of Retail Dollar by Beverage, 1988-1991, *Jobson's Liquor Handbook*, 1992, p. 233.

Riding, Alan, "Perrier Asserts Source of Water Is Unaffected," *New York Times*, February 13, 1990, sec. D, p. 6.

Rossant, John, "Perrier's Unquenchable U.S. Thirst," *Business Week*, June 29, 1987, p. 46.

Rothenberg, Randall, "The Media Business: Advertising; Perrier Plans Return with a New Voice," *New York Times*, March 29, 1990, sec. D, p. 22.

Schnorbus, Paula, "Water, Water Everywhere," *Marketing & Media Decisions*, September 1987, pp. 97-103.

Seaman, Debbie, "An American in Paris: Bird on a Wire," *Advertising Age*, December 2, 1991, p. 22C.

"Old Yeller," *Advertising Age*, April 1, 1991, p. 26C.

Selinger, Iris Cohen, "Why Perrier Turned to a PR Agency for Advertising," *Adweek*, April 23, 1990, p. 6.

Sellers, Patricia, "Perrier Plots Its Comeback," *Fortune*, April 23, 1990, p. 277.

Sfiligoj, Eric, "The Beverage Market Index for 1992," *Beverage World*, May 1992, pp. 30-41.

"The Beverage World Top 50," *Beverage World*, July 1992, pp. 38-41.

"The Beverage Market Index for 1992," *Beverage World 1992-1993 Databank*, p. 6.

Simmons, Tim, "Perrier Pulling Out Stops to Regain Its Lost Sparkle," *Supermarket News*, April 30, 1990, p. 16.

Smith, Melody, "Message in a Bottle," *Arkansas Business*, November 19, 1990, p. 25.

"The Return of Perrier: EauKay," *Economist*, March 24, 1990, p. 70.

Toy, Stewart and Lisa Driscoll, "Can Perrier Purify Its Reputation?" *Business Week (Industrial/Technology Edition)*, February 26, 1990, p. 45.

"Volumes and Market Shares of Bottled Water by Type, 1990-1991," *Jobson's Liquor Handbook*, 1992, p. 237.

"Water Hits 2.2 Billion Gallons as Growth Slows to *Just* 9.4%," *Beverage Industry Annual Manual 1991/92*, p. 46.

"Water's Rise: A Sales Torrent," *Business Week*, January 11, 1982, p. 97.

Weaver, Jane, "Perrier: Fighting Crisis with Laughter; Ads Aim to Keep Awareness High Till Product Reappears," *Adweek Western Advertising News*, March 19, 1990, p. 12.

Winters, Patricia, "Perrier Rivals Refuse to Make Waves," *Advertising Age*, March 12, 1990, p. 74.

"Perrier's Back: Whimsical Campaign to Support Its Return, " *Advertising Age*, April 23, 1990, p. 1.

"Perrier Springs Back, *Advertising Age*, July 23, 1990, p. 38.

"Perrier, Other Waters Facing New Scrutiny," *Advertising Age*, April 30, 1990, p. 2.

—Maxine Gold

PHILADELPHIA® BRAND CREAM CHEESE

One of the most recognizable products in the supermarket aisle, Philadelphia Brand cream cheese is packaged like a dairy present, wrapped in shiny aluminum foil and encased in a silver, cardboard box. An industry leader since the invention of cream cheese in the late nineteenth century, Philly, as many consumers have come to know the product, has successfully negotiated the peaks and valleys of the multi-billion-dollar cheese industry. Kraft General Foods, Inc., which in various corporate incarnations has engineered the product's market ascension over the years, used strong multi-media advertising to insinuate the cream cheese into the staple American menu, and consistently revised the production process to expand the product's shelf life in a market where spoilage is an ever-present adversary. When Kraft, which also makes Velveeta cheese pasteurized process cheese spread, Miracle Whip salad dressing, and Kraft mayonnaise, was purchased by Philip Morris Companies, Inc., in 1988, and was subsequently merged with the General Foods Corporation, Philadelphia Brand cream cheese fell among a dizzying array of products under one of the largest corporate umbrellas in the world. In the early 1990s, as Philly faced fierce competition from less expensive generic and store-brand cream cheeses, Kraft General Foods banked on a synergy among its many foodstuffs and an aggressive advertising campaign to buoy sales and to sustain a rich history of cream cheese leadership.

Brand Origins

Kraft company records place the invention of cream cheese in the hands of a New York dairyman named William A. Lawrence, who first experimented with and saw the potential in the mixture he fashioned from milk and cream in 1872; he called the product Star Brand. The cream cheese became so popular that other dairies in the New York area began manufacturing a similar product. In 1880 a cheese distributor named C. D. Reynolds forged a deal with Lawrence for the latter to supply a steady flow of cream cheese. At the same time, Reynolds purchased another cream cheese production facility, the Empire Cheese Company of South Edmeston, New York. The name ''Philadelphia'' was adopted for the product because the Pennsylvania city was treasured as the seat of high-quality foods, particularly dairy products.

Tragedy struck in 1900, when the Empire Cheese plant burned to the ground. From its ashes arose the Phenix Cheese Company, a cooperative firm founded by farm businessmen who found inspira-

tion in the fabled bird of Greek mythology that burned itself on a funeral pyre and spawned a renewed, stronger Phoenix. Though the businessmen captured the spirit of the myth, they had less success with the spelling. Sticking with the name Phenix, they speeded up production of the cream cheese and expanded distribution beyond the New York area. In 1924 J. L. Kraft & Bros. Co., which had produced and provided processed cheese to the U.S. government for the armed forces in World War I, went public as Kraft Cheese Company and entered the cream cheese market. Four years later, Kraft merged with Phenix, continuing the production of Philadelphia Brand cream cheese and introducing new products like Velveeta pasteurized process cheese spread. The corporate name would revert to the Kraft Cheese Company in 1940.

Compared to Camembert and other rich, soft cheeses of Europe, Philadelphia Brand cream cheese was originally made in U.S. locations that could easily provide production plants with fresh milk and cream. Under strict monitoring, cream and milk are blended and the mixture is pasteurized to destroy any harmful micro-organisms. A starter culture is added, and the mixture is matured for enough time to allow the harmless lactic microorganisms to develop the characteristic cream cheese flavor and texture. After the curd is separated from the whey, and several ingredients, including salt and vegetable gum, are added, the cheese is cooled quickly in rooms where the air pressure is carefully controlled to reduce the danger of introducing molds. The cheese is wrapped and packaged by high-speed machines to ensure that the freshest possible product is delivered to market. Because of several patented adjustments to the production process in the mid-1940s, the life span of the cheese jumped from an original couple of weeks to about four months. Although Philadelphia Brand cream cheese was originally manufactured just in the United States, Kraft quickly set itself up for international sales by establishing production plants in Germany, Australia, and Venezuela, among others.

The packaging, with the duel purpose of protecting the freshness of the cream cheese and making Philly an attractive, eye-catching product on the store shelf, has changed several times over the years. Connie Larkin, on the occasion of the 100th anniversary of the cream cheese, wrote in a Kraft publication that, ''when first introduced, Philadelphia Brand cream cheese came in parchment paper-lined tin foil. In 1934, aluminum foil replaced that wrapper. Kraft developed new parakote packaging—a cellulose product coated with amorphous wax—for Philadelphia Brand in 1941,

AT A GLANCE

Philadelphia brand cream cheese introduced in 1880 in South Edmeston, NY, by Empire Cheese Company; in 1928 company merged with Kraft Cheese Company to form Kraft-Phenix Cheese Corporation, which became a subsidiary of the National Dairy Products Corporation, 1930; Kraft-Phenix changed name to Kraft Cheese Company, 1940, and then to Kraft Foods Company, 1945; in 1969 National Dairy Products Corporation changed its name to Kraftco Corporation, which became Kraft, Inc., 1976; Philip Morris Companies, Inc., acquired Kraft, Inc., 1988, and combined Kraft, Inc., and General Foods Corporation in 1989 to form Kraft General Foods, Inc.

Major competitor: Generic, private label, and store brands of cream cheese.

Advertising: *Agency*—J. Walter Thompson, New York, NY. *Major campaign*—"As always, half the calories of butter or margarine."

Addresses: *Parent company*—Kraft General Foods, Inc., Kraft Court, Glenview, IL 60025; phone: (708) 646-2000. *Ultimate parent company*—Philip Morris Companies, Inc., 120 Park Ave., New York, NY 10017; phone: (212) 880-5000; fax: (212) 878-2167.

when it became apparent that the war effort would create shortages of both tin and aluminum." The foil was reissued after World War II, and in 1970, Kraft introduced the signature rigid carton for its eight-once cream cheese brick, a packaging model that competitors in the cream cheese industry would emulate.

Aggressive Advertising Approaches

Central to Kraft's success at positioning Philadelphia Brand cream cheese as one of the most recognizable products in the American marketplace was the company's unflappable commitment to media saturation and advertising. Early print campaigns in the 1930s concentrated on exploiting the versatility of the product. A 1931 display ad featured the copy: "Cream Cheese for breakfast, whoever heard of that? Oh, with strawberry jam—that's different, ought to go pretty well." Another means of boosting sales was the tie-in campaign, in which Philadelphia Brand cream cheese was sold alongside other items, such as a package of crackers or a jar of jam, again to boast the product's versatility. In 1933 the high-profile magazine and newspaper promotions were supplemented with Kraft's radio broadcasts, the first coast-to-coast radio forum used to sell cheese. All-stars in the music business, including Al Jolson, Paul Whiteman, and the Rhythm Boys, sang the praises of Philly in a series of weekly Thursday night broadcasts.

In the 1950s Kraft launched its advertising campaign targeting the housewife, suggesting easy, delicious recipes with the cream cheese, unsurprisingly, as the central ingredient. Kraft also jumped on the television bandwagon, sponsoring Perry Como's Kraft Music Hall TV program as a means of flashing the company's products, including Philly, into millions of American homes. In the 1990s Kraft has not subsided in its aggressive efforts to expose Philadelphia Brand cream cheese, using TV ads to present the

product as an attractive alternative—with only half the calories—to more staid spreads such as butter or margarine.

Adjustments to Market Changes

Despite consistently high sales of its original cream cheese, Kraft has not allowed itself to rest on the success of one formula or flavor, recognizing that consumer tastes fluctuate wildly. The company introduced Philadelphia brand cream cheese flavored with chives, pimento, bacon, onion, and smoked salmon. Around 1980 Soft Philadelphia Brand debuted, nearly identical in flavor to the original but, as the name implies, softer directly from the refrigerator to enable easier spreading on bread and crackers.

To capitalize on a health-conscious craze in the 1980s, Kraft introduced Philadelphia Light cream cheese. By 1991, Philadelphia Light was a stand-out success, representing a substantial share of the cream cheese business. That same year, Philadelphia Free fat-free cream cheese began test marketing, and in 1992, Kraft implemented a national roll-out of the product to further tighten its hold (the company, according to Julie Liesse in *Advertising Age*, puts it at 60 percent) of the $500 million light cheese industry. By expanding its offerings of Philadelphia variations, Kraft is hoping to protect itself from the slump in the general $5 billion cheese industry by continuing to dominate the industry's star segment: light cheese. The challenge for Kraft, according to some industry observers, is that in peddling flavor without the fat, the newer health-conscious products will not cannibalize their fattier cousins from which they have been spun off.

To counter an industry-wide sales slowdown, Kraft General Foods, as indicated by Joanne Lipman in a 1989 *Wall Street Journal* article, has increased its marketing presence by relying on the ways in which certain foods complement others. Lipman reported that then division president Michael A. Miles advocated "a 'breakfast' promotion in which coupons and in-store signs push [company owned brands such as] Post cereals, Oscar Mayer bacon, Lenders bagels, Philadelphia cream cheese, Maxwell House coffee and Kraft margarine, all at once." And in 1992 Stuart Elliot stated in the *New York Times* that "advertising and marketing efforts for Kraft's cheese brands are expected to intensify to counter sales declines suffered at the expense of lower-priced supermarket and store brands."

Further Reading:

A Chronological History of Kraft General Foods, Glenview, IL: Kraft General Foods, 1992.

Dreyfack, Kenneth, "Kraft, Minus Some Extra Baggage, Is Picking Up Speed," *Business Week,* March 9, 1987, p. 42-43.

Elliot, Stuart, "Kraft Natural Cheese Shifted to Thompson," *New York Times,* May 14, 1992, sec. D, p. 6.

The Kraftsman, Glenview, IL: Kraft, 1962.

Larkih, Connie, "Philly 100th Anniversary," *Kraft Ink,* vol. 5, no. 1.

Liesse, Julie, "ConAgra, Kraft Start Cheese War," *Advertising Age,* July 6, 1992, p. 3.

Lipman, Joanne, "Kraft Plans to Boost Spending on Ads Significantly This Year," *Wall Street Journal,* February 24, 1989.

Sweeda, Gerry, "Our 'Golden Oldies'," *Kraft Ink,* vol. 4, no. 2.

Thefrien, Lois, "Kraft Is Looking for Fat Growth from Fat-Free Foods," *Business Week,* March 26, 1990, p. 100.

—Isaac Rosen

PILLSBURY®

Instantly recognizable for its dough and dessert products, Pillsbury has been one of the most reputable brand names in the food industry for more than a century. It has been the Pillsbury Company's premier brand name since 1869, when the company began in flour milling and, over the course of more than a hundred years, has been identified with baking mixes, refrigerated bread dough, all-ready pie crusts, refrigerated and toaster pastry, and cookies. With sales in excess of $500 million, the Pillsbury brand name dominates the refrigerated dough segment with nearly 70 percent of the market share (in volume). Pillsbury's trademark—a doubled-dotted circle representing the nails in a barrelhead of flour—is one of corporate America's most respected symbols. Synonymous with the brand and even more easily recognizable, is the Pillsbury Doughboy, called Poppin' Fresh, featured in the Pillsbury commercials for prepared dough products since 1965. With the traditional poke in his belly followed by his customary giggle, the Pillsbury Doughboy is America's most popular and adorable advertising symbol.

When Pillsbury diversified into other industries in the 1970s and 1980s, it became an attractive takeover target. Grand Metropolitan PLC, a diversified British beverage company, acquired the company in 1989 and set about realigning the company with its profitable core business in consumer foods. New innovative products rolled out under the Pillsbury aegis and, with the ever-popular Pillsbury Doughboy omnipresent in most introductions, the brand continued to prosper with sales of $1 billion in its bakery division.

Brand Origins

The Pillsbury brand name owes its existence to Charles A. Pillsbury, who bought one-third of a local flour mill in 1869 and began the Pillsbury Company in Minneapolis, Minnesota. Within 20 years he owned six mills, including what was then the world's largest flour mill, and the famous trademark, Pillsbury's Best XXXX. The origins of this trademark go back to the early Christian era, when millers and bakers adopted an XXX symbol for bread, each X representing one of the crosses on Calvary. Medieval millers continued using the symbol as a mark of quality for their flour, a practice subsequently adopted in 1872 by Charles Pillsbury with a slight modification: an additional X was added, signifying that Pillsbury flour was the best.

In 1889, a group of English investors took over the company. However, bad management damaged the company's profits and image, and by 1923 the Pillsbury family repurchased the company and went on to build the corporate food giant. In the 1930s and 1940s, the company expanded into specialized grain products like cake flour and cereals and began to export its flour. Pillsbury then introduced innovative food products like Yellow Cake Mix, Pancake Mix, Pie Crust Mix, and Hot Roll Mix. Higher margin convenience products, such as cake mixes in 1948 and refrigerated foods in the 1950s, followed. Unprecedented growth in the 1950s resulted in the Pillsbury name appearing on 127 different products by 1963. The company's diversification into fast-food restaurants, frozen foods, ice cream, etc. meant that though profits were booming, the company was slowly losing focus on its core business: flour and bakery related products. By the mid-1980s the company was no longer exporting flour, since local mills could produce it more efficiently. Additionally, the restaurant business was doing badly and the bakery products unit was subsidizing losses in other segments. It took Grand Metropolitan's takeover and its subsequent streamlining of Pillsbury's businesses for the bakery products to reclaim their preeminent position in the company.

Prepared Dough

The story of Pillsbury's refrigerated dough begins in 1930 with a baker in Louisville, Kentucky. Lively Willoughboy, as he was called, sliced and stacked unbaked biscuits, wrapped them in foil, and packed them in cardboard tubes before storing them in an icebox. When the compressed dough was removed from the icebox, it exploded, converting the Willoughboy kitchen into a shooting gallery. Lively's son had to stand on a ladder to scrape the dough off the ceiling with a putty knife. Consistent efforts by Lively to eliminate the explosive character of his refrigerated dough eventually paid off and he sold his process to the Ballard and Ballard Flour Company. Pillsbury obtained this process in 1952 when it acquired Ballard.

Pillsbury launched its crescent rolls in 1965, first approaching Leo Burnett, its ad agency, which came up with the idea of the animated Pillsbury Doughboy. Poppin' Fresh, a revolutionary figure in advertising, launched the crescent rolls in 1965 and went on to symbolize Pillsbury's products in a vast number of commercials.

During the 1970s, sales of the refrigerated dough category fell by two to three percent annually. The decreased consumption was attributed to changes in lifestyle, as people began to move away from the basic biscuit as a breakfast item, especially in the Southeast and Southwest, Pillsbury's chief markets. General Mills and Borden, Pillsbury's principal competitors in the market, had dropped out by the early 1970s, leaving private-label refrigerated products as the only other contenders. By 1981, Pillsbury decided to reverse the sales decline in the refrigerated dough market, perceiving the dough products as offering greater growth potential than Pillsbury's older dessert baking mixes. Advertising, handled by the company's long-standing agency, Leo Burnett, was beefed up more than 40 percent from earlier levels, with increased TV and print support and coupons. As Janet Neiman reported in *Advertising Age,* "most (70 percent) of the sales of refrigerated dough products are impulse buys, made when the consumer goes to the case for biscuits and then picks up dinner rolls and cookie dough. But as the only advertiser in the category, Pillsbury must rely heavily on ads to get consumers to the case." In addition, Pillsbury product quality grew with increased butter levels; price, however remained unchanged.

New product introduction was also part of the game plan to revitalize the refrigerated dough market. Noteworthy new product introductions included refrigerated All Ready Pie Crust and Pipin' Hot Loaf. The All Ready Pie Crust, launched in September 1982, was a refrigerated product, contained in a package instead of the familiar Pillsbury dough can. It was designed to appeal to two basic consumer segments: those who were nervous about attempting a pie crust from scratch, and those who sought convenience. The product contained a large proportion of shortening, giving it a homemade taste. The advertising campaign with the theme, "Good enough to call your own," was handled by BBDO. Pies, being a seasonal product, were principally advertised between September 15 and January 1—fall fruit and holiday baking time.

Pipin' Hot Loaf was a yeast-character bread dough, which was developed using new technology, and provided a loaf of bread after 30 minutes of baking. It appealed to a wide range of consumers, from bakers to working women. It was launched with a $10.5 million introductory campaign under the theme, "There's a

new loaf coming," developed by Leo Burnett. The loaf was a roaring success and soon a whole wheat version was also introduced to take advantage of its popularity. The new pie crust and loaf helped increase unit sales in the refrigerated dough segment by 3.5 percent in 1982, reversing a ten-year decline and creating a new consumer category in the process, called bake-off. This consists of frozen and refrigerated items that are partially baked before consumers buy them from the stores, the baking to be completed in consumers' homes.

By 1992, Pillsbury continued to be a market leader in prepared dough with established products like Pillsbury cookie dough, sweet rolls, crescent dinner rolls, Hungry Jack, and Ballard biscuits. New products, combining quality and convenience included Grands! biscuits, Hearty Grains, Toaster Strudels, Soft Breadsticks, and Cornbread Twists. Grands!, a large, high quality biscuit, is the most successful product in Pillsbury's history. It was introduced regionally in 1991, and launched nationally in 1992.

Cake Mixes, Microwave Products

Originally introduced in 1948, Pillsbury's cake mixes were a major player in the market and expanded into a variety of cake mix segments. In January 1977, Pillsbury began a national rollout of its new Pillsbury Plus cake mixes, aimed at reestablishing brand presence in the two-layer segment of the market. The product was an improved cake mix; it included pudding to enhance moistness and firmness. The flavors that were test marketed were yellow, devil's food, white, lemon, German chocolate, and dark chocolate. A $6 million advertising budget positioned Plus against scratch cakes, with the theme, "Scratch has met its match," indicating that the cake mixes were as good as ones baked in ovens at home from scratch. Accompanying the launch of Pillsbury Plus, the company also introduced a line of ready-to-spread frostings, Frosting Supreme, which replaced an existing line of canned frostings that were in limited distribution and unadvertised.

By 1977, Pillsbury had decided to diversify into higher-growth areas like convenience foods, some aimed at microwave oven users. Management was convinced that fundamental changes in the American lifestyle, especially the increasing number of women entering the work force, would make convenience foods extremely important. Soon Pillsbury began test marketing a wallet-sized pack of popcorn, palm-sized ready-made pancakes, and microwave cake mixes. A corporate cash crunch came to Pillsbury at an unfortunate moment—just as cross-town rival General Mills was rolling out its own line of Betty Crocker microwave mixes. With Pillsbury unable to defend its products due to limited funds, Betty Crocker captured the lead and continued to hold it thereafter. The microwave popcorn did not fare any better—stronger rivals had edged out Pillsbury's leading position, and it fell to fifth place by 1989. Pillsbury's microwave pancakes, however, were very successful.

Promotional Activities—The Bake-Off

In 1949, Pillsbury staged the first national cooking competition at New York City's Waldorf-Astoria Hotel and called it the Grand National Recipe and Baking Contest. Originally planned as a one-time event, "the Pillsbury BAKE-OFF Contest," as it came to be known, went on to become an American institution. Entrants to this contest developed recipes for specified types of baked goods, incorporating some Pillsbury products. Tens of thousands of entries were evaluated, with the winners receiving prizes and having their recipes published. Although primarily a publicity medium, the Bake-Off has brought several user-developed products that Pillsbury has commercialized. One of its four cake mix lines and several variations of another have been derived directly from the recipes of Bake-Off winners, and, in 1993, an entire line of ready-to-eat products were launched under the Bake-Off name.

Ready-To-Eat Products—The Bake-Off Collection

As time limitations and the desire for convenient foods exerted ever stronger influences on consumer purchases in the 1980s and 1990s, Pillsbury found that its flour, cake mixes, and frostings were frequently relegated to the back shelves of pantries. A possible solution emerged in the form of a range of products that were already baked and ready to eat. In January 1993, Pillsbury began testing its ready-to-eat snack cakes. Raspberry Ribbon Brownies, Cinnamon Streusel Coffee Cake, and Tunnel of Fudge Bundt Cakes were among eight varieties offered on supermarket

Poppin' Fresh, the Pillsbury Doughboy, made his advertising debut in 1965.

shelves. This diversification strategy, under development since 1990, put Pillsbury head-to-head against desserts like Twinkies and Sara Lee.

To ease the task of individual product introductions, Pillsbury launched its ready-to-eat line under the name, The Bake-Off Collection, appealing to its legendary Bake-Off national recipe contest. Though Pillsbury sold a recipe magazine in supermarkets under that name, it had never used it on a product. Leo Burnett's broadcast, print, and in-store campaign, under the slogan "Everyone's a winner," also stressed that the snack cakes were "inspired" by successful Bake-Off entries. The ads went to great length to explain that the products were not baking mixes. Tar-

geted at dessert lovers, the product line was produced by an independent commercial bakery and marketed and distributed by Pillsbury.

Advertising—Poppin' Fresh, The Pillsbury Doughboy

American advertising's most popular character traces its origins to Leo Burnett, Pillsbury's ad agency in the 1960s. In 1965, Pillsbury approached the Leo Burnett agency for help in marketing its refrigerated dough. Leo Burnett's creative director Rudy Perz obliged by creating the animated Doughboy with bright blue eyes, a giggle, and an ideal tummy for playful poking. Named Poppin' Fresh, the Doughboy made his debut by springing out of a tube of Pillsbury's refrigerated Crescent Dinner Rolls and performing a two-step on the kitchen counter. He went on to deliver the famous slogan, "Nothin' Says Lovin' Like Something from the Oven, and Pillsbury Says It Best." By 1990, after 25 years of playful poking and giggling, the Doughboy had appeared in 611 commercials, been poked 32,500 times, and popped out of a can 5,760 times. The Doughboy's major advertising roles consisted of being a kitchen helper, musician, skateboarder, poet, and business executive, among other things. His impressive résumé boasts of finishing first in *Advertising Age's* 1987 "Whom Do You Love?" contest and being declared "1972 Toy of the Year" by *Playthings Magazine.*

A Pillsbury press release says, "White, short and pudgy, wearing a chef's hat and a white neckerchief, Americans have described the Doughboy as cute, cuddly and irresistible . . . the Doughboy is used to represent warmth and humanity, science and technology. At all times he represents what a Pillsbury product can do at a homemaker's command. He symbolizes good-tasting, easy-to-prepare food." He delivers to the consumers a message of convenience—that they can have the pleasure of home-baked goods without the time-consuming efforts required to prepare foods from scratch. Consumers, in turn, perceive the Poppin' Fresh character as having human qualities, representing the nurturing value of home-baked goods. Consumer involvement with the lovable character has been unprecedented. In 1969, just four years after the Doughboy was introduced, a study revealed that 87 percent of the people surveyed could identify an unmarked Doughboy as the symbol of the Pillsbury Company. Twenty-five years after his launch in 1965, Poppin' Fresh's popularity continued unabated: he received 200 love letters a week in 1990. Poppin' Fresh has remained contemporary, singing, dancing, rapping, painting, and playing the harmonica in Pillsbury advertising. Created as the essence of soft, fresh, ready-to-bake dough, the Doughboy has gone on to typify the wholesome warmth of Pillsbury products.

Further Reading:

"Amazing Facts and Figures on the Pillsbury Doughboy," "The Pillsbury Doughboy Is a Symbol of American Culture," "Poppin' Fresh—The Pillsbury Doughboy," "Prepared Dough," and "Where We've Been," *Pillsbury Corporate Communication Services.*

Edwards, Larry, "Pillsbury Puts $6 Million Behind New Two-layer Cake Mix Line," *Advertising Age,* January 10, 1977, p. 3.

Elliott, Stuart, "Pillsbury, That Staple of Home Pantries, Tries Entering the Market for Store-bought Goods," *New York Times,* January 20, 1993, section D, p. 17.

Grand Metropolitan, *Annual Report 1992,* p. 15.

Kirkland, Richard, "Grand Met's Recipe for Pillsbury," *Fortune,* March 13, 1989, pp. 61-68.

Neiman, Janet, "Execs Say 'New Day Is Coming' at Pillsbury's Refrigerated Unit," *Advertising Age,* March 15, 1982, p. 37.

"Pillsbury Company," *International Directory of Company Histories,* pp. 555-57.

Riddle, Judith, "Pillsbury Combines Logos to Capitalize on Familiarity," *Supermarket News,* September 28, 1992, p. 47.

Riddle Judith, "Pillsbury Will Purchase McGlynn Frozen Division," *Supermarket News,* January 20, 1992, p. 56.

Shapiro, Eben, "The Doughboy Gets A Streamlined Look," *New York Times,* April 22, 1990, section 3, p. 5.

Sobczynski, Anna, " 'Half-baked' Idea Gets Off to a Full-baked Start," *Advertising Age,* May 9, 1983, pp. M24-26.

—Ashish Patwardhan

PLANTERS®

Peanuts were not a popular food in America until Planters brand peanuts came on the market in 1906. Today peanuts make up a large segment of the U.S. snack food market, and the best known brand remains Planters. The Planters company was the first to successfully market large, whole roasted Virginia peanuts in conveniently priced and sized individual bags. Founder Amadeo Obici first sold roasted peanuts in two-ounce glassine packages, the product of a peanut roaster he perfected at his Wilkes-Barre, Pennsylvania, fruit stand. Although his five-cent bags were about four times more expensive than the bulk price of loose peanuts, customers enjoyed the guaranteed quality of the neatly packaged product.

Planters, owned by Nabisco Foods Group, currently sells several peanut and nut products in salted, unsalted, lightly salted, honey roasted, and other varieties, in sizes ranging from small vending machine packets to large vacuum-packed jars and cans. Planters products bear one of America's most successful advertising logos, Mr. Peanut, the dapper peanut man with top-hat, cane, and monocle who has been pictured on Planters products since a school child dreamed him up in 1916.

Brand Origins

Planters' first president and founder, Amadeo Obici, came to America from a village in Italy in 1889 at the age of 12. Alone and unable to speak English upon his arrival, his rise to the top of America's leading peanut company is a classic immigrant success story. Young Obici was taken in by an uncle in Pennsylvania. He attended school there for only three months before, unhappy with school, he quit and went to work. He eventually secured a job working for $6 a month at a fruit stand in nearby Wilkes-Barre, Pennsylvania. Obici later worked as a barkeep, and along the way met another Italian immigrant, a wholesale grocer named Mario Peruzzi, who later became his partner in Planters. The original peanut inspiration, however, is credited to Obici himself. Armed with modest savings from his work as a barkeep, Obici opened his own small fruit stand. An investment of $4.50 allowed him to add a peanut roaster to his stand.

Roasted peanuts were something of a novelty at that time. P. T. Barnum had sold them at his popular circus shows, which flourished at the end of the nineteenth century. Outside such venues, though, they were not widely available. Obici decided that since peanuts did not rot quickly like fruit, there was little risk to inventory in trying out this new line. He also tinkered with the roaster he had bought, equipping it with automatic pulleys so it did not need to be turned by hand. He salted the nuts, and even experimented a little, coating some batches with chocolate.

The young entrepreneur soon expanded beyond the simple fruit stand and bought a restaurant. He continued with his successful trade in peanuts, though. He installed a large peanut roaster above the restaurant and hired a few young women to package peanuts in five-cent, two-ounce glassine bags. Obici thus became "The Peanut Specialist." In a horse-drawn wagon bearing this logo, he jobbed his packaged product to groceries all around the Wilkes-Barre area.

First Commercial Success

It was not long before "The Peanut Specialist" became known as "The Peanut King." Business was so good that Obici was able to buy peanuts by the carload, making quite a spectacle as he paraded his vast purchases through Wilkes-Barre. In 1906 Obici put all his faith into peanuts. In partnership with his old friend Mario Peruzzi, Obici incorporated the Planters Nut & Chocolate Company. The name Planters was chosen for its impressive ring—the company had no actual connection to any peanut planters or plantations.

The new company concentrated its sales on blanched, salted Virginia peanuts. Virginia peanuts were larger than Spanish peanuts, and more expensive, but also more attractive. Spanish peanuts were small, round and red-skinned. Obici discovered a process for removing the skin from the long Virginia peanut in a way that left the nut whole. These blanched peanuts, packaged in clear, two-ounce bags, were aesthetically quite a different product than the loose red peanuts a customer might buy in bulk at a grocery from an open barrel. Extensive house-to-house sampling proved to the two peanut entrepreneurs that theirs was a preferred product. People proved willing to pay about four times the going per pound price for peanuts to enjoy the neat little bag of Planters.

In three years demand for Planters Peanuts grew so quickly that the company spent thousands of dollars to expand its nut processing plant, for which they had not yet fully paid. This expenditure put the firm in the red, and only a second mortgage on the plant pulled the firm through. In 1910, however, the company made its first net profit—$4,000 on sales of about $100,000—and sales continued to expand. In 1913 Planters established a large peanut processing plant in Suffolk, Virginia, to increase their proximity to the peanut crop source. Planters was also able to buy two existing peanut processing companies, open a San Francisco branch for the West Coast market in 1921, and set up a Canadian subsidiary in Toronto in 1925. Though profits were influenced by changes in production costs and raw material prices, Planters was able to remain stable by altering—even by two peanuts per bag—the number of nuts that went into its individual snack size packages. Obici and Peruzzi paid themselves only meager salaries, but made up for it by taking a commission based on the company's net profits.

The rapidly growing company took on a multitude of responsibilities. It made its own bags, boxes, and tins, and found new uses for peanut wastes such as the skins and shells. The company also manufactured three brands of peanut oil—an Italian version, a kosher brand, and one for "the world at large"—made peanut bars, chocolate-covered peanuts, and other confections, and processed and cleaned peanuts for peanut butter makers and others in the peanut trade. In spite of all these peripheral activities, the core product and biggest seller by far was always the classic Planters nickel bag of salted peanuts. This tried and true product was sold

AT A GLANCE

Planters brand of nuts first produced in 1906 by the Planters Nut & Chocolate Co., founded by Amadeo Obici and Mario Peruzzi; in 1961 Planters acquired by Standard Brands, Inc., which in turn merged with Nabisco to form Nabisco Brands, Inc., in 1981; Planters Nuts and Life Savers divisions of Nabisco consolidated in 1987 to form the Planters Life Savers Company, which was later dissolved; in the early 1990s, Planters Nuts became a product of the Planters Nuts Division of Nabisco Foods Group, which is held by RJR Nabisco, Inc.

Performance: *Sales*—$93.4 million (entire Planters brand).

Major competitor: Fisher Foods' brand of nuts; also Anheuser-Busch, Inc.'s Eagle brand snacks.

Advertising: *Agency*—Lintas, New York, NY. *Major campaign*—"Mr. Peanut" icon; slogan "Everybody loves a nut."

Addresses: *Parent company*—Nabisco Foods Group, 1100 Reynolds Blvd., Winston-Salem, NC 27102-0064; phone (919) 741-2000; fax: (919) 741-6602. *Ultimate parent company*—RJR Nabisco, Inc., 1301 Avenue of the Americas, New York, NY 10019-6013; phone: (212) 258-5600.

at grocery and candy stores all across the country, and also became a top-selling vending machine item.

Advertising

A writer for *Fortune* magazine claimed in 1938 that the Planters company believed that "any one with teeth is a potential customer." At that time, Planters was the only peanut company in America that advertised nationally. The company's charming advertising reached out to children and adults alike, and gave the Planters brand high visibility.

An early trademark for Obici's peanuts, before Planters was incorporated, showed a handsome, mustachioed man—"The Specialist" himself—supported by two elegant peanut halves. Mr. Obici also traded on his own name recognition around Wilkes-Barre by inserting a letter of his name into each peanut bag, and the customer who collected enough letters to spell out Amadeo Obici won a prize, at first a large bag of peanuts, later a watch.

Early slogans, such as "The Nickel Lunch" and "2 1/2 Hours' Extra Pep," also promoted Planters' nutrition and convenience. A magazine ad showed a languid young lady sipping an iced drink and reaching into a jar of peanuts, under the banner "A Dainty Summer Food." Easily the most successful Planters advertising involved the famous Mr. Peanut. Mr. Peanut came to life in 1916, when Obici held a contest among Suffold school children to make a new trademark for Planters. A 14-year-old boy named Antonio Gentile won the five-dollar prize with his drawing of a peanut-shaped man with face, arms, and legs. A commercial artist then improved the design by giving Mr. Peanut a top hat, monocle, cane, and jauntily crooked legs. Mr. Peanut soon appeared as the hero of comic strips portraying historical events, travel, and adventure. Sightings of Mr. Peanut became more frequent as well. He could be seen walking the streets distributing samples or sitting on top of Planters delivery trucks, and his likeness was made into all sorts of toys and gadgets. Invented by a child, Mr. Peanut clearly attracted juvenile followers. His picture books were given away as premiums to customers who saved up their wrappers, and these hoarders were presumably mostly children. Planters, though,

believed that if a person was hooked on peanuts as a child, that person would continue to buy them as an adult. Moreover, Mr. Peanut had such panache that he did not seem an exclusively childish symbol.

The appearance of Mr. Peanut was revamped several times. The hand in which he held his cane was changed, he became stouter and more detailed, and eventually was made to appear taller and more streamlined. But he was always Mr. Peanut, and he still appears on Planters packaging, winking through his monocle.

Corporate Changes

By 1960 Planters Nut & Chocolate Co. was earning close to $2 million on sales estimated at approximately $55 million. The nut business had become highly profitable following World War II, with an expanding younger population and a rise in disposable income. Yet no other nut company had the name recognition of Planters. Several smaller nut companies such as Circus Foods and the Crown Nut Co. had been bought up at the end of the 1950s by bigger food companies eager to get a piece of a profitable market. Planters itself was bought out by Standard Brands, Inc., in 1961 after a bitter court battle. Though some of the Planters trustees had opposed the sale, a court-ordered settlement gave the large food conglomerate control of the nation's oldest and largest peanut company.

Standard Brands sold many popular products such as Fleischmann's and Blue Bonnet margarine, Fleischmann's gin, Chase and Sanborn coffee, and Tender Leaf tea. The company had strong national and international distribution systems for these brands, and Planters fit in well. Standard Brands grew profitably after acquiring Planters, with sales increasing every year of the 1960s until total sales reached more than a billion dollars.

In 1981 Standard Brands merged with another food giant, Nabisco, and Planters continued as a division of the new Nabisco Brands, Inc. In 1985 Nabisco management moved to consolidate Planters with another strong snack food division it had acquired, Life Savers. The new Planters Life Savers Co. was headquartered in Winston-Salem, North Carolina. This company had remained stable despite changes in its parent organization when Nabisco Brands merged with tobacco giant R.J. Reynolds Industries, Inc., in 1988 to form RJR Nabisco, Inc.; in the early 1990s, the Planters Life Savers Company was dissolved and the Planters brand came to be handled by the Planters Nuts Division of Nabisco Foods Group. Though Planters is currently under the umbrella of one of the largest food and consumer product manufacturers in America, the brand has not lost its unique identity or substantially altered the formula created at the beginning of this century by Amadeo Obici.

Brand Development

The original formula for Planters Peanuts has withstood the test of time, but many new varieties were added to the brand line after Planters became part of Standard Brands. Changes in packaging also affected the brand's performance. In 1961 Planters Peanuts had a large sales volume from the vending machine market. Planters was second only to one other candy product in national candy vending machine sales, and nearly 30 percent of the brand's total sales came from its ten-cent peanut bags and peanut bars. By the early 1980s, Planters had made a successful move toward marketing larger packages that were sold through drug stores and mass merchandise outlets. A new kind of salted peanut, dry roasted, was also selling well around this time. Dry roasted peanuts became the subject of a $20 million television ad campaign in 1990 that featured Mr. Peanut.

Rising consumer health consciousness in the 1980s led Planters to market a product that was a departure from Amadeo Obici's original recipe: unsalted peanuts. A new line of unsalted nuts, including peanuts, cashews, and mixed nuts, was released for national sale in 1981, after marketers noticed an almost 30 percent increase in sales of unsalted nuts in 1980. Advertising for the unsalted line emphasized the health benefits of the new product. Planters unsalted nuts met federal dietary recommendations for low-sodium and no-sodium diets, a fact that was publicized through a national print media campaign aimed at medical and health professionals as well as the general public. In 1991 Planters introduced a Lightly Salted line of peanuts and mixed nuts, also intended for consumers on low-sodium diets.

Not all the Planters line extensions were so health conscious, however. Honey-Roasted Peanuts came out in the late 1980s, a sweet snack. These soon became available as Honey-Roasted Mixed Nuts and Honey-Roasted Pecans, selling in large tins as well as snack-size foil packets. Other Planters products bore the Planters logo but were not nuts at all. Cheez Curls, Cheez Balls, and Kick Stix sesame sticks were all salty snack products, but with no nut element about them. By the early 1990s, the Planters line had grown to include a spectrum of products, from the old standard Planters Peanuts, to its Gold Measure line of cooking and baking nuts, to low- and no-salt nuts, to sweet and salty snack foods.

Performance Appraisal

No other brand of peanuts has enjoyed the visibility garnered by Planters. The brand's success is probably due in part to the marketing acumen of founder Amadeo Obici, who recognized the potential size of the peanut market and who offered his product in an attractive, conveniently sized and priced package. Obici paid attention to the look of his product by using the long, blanched, whole, white Virginia peanut instead of the small, red-skinned Spanish variety, and he also developed the proper salty taste of his nuts. Without formal education, Obici nevertheless had the mechanical skill to modify existing roasting technology to produce exactly the kind of nuts he wanted. Planters Peanuts were thus a high quality product from their inception.

Population growth and American eating habits also fostered the growth of the Planters brand. A burgeoning younger population after World War II, coupled with consumers' increasing interest in snack foods, enabled the market for Planters to continue to grow in the second half of this century.

Planters' marketers also proved able to keep up with shifting fads in the snack market without substantially altering the original brand's successful formula. Line extensions such as low- and no-salt varieties took advantage of rising health consciousness among consumers, yet a place in the market remained for saltier and sweeter versions, too. Planters Peanuts have proved to be an enduring item in the American marketplace, and there is no reason to doubt that they will continue to be so.

Further Reading:

"$10,000 Worth of Peanuts," *Fortune,* April 1938, p. 78.

"Analysis of Snacks," *Food Engineering,* August 1980, p. 83.

Du Bois, Peter C., "Goobers to Cashews," *Barron's,* June 19, 1961, p. 11.

McGrath, Molly, *Top Sellers, U.S.A.,* New York: William Morrow and Company, Inc., 1983, p. 70.

"Standard Brands: Solid Achievement," *Financial World,* April 22, 1970, p. 20.

—A. Woodward

POST® GRAPE-NUTS®

Since its 1897 introduction as one of the first ready-to-eat cold cereals available to the public, Post Grape-Nuts Cereal has remained a leading brand in both sales and nutritional value. Its blend of wheat and malted barley provides a uniquely dense, crunchy, and flavorful product that is fat-free and high in complex carbohydrates. Grape-Nuts cereal was invented by C. W. Post, founder of the Postum Cereal Company, which was renamed General Foods Corporation in 1929.

While the company that produced Grape-Nuts evolved, so did the Grape-Nuts product line: Grape-Nuts Flakes were introduced in 1932, Grape-Nuts Wheat-Meal appeared in 1936, and Raisin Grape-Nuts entered the market in 1981. Less direct relatives also proliferated as Post cereals expanded under the ownership of the General Foods Corporation and eventually under Kraft General Foods. By the late 1980s, Post was slipping from its third place in the multi-billion-dollar ready-to-eat cereal market, trailing top-ranked Kellogg Company, Inc., and General Mills, Inc., in second place. After Philip Morris merged Kraft Inc., and General Foods Corporation (the owner of Post cereals) into Kraft General Foods, Inc. in 1989, Grape-Nuts and its Post cereal siblings gained the financial security of the largest food company in the United States. By 1990 Grape-Nuts and other Post cereals recorded the first category share gain in a decade, increasing hopes of continued success in an increasingly competitive cereal market.

Brand Origins

The history of Grape-Nuts dates back to the entrepreneurial spirit of Charles William Post, an eighth generation American of Welsh ancestry, who was born in 1854 in Springfield, Illinois. In tireless efforts at developing a nutritious cereal beverage, C. W. Post bought a small farm in the outskirts of Battle Creek, Michigan, where he and his helper, Clark Bristol, experimented with grain combinations for two years. On New Year's Day of 1895, the partners introduced Postum cereal beverage, the Postum Cereal Company's first product and the precursor to Grape-Nuts and eventually a whole line of cereals and foods.

Though Postum generated profits after the first year, Mr. Post continued to innovate. One problem with the cereal beverage was that its sales were seasonal, peaking during the winter and slacking off during the summer. In order to even out the success of Postum, the fledgling company developed a cereal food made of wheat and malted barley and introduced it in 1897 as Grape-Nuts. In a 1913

company brochure, C. W. Post explained that, "Thoughtful people desire a food that is clean, pure and palatable; easily digested and healthful; and withal economical."

In order to maintain its success, Postum Cereal Company engineered production facilities that would ensure consistent quality and supply. Despite modernization of its facilities over time, the manufacturing process at Postumville—as the plant was called—remained essentially the same. The first step involved preparation of modified bread dough, for which wheat and malted barley grains were cleansed, ground, combined by automatic weighing devices, and mixed with yeast, salt, and artesian well water. The so-called "sponge" was then conditioned with water and flour and kneaded into dough. The risen dough then underwent a preliminary baking of about two hours, during which the diastase of the malt would convert part of the starch into sugar and dextrin. The Grape-Nuts loaves were then trimmed, sliced, and baked a second time for many hours in ovens heated to over 200°F to complete the evaporation of all moisture and the dextrinization of the cereal starch (sugar thus formed is commonly referred to as dextrose, or "Grape-sugar," a digestible derivative of starch). In a publication titled, *Elements of Dietetics and Nutrition,* published by Postum Cereal Co. in 1914, the double baking process was summarized: "It is the purpose in making this food to concentrate the food elements in the smallest bulk and to eliminate the non-essentials." That "smallest bulk" was finally realized by grinding the hard-baked slices into granules that were then ready for packaging.

Early Marketing

Early packaging for Grape-Nuts promoted the cereal's healthfulness. A small black and yellow container featured C. W. Post's signature, lending and air of authenticity. Each box also contained a pamphlet entitled, *The Road to Wellville,* emphasizing the cereal's nutritional benefits. There were even those doctors who prescribed Grape-Nuts as medicine.

In addition to health appeals, less specific benefits were tied to the cereal in early advertising campaigns. The slogan, "There's a Reason," which had been originally used to promote Postum cereal beverage, was transferred to the service of Grape-Nuts. Even though the promised "reason" remained infinitely vague, the slogan produced tangible effects on sales in 1898. Other ads related indirectly, if at all, to the product. A little girl, for example, was pictured alongside a St. Bernard in front of a cottage, with the

AT A GLANCE

Post Grape-Nuts brand of cereal was developed by C. W. Post, the 1892 founder of Battle Creek, Michigan's Postum Cereal Company; Postum Cereal Company, Inc., was incorporated in 1922; the company changed its name to Postum Company, Inc., in March of 1927 and to General Foods Corporation in July of 1929; after acquiring General Foods in 1985 and Kraft, Inc., in 1988, Philip Morris Companies, Inc., combined the two subsidiaries to form Kraft General Foods, Inc.

Performance: *Market share*—2.9% of ready-to-eat cereal category (*Advertising Age*, May 11, 1992, p. 72).

Major competitor: Kellogg's Corn Flakes, Raisin Bran, Rice Krispies, and All-Bran; also General Mills Inc.'s Cheerios.

Advertising: *Agency*—Grey Advertising, Inc., New York, 1960s—. *Major campaign*—"Try it for a week."

Addresses: *Parent company*—Kraft General Foods, Inc., 250 North St., White Plains, NY 10625; phone: (914) 335-2500; fax: (914) 335-1786. *Ultimate parent company*—Philip Morris Companies, Inc., 120 Park Avenue, New York, NY 10017; phone: (212) 880-5000; fax: (212) 878-2167.

label, "Playmates" and the copy following, "Off to School Well-Fed with Grape-Nuts and Cream."

Brand Development

Until the early 1900s, Grape-Nuts and Postum were the only two products offered by Postum Cereal Company. Their production was extremely cost-efficient, as the bran removed from wheat when making Grape-Nuts served as a key ingredient in Postum. In addition, the two foods were marketed as accompaniments to each other. A 1906 company booklet suggested "A delicious breakfast dish made by placing one or two teaspoons of Grape-Nuts breakfast food in the cup of Postum." By the 1920s, the company was also expanding market share by promoting new uses for Grape-Nuts: the cereal could be sprinkled on sundaes or fruit to add crunch or heated and prepared as a hot cereal.

The symbiotic relationship between Grape-Nuts and Postum continued even after the company introduced several new products. A corn flakes cereal was introduced in 1904 as ELIJAH'S MANNA. The religious tenor of the name caused more controversy than Mr. Post could have anticipated, including the English Government's refusal to register the trade-mark. In 1907 the name was changed to Post Toasties. In December of 1911 an instant Postum variety was introduced. Post's 40% Bran Flakes appeared in 1922 and became the world's best-selling bran cereal, according to company records. By 1929, the Postum Company, Inc., had diversified its cereals and other products to the point where General Foods Corporation was adopted as a more suitable name.

Bran Development

Though Grape-Nuts had always been marketed for his health benefits, the 1970s and 1980s brought a new wave of public health-consciousness that effected renewed interest in Grape-Nuts and other high-fiber cereals. The concerns of scientists and doctors that people were not getting the proper amounts of fiber to stay healthy filtered down to consumers, contributing to a boom in bran and related cereals. Between 1975 and 1979, the bran segment of the ready-to-eat cereal category rose 20 percent each year to reach

15 percent of the market. SAMI/Burke Inc. reported that by 1986, market share of bran/fiber cereals had reached 17 percent of the category. Grape-Nuts and its kin benefited from the fiber rage—Post reached its peak category share of 29 percent in the early 1970s according to Tim Ramey, a County NatWest Securities analyst in a *Battle Creek Enquirer* report, while Grape-Nuts cereal sales increased through the 1980s, riding the crest of the wave with its introduction of Raisin Grape-Nuts in 1981.

Competition: Roughing the 80s

Grape-Nuts was only one of numerous cereals to join the fiber craze. In the early 1980s, competition stiffened as Kellogg, the industry leader, stepped up advertising spending and new product introductions. According to an October 7, 1985, *Forbes* article, in the previous year Kellogg's market share rose 2 percent, to 40 percent. The number two player, General Mills, held its ground at about 20 percent, while General Foods, in third place, dropped 2 percent to hold 14 percent of the $4 billion market. By 1987, Post slid further to 12 percent of the $4.5 billion cold cereal category, as reported in a September 24, 1987 *Advertising Age* article, still ranking third behind Kellogg with 42 percent and General Mills with 24.1 percent.

In an October 7, 1985, report for *Forbes*, Pamela Sherrid attributed much of Post's decline to its advertising strategy. In 1983 Post decreased ad spending by 24 percent, to $44 million. Then in 1984 Kellogg's ad budget soared 49 percent, to $160 million, while General Foods increased spending only 16 percent, to $52 million. Many analysts attributed Post's low spending to attempts at short-term profit. A General Foods executive explained that the cause was not short-term profit motives, but lack of effective campaigns, especially for the cereal leader, Grape-Nuts.

With reduced advertising spending, General Foods tried diverse strategies to increase sales. Introducing new products yielded mixed results. Post Fruit & Fiber was introduced in 1980, to appeal to adult health concerns as well as good taste. The success of that cereal was quickly marred by the failure of Smurfberry Crunch, a heavily promoted children's cereal that appeared in 1983 and fizzled soon thereafter. The company also tried heavy promotional spending, offering cents-off coupons and discounts to grocers, a tactic that encouraged more one-time sales than brand loyalty, according to Sherrid. Finally, a campaign for Grape-Nuts appealed to the competitive edge of upwardly mobile customers. The tag line read, "The question isn't whether Grape-Nuts is right for you, it's whether you're right for Grape-Nuts." Though Sherrid reported that it offended some customers, the campaign spurred unit sales by about 10 percent during the year it ran, compared with industry growth of 3 percent.

Advertising Innovation

With increased competition raging between leading companies, Grape-Nuts depended more than ever on its marketing efforts to set it apart. With the 1984 promotion of David Hurwitt to general manager of the breakfast food division and corporate vice president of General Foods, a period of active advertising innovation had begun. Hurwitt planned not only to increase ad spending, but to rigorously increase its effectiveness. "It costs just as much to run a lousy commercial as a good one," he remarked in an October 7, 1985, article in *Forbes*. Following along the lines of his predecessor, Hurwitt's strategy would focus primary market support on the company's core brands—Raisin Bran, Grape Nuts,

Fruit & Fiber, Super Golden Crisp, and Pebbles—which accounted for roughly 75 percent of cereal sales.

In 1985 Hurwitt expanded those core brands with the introduction of Horizon cereal, supported by nature-oriented advertising that would supplement similar marketing for Raisin Bran, Grape-Nuts, and other Post cereals. Horizon was based on the "trail mix" concept, offering chunks of peanuts and grains and evoking images of hardy treks through nature. In 1986 the all-natural appeal was extended to Post Natural Raisin Bran, from which preservatives and sugar coating on the raisins had been completely removed, and for which John Denver served as spokesperson for about a year. In addition, Post donated $250,000 to the national park system. "We were helped along by consumers through proofs of purchase to order materials we had written [about various parks]," stated Ken Defren, director of communications at General Foods in the April 1987 *Marketing & Media Decisions.*

These advertisements continued a tradition that had been well established in the early days of Grape-Nuts. Before cholesterol and nutritional fiber had even become issues, Grape-Nuts commercials featured naturalist Euell Gibbons dispensing health advice over his box of Grape-Nuts, and saying things like, "I love the taste of Grape-Nuts, it reminds me of wild hickory nuts." According to a *Crain's Chicago Business* article, after his 1975 death, the cereal lost momentum, a pattern that worsened as Kellogg's Nutri-Grain Nuggets and the whole oat bran category occupied more "natural" territory. Gibbons's spirit returned to its beloved cereal, however, and by the late 1980s Grape-Nut commercials showed outdoorsy types in their woodsy yards, drinking the left-over milk directly from their cereal bowls.

Post's advertising initiatives for its core brands, however, extended well beyond the appeals of nature. Starting in 1985, Grape-Nuts sponsored the annual Grape-Nuts Bike Festival, one of the largest cycling events in the state of Florida, according to the *St. Petersburg Times.* An April 1987 *Marketing & Media Decisions* report stated General Foods had spent $13.8 million to advertise Grape-Nuts, with ads ranging from the ridiculous to the conceptually clever. According to an August 8, 1989, *Los Angeles Times* article, one of the ads provoked the ire of Men's Rights, a group that compiled a list of that year's ads it deemed particularly offensive to men. The ad portrayed a woman trying to explain to her less-than-witty husband why Grape-Nuts was good for him. When she referred to "complex carbohydrates," he was utterly bewildered.

In an attempt to attract additional attention to Grape-Nuts, marketers in the late 80s drew on shear novelty. One campaign used a technique known as cliffhanging to highlight a woman asking how long the cereal would remain crunchy in milk. After several commercials for other products, she returned with, "After all this time, it's still crunchy." A 1989 campaign exploited the physical-craze by referring to the actual act of eating Grape-Nuts. A woman explained that "just chewing it feels like exercise." In a male variation, a man tells the camera that he is 35 and that he "really looks forward to the crunch . . . just chewing it feels healthy."

The January 2, 1989, *Advertising Age* reported that same crunchy appeal prompted a $5 million campaign in which Grape-Nuts was promoted as a mix-in for hot oatmeal. The TV spot rode on the coat-tails of the hot cereal, which grew about 24 percent in 1987 to $606 million, and continued to rise. Consumers were urged to "ooooomph up" their oatmeal by adding "the crunchy, nutty taste" of Grape-Nuts. In a similar attempt at crossing categories, Orowheat Grape-Nuts Bread was introduced in August of 1989 for test marketing in Oregon and Washington.

Merging Companies, Emerging Cereals

In February of 1989 Philip Morris Companies merged Kraft Inc. and General Foods Corp. to form the $22.5-billion Kraft General Foods, Inc. With the backing of its massive parent, Post was in a new position to benefit from better corporate discounts for large-quantity purchase of staples, similar discounts in advertising spending along with greater ad support, and possibly increased market share due to price slashing. Michael A. Miles, Kraft General Foods's president and CEO, told analysts that the company would seek ways to translate its position "into greater visibility if not influence, with the trade," according to Judith Crown's March 13, 1989 article in *Crain's Chicago Business.*

The turnaround was anything but instant. *United Press International* reported that by November of 1989, continued market losses in Post's core line—Grape-Nuts and Raisin Bran—prompted cutbacks in operations, which, in turn, caused a union strike at the company's main plant in Battle Creek, Michigan. While a resolution to the labor dispute was negotiated, a resolution to Grape-Nuts's slide—from 3.1 percent of the market in 1980 to 2.1 percent in 1989—proved more elusive. By 1989, as reported by *Advertising Age,* Post's overall share of the ready-to-eat cereal category had plummeted to 10.9 percent.

By 1990, however, prospects began to lighten. The *Advertising Age* article went on to report that Post's market share improved slightly to 11.1 percent in pound volume for the nine months ended September 30, 1990. Grape-Nuts jumped 20 percent in volume, reflecting the company's efforts at core line development and, more particularly, the success of an advertising campaign urging consumers to "Try it for a week."

In January of 1993 Kraft added approximately three additional market share points to its cereal division by acquiring RJR Nabisco's cereal division, which included Shredded Wheat cereal. Robert Abrams, New York attorney general, opposed the move as a breach of anti-trust law and as a sure way to reduce competition and increase prices of cereals such as Grape-Nuts and Shredded Wheat. After performing a thorough investigation, however, the Federal Trade Commission offered no objections to the acquisition.

Future Growth

From its origins on a small farm near Battle Creek, Michigan, Grape-Nuts peaked as a cereal leader in the early 1970s, claiming 29 percent of the ready-to-eat market with other Post brands. Post's market share gradually slipped until August of 1990, when it reached 10.5 percent, its lowest mark ever. Under the parentage of Kraft General Foods, however, Post, and more specifically Grape-Nuts, began to show renewed promise. The cereal's early motto, "There's a Reason," would take on new meaning as Kraft persuaded more customers to fill their bowls with Grape-Nuts.

Further Reading:

Advertising Age, May 11, 1992, p. 72.

Blake, Judith, "Cereal Sticker Shock—My-Grain Headache: Morning Crunchies have Soared in Price," *The Seattle Times,* March 31, 1993, p. F1.

Burros, Marian, "Fighting For a Bran New Way," *The Washington Post,* May 17, 1979, p. E1.

"Cereals: Which Belong in Your Bowl?" *Consumer Reports,* November, 1992, Vol. 57, No. 11, P. 688.

Colwell, Carolyn, "Bowled Over by Cereal Merger; Abrams Antitrust Suit Names 2 Food Makers," *Newsday,* February 11, 1993, p. 47.

Crown, Judith, "Why New Kraft Must Wake Up Sleepy Brands," *Crain's Chicago Business,* March 13, 1989, p. 17.

Dagnoli, Judann, "Riding Oat Craze; GF Touts Grape-Nuts for Hot Cereals," *Advertising Age,* January 2, 1989, p. 2.

Dagnoli, Judann, and Julie Liesse, "Post Marks First Gain in 10 years," *Advertising Age,* December 3, 1990, p. 4.

Deck, Cecilia, "Post Cereal Plagued by 6-Week Strike," *United Press International,* December 12, 1989, BC Cycle.

De Silva, Cara, "The Cereal Crunch; Antitrust Suit Focuses Attention on Something Consumers Have Known For Years: Cereal Prices are Sky-High," *Newsday,* February 24, 1993, p. 61.

Elliott, Stuart, "A Big Spender Finds Fault With Agencies and Clients," *The New York Times,* April 13, 1992, p. D8.

Gorman, Tom, "Oats are 'Hot' in Breads, Plus New Selling Ideas," *Bakery Production and Marketing,* Vol. 24, No. 1, p. 78.

Hines, Nathaniel, "Biking Festival Draws 4,200 Plus," *St. Petersburg Times,* November 9, 1987, p. 5.

Kalish, David, "Ads as Cliffhangers; Advertising Technique," *Marketing & Media Decisions,* October, 1988, Vol. 23, No. 10, p. 32.

Levine, Joshua, "The Last Gasp of mass Media," *Forbes,* September 17, 1990, p. 176.

Liesse, Julie, and Judann Dagnoli, "Kellogg's Golden Era Flakes Away," *Advertising Age,* August 13, 1990, p. 4.

Lippert, Barbara, "Something to Chew On; Grape-Nuts Commercials Stress the Crunch," *Chicago Tribune,* October 20, 1989, p. CN2.

"Post Grape-Nuts: A 95-Year-Old Cereal With a Rich History," White Plains: Kraft General Foods, Inc., 1992.

Sherrid, Pamela, "Fighting Back at Breakfast," *Forbes,* October 7, 1985, p. 126.

Schnorbus, Paula, "Brantastic; Brand Report," *Marketing & Media Decisions,* April, 1987, No. 141.

Stern, Michael, and Jane Stern, "Help Solve Mystery That is Grape-Nuts," *St. Petersburg Times,* march 24, 1988, p. 2D.

Sterrett, R. M., M.D., *Elements of Dietetics and Nutrition,* Battle Creek, MI: Postum Cereal Co., Ltd., 1914.

Strauss, Gary, "RJR, Philip Morris in Cereal Deal," *USA Today,* November 17, 1992, p. 1B.

A Trip Through Postumville, Battle Creek, MI: Postum Cereal Company, Inc., 1920.

—*Kerstan Cohen*

PROGRESSO® SOUP

Progresso ready-to-serve soups originated along with a large family of products in the kitchens of Italian immigrants who came to the United States in the late 19th and early 20th centuries. Progresso's range of products includes more than 150 items, featuring tomatoes, sauces, olive oil, vinegar, bread crumbs, olives, peppers, and many other items along with its more than 40 soups and new line of healthy soups. The Progresso brand has been owned by several different companies. Pet Incorporated, which has owned Progresso since 1986, has emphasized the taste as well as the healthy content of Progresso soups. Their method has proven successful, and the soups have held onto a solid second-place position in their market.

Brand Origins

Progresso soup began as a product of two Italian immigrant families. Vincent Taormina, who came from Italy to New Orleans in the late 19th century, opened a company to import Italian olive oil and tomato products aimed at the local Italian-American community. He called it V. Taormina & Company. Other members of his family joined Taormina in the United States, including Giuseppe Uddo. Uddo formed a business called Uddo Brothers in 1913. Vincent Taormina moved to California and opened a branch of his business called La Sierra Heights Canning Company. His New Orleans company continued operation under the direction of Vincent and others, and in the 1920s he merged with Uddo Brothers. The new company, with branches in New Orleans and California, was known as the Uddo & Taormina Corporation.

The Uddo & Taormina Corporation bought the Progresso logo and brand name from a New Orleans shop called the Progress Grocery Store for under $50. Another branch of the company was opened in Brooklyn, New York, by Frank Taormina. In the late 1920s all of the branches in New York, Louisiana, and California consolidated under the name Progresso Foods Corporation, although the name Uddo & Taormina was still used until 1969.

The company opened a manufacturing plant in Vineland, New Jersey, in the 1940s. Vincent Taormina, Jr., served as its plant manager until his death. He was succeeded by Eugene Taormina. After World War II Progresso Foods met with tremendous success. They expanded into large supermarket chains from the Italian-American food stores that they had served before. Soon Progresso Foods was the largest manufacturer of Italian foods in North America.

In 1969 a Canadian conglomerate, Imperial and Associated Companies (IMASCO), bought the family business. It became the Progresso Quality Foods Division of IMASCO. While it was owned by IMASCO, the Progresso division was given a boost with the construction of a large, modern manufacturing facility in Vineland. Ten years later, in 1979, the division was bought by Ogden Corporation. Ogden operated Progresso as part of its Ogden Food Products Company. Several family members were still actively involved with Progresso, including Gasper Taormina, who remained in office as president of Progresso until 1986.

In 1986 Pet Incorporated bought the Ogden Food Products Company under which Progresso had been flourishing. Pet at that time was a wholly-owned subsidiary of IC Industries, a Chicago-based company built on the success of the Illinois Central railroad. In 1988, after spinning off the railroad, IC Industries was renamed Whitman Corporation. Whitman itself was still a large corporation, and in 1991, Pet was spun off, and again became its own publicly-held and traded company. By that time, Progresso was already one of Pet's most important money-making product lines.

When Pet bought Progresso, the brand was integrated into Pet's grocery group. The product line has expanded and currently features more than 40 varieties of soup. A new line of Progresso soups, known as Progresso Healthy Classics, with lower sodium and less fat, was introduced in 1993 in 21 markets.

More than Forty Varieties

Progresso soups come in three basic sizes and types. The 10.5 ounce size is considered single-serving. There are 10.5 ounce vegetable soups, chicken soups, beef soups, chowders, and specialty soups. The larger size, at 19 ounces, has the most flavor variety. Like the smaller size, the 19 ounce size includes vegetable, chicken, beef, chowder, and specialty soups, as well as several cream soups. The 16 ounce size is reserved for the Healthy Classics. These are available in vegetable and chicken flavor varieties including minestrone, lentil, chicken noodle, and chicken rice.

How Progresso Fits into Pet

When Pet was spun off from Whitman in April 1991, Progresso soups together with Old El Paso Mexican foods brought in much of Pet's revenues. Analyst Michael Branca, as quoted in *The*

AT A GLANCE

Progresso brand of soup originated by Italian immigrants at the turn of the century; manufacturer founded in 1920s as Uddo & Taormina Corporation in New Orleans, LA, a consolidation of Uddo Brothers, founded by Giuseppe Uddo in 1913, and V. Taormina & Company, founded by Vincent Taormina; renamed Progresso Foods Corporation with branches in New Orleans, Brooklyn, NY, and California; acquired by Imperial and Associated Companies (IMASCO), a Canadian conglomerate, and became Progresso Quality Foods Division, 1969; division purchased by Ogden Corporation and operated as part of Ogden Food Products Company, 1979; Ogden Food Products Company and Progresso acquired by Pet Incorporated, a wholly owned subsidiary of Whitman Corporation, 1986; Whitman, a $2.4 billion conglomerate, was known as IC Industries until 1988; Pet Incorporated spun off from Whitman Corporation, 1991; Pet Inc. currently handles Progresso brand.

Performance: *Market share*—25% (second-highest share) of ready-to-serve soup category. *Sales*—$150. million.

Major competitor: Campbell's Soup.

Advertising: *Agency*—D'Arcy Masius Benton & Bowles, St. Louis, MO, 1991—. *Major campaign*—(for Healthy Classics varieties introduced 1993) "The label says Healthy, the taste says Progresso."

Addresses: *Parent company*—Pet Incorporated, 400 South Fourth Street, St. Louis, MO 63102; phone: (314) 622-7700; fax: (314) 622-6525.

New York Times, said that Old El Paso and Progresso foods together accounted for about 45 percent of Pet's operating profits. Pet Inc.'s sales were about $1.9 billion. The ready-to-serve soup market is a huge business in this country. Sales in the category are estimated at $780 million per year, and are growing at a rate of 7 to 9 percent each year.

Evelyn Tribole, writing in *Consumers Digest,* noted that the "$2.7-billion prepared-soup market is beginning to reflect the nation's health consciousness." As Pet introduced its new healthier line of soups, the company also showed its intention to concentrate on Progresso, Old El Paso, and its other grocery lines. In June 1992 Pet announced that it was selling Whitman's chocolates. The actual sale to Russell Stover took place in March 1993, for $35 million. Whitman's annual sales were about $85 million and had been flat for several years. Other grocery products under Pet's umbrella were Downyflake waffles and Van de Kamp's seafood. Sales of Downyflake waffles had been growing quickly, with 1992 sales almost 32 percent higher than those in 1991. The waffles, like Progresso soups, were a brand on which Pet wanted to concentrate.

Marketing Strategies

Progresso soups had their early successes on the east and west coasts of the United States. It took strong marketing to encourage distribution and sales in the rest of the country. In 1988 and 1989 Pet's marketing strategy was far more focused on discounts, store displays, coupons, and other promotions than on media and advertising. In fact, Pet was spending 90 percent of its marketing budget on these promotions. Waring & LaRosa of New York, NY, handled the Progresso account until the 1991 spinoff.

When Pet was spun off, its chief executive officer Miles Marsh promised to increase advertising for Progresso. Progresso's first national television advertising campaign was unveiled in the fall of 1991. D'Arcy Masius Benton & Bowles had the Progresso soup account as well as many other of Pet's brands by mid-1991. Progresso's first network television campaign, unfortunately, could not help slumping sales of soups, which suffered in part because of the unusually mild weather in the winter of 1991-92. During 1991 Progresso's market share dropped several percentage points.

Pet invested a total of $43 million in media advertising in fiscal 1992. Much of this was spent on Progresso as well as on the Old El Paso and Van de Kamp's brands. The company also increased its consumer marketing by 24 percent, spending $93 million in fiscal 1992. The effective marketing program helped Progresso's market share to stabilize in 1992. An aggressive campaign featured everyday people doing taste comparisons. Progresso soups were preferred by testers because of their good taste. The advertisements emphasized the great taste and healthy content of Progresso soups. In fact, 82 percent of Progresso soups qualified for low-fat and low-cholesterol designations. New labeling on the soup cans highlighted low levels of both cholesterol and sodium.

Below-average temperatures helped soup sales in late 1992, and a 7 percent price increase over the previous year aided Progresso's profits. In September 1992, when the campaign began, sales were up 10 percent over September 1991. The cool, wet weather also contributed to the increase, however, and Pet's competitors also showed improved numbers for the same period.

New Products

In early 1991, before it came out with Healthy Classics, Pet had tested Progresso Sodium Watch, a lower-sodium version of its soups. The five varieties contained about 250 to 330 milligrams of sodium per serving, which was about half the amount in their regular soups. Healthy Classics have more sodium than the early Sodium Watch soups, but still one third less than regular Progresso soups. The five varieties of Sodium Watch, all packaged in single-serving 10.5 ounce cans, were test marketed in Arizona and Florida, and were supported by advertising separate from that for their regular soups. Waring & LaRosa of New York was the advertising agency handling Progresso soups at the time.

Progresso sales were hurt in 1991 to 1992 while Campbell and ConAgra introduced "healthy" soups. ConAgra had been testing its Healthy Choice soups at the same time as Pet was working on Progresso Sodium Watch. Healthy Choice, Campbell's Healthy Request, and Pritikin soups were all introduced in September 1991. These featured less sodium and less fat per serving. Pritikin had the lowest fat and sodium content of the three.

In 1993 Pet introduced Progresso Healthy Classics soups. They were available only in 16 ounce cans—a size between the sizes of regular Progresso soups. The labels featured the familiar Progresso logo with a picture of the enclosed soup. A bright yellow flag on the label trumpeted the low number of calories, the percentage per serving that was fat free, and the presence of low cholesterol and low sodium.

Personalities that Influenced Progresso

Beginning with the Taormina and Uddo families, there have been many people who have shaped the success of Progresso soups. Gasper Taormina, who first worked at Progresso's Vineland plant at the age of 10, rose to become secretary/treasurer, vice president for finance, and later president of Progresso. His father had been plant manager in Vineland when Gasper was a child. Gasper, an avid cook, was quoted in a company profile explaining his philosophy, which illustrates much of Progresso's success. He said that Americans are rediscovering home cooking, and "when the recipe is to be Italian, they want the real thing."

More recently, Miles Marsh has guided Progresso through some major changes. The South African-born executive had spent five years at McKinsey & Co., a consulting company, and eight years at Kraft, remaining after Kraft was purchased by General Foods. In 1989 he joined Whitman Corporation and in 1991, with the spinoff of Pet from Whitman, Marsh became Pet's chairman and chief executive officer. With a Ph.D. in finance from Northwestern University, Marsh was well respected in the industry.

In 1993 Francis Florido, group vice president of Progresso, began reporting to Marsh on the ups and downs of Progresso soups. Florido joined Pet in 1992 as vice president of corporate marketing and strategy. Preceding Florido was Raymond N. Felitto, who resigned in 1993 following a consolidation of group and division layers and a restructuring to focus on Pet's core businesses, including Progresso.

Technological and Ecological Improvements

Pet centralized its purchasing operations in fiscal 1992. Until then, each of the three Progresso soup plants had different soup can specifications, and different suppliers. The company called for competitive bids and standardized can specifications. Pet saved an estimated $2 million for the year on soup cans alone.

The company was intent on improving its conservation efforts. In the Vineland plant, a team of Progresso employees found that more than 400 gallons of water were being discarded in the preparation of each batch of vegetables for canning. By recalibrating pumps, installing signal lights, and rerouting process water, Pet estimated it saved more than six million gallons of water annually. Costs were also reduced by more than $17,000.

Pet introduced a computerized shipping system at several of its locations. The Progresso plant in Vineland, New Jersey was one of the first to have its trucking operations simplified, thereby improving productivity and lowering costs. It enabled the company to evaluate the performance of some of its carriers, and also to respond to customer inquiries more quickly. The shipment management software of Optimal Decision System used a network linking customers, carriers, and the processor. Using the software,

Pet was able to schedule truckloads of Progresso soup and other products so that smaller orders were combined for single deliveries.

With Marsh at the helm of Pet, and Progresso soups still commanding a large market share, the outlook was bright in the early 1990s. By introducing its new healthier varieties of soup, Pet showed an ability to accommodate the needs of its customers. The company's emphasis on natural, healthy ingredients for its soups, and great taste, seemed to fit easily with the changing American palate.

Further Reading:

Belsky, Gary, "How Investors Can Put a Fresh Spin on Profits," *Money,* October 1991, p. 78.

Brunelli, Richard, "Pet Drops Buying Shop," *Mediaweek,* May 6, 1991, p. 3.

Desloge, Rick, "Esco, Venture, Spun Off by Parent Firms; Pet to Follow," *St. Louis Business Journal,* December 24, 1990, p. 6A.

Desloge, Rick, "Pet's Top Five Earn $1.8 Million in '90," *St. Louis Business Journal,* March 25, 1991, p. 1A.

Desloge, Rick, "Pet Takes on General Foods Air," *St. Louis Business Journal,* January 21, 1991, p. 1A.

"Dividend Linked to Pet Inc. Spinoff," *The New York Times,* March 16, 1991, pp. 1, 33.

"Felitto Heads Pet USA," *Advertising Age,* September 21, 1992, p. 40.

Lubove, Seth, "On Their Own," *Forbes,* March 16, 1992, pp. 68-69.

"Pet Appoints Felitto to Post of President at Pet USA," *The Wall Street Journal,* September 16, 1992, p. B7.

"Pet Inc. Grocery Unit's Head Quits in Shake-Up," *The Wall Street Journal,* July 8, 1992, p. B6.

Pet Incorporated Annual Report, St. Louis: Pet Incorporated, 1992.

Pet Incorporated Brands & Businesses, St. Louis: Pet Incorporated, September, 1992.

Pet Incorporated Highlights, St. Louis: Pet Incorporated.

"Pet Plans to Divest Itself of Whitman's Chocolate," *The New York Times,* June 20, 1992, pp. 1, 37.

"Pet Testing Low-salt Soups," *Advertising Age,* January 7, 1991, p. 38.

"Pet to sell Whitman's Chocolates Unit as New Managers Fail to Revive Line," *Wall Street Journal,* June 22, 1992, p. B3.

Progresso: Historical Overview, St. Louis: Pet Incorporated, February 1987.

Progresso Soup Item Portfolio, St. Louis: Pet Incorporated, February 4, 1993.

Tribole, Evelyn, "Which Soups Are Best?" *Consumers Digest,* January/February 1992, pp. 71-73.

Willis, Clint, "Board These Stocks at the Bottom and Soar 14% to 65%," *Money,* October 1992, pp. 83, 91.

—Francine Shonfeld Sherman

PURINA® PET CHOW®

Purina Dog Chow and Purina Cat Chow are the leading pet foods in America. For almost a century, the Ralston Purina Company has made itself known as a leader in nutritional research in the area of feeds for a variety of animals, ranging from hogs to wild birds to laboratory cockroaches, as well as marketing such other grocery items as Chex cereal, Hostess cupcakes, and Energizer batteries. The Ralston Purina Company has led the industry in nutritional research and has remained consistently at the head of the pack due to both its research and aggressive marketing.

Dog Chow Origins

The Ralston Purina Company had been already well known as a producer of feed for farm animals and breakfast cereals when it introduced Purina Dog Chow in 1957, having begun test-marketing the product in 1954. It committed a great deal of research and advertising to this venture, which were to pay off with a handsome market share from the product's first months.

The famous checkerboard logo had been with Ralston Purina since 1900. William H. Danforth, the company's head, got the idea for this device from a family in St. Louis, whose economical mother had outfitted them in red and white checks, making the children easily identifiable. Danforth wanted his products to stand out, so this struck him as an appropriate—not to mention wholesome—symbol. He settled on the term "chow" after visiting U.S. Army troops in France during World War I and hearing them use the word as a term of endearment for victuals. Danforth henceforth used the name "Chow" to apply to all of his company's feeds.

Six hundred dogs from 30 different breeds were involved in Purina's five-year research for its Dog Chow. Although Purina had fed farmers' dogs since the 1930s and once even supplied food for Admiral Richard E. Bird's huskies, it found the household pet to be more finicky. However, in part due to the increasing predominance of packaged foods on the dinner table, these dogs were less likely to get table scraps than farm dogs.

The size of the market was very attractive to Purina. In 1960 there were about 25 million dogs in America, as well as 22 million cats, which together consumed about a $500 million worth of food—more food, dollar-wise, than was consumed by babies that year. Since World War II, sales had increased 5 percent per year; during the 1960s, that growth rate would double. The number of pets grew as the dog came to be associated with the suburban family ideal—a house, two kids, and a dog. By 1964 the dog food market would be worth an estimated $415 million. And in bigger cities, people acquired dogs for protection as well as for emotional reasons. By 1970 32.6 million dogs were kept in the United States as pets.

Using a new process of extrusion developed by mechanical engineer Douglas Hale, Purina created its new Dog Chow in the form of puffed biscuits, which were less messy and cheaper than canned dog foods such as Alpo. The Purina recipe, of which over 100 variants were tested, included cereal grains, meat, bone meal, and vitamins and minerals.

In order to introduce consumers to the new product, Purina put an unprecedented $3 million into advertising supporting the introduction of Dog Chow, which featured the slogan, "Is your dog an eager eater?" It offered 18 million coupons and redeemed 3 million of these for free bags of Dog Chow.

Within fifteen months, the brand led the dog food category with an estimated 20 percent market share. In two years, that increased to 30 percent. This success came at the expense of General Foods, which had owned the Gaines brand of dog food since 1943. Purina Dog Chow cut into about half of its business, which would return to Gaines only after the product launches—supplemented by millions of dollars in advertising—of its Gravy Train dog food, a dry dog food that "makes its own gravy" when water is added, and later, its Gainesburgers, a moist dog food product.

The other major leader was Ken-L Ration, owned by Quaker Oats since 1942. This brand had approximately a 15 percent share of the canned market in 1960. Approximately 3,000 other regional brands included leaders Rival in the East, Jim Dandy in the South, and Skippy and Kal Kan in the West.

One regional supermarket chain reported carrying 32 different brands of pet food in 1962. However, Purina's largest rival was perhaps the owner who fed his pet table scraps. It was estimated in 1965 that the pet food market had a potential of being worth over $1 billion a year if owners didn't feed pets scraps. In 1970 it was estimated that less than half the cats and dogs in America were fed prepared pet foods, though the size of the market had doubled in five years to $1.4 billion per year.

Since 1950, the Quaker Oats Company had owned the leading brand of cat food, Puss 'N Boots, which had an estimated 70 percent market share. Purina entered the $100 million cat food market in 1962 with its Cat Chow, which it began testing in 1960, using a strategy similar to that used in its debut of Dog Chow. It offered millions of coupons and supported the product launch with millions of dollars worth of advertising.

Purina claimed to have attained a 17 percent market share with Cat Chow within a year after it was introduced nationally. However, Quaker retained its lead in combined dog and cat food sales into the 1960s. By 1965 it was estimated that General Foods led the field with combined sales of $80 million per year, with Ralston Purina following at $50 to $60 million, and Quaker not far behind that. Ralston Purina's total sales in 1964 were $864.8 million, compared to $585 million in 1960. Earnings were $24.3 million. In 1966, Ralston Purina's total sales reached $1.5 billion, with profits of $44.9 million. In 1970 the company's pet food sales were $290 million, accounting for 17 percent of total sales and $22 million, or 40 percent, of the company's profits.

Dry, Moist, Semi-Moist

The industry branched out into new directions from the basic dry and canned dog and cat foods. Gravy Train, by General Foods,

AT A GLANCE

Purina brand founded in 1902 in St. Louis, MO, by Robinson-Danforth Commission Company founder William Danforth in association with Dr. Albert Webster Edgerly (a.k.a. "Dr. Ralston"); Purina Dog Chow introduced in 1957, and Purina Cat Chow in 1960.

Performance: *Market share*—25.8% (top share) of pet food category. *Sales*—$283.8 million.

Major competitor: Nestlé's Friskies Pet Care; also Mars's Kal Kan.

Advertising: *Agency*—Centra Advertising, St. Louis, MO. *Major campaign*—Actor Robert Urich and golden retriever with slogan, "O.N.E.—Second to none."

Addresses: *Parent company*—Ralston Purina Company, Checkerboard Square, St. Louis, Missouri 63164; phone: (314) 982-1000; fax: (314) 982-2752.

was a dry dog food which made a gravy sauce upon adding water. In 1962 Rival introduced a similar food for cats called Mil-Kit, a dry food which made a milk sauce. Purina brought out its own variations on this theme with its Gravy Dinner and its Dairy Dinner, both for cats. In 1987 it introduced the dog food Grrravy: "The name says it all."

Moist dog foods were introduced by General Mills, with its Speak brand, and Gaines, with Gainesburgers. Both of these products required no refrigeration. Speak was packaged in six disposable feeding dishes per pack. Gainesburgers were shaped like hamburger patties and individually sealed in plastic.

In 1970 Ralston Purina introduced Tender Vittles, the first semi-moist cat food, which Robert K. Mohrman spent four years developing for the company. The product was packaged in airtight foil, came in four flavors, and sold for quite a bit more than dry food—39 cents for six ounces, compared to 49 cents for 22 ounces of dry cat food. The company diversified this product somewhat with its Choice Morsels, introduced in 1974.

Ralston Purina made a direct attack on the successful Alpo line of canned dog foods in 1972. In newspaper ads, it compared Alpo to a new high-protein dry dog food called Purina High-Protein Dog Meal, which the advertisements featured as having twice the protein and being half the price of Alpo. Purina had a canned dog food in the 1950s and introduced a mid-priced canned cat food, Lovin' Spoonfuls, in 1974.

Eventually, dog snacks appeared in such forms as Doggie Donuts and People Crackers, a play on animal crackers shaped like postmen and dogcatchers. Purina challenged Milk-Bone's domination of the category with Bonz, a snack shaped like a meat-filled bone, and Purina Biscuits. In 1990 the dog snacks market was worth $500 million.

Flavor Variation

Much of the variation in new products came in flavor, especially in cat foods, since it was perceived that cats needed variety in their dinners. Quaker Oats' cat foods included such flavors as chicken parts in liver. Carnation offered moist cat food in flavors including turkey with bacon. In 1967, Purina introduced a new canned cat food in seven flavors, one for every day of the week:

chicken and tuna liver, mackerel, liver and tuna, beef by-products, chicken and kidney, and country dinner with fish, chicken, and liver. The cans were labeled with the numbers one through seven to reinforce the point. Later that year, in a development a Purina representative called "flattering but disconcerting," Puss 'n Boots offered seven flavors in numbered cans, calling them the "seven wonders of the cat world."

Dogs had their day, too. Alpo offered a great variety of flavors in its canned products, including Meat Balls with Gravy and Eggs 'n Beef. A small "gourmet" brand, Voila, offered Burgundy Beef in Gravy. The Purina Dog Chow line came to include such flavor extensions as Butcher's Blend and Homestyle Blend. Flavoring ingredients common to almost all the foods were garlic and onions, flavors said to encourage dogs to eat almost anything.

Price

The many varieties in pet foods have spanned a wide range of prices. Purina's chows entered the market at the low end of the spectrum. Voila was successful in the gourmet "specialty" market of dog foods. In 1968 a 6 1/2 ounce can of Voila sold for 39 cents; a 14 1/2 ounce can of regular dog food sold for 6 to 17 cents. Alpo marketed cans of veal and lamb for approximately 30 cents per 14 1/2 ounce can.

In 1988 Purina introduced its O.N.E. (Optimum Nutritional Effectiveness) dog food, which by 1992 it had expanded from two to 17 items covering cats and different aged pets. This was a superpremium line expanded to challenge the successful brands sold outside the supermarket. By 1992 the O.N.E. line was bringing in $67 million a year for Purina.

Lean and Green

The 1970s saw the creation of new categories of pet food, mostly concepts borrowed from people food marketing. The Ralston Purina Company created a diet dry dog food called Fit & Trim in 1976, apparently in response to General Foods Cycle concept: four different canned foods for different growth stages in a dog's life. Cycle 3 was for older, less active, potentially overweight dogs. As with other Purina launches, the launch of Fit & Trim was preceded by extensive marketing research and accompanied by discount coupons and heavy advertising. Purina has also offered Tender Vittles semi-moist cat food in a diet version. In 1990 Cat Chow Mature debuted, "specially formulated for mature cats."

In 1980 Purina specifically targeted large breeds of dogs with its Hero brand. Nature's Course, an organic dog food packaged in recycled paper boxes, was introduced by Purina in 1991. Made from grains grown without pesticides, the product boasted having no artificial colors or flavors.

Marketing Pet Foods

After Purina entered the pet food arena, the business became very competitive, requiring contenders to back the many new products they introduced with millions of dollars in advertising in order to gain shelf space. A seemingly integral part of promoting the new foods was the dissemination of stories demonstrating the acceptability of the product to human palates. When Purina Dog Chow was introduced, it was reportedly consumed with gusto by an unknowing industry insider who mistook it for a breakfast food. The moist dog food Speak, put out by the unsuccessful General Mills, was reportedly successful as an undercover hors d'oeuvre.

Another typical feature of Ralston Purina advertising was the coupon. New Purina products were typically accompanied by either coupons for a free sample, as with the original Dog Chow, or, more typically, for a discount off the purchase price. In 1979 the company for the first time coordinated coupons for all of its pet food products in its "Circus of Savings" promotion.

In the 1980s new channels of distribution developed for pet food sales besides the grocery store. Pet shops and veterinary clinics were targeted for Purina's Pro Plan line of pet foods not sold in supermarkets. By 1991 these alternative vendors were worth $1.1 billion dollars a year in pet food sales. In 1990 Purina challenged Hill's Prescription Diet, a "prescription" dog food sold only through vets, with its Clinical Nutrition Management brand.

Packaging

Ralston Purina has been on top of the packaging scene, too. While other brands risked alienating possible buyers by illustrating their packages with pictures of a single breed, Purina Dog Chow packaging featured fifteen different dogs. Gaines presented the ideal dog, Rin-Tin-Tin, on its packages. Lassie sponsored a Campbell Soup Company entry. Eventually Purina, too, featured a celebrity endorsement: the dog film star Benji sponsored Benji's Moist 'n Chunky, Purina's renamed soft-dry dog food, in 1987. Ibco Products tried the cartoon dog Snoopy on its entry, which was unsuccessful.

Ralston Purina introduced innovative packaging for its Deli-Cat premium cat food in 1990. The product was packaged in 18-ounce and 3 1/2–pound recyclable and reusable transparent plastic jugs. It also has offered its Cat Chow in a self-feeder and its Happy Cat in resealable cardboard cartons.

Strategies in Advertising

Purina used a two-pronged approach to winning the heart of the pet food buyer. Purina eventually developed the slogan "All you add is love," addressing both the emotional and nutritional factors involved in purchasing dog food. In the 1980s, Ralston Purina benefited from reports that owning a pet is beneficial to one's mental and physical well-being, lowering one's blood pressure, for example.

From the very beginning, Purina emphasized the nutritional value of its products. However, this brought the company some trouble when in 1986 the company was sued by competitors over claims that its puppy foods could reduce the severity of the crippling disease canine hip dysplasia. Ralston agreed to remove the claims from its advertising without admitting wrongdoing. However, in 1991 the company was ordered to pay Alpo $12 million to reimburse it for response advertising, lost revenue, and other damages to its puppy food marketing effort.

An innovation Ralston Purina introduced in dog food advertising was the use of "scratch 'n sniff" in its advertising for its relaunch of Butcher's Blend in 1987. 1989 saw another advertising first, when the Energizer bunny, the tireless battery mascot known for its appearances in parodies of tiresome television commercial genres, marched across a Purina Cat Chow spot revived from the early 1980s. The well-known commercials featured a woman singing and dancing the "chow chow chow" with her cat. A Purina mascot made a guest appearance of its own when

Ike, the Lucky Dog, appeared on The Family Channel's "Maniac Mansion" series in 1991 as part of a joint promotion deal.

Ralston Purina has also gotten involved in improving community relations for dogs. In 1965, the company distributed millions of brochures containing tips on training dogs to behave properly in the suburbs. Of course, the brochures also included ideas on what to feed these dogs—i.e., Purina Dog Chow. Later, through the Pets For People Program, Purina has provided senior citizens with free pets from animal shelters. In the 1990s, the company set aside funds from its cat foods to support the Purina Big Cat Survival Fund, which funds efforts in breeding endangered species through zoos.

Performance and Predictions

Ralston Purina had the top share of the $7.5 billion pet food market in 1990 with a market share of 25.8 percent, down from 27 percent the previous year. Dog Chow was the top selling dry dog food, with sales of $257 million, followed by Puppy Chow at $155 million and competitor Alpo's Regular Dinner at $110 million. Kal Kan Pedigree was the top-selling canned food with $265 million in sales. Purina also had the top-selling dry cat food, Purina Cat Chow, which sold $145.6 million. Carnation's Friskies was second at $114.9 million in sales. Purina also led the moist cat food category with its Tender Vittles, worth $98.5 million in sales.

Ralston Purina's International expanded operations in 1992, entering new markets in China, the Philippines, and Thailand. The company now sells its products in more than fifty countries. Its international pet food sales have increased at a compound rate of fifteen percent since 1987. With its continued success in pet foods and grocery products in expanding markets, the Ralston Purina Company appears poised to have another profitable century.

Further Reading:

Austin, Beth, "Dog Days of Summer: Purina Beefs Lineup to Remain Top Dog," *Advertising Age,* August 31, 1987, p. 12.

"Back Up Ad Claims, FTC Tells a Dozen Makers of Pet Foods," *Wall Street Journal,* November 27, 1972, p. 4.

"Catering to the Cats and Dogs," *Business Week,* November 9, 1961, pp. 64-68.

Colford, Stephen W., "Thomas Ruling Shows Support of Advertising," *Advertising Age,* July 8, 1991, p. 4.

Colford, Stephen W., "$12 Million Bite: Purina Hit In Latest False-Ad Ruling," *Advertising Age,* December 2, 1991, p. 4.

"Did AT&T Mailing Reach Out Too Far? One of Five to Modify After NAD Review," *Advertising Age,* December 15, 1986, p. 12.

"Dogs Are More Reliable Than People," *Forbes,* July 1, 1964, pp. 15-16.

"Dry Cat Food Field Attracts New Activity," *Advertising Age,* February 10, 1975, p. 8.

Edwards, Larry, "Purina Eyeing Position in Expanding Cat Litter Area," *Advertising Age,* April 3, 1978, p. 2.

Edwards, Larry, "Purina Sets 'Major' New Dog Food," *Advertising Age,* August 13, 1979, pp. 1, 77.

Edwards, Larry, "Purina To Originate New Pat Category—Low-Calorie Dog Food," *Advertising Age,* September 27, 1976, pp. 1, 79.

Edwards, Larry, "Spoonfuls National Roll Tops Purina Pet Parade; See 20% Ad Budget Hike," *Advertising Age,* April 29, 1974, pp. 1, 80.

Fahey, Alison, "Dogged Determination: Ralston, Cable Net Make 'Value-Added' Come to Life," *Advertising Age,* July 22, 1991, p. S-22.

"Fido and His Friends," *Barron's,* March 22, 1965, pp. 11, 24-27.

Garino, David P., "Sales of Pet Food Boom as Ads Emphasize Human Traits and Push "Gourmet" Treats," *Wall Street Journal,* April 19, 1971, p. 36.

Kreisman, Richard, "Dog Snacks Tempt Majors," *Advertising Age,* September 8, 1980, pp. 3, 79.

"Last Minute News," *Advertising Age,* January 21, 1991, p. 8.

Liesse, Julie, "Purina Bites Back Into Pet Food," *Advertising Age,* April 20, 1992, p. 45, 48.

Liesse, Julie, "A Clear Advantage? New Deli-Cat Comes in Plastic Jugs," *Advertising Age,* March 12, 1990, p. 75.

Liesse, Julie, "Purina Dishes Up Organic Dog Food," *Advertising Age,* January 28, 1991, p. 30.

Liesse, Julie, "Purina's Latest Target Is 'Mature' Cats," *Advertising Age,* June 18, 1990, p. 81.

Liesse, Julie, "Purina O.N.E.," *Advertising Age,* July 6, 1992, p. S-23.

Liesse, Julie, and Judann Dagnoli, "Gnawing Milk-Bone: Purina, Heinz Nip at Leader's Share," *Advertising Age,* April 2, 1990, p. 40.

Liesse, Julie, and Bradley Johnson, "New Pet Food Scrap In Supermarkets: Purina, Kal Kan, Quaker Try High-Price Lines," *Advertising Age,* January 28, 1991, p. 3.

Maidenberg, H. J., "Ralston Has Outgrown Tom Mix," *New York Times,* March 12, 1967, p. 1.

Margulies, Walter P., "Packaging Plays an Important Part in New Pet Food Boom," *Advertising Age,* December 14, 1970, pp. 43-53.

"Marketing Briefs," *Business Week,* December 4, 1966, p. 66.

Maxwell, John C., Jr., "Lucky Dogs: They, At Least, Are Eating Better Than Ever These Days," *Barron's,* April 9, 1973, pp. 11, 20.

Maxwell, John C., Jr., "Pet-Food Sales Up Slightly," *Advertising Age,* June 26, 1989, pp. 43, 53.

Maxwell, John C., Jr., "Specialty Shops Spice Up Sales For Pet Foods," *Advertising Age,* September 25, 1991, p. 59.

Maxwell, John C., Jr., "Pet Food '78 Growth," *Advertising Age,* June 18, 1979, p. 39.

"One of the Family," *Barron's,* March 3, 1969, pp. 11-29.

"The Pet Food Business: A Revealing Scoreboard," *Barron's,* March 8, 1971, pp. 13, 22.

"Purina Ads Compare New Dry Dog Food With Alpo," *Advertising Age,* October 2, 1972, p. 10.

"Purina Sets $25 Million for Hero," *Advertising Age,* July 21, 1980, pp. 2, 86.

"Purina Sets 'Circus of Savings' For Cat Food," *Advertising Age,* June 25, 1979, p. 6.

"Ralston Broadens Distribution of Its 7-Day Feline Menu," *Advertising Age,* September 25, 1967, p. 42.

Ralston Purina Company Annual Report, St. Louis: Ralston Purina Company, 1992.

"Ralston Tests Tender Vittles For Fussy Cats," *Advertising Age,* August 17, 1970, p. 3.

"Ralston Ties on a Bigger Feedbag," *Business Week,* December 3, 1966, pp. 77-82.

Sederberg, Kathryn, "In-House Stretches Ralston Media Dollars," *Advertising Age,* October 8, 1979, pp. S20-22.

"Success Story," *Forbes,* August 1, 1968, pp. 23-25.

Tracy, Eleanor Johnson, "Lush Times For the Pet-Food Producers," *Fortune,* December, 1971, pp. 110-113, 172-177.

"We Had Number Idea For Cat Food First," *Advertising Age,* October 23, 1967, p. 6.

"100 Leading National Advertisers," *Advertising Age,* September 25, 1992, p. 59.

—*Frederick Ingram*

QUAKER® OATS OATMEAL

The Quaker Oats brand of oatmeal, in its original rolled oats formula, quick cooking style, and flavored instant varieties, is the top-selling hot cereal in the United States. Packaged in the trademark red, blue, and yellow cylindrical carton brandishing a stout man in Quaker clothing, Quaker oatmeal has been offering purity and basic nutrition to consumers for more than a century. Oats have gone from merely inexpensive feed for livestock in the mid-nineteenth century to the trendy food of the late 1980s, when studies indicated that eating oat bran reduces cholesterol levels in humans. While consumer interest in hot cereals has waned during the early 1990s, Quaker has consistently out-muscled would-be competitors in the hot cereal market. Just one product put out by The Quaker Oats Company, which also manufacturers such other popular brands as Aunt Jemima breakfast foods, Gatorade thirst quencher, and Cycle dog food, Quaker Oats oatmeal has remained a market share leader due to years of quality assurance and innovative advertising.

Brand Origins

The Quaker brand was created in 1877, when four men organized the Quaker Mill Company in Ravenna, Ohio, and registered Quaker's famous trademark, the "figure of a man in Quaker garb." According to one story, Henry O. Seymour, one of the four partners, chose the Quaker name after perusing an encyclopedia for trademark ideas and being struck by the entry on Quakers, which described "the purity of the lives of the people, their sterling honesty, their strength and manliness"; Seymour thought these attributes neatly paralleled the qualities necessary for a new business. But William Heston, another of the partners, also claimed credit for the Quaker name. Heston said that he was prompted by a picture of William Penn he saw while walking one day in Cincinnati. Although Seymour is usually given credit for the inspiration, Heston, a Quaker himself, cannot be totally discounted.

Whatever the origins of the name, the Quaker Mill failed to thrive, and in 1881 Henry Parsons Crowell bought it for a small sum. Crowell was an energetic and talented businessperson. In the course of only ten years, he turned the $25,000 Quaker Mill into a $500,000 business. But Quaker was still dwarfed by the operations of Ferdinand Schumacher in nearby Akron, Ohio. Schumacher was known as the Oatmeal King, not only because he was the nation's largest oatmeal miller but because he quite literally cre-

ated the oatmeal industry in America. When Schumacher, a German immigrant, entered the grocery business in Akron in 1884, he noticed that one item he had known in Germany was missing in American stores: oatmeal. Oats were widely grown in America but used primarily as an animal feed; humans ate the grain only as a thin gruel for invalids.

Early Marketing Strategy

Schumacher decided to offer hand-milled oats in his store as an experiment. His oatmeal became popular so quickly that in 1856 he entered the oatmeal business full time. By the 1880s Schumacher was selling his oats throughout Ohio, as far east as New York and Philadelphia, and as far west as Denver, Colorado—wherever a concentration of German, Scottish, or Irish immigrants created a market. Oatmeal's popularity among these immigrants, who were accustomed to eating oats in their native countries, took quite some time to spread through American society. Jokes about oatmeal-eaters stealing from horses or whinnying abounded for many years. But oatmeal's status gradually rose as its virtues as an inexpensive and nutritious food became better known.

The introduction of rolled oats in the early 1880s also helped to popularize oatmeal. Before that time oats were ground or cut into a coarse meal that required long and careful cooking. The rolling process dramatically shortened the cooking time required to prepare oatmeal (from three or four hours down to one) and greatly improved the cereal's taste and texture. Rolled oats quickly became the staple of the industry. Since then, the only marked improvements in oatmeal have been further reductions in cooking time.

The growing popularity of the cereal led many a miller into oatmeal, and soon the industry was overcrowded. Prices fluctuated wildly. To solve this problem, Crowell and Robert Stuart, who ran another very large milling operation in Cedar Rapids, Iowa, and Chicago, Illinois, formed the Oatmeal Millers Association in 1885. This association, organized only five years before the Sherman Antitrust Act was passed, aimed to regulate the price of oats and improve profits, and most millers readily joined—but not Schumacher, who considered it a waste of time. Without Schumacher, the association lacked sufficient clout, and its price structure soon collapsed.

AT A GLANCE

Quaker Oats brand of oatmeal founded in 1877 in Ravenna, OH, by Quaker Mill Company owners, including Henry O. Seymour and William Heston; later developers include American Cereal Company operators Henry Parsons Crowell, Ferdinand Schumacher, and Robert Stuart; American Cereal Company renamed The Quaker Oats Company, 1901.

Performance: *Market share*—63% (top share) of hot cereal category. *Sales*—$378.2 million.

Major competitor: Nabisco Foods Group's Cream of Wheat.

Advertising: *Agency*—Jordan, McGrath, Case & Taylor, New York, NY. *Major campaign*—Veteran actor Wilford Brimley proclaiming, "Every day should feel this good."

Addresses: *Parent company*—The Quaker Oats Company, P.O. Box 9003, Chicago, IL 60604-9003; phone: (312) 222-7843.

But when a fire destroyed Schumacher's mills the next year, his situation changed considerably, and he joined forces with Crowell and Stuart. Their next two attempts at organizing the industry also failed, but in 1888 seven major oatmeal millers, including Schumacher, Stuart, and Crowell, joined together to form the American Cereal Company. When that company was reorganized in 1891, a stable entity finally emerged. American Cereal, renamed The Quaker Oats Company in 1901, has survived now for a full century. Schumacher, Crowell, and Stuart were the leaders of American Cereal. Unfortunately, however, Schumacher, a stern and autocratic leader, did not take kindly to sharing power and thought little of his younger partners and their newfangled ideas. The struggle between the two factions continued until 1899, when Crowell and Stuart ousted Schumacher and won complete control of the company. Under them, the company began a twenty-year growth streak.

Quality Assurance in Packaging

One of the company's most important assets was the Quaker reputation. First and foremost, this was a reputation for purity—the original "man in Quaker garb" even held a scroll with the word "pure" written on it. Quaker's claim to purity lay in a radical innovation: its oats were sold in cardboard packages. In the late nineteenth century oats (and many other products) were generally sold out of open barrels from which a grocer scooped customers' purchases on request. There were no brands: oats were oats, flour was flour, crackers were crackers. Grocers bought their goods according to price, and customers bought whatever their grocer stocked. Under this system, neither the customer nor the manufacturer had any control over quality. Oats might leave the mill clean and pure, but Quaker salespeople cited spectacular examples of the unsanitary treatment of bulk oats after that: grocers who sat on oats and trimmed their nails, adding the nails to the oats; cats who regularly napped in open sacks of oats; oats that were spilled into the street and swept up to be sold, dirt and all; even rat traps set on top of open oat barrels, the better to bait the rats with. Prepackaged Quaker oats held a distinct advantage in cleanliness.

But packaging oats held other advantages, too. The package itself could attract customers. Crowell designed Quaker's famous red, yellow, and blue packages soon after the 1891 reorganization

of the American Cereal Company. In 1893 the original black-suited and somber "man in Quaker garb" acquired a round belly and a smile, and, thanks to color printing, a blue coat, red vest, and gold buckles on his shoes. The bright colors and cheerful "Quaker Man" helped to catch shoppers' eyes and made it expensive for competitors to imitate Quaker. The original package was rectangular (unfolded, it passed easily through a printing press), but Quaker's distinctive round canister was in use by 1915. In addition, the package itself was an opportunity to make direct sales pitches to the customer. Quaker packages were printed with paeans to the nutritiousness and purity of the product. They also carried cooking directions to lure customers who were unfamiliar with oatmeal.

Advertising Innovations

Quaker's most important innovation, however, was not packaging but advertising. Crowell was a fervent believer in advertising at a time when it had such a bad reputation that many banks wouldn't lend to companies that advertised. Overt sales pitches were associated with quacks and fakes. Undeterred, Crowell set out to make Quaker Oats the first nationally—and internationally—advertised food brand. His strategy was to bypass the grocer, who only cared about his profit, and appeal directly to consumers, who cared about quality and could be impressed by advertising claims.

Name recognition was the first essential element of Quaker's strategy. The company plastered its name on buildings, billboards, streetcars—even, in 1897, on England's famous white cliffs of Dover. When Quaker's British sales agent placed a sign there so large that it could be read by ships three miles at sea, he generated an instant public outcry in England—but also several weeks of invaluable publicity for Quaker before the British House of Commons finally ordered the sign removed.

When introducing the Quaker brand to a new area, Quaker often blanketed a city with free samples. These half-ounce samples were packed in replicas of the standard Quaker Oats package, helping to connect the free sample with the product that shoppers would see on the grocery shelf. One of the most famous examples of this strategy was the introduction of Quaker Oats to the Northwest in 1891. Crowell first supplied the city of Portland, Oregon, with samples and then rushed a highly publicized special train to the city to answer the "sudden" demand for Quaker Oats. It was a carefully orchestrated performance: the train stopped in town after town along the way to distribute free samples and stage a little production.

But awareness of the Quaker brand was only the first step. Puzzles, rhymes, comic books, and endorsements from stars like Babe Ruth and Roy Rogers appealed to children, while premiums packed into the oatmeal itself or available for "proofs of purchase" (in the early days, the Quaker man cut out of the package) attracted parents. The earliest of these prizes were pieces of china and silverware packed into the oatmeal package. It was no accident, of course, that it was necessary to eat great quantities of oats to acquire an appreciable silverware or china collection. Other premiums packed right into the oats included coupons, novelty rings for children, and kitchen gadgets. Some of the most popular "box top" premiums (ones that required proofs of purchase and usually a small sum of money) included a double boiler (for cooking oats, of course), offered in 1915; a radio set that mounted on a Quaker Oats canister, offered in 1921; and a Lionel train set, offered at Christmastime in 1961. In time, radio and television advertisements augmented Quaker's original newspaper and magazine campaigns. For example, Roy Rogers sang to children that Quaker Oats, "the giant of cereals," was "delicious, nutritious, makes you feel ambitious" on radio shows sponsored by Quaker.

Health Claims in Advertising

Quaker further sought to convince consumers to increase their oat consumption—specifically their Quaker oat consumption—by attaching health benefits to eating the hot cereal. Health claims were one of Quaker's earliest strategies, and they have remained the backbone of the company's advertising ever since. An advertisement on the back cover of the *Saturday Evening Post* in 1899 admonished, "How foolish to keep on eating meat to the exclusion of Quaker Oats when dietary experts agree that Quaker Oats is more nourishing and wholesome." In the 1930s the discovery that oats were a good source of vitamin B-1 sent Quaker's sales soaring 35 percent. A half a century later, studies reporting that oat bran could lower cholesterol levels boosted sales 23 percent between 1987 and 1988, and up a further 15 percent in 1989. Suddenly "the lowly oat has become *haute,*" asserted Annetta Miller in *Newsweek*. "Health-conscious consumers are rushing to buy oatmeal." Signing on veteran actor Wilford Brimley as spokesperson in its famous "It's the right thing to do" advertising campaign, Quaker ran ads featuring Brimley also saying, "It's right for your heart. Right for your blood. Right for a lot of things." "It's a product, suggests the commercial, that can not only make people happy, healthy and regular, but improve their moral fiber, too," Miller said of the award-winning advertisement. The commercial's tag line was later changed to "Every day should feel this good."

But The Quaker Oats Company ran into some opposition when nutritionists and consumer activists challenged Quaker's health claims. In 1988 a task force of attorneys general from several states attacked the company's assertion that, as part of a low-fat, low-cholesterol diet, oats help reduce serum cholesterol levels an average of 10 percent and in some cases as much as 20 percent. The state of Texas later sued Quaker, accusing the company of leading, as quoted by *Business Week,* "a campaign of deception." Striking another blow to Quaker's advertising claims was a 1990 study published in the New England Journal of Medicine determining that oat bran has little specific cholesterol-lowering effect.

In the midst of the controversy, Quaker has responded by both admitting, according to Janet Key in the *Chicago Tribune,* that "eating oat bran is no miracle worker in dramatically reducing cholesterol" and funding subsequent studies that support oat bran's ability to lower cholesterol levels. While the specific health benefits of eating oats may never be proven, Quaker will always be able to pitch its product as a nutritional breakfast food rich in fiber and B vitamins. Discussing Quaker's advertisements featuring Brimley, Bob Garfield in *Advertising Age* praised the spots for "focus[ing] on how substituting oatmeal for bacon and eggs is a vast dietary improvement. . . . Now *that* is a powerful campaign. And it's the right thing to do."

International Growth

One of the most remarkable aspects of Quaker Oats is how early, and how thoroughly, it became a worldwide brand. Quaker's tradition of international trade began as far back as Schumacher, who had the audacity to try to sell his oats in Scotland, the home of oatmeal. Under Crowell, Quaker began a vigorous international marketing effort before the turn of the century (as the Dover cliffs were witness). In 1906 Crowell claimed in Quaker's annual report that "the Quaker brand is registered, and Quaker products are sold, in more countries in the world than any other brand of goods of any character."

Before World War I Quaker Oats were sold not just across Europe but throughout Latin America and in China, India, Japan, Egypt, and many other countries. Quaker devised such a sturdy container to keep its exported oats fresh and pure that Quaker Oats were even carried by explorers to both the North and the South Poles. Quaker's flexibility in marketing was an important part of this international success. For example, in Asia the recipe on the box made a thicker oatmeal, suitable for eating with chopsticks, while in countries that ate little or no breakfast, Quaker marketed oats as a general baking item. In 1991 Quaker oatmeal experienced one percent category growth in the company's international grocery products division.

Brand Development

Whatever Quaker's advertising and marketing strategies, the oats themselves have not gone through many changes. Quaker introduced its first quick-cooking oats in 1919, under the name Two-Minute Oats. This product failed, but two years later, renamed Quick Quaker and reformulated to cook in three to five minutes, the product thrived. As an inexpensive and high-protein food, oatmeal was a steady seller during the Great Depression as well as during both world wars, when consumers were forced to find alternatives to meat.

After World War II, however, oatmeal's place at the breakfast table was steadily eroded by ready-to-eat cold cereals. Quaker countered this trend in two ways. It enhanced its ready-to-eat cereal line, but it also introduced Instant Quaker Oatmeal in 1965. Instant Oatmeal was distributed nationally by 1967, and was available in four flavors—plain, maple and brown sugar, apples and cinnamon, and raisins and spice—by 1969. Sales were strong from the start, giving a needed impetus to the "mature" oatmeal line. By 1982 sales of Instant Quaker Oatmeal had topped those of Old Fashioned Oats and Quick Quaker Oats combined. In 1986 Quaker introduced a premium "Fruit and Cream" flavored instant line, and in 1988 Quaker Extra, a fortified instant oatmeal designed to challenge General Mills' entrance into the hot cereal category, was introduced. In late 1991 Quaker tested microwaveable single-serving cups of oatmeal that can be eaten on the run, without milk. And the following year the company introduced two new versions of its hot cereal, Quaker Multigrain and Quaker Oats Plus Fiber.

Performance Appraisal

In 1901, the year American Cereal became Quaker Oats, the company's total sales were $15.8 million; oatmeal made up $4.8 million, or 30 percent of that total. By 1910 total sales had reached $25.6 million and $5.6 million of that total, or 22 percent, was oatmeal. Oatmeal later declined as a percentage of the company's total sales due to Quaker's enormous growth and diversification since the late 1960s; in 1991 hot cereal made up just under a quarter of Quaker's total North American sales in breakfast foods only. That same year, Quaker reported sales of oatmeal at a high $378.2 million, but hot cereal volumes were 4 percent lower than the previous fiscal year, and down 4 percent and 16 percent in the first and second quarter of 1992, respectively. Analysts agree that the decline is due to both the fizzled fervor over oat bran and the vast amount of ready-to-eat cereals on the market pitching aggressive health messages.

Despite dwindling consumption of their hot cereal, Quaker continually benefits from reduced competition in the market. Such hot cereals as Cream of Wheat, Maypo, and Malt-O-Meal have posed little threat to the hot cereal leader. And even larger contenders have succumbed to Quaker's superior performance in the category. When food giant General Mills entered the hot cereal market in 1987 by introducing Total Oatmeal, Steve Weiner in *Forbes* speculated that, in competing against Quaker, "General Mills is in for a grueling time of it." In June of 1991 the competitor, which only attained an 8 percent market share, "finally faced the numbers and announced that it was dumping Total oatmeal and sibling kiddie brands Undercover Bears and Oatmeal Swirlers," reported Fara Warner in *Adweek's Marketing Week*. And, commenting on an even earlier Quaker victory, Weiner wrote that the Ralston-Purina Company "saw its Sun Maid brand of instant [hot] cereal crushed in just two years when Quaker Oats introduced directly competitive oatmeal flavors and intensified its push to gain more supermarket shelf space." In 1991 Quaker oatmeal held 63 percent of the market share in the $770 million hot cereal industry.

Future Predictions

Quaker has not kept "Oats" in its name for nearly a century without a reason. Yet the company's original name, the American Cereal Company, was actually a more accurate title. From its earliest days, Quaker has done a healthy trade in other cereal grains, marketing not only oatmeal but corn meal, grits, a hot wheat cereal (Pettijohn), mixes (Aunt Jemima), and of course many cold ready-to-eat cereals (beginning with Puffed Rice and Puffed Wheat, "the food shot from guns," and including Cap'n Crunch and Life cereals). Animal feeds, pet foods (Ken-L-Ration and Cycle), chemicals (furfural), and toys (Fisher-Price) have also played an important part in the company's history. But oats were its starting point, and as the company's most profitable product, they retain a central role today. "Looking ahead, Quaker expects

the hot cereal market to return to its pattern of steady, more modest sales growth experienced prior to the 'oat bran boom,' " asserted Quaker's 1991 annual report. "We believe that the health and nutritional benefits of hot oat cereals are in line with the needs of today's consumer. With our leadership position in hot cereals, we have aggressive plans to drive growth in the hot cereals category."

Further Reading:

Bishop, Jerry E., "Quaker Gets Boost for Oat Bran Lines as Study Shows Declines in Cholesterol," *Wall Street Journal*, April 10, 1991, p. B4.

Carey, John, "Snap, Crackle, Stop," *Business Week*, September 25, 1989, pp. 42-43.

Erickson, Julie Liesse, "Quaker Not Backing Down as Oatmeal Wars Escalate, *Crain's Chicago Business*, August 22, 1988, sec. 1, p. 29; "Hot-Cereal Sales May Be Cooling Down," *Advertising Age*, October 2, 1989, p. 16.

Garfield, Bob, "Quaker Oat Bran Ad Lacks Moral Fiber," *Advertising Age*, June 26, 1989, p. 78.

Gershman, Michael, *Getting It Right the Second Time*, Reading: Addison-Wesley, 1990, pp. 95-99.

Key, Janet, "Oat Bran No Miracle, Quaker Says," *Chicago Tribune*, February 8, 1990, sec. 1, p. 2.

LaGanga, Maria L., "Cereal Firms Are Defiant, Stick by Their Oat Bran," *Los Angeles Times*, January 18, 1990, p. D1.

Liesse, Julie, "Quaker's New Cereals Run Hot and Cold," *Advertising Age*, July 20, 1991, p. 3.

Marquette, Arthur F., *Brands, Trademarks, and Good Will: The Story of the Quaker Oats Company*, New York: McGraw-Hill, 1957.

Miller, Annetta, "America Feels Its Oats," *Newsweek*, July 11, 1988, p. 53; "Oat-Bran Heartburn," *Newsweek*, January 29, 1990, pp. 50-52.

The Quaker Oats Company Annual Reports, Chicago: The Quaker Oats Company, 1904-1989, 1991.

Snyder, David, "Quaker Ads' Health Claims Draw Fire from State Officials," *Crain's Chicago Business*, October 3, 1988, sec. 1, p. 67.

Thornton, Harrison John, *The History of the Quaker Oats Company*, Chicago: University of Chicago Press, 1933.

Warner, Fara, "Oatmeal Blues," *Adweek's Marketing Week*, June 24, 1991, pp. 18-19.

Weiner, Steve, "Food Fight!," *Forbes*, July 27, 1987, pp. 86-87.

RAGÚ®

Ragú is considered the giant of the jarred spaghetti sauce industry, holding approximately 40 percent of the $1.2 billion market. Its market share, however, was formerly as high as 60 percent. Rival sauces introduced into the expanding industry have significantly cut into Ragú's lead. To stay ahead of its ever-growing competition, Ragú introduces new varieties of sauce with frequent regularity. The Ragú line has expanded to include original Old World Style, Slow-Cooked Homestyle, Chunky Gardenstyle, and Fino Italian varieties, as well as a number of related products such as Ragú Pasta Meals (pasta and sauce in a jar) and Classic Value (a canned sauce introduced in 1992). Ragú products have been sold nationwide, in Canada, Puerto Rico, and South America since the 1950s. In September 1989 Ragú Foods, Inc. became an independent unit within Unilever, its longtime parent company. Ragú products were introduced in European markets within the year. In 1992 Ragú was merged into Unilever's Van den Bergh Foods Company.

Origins

Ragú sauce began as a family favorite, a recipe brought to the United States by Assunta Cantisano when she and her husband Giovanni emigrated from Italy near the turn of the century. The Cantisanos settled in Rochester, New York, where Giovanni set up an import business. Assunta's sauce soon became a favorite among friends and neighbors who liked it so much they offered to purchase it. Giovanni Cantisano decided to sell his sauce as a business venture and in 1937 he incorporated the Ragú Packing Co., headquartered at their home at 35 Avery Street in Rochester.

Production and marketing of Ragú (which means sauce in Italian) was a family affair. Assunta supervised cooking in the Cantisano's "summer kitchen" while their six sons helped seal the cans, pack them, and, along with their father, distribute them to local food chains. Distribution of the sauce (in plain, meat, or mushroom varieties) eventually expanded beyond the Rochester area. Sauce sales grew and the family moved to larger facilities in 1946 to accommodate increased demands. Three years later, the company moved again, to its present site on Lyell Avenue in Rochester.

The Ragú line expanded to include Spanish Rice, shell macaroni and ravioli dinners, pizza sauce, and romano cheese, but Assunta's spaghetti sauce remained the leading product. The company exported Ragú to Puerto Rico and South America. Sales continued to grow slowly but steadily and hit the $150 thousand mark in 1953. In the years that followed, sales doubled almost annually. In 1958 Ragú was launched on a more ambitious scale via a newspaper campaign in markets in New York City, Philadelphia, Cleveland, and Detroit. Ten years later Ragú was the nation's largest producer of spaghetti sauce, with sales of $23 million and a market reaching as far south from Rochester as Georgia and as far west as Fargo, North Dakota.

Going National

In 1968 Ragú Packing Co. reached an agreement to merge into Liggett & Myers, Inc., then the sixth largest cigarette manufacturer in the United States. Had the deal been completed, Ragú would have become a fully owned subsidiary of Liggett & Myers. The merger, however, fell through. The following year, Ragú was purchased by the drug and cosmetic giant Chesebrough-Pond, Inc., in a $43.8 million stock swap. The Ragú Packing Co. changed its name to Ragú Foods, Inc. and became a wholly-owned subsidiary of Chesebrough-Pond. Ralph Cantisano, who had succeeded his father as president of Ragú, continued in that role until 1975.

Ragú was Chesebrough-Pond's first foray into the food business, part of the company's "long-term policy of diversification in packaged goods and specialty products." Although Ragú held a 60 percent share of the market at the time of acquisition, distribution was concentrated in the Northeast and Midwest. Chesebrough-Pond's first order of business was to expand distribution to include the West Coast by the end of 1970.

Ragú can be credited, at least in part, with creating the commercial sauce market of the 1970s. It had already captured a 60 percent share of the U.S. market and carried with it a 25-year history of name recognition. Chesebrough-Pond started a nationwide promotional and advertising blitz to further solidify Ragú's standing as the preeminent spaghetti sauce on the market. However, its share was about to be challenged by an invasion of new products into the rapidly growing Italian food market.

Competition Heats Up: Marketing Strategies

In a 1971 *Advertising Age* article, writer Walter Margulies noted that, since the end of World War II, the United States had undergone "what might be considered a culinary flip-flop." A nation of strictly meat and potato eaters had become more cosmopolitan in their culinary interests. "Ethnic" foods such as French, Chinese, German, and Mexican fare were enjoyed by people outside those specific cultures. Leading the pack was Italian cuisine. Total sales for all Italian food products reached $600 million by 1971. Ragú's expanding distribution, supported by a massive media blitz, was in part responsible for triggering the commercial sauce boom.

Sensing a lucrative market, well-established corporations such as H.J. Heinz, Hunt-Wesson, and Del Monte began introducing new products, providing some heavy competition for more traditional Italian food manufacturers. Smaller regional manufacturers were also trying to break into the market. As one supermarket buyer commented in a 1971 issue of *Chain Store Age*, "I think we saw 5,000 lines (sic) of new spaghetti sauce last year. Every one was a duplicate of something else. How far can you go with spaghetti sauce?"

By 1973, Chesebrough-Pond had boosted Ragú sales to $70 million. Ragú's Old World Style sauce continued to hold its strong market share, but the national spaghetti sauce market was growing 20 percent annually—a rate faster than Ragú sales were growing. It became evident to Chesebrough-Pond executives that consumers were increasingly buying other sauces besides Ragú.

One sauce that threatened to cut into Ragú's market share was Prima Salsa, introduced in the mid-1970s by Hunt-Wesson Inc. Advertising promoted this new, spicy sauce as "extra thick and zesty." Chesebrough-Pond's strategy was to wait several months to make its move, then fight back with a new spaghetti sauce which, like Prima Salsa, was thicker than Old World Style and contained more spices. They called this sauce Ragú Extra Thick and Zesty. Ragú Extra Thick and Zesty was immediately successful, capturing the number two position nationally (after Ragú Old World Style).

In 1976 Hunt-Wesson filed charges against Ragú Foods, alleging that Ragú was attempting to monopolize the spaghetti sauce market in violation of the Sherman Act, a major antitrust law. Hunt-Wesson objected to Ragú's use of the term "extra thick and zesty." The suit demanded an injunction against the use of the term and payment for any damages incurred by Hunt-Wesson. The suit dragged on, ultimately reaching the U.S. Supreme Court in 1981. By that time, although Prima Salsa was the number two brand nationally, its market share was only five percent.

In 1978 Ragú introduced Ragú Classic Combinations, prompted in part, according to industry analysts, by the growing popularity of Aunt Millie's spaghetti sauce. Ragú used the same strategy when the Campbell Soup Co. launched its Prego brand spaghetti sauce in 1981. Campbell introduced Prego to 60 percent of the national market with the advertising theme, "We put homemade taste in every jar." Ragú's market share dropped noticeably in the months following Prego's introduction. Chesebrough-Pond held back for several months, then introduced a new Ragú Homestyle version, positioned identically to its new rival Prego.

Supported by heavy advertising and promotional spending, the company targeted Ragú Homestyle to capture the 40 to 45 percent of households who continued to prepare homemade sauces. Ragú

estimated that the homemade sauce market had sales of approximately $500 million, the same level garnered by prepared spaghetti sauces.

"Obviously we're aware of their (Campbell's) efforts," George Goebler, president of Chesebrough-Pond's package foods division, told *Advertising Age* in early 1982. "But with Homestyle we went after the market. We saw the numbers on the people who still make homemade spaghetti sauce and went after it. They're going after it too, but we're not a defensive company. We're just very aggressive advertisers and marketers." Prego proved to be a formidable competitor, with a $12 million advertising and promotion budget. By 1991 its share of the ever rising $1.2 billion spaghetti sauce industry had risen to 26.1 percent, while Ragú's dropped to 41.1 percent.

Ragú entered into battle with Hunt-Wesson again in 1991 in a race to be the first to introduce "healthy" sauces. Ragú introduced Today's Recipe in December 1991, one month before Hunt-Wesson introduced a similar sauce. Today's Recipe was promoted as a cholesterol-free, sugar-free sauce that has "50% less fat" than Old World Style. The new sauce was introduced through national television ads, print, in-store advertising, and distribution of 375 million coupons. Ragú Foods stated in *Advertising Age* that advertising spending to introduce Today's Recipe was, "higher than both Hunt's and (Borden's) Classico combined and comparable to Prego."

In 1992 Ragú began test marketing Classic Value spaghetti sauce in a can, following the lead of Campbell and Hunt-Wesson The jarred spaghetti sauce market had become much more crowded than it was in 1973. According to John Gennari, marketing manager for Ragú Foods, more new pasta sauces were introduced in 1992 alone than in any year since Ragú distribution went national. Some of Ragú's attempts at line extension, such as its Homestyle, Fino, and Thick & Hearty brands, registered sharp sales declines in 1991. Ragú's introduction of its canned Classic Value may be an attempt to tap in to the 30.9 percent growth in the canned sauce market that Hunt-Wesson experienced in 1991.

Advertising

In 1969 Ragú dominated the market with a 60 percent share and a 41-year history—far longer than that of its competitors. That year, national companies descended on the upstate New York region, where Ragú sales were strongest, to begin marketing their new sauces. In response, a television commercial developed by Finnegan Advertising Agency in Rochester, New York, capitalized on Ragú's well established popularity, not even mentioning the name Ragú until the closing six seconds. The ad featured a Ragú spokesman, tenor Enzo Stuarti, singing an Italian lullaby to his nine-year-old daughter Andrea. Andrea spoke the tag line, "Thats-a nice!"

That tag line prompted a protest from the New York office of the Italian-American Civil Rights League, which claimed the usage of the Italian dialect was defamatory towards Italian-Americans. Ragú president Ralph Cantisano said the company had no plan to abandon the commercial. Asked if he thought the commercial presented a negative image of Italian-Americans, Cantisano responded, "If I did, I wouldn't be doing it."

After Chesebrough-Pond acquired Ragú in 1969, advertising was transferred to New York-based Waring & LaRosa. Waring & LaRosa remained Ragú's primary agency for Ragú accounts until

1989. That year, Ragú called in J. Walter Thompson USA to assist with creative ideas on its $25 million main sauce account. Ragú was reportedly frustrated by Prego's growing market share and displeased with Waring's earlier campaign, a sitcom-style ad, complete with laugh track. That ad was ultimately pulled off the air. By December 1989 Ragú had completely transferred its sauce account to J. Walter Thompson. Industry analysts cited three reasons for the transfer: Prego's growing encroachment on Ragú's share; a shake-up in Ragú's top management; and a decision by Ragú's new parent company Unilever to consolidate all its advertising at a small number of multi-national agencies.

Product Development

Consistent with its marketing strategy was the company philosophy to "provide new variants without eroding its original sauce sales." Since 1973, Ragú has introduced over eight different varieties of pasta sauce. Ragú has also made several forays into other markets with Ragú Table Sauce in 1978, Pasta Meals in 1985, and Chicken Tonight in 1991.

Ragú Table Sauce, marketed as "ketchup's Italian cousin," was bottled to resemble ketchup packaging, and was sold in the ketchup section of supermarkets. Television commercials developed by Waring & LaRosa for test markets in Milwaukee and New England suggested that Ragú Table Sauce be used as a "zippy" alternative to ketchup. The new sauce was so successful in its Milwaukee test market that retailers temporarily ran out of stock. It was slated for national rollout by late 1979, but despite the sauce's test market success, it was never distributed nationally.

Ragú Pasta Meals, prepared pasta and sauce in a jar, hit the market in 1985 with a $24 million annual ad campaign developed by Waring & LaRosa. The campaign employed print and television ads to convince parents that canned pasta was not just kid's food. Print media compared Pasta Meals with a generic fictitious canned pasta. "A good idea, 1949," stated a banner above a photo of generic canned pasta; "A fresh idea, 1986," stated the banner above a jar of Ragú Pasta Meals. Underneath the visuals was placed a paragraph, headed, "Introducing fresh taste you don't get from a can."

The Can Manufacturers Institute objected to the ads, and petitioned the Better Business Bureau to delay printing of the ads (slated for April 1986), which they said implied that glass jars are inherently better than cans. Chesebrough-Pond defended Waring & LaRosa and refused to change the ads, saying the ads were supported by scientific research. As with Ragú Table Sauce, Pasta Meals never reached the national distribution stage.

Unilever desired to move the Ragú name into other food categories.In 1991 Ragú introduced Chicken Tonight, a six-item line of jarred sauces designed to accompany chicken. Chicken Tonight was positioned to compete with the $830 million dry dinner category, led by General Mills' Hamburger Helper line. Chicken Tonight was introduced with the largest media expenditure by Ragú to date. Television advertising alone totaled over $24 million.

International Market

Ragú has been distributed in Puerto Rico and South America since the 1940s, when the Cantisano family owned the business. However, little other attention was paid to international markets until 1988. When Chesebrough-Pond was acquired by Unilever,

Ragú was transferred to Unilever's international foods operation. In 1988 Unilever-owned Brooke Bond Oxo orchestrated a Christmas introduction of Ragú in Great Britain. Ragú's largest competitor was Dolmio jarred sauce, owned by Master Foods. Marketing strategy for Ragú was to "arrive in force" and inundate the market during a traditionally slow season, aiming to attract new users in England's rapidly growing sauce market. According to Unilever materials, UK sales in the first two years were "excellent."

Performance Appraisal and Future Growth

Ragú can be credited with creating the pasta sauce boom that began in the 1970s. Although a number of competitors have presented challenges to its market position, Ragú sauces continue to hold a majority share. Despite its aggressive marketing strategy, Ragú's share has been slowly eroding, from around 60 percent in 1973 to just over 40 percent in 1992. This is due in large part to increased competition from Campbell's Prego, but it's also due to smaller regional sauce manufacturers whose sales chip away at Ragú's market base.

The pasta sauce market has grown at rate of about 20 percent a year since the 1970s. A 1992 *New York Times* article predicted that sauce sales will continue to grow, but that larger brands such as Ragú will only see a small percentage of that growth.

While the U.S. market is flooded with new sauces, foreign markets seem to present greater growth opportunity. Ragú has been successfully introduced in British markets and the company is reportedly eyeing other foreign market opportunities.

Further Reading:

"Chesebrough: FInding Strong Brands to Revitalize Mature Markets," *Business Week,* November 10, 1980, p. 73.

Conway, Linda, "Spaghetti Sauce States Style," *Unilever Magazine,* p. 22.

Dagnoli, Judann, "Ragú Shop May Be Waring Out," *Advertising Age,* September 4, 1989, p. 3.

——, "Ragú Serves Sauce for Chicken," *Advertising Age,* January 14, 1991, p. 4.

Dougherty, Philip E., "Spaghetti-Sauce War Takes Aim at Ragú," *Rochester Times Union,* June 9, 1969.

Fabricant, Florence, "Sauce Makers Are All Smiles at the Rage for Pasta," *New York Times,* October 28, 1992.

Giges, Nancy, "Simmering Ragú Cooks Up Defense against Prego," *Advertising Age,* October 19, 1981, p. 119.

Heller, Karen, "In the Sauce," *Rochester Democrat and Chronicle,* April 4, 1982, p. 1C.

Hoggan, Karen, "Ragú Sparks Pasta War," *Marketing* (United Kingdom), October 13, 1988, p. 5.

Hulin-Salkin, Belinda, "Would Mother Approve?," *Advertising Age,* March 15, 1982, p. M26.

Levin, Gary, "JWT Eats Up $25M Ragú Account," *Advertising Age,* December 18, 1989, p. 40.

Liesse, Julie, and Pat Sloan, "Hunt's, Ragú Spread Across Aisles in Spaghetti Sauce Wars," *Advertising Age,* November 16, 1992, p. 4.

Margulies, Walter P., "Mama Mia, Thassa Some Heavy Competition in Italian Food Packaging," *Advertising Age,* February 8, 1971, p. 46.

Record, Don, "Spaghetti Sauce Started Firm," *Rochester Democrat and Chronicle,* February 3, 1957.

"Ragú Foods Inc.," *Rochester Democrat and Chronicle,* March 25, 1973.

"Ragú Agrees to Purchase by L&M," *Rochester Times Union,* August 1, 1968.

"Ragú Table Sauce out to Ketchup with Leaders," *Advertising Age,* July 10, 1978, p. 4.

"Ragú May Merge with Tobacco Firm," *Rochester Democrat and Chronicle,* August 2, 1968.

Sloan, Pat, "New Ragú Line Jars Canned Pasta Brands," *Advertising Age,* December 2, 1985, p. 36.

Stear, James R., "Ragú Defends Italian-Dialect TV Ads," *Rochester Democrat and Chronicle,* March 27, 1971, p. 4B.

"Suit: Ragú Monopolizes Sauce Sales," *Rochester Times Union,* July 19, 1976.

"Vaseline Tomato Sauce?" *Forbes,* October 1, 1974, p. 69.

—Maura Troester

RC® COLA

The earliest carbonated beverage makers were pharmacists who had the knowledge to make process carbonated water. After commercially prepared carbon dioxide became available, the soda fountain became a drugstore fixture. The pharmacists claimed that the drinks they dispensed at their soda fountains could cure any number of ailments; but because carbonated or soda water did not taste very good, they added flavorings selected for their ability to improve the drink's curative properties. The first flavorings were roots and herbs, such as raspberry leaves, nettles, dandelion, birch bark, and sassafras. However, since the flavorings had no color, formulators later added dyes to soft drinks to increase their appeal.

Like many other soft drink inventors, Claud A. Hatcher was a pharmacist who experimented with various flavorings to come up with a combination that customers would like to drink in a carbonated beverage. However, Hatcher did not experiment at a drugstore soda fountain, he worked in the basement of the Hatcher Grocery Company, a wholesale grocery business he owned with his father in Columbus, Georgia. His first product was a ginger ale sold under the brand name Royal Crown. A line of flavors followed. The soft drinks sold so well that Hatcher and his father organized the Union Bottling Works in 1905 to literally get the soft drink operation out of the basement.

One of Union Bottling's most popular drinks was Chero-Cola. In 1912, the company reorganized and became the Chero-Cola Company. By 1925 the company had 315 franchised bottlers, of which 310 bottled Chero-Cola and 263 produced the company's other products under the Nehi trademark. (Nehi was such a popular brand that the Chero-Cola Company became the Nehi Corporation in 1928.)

Following financial difficulties caused by a backfired Cuban sugar plan during World War I and the Depression, plus the death of Claud Hatcher in 1933, the company was ready to move forward again. It was decided that Nehi Corporation needed a different, better cola product than Chero-Cola. Six months later company chemist Rufus Kamm had formulated a new cola concentrate to send to selected bottlers for test marketing. The new cola product was an instant success. It was honored with the brand name of Hatcher's original ginger ale creation, Royal Crown. Depression-era consumers, who could buy a 12-ounce bottle of Royal Crown Cola for just five cents, paid the new soft drink the

highest compliment when they shortened the name to RC Cola, an appellation still used.

The search for a new cola may also have had something to do with a legal action taken by the Coca-Cola Company. The U.S. Patent Office registered the Coca-Cola name in 1893. Soon there were numerous companies trying to imitate Coca-Cola because it was such a big success. Stockholders urged Coca-Cola management to take legal action against these imitators. Chero-Cola was one of the companies against which a lawsuit was filed. The issue was settled in 1933 when Chero-Cola became Royal Crown Cola.

Brand Identification

Royal Crown Cola came in a 12-ounce bottle in the 1940s. The label had an Egyptian look: two pyramids flanked the letters *RC* on each side. The "sand" and pyramids were yellow, outlined in black. The "sky" was orange and had the words *Royal Crown* and a star below them in yellow. *RC* was embossed on the bottle. RC Cola initially proved to be more competition for Pepsi-Cola than Coca-Cola because it sold in the same size bottle and tasted very much like it. In 1958, the RC logo changed to a red and white diamond design.

By the end of 1940, Nehi Corporation was selling its products in 47 of the then 48 states. In 1959, the company made its third corporate name change to Royal Crown Cola Company. A final name change was made in 1978 to Royal Crown Companies, Inc., to reflect the company's diversification; the soft drink division retained the Royal Crown Cola Company name. Chesapeake Financial Corporation, a Victor Posner affiliate, acquired the companies in 1984.

In 1989, Royal Crown Cola Company changed the RC logo and all packaging design. The logo has large red *RC* letters, positioned at a right upward angle, underlined with a red brush stroke. The word *Cola* is written underneath in blue. Both *RC* and *Cola* are in script. The lower portion is on field of wide blue and narrow white stripes. The Diet RC Cola logo includes the word *Diet*. Royal Crown also updated the logo and package design for Diet Rite the same year, also using blue and red for lettering.

AT A GLANCE

RC Cola brand soft drink founded originally as a ginger ale bottled by Union Bottling Works, Columbus, GA, by Claud A. Hatcher; name given to cola product in 1933; company made third corporate name change to become Royal Crown Cola Company, 1959.

Performance: *Market share*—3% of soft drink category. *Sales*—$1.1 million.

Major competitor: Coca-Cola; also Pepsi-Cola.

Advertising: *Agency*—In-house. *Major campaign*—Revival of taste tests with slogan "Take the RC Challenge."

Addresses: *Parent company*—Royal Crown Cola Company, 6917 Collins Ave., Miami Beach, FL 33141-0210; phone: (305) 866-3281.

Soft Drink Industry Innovations

Royal Crown Cola is renowned for its promotional and product-related innovations. It was the first soft drink beverage company to conduct independent, certified taste tests. The tests found RC Cola the unquestioned winner. The company used the results to launch the product with a nationwide newspaper advertising campaign using the slogan "Best by Taste Test." A later campaign, "The RC Challenge," revived the taste test in 1989.

Royal Crown broadened its market base with the development of Diet Rite Cola, which had originally been offered as a dietary soft drink to a limited market in the mid-1950s. The artificial sweetener cyclamate had made it possible for the product to be reformulated to improve its taste, eliminate the somewhat metallic aftertaste associated with artificial sweeteners, and reduce its caloric content. When Diet Rite Cola was introduced in 1962, it was the first nationally marketed good-tasting diet soft drink, creating a whole new segment in the beverage industry. (Coca-Cola did not introduce Tab until 1963). Consumer response was phenomenal; within eighteen months Diet Rite Cola was the number four cola in the United States.

Diet Rite was enjoying sustained success, even though competitive products were on the market, when the safety of cyclamates became a health concern. *Soda Poppery* says, "Diet Rite suffered the most. Royal Crown claimed that the government's tests were 'pseudo-scientific.' The company even claimed that other soft-drink companies, jealous of Diet Rite's success, had financed the research, but nothing along those lines was ever proven."

The U.S. Department of Health, Education & Welfare banned the use of cyclamates in soft drinks on October 18, 1964. Although a reformulated Diet Rite concentrate sweetened with sugar and saccharin was available for shipment to bottlers within 48 hours of the ban, RC and the sugar industry (which had feared a loss of sales due to diet drinks) still waged an advertising battle. According to *Soda Poppery,* the sugar companies ran an ad with the picture of a healthy-looking, energetic boy with copy that claimed he just "delivered 82 morning papers, swam half a mile, hit a home run [and] needs a sugarless, powerless soft drink like a moose needs a hatrack." The book goes on to say that Royal Crown Cola Company "responded with an ad of its own: 'Have you tried the soft drink that's got the "Sugar Daddies" howling mad?' The sugar people retorted by attacking the notion that diet colas will slim one down. Soft drinks, they said, contain only

about 2 percent of an average person's caloric intake. Cutting out soft drinks, they said, will never make fat people skinny."

When the effects of caffeine became a concern to consumers, Royal Crown responded in 1980 by introducing the industry's first caffeine-free diet cola, RC100. Its Decaf.RC (launched in 1982 and later renamed RC100) was the first caffeine-free regular cola. The company also was the first to offer a salt-free diet cola (Diet Rite Cola, 1983); the first to offer a diet cherry cola (Diet Cherry RC Cola, 1985); and the first to offer no-salt, no-sodium, caffeine-free flavored soft drinks with 100 percent NutraSweet (Diet Rite, 1988).

Royal Crown Cola Company was the first to distribute soft drinks nationally in cans in 1954, the first to introduce the 16-ounce bottle in 1958, and the first to introduce the all-aluminum can in 1964.

Star-Studded Advertising

Over the years, Royal Crown has employed celebrities and stars of the stage, airwaves, beauty pageants, sports, and other arenas to promote its products. The trail of celebrity endorsements started with sponsorship of one of the top-rated radio shows in America, Robert Ripley's "Believe It or Not" in 1939-40. The theme line was "Royal Crown is tops in taste!"

Royal Crown Cola Company featured Hollywood celebrities and starlets in product endorsements in magazine ads and point-of-purchase materials beginning in the 1940s and continuing through 1955. The long list of endorsers included Bing Crosby, Joan Crawford, Lizabeth Scott, Hedy Lamarr, Joan Bennett, Rita Hayworth, Carole Landis, Merle Oberon, Dorothy Lamour, Irene Dunne, Alexis Smith, Claudette Colbert, Loretta Young, Gene Tierney, Virginia Mayo, Mary Martin, Betty Hutton, Gary Cooper, Shirley Temple, Ronda Fleming, Arlene Dahl, Jeanne Crain, June Haver, and Shelly Winters. The 1941 RC Calendar Girl was Jinx Falkenburg of the "Tex and Jinx Show."

During the 1950s, Royal Crown used the slogan "Better Taste Calls for RC!" for two years, combined with appearances by TV starlet Bunny Cooper as "Miss Royal Crown Cola" and local "Miss Royal Crown Cola" competitions. Later, a new, faster way to deliver concentrate to bottlers inspired the slogan "RC—The Fresher Refresher!"

In 1961, TV and radio personality Art Linkletter became the brand's spokesperson, along with Miss Universe. Through 1966, RC Cola was a major sponsor of the Miss Universe Pageant, while continuing the freshness theme with the slogans "Go Fresher With RC" and "Go Fresher: Go RC." Linkletter got a partner in TV commercials in 1965, a cartoon character named "Zippy." Zippy was an extension of the latest slogan, "You'll Flip at the Z-Z-Zip in RC Cola!" Zippy moved aside in 1967 as Jill Hayworth, Joey Heatherton, Robie Porter, and the group Dino, Desi & Billy began appearing in TV commercials with the theme "Escape—Come on Over to RC Cola—The One with the Mad, Mad Taste!" During the next two years, the "RC Cola: the Comer" advertising tied in with the careers of TV stars Meredith MacRae of "Petticoat Junction" and Pamela Austin of "Laugh-In," and stage star Emily Yancy of "Hello Dolly."

Royal Crown used the advertising themes "We Cool Off the Hot Towns" and "RC: Its just right for you" in the early 1970s, but it was the slogan "Me and My RC" and its catchy jingle that sent RC sales soaring. "Fifty Years of RC Advertising" states, "Half the country sang the tuneful RC jingle: 'Me and My RC, Me and My RC: What's good enough for other folks ain't good enough for me!' " One of the most memorable "Me and My RC" TV spots was the skateboard girl delivering pizza while the jingle played. A variation of the jingle played in the early 1980s, "Here's to you and me and my RC: Here's to fun—You know a good time when you taste one," and featured real life people.

The "Me and My RC" slogan was followed by campaigns based on the slogans "Cola Lovin' Woman—Cola Lovin' Man" and "Some People Go Out of Their Way for the Taste of RC" from 1985 to 1987. The company later shifted to newspaper ads and became a broadcast sponsor of the New York Mets and the official soft drink at Shea Stadium and the Los Angeles Forum. The Royal Crown Cola Company in the early 1990s continued displaying signage in both stadiums and sponsored the Los Angeles Lakers home basketball games on TV and Los Angles Kings home hockey games on radio.

From 1988 through mid-1989, Royal Crown continued the "celebration of the individual" theme developed in the 1970s with the slogan "Decide for Yourself." According to "Fifty Years of RC Advertising," the "attention-getting TV spots [showed] people who make their own decisions about 'what's right for them' and decid[e] on RC." The most recent campaign used the slogan "C'mon, say yes to RC."

Diet Rite Cola also had some notable advertising and promotional campaigns. Early on, the brand had a distinct advantage; it created the diet soft drink category, was the uncontested number one in the category and the fourth best-selling cola in the country. Diet Rite built on its status by using the themes "Overnight—America's Number One," "America's Most Modern Cola," and "America's No. 1 Low-Calorie Cola." Diet Rite was a major sponsor of the Miss U.S.A. Pageant at the same time RC Cola sponsored the Miss Universe Pageant. Pageant winners from 1963 to 1966 became Diet Rite spokespersons and were featured in TV spots for local bottlers and in newspaper, radio, and point of purchase programs. The brand's first network TV advertisement, shown in 1967, had the theme "What've You Got to Lose."

After the ban on cyclamates in 1969, the reformulated Diet Rite was a tougher sell. Fashion model Twiggy, basketball star John Havlicek, and singer Lena Horne promoted the brand with the slogan "Diet Rite: tastes so good even non-dieters drink it." During the years 1971 and 1973 the brand's advertising claimed "Everybody likes it!" Diet Rite used the slogan "The One You Loved is Back" in 1974 after it was reformulated to become a sugar-free cola again. Royal Crown Cola commissioned certified taste tests of Diet Rite versus Tab and Diet Pepsi to prove that consumers preferred Diet Rite. The results gave them the right to say "Taste The One That Won!" Another reformulation of the brand made it the first and only nationally marketed diet cola that was sodium and caffeine free and that replaced saccharin with a NutraSweet and saccharin blend. "It's the *only* one!" TV spots stressed the uniqueness of the new Diet Rite formula.

The brand capitalized on the fitness craze of the 1980s by hiring TV and motion picture star Lee Majors as the spokesperson. "Diet Rite Cola Advertising: Textbook Study in Enhancing Brand Image" says, "The theme, 'Everybody's Gotta Diet Rite,' gave rise to a series of TV spots showing Majors laboring mightily to keep in shape and ending his workouts with refreshing salt/so-

dium-free Diet Rite." Tony Danza was the brand spokesperson from 1987 through mid-1989. Subsequent marketing slogans were "Do Right. Diet Rite," "Living Right with Diet Rite," and "Live Right, Diet Rite."

Controversy and Continuance

After the 1984 acquisition of Royal Crown by Chesapeake Financial Corporation, the company experienced turmoil. While bottlers clung to Royal Crown's history of product and promotion innovativeness, many became increasingly disgruntled with company management. A 1991 survey of bottlers by *Beverage World* found that although Royal Crown Cola Company was not responsive to their needs, had not been innovative, was only average in its concentrate pricing, and did not produce quality consumer advertising, the bottler network had somehow endured over the years to keep the brand the number-three cola. The article quoted one bottler as saying, "We have always bragged that no matter how bad RC has been run, it's always recovered. This time it won't. The RC bottling network is in total shambles. There are signs that bottlers have given up. They don't have the fight anymore, and that was always our strongest suit. The RC Cola Company is in full hemorrhage. It's the final and ultimate demise."

Business Week ran an article titled "Three Sparkling Turnarounds: Can This Really be Victor Posner?" in 1987. By 1992 the sparkle was off him and his control of DWG Corporation, which holds Royal Crown. A U.S. District Court in Cleveland agreed with Posner plaintiff Granada Investments over potential control of Posner-pillaged DWG Corporation. Larry Jabbonsky reported in *Beverage World* (March 1992) that the judge opined that "Victor Posner is engaged in the flagrant and systematic diversion of DWG assets for his own benefit. His acts of corporate waste and self-dealing compel the immediate intervention of this court." How this would ultimately affect Royal Crown Cola was not known.

However, not all of Posner's management activities were detrimental to the company. In 1986 Royal Crown took out full page newspaper ads charging that proposed acquisitions by Coca-Cola and Pepsi-Cola would give the two companies 80 percent market share, a violation of antitrust law. The Federal Trade Commission and a federal judge agreed with Royal Crown, forcing Coke and Pepsi to abandon their proposed buyouts.

Royal Crown Cola Company operates through 266 franchises and distributors in the United States and 53 foreign countries.

Further Reading:

Davis, T., "Put the Prinicipal on Detention," *Beverage World,* October 1991, pp. 44-46.

Diet Rite Cola Advertising: Textbook Study in Enhancing Brand Image, Miami: Royal Crown Cola Company typescript.

Dietz, Lawrence, *Soda Pop: The History, Advertising, Art and Memorabilia of Soft Drinks in America,* New York: Simon & Schuster, 1973.

Engardino, Peter, "Three Sparkling Turnarounds: Can This Really be Victor Posner? Surprise—Some Talented Managers Are Minding His Business," *Business Week,* July 27, 1987, p. 56.

Fifty Years of RC Advertising, Miami: Royal Crown Cola Company typescript.

Jabbonsky, Larry, "Sex, Lies and Red Tape," *Beverage World,* March 1992, p. 6.

Jacobs, Morris B., Ph.D., "Introduction," *Manufacture and Analysis of Carbonated Beverages,* New York: Chemical Publishing, 1959.

RC Histories, Miami: Royal Crown Cola Company typescript.

The Royal Crown Cola Company: Brief Fact Sheet, Miami: Royal Crown Cola Company typescript.

The Royal Crown Cola Co. Story, Miami: Royal Crown Cola Company typescript.

Tchudi, Stephen N., *Soda Poppery: The History of Soft Drinks in America; with Recipes for Making & Using Soft Drinks PLUS Easy Science Experiments,* New York: Scribner, 1986.

Wolf, Alan, ''That Was the Year That Was (But Some Soft Drink Franchisors Wished It Wasn't),'' *Beverage World 1992/93 Databank: Sourcebook for the Beverage Markets,* Shepherdsville, KY: Keller International Publishing Corporation, pp. 20-25.

—Doris Morris Maxfield

REESE'S® PEANUT BUTTER CUPS

The top-selling candy bar in the United States and Canada, Reese's Peanut Butter Cups are a staple of the American snack diet. Manufactured by Hershey Chocolate U.S.A., Reese's recently surpassed the rival Snickers bar for the number one position after a period of pursuit that began in the early 1970s. The now famous Reese's candy bar, with its well-known orange, yellow, and brown wrapper, has been used to develop spinoff products, including Reese's Crunchy Peanut Butter Cups, Reese's Miniature Peanut Butter Cups, Reese's Pieces, Reese's Peanut Butter Chips, and Reese's Peanut Butter. The last of these was introduced in 1992.

Brand History

Harry B. Reese was born in York County, Pennsylvania, in 1879. He did not enjoy the farm life to which he had been born, so he embarked on several other career paths. He worked as an oil burner salesman and as a country butcher before moving to Hershey, Pennsylvania, in 1917, where he secured employment on one of Milton Hershey's dairy farms. H.B., as his friends called him, admired the achievements of Milton Hershey. While employed at the dairy farm, he observed the town and its remarkable growth, which had resulted from one man's vision and hard work. He decided to strike out on his own in the confectionery industry.

Like Hershey, Reese pursued a slow and difficult path to success. He began creating different confections in nearby towns. Reese lived briefly in Hummelstown, Harrisburg, and Palmyra. While in these towns he invented such candies as Johnny Bars and Lizzie Bars. His first real success did not come until he moved back to Hershey.

Reese's and Hershey

By 1923 H.B. Reese was back in Hershey, Pennsylvania, producing what is now known as the Reese's peanut butter cup. It was made with Hershey's milk chocolate surrounding specially processed peanut butter, and it was originally made to be sold as part of candy assortments. In 1933 Reese added the penny peanut butter cup, and the business was on solid ground. The peanut butter cup had been suggested to Mr. Reese by one of his early customers in Harrisburg. When Reese developed the formula, he sold the peanut butter cups in five-pound boxes so that they could be combined with other candies for sale in stores.

While Reese was still a young man, Milton Hershey had built the world's largest chocolate manufacturing plant in Derry Church, Pennsylvania, which was later renamed Hershey. The plant opened in 1905, and Hershey established an entire community around it. The building boom in those years included construction of a trolley to bring Hershey workers into the town from surrounding areas, as well as a zoo, department store, bank, park, golf courses, the Milton Hershey school for boys, and churches.

During the Great Depression, Milton Hershey went against the common wisdom of the day. He vowed not to lay off any workers, and kept them busy with another construction boom. In the 1930s he started construction of a sports arena, community center, large hotel, stadium, a new building for the Milton Hershey School, and an office building. Meanwhile, the H.B. Reese Candy Company was struggling, and Reese discontinued all of his product lines except for the peanut butter cup. Reese never went back to any of the other lines, instead concentrating all of his energies on making and selling one distinctive product. During the 1940s and 1950s H.B. Reese's six sons joined him in the top management of the company and they prospered as the peanut butter cups became popular nationwide.

The Reese brothers saw a need for a larger, more modern facility, and they began construction of a highly automated plant on Chocolate Avenue in Hershey. H.B. died in 1956, just a year before the new factory began production of peanut butter cups. The business continued to flourish after his death, and in July 1963 the H.B. Reese Candy Company was bought by the Hershey Chocolate Corporation. It was the first significant acquisition by Hershey, and proved to be a major asset for the larger company.

The Hershey Chocolate Corporation took on a new direction in the 1960s and 1970s as Reese's peanut butter cups became an integral part of the company. In 1968 Hershey Chocolate Corporation reorganized into Hershey Foods Corporation, and the manufacture of Reese's peanut butter cups came under the newly-created division called Hershey Chocolate U.S.A.

During the same year that Hershey acquired H.B. Reese Candy Company, Hershey opened its second manufacturing plant. This one was in Smiths Falls, Ontario, Canada. The plant operation was originally known as Hershey Chocolate Corporation of Canada, Ltd., but in 1981 the name was changed to Hershey Canada Inc. Its headquarters were moved closer to Toronto, but the plant in

AT A GLANCE

Reese's brand peanut butter cup founded in 1923 by Harry B. Reese; first produced by the H. B. Reese Candy Company in Hershey, PA; company discontinued all other product lines to concentrate on peanut butter cup production during World War II; in July of 1963 the H. B. Reese Candy Company was sold to Hershey Chocolate Corporation, which was renamed Hershey Foods Corporation in 1968; Reese's peanut butter cup later manufactured by Hershey Chocolate U.S.A. and Hershey Canada Inc., divisions of Hershey Foods Corp..

Performance: *Market share*—5.2% of candy market (top share). *Sales*—$357 million.

Major competitor: Snickers, a product of M&M/Mars.

Advertising: *Agency*—Ogilvy & Mather, New York, NY, 1969—. *Major campaign*—"There's no wrong way to eat a Reese's."

Addresses: *Parent company*—Hershey Chocolate U.S.A., P.O. Box 815, Hershey, PA 17033-0815; phone 800-468-1714. *Ultimate parent company*—Hershey Foods Corporation, 100 Crystal A Drive, P.O. Box 810, Hershey, PA 17033-0810; phone: (717) 534-7631; fax: (717) 534-7896.

Smiths Falls remained in operation. The Canadian plant was kept busy, especially when Hershey acquired Y & S Candies Inc., the makers of Twizzlers licorice. Both Y & S and Reese's candies are now manufactured by Hershey Chocolate U.S.A. and Hershey Canada.

The Canadian versions of Hershey's and Reese's products featured a reformulated chocolate designed to appeal to the Canadian palate. In Canada, Reese's peanut butter cups are known as Reese peanut butter cups, and the familiar orange, brown, and yellow wrapping features the French translation *moules au beurre d'arachides*. In 1991 Reese peanut butter cups reached record market shares in their category in Canada.

The manufacture of Reese's peanut butter cups involves an operation that seems quite simple. Brown paper cups are lined up on conveyor belts in Hershey; Oakdale, California; and Smiths Falls, Ontario. Hershey's chocolate is the first ingredient poured into the cups. The chocolate is followed by Reese's special peanut butter, which is then topped with a covering of chocolate. The peanut butter cups are then shaken so the chocolate fully coats the sides of the cup, and to ensure that the top of the cup has no bubbles. The peanut butter cups then spend 30 minutes in a cooling tunnel before being packaged in the orange, yellow, and brown wrappers and boxed or bagged for shipping.

In 1970 Hershey invested additional money into the manufacture of Reese's peanut butter cups by building an addition to the Reese plant in Hershey. It doubled the size of the former plant and enabled Hershey to domestically produce Kit Kat candy bars as well as increase production of peanut butter cups.

Product Innovations

As H.B. Reese discovered, the peanut butter cup established itself as a popular product not in need of radical change. However, Hershey has slowly found ways to create innovations in its perennially winning product. In 1976 Hershey introduced Reese's crunchy peanut butter cups. By the next year, demand required yet another expansion of the Reese's factory. The crunchy peanut butter cups were very similar to the original peanut butter cups, but the chocolate on top of the peanut butter contained chopped peanuts. The crunchy peanut butter cups were reformulated in 1991 to contain three times as many chopped peanuts. Hershey expanded its advertising efforts to tout the reformulated peanut butter cups. In the same year, holiday varieties were added to the Reese's family. For Easter, Reese's displayed peanut butter eggs, and for Christmas Reese's peanut butter trees were made available.

In addition to its confectionery goods, Reese's products expanded into grocery goods. Reese's peanut butter chips were the first products with the Reese's label to appear outside the candy aisle. It was several years before Hershey made the far more adventurous foray into the peanut butter aisle.

Reese's peanut butter was nationally introduced in January 1992. Timing for the release of the new product was favorable. Peanut prices surged from the end of 1990 through 1991, but the prices moderated by 1992, when Reese's peanut butter was introduced. The advertising for the peanut butter relied heavily on the Reese's peanut butter cup image. Using the same brightly colored orange and yellow Reese's label, print ads said: "Everything we know about peanut butter is now available in jars. Introducing Reese's peanut butter in creamy or crunchy style. Spread the word." A report in *Wall Street Journal* in October 1992 listed the new peanut butter's market share as 3.5 percent.

Another item in test marketing in the early 1990s was a new Reese's peanut butter and caramel cup. Given Hershey's extended rivalry with M&M/Mars, the new candy bar was well positioned to compete directly with the competition's flagship candy bar, Snickers. Called Reese's Caramel & Peanuts, the new product's performance was being evaluated in Ohio. M&M/Mars had previously enjoyed success with their peanut butter M&M's, which competed directly with the Reese's peanut butter cups. The rivalry between the two companies is obviously still a healthy one.

Marketing Strategy

Milton Hershey did not believe in advertising his products in the conventional way. His theory was, "Give them quality. That's the best advertising in the world." Because of this, Hershey did not begin consumer advertising until 1970. The only advertising agency responsible for Reese's peanut butter cups has been Ogilvy & Mather in New York. They were signed on in 1969. In 1991, according to *Advertising Age*, Hershey spent $13,014,000 advertising Reese's candy alone. This represented a 34 percent increase over the previous year.

Sales of the Reese's peanut butter cup have continued to improve despite, or perhaps because of, the lack of major changes in the product. Writing in *Forbes,* Janet Novack explains: "Hershey has boosted cup weights, improved product freshness, and now dresses miniature cups in red and green for Christmas. Result: a five-year compound annual dollar sales growth of 17%." Such attention to the cups make the 70-year-old product seem like a brand new discovery.

A promotion in the 1980s helped increase Reese's sales by double digits. The contest offered prizes, including televisions and computers. Winners were those who found two matching wrappers of Reese's peanut butter cups.

In February 1991, Hershey had its first price increase in five years. The 12 percent increase (five cents per regular-sized candy bar), affected all Hershey candies. Although all of the other major companies in the industry followed suit almost immediately, unit volumes dropped. But dollar sales were up four percent. In March 1992 Hershey introduced another increase of five percent to the wholesale prices.

While the competitors watched each other's price increases, they also followed each other's promotions. Early in 1992, M&M/Mars began a price rebate promotion. The program was matched soon afterwards by Hershey, and ran through October 1992. Both companies offered a five cent refund for each wrapper mailed to the company. Hershey accepted wrappers from any Reese's, Hershey, or Peter Paul/Cadbury candy bar. The company also sent coupons for four free candy bars to those who responded by July 31.

Health Food?

Hershey Foods has always been concerned about the image of its products with the American public. As Americans have become more health conscious, Hershey has emphasized the American Dietetic Association's view that there is room in a well-balanced diet for snacks. Hershey was among the first confectionery companies to provide nutritional labeling on its products in the early 1970s. Scientific research has often supported the company's assertions regarding chocolate and tooth decay, chocolate and hyperactivity, chocolate and caffeine, chocolate and cholesterol, and chocolate and acne.

Hershey points out that granola bars and raisins may cause more tooth decay than chocolate because chocolate melts quickly and because it has a component that blocks the production of plaque. The FDA concluded there was no scientific evidence linking sugar to hyperactivity in 1986. Milk chocolate has been found to be low in caffeine: there are only ten milligrams of caffeine in a Hershey's milk chocolate bar, while a can of Coca Cola contains thirty milligrams, and even a five-ounce cup of decaffeinated coffee contains three milligrams. Stearic acid, a saturated fat found in chocolate, may actually lower blood cholesterol, unlike other saturated fats. Milk chocolate is low in cholesterol, and cocoa is cholesterol-free. A 1.55-ounce chocolate bar has less than half the cholesterol found in a one-ounce piece of cheddar cheese. Researchers have also found that chocolate does not cause acne unless it is rubbed directly onto the skin.

Also helpful to the growth of Reese's peanut butter cups has been the peanut content. Joan Steuer, president of Chocolate Marketing Inc., quoted in the *New York Times*, stated that "[n]uts in chocolate, toffee and peanut butter are very big because there is a perceived wholesomeness there."

Hershey Chocolate U.S.A. uses hundreds of tons of peanuts annually for peanut butter cups and other products. The peanuts come from the southern and southwestern United States, and Hershey has always been a very good customer for the industry. The company also suffers with the industry, as it did during the bad weather in 1991 that drastically reduced the peanut harvest and brought the market price for peanuts to a record high that year.

Reese's peanut butter cups are one of five Hershey brands consistently on the industry's best-seller lists. However, the candy industry in the 1990s was being forced to consider that while they may be recession-resistant, they were not recession-proof. Suein Hwang, writing in *Wall Street Journal*, noted that "consumers are increasingly preoccupied both with their wallets and their waistlines . . . And the aging of the population hasn't helped matters." Joan Steuer of Chocolate Marketing was less pessimistic, however, and stated that "people see [chocolate] as an affordable indulgence . . . It's the ultimate feel-good food."

Further Reading:

"Candy Is Dandy: Some Facts about America's Sweetest Industry," *MetroKids*, October 1992, pp. 5-6.

Dagnoli, Judann, "Reese's brand spreads," *Advertising Age*, February 17, 1992, p. 56.

Federal Reserve Bank of Boston, "How Sweet It Is!," *The Ledger: Economic Education Newsletter*, June 1988, pp. 1-2.

The H.B. Reese Candy Company Inc.—A Brief History, Hershey, PA: Hershey Foods Corporation.

Hershey Foods Corporation 1991 Annual Report, Hershey, PA: The Hershey Foods Corporation, 1992.

Hwang, Suein L., "Peanuts and Caramel Combine to Create Sticky Competition," *Wall Street Journal*, April 14, 1992, p. B11.

Koselka, Rita, "Candy Wars," *Forbes*, August 17, 1992, pp. 76-77.

Kupfer, Andrew, "The Sweet Smell of Success," *Fortune*, April 24, 1989, pp. 31-32.

Lawrence, Steve, "Bar Wars: Hershey Bites Mars," *Fortune*, July 8, 1985, pp. 52-57.

Novack, Janet, "The High-Profit Candy Habit," *Forbes*, June 29, 1987, p. 76.

A Profile of Hershey Foods Corporation, Hershey, PA: Hershey Foods Corporation, 1992.

Reitman, Valerie, "Hershey Stirs Up Peanut-Butter Market," *Wall Street Journal*, October 27, 1992, p. B1.

Shapiro, Eben, "Hershey Follows Mars on 5 cent Refund," *New York Times*, April 21, 1992, p. D9.

Steinhauer, Jennifer, "America's Chocoholics: A Built-in Market for Confectioners," *New York Times*, July 14, 1991, p. III, 10.

Warner, Fara, "Sweet Rewards of Competition," *Superbrands, 1991*, pp. 95-96.

—Fran Shonfeld Sherman

RICE-A-RONI®

Since its introduction in 1958, Rice-A-Roni, a convenient blend of rice, vermicelli, and flavored broth advertised as the "San Francisco Treat," has offered American consumers a tasty, easy-to-prepare alternative to ordinary rice, pasta, and potatoes. Despite fierce competition from other products, it remains the best-selling brand in the rapidly growing prepared-rice category. Over the years, the Rice-A-Roni product line has expanded to include a number of other specialties, such as Noodle Roni and Savory Classics, all of which have captured a substantial share of the prepared side-dish market. Now owned by the Quaker Oats Company, maker of dozens of other popular brands, including Aunt Jemima waffles, Gatorade thirst quencher, and Van Camp's pork and beans, Rice-A-Roni maintains its top position based on timely product innovations, trend-setting advertising, and continued responsiveness to consumers' needs for value and convenience.

Brand Origins

The Rice-A-Roni brand was created in 1958 when Vincent de Domenico, one of four sons of Domenico de Domenico, founder of San Francisco's Gragnano Products (later known as Golden Grain Macaroni Company) adapted a favorite Armenian-style rice pilaf recipe for the consumer market. For ten years the original recipe, borrowed from an Armenian neighbor, had appeared on the back of one of Golden Grain's pasta packages, and de Domenico and his wife, Mildred, had often prepared it from scratch in their own kitchen. In 1958 de Domenico decided to substitute dehydrated chicken soup—the company had developed its own soup mix for the U.S. Army during World War II—for the can of Swanson's chicken broth the recipe called for. Before long he had worked out the proper proportions of soup mix, long grain rice, and broken vermicelli, and named the product "Rice-A-Roni" (a combination of rice and macaroni).

Once he had registered the trademark, de Domenico approached a local design firm for packaging suggestions. Finding that none of their ideas appealed to him, he took out a pair of scissors and, using the red and white tablecloth background from a Lipton soup package and an original blue and white Rice-A-Roni logo, designed his own eye-catching box, which he then presented to the designers for refinements.

His next step was to find an advertising agency willing to test the product at a reasonable cost. The only large agency that agreed to accept the assignment was San Francisco-based McCann Erickson. Although they liked the product, they suggested that it be prepared as a casserole rather than as a side dish. De Domenico quickly rejected the casserole idea, but agreed to radio and newspaper test campaigns in Oregon and television and newspaper campaigns in Sacramento—as long as the radio and newspaper advertisements featured a memorable jingle. Before long, McCann Erickson had come up with a catchy tune which, combined with the image of a San Francisco cable car and the sound of its tinkling bell, became the unmistakable symbols of Rice-A-Roni for generations of American TV viewers. The "San Francisco Treat" tag line was soon added to provide additional product recognition.

Rice-A-Roni, viewers learned, was a tasty and convenient side dish—a welcome "change from potatoes"—that could also be used as a base for casseroles. Although the Oregon advertising campaign failed, the product took off in Sacramento. Test-marketing in California and the Pacific Northwest continued through 1958 and 1959. By the end of the decade, a broker organization set up by Vincent de Domenico's younger brother, Tom, and product salesman Paul Mighetto had expanded throughout the West and into the major eastern markets.

Early Marketing Strategies

During the nationwide launch of Rice-A-Roni, the Golden Grain marketing team devised a unique strategy to attract the attention of buyers in the major markets. Company brokers would schedule appointments with chain store owners, wholesalers, and independent buyers across the country. Shortly after their arrival, a hired bus fitted out as a traveling kitchen, complete with a home economist to prepare and serve Rice-A-Roni, would pull up outside, and the buyers would troop out to sample and purchase the product. In New York, more than 300 people attended a special product introduction party held aboard the Circle Line 'Round Manhattan tour boat. The launch was a resounding success.

For the stores themselves, the company introduced "square footer" wire display racks which could be moved from place to place to attract customers' attention. These were labeled with the slogan, "Take a break from potatoes, serve Rice-A-Roni." In large supermarkets, Golden Grain salesmen would stand in front of the checkout counters and give a free sample to every customer with a full basket of groceries. Word-of-mouth advertising also helped to boost the product's sales. Within two years, however, competitive brands, such as American Beauty's Rice-A-Bongo,

AT A GLANCE

Rice-A-Roni brand founded in 1958 in San Leandro, CA, by Vincent de Domenico of Golden Grain Macaroni Company (formerly Gragnano Products, later the Golden Grain Company), which in 1986 became a division of the Quaker Oats Company.

Performance: *Market share*—36% (top share) of prepared-rice category. *Sales*—$135.0 million.

Major competitor: Lipton Golden Sauté; also Uncle Ben's Country Inn.

Advertising: *Agency*—Goldberg, Moser, O'Neill, San Francisco, CA, 1990—. *Major campaign*—San Francisco cable car motif with jingle describing the product as the "San Francisco Treat."

Addresses: *Parent company*—Golden Grain Company, 1111 139th Ave., San Leandro, CA 94578; phone: (510) 357-8400; fax: (814) 667-6126. *Ultimate parent company*—The Quaker Oats Company, Quaker Tower, 321 North Clark St., Chicago, IL 60604-9001; phone: (312) 222-7111.

began to appear on the shelves, forcing Golden Grain to invest in national TV advertising. To cover the cost of an intensive forty-week campaign on ABC-TV, the company raised the price of Rice-A-Roni from 19 to 29 cents per package. The strategy soon paid off, and before long advertising and product distribution had expanded northward to include the Canadian market. In 1962 Golden Grain's total advertising budget was $1.5 million, of which Rice-A-Roni accounted for $1.4 million.

Brand Development

One year after the launch of chicken-flavored Rice-A-Roni, Golden Grain added two new flavors to the product line: Beef and Spanish Rice-A-Roni. Both achieved considerable success, and in 1962 many more varieties, including Chinese Style Fried, Long Grain & Wild, Cheese, Pilaf, Rissotto, Turkey, Herb & Butter, and Rice Custard Pudding, were introduced to the national market. Many more flavors were added following Quaker Oats' acquisition of Golden Grain in 1986. By 1988 the product was available in 30 different varieties—one for every day of the month.

In an effort to capitalize on the success of Rice-A-Roni, a dish which had proved especially popular among busy families seeking both flavor and convenience, Golden Grain introduced a similar product called Noodle Roni in 1964. While vacationing in Italy, Vincent and Mildred de Domenico happened to sample a tasty dish made out of cheese, butter, cream, and thin noodles. Upon his return to the United States, de Domenico copied the recipe and came out with a product he called Noodle Roni Parmesano. This was quickly followed by Scallop-A-Roni, which featured a shell-shaped pasta and a cheese flavor sauce, and Twist-A-Roni, which had a chicken flavor sauce. Although Scallop-A-Roni and Twist-A-Roni received scant advertising support and were soon discontinued—most of the company's advertising money was still going to support Rice-A-Roni—Noodle Roni caught on quickly. Now available in 16 flavors, it is the number two product in the $285 million pasta side-dish category.

By the mid-1960s, a number of well-known companies, including Minute Rice, Lipton, Near East, and General Mills, had test-marketed rice and noodle mix products to compete with Golden

Grain's successful entries. According to Vincent de Domenico's memoirs, General Mills got the idea for several of its new products after taking a firsthand look at the Golden Grain/Rice-A-Roni line-up. In 1966, one year after meeting with de Domenico and touring the company's San Leandro manufacturing facility, product managers from General Mills introduced Betty Crocker Noodles Romanoff and Noodles Stroganoff. These were later upgraded from side-dish entries to main-dish items and marketed under the name Hamburger Helper. However, it was not until the late 1980s that the flavored rice battle really got going.

According to a report compiled by the United States Department of Agriculture, per capita rice consumption in the United States stood at 20.5 pounds per year in 1992—more than double what it had been in 1980. Experts suggested that this dramatic growth in popularity was linked in part to consumers' increasing demands for fat-, sodium-, and cholesterol-free foods, and in part to the active promotion of rice as a versatile alternative to potatoes. However, consumers did not seem willing to sacrifice flavor and diversity just to avoid calories. A June 1990 article in *Consumer Reports* identified rice mixes, such as Rice-A-Roni, as the "fastest growing segment of the rice marketplace."

In 1984 Lipton introduced a product it called Rice and Sauce (later renamed Lipton Golden Sauté) in an effort to unseat market leader Rice-A-Roni. That same year, Mars Inc. launched Uncle Ben's flavored rice. Then in 1988, H.J. Heinz Company purchased Near East brand flavored rice and re-packaged it to catch consumers' attention. "Indeed," wrote David Kalish of *Food & Beverage Marketing,* "the figures tell a story of a category that is feeding on itself. In 1986 unflavored rice sales totaled $426 million, easily surpassing flavored rice sales of $286 million, according to SAMI/Burke. But last year [1987] flavored rice sales jumped 11 percent to nearly $320 million, while unflavored rice sank 8 percent to $390 million. While cannibalization is evident, food marketers have had no choice but to respond to America's growing appetite for value-added rice."

When the Quaker Oats Company bought Golden Grain in 1986, it quickly introduced a string of new Rice-A-Roni flavors. The following year it launched Rice-A-Roni Savory Classics, a premium line of flavored-rice products intended to compete with Uncle Ben's. Microwave versions of Rice-A-Roni and Noodle Roni, originally introduced in 1986 in selected western markets, were launched on a nationwide basis in 1991. To meet the needs of health-conscious consumers, the company introduced Rice-A-Roni with 1/3 Less Salt in 1992. Although the original rectangular box endures, over the years a number of packaging variations have been introduced, including mini-packs, featuring two separate envelopes—enough for two, with no leftovers—and a resealable canister pack.

Innovations in Advertising

During the late 1980s, the battle for supremacy in the flavored-rice arena reached its peak. The Thomas J. Lipton Co. proved a formidable adversary, resorting to what David Kalish of *Food & Beverage Marketing* described as "unusually aggressive tactics" in its efforts to undermine Rice-A-Roni's position. "Nothing is sacred," Kalish wrote. "Not only is Lipton using an ad medium made famous by Rice-A-Roni—cable car boards—but the food giant also dares to challenge Rice-A-Roni's time-honored claim to being 'The San Francisco Treat.' Proclaims recent cable car advertising touting Lipton's Rice and Sauce: 'Now for a real treat.' "

Lipton, wrote Victor F. Zonana of the *Los Angeles Times*, "may have been taking advantage of the year-and-a-half hiatus in TV ads for Rice-A-Roni after Quaker unveiled—and quickly abandoned—a new campaign that played down the cable cars."

In July 1990, following several less successful advertising campaigns, the Golden Grain Co. resurrected the old cable car imagery and introduced a somewhat up-tempo version of the "San Francisco Treat" jingle it had used so successfully in the 1960s and 1970s. "The cable cars are an integral part of our heritage and our advertising position," Golden Grain's Sandy Posa told Zonana. "We consider them ours." In late 1991 the company launched a $2 million TV ad campaign focusing on Rice-A-Roni's Broccoli Au Gratin. One of the key elements of the campaign was a 15-second spot which showed a picture of the White House and alluded to President George Bush's outspoken disdain for broccoli in a humorous attempt to promote the latest in a long line of flavors. Although the Rice-A-Roni brand has had no long-term association with a particular celebrity or celebrities, the company takes an active part in San Francisco's annual cable car bell-ringing contest.

Performance Appraisal

In June 1986 Golden Grain Co. became a subsidiary of the Quaker Oats Company. Since that time, Quaker has introduced a host of new Rice-A-Roni and Noodle Roni flavors, as well as a number of innovative packaging concepts. In 1992 total sales of Rice-A-Roni were $135 million. Its 36 percent market share gave it the number one position in the rapidly growing $540 million prepared-rice category. "Both Rice-A-Roni and Noodle Roni meet consumer needs for convenience and value while providing a light dinner alternative that is a good source of complex carbohydrates," reads the Quaker Oats Company's 1992 annual report. "These factors lead us to believe that Rice-A-Roni and Noodle Roni volumes will continue to grow as we improve profits and returns, driven by tight cost control, innovative marketing and new products."

Further Reading:

Berry, Jon, "Winner's Query: Chiat/Day Asks, 'What's a Roni?'" *Adweek: Western Advertising News*, January 25, 1988, p.1.

Cuneo, Alice Z., "Give Broccoli Another Try, George," *Advertising Age*, October 14, 1991, p. 62.

De Domenico, Vincent, *Golden Grain: The Story of a Family-Owned Company*, Chicago: The Quaker Oats Company, 1989.

Kalish, David, "Rice Revolution," *Food & Beverage Marketing*, August 1988, p. 8.

Lowry, Brian, "Quaker's Rice-A-Roni Sparks Microwave Bout with Pillsbury," *Advertising Age*, September 29, 1986, p. 3.

"Mixes Rate a Mixed Review," *Consumer Reports*, June 1990.

The Quaker Oats Company Annual Report, Chicago: The Quaker Oats Company, 1992.

"Revived Jingle," Ad Notes, *Wall Street Journal*, July 13, 1990.

"Rice Advice," *Consumer Reports*, June 1990.

"Rice and Dried Vegetables," *The 1992 Supermarket Sales Manual: Progressive Grocer*, July 1992, p. 74.

Zonana, Victor F., "Boiling Battle," *Los Angeles Times*, March 29, 1988.

—Caroline Smith

RICHARDS WILD IRISH ROSE®

When Richards Wild Irish Rose brand of wine was introduced in 1954, it faced hundreds of competitors in the U.S. dessert wine market. By the 1980s, however, Wild Irish Rose had outlasted and outsold many of its competitors to become the top-selling dessert wine and, according to the 1992 *Business Rankings Annual,* the eighth best-selling wine brand in the country. Wild Irish Rose is a sweet, light-red wine produced by mixing five kinds of grapes and fortifying the wine to boost its alcohol content to 18 percent. The Wild Irish Rose fortified wine line was extended in 1977 with Wild Irish Rose Light, in 1980 with the introduction of Wild Irish Rose White Label, and in 1992 with Wild Irish Rose Platinum. Wild Irish Rose, sold by the Canandaigua Wine Company, Inc. in Canandaigua, New York, has become the top seller in its class because it appeals to a stable market segment, is reasonably priced, and has maintained a consistent standard of quality.

Brand Origins

"In 1954 we eyed the huge U.S. dessert wine market," Canandaigua chief executive Marvin Sands told contributor Tom Pendergast in an interview, "and decided that we were ready to produce a brand of our own." The competition was formidable. E & J Gallo dominate the dessert wine market, followed by Italian Swiss Colony, Roma, and more than 200 other bottlers—at least one in each state. These companies produced many types of dessert wines, including port, white port, muscatel, sherry, and tokay. But Sands did not want to produce just another varietal. "We wanted to develop a unique product—" Sands told Pendergast, "one that would be recognizable on its own terms and not just as another brand of port or sherry. That is why we gave the product a proprietary name—Richards Wild Irish Rose—rather than a varietal name." The brand is sold under the name of the Richards Wine Company and is produced at both the Canandaigua headquarters the Tenner Brothers Wine Company in Patrick, South Carolina.

Irishman Robert Meenan, Canandaigua's lone sales manager in 1954, suggested naming the new product Wild Irish Rose. Sands added the name of his first son (for whom he had also named a company-held winery in Petersburg, Virginia) to the complete the product's name. Canandaigua winemaker Max Appelbaum developed the brand's sweet combination of five New York grapes. The wine was packaged in a unique square bottle with a red rose on its label, and Canandaigua test marketed its new product in Buffalo,

New York, the closest large city. It met with immediate success, and soon Canandaigua began marketing its product to other cities—including Cleveland, Ohio, and Boston—within the target radius of 300 miles.

Canandaigua Wine Company

Marvin Sands purchased the Canandaigua Wine Company in December of 1945. Canandaigua's production facilities, located in the Finger Lakes district near Rochester, New York, were once used to produce sauerkraut, but they were reconfigured to take advantage of the state's growing wine industry. Initially, Canandaigua's primary business involved producing and selling bulk wine to bottlers owning their own labels. There were more than 200 independent bottlers at the time, but none existed in the early 1990s. Canandaigua specialized in Concord grape wine but also produced many of the other wines for which New York state is known: sweet wines made from apples, cherries, raspberries, and other fruits, and kosher wines. Mack Sands, who had helped his son launch the business with a $10,000 down payment, was himself a wine bottler and one of Canandaigua's early customers.

According to *Forbes* contributor William Baldwin, the 21-year-old Sands soon found himself saddled with more than $250,000 in inventory when the wine business suffered a postwar decline. Eight years later Canandaigua was out of debt, and in 1973, wrote Baldwin, Sands "took Canandaigua public, selling a fourth of the company for $10 million, or $20 a share." Sands, first alone and later with his two sons, Richard and Robert, pursued a dual strategy of developing proprietary brands of wine and purchasing existing wineries and their brands to build a company that could compete in a changing wine market. By 1990 Canandaigua had surpassed the Taylor Wine Company as New York's largest winemaker; by 1993 Canandaigua owned more than 100 brands of wine and operated 11 different wineries, seven of which were located in California.

Early Marketing Strategies

"Wild Irish Rose began as one among hundreds of brands," Sands told Pendergast, "so we had to develop careful marketing and pricing strategies to succeed." One strategy was to price its product slightly higher than the competition; a fifth of Wild Irish Rose cost $1.15 as opposed the $1.00 for competing brands. Such a strategy indicated to the consumer that there was some differ-

AT A GLANCE

Richards Wild Irish Rose brand of dessert wine founded in 1954 in Canandaigua, NY, by Canandaigua Wine Co. Inc. executive Marvin Sands and winemaker Max Appelbaum; produced by the Canandaigua Wine Co. under the name of the Richards Wine Company at production facilities in Canandaigua, NY, and Patrick, SC; brand extensions include Wild Irish Rose White Label and Wild Irish Rose Platinum.

Performance: *Market share*—Top share of dessert wine category. *Sales*—$36 million (1991 figures).

Major competitor: E & J Gallo's Winery's Night Train and Thunderbird brands, as well as their port and white port; Mogen David 20/20.

Advertising: *Agency*—Eric Mower, Buffalo, New York City, Rochester, and Syracuse, NY, 1990—. *Major campaign*—Last major television campaign aired on CBS broadcasts of National Football League games; extensive radio and point-of-sale advertising.

Addresses: *Parent company*—Canandaigua Wine Co. Inc., 116 Buffalo St., Canandaigua, NY 14424; phone: (716) 394-7900; fax: (716) 394-6017.

ence in the quality of the products, yet it did not put the higher priced product out of reach. This method became common among marketers of premium products—especially alcoholic goods—in the 1980s, but was considered innovative at the time. Canandaigua also familiarized consumers with Wild Irish Rose by displaying sample-size bottles in woven baskets that on a retailer's counter. For just 25 cents the consumer could try a sample size and decide whether they were ready to purchase the larger bottle.

When breaking into the Buffalo market, Canandaigua used a small number of local radio spots to advertise its product, but the company moved to heavier radio advertising as it proved an efficient and cost effective way of making its product known. The company's advertising agency in the early years, Helfgott, Towne, & Silverstein, worked with local distributors of Wild Irish Rose to coordinate point-of-sale displays and to offer retailer promotions during periods of heavier advertising. Point-of-sale promotional materials have remained one of the company's most effective means of advertising.

Changing Strategies for Changing Markets

For its first 25 years, Wild Irish Rose was primarily a regional brand. According to Sands, a number of factors kept the product off the national market. The low profit margin available to dessert wine producers forced them to do what they could to keep costs down. However, regulations in the trucking and shipping industry—especially in California—favored companies who shipped larger amounts, and Canandaigua found the cost of shipping its comparatively small amounts prohibitive. Canandaigua decided that the way to keep costs down was to operate its own fleet of trucks, select distributors who would take an interest in the product, and stay within a 300 to 500 mile radius.

Canandaigua's distribution strategy was modified, Sands told Pendergast, "when we began to follow the lead of the soft drink companies that shipped syrup to independent bottlers and distributors. We didn't ship syrup, but it was far cheaper to send one tanker truck full of wine across the country than a truck carrying

six hundred cases of wine." There were several benefits to contracting with independent bottler/distributors. Sands explained, "First, we didn't have to add more bottling facilities to our operation; second, these companies now had an interest in promoting Wild Irish Rose within their existing distribution network; third, we reduced freight costs and extended our distribution area to the whole United States." Canandaigua's first bottling arrangement was with a Chicago, Illinois firm, but the company soon worked with bottlers in Indiana, Texas, Florida, Maine, and Missouri.

In addition to selling to several hundred spirit/wine/beer distributors directly, Wild Irish Rose also relied on independent bottler/distributors in selected markets from 1960 until the early 1980s. In the early 1980s, however, changes in bottling technology and capacity allowed Canandaigua to centralize its bottling operations. With the older equipment, a bottler could produce approximately 30 bottles a minute; the new high-speed bottling equipment allowed production levels of between 300 and 500 bottles a minute. Moving bottling in-house allowed the company gain greater control over the quality of the product and save money by consolidating a step in the production process. During this same time, deregulation of the trucking industry under President Ronald Reagan meant that Canandaigua could save money by using its own fleet of trucks to deliver wine to its distributors and return with empty bottles picked up at designated glass factories.

Reshaping a Wine

In the 1960s, Canandaigua's Indiana bottler found that the trademark square Wild Irish Rose bottle was comparatively expensive, and suggested that the company consider a bottle that would be cheaper to produce. "We were leery about changing our packaging," Sands remarked, "but decided that it would be worthwhile to give a new bottle a chance." They experimented with an hourglass-shaped bottle for several years and later changed to a slender, rectangular shaped bottle with a long neck that was significantly less expensive. After test marketing the new bottle in Washington, D.C. and finding that customers' buying habits remained the same, they switched to the new bottle and have stayed with it ever since.

Canandaigua also modified the ingredients of Wild Irish Rose in the 1960s. Originally the product was a blend of five New York grapes, but in an effort to improve the taste, the winemaker tried a blend with California grapes and finally settled on a blend of grapes from both states. Canandaigua also adjusted the sweetness level from eight balling (a measure of sweetness) to between five and six balling. Such adjustments, noted Sands, were aimed at making the product more palatable to the largest possible market.

Surviving in a Shrinking Market

In its first decade, Wild Irish Rose was the mainstay of Canandaigua's business, representing as much as 95 percent of the company's gross sales. In the late 1960s, however, Americans' tastes in wine began to change from dessert wines to table wines. "Sweet dessert wines were 70 percent of total U.S. wine consumption not long ago," Canandaigua president Richard Sands told *American Demographics* contributor Brad Edmondson. "Now they're 10 percent." Such drastic changes in the wine market have meant equally drastic changes in wine producing strategies. Many producers of dessert wines simply dropped out of the market; others, like Canandaigua, diversified its product portfolio and continued to produce dessert wines for an admittedly shrinking market. By the late 1980s, Wild Irish Rose represented only 20 percent of Canandaigua's roughly $250 million in gross sales, though it was the number one selling wine in its class.

Wild Irish Rose has stayed strong in part because it is a wine without pretension. Marvin Sands described Wild Irish Rose drinkers to Pendergast as "blue collar workers who are not interested in nuance. We make a wine that people drink like they do a beer, not because it is gourmet but because it is refreshing and tastes good." Richard Sands indicated to Edmondson that the company sells its product to "blacks, Hispanics, 'little old ladies,' rural and blue-collar people, and 'the metropolitan market.' " Canandaigua's advertising has long reflected the interests of that market: commercials aired on nationally televised football games in the early 1970s featured an ethnically-diverse group of musicians playing popular music and bore the slogan "Everybody Knows Wild Irish Rose." This campaign was backed up by extensive in-store advertising, according to Canandaigua's 1976 annual report. Television commercials in the late 1970s and early 1980s featured bouncing cheerleaders in tiny red shorts. By 1982 the advertising theme for Wild Irish Rose had switched to "There's No Taste Like the Rose."

Canandaigua has also used more unconventional ways of reaching out to potential customers. In September of 1984 the company introduced a sweepstakes promotion. In 1985 a second sweepstakes offered a $65,000 automobile as the grand prize. Furthermore, Sands told Forbes contributor Baldwin, "We were the initiators of coupons in the wine industry." "We've always appealed to a broad market," Sands told Pendergast, "a group of people who were less interested in what variety of grape went into the wine than in whether they liked the product or not."

Facing Criticism

Many wine connoisseurs look down on Canandaigua's lower priced products, especially Wild Irish Rose. "When New York wines are good, they're among the best in the world," International Wine Review publisher Craig Goldwyn told Edmondson. "But when they're bad, they're among the worst. New York wine makers must struggle to disassociate themselves from Mogen David and Wild Irish Rose." However, Canandaigua executives seem to recognize that consumers are not choosing between Wild Irish Rose and the more expensive and sophisticated Californian or French wines. "Wild Irish Rose appeals to a less sophisticated taste that hasn't changed with the times," Richard Sands told Edmondson. Furthermore, Canandaigua's annual report for 1977 boasted that Wild Irish Rose had received the Gold Award as "best in category" for dessert wines for three straight years at the International Wine and Spirits Competition in Surrey, England. And, Marvin Sands reminded Baldwin, "A lot of [California wine makers] make nice wine, but they don't make money."

More damaging criticism has come from those who insist on calling Wild Irish Rose a "wino wine." Community groups in Los Angeles, San Francisco, Seattle, and Portland have urged makers of fortified wines such as Wild Irish Rose and E & J Gallo's Thunderbird and Night Train brands to pull their products from the shelves of liquor retailers in skid-row areas. In Nashville, Tennessee, one liquor store owner told Nashville Business Journal reporter Julie Hinds that police warned him to stop selling his biggest selling product, Wild Irish Rose, because it encouraged homeless people to linger in the area. However, there is little solid evidence to point to these brands as contributing to the rise of homelessness and indigence that many cities experienced in the 1980s. An E & J Gallo spokesman told Wall Street Journal reporter William Celis III that "history shows that if alcoholics are deprived of one source of alcohol, they will simply find another, regardless of difficulty or cost." And, in markets where fortified wine products have been withdrawn from liquor stores, there has been no noticeable decrease in the number of indigents.

Thomas King, writing in the Wall Street Journal, echoed a commonly-held sentiment when he claimed that fortified wines "have long been associated with the shadowy market of low-income alcoholics and indigents." But this perception is just not accurate, Sands told Pendergast: "Neo-prohibitionists have been looking for easy solutions to the problems of drunkards and indigents on the streets of big cities, but their publicity efforts make some products appear more responsible than they actually are. We know that a wide variety of Americans consume our products for a wide number or reasons, and that these so-called problem drinkers consume approximately one percent of the Wild Irish Rose that is sold." And, investor Richard S. Strong told Barron's National Business and Financial Weekly contributor Jay Palmer, "It's unfair to call [Canandaigua] a wino's winemaker." Instead, Strong said that people should recognize that the company is "oriented downmarket. It makes common ordinary wines for the average blue-collar worker. This is stuff that the average Joe can buy and enjoy."

Healthy Future for Canandaigua

Marvin Sands recognized early on that the Canandaigua Wine Company would succeed by making sound business decisions first, and fine wines second. "When we started, there was just myself and Max Appelbaum, our wine maker, making all the decisions," Sands told Pendergast. "Now, even though we are a much larger company, we are still fairly centralized and efficient—there are ten people on our management team, and they include my sons Richard, who is company president, and Robert, who is the company's lawyer. We currently have 900 employees nationwide with 11 wineries in New York, California, and South Carolina. Of course we have expanded our sales staff, building up a state-by-state network until we reached our present level of 100 salespeople. Our strategy throughout the years has been to develop both internally and externally. We always want to have horses in the race."

Canandaigua developed many of its own brands, including the kosher wine Manischewitz, a white wine called Rhinelieben with a German-looking label, and a New York champagne called J. Roget, which sold over 100,000 cases soon after its introduction in the early 1980s and in recent years reach one million cases. Canandaigua also plunged into the wine cooler market with its Sun Country Wine Cooler, but soon discovered that to compete in the cooler market required massive advertising. In 1987, a year of record sales for the company, the costs of running ads on MTV and of hiring ex-Beatle Ringo Starr to promote the product forced the company to post a loss. To supplement its own brands, Canandaigua has also been aggressive in acquiring outside wineries. The company purchased the Bisceglia Brothers Wine Company in 1974, and in 1991 paid $55 million dollars for the California-based Guild Wineries, makers of the popular Cook's champagne and of Cribari wine, which posts sales of over a million cases annually for each brand. In 1992 a 40-percent earnings increase capped three years of strong growth and prompted Strong to call the Sands's strategy a "hard core approach that works. They go out and buy the small family wineries, take their sales, close surplus facilities and then reap the benefits in margins."

Wild Irish Rose remains a top seller for Canandaigua, selling four to six million cases annually. More recent additions to the Wild Irish Rose line promise that the brand will continue to be a major player in Canandaigua's increasingly diverse family of wines. Wild Irish Rose Light was introduced in 1977, though the "light" designation referred to the alcohol content rather than the calories. In 1980 Wild Irish Rose White Label was introduced, and by the early 1990s it was selling over one million cases annually. This wine contained a blend of New York State Aurora and Elvira grapes and California Thompson and French columbard grapes. 1992 saw the addition of Wild Irish Rose Platinum, a blend of New York and California varietal grapes with a more brandy-like, slightly burnt flavor. Astute management has made Wild Irish Rose the dominant brand in the dessert wine category, despite a market that has gone through years of decline, and Canandaigua shows every sign of continuing the success of the brand.

Further Reading:

Baldwin, William, "New Wine in New Bottles," *Forbes,* January 30, 1984, p. 50.

Business Rankings Annual, Detroit: Gale Research, 1992, p. 655.

Canandaigua Wine Company Annual Reports, Canandaigua, NY: Canandaigua Wine Company, 1973-85.

Celis III, William, "Gallo to End Skid-Row Sales, but Plan May Not Work," *Wall Street Journal,* September 22, 1989.

Dougherty, Timothy R., "Vintners International to Sell its Taylor Wine Unit," *New York Newsday,* April 18, 1990, p. 45.

Edmondson, Brad, "In Vinifera Veritas," *American Demographics,* October, 1988, pp. 49-50.

Gardiner, Christine, "Canandaigua Wine Will Report Jump in Quarterly Net Despite Flat Industry," *Wall Street Journal,* June 7, 1991, sec. B, p. 4.

Hinds, Julie, "Lower Broad Liquor Store Owner Says He's Victim of Cleanup Effort," *Nashville Business Journal,* August, 1990, sec. 1, p. 1.

King, Thomas, "Marketing and Media: Canandaigua Faces Pressure to Drop High-Alcohol Wine Groups, Claim Consumers May Mistake Cisco Brand for Regular Wine Cooler," *Wall Street Journal,* September 12, 1990, sec. B, p. 6.

Palmer, Jay, "Sampling Chateau Screwcap," *Barron's National Business and Financial Weekly,* July 20, 1992, pp. 36-37.

Sands, Marvin, interview with Tom Pendergast for *Encyclopedia of Consumer Brands,* March 2, 1993.

—Tom Pendergast

RITZ®

Ritz, pride of the Nabisco cracker fleet, has been the premium cracker of choice since its inception in 1934. But its history dates back to early in the nineteenth century. It was in 1801, in fact, that the Ritz cracker got its beginnings. It was in that year that John Bent, a retired sea captain, adapted a hardtack recipe into a product more palatable to the general public. He took the hardened "biscuit" (an English designation used at that time) and added leavening agents until the product was a flat, crisp biscuit. Bent's family handled the baking chores while he travelled the countryside selling crackers from his wagon. The basic cracker recipe was refined four years later by the Kennedy Biscuit Works, which used sponge dough for a lighter consistency.

In 1898 the Bent bakery, Kennedy Biscuit Works, and dozens of other bakeries across America joined forces to form the National Biscuit Company. The company was highly successful. By the early 1930s, however, America was ready for a new kind of cracker. Bakers at N.B.C. (as the National Biscuit Company was still known at that time; the amalgam "Nabisco" wouldn't appear as an official name until 1971) experimented with a recipe that used more butter and no yeast. Early trials met with spotty success.

A Formula Perfected

In 1934 the recipe was perfected, resulting in a smooth, flaky cracker hinting of butter. Contrary to the pale, square crackers widely sold, these creations were golden and rounded, with serrated edges. A company-wide cracker-naming contest yielded the name Ritz. Mass production of Ritz crackers began in Nabisco's North Philadelphia bakery and on November 21, 1934, the new product was introduced at markets in Philadelphia and Baltimore.

Consumers responded to this new type of cracker, one that satisfied as much by itself as it did with toppings. By 1935 Ritz was distributed nationally. It was initially marketed as a taste of affordable luxury, no small claim during the Depression years. The positioning worked, with Ritz selling in the five-billion volume area (about 40 crackers for every American in 1935) during its first year of nationwide distribution. Some of this success can be attributed to the product's relatively low price; mass production by Nabisco, the only baking manufacturer with the facilities to distribute nationwide at that time, kept the price of a box of Ritz crackers to an affordable 19 cents.

Within a few years, Ritz had established itself as a dominant presence in the cracker market in both volume and image. In addition, its popularity quickly spread beyond American shores. According to Nabisco company history, in Europe of the late 1930s, young men carried boxes of Ritz crackers as courting gifts, much the way they used to carry chocolates. The luxury liner *Queen Mary* featured the product on their menu, as did the "ritzy" Waldorf-Astoria hotel. Ritz's popularity continues to this day, with volume up to 16 billion crackers per year, sales topping $264 million (1991 figures), and several spinoff brands on the market. But the basic Ritz still retains the same size, shape and flavor.

Themes and Variations

Classic Ritz still heads Nabisco's cracker line—according to *Adweek*, it is the top-selling cracker in America and one of the 40 top brands among all food in 1991. But recent variations to the original cracker have helped to diversify the Ritz name. First to appear was the Ritz Bits product, introduced in 1987. These quarter-sized crackers were made for munching by the handful. Ritz Bits Sandwich followed in 1989, based on the belief that peanut butter was a popular spread on Ritz crackers. Ritz Bits sandwiched a bite-size helping of peanut butter between two miniature crackers. In 1990 Nabisco introduced the Ritz Bits Cheese Sandwich, a dollop of real cheddar cheese tucked between the two small crackers. Jalepeno and Pizza Cheese variations followed soon afterward. Nabisco also introduced two additions to the product line that address the growing market for health foods. Low Salt Ritz crackers were marketed to consumers concerned with their sodium intake, while Whole Wheat Ritz was created for grain-conscious snack seekers.

People have found a variety of imaginative uses for Ritz crackers as snacks, but one recipe has withstood the test of time and become a Ritz classic. Mock Apple Pie, which contains no apples, is the best-known Ritz recipe. The concoction is so popular, in fact, that Nabisco periodically reprints the recipe for new generations of consumers.

"Gooo-ood Cracker"

In its constant efforts to maintain the primacy of Ritz in the snack cracker marketplace, Nabisco has promoted the product in several ways over the years, utilizing both print and electronic media outlets. Always positioned as a premium product, the brand also reminds consumers that Ritz is available for snacks anytime (an early print ad urges, "BUY TWO [boxes] . . . and have *enough!*").

In the field of direct marketing, Nabisco has long utilized coupons and "free-standing inserts" as part of Ritz advertising campaigns, which unfailingly stress the high quality of the cracker. This is demonstrated in a series of television commercials that date back to the 1970s.

The mid-1970s brought one of Ritz's best-known spokesmen, actor Andy Griffith, into the spotlight. In a series of ads, Griffith employed his down-home appeal—"Gooo-oood cracker," he'd inevitably drawl—and interacted with other characters to showcase Ritz's versatility. It was Griffith who suggested to America such popular toppings as peanut butter, cold cuts, and cheeses. "Everything's great when it sits on a Ritz," was his tag line.

In the 1980s commercials emphasized the way Ritz embodied class. A new series of commercials were prepared that featured young, upscale types entertaining guests with Ritz spreads—or just treating themselves to a better-than-average snack. "Inviting" Ritz to parties was the focal point of these ads. Other commercials during this period reminded consumers that Ritz had a "lighter, crispier taste" than other crackers.

Children, being inveterate snackers, were often featured in Ritz commercials. In one, a little boy catches his father in the act of a

Ritz Bits Sandwiches made with cheese were introduced in 1990.

midnight raid on the kitchen—but they make amends by sharing a Ritz snack. In another spot, a child confined to bed with a cold uses her suction-gun to snare a box of Ritz.

A series of mid-1980s commercials featured kids in brief, question-and-answer type commercials, shot on simple sets with a soft jazz score in the background. One child (Raven-Symone, who would later star on the sitcom *Cosby*), is asked who in her house liked Ritz crackers. "Everybody," she replies. "Even the goldfish?" prompts the interviewer. Caught in that trap, Raven admits that everybody *else* likes Ritz. Other children recited the kinds of toppings they liked on their Ritz crackers—as well the kinds they didn't, such as brussels sprouts.

To introduce the specialty Ritz products, several animated commercials were created that depicted tiny Ritz Bits flying to the moon (cheese flavor), cavorting with a cactus (jalepeno flavor), or partying with a pizza (pizza flavor).

Ritz was also featured on the big screen as a plot device in the 1991 drama "Regarding Henry." In that movie, Harrison Ford played a heartless, ruthless attorney who suffers a gunshot wound to the head during the course of a robbery. The resulting brain injury transforms Henry into a more caring, compassionate character—and during his months of amnesia-tinged convalescence, he is taken with the word "Ritz" and paints several canvases with the cracker label's distinctive features. It is only later that we learn his obsession with "Ritz" refers to Manhattan's Ritz-Carlton hotel, where the pre-accident Henry conducted an extramarital affair.

A Line of Quality

For the new generation of quality- and health-conscious snackers, Ritz continues to fulfill a promise of value. Today's manufacturing methods include mechanized mixers to blend the shortening, water, and other ingredients into just the right level of consistency; the wide sheets of dough then pass under specialized cutters. Ovens subsequently bake the crackers to the requisite golden color, and stacks are packaged into 12-oz and 16-oz boxes, each containing rows of Ritz crackers sealed securely in stay-fresh packs. This same attention to detail highlights other Nabisco products. Today, a partial listing of what Nabisco still calls its "biscuit" line—crackers and cookies and pastries—includes not only the Ritz Bits sandwiches, but Wheat Thins, Vegetable Thins, Premium, Uneeda, Escort, Wheatsworth, Waverly, Royal Lunch, Sociables, Twigs, and Triscuits. Nabisco also produces related products such as Doo Dads, Honey Maid Graham Crackers, Cracker Meal, and Nips cracker snacks.

Further Reading:

Petersen, Laurie, "Groan . . . I Don't Find This Funny," *Adweek's Marketing Week,* April 22, 1991.

RJR Nabisco Annual Report, 1991, New York: RJR Nabisco, 1991.

"The Tug of War for America's Tastebuds," *Superbrands 1991,* p. 91.

—Susan Salter

ROLD GOLD®

Rold Gold brand pretzels, manufactured and marketed by Frito-Lay, Inc., were the best-selling pretzel brand in 1992 and 1991. Pretzels are the third-largest salty snack category in the nation, and while they are classified as snack food, they are generally considered to be healthy snack items. Consumers perceive pretzels as nutritious and healthful not only because they are low in fat (pretzels are baked, not fried) but because they are made from wheat flour and contain protein, calcium, phosphate, and other minerals. In addition, most pretzel brands contain no cholesterol or sugar, and may be found in low-salt or no-salt varieties. Surveys show that when consumers decide to make health-related dietary changes, they make cutting back on fat intake a top priority.

It can be said that Rold Gold pretzels accommodate consumers' concerns: each one ounce serving of Rold Gold contains one gram of fat, 110 calories, three grams of protein, 22 grams of carbohydrate, 55 milligrams of potassium, and 620 milligrams of sodium. Pretzels in general have the lowest fat content of all salty snacks, including potato chips, popcorn, corn chips, and peanuts. Pretzels also have the lowest amount of calories from fat—8 percent—of all these salty snacks.

With all these advantages perceived by consumers, particularly as the trend toward healthy eating took hold in the late 1980s, pretzel sales outpaced the modest gains in sales for snack foods as a category. From 1989 to 1992 pretzel sales grew at the rate of 10 percent per year. In fact, The Snack Food Association reported in 1992 that pretzel tonnage in supermarkets increased by almost 18 percent over 1991—more than five times the increase of all snacks—with Rold Gold leading the pack.

Origins

Pretzels have a long and illustrious history. They were known as early as 600 A.D. in southern France and northern Italy, when a monk reportedly made them using leftover bread dough. Children received them as rewards for reciting their prayers. The monk called the pretzel ''pretiola,'' which is Latin for little reward. The popularity of pretzels spread to Austria and Germany, and the product was brought to the United States when people from those countries immigrated to America. Throughout the years, the name evolved as the food was accepted by people speaking different languages, from the Latin pretiola to the Germanic bretzel, to its current appellation, pretzel.

The product that would become Rold Gold pretzels was originally made by the Oakdale Baking Company, founded in 1905. In 1916 the company merged with several other pretzel bakeries and specialty food firms to form the American Cone and Pretzel Company. The original name of the pretzels sold was Halters pretzels and later was changed to Rold Gold. In June of 1958 American Cone and Pretzel Company officially changed its name to Rold Gold, Inc., after its best known trademark. In 1961 Frito-Lay, Inc., purchased Rold Gold from American Cone and Pretzel and began marketing the already well known brand name.

Pretzel Demographics

Frito-Lay came to operate four manufacturing plants around the country that produce one to one and a half million bags of Rold Gold pretzels every week. The majority of Rold Gold pretzels, however, are made in the facility at Canton, Ohio. The facility began production in 1967 and in the early 1990s produced 35 million bags annually to serve its largest market.

The Northeast and North Central regions of the country are known as Pretzel Heartland, and about 60 percent of Rold Gold sales take place there. Philadelphia is considered to be the Super Heartland, and ranks as the city with the nation's highest per capita consumption of pretzels, three pounds per person per year. The increasing popularity of pretzels nationwide is aided, in part, by population shifts taking place. As people move from the Mid-Atlantic and East Central regions to the Southeast and Southwest, they take their regional taste with them, and sales have increased in those regions.

Quality Assurance in Packaging

The widespread popularity of pretzels may also be attributed to modern packaging techniques, which have allowed the national distribution of pretzels. Such packages as air-tight glassine and wax inner bags, strong boxes with cellophane, and foil and wax overwraps have enabled pretzels to stay fresh and crisp during transport and storage.

Typically, Rold Gold pretzels are shipped out of a warehouse within two and a half days and sent to distribution centers and retail store shelves. At the Canton, Ohio, facility alone, 12 packaging machines fill 13 to 56 bags per minute, depending on the size of the bag.

AT A GLANCE

Rold Gold brand pretzels are an outgrowth of the Oakdale Baking Company, founded in 1905; company merged with several other pretzel bakeries and specialty food firms to form the American Cone and Pretzel Company, 1916; the company's original pretzel brand called Halters, and name was later changed to Rold Gold; in 1958 American Cone and Pretzel Company changed its name to Rold Gold, Inc., which was bought by Frito-Lay, Inc., in 1961; the Pepsi-Cola Company acquired Frito-Lay and formed PepsiCo, Inc., 1965.

Performance: *Market share*—12.6% (top share) of U.S. pretzel category. *Sales*—$122 million.

Major competitor: Regional brands of pretzels.

Advertising: *Agency*—DDB Needham /Chicago, Chicago, IL.

Addresses: *Parent company*—Frito-Lay, Inc., 7701 Legacy Dr., Plano, TX 75024; phone: (214) 334-7000; fax: (214) 334-2019. *Ultimate parent company*—PepsiCo, Inc., Purchase, NY; phone: (914) 253-2000; fax: (914) 253-2070.

Pretzel Make-Over

Beginning in 1989, Frito-Lay reformulated the Rold Gold line, and introduced Bavarian Pretzels, among other variations. The reformulation was part of Frito-Lay's new policy of breathing new life into some of the company's old snack brands. As Steve Liguori, former Frito-Lay vice president of brand marketing, told *Advertising Age:* "We are having a renaissance of our brands. During the 80s, we didn't do a whole lot of feeding and caring for our existing brands. We almost had an attitude if it was an old brand, it was a tired brand and it wasn't exciting and we wouldn't put a lot of effort against it. We've radically changed that frame of mind."

In the ensuing years, the Rold Gold brand changed its size and shape. In the early 1990s the Rold Gold line had come to include a total of six products: Bavarian Pretzels, Pretzel Twists, Pretzel Sticks, Pretzel Rods, Tiny Twists, and Sourdough. As part of the plan to give a new image to the brand, the reformulated Bavarian Pretzels were packaged in a new yellow package in 1989. In the same year, the Heartland region was given an exclusive Blue Harvest packaging. The following year, 1990, Rold Gold brand pretzels were introduced in canisters.

Marketing

Pretzel manufacturers attributed the robust growth of pretzel sales beginning in 1989 partly to Frito-Lay's heavy promotion of Rold Gold. The promotional efforts gave the whole pretzel category a boost and increased consumer awareness of the snack food.

Frito-Lay's aggressive merchandising was also cited as a reason for Rold Gold becoming the leading pretzel brand. In the late 1980s and early 1990s a host of new and different salty snack items were introduced, and space on store shelves became a precious commodity. If a certain brand sold out, there would be empty shelf space. In order to remedy this situation, it became

Frito-Lay's policy to have salesmen visit supermarkets seven times a week—compared to three times a week in less competitive times—to re-stock its salty snack products. As one supermarketer explained, "The national brands, such as Frito-Lay, are dominating the section more today because of aggressive merchandising."

Another marketing strategy that raised sales was the price war that erupted during this same period among snack manufacturers. The proliferation of so many new salty snack products, coupled with the early-1990s' recession that saw people staying home more, causing snack consumption to rise, resulted in price discounts as an incentive to consumers. One supermarket buyer told *Supermarket News,* "I've seen deeper discounts than I've ever seen before."

Performance Appraisal

In 1993 pretzels were cited in *Advertising Age* as one of 1992's hottest food categories, and Rold Gold topped the list for the second straight year with a 12.6 percent market share. For all brands of pretzels in 1991, the fastest-growing types were the low-salt and no-salt varieties, although together they made up only about ten percent of total pretzel pound volume. This is further indication of the continuing trend toward consumption of healthy snacks.

For all brands of pretzels, the most popular type is hard/sourdough, which make up an estimated 21 percent of total pretzel sales, followed by twists at 14 percent, minis at 13.8 percent, sticks at 13.2 percent, rods at 8.5 percent, rings at 1 percent, and nuggets at 0.3 percent. The remaining 6 percent is made up by all other types. Since the new stated policy of Frito-Lay is to periodically reevaluate existing brands, consumers might see some new Rold Gold pretzel variations in the future.

Further Reading:

Elson, Joel, "Health Trends Put a New Twist in Pretzel Sales," *Supermarket News,* March 18, 1991, p. 20.

"The Evolution of Rold Gold," *The Lay o' the Land,* July, 1961, pp. 6, 15.

"Five Top Brands in 1992's Hottest Categories," *Advertising Age,* January 4, 1993, p. 21.

Kiley, David, "From Potato Famine to a Pretzel Feast," *Adweek's Marketing Week,* July 9, 1990, p. 8.

Klepacki, Laura, "Salty Snack Wars," *Supermarket News,* September 2, 1991, pp. 13-14.

Lawrence, Jennifer, "Enrico Makes His Mark on Frito-Lay," *Advertising Age,* May 18, 1992, p. 26.

Lenius, Pat M., "Stores Find More Space for Salted Snack Displays," *Supermarket News,* September 3, 1990, pp. 14-15.

PepsiCo., Inc., Annual Report, Purchase, NY: PepsiCo, Inc., 1991.

The Pretzel Story, Pottstown, PA: National Pretzel Bakers Institute.

Rold Gold Information Fact Sheet, Canton, OH: Frito-Lay, Inc.

"Solid but Not Spectacular," *Progressive Grocer,* July 1992, pp. 63-70.

"Who Makes the Best Potato Chip?," *Consumer Reports,* June 1991, pp. 380-81.

Zbytniewski, Jo-ann, "A Snack Food Free-For-All," *Progressive Grocer,* September 1992, pp. 121-22.

—Dorothy Kroll

RUFFLES®

Ruffles brand potato chips, the ridged potato chip created in the late 1940s and purchased in 1958 by what would later become Frito-Lay, Inc., was one of only a few brands of potato chips to be distributed nationally, helping to make Ruffles one of the top-selling potato chip brands in the United States with more than $1.3 billion in sales in 1992. In addition to its regular variety, Ruffles came to be sold in popular flavors, including Cheddar & Sour Cream, Mesquite Grille Bar-B-Q, Ranch, and Sour Cream & Onion. A Cajun Spice variety introduced in 1987 has since been dropped from the lineup.

Invention of the Potato Chip

Potato chips are an American original. According to legend, they were created accidentally in 1853 by an irate chef at a trendy restaurant in Saratoga Springs, in upstate New York. As the story goes, Cornelius Vanderbilt, the most powerful American business-man of his time, was dining at Moon's Lake House, and subse-quently became unhappy with the thickness of his fried potatoes. He kept sending them back to the chef, demanding that they be sliced thinner and thinner. After several unsuccessful attempts to please the fussy Vanderbilt, the chef, an American Indian named George Crum, cut a potato into paper-thin slices. He then boiled them in fat until they were crisp, and layered them with salt. He was sure that Vanderbilt would hate them. But to the contrary, Vanderbilt loved the taste of his ''crunch potato slices.'' Potato chips—or ''Saratoga chips'' as they were known for many years—were born. (According to one version of the story, the chef's real name was George Speke. He changed his name to Crum after his Saratoga chips became famous, because Vanderbilt had screamed, ''Get that crumb in here.'')

Early Marketing

Although ''Saratoga chips'' quickly became a popular restau-rant item, especially in the East, they were difficult to manufacture for commercial marketing. Both the supply of potatoes and the cooking process were erratic, making it impossible to ensure consistency in the texture or the taste. The chips also crumbled easily, and because of the fat used in the cooking process, they quickly became rancid, making it difficult to distribute potato chips very far from the ''plant,'' which in the early days was often a kitchen stove.

It wasn't until the turn of the century that true potato chip factories began appearing. The chips were sold to local grocers, who, in turn, dispensed them in bulk from cracker barrels or glass display cases. In 1929 the first continuous cooker was installed at the Ross Potato Chip Company in Richland, Pennsylvania, and in 1933 the Dixie Wax Paper Company of Dallas, Texas, introduced the first pre-printed waxed glassine bags, which allowed potato chip makers to brand their potato chips. In 1992 potato chips represented the largest segment of the $13.4 billion snack food market in the United States with more than $3 billion in sales.

Creation of Ruffles

Ruffles brand potato chips were apparently created in the late 1940s by Bernhard Stahmer, who held patents on several potato-slicing machines, including the slicer that gave Ruffles their dis-tinctive ridges. In 1952 Stahmer leased potato-slicing machines to the Chesty Company, a small, Midwestern potato-chip company. In 1954 Stahmer gave Chesty a license to manufacture and sell Ruffles in Indiana and Illinois.

The Chesty Company had been founded in 1943 by George Johnson in Milwaukee, Wisconsin, but in 1945 he moved the company to Terre Haute, Indiana. Johnson had not been very imaginative in naming his potato chip company. According to the Snacktime Company, which purchased Chesty from Fairmont Foods in 1978, Johnson had been inspired by a pack of Chester-field cigarettes. However, the Chesty Company was an early leader in promotional marketing. Throughout the 1950s Chesty potato chips were a sponsor of the annual ''March Madness'' high school basketball tournaments in both Indiana and Illinois. The Chesty boy, a fair-haired youth in a striped shirt who proudly wore a big ''C'' on his chest, and Ruffles the Clown were well-known symbols of the Chesty Company.

Ruffles Purchased by Frito Company

In 1958 Stahmer assigned all his assets, including the Ruffles brand name, to the Frito Company, the corn chip maker that would merge three years later with potato-chip manufacturer H. W. Lay & Company to become Frito-Lay, Inc. Under the agreement, the Chesty Company continued to manufacture and sell Ruffles in Indiana and Illinois until 1964, when the contract was canceled.

AT A GLANCE

Ruffles brand potato chips created in the late 1940s by Bernhard Stahmer; the Chesty Company became licensed to manufacture and sell the chips, 1954; the Frito Company acquired the Ruffles brand from Stahmer, 1958 (Chesty Company continued to make and sell the chips until 1964); Frito Company merged with H. W. Lay & Company, 1961, to become Frito-Lay, Inc.; merged again in 1965 with Pepsi-Cola Company, forming PepsiCo, Inc.

Performance: *Sales*—$1.3 billion.

Major competitor: Regional brands of potato chips.

Advertising: *Agency*—BBDO, New York, NY, 1992—. *Major campaign*—"Get Your Own Bag."

Addresses: *Parent company*—Frito-Lay, Inc., 7701 Legacy Dr., Plano, TX 75024; phone: (214) 334-7000; fax: (214) 334-2019. *Ultimate parent company*—PepsiCo, Inc., Purchase, NY; phone: (914) 253-2000; fax: (914) 253-2070.

The Chesty Company would eventually disappear in a series of purchases and consolidations. Borden, Inc., which had purchased Snacktime in 1987, closed the Chesty plant in Terre Haute in 1993. But Frito-Lay, which merged with the Pepsi-Cola Company in 1965 to form PepsiCo, Inc., would become the largest salty snack-food company in the world with an estimated 50 percent of the $13.4 billion market. In 1992 Ruffles brand potato chips were Frito-Lay's biggest seller.

"R-R-Ruffles Have R-R-Ridges"

In 1965 Frito-Lay launched an advertising campaign for Ruffles that would become part of the national lexicon. Baby Horton, a cartoon character, trilled his "R"'s, creating the phrase "R-R-Ruffles have R-R-Ridges." That phrase would be the central advertising theme for Ruffles until 1969. Frito-Lay then began to promote Ruffles as a compliment to meals or for between-meal snacking, rather than strictly a chip for dips, with the new theme, "It's Ruffles or Nothing." That was followed by, "The taste won't leave you flat," as the company began introducing new flavored varieties in the 1980s.

Then, in 1989, the theme "R-R-Ruffles have R-R-Ridges" was revived in a major, nationwide television advertising campaign in conjunction with the introduction of Ranch-flavored Ruffles and reformulation of a barbecue version under the name Mesquite Grille. In an article about the new Ruffles campaign, *Advertising Age* quoted then Frito-Lay advertising director Jeff Myers: "Ruffles have ridges" is "a fun thing for consumers to say. Three quick words differentiate what we're all about." Instead of Baby Horton, Warner Bros. cartoon character Porky Pig appeared at the end of the commercials.

New Flavors

In the mid-1980s Frito-Lay introduced several new snack products, many of which failed in the marketplace. The company also drastically reduced advertising support for many of its most popular brands, apparently because Frito-Lay viewed them as "mature" products with little room for growth. However, in 1986, more than 40 years after Ruffles were introduced, Frito-Lay revi-

talized the Ruffles brand with the introduction of a new flavor, Cheddar and Sour Cream.

A year later Cajun Spice was added to the Ruffles family of flavors, followed by Mesquite Grille B-B-Q and Ranch-flavored chips in 1989 and Monterey Jack Cheese-flavored chips in 1991. Steve Liguori, then Frito-Lay vice president of brand marketing, told *Advertising Age* in 1992, "We are having a renaissance of our brands. During the 80s, we didn't do a whole lot of feeding and caring for our existing brands. We almost had an attitude if it was a old brand, it was a tired brand and we wouldn't put a lot of effort against it. We've radically changed that frame of mind."

Nutritional Changes

In 1942, with wartime restrictions on everything from shortening to tires threatening to shut down the potato chip industry, the National Potato Chip Institute (which has since become the Snack Food Association) drafted a paper entitled, "32 Reasons Why Potato Chips Are an Essential Food." The institute argued that potato chips were nutritious, "practically the only ready-to-eat cooked vegetable," and "an economical energy lunch for children." The argument succeeded, and potato chip makers were able to obtain raw materials and continue operating during the war years. Afterwards, manufacturers continued to promote the nutritional value of potato chips, and dozens of other food companies began to link their products to the growing demand for chips, marketing chips and dips, chips and soft drinks, chips and soups, and chips in dozens of recipes printed in national magazines.

By the late 1970s, however, Americans were becoming more health conscious, and potato chips were being criticized by nutritionists because of their high fat content. As an article in *Consumer Reports* stated in 1991, "Potato chips, like potatoes, do supply some vitamins and minerals. . . . Mostly, though, potato chips offer fat."

Frito-Lay began providing nutritional information for its potato chip brand in 1980, and later stressed that its chips were cholesterol-free and only vegetable oils were used in the cooking process. The nutritional label on the distinctive red and blue Ruffles potato chip bag said the chips contain "nine widely recognized nutrients," and added that "Ruffles brand Potato Chips add fun and variety to a well-balanced diet. While our products are not meant to be a basic source of nutrients, they can be enjoyed as part of a healthy diet."

In 1990 Frito-Lay introduced Ruffles Light and Ruffles Light Sour Cream & Onion-flavored potato chips, which the company said contained 33 percent less oil and were at least 10 percent lower in calories. In 1991 *Consumer Reports* said Ruffles Light contained the fewest calories of any brand tested. Frito-Lay also introduced "light" versions of its Doritos brand tortilla chips and Chee-tos brand cheese-flavored snack, and promised more. "The trend toward healthier foods is the most important trend in the industry," reported *Supermarket Business* in 1990.

"Get Your Own Bag"

In 1992 Frito-Lay announced that Ruffles and Lay's potato chips had been reformulated "so that each and every ridge packs more taste and crunch." A Frito-Lay spokesperson told *Progressive Grocer* magazine that "the competition was getting almost as good as us. In order to retain our leadership position, we had to become more unbeatable.'' Ruffles were also back on network television with a new advertising campaign built around the theme, ''Get Your Own Bag.'' Advertising on the bag told potato chip lovers, ''Go ahead. Keep this bag of Ruffles brand Potato Chips all to yourself . . . and hold on tight! You never know who might want your bag of tastier, crunchier Ruffles brand Potato Chips for their very own.''

Overseas Distribution

Ruffles were introduced in the United Kingdom, where potato chips are known as potato crisps, in 1991, giving Frito-Lay the right to claim Ruffles as one of the biggest-selling potato chip brands in the world, as well as in the United States. Kyle Mac-Lachlan, who starred as Dale Cooper in the nighttime TV soap opera *Twin Peaks,* was brand spokesperson in the £3.5 million TV advertising campaign overseas.

Further Reading:

50 Years: A Foundation for the Future, Snack Food Association, 1987.

Berry, Jon, ''The Big Brawl in Snack Food,'' *Adweek's Marketing Week,* September 23, 1991, pp. 4-5.

''Frito-Lay's Cooking Again, and Profits Are Starting to Pop,'' *Business Week,* May 22, 1989, pp. 66-67.

Hoggan, Karen, ''Twin Peaks Star in Double Ad for Ruffles,'' *Marketing,* February 7, 1991, p. 5.

Lawrence, Jennifer, '' 'Rrr-ridges' Rule New Ruffles Ad,'' *Advertising Age,* April 24, 1989, p. 3.

Lawrence, Jennifer, ''Enrico Makes His Mark on Frito-Lay,'' *Advertising Age,* May 18, 1992, p. 26.

''Snack Foods,'' *Supermarket Business,* September 1990, pp. 183-84.

''Who Makes the Best Potato Chip?,'' *Consumer Reports,* June 1991, pp. 379-83.

Zbytniewski, Jo-ann, ''A Snack Food Free-for-All,'' *Progressive Grocer,* September 1992, pp. 121-22.

—Dean Boyer

SALADA®

For more than one hundred years, Salada tea has been promoting quality tea throughout Canada and the northeastern United States. In 1992 in Canada, Salada was the third-best-selling brand of tea, and in the northeastern United States, Salada's largest market area, Salada held a 14.2 percent market share. Salada's regular tea in bags, the tea that built the brand, accounts for 80 percent of the Salada tea line in the U.S. market. In the United States, Redco Foods Inc. manufactures and distributes both Salada and Red Rose teas, whereas in Canada, Salada and Red Rose are owned by Thomas J. Lipton, a subsidiary of UL Canada Ltd. In 1992, *Consumer Reports* rated Salada's black tea as first in taste, along with Red Rose tea, describing Salada as a "well-blended, floral and full body" tea.

Brand Origins

The Salada Ceylon Tea Company was established in Toronto, Canada, in 1892 by Peter C. Larkin, a Canadian wholesale grocery salesman with a flair for marketing and a long-standing interest in tea. In 1888, he entered the wholesale grocery business with the intent of marketing Ceylon teas throughout Canada and the United States. At the time, Ceylon teas were virtually unknown in North America, but in England, they had displaced Chinese teas and dominated the tea market. Larkin believed that Ceylon teas were far superior to the Chinese teas, and if he could induce the public to try a superior product, they would inevitably want to switch to it.

Larkin chose two names for the brand: "Golden Tea Pot Blend" and "Salada," a melodic name of a small tea garden in Northern India, taken from a directory of all the tea gardens in India and Ceylon. Both names appeared on the original package label. Within six months of its introduction to the Canadian market, Larkin dropped the "Golden Tea Pot Blend" name and adopted the "Salada" name exclusively because the two names were confusing grocery orders. He liked the euphonious sound of "Salada" and was convinced that the "Salada" name would best distinguish the tea.

Larkin was the first tea marketer in North America to prepackage loose tea in metal foil packages. Larkin introduced the packaged tea to insure that the public got Ceylon tea and not lower grade tea and to save labor for consumers.

Early Marketing

The business began as a two-man operation, with Larkin handling sales. Larkin's credit was so limited at first that he could only buy what he could quickly sell. According to Larkin's son Gerald, sales in Ontario rose rapidly in the early days, from 12,000 pounds in the first six months of the business to nearly 150,000 pounds three years later, in 1895. Larkin's direct contact with the merchants and his awareness of the competition enabled him to develop a pragmatic marketing strategy. For instance, when he learned that a store clerk believed that a competing tea, Mazawatte, was superior to Salada because it was priced higher, Larkin promptly set his price higher than Mazawatte.

Salada soon expanded beyond Ontario, reaching Montreal in 1895. Salada was sold throughout Canada by the turn of the century. U.S. distribution began in 1896, when Larkin contracted with an agency in Buffalo to distribute Salada throughout New York and Pennsylvania. Within two years, Salada had become popular in Pittsburgh, Cleveland, Syracuse, and Rochester. Larkin established Salada's U.S. headquarters in Boston and built the Salada Tea Company Building, which accommodated the company's administrative, tea manufacturing, and packing operations. The building was well known for its luxurious, aesthetic surroundings and its distinctive bronze doors depicting the history of tea cultivation. Boston quickly became one of Salada's most successful market areas in the United States. By 1916, Larkin incorporated the U.S. part of Salada separately as the Salada Tea Company Inc., and in 1920, he appointed his son Gerald as president of the Salada Tea Company of Canada, Ltd.

Innovative Promotions

From the brand's inception, Larkin believed in using the public to promote the Salada name. When the tea first went to market in Canada, Larkin planned to ask the public which brand name they preferred ("Salada" or "Golden Tea Pot Blend") as soon as the tea gained sufficient visibility. He felt that if the public helped to name the product, they would be more drawn to buying it and staying with it. Although Larkin felt compelled to drop the longer "Golden Tea Pot Blend" name from the package before he could stage this publicity stunt, he used public participation effectively to promote the Salada name in years to come.

AT A GLANCE

Salada brand tea created in 1892 in Toronto, Canada, by the Peter C. Larkin's Salada Ceylon Tea Company, Ltd.; brand first marketed in the United States in 1896; distinctive tea tag sayings introduced into U.S. brand by John Colpitts in 1956; in 1957, company merged with Shiriff-Horsey and renamed Salada-Shiriff Horsey; in 1962, renamed Salada Foods Inc. in the United States and Salada Foods Ltd. in Canada; company purchased by Slater's Steel of Canada in 1967; in 1969, Salada U.S. and Canada divisions split into two separate business operations, both bought by the Kellogg Co.; in 1988, both divisions purchased by Redco Foods Inc.; in 1990, Canadian division sold to Thomas J. Lipton, subsidiary of UL Canada Inc.

Performance: *Market share*—(U.S) 1.7% of tea category. *Sales*—$10.4 million.

Major competitor: Lipton brand of tea.

Advertising: *Agency*—Clark and Pope, New York, NY.

Addresses: *Parent company*—Redco Foods Inc., 100 Northfield Drive, Windsor, CT 06095; phone: (203) 823-1300; fax: (203) 823-2069.

In the brand's earliest days, Larkin attached enormous importance to newspaper advertising and outdoor enamel signs. Early advertising emphasized the introduction of fine Ceylon Tea and often gently coaxed the public to try a higher quality product. Advertising in the 1920s often used repetition of the Salada name in the same ad, along with provocative slogans emphasizing the benefits of the brand. Slogans such as " 'SALADA' TEAS are most Delicious and Refreshing," " 'SALADA' TEAS are drunk by thousands daily," and " 'SALADA' TEAS are most grateful and comforting," aimed to establish the tea as an everyday luxury. Newspaper ads often offered inducements to buy Salada, including coupons for the product, a tea pot, or a cup and saucer. Larkin also advertised in the trade journals, believing that it was important to increase Salada's visibility in the industry.

Larkin also offered tea demonstrations and samples as a strategy to create demand for the tea. In the early 1900s in the United States, Salada tea was introduced at exhibitions, cultural events, and in stores. Larkin invited the public to the Salada Tea Building in Boston to learn about tea manufacture and production and to enjoy the artistic amenities. A 1919 newspaper story in the *Boston Evening Record* urged the public to write essays titled "What I Learned at the Salada Plant" and win $50 or one of the other $150 worth of prizes.

In 1962, Salada moved its entire advertising budget from newspaper advertising to radio. According to Bob Palmer, Media Supervisor at Cunningham and Walsh, Salada's ad agency, "We felt the need to generate excitement around tea." Radio offered repeated exposure, considerable listener loyalty, and reasonable advertising cost. Since radio stations at the time were actively involved in promotional campaigns based on listener participation, the medium offered Salada the opportunity to dynamically involve the public in Salada promotions. Cunningham and Walsh suggested to broadcasters that they come up with station promotions and link them to promotions for Salada.

Stan Freberg, a noted comic and songwriter, was chosen to do radio commercials. Freberg sang off-beat, funny songs that directly addressed the problems of marketing tea in the United States, especially Salada. Freberg took on the American preference for coffee and the public's unwillingness to take the time to brew Salada tea. The Salada commercials poked fun at rivals' use of "tea dust" to quickly create an orange water lacking in flavor. Songs such as "Take Tea and See," "Take Tea and Wait," and "Well Worth the Dangling" made listeners laugh. Stations invited listeners to write one-line jokes or sayings for Salada's tea tags and compete for prizes. These commercials ran in 25 markets, with many stations receiving hundreds of listener entries.

When Kellogg purchased Salada in 1967, advertising returned to more conventional forms. Emphasis shifted to cereal box promotions, newspaper coupons, and supermarket sales. After Redco Foods Inc. bought Salada, newspaper coupons and supermarket sales became the mainstay of Salada's advertising. According to Leading National Advertisers' *Ad Dollar Summary*, $137,000 was spent on advertising in magazines and spot TV for Salada in 1991.

Brand Development

Until World War I, regular green tea in bags was the cornerstone of the Salada brand. By the 1920s, black tea had become widely used in England, and Salada was quick to introduce it in place of green tea. Between the 1920s and the 1990s, regular black tea in bags was the mainstay of the Salada brand of tea. In 1992, regular black tea in bags still accounted for approximately 80 percent of Salada's sales. Although green tea continued to be produced throughout the years, it represented a negligible part of Salada's business.

In 1956, Salada incorporated its distinctive tag lines, or fortune cookie type sayings, on tea tags for the U.S. brand. According to advertising manager John W. Colpitts, who introduced the tag lines, "We felt that good thoughts were very compatible with good tea, and that our tag lines could become conversation pieces on all tea drinking occasions. We could add to Salada Tea Bags something that was novel, unique, interesting, and exclusive." Popular examples of the early tag lines include: "Chop your own wood and it will warm you twice," "Be careful of your thoughts; they may break into words at any time," "If you have plans for tomorrow, drive carefully today," and "About the time you think you can make ends meet, someone moves the ends." Salada frequently added new tag lines and also used a wide variety of types of sayings. Eventually, Salada began to have tag line contests with winners receiving prizes. (The tag lines were never introduced into the Canadian market.)

In 1984, just a year after decaffeinated black teas were introduced into the U.S. market, Salada introduced a "Caffeine-Reduced" tea produced with a water-processed decaffeination technique. By 1989, the decaffeination process was changed to an ethyl acetate process and a reformulated "Naturally Decaffeinated" tea was introduced. In 1992, Redco Foods Inc., Salada's parent company, estimated that the "Naturally Decaffeinated" black tea accounted for 15 percent of Salada tea sales.

Anticipating a shift to convenience cold beverages, Salada got the first patent for ready-to-drink iced tea mix in the United States in 1966. Salada still manufactured the ready-to-drink iced tea in 1993, but it had not gained wide distribution. A family-size tea bag for making large quantities of iced tea has been produced for a southern market, where iced tea made from tea bags is popular. As of 1993, a canned ready-to-drink iced tea in regular and diet formulas was being test marketed, but Redco's plans for broader distribution remained unclear.

Performance Appraisal

In its youth, Salada achieved a strong market position in Canada and the northeast United States. However, by the 1990s, Salada's market share position in the Canadian and U.S. markets was slipping. At the end of 1988, *The Financial Times of Canada* reported that although Salada remained the third-top-selling national brand in Canada, its market share had slipped from 20.9 percent in 1986 to 18 percent in 1987. By the end of 1993, the *Wall Street Journal* reported Salada's $10.4 million annual sales and 1.4 percent market share were the lowest of the nine best-selling supermarket tea brands in the United States, with Salada showing the largest (14.2%) percentage drop in sales from the previous year.

Despite declining sales and market share figures in the 1990s, taste appraisals by *Consumer Reports* in 1977 and 1992 were consistently high. The 1977 report gave Salada the top rank of all teas reviewed, describing it as "mellow, well-balanced, with fragrant flavor and aroma." In the 1992 report, Salada was one of two top-ranked teas by taste quality and was described as a "well-blended, floral and full body" tea.

Predictions

As the early 1990s began, the future of Salada tea remained unclear. The national tea market had shown persistent declines in consumption from the mid-1960s through the early 1990s. *The 1992 Beverage Marketing Directory* reported that 1991 national tea consumption was 1.636 million gallons, down from 1.790 million in 1981. In the early 1990s, *Progressive Grocer* had reported that sales of regular tea in bags showed small yearly declines or, at best, remained soft.

Industry analysts in the early 1990s argued that the tea industry must become more diverse. The black-tea market was shrinking and consumer demand for specialty, decaffeinated, and herbal teas was growing. In 1992, tea industry analyst M. Gill predicted that the regular black tea market would shrink from 90 percent in 1990, to 65 percent by the year 2000, down to 33 percent by the year 2010. This decline would be paralleled by rising consumption of specialty black, decaffeinated, organically grown, and herbal teas.

The whole tea market was threatened by a continuing shift in demand from hot to cold drinks. Analysts predicted an expanding market for cold convenience drinks. In the early 1990s, the larger tea manufacturers attempted to enter the convenience cold beverage market. In commenting on the entire tea industry in 1992, analyst Denys Forrest stated "The question remains whether the sellers of 'real' tea—specialty or otherwise—carry enough clout to resist the tendencies which might seem to be turning the beverage into one more 'soft drink'." By 1992, several mergers for the manufacture of ready-to-drink canned iced tea were announced, including Coke and Nestlé, Pepsi and Lipton, Tetley and A&W, Luzianne and Barq's, and Celestial Seasonings and Perrier.

By 1993, Lipton and Tetley were engaged in a price war, with aggressive couponing strategies that a smaller brand like Salada could not match. Americans based buying on price and did not show much brand loyalty. As the 1990s began, Lipton and Tetley aggressively promoted new herbal and premium teas. By 1993, the continuing price wars launched by Tetley and Lipton and the giant tea-and-soft-drink distribution systems placed increasing competitive pressure on smaller companies like Salada. Salada's capacity to resist these forces remained uncertain.

Further Reading:

Ad Dollar Summary January-December 1991, New York: Leading National Advertisers Inc., Publishers Information Bureau, and The Arbitron Company, 1991.

Brody, Jane, "Scientists Seeking Possible Wonder Drugs in Tea," *New York Times,* March 14, 1991, p. B8.

"Canada Pursues Tea Marketing Ideas," *Tea & Coffee Trade Journal,* August 1992, pp. 18-23.

Deveny, Kathleen, "Marketscan: Tetley Hopes to Reshape the Tea Market," *Wall Street Journal,* February 16, 1992, p. B1.

Forrest, Denys, *The World Tea Trade: A Survey of the Production, Distribution and Consumption of Tea,* Cambridge: Woodhead-Faulkner, 1985, pp. 168-71.

Gill, M., "Specialty and Herbal Teas," published in *Tea: Cultivation to Consumption,* edited by K. C. Willson and M. N. Clifford, London: Chapman & Hall, 1992, pp. 513-28.

"Larkin, Peter C., P.C. (Can.)," *Who's Who in Canada 1928-29,* 20th ed., pp. 613-14.

Moore, Wendy Rasmussen, "Tea Moves Towards the 90's," *Tea and Coffee Trade Journal,* October 1990, pp. 14-18.

Morgan, Hal, *Symbols of America,* New York: Penguin, 1986.

The 1992 Beverage Marketing Directory, Beverage Marketing Corporation, 1991.

"The 1991 Supermarket Sales Manual: Coffee and Tea," *Progressive Grocer,* July 1991, pp. 46, 48.

"The 1992 Supermarket Sales Manual: Coffee and Tea," *Progressive Grocer,* July 1992, p.86.

The 1978 Buying Guide of Consumer Reports, Mt. Vernon, New York: Consumers Union of the United States, 1977, pp. 85-87.

Pouschine, Tatiana, "Tea for Two, but Make It Decaf," *Forbes,* July 14, 1986, p. 89.

Prince, Greg W., "Tea for All," *Beverage World,* April 1992, pp. 24-32.

"Salada Inspires Radio to Sell Itself—and Tea," *Printer's Ink,* January 12, 1962.

Saltmarsh, M., "Instant Tea," published in *Tea: Cultivation to Consumption,* edited by K. C. Willson and M. N. Clifford, London: Chapman & Hall, 1992, pp. 535-54.

Shalleck, Jamie, *Tea,* New York: Viking Press, 1972.

Sisto, Joanne, "Beverages: Who's On First?," *The Financial Times of Canada,* December 31, 1988.

"Tea," *1990 Study of Media and Markets,* Simmons Market Research Bureau Inc., 1990.

Ukers, William H., *All About Tea,* New York: Tea and Coffee Trade Journal, 1935.

"Which Tea Is Best?," *Consumer Reports,* July 1992, pp. 468-74.

Wyman, Carolyn, *I'm a Spam Fan: America's Best Loved Foods,* Stamford, Connecticut: Longmeadow Press, 1992.

—Laura Newman

SALEM®

Salem, the first menthol-flavored, filtered cigarette, was introduced in 1956 by the R. J. Reynolds Tobacco Company (RJR). RJR also marketed Winston cigarettes, and the two brands, named after the corporation's hometown of Winston-Salem, North Carolina, were considered twins in the industry. Salem followed closely on the heels of the hugely successful Winston brand, maintaining a respectable market share and becoming the leading brand in the menthol category in 1992. Pioneering advertising approaches that highlight the "lighter, brighter, and fresher" aspects of smoking, Salem also markets light and ultra light brands.

Brand Origins

Salem appeared two years after the very successful introduction of the Winston brand. Unlike Winston, however, Salem was sprung on the market to complete surprise of its competition. All of the matters surrounding the production of the Salem cigarette were well guarded secrets, more so than any other brand introduced up until that time, in order for the product to get a jump on the competition. As Nannie Tilley points out in *The R.J. Reynolds Tobacco Company,* the basic production technology was already in place from the manufacture of Winston. Thus, the company was very familiar with filter-tip cigarette production and needed only to obtain the menthol to make Salem a new, marketable product.

By the mid-1950s, the menthol market was dominated by Brown and Williamson's Kools, which accounted for four percent of total cigarette sales. Originally, RJR had scheduled the distribution of Salem to begin in January 1957. However, industry rumors indicated that Philip Morris was also ready to release a mentholated cigarette under the Spud brand name. Thus, by moving up its introduction of the Salem brand by nine months, RJR beat Philip Morris to market. This was key to Salem's early success.

National distribution was the company's goal and, after bringing together sales distributors from across the country, it was only a short time before orders for Salem cigarettes came pouring in. As a company experienced in filter cigarette production, RJR was quick to respond to the growing demand for the new cigarette, which reached nationwide markets very quickly. The factory added a third production shift as employment soared and output was expanded to meet the escalating demand.

Early Marketing Strategy

While there were many menthol cigarettes on the market at the time of its introduction, Salem was the first filtered menthol cigarette. Thus, in an industry where products were distinguished mainly by their brand logo, capitalizing on Salem's claim as the "first" of its kind was clearly its best marketing strategy. Head salesperson Frederick Carter took this approach in Salem's initial advertising, spending $2 million to promote Salem as a cigarette which combined "the trend of king size, improved filter, and a new idea in menthol freshness."

The Salem name was initially marketed as being associated with springlike freshness, and this approach was enhanced by the brand's print advertising, primarily in magazines, portraying outdoor scenes and text extolling the cool green menthol feeling. This advertising campaign, along with Salem's reputation as the "best kept secret in the tobacco industry," proved very successful for brand sales in the early years. Salem soon came to dominate the menthol segment of the market and began winning an increasing share of the market.

Salem was clearly a threat to the mentholated cigarette market. However, according to its developers, the product's initial marketing push would not be directed only at the consumer who preferred menthol cigarettes. The company also speculated that a light, pleasant-tasting cigarette might appeal to other smokers and non-smokers. Emphasizing the "lightness" of smoking a Salem, the brand achieved supremacy in sales very quickly, selling four billion cigarettes in its first 12 months. By the end of Salem's second year, sales reached 11 billion cigarettes, and from there they rose from 19.1 billion in 1959 to 44.8 billion by 1963. Bowman Gray, president and later chair of the board at RJR, in an article entitled "The Change to Filter Cigarettes" for *The Strategy of Change for Business Success,* attributed the success to a combination of circumstances, timing, and marketing strategy. Essentially, all components of a successful product came together: manufacturing costs, due to a facility well established from the production of the Winston brand, were so low that no company could compete; marketing research had kept track of the competition, facilitating Salem's early introduction into the market; and the successful promotion of the trend toward lighter, "fresher" cigarettes cracked a market that would be a mainstay of RJR's business for years to come.

AT A GLANCE

Salem brand of filtered menthol cigarette introduced in 1956 by R. J. Reynolds Tobacco Company; became a registered trademark, 1956; company, along with Reynolds Industries, became a subsidiary of RJR Nabisco, Inc., 1986.

Performance: *Market share*—4.8% of cigarette category. *Sales*—$24.6 billion.

Major competitor: Brown & Williamson's Kool; also Lorillard Tobacco Co.'s Newport.

Advertising: *Agency*—Trone Advertising, Greensboro, NC, 1992—. *Major campaign*—"Escape to the Fresh Side."

Addresses: *Parent company*—R. J. Reynolds Tobacco Company, P.O. Box 2959, 401 North Main St., Winston-Salem, NC 27102; phone: (919) 741-5000. *Ultimate parent company*—RJR Nabisco Inc., 1301 Avenue of the Americas, New York, NY 10019; phone: (212) 258-5600. *Ultimate ultimate parent company*—RJR Nabisco Holdings Corp.

Packaging

Salem's bright green and white label (as well as Winston's brilliant red and white package design) contrasted sharply with the dull packaging of other brands at the time, decidedly commanding the attention of consumers. Compared with the plain packaging of such established brands as Camels, Lucky Strikes, and Chesterfield Kings, Salem's packaging offered a bright, fresh alternative.

Of course, the company stressed the package's appearance in its advertising. Gothic lettering of the Salem name was meant to give the package a classic look, while the bright green label color recalled both the cigarette's menthol flavor and the hoped-for association of the cigarette with springtime, the outdoors, and light clean refreshing flavor. This packaging got Salem a leg up on the competition. In Bowman Gray's hyperbole: Salem's "delightful green package suggests perennial green buds that draw the whole of America outdoors. It suggests gentle waters, a shoreline, a breeze permeated with pine scents, the aroma of apple blossoms, and the myrrh of the first roses—in a word, springtime."

Furthermore, RJR's innovation in moisture proof packaging set industry standards for sealing in tobacco freshness. In 1991 RJR introduced "The Wrap" (TM) arguably the most important breakthrough in cigarette packaging since the 1931 cellophane "Humidor Pack" also introduced by RJR. With the trademark name of Flavor Seal, The Wrap is a major improvement on cellophane seal, retaining moisture, critical to cigarette quality, ten times better than the traditional clear film wrap. The Wrap is also better at keeping water *out*, as well as keeping air from seeping into the package, which changes the taste of the cigarette.

Advertising Innovations

Salem's advertising has relied on the green package and visual media focusing on images of springtime and the outdoors. In contrast to Winston, which was marketed mainly through radio advertising, the Salem advertising program made use of print ads featuring photographs of outdoor scenes recalling softness, mildness, and freshness. Campaigns have, throughout the years, continued to identify Salem with springtime, using such slogans as "Springtime Fresh" and "Springtime Softness in Every Puff." The latter campaign was begun after RJR introduced high porosity

cigarette paper in 1959, another innovation that became an industry standard.

In general, Salem advertising during its ascendance was much more visually oriented than Winston's. Although it placed a greater emphasis on magazine ads, Salem did employ some radio advertising and is believed to have been the first to use "mood music" in radio advertising. In 1968, Salem ads began featuring the famous jingle "You can take Salem out of the country but . . . you can't take the country out of Salem." Advertising of that period began to emphasize the "country" and, later, in the 1970s, ads appealed to the consumer's focus on "enjoyment" and "satisfaction."

In recent years RJR has looked to expand in new markets, especially among younger people and, of course, in the global market. Salem's 1991 advertising budget was $7.9 million compared to $41 million spent by Lorillard Tobacco Co. to advertise Newport cigarettes, one of Salem's closest competitors. One campaign, to be launched in test market by Trone Advertising—the company that replaced FCB/Leber Katz Partners as Salem's agent in 1992—is an attempt to attract contemporary smokers called "Escape to the Fresh Side," which will include popular music and entertainment tie-ins.

In 1989 RJR received unfavorable media attention when it began a test introduction of Uptown, a cigarette brand that the company admitted was targeted specifically toward African Americans. Protests from special interest groups as well as from U.S. Health and Human Services Secretary Louis Sullivan prompted RJR to discontinue the test and the Salem Uptown brand. Shortly after this controversy, RJR introduced Salem Gold which used, some industry experts claim, the same advertising pitch as the failed Uptown brand. RJR disputes the claim that Gold is a clone, claiming that each brand has a different tar and nicotine content. In any case, the Salem Gold brand did help Salem gain market share (7.4 percent in the first quarter of 1990 compared to 7.3 percent in the first quarter of 1989), maintaining its lead over other major menthol leaders Kool (which held 3.8 percent of the market in 1990) and Newport (which lost market share, dropping from 4.3 percent to 3.8 percent over 1989).

Health Issues

Smokers wanted a lighter cigarette with less tar and nicotine and Salem was one of the earliest brands to market one. While the cigarette industry has never claimed health benefits of smoking, it has responded to requests from smokers over the years by marketing cigarettes that contain less tar and less nicotine, brands which give the impression of being less harmful to the smoker's health. The Salem brand family includes light and ultra light brands in accordance with this trend.

International Development

RJR continues to explore international markets for its cigarette industry. Since the end of World War II, export markets have been open and developing. Government development assistance included tobacco exports to the third world under the Food for Peace Program, also known as P.C. 480, the "Agricultural Trade Development and Food Assistance Act" which created markets in Thailand, Philippines, Taiwan, among other countries. Furthermore, since the release of the U.S. Surgeon General's report in the 1960s on the health hazards of smoking, the U.S. tobacco industry, in general, has had to resort to export markets in the face of declining domestic consumption. Despite much opposition to cigarettes as a health risk, legal imbroglios, and anti-smoking legislation, the industry has many things going for it to ensure its survival; according to an interview in the *Multinational Monitor:* "The cigarette is an incredible cash cow. It is the most profitable product ever conceived of, and the reason lies in the very truthful words of the former R. J. Reynolds board member, Warren Buffet . . . 'Tell you what I like about the cigarette business. Costs a penny to make, sell it for a dollar. It's addictive.' "

After World War II, not only were export markets opened but cigarette manufacturing itself became multinational, and Salem was a key brand developed overseas. With markets expanding throughout the 1950s, Salem reached the German market by 1960, when RJR announced formation of Neuerburg G.m.b.H., which manufactured a menthol-flavored filter-tipped cigarette called Reyno, which was actually Salem by another name. This new division of RJR established a base within the European Common Market, which was ripe with purchasing power after the war.

International expansion continues into the 1990s. Again, according to *Multinational Monitor*, for the past decade, operating under the authority of Section 301 of the 1974 Trade Act, the U.S. Trade Representative has threatened to impose severe trade sanctions against countries which deny U.S. tobacco companies market access. The opening up of the Eastern European market is pointing toward new ventures in the infant capitalist societies, with RJR planning production facilities in Poland. The Salem brand will perhaps play a role in these plans.

Brand Development

Strong growth throughout the 1960s, coupled with the popularity of Winston, forced the company to construct a new production facility. The Whitaker Park Manufacturing Center, which went into production in 1961, provided a large enough facility to meet the demand for both products. In 1989 the center was completely renovated and equipped with computerized controls and robotic vehicles that allow it to produce up to 275 million cigarettes per day.

As the trend toward lighter brands continued into the 1970s, the company began to experiment with versions of the Salem brand which were of different length, box packaging, and light and ultralight variations. The 100mm softpack was introduced in 1967; Salem Lights came on line in 1975; Salem Ultra Lights in 1980; Salem Slim Lights in 1981; Salem Gold and Salem Box, both introduced in 1990.

Salem's market share, though consistently strong, declined to 5.2 percent in 1992, and the brand is in a constant battle with menthol leaders Kool and Newport. In the face of declining sales of its largest brands, RJR has undertaken ambitious and risky packaging and advertising innovations. One of the reasons for

sagging sales has been the fact that cigarette prices keep rising, due in no small part to the increases in government "sin taxes" on cigarettes. As a result, full price brands such as Salem have been losing market share to discount brands. Now RJR also sells discount brands such as Doral, but full-price brands can be two to three times more profitable (according to David Adelman, a food and tobacco analyst at Dean Witter). Therefore, brands like Salem must maintain consumer loyalty through advertising. RJR hopes that expensive innovations such as the new "Flavor Seal" packaging and billboards proclaiming "Escape to the FreshSide" will continue to help broaden the appeal of Salem.

Performance Appraisal

When Salem burst upon the market in 1956 menthol-flavored cigarettes were already a solid market. RJR's ability to sneak its new product on the market before the competition gave it an initial advantage that would help it well into the future. However, with the cigarette market dwindling over the past two decades, new product innovation, fueled mostly by innovative, expensive advertising campaigns, has kept Salem in the top five in market share.

As with almost all of the nearly 450 brands on the market, brand loyalty generated by expensive advertising campaigns is the key to high profit margins. Thus, although threatened by price competition from lower priced discount brands, ultimately, Salem's new "Escape to the Fresh Side" ad campaign will be a key to its ability to expand its markets.

Further Reading:

Cleary, David Powers, *Great American Brands,* Fairchild Publications, New York, 1981.

Dagnoli, Judann, "RJR's New Smokes Look Uptown," *Advertising Age,* June 25, 1990, p. 6.

Dagnoli, Judann, and Jon Lafayette, "Salem Turns Up the Heat," *Advertising Age,* February 3, 1992, p. 41.

Elliott, Stuart, "Sealing Up Salems to Sell Them," *New York Times,* December 19, 1991, p. C13.

Gray, Bowman, "The Change to Filter Cigarettes," in Furst, Sydney and Milton Sherman, eds., *The Strategy of Change For Business Success,* Clarkston N. Potter, 1969.

Miller, Barry, "History of Salem Cigarettes: Notes From the Archives," R. J. Reynolds, 1993.

"Salem Returns to North Carolina," *ADWEEK Eastern Edition,* April 13, 1992, p. 44.

Tilley, Nannie M., *The R.J. Reynolds Tobacco Company,* University of North Carolina Press, Chapel Hill, 1985.

"Tobacco Buster," *Multinational Monitor,* January/February, 1992, pp. 27-30.

"Tobacco Lords," *Multinational Monitor,* January/February, 1992.

Warner, Fara, "RJR Plans Escape to Make Menthol Hip," *Brandweek,* October 19, 1992, p. 2.

Wheatfirst Securities, Inc., "Maxwell Report" (quarterly), 1992 issues.

—John A. Sarich

SANKA®

Sanka, a roasted blend of arabica and robusta beans, is said to be the world's oldest brand of decaffeinated coffee. First sold in Europe in the early 1900s, Sanka decaffeinated coffee has long been popular among people wanting the flavor of coffee without the stimulation of caffeine. Not until 1923 was the brand introduced in the United States, where it eventually achieved a remarkable level of name recognition, leading some customers to mistakenly use Sanka as a generic term for any decaffeinated coffee. By the early 1990s, Sanka brand coffee is just one of many coffee brands produced by its parent company, Kraft General Foods, Inc., which, according to a 1989 *New York Times* article, controls more than 30 percent of the total U.S. coffee category. Among its other coffee brands are Maxwell House, Maxim, Yuban, Brim, and General Foods International Coffees.

Brand Origins

Although coffee was consumed earlier as a stimulant and a medicine, it was not until the 13th century, or perhaps as late as the mid-15th century, that a beverage was made from roasted coffee beans. First brewed in Arabia, this drink eventually spread to Turkey and, by the 17th century, to Italy, France, and other European countries.

By the late 1800s coffee was a popular drink in many parts of the world, although for a variety of reasons it also had its detractors. Many people, though fond of the flavor, abstained from coffee because it made them nervous or fidgety or because it kept them from sleeping at night. In the United States, where per capita coffee consumption greatly surpassed that of tea in the 1800s, a cereal beverage called Postum was introduced in 1895 as a coffee alternative.

Dr. Ludwig Roselius, the founder of Sanka, emerged as a major coffee producer during this era of rising coffee consumption and growing concern about caffeine. In 1901 he inherited his father's successful coffee business, located in Bremen, a city in northern Germany, and soon afterward began looking into the possibility of removing caffeine from coffee beans. The challenge was to do this without destroying the coffee's delicate flavor and aroma. According to company lore, Roselius was unsuccessful until he gained an unexpected clue in 1903. That year a ship destined for his Bremen business was caught in a heavy ocean storm, leaving the ship's load of coffee beans soaked in brine. When the cargo arrived, Roselius had no commercial use for the ruined beans, so he sent them to his company's researchers for testing. It was soon learned that brine-soaked coffee beans "reacted" differently than ordinary beans, a difference that apparently suggested a new extraction process for caffeine that would not significantly harm the quality of the beans.

The soaked beans, in fact, mimicked the first stage of what became the standard decaffeination process of the 20th century. To extract caffeine, green, or unroasted, coffee beans were steamed under high pressure, thus raising the bean's moisture content and forcing the caffeine to the surface. The beans were then washed with a solvent that extracted the caffeine. Once the beans were decaffeinated, they could be roasted and packaged like regular coffee.

Roselius spent three years refining what became his patented decaffeination process, and in 1906 he was ready to introduce the world's first decaffeinated coffee to Germany and France. Although he already owned a coffee business, he established for this purpose a new company—Kaffee-Handels-Aktiengesellschaft ("Coffee Trading Corporation"), or simply Kaffee HAG—which eventually became one of Europe's largest coffee concerns. In France the new decaffeinated coffee was given the name Sanka, an appellation some speculate is a contraction of the French words *sans* ("without") and *caféine* (caffeine).

Introduction to the United States

Roselius initially marketed his decaffeinated coffee only in Europe, but soon he turned his attention to the rapidly expanding population of North America, where such coffee substitutes as Postum had attracted customers wishing to avoid caffeine. The decaffeinated coffee was introduced in the United States in 1909, and by 1914, just prior to World War I, it was being marketed under its corporate name, Kaffee HAG. Sales of Kaffee HAG coffee, however, were soon interrupted when war broke out between the United States and Germany.

After the war, with Germany defeated, Roselius remained a major business leader in his country, but before long he turned his attention again to the United States, which consumed more than a billion pounds of coffee each year and about half the total world production. In 1923, in order to reenter the U.S. market, Roselius established Coffee Product Corporation in New York, but this time his decaffeinated coffee was sold under the brand name

AT A GLANCE

Sanka brand decaffeinated coffee introduced in 1906 by Dr. Ludwig Roselius of Bremen, Germany; brand first sold in the United States in 1923; beginning in 1927 Sanka marketed by Postum Company, Inc.; Postum, renamed General Foods Corporation in 1929, purchased the Sanka brand in 1932; General Foods became a subsidiary of Philip Morris Companies, Inc., in 1985 and merged in 1989 with Kraft, Inc., to become Kraft General Foods, Inc.

Performance: *Market share*—Top share of instant decaffeinated coffee category; 7.1% (third share) of ground decaffeinated coffee category. *Sales*—$6.1 million (supermarket sales; figures according to a 1993 *Wall Street Journal* article).

Major competitor: Other brands of decaffeinated coffee, such as Procter & Gamble Company's Folgers and Nestlé Beverage Company's Taster's Choice and Nescafé Decaf.

Advertising: *Agency*—Young & Rubicam, New York, NY. *Major campaign*—"Everything you love about coffee."

Addresses: *Parent company*—Kraft General Foods, Inc., 250 North St., White Plains, NY 10625 (914) 335-2500. *Ultimate parent company*—Philip Morris Companies, Inc., 120 Park Ave., New York, NY 10017; phone: (212) 880-5000; fax: (212) 878-2167.

Sanka (the name Kaffee HAG was eliminated from U.S. marketing efforts).

Sanka Coffee Corporation, as the U.S. firm came to be called, was sufficiently optimistic about Sanka's prospects that just four years later, according to a May, 1927, *New York Times* article, it leased a 46,500 square-foot building in Brooklyn to begin decaffeinating coffee in the United States. This building, located on Joralemon Street, was equipped with a private siding to provide easy access to the country's major railroads.

According to a series of other 1927 *New York Times* articles, the U.S. firm also signed a contract with Broadway Subway Advertising Company (BSAC) that allowed it to launch a new marketing campaign for Sanka in the city's subway cars. With the hope of catching the wandering eyes of New York commuters, Sanka Coffee Corporation began putting up advertisements on May 1, 1927, but, unexpectedly, the cards were removed by BSAC just a little more than three weeks later. The advertisements, BSAC said, were considered "unethical" by a Sanka competitor whose products were criticized in the subway cards, and the advertising company claimed it had a responsibility to be considerate to all its clients. Charging conspiracy by "certain large interests," Sanka Coffee Corporation, according to a *Times* article, filed suit against BSAC on June 24, and the following month it won a temporary injunction forbidding the removal of Sanka advertisements from the subway system.

In late 1927, amid this change and controversy, Postum Company, Inc., producer of not only the coffee substitute Postum but also Grape-Nuts, Jell-O, and other food products, signed an agreement to take over the U.S. marketing of Sanka, and by March of 1928 the Postum Company was in full control of the coffee's sales and production. Under the direction of Postum, renamed General Foods Corporation in 1929, the distribution of Sanka was greatly expanded, and by 1930 the product was being sold nationally. Apparently pleased with the decaffeinated coffee, General Foods

purchased Sanka Coffee Corporation from Kaffee HAG in 1932. Roselius, who according to a *New York Times* article gave up his seat on the New York Coffee and Sugar Exchange in 1929, continued to sell Kaffee HAG decaffeinated coffee in Europe. Fifty years later, as reported in a 1979 *Advertising Age* article, General Foods bought the European company, then called HAG AG, from the founder's son, Ludwig Roselius, Jr.

Product Development and Advertising

Under the ownership of General Foods Corporation, Sanka became one of the best-known coffee brands in the United States, and its dominance of the decaffeinated market was reflected by the common use of Sanka as a generic term for any decaffeinated coffee. The problem of genericness—also experienced by other successful brands, such as Coke and Xerox—was eventually confronted by General Foods by having the phrase "Sanka brand coffee" emphasized in its television commercials.

Over the years the company built on its success by developing new types of Sanka products. During World War II General Foods developed soluble, or instant, coffee for sale to the U.S. government for military use, and soon after the war introduced soluble coffee to the general public. In 1946 General Foods marketed Sanka instant coffee in Chicago, and the following year the product was introduced nationally. Two decades later, in 1968, the company came out with its Sanka freeze-dried coffee. The process of freeze-drying, used during World War II for preserving plasma, involved freezing the coffee and then removing its moisture. The moisture was transformed from ice to vapor without first becoming liquid, thus causing fewer adverse effects to the flavor of the coffee. Later innovations included the introduction of a stronger, or high-yield, ground Sanka in 1983 and a darker, more uniform, fresher tasting instant Sanka in 1985.

Along with these innovations, Sanka benefited from a marketing strategy focused on health concerns about caffeine. For example, in 1931, one year after the product reached national distribution, a Sanka advertisement highlighted the problem of insomnia. Featuring an illustration of a woman sitting up in bed, the advertisement announced, "Never again need you exclaim 'Oh, why did I drink that coffee.' " Instead, the advertisement continued, "Why, oh why don't you drink Sanka Coffee—with 97 percent of the caffeine removed. And caffeine is the one thing in coffee that can steal your sleep." Any customer that did not find Sanka "delicious" could ask for a refund.

Some 40 years later health claims were central to Sanka's famous advertising campaign featuring Robert Young, star of the popular television show *Marcus Welby M.D.* Run during the 1970s, these commercials did not identify Young as a physician, but the actor nevertheless was likely seen as lending medical authority to the Sanka advertisements. In the commercials, Young recommended Sanka for people who either felt nervous or suffered from sleeplessness after drinking regular coffee. In 1979, however, the U.S. Federal Trade Commission, according to a *Wall Street Journal* article, publicly stated that the commercials were placing too much emphasis on the relation between nervousness and consumption of caffeinated coffee.

The exact health effects of caffeine, in fact, were not known, and studies showing a possible connection between caffeine use and a series of major health problems were hotly debated. Even so, in the United States, health concerns were likely a major cause for the steady decline in per capita coffee consumption, which, coupled with increased sales of decaffeinated coffee, began in the early 1960s. According to Corby Kummer in an *Atlantic* article, when daily coffee consumption reached its peak in 1962 at 3.12 cups per person, decaffeinated coffee represented just 3 percent of the coffee market. By the late 1980s per capita coffee consumption had fallen below two cups a day, but the market share of decaffeinated coffee had risen.

Change in Sanka's Decaffeination Process

Sales of Sanka and other brands of decaffeinated coffee were carried along on this wave of changing consumer preference, but lurking behind this success were health concerns about the decaffeination process. According to Kummer, most brands were decaffeinated by first raising the moisture level of green coffee beans and then using a chemical solvent, such as methylene chloride, to extract the caffeine. The beans were then roasted at a temperature usually between 350 and 425 degrees Fahrenheit, but because the solvent evaporated at a much lower temperature, little if any residue was thought to remain. Kummer reported that in 1985 the U.S. Food and Drug Administration called the health risks of methylene chloride, the most common solvent, "essentially non-existent," although the chemical was also challenged as being harmful to the Earth's ozone layer.

In response to the controversy, Sanka competitor Nescafé Decaf, owned by Nestlé Beverage Company, began in the mid-1980s to be processed with what was called a "natural" solvent; according to Patricia Winters in *Advertising Age*, advertisements for the product in 1986 seemed to question the safety of the chemical decaffeination method used by other brands. Soon, however, General Foods began decaffeinating Sanka with its own natural solvent, "pure mountain water and natural effervescence," a change announced to television viewers in a January, 1987, commercial featuring a woman speaking directly into the camera. "They say decaffeinated coffee is good for you," Winters quoted the commercial as saying, but "then they turn around and get you wondering about the way it's decaffeinated. Well, the people who make Sanka want you to know that you can enjoy cup after cup of Sanka without a drop of worry." The commercial ended with the question, "Now what are they going to say about that?"

Although the phrase "pure mountain water and natural effervescence" suggested a simple, traditional method, General Foods had actually adopted a highly sophisticated process of decaffeination. All decaffeination methods could be said to use water, whether from a "pure mountain" source or some other origin, but what made the company's new process interesting was its use of supercritical carbon dioxide, referred to in the Sanka commercial as "natural effervescence." Created within a small range of high pressure and temperature, this type of carbon dioxide was neither a gas nor a liquid, but rather in the hazy "supercritical" state between the two, in which gas could not be distinguished from liquid. In the decaffeination of Sanka, it was used as a solvent that could pass through the coffee beans, remove most of its caffeine,

and then vaporize without a trace of residue. Moreover, it did not extract other important, flavor-producing solids in the coffee.

Brand Outlook

The rising sales of decaffeinated coffee began to taper off by the late 1980s, and by 1990 the decaffeinated category appeared to be declining. According to Information Resources Inc., in 1990 alone sales of ground decaffeinated coffee decreased 14 percent, while the drop in instant decaffeinated sales, the category that Sanka led, was a remarkable 24 percent. These declines were three times as large as those in the sales of regular coffee.

Explanations for the decline were varied. In 1993, as reported in the *Wall Street Journal*, a spokesperson for Kraft General Foods, Inc., suggested that the drop in ground decaffeinated sales resulted from two trends: a growing consumer interest in gourmet beans and the recently introduced blends of regular and decaffeinated coffee, such as Maxwell House Lite and Hills Bros. Perfect Balance. Young people, claimed a representative from Nestlé, were no longer impressed with instant coffee the way that previous generations were. In addition, decaffeinated coffees were frequently cited as having an inferior flavor to the regular brews.

During this period of uncertain sales, Sanka was advertised with an ambiguous but inclusive tagline, "Everything you love about coffee." Coupons were also offered in an effort to attract customers. Despite the general fall of the decaffeinated market, the long-term outlook of the brand seemed far from bleak. The Sanka name continued to be the best recognized of the country's many decaffeinated coffee brands.

Further Reading:

"20,000 for Coffee Exchange Seat," *New York Times*, January 19, 1929, p. 30.

"Coffee Concern in Brooklyn Lease," *New York Times*, May 13, 1927, p. 41.

Deveny, Kathleen, "Decaf Loses Favor with Seekers of Flavor," *Wall Street Journal*, February 25, 1993, p. B1, B6.

Kummer, Corby, "Is Coffee Harmful? What Science Says about Caffeine and Decaffeination," *Atlantic*, July 1990, pp. 92-96.

"Marcus Welby Sanka Ads Making FTC Nervous," *Wall Street Journal*, September 5, 1979, p. 22.

Maxwell, John C., Jr., "Coffee Brands Fail to Heat up a Tepid Market," *Advertising Age*, April 17, 1989, p. 62.

Mussey, Barrows, "Uphill Battle Ahead for GF after Buy into HAG," *Advertising Age*, October 8, 1979, p. 18.

"Must Display Sanka Cards," *New York Times*, July 7, 1927, p. 39.

New York Times, October 29, 1989, p. F11.

"Sues Over Subway Ads," *New York Times*, June 25, 1927, p. 22.

"Upsets Ad Injunction," *New York Times*, November 5, 1927, p. 31.

Ukers, William H., *All About Coffee*, New York: The Tea & Coffee Trade Journal Company, 1935, pp. 258-261, 405.

Winters, Patricia, "Sanka Going Natural; Decaf War Perking Up," *Advertising Age*, January 12, 1987, pp. 1, 56.

—Thomas Riggs

SARA LEE®

Sara Lee Bakery Company is one of the largest baking companies in the world and a familiar name to the vast majority of Americans. Sara Lee bakery products have maintained an image of high quality over the years, consistent with founder Charles Lubin's belief that people will pay for premium goods baked with the best ingredients. According to the book *World's Greatest Brands,* Lubin said that he named the company after his daughter because "Sara Lee sounds wholesome and American."

The strength of the Sara Lee brand name was underlined in 1985 when its parent company, Consolidated Foods Corporation, changed its name to Sara Lee. The multi-billion Sara Lee Corporation runs a variety of businesses producing other well-known products, including Coach leatherware, Hanes clothing, Isotoner gloves, Kahn's foods, and L'eggs pantyhose.

Baker Charles Lubin

Charles Lubin began baking as an apprentice in Decatur, Illinois, just after the First World War. Lubin and his brother-in-law Arthur Gordon became partners in 1935 to buy and manage three Chicago bakeries. During the next fourteen years, while the pair ran the Community Bake Shops, Lubin considered the possibility of creating bakery products to sell through supermarkets. In 1949 he created Sara Lee Original Cream Cheese Cake, then founded Kitchens of Sara Lee upon the cheesecake's great success.

By 1951 Lubin was selling his cream cheesecake via delivery trucks that made daily stops; within two years Sara Lee reached a 350-mile radius of the greater Chicago area. Refrigeration was introduced in 1954, and warehouses were set up at various points. On each box founder Charles Lubin printed the words "Keep cool." Some grocers stocked the cheesecake in the cold-cuts and meat cases, while others stored them in the freezer.

Experimenting with a franchise in New York city, Lubin quickly decided he was not comfortable with the situation, since he was unable to constantly check on the quality of the products being produced there. The only other way to distribute nationally was to freeze the product. In January 1952 Lubin bought a number of full-page ads in the trade magazine *Quick Frozen Foods.* The first non-local advertisement copy read, "Now Available for the First Time for Frozen Food Distribution, Sara Lee Cream Cheese Cake. Distributor Inquiries Invited for Available Choice Territories." Lubin also worked with Kraft Cheese Company on a formula that would eliminate surface cracking on the cheesecake during the quick-freeze process.

According to *Quick Frozen Foods,* "Progress with frozen cheese cake was great, but Charlie Lubin soon found out that you couldn't launch any sort of a promotional drive with a single item." Lubin baked items and tested them in the freezer, settling on an all-butter pound cake and an all-butter coffee cake with pecans. Together with the original cheesecake, the three formed the flagship Sara Lee product line.

Price and Packaging Innovation

Charles Lubin did a number of unusual things in his burgeoning business. He printed the price—*his* price of 79¢—on the lid of every frozen cake sent out. Not only were fresh coffee cakes selling for 29¢ at the time; retailers, according to general industry standards, shouldn't be told what price to sell the product for. And Sara Lee cakes were packed in a large tray, which many grocers didn't have freezer space for in the early 1950s. Nevertheless, the product sold in corner stores so well that supermarkets were soon convinced to order Sara Lee.

Production was forced to move to larger spaces several times during the 1950s due to increased demand. Lubin's experiments during this time led him to several discoveries. First, he developed a method to freeze baked goods immediately out of the oven, better preserving their freshness. Second, Lubin packed his baked goods in aluminum foil pans so that the desserts could be baked, sold, and warmed up in the same package.

Sara Lee grew from a $400,000 company in 1951 to a $5 million force by the end of 1955, while the prices on Sara Lee products held steady. In fact, prices remained stable until the late 1960s when inflation finally forced an increase.

Enter, Consolidated Foods

Sara Lee sales, though astronomical—doubling to $10 million in 1956—were in only a few markets. Charles Lubin hired Mandall Kaplan as vice-president and general sales manager in 1955; within months, Sara Lee was distributed in 90 percent of its potential outlets in New York. Yet Lubin had a problem. He didn't have enough space to fill the demand for Sara Lee products, nor did he have enough capital to borrow or build facilities that could do the job. In 1956 he sold Sara Lee to Consolidated Foods Corporation, joining the company as a vice-president, and remaining president of the Sara Lee Bakery division. "A $2.8 million stock arrangement," as reported the April 15, 1960, *Printer's Ink,* "provided a stronger capital base for even further expansion." Through this one move, Sara Lee secured the necessary funds for large manufacturing facilities, product line extensions, and big-league advertising.

Motivational Advertising

Ivan Hill was Sara Lee's original advertising agency. When Hill merged with Cunningham & Walsh in 1955, he took the Sara Lee account with him. Soon after the Consolidated Foods merger, new ads, based on market research, were drawn up to move from what was an introductory campaign to a more sophisticated angle. The market study showed that those who bought Sara Lee cakes associated them with social status and pride, so the company designed the new ads around this theme. As the sub-heading of a 1958 article in *Advertising Age* stated, "Motive Study Guided Shift of Ad Stress from Ingredients to 'Status'." Or, as another caption succinctly stated, the emphasis went from "eggs to ego." The ads pictured a sophisticated dinner party in the background with a woman in the foreground handing out slices of dessert. The copy read: "She's the best cook in her circle—yet she still serves Sara Lee cakes!"

Playing Catch-up

Sara Lee lost no time introducing new baked goods. Cunningham & Walsh planned to hit newspaper, radio, and television audiences in the first national drive introducing two new products simultaneously. In New York, a newspaper ad campaign introducing Sara Lee orange and banana cakes reached 92 percent of its readership, according to a study conducted at the time by the Bureau of Advertising. Long Island stores ran out of the products. Sara Lee placed follow-up ads, as reported in the April 15, 1960, *Printer's Ink,* that showed a few crumbs on an empty plate with the copy: "We're so embarrassed—yet real pleased too. We simply could not bake nearly enough cakes to meet this instantaneous demand." Experts—who Charles Lubin had safely ignored in the past—had advised that banana cake didn't sell. In six months it was Sara Lee's number-two seller, at 12 percent of volume, behind pecan coffee cake, which accounted for 25 percent of total sales. The original cheesecake and pound cake each stood at 10 percent.

The company was better prepared for the year-end 1960 launch of two improved products, chocolate and yellow cake. Large quantities of cakes were baked, frozen, and stored in anticipation of the next campaign. However, Sara Lee ran into the excess demand problem again four years later when introducing frozen rolls. This time the company was represented by a different agency, Chicago's Foote, Cone & Belding. Follow-up ads were once again placed in trade journals asking retailers to be patient until production could meet demand.

"Going Frozen"

For Sara Lee, business had been booming since the company's inception. Although fresh baked goods were selling up to $10

million a year in 1954, Lubin decided to switch to all frozen products. As quoted in the December 1976 *Quick Frozen Foods,* "It was ridiculous," Lubin said. "People in New York were getting a fresher Sara Lee product than a customer in Chicago."

In 1961 the company was ready for the change. Not only did Sara Lee have the best method for quick freezing directly from the oven; marketing evaluations demonstrated that the greatest growth came from the bakery's frozen goods. Converting to all frozen products gave Sara Lee the basis for mass distribution of a consistently fresh product, and all baked goods came out of a single production facility that upheld rigid quality control standards.

A campaign headed by (Ivan) Hill, Rogers, Mason & Scott explained to customers that all ten Sara Lee cakes were " 'oven fresh' every day—and in your grocer's freezer!" A new pineapple cream cheesecake was introduced with the second wave of ads on television's "Judy Garland Show." Within three years the Sara Lee line had seventeen items, and other high-profile TV sponsors included Bob Hope, Art Carney, and Jack Parr. By 1965, advertiser Foote, Cone & Belding had taken over the account.

Distribution

Advertising was only one part of the consistent fine-tuning Charles Lubin gave to Kitchens of Sara Lee. A $22 million, 52-acre, state-of-the-art plant built in Deerfield, Illinois, ensured that quality, consistency, and quantity remained the name of the baking game. The March 1965 *Forbes* described the Sara Lee marvel, a Honeywell computer system which was "the first in the food-processing industry to be applied to plant-wide central processing and quality control." Humans were still needed, however, to ice the cakes, braid Danish pastry, and perform the final taste tests. The plant also hosted a superior distribution system, including an enormous freezer, controlled by the Honeywell computer, that could store up to 8.2 million cakes. Visitors to the plant included delegations from England, France, Germany, Japan, and Russia—Soviet premier Nikita Khrushchev's son-in-law made the trip to suburban Chicago.

Quality Image a Double-Edged Sword

Sara Lee's nationwide marketing success was in full stride by 1970. Although Sara Lee had maintained the same prices on its products for fifteen years—due to superior automation and consistent growth—the company still stressed high quality over competitive pricing. As quoted in the September 28, 1970, *Advertising Age,* Richard Mier, general product marketing manager, explained: "We're worried about the competitor with the higher price, not the guy who underprices." Perhaps because Sara Lee commanded a 70- to 80-percent market share, competition wasn't a great worry. The company's high-quality image, however had "overtones of self-indulgence," as ad agency Doyle Dane Bernbach (DDB), who joined Sara Lee in 1967, quickly pointed out. The same *Advertising Age* article reported that Sara Lee's advertising effort began to focus on persuading customers to overcome "the psychological resistance to buying." The Sara Lee image carried many more advantages than disadvantages, however. The company's association with quality—not restricted to any particular item—was easily extended to any new product offering.

Market Forces

While Sara Lee maintained a commanding market share during the 1970s, the decade presented challenges that foreshadowed more competitive times ahead. To get a jump on any possible challengers, in the fall of 1971 Sara Lee began an intense campaign designed to take business away from neighborhood bakeries. The thrust was directed at retail marketers, in the attempt to convince them that bake shops were cutting into supermarket profits, and they could solve the problem by placing a baked goods freezer next to the fresh bakery section.

The years 1973-75 were rough for Sara Lee due to a nationwide recession and higher costs for bulk products. Producing goods like an all-butter pound cake left the massive bakery little room to maneuver (through the substitution of less expensive margarine, for example). In an interview published in the June 21, 1976, *Advertising Age,* president Thomas Barnum admitted that adhering to the Sara Lee promise of quality, "really hurt, and at times we asked ourselves, 'How good do we want to be?' But we stuck." Sara Lee did drop some items that had not been pulling their weight in the product line-up.

As early as 1959 the company had introduced a dinner item, Chicken Sara Lee. The entree was packaged in a bag, easily dropped into hot water for boiling. A year later, Sara Lee tried a new ad approach with the chicken, concentrating on showing faces and pleased expressions, rather than featuring the food item itself. The product received very little press coverage through the 1960s. In 1972 the company entered the frozen entree market, only to bow out in October 1975. The quality of flour was consistent, the company knew; meat quality, in contrast, could vary even on the same cow.

Line Extensions

In a bold move founder Charles Lubin could be proud of, Sara Lee turned convention on its head with an unusually timed investment. Rather than wait for the economy to bounce back, the company introduced a new line of desserts in July 1974. A combination of careful test marketing (Sara Lee hit 13 percent of the total; most tests reached 6 percent maximum) and phased product expansion proved a great success. Sara Lee presented "Internationals" as a new product line, convincing retailers that the hefty price tag would yield high profit margins.

Other segments of Sara Lee markets were hurt, however, by a combination of the recession and stepped-up competition. By March 1981 Sara Lee's market share in frozen baked goods was 45 percent—a decisive share, yet 30 percent less than a decade previously. Losses were in the subcategories of frozen pies, cookies, and donuts. The problems resulted in management changes and a number of layoffs at the Deerfield headquarters and an Iowa plant. The president and chief executive of Sara Lee's domestic group resigned; the position was then eliminated. Sara Lee's parent company also rearranged executive-level positions, giving Consolidated staff more control over Sara Lee. Ad agency changes occurred as well: Benton & Bowles, with Sara Lee for the past eight years, was replaced by Foote, Cone & Belding. The budget for advertising, however, was one-third what it had been ten years earlier.

Sara Lee began offering frozen croissants in 1983, and introduced a breakfast sweet roll the following year. In 1985 the company returned to the frozen entree market with Le San*wich in 1985. The late 1980s and early 1990s promised more of the same for Sara Lee and its competitors: a rash of new products and heavy advertising in the attempt to define niche markets. Sara Lee went

after the food-service market, making headway in the fast-food sector with products such as croissants, cobblers, snack-size cakes, and gourmet muffins. Breakfast items and cholesterol-free foods were popular as well.

In late 1989 the company invited Charles Lubin's daughter Sara Lee to serve as a spokesperson. Ad agency Chiat/Day/Mojo wanted to focus on the Sara Lee Bakery again, with Sara Lee stressing her father's perfectionism. The company invested $20 million in the campaign. Relying on tradition, the company chose to incorporate their well-known melody and tag line, "Nobody doesn't like Sara Lee."

Forecast

A number of management changes were made in the early 1990s. Most significantly, Sara Lee closed its Deerfield plant, shifting production to other modern facilities capable of turning out a number of food products in addition to the company's traditional desserts.

As with all companies of national stature, the 1990s proved even more competitive as worldwide markets were explored. Sara Lee had a strong base in the United Kingdom and worked to improve its market presence in Australia, Hong Kong, Singapore, and New Zealand. In France, the company introduced a number of cheesecakes, gateaux, and pies. Via a $21 million investment in the production capacity of its plant in Bridlington, England, Sara Lee planned further expansion through the United Kingdom and continental Europe.

Further Reading:

Brown, Kevin V., "Pricing: Sara Lee Beats the Recession with Costly Cakes," *Product Marketing,* April 1977, p. 21.

"Charles Lubin—The Man Who Made Frozen Baked Goods," *Quick Frozen Foods,* December 1976, p. 26.

Edwards, Larry, "Sara Lee President Says 'Convenience' Still Sells," *Advertising Age,* June 21, 1976, p. 69.

Giges, Nancy, "Continental Baking, Sara Lee Seen Declaring War on Little Bake Shops," *Advertising Age,* December 31, 1971, p. 3.

Liesse Erickson, Julie, "Sara Lee Touts Sara Lee," *Advertising Age,* August 28, 1989, p. 4.

Liesse, Julie and Judann Dagnoli, "Desserts Don't Wait for Fat Substitutes," *Advertising Age,* February 5, 1990, p. 3.

"Making a Cake as Fast as You Can," *Fortune,* March 1965, p. 134.

"Motif in New Sara Lee Ads Is Pleased Eaters," *Advertising Age,* September 12, 1960, p. 4.

Neiman, Janet, "What's Ailing Sara Lee?" *Advertising Age,* March 23, 1981, p. 4.

"Sara Lee Ads Promise Pride of 'Home Baking,' " *Advertising Age,* April 14, 1958, p. 80.

Sara Lee Corporation Annual Reports, Chicago: Sara Lee Corporation, 1985, 1990.

"Sara Lee Postpones Ads as Production Lags Behind Demand," *Advertising Age,* November 9, 1964, p. 3.

"Sara Lee: Selling Like Hotcakes," *Printer's Ink,* April 15, 1960, p. 54.

"Sara Lee Sets Ads in Three Media in Push for New Cakes," *Advertising Age,* August 31, 1959, p. 2.

"Sara Lee's Continuity Blanket Puts Shoppers in Frozen Frame of Mind," *Progressive Grocer,* April 1965, p. 239.

"Sara Lee's Recipe: Uni-Marketing," *Printer's Ink,* December 7, 1962, p. 42.

"Sara Lee: Success Is a Piece of Cake," *Railway Age,* April 24, 1967, p. 40.

Sederberg, Kathryn, "Sara Lee Finds High Quality, Good Pricing, Volume Efficiencies Are Keys to Success," *Advertising Age,* September 28, 1970, p. 6.

Wylie, Kenneth, "Sara Lee Recipe for Proper Introduction," *Advertising Age,* February 13, 1986, p. 27.

—*Frances E. Norton*

SCHWEPPES®

A worldwide leader in mixers and soft drinks, Schweppes pioneered the industry in the 18th century. Ranked among the world's 25 most valuable brands, the Schweppes name has virtually complete awareness in Europe and North America, and is Europe's largest bottler. The brand has long dominated the tonic market, and has established a significant niche in the overall soft drink industry. Now owned by Cadbury Beverages Inc., Schweppes defined the mixer category with its tonic, bitter lemon, bitter orange, quinine, club soda, and ginger ales.

Brand Origins and Early Marketing Strategies

Schweppes mineral waters were created in 1783 by Jacob Schweppe, a German-born Swiss jeweler and amateur scientist. Schweppe invented a process of artificially suffusing water with gas to produce mineral waters. Schweppe emigrated to 141 Drury Lane in London, England, where his newly developed "Geneva System" was a closely guarded secret. Schweppe even designed special bottles with rounded ends and wire bound corks to contain the drink's carbonation. The so-called "drunken" bottles are now collectors items.

The market for Schweppes pure bottled waters was enormous. Many people recognized that the polluted drinking water of eighteenth-century England was a source of disease, even though that fact wasn't proved for almost 50 years. Middle- and upper-class Britons were Schweppe's primary market, as they could afford the beverage. Schweppes would retain a premium image and price throughout its history.

After Schweppe retired in 1799, the company continued to concentrate its efforts on table waters. In the early 1800s, Schweppes began to expand its range of products to include aerated lemonade and seltzer waters. Over time, the brand was identified with such honorary designations as: "By Appointment to the King," or "Purveyors to the King," and a gold medal. In 1851 Schweppes was selected as the official refreshment caterer at The Great Exhibition in London, a precursor of the World's Fair. A fountain, the symbol of the exhibition, was incorporated into the Schweppes trademark and remains a part of the brand's identification.

The American Introduction

In 1952 Commander Edward Whitehead flew across the Atlantic Ocean to introduce "Schweppervescence" to America. David Ogilvy of Ogilvy, Benson & Mather, then Schweppes' advertising agency, made the Commander Schweppes' symbol and model. He coined the term "Schweppervescence" to describe the distinctive carbonation of the beverage, which was still a trade secret.

With his scruffy beard and crusty, eccentric image, Whitehead came to represent "the model of a gin-and-tonic man," as a 1970 *Forbes* article put it. The article noted that Americans identified Whitehead so closely with Schweppes that most assumed Whitehead invented the drink as well. The campaign was a marketing coup, one of the most successful ever undertaken, as Schweppes made a solid entry into the vital American soft drink market with a positively British product that was more expensive than consumers had come to expect. The Commander introduced Americans to bitter lemon and bitter orange, and was proud that he came up with the bitter lemon slogan: "The only soft drink that children don't like."

But Whitehead was more than an advertising character. As Chairman of Schweppes, U.S.A., he helped negotiate franchise agreements with the Pepsi-Cola Company. The "essence" of Schweppes products was prepared in England, and Pepsi bottled and sold Schweppes products in the United States and Canada. Under Whitehead's leadership, Schweppes soon became the top tonic brand in America—a rank it continues to enjoy today.

Corporate and International Expansion

Schweppes merged with Cadbury in 1969. The two companies had similar patterns of development and, perhaps more importantly, products that were sold side by side with little overlap or competition. The combined financial strength of the two companies helped provide capital for international expansion. With a market one-third the size of the United States, British companies focused on the international market out of sheer necessity. In the 1960s, one-third of Cadbury Schweppes' profits were made outside the United Kingdom, and foreign sales were expected to grow twice as fast as domestic sales. By the end of the 1960s, Schweppes had expanded into Australia and South Africa.

Schweppes entered the continental European market in late 1971, and made beverage sales the conglomerate's number one

AT A GLANCE

Carbonated mineral waters created in 1783 by Jacob Schweppe in London, England; introduced to the United States in 1952 by Commander Edward Whitehead; Schweppes merged with Cadbury to form Cadbury Schweppes plc in 1969.

Performance: *Market share*—40% of tonic water category.

Major competitor: Canada Dry.

Advertising: *Agency*—Ammirati & Puris, New York, NY, 1983—. *Major campaign*—Comedian John Cleese proclaiming, "The world's only source of Schweppervessence."

Addresses: *Parent company*—Cadbury Beverages Inc., 6 High Ridge Park, Stamford, CT 06095, U.S.A.; phone: (203) 329-0911; fax: (203) 968-7854. *Ultimate parent company*—Cadbury Schweppes plc, 25 Berkeley Square, London W1X 6HT, England.

priority. The company launched Schweppes Cola in Spain and Israel that year, but wanted to concentrate on fruit-based drinks. One Cadbury Schweppes executive commented that the best-selling soft drinks in Germany, France, and Italy contained between 25 percent and 35 percent fruit juice in the 1970s. He noted that, in Europe, cola was "a bit passe—very sweet, very filling. . . ." His comment foreshadowed the worldwide popularity of fruity, natural, "New Age" soft drinks.

The merger of Cadbury and Schweppes was successfully completed in 1972. The company spent over $12 million on soft drink ads worldwide that year, and began to position itself as a healthy product. Overseas sales contributed 40 percent of profits that year, and the company began to leverage its successful merger into investment in Germany, France, Switzerland, Italy, Sweden, and Austria, as well as franchises. Despite an unseasonably cold summer in 1972, Schweppes soft drink sales continued to grow, to the point that production capacity had to be increased.

By 1975 Schweppes Tonic Water dominated the European mixer market, and had nine varieties of soft drinks: Tonic Water, Dry Ginger Ale, American Ginger Ale, Soda Water, Bitter Lemon, Sparkling Orange Lemonade, Ginger Beer, Shandy, and Slimline Range; and 28 franchisees throughout Europe. The brand had also added New Zealand, India, Malaysia, Nigeria, Ghana, Kenya, South Africa, and Zambia to its territory by that time, and had penetrated the Japanese market.

Schweppes' Identity Crisis

After the Cadbury Schweppes merger, Commander Whitehead was elected to the new conglomerate's board of directors. As the Commander neared 60, his advertising roles grew too time-consuming, conflicting with his higher-ranking responsibility as a Cadbury Schweppes director. In order to phase out the Commander, Ogilvy & Mather created an ad campaign that placed Whitehead's mythical ancestors at key events in British history proffering Schweppes to famous figures. The ads capitalized on Whitehead's image and appearance without actually using him, and helped Schweppes achieve national distribution in the United States and Canada.

But during the late 1970s, the brand struggled for a new identity. Beginning in that decade, mainstream soft drinks were advertised primarily to teens. Schweppes, which had always been

positioned as an adult beverage, was faced with a marketing dilemma: should it jump on the teen bandwagon, or keep its mature image?

Ted Bates & Co., an agency employed in the late 1970s and early 1980s, tried to merge the "Britishness" with youthful images. In their campaign, a distinctly British voice described Schweppes as "The Tastemaker" or "a refreshing change from the ordinary," while young, action-oriented people (a ballerina, a pole vaulter, and a couple dancing to disco music) emerged from carbonation bubbles. Versions of the ad appeared on television and radio, in magazines and on billboards, and although it had "Schweppervescence," the campaign soon fizzled.

As the brand struggled with a nebulous image at the end of the decade, Schweppes tonic water dropped from the number one position to number three, and Canada Dry (acquired by Cadbury Schweppes in 1986) achieved domination over Schweppes' ginger ale. Marketers bandied about options "from butlers to bikinis," as one Ammirati & Puris executive recalled in a 1987 *Marketing News* interview.

Advertising Innovations

Schweppes finally realized that the brand needed to regroup and consolidate its efforts to reconstruct its original image. Ammirati & Puris, Inc., was hired to handle the account in 1983, and the agency immediately set work on a "finely tuned brand character." The agency examined Schweppes' history in an effort to find a basis for a new character. Despite a near 20-year gap, Ammirati & Puris' research revealed that consumers still strongly associated Schweppes with the image of Commander Whitehead.

But other images had encroached upon the sophisticated British brand: expense, stuffiness, a special occasion drink. Ammirati & Puris worked to emphasize the sophistication and cosmopolitan Britishness and inject warmth and contemporary humor to offset the stuffiness factor. The results were an ad theme line labeling the brand as "Schweppes, The Great British Bubbly," and a new spokesman known as "The Duke." Not to be confused with John Wayne, the Duke projected an appealing combination of class and humor that quickly communicated the Schweppes brand character to consumers.

By 1987 the character had helped the brand regain its number one position in the tonic water category, earn 13 percent of the ginger ale market, and make flavored seltzer waters a success. In short, the Duke "revitalized" Schweppes' performance.

In 1989 Schweppes Great Britain employed comedian John Cleese as spokesman. Cleese was featured in advertisements that parodied subliminal sales ploys. One 90-second ad preceded the home video of Cleese's 1989 movie, "A Fish Called Wanda." As he railed against subliminal techniques in advertising, the word "Schweppes" appeared inside Cleese's jacket, on the bottom of his shoe, and on the blinds behind him. Research showed that some consumers actually watched the ad two or three more times for the entertainment value. Cleese continued to serve as Schweppes' spokesman into the 1990s.

Finding a Soft Drink Niche

In the late 1980s, Schweppes resolved to disregard cola giants Coca-Cola Company and PepsiCo and their teenage market to concentrate on the "adult soft drinker," as Ammirati & Puris termed the target market. The competition, with 40 percent and 31 percent of the soft drink industry respectively, was daunting: Cadbury Beverages held only 3.4 percent of the market, and that figure included sales of Canada Dry.

But with the steady decline of liquor consumption in the second half of the twentieth century, promoters had no choice but to reposition the brand, noting that 50 percent of tonic was consumed straight. A subtle, but revolutionary, change put tonic in single-serve cans for the first time in Schweppes' history. The move was designed to bring tonic out of the mixer category, which grew half as fast as carbonated beverages.

Research in the United Kingdom revealed that soft drinkers aged 16 to 34 accounted for 38 percent of carbonated beverage consumption. Other market research indicated that, although adult soft drinks constituted a small market, a variety of trends relating to lifestyles, gender, affluence, and consumption suggested that the market would grow.

The "New Age" soft drink trend centered on lighter, healthier beverages with natural flavors and fruit juices, reflecting consumer interest in health and fitness. In the 1990s, New Age beverages offered one of the few opportunities for development in carbonated beverages, growing at 15 percent per year compared to an overall increase of only 2 percent.

In response to the New Age phenomena, Schweppes has positioned its tonic water as a diet drink, emphasizing its sugar- and saccharine-free qualities and refreshment value. Schweppes also led the flavored ginger ale movement with its Raspberry Ginger Ale, which revitalized consumer interest in ginger ale and helped Schweppes gain valuable shelf space in supermarkets.

Performance Appraisal

Schweppes has been involved in the international soft drink arena since the mid-twentieth century, but faced the challenge and opportunity in Eastern Europe and Asia in the 1990s. And although Schweppes is a worldwide leader in mixers, the brand has struggled in recent years to expand into the mainstream soft drink arena. While its competition ranges from giants like Coca-Cola and Pepsi to "lean and mean" regional and private labels, Schweppes has a commodity that many challengers and competitors may never develop: a powerful brand identity that relies on a sense of history, premium quality, and class.

Further Reading:

"Brand power and determination," *Directors & Boards,* Fall 1991, 26-28.

Horovitz, Bruce, "Parodies of Subliminal Advertising Play on the Public Imagination," *Los Angeles Times,* v. 109, August 24, 1990, D6(1).

Houndslow, Stephen, "John Cleese Acts as a Tonic for Schweppes," *Marketing,* May 3, 1990, 3.

Interbrand, *World's Greatest Brands,* New York: John Wiley & Sons, Inc., 1992, 35.

Johnson, Mike, "Cadbury Conquers the World . . . " *Marketing,* January 24, 1991, 20-21.

Kreitzman, Leon, "Food and Drink: Going Soft," *Marketing,* January 12, 1989, 33, 36.

Meller, Paul, "Britvic Takes on Schhh . . . You Know Who," *Marketing,* June 18, 1992, 4.

Ourusoff, Alexandra, "What's in a Name? What the World's Top Brands Are Worth," *Financial World,* September 1, 1992, 32-49.

Sambrook, Clare, "Britain's Biggest Brands," *Marketing,* June 20, 1991, 19-23.

Shapiro, Eben, "A Dowdy Soft Drink in Search of a New Age remake," *New York Times,* May 3, 1992, sec 3, F10(L)(1).

"Schweppes Has 'A Socially Correct Image,' . . . ," *The Marketing Magazine,* April 1, 1969, 39-40, 42, 44, 46.

"Schweppes Rolls Out New TV Commercials," *Beverage Industry,* April 11, 1980, 4, 29.

"Schweppes Sees 'Double' Success," *Beverage Industry,* May 1991, 4, 46.

Thomas, Hester, "Mixed Blessings," *Marketing,* March 28, 1991, 28-29.

——, "New Product Development: Fledglings," *Marketing,* November 10, 1988.

Toor, Mat and Andy Fry, "All Quiet on the Ad Front," *Marketing,* January 24, 1991, 2-3.

Winters, Patricia, "Cadbury Schweppes' Plan: Skirt Cola Giants," *Advertising Age,* August 13, 1990, 22-23.

—April S. Dougal

SEAGRAM'S®

Ranked at number 225 in the 1992 *Fortune* 500 and the largest distilled spirits and wine marketer in the world, The Seagram Company Ltd. is the parent company of such popular liquors and spirits as Crown Royal, Seven Crown, The Glenlivet Scotch, and Chivas Regal, all of which bear the Seagram's brand name. Incorporated in Canada in 1928 as Distillers Corporation-Seagrams Ltd., the company subsequently expanded geographically into the United States, Europe, and the Far East. It also has diversified its holdings to include interests in oil, gas, textiles, and non-alcoholic beverages. The world headquarters of The Seagram Company Ltd. is located in Montreal, Quebec; the U.S. division is based in New York City.

Early History—Canada

Joseph E. Seagram & Sons, Ltd., a small distillery on the Grand River in Waterloo, Ontario, was founded in 1857. A sideline of a grain millery, the distillery used leftover grain to produce alcoholic beverages. Joseph E. Seagram, who began his working career as a miller, became the sole owner of the firm in 1883. The company expanded rapidly, and by 1900, it was producing a number of popular liquors, including the ''83'' blend, named to commemorate the year in which Joseph purchased the company, and Seagram's V.O., a Canadian whisky launched shortly before Joseph's death in 1919.

A Conservative member of Canada's Parliament and an avid horseman, Joseph Seagram was a more common figure in the stable than the boardroom. When he died, his eldest son, Edward Frowde Seagram, took over the distillery, but the company fared poorly under Edward's stewardship. In 1926 it was purchased by Doherty, Easson, a stock brokerage concern in Toronto.

Meanwhile, in 1925, Samuel ''Mr. Sam'' Bronfman, scion of a family of Russian-Jewish emigrants who arrived in Canada in the 1890s, built a distillery in LaSalle, a suburb of Montreal. The company, known as Distillers Corporation Ltd. (DCL), produced Canadian whisky and other alcoholic beverages. DCL purchased Seagram's in 1928, and the new company was incorporated under the name Distillers Corporation-Seagrams Ltd.; the name Seagram Company Ltd., was adopted in 1975.

During the tenure of the flamboyant ''Mr. Sam,'' the company enjoyed a certain amount of notoriety and fame. While Prohibition made the production, selling, and consumption of alcoholic beverages illegal in the United States from 1920 to 1933, such laws did not exist in Canada. In fact, the distilling of alcoholic beverages was actively encouraged by the Canadian government, and the Bronfmans were able to take advantage of ambiguous customs regulations to spirit their products over the Canadian-American border and into the hands of liquor-starved U.S. consumers.

Anecdotal history credits Bronfman with gaining a sure grip on the U.S. market by his decision to stop exporting whisky shortly before the end of Prohibition. He reasoned that if he could stockpile the product, he would then have a large supply of smooth, properly aged whisky to sell legally south of the border. In this way he could establish the Seagram's name on a superior product long before American distillers could get their factories up and running efficiently.

Success in the United States

When Prohibition was repealed on December 5, 1933, Seagram's products became Americans' alcoholic drinks of choice. Immediately upon entering the U.S. market, Bronfman established Joseph E. Seagram & Sons, Inc., headquartered in New York City, and acquired a distillery in Lawrenceburg, Indiana. In 1934 Seagram purchased the Calvert Distillery in Relay, Maryland, and subsequently began production of Calvert Extra blended whisky and Lord Calvert Canadian Whisky, which became two of the top-selling brands on the market.

Bronfman's gambit to take the United States by storm had paid off handsomely: by the end of 1934, Seagram's Five Crown blended whisky was the best-selling brand in the United States, and the popular Seven Crown was not far behind. According to Bronfman's personal narrative, published as a company history in 1970, ''In just 60 days [in the fall of 1934], we were able to tell the public that these blended whiskys were outselling all others throughout the country. 'THANKS A MILLION,' we told our American consumers in newspaper advertisements in early November, 'you have made the Seagram's Crown Whiskys Number One in America.' ''

Seagram continued to acquire distilleries throughout the country. In 1937 it purchased Carstairs Brothers Distillery Co. and in the 1940s, it acquired three other distilleries as well as the Paul Masson Vineyards in California, the company's first foray into the wine industry.

AT A GLANCE

Seagram's brand of alcoholic beverages, including Seven Crown, V.O., and Crown Royal, founded in 1857 by Joseph E. Seagram, president of Joseph E. Seagram & Sons Ltd. distillery; company purchased by Distillers Corporation Ltd. and incorporated under the name Distillers Corporation Limited-Seagrams Ltd., 1928; renamed The Seagrams Company Ltd., 1975.

Performance: *Market share*—(Seagram's Coolers) 30% of wine cooler category. *Sales*—(Seagram's Seven Crown; 1991) $426.1 million; (Seagram's Gin; 1991) $334.7 million.

Major competitor: (for Seagram's Coolers) Gallo's Bartles & Jaymes; (for Seagram's V.O.) Canadian Mist; (for Myer's Rum) Bacardi Rum.

Advertising: *Agencies*—(Seagram's Seven Crown and Seagram's Gin) Ogilvy & Mather, New York, NY; (Seagram's Coolers) Wells Rich Greene BDDP, New York, NY. *Major campaign*—(Seagram's Coolers) Supermarket point-of-purchase displays.

Addresses: *Parent company*—The Seagram Company Ltd., 1430 Peel St., Montreal, Quebec, Canada H3A 1S9; phone: (514) 987-5209; (U.S. distributor) The Seagram Company Ltd., 375 Park Ave., New York, NY 10152; phone: (212) 572-7000.

In the 1950s and 1960s, The Seagram Company diversified again, organizing the Frankfort Oil Company in 1953 and the Texas Pacific Coal and Oil Company in 1963. In the same year, it merged the two companies to form Texas Pacific Oil Company, Inc. American expansions were limited in the 1970s to the acquisition of Gold Seal Vineyards in 1979.

One of the most active decades since the 1930s, the 1980s saw the acquisition, merger, and sale of a number of Seagram holdings. In a 1980 reorganization of its oil and gas division, the company sold Texas Pacific U.S. Oil for $2.3 billion. It also sold its Canadian and North Sea oil and gas properties in 1985 and its Thailand gas properties in 1988.

In another move to diversify the company's holdings, The Seagram Company acquired 27.9 million shares of Conoco Inc. for $2.6 billion. It tendered the shares to E. I. du Pont de Nemours and Company for 20.2 percent interest in Du Pont common shares in 1981. Du Pont has interests in industrial products, fibers, polymers, petroleum, coal, and such diversified businesses as agricultural products, electronics, imaging systems, and medical products.

In the alcoholic beverage category, Seagram acquired the Wine Spectrum—comprising Taylor, Great Western, Taylor California Cellars, Sterling Vineyards and The Monterey Vineyard wines and champagnes—in 1983. It sold Paul Masson, Taylor California Cellars, Taylor, Great Western, and Gold Seal Vineyards in 1987, and in 1989 it divested 24 non-premium American distilled spirits brands, deciding instead to focus on premium products. In the nonalcoholic beverage market, Seagrams bought Tropicana Products, Inc. in 1988, and the American Natural Beverage Corp., manufacturer of Soho all-natural soft drinks, in 1989.

In a 1989 corporate reorganization, Seagram USA was formed to allow for an integrated beverage strategy within the United States. This organization included The House of Seagram, Tropi-

cana Products, Inc., The Seagram Beverage Company, Vie-Del Company of Fresno, California—a producer of grape juice, brandy, and wine—Premium Beverage Company of Fairfield, Connecticut—a producer of Seagram's Mixers and Seagram's Seltzers—and the company's central research and development group.

At the end of 1991 Seagram sold the trademark rights to seven of its mid-priced brands. Jim Beam, a subsidiary of American Brands, Inc., acquired for an estimated $372.5 million Lord Calvert Canadian Whisky, Calvert Extra, Kessler Blended American Whiskys, Calvert Gin, Wolfschmidt Vodka, Ronrico Rum, and the Leroux cordials. Following the same marketing strategy that influenced the selling off of mid-range brands in 1989, Seagram preferred instead to concentrate its efforts on its premium business.

As of 1990 The Seagram Company Ltd. had four major divisions: Seagram Spirits and Wine Group (New York); Seagram Classics Wine Company (San Mateo, California); Seagram Chateau & Estate Wines Company (New York); and Seagram Beverage Company (New York).

Seagram Spirits and Wine Group

Based in New York City, the Seagram Spirits and Wine Group includes all Seagram-owned spirits and wine brands—except The Sterling Vineyard and The Monterey Vineyard—worldwide. It is also in charge of both producing the company's U.S. distilled spirits brands and importing and marketing both Seagram and select premium brands of other companies.

The most popular domestic brand produced by Seagram is Seven Crown (also known as Seagram's 7), which in 1991 had total retail sales of $415.8 million. Seagram's Gin, with 1991 sales of $334.7 million, was also among the leaders in its category. Other important and profitable labels controlled by the Spirits and Wine Group include Crown Royal Canadian whisky, Chivas Regal, The Glenlivet Scotch, Captain Morgan Original Spiced Rum, John Jameson Irish Whisky, Myers's Original Dark Rum, and Martell Cognacs.

Seagram Classics Wine Company

Seagram's domestic wine holdings are comprised of the products of Sterling Vineyards and The Monterey Vineyard. The company also imports and markets Seagram-owned Mumm Champagnes and Barton & Guestier (B&G) Wines, which are the leading A.O.C. (*appelation d'origine contrôlée*) wines in America. In addition, the Seagram Classics Wine Company acts as worldwide sales agent for Bandiera, Charles Krug, and C.K. Mondavi, among others. A 1990s venture by the company involved a partnership with G.H. Mumm to use the *méthode chanpenoise* to produce Mumm Cuvée Napa Sparking Wines.

Seagram Chateau & Estate Wines Company

As an importer of fine wines, Seagram Chateau and Estate Wines Company is responsible for bringing nearly 35 percent of all chateau-bottled Bordeaux and 25 percent of all estate-bottled burgundy from France to the United States. Among the products imported by this subsidiary are Perrier-Jouët Champagne, Sandeman ports and sherries, Janneau armagnac, and such wines as Domaines Barons de Rothschild, Domaines Cordier, F.E. Trimbach, and Miguel Torres.

Seagram Beverage Company

Based in New York City, Seagram Beverage Company pro
duces and markets the category-leading Seagram's Coolers, which
were introduced in 1983. Product extensions include malt-based
beverages, launched in 1989, and Light Coolers, introduced in
1992. Seagram Beverage Company also produces and markets a
line of premium, all-natural sparkling soft drinks produced under
the Soho Natural Soda label.

Tropicana Products, Inc.

Since its acquisition by The Seagram Company in 1988, the
Bradenton, Florida-based Tropicana Products, Inc. has enjoyed
enormous growth. Its full product line is distributed throughout the
United States, and in 1989, Tropicana International was founded
to implement expansion into worldwide markets. Tropicana holds
the leading share in the not-from-concentrate orange juice segment in France, the first European country in which it has been
introduced. It also holds a commanding lead in the domestic
ready-to-drink orange juice category, with a 38 percent share of
the $2 billion market.

Tropicana has expanded its juice offerings to include other fruit
juice beverages such as well as Tropicana Twisters, which were
launched in 1988. Originally comprising eight flavors marketed in
46-ounce and 10-ounce glass bottles, the Tropicana Twister line
was extended in 1990 to include four flavors in frozen concentrate
form, and again in 1991 to include eight light varieties.

Early Advertising Strategies

In the early years of The Seagram Company Ltd., Samuel
Bronfman did not just direct the organizational aspects of the
company, but he also retained creative control over the company's
advertising campaigns. The most famous of his early strategies,
and one which is still used by the company, is the print ad stressing
the need for moderation. As he recalled in his 1970 narrative . . .
*From Little Acorns . . . The Story of Distillers Corporation-
Seagrams Ltd.,* Bronfman was shocked at the level of social
drinking being undertaken by Americans shortly after the repeat of
Prohibition. "I observed men and women enjoying too freely the
new liberty of legal drinking. This disturbed me greatly. As distillers, I felt that we should issue a warning. Accordingly, I asked our
advertising agency to prepare an advertisement, the heading of
which was to state, 'We who make whisky say: Drink moderately.' "

Copy for the body of the ad read, "The real enjoyment which
whisky can add to the pleasures of gracious living is possible only
to the man who drinks good whisky and drinks moderately. The
House of Seagram does not want a dollar that should be spent on
the necessities of life." The campaign was incredibly successful—bringing the company praise in newspaper editorials, church
sermons, and letters from private citizens—and Seagram's whisky
sales in the United States topped $60 million by 1936. The com-
pany's dedication to promoting responsible drinking has continued—Seagram still runs holiday ads exhorting liquor consumers
to exercise moderation.

Another successful ad campaign devised by Bronfman was
designed to improve the image of whisky, raising it from an
"everyman" drink to one with appeal for the upper classes.
Consequently, Bronfman created the series of "Men of Distinction" ads, which used as its spokespersons men and women with
high-profile personalities. The campaign was used to promote
Lord Calvert whisky and set the tone for the brand.

So dedicated was the company to promoting its products that
its advertising budget for 1936 was an astounding $2.5 million. In
the early 1990s Seagram's worldwide ad budget is more than 100
times that amount, but for its time, the 1936 figure stands out as
one of the highest for any product line in the country.

Marketing Successes—Wine Coolers

In the late 1980s and early 1990s, Seagram has enjoyed a
number of successes with several of its products. Its line of wine
coolers, marketed under the Seagram's Coolers label, has been
particularly successful. Recognizing the trend away from "hard"
alcohol that has been growing in America through the health-
conscious 1980s and 1990s, the company developed a number of
lowered alcohol beverage alternatives.

Wine coolers, a 1981 California invention, took the country by
storm as a lighter, alcohol-based beverage perfect for summer
drinking. The Seagram Company was slow in entering the wine
cooler market—its first product, a citrus-flavored beverage, was
launched in 1983. It was not until 1986 that competition between
the established brands escalated. In that year, Seagram introduced
its Seagram's Premium Wine Cooler, a new formulation with new
flavors and package graphics. Also in 1986, Seagram introduced
the more sophisticated Golden Wine Coolers, a less-sweet product
aimed at the upscale market, and the Natural Peach-Flavored Wine
Cooler, which immediately gained favor among cooler drinkers.

By 1986 the wine cooler category had grown to some 60
million cases, up one-third from the previous year. The industry
leader, E&J Gallo's Bartles & Jaymes, held a 25 percent market
share, but Seagram was gaining ground quickly. Taking into account the seasonality of wine coolers as a summertime favorite,
The Seagram Company timed its launch of two new flavors—
Original Wild Berries and Apple Cranberry—for the spring of
1987, at which time it employed a number of successful marketing
tactics, especially well-conceived point-of-sale devices, to promote all five Wine Coolers.

The Seagram's marketing strategy began to see quick results.
By the summer of 1987, Seagram had topped Bartles & Jaymes in
market share, gaining nearly 30 percent of the market, as opposed
to the rival's 27 percent, a position of strength it continued to hold
in the early 1990s. The cooler line was expanded in the ensuing
years to include Natural Black Cherry and Island Tropics flavors,
launched in 1989, and two "light" offerings—Strawberry Splash
and Tropical Twist—both containing only 2 percent alcohol and
launched in 1992.

Other Marketing Successes

Seagram also actively promoted its "white," or more accu-
rately, clear, alcoholic beverages in the 1980s. Such offerings as
vodka, light rum, liqueur, and wine had not been among
Seagram's strongest sellers, but campaigns during the 1980s for
Seagram's Imported Vodka have taken aim at Smirnoff's and
Absolut's market share.

The Seagram Company has also taken a stab at Bacardi's
secure place as number one in the rum market by actively promoting its Myers's Rum. The most popular print ad campaign for
Myers's touts the product as a Jamaican, rather than Puerto Rican,
rum. The ad's copy stresses the difference by identifying the

Myers's product as a step up, to appeal to the more sophisticated palate. "We used to drink Puerto Rican rum. Then we graduated to the flavor of Myers's Jamaican Rums," read the copy for a 1982 ad campaign that was designed to attract the discerning consumer.

Seagram's alcoholic offerings have consistently remained among the top-selling and most profitable brands on the market. According to the 1992 *Business Rankings Annual,* among the most profitable spirits brands ranked by 1989 profit contribution, in millions of dollars, Seagram's Crown Royal was ranked at number one, with a profit contribution of $88 million; Seagram's V.O. was listed at number five, with a contribution of $61 million.

The Future of Seagram's

According to *Adweek's Superbrands* of 1991, spirits manufacturers were feeling the pinch of the economic recession to a much greater extent than they had anticipated. The $16 billion industry had to respond to the "new sobriety" of the 1990s as well as to the potential for increased taxes on its products. Brands that were expecting great growth were posting negligible increases, and some saw their sales decline as Americans turned away from traditional hard liquor offerings.

In January of 1991 an 8 percent federal excise tax (FET) was imposed on liquor, and combined with producer, wholesalers, and retailer price increases, caused a jump in the price of every bottle of alcohol sold in the United States. The early 1990s recession, which forced a change in consumers' buying habits, also took its toll on liquor sales. In addition, analysts believed that government regulation and social criticism of spirits marketing, both of which are perhaps at their strictest since Prohibition, have taken a huge bite out of the market. Seagram's weathered the storm, boasting three of the top ten sellers in the spirits category—Seagram's Seven Crown, which was ranked at number five with total retail sales of $426.1 million; Seagram's Gin, falling in at number seven with $334.7 million in sales; and Crown Royal, listed at number nine with total retail sales of $310.9 million.

Wine coolers, which gained in popularity since their introduction in the late 1980s, is one area in which Seagram maintains its lead. Other companies, however, were moving into the spirit-based "cocktail" beverage market, one that was yet to be tapped by The Seagram Company. Bacardi Breezers, a four percent alcohol rum cooler introduced to test markets in 1988, were posting sales of $134 million by 1991. Also, Jack Daniel's entered the market with bourbon whisky-based Jack Daniel's Country Coolers.

In general, however, the multinational Seagram Company Ltd., with its diverse range of holdings, seemed poised to retain its position on the Fortune 500 list for many years to come. According to the company's 1992 annual report, Seagram's racked up worldwide beverage sales totalling $6.3 billion in 1991. Despite the recession of that year, Seagram's top 50 brands combined saw only a modest 3.2 percent decline, according to Standard and Poor's 1992 *Industry Survey.* With interests in the United States and Canada and affiliates in more than 28 countries in Europe and the Far East, The Seagram Company, producing a lucrative line of alcoholic beverages bearing the Seagram's label, has a very secure position among the top corporations of the world.

Further Reading:

Bird, Laura, "A Scary Outlook for the Spirit World," *Adweek's Superbrands,* 1991, p. 61.

Bronfman, Samuel, . . . *From Little Acorns . . . The Story of Distillers Corporation-Seagrams Ltd.,* Montreal, 1970.

"Food, Beverages, and Tobacco," Standard and Poor's *Industry Surveys,* August 6, 1992, p. F29.

Kraar, Louis, "Seagram Tightens Its Grip on Du Pont," *Fortune,* November 16, 1981, pp. 75-78.

Leinster, Colin, "The Second Son Is Heir at Seagram," *Fortune,* March 17, 1986, pp. 27-31.

Marrus, Michael R., *Mr. Sam: The Life and Times of Samuel Bronfman,* Toronto, Ontario: Viking Books, 1991.

McCann, Thomas, "How Seagram's Uncorked Its Wine Cooler Marketing," *Marketing News,* October 10, 1988, p. 22.

McCann, Thomas, "Where the Fun Started: A Merchandising Case History on the Rise of Seagram's Coolers," *Beverage World,* May 1988, pp. 52-57.

Meyer, Priscilla S., and Aaron Bernstien, "Hello Wilmington? This Is Montreal," *Fortune,* June 21, 1982, pp. 46-47.

Newman, Peter C., *King of the Castle. The Making of a Dynasty: Seagram's and the Bronfman Empire,* New York, NY: Atheneum, 1979.

Sawyer, Deborah C., "Seagram Company Limited," *The Canadian Encyclopedia,* 1968.

"The Seagram Company Ltd," *Dollars & Sense,* August/September 1983, pp. 53-63.

The Seagram Company Ltd. Fact Book, May 1990.

The Seagram Company Ltd. annual reports, 1991 and 1992.

"Seagram Puts Its Money Where Your Mouth Is," *Ad Forum,* November 1983, pp. 29-32.

Shapiro, Eben, "Tropicana Squeezes out Minute Maid to Get Bigger Slice of Citrus Hill Fans," *Wall Street Journal,* February 4, 1993, p. B1.

Thompson, Tony, "For Seagram, Sam's Savvy Was 100 Proof," *Advertising Age,* October 4, 1982, pp. M16-M18.

"What Edgar Bronfman Wants at Seagram," *Business Week,* April 27, 1991, pp. 135-142.

—*Marcia K. Mogelonsky*

7UP®

7UP brand (formerly 7-Up), a clear soda with a lemon-lime flavor in a heavily carbonated base, has endured as one of the top ten soft drinks for more than half a century. Rising in the soft drink market during the Great Depression by touting its medicinal benefits, 7UP continued to hold a formidable market share by advertising its refreshing qualities into the 1990s. In 1992, 7UP ranked eighth among competing soft drinks.

The inventor of 7UP, Charles L. Grigg, was an advertising and merchandising man who formed the Howdy Company in St. Louis, Missouri, in 1920. Grigg's first product was Howdy orange drink, which he marketed across the United States. Manufacturing an artificially-flavored orange drink became less practical when citrus growers pushed for government regulations that insured that orange drinks contain some real orange juice. The use of real orange juice, however, presented the problem of spoilage and raised production costs. As several states adopted the regulations, bottlers had to find a way to comply. Grigg decided to diversify.

He searched for an alternative soft drink to market. After testing eleven different formulas of lemon-flavored soft drinks, he chose one that was caramel-colored and contained some of the antidepression chemical lithium. Just two weeks before the October 1929 stock market crash, the Howdy Company introduced Bib-Label Lithiated Lemon-Lime Soda into a market that already contained more than 600 similar brands.

Even though the beginning of the Great Depression was an inopportune time to launch a new product, consumers did not view soft drinks as luxury items. The benefits of naturally occurring bubbling mineral waters had been espoused for centuries, and it was a short leap to make the same medicinal claims for processed soda water. To make carbonated waters more palatable and to increase their "health benefits," pharmacists had added a variety of herbs and flavors. Pre-bottled soft drinks were a more convenient form of the pharmacist-flavored soda water. The curative powers of soda pop were still of prime importance to consumers when Bib-Label appeared. Bib-Label's lemon-lime flavor, lithiated content, and extra fizz allowed it to market itself as the best cure for a hangover or an upset stomach. The tag line used in the early 1930s advertising was that it "Takes the 'Ouch' Out of Grouch." It was also presented as a healthful drink for babies, claiming it "tunes tiny tummies."

Shortly after Bib-Label was introduced, Grigg changed the name to 7UP. How Grigg arrived at the 7UP name is ambiguous. One story maintains the drink was a blend of seven flavors. A company report titled "Seven-Up: Still the Uncola" noted that the "earliest 7UP advertising featured a winged 7UP and described 7UP as 'A glorified drink in bottles only. Seven natural flavors blended into a savory, savory drink with a real wallop.' " It goes on to say that "an early 1929 sales bulletin said consumers 'are tired of insipid flavors, and the aftertaste of the heavy synthetic flavors is more objectionable. . . . So, in Seven-Up, we have provided seven natural flavors so blended and in such proportion that when bottled, it produces a big natural flavor with a real taste that makes people remember it. . . .' " Another explanation for the 7UP name is that the drink was bottled only in seven-ounce bottles, the 7, and that the up was borrowed from another popular lemon-lime drink made in St. Louis since 1917, Bubble Up. The drink's heavy carbonation may also have had something to do with the up. According to Michael Gershman in *Getting It Right the Second Time,* Grigg "emerged from the Depression with the decision that a name change would solve his problems and promptly bought the name 7UP from a Minnesota candy company that made a chocolate candy bar with seven different fillings." Whatever the reason, the switch to the 7UP trademark proved so successful that Grigg changed the name of the Howdy Company to the Seven-Up Company in 1936.

Pop Advertising History: The Uncola Campaign

During the 1930s, 7UP started to use the tag line "fresh up." The company put out a 14-page advertising booklet to explain the restorative powers of 7UP. It contained vignettes with titles like "Ma's Metabolism," "Riled Up' from Riding," "Mental Lassitude," "Slenderizing?," "Now Grandma Laughs," and "What Does Hang-Over Mean to You?" The vignette on entertaining offered the advice, "Drink 7-Up freely. Being highly carbonated, 7-Up tends to activate the stomach and is an aid in relieving the distressed feeling after heavy meals. In the evening, along about yawning time, open a cool bottle and 'Fresh Up' with 7-Up."

By the 1940s, 7UP was the third largest selling soft drink in the world. The advertising shifted from medicinal claims to family themes and good clean fun. The "fresh-up" slogan continued to be used and became part of the name of an anthropomorphic character. The company's advertising agency commissioned Walt

AT A GLANCE

7UP brand soft drink (formerly 7-Up) founded in 1929 by Charles L. Grigg, owner of the Howdy Company in St. Louis, MO; the brand's success prompted the company name change in 1936 to the Seven-Up Company; through a buyout, the Seven-Up Company merged with the Dr Pepper Company in May, 1988.

Performance: *Market share*—3.0% of soft drink sales. *Sales*—$1.8 billion.

Major competitor: Coca-Cola Company's Sprite; also Pepsi-Cola Company's Lemon-Lime Slice.

Advertising: *Agency*—Leo Burnett, Chicago, IL, 1985—. *Major campaign*—The Uncola theme emphasized the brand's characteristics that were opposite those of cola drinks.

Addresses: *Parent company*—Seven-Up Company, 8144 Walnut Hill Lane, Dallas, TX 75231-4372; phone: (214) 360-7000; fax: (214) 360-7980. *Ultimate parent company*—Dr Pepper/Seven-Up Companies Inc., P.O. Box 655086, Dallas, TX 75265; phone (214) 360-7000; fax: (214) 360-7980.

Disney Studios in 1959 to create Fresh-Up Freddie. The character had the Disney style, but he did not increase 7UP sales.

The company replaced the family theme in the 1960s with a "Wet and Wild" campaign, which Stephen N. Tchudi noted in *Soda Poppery,* may have been the most youth-oriented campaign carried out by a soda drink company. The youth orientation continued into the 1970s with the theme "America's Turning 7-Up." The company invested $40 million on broadcast and print advertising and on grocery-store displays that featured youthful, athletic types in vigorous pursuits.

Although 7UP was a big seller, it had a persistent image problem. Gershman noted that research found that consumers thought 7UP was a specialized drink for special occasions; a mixer that "played the caboose in the most popular mixed drink in America at the time—Seven & Seven" (Seagram's Seven Crown whiskey and 7UP); and a medicine (people still remembered the ads promoting 7UP as an upset stomach and hangover reliever). Another problem was that 7UP was not brown, the accepted color for carbonated soft drinks.

7UP's advertising agency, J. Walter Thompson, worked on a solution to reposition the brand "in the middle of the soft drink spectrum," while keeping its mixer business from other "green bottle goods" and from "white goods" (diet drinks and drinks featuring vodka) competition. 7UP was not a cola, but it competed for cola sales. The agency tackled the problem head-on. William E. Ross, a Thompson vice-president, coined the phrase "The Uncola." The new slogan engendered skepticism from some bottlers who thought it might reduce sales of their cola brands, but brought an immediate positive response from the public. 7UP sales skyrocketed. The first ad in the Uncola campaign called 7UP "Fresh. Clean. Crisp. Never too sweet. No aftertaste. Everything a cola's got and more besides. 7UP . . . The Uncola. The Un and Only."

The Uncola tag soon became part of the popular vernacular, and it remained synonymous with 7UP despite subsequent marketing campaigns. The Uncola theme fit right into the youth and antiestablishment attitude of the 1960s. 7UP was uniquely posi-

tioned to capture the youth soft drink market. The Uncola theme related to the current view of "them" against "us"; in this case, cola drinks were "them." The company put out a poster with the caption "Hear no cola; see no cola; drink Uncola." The positioning paid off. Sales increased 50 percent between 1968 and 1973.

Commercials for the Uncola campaign made advertising history. They broke advertising traditions by speaking directly to consumers and, except for one ad, had no music. A company publication noted that Charles Martell, the creator of the original campaign, said, "we actually mentioned the competition. Common as that is today, it just wasn't done in 1967." The narration commented on 7UP's competitors in humorous fashion, and always emphasized that 7UP was not a cola, but was a soft drink—not just a cocktail mixer. In one ad, as the narrator read copy, brown bags were lifted to reveal Cola No. 1, Cola No. 2, and The Uncola. Another ad showed a white-gloved hand emerging from a plain black box and pouring 7UP into what was considered a cola soda fountain glass. Later a series of ads displayed the Uncola soda fountain glass, shaped to look upside-down compared to the cola glass. Although the cola companies had sold merchandising tie-ins for years, the Uncola glass was an opportunity for the Seven-Up Company to enter the arena. The company reportedly sold 20 million Uncola soda glasses and 60,000 Uncola lamps.

Geoffrey Holder, a stage actor with a deep, rich voice, portrayed a tropical island plantation owner in the memorable "Uncola Nuts" commercial. In it, Holder showed cola nuts and said they were grown there. Then he showed a lemon and lime and declared, "These are Uncola Nuts; we grow them here, too." He noted that Uncola Nuts are juicier, more refreshing, and prettier, then tasted 7UP and proclaimed the Uncola "mahhhhvelous, simply mahhhhvelous."

Radio, print, and outdoor Uncola advertising were innovative, too. Radio advertising featured live interviews with consumers. 7UP commissioned various illustrators who created a series of billboards using bright, modern images, which became collector's items.

The popularity of the campaign led 7UP to protect the Uncola name. For nearly four years the Coca-Cola Corporation challenged the concept. The slogan received trademark status on June 20, 1974, settling the matter. Two years later 7UP sent out trucks painted with "The Uncola Salutes 200 Years of Un-Britain" to celebrate the United States Bicentennial of "Undependence." The company retired the original thematics of the Uncola campaign and the focus on 7UP as "The Uncola" at the end of the 1970s. (Although the Uncola theme and ads featuring Geoffrey Holder—"The Un's The One"—were brought back briefly in the mid-1980s.) The themes "America is Turning 7UP" and "Feelin' 7UP." followed.

An emerging fitness and health consciousness gave the Seven-Up Company the opportunity to reposition the brand. In 1970 the company introduced Diet 7UP. The Seven-Up Company again dealt with a problem by using a direct statement. Diet drinks with artificial sweeteners had a somewhat metallic taste and a noticeable aftertaste. The company advertised that Diet 7UP was "a diet drink that doesn't taste funny." (Diet 7UP switched from saccharin to 100 percent aspartame in 1984.)

Spot

The Seven-Up Company debuted "Spot," a cartoon character derived from the red dot in the 7UP trademark, in 1988 to expand awareness of 7UP to the nation's youth market. The frisky character appeared popping around in vignettes entitled "Refrigerator," "Football," and "Fire Truck." Spot also floated across the Pacific on a 7UP bottle containing a message and washed ashore at a wedding. Wearables and stuffed toys sold in retail stores across the country pictured the popular Spot. Another 7UP tie-in featured Spot on a game cartridge for the Nintendo video system.

Spot's appeal, however, did not translate into market share. In 1991, the Seven-Up Company decided to bring back the Uncola theme for Diet 7UP. It modified packaging for 7UP and Diet 7UP in 1992 to include the tag "The Uncola." (In addition, Diet 7UP's label read "The One Calorie Uncola," and Cherry 7UP's and Cherry Diet 7UP's labels added that they had "No Caffeine".) The company also started to use a combination of the Spot character with the Uncola theme in advertising. The advertisements showed two Spots approaching a glass of diet cola as it transformed into a glass of Diet 7UP. Daniel Stern, the adult voice of ABC-TV's *The Wonder Years* character Kevin Arnold, narrated them. The brand posted its first market share gain in a decade within a year after Uncola was brought back. Other ways in which the Seven-Up Company promoted its brands were sweepstakes, an annual promotion during the National College Basketball Championship, and NASCAR sponsorship of race car driver Davey Allison and his Havoline/Texaco car.

Variations Yes, Caffeine No

Concern about the effects of caffeine in soft drinks, especially on children, led several cola brands to introduce caffeine-free versions in the early 1980s. 7UP merely had to launch its "No Caffeine" campaign with the slogan "Never Had It, Never Will." In 1982, the Seven-Up Company introduced a 99 percent caffeine-free cola, LIKE, and Sugar Free LIKE in select markets, but strong competitive reaction from major cola markets stunted the market opportunities for the brands.

7UP was able to extend market share after introduction of Cherry 7UP and Cherry Diet 7UP in early 1987. The advertising theme "Isn't it cool in pink!" helped the products become instant successes. *USA Today* and several other national publications named Cherry 7UP one of the "in" new products. Additionally, the American Marketing Association named it one of the best new products to appear in 1987.

In 1988, the Seven-Up Company introduced 7UP Gold and Diet 7UP Gold. The products, intended to appeal to men aged 18 to 34, were amber in color and, according to the publisher of *Beverage Digest* newsletter, tasted like "cinnamon and ginger with a cola top note." The drink's bland flavor did not capture consumer interest, however, and production was discontinued before 1990.

To boost 7UP's lost market share, the company relaunched reformulated versions of Cherry 7UP and Diet 7UP in 1990 with new packaging graphics and advertising support. Cherry 7UP received an extra "splash of cherry taste," and Diet 7UP was given a slightly sweeter taste.

Clear and Clean in a New Age

The reinvigoration of the Uncola theme in 1992 coincided with the introduction of clear "new age" beverages, the fastest growing segment of the beverage industry in the early 1990s. 7UP had a distinct advantage as cola and beer producers strove to prove their purity by removing dyes and coloring to become clear. Actually, many products like detergents and gasoline were reformulated at that time to be clear, hoping to impart the idea that they too were more "clean." 7UP's advantage lay in the fact that it had been clear most of its existence.

Additionally, during the 1992 U.S. presidential campaign, the Uncola theme was ideally positioned. Patricia Winters wrote in *Advertising Age,* that "independent candidate Ross Perot was often referred to in the media as the 'uncandidate,' and his efforts were called the 'uncampaign,' an expression of change from past political traditions."

Company and Brand Prospects

The Seven-Up Company remained in the hands of its original owners until it became publicly owned in 1967. Philip Morris Incorporated owned the company from June of 1978 until 1986, when the leveraged-buyout firm of Hicks & Haas arranged the sale of domestic operations to a private investment group for $240 million. The Seven-Up Company and Dr Pepper Company returned to private ownership, owned by two separate investment groups. The new company was operated under a joint management team headed by chief executive officer John R. Albers, but sales and marketing staffs remained separate.

Although 7UP usually is priced higher than competitive brands Sprite, Diet Sprite, Lemon-Lime Slice, and Diet Slice, its sales are steady. The *Beverage World Databank: Sourcebook for the Beverage Markets* noted that in 1992 Diet 7UP had experienced its best sales since 1986. The March 1992 issue of *Beverage World* stated that while Sprite has been the leading overall lemon-lime soft drink sales since 1988, 7UP had foodstore superiority.

Throughout its history, the Seven-Up Company has been successful in repositioning the 7UP brand using themes emphasizing "what it wasn't" and by introducing brand extensions, such as Diet 7UP, Cherry 7UP, and Cherry Diet 7UP. In a 1992 *Beverage World* article, Russ Klein, senior vice-president of marketing for the Seven-Up Company, said consumers bought 7UP as an incremental purchase (along with cola or other flavors). Unlike cola brands that relied heavily on promotions to get sales, 7UP products sold at about the same rate whether a special promotion was on or not. The magazine quoted Klein as saying that "people find colas and 7UP to be the ultimate in terms of complementary drinks: dark versus clear, caffeine versus caffeine-free, sweeter versus less sweet." The four core Seven-Up brands—7UP, Diet 7UP, Cherry 7UP, and Cherry Diet 7UP—provide consumers with alternatives to cola brands. The company continues to attune itself to current sentiments and reposition its 7UP brands accordingly.

Further Reading:

Broekel, Ray, *The Chocolate Chronicles,* Lombard, IL: Wallace-Homestead Book Company, 1985.

"Coke Is Sued by Seven-Up," *New York Times,* February 28, 1992, sec. D, p. 5.

Davis, Tim, "Hitting the Spot; The Seven-Up Company Plans a Renewed Effort to Secure Its Lemon-Lime Station," *Beverage World,* October, 1990, pp. 66-70, 149.

Davis, Tim, "The Many Moods of John Albers," *Beverage World,* January, 1992, pp. 20-27.

Davis, Tim, "Seven-Up Takes Light Approach in Spotty Return of Uncola Ads," *Beverage World* (Periscope Edition), October 31, 1991, p. 10.

Dietz, Lawrence, *Soda Pop: The History, Advertising, Art and Memorabilia of Soft Drinks in America,* New York: Simon & Schuster, 1973.

Gershman, Michael, "7-UP The Un and Only," *Getting It Right the Second Time,* Reading, Massachussetts: Addison-Wesley Publishing Co. Inc., 1990, pp. 74-78.

Jabbonsky, Larry, "Sex, Lies and Red Tape," *Beverage World,* March, 1992, p. 6.

Jacobs, Morris B., "Introduction," *Manufacture and Analysis of Carbonated Beverages,* New York: Chemical Publishing Co., Inc., 1959.

Kelly, Kevin, and Walerna Konrad, "Seven-Up: Where Have All the Bubbles Gone?" *Business Week,* January 29, 1992, p. 85.

"New Seven-Up Soft Drinks," *New York Times,* February 23, 1988, sec. D, p. 5.

"Seven-Up: Still the UNCOLA," The Seven-Up Company.

"7UP The Uncola: 25 Years of UN," The Seven-Up Company press release, 1992.

"A Tale of Two Non-Colas: The Uncola's Modus Operandi," *Beverage World,* September, 1992, pp. 63, 70-72.

Tchudi, Stephen N., *Soda Poppery: The History of Soft Drinks in America; with Recipes for Making and Using Soft Drinks PLUS Easy Science Experiments,* New York: Charles Scribner's Sons, 1986.

Winters, Patricia, "7UP Logs 'Un'-Usual Gains in Market Share," *Advertising Age,* November 16, 1992, p. 43.

Wolf, Alan, "That Was the Year That Was (But Some Soft Drink Franchisers Wished It Wasn't)," *Beverage World Databank: Sourcebook for the Beverage Markets,* Shepherdsville, KY: Keller International Publishing Corporation, 1992, pp. 22-25.

Worthy, Ford S., "Pop Goes Their Profit," *Fortune,* February 15, 1988, p. 68.

—Doris Morris Maxfield

SHASTA®

SHASTA

Shasta soda has a grand vision that it will one day recapture the glory it enjoyed in the early years of the twentieth century to become—at least—the number three soft drink company in the United States, led only by Coke and Pepsi. This is a major challenge for a product that was on the verge of extinction just a few short years ago, and which today controls a mere two percent of the national soft drink market. To achieve its goal, Shasta would have to first surpass such firmly established brands as Dr. Pepper, Sprite, Mountain Dew, 7UP, and Royal Crown (RC), all of which are well ahead both in sales and in name recognition. However, Nick Caporella, head of Florida-based National Beverage Corp., the parent company of Shasta, has been optimistic, determined, intuitive, and committed to once more building Shasta into a soft drink behemoth.

Brand Origins

More than a century old, Shasta was originally a naturally carbonated mountain spring water accidentally discovered by a lumberjack named J. J. Scott in the 1880s and named for Mt. Shasta, in California. Initially, Scott did little to promote and market the water, but he was eventually joined by a group of enterprising businessmen who proposed the development of a health and vacation resort on the spot where the spring was discovered at the base of Mt. Shasta. They planned to call the operation the Shasta Mineral Springs Company and tie the resort in with the water and its alleged therapeutic qualities.

Guests to the resort raved about the quality and taste of the water, and its fame soon spread along the West Coast. Inevitably the resort took a back seat to the water, which the company began packaging and distributing throughout California and neighboring states. By the 1920s Shasta mineral water had grown so popular that the company's operators renamed the firm The Shasta Water Company. They then opened two bottling plants in Los Angeles and began distributing the product to their growing numbers of customers in glass-lined redwood containers.

History does not reveal whose idea it was to add flavors to the water, but by the end of the 1920s Shasta had introduced flavored beverages. The line was also expanded to include flavored carbonated soft drinks, with ginger ale and club soda among the popular early flavors.

By the 1950s Shasta was well established in most of the United States, and the line's early flair for innovation was becoming part of its hallmark. It was in that decade that Shasta became the first American soft drink company to package its products in cans. It also introduced the first low-calorie soft drink, and, using a network of wholesalers, developed a direct-to-the-grocer distribution system.

Ten years later Consolidated Foods of Chicago, better known as the Sara Lee company, acquired Shasta, and for the next 20 years aggressively marketed the line by adding new and more exotic flavors and introducing sugar-free and no-calorie soft drinks.

During the 1970s Consolidated Foods established a Food Services Division through which it pursued further market share for Shasta with eight-ounce cans and returnable bottles. Then, with Americans growing increasingly health conscious, it switched from conventional cane sugar to corn sweeteners, thereby establishing what has since become an industry standard.

By then the company was up to 34 flavors, and was considered the Baskin-Robbins of the flavored soft drink market. However, Shasta's downward spiral began when Consolidated Foods began to neglect its rich array of flavors to concentrate almost exclusively on an aggressive promotion of Shasta cola, in a futile bid to win market share from Coke and Pepsi.

In 1985, with Shasta sales down to about 1.4 percent of market share, Consolidated Foods welcomed the arrival of Nick Caporella and his newly formed National Beverage Company as a suitor for the brand. National Beverage acquired Shasta for $67 million dollars in cash and promissory notes.

Marketing Strategy

Until National Beverage's acquisition of Shasta, Caporella, 56, had had no experience in the soft drink business. He had recently headed Burnup & Sims, National Beverage's parent company, and a corporation with strengths in the manufacture, installation, and maintenance of lines for telephone, utility, and cable TV companies. Caporella moved dramatically to alter the unsuccessful marketing philosophies of Consolidated Foods. Known as a savvy businessman with a wealth of fresh ideas, he first established the company's motto of innovation, responsiveness, and quality.

AT A GLANCE

Shasta brand founded in 1889 in Mount Shasta, CA, by J. J. Scott; early enterprises under the name the Shasta Mineral Springs Company; renamed The Shasta Water Company in the 1920s; acquired by Consolidated Foods in the 1960s and by the National Beverage Corp. in 1985.

Performance: *Market share*—Eighth best-selling soft drink in the United States. *Sales*—$699 million.

Major competitor: Pepsi; also Coke, Mountain Dew, Sprite, RC Cola, Dr Pepper, and other major soft drinks.

Advertising: All advertising done in house with the exception of special projects such as the brand's 1989 centennial celebrations.

Addresses: Parent company—The National Beverage Corp., One North University Drive, P.O. Box 16720, Fort Lauderdale, FL 33324; phone: (305) 581-0922; fax: (305) 473-4710.

Caporella then acted to reverse Shasta's fortunes and return it to profitability by re-emphasizing its vast array of flavors, said to be the greatest number in the world for a single company. He also established a national distribution network based on data demonstrating that in spite of strong regional competition for flavored sodas—such as Canfields in Chicago and Franks of Philadelphia—the national market remained largely untapped.

Decentralization of National Beverage's operations became Caporella's next goal. He created eight autonomous geographic regions and established National BevPack, a 12-plant bottling facility with autonomous operations across the country. Strategically locating plants, warehouses, and regional office facilities allowed better control over production, and provided regional managers with easy access to BevPack's research and development facilities and data. It also allowed the managers to tailor purchasing, production, and marketing operations to the specific needs of their region.

To further strengthen the operation, Caporella introduced a two-tier system of distribution, one through direct store delivery and the other through warehouse disbursements. In so doing he skillfully sidestepped the pitfalls of exclusive warehouse distribution, which, while facilitating large supermarket chains, was not designed to efficiently and expeditiously address the needs of the lucrative convenience store and vending machine market. Caporella sought to create a national soft drink company responsive to regional market needs while retaining the financial and purchasing power of a national company.

Quality Assurance in Packaging

Shasta makes its own flavor concentrates, avoiding the price hikes in sweeteners, limited range of flavors, and inconsistency in syrups that other manufacturers are subject to. According to Caporella, Shasta can better control quality and deliver more flavors faster than any other soft drink manufacturer in the world. With the fundamental components for success firmly established, and with operations, supported by more than 1,000 dedicated employees, in high gear, Shasta unveiled a far-reaching blueprint for adding product lines and expanding its market share.

Health Claims

In 1989 the company introduced Shasta Plus, a juice-based non-carbonated drink which it sold, through its Food Services Division, to health food stores, schools, hospitals, and other institutions. The premium-priced line featured 10 percent real fruit juice, 15 percent of the daily recommended allowance (DRA) of calcium, and 100 percent DRA of Vitamin C. It was available in 12-ounce cans. The company used trade shows and advertisements in the National Food Service Journal, as well as one-on-one meetings with school and hospital dieticians, to promote the nutritional benefits of the product.

With an eye on the burgeoning athletic market, the company launched Shasta BodyWorks in 1992 and aimed its marketing strategy squarely at consumers of Gatorade, confident that it could successfully erode that beverage's stranglehold on the market. Shasta officials describe BodyWorks as "an isotonic sports drink formulated to quickly replace body salts and minerals lost through exertion."

All this effort has paid encouraging dividends to National Beverage. In the fiscal year ending in May 1992, the company realized net sales of close to $336 million, up from $307 million in 1991 and just over $300 million in 1990 for an annual growth rate of about two percent. Industry experts consider this to be a very respectable growth figure when considered in terms of the highly competitive nature of the business and the fact that National Beverage is dwarfed by industry giants such as Coke and Pepsi.

Advertising Innovations

Still, the innovative drive for excellence and a place of prominence for Shasta in the industry continues, reaching well beyond new flavors, designer packaging, upscale lines, and clever distribution. A very publicity-minded company, National Beverage remains an aggressive advocate of Shasta. Promotions range from conventional radio and newspaper advertising, billboards, and point-of-purchase displays to sponsorship of athletic events and strong community involvement built around a Shasta theme.

In the past it has launched an active program to help the hungry and homeless following the devastating effects of Hurricane Andrew, and has provided unlimited thirst quenchers for exhausted firefighters during the destructive fires of 1991 in Oakland, California.

Most of Shasta's promotions are created at the company's Fort Lauderdale headquarters, with input from managers of the particular regions to which the promotions are targeted. However, on special occasions, like the brand's centennial celebration in 1989, when a major national promotion was undertaken, the company seeks the help of an independent advertising company. An outside firm was targeted in the summer of 1993 to design a major campaign using celebrity spokespeople.

National Beverage became a publicly held company on September 3, 1991. On that day its stock offering opened at $25 a share. Today it is traded at around $20 a share, but has reached heights as dizzying as $50 a share. National Beverage's stocks are traded on NASDAQ under the code name POPS.

Further Reading:

Linden, Brayden, "For These Two Sodaholics, a Big Thirst Never Fizzles Out," *People Weekly,* February 22, 1988, p. 88.

"More Quality Controls Than Any Other Soft Drink Brand: Shasta's Sanitation Program Key to Standard of Excellence," *Beverage Industry,* May 4, 1979, pp. 28-29.

Pendleton, J., "Shasta Fights Crowding in Juice Market," *Advertising Age,* September 3, 1984, p. 55.

Revett, J., "Colas Lead the Way in National Shasta Effort," *Advertising Age,* April 24, 1978, p. 2.

Selinger, C., "Shasta Sees New Markets for Returnable Packaging," *Beverage Industry,* January 27, 1978, p. 14.

"Shasta: Anatomy of a Maverick Firm," *Beverage Industry,* November 4, 1977, pp. 40-41.

"Shasta's Difficult Sales Goal," *Business Week,* December 5, 1977, p. 125.

"Shasta Pops up as Contender in Soft Drink Major Leagues," *Advertising Forum,* June 1983, p. 15.

"Who's Got the Right One?" *Consumer Reports,* August 1991, p. 518.

—Radcliffe A. Joe

SKIPPY®

Skippy peanut butter, manufactured by CPC International, has been the number one or number two top seller in its category since its introduction in 1932. Competition through the 1970s and 1980s pushed Skippy to number two behind Proctor & Gamble's Jif; the entry of the Hershey Food Corporation's Reese's peanut butter added another new competitor with a popular brand name to the ever tightening food products market, dominated by giants in the industry.

According to the U.S. Food and Drug Administration's (FDA) Standard of Identity, peanut butter must contain at least 90 percent peanuts and no more than 10 percent of seasoning and stabilizing ingredients such as salt, sugar, or partially hydrogenated vegetable oil. No lard or other animal fats, artificial flavorings, artificial sweeteners, chemical preservatives, vitamins, or colors may be added.

Brand Origins

The first credited peanut butter producer was a St. Louis doctor who was searching for an easily digestible, high-protein food for his patients. Around 1880 this physician used a food grinder to mix peanuts with a bit of added salt. This first effort resulted in a very chunky-style peanut butter.

News of the product quickly spread. Riding the crest of peanut butter's popularity, J. L. Rosefield, president of his own manufacturing company, began producing the spread at his plant in Alameda, California. While the product was similar to the original St. Louis physician's recipe, it differed noticeably in texture. Rosefield employed a churning process which not only prevented oil separation, thus eliminating the consumer's need to stir the product—it resulted in a much smoother and creamier peanut butter.

In 1927 the E.K. Pond Company of Chicago licensed Rosefield's process, producing a brand called "Peter Pan." The contract was quickly dissolved, and in 1932 Rosefield marketed his own brand of peanut butter, called "Skippy." From its introduction in 1933, Skippy peanut butter was well received; within three years the product was distributed nationwide. The first Skippy label pictured a young boy in front of a fence on which the word "Skippy" had been painted in bright red. In the lower right of the label was the paint can, evidence of the boy's mischief. Skippy appealed to children in its early days of production, and it steadily grew more popular through the 1940s.

A New Parent Company

In 1955 the Best Foods Company acquired the Skippy peanut butter brand. Three years later the Corn Products Company acquired Best Foods, which remained operating as the large firm's consumer products division. The new parent company, one of the nation's largest corn refiners, had transformed itself into a major food manufacturing company through a number of recent large-scale acquisitions. Skippy was in capable hands. The Corn Products Company brought brand expertise; it had been producing Argo starch and Karo syrup for three decades and Mazola corn oil for nearly five. Best Foods, as well, had been successfully producing and promoting well-known brands, with Hellmann's mayonnaise and Knorr soups among them.

With experience overseeing a variety of grocery and household items, Best Foods decided to promote Skippy peanut butter and Hellmann's mayonnaise together, displaying them next to one another on supermarket shelves. In the early 1960s, print ads were scheduled for the two brands in popular magazines of the day, such as *Good Housekeeping, Ladies' Home Journal, Sunset Magazine,* and regional editions of *American Home, Better Homes & Gardens, Family Circle, McCall's, Redbook,* and *Woman's Day.*

Early Advertising

Credit for upping the visibility of Skippy through the years 1955 to 1965 was given to the New York office of advertising agency Guild, Bascom & Bonfigli, headquartered in San Francisco. From the beginning of their relationship, both client and agency decided against gimmicky and short-lived promotions which sometimes caused distributors and supermarkets to over-order the product. This resulted in a less-than-fresh peanut butter being stocked on grocers' shelves. In addition, Guild, Bascom & Bonfigli had experience in sticking to a basic approach which had been working successfully with Best Foods' Knorr soups and Mazola corn oil accounts.

Based on research findings, Best Foods and Guild determined that when peanut butter was chosen, adults were the consumers 45 percent of the time. Accordingly, a family audience was targeted, in the majority of cases via television. Best Foods ran commercials during programs beginning at 7:30 p.m. The company ran ads during "You Asked for It" for eight years, "Dennis the Menace" for three years, and beginning in 1965, Best Foods added "The Flintstones" to its prime-time roster.

In working with Guild, Best Foods offered seventeen points it viewed as essential advantages of Skippy peanut butter, among them flavor, freshness and quality of ingredients, and the product's reusable jar. The link of Skippy with these fundamentals was so strong that in the early 1960s, when Best Foods sought to lower production costs, the company felt comfortable re-airing ten of fifteen previously shown commercials.

Market Research

In the spring of 1963 Corn Products tried a new approach with Skippy, in an advertising campaign called Whispering Sweepstakes. Allocating $200,000 for spending, the company placed ads in three Curtis magazines, the *Saturday Evening Post, American Home,* and *Ladies Home Journal.* Continuing its connection with the television show "Dennis the Menace," Corn Products advertised the same promotion during that CBS program. Using drawings by Norman Rockwell, the copy, as reported in a 1963 *Advertising Age* article, explained that although for years the company had been "shouting the merits of Skippy . . . a small segment of the population has paid absolutely no attention to our advertising." The ad went on to ask customers to "whisper to just one person how great Skippy is. In return, we'll enter you in our Whispering Sweepstakes." Prizes available were tours around the world and to selected U.S. cities, as well as 100 extension telephones—"to whisper to friends and neighbors about how delicious Skippy is." The company planned to spend $1.5 million for the year in the Curtis magazine campaign.

Best Foods also used radio advertising to market Skippy, in an attempt to double the product's market share of 23 percent. From June through December of 1963 the company aired 92 sixty-second commercials on three Nashville stations. The effort was to get customers to hear a Skippy spot once every half-hour, four days a week. The campaign was planned for three weeks on, and two weeks off the air schedule, with print ads and coupons run during the "off" weeks. Best Foods based its Nashville blitz on marketing information gathered in the Buffalo-Rochester area, which the company had been studying since January. Radio ads in those cities would continue through year-end 1963. The company's goal was to boost the overall market share for Skippy to the 40-plus percentage it enjoyed in New York state.

The successful marketing of Skippy was a result of sticking to the basics as well as the use of carefully planned new approaches.

To illustrate the former tactic: along with its warm, homey commercials aimed at family audiences, Best Foods ran a nationwide campaign, once again connecting its product with the homespun values of Norman Rockwell. The first-prize winner won a family portrait by the popular artist. A more unusual, award-winning ad Guild created showed an elephant couple in bed, eating first peanuts, then Skippy peanut butter.

Best Foods and Guild went even farther to capture a market that had been neglected. While commercials aired during "You Asked for It," the Skippy product was funneled only to the areas whose networks carried the show. It was discovered that in Albany, New York, the market share for Skippy was 60 percent, while in Syracuse sales were quite low, since the region didn't have network coverage of "You Asked for It."

To get a pointed message across, Best Foods blanketed Syracuse radio with 150 commercials a week. The ads, according to *Progressive Grocer,* were "advising housewives that the 'Freshmen' were on their way, ready to give up to $8 when they knocked on a door." Thirty Syracuse students were sent out in pairs, wearing bright red Skippy blazers and hats, making a total of 17,000 house calls. Customers received one dollar if they remarked about Skippy on a tape recorder, two dollars if they had a jar of Skippy at home, and five dollars if their stated comments were used in a commercial. As a result of the campaign, Skippy distribution was solidly established in the Syracuse market. By 1965 Skippy peanut butter was the market leader, with a volume twice that of the two closest competitors combined.

Best Foods continued its push with another advertising campaign to promote Skippy in 1966. With a 13-page color series in *Life* magazine, Skippy was popularized with a new cast of characters. Standing peanuts, perched vertically on one end, were pictured with large eyes, perky facial expressions, and various hats. The caption under one read: "Are you a nut nut?" Under another peanut, with a gangster-style 1930s beret, the copy read: "Capture America's most wanted nut!" After blanketing selected U.S. regions with print, radio, and television advertising to increase the already dominant market share enjoyed by Skippy, Best Foods looked to lock onto other markets.

Old History, New Image

The ultimate owner of the Skippy brand, the Corn Products Company, changed its name to CPC International in the mid-1960s. After one brief return to the old name (initiated in 1975), the company remained CPC International. Skippy peanut butter, along with CPC's Hellmann's mayonnaise brand, was already selling well in Mexico by 1962. These products were moved easily into Mexico due to CPC's prior presence in international markets.

Beginning in 1956, when William T. Brady was named president of the Corn Products Company, the corporation changed its emphasis. Not only did CPC move from corn milling and refining to aggressive marketing of consumer goods, the company also planned increasing overseas expansion. International expertise at CPC had a long history. The original Corn Products, formed as a monopoly in 1906 and broken up by an antitrust decision in 1916, was "internationally minded and from 1919 on expanded its foreign manufacturing facilities and investments," according to *Fortune.* The article went on to list names and sites of Corn Products sites operating at that time in Germany, Britain, France, Brazil, and Latin America.

By 1958, when Corn Products merged with Best Foods through a stock swap, the company was established in various manufacturing sites and joint ventures in eighteen countries. Earnings rose from $21 million in 1956 to $41 million only five years later. Corn Products stock quadrupled in the same five-year stretch. All this combined to place the formerly "somnolent giant"—as described in a 1958 *Business Week* article—in the forefront of successful American food companies.

By the late 1960s, CPC focused less on its solid food brands like Skippy and Hellmann's, diversifying into management consulting, computer programming, and training and development. The company also burned through five chief executives in one decade. By the 1970s CPC recognized that it was time to move back to the basic consumer products businesses William Brady had steered the company toward nearly twenty years earlier.

Line Extensions

CPC International planned to introduce 21 new products in the late 1960s. In keeping with lessons learned through the active period in its growth, however, the company created many of those products through line extensions on its most successful and well-known brands. CPC devoted more than $30 million to advertise a range of new products in 1966, a 10 percent increase over the previous year's budget.

Traditional Skippy peanut butter was still a strong seller, and Best Foods decided to offer Skippy peanut butter with smoky crisps, a non-meat protein additive. Production was problematic early on, but the new Skippy item was available in Best Foods' central region and in several western and eastern markets. The company hoped for national distribution by 1967.

By the 1970s Proctor & Gamble's competitor, Jif, was beginning to outstrip Skippy in the national market. In 1973 CPC's Best Foods division brought out Skippy Super Chunk, a thicker peanut butter, to further extend the product line. Attempting to capture new markets, CPC introduced Skippy in Canada in 1976, which held second place in that country's peanut butter sales.

Sales of Skippy continued on a steady increase; according to CPC International's 1980 annual report, Skippy was "the largest selling peanut butter in the United States." This was despite a shortage in the peanut crop, which caused company buyers to have to juggle their purchasing programs and allocation limits that year. Skippy held 25 percent of the still rapidly growing market.

Back to Basics

Skippy television advertising during this time once again zeroed in on the basics, as CPC Chairman James W. McKee focused on his company's bottom line—profitability. CPC entered the 1980s in great shape. According to James Cook in *Forbes,* CPC was "second in profitability only to Kellogg among major companies and ahead of both General Foods and General Mills." A subheading of the article title stated that CPC International was "one of the best managed outfits in the United States."

Thus, to keep it simple, the nutritional advantages of Skippy were touted; peanut butter, as always, was high in protein and contained no cholesterol. To the health-conscious consumer, this was good news. An unhomogenized version of "old-fashioned" Skippy peanut butter was brought out in the late 1970s. In 1984 Best Foods introduced a new five-pound container for the food-service market. To indicate its products were the freshest and

safest available, in 1985 Best Foods provided tamper-evident seals for Skippy jars.

The Conscious Consumer

Consumers, in fact, were becoming much more conscious not only of their health but of advertising schemes. The simple hard sell used to push Skippy in the early 1960s was obsolete by the 1980s. Catering to the more sophisticated consumer, Best Foods created a multibrand promotion linking the company's most popular products with a high-profile event.

In August 1986 the Best Foods Consumer Promotion Group, after viewing four presentations, chose to work with Glendinning Associates of Westport, Connecticut. Their theme, "Brands Across America," was to coincide with Hands Across America, a non-profit organization aiding the homeless. Best Foods pledged one dollar for every refund certificate mailed in to Hands Across America, up to a maximum of $100,000. Consumers could receive refunds ranging from one to ten dollars if they mailed in the UPC codes (as proof of CPC items purchased) by certain deadlines. Skippy peanut butter was one of the three strongest participating brands included in the promotion. Some brands enjoyed a 20 percent sales increase over the previous year; all brands reported an increase in varying amounts.

To emphasize an association with health and fitness, Skippy peanut butter was an official sponsor of the 1988 U.S. Olympic team. The consumers sought by Best Foods were women aged 18 to 49, who tuned in to the Olympics by the millions. According to research cited in CPC International's 1987 annual report, for this targeted audience "the Olympics is the single favorite sports viewing event." Forty-five Skippy commercials were run prior to and during the winter games. Skippy was the only Best Foods brand to improve its market share by 1.5 points in 1987.

Since the early 1980s, ads stressed that Skippy peanut butter contained less sugar than other brands. One of these sweeter competitors, Proctor & Gamble's Jif peanut butter, had been slowly increasing its market share since the early 1970s. In early 1988 a reformulated, sweeter Skippy was launched in an attempt to hang on to customers with sweeter tastes. Another move Best Foods made was to license the use of the Skippy name on products such as Skippy Ice Cream bars and Skippy peanut butter cookies. The company also focused once again on the adult consumer in its advertisements, "the fastest growing segment of peanut butter-eaters" according to *Adweek's Marketing Week.*

CPC's chief competitor in the peanut butter category commanded a 30 percent market share by 1989, however, compared to the 22 percent Skippy had maintained through the 1980s. Focusing on another means to combat Jif's gains, Best Foods brought out Roasted Honey Nut Skippy and a new nuttier version, Super Chunk, in 1990.

In 1991 CPC International acquired Canada's Squirrel brand peanut butter, which made CPC the largest producer in the Canadian market. In addition to its solid presence in Mexico and Japan, Skippy and CPC's Lady's Choice brand peanut butter were either manufactured in or imported into all Asian markets where the company pursued joint ventures.

Skippy, a favorite for more than six decades, appeared likely to maintain its strong presence in its category. The international market, however, was a necessary playing field for Skippy, along with brands by other major American food companies, as competition in the United States crowded. CPC, once opting for overseas expansion in the beginning of the century, found itself depending on the international market for growth at the century's close.

Further Reading:

Cook, James, "Handsome Is as Handsome Does," *Forbes,* March 3, 1980, p. 43.

"Corn Products Finds Other Fields Green," *Business Week,* July 5, 1958, p. 76.

CPC International Annual Reports, Englewood Cliffs, N.J.: CPC International, 1980-1992.

Crain, Rance, "At Best Foods It's New Wares, Old Names," *Advertising Age,* May 16, 1966, p. 3.

"How Best Foods Keeps a No. 1 Product on Top," *Progressive Grocer,* April, 1965.

Koeppel, Dan, "Skippy Launches Three-Pronged Bid to Catch Jif," *Adweek's Marketing Week,* July 31, 1989.

Lawrence, Jennifer, "P&G's Peanut Butter Share Gets Boost with Simply Jif," *Advertising Age,* September 14, 1992.

"New Whispering Sweepstakes to Push Skippy Peanut Butter," *Advertising Age,* May 27, 1963, p. 10.

"Q&A about Skippy Peanut Butter," Englewood Cliffs, NJ: CPC International, 1988.

"Skippy Peanut Butter History," Englewood Cliffs, N.J.: CPC International, 1992.

Telzer, Ronnie, "Single Event Is Better Way for Best," *Advertising Age,* November 16, 1987, p. S-11.

"Uncommon Market," *Fortune,* March, 1962, p. 98.

—Frances E. Norton

SLICE®

Credited with creating an entirely new segment in the soft drink market, Slice is Pepsi-Cola Company's fifth-biggest brand name. Though the segment that lemon-lime Slice pioneered, juice-added soft drinks, has dwindled to about 3 percent of the soda market, the brand extension Mandarin Orange Slice is the leader in the orange soda market with about 20 percent of the market. Considered to be a marketing coup when originally introduced in 1984, Slice went on to capture an impressive 3.2 percent of the $40 billion cola-dominated market by 1987. *Fortune* magazine ranked lemon-lime Slice as one of its "Products of the Year" in 1986. Three new brand extensions were rushed into the market to take full advantage of Slice's leading position in the juice-added soft drink market. Competitors followed suit by introducing their own juice-added products, including Coca-Cola's Minute Maid soda. By 1988 however, consumers had grown disenchanted with juice-added soft drinks, and sales for that category began to plummet. Despite parent company PepsiCo's marketing muscle and constant reformulations of the brand family, sales continued to decrease. By 1989, Slice was no longer considered a juice-added product. The brand nevertheless continues to fill a profitable niche thanks mainly due to Mandarin Orange Slice's dominant position in the orange soda category.

Brand Origins

By the mid 1980s, PepsiCo was a very close second to Coca-Cola in the soft-drink market. The one product PepsiCo lacked was a significant lemon-lime drink. Teem, its earlier lemon-lime soda, had flopped and was available only in a few markets. Repositioning the product would be a futile and uphill task. Being a late entrant into the lemon-lime soda market, the company needed a product that was different from Philip-Morris's 7UP and Coca-Cola's Sprite. Jennifer Lawrence wrote in *Advertising Age,* "Pepsi's consumer research in the early 1980s indicated that consumers were looking for added value in products. Soft drinks had been busy removing caffeine and calories, but had not introduced a 'value-added' beverage. Pepsi chose to add value by adding juice—a popular marketing twist overseas." Another fact Pepsi gleaned from its research was that consumers did not realize that lemon-lime drinks, while fruit-based, lacked any real fruit juice—and this was going to be Slice's unique selling characteristic. The drink was targeted at "active adults from 18-34—trend-setters who are willing to try new experiences and products," according to a PepsiCo fact sheet.

Focus-group research yielded a high degree of interest in a juice-added lemon-lime soft drink. After 18 months of testing and development, lemon-lime Slice was introduced in test markets in 1984. In addition to lemon and lime juices, Slice contained white grape and pear juices. The diet version contained 14 calories, almost all from the juices. Both the regular and diet versions were tested in Tulsa, Oklahoma; Phoenix; and most of Wisconsin. Test marketing was done in house, and New York–based J. Walter Thompson brought out a multimedia ad campaign with the "We Got the Juice" tag line, emphasizing Slice's unique selling attribute. From the beginning, Slice was positioned head on against 7UP and Sprite because consumers were not aware that those products did not contain real fruit juice. Slice's fruit content was emphasized in ad copy and visuals. When the test market results came in, Slice had done much better than originally anticipated; moreover, it had also strongly attracted consumers to its diet version. Working on the strong reception that Slice got in the three test markets, Pepsi decided to expand into another 15 percent of the country by the fourth quarter of 1984. The West Coast, with its highly developed lemon-lime market area, was seen as a demanding test for the introductory product, and the late 1984 expansion was concentrated in this region. With a successful debut in the West Coast, Slice began a gradual national roll out in January 1985.

Six months after Slice had entered test markets in 1984, Pepsi had already begun developing Mandarin Orange Slice to tap the third-largest soft drink segment after colas and lemon-lime. Diet and regular versions of the orange juice-based product began testing in November 1985—the off-season for orange soft drinks. Hartford, Connecticut, and Phoenix, two well developed orange soft drink markets, were chosen as the test markets. Pepsi wanted to learn whether Mandarin Orange Slice sold more quickly in an established Slice market like Phoenix and whether a new market like Hartford would require more time to develop the Slice brand name. Slice's orange-based extension did equally well in both markets, and Pepsi began quickly rolling out Mandarin Orange Slice in January 1986, achieving 80 percent national distribution by July 1986. Within six months and with only 50 percent distribution, it became the leading orange soft drink, a position it has not relinquished since.

AT A GLANCE

Slice brand soda founded in 1984 in Somers, NY, by Pepsi-Cola Company. Brand extensions include Mandarin Orange Slice, regular and diet, introduced in 1985; Apple Slice and Cherry Cola Slice, regular and diet, introduced in 1986; Fruit Punch, Red, Grape and Strawberry, introduced in 1992.

Performance: *Market share*—1.2% (all Slice brands) of U.S. soft drink market. *Sales*—100.5 million cases (all Slice brands).

Major competitor: Minute Maid; also Sprite, 7UP, Sunkist, Crush.

Advertising: *Agency*—BBDO Worldwide, New York, NY, 1987—. *Major Campaign*—"Slice is clearly the one."

Addresses: *Parent company*—Pepsi-Cola Company, 1 Pepsi Way, Somers, NY 10589-2201; phone: (914) 767-6000; fax: (914) 767-7762. *Ultimate parent company*—PepsiCo, Inc., Purchase, NY 10577; phone: (914) 253-2000; fax: (914) 253-2070.

Marketing Strategy

Slice's initial phenomenal success is considered to be one of the greatest marketing achievements in the beverage industry. In two years on the market, Slice had hit $1 billion in sales and pioneered a completely new segment of soft drinks with juice in them. Its meteoric rise created high hopes in the company that Slice would capture 10 percent of the immensely competitive soft-drink market. PepsiCo president Roger Enrico went on to say in his 1986 book, *The Other Guy Blinked,* that Slice would become the third-largest trademark in the soft-drink industry. But Slice's success was too good to last; with changing market tastes, Slice sales soon plunged. With a lot of money and time invested and reputations on the line, Pepsi brought out its formidable marketing power to regain lost momentum and pride. Efforts to salvage the brand met with mixed success: the juice-added soda segment continued to decline, but the Mandarin Orange Slice brand continued to command the orange soda segment. According to Doron Levin in the *New York Times,* " It (Slice) is starting to look like a case study of how difficult it is to create a new consumer brand with staying power--especially in a market in which consumers are fickle and competitors are quick to copy any successful product."

By 1986, the Slice brand name had become hugely successful, being named by *Fortune* magazine as one of its 1986 "Products of the Year." Slice also began to make substantial inroads into the food-service channel through Wendy's International decision to serve it in its 1,050 company-owned restaurants. The stunningly fast evolution of the Slice brand continued with the rolling out of Apple Slice and Cherry Cola Slice without prior testing. *USA Today* named Diet Apple Slice as one of the best new products of 1986. While the Slice brand was a huge success initially, the apple and cherry cola flavors led to some amount of cannibalization. By the end of 1986, the Slice line had 2.5 percent of the total soft drink market.

Meanwhile the competition in the newly created juice-added segment began to heat up. Competitors countered with their own juice-added drinks, choosing names for their products that consumers already associated with juice, like Coca-Cola's Minute Maid orange soda, Procter & Gamble's Crush, and Canada Dry's Sunkist brand, thus making market barriers easy to penetrate. By 1987, the novelty of the juice-added segment began to wear off.

Consumers began to switch back to real juice for the nutrition and regular soda for the taste. Slice sales began to fall, and Pepsi executives reacted by reformulating Slice in November 1987, making it lighter and crisper, but keeping the same juice content. Coca-Cola, whose research showed that consumers cared more about taste than the juice content, cut down the juice content in its Minute Maid orange soda from 10 percent to 2 percent. Another rival, Sunkist soda, which had also contained 10 percent juice, began selling an "original" Sunkist with no juice.

While the orange version of Slice was doing very well, its apple and cherry line extensions fared poorly on a national basis. The rapid introduction of these two new flavors after the earlier two lemon-lime and orange products, in both regular and diet versions, were too much to handle for bottlers and consumers alike. Some bottlers were reportedly unhappy after the introduction of the juice-based category in the first place. Adding juice to a soft drink is an expensive proposition, and bottlers could not pass on the added cost to the consumers, who would have been unwilling to pay a premium for juice content. Moreover, bottlers had a tricky time with the manufacturing process because the juice would ferment quickly if it came into contact with yeast, forcing them to adopt more rigorous and stringent sterilization standards. By 1988, with the Slice sales dropping, a number of bottlers in upstate New York dropped lemon-lime Slice to become 7UP bottlers.

Slice saw its 3.8 percent share of the 10.5 billion gallon soft-drink market drop to 2.7 percent by 1987. Slice, even then, was worth $1 billion to PepsiCo and ranked among the top ten brands. In an effort to revive the struggling brand, Slice shifted advertising agencies. J. Walter Thompson, New York, who gave Slice the once-triumphant "We got the juice" campaign, lost the $30 million Slice account to cross-town rival BBDO, which had created the tremendously successful Michael Jackson campaigns for the Pepsi brand. In an extension of the earlier campaign, BBDO came out with the lines, "Who's Got the Juice?" and "Either you've got it, or you don't," shifting the focus of the ad from popularizing the brand to who should be drinking it. Implicitly acknowledging that the juice-added segment Slice created had failed to materialize into the predicted 10 percent of the soda market, Slice reduced the juice content to 2 percent from the earlier 10 percent in the regular lime-lemon and Orange Slice, and halved the juice content in the diet versions to 5 percent. Bottlers were pleased with the change— the reduced juice-content meant lesser manufacturing headaches and decreased costs.

In early 1989, Slice launched the reformulated drinks with the ad campaign, "Slice is clearly the one," positioning Slice as a mainstream lemon-lime soda pitted against category leaders Sprite and 7UP. Lemon-lime was the nation's second best-selling flavor after cola, with about 12 percent of the $40 billion retail market-- precisely the segment in which PepsiCo had aimed to establish a presence when it first introduced Slice. The lemon-lime drink, however, had lost precious momentum to its established rivals, and by the end of 1989, the Slice brand's sales plunged 11 percent, giving it 1.6 percent of the market. The Mandarin Orange Slice, on the other hand, continued to be the largest selling orange drink in the orange soda market, which had increased to 2.4 percent of the soft-drink industry. PepsiCo began running separate ads for the orange-flavored drink, now the brand family's principal trademark, giving it a chance to distance itself from its lemon-lime brethren's possible failure. In 1990 PepsiCo shifted its focus to Diet Pepsi and Caffeine-Free Pepsi; advertising allocation to Slice went down by 24 percent. Caffeine-Free Pepsi had already replaced Slice as PepsiCo's fourth-largest brand after Pepsi, Diet Pepsi, and Mountain Dew. Buoyed by a distinct advertising identity and the Magic Johnson commercials, Mandarin Orange Slice continued to lead the $650-million-dollar orange soda segment, with a 20 percent share in 1991. By November 1992, PepsiCo had extended its Slice brand line further by adding Fruit Punch, Red, Grape, and Strawberry.

Advertising and Other Promotional Activities

J. Walter Thompson introduced the multimedia "We Got The Juice," campaign in Slice's three introductory markets. Commercials featured citrus slices splashing through water, announcing Slice's 10 percent fruit juice ingredient, and targeted consumers in activities that captured contemporary lifestyles, beach scenes, and aerobics. The ad copy, tag line, and visuals emphasized Slice's juice content, its point of difference. When the diet version began to show immense promise in tests, PepsiCo began advertising Diet Slice in separate TV spots in May 1985; initial ads included only a tag for the diet version. By 1986, the company was spending about $32 million in advertising its Slice brand, keeping up a heavy ad schedule for the Slice flavor extensions, promoting them individually in TV, radio, and print. While lemon-lime spots were also tagged with the announcement of the new flavors, Pepsi used split 30-second commercials to advertise more than one flavor. In June 1987, J. Walter Thompson won the American Marketing Association's gold Effie for ad effectiveness for the introduction of Slice with the "We Got The Juice," campaign.

But the ad agency that created one of the most effective advertising campaigns in history was to lose the prestigious $30 million Slice account to BBDO by November 1987. The brand had begun to falter in the market and Pepsi, after spending below $30 million in advertising the brand in 1987 from a high of $40 million in 1985, wanted a new ad approach. JWT worked frantically to save the account, even trying to sign up comedian Robin Williams as pitchman. Pepsi went ahead with BBDO, maintaining that Slice had moved to a new stage in its life—from a new product to an established brand—and hence required a new ad approach. The JWT ads had managed to establish Slice in the preliminary phase but were unable to differentiate it from the others as the segment grew more crowded.

BBDO's new ads used the line, "Who's Got The Juice?" In fleeting visuals, the ads told the viewer who's "got it"—an athlete diving for a volleyball—and who doesn't—arch rivals Sprite, 7UP, and man with a bad toupee. The theme of the ads had changed to focus both on juice and taste in a campaign tagged, "Either you got it or you don't." On the orange end, meanwhile, a "Taste the Biggest Orange" ad campaign was launched in summer 1988 to herald Mandarin Orange Slice's rise to the nation's biggest-selling orange drink.

Beginning in 1987, PepsiCo began renting the world's largest blimp to promote the Slice brand. It made its first appearance as the "official" blimp for CBS's coverage of the Super Bowl in Pasadena, going on to promote a win-a-ride in the Slice blimp contest, and eventually requiring the services of a full-time "blimp coordinator," whose job was to schedule promotions with local bottlers and rides for journalists and consumers. Other promotions, however, served in bringing down Slice's image. For instance, at the 1989 Rose Bowl, Slice's prize-winning parade float broke down, and rowdy fans brought the football game to a

halt with a fusillade of Slice promotional seat cushions. Much time and money had gone into preparing the float, and eventually, Slice failed to get the supreme bonus on an award-winning float: TV exposure that could have reached more than 300 million viewers.

1989 had a more positive note to it with its new campaign "Slice is clearly the one," featuring *Saturday Night Live* comedian Phil Hartman. The offbeat, humorous commercial was a parody of late-night TV advertising and went on to become a big hit. Unfortunately, it did little for the brand's sales, and with PepsiCo opting to put more of its advertising strength into Diet Pepsi, Slice spent a relatively low $11 million in advertising for that year. In 1990 Slice chose NBA star Earvin "Magic" Johnson to advertise the Mandarin Orange Slice brand, by then the best performing product in the brand family. "The Magic is Mandarin" ad campaign displayed Johnson's shooting prowess in two commercials and represented the company's renewed emphasis on the brand. The campaign also featured a consumer promotion with a first prize that included an all-expenses paid trip for two to Los Angeles to meet Johnson and a chance to play "One-On-One" with the celebrity. Animation also played a role in Slice advertising when the popular character Fido Dido starred in a commercial for Lemon-Lime Slice in summer 1990. Perceived as "cool," the animated star was considered to be a perfect spokesman for the lime drink.

Competition

Originally slated as PepsiCo's entry into the lemon-lime market, Slice did take on Coca-Cola's Sprite and Philip Morris's 7UP. Initial market share gain was entirely at the expense of 7UP; Sprite did not lose sales with Slice's entry. But as the juice-added soda category began to fade, much to 7UP's relief, Slice cut down its juice content, which, ironically, was its distinguishing feature. Result: a drink more like 7UP. Meanwhile, Cherry 7UP's success had rejuvenated the 7UP franchise, and bottlers switched back to 7UP, with whom they had a long-standing association. As lemon-lime Slice's sales fell, Coca-Cola's Sprite continued to hold on to its 25 percent share of the lemon-lime market. By 1990, Sprite's share of the pie had increased to 30 percent and 7UP's to 25 percent, while lemon-lime Slice's was at 8 percent.

The early success of the Slice brand attracted many competitors—notably arch-rival Coca-Cola's Minute Maid juice-added soft drinks. Existing brands in the orange soda market, like Sunkist and Crush, at first added juice-content in their beverages, only to take them out altogether as the segment started waning. Mandarin Orange Slice had by then surpassed them as the largest selling orange soda and by 1990 had 20 percent of the segment, followed by Minute-Maid with 15 percent and Sunkist and Crush with 13 percent and 10 percent respectively.

Further Reading:

"Packaging Promotions Push U.S. Sales up 3%," *Beverage Industry/Annual Manual 1991/92,* 1991-92, pp. 14-34.

"Soda Sales Going Flat," *Standard & Poor's Industry Surveys,* August 6, 1992, pp. F24-F28.

Dugas, Christine, "Slice Fails to Carve Out More Than a Small Niche," *Newsday,* February 5, 1989, p. 67.

Dunkin, Amy, and Ticer, Scott, "Can a New Ad Blitz Put the Fizz Back in Slice?" *Business Week,* February 8, 1988.

Giges, Nancy, "Orange Slice Tops Soft-Drink Market," *Advertising Age,* September 22, 1986, p. 4.

Lawrence, Jennifer, "Testing Juices up Slice's Performance," *Advertising Age,* August 24, 1987, p. S2.

Levin, Doron, "Slice: Case Study of a Setback," *New York Times,* July 15, 1988, section D, p. 1.

Winters, Patricia, "Orange Hoops It Up; NBA Stars Tout Minute Maid, Slice," *Advertising Age,* February 19, 1990, p. 62.

Winters, "Pepsi Re-Aims Slice," *Advertising Age,* December 12, 1988, p. 3.

Winters, "Pepsi Slices JWT; BBDO Gets Call to Help Struggling Soft Drink," *Advertising Age,* November 30, 1987, p. 3.

—Ashish Patwardhan

SMIRNOFF®

The most popular vodka in America, Smirnoff can trace its history back to the days when it was the vodka of the czars. Heublein, Inc., who acquired the brand from its American franchisee in 1939, originally had difficulty selling the Russian liquor to Americans. Its innovative strategy of marketing Smirnoff as a liquor with which to make mixed drinks, rather than as a liquor to drink straight, propelled vodka from obscurity to its position as the best-selling liquor in the United States.

Brand Origins

Peter A. Smirnoff opened his vodka distillery in Moscow in 1864 and established the brand's reputation for quality. In 1877 his vodka won its first double eagle, Russia's highest industrial honor, distinguishing it as the best in its field. Upon its award of a third double eagle in 1886, Smirnoff became the purveyor to the Court of His Imperial Majesty, Czar Alexander III. Although for a time this distinction contributed to Smirnoff's popularity—the company was said to be producing one million bottles a day by the end of the century—being associated with the Imperial Court did not recommend the distillery to the revolutionaries in 1917. Vladimir Smirnoff, one of the only members of the Smirnoff family to escape Russia during the revolution, emigrated to France and attempted to re-create the secret Smirnoff distilling process in Paris.

Meanwhile, Rudolph Kunett, whose father had supplied the Smirnoffs with the raw spirits they used in making vodka, left Russia for the United States. In 1933, Kunett convinced Vladimir Smirnoff to sell him the American rights to Smirnoff for $2,500. With money saved from working in sales for Helena Rubinstein and Standard Oil, Kunett established Ste. Pierte Smirnoff Fils in Bethel, Connecticut, in 1934.

Initial Marketing Difficulties

Standing as America's first vodka distillery, Smirnoff was also nearly the country's last. Five years after its establishment, the company was selling only six thousand cases a year at $6 a case. "All was tragedy," Kunett said of the year 1939 to the *New Yorker*. "My partner, Vladimir Smirnoff, fourth generation in the company, had just died, and I decided I would have to sell out." He turned to John G. Martin, president of G. F. Heublein and Brothers, Inc., who had saved Kunett a $1,600 licensing fee expense in 1934 by agreeing to sell Smirnoff under his company's

name. Kunett sold Smirnoff to Heublein for $14,000, a small royalty on sales of the vodka, and a job.

Heublein, which sold liquor and wine before Prohibition, survived those dry years with sales of A1 Sauce. Essentially a one-product company, Heublein found it difficult to sell what was considered a luxury item during the Depression. Although the company produced several brands of whiskey, including Heublein Private Stock, Old Waverly, Powderhorn, and Forest Park, their sales were negligible. With Smirnoff, the company hoped to break back into the liquor industry with a new type of liquor.

"Martin's folly," as some colleagues referred to the acquisition of Smirnoff, seemed to be just that. Demand for vodka in the United States was almost nonexistent. "Even the Russians in this country weren't drinking vodka then," Martin reported to *Nation's Business*. Despite Heublein's greater sales staff and advertising resources, sales in the next few years rose no higher than 10,000 cases per year.

The problem was not Americans' unfamiliarity with vodka, but their false impression of it. Kunett explained to the *New Yorker*, "Vodka, it was said, is lethal, gives you exceptionally bad hangovers, and is made from moldy potatoes. None of this is true." Vodka is made from pure grain alcohol. The raw spirits are filtered through charcoal and sold without aging. Smirnoff Vodka is continuously filtered for more than eight hours; this process was developed by Peter Smirnoff in nineteenth-century Russia and is one Heublein continues to stand by. Smirnoff is only filtered through charcoal made from hardwoods such as maple, birch, ash, and oak, which Heublein cites as a vital ingredient in producing Smirnoff.

First Commercial Success

Soon after taking over Smirnoff, Martin had a marketing idea that he felt would overcome Americans' aversion to vodka. Kunett's distillery in Bethel had provided Heublein with 2,000 cases of vodka before shutting down operations. Because they had run out of vodka corks, the foreman substituted whiskey corks left over from a failed attempt to market Smirnoff whiskey. Since the labels said Smirnoff Vodka and the corks would be covered with tax stamps, he thought no one would be the wiser. However, when the Heublein salesman in the South received his initial 25 cases, he

AT A GLANCE

Smirnoff brand of vodka founded in 1864 in Moscow by Peter A. Smirnoff of the P. A. Smirnoff Vodka distillery; brand reestablished in Paris after the Russian Revolution in 1917 by Vladimir Smirnoff; Rudolf Kunett bought American rights to brand in 1933 and set up a distillery in Bethel, CT, in 1934; brand sold to Heublein, Inc., in 1939; Heublein acquired by Grand Metropolitan PLC in 1988.

Performance: *Market share*—19% (top share) of U.S. vodka category.

Major competitor: Gilby's; also Absolut.

Advertising: *Agency*—McCann-Erickson, New York, NY. *Major campaign*—"It leaves you breathless"; mixer suggestions; "Home is where you find it."

Addresses: *Parent company*—Heublein, Inc., 16 Munson Road, Farmingtion, CT 06034-0388; phone: (203) 231-5000. *Ultimate parent company*—Grand Metropolitan PLC, 20 St. James Square, London SW1Y 4RR England; phone: 071 321 6000; fax: 071 321 6001.

sampled the "whiskey" and found it had no taste or smell. His next sale was 50 cases, and the next, 500.

Martin investigated this extraordinary jump in sales and found that the salesman had ordered streamers made with the slogan, "Smirnoff's White Whiskey. No Taste. No Smell." The scheme, as Martin told *Nation's Business,* was "rather ingenious but totally illegal." However, Martin noticed that people were not drinking the "white whiskey" chilled and neat, as vodka is traditionally, but with a variety of mixers. The incident provided the germ of Smirnoff's future marketing strategy.

Unfortunately, World War II intervened before Martin could implement his idea. Because grain was needed in more crucial areas, the production of alcohol was restricted. Heublein made no vodka for four years. When the company resumed production of Smirnoff after the war, Martin decided to try his idea of marketing the vodka by piggybacking onto mixed drinks such as gin and tonic or Scotch and soda. He joined forces with two colleagues who were also having trouble marketing their products: Jack Morgan, who was unable to sell his Cock 'n' Bull Ginger Beer, and Susan Brownell, who had few buyers for her copper dishes. They decided to entice the public with a new drink, the Moscow Mule, a combination of Smirnoff vodka and Cock 'n' Bull Ginger Beer, served in a copper mug.

Martin promoted the drink by presenting a bartender with a free bottle of Smirnoff. He then offered to take the bartender's picture with one of the new instant Polaroid cameras if the bartender would sample the drink. Martin would pose the bartender with a Moscow Mule in his hand and a bottle of Smirnoff in the background and then take two pictures: one for the bartender and one for Martin to take to the next bar as evidence of Smirnoff's growing popularity.

The Long-Term Strategy

Smirnoff and the Moscow Mule became the latest rage, but Heublein did not rest on its laurels. Worried that Smirnoff would become a one-drink sensation and fade with the inevitable passing of the Moscow Mule fad, Heublein repeated its successful strat-

egy. The company promoted mixed drinks made with vodka in joint campaigns with soft drink manufacturers and fruit and vegetable trade organizations.

In the early 1950s Heublein initiated its first advertising campaign for Smirnoff. Print ads with color photographs by Bert Stern featured mixed drinks in a variety of exotic locations, such as the Sahara and the South Seas. The campaign's slogan, "It leaves you breathless," not only implied that Smirnoff was exciting, but also subtly suggested that the liquor, with its lack of taste or smell, would be difficult to detect on one's breath.

Each ad suggested a new mixer to drink with Smirnoff, creating enduring drinks: the Black Russian, made with Smirnoff and coffee liqueur; the Bloody Mary, made with Smirnoff, tomato juice, Worcestershire sauce, and lemon juice; and the Screwdriver, made with Smirnoff and orange juice. Heublein also suggested using Smirnoff in drinks traditionally made with other liquors, creating such mainstays as the vodka martini, vodka and tonic, the vodka gimlet, and the vodka collins.

The ad campaign also promoted the new mixed drinks by featuring celebrities, including Groucho Marx, Brian Donlevy, and Robert Morse. One of the campaign's first ads pictured the comedian George Jessel stating, "I, George Jessel, invented the Bloody Mary." Although Fernand Petiot was the rightful creator of the Bloody Mary, having first made the drink in Harry's New York Bar in Paris in 1921, the ad made a Smirnoff mixed drink once again the hottest drink in the country. The ad campaign proved so successful that Heublein continued to use the same formula for more than a decade. In a 1969 joint promotion with The Coca-Cola Company, Johnny Carson appeared in an ad drinking a Blizzard, a combination of Smirnoff and Fresca.

Advertising Innovations

Heublein's sophisticated and expensive advertising for Smirnoff changed the liquor industry's marketing focus. Stuart D. Watson, Heublein's chief executive officer in 1968, explained to *Forbes:* "Traditionally, the other companies have been production-distributor oriented. Heublein is consumer-oriented. We want to give the consumer what he wants." Heublein appealed directly to the customer with its ads and concentrated on specialty products, advertising a plethora of mixed drinks to appeal to a wide variety of tastes. In addition, Smirnoff broke away from the traditional advertising that was then common in the liquor industry. According to *Business Week,* Smirnoff introduced "to the stodgy liquor business a catchy new style of advertising and promotion. Now, the sophisticated humor that made Screwdrivers and Bloody Marys into favorite mixed drinks is being applied to the growing list of wines, pre-mixed cocktails, liquors, sherry, rum, and cordials."

Smirnoff also started the trend toward increasingly large ad budgets. Heublein spent $1 million on advertising in 1954 and $1.25 million in 1955. In 1968 the company spent ten percent of its sales on advertising—almost twice the industry norm. These exorbitant yet successful advertising campaigns pressured other major distillers to follow suit with expensive campaigns of their own.

A Market Created, a Monopoly Lost

Vodka proved to be much more palatable to Americans when mixed with something else. By 1955, Heublein was selling more than one million cases of Smirnoff a year, but success bred competition. Eager to win part of the growing vodka market, liquor companies had little trouble producing their own brand of vodka. Because vodka requires no aging, companies could produce the finished product with little investment (especially compared to the effort needed to make liquors with a prolonged aging process, such as scotch or bourbon). As a result, vodka brands soon flooded the market. In 1946 six brands competed in the American market; ten years later, 40 brands were vying for a market share.

Smirnoff's illustrious history as purveyor to the czar helped it maintain its lead. According to *World's Greatest Brands,* "Consumers are remarkably conservative in their drinking habits; they like their drinks to have heritage and tradition and do not like to think of themselves as pawns being manipulated by faceless marketing people. Smirnoff possesses genuine heritage and reassurance." Because of Smirnoff's extensive advertising and the brand's standing as the first vodka Americans drank, the name Smirnoff became virtually synonymous with vodka. In 1956, against 40 competitors, Smirnoff accounted for more than half of all the vodka sold in the United States. By 1968, Smirnoff still solidly held the largest market share, selling four cases to every one of Gilbey's, its closest competitor.

International Market

In the early 1950s Smirnoff expanded overseas, opening plants in England, France, and Mexico. The brand's success seemed to translate well; between 1953 and 1955, sales quadrupled in France. In 1955 Heublein had plans to open Smirnoff distilleries in Australia, South Africa, Spain, Italy, and Canada. In 1968 Heublein had Smirnoff licensees in 35 countries. The company steadily expanded internationally and by 1991 Smirnoff was manufactured in 25 countries, including Botswana, Ireland, and Venezuela, and was sold in more than 100 countries worldwide.

Vodka's popularity continued to grow in the United States. In 1974 vodka outsold any other type of spirit, including bourbon, the traditional favorite of Americans. However, because producing vodka required so little investment, companies continued to enter the vodka market, driving prices and profits down. An executive at National Distillers and Chemical Corporation claimed in an interview with *Business Week* that "only Smirnoff is making a profit." With his own Old Crow bourbon suffering from the decline in bourbon sales, he said, "We've got some suspicions that the fad for 'white goods' [vodka and gin] is at the top of its curve." Unfortunately for bourbon distillers, his suspicions were unfounded. By 1980 vodka was firmly entrenched as one Americans' favorite liquors, and Smirnoff was the best-selling spirit in the world.

Smirnoff sales suffered in the 1980s from vodkas that presented themselves as prestigious, such as Absolut. Smirnoff's sales in the United States fell from 7.45 million cases in 1980 to 6.55 cases a decade later. Although Heublein tried to play upon Smirnoff's long history and status as the drink of Russian royalty,

a significant portion of its customers defected to more expensive, flashy vodkas.

Advertising Changes

In the 1990s Heublein attempted to change Smirnoff's image from a party drink to a "cozy staple of family life," according to the *Wall Street Journal.* Hoping to take advantage of Americans' renewed focus on traditional values and family, Heublein chose "Home Is Where You Find It" as their new slogan for Smirnoff. Heublein spent $9.6 million on advertising for Smirnoff in 1990 and planned to double its budget for the new advertising campaign.

Interpublic Group's McCann-Erickson agency designed the campaign, producing print ads and a commercial that aired on MGM Grand Air flights. The commercial, which is prohibited by federal regulations from being aired on television, includes shots of farms, firemen, and clapboard houses, but no drinking. The print ads likewise show homey scenes—a Thanksgiving dinner, a home wedding with the bride wearing her mother's dress, and a couple eating take-out Chinese food. Martin Pazzani, a Heublein vice-president of marketing, told the *Wall Street Journal* that the ads intentionally try "to get away from some of the things that made brands kick in the eighties—glitz and flash and things that were superficial and showy."

Heublein made its fortune off Smirnoff vodka and used that fortune to expand the company's product line. A diversified company with substantial revenues from other products, Heublein still depends on Smirnoff for a major portion of its income. The company's "Home Is Where You Find It" campaign was designed to raise Smirnoff sales to their previous heights. Although the company was concerned about Smirnoff's loss of market share in the 1980s, Smirnoff remained the best-selling brand of vodka in the United States and the leading vodka in the world market in the early 1990s.

Further Reading:

Gershman, Michael, *Getting It Right the Second Time,* Reading, MA: Addison-Wesley Publishing Co., 1990, pp. 37-42.

"Heublein Pours a Potent Sales Mix," *Business Week,* June 14, 1969, pp. 76-79.

"Heublein Promotes 'Home and Hearth'," *Wall Street Journal,* October 11, 1991, p. B8.

"Little Water," *New Yorker,* September 24, 1955, p. 36.

Martin, John G., "Riding High on a 'Moscow Mule,' " *Nation's Business,* January 1971, pp. 66-67.

"The New Talents Test Their Mettle," *Business Week,* January 3, 1970, pp. 33-34.

"That Yankee Vodka," *Newsweek,* June 27, 1955, p. 68.

"Vodka Gets High at Bourbon's Expense," *Business Week,* January 13, 1975, p. 34.

" 'Without Excitement, a Management Dies'," *Forbes,* November 1, 1968, pp. 51-52.

—*Susan Windisch Brown*

SMUCKER'S®

Since its birth nearly a century ago—as a "secret recipe apple butter peddled from the back of a farm wagon"—Smucker's has become today's largest-selling brand of jams, jellies, and preserves. As of 1992, Smucker's had gobbled up 38 percent of the $650 million U.S. domestic market, positioning itself at a comfortable distance from its strongest competitors, Welch's and Kraft, which control a mere 12 percent and 4 percent, respectively. (Store brands claim about 19 percent of the market.) While some portion of The J. M. Smucker Company's generous market share derives from sales of company-owned non-Smucker's brand products, analysts ascribe the lion's share to sales of the Smucker's brand itself. Those familiar with the company and the industry attribute the brand's unchallenged success to the Orrville, Ohio-based jelly-maker's unflagging commitment to quality. A 1980 *New York Times* report summed up the Smucker's marketing philosophy like this: "[It's] . . . as simple as it has been successful: Stay committed to the jam and jelly market and make the Smucker's name synonymous with quality. And don't worry if it is the most expensive jam and jelly on the grocery store shelf."

Smucker's has relied for nearly 30 years on a single advertising agency—Wyse Advertising Inc. of Cleveland, Ohio—to drive its quality message home. Wyse, the first and only agency to represent Smucker's, is responsible for the trademark slogan that helped propel the Smucker's label to national fame in the early 1960s: "With a name like Smucker's, it has to be good." Smucker's trademark gingham cap, strawberry logo, and crock-shaped jar are symbolic of the brand's humble, wholesome, down-home image. Strict adherence to quality standards has enabled Smucker's to continue chipping away at market share each year, despite having to compete in a mature market plagued by an annual growth rate of less than 2 percent.

Brand Origins

The Smucker's brand was founded in 1897 by Jerome M. Smucker. Smucker operated a steam powered cider mill for farmers in his rural hometown of Orrville, Ohio, about 45 miles south of Cleveland. However, it was his off-season business—making apple butter from a secret recipe handed down through generations of Smuckers—that eventually led Smucker and his descendants into the jam, jelly, and preserves business. A devout Mennonite, Smucker believed in delivering honest value to his customers in exchange for their loyal patronage. So firm was his

conviction that he personally hand-signed the paper lid of each individual crock of apple butter he sold, after guaranteeing in writing that the product was "manufactured and personally guaranteed by J. M. Smucker." Nearly a century later, third- and fourth-generation Smuckers no longer hand-sign Smucker's labels. However, as the controlling powers behind the now publicly held company, they are no less zealous than Jerome Smucker himself when it comes to preserving the Smucker image of honesty and value.

Jerome Smucker's foray into the apple butter business proved so prosperous that he began experimenting with other fruit-based products. By the early 1920s, The J. M. Smucker Co. was marketing a complete line of preserves and jellies. Recognizing the need to expand his operations beyond the small-town boundaries of Orrville, Smucker acquired his first fruit processing operations in Washington in 1935. The Smucker's brand enjoyed a strong local following before going national in 1942, when the first Smucker's-brand jams and jellies were shipped from Orrville to Los Angeles, California. The company continued to grow, both through expansion of its own facilities and acquisitions. Widespread national distribution was achieved in the early to mid-1960s, according to the company's 1967 *Annual Report*. Today, the Smucker's label appears not only on jams, jellies and preserves, but also on fruit spreads and ice cream toppings, juice beverages, peanut butter, fruit syrups, and whipped fruit dessert products.

In addition, The J. M. Smucker Co. markets similar products under a variety of acquired labels, including Mary Ellen, R. W. Knudsen Family, Goober, Elsenham, Dickinson's, Lost Acres, Good Morning (Canada), and IXL (Australia). The largest percentage of Smucker's products are sold to consumers, although products also are distributed to the food service, industrial, and specialty food markets. The company operates facilities in Ohio, California, Tennessee, Wisconsin, Pennsylvania, Oregon, Washington, England, and Australia.

Product Evolution

Jerome Smucker's apple butter recipe has changed little since 1897. And Smucker's patented essence recovery process, in use since 1953, continues to set the brand apart from its competitors. Paul Smucker, grandson of the firm's founder and current CEO, described the brand's formula for success to a *New York Times* reporter in 1980: "We buy the best fruits and berries we can

AT A GLANCE

The Smucker's brand of jams, jellies, and preserves founded in 1897 by Jerome M. Smucker in Orrville, OH; The J. M. Smucker Company went public in 1959, but family members, who continue to run the company, control about 30 percent of its stock.

Performance: *Market share*—Approximately 38% (top share) of the domestic jam, jelly, and preserves market. *Sales*—$483 million.

Major competitor: Welch's; also Kraft jams and jellies.

Advertising: *Agency*—Wyse Advertising Inc., Cleveland, OH, 1959—. *Major campaign*—"With a name like Smucker's it has to be good."

Addresses: *Parent company*—The J. M. Smucker Company, Strawberry Lane, Orrville, OH 44667; phone: (216) 682-3000; fax: (216) 684-3370.

obtain, cook under pressure at the lowest temperature possible, recover the essence and add it back to the preserves before the cap goes on." He added: "There is no way you can do it as well at home." For nearly 60 years, consumers were content with Smucker's jams and jellies, happy to pay a little more for guaranteed quality. However, by the early 1970s, the pressure was on to respond to changing consumer demands. Beginning in 1971, Smucker's introduced a lower-priced jelly line—Smucker's for Kids—to compete directly with a similar product already being marketed by Kraft. By 1978, consumers were more interested in lower sugar intake than lower prices. Smucker's responded with its Low Sugar Spreads—sweetened with sugar, but containing only half the calories of regular jams and jellies. The product, according to The J. M. Smucker Co.'s 1977 *Annual Report,* was directed to the traditional light or non-user of fruit spreads who was concerned about sugar intake.

Consumer trends also spurred the 1973 introduction of Smucker's first two-pound jar of grape jelly, followed in 1974 by a two-pound jar of strawberry jam. Though the products themselves were no different than the traditional Smucker's jellies and jams, packaging and marketing were aimed at the growing number of young families. By 1976, the jelly-maker had introduced a three-pound jar of its best-selling grape jelly and was now concentrating much of its marketing efforts on the new large sizes, according to the 1977 *Annual Report.* Emphasizing "good value for the dollar," Smucker's backed the products with advertising that promised, "Thirty-six sandwiches from now, you'll like the price of Smucker's."

While Smucker's product introductions have most often been consumer-driven, it took a little company in New Jersey to push the giant jelly-maker into at least one new market segment. Sorrell Ridge took the New York market by storm in 1987 with a line of no-sugar, all-natural fruit spreads in 20 flavors. The product was packaged in tall, slender jars to contrast with Smucker's short, crock-like packaging. Smucker's had yet to offer consumers anything like the Sorrell Ridge product, which was sweetened with white grape juice instead of sugar. Smucker's was "embarrassed and stung," according to a 1989 *Forbes* magazine report. According to *Forbes,* the all-fruit jams and jellies niche was "the fastest-growing segment of the market, and Sorrell Ridge got there first. Adding insult to injury, Sorrell Ridge took direct aim at Smucker's

with an advertising campaign that lampooned Smucker's own famous "With a name like Smucker's, it has to be good" slogan. Sorrell Ridge challenged Smucker's with TV ads that said, "With a name like Smucker's, is it really so good? Sorrell Ridge—with 100 percent fruit, it has to be better."

Sorrell Ridge officials said at the time that Smucker's tried to squelch the TV ads and buy the New Jersey company. Smucker's never confirmed those reports, and as late as November 1992, told the *Cleveland Plain Dealer*: "Our position then and now is not to comment on that." Revenge was sweet, nevertheless. In 1988, Smucker's retaliated with its own Simply Fruit line. And when Sorrell Ridge launched its product in the Los Angeles market, Smucker's ran a coupon campaign offering buyers of the Sorrell Ridge product a free jar of Smucker's Simply Fruit. Margins on Simply Fruit are narrower because of the higher cost of sweetening fruit with white grape juice, compared with sugar. However, the product was necessary if Smucker's wanted to address the all-fruit niche. According to a 1992 report by Cleary, Gull, Reiland & McDevitt Inc., a Milwaukee investment banking firm, Simply Fruit has "experienced widespread acceptance and has helped nudge Smucker's nearer its goal of increasing market share to 50 percent." In its 1992 *Annual Report,* Smucker's acknowledged that "new branded and private label entrants into the all-fruit segment, combined with deep, ongoing promotions by all competitors, made for a difficult year for our Simply Fruit line. Nonetheless, we have retained our position as the share-of-the market leader in this maturing segment, while improving the line's overall profitability."

In 1990, Smucker's expanded on the no-sugar theme by introducing Smucker's Light—similar to its Simply Fruit line, but sweetened with a combination of white grape juice concentrate and NutraSweet-brand sweetener. In 1992, the company debuted Extra Fruit, a home style fruit spread made with more fruit than regular preserves. The company said it anticipated expanding distribution of the new product in 1993. Several product introductions never made it past the test-market stage. Those include Fresh Frozen Preserves, a frozen, spreadable fruit product requiring refrigeration, introduced in 1985; and a line of squeezable containers, tested in 1987 and subsequently abandoned.

Advertising

Few companies have remained as loyal to an advertising firm as Smucker's has to Wyse Advertising. According to a 1982 *Crain's Cleveland Business* report, Mark Wyse first approached Smucker's in 1959 about doing some work for the jelly-maker. Though initially turned down, Mr. Wyse was invited to stop by the Orrville facility next time he was in town, which just happened to be a week later. Mr. Wyse was invited back to make a presentation. The agency's pitch led to a request for help with an advertising campaign that would boost sales enough to keep the just-opened Salinas, California, plant running a full five days a week. Wyse built Smucker's first radio campaign around the brand's honest, humble image—a strategy that would survive three decades.

In 1962 Wyse dreamed up the now-famous tag line that accompanies all Smucker's advertising—one of the longest-running slogans in advertising history. The story behind the slogan is that Smucker's needed a strong campaign for its entry into New York City—a market that contrasted sharply with Smucker's down-home image. When Lois Wyse, the agency's cofounder, explained to Paul Smucker that his last name evoked a negative meaning in Yiddish, Smucker asked her to try to come up with something positive. When he first heard the new slogan, "With a name like Smucker's, it has to be good," Smucker reportedly fretted over how family members, who made up the company's board of directors, would react. It was his Aunt Winna who is said to have asked if the slogan would help increase dividends in the future. When told that it would, she said, "Then I'm all for it."

Poking fun at the Smucker's name led to a later series of ads that used the unusual names of employees to sell Smucker's products. First, there was Clarence Marlin Icenogle. According to advertisements, he was the fellow who decided which fruits were good enough for Smucker's preserves and jellies. The tag line read: "No, Icenogle. Only Mr. Smucker's name goes on the jar." A similar ad heard on a Los Angeles radio station in 1968 told listeners that Mrs. Louella Just, switchboard operator for The J. M. Smucker Co., could name all 43 flavors of Smucker's jellies and preserves. According to a 1968 *Advertising Age* piece, a Los Angeles disc jockey decided to test the veracity of the ad—right there on the air. He dialed the Smucker's switchboard and asked Mrs. Just to name all 43 flavors. She rattled them right off— unaware that she was being broadcast live to thousands of the station's listeners. That episode served to underscore Smucker's commitment to honesty. In 1975, William P. Boyle, Jr., then marketing vice president, reconfirmed that commitment when he told the *Wall Street Journal* that Paul Smucker "takes great interest in the tenor of our advertising." Mr. Boyle added, "Paul's only requirement is that we must be absolutely truthful. We've never even stretched a point."

From the outset, Smucker's advertising strategy has played heavily on the brand's humble, Midwest farm-country roots. Ad campaigns have consistently linked the Smucker name to good, old-fashioned values such as honesty, wholesomeness, and above all, quality. Early ads went so far as to feature pastoral scenes from Orrville, intended to showcase Smucker's "pure and simple heritage." As Paul Smucker told the *New York Times,* "I'd rather buy my preserves made in Orrville than some large city. Seems like it would taste better to me." In 1963, Smucker's cosponsored the Garry Moore show with its first national advertising program, which ran on 210 CBS Radio Network stations. Then in 1965, Smucker's teamed up with Hugh Downs and Johnny Carson to run live 60-second spots on NBC's *Today* and *Tonight* shows. Advertisements in the 1980s included themes such as "Smucker's takes the best in American life and preserves it," and "If you could taste tradition." The company said that during fiscal 1993 it would stress the potential variety of uses for Smucker's fruit spreads to remind those consumers who no longer breakfast at home that there are other ways to enjoy Smucker's preserves. The ads will also reinforce the message that fruit spreads are lower in calories than most people think.

Marketing

Smucker's marketing efforts are structured around five strategic business areas: consumer, food service, industrial, specialty foods, and international. A review of 30 years' worth of The J. M. Smucker Co. Annual Reports reveals two predominant recurring themes at the consumer level: commitment to product quality and an ever-increasing emphasis on marketing and advertising support. The Smucker's brand has always been marketed as the cream-of-the-crop in its category. Strong brand identification and consumer loyalty have been carefully cultivated by aligning the

Smucker name with a tradition of consistent product quality. "This company has maintained a quality image over all its years," said Marty McDevitt, an analyst with Cleary, Gull, Reiland & McDevitt. While the brand is priced a little higher than its competitors, McDevitt said, "people are always willing to pay for quality, and Smucker's delivers consistent quality."

Continuity in management—third- and fourth-generation Smuckers have a tight rein on all marketing, public relations and advertising efforts—has minimized shifts in marketing strategies. However, on several occasions, the jelly-maker has significantly expanded its marketing program. Prior to the early 1970s, Smucker's jams, jellies, and preserves were marketed primarily to older, upper-income households. The products were packaged in small, adult-size jars. However, Smucker's broadened its marketing approach—and its consumer base—with the introduction of the larger, family-size products aimed at the growing number of families with children. According to the 1975 *Annual Report,* that year Smucker's launched its strongest multi-media campaign, designed specifically to appeal to younger families with small children, prime users of the two-pound jars of grape jelly and strawberry jam. Smucker's expanded its marketing program again in 1977, moving beyond traditional grocery store channels by introducing the brand to major retail chains offering general merchandise as well as food.

Smucker's made a strategic marketing move by winning the jelly and preserve contract for Florida's Walt Disney World. The contract put Smucker's products in all Walt Disney World restaurants. Smucker's gift-boxed products are also the only ones of their kind sold in Disney World's Market House.

International

While The J. M. Smucker Co. remains committed to increasing its share of the domestic market, much of its future growth is expected to be achieved through increased participation in the global market. In 1983, the company said it planned "to move slowly in the international market," but made it clear by filing for foreign registration of some of its trademarks that it planned to increase its presence overseas. Throughout the 1980s, Smucker's placed increasing emphasis on foreign markets, according to company reports. In 1988, The J. M. Smucker Co. acquired the "Good Morning" label in Canada. That acquisition was followed by the purchase of Elsenham Quality Foods Ltd. in England and Henry Jones Foods, makers of IXL-brand preserves, in Australia. In 1989, Smucker's created its first international business area and by 1991, told shareholders that senior management was committed to making foreign business the fastest-growing segment of the 1990s. As of fiscal 1992, international sales accounted for less than 10 percent of total sales and the segment was still operating at a loss. However, the company said it remained "confident that the area will become profitable in the near term," and cited significant sales gains in the Canadian market.

Further Reading:

Clark, Sandra, "Living Up to Its Name: Smuckers Delivers on Its Promise, *Cleveland Plain Dealer,* November 1, 1992, p. 1E.

Groseclose, Everett, "The Scions: Paul H. Smucker Takes Great Pains to Preserve His Products' Quality, *Wall Street Journal,* February 3, 1975, p. 1.

Levine, Joshua, "Sorrell Ridge Makes Smucker Pucker," *Forbes,* June 12, 1989, p. 166.

McDevitt, M. A. Jr., *The J. M. Smucker Company—Company Report,* Milwaukee: Cleary, Gull, Reiland & McDevitt Inc., March 2, 1992.

Miller, Jay, "Wyse, Smucker's Stuck on Each Other, *Crain's Cleveland Business,* June 21, 1982, p. T-1.

The J. M. Smucker Company: An Introduction, Orrville, Ohio: The J. M. Smucker Co.

The J. M. Smucker Company's Annual Reports, Orrville, Ohio: The J. M. Smucker Co., 1960-92.

"The Savvy Saleslady of Strawberry Lane," *Sales and Management,* September 1, 1971.

"Smucker's Ads Prove They're Solid: Skeptical Angelenos Put 'em to Test," *Advertising Age,* April 22, 1968, p. 50.

"Smucker's Jellies Gets Campaign on NBC: Warner-Lambert Sponsors News on Radio," *Advertising Age,* October 2, 1967, p. 2.

"Smucker's Recipe Paying Off," *New York Times,* Sept. 13, 1980, p. L27.

—Katherine J. Paul

SNICKERS®

A hit since it was first widely marketed in the 1930s, Snickers brand of candy bar is a favorite of people of all ages—so much a favorite that it has been the number one selling candy bar in the United States since the early 1970s. Considering how crowded the candy market is with products, and that chocolate bars account for 70 percent of the candy market, it is remarkable that Snickers has held the coveted top spot for decades. Produced by the M&M/Mars division of Mars, Inc., the positioning of the product is partly due to the manufacturer's commitment to using high quality ingredients and guaranteeing that the product will always meet consumers' standards. Buyers know that when they open the familiar brown wrapper with the Snickers logo emblazoned in bold blue letters on a white background bordered in red, they will enjoy the same taste they enjoyed the last time they ate one of the bars. M&M/Mars also continuously keeps the Snickers bar in consumers' minds through advertising and promotional campaigns.

The Perfect Candy Bar

For the founder of the Mars Company, Franklin "Frank" C. Mars, the journey from being a candy salesman to being a candy giant was not always sweet. After marrying his second wife, Ethel V. Healy, he decided to move to Seattle and go into the candy business. His previous experience as a candy salesman did not guarantee him success; the business failed. The couple, however, remained undaunted. They moved to Tacoma, Washington, in 1911, and started making big batches of butter cream candies in the kitchen of their home. The candies were so popular they opened a candy factory. But again, success proved elusive. This time the Oriole Candies Company proved to be too much competition, and, according to Ray Broecket in *The Chocolate Chronicles,* Mars filed for bankruptcy. Broecket further states that Frank Mars was thirty-seven when he moved his family and candy-making operation back to Minneapolis, Minnesota, in 1920. The family lived over a one-room factory where Frank began trying to create the ultimate candy bar that might have national appeal. Ethel sold Frank's candy to retail stores.

Mars named his next candy company the Mar-O-Bar Company after his first candy bar. The Mar-O-Bar itself was not a success in the marketplace, but Mars struck gold with his second try— Snickers. The bar, brought out in 1921 without a chocolate coating, became popular as a cool treat in hot weather. Consumers just needed to chill them in ice units to have a refreshing snack. In 1923, the company introduced the Milky Way candy bar, which also quickly became a national success. To meet the demand for increased production, Mars built a new plant in Chicago, Illinois, where operations began in 1929 and continue today. Frank Mars continued to develop other quality candy products, including the chocolate-coated (enrobed) version of Snickers bar that exists today.

Frank Mars only enjoyed a few years of his long-sought-after success in the candy bar business before he died in 1934. His wife, Ethel, was company president until her death in 1945.

Fluffy Nougat

Most of the candy bar formulas Frank Mars created used the fluffy nougat center that was to become a Mars hallmark. Nougat is an important ingredient in such "filled" brands as Snickers, Milky Way, and other M&M/Mars candy bars. It is made by whipping egg whites until they are light and frothy, then adding sugar syrup to stabilize the foam and create a "frappe." A number of other flavoring ingredients are added to the frappe; each ingredient creates a nougat with a different taste. It was at the Chicago plant that Mars developed the new version of the Snickers, with its peanut butter nougat, caramel and peanut topping, and milk chocolate coating. The Snickers bar appealed to all ages.

M&M/Mars

After graduating from Yale University, Forrest Mars, Sr., who was Frank Mars' son from his first marriage to Ethel G. Kissack, tried to join his father in the candy business. There is a frequently published legend that father and son disagreed on how to run the business, and that therefore in 1932, Frank gave the thirty-year-old Forrest fifty thousand dollars, the foreign rights to Milky Way and other Mars bars, and told him to go overseas and sell Mars candy. Spokespersons for Mars, however, have repeatedly rejected this legend.

Forrest launched European operations with the establishment of Mars Confections in Slough, in the United Kingdom. He started his business by reformulating the American bars to suit British tastes; he created the Mars Bar, a sweeter version of the Milky Way. He soon was a leading confectioner. He also diversified his business by establishing the first canned pet foods business in

AT A GLANCE

Snickers brand candy bar founded in 1921 by Franklin "Frank" C. Mars, president of the Mar-O-Bar Company; company changed name to Mars Candies in 1926, and later to Mars, Inc.; Snickers first coated in chocolate in 1930 when Mars opened candy manufacturing plant in Chicago, IL.

Performance: *Market share*—9.5% (top share) of chocolate candy products; 53.5% of top 10 selling chocolate candy products. *Sales*—$600 million.

Advertising: *Agency*—Backer Spielvogel Bates, New York, NY. *Major campaign*—"Packed with Peanuts, Snickers Really Satisfies" slogan; also, campaigns that show active people at work and play eating Snickers bars to satisfy their appetites until mealtime.

Addresses: *Parent company*—M&M/Mars, High St., Hackettstown, NJ 07840; phone: (908) 852-1000. *Ultimate parent company*—Mars, Inc., 6885 Elm St., McLean, VA 22101; phone: (703) 821-4900.

England and, subsequently, many other food companies around the world.

Forrest Mars brought his business expertise to the United States in 1940, where he founded M&M Limited in Newark, New Jersey, to manufacture what are now known as M&M's Plain Chocolate Candies. He and Bruce Murrie, the son of the president of Hershey's and a business associate of Forrest Mars in this enterprise, created the M&M's name for their company by combining the initials of their last names. M&M's merged with Mars, Inc. in 1964. The various U.S. confectionery businesses of Mars, which includes the manufacture of the Snickers bar, were consolidated in 1967 to form the M&M/Mars division of Mars, Inc. in Hackettstown, New Jersey. Forrest Mars was at the helm of Mars until 1973. His children, Forrest, Jr., John, and Jacqueline, now run the company.

The mission statement of M&M/Mars is: "Quality is our cornerstone; value for money our goal." Quality has always been an integral part of M&M/Mars products and is a primary characteristic of the company's practice of "branding." Branding enables M&M/Mars customers to easily recognize products when they want to make repeat purchases. Each brand marketed by M&M/Mars carries a registered brand name that communicates its unique character to consumers. Variations of the brand are allowed to carry the brand name only if they can deliver the brand's specific benefit or quality to the customer. M&M/Mars did not extend the Snickers brand name to any other products until 1990.

Market Leverage

Americans love nuts and chocolate, and that is the major reason why millions of Americans of all ages snack on Snickers bars. M&M/Mars ensures that Snickers will stay a perennial snack favorite by providing its consumers with consistent quality and by offering the product in a variety of bar and package sizes. The company made Snickers bars in king size and full size and sold them individually and in packages of six or ten. It also reduced the bars so consumers could buy Snickers in bags of snack size, fun size, and bite-size miniatures ("One Bite, Just Right").

The candy business—especially the candy bar category—is a tough market in which to hold share. Because the chocolate candy products market is so competitive, large chocolate bar manufacturers sometimes save themselves the costs of research and development of new products and instead come out with new products under an established brand name. M&M/Mars leveraged its brand equity in the Snickers name in 1990 through the introduction of two line extension products. The Peanut Butter Snickers bar contains a caramel and peanut layer with peanut butter cream and peanuts. It is packaged in an orange wrapper with the words peanut butter in a red banner above the familiar Snickers blue and white logo. The Peanut Butter Snickers Bar was M&M/Mars' first variation of Snickers.

Dove International, which became a sister company of M&M/Mars in 1986, also introduced a variation of Snickers in 1990, the Snickers ice cream bar. Leo Stefanos, a Greek immigrant, started the Dove company in 1939 when he first introduced Dove candies in the south side of Chicago. Dove created the frozen snack category by producing uniquely designed brands that are linked directly to the original Dovebar, an ice cream bar first made in 1956. It was only natural that when Mars, Inc. bought Dove International, the companies would combine their expertise in candy bars and ice cream to create new frozen snacks. When Dove International introduced the Snickers Ice Cream Bar, it quickly became a top ten seller in the crowded frozen novelties market. The ice cream snack reached the number one slot, toppling—without advertising—Sugar Free Eskimo Pie and Original Klondike. The Snickers Ice Cream Bar is a blend of premium peanut butter ice cream, roasted peanuts, caramel, and milk chocolate.

Packed with Peanuts

Although a brand name as recognized as Snickers can sustain itself for years, Mars protects its products through tremendous advertising campaigns and by being a powerful marketing force. M&M/Mars has been among the top U.S. advertisers for years, with Snickers receiving major support. Mars advertises the brand on television, in magazines and newspapers, on radio, and in a variety of special media, including the sponsorship of events such as the 1992 Olympics and the 1994 Soccer World Cup. The company also uses coupons, refunds, sweepstakes, and other special promotions to keep Snickers' buyers interested in the product.

The advertisements created for M&M/Mars focus on a short and memorable theme or proposition, which communicates the product's unique consumer benefit and why it is the best available alternative for getting that benefit. Snickers' advertising campaigns have focused on active people eating Snickers bars to appease their hunger until they can have a meal, using the slogan: "Packed with Peanuts, Snickers Really Satisfies." The wrapper of each Snickers bar also features this slogan with the Snickers logo in the middle of it.

The Competitive Candy Market

According to Avanstar Communications, publishers of *Candy Marketer* and *Candy Industry* trade publications, the Snickers bar enjoys a 53.5 percent of the market share of the top ten selling chocolate candy products. That translates into 9.5 percent of the market share of all chocolate brands. The *Confectioner* puts the Snickers bar in the $600 million of sales category on its list of

"The Confectionery Elite 1991." M&M's Chocolate Candies tops Snickers in the report, but only because the category included all varieties of M&Ms—plain, peanut butter, and peanut.

Mars and Hershey Foods Corp. have been locked in a chocolate war for years. In 1988, Hershey gained the edge when it bought Peter Paul/Cadbury. Mars instituted an aggressive advertising attack and introduced several new products to quickly regain the lead in the chocolate confection category. In 1992, Hershey began test marketing a new Peanuts and Caramel Reese's cup. In spite of some similarities to Snickers, it is doubtful that Hershey can wrest the market from Snickers, which has built brand recognition since its inception in 1930 and has been the best-seller in the overall candy segment since the early 1970s. However, the competition remains tough. According to Nielsen Marketing Research, in the 52-week period ending in November 1992, Reese's peanut butter cups took over Snickers' number one position in store candy sales, with 5.2 percent of the $6.0 billion dollar market, compared to Snickers' 5 percent. Snickers remained number one in overall candy sales because of its continuing strength in vending machine sales, which are not calculated into the Nielsen store candy sales category.

M&M/Mars carries on Forrest Mars, Sr.'s, determination to manufacture products of the highest quality ingredients in spotless plants. The Snickers name, associated with its long-standing popularity, will continue to propel the brand's success in the competitive chocolate candy market, as will M&M/Mars' advertising programs and product innovation and the strong consumer loyalty to that special combination of milk chocolate, peanut butter nougat, caramel, and peanuts.

Further Reading:

Brockel, Ray, *The Chocolate Chronicles,* Lombard, IL: Wallace-Homestead Book Company, 1985, pp. 22,31-34.

"Definitely Not the Same Old Chocolate Bar Scene," *Candy Marketer,* January/February 1992, pp. 44-50.

Fisher, Christy, "Reese's Tops Snickers to Rule as Candy King," *Advertising Age,* March 22, 1993, p. 42.

Fucini, Joseph J., and Suzy Fucini, *Entrepreneurs: The Men and Women behind Famous Brand Names and How They Made It,* Boston: G. K. Hall & Co., 1985, p. 219.

Hwang, Sueis L., "Peanuts and Caramel Combine to Create Sticky Competition," *Wall Street Journal,* April 14, 1992, sec. B, p. 11.

Katayama, Frederick H., "Snickers Ice Cream Bar," *Fortune,* August 13, 1990, p. 102.

Koselka, Rita, "Candy Wars," *Forbes,* August 17, 1992, pp. 76-77.

Meyers, Janet, "Mars Opens Umbrella for Candy Bar Pitch," *Advertising Age,* March 26, 1990, pp. 3, 52.

Morgan, Hal, *Symbols of America,* New York: Viking Penguin Inc., Steam Press, 1986, p. 144.

Moskowitz, Milton, Robert Levering, and Michael Katz, editors, *Everybody's Business: A Field Guide to the 400 Leading Companies in America,* New York: Doubleday, A Currency Book, 1990, pp. 54-56.

"100 Leading National Advertisers," *Advertising Age,* September 23, 1992, p. 44.

"100 Leading National Advertisers," *Advertising Age,* September 25, 1991, pp. 47-48.

Saporitz, Bill, "Uncovering Mars' Unknown Empire," *Fortune,* September 26, 1988, pp. 98-104.

Sharp, Harold S., *Advertising Slogans of America,* Metuchen, NJ: Scarecrow Press, Inc., 1984, p. 433.

—Doris Morris Maxfield

SOUTHERN COMFORT®

Southern Comfort brand liqueur is one of the best-selling premium brand cordial and liqueur spirits sold in North America. Since 1979, its foreign sales have experienced considerable growth as the distilled spirits industry has become increasingly global in scope. The liqueur's trademark label was introduced in 1945. Designed with black and white picture graphics that recall a time before the contemporary age of slick, computer-aided visuals, it depicts a bucolic, late-19th-century southern Mississippi River scene, complete with a paddle-wheel steamboat and horse-drawn carriage. From its rather humble, late-19th-century beginnings in the city of New Orleans, Southern Comfort's marketing themes have traditionally highlighted the brand's regional heritage as a down-home product of a bygone era of Southern culture, even while its popularity has spread worldwide. The label's boldface handwriting greets the consumer and declares that Southern Comfort is "The Grand Old Drink of the South." And, directly below the picture graphic, the consumer is informed that Southern Comfort is "Made on the Banks of the Mississippi in St. Louis, Missouri, U.S.A." Ever vigilant for expanding its share of the export market, most overseas marketing campaigns for Southern Comfort are foreign productions. Though the ads are designed to appeal to their native audience, they typically incorporate a healthy dose of "American imagery," a theme that plays up the brand's unique southern American cultural heritage.

Southern Comfort whiskey was acquired by the Louisville-based Brown-Forman Corporation in 1979. Brown-Forman has a longstanding reputation as a producer and marketer of fine quality alcoholic beverages dating back to 1870. Besides Southern Comfort, the corporation also produces a prominent line of wines and spirits that includes Jack Daniel's whiskey, Canadian Mist, Korbel champagnes, and Bolla wines. Based on market shares for the year 1991, Southern Comfort's major rivals in the cordials and liqueurs category are: DeKuyper at 14.08 percent; Kahlua at 10.15 percent; Hiram Walker at 8.89 percent; and Baileys Irish Cream at 5.12 percent.

Brand Origins

The Southern Comfort brand of whiskey-based liqueur was created by M. W. Heron, a bartender in the busy Mississippi River port of New Orleans in the 1880s. In 1889 Heron relocated to Memphis, Tennessee, another thriving Mississippi River port town, where he first began to bottle his drink for commercial purposes. Not long after, Heron moved further north along the Mississippi River to St. Louis, Missouri, where he eventually settled to become the proprietor of a bar. At that time Southern Comfort was referred to as the "St. Louis Cocktail" whose preparation was "made with Southern Comfort." Customers where limited to two drinks only since, as a sign in Heron's bar noted, "No gentlemen would ask for more."

The 20th-century development of Heron's early entrepreneurial creation gave rise to the emergence of the Southern Comfort Corporation. The corporation was sold to Brown-Forman on March 2, 1979, for $89.5 million. Among the factors motivating Brown-Forman's purchase of Southern Comfort was the liqueur's historically impressive return on capital and on common stockholders' equity, along with the brand's large and diverse consumer franchise and its extensive marketing and distribution facilities. Under Brown-Forman's ownership, Southern Comfort has enjoyed a continued legacy of prosperity. According to the corporation's 1992 annual report, Southern Comfort has perennially maintained or increased its market share of the total distilled spirits category and remained an important contributor to company profits.

In the late 1960s, Southern Comfort received some unsolicited notoriety and was brought to the attention of the baby boom generation when the popular blues-rock singer Janis Joplin performed live with a bottle of Southern Comfort. Taking its cue from shifting social mores that associate negative health consequences with the consumption of alcohol, the distilled spirits industry, since the early 1990s, has incorporated promotional advertising themes that signal a message of responsible drinking and moderation.

Brand Development

The North American wine and spirits industry, in which the whiskey-based Southern Comfort brand participates, competes in a highly regulated market in both the United States and Canada. To a considerable extent, these regulations define much of the economic latitude the companies encounter when producing and marketing their product. At the federal level in the United States, the Bureau of Alcohol, Tobacco, and Firearms of the United States Treasury Department serves as the regulatory agency. The Bureau sets standards concerned with the production, blending, bottling, sales, advertising, and transportation of the products under its

AT A GLANCE

Southern Comfort brand of whiskey-based liqueur founded in the 1880s by M. W. Heron in New Orleans, LA; commercially bottled and sold in Memphis, TN, 1889; business relocated to St. Louis, MO, and later emerged as the Southern Comfort Corporation; acquired by the Brown-Forman Corporation, 1979.

Performance: *Market share*—7% (4th-largest share) of the U.S. cordials and liqueur category; ranks 26th in the overall U.S. distilled spirits category.

Major competitor: DeKuyper; also other liqueur brands, including Kahlua.

Advertising: *Agency*—Altschiller-Reitzfeld, New York, NY, 1992—. *Major campaign*—"Take it easy."

Addresses: *Parent company*—Brown-Forman Corporation, P.O. Box 1080, Louisville, KY 40201-1080; phone: (502) 585-1100.

jurisdiction. Federal regulations require that all whiskey designated as "straight whiskey" should be aged for at least two years prior to its being sold for U.S. domestic consumption. In order to ensure its premium standards, company policy at Brown-Forman goes one step further and ages its whiskeys for a minimum of three to five years.

State regulations duplicate many of the regulatory aspects mandated at the federal level. Besides these, they grant liquor licenses and also determine the distilled spirits' alcoholic content level. This explains why it is not unusual to find that the alcoholic content of Southern Comfort, and other distilled brands, may vary in different states. In certain states, the agencies are the sole legal distributors of all distilled spirits and have enacted statutes that restrict the ability of companies like Brown-Forman to terminate their contracts.

Whiskey production is planned to connect with demand three to five years in the future. For this reason the level of inventories to total sales and total assets is above what is considered normal in most non-whiskey related business. The main ingredients used in the production and packaging of distilled spirits are corn, rye, malted barley, glass, cartons, along with sugar for the production of liqueur and cordials.

In March of 1993 Southern Comfort introduced three new flavors of "Comfort Cocktails " in 25 markets across the United States. These drinks are intended to compete in the rapidly emergent single serve, premixed, low-proof spirits-based category. Called Laidback Lemonade, Dixie Jazzberry, and Big Easy Punch, these low-proof cocktails are designed to appeal to "today's lifestyles"—having fun but with an eye toward moderation. The cocktails are marketed in single-serve, 200-milliliter bottles that are miniature replicas of the 750-milliliter Southern Comfort bottle and are sold as singles or four-packs. Company officials at Brown-Forman anticipate that Comfort Cocktails will have a "synergistic effect" on Southern Comfort and serve to enhance the brand's name recognition and consumer loyalty.

Marketing Structures and Strategy

Brown-Forman's policy for marketing Southern Comfort extends to programs that are intended to boost the brand's interna-

tional, and national, exposure. To implement this goal, Brown-Forman undertook a significant internal reorganization in 1992. It decentralized the core group of its wine and spirits segment into three groups: the Wine Brands Group, which markets all Brown-Forman wines and brandy; the Select Brands group, which markets spirits sold in regional and niche markets; and the Spirits group, which includes Southern Comfort and their other major spirits brands.

In 1992 consumer research conducted by Brown-Forman indicated that Southern Comfort's exposure among consumers had increased over previous years. The programs employed included trial usage, 30-day usage, unaided awareness, and purchase intent campaigns. Efforts targeting sports-oriented consumers and consumer participation merchandising programs that emphasized on-premise trade also served to extend brand recognition.

To support the 1993 introduction of Comfort Cocktails, Brown-Forman launched a major promotional campaign complete with radio and outdoor advertising based on contemporary themes and imagery in line with the industry's emphasis on moderate drinking. At establishments where the Comfort Cocktails are sold, the brand's promotion was to make use of cold box signs, bottle case cards, soft sheet banners, price cards, bull's eyes, and specially designed shelf strips that highlight the cocktail's presence so as to stimulate single and four-pack sales.

Southern Comfort's U.S. marketing structure encompasses sales managers and agents or brokers who represent the brand throughout the country. Contracts for domestic distribution are undertaken with state agencies or wholesale outlets. The location and types of retail sale establishments are determined according to laws specific to each state. Should Brown-Forman decide to terminate a contract, the distributors are reimbursed according to legally enforced formulas calculated on the basis of the distributor's length of service and the percentage of purchases over time.

Southern Comfort sales in foreign markets are conducted through contracts with brokers and distributors. Retail sales, however, face numerous outlet restrictions and are typically confined to Duty Free shops, a small number of stores that deal in foreign currency, and large tourist hotels, reported Nancy Madlin in *Adweek*. In 1992 Brown-Forman was "actively involved" in negotiations with a host of government agencies in order to broaden market access and eliminate what they consider barriers to free trade.

Recent Advertising Strategies

Since 1986, as cited in *Jobson's Liquor Handbook,* overall U.S. sales of cordials and liqueurs have steadily declined. Southern Comfort has not been immune from this trend. In fact, the brand's annual level of U.S. sales has been in decline since 1979, noted R. D. Burry in a *Kidder, Peabody & Company* report on the Brown-Forman Corporation. In an attempt to jump-start sales, Brown-Forman initiated several large scale advertising campaigns that targeted increased expenditures for consumer awareness along with promotional sales programs based on the theme that "Everything Is More Delicious with a Touch of Southern Comfort." Another innovative program was meant to refocus emphasis on merchandising to on-premise trade, such as the "Finger Flick Football" bar promotional strategy.

In 1992, in a rather highly publicized affair, Brown-Forman parted company with its old advertising agency of Ally & Gargano in New York City, which had previously handled the corporation's account with billings estimated at $10 million per year. Five finalists were chosen and the agency of Altschiller-Reitzfeld was awarded the account. The selection of Altschiller-Reitzfeld, noted as an industry leader in print work, according to *Adweek,* was consistent with Brown-Forman's traditional focus on magazine and outdoor print media. No doubt the successful relationship Altschiller-Reitzfeld had with other beverage accounts, like Campari, also worked to the ad agency's favor.

But the fallout with Ally & Gargano and the selection of Altschiller-Reitzfeld signaled Brown-Forman's dissatisfaction with these promotional efforts and their results. The arrival of Altschiller-Reitzfeld marked a departure from the business as usual approach of past marketing themes. Instead a sense of coming to grips with the general public's growing impatience with excessive drinking was clearly recognizable in Brown-Forman's 1993 "Take it Easy" advertisements for Southern Comfort. Similar promotional campaigns, which convey a message of moderation and responsible drinking, are scheduled for the brand's premixed Comfort Cocktails line.

Discussing Brown-Forman's commitment to moderate drinking messages in the *New York Times,* John V. O. Kennard, senior vice president and executive director of the corporation's spirits marketing segment, commented that "it's clear to anyone who ever had Southern Comfort that because it's sweet and palatable, you can drink too much of it and have a hangover." To which he added, "That doesn't help our business at all, because all that's left is a bad memory." Perhaps even more salient was the fact that Brown-Forman targeted their moderation message at drinkers in their mid- to late-20s, among whom Southern Comfort is a popular favorite.

International Growth

In contrast to the declining fortunes Southern Comfort has experienced in the United States, its overseas growth has encountered remarkable success. According to a report on Brown-Forman by *Kidder, Peabody & Company* for the period of 1979 to 1984, Southern Comfort's international sales grew at an annual rate of 25 percent, and for the period between 1984 and 1989, the rate was 24.8 percent. Forces generating this trend were attributed to: export profit margins that outperformed their U.S. counterparts, the globalization of "American Culture" via print, cinema, and television, and the phenomenon of "brand image," which allowed Southern Comfort to charge prices overseas that are two to three times what they charge in U.S. markets.

Sales of Southern Comfort have achieved record performance levels in the English speaking countries of Australia and the United Kingdom. In the 1980s Southern Comfort also has enjoyed considerable growth in Germany, New Zealand, and Ireland.

Future Trends

Like the high-proof distilled spirits industry in general, the continued slowdown in U.S. sales of Southern Comfort has been affected by several factors. Throughout the 1980s a shift in social norms occurred that de-emphasized the consumption of alcoholic

beverages at business and social events. For the period of 1981 to 1991, this trend has resulted in an overall decline in distilled spirits consumption of about three percent a year, according to a 1992 beverage industry report issued by *Merrill Lynch Capital Markets.* A consumer preference shift to lower-proof premixed alcoholic beverages that are marketed with a message of "drink to be cool but stay in control" theme, have steadily eroded the consumption of high-proof distilled spirits. In the early 1990s the unyielding persistence of recessionary forces, both in the United States and abroad, has slowed the upward movement of Southern Comfort export sales and further dampened its U.S. sales.

In the early 1990s a number of long-term factors were at work that may have a favorable impact on Southern Comfort's future. Rising export prices for distilled spirits showed no indication of turning downward. An aging baby-boomer population with "eclectic tastes" showed some signs of turning away from the consumption of lighter alcohol products (such as light beer, white wines, and wine coolers), while a renewed interest in alcoholic beverages with a "distinctive" taste quality (i.e., higher-proof) may be gathering momentum. In the United States, a growing challenge by consumer, industry, and agricultural constituencies to repeal the "sin taxes" levied by the George Bush administration in January of 1991 is underway, which may limit the use of this tax as a measure to balance the budget in the future. And recent medical reports that point to the alleged value of alcoholic beverages in the prevention of heart disease may cause the media to approach the subject of alcoholic consumption in a more even-handed manner than in times past.

Over the last 100 years, Southern Comfort has pushed beyond the narrow boundaries of its early Mississippi River market as the "Grand Old Drink of the South," going from crossing rivers to oceans. And, while more turbulent days may still lie ahead, the long tradition of this river-town product would seem to ensure its continued appeal to consumers.

Further Reading:

"Accounts in Review/2," *Adweek,* July 27, 1992, p. 9.

Brown-Forman Annual Reports, Louisville, KY: Brown-Forman Corporation, 1979-92.

Burry, R. D., "Brown-Forman Corporation-Company Report," *Kidder, Peabody & Company,* August 11, 1992.

"Cordials and Liqueurs," *Jobson's Liquor Handbook 1992,* 1992, pp. 127-133.

Elliott, Stuart, "Southern Comfort Adopts Moderation as Its Byword," *New York Times,* January 12, 1993, p. D21.

"Family Fortunes," *Forbes,* October 21, 1991, p. 276.

"Finalists Chosen by Brown-Forman," *New York Times,* May 20, 1992, p. D17.

"For the Record," *Advertising Age,* April 6, 1992, p. 17.

Kaplan, A., "Beverages—Industry Report," *Merrill Lynch Capital Markets,* December 8, 1992.

Madlin, Nancy, "Selling the Spirits of America Overseas," *Adweek,* September 19, 1985, pp. 22-23.

Morgan, Hal, "Southern Comfort," *Symbols of America,* Penguin, 1986, p. 98.

—Daniel E. King

SPAM®

Since its introduction in 1937, Spam has been one of Geo. A. Hormel & Company's most profitable brands. Though it has served as the butt of endless jokes, its success is a serious matter: by 1993, 5 billion cans had reached the market. According to company statistics, an average of 3.8 cans of Spam were consumed in the United States every second, by nearly 30 percent of U.S. households. These are just a few of the many popular trivia facts emphasizing the degree to which the brand has become entrenched in American popular culture. Nor has its market been limited to the United States. Spam has been sold in more than fifty countries and produced in seven: England, Australia, Denmark, Philippines, Japan, Taiwan, and South Korea. It has assumed a high priority in Hormel's promotional spending—about 2.7 percent of gross dollar sales were spent on advertising the brand in 1985. Such attention to Spam emphasized the company's change in strategy since 1979, when Richard Knowlton became president and shifted focus from sales of raw meat commodities to branded consumer products. Results were positive, with sales in 1991 reaching $2.8 billion, up from $1.3 billion in 1980, while profits over that period shot to $86.4 million from $32.8 million. Spam contributed substantially to such figures.

Brand Origins

"Innovate—don't imitate," one of George A. Hormel's mottos, became a key slogan of the company he founded in 1891, in an Austin, Minnesota, creamery. His son, Jay C. Hormel, followed the advice and came up with a product that combined the company's surplus of pork shoulder with ham. Though Hormel had developed America's first canned ham—Hormel Flavor-Sealed ham—in 1926, the pork shoulder product was less expensive, required no refrigeration, and had a virtually unlimited shelf life. Packaged as Hormel spice ham, the mixture became Spam luncheon meat in mid-1937, after the company launched a competition for a catchy brand name to distinguish its new product from other canned meats. Kenneth Daigneau, the brother of a Hormel executive, won with his coinage of Spam, a foreshortening of spiced ham. The distinctive blue and yellow can was developed, and Spam was officially launched. The product's convenient lifespan and high quality—consisting of pork shoulder and ham, with no fillers, cereals or meat byproducts—were not, however, solely responsible for its success. From the outset, Spam was promoted with rigorous advertising and promotional campaigns.

Early Advertising

Radio played an instrumental part in Spam's early history. Hormel sponsored a weekly promotional performance by an 18-piece orchestra called "Swing with the Strings." In 1940, the company made media history with one of the first singing commercials, setting Spam-related lyrics to the tune of "Bring Back My Bonnie to Me." That same year, a contract was signed with George Burns and Gracie Allen whose weekly radio show promoted "the miracle meat" to the accompaniment of Artie Shaw and his 23-piece band. National airing of the Burns and Allen show on the NBC Red and Blue Networks was reinforced by a series of print advertisements also featuring the celebrities. "Cold or Hot, Spam hits the Spot!" was just one of several mottos in wide circulation. In the late 1940s and early 1950s, the 60-member Hormel Girls troupe performed throughout the country, distributing Hormel samples door to door and in supermarkets, and hosting a Sunday night national radio show. It is not surprising that Spam quickly became a household word.

Military Spam

Possessing an indefinite shelf life without refrigeration, Spam became a military staple food served in wars since the 1940s. The United States sent 100 million pounds of the canned meat to feed Allied troops in the Second World War. As documented in the Hormel archives, one squadron of American soldiers named their overseas post Spamville, established Dec. 8, 1942. But Spam made its way into the civilian population as well. Reporting from London in 1942, Edward R. Murrow underlined the plentitude of the pork: "This is London. Although the Christmas table will not be lavish, there will be Spam for everyone." It also made its way into hundreds of war cartoons as an emblem of the American presence. In a 1966 letter to Hormel, Dwight D. Eisenhower summarized the prevalence of Spam, and its mixed reception: "During World War II, of course, I ate my share of Spam. . . . As former Commander in Chief, I believe I can still officially forgive you your only sin: sending us so much of it." In his memoirs, *Khrushchev Remembers,* the late Soviet Premier remarked that "without Spam, we wouldn't have been able to feed our army." In that tradition, former Soviet leader Mikhail Gorbachev was offered a can of Spam during his 1990 visit to Hormel headquarters, and Russian President Boris Yeltsin received a can of Spam following a tour of a Hormel plant facility in Wichita, Kansas, in June of 1992. David Letterman, hosting his popular late-night

AT A GLANCE

Spam brand of canned meat developed in 1937 in Austin, MN, by Jay C. Hormel, son of the founder of Geo. A. Hormel & Company, as a productive way to use excess pork shoulder; name originally Hormel Spiced Ham (name changed to Spam, 1937).

Performance: *Market share*—73% (top share) of canned luncheon meat category. *Sales*—Approximately $200 million.

Major competitor: Armour's Treet.

Advertising: *Agency*—BBDO, Minneapolis, MN, 1937—. *Major campaign*—"Spamburger."

Addresses: *Parent company*—Geo. A. Hormel & Company, 501 16th Ave. NE, Austin, MN 55912; phone: (507) 437-5611.

comedy show, remarked that, "It was inevitable that Yeltsin learn about the dark side of capitalism."

After World War II, Spam continued its military service in both Korea and Vietnam. The Pentagon maintained interest, ordering 3.3 million pounds of Spam in 1989, and $8 million of canned foods—including Spam—in January of 1991, according to Hormel spokesperson V. Allen Krejci. Due to dietary strictures forbidding pork in the Islamic religion, however, Spam was not sent to participants in the 1991 Persian Gulf War.

Advertising Innovation

Spam gained valuable public exposure as a military staple food, even if it was commonly called "ham that failed its physical." Advertising and promotional campaigns have tried to capitalize on Spam's reputation and on positive images established in its earliest promotions. BBDO, the Minneapolis agency that has been with Spam from the beginning, returned to the radio tradition in 1983, intent on appealing to new consumers. According to Radio Expenditure Reports for 1984, Spam accounted for $1.1 million of Hormel's $4.4 million radio spending. Jerry Figenskau, director of marketing and advertising for Hormel's grocery product division, explained in the October, 1985, edition of *Marketing & Media Decisions* that, "A lot of the consumers of Spam are becoming older . . . we're trying to pick up new users, the 25-45 age group." A new series of national radio ads was launched. Stands were set up in California shopping malls in order to dispense Spam recipes and record the reactions of consumers unsuspectingly eating the product. The ads capitalized on Spam's reputation, both good and bad, and tried to correct misconceptions, according to Bob Jackson, account supervisor for Spam at BBDO. A slogan reinforced that objective: "Spam—it just might surprise you," and the subtext, "C'mon, America, try it. You might like it."

The product's 50th anniversary in 1987 brought on invigorated media spending. Funding for Spam-related events and brand promotions contributed to the company's growing advertising outlay. The list was extensive. Since 1987, Hormel funded the Austin, Texas, Spamorama, a yearly food festival with delicacies from Spamales to Spamoni ice cream and activities such as the Spam Eat, a speed-eating contest; donations were made to the Maui Mall's annual Spam cook-off in Hawaii, and to varied Spam parties, increasingly popular at American colleges. Hormel marked its centennial celebration with the Spam Jamboree, a festi-

val of Dionysian proportions that has become an annual event at the Austin, Minnesota, plant. Promotions also grew significantly after the 1980s. In March, 1985, the "Out of the Blue" sweepstakes began, offering registrants a "Big Blue Coupon Book" toward future purchases. The promotion generated 290,000 responses. Later in 1985, the Spam "Instant Winner Game" circulated 100 cans containing secret phrases worth $1000. In 1991 Hormel used newspaper ads in North Carolina and South Carolina to promote "Breakfast Carolina Style: Buy Spam and get free eggs!" In 1992 Joel Johnson replaced Richard L. Knowlton as acting president of Hormel, and not only expanded Spam advertising, but changed its timber. He instructed BBDO to discontinue its jokes in so-called "backswing" campaigns and to focus, instead, on a new generation of television ads. The result was the "Spamburger" campaign, suggesting quick and easy cooking alternatives to busy consumers. These and other incentives helped prop up Spam shipments, which increased by 8.9 percent in 1992.

Brand Development

In the 1980s, Hormel chief executive, Richard Knowlton, appointed teams to develop new products and expand existing brand lines. This strategy marked a tendency toward change and development, features characteristic of Spam's development. In 1962, the standard 12-ounce can was supplemented by a 7-ounce version designed for smaller families; in 1971, Smoke-Flavored Spam entered the market; in 1986, a Less Salt/Sodium Spam was introduced to meet health-conscious consumer demands; and in February, 1991, Spam Lite,, a variety with reduced fat and reduced salt was launched. Spam Lite was bolstered by the most extensive television advertising campaign in the history of the brand.

Health Issues

Though Spam Lite was designed to appeal to more health-conscious consumers, it also caught the attention of health specialists and media experts interested in the legal and ethical aspects of health claims in advertising. The trend since the 1970s, virtually exploding in the 1990s, was toward low-sodium, low-fat, low-cholesterol meats, forcing red meat producers to focus increasingly on leaner product. The National Pork Board and the National Pork Producers Council (NPPC) even broke a 1991 television advertising campaign for "Pork. The Other White Meat."

At the same time, however, the media were brimming with stories relating false health claims to advertising, partly in response to new labeling laws. Though Spam Lite made no false claims concerning its contents or healthfulness, it prompted critics like David Jacobson of the Hartford Courant to observe that "the mostly unregulated lite, or light, food labeling rage is reaching new peaks (or lows, depending on your view)." Jacobson pointed out that Spam Lite, despite its 25 percent reduction in fat by weight, still derived 77 percent of its calories from fat, as opposed to 85 percent in regular Spam.

Labor Dispute

In addition to health controversies, Spam and Hormel had their share of labor-related problems as well. In 1984, after an annual profit of just $29 million, Hormel offered the meat packers in its Austin, Minnesota, plant a roll-back in wages from $10.69 to $8.25 an hour. In response, members of the local union P-9 began a 13-month strike that resulted in a breach with the parent union— the United Food and Commercial Workers International Union (UFCW)—the loss of 1,000 jobs, and a decrease in pay for remaining workers. The company was relatively unscathed, moving into the 1990s with a 1 percent increase in net margins. The story of the labor dispute spawned numerous books and was turned into a documentary film, *American Dream,* directed by Barbara Kopple and released in April, 1992.

International Growth

By 1992 Spam was shipped to over 37 countries. Licensing agreements established in the 1950s granted foreign companies the rights to produce certain foods, including Spam, under the Hormel label. Such arrangements applied to companies in South Korea, Australia, Panama, and England. Joint ventures for sales and distribution were held with Pure Foods Corporation, located in the Philippines, and Hormel Limited (Japan). Ron Plath, Hormel's president of international operations, said in 1992 that the company was aiming to double its international sales within five years. According to Hormel's 1992 annual report, to meet these objectives the company began initiatives in the Commonwealth of Independent States, Poland, Hungary, The Czech Republic, Slovakia, Romania, and other newly opened markets. Free-trade agreements with Canada also began to reopen that market. While Spam was typically American, it was by no means limited to the American continent.

Predictions

As new president of Hormel in 1992, Joel Johnson was most immediately credited with a renewal of Spam, the company's flagship brand, after 1990 sales had declined 10 percent from their 1982 peak. By 1993, the brand had regained lost market share and once again filled radio and television broadcasts. In addition, the brand had a solid parent: in 1991 Hormel sales reached $2.8 billion, up from $1.3 billion in 1980, while profits nearly tripled to $86.4 million from $32.8 million.

Until 1992, the company seemed an unlikely target for the kinds of hostile takeovers that rocked the rest of the market. The Hormel Foundation and other insiders held over half of the company's assets. But in April of 1992, there was a conflict. George A. Hormel's three grandsons, George Hormel II, James Hormel, and Thomas Hormel, decided that they wanted the foundation to sell off virtually all its assets and diversify its portfolio. They sued, and in December of 1992 a judge ordered the Hormel Foundation to

reduce its control of the company to between 30 percent and 35.7 percent. The foundation had held about 41.7 percent of Hormel's 76.7 million outstanding shares. According to a June 8, 1992, article in *Forbes,* however, the heir's move did not threaten Hormel's life as an independent company. According to the article, the brothers were ready to make a compromise, perhaps separating ownership of the heir's stock from voting rights. Regardless, by the end of 1992 Hormel had $500 million in reserves and was looking for expansion possibilities. The prospects for Spam looked promising. With an indefinite lifespan, it had been technically referred to as "shelf-stable." Its sales dependability had proven it market-stable, as well.

Further Reading:

Berss, Marcia, "This isn't Ross Perot and GM," *Forbes,* June 8, 1992.

"Pork Industry to join forces with CBS-TV," *Business Wire,* Nov. 19, 1991.

"Hormel Hunts Out Options for Expanding Sales Overseas," *CityBusiness/Twin Cities,* Vol. 10, No. 17, Sec. 1, p. 15.

Haeseker, Fred, "Documentary Looks at Workers' Struggle," *Calgary Herald,* July 20, 1992, p. D6.

Hage, Dave, *No Retreat, No Surrender: Labor's War at Hormel,* New York: W. Morrow, 1989.

Hardy, Green, *On Strike at Hormel: The Struggle for a Democratic Labor Movement,* Philadelphia: Temple Univ. Press, 1990.

Geo. A. Hormel & Co. Annual Reports, Austin, MN: Geo. A. Hormel & Co., 1991-92.

Jacobson, David, "A Lite Hot-fudge Sauce?" *The Hartford Courant,* Aug. 7, 1991, p. E1.

Kelleher, Terry, "Punchlines," *Newsday,* Nassau and Suffolk Ed., Viewpoints, p. 66.

Kennedy, Tony, "Something Smells . . . " *Star Tribune,* Sept. 21, 1992, p. D2.

Maclean Hunter, Ltd., "Spam-O-RAMA," *Maclean's,* Sept. 4, 1992, p. 9.

Meyer, Marianne, "Spam's Media Plan: It Might Surprise You," *Marketing & Media Decisions,* Oct., 1985, pp. 68-70, 152.

Simon, Ruth, "And This Little Pig Processor Does Nicely," *Forbes,* Feb. 23, 1987, p. 93.

Smith, Rod, "Geo. A. Hormel & Co. Begins Second Century 'at Ravine's Edge'," *Feedstuffs,* May 27, 1991, p. 28.

News World Communications, Inc., "Group to Sell Spam-maker Shares," *The Washington Times,* Dec. 14, 1992, p. C4.

—Kerstan Cohen

SPRITE®

Sprite is the largest selling lemon-lime soft drink in the United States and the seventh largest in the entire soft drink industry. In an effort to diversify its product portfolio and compete effectively against PepsiCo, Coca-Cola launched Sprite in the 1960s. Within a decade of its introduction, Sprite went head-on against segment leader 7UP. By 1988 Sprite had garnered the prestigious top spot in the lemon-lime soft drink segment, ahead of rivals 7UP and Slice. Propelled by the now-famous campaign slogan, "I like the Sprite in you," Sprite went on to become the fastest growing lemon-lime soft drink and Coca-Cola's third largest selling brand by the 1990s.

Brand Origins

In 1956 the Coca-Cola management committee decided to develop a tart, light, highly carbonated drink. The beverage was to be developed and administered through the Fanta Beverage Company. Developed originally as a mixer and targeted at the 18-25 age group, the brand was positioned to compete against 7UP. By 1958 blind taste tests were being conducted and, in 1960, the test marketing of Sprite began in Lansing, Michigan, and Sandusky, Ohio. The packaging used in tests consisted of 7-ounce and twelve-ounce bottles. In January 1961, distribution in the cold bottle market began in Ogden, Utah. A month later, Sprite was made available to all bottlers in seven-, ten-, 12-, and 16-ounce bottles, with the Houston bottler becoming the first to launch Sprite. Sprite cans entered the market in the summer of 1961, and by October of that year, Sprite was available in 40 states through 214 bottlers. The advertising campaign that accompanied the national launch invited consumers to "Taste Its Tingling Tartness."

Marketing Strategy

During most of the 1960s and 1970s Coca-Cola did not emphasize its Sprite brand. The cola business was the company's bread-and-butter segment and naturally received greater attention. By the late 1970s, however, Coca-Cola began to move its Sprite brand more aggressively against 7UP. In the meantime, 7UP doubled its advertising expenditure. Coca-Cola responded by cutting the price of its syrup early in 1980, when consumers exhibited increasing price awareness, and by enlarging its distribution area. Advertising support tripled over the course of four years to reach $11.5 million in 1981. The state of the soft drink market in the mid-1980s made it imperative for Coca-Cola to push Sprite even more.

Growth in the cola segment, hitherto boosted by the diet sodas, had begun to slow. Coca-Cola saw the lemon-lime segment as an undermarketed niche that would help increase growth in an otherwise maturing business.

The market leader in the lemon-lime soft drink segment had long been Philip Morris's 7UP. With its memorable "Uncola" campaign, 7UP had managed to differentiate itself from the colas and continued to dominate its particular market segment. Maintaining its interest in the lemon-lime category, though, Coca-Cola more than doubled Sprite's advertising budget from 1982 to 1985, increasing its expenditures from $17 million to $40 million during that time. This increased marketing muscle, coupled with Coca-Cola's influence with bottlers, cast 7UP in an unenviable position. While a Coca-Cola bottler could diffuse the cost of discounting Sprite over a high percentage of other Coca-Cola brands it distributed, the independent bottlers that 7UP relied heavily upon did not have that alternative because the 7UP brand constituted 75 percent of the bottler's volume. In discussing Sprite in *Marketing & Media Decisions*, Rebecca Fannin noted that "Aggressive price discounting, sharp ads proclaiming superior taste, and ad funds double the size of two years ago have helped spin the drink out from its lethargic past. . . . The gains helped Sprite advance from the eighth most popular beverage overall to sixth."

By 1988 Sprite had displaced 7UP from the top spot in the lemon-lime category, a position it has not relinquished since. Backed by the memorable advertising campaign, "I Like The Sprite In You," Sprite became the best-selling non-cola brand in 1989, claiming 3.6 percent of the enormous soft-drink market. With the advent of the 1990s, Sprite became an increasing presence in the 800,000 vending machines that stock Coca-Cola products. Management showed an increasing propensity to treat Sprite as a core brand in the company's product portfolio. In 1990, for the first time in the brand's history, it was advertised on a pregame segment on Super Bowl Sunday. Promotions and advertisements featuring the popular comedian and talk-show host Arsenio Hall were launched in 1990. In 1991 Sprite maintained its 3.6 percent market share of the soft drink market.

Advertising and Promotional Activities

Sprite's earlier advertisements supported its introduction as a tart, highly carbonated drink. The 1961 campaign, "Taste Its Tingling Tartness," was followed by "Taste Sprite—Tart and

AT A GLANCE

Sprite brand introduced nationally in 1961 by The Coca Cola Company in Atlanta, GA.

Performance: *Market share*—(Sprite) 3.7% of domestic soft drink market; (diet Sprite) 0.9% of domestic soft drink market. *Sales*—(Sprite) $1.5 billion.

Major competitor: 7UP; also, Lemon Slice.

Advertising: *Agency*—Lowe & Partners, New York, NY, 1991—. *Major campaign*—"I Like The Sprite In You."

Addresses: *Parent company*—The Coca Cola Company, 1 Coca Cola Plaza, N.W., Atlanta, GA 30313; phone: (404) 676-2121.

Tingling," in 1964 and "Taste Sprite! It's Naturally Tart," coupled with "Naturally Tart for Adult Tastes," in 1965. The product's lemon aspect became a part of the advertising in 1974 with "Sprite. It Tastes Like a Lymon," followed ten years later by "Enjoy Sprite—Great Lymon Taste." The 1986 advertising campaign, "Great Lymon Taste Makes It Sprite," featured Jim "Ernest P. Worrell" Varney.

1989 was a big year for Sprite promotions, with Sprite taking on 7UP in its biggest ad promotion effort ever. The aim was to garner a greater share of food store sales, the only channel in the lemon-lime market in which Sprite was not the leading brand. The marketing blitz started off with a Sprite sponsored "Comedy Week" in which Sprite was advertised on a number of popular comedy shows on network television, including *The Cosby Show*, *The Golden Girls*, *Roseanne*, and *Arsenio Hall*. Radio advertising was also utilized in the form of "Sprite Presents The Saturday Night Live Radio Network," which featured 60-second audio highlights of the best material from the legendary television program and a 30-second Sprite commercial. Another component of the marketing activity was the "$75,000,000 Scrabble Game at McDonald's," launched in collaboration with the McDonald's restaurant chain—the first time that the fast-food restaurant leader conducted a national promotion for a non-cola soft drink. Massive use of coupons was also a part of the promotional effort, as Coca-Cola placed 40 million Sprite coupons on diet Coke bottles and another 40 million in consumer magazines. The "I Like The Sprite In You" campaign was launched by Lowe Marschalk and proved to be enormously popular. In the spring of 1990, Sprite signed popular comedian Arsenio Hall for the "I Like The Sprite In You" campaign, linking it with his talk show. Arsenio Hall was supposed to personify the campaign, especially the accompanying lyric, "I like the way you make me laugh."

Competition

Until the 1980s, the lemon-lime market had been dominated by Sprite's traditional rival 7UP. Even though Sprite was positioned against 7UP from the day it was launched in 1961, 7UP was the undisputed leader in the lemon-lime segment through the mid-1980s. Mindful of the fast-growing lemon-lime segment of the industry, however, The Coca-Cola Company set its sights on the lemon-lime business, hoping to make Sprite the largest selling soft drink in that segment by 1990. Coca-Cola's mighty distribution and advertising power was more than a match for the struggling 7UP, which feared relegation to regional status. With its renewed marketing push, Sprite achieved the top position in the lemon-lime

market in 1986, four years ahead of schedule. Even though 7UP had an edge in grocery store sales, Sprite's huge vending machine and fountain/food-service network enabled it to outsell 7UP.

In what came to resemble a David versus Goliath fight, 7UP tried to strike back with its Like and Gold brands, both of which flopped. Turning to the advertising theme that had made it a nationally prominent brand, 7UP revived the noteworthy Uncola campaign, replacing the earlier comparative ads that had pushed differences in product characteristics such as caffeine content. 7UP began to emphasize advertising targeted toward teenagers, who were already exhibiting a switch of allegiance to Sprite; by 1990, Sprite had 31 percent of the lemon-lime market to 7UP's 25 percent.

The creation and rapid initial success of the juice-added segment that PepsiCo's lemon Slice brand pioneered in the mid-1980s added another dimension to the competition, which the media dubbed the "lemon-lime wars." Though the juice-added segment was considered distinct from the citrus soda segment, Slice's success had clear repercussions on the lemon-lime market. Within a year of its introduction in 1985, Slice had captured 12.5 percent of the $3.2 billion lemon-lime market, with most of the gain at 7UP's expense. Even though 7UP sales suffered under the Slice onslaught, Sprite sales continued to increase. Preferring not to tackle Slice head-on by changing Sprite's formulation, The Coca-Cola Company chose instead to compete under its popular juice brand name Minute Maid. By 1989 the juice-added segment had suffered several setbacks. Lemon-lime Slice cut its juice content and entered the lemon-lime market segment. By 1990 Slice's share of that market was eight percent.

In March 1992 7UP filed a suit against Coca-Cola in a Dallas state district court accusing Coca-Cola of using false statements to entice bottlers to switch from 7UP to Sprite. The suit claimed that Coca-Cola interfered with 7UP's contractual business relationships with independent Coca-Cola/7UP bottlers, and asked for $500 million in punitive damages. Coca-Cola has denied all allegations of wrongdoing and the matter is currently in litigation.

International Market

Sprite is available in 155 markets, approximately 80 percent of the countries where Coca-Cola products are available. The list of countries includes Australia, Argentina, Belgium, Bulgaria, China, Czechoslovakia, Djibouti, Ivory Coast, Japan, Mexico, Russia, and Romania. In 1989 Sprite was introduced in Great Britain in association with Cadbury Schweppes. In April 1992 the Korean subsidiary of The Coca-Cola Company filed a trademark infringement suit against a local company for marketing a soft drink similar to Sprite. The local company had launched a similar beverage named "Sprint" with a package design resembling that of Sprite. The drink was subsequently renamed "Sprinter."

Further Reading:

Giges, Nancy, " 'Feisty' Reid: Coke's Marketing Chief Mounts 'Integrated' Effort," *Advertising Age,* November 24, 1986, pp. 3, 82.

Fannin, Rebecca, "Who's Squeezing Whom in the Lemon-lime Wars?" *Marketing & Media Decisions,* July 1985, pp. 125-127, 166.

Kelly, Kevin, and Konrad Walecia, "Seven-Up: Where Have All The Bubbles Gone?" *Business Week,* January 29, 1990, p. 95.

Lawrence, Jennifer,"Seven-Up Puts New Fizz in Ads," *Advertising Age,* October 17, 1988, p. 34.

"Packaging Promotions Push U.S. Sales up 3 Percent," *Beverage Industry/Annual Manual 1991/92,* 1991-92, pp. 14-34.

Rieser, Robyn, Interview with Ashish Patwardhan for *Encyclopedia of Consumer Brands*, April 1993.

Scredon, Scott, and Amy Dunkin, ''Pepsi's Seven-Up Deal: Shaking up the Soft-Drink Wars,'' *Business Week,* February 3, 1986.

''Soda Sales Going Flat,'' *Standard & Poor's Industry Surveys,* August 6, 1992, pp. F24-F28.

Winters, Patricia, ''Sprite Shops for Share; Brand Challenges 7-UP for Grocery Sales Lead,'' *Advertising Age,* April 3, 1989, p. 43.

—Ashish Patwardhan

STARKIST®

StarKist

The StarKist (formerly Star-Kist) brand of tuna has the biggest market share of tuna sales, more than 40 percent in the United States, which accounts for 50 percent of the world's consumption of tuna. StarKist was the first tuna brand in the world to adopt the "Dolphin Safe" label, and prior to that, the first to be canned in spring water. StarKist Seafood Company of Long Beach, California, the parent company of StarKist and a subsidiary of H.J. Heinz Company, is the world's largest processor of canned tuna.

Brand Origins

Tuna accounts for nearly half of American fish consumption. Americans developed a taste for tuna after World War II; prior to the war, tuna was consumed in the coastal regions, and the tuna industry was in its infancy. Tuna was first processed and marketed in 1903 in California, the year the sardine catch suddenly dwindled. An enterprising fisherman processed the little known tuna fish in San Pedro, California, the birthplace of the world's tuna industry. While his 700 cases of tuna sold out quickly, still there were inefficient means of preparing tuna for market. The fish were not refrigerated so they had to be caught close to shore and the boats could only stay out as long as the catch remained fresh. These conditions made fishing difficult, because tuna is one of the ocean's most migratory fish, traveling at speeds up to 45 miles per hour.

Immigrant Martin J. Bogdanovich revolutionized the seafood industry by founding the predecessor of the StarKist Seafood Company. A seasoned fisherman from the Dalmatian island of Viz, the 26-year-old Bogdanovich arrived in California with his bride in 1908, lured there by tales of abundant fishing and a newfangled technique for preserving fish: canning. Bogdanovich joined fellow Dalmatians in San Pedro in the hunt for the elusive tuna. The enterprising Bogdanovich soon owned his own boat, giving him the incentive to implement radical ideas about fishing. On a visit to an ice plant in Santa Barbara in 1910, it occurred to him that fishing could be extended by refrigerating fish on board immediately after their capture. To the amazement of his fellow seamen, he equipped his boat with the world's first ice box. Chilling the fish greatly increased his yield. He marketed his ice box idea, and began to focus on processing the fish as close to shore as possible. In 1917, Bogdanovich plowed the profits from his shoreline seafood stand into his own company, the French Sardine Company. The country had just entered World War I in

Europe and profits for food processors promised to be lucrative. Moreover, food shortages encouraged the search for substitutes for beef and pork, and Bogdanovich put his faith in tuna. The health benefits of tuna as a high protein, nutritious food were emphasized by nutritionists, and Americans' consumption of tuna increased accordingly.

Tuna consumption declined in the heartland after the war, but remained steady in the coastal areas. After weathering the Great Depression of the 1930s, Bogdanovich turned over management of the company to his son Joseph, a young man with fresh ideas. If his father had revolutionized the tuna industry, Joseph Bogdanovich would turn tuna into a household word: StarKist.

First Commercial Success

When Joseph Bogdanovich became director of the French Sardine Company in 1937, he felt the company could prosper only if it overcame an ingrained aversion, especially among the old timers within the firm, to marketing tuna nationwide. With that end in mind, the company's tuna product was christened with the lyrical name of StarKist to identify it in the public mind.

The company's reluctance to engage in the innovations and expense of turning a coastal seafood into a national household item was largely overcome during the World War II years, which saw the death of Martin Bogdanovich and his son's rise to presidency of the company in 1944. Once again, as in the First World War, widespread food shortages created a huge demand for tuna, and the demand for tuna exceeded the supply. Many of the 15.5 million American soldiers got their first taste of tuna when they entered the service.

With the war's end, Joseph Bogdanovich was determined that the gains made during the war would not be eroded, as after World War I, when the market for tuna once again declined nationwide. He felt the public must be kept informed of the nutritional value and versatility of tuna. Using all advertising media, including storewide taste tests and famous Hollywood stars, StarKist was introduced in an advertising blitz that the French Sardine Company had never before witnessed.

Demand for tuna rose, and by 1952 StarKist became the best known tuna brand in the country. The company, at its new facilities on Terminal Island, California, was producing 960,000

AT A GLANCE

StarKist brand of canned tuna founded as Star-Kist in San Pedro, CA, by Martin J. Bogdanovich and partner, Nicholas Vilicich, owners of the French Sardine Company; first appeared on the market in 1942 as Star-Kist brand of tuna; The French Sardine Company renamed Star-Kist Foods, Inc., by Joseph M. Bogdanovich, son of original founder, 1953; H. J. Heinz Company acquired Star-Kist Foods, Inc., as a subsidiary, 1963; renamed StarKist Seafood Company, 1988.

Performance: *Market share*—42% (top share) of canned tuna sales.

Major competitor: Chicken of the Sea; also Bumble Bee.

Advertising: *Agency*—Leo Burnett USA, Chicago, IL. *Major campaign*—Charlie the Tuna, animated television character who repeatedly tries to get caught by StarKist.

Addresses: *Parent company*—StarKist Seafood Company, 180 East Ocean Blvd., Long Beach, CA 90802-4797; phone: (310) 590-9900; fax: (310) 590-3799. *Ultimate parent company*—H. J. Heinz Company, P. O. Box 57, Pittsburgh, PA 15230-0057; phone: (412) 456-5700.

cans of tuna a day. In 1953, the French Sardine Company decided to adopt the name of its famous product, and call itself StarKist Foods, Inc. Several years later, StarKist was the biggest selling brand of tuna in the world.

Advertising Innovation

Because production facilities lagged so far behind the high demand created by the company's mass advertising campaigns, Bogdanovich oversaw the construction in 1952 of the most modern canning facility in the world on Terminal Island. With the success of StarKist well launched, and demand for the tuna being met, it was necessary to develop a strategy for marketing the brand more successfully than any of its domestic and foreign competitors. That strategy would have to take advantage of the new television medium as well as plant a love of StarKist in the palates of million of suburbanites and the postwar baby boomers.

What StarKist lacked was an identifiable logo or trademark. The combined creative efforts of both the company and their new advertising agency, Leo Burnett USA, produced the nationally identifiable Charlie the Tuna. Goofy, funny, and dressed in a necktie and hat, Charlie the Tuna debuted in 1961 in national television commercials that capitalized on the StarKist name and, especially, the quality of the product. In escapade after escapade, Charlie endeavors—what one would least expect from a tuna fish—to be captured by StarKist Foods, the best tuna processor. After each of Charlie's attempts, StarKist refuses to catch the hapless Charlie for canning. Keeping him alive in this way soon made him one of the most famous trademarks in business, as well as the company's spokesman and chief product advertiser. Whether StarKist Foods is introducing Albacore Fettucine, Charlie's Lunch Kit, or "Dolphin Safe" tuna to the world, it is the adorable Charlie, in cap and glasses, who "sells" the product and identifies the company, a feat neither one of StarKist's competitors has come close to matching.

Product Changes

StarKist has long led the tuna industry in innovations as well as sales. StarKist engaged the first research and quality control group in the tuna industry. By 1954, StarKist Foods came out with its first new tuna product, the popular 9-Lives Cat Food, made from the red meat skimmed from tuna loins during processing. Shortly afterwards, the company introduced its first frozen product, Frozen Tuna Pie, the first in a long line of frozen foods that later grew to feature low fat, low cholesterol Albacore Fettucine.

Canned StarKist also lead the tuna industry in product changes. New cans were introduced: the nine-and-a-quarter-inch large and the twelve-and-a-half-inch giant cans, as well as the flip-top can. StarKist was the first to can tuna in spring water, and to market low-sodium, low-fat canned tuna. Another innovation was Charlie's Lunch Kit, which consisted of a single serving can of tuna, Heinz mayonnaise and relish, crackers, plastic cups and a wooden spoon, all wrapped in a recyclable plastic lunch-sized package.

The Dolphin Controversy

In June of 1990, StarKist was the first tuna company in the world to come out with "Dolphin Safe" tuna (quickly followed by its main competitors, foreign-owned Bumble Bee and Chicken of the Sea tunas). Prompting this move, much heralded by environmental groups, was a public letter writing campaign to major tuna processors threatening to boycott their tuna products unless the companies adopted a "dolphin safe" fishing policy and stopped buying tuna from fishing vessels that slaughtered dolphins. Since the early 1970s, millions of dolphins had been killed by fishing boats. In 1988, an environmental group's eleven minute video, depicting the tragedy, triggered a national public outcry against dolphin killing, which occurred mainly in the eastern Pacific Ocean.

Rather than dismissing the protest, StarKist managers adopted an enlightened, though costly, approach. Henceforth, the company would not only refuse to buy tuna caught by "intentional encirclement of dolphins" but any tuna caught in drift net fishing. The company itself, however, did not determine whether the tuna caught was dolphin safe; U.S. government inspectors from the National Marine Fisheries Service decided whether the tuna was dolphin safe.

Though the changeover to "Dolphin Safe" canned tuna proved costly for the Starkist Seafood Company, in the long run it has paid off. StarKist remained the best-selling tuna in the country, and in 1991, StarKist Seafood Company won the coveted Global 500 Award from the United Nations' Environment Program in recognition of its enlightened stand in the dolphin controversy.

International Growth

StarKist Seafood Company has been a global company every since Joseph Bogdanovich established overseas bases in South America and Africa, a necessity given the volatile domestic tuna market. StarKist maintained processing facilities on five continents, including the island of Puerto Rico and Ecuador. StarKist produced tuna for the European community and Latin America without the StarKist label. StarKist tuna is not, however, represented in Canada. The most important market for StarKist tuna is the United States, and the company's worldwide processing facilities enable the tuna to reach the American market quickly and efficiently.

Future

StarKist tuna has grown in popularity steadily since it first appeared on the market in 1942, despite growing competition that forced the shutdown of the company's impressive Terminal Island facility in 1984. However, the fact that 43 percent of all fish consumed in the United States is tuna, and that sandwiches and salads are Americans' favorite foods (some restaurants are even featuring "tuna pizza" on their menus, according to *Restaurant Hospitality*), and that the consumption of meat is steadily declining, all mean that StarKist will at least hold its own, which translates into the biggest domestic market share in the United States. StarKist continues to capitalize on its instantly recognizable name, and the popularity of Charlie the Tuna continues undiminished.

Further Reading:

Aspin, Chris, "The Embargo That Won't Go Away: Tuna," *Business Mexico,* March, 1992, p. 24.

Conan, Kerri, "Menu Ideas: Flounder No More," *Restaurant Business,* March 1, 1992, pp. 129-133.

"A Fishy Story (Killing of Dolphins Caught in Tuna Fishing Nets)," *The Economist,* May 4, 1991, p. 69.

Fuhrman, Peter, "Strange Bedfellows," *Forbes,* December 9, 1991, pp. 94, 98.

Hannon, Kerry, "The King of Ketchup," *Forbes,* March 21, 1988, pp. 58-65.

"Healthy Option," *Restaurant Hospitality,* February, 1991, pp. 95, 98.

H.J. Heinz Company Annual Report, Pittsburgh, PA: H. J. Heinz Company, 1992.

Holland, Kerry L., "Exploitation on Porpoise: The Use of Purse Seine Nets by Commercial Tuna Fishermen in the Eastern Tropical Pacific Ocean," *Syracuse Journal of International Law & Commerce,* spring, 1991, pp. 267-280.

Magnusson, Paul, and Peter Hong, "Save the Dolphins—Or Free Trade?" *Business Week,* February 17, 1992, p. 130.

Mallory, Maria, "Heinz's New Recipe: Take a Dollop of Dollars," *Business Week,* September 30, 1991, pp. 86, 88.

"Media Wise and Dolphin Free (StarKist Marketer H. J. Heinz Stops Buying Tuna Caught Using Methods That Kill Dolphins)," *AdWeek's Marketing Week,* July 23, 1990, p. 21.

Page, J. D., et al. "H. J. Heinz—Company Report," *Investext,* July 20, 1992.

Rice, Faye, "How to Deal with Tougher Customers," *Fortune,* December 3, 1990, pp. 38-48.

Rose, Merrill, "Activism in the 90s: Changing Roles for Public Relations," *Public Relations Quarterly,* fall, 1991, pp. 28-32.

StarKist, A Quality Driven Success Story, Long Beach, CA: StarKist Seafood Company, 1991.

StarKist Dolphin Safe, Long Beach, CA: StarKist Seafood Company, 1992.

The Star-Kist Story, Long Beach, CA: Star-Kist Foods, Inc., 1963.

Star-Kist: World Famous Processors of Food from the Sea, Long Beach, CA: Star-Kist Foods, Inc., 1976.

Stiling, Marjorie, *Famous Brand Names, Emblems, Trademarks,* Newton Abbot, VT: David & Charles, 1980.

Weinstein, Steve, "The 1991 Supermarket Sales Manual: Main Courses & Entrees," *Progressive Grocer,* July, 1991, pp. 50-55.

—Sina Dubovoj

STOUFFER'S®

The Stouffer's brand of frozen entrees is both pioneer and leader in its $3.4 billion category of the U.S. frozen dinner/entree industry. Introduced in the early 1950s, Stouffer products—considered a novelty at first—were hungrily snatched up from grocers' freezers by consumers with a healthy appetite for convenience. By the late 1950s, price-cutting competitors crowded into the market and a threatened Stouffer Foods Corporation retaliated first by dropping prices, then by revamping its marketing strategy. The company was forced to compete on price twice—in 1957, and again in 1991, on its Lean Cuisine brand. However, Stouffer has consistently relied less on price and more on quality, new product development, and innovative advertising to carve out its role as market leader. In 1961 Stouffer revolutionized food advertising by placing the first grocery ad to appear in *Time* magazine. During its 38-year history Stouffer Foods has introduced more than 150 frozen food products. Brand ownership has changed twice—in 1967, when Litton Industries acquired Stouffer Foods, and again in 1973, with the firm's purchase by Swiss-owned Nestlé S.A., holding company of parent firm Nestlé USA, Inc. New owners never tampered with Stouffer's brand image, however, which remains a blend of the contemporary and traditional, supported by advertising that emphasizes quality, taste, and homespun warmth. Carton designs have been upgraded periodically, including in 1971, when Stouffer became the first frozen entree marketer to include microwave cooking instructions on select items. However, it was not until 1992 that the company traded its original logo—a quaint Dutch oven containing the Stouffer name—for a sleeker, more contemporary design. The move coincided with a campaign to emphasize the Stouffer name on all its brands. Stouffer preserved its trademark coral red and black colors in the new logo, but replaced the Dutch-oven design with a black oval against a red sash.

Brand Origins: From Table to Oven

It is perhaps ironic that Stouffer frozen entrees—commercially prepared for those who prefer to dine at home—were created by the owners of a restaurant chain. The Stouffer saga began in 1922 when Abraham and Mahala Stouffer opened a small, stand-up dairy counter in downtown Cleveland. The Stouffer name soon came to be associated with home-baked pies, fresh sandwiches, and wholesome ingredients. In 1924 the Stouffers opened a full-service restaurant—Stouffer Lunch—which quickly built a local reputation for serving well-prepared food in a warm, friendly

setting. By 1937 the Stouffers, aided by their business-minded sons, had expanded the restaurant chain to Detroit, Pittsburgh, and New York. As the population migrated to the suburbs after World War II, the Stouffers followed, opening their fifteenth restaurant in the Shaker Heights suburb of Cleveland in 1946.

In Shaker Heights customers began asking restaurant manager Wally Blankenship to freeze some of the popular menu items for home consumption. Convinced that he had discovered a new market for frozen take-home dinners, Blankenship opened, in the late 1940s, the 227 Club, a retail outlet adjacent to the Shaker Heights restaurant. Here hungry customers could select from a wide variety of frozen entrees, including braised swiss steak, shrimp curry, macaroni and cheese, and roast beef hash. Despite Blankenship's enthusiasm for the new project, the Stouffers tiptoed warily into the frozen entree business, lest they damage the Stouffer reputation for taste and quality if the product proved inferior to their restaurant fare. Even before the 227 Club opened, restaurant staffers experimented with a variety of freezing methods in the restaurant's test kitchen, in search of the perfect means of preserving flavor for take-out customers. This quest for quality assurance has been a hallmark of the Stouffer brand since its origin.

Early Marketing Milestones

Local interest in Stouffer frozen entrees proved so strong that in 1954 the Stouffers forged full-speed ahead into a new business venture with the opening of Stouffer Frozen Cooked Foods, a 20,000-square-foot operation in Cleveland. From the outset, the Stouffer brand distinguished itself from existing frozen food brands, most of which included a mix of meat pies, fish sticks, and blanched vegetables. Instead, Stouffer's initial product launch featured 18 items ranging from prepared entrees and vegetable side dishes to soups and desserts. The products were so unique that Macy's department stores at one time carried them in their specialty food departments, according to the company's 1984 Stouffer Foods Annual Report to Employees.

Consumer demand grew steadily, prompting Stouffer in 1956 to add another 55,000 square feet to its Cleveland plant in order to fill orders from distributors in Pittsburgh, Detroit, Chicago, and Philadelphia. By 1957 Stouffer entrees were available throughout the United States as well as in Toronto, Ontario. However, despite such rapid expansion into new markets, Stouffer ran into trouble

AT A GLANCE

Stouffer's brand frozen foods founded in 1954 by Stouffer Foods Corporation owners Abraham and Mahala Stouffer, who had previously founded the Stouffer's restaurant chain; acquired in 1967 by Litton Industries; purchased from Litton Industries in 1973 by Nestlé, S.A., of Vevey, Switzerland; merged into newly formed Nestlé USA, Inc., in January 1991.

Performance: *Market share*—14.5% (top share) of frozen dinner/entree category. *Sales*—$450 million.

Major competitor: Kraft's Budget Gourmet; also Campbell's Swanson, ConAgra's Healthy Choice.

Advertising: *Agency*—Ruder-Finn, Chicago, IL. *Major campaign*—"Nothing comes closer to home."

Addresses: *Parent company*—Stouffer Foods Corporation, 5750 Harper Rd., Solon, OH 44139; phone: (216) 349-5757; fax: (216) 248-6413. *Ultimate parent company*—Nestlé USA, Inc., 800 North Brand Boulevard, Glendale, CA 91203; phone: (818) 549-6000; fax: (818) 549-6952. *Ultimate ultimate parent company*—Nestlé S.A.

late in 1957. Asked by *Frozen Food Age* editors in 1979 to describe the late 1950s dilemma, Gerald DeCroce, vice president of marketing, put it this way: "We began by spreading marketing funds too thin. We fired inexpensive marketing 'buckshot' into the air and hoped some of it would fall on customers. If this didn't get us the volume we were looking for in a city, we added markets to keep our production plant going. The result was we started losing distribution in middle income stores, and we were actually getting into real trouble, even though our sales volume was steadily increasing."

The company reacted by slashing prices on its entire product line. However, when this short-term solution failed to produce the desired long-term results, Stouffer's marketing strategy took a drastic turn. In 1960 Stouffer executives James M. Biggar, Don Stover, and Denny Studer teamed up with William Sprague, a Pittsburgh advertising expert, to prove to retailers that they could reap substantial profits with moderate unit sales by targeting a select audience and charging higher prices. Stouffer convinced retailers that certain consumers would pay up to $1.99 for items in a category where 79 cents was considered the top asking price, provided consumers believed they were buying superior-quality products. In tandem with the pricing philosophy, Stouffer adopted the untested strategy of marketing its entire 25-product line in a select few stores in high-income areas. This was in stark contrast to its previous policy of relying exclusively on the brand's fastest-selling items—marketed in as many stores as possible—to generate profits. Stouffer backed its about-face strategy with an unprecedented advertising campaign, committing most of its 1961 advertising budget of $332,000 to the first grocery ads ever to appear in *Time* magazine. Rather than try to reach everyone, the ads targeted upper-income families in 10 key markets.

The selective distribution method worked. The 1984 Stouffer Foods Annual Report to Employees stated: "In the '60s, 10 percent of the nation's grocery stores were responsible for 75 percent of our business. We had a choice to make—should we lower the cost or keep the quality high. Obviously, we opted for the latter." But once profitability was restored, Stouffer went shopping again for new markets. This time, the company focused

its attention on middle-income consumers—a market segment that was growing by leaps and bounds in the early and mid-1960s. Biggar told *Frozen Food Age* in 1962 that the company's goal was to have 40 percent of the market buying the greater share of Stouffer products. Once again, Stouffer convinced retailers that the more high-ticket Stouffer items they stocked, the more profits they would reap per square foot of display space. Stouffer even went so far as to guarantee retailers that within 90 days, a 21-inch display with 13 Stouffer items would generate weekly profits of $15 on sales of $51. The guarantee strategy worked so well that the company returned to variations on the same theme many times throughout its trade advertising history.

Product Innovations

Having defined its market and established preeminence, Stouffer channelled its energies into developing new products and expanding operations. Some product innovations, such as french bread pizzas, side dishes, and home-style entrees—all considered part of the "red box" line—have endured. Others have not. In 1968, banking on company research that revealed a significant percentage of Stouffer sales came from larger families, the firm debuted its Family Casserole line. Reception was cool. The product flopped, but its creators learned a lesson: Consumers preferred split-menu dining, which allows individual family members to eat what they want, when they want. Family Casserole wasn't a total loss, however, according to DeCroce, who told *Business Reports:* "Frozen lasagna, one of our biggest selling items, was first introduced in our family casserole size. When Family Casserole failed, we came back with lasagna in a two-serving size and had an overnight success on our hands." In 1992 Stouffer returned to the family-size theme, but on a smaller scale. The company introduced two of its entrees in 40-oz. sizes designed to serve four or more people.

New products continued to emerge in the late 1960s and early 1970s as Stouffer experimented with a line of soups and bakery items. The company introduced soup lines on two different occasions, only to pull the item from the shelves both times. Then in 1981, Stouffer launched its Lean Cuisine brand. For nearly a decade, Lean Cuisine ruled the industry's healthy entree category, until being bumped briefly from the top spot in 1991 by competitor ConAgra Inc.'s Healthy Choice brand. Lean Cuisine also led to the creation of a new red box line—Right Course. In 1989 Stouffer made a play for the over-50 crowd with the Right Course line, touting the products' lower salt, fat, and cholesterol levels. The strategy that had worked for Healthy Choice bombed for Stouffer. Right Course "failed miserably" according to *Adweek* magazine, which claimed the product eked out a slim one percent of the market. Admitting defeat, Stouffer pulled the plug on Right Course after only two years, claiming the product had cannibalized sales of its Lean Cuisine brand.

In 1986 the Dinner Supreme line hit the market, surviving until 1990. Dinner Supreme performance peaked in 1988 with sales of about $75 million, or 7 percent of the frozen dinner market. Irrezestables—a line of spicy entrees—debuted in 1989. Instead of sizzling, they fizzled, and Stouffer abandoned the product without ever expanding beyond the initial Midwest test markets. In 1990 Stouffer targeted the consumer with a taste for the traditional when it launched a new eight-item red box line under the Homestyle label. The two-compartment entrees featured traditional consumer favorites, including beef and poultry main dishes with pasta, potato, or vegetable sidelines.

Steady Growth

Early product acceptance and ongoing product development drove expansion. By 1968 Stouffer had outgrown its Cleveland facility. The company moved to a brand new high-rise warehouse, plant, and headquarters on a 42-acre site in Solon, Ohio. A 21,000-square-foot office building was added in 1969, along with new research and development kitchens. In 1971 Stouffer added a $1.7 million technical center to the Solon complex. Soon afterward, the company struck a deal with Robin Hood Multifoods Ltd. of Canada to produce Stouffer entrees for the Canadian market. The Stouffer brand has not expanded beyond North American boundaries, despite its purchase in 1973 by Nestlé. It has continued to grow under Nestlé, however, necessitating the addition of a new production plant in Gaffney, South Carolina, in 1980, and a third plant, in Springville, Utah, in 1986.

Advertising Strategies

In 1979 *Frozen Food Age* noted that Stouffer's advertising "has been distinguished by a keen perception—often an anticipation—of changing consumer attitudes, interests, and needs. And the thrust is invariably contemporary, often featuring spectacular product graphics to convey a high quality image." In the 1950s, Stouffer's ads promised consumers more of what they most craved—leisure time. One ad read, "Golf, swimming, sunning . . . I have time for everything since Stouffer came into my life." Then in 1961, Stouffer unveiled its *Time* magazine campaign and rewarded its creator, Sprague, by sticking with him for nearly two decades. Believing that *Time* readers matched the profile of the Stouffer-brand consumer—a high income-earner—Stouffer's early *Time* ads played up the ideas of taste and quality. They were designed to evoke images of warmth and home, and carried the message: "You taste a priceless difference in Stouffer's frozen cooked foods." The first campaign was so successful that in 1963 Stouffer spent $1.2 million on a similar campaign to reach 23 million homes through national publications such as the *New Yorker, McCalls,* and *Ladies Home Journal,* in addition to local media, such as Sunday supplements, radio, television, and billboards.

Stouffer stood by its broad-interest publication strategy as it rode the waves of consumer whims. In the mid-1970s when meat prices skyrocketed, Stouffer took a "value-added" tack, pointing out that 13 of the brand's main dishes cost $1 or less per serving. "If you think you can't afford Stouffer's, look again," Stouffer told consumers. In 1979 the company embarked on its largest campaign to date, spending $14.8 million to promote its line of single and two-serving entrees. The campaign addressed new technology—namely, the microwave—and changing lifestyles that included a steady procession of women into the workplace and increasing numbers of one- and two-member households. Advertising shifted its focus to convenience as a necessity, rather than a luxury, with ads that asked, "After a hard day at the office, who needs a hot night over the stove?" When "women's liberation" became a prevalent topic, Stouffer turned to its male audience with ads depicting a steaming, tempting helping of lasagna under the simple heading: "Men's liberation." Both ads were also designed to keep consumers out of fast-food restaurants, considered direct competition by Stouffer.

In rare instances, Stouffer has deviated from its home-centered theme to capitalize on current events or unique marketing opportunities. Most noteworthy is a 1969 campaign, born out of NASA's selection of Stouffer products for consumption by the Apollo 11 crew. The astronauts dined on 14 Stouffer entrees during a quarantine period immediately following a lunar flight. In large, bold type, Stouffer proclaimed: "Everybody who's been to the moon is eating Stouffer's." While home did not figure in these ads, quality played prominently: "Of all the foods on earth, Stouffer's Frozen Foods met or exceeded every NASA specification," the ad claimed. In another departure from standard strategy, Stouffer played on the popularity of the film *The Godfather* with ads featuring lasagna and "Our Gang." The award-winning 30-second television spots ran in 35 markets from 1972 to 1974.

In the 1980s, Stouffer committed much of its advertising budget to promoting its new Lean Cuisine brand. Meanwhile, advertising for the Stouffer red box line continued to reflect consumer interests and emphasize home and quality. In 1992 Stouffer picked up on the "back to the family" movement and the concept of home as a haven by introducing a comforting campaign claiming, "Stouffer's: nothing comes closer to home." The ads featured "coming home" vignettes and the company's newly designed logo. Before introducing the new logo, Stouffer hinted at the possibility of unifying all Stouffer brands under a single, umbrella campaign. Instead, the company stuck with separate campaigns for the Lean Cuisine and Stouffer brands, but initiated plans to play up the Stouffer name more in all brand advertising. In announcing the logo change in August 1992, president E. Michael Moone said the company's foremost concern was to preserve Stouffer's strong brand identity. "The new logo works to unify our brands under a common name in a simple design that is still recognizable as Stouffer's, but delivers a modern feel to the product lines."

Future Directions

Industry observers forecast continued emphasis on product development and brand awareness at Stouffer, with no drastic changes in marketing philosophy. Products will continue to flow in and out of the market, a reflection of changing consumer tastes and lifestyles. While Stouffer's leading position in the healthy entree category may have been threatened in 1991 by ConAgra's Healthy Choice, the Stouffer brand remains the undisputed leader in its category. Alone, it accounts for about 14.5 percent of the market in dollar sales, according to Chicago's Information Resources Inc. 1992 statistics. However, all Stouffer products combined, including Lean Cuisine, give the company close to 25 percent of the market, according to industry experts. Competitors such as Kraft General Foods Group, which markets Budget Gourmet and a "blue box" frozen entree line, Campbell Soup Co., creator of Le Menu, and H.J. Heinz with its Weight Watchers brand, have heated up the competition, but never won the race. "Stouffer's plain-Jane dishes—including Chicken a la King and Macaroni & Cheese—still dominate," reported *Adweek's Marketing Week* in 1992. "Quiet Stouffer, it seems, has solid clout with consumers who eat healthy or hearty."

Further Reading:

Dagnoli, Judann, "Weight Watchers Gaining: Heinz Unit Builds Share as It Leans on Stouffer," *Advertising Age,* 1987, p. 4.

Dagnoli, Judann, "How Stouffer's Right Course Veered off Course," *Advertising Age,* May 6, 1991, p. 34.

Frozen Food Age, reprint of 1979 feature on Stouffer's Foods, Solon, Ohio: Stouffer Foods Corporation, Solon, Ohio.

Kirk, Jim, "Stouffer Veers from 'Right Course,' Plans to Emphasize Company Name," *Adweek,* February 25, 1991, p. 2

Liesse, Julie, ''Heat's on Stouffer: Kraft Rolls Out 'Blue Box' Entrees,'' *Advertising Age,* February 5, 1990, p. 2.

Lloyd, Ann, ''The Lean Cuisine Story,'' *Business Reports,* 1984, p. 16.

''Our 30th Year,'' excerpts from *Stouffer Foods Annual Report to Employees,* Solon, Ohio: Stouffer Foods Corporation, 1984.

''Powerful Brand 'Families' Key to Growth,'' *Adweek's Marketing Week Superbrands,* 1990.

Warner, Fara, ''Stouffer Defends Its Lead in Frozen Meals,'' *Adweek's Marketing Week,* April 20, 1992, p.7.

—Katherine J. Paul

SUNKIST®

The Sunkist trademark stamped on navel and valencia oranges, grapefruits, lemons, and tangerines is one of the most widely recognized brand names in the world. The brand, which is also marketed extensively by licensed retailers in other related industries, is still most closely tied to its original product, the Sunkist navel orange, which controls around 60 percent of the domestic orange market. Sunkist's parent, Sunkist Growers, Inc., is the world's largest citrus cooperative and consists of some 6,500 grower members who trace their business heritage back over 100 years, to a period when California was emerging as one of the world's foremost agricultural regions. The Sunkist name materialized in 1908, and ever since it has been the driving force behind the company's sales and is its major marketing apparatus. Like another fruit frontrunner, Chiquita, Sunkist represents a pioneer brand name in the commodity business and stands as the first of its kind to be affixed to an agricultural product.

The Birth of a Cooperative

As early as 1880 California was producing more citrus fruits than surrounding markets could support. For a grower, continued survival meant being able to transport fruit nationwide. Smaller growers, which accounted for almost 90 percent of all orange farmers, were forced to rely on produce brokers and shipping agents in order to accomplish this. Unfortunately, because of the inadequate methods of shipping available (produce traveled by rail with no refrigeration, resulting in a high percentage of spoilage), brokers soon placed the full financial risk on the grower. "Broker wars," questionable business practices, and secret deals abounded, and some markets were intentionally flooded with fruit while others were left wanting. Desperate to save their farms, such growers as T. H. B. Chamblin and P. J. Dreher convinced their associates to form a "pool" and sell their fruit cooperatively. Chamblin and his Riverside, California, associates named themselves the Pachappa Orange Growers and were the first to attempt to control their citrus crop entirely, from grove to wholesaler. Dreher and ten other Claremont growers formed the Claremont California Fruit Growers Association to serve as their own brokerage firm in dealings with eastern merchandisers.

The first year's return for growers in the "pools" was almost twice that of any past year. Soon other smaller exchanges sprang up. In 1893 a landmark citrus grower's conference was held in the city of Los Angeles. Five men, among them Chamblin and Dreher, were chosen to devise a statewide cooperative. Several months later, 60 growers reconvened to hear the plan for the new cooperative and on August 29, 1893, the Southern California Fruit Exchange (SCFE) was born.

Brand and Marketing Origins

At the turn of the century, people prepared oranges in one way only: they peeled, divided, and ate them. Oranges simply did not appear to lend themselves to baking or inclusion in other dishes as did, say, apples. Yet, early in its history, the SCFE realized it would have to find new uses for its product if it were to remain competitive in the food industry. An early result of this strategy was the design and marketing of a glass hand-reamer to allow consumers to squeeze their own fresh citrus juice. The cooperative made this new product available to the public in 1916 and the "Drink an orange" slogan was born. Years later, the slogan "Best for juice and every use" would be adopted. Such use-oriented campaigns greatly furthered the marketability of oranges.

However, none was to prove nearly as successful as that originated in 1908 by the Lord & Thomas advertising agency (later to become Foote, Cone & Belding). In an effort to accentuate the qualities of California citrus following an "Orange week in Iowa" newspaper ad, an agency copywriter coined the name "Sunkissed." The evocative name stuck, though the spelling was changed shortly thereafter to strengthen the trademark. The steady repetition of the Sunkist name in subsequent advertising campaigns to promote the collective was a revolutionary concept when it began, and soon caught on with other produce marketers. In 1952 the Fruit Exchange voted to rename itself Sunkist Growers (which became Sunkist Growers, Inc., in 1958) to more closely identify with the brand that now appears on 65 percent of the citrus crop produced in California and Arizona.

Packaging and Advertising Innovations

The Sunkist brand name was originally printed on tissue that covered each piece of fruit, with promotional recipes and premiums such as "Orange Blossom" silverware for collectors also prominently featured. In 1925, however, the Sunkist trademark was stamped directly onto the fruit, and innovation soon extended to other areas of marketing. In 1926 the first national radio series began airing from the West Coast, featuring popular movie stars. In later years, Sunkist's sponsorship of nationally televised events became a part of a premium-brand advertising strategy. Surprisingly, however, most of Sunkist's marketing is directed at the retailer, with whom the cooperative has tried to foster a relationship emphasizing both product and service quality.

Despite efforts at diversifying its product line (beginning with its pioneering marketing of bottled orange juice in 1933), Sunkist is first and foremost a marketer of fresh citrus fruit. In 1956, in a variation of its 1916 marketing strategy, Sunkist sold 1,500 commercial electric juicers to the food service industry, and 32,000 household models to consumers. The benefits of fresh over frozen or processed juice were clearly stated in the company's ads. Sunkist was first to mention the importance of vitamins in another national ad campaign, and they funded early research into Vitamin C in an effort to strengthen advertising claims. As a further reflection of the company's desire to educate the public about the benefits of Vitamin C, Sunkist became the first citrus products processor to market frozen concentrated orange juice with nutritional labeling.

Although much of its consumer advertising has been aimed at the orange, Sunkist has also developed successful campaigns for its other products. In 1950 Sunkist Frozen Lemonade was introduced to overwhelmingly favorable response by consumers. The company has also marketed lemons as a garnish for fish and seafood and has promoted the idea of flavoring water with slices of the fruit as a low-cost, low-calorie flavor enhancer, employing the slogan "Three calories a squeeze." As Sunkist entered the 1990s it began to renew efforts at promoting the Sunkist brand name to consumers. The cooperative also began a series of promotional campaigns for new produce bearing the Sunkist name. After the introduction of Minneola tangelos and Kinnow mandarin oranges, Sunkist supported these specialty fruits by offering videos for in-store display to educate consumers, as well as a leaflet with recipes for the new fruits.

"Go Nuts. Get a Cooler" was the slogan behind the promotional campaign to introduce Sunkist's new line of pistachio nuts during the summer of 1992. A Coleman cooler was offered at a discount price with the purchase of one pound of Sunkist Pistachios. At the same time, a traditional product, Sunkist's fresh lemons, was given a new boost through a television commercial depicting lemons as a perfect addition to light summer dining and

through various packaging innovations. Like lemons, grapefruits were also repackaged in five-pound bags and accompanied by the logo "5 a day" to encourage consumption in July, the start of the summer grapefruit season. In the majority of its advertising, the company wisely incorporates the slogan that reflects the quality associated with its brand name: "Sunkist—You have our word on it."

New Products

The demand for citrus fruit, as one might suspect, has extended far beyond the produce aisle. Sunkist Growers, for several decades, has supplied its products to beverage, food, flavor, and fragrance manufacturers around the world. The company's continuing research into new uses for citrus and production byproducts in both food and nonfood items, such as lemon oil for furniture polish, citric acid, and citrus pectin, have helped the cooperative's sales. In the early 1950s Sunkist decided to license its name to other companies, and thereby branched out from the breakfast juice market into soft drinks, then a new industry posting annual sales of $2 million. They attempted a marketing strategy designed to bring their new products, quite literally, to the consumer's door. The Sunkist brand appeared on three new ready-to-drink beverage products: lemonade, fresh orange juice, and orangeade. Distributed by dairies along with the customary milk and cream, the new products quickly became profitable for the company.

In 1951 Sunkist added to their product line again and began producing orange juice in frozen concentrate form. Its initial entry into the frozen concentrate market was late, and the expected brand recognition was not enough to prompt consumers to pay the premium price that Sunkist charged. Florida oranges, Sunkist's major competitor, while less pleasing to the eye than the more expensive California naval orange, are the most suitable type of orange for frozen juice, and the lower production costs afford the Florida orange growers an additional edge.

Despite Sunkist's efforts at touting the benefits of fresh juice over its frozen counterpart, by the 1970s the frozen concentrate market had overtaken that of fresh fruit. The California cooperative decided to retaliate against Florida growers in 1972 by reserving the bulk of its advertising budget for television ads designed to increase the purchase of oranges as a natural, healthy snack. "The good Lord made oranges, and we do an absolute minimum to them," *Business Week* quoted a Sunkist executive as saying. In support of this statement, the company designed a series of 60-second commercials featuring its growers. Yet, by the fall of the following year, Sunkist decided that it was fighting a losing battle.

In 1990 Sunkist introduced Sunkist Grapefruit Juice and Juice Cocktail, and expanded its line of frozen concentrate juices to include grapefruit. 1992 saw the introduction of Sunkist Freshly Peeled Citrus, marketed to the institutional food trade.

Agriculture in Southern California

California and Arizona are among the world's finest areas for the cultivation of citrus. Yet, weather has proved to be the one factor that agricultural scientists have been unable to control, and it has caused severe losses throughout Sunkist's century of operation. Disaster struck during the Christmas season in 1990 when temperatures plummeted to below-normal levels in areas where much of Sunkist's orange crop was cultivated. The worst freeze on record for California's citrus-producing region damaged more than half the orange crop for that year; almost 50 percent of the fruit was destroyed. The cost of navel oranges to wholesalers soon doubled. Fortunately, farmers combatted the low temperatures with water, heaters, and wind machines to save the trees on which the fruit had failed.

By the following spring, crop levels again approached normal, and after heavily advertising the return of oranges to the stores, sales followed suit. The 1992/1993 navel orange crop turned out to be the largest in Sunkist's history, and the quantity of the new fruit compensated for the unusually small oranges produced by the recovering trees.

Crop fluctuations have caused other problems from a marketing standpoint. For example, 1992's valencia orange crop matured early in California and resulted in a greenish cast to the orange skin. "Regreening" happens when a mature orange is allowed to stay on the tree, and is normal with summer oranges. "The regreening creates retailer problems because consumers think the green-tinged fruit is not ripe," Sunkist's consumer affairs manager told Lisa Saxton of *Supermarket News*. The cooperative designed a TV commercial to explain the regreening process to consumers, and designed a point-of-sale card to aid supermarket retailers in counteracting consumer shyness. These measures, combined with offering consumers a taste of the off-colored fruit, allowed the season to pass without a dip in valencia orange sales.

Brand Name Licensing

Oranges, lemons, and grapefruit are but a few of the products that carry the Sunkist brand name. In the early 1960s Sunkist began licensing its trademark to other companies, and the brand now appears on everything from children's vitamins and candies to fruit snacks and soda pop. However, the company limits the products it allows to bear the Sunkist brand to three basic categories: beverages, other food-related items, and wellness products. 1992 royalties from such products yielded $12 million for the cooperative on consolidated licensed sales in excess of $1.1 billion.

"People immediately associate 'Sunkist' with summer's attributes," a representative of Cadbury Schweppes told Cara S. Trager in *Beverage World*. Cadbury Schweppes purchased the licensing rights for Sunkist Orange Soda from former owner General Cinema, confident that their strong national marketing network could more effectively bring the citrus-flavored soft drink to public notice. The Sunkist Vitamin C tablets, produced by Ceiba-Geigy Pharmaceuticals, was so successful that Sunkist has actively sought other health-related products on which to place its name. The Thomas J. Lipton Company, purveyors of the well-known Lipton tea, put the Sunkist brand on their own line of juice drinks, juice bars, frozen desert items, as well as the popular Sunkist Fun Fruits, a line of fruit snacks for children. "Licensing supports the core branded fresh-fruit business by allowing us to take the Sunkist message to the consumer all year round," Sunkist's manager of licensed products told Lori Kesler of *Advertising Age*. Such products as Sunkist Orange Soda have indeed taken the Sunkist brand far from the produce aisle. The Sunkist brand is now licensed for use on more than 400 products and can be found in 30 countries.

Sunny Future?

Despite the damage to crops by frost in 1990, Sunkist set new sales records for that year, posting revenues of $931 million. Diversification into real estate, electronic packers, electronic grading systems, and other areas have also accounted for some of the cooperative's profits, as well as the lucrative licensing of its brand name. Even with a stable financial picture, Sunkist continues to look for ways to expand its product line. "We're searching for new things to offer to the consumer," Sunkist Vice-President Curtis W. Anderson told Marc Millstein in *Supermarket News*. "We're seeking other new product lines to concentrate on. It's a way of using our expertise and manpower to reach a growing segment of consumers." Sunkist has entertained no thoughts of abandoning its traditional base as a seller of fresh produce, however. In the past several years the company has expanded into grapes and other varieties of citrus. The market for specialty citrus such as Kinnow and Minneola oranges is growing, and other increasingly popular citrus varieties include the Orlando Tangelo and the Pomello, an expensive fruit from China that is about the size of a soccer ball and has a sweet, unusual flavor. Sunkist is expanding its product line to meet consumer requests.

Unfortunately, Sunkist's recent defeat in the legal battle to continue volume restrictions in the navel orange market has left them in a precarious position. From 1937, the year in which the U.S. Congress passed the Agricultural Marketing Agreement (AMA), until the early 1990s, Sunkist and other large cooperatives have enjoyed almost unchallenged control over production and marketing quotas within their niche industries. "Suspending the marketing orders was a case of fixing a system that wasn't broken, and growers will pay for it with lost revenue," a Sunkist representative told Guy Gugliotta in the *Washington Post*. Further problems include corporate infighting that has led to a lawsuit by company director Berne Evans, which alleges that a cover-up existed within the company. In 1992 four other lawsuits were filed accusing Sunkist of violating quotas in the late 1980s on the sale of lemons established by the AMA. While the results of the lawsuits are still forthcoming, such litigation could place the citrus giant's reputation in jeopardy, according to Don Lee of the *Los Angeles Times*. In *Business Week*, Amy Barrett declared that "Sunkist's image has been battered, and its members say they're disgusted with the controversy."

To make matters worse, Sunkist has also been the target of increasing international competition. Grapes, peaches, plums, strawberries, and oranges have begun arriving from Spain, Morocco, Brazil, Chile, and Israel to compete for sales traditionally garnered by domestic producers. By 1987, Sunkist's share of the fresh citrus fruit market had fallen from a high of 75 percent in 1970 to just 62 percent (its share of navels alone fell from 72 to 49 percent in the same period). At the same time, the number of growers in the Sunkist cooperative has been decreasing.

Although the Sunkist brand has always commanded a premium price in grocery stores, many growers began selling at least a portion of their crop to independent packers to help offset expenses. Considering the turmoil currently underway in the California citrus industry, one cannot help but wonder at the future of the Sunkist brand. Yet, with the popularity it has built up over a century in the public eye, Sunkist may well be a trademark that has, like Kleenex and Q-tips, irrevocably evolved into a consumer staple whose success is independent of the business that created it decades ago.

Further Reading:

"Ade on Wheels," *Business Week,* February 14, 1953, p. 73.

Barrett, Amy, "Something Shady at Sunkist?," *Business Week,* May 17, 1993, p. 40.

Brown, Paul B., "Technology Isn't Everything," *Forbes,* October 12, 1981, pp. 55-57.

"Despite Difficulties, Sunkist Established New High Last Year," *Los Angeles Business Journal,* February 12, 1990, p. 12.

"End of the Citrus Cartel" (editorial), *Wall Street Journal,* December 15, 1992, p. A18.

"Florida Squeezes Sunkist," *Business Week,* August 18, 1973, pp. 84-85.

Glover, Kara, "Sunkist Assessing Damage from Crop-Killer Freeze," *Los Angeles Business Journal,* January 7, 1991, p. 3.

Gugliotta, Guy, "Orange Growers in a Policy Squeeze," *Washington Post,* December 21, 1992, p. A19.

Gugliotta, "USDA Cleared to Lift Orange Sales Quotas," *Washington Post,* December 30, 1992, p. A3.

Kesler, Lori, "Wider Market Awareness a Tempting Enticement," *Advertising Age,* June 1, 1987, pp. S2, S4.

Kiley, David, "VegiSnax Is Ready to Roll This Spring with Sunkist Signed up as Distributor," *Adweek's Marketing Week,* February 12, 1990, p. 35.

King, Ralph T., Jr., "Sunkist Could Be Sunk in Navel Battle, But Consumers Could Win Lower Prices," *Wall Street Journal,* March 18, 1993, p. A2.

Koenig, Richard, "Sunkist to Market New Produce Bred by Du Pont, DNA," *Wall Street Journal,* January 24, 1990, p. B4.

Lee, Don, "Lawsuits Threaten to Sour Image of Sunkist Growers," *Los Angeles Times,* September 29, 1992, pp. D1, D7.

Mejia, John, "Sunkist to Handle Sales of VegiSnax," *Supermarket News,* February 5, 1990, p. 12.

Millstein, Marc, "Sunkist Sees Growth Ahead for Value-Added Products," *Supermarket News,* July 9, 1990, p. 29.

Paris, Ellen, "Sunset in the Groves," *Forbes,* March 23, 1987, pp. 35-36.

Processed Citrus Product from Sunkist Growers, Inc.: A World of Difference, Sherman Oaks, CA: Sunkist Growers, Inc., 1985.

"Pyramid in the Sun," *Time,* November 16, 1953, pp. 102, 104-05.

Ramey, Joanna, "Orange Quotas Pit Sunkist, FAIR in Navel Confrontation," *Supermarket News,* January 13, 1992, p. 40.

Saxton, Lisa, "Sunkist to Offer Peeled Citrus Packs to Clubs," *Supermarket News,* December 31, 1990, p. 18.

Saxton, "Specialty Citrus' Peel Gains Appeal," *Supermarket News,* February 3, 1992, p. 32.

Saxton, "Greenish Oranges Pose Challenge," *Supermarket News,* August 31, 1992, p. 41.

Stroud, Ruth, "Sunkist a Pioneer in New Products, Promotions," *Advertising Age,* November 9, 1988, pp. 22, 140.

"Sunkist 'Goes Nuts' with Promotion," *Supermarket News,* June 8, 1992, p. 36.

Sunkist Growers, Inc., Annual Report, Sherman Oaks, CA: Sunkist Growers, Inc., 1992.

"Sunkist Offers New Fruit Bag," *Supermarket News,* July 6, 1992, p. 32.

"Sunkist Offers Two New Videos, *Supermarket News,* February 3, 1992, p. 30.

"Sunkist Oranges Blossom on TV," *Business Week,* December 23, 1972, p. 23.

"Sunkist Promoting Fresh Lemons," *Supermarket News,* June 29, 1992, p. 50.

"Sunkist's Strategy," *Business Week,* June 1, 1957, p. 160.

"Sunkist Unbottles Juices," *Advertising Age,* August 29, 1991, p. 23.

"Sunset in the Groves," *Forbes,* July 25, 1988, p. 10.

"The Revolution of 1893," *Sunkist Magazine,* August/September 1988, pp. 1, 10-12.

Tobenkin, David, "Sunkist: Citrus Co-op Keeps the Juices Flowing," *Los Angeles Business Journal,* February 5, 1990, pp. 16-17.

Trager, Cara S., "Let the Sunshine In," *Beverage World,* October 1990, pp. 74, 76, 78, 104.

Walters, Donna K. H., "Growers to Appeal Halt on Lifting Quotas," *Los Angeles Times,* December 23, 1992, p. D2.

Watanabe, Teresa, "Sunkist Squeezing out Higher Sales in Japan," *Los Angeles Times,* March 25, 1991, p. D3.

—Jay P. Pederson

SUN-MAID®

The Sun-Maid raisin brand is one of the most durable and recognizable trademarks in the world. Created in 1915, Sun-Maid brandishes one of the few brand designs that has survived the twentieth century almost unchanged. Although 75 percent of Sun-Maid raisins are consumed in the United States and Canada, the branded product, owned by Sun-Maid Growers of California, is sold in more than 25 countries around the world, with packaging produced in 9 different languages. Sun-Maid's groundbreaking sales efforts have benefitted the entire raisin industry by raising consumer awareness and thereby opening new markets for California's dried fruit products.

Brand Origins

The Sun-Maid story began more than 80 years ago with a raisin growers' cooperative created to manage raisin sales and initiate assertive marketing programs to encourage raisin consumption. The basic organization, California Associated Raisin Company, has remained constant since its foundation in 1912. It has been owned and managed by its grower-members who agreed to sell their produce exclusively through the co-op. The arrangement stipulated that, rather than receiving a lump sum payment for their crop, the co-op members were paid in installments throughout each year. The growers were "shareholders" in the packing and distribution organization, and upon the completion of selling a particular crop, any profits generated were distributed to the growers.

Under optimal circumstances, the cooperative's payments were higher than what an independent grower would earn. As an added benefit, the cooperative provided a home for member-growers' crops, and guaranteed that their harvests would not be turned down due to oversupply or other market-related conditions.

Early Marketing Strategies

In search of a brand name for its product, California Associated Raisin's in-house advertising department first floated the Bear Brand as a raisin identity, then developed a "Sun-Made" logo with a sunburst in reference to the sun's influence on the raisin-making process. Even into the 1990s, 97 percent of Sun-Maid's raisins were naturally sun-dried.

Associated Raisin's first campaign, in 1914, centered around a 60-car freight train that carried Associated raisins to Chicago,

Illinois. Banners emblazoned with "Raisins Grown by 6,000 California Growers" graced each car. The campaign constituted the first advertisement using the Sun-Made trade name, and featured a free recipe book for consumers.

The First Sun-*Maid*

With many young women working throughout Associated Raisin's processing and packaging plant, the play on words seemed all too obvious. The change to Sun-Maid was simple, but it lacked a distinguishing image. The cooperative needed a real Sun-Maid, and found her in Lorraine Collett.

Collett was working in Fresno, California, packing raisins when she was asked to join two other young women for a Sun-Maid promotion at the Panama-Pacific International Exposition in San Francisco. The attractive, black-haired girl and her co-workers wore the traditional uniform of packing house employees—white blouses trimmed in blue and matching blue bonnets—as they walked about the fairgrounds passing out raisin samples. Each afternoon, Collett was flown over the Exposition crowd dropping raisins on the fair-goers.

One Sunday morning during the Exposition, Collett returned to Fresno to take part in the annual Raisin Day Parade. She put on her favorite red bonnet while she waited for the parade to begin. Before she could change into the familiar blue hat, Collett was joined by Leroy Payne, an Associated Raisin executive. Payne was struck by the way the red bonnet flattered the young woman and asked all of the "Sun-Maids" to wear that color for the remainder of the Exposition.

Upon returning to the Exposition, Collett was asked to pose for the Sun-Maid trademark. San Francisco artist Fanny Scafford tried several poses of Collett before finally settling on a scene with the Sun-Maid in front of a radiant sunburst and holding a wicker tray overflowing with green grapes. Scafford's final painting was then displayed at the Exposition's horticulture building and later presented to Collett.

When first transformed into packaging, the design featured a blue background with white lettering for Sun-Maid's traditional raisin variety, Muscats. The Muscats, which had seeds, went through a seed removal process that left a sticky, but sweet raisin. In the 1990s these large, sweet raisins were still used for baking,

AT A GLANCE

Sun-Maid brand created in 1915 by raisin cooperative formed in 1912 in California's San Joaquin Valley; the cooperative, originally named California Associated Raisin Company, changed its name to Sun-Maid Raisin Growers, 1922, and later to Sun-Maid Growers of California; company owns and operates the largest raisin processing and packing facility in the world.

Performance: *Market share*—50% of raisin category. *Sales*—$181.75 million.

Major competitor: Dole Food Company, Inc.'s Sun Giant (15% market share).

Advertising: *Agency*—Grey Advertising, Los Angeles, CA, 1989—. *Major campaign*—"Rise and Shine."

Addresses: *Parent company*—Sun-Maid Growers of California, 13525 South Bethel Ave., Kingsburg, CA 93631-9232; phone: (209) 896-8000; fax: (209) 897-2362.

and seeded Muscats were still available in the blue box. The color scheme of the box was varied so that each raisin type was designated by the background color.

After the Thompson Seedless grape was introduced to California growers, it quickly became the primary variety of Sun-Maid vineyards, constituting 95 percent of production. Always the most abundant type of raisins under the Sun-Maid brand, Thompson Seedless boxes were given the now-familiar red background. The raisins came to be processed into special varieties, including natural seedless select, natural seedless midgets, and cereal-size (which are coated with sugar). Some Thompson Seedless are chemically processed to produce golden fancy and extra choice raisins for fruit cakes and confections. Zante Currants, a traditional ingredient in hot cross buns, are made from Black Corinth grapes, and come in a bright orange box. It is said that the many-colored boxes make for striking grocery displays.

First Commercial Success

The success of the new trademark was evidenced by raisin sales that grew markedly until about 1920, bringing profits to co-op members. By the outbreak of World War I, California raisin production had more than doubled, and Sun-Maid raisins achieved international distribution as early as 1917. By 1918, more than 85 percent of California's raisin growers were members of the California Associated Raisin Company. In 1922 the cooperative changed its name to Sun-Maid Raisin Growers to identify more closely with its nationally recognized brand.

Raisin advertisements of the 1920s capitalized on the decade's emphasis on youth and beauty. The introduction of the 1.5-ounce box encouraged healthy snacking, and advertising was expanded to print media and billboards. That decade, Sun-Maid commissioned the popular artist Norman Rockwell to create scenes for print ads. His paintings always included the familiar Sun-Maid. Over the course of the decade, Sun-Maid spent more than $16 million on promotion, a sum that helped establish the cooperative's product as "America's Favorite Raisin."

Brand Development

By the onset of the Great Depression, huge raisin crops left the cooperative with excess raisin inventories. Sun-Maid joined other industry leaders in a call for the creation of the Agriculture Marketing Adjustment Act of 1937 under the auspices of the United States Department of Agriculture. The economic havoc of the 1930s and near financial collapse prompted Sun-Maid to reduce its advertising. During the 1940s, though, raisins became part of the World War II soldier's diet for high energy, and demand exceeded production throughout the war years.

In the 1950s some multi-purpose advertisements were used in magazines and for in-store displays. Sun-Maid also embraced radio advertising in the 1950s and 1960s. Arthur Godfrey, a popular radio personality, plugged Sun-Maid raisins over the radio and on television.

Around this time, marketers tampered with the tried-and-true Sun-Maid image by creating a two-tone box, but switched back to the all-red box in the late 1960s. Artists and advertising directors have made slight changes in the renderings of the Sun-Maid over the years, but she's essentially the same as she was when first created.

Intra-Brand Cooperation

In the mid-1950s Sun-Maid began to foster a relationship with other dried fruit producers in California. In 1955 Sun-Maid and Sunsweet branded products were represented by the same broker, and were featured together in print and grocery advertisements. The partnership saved the two cooperatives advertising costs, and was the beginning of a relationship that continued into the 1990s.

In 1980 Sun-Maid provided the impetus for a cooperative sales organization to market the produce of Diamond Walnut Growers, Sunsweet Growers, and Valley Fig Growers. The resulting group, Sun-Diamond Growers, supplied marketing, sales, and distribution expertise for a full line of dried fruits and nuts.

Sun-Maid undertook licensing contracts with several bakeries in the early 1980s. The agreements gave bakeries and dairies permission to use the brand name on raisin bread, English muffins, and even raisin ice cream. Cross-couponing—offering cents off of one product when another is purchased—among Sun-Diamond's members encouraged consumers to buy more than one of the group's products at a time.

Despite these successful efforts, alleged unfair practices within the European Community's wine and raisin trade in the early 1980s dealt a sudden economic blow to the California raisin industry; revenue to California growers was reduced, as were raisin export sales. While California growers endured economic hardship through this period, by the mid-1980s better days were on the horizon for the industry and Sun-Maid.

A New Era of Raisin Advertising

In 1986 the California Raisin Advisory Board introduced its successful "dancing raisin" campaign. The independent board's first advertisement, created by Foote, Cone & Belding, featured Claymation raisins in sunglasses and sneakers. The series of advertisements, and the raisin characters themselves, constituted one of the most successful promotional campaigns of the decade: in just one year, more than $400 million worth of raisin paraphernalia was sold.

In 1987 Sun-Maid adapted the spot for use in the United Kingdom by adding a box of branded raisins to the ad's conga line of "finger-snapping, hip raisins." It was hoped that the television advertisement would help Sun-Maid—the only California raisin sold in the United Kingdom—increase its 15 percent market share there. At the time, 47 percent of the country's raisin sales went to supermarket brands, making Sun-Maid the largest single brand in the country.

Sun-Maid launched its biggest advertising effort to date in the fall of 1988 in conjunction with a 30-minute television special, "Meet the Raisins," designed to capitalize on the now-famous California dancing raisins. Sun-Maid's spots had three Claymation raisins serenading the Sun-Maid, who was brought to life in clay. Extensive print advertisements also promoted the campaign theme "Sun-Maid. America's Favorite Raisin." Normart Advertising of Fresno prepared the television ads, and D'Arcy Masius Benton & Bowles of San Francisco created the print ads.

Sun-Maid began to define and target specific groups for promotional efforts in the 1990s. Segmentation studies led to successful campaigns directed at Jewish and Hispanic consumers. As minority groups in America continued to grow in numbers and market influence, Sun-Maid planned to continue offering specialized advertising.

A Sunny Future

Growing consumer interest in a healthy, fat-free diet has raised hopes for increased raisin consumption in the early 1990s. In 1991 the U.S. Department of Agriculture's Human Nutrition Information Service announced its new Food Pyramid Guidelines to encourage increased consumption of cereals, fruits, and vegetables. As one of the most concentrated fruit sources, raisins have been promoted as an easy way to comply with the new guidelines: just one ounce of raisins is the equivalent of a full serving of fresh fruit.

Also in the early 1990s, with heightened interest in ecologically friendly products, Sun-Maid pursued making raisin packaging recyclable. To that end, the cooperative converted its 15-ounce bag-in-the-box to recycled cardboard, and introduced an environmentally friendly six-pack display case.

To attest to the brand's enduring popularity, Sun-Maid entered the *Guinness Book of Records* in 1992 when students from California State University at Fresno constructed a twelve-foot-tall raisin box filled with more than eight tons of raisins to honor the cooperative's 80th anniversary. The Sun-Maid brand continues to prove more valuable than ever, having laid a firm foundation for future growth. Consumer buying trends place it—and the raisin industry it helped found and promote—in good stead.

Further Reading:

The Brands, Stockton, CA: Sun-Diamond Growers of California.

Cuneo, Alice Z., "Sun-Maid, Dole Boost Raisins," *Advertising Age,* October 10, 1988, p. 44.

Goble, Ron, "Sentimental Journey," *Sun-Diamond Grower,* spring 1992, pp. 6-7, 21.

Paris, Ellen, "Growing Pains," *Forbes,* June 30, 1986, p. 92.

Tanasychuk, John, "Calling All Raisins," *Detroit Free Press,* August 12, 1992.

Wentz, Laurel, "Raisins Dance in U.K. to Promote Sun-Maid," *Advertising Age,* July 27, 1987, p. 4.

"What Makes Sun-Diamond Grow," *Business Week,* August 9, 1982, p. 83.

The World's Favorite Raisin, Kingsburg, CA: Sun-Maid Growers of California, 1989.

—April S. Dougal

SUTTER HOME®

Sutter Home wines, most famous in the blush-colored white zinfandel variety, are the top-selling premium wines in the United States. The Sutter Home Winery, Inc., introduced its brands of cabernet sauvignon, sauvignon blanc, and chenin blanc in 1987, quickly becoming a top-five selling brand of each of these varietal wines (wines made from one specific grape variety). In the early 1990s the winery was also the largest red zinfandel producer. The company's most outstanding success story, however, remained its Sutter Home white zinfandel.

Brand Origins

The story of the Sutter Home Winery is a distilled version of the melting-pot origins of America. In 1874 a Swiss-German immigrant named John Thomann founded a small winery in the Napa Valley in California. After his death in 1900, the Leuenberger family of Swiss immigrants who had already established the Sutter Home brand name at a different winery, bought his estate and called it Sutter Home, after Lina Leuenberger's father, John Sutter. John and Mario Trinchero, brothers whose family owned a wine business in their native Italy, bought Sutter Home in 1947 and began production of a diverse array of Napa Valley wines under the motto, "A great product for a fair price."

In the late 1960s and early 1970s, the three successors to the Trinchero brothers—all children of Mario Trinchero—introduced the change in production from generic wines to premium varietal wines. After tasting a homemade zinfandel produced from grapes grown in the Sierra foothills in 1968, Bob Trinchero began producing Amador County Zinfandel. This move distinguished Sutter Home as the first post-Prohibition North American winery to produce a commercial wine from Sierra foothill grapes.

Brand Development

Sutter Home produced its red 1968 Amador County zinfandel from 85-year-old vines grown at the Deaver Ranch in the Shenandoah Valley. The new wine renewed enthusiasm in the winemaking potential of the Sierra foothill region and reawakened the taste for the zinfandel grape. In 1972, almost by accident, Bob Trinchero created what was to become the trademark wine of Sutter Home. Seeking a way to make the red Amador zinfandel more robust, he drew off some of the free-run juice immediately after the crushing of the grapes to increase the ratio of the skins that give a red wine most of its color and body. On the side, he fermented the extra juice to produce a "white" wine, actually pale pink in color. First called Oeil de Pedrix (Eye of the Partridge), the new wine had a lighter body and more delicate flavor than the "normal" red zinfandel, and it made a big splash with clients in the tasting room.

After customers complimented the wine's fruitiness, Trinchero decided to refine the wine by leaving in small amounts of residual sugar to bring out its fruity qualities. While wine critics dismissed the wine as insipid and too sweet, the public loved it. Production went from 25,000 cases in 1981 to 850,000 in 1985. In 1987 Sutter Home white zinfandel became the top-selling premium wine in the United States. Because this wine was easy to produce and needed little aging, profits poured in soon after harvest. The quick cash-flow potential of the product encouraged a host of emulations by other wineries. But Sutter Home's white zinfandel remained at the top of the heap; in 1989 Sutter Home sold 2.9 million cases of its star wine.

White zinfandel became popular in the early 1980s, because the wine was sweet, visually appealing, refreshing—and not very expensive. According to Lawrence M. Fisher in the *New York Times,* "While most of its neighbors were striving to prove that California cabernets could beat the best Bordeaux in blind tastings, the Trinchero family of Sutter Home was happy to show that white zinfandel could stand up to beer with a barbecue." White zinfandel also gained some customers in the American market partly because the wine had a low alcohol content and appealed to American consumers drenched in campaigns for responsible alcohol consumption.

Other Sutter Varietals

Because Sutter Home's white zinfandel became so popular and because other wineries had staked out territory in the Napa Valley, in the early 1980s the winery faced the challenge of assuring its future grape supply. The Trinchero family purchased a 300-acre vineyard in 1984 in Lake County, an area to the northeast of Napa Valley. While the original idea was to cultivate zinfandel grapes there, the quality of the varieties already growing in the vineyard's soil convinced Sutter Home to expand its range of premium varietal wines to include chenin blanc, sauvignon blanc, and cabernet sauvignon. Each of these Sutter Home wines was eventually among the best sellers in its varietal category.

AT A GLANCE

Sutter Home brand name founded in 1890 by the Swiss Leuenberger family; wine produced at the former John Thomann Winery and Distillery, founded in 1874 in California's Napa Valley by the Swiss-German immigrant John Thomann; bought by Leuenberger family in 1906; Sutter Home Winery purchased in 1947 by the Italian immigrant brothers John and Mario Trinchero.

Performance: *Market share*—9.2 percent (top share) of U.S. premium varietal wine category. *Sales*—$215 million.

Major competitor: Gallo; also Glen Ellen, Robert Modavi, and Sebastiani.

Advertising: *Agency*—Goldberg Moser O'Neill, San Francisco, CA, 1988—. *Major campaign*—Five full-color ads in 16 major national publications focusing on varieties within food groups, including pasta, mushrooms, and peppers; after a humorous paragraph explaining how to use the food is a photo of a Sutter Home Wine that "goes well."

Addresses: *Parent company*—Sutter Home Winery, Inc., Box 248, St. Helena, CA 94574; phone: (707) 963-3104; fax: (707) 963 2381.

Another force, the rising tide of "fighting varietals" on the American wine-market scene, was probably behind the company's decision to expand its product range. While varietal wines were historically top-of-the-line products, premium wines that sold in a lower price range mounted a challenge. Frank J. Prial of the *New York Times* noted that fighting varietals "made good wine accessible to almost everyone and they raised the standards of inexpensive wine forever." These wines hit America's shelves in full force after acres of grapes planted in California during the 1970s were harvested in the mid-1980s, just when wine consumption in America began to decrease. The Glen Ellen winery was the first to use these excess premium grapes to put out low-priced cabernet and chardonnay wines. Other wineries—including Sutter Home—jumped into the fray.

The Sutter Home name continued to be most closely associated with white wines into the 1990s. By 1992 Sutter Home white wines included a chenin blanc, sauvignon blanc, chardonnay, and muscat Alexandria. All were produced with the broad American market in mind; instead of being dry, they were fruity and crisp. The winery described its chenin blanc as a "light, fruity white wine" with a "floral aroma redolent of fresh-cut melons, and juicy flavors suggesting melons, peaches and apricots." The Sutter Home chardonnay, introduced in fall of 1990, attempted "fresh, well-defined appley aromas and crisp, fruity flavors." Because the word "chardonnay" had become synonymous with white wine in America, the company was once again catering carefully to the tastes of the American consumer. According to Anthony Roe of the *Independent,* chardonnay had become "the sophisticated way of weaning the U.S. public off Coke and iced tea."

In an attempt to stay closely attuned to consumer tastes and desires, in October of 1992 Sutter Home became the first U.S. winemaker to offer nonalcoholic wine, in the form of de-alcoholized versions of its white zinfandel and chardonnay varieties. Seeking to win over pregnant women, dieters, designated drivers, business luncheners, those who opposed alcohol on religious

grounds, and others, Sutter Home imported a "spinning cone column" production method from Australia to extract the wine's alcohol.

Sutter Home Reds

In the red-wine category, Sutter Home produced only full-bodied zinfandels from 1968 to 1977. In response to the requests of restaurateurs for lighter-bodied wines that appealed to the tastes of their typical customers, Sutter Home began producing two types of its red zinfandel in 1980: "old-style" Deaver Ranch wine, rechristened Amador County Reserve zinfandel; and a lighter-bodied wine called California zinfandel, produced from grapes grown both in northern-California-coast vineyards and in the Sierra foothills.

For the Amador County Reserve zinfandel, the winery continued to use only grapes grown on the Deaver Ranch in the Shenandoah Valley, and aimed for "berry-spice aromas and flavors typical of the finest Sierra foothill red wines." Grapes for this wine were harvested at the end of the season to give the wine a full flavor; the wine's aging lasted up to 18 months in 135-gallon oak puncheons. Sutter Home also became a leading producer of cabernet sauvignon, describing its brand of the varietal as "a smooth, fruity red wine with round, forward flavors, mild tannins, and the accent of French oak aging."

Finally, the winery introduced a light red wine called Soleo in 1991, made from a combination of zinfandel, barbera, pinot noir and Napa gamay. Sutter Home described it as "light, fruity, easy-drinking wine tailored to those consumers who find most red wines too heavy." In the first three months of 1992, the winery claimed to have sold out of 250,000 cases of the new wine. One factor thought responsible for the product's quick success was the November 1991 airing of a *60 Minutes* documentary called "The French Paradox." The show linked lower rates of heart disease in France to the consumption of red wine; health-conscious, heart-disease-prone America pricked up its ears—and pulled out its wallet.

Continued Land Acquisitions

In 1986, two years after its first vineyard purchase, Sutter Home bought a 640-acre vineyard near the Sacramento Valley town of Artois, in Glenn County. The vineyard originally cultivated various black grape varieties, but Sutter Home grafted about a third of the land to zinfandel. In 1988 the winery purchased another 1200 acres, located near the Sacramento Valley town of Arbuckle, in Colusa County. Bought as bare land, the plot was planted with a clone of the zinfandel grape especially suited to producing white zinfandel wine.

Other land purchases by the winery included the 1989 acquisition of 600 acres of uncultivated land in the Sacramento Delta, eventually used to grow chardonnay and cabernet sauvignon grapes. In 1991 Sutter Home purchased 1,000 acres in Santa Barbara County with the intention of planting it entirely with chardonnay grapes. By the beginning of the 1990s, Sutter Home had purchased a total of 3,500 vineyard acres. The original Thomann winery was still in operation in the 1990s and continued to house Sutter Home's offices and tasting room. Most production, shipping, and warehousing were moved to better-equipped facilities also located in the Napa Valley.

Advertising and Packaging Innovations

In 1989 Sutter Home introduced the classic single, a 187-milliliter single serving of white zinfandel, sauvignon blanc, cabernet sauvignon, and chardonnay. The bottle was from an upscale, Bordeaux-style mold; thus it appealed not just to airline and cold-box buyers, but to demanding wine consumers determined to drink in moderation but wishing to avoid wasting undrunk wine in the process. In addition, the new packaging gave restaurant and bar owners many advantages: a classy alternative to standard house wines poured from a jug, easier inventory control, reduced spoilage, and easier handling. In 1990 sales of the classic single topped one million cases.

Also in 1989, *Advertising Age* chose Sutter Home's radio commercial "Gorbachev" as a finalist in the magazine's competition for best radio commercial of 1988. The ad offered humorous advice on what to do when Gorbachev pops in for a visit. Another attention-getting promotional strategy was the 1990 "build a better burger" recipe contest. The winery offered a grand prize of $10,000 for the best original, previously unpublished recipe with ingredients and condiments that "fit into a bun."

Performance Appraisal

In 1980 Sutter Home's total sales were 34,000 cases. The wild success of its white zinfandel shot sales up to 3.7 million cases by 1989. Even after producers of the white zinfandel varietal numbered a fiercely competitive 120 wineries in 1990, Sutter Home maintained a market share of 28.4 percent, or nearly three times the share of Beringer, the second-place producer. Sutter Home was the only winemaker whose retail sales topped $200 million in 1990; it was also the only fighting varietal brand among the top five producers. The company's dollar sales performance was particularly impressive since Sutter Home placed only twelfth in unit volume sales.

Savvy marketing techniques were in part responsible. For wine-selling supermarkets, for example, the company provided display materials that encouraged managers to put Sutter Home wines in meat, produce and cheese departments, where customers are more prone to succumb to impulse buying. Sutter Home distributed a display for its "build a better burger" campaign to be used for stacks of ketchup, mayonnaise—and red and white zinfandel posing as necessary hamburger accessories. As a result of Sutter Home's marketing efforts, the company's production reached 4 million cases by 1990.

Future Growth

At the start of the 1990s, jug wine and coolers had lost some popularity. In 1991 wine consumption in the United States, sobered by a recession, was down by roughly three percent. "Generic" wines such as Carlo Rossi, Gallo, Almaden, and Inglenook took a steep downhill slide; premium, mid-priced wines or "superbrands" gained momentum. In the 1990s, Sutter Home promised continued commitment to high-quality varietal wines at accessible prices—exactly the kind of wines that passed marketing muster as the decade began. This winery, steeped in American marketing traditions and keen to please American tastes, seemed to follow a secondary company credo that could be worded, "Give the public what it wants." The American public, even in a cost-conscious, health-conscious, morality-conscious era, continued to want Sutter Home wines.

Further Reading:

Berger, Dan, "The Wine List," *Los Angeles Times Magazine,* October 20, 1991, p. 46.

"Best of '88," *Advertising Age,* April 3, 1989, p. 42.

"Big Wineries Begin Phasing Chemicals Out of Vineyards," *Business Journal—Sacramento,* October 12, 1992, p. 4.

Bird, Laura, "Losing Ground, Vintners Till New Soil," *Adweek's Marketing Week,* p. 60.

Boyd, Gerald D., "A Look at Quaffable White Zinfandels," *San Francisco Chronicle,* September 4, 1991, p. 7/ZZ5.

A Brief History of Sutter Home Winery, St. Helena, California: Sutter Home Winery, Inc., 1992.

A "Classic" Idea, St. Helena, California: Sutter Home Winery, Inc., 1992.

Ellis, Leslie, "Buying Power," *Gannet News Service,* September 4, 1992.

Fisher, Lawrence M., "A Clink Heard Round the Valley," *New York Times,* September 1, 1990.

Fisher, Lawrence M., "Organic Wines Enter the Mainstream," *New York Times,* November 19, 1991.

Hochstein, Mort, "Home 'fre' [sic] Sutter Winery Uncorks Non-Alcoholic Duo," *Nation's Restaurant News,* October 26, 1992.

Lonsford, Michael, "Save Your Money: Sutter Home Offers Inexpensive, Balanced Zin," *Houston Chronicle,* May 13, 1992, p. 12.

Lonsford, Michael, "DuBoeuf Beaujolais Is Fine Now—or Later," *Houston Chronicle,* p. 2.

Martin, Glen, "New Refuge Could Be a Winner," *San Francisco Chronicle,* March 25, 1991, p. C11.

Martin, Glen, "Winemakers Might Sink Refuge Plan," *San Francisco Chronicle,* December 3, 1990, p. E1.

Prial, Frank J., "Flights of Chardonnay," *New York Times,* July 28, 1991, section 6, p. 42.

Prial, Frank J., "Wine Talk," *New York Times,* April 18, 1990, p. C9.

Prial, Frank J., "Wine Talk," *New York Times,* January 10, 1990, p. C12.

Rice, William, "Add These 2 Novel Events," *Chicago Tribune,* June 28, 1990, p. C4.

Roe, Anthony, "Food & Drink: America's ABC—Anything But Chardonnay," *The Independent,* July 25, 1992, p. 739.

Seligmann, Jean, "Zinfandel Without the Zing," *Newsweek,* September 28, 1992, p. 37.

"Soleo Act," *Beverage World,* April 1992, p. 22.

"Sutter Home Is No. 1 U.S. Premium Wine Brand in Retail Dollar Sales," *PR Newswire,* November 5, 1992.

"Sutter Home Is No. 1 U.S. Wine Brand in Retail Dollar Sales," *PR Newswire,* October 11, 1991.

Sutter Home Red Wines, St. Helena, California: Sutter Home Winery, Inc., 1992.

Sutter Home Vineyards, St. Helena, California: Sutter Home Winery, Inc., 1992.

Sutter Home White Wines, St. Helena, California: Sutter Home Winery, Inc., 1992.

Sutter Home White Zinfandel, St. Helena, California: Sutter Home Winery, Inc., 1992.

"Sutter Stays In with the Inn Crowd," *Beverage World,* November 1989, p. 18.

"Sutter's Big Push," *Beverage World,* May 1989, p. 12.

"Sutter's Illusion," *Beverage World,* June 1991, p. 12.

Vigoda, Arlene, "In Spirits of Good Health Comes Alcohol-Free Wine," *USA Today,* September 17, 1992, p. 1D.

Walker, Larry, "Under $10 Wines Prosper Amid Tumult in Industry," *San Francisco Chronicle,* December 28, 1992, p. B3.

—*Dorothy Walton*

SWANSON®

The Swanson brand of home style frozen foods, with its ease of preparation, commitment to quality, and variety of products, is one of the most innovative and enduring lines of frozen foods in the United States. Packaged in spoilage-retardant paraffined boxes with the trademark red Swanson logo in the upper left-hand corner, Swanson frozen dinners and entrees have been offering efficiency, economy, and basic nutrition to consumers for almost 40 years. Premiering with a line of humble yet hearty chicken, meat, and turkey pot pies in 1951, they produced the first frozen TV dinners—classic turkey and chicken dinners—three years later; these have become the top-selling frozen dinners in the United States.

In 1969, perceiving yet another need of busy, budget-minded Americans—that of a quick, tasty, well-balanced morning meal—C. A. Swanson & Sons, Inc., which had been absorbed in 1955 into the Campbell Soup Company in Camden, New Jersey, introduced its frozen breakfast line, which it relaunched in 1982 under the "Great Starts" name. Over the years, Swanson's frozen dinners and entrees have out-muscled such hefty competitors as Banquet Healthy Choice in the frozen dinners category and Fleischmann's Egg Beaters and Jimmy Dean in the frozen breakfasts category. Just two of the lines of products put out by the Campbell Soup Company, which also manufactures such other popular brands as Godiva chocolates, Mrs. Paul's fish sticks, and Pepperidge Farm bread, Swanson's frozen dinners and entrees have consistently kept current with the desires and demands of an ever-busy and budget-conscious population. Designed to economical as well as palatable, Swanson frozen dinners and entrees have remained market share leaders due to years of nutritionally balanced content and value pricing.

Brand Origins and Early Marketing Strategy

The year was 1954, and the United States was flourishing in the postwar economy. With women joining the labor force in increasing numbers, emulating the 19 million other women who had taken jobs outside the home during World War II and who had continued working after the war had ended, housewives were suddenly finding themselves with less time and energy to spend preparing meals for their growing families. Television had just emerged as a major entertainment medium which was engaging the attention of a population seeking a relaxing, at-home leisure activity. And work-weary women were searching for an efficient,

economical way to prepare tasty, well-balanced meals. Striving to meet that need, as well as realizing the advertising potential of the untapped television medium, C. A. Swanson & Sons, Inc., frozen food packers in Omaha, Nebraska, gambled and won with a major innovation in food manufacturing—the frozen TV dinner.

First Commercial Success

Swanson's frozen chicken, meat, and turkey pot pies had already debuted in 1951. Three years later, Swanson's first frozen dinner, consisting of turkey, cornbread dressing, gravy, peas, and sweet potatoes in a three-compartment tray, premiered and was soon followed by a frozen fried chicken dinner. At first considered a risky proposition by food analysts, Swanson's initial stock of 5,000 frozen turkey dinners, which retailed for only 98 cents each, sold out immediately, quickly capturing the label "TV dinner" and a huge market. By 1955, about the time The Campbell Soup Company purchased C. A. Swanson & Sons, production had skyrocketed to 25 million frozen packages a year and continued to grow.

Brand Development

In addition to its traditional pot pies and TV dinners, Swanson's frozen foods still sought to offer delicious, well-balanced meals to satisfy a wide spectrum of tastes and budgets. In 1973, Hungry-Man Dinners premiered. Featuring such wholesome, healthy favorites as salisbury steak and fried chicken (both white and dark meat versions), with heartier portions of meat for heartier appetites, Hungry-Man rapidly became a leader in the extra-portion market. Other selections in this line included boneless chicken, chopped beef steak, Mexican meals, sliced beef, turkey, and veal parmigiana.

In 1987, Swanson Homestyle Recipe Entrees debuted in direct response to the demands of consumers for a wider variety of high quality, quick to prepare meals. This line included such favorites as macaroni and cheese and lasagna, as well as fancier fare such as seafood creole with rice, sirloin tips in burgundy sauce, veal parmigiana, chicken cacciatore, and scalloped potatoes and ham. Also during this time, Swanson's frozen breakfast food line, originally introduced in 1969, was launched again, offering a wide variety of "Great Starts" breakfasts. The ultimate traveling breakfasts, Great Starts Breakfast Burritos and Mini-Breakfast Sandwiches were particularly popular.

Swanson also marketed breakfasts and dinner entrees especially for children. Swanson's Kids Breakfast Blast line and Fun Feast Dinners made their appearance in 1992, addressing the need for quickly prepared, well-balanced children's meals. Designed to help parents provide their children with fun and nutritious food fresh from the microwave in just over one minute, Breakfast Blast Entrees were competitively priced at under one dollar. All four varieties—pancakes, French toast sticks, waffle sticks, and mini-French toast—were smaller versions of popular adult breakfast foods, and each breakfast featured a convenient syrup cup which heated up warm, not hot, so that children could dip their food. The colorful design of each portable heat-and-serve box featured one of four different cartoon characters and easy one-step microwave directions. Since the Swanson children's breakfasts were designed as "finger food," there were no dishes or silverware to wash after the meal.

The Fun Feast Dinner line offered traditional children's favorites such as pizza, fish sticks, and breaded chicken nuggets, in addition to a unique lift-out dairy dessert called "Arctic Freeze," which tasted like ice cream and could either be eaten right away or saved for later. Other varieties offered brownies or fruit cocktail for dessert. Besides the popular food products and whimsical cartoon characters featured on the boxes, Fun Feast Meals were typified by a "surprise inside." Each meal contained one of four different surprise packs containing activities, games, and stickers. The economical Fun Feast Meals were prime contenders to conquer the $120 million children's meal segment.

Product Changes

Long committed to addressing the changing palates and lifestyles of consumers, the Swanson line, keeping in stride with the microwave revolution, retired its aluminum TV dinner tray in 1986, introducing a new tray composed of CPET (crystallized polyethylene terephthalate) for microwave ovens. Attesting to its stature as a leader in American food trends, an example of the original three-compartment metal tray for the Swanson's frozen turkey TV dinner was featured in an exhibit in the Smithsonian Institution.

Because Swanson's frozen foods have become such family favorites over the years, consumers often wax nostalgic for the Swanson varieties of yesterday. When the brownie, introduced with the original fried chicken dinner in 1954, was discontinued in 1986, disgruntled consumers across the nation bombarded The Campbell Soup Company with requests for its return. In response, the brownie was reintroduced in the following year.

The Swanson line was always a diversified line. In 1992, varieties of chicken entrees included chicken "nibbles," chicken nuggets, fried chicken (breast portions), one-pound pre-fried chicken parts, and chicken thighs and drumsticks. Three-compartment dinners boasted beans and franks, macaroni and beef, macaroni and cheese, noodles and chicken, and spaghetti and meatballs.

The first TV dinner, 1954.

By adapting to the changing tastes and lifestyles of consumers, Swanson's frozen dinners and entrees remained American favorites for almost 40 years. Those 5,000 turkey dinners sold in 1954 rose to a figure of nearly 82 million dinners consumed in 1992.

Dietary and Health Considerations

In order for foods to be frozen and preserved for long periods of time, extra sodium had to be added. Health-conscious consumers voiced their fears that the excessive salt content in the food might elevate their blood pressure and contribute to weight gain.

In 1990, questions, too, began to arise concerning the fact that microwaving did not heat the centers of the foods—in particular, heavily salted foods—sufficiently to destroy toxic bacteria. In England, Richard W. Lacey and Stephen F. Dealler of Leeds University conducted experiments on foods and determined that increasing concentrations of sodium chloride, potassium chloride, ammonium chloride, and monosodium glutamate contributed to lowering core temperatures. The core temperatures of unsalted samples tested uniformly throughout the scientists' experiments. Professor Dealler then conjectured that if the food contained major causes of food poisoning in the form of *Salmonella* or *Listeria* bacteria, microwaving might heat the microorganisms to a temperature that spurred rather than subdued their growth.

When the researchers recorded similar results in measuring the core temperatures of frozen dinners microwaved according to package instructions, they published a report in the April 5, 1990 issue of *Nature,* showing how the core temperature increase of dinners containing 200 to 1,000 milligrams of salt averaged 62 percent that of comparable unsalted foods. The team postulated that since microwave radiation encouraged the flow of the ionic current on the surface of foods with high sodium concentrations, the ions might absorb the microwave energy and function as a shield, diminishing the waves' penetration. Professor Dealler believed that this theory would explain why microwaved food often boiled on its surface but remained cool inside.

Researchers in the United States concurred with their British counterparts. Theodore Labuza, a food scientist at the University of Minnesota in Saint Paul, maintained that other studies indicated that significant amounts of salt and sugar tended to change the way food absorbed microwave energy and suggested that the chemical mechanisms might even prove more complex than the British team had hypothesized.

Swanson answered these dietary and health challenges by first maintaining that salt was as necessary to the metabolism of the body as it was to the preservation of food, and secondly by recommending that consumers follow the advice of professors Labuza and Dealler to microwave the frozen dinners and entrees longer and at lower power than the package instructed, and then to let them sit for a few minutes to help make certain that harmful bacteria had been killed.

Performance Appraisal

That frozen dinners and entrees were here to stay was incontestable. In 1987, sales of frozen breakfasts approached $500 million, and in 1990 alone, sales of these products topped $4 billion. One reason for Swanson's enduring popularity was the brand's philosophy: basic nutrition at a reasonable price. Through the years, the Swanson line kept up with the times but never indulged in faddism. While competitors attempted to capitalize on consumers' concern for their weight, Swanson adhered to its credo of well-balanced, nourishing meals. In 1989, ConAgra launched the first frozen "healthful meals" with its Healthy Balance Frozen Dinners, and other rival brands such as Healthy Choice Budget Gourmet Light and Healthy, and Budget Gourmet Hearty and Healthy soon followed. Nevertheless, Swanson not only kept the top share of the frozen dinners category, but market share increased from 22 percent in 1991 to 23.1 percent in 1992. Sales for this Swanson line in 1992 were $262.6 million.

In the frozen breakfasts category in 1992, Swanson's Great Starts again triumphed, out-flanking the sluggish low-calorie leaders Healthy Choice and Weight Watchers with a market share of 29.1 percent (top share) in 1991 and 25.9 percent (top share) in 1992. Sales that year for this Swanson line were $89.9 million.

In the frozen entrees category, Swanson pulled a market share of 6.5 percent in 1991 and 5.4 percent in 1992. Sales for the line that year were $174.3 million. In the period between 1986 and 1991, lowfat frozen dinners' share of the market increased by 4 percent, an increase derived from a market study conducted by Find/SVP. Weight-conscious consumers, predominantly working women and overweight men of the baby boom generation, formed the 124 million Americans who included lowfat frozen foods in their diets.

Although "healthful meals" in 1992 accounted for 26 percent of the frozen meal market, consumers as well as nutritionists evidently felt that these low-calorie versions did not adequately represent all basic food groups in the diet and so voted with their food dollars for the Swanson brand, which had never compromised on nutrition. Indeed, according to The Campbell Soup Company's Annual Report for 1992, Swanson frozen dinners turned in an extraordinary performance in 1991.

International Growth

1992 marked the year in which the vision of The Campbell Soup Company turned to the global marketplace. That year, with the implementation of the aggressive global marketing strategy "Campbell Brands Preferred Around the World," company executives redefined their priorities, deciding to focus attention on becoming competitive in the global economy. The groundwork for the role of Swanson's frozen dinners and entrees in this inspired vision had already been laid: in addition to frozen food operational facilities in the United States—in Fayetteville, Arkansas; Miami, Florida; Modesto, California; Philadelphia, Pennsylvania; Salisbury, Maryland; and Omaha, Nebraska (the home of the original frozen TV dinner), an affiliate had also been established in Listowel, Ontario, Canada. And in Europe, subsidiaries had been set up in England (Braintree, King's Lynn, Peterlee, and Salford), Ireland (Middleton), in Scotland (Glasgow), and The Netherlands (Zundert).

Drawing upon the driving force of the fame of the Swanson line, Campbell's strategy was to make the brand even more powerful by leveraging the clout of its name to build profitable volume through the evolution of innovative additions to the line. In 1992 also, The Campbell Soup Company led the food industry in utilizing the North American Free Trade Agreement; it reorganized itself into three multinational profit-focused divisions to develop brand and brain power across continents. Realizing that in the global marketplace a company must relentlessly surge forward to improve operating efficiency, Campbell launched a global drive to remove barriers to productivity, to downsize bureaucracy, to hasten decision-making, and to blaze new paths of excellence. Emphasizing teamwork, Campbell employees worldwide in 1992 were able to deliver savings in manufacturing and purchasing. For instance, at the Modesto, California, plant, employees challenged themselves to invent a product which made use of spare plant capacity. That year, too, teams created and developed "Swanson Fiesta" breakfasts, which became a consumer success due to their distinct "Southwestern" taste appeal. As the years progressed, Swanson food engineers around the world made plans to develop products uniquely suited to the tastes and lifestyles of each country.

Future Predictions

Campbell readily acknowledged that it was still an infant in the competitive global economy. But it was ready for the challenge— ready to think, ready to build, ready to grow. And Swanson's Frozen Dinners and Entrees were ready, too, to adapt to the changing palates of a diverse population—from youngsters scurrying off to school, to parents bustling home to make supper, to older adults seeking an easy-to-prepare, well-balanced meal at a reasonable price. If the years from 1954 to 1992 were any indication of success, the coming years should see even greater growth as new ideas and new technology burst upon the 21st century. The products might change, but the quality should always stay the same.

Further Reading:

Adams, Anthony J., and Margaret Henderson Blair, "Persuasive Advertising and Sales Accountability: Past Experience and Forward Validation," *Journal of Advertising Research*, March-April, 1992, pp. 20.

Anthony, Sterling, "Dual-Ovenable Trays: A 'Choice' Market," *Prepared Foods*, April, 1986, p. 27.

Appelbaum, Cara, et al., "Dinosaur Brands (Marketing Strategies of America's Top Consumer Products)," *Adweek's Marketing Week*, June 17, 1991, p. 17.

Blackburn, George L., "How to Choose (and Use) A Frozen Dinner," *Prevention*, January, 1989, p. 30.

"Brand Scorecard," *Advertising Age*, November 2, 1992, p. 16.

"Campbell Consolidates Frozen Foods at BBDO," *Adweek* (Eastern Edition), January 20, 1992, p. 52.

"Campbell Launches Regional Marketing Event with NFL," *U. S. Distribution Journal*, October, 1989, p. 52.

"ConAgra Tries Health Claims," *Advertising Age*, October 2, 1992, p. 4.

Decker, C., "Microwaving Microorganism: Salty Shield?", *Science News*, April 7, 1990, p. 215.

"Dueling Dinners Pays Dividends (Doubling-Up Packaging Lines for Two Brands of Frozen Dinners at Campbell Soup Co.)," *Packaging Digest*, September, 1987, p. 102.

"Foil's Swan Song at Swanson: Crystallized Polyethylene Terephthalate Trays Replace Aluminum Ones," *Packaging Digest*, June, 1986, p. 34.

"Frozen Breakfast Appetite Still Hearty As Boom Category Approaches $500 Million," *Quick Frozen Foods International*, October, 1987, p. 180.

Hanlin, Elizabeth, "Swanson Frozen Dinners—Evolution of a Classic," The Campbell Soup Company, March 1, 1993.

Iezzi, R. A., and D. F. Toner, "How Campbell Tests CPET (Crystallized Polyethylene Terephthalate) Trays," *Packaging*, April, 1987, p. 102.

Karolefski, John, "New Technology Expected to Increase Market Share," *Supermarket News*, March 5, 1990, p. 37.

Kemp, Gordon, "Listeria Hysteria Hands FF Industry Another (Missed) Opportunity in U. K. [Food Poisoning Bacteria]," *Quick Frozen Foods International*, April, 1989, p. 135.

"Large Market Potential for Frozen Meals in Elderly Nutrition Program, Says Study," *Quick Frozen Foods International*, April, 1989, p. 116.

Leblang, Bonnie Tandy, "Frost Bites: Is Lean Cuisine's Healthy Choice for Weight Watchers?", *American Health: Fitness of Body and Mind*, April, 1992, p. 58.

Levitt, Alan, "The Microwave Revolution: Zap-Happy Consumers Love This Kitchen Companion, Spawning a Wave of Opportunities," *Dairy Foods*, July, 1988, p. 21.

Losee, Stephanie, "Weight Watchers Lite (Weight Watchers Frozen Foods Entrees to Contain Less Sodium and Cholesterol)," *Fortune*, March 11, 1991, p. 76.

McNichols, Megan, "Novel Features and Plenty of Fun Highlight Swanson's New Fun Feasts for Kids," *Campbell Soup Company News*, April 30, 1992.

McNichols, Megan, "Swanson Prepares Its New Breakfast Blast Entrees for Takeoff," *Campbell Soup Company News*, April 30, 1992.

Moskowitz, Milton, *Everybody's Business*, New York: Doubleday Currency, Inc., 1990, p. 19.

"New Packaging for Microwave Ovens," *Packaging*, January, 1988, p. 75.

"1992 Proud Performance: Campbell Soup Company Annual Report," Camden, NJ: The Campbell Soup Company, 1992.

"The 100 Most Healthful Frozen Dinners You Can Buy," *Tufts University Diet and Nutrition Letter*, October, 1992, p. 3.

"Plastics Here to Stay As Aluminum Gets Foiled," *Quick Frozen Foods International*, January, 1986, p. 53.

Rice, Judy, "MAP Chinese Entrees in Dual-Oven CPET Trays," *Food Processing*, January, 1990. p. 28.

"Sales of Frozen Dinners and Entrees Top $4 Billion in 1990," *Frozen Foods Digest*, April-May, 1991, p. 80.

Schwartz, Joe, "Fat Flees from Frozen Foods," *American Demographics*, June, 1992, p. 21.

Semling, Harold V. "Labeling Proposals for Frozen Pizzas and Tropical Oils Spark Heated Hearings Debate," *Foods Processing*, November, 1987, p. 10.

Shapiro, Laura, "The Zap Generation," *Newsweek*, February 26, 1990, p. 56.

Webb, Denise, "Rating the Winners in Frozen Dinners," *New Choices for the Best Years*, June, 1990, p. 82.

"What's Cooking in Frozen Breakfasts," *Tufts University Diet and Nutrition Letter*, February, 1992, p. 3.

—Virginia Barnstorff

TABASCO®

"It traveled to Khartoum with Lord Kitchener and was carried on Himalayan expeditions, in the mess kits of World War I dough-boys, and aboard Skylab," noted Pat Mandell in an *Americana* article. "It is the quintessential ingredient in Bloody Marys. Its pungent flavor enlivens gumbos, eggs, steaks and stews, salads, chicken a la king, French onion soup, and jambalaya." *It* is the McIlhenny Company's Tabasco brand of pepper sauce, known more familiarly as just Tabasco sauce, and it has become the stuff of legend in the world of spice and flavor.

"For about a century and a half," as William Rice declared in an article reprinted in the *Detroit Free Press,* "Tabasco has represented one of the most effective cures for blandness in food. Remarkably pure and flavorful . . . it can be applied either by a diner, who uses it as a condiment at table, or by a cook, who may employ it as an ingredient in the kitchen." In its characteristic tiny bottle (just a few drops of Tabasco sauce go a long way), the peppery flavoring has proved singular enough to earn the distinction of being almost a generic description of a hot-tasting liquid condiment.

Birth of a Brand

The history of Tabasco sauce is the history of a family—the McIlhennys of Avery Island, Louisiana. It was in the mid-1800s that Edmund McIlhenny, a self-made banker and vegetable-garden hobbyist, married Mary Eliza Avery, whose family owned 2,300 acres in the bayou of south Louisiana. (The Averys were something of condiment experts themselves, as patriarch Daniel Dudley Avery had cultivated native rock salt and built his fortune on selling it as a meat preservative.) For a long time, McIlhenny had been interested in some extra-spicy pepper seeds a friend had brought back from Mexico, and he experimented with their plant-ing. But the Civil War interrupted this line of thought; the invading Union Army forced the Averys and the McIlhennys to take refuge in Texas. At the war's end, the family returned to their home to find almost all of the crops destroyed—except the pepper plants. Around 1866, McIlhenny resumed his gardening research, finding that Avery Island was a prime place for the potent *Capsicum frutescens,* which thrived in the humid atmosphere.

McIlhenny knew that these red peppers could be turned into a flavoring sauce. He mashed a number of them, mixed them with native Avery Island salt, then aged the concoction in wooden barrels. After some time he added vinegar, then strained the liquid to produce pure pepper concentrate, with a naturally bright red color. Friends raved about the sauce, which could enhance the flavor of food as subtly or as extravagantly as taste demanded. McIlhenny poured samples into some small cologne bottles, and added a sprinkler top to regulate the portions into drops. He called it "Tabasco," which, according to company history, is a Mexican moniker meaning "land where soil is humid."

In 1868 McIlhenny sent 350 bottles to a group of handpicked wholesalers. By 1869 he had received orders in the thousands of bottles at the premium price of $1.00 apiece. The McIlhenny Company was born. The former banker went into pepper-sauce production full time, and by 1870 had secured a patent for his Tabasco brand pepper sauce. Tabasco sauce went international as early as 1872, when McIlhenny opened an office in London to accommodate European buyers. In the early 1990s, Tabasco sauce sales stood in the millions, with labels printed in 15 different languages. "The shape of the bottle has changed little, as has the process of making the sauce," noted *Wall Street Journal* reporter Mark Robichaux. "From August to about November, workers cull [Avery Island's] 75 acres of peppers. A mechanized picker was tried years ago but today sits idle in a warehouse." Human pepper-pickers are equipped with a *baton rouge,* or small red stick, by which to judge the redness of the plant. The McIlhenny Company, still family-owned and operated, acknowledges that to lessen the risk of losing the entire crop to disease, some 90 percent of its pepper seeds are sown in Columbia, Honduras, and Venezuela.

When it comes time to make the sauce, the chopped peppers are packed with salt in 50-gallon oak casks and are aged three years. "The company experimented with plastic vats once, but tossed them aside," added Robichaux. Nearly the only bow to new technology comes when a large mechanical arm stirs the pure liquid to blend the spices—thus eliminating the need for the hand-held wooden paddles of the past. In keeping with Edmund McIlhenny's original formula, only peppers, salt, and vinegar go into the little shaker bottles; no artificial colors, flavors, or additives appear in Tabasco sauce. A member of the McIlhenny family personally inspects the vats to determine if the sauce is ready for bottling.

The success of Tabasco sauce can be credited to its versatility in the kitchen. Not merely "hot stuff," Tabasco sauce describes itself as a "piquancy" agent; it produces a spicy flavor, not just heat. The condiment has always been popular in meat drippings and gravies and also appears regionally in egg dishes, soups, and salad dressings. A new appreciation of the cajun and creole cooking of Louisiana further promoted Tabasco sauce beginning in the mid-1980s. Chef Paul Prudhomme praised the condiment's properties, telling the *Wall Street Journal:* "I may use 10 drops of Tabasco, but I can trust those 10 drops. It pushes the natural flavor of the food. There's an afterglow in your mouth." Tabasco sauce is also a favorite spice of those watching their dietary intake, because the concentrated pepper mash is low in sodium and free of fat and calories. And while Tabasco didn't invent the Bloody Mary, it is perhaps the drink's best-known ingredient.

Cool Promotion for a Hot Sauce

But for all of the sales of Tabasco sauce, the company's marketing efforts have traditionally remained low-key. McIlhenny Co. concentrated its advertising almost exclusively in print for the brand's first 125 years, primarily running ads in trade and consumer publications. Only in 1985, as Robichaux pointed out, did Tabasco sauce first air a television commercial. By 1990 "various 30-second spots [showed] Avery Island natives topping all sorts of foods with Tabasco sauce. In print ads pushing a 'power breakfast,' the company suggests adding a few drops to hash browns, grits and omelets. 'That'll get your engine started,' the ad says." Tabasco influence has even pervaded other advertisers: a two-column 1992 print ad began, "What's Red-Hot, Plenty Powerful, and Perks Up Anything?" while the photo below showed an unmistakable, though unlabelled, Tabasco sauce bottle with partial lettering of the product name circling the bottleneck. The other column of the ad was headlined "Guess Again," revealing a similarly-shaped, cherry-red Dirt Devil vacuum cleaner.

Tabasco sauce has found marketing success in other areas. Avery Island itself is a tourist attraction, boasting a lush bayou atmosphere populated by snowy egrets (a species almost extinct until the McIlhennys reintroduced them to the island) as well as alligators, deer, and armadillos. Visitors can walk through the Tabasco factory, which is virtually unchanged from its 19th-century appearance. A highlight of Avery Island is the Tabasco country store, located on the factory grounds. Here all manner of Tabasco-themed items are sold; the company also prints a catalog for phone and mail order. Fans of the sauce can find posters featuring the familiar red, white, and green bottle as interpreted in the styles of surrealism, impressionism, and even cubism. There

are 125th-anniversary pewter bottle holders, replica bottles, cookbooks, t-shirts, jewelry, key rings, "pepper" refrigerator magnets, coasters and trivets, drinking glasses, aprons, and more.

For the chef, Tabasco sauce has expanded its name into a line of dry condiments including chili powder, seasoned salt, red pepper, herb and spice, and popcorn seasoning. The company sells ready-made Bloody Mary mix in both 8-ounce and 32-ounce bottles. A notable recent addition is Tabasco 7-Spice Chili recipe (by 1992 "limping along with limited distribution," according to the *Wall Street Journal*), and Tabasco picante sauce. "We've been a one-product company long enough," explained company president Edward McIlhenny Simmons, a grandson of the founder, in *Americana.* The relatively slow rollout of new products in the past and their careful test-marketing represent sound business practice to Simmons. As he told Robichaux, "We could wash the chili sauce out tomorrow, and we'd have a few gray hairs, and we'd have spent a few dollars, but we're not going to have bankers crawling all over us." In 1991 Tabasco "made its first-ever acquisition, buying rival Trappey's Fine Foods," maker of Red Devil pepper sauce, noted *Wall Street Journal* reporter Kathleen Deveny. Under the newer line name McIlhenny Farms, the roster of food products varies more widely. Spicy specialties like pepper jelly are available, but so are ketchup, mayonnaise, molasses, and honey. All jars and bottles are packaged individually or in collected gift boxes.

The low-key sales approach has evidently worked for the McIlhenny family. While some 150 brands of pepper sauce exist, the Tabasco brand stands virtually alone in name recognition and controls more than a third of the total market share. (The sauce has even been mentioned in such comic strips as "Heathcliff," "Blondie," "Shoe" and "The Wizard of Id.") Even though Tabasco sauce is the reigning market leader, exact sales numbers for the sauce and its other brands are kept confidential. But the overall market for pepper sauces has seen growth. According to a 1992 *Wall Street Journal* article, the market has risen to $58 million. At the same time, Tabasco sauce's competitors have attempted to heat up their sales. Tabasco sauces's leading rival, Durkee's Red Hot, claimed in Robichaux's article to have sold more bottles by volume than did the more expensive Tabasco sauce. But even Cal Garrett, a Durkee manager, admitted that "McIlhenny is laughing all the way to the bank. They've built a great niche." That niche has been threatened in the past few years by new and varying rivals. As Deveny pointed out, "During the 13 weeks ended Nov. 12, 1989, Tabasco's share of the market averaged an impressive 32.5 percent. By the end of a comparable 13-week period in 1992, however, it had tumbled to 27.5 percent." The main threat has come not only from Durkee's Red Hot, but also from sauces that frankly don't match Tabasco sauce's potency—and it works to their advantage: "The trend toward milder sauces," Deveny wrote, "may also reflect the fact that they appeal to pepper-sauce neophytes." But Tabasco sauce's reputation stands firm. Robichaux noted that the company "still profits every day from developing the first widely sold hot sauce and, in essence, creating the market."

Tabasco Sauce Now and Tomorrow

Tabasco sauce seems to have weathered every obstacle in its path. It even stood up to a hurricane. When Hurricane Andrew slashed through the Gulf Coast in August of 1992, Avery Island was one of its final targets. But no lasting damage came to the factory or the fields, and business eventually resumed as usual.

Much of that business goes to Japan—the highest overseas consumer of Tabasco Sauce. There, Tabasco sauce spices not only sushi, but spaghetti and pizza. Worldwide, fans of Tabasco include members of Britain's royal family. According to *My Twenty Years in Buckingham Palace,* the Queen Mother is fond of a lobster cocktail that includes the condiment. "In wartime it was not always possible to obtain the necessary ingredients, especially the Tabasco sauce, which is an essential item of the cocktail mixture," a palace staffer told author F. J. Corbitt. "I was able to send a message to the Queen that enough bottles of Tabasco sauce had arrived to last for years, as only a few drops of it are used in making the lobster cocktail." Tabasco sauce's appeal goes even beyond earthly boundaries—supplies of the sauce went into space with two Skylab missions during the 1970s.

None of this is surprising to the McIlhenny family, whose members still make up Tabasco's major shareholders. The popularity of salsa has helped Tabasco sauce, and Edward M. Simmons thinks his condiment can become at least as visible as salt or pepper. "We'd like one [bottle] in your kitchen and one on your dining room table," he told the *Wall Street Journal.* And Paul McIlhenny added that he thinks the pace of the 125-year-old company will pick up in the future. "We've gotten more aggressive than previously, and I think the next hundred years will see us trying even more new things."

Further Reading:

Deveny, Kathleen, "Rival Hot Sauces Are Breathing Fire at Market Leader Tabasco," *Wall Street Journal,* January 7, 1993, p. B1.

Mandell, Pat, "Louisiana Hot," *Americana,* February 1991, pp. 26-32.

Moore, Diane M., "The Treasures of Avery Island," Lafayette, LA: Acadian House Publishing, 1990.

Rice, William, "Tabasco Sauce Stands up to a Hurricane," *Detroit Free Press,* November 18, 1992.

Robichaux, Mark, "Tabasco-Sauce Maker Remains Hot After 125 Years," *Wall Street Journal,* May 11, 1990.

—Susan Salter

TANQUERAY®

Manufactured by Charles Tanqueray & Co., Tanqueray brand of gin is instantly recognizable for its barrel-shaped green bottle with the red Tanqueray seal. Tanqueray stands as the number one imported premium gin in the United States, outselling all other imported gins combined. Formulated in England in 1830 by Charles Tanqueray, the 94.6 proof gin is sold in more than 100 countries around the world in sizes ranging from 50 milliliters to 1.75 liters. Like all premium gins, Tanqueray has a smooth, dry taste. However, Bruce Weber writes in *Esquire* that "Tanqueray has a sting, a nifty little bite" that distinguishes it from competitors such as Bombay, Boodles, and Beefeater. In 1989 Tanqueray leant the strength of its name to a new premium vodka, Tanqueray Sterling Vodka. Within a few months of its introduction, the brand was the number-four seller in the highly competitive premium imported vodka market.

Distinguished History

Gin is widely known as an English drink, but the juniper-based spirit was actually invented in the seventeenth century in the Netherlands by Dr. Franciscus Sylvius. Sylvius, a professor of medicine at the University of Leiden, was convinced of the therapeutic effects of the juniper berry but realized that his patients would be more likely to take their medicine if he could combine it with alcohol. The doctor was partially right: the concoction, which he named *genievre* after the French word for juniper, proved quite popular among his patients, though its medicinal value was dubious. Soon the drink was popular throughout the country, perhaps most clearly aboard Dutch sailing ships. "A little of this new juniper water not only helped prevent scurvy by contributing a smidgen of vitamin C . . . to [the sailors'] diets," wrote Henry McNulty in *Gourmet*, "but also provided a shot of instant courage when the enemy heaved in sight." English sailors, who later made their gin more palatable by squeezing in limes, became known the world over as "limeys."

Gin made its way to England as the result of a political alliance between the English and the Dutch. Production boomed in the late seventeenth century when William of Orange discouraged the importation of French spirits in favor of domestic distillation. "Gin was the cheapest and easiest liquor to produce," Emanuel and Madeline Greenberg wrote in the *New York Times Magazine,* "and the English went at it with gusto." In fact, that gusto soon led the popular drink into ill repute. Gin was widely linked to the public drunkenness made famous by engraver William Hogarth's "Gin Lane," which depicted people lying in the streets drunk on gin. By 1736 the English Parliament had passed the Gin Act, restricting sales.

The improvement of gin's taste and production through the development of the column still, a tall curvaceous kettle, rescued gin from disrepute in England. The new concoction was dubbed "dry gin," and later "London dry gin," which has remained the standard name for this type of gin made all over the world. London dry gin achieves a clean, crispness by adding botanicals such as coriander, orange peel, and other types—the combination varies with the recipe—to the second distilling of the purified alcohol, or by hanging the botanicals in the alcohol's steam to infuse the flavor. In 1830 Charles Tanqueray combined Finsbury Spa water, known for its purity, and malted barley that had been rectified into a neutral spirit with a secret combination of herbs and botanicals to make his premium gin. His recipe continues to be followed and is Charles Tanqueray & Co.'s "most treasured secret." London dry is the most popular type of gin because of its ability to mix well. The other two types of gin are far less popular. Amber-colored Dutch gin's pungent taste doesn't mix well, according to Henry McNulty in *Gourmet*. And Plymouth gin, which was once favored by the British Navy, has not kept or increased its following. It is only made in the port town of Plymouth, England.

Marketing a Premium Product

Britain, known as the "guardian of the 'original' formula" of gin, has long dominated the world's exported gin business. Tanqueray followed Beefeater brand gin, another British product, into the U.S. market where both were known as exclusive British London dry gins. Charles Tanqueray & Co. reported that Tanqueray "came into its own in America" during the 1950s, nurturing its premium image in Hollywood before gaining popularity in the East. Even though Tanqueray was the second best-selling imported gin in 1973, it didn't rank in *Business Week*'s rankings of the top 40 liquors; it lagged far behind Beefeater, the imported gin benchmark of the time. By the early 1980s, however, Tanqueray had edged its way into the top 40 rankings, hovering in the upper thirties from 1981 to 1983. By 1984, Tanqueray surpassed Beefeater in case depletions to become the top-selling imported gin, according to John W. Heilmann, chairman of the board, chief executive officer, and president of the Distillers Somerset Group,

AT A GLANCE

Tanqueray brand of gin founded in 1830 in England by Charles Tanqueray; produced by Charles Tanqueray & Co., a subsidiary of Guinness PLC; brand extensions include Tanqueray Sterling Vodka, introduced in 1989.

Performance: *Market share*—Top share of U.S. imported gin category.

Major competitor: Beefeater; also, Boodles, Bombay Sapphire, Gilbey's, Gordon's, and Seagram's Extra Dry.

Advertising: *Agency*—Smith/Greenland, New York City, NY. *Major campaign*—Major print campaign for 1993 featured Tanqueray twirling out of the bottle into a lemon garnished glass; caption read, "Perfect backflip with a twist."

Addresses: *Parent company*—Charles Tanqueray & Co., 260-66 Goswell Rd., London EC1V 7EE, England; phone: (01) 253-2060. *U.S. importer*—Schieffelin & Somerset, 2 Park Avenue, New York, NY 10016; phone: (212) 251-2008. *Ultimate parent company*—Guinness PLC, International House, 7 High St., London W5 5DB, England; phone: (71) 486-0288.

Tanqueray's U.S. importer, in *Advertising Age.* Tanqueray continued to hold the leading imported gin market share into the 1990s.

Tanqueray relies on price differentiation, taste, and product identification to maintain its loyal following. Premium gins appeal primarily to drinkers who are willing to pay for a product that stands apart from the competition. One way to make that difference clear to purchasers has been price differentiation. Richard Vreeland, a Somerset marketing executive, told *Advertising Age* that "we always try to be between 25 cents to 35 cents higher than Beefeater." *Harper's Bazaar* contributor William Clifford noted the connection between price and taste in a market where cost reflects quality. "Buy the best you can afford," he wrote, noting that devoted gin drinkers would rather go without lunch than without a good gin. "The taste of the most sophisticated Londoners leans toward" the "clean, light, dry, well-balanced" flavor of Tanqueray, he continued. Yet, John Tanqueray, part of the gin's founding family's fifth generation, told *Gourmet* that Tanqueray's success is based on something quite different: its "funny bottle." Indeed, Tanqueray's bottle is tied closely to its success because its bottle has been the main feature in Tanqueray ads for years. Mark Dolliver in *Adweek*'s Midwest edition dubbed ads for Tanqueray as part of the "old bottle-and-glass genre" typical of liquor marketers during gin's rapid rise in popularity in America. Doug Rubbra, an executive at the Association of Canadian Distillers, told *The Financial Post* that "consumer identification of labels and bottles is a cornerstone of liquor marketing." The combined appeal of price, taste, and identifiability allows Tanqueray to command a large share of the market.

Advertising Innovations

During the 1980s, U.S. liquor consumption began to decline and liquor marketers scrambled to maintain a share of the market. Victor Macoll, a liquor analyst at Kleinwort Grieveson Securities in London, told *Business Week* that aggressive advertising could capture growth, thereby counteracting a market decline. To achieve growth, Tanqueray adjusted its marketing techniques and advertising budget to focus on brand image and target marketing. *Business Week* reported that Guinness PLC, Tanqueray's corporate owner, increased its advertising budget for Tanqueray and

other high-profile brands by 26 percent in 1988. The increased advertising budget, according to Barbara Toman, a staff reporter at the *Wall Street Journal,* was used to "persuade drinkers to 'trade up'—that is, to pay fancy prices for premium brands with snob value." Guinness wanted to persuade consumers to purchase more expensive brands because, as Anthony Tennant, chief executive of Guinness PLC, told *Forbes,* "people are drinking less by volume and more by value." Focusing on premium images worked: by the late 1980s, Tanqueray sales had grown in the face of a waning gin market.

Tanqueray's sales jump also resulted from its targeting the "young, affluent urbanites just starting to form brand loyalties," said Clint Rodenberg, a Schieffelin & Somerset executive, in the *Wall Street Journal.* Print ads were splashed throughout magazines with "trendy readerships," such as *Spy, L.A. Style, GQ,* and *Details.* To reinforce the print campaign, 14,000 posters were sold. Tanqueray's strategy won over 2.7 million consumers between the ages of 25 to 35 in 1990, a fifteen percent rise since 1985, according to the *Wall Street Journal.*

In the search for what Guinness called "better ads," Tanqueray's agency, Smith/Greenland Inc., toyed with the consumer's sense of smell. Tanqueray's 1989 "Spruce up their holiday. Give Tanqueray" ads, that ran in *USA Today,* were impregnated with pine scent and showed cars driving through the snow, one with a bottle of Tanqueray tied to its roof. But by December of 1991, with the United States in a recession, Schieffelin & Somerset thought it wise to repeat Tanqueray's 1990 "straightforward" print ads instead of using scented gimmicks, noted Laura Bird in the *Wall Street Journal.* In 1992 Tanqueray's holiday ads continued to be low-key. One ad featured a wreath made of Tanqueray bottles with the caption, "Share the wreath. Give friends a sprig of imported greenery." Even Tanqueray's nonseasonal ads aimed to be "visually arresting," according to Mark Maremont in *Business Week.* Playing on Tanqueray's bottle's dark green color, early 1990s ads featured a man with hair dyed green to match the hue of the Tanqueray bottle and a woman wearing Tanqueray-bottle-green lipstick in ads with the caption "Imitation is the sincerest form of flattery." *Sports Illustrated*'s 1990 swimsuit issue featured "The perfect tan" ad, showing a sunbathing woman tanned with Tanqueray's script lettering.

Under the directorship of Anthony Greener, Guinness's chief executive in 1992, Guinness's premium brand images remained important. Greener told the *New York Times* that "the brand you drink is very much a demonstration of your lifestyle, of your affluence." Guinness's sales continued to rely on people wanting to associate themselves with exclusive, quality brands. Tanqueray's 1993 ads highlighted the fresh, zestiness of citrus fruits and promoted their perfection when mixed with Tanqueray. One ad featured a picture of the Tanqueray bottle underneath a freshly washed lime. The copy read, "We didn't invent the lime. We just perfected it." Another ad read "Perfect backflip with a twist." It showed Tanqueray twirling out of the bottle into a lemon garnished glass.

Building on Tanqueray's Heritage

In the mid- and late-1980s, premium vodkas were the top performers in a sluggish liquor market. Hoping to take advantage of the 22 percent jump in imported vodka sales in the wake of an overall drop in liquor consumption, Tanqueray used its name and premium image to introduce Tanqueray Sterling Vodka. A Smith/

Greenland executive told *Marketing and Media Decisions* that they hoped to "snare the 'elegant' niche that Absolut and Stoli have ignored," and to make their product a "strong number three." The Tanqueray brand name was used because 25 percent of those who drank Absolut and Stolichnaya, the leading competitors, also drank Tanqueray gin, according to the *Wall Street Journal.* The established Tanqueray brand image, good rankings in taste tests, and an enormous $10 million rollout campaign were the three key ingredients fueling Tanqueray Sterling's strong sales. "It's all image," according to Warns Roy Burry, an executive at Kidder Peabody & Co. Government regulations state that vodka is an alcohol without taste, color, or odor. So, Mr. Burry said, "if you are going to import something across the ocean, you had better have an image."

To establish Tanqueray Sterling's premium image, Schieffelin & Somerset courted the young "fashion trend setters" by sponsoring a benefit for the People with AIDS Coalition at a trendy New York dance bar. Irma Zandl, a consultant who follows the trends of the young, told the *Wall Street Journal* that the group Tanqueray Sterling targeted was "the power brokers of trends. It's a very small but powerful group." With all its backing and promotion, Tanqueray Sterling's image started "leaps and bounds ahead" of the competitors, noted JoAnn Craner, Schieffelin & Somerset marketing brand manager, in *Marketing & Media Decisions.* This image fueled sales of more than 100,000 cases before the end of its first year.

Tanqueray Sterling's print ads were reminiscent of Absolut's, the leading vodka, featuring a lone bottle with a confident caption. Tanqueray Sterling's rollout theme was "At last, perfection in a vodka." In addition to advertising similarities, Tanqueray Sterling's frosted bottles also mimic Absolut's color scheme: the 80 proof bottles have blue lettering, the 100 proof bottles have red lettering, and the citrus flavored vodka bottles have bright yellow lettering. If positioned close enough on a shelf, the consumer may inadvertently choose Tanqueray Sterling over Absolut. However, Frank Walters, a researcher for M. Shanken Communications, told the *Wall Street Journal* that he did not expect Tanqueray Sterling to "take anything away from Absolut or Stoli." Nevertheless, Tanqueray Sterling's U.S. importer expected sales to reach "500,000 cases a year by 1992, at a price equal to Absolut's," according to the *Wall Street Journal.* Sales of such magnitude would rival the top sellers.

Corporate Ownership

Although Tanqueray has always been made by the venerable Charles Tanqueray & Co., the 1980s saw the brand's U.S. distributorship and corporate ownership go through a dizzying series of changes. The U.S. importer of Tanqueray, Somerset Importers Ltd., which was owned by Esmark Inc., became Distillers Co. PLC in June of 1985. Distillers Co. was then taken over by Guinness PLC in April of 1986 under then chief executive officer Ernest Saunders. The $4.6 billion takeover was the largest in England's history, and provoked one of England's largest financial scandals when it was found that the takeover was made possible through illegal stock manipulations that cost Saunders and others their jobs. Under the leadership of Anthony Tennant, Guinness survived the controversy. Tennant told *Forbes* that "it's the only job I've ever taken where there was no briefing by my predecessor and no access to his files. I had to start from scratch." During his tenure Tennant pared down acquisitions to the main line of business: alcohol. Guinness focused on controlling distribution and

marketing premium brand images, according to *Forbes.* Tennant masterminded a 1988 investment in the French company Moet Hennessy Louis Vuitton S. A. (LVMH), a spirit house known for the world's number one cognac and some premium champagnes, which aided Guinness in becoming a powerful European distribution company.

Under Tennant's leadership, Guinness assumed a leading position in world liquor marketing. William Pietersen, a Distillers' executive, told *Business Week* that the joint venture with LVMH gave U.S. importers Schieffelin & Somerset the opportunity to offer "a must-stock portfolio for wholesalers and retailers," because Tanqueray and Johnnie Walker were sold in conjunction with Moet champagne and Hennessy cognac. In 1992 Anthony Greener succeeded Tennant as Guinness chief executive officer, promising he would carry on Tennant's focus on the spirit and beer business. "We intend to remain as single-minded as ever. The success of this company is dependent on how well we develop these brands," Greener said in the *New York Times.* The continued financial strength of Guinness, and the priority it places on premium brands bodes well for the future of Tanqueray gin and Tanqueray Sterling vodka. Both brands are made of the white alcohol that weathers the storms of moderation with ease. Tanqueray gin has aged well, in keeping with the Tanqueray family motto, "Qui Perstat Obtinet—He Who Persists Obtains." And Tanqueray Sterling vodka shows every sign of similar success.

Further Reading:

Bird, Laura, "Many Liquor Firms Shun Splash in Ads of December Magazines," *Wall Street Journal,* October 30, 1991, p. B5.

Charlier, Marj, "Youthful Sobriety Tests Liquor Firms," *Wall Street Journal,* June 14, 1990, p. B1.

Clifford, William, "Enjoying the Gin Game," *Harper's Bazaar,* April, 1983, pp. 180-181, 232.

Deveney, Kathleen, "Aiming High, Some Ads Shoot for the Hip," *Wall Street Journal,* January 10, 1990, p. B1.

Deveney, Kathleen, "Middle-Price Brands Come Under Siege," *Wall Street Journal,* April 2, 1990, p. B1.

Dolliver, Mark, "Schieffelin & Somerset: Running Magazine Ads for Tanqueray Gin Brand," *Adweek* (Midwest edition), June 29, 1992, p. 30.

Dunkin, Amy, "In Sales, Liquor Isn't Quicker," *Business Week,* June 22, 1987, pp. 120-121.

Dunkin, Amy, "What Stirs the Spirit Makers: Vodka, Vodka, Vodka," *Business Week,* June 12, 1989, pp. 54-55.

Egerton, Judith, "Glenmore is Sold to British Distillery," *Courier-Journal* (Louisville, KY), July 12, 1991, p. A1.

Ellis-Simons, Pamela, "Vodka Chasers," *Marketing and Media Decisions,* November, 1989, pp. 50-54.

Fennell Robbins, Sally, "Somerset Gets Shot in Arm from Distillers Company," *Advertising Age,* July 18, 1985, p. 42.

Freedman, Alix, "With Yuppies Fading, Absolut May Too," *Wall Street Journal,* December 17, 1990, p. B1.

Fried, Eunice, "A Drink Fit for a King: Let Good Taste Rule with the Regal Flavor of Gin," *Black Enterprise,* October, 1989, p. 144.

Greenberg, Emanuel, and Madeline Greenberg, "Gin: A Summertime Tonic," *New York Times Magazine,* August 7, 1983, p. 52.

Hogarth, Don, "Distillers Issue Ultimatum," *Financial Post* (Windsor, Ontario), April 27, 1991, p. 1.

"It May Be Hard Times in the Hard-Liquor Industry; Seagram & Sons Plans to Enter Premium Gin Market," *Adweek* (Eastern edition), August 19, 1991, p. 9.

Kalish, David, "New Vodkas Vie for Classy Cachet," *New York Newsday,* December 11, 1989, section 3, p. 6.

Lipman, Joanne, "Tanqueray Brand to Join the Vodka Wars," *Wall Street Journal,* August 16, 1989.

Lipman, Joanne, "More Firms Are Spending Less on Campaigns to Hone Images," *Wall Street Journal,* November 26, 1991, p. B12.

Lipman, Joanne, "Carriage House Seeks Status for a Dry Rum," *Wall Street Journal,* September 20, 1991, p. B1.

Lipman, Joanne, "Ad Industry Debates About Line between Patriotism, Opportunism," *Wall Street Journal,* January 30, 1991, p. B6.

Mabry, Marcus, "A Thirst for Slicker Liquor: Now, 'Superpremiums,' " *Newsweek,* October 16, 1989, p. 60.

Marcom, Jr., John, "The House of Guinness," *Forbes,* June 12, 1989, pp. 85-91.

Maremont, Mark, "Guinness: A Lesson in Dealing with Drier Times," *Business Week,* June 27, 1988, pp. 52-54.

McNulty, Henry, "Gin," *Gourmet,* November, 1982, p. 26-29, 182-185.

"Model Sports Tanqueray Tan," *U.S.A. Today,* January 17, 1990, p. B4.

Sanchez, Jesus, "Liquor Advertising Flows Freely during Holidays, but Some Call for Temperance," *Los Angeles Times,* December 23, 1989, p. D1.

"Schieffelin & Somerset: Running Magazine Ads for Tanqueray Gin Brand," *Adweek* (Midwest edition), June 29, 1992, p. 30.

Silver, Jonathan, "Guinness Engages in Spirited Campaign to Upgrade the Image of Scotch Whiskey," *Wall Street Journal,* April 27, 1990.

Stewart, James, "The Vodka Challenge," *Wall Street Journal,* December 13, 1989, p. A12.

"Tanqueray Ad Makes Scents," *U.S.A. Today,* December 13, 1989, p. B9.

"Tanqueray Vodka Goes Nationwide," *Beverage Industry,* December 1990, p. 14.

Toman, Barbara, "Guinness Learns to Keep Up its Spirits Surviving Scandal, Firm Brews Recipe for Success," *Wall Street Journal,* December 20, 1990, p. A12.

Waggoner, Glen, "Gin as Tonic," *Esquire,* February, 1990, p. 30.

"Watch Out Seagram," *Forbes,* May 19, 1986, pp. 200-201.

Weber, Bruce, "Cottoning to Gin," *Esquire,* July, 1984, p. 46.

Winters, Patricia, "U.S. Vodka Volley: Upscale Line Extensions Fight to Fend Off Imports," *Advertising Age,* August 7, 1989, pp. 3, 60.

—Sara and Tom Pendergast

TASTER'S CHOICE®

Taster's Choice is the top-selling brand of 100 percent freeze-dried instant coffee sold in the United States. Marketed by the Nestlé Beverage Company, Taster's Choice is the only nationally distributed instant coffee that is produced using the process of freeze-drying, an expensive method of preserving coffee aroma and flavor. Nestlé, a multinational food manufacturer headquartered in Switzerland, also manufactures Nescafé, the most popular brand of instant coffee outside the United States. In addition to Taster's Choice and Nescafé, Nestlé owns Hills Brothers, MJB, and Chase & Sanborn coffee brands, all of which are handled by the Nestle Beverage Company, which derives approximately 20 percent of its sales from coffee. While distributed in Canada and in several international markets, Taster's Choice enjoys its greatest popularity in the United States.

Brand Origin and Early Marketing Strategy

Nestlé launched Taster's Choice nationally in 1967, almost three decades after the introduction of Nescafé, the first instant coffee. During the early 1960s, Nestlé and General Foods Company had been concurrently working on freeze-dried instant coffee products and were competing to be the first company to the market. Up until that time, instant coffee was produced primarily through spray-drying, a hot air drying technique that caused brewed coffee to lose much of its aroma and flavor. The freeze-drying process, which required only mild heat, resulted in what independent consumer taste tests deemed a superior-tasting instant coffee.

General Foods had test-marketed its new freeze-dried instant, Maxim, in Albany in 1964 and had expanded distribution throughout Upstate New York and into parts of Arizona and Indiana. Nestlé had been marketing Taster's Choice in Canada and was positioned to begin distribution in the United States. In December of 1966, Nestlé beat General Foods to supermarkets in the Cleveland area by three to four days. In the fierce advertising battle that ensued, each company spent approximately $20,000,000 to promote its new coffee. Nestlé selected advertising firm Leo Burnett USA of Chicago to handle the Taster's Choice campaign. Ogilvy & Mather promoted the General Foods Maxim label. Nestlé distributed 120,000 two-ounce sample jars of Taster's Choice to homeowners, hired spokeswomen to discuss the flavorful and aromatic advantages to Taster's Choice, and served samples in area shopping centers. General Foods deposited six-cup cans of

Maxim in the shopping carts of patrons at local supermarkets and distributed coupons at Cleveland train stations. Both companies offered additional coupons and ran television, radio, and newspaper ads. By March of 1967, Maxim had earned a 13.4 percent share of the Cleveland area market, edging out Taster's Choice by a single percentage point.

Early Marketing Strategy

Although it placed second to Maxim during its initial U.S. marketing effort, Taster's Choice enjoyed almost immediate success upon its national debut in 1967. Nestlé devoted extensive resources to promote its latest product, and Taster's Choice continued to gain market share. Nestlé capitalized on the distinction between Taster's Choice and most other instant brands, promoting the idea that Taster's Choice was *the* freeze-dried instant coffee. Early advertisements focused on the uniqueness of the manufacturing technology, explaining what the freeze-drying process entailed and why it resulted in the best possible instant coffee.

Beginning in the 1970s, Nestlé shifted its advertising strategy away from the technical attributes of Taster's Choice and instead appealed to the emotions of its consumers by highlighting the role coffee played in their lives and relationships. This tactic proved successful, and Taster's Choice strengthened its position in the instant coffee market. In 1973, Nestlé introduced Taster's Choice Decaffeinated and proceeded to promote it in conjunction with Taster's Choice regular. By 1974, Taster's Choice regular was the leading brand in the soluble coffee market, and by the following year, Taster's Choice decaf had earned first place in the decaffeinated instant coffee market. The 5 percent market share earned by Taster's Choice decaf in 1975 was almost equal to the combined share of its two primary decaf competitors, Brim and Sanka, both of which were also produced using freeze-drying technology.

Brand Revitalization

Sales of Taster's Choice regular and decaf declined during the late 1970s and Taster's Choice slipped to the number two position in the soluble coffee market behind General Foods' Maxwell House brand. Nestlé's initial response was to substantially cut the Taster's Choice advertising budget in 1980 only to increase it again in 1981. The decline in coffee sales was due in part to the rising cost of raw materials and in part to an increasing preference by consumers for cold, sweet drinks. In an effort to reinvigorate the Taster's Choice line and regain market share captured by the cold beverage industry, Nestlé technicians worked to improve the freeze-drying process The new technology was designed to extract and seal in more of the coffee's aroma and flavor and result in a darker color and richer flavor. The end product represented what Nestlé considered to be a ''major break-through'' in freeze-drying technology. Taster's Choice regular and decaf were relaunched in 1982 with updated labeling and a new marketing strategy.

In conjunction with the reintroduction of Taster's Choice regular and decaf, Nestlé implemented an advertising campaign featuring the tag line ''Times like these are made for Taster's Choice.'' The television commercials depicted the integral part coffee plays at important moments in consumers' lives. In the first ad, a woman anxiously waited for her husband to come home on a stormy night and then, over a cup of Taster's Choice, expressed her relief at his return. Nestlé hoped the ads, again handled by Leo Burnett USA, would create a bond between the public and Taster's Choice. But Taster's Choice faced stiff competition from rival Folgers, whose restaurant switch promotion proved effective in gaining Folgers widespread brand recognition and increased market share. While the Taster's Choice decaffeinated instant coffee sales increased from a 6.0 percent market share in 1981 to 7.1 percent in 1982, Taster's Choice regular remained at 9.5 percent, down 2.2 percent from 1980. The ''Times Like These . . .'' campaign was less successful than anticipated, and Nestlé thereafter concentrated its efforts on promoting the ''fresh-brewed'' advantages of the improved freeze-drying process.

Brand Expansion

Coffee consumption in general continued to decline in the 1980s, and one market study revealed that the percentage of coffee drinkers in their 20s had dropped from 80 percent in 1963 to only 40 percent in 1986. Coffee producers were faced with countering aggressive marketing strategies by the soft drink industry, which had captured a wider segment of the beverage market through expanding its product line with new cold beverages, such as caffeine-free cola.

After the introduction of Taster's Choice decaf in 1973, the Taster's Choice product line had remained unchanged for fifteen

years. Responding to the challenge of soft drink competitors, in 1987 Nestlé introduced two new products to the Taster's Choice line: Maragor Bold, a dark roasted coffee, and Colombian Select, a 50/50 blend of regular and decaffeinated coffee. Neither brand was successful in capturing the public's attention, and both were subsequently dropped from the Taster's Choice line. Maragor Bold failed primarily because few consumers had ever heard of the maragor coffee bean. Maragor Bold was replaced by Gourmet Roast and Decaffeinated Gourmet Roast in 1990, both of which were also dark roasted coffees. Caff-Lite, another brand containing 50 percent less caffeine than regular coffee, replaced Colombian Select in 1991. Product line extensions in general earned less than 2 percent of the market share of coffee sales, and Nestlé chose not to invest heavily in marketing the new products. Taster's Choice regular and Taster's Choice decaf continued to account for the large majority of sales for the product line.

To streamline its operations, in 1990 Nestlé combined its beverage operations, including Taster's Choice, MJB, and Chase & Sanborn coffee brands, all Nestlé beverage products, and Hills Brothers Coffee Company, which Nestlé had acquired in 1985, under the management of the Nestlé Beverage Company.

Advertising Innovations

During the restructuring process, Nestlé selected McCann-Erickson of New York to handle advertising for all Nestlé beverage products. In late 1990, McCann-Erickson launched the first in a series of advertisements that were to earn Taster's Choice a sizable market share increase. The ads, presented in an episode format, focused on the developing romance between two charming neighbors. In each episode, the couple (British actors Sharon Maughan and Anthony Head) grew closer, brought together as a result of their mutual love of Taster's Choice. The ads were taken from an immensely successful promotion of Nescafé s Gold Blend that was launched in 1987 in the United Kingdom by McCann-Erickson Worldwide and resulted in a 40 percent increase in Gold Blend sales between 1987 and 1992. The British public's continued enamoration with the commercials evolved to the point that in 1992, Corgi Books, a subsidiary of Bantam Doubleday Dell, announced its plan to publish a 300-page romance novel telling the couple's complete story.

The Taster's Choice version of the ads enjoyed similar popularity in the United States. By early 1993, six episodes had been released and market share had increased by 10 percent—indicating a strong resurgence of interest in the product. Indeed, Nestlé offices were flooded with calls and letters of admiration for the campaign. Taster's Choice announced it would continue the ads as long as the public remained interested, but no plans were made to publish a U.S. version of the romance novel. Nestlé did, however, run a ''Most Romantic First Date'' contest in conjunction with ABC and featuring ABC soap opera stars, as a promotion for its product.

The coffee market has faced the increasing challenge of competing successfully with the soft drink industry for consumers. Continual fluctuation of coffee sales and consumption in the U.S. has forced Nestlé to be innovative and aggressive in promoting its coffee products. With its latest advertising strategy and long-term consumer brand loyalty, Taster's Choice is well positioned for continued success in the instant coffee market.

Further Reading:

Bowers, Elana, "Coffee Couple's Story to Percolate in Book," *Advertising Age,* December 14, 1992, p. 6.

Brunelli, Richard, "Taster's Choice Flirts Take a Lot of TLC," *Mediaweek,* September 16, 1991, p. 2.

"GF-Nestlé Coffee Battle Rages in Cleveland Market," *Advertising Age,* January 9, 1967, p. 1, 84.

Heer, Jean, *Nestlé: 125 Years 1866-1991,* Vevey, Switzerland: Nestlé S.A., 1991.

"Instant Coffees," *Consumer Reports,* May, 1985, p. 264-68.

Jervey, Gay, "Will Nestlé Face New P&G Entry? Taster's Choice Wakens," *Advertising Age,* March 22, 1982, p. 2, 88.

Johnson, Bradley, "What's Next? A Brew-Haha?" *Advertising Age,* September 14, 1992, p. 4.

Maxwell, John C., Jr., "Changing Tastes Grinding Away at Coffee Sales," *Advertising Age,* September 15, 1986, p. 82.

—Shannon J. Young

TETLEY®

Tetley brand of tea, a blend of pekoe and orange pekoe cut black teas, is the top-selling packaged tea in the United Kingdom and number two in the United States, where tea is not as popular. Tetley was among the first brands of tea sold in individual teabags, and its popularity began to climb further when it introduced round tea bags in Britain and the United States in the early 1990s. By this time Tetley had moved into marketing instant teas, and had also introduced bottled cold teas in eight flavors to keep pace with changing consumer preferences.

Brand Origin

Tetley tea got its start in 1837 when Joseph and Edward Tetley began selling tea from the back of a horsecart in Yorkshire, England. The Tetleys had been selling salt from their horse, and tea was initially a relatively minor addition. At that time, tea was regarded as an expensive luxury item, and selling tea in this fashion was unique. Their success was moderate at first, but the two wisely invested their profits in railroads. With money from this investment, and with their brand of tea still selling reasonably well, the Tetleys brought their business to London, setting up an office there in 1856.

Tea was becoming far more popular and far less expensive as more of it was imported to England on British and American tea clippers, which raced each other from the East, making the journey in about 100 days. Teas from all over the world passed through London, and Joseph Tetley & Company created different blends to meet growing public demand. Tetley imported tea from India and Ceylon, but remained a wholesaler in England.

Early Marketing Strategy

Tetley became a consumer brand in the United States in 1888, when Robert G. Cather, who had become a partner with the Tetleys, arranged for an American firm, Wright & Graham, to distribute Tetley's Teas in the United States. A U.S. headquarters was set up on White Street in New York City, and the brand was sold primarily through department stores. Tetley's teas were publicized during the Chicago World Fair in 1893 and through newspapers, posters, and later by radio, building up the brand's name recognition east of the Mississippi River, its primary sales area.

The years before World War I were prosperous for the brand as it expanded throughout the eastern half of the United States, and

tea drinking became more popular. The invention of iced tea in the early 20th century and the tea bag in 1910 increased tea's appeal as a consumer commodity. In 1913 Joseph Tetley & Co. was incorporated in the United States, maintaining close ties with its British parent company. Offices and manufacturing facilities were set up on Greenwich Street in New York City.

World War I disrupted the Tetley's business, because it was difficult to get tea leaves from India and Ceylon to London or New York during that time. After the war, tea became more popular in the United States, and Tetley's sales rose. Tea rooms were opened in many hotels, and tea began to shed its image as a less "manly" beverage than coffee. World War II was even more devastating to Tetley's trade. Tea had been packaged in tins, but in 1942 a tin shortage caused by the war forced Tetley to begin using cardboard tea boxes. Tea tins were resurrected after the war, but discontinued again in 1969.

Tetley went from strictly being a wholesaler to becoming a consumer brand in Britain after World War II. British tea consumption per capita was five times that of the United States, but consumption patterns were different. The British made their tea from loose leaves, and tea bags were virtually nonexistent until Tetley began marketing them in England in 1955. The tea bags were barely promoted, however, and sales were slight.

Competition increased in the U.S. tea market after World War II, and by the early 1950s, Tetley found itself fighting with Salada and Tenderleaf teas for second place. All three lagged behind Lipton, the leading U.S. tea brand with national distribution.

Despite the competition, sales were growing, and in 1950 Tetley opened a plant in Savannah, Georgia, to produce more Tetley Tea. In 1958, another plant was opened, in Williamsport, Pennsylvania, and the outdated Greenwich Village site was phased out.

Product Manufacture

Tetley Tea was bought on direct consignment from factories in Ceylon and India, where green tea leaves were withered, rolled, fermented, and fired to produce brittle, dark brown leaves ready for transport. Arriving at a Tetley warehouse, tea was tasted and sorted by blend of leaf. Highly trained tea blenders then blended different types of teas to produce teas with the right body, flavor,

AT A GLANCE

Tetley brand tea founded in 1837 by Joseph and Edward Tetley; product entered the United States as a packaged brand, 1888; bought by Beech-Nut Life Savers, Inc., 1961; parent became Squibb Beech-Nut Inc., 1968, which was bought by J. Lyons & Co. Ltd., 1972; Lyons bought by Allied Breweries Ltd. to form Allied-Lyons PLC.

Performance: *Market share*—15% (second-place share) of packaged black tea market.

Major competitor: Lipton.

Advertising: *Agency*—Rotando, Lerch & Iafeliece, Stamford, CT. *Major campaign*—"Why is it round?"

Addresses: *Parent company*—Tetley, Inc., 100 Commerce Dr., Shelton, CT 06484; phone: (303) 929-9200. *Ultimate parent company*—Allied-Lyons PLC, London, England.

and color. The blending of mass quantities of tea was then done mechanically. Various types of tea were fed into giant hoppers at the top of a Tetley tea plant, where any debris from packing chests was removed. The tea leaves then went into drums with a capacity of 2,500 pounds, where they were blended for about eight minutes. Tea destined for consumers then went into elaborate packing machines that filled and sewed tea bags, while also labeling and cartoning them. Thus, tea leaves were not touched by human hands between being picked and reaching the tea cup.

Advertising Strategies

In 1956 Tetley hired Ogilvy, Benson & Mather as its advertising firm and began relying primarily on radio ads to increase its U.S. market share. Radio sports were favored because radio allowed advertising to be flexible, reducing or increasing spots as market requirements changed. Radio also reached all segments of the public, bringing Tetley's ads into seven out of ten target households each week. The ads were broadcast in city, suburban, and rural locations frequently, reaching consumers several times a day on shopping days, considered to be the later days of the week.

The first year results of the radio campaign were mediocre, and Tetley increased radio spending and began to pull away from its closest competitors. By 1959, spot radio accounted for 80 percent of its $1.4 million advertising budget. Tetley had pulled securely into the second-place slot.

Radio ads featured dialogues between a Tetley's Tea taster and his assistant. The characters used humor and pushed key selling points such as the fact that Tetley only used tiny leaves from the top of tea plants, and that each tea bag contained a blend of leaves from 22 plantations. The ads also promoted the "rejuvenating lift" of tea and attacked lingering doubts about its being a "sissy drink."

Hot tea was promoted in the northern United States during the fall and winter, with some attention devoted to iced-tea during the summer. Tetley Tea was promoted more heavily in the South during the warmer months, when attention was put on iced tea. The advertising budget for a particular region was determined by Tetley's sales in the area. Print ads and spot TV were also used in the company's promotions.

In 1961 Tetley was bought by Beech-Nut Life Savers, Inc. One of the new firm's first decisions was to begin promoting Tetley tea bags in Britain using British agency Smith-Warden Ltd. Ads began in late 1964, primarily 30-second TV commercials using Megs Jenkins, a well-known British character actress. British tea bag sales rose 40 percent in less than a year, with Tetley accounting for 80 percent of the new sales. Smith-Warden then began a research campaign to identify tea bag buyers and potential tea bag buyers.

While it still barely existed west of the Mississippi, by the early 1960s Tetley was a huge presence in many eastern cities, sometimes holding as much as one-third of a given market. In order to increase that percentage, the brand was sometimes promoted through large events like television contests. In 1964, for example, in Philadelphia, where Tetley already held 32 percent of the market, the brand was extensively advertised on a local TV station. The brand was then promoted heavily on one of that station's live daytime programs for women, with the host explaining the rules of a four-week Tetley contest.

Product Innovations

In the 1970s and 1980s when convenience in beverages became more important, and consumers moved toward cold, sweet drinks, many companies introduced instant drink mixes, particularly for making iced tea. Tetley's Iced Tea Crystals were introduced in 1985 in the United States. Though the brand entered the market late, Tetley claimed to sell a superior product with crystals

Various antique tea tins in which Tetley products were originally distributed, and the revolutionary tea bag from 1930.

that dissolved more rapidly and did not create the foam that other instant teas often produced. In 1988 Tetley began test marketing Tetley Real-Brewed Iced Tea in ten-ounce bottles.

Meanwhile Tetley was pushing hard in the United Kingdom, through ad campaigns that depicted it as a fun and lively modern brand that was also a good value. From 1990 to 1991 Tetley was the most heavily advertised brand in the United Kingdom. In 1991 Tetley introduced Tetley's Round Teabags in Britain. Tea consumption had been declining for a decade, and tea companies were searching for ways of making tea more marketable. The round bag was seen as a way to differentiate the brand from the competition and was seen as "friendly" and "feminine."

The round teabags were heavily promoted in print ads that depicted it as simpler and more elegant than square bags with their strings, tags, and staples. The new teabags were promoted with round teatowels and radios. Tetley also claimed that the round bags made a better cup of tea. Tetley Round Teabags contained a blend of orange pekoe and pekoe cut black tea that was slightly different than Tetley's other teas. They were also made of more porous paper and contained more tea than square teabags. The result was large gains for Tetley in Britain as the brand soared from the number two tea at a 17 percent market share in 1988, to the number one brand with 21 percent in 1991.

In 1991 Tetley introduced Tetley Freeze Dried Instant Tea in Britain. As in the United States, instant teas had been introduced as early as the late 1960s, but not had done well because their taste was considered inferior. Tetley had put considerable effort into research and development and believed that it had finally created a good tasting instant tea.

By 1992 Tetley Round Teabags were regarded as Britain's favorite brand of teabag. Tetley's sales had risen 30 percent in two years, and it continued to be one of the most heavily advertised grocery brands in Britain.

In 1992 Tetley introduced eight ready-to-drink iced teas in flavors like Peach Chiller and Raspberry Blizzard. The teas were distributed by A&W Brands and backed by a $5 million to $10 million advertising campaign.

The same year, Tetley set its sights on reproducing the success of its round teabag in the U.S. market, test marketing the teabags in the Northeast. The bags did extremely well there, increasing the brand's market share by 60 percent in some markets. Round teabags were introduced nationally in 1993, backed by a $35 million annual ad campaign, most of it on TV. The TV ads featured a waitress who could not understand why a teabag should be round. In an unusual move, Lipton, Tetley's main competitor in the United States, began a large counter-campaign, faulting the round teabags for lacking a string and tag to pull them from hot water. Lipton had a 41 percent share of the $500 million U.S. teabag market, while Tetley had 15 percent.

Tea sales on the whole were growing in the United States as health-conscious consumers turned away from coffee, which has about three times as much caffeine. With its new round bags, Tetley seemed poised to reap benefits from this expansion.

Further Reading:

"Lyons Tetley Innovation Livens Up Tea Market," *Co-Operative News,* April 7, 1992.

Deveny, Kathleen, "Tetley Hopes to Reshape the Tea Market," *Wall Street Journal,* February 16, 1993.

"Can Tradition be Shattered?" *Printers Ink,* June 10, 1966.

"Tetley's Tastes Best with Spot Radio," *Sponsor,* November 21, 1959. "Tea For TV," *Sponsor,* October 12, 1964.

"Tetley's Centenary History," *Tetley's World Newsletter,* Fall, 1988.

Winters, Patricia, "Tetley Round Tea Bags Challenge No. 1 Lipton," *Advertising Age,* February 1, 1993.

—*Scott M. Lewis*

TOOTSIE ROLL®

Tootsie Roll brand of candy, in its brown, white, and red wrapped cylinder, has been a candy-counter staple for nearly a century. Indeed, a consistent industry performer, Tootsie Roll is virtually an American icon. Like many American icons, of course, Tootsie Roll was created by a newly arrived immigrant.

In 1896 Leo Hirschfeld, who had settled in Brooklyn, New York, from his native Austria, began experimenting with a recipe from his homeland. Hirschfeld had already produced such food products as Bromangelon, a jelling powder that prefigured today's gelatin desserts. The scientist created a thick, chewy chocolate, fashioning it into bite-size rolls and—more distinctively—wrapping each piece in an individual paper. The hand wrapping is believed to be a first for the candy trade: in turn-of-the-century America, sweets were still primarily sold by the scoop out of large barrels or jars.

Brand Growth

Hirschfeld's penny apiece confection—dubbed "Tootsie Roll" in honor of his daughter, Clara "Tootsie" Hirschfeld Ludwig—was an instant success Brooklyn. As demand outgrew supply, the production was moved to a New York City company called Stern & Staalberg, where Hirschfeld himself was a partner. "Here was a treat for everyone," as Nancy Boas writes in *Across the Board.* "Sales at Stern & Staalberg swelled, and by 1922 the company, renamed Sweets Company of America, was listed on the New York Stock Exchange."

The Great Depression bit into Tootsie Roll sales, but by 1938, with recovery at hand, Sweets Company of America had enough orders to again expand, this time into a modern, 120,000-square-foot plant in Hoboken, New Jersey. Such innovations as the conveyer belt sped up Tootsie Roll production, to the tune of increased sales. By 1941, it was again necessary to expand facilities, with a 40,000-square-foot addition to the plant.

World War II ushered in an era of austerity for seemingly everyone *but* Tootsie Roll. In fact, the candy was one of the few confections to stay in full production throughout the war and, because of its ability to "keep" in most conditions, was shipped to servicemen overseas. During this time Tootsie Roll was even part of standard G.I. rations, valued for its "quick energy" properties.

The postwar years saw an increase in raw materials like cocoa and sugar, allowing Tootsie Roll to expand even further. In 1948 business executive William B. Rubin became company president. He concentrated on increased marketing and advertising, resulting in 15 consecutive years of record growth. A second operating plant, in Los Angeles, opened to accommodate more demand.

Under Rubin's direction, Tootsie Roll advertising was venturing into the fledgling medium of television—sponsoring the Howdy Doody show and other programs with high "child appeal"—while increasing its presence in print, radio, and other media. One print piece in particular is legendary to Tootsie Roll: the 1950 *Life* magazine ad showed a beaming young woman posing with a Tootsie Roll while the words *Sweet!, Popular!* and *Wholesome!* danced around her head. The woman was 18-year-old Ellen Rubin, daughter of the president; later on, as Ellen Gordon, she would assume the presidency of the company.

Tootsie Roll entered the 1960s with a healthy profit, nearly tripling its net earnings through 1966. That year proved to be a significant one: 1966 saw the company's name changed to Tootsie Roll Industries, Inc. At the same time, the company opened a large Midwest facility in Chicago's South Side. This plant would eventually become Tootsie Roll headquarters; by 1970 both the Hoboken and Los Angeles plants had transferred their resources to Chicago.

Tootsie on a Roll

Through all the corporate changes and marketing plans, though, the basic Tootsie Roll never lost its familiar appearance, flavor, or texture. And that, suggests financial analyst David Leibowitz, is one secret to its success. "Name me an alternative to a Tootsie Roll," he states in a *Chicago Tribune* article by John Gorman. "They don't exist. Who else has a 1-cent product? Who else has the Tootsie Roll variety? It's a household name."

And it's a name that turns up in some unusual places. In another *Chicago Tribune* piece, writer John Blades lists the books in which the candy has made cameo appearances. They include Ken Follett's novel *Triple,* which includes the line "Girls will do anything for a Tootsie Roll"; *The Eighth Dwarf,* by Ross Thomas ("Can you imagine a conquering nation with a sweet called Tootsie Rolls?"); and even the cover of a thriller, *Pocock and Pitt,* by Elliot Baker. But Tootsie Roll president Ellen Gordon "wasn't

AT A GLANCE

Tootsie Roll brand of candy invented in 1896 in Brooklyn, NY, by Leo Hirschfeld; produced in New York City by Stern & Staalberg; company used the name Sweets Company of America, 1922-66; renamed Tootsie Roll Industries, Inc., 1966.

Performance: Market share—2% of total candy market; 50% (top share) of candy subsegment that includes taffies and lollipops; current leader in lollipop manufacturing. *Sales*—$207 million.

Advertising: Agency—In-house. *Major campaign*—A long-running animated commercial with the theme "How many licks does it take to get to the Tootsie Roll center of a Tootsie Pop?"

Addresses: Parent company—Tootsie Roll Industries, Inc., 7401 South Cicero Avenue, Chicago, IL 60629; phone: (312) 838-3400.

exactly thrilled by the devious use that Baker's hero makes of the company candy," notes Blades. "He leaves a trademark Tootsie Roll in the hand of an enemy agent after breaking his neck."

In the field of autobiography, Tootsie Roll proves heroic. In *Doorknob Five Two,* the memoirs of World War II fighter pilot Frederick Arnold, the author describes the time he was shot down over the Sahara with little more than Tootsie Rolls to sustain him. "I carried Tootsie Rolls with me on every mission," Arnold told interviewer Nancy Boas. "I would divide up a mission by rewarding myself: If I made it, I'd reward myself with a segment." Arnold, stranded for three days, survived by eating Tootsie Rolls and using them as gifts for a friendly native tribe that took him in.

Though it has traditionally captured only about two percent of the $8 billion candy market (outdrawn by corporate giants like Nestlé and Hershey), Tootsie Roll has been a leader in its own segment (taffies and lollipops), enjoying a 50 percent market share. As Stephen Wilkinson, writing in *Working Woman,* elaborates, Hershey and Nestlé "control virtually all the chocolate-bar display space in shops and supermarkets. [But the] great strength of Tootsie Rolls is that they stand entirely alone in their field—unlike chocolate bars, chewing gum, LifeSavers or a lot of other familiar favorites."

The company made some acquisitions beginning in 1972, when Tootsie Roll Industries purchased the Mason Division of Candy Corporation of America. This added such items as Mason Mints, Mason Dots, Mason Licorice Crows, and Mason Spice Berries to the Tootsie Roll family. Another addition was Bonomo Turkish Taffy. In 1978 the company bought Cella's Confections, Inc., which had been manufacturing chocolate-covered cherries since 1864. Tootsie Roll purchased the Charms Company in 1988, a manufacturer best known for the Charms Blow Pop. The addition of Charms makes Tootsie Roll the current leader in lollipop manufacturing.

Brand Development

Within the Tootsie Roll line itself, several variations on the original theme have proven popular. Best known is the Tootsie Roll Pop (also known just as the Tootsie Pop), a lollipop fashioned from a round hard-candy shell. Within the shell—which comes in such flavors as cherry, grape, orange, and chocolate—is a bite-

sized portion of Tootsie Roll. The Tootsie Pop Drop is essentially a smaller version of the lollipop, but without the stick. Flavor Rolls retain the Tootsie Roll texture but feature flavors like lime, vanilla, and orange rather than chocolate. Tootsie Frooties are chewables in cherry, banana, and grape. And for those who grew up on the candy but now "find traditional Tootsies a challenge for dentalwork," as Blades puts it, there are Tootsie Bars, a chocolate-covered softer version of the original.

Tootsie packaging has also evolved over the years. A Tootsie Roll, Flavor Roll, Frootie, or Bar may now range in size from a penny-nip (called a Midgee) to the more daunting "foot of Tootsie." Different combinations of the candies are packaged as Tootsie Bunch Pops and Child's Play Assortment. Tootsie-theme banks and decorative boxes can also be purchased.

"How Many Licks?"

A large part of Tootsie Roll's continuing appeal lies in the area of creative advertising. One spot from the early 1970s has run in continuous cycle, reaching both nostalgic baby-boomers and their young children. In one animated spot for Tootsie Roll Pops, a little boy's quest for the answer to an important question brings him to a wise old owl. "Mr. Owl," says the boy, "how many licks does it take to get to the Tootsie Roll center of a Tootsie Pop?" In order to find out, the owl takes the boy's Tootsie Pop in his wing and begins licking it, counting "One, two, three," and then with a rattling *crunch,* bites open the lollipop and proclaims "three" to be the correct answer. "How many licks does it take? The world may never know," intones a voice-over. Actually, many consumers have taken it upon themselves to answer the question.

A vehicle used in the 1920s to transport Tootsie Rolls.

According to Boas, some 10,000 children have responded to the campaign; and during Operation Desert Storm, when Tootsie Pops saw active service, two soldiers came up with their calculations: around 1,635 licks. Another television spot plays on the theme "Whatever it is I think I see, becomes a Tootsie Roll to me," as ordinary objects in the ad take on the appearance of the candy. This too has become a memorable campaign.

Performance Appraisal

In addition to producing a quality product, Tootsie Roll Industries, Inc. has won praise for its business savvy. Virtually free of long-term debt, the company "is nearly impervious to economic cycles,'' according to Malcolm Berko in an *Akron Beacon Journal* column. As Berko relates, the company has seen its dividends increase threefold, its sales triple, its book value increase five times, and its net margins double between 1979 and 1991. With sales reaching $207 million in 1991, overall profit peaked at more than $25 million in that year.

This is not to say that Tootsie Roll hasn't weathered its share of setbacks, however. Like all confectioners, the company was hard hit in 1974 by a 600 percent jump in sugar prices, the same year that cocoa prices also rose dramatically. The result was a shift in size of some Tootsie Roll products. And in 1982, like many other companies, Tootsie Roll suffered slightly in the wake of a national scare involving the poisoning of Tylenol tablets. Because Tootsie Rolls are individually wrapped, they, like many other candies, came under suspicion as parents worried over the safety of their children's Halloween treats. By the next year, however, sales had bounced back to their normal momentum.

A family-owned concern, Tootsie Roll remains firmly in the hands of president Ellen Gordon and her husband, chairperson Melvin Gordon. Their cooperative management approach has resulted in Tootsie Roll's being named to *Forbes*' honor roll of small companies—those with annual sales between $5 million and $350 million)—as well as a mention in *CFO* magazine's list of America's strongest companies. ''It's easy to increase sales and to increase market share,'' Gordon told *CFO*, ''but not profits.'' Nonetheless, according to the article, ''Tootsie Roll has consistently achieved a healthy 18 percent return on equity and an 11 percent net return on sales.''

As a small but prosperous company, Tootsie Roll has been considered a prime target for purchase by a corporate giant. But that's unlikely in the near future, as the Gordon family controls 63 percent of the voting power. And Ellen Gordon, for one, doesn't see too much of a threat from Hershey or Nestlé. ''What we have here is nostalgia, and the nostalgia has been perpetuated,'' she told *Financial World* reporter Kathleen Morris in January 1992.

''People ask us how we can compete against the giant candy corporations,'' adds Melvin Gordon in an interview with *Midway* reporter Jack Klobucar. ''We wonder how they can compete against us. We can make decisions on the spot; we have hands-on management that's impossible in most billion-dollar companies; we know all our employees . . . by name and take an interest in

their families. And we encourage input from the bottom—the door is open to anybody with an idea.''

Such hands-on management has resulted in what Klobucar calls ''vertical integration'': Tootsie Roll Industries, Inc. ''designs its own packaging, prints its own retail displays and promotional literature, refines its own sugar, transports its own raw materials, owns its own New York ad agency, and has the capability to generate all of its own power. By controlling these services, they not only reduce operating costs but also reinforce their independence—a commodity almost as precious as chocolate.''

The Gordons have also put their minds toward expansion. Starting in the 1960s the company began foreign investment, beginning with a subsidiary in Mexico. Known as ''Tutsi,'' the candy proved a hit there, so Tootsies traveled north to Canada, in 1971. Next came a Philippines licensing and distribution concern. According to Berko, Tootsie Roll is also ''targeting the Far East and Europe for export growth, where per capita consumption of confectionery is 40 percent higher than in the United States.''

Further Reading:

Berko, Malcolm, ''A Sweet Deal for Long-Term Investors,'' *Akron Beacon Journal,* August 4, 1991.

Bettner, Jill, ''Sticky Business,'' *Forbes,* February 13, 1984, p. 112.

Blades, John, ''Tootsie's on a Roll,'' *Chicago Tribune,* December 6, 1990.

Boas, Nancy, ''How Sweet It Is,'' *Across the Board,* vol. 21, no. 1, December 1984.

Driscoll, Mary, and Maile Hulihan, ''America's Strongest Companies,'' *CFO,* April 1991, p. 17.

Gorman, John, ''Tootsie Roll Turns Chocolate into Gold,'' *Chicago Tribune,* June 24, 1985, sec. 4, p. 1.

Klobucar, Jack, ''How Sweet It Is: Tootsie Roll Industries Posts Record Sales,'' *Midway,* May 1986, p. 24.

Lappen, Alyssa A., ''Tootsie Rolling in Money,'' *Forbes,* January 21, 1991.

Magee, Patricia, ''Ellen Gordon Reaches 'Top of the Mountain','' *Candy Industry,* September 1985.

Morris, Kathleen, ''Tootsie Roll: Cashing in on Closet Candy Eating,'' *Financial World,* January 21, 1992, p. 16.

Ryan, Nancy, ''Tootsie on a Roll in Forbes Magazine Survey,'' *Chicago Tribune,* October 29, 1991.

Wilkinson, Stephen, ''The Practical Genius of Penny Candy,'' *Working Woman,* April 1989.

—Susan Salter

TOTAL®

Total means nutrition. Marketed under the banner "Total nutrition," all three Total cereal varieties—the original whole wheat Total, Corn Total, and Total Raisin Bran—provide in each one-ounce serving 100 percent of the U.S. Recommended Daily Allowance (RDA) for nine vitamins and iron and 20 percent of the U.S. RDA for calcium. For consumer advocacy groups and some competitors, however, the definition of Total as nutrition has seemed exaggerated, and Total has drawn criticism for its claims. Nonetheless, since its introduction in 1961 Total has become one of the central brands in the ready-to-eat breakfast cereal line-up of General Mills, Inc., which ranks second in the industry after Kellogg. General Mills brought Total to prominence with its distinctive marketing of the brand as a nutritional cereal and with its strategy of continual brand innovation and aggressive advertising. To achieve continued growth in the ready-to-eat cereal category, General Mills has focused upon constantly improving its established brands and advertising fiercely, rather than on launching new products. In the early 1990s Total Raisin Bran represented a major domestic offensive for General Mills against its arch-rival, the Kellogg Company, in a worldwide battle between the two leading cereal companies. General Mills continued to improve the original Total during the 1990s as well.

Brand Origins and Initial Commercial Success

General Mills introduced Total in the midst of a rapid expansion of the ready-to-eat breakfast cereal market during the 1950s and 1960s. *Forbes* reported in 1966 that during the past decade the number of cereal brands had virtually doubled, from about 50 to almost 100. Half of the new cereals were "kid-oriented," and in all, the new brands accounted for almost one-quarter of overall cereal sales, partly as the result of television advertising directed toward children. "Healthy" cereals also debuted during this period, and Total capitalized on this industry trend. The cereal offered 100 percent of the officially established U.S. RDA of all vitamins and iron mandatory for a multi-vitamin and iron supplement.

Total contributed to phenomenal success for General Mills. From 1960 through 1965, *Forbes* reported, General Mills's sales of cereal rose 90 percent to $143 million. Acquiring about 22 percent of the market by 1965, General Mills had by then over-taken General Foods for second place in the category. *Forbes*

attributed much of General Mills's success to its steeply rising cereal sales.

General Mills had been manufacturing breakfast cereal for almost four decades before it introduced Total. In 1924 it introduced Wheaties, a whole grain flake cereal based on an accidental discovery by a Minneapolis health diet clinician. Thirteen years later, General Mills brought out Corn Kix, and four years after that, Cheerioats (now Cheerios). These three cereals formed the backbone of the company's market share until the 1950s.

Of all General Mills cereals, Total is most closely related to Wheaties, and both cereals are made by the same process: two rotating rollers flatten wheat pellets to make the flakes; heated air then toasts the flakes to specific moisture levels for maximum crispness and flavor. Total is additionally fortified with vitamins and iron.

Total Innovation

The first Total line extension premiered in 1971 when General Mills offered the vitamin supplement of Total on a corn flake instead of a wheat flake. Named Corn Total, the cereal appeared under the same advertising slogans that the original Total had ten years earlier. The ads boasted the high vitamin and iron content while appealing to dieters: "Watches your vitamins while you watch your weight."

In 1988 General Mills took the bran flakes from its Raisin Nut Bran cereal, substituted natural, uncoated raisins, and added the vitamin and mineral supplement from Total to create Total Raisin Bran, proclaimed "the most nutritious raisin bran in the market." Advertisements comparing the nutritional content of Total Raisin Bran with similar raisin brans from Kellogg's and General Foods Corporation's Post division soon followed. As a result of Total Raisin Bran and extensions of other major brands, General Mills had by 1991 achieved a 29 percent market share in the dry cereal category, an all-time high. Meanwhile, Kellogg was down to 38 percent in 1991 from 41 percent in 1988, according to Patricia Sellers writing in *Fortune*. In a $7.4 billion industry in 1991, each market share percentage point represented $74 million of sales. Kellogg responded to General Mills' direct offensive against Kellogg's Raisin Bran with large advertising expenditures of its own. As a result, by mid-1992, Kellogg was able to stabilize its core brands, including Raisin Bran.

AT A GLANCE

Total brand of cereal founded in 1961 by General Mills, Inc., in Minneapolis, MN; brand extensions include Corn Total in 1971 and Total Raisin Bran in 1988; beta carotene, the base of vitamin A, was added to Total in 1991.

Performance: *Market share*—1.9% of ready-to-eat cereal category (1990). *Sales*—$124 million (1990 estimate).

Major competitor: Kellogg's Just Right; also Kellogg's Raisin Bran.

Advertising: *Agency*—Saatchi & Saatchi DFS Compton, New York, NY. *Major campaign*—"Total nutrition."

Addresses: *Parent company*—General Mills, Inc., P.O. Box 1113, Minneapolis, MN 55440; phone: (612) 540-2311; fax: (612) 540-4921.

In 1992 General Mills brought to the market an innovation in its original Total, offering 20 percent of Total's vitamin A content in the form of beta-carotene, the vitamin A precursor. The cereal then provided 100 percent of the RDA for vitamin A and 11 other vitamins and minerals, positioning itself yet more solidly as the cereal with the most complete vitamin and mineral supplement available.

Some of General Mills' brand extensions were less successful. In the 1980s, the company attempted to enter the hot cereal market with products marketed under the Total brand name. According to Steve Weiner in *Forbes,* in 1987 General Mills spent $12 million introducing its line of vitamin-enriched instant and quick oatmeals. The hot cereal category was dominated at the time by the Quaker Oats Company, with 68 percent of the market, and Quaker defended with a $35 million advertising campaign in 1987 and $46 million in 1988. Quaker's defense successfully beat back General Mills' attack: in 1991 General Mills announced withdrawal from the market of Total Oatmeal, as well as two other recent introductions, Under Cover Bears and Oatmeal Swirlers.

Aggressive Advertising and Related Controversies

General Mills' aggressive advertising campaigns for Total have drawn a fair amount of criticism and controversy to the brand over the years. While the specific claims for Total have been unique, the aggressive marketing approach has not been unusual for General Mills or for the cereal industry as a whole. The most pointed criticism has been fired from a consumer group, the Center for Science in the Public Interest. *Broadcasting* reported in 1978 that the Center requested an investigation by the Federal Trade Commission of General Mills' Total television ads. The Center accused General Mills of "false, misleading and deceptive" advertising; in addition, the group believed that General Mills overcharged consumers $31.6 million from 1973 to 1978. Advertising that Total provided 100 percent of the RDA for "all these important vitamins and iron," General Mills had wrongly implied to consumers that Total could provide all the daily nutrients needed, the Center argued. General Mills had overcharged consumers by requiring 30 cents more per box for Total than Wheaties when the added nutrients in Total cost General Mills only 2 cents more per box.

The Center's accusations were not particularly new for Total; competitors had forced General Mills to scale back some of its

comparative nutrition claims, and the Commission had already heard arguments about Total overpricing five years earlier. In addition, the Commission was in the midst of what turned out to be a ten-year lawsuit against all of the major cereal manufacturers, including General Mills, for sharing an illegal monopoly and overcharging consumers. The case was dropped during President Ronald Reagan's first term in office.

In 1975 Quaker had also challenged a General Mills television ad comparing the nutrition of Total with that of Quaker's 100% Natural cereal. General Mills claimed that it took 25 ounces of Quaker's cereal to match the nutrition in one ounce of Total. The spokesperson poured out 25 ounces (more than one box) into a bowl, letting the extra spill out onto the table. After charges by Quaker that the ad was "deceptive and misleading" and "disparaging" to its product, ABC-TV required revisions of the commercial. The new version limited its claims to those vitamins fortified in Total and spotlighted the enlarged slogan, "100% vs. 6%."

Such aggressive marketing was not unusual for either General Mills or the cereal industry as a whole, and throughout the early 1990s, the industry aggressively promoted nutritional claims that the FDA and state governments then moderated. In 1991 the U.S. Food and Drug Administration (FDA) supported suits by state governments against several companies, including Kellogg, Ralston Purina, and Quaker Oats, for false health claims, including those based on the benefit of psyllium. Taken from the seed husk of a grain grown primarily in India, psyllium contains more than eight times the soluble fiber of oat bran. General Mills withdrew its psyllium-based Benefit cereal within one year after introducing it, after controversy erupted over the cereal's cholesterol-reducing claims and over psyllium's possible allergic side effects for some people. Kellogg left its psyllium-based Heartwise cereal on the market.

Thriving on Competition in U.S., World Markets

Despite such controversies, General Mills and Total continued to perform well. General Mills entered into a joint venture with Nestlé called Cereal Partners Worldwide (CPW) to market General Mills cereals outside the United States. Kellogg currently dominates the world cereal market, but by 1992 the fledgling joint venture reached sales of $250 million, passing Europe's second-largest cereal marketer, Quaker, in several European countries. Total is not currently marketed overseas, but as CPW establishes itself worldwide, it will be in a position to introduce more brands. At the same time, Total is in a strong position to continue growing in the domestic market. What Lois Therrien and Charlie Hoots of *Business Week* wrote in August 1992 about General Mills's recent success applies equally well to Total's: "General Mills continues to deliver dazzling results, even as most other foodmakers struggle through the recession."

Further Reading:

"500,000 Push Set for Corn Totals," *Advertising Age,* April 12, 1971.

Bender, Marylin, *New York Times,* June 17, 1973, p. F1.

Berry, Kathleen M., "The Snap Has Turned to Slog," *New York Times,* November 18, 1990.

Biesada, Alexandra, "Life After Oat Bran," *Financial World,* June 11, 1991, pp. 46, 49.

Big 'G' Cereals, Minneapolis: General Mills, Inc., 1993.

"Consumer Group in a Stew Over Cereal Ads," *Broadcasting,* October 23, 1978, pp. 50, 52.

"Don't Underestimate the Power of a Kid," *Forbes,* October 15, 1966, p. 66.

Edwards, Larry, "General Mills Revises its Total Comparison Spot," *Advertising Age,* April 28, 1975, pp. 1, 74.

Erickson, Julie Liesse, "General Mills Refills Cereal Bowl," *Advertising Age,* October 10, 1988, p. 30.

"General Mills," *Advertising Age,* September 25, 1991.

Hill, D. M., Brown Brothers Harriman & Co., "Kellogg—Company Report," Thomson Financial Networks Inc., November 12, 1992.

Liesse, Julie, "Kellogg Sees Return of 40% Share as Core Brands Rise," *Advertising Age,* June 15, 1992, pp. 1, 54.

Sellers, Patricia, "A Boring Brand Can Be Beautiful," *Fortune,* November 18, 1991, pp. 169-70.

Shon, Melissa, "Beta-Carotene a Winner with Debut of GM's 'Total'," *Chemical Marketing Reporter,* August 31, 1992, pp. 3, 14.

Therrien, Lois, and Charlie Hoots, "Cafe au Lait, a Croissant—and Trix," *Business Week,* August 24, 1992, pp. 50-1.

Weiner, Steve, "Food Fight!" *Forbes,* July 27, 1987, p. 86.

"When a General Takes the Controls," *Business Week,* December 9, 1961, pp. 53, 57-8.

Willatt, Norris, "Bottomless Bowl: Makers of Breakfast Foods Keep Pouring Out New Products," *Barron's,* June 21, 1965, pp. 5, 15.

—Nicholas Patti

TRIDENT®

Trident brand of chewing gum is the second-best-selling sugarless gum in the United States, and the second best selling chewing gum of any type. It is also the top-selling brand of chewing gum for its owner, the Warner-Lambert Company. When Trident was introduced as the first sugarless gum, it not only revolutionized the chewing gum industry but also began a totally new type of industry—that of sugarless gum. Thirty years after Trident was launched, sales for the sugarless gum industry were estimated to be equal to that of the sugared gum industry.

The popularity of Trident has always been due to its ability to deliver pleasant taste, sweetness, and a health bonus—protecting teeth from the detrimental effects of sugar. Consumers could still indulge in the practice of chewing gum without adding to the risk of tooth decay. Even the federal government recognized Trident's value when, in 1964, Trident was selected as the official chewing gum for the Gemini Space Flights.

The combination of great taste and health benefits was the product's initial selling point, a claim no other gum could make at that time. In the ensuing years, as other types of products also prevented cavities, Trident shifted its advertising focus to its new flavor line and the brand's power to freshen breath. Still, the message that Trident had the ability to fight cavities was never totally eliminated from the Trident's advertising: consumers have always been informed of the gum's extra value.

Brand Origins

In 1953 the American Chicle Company (which later became known as the American Chicle Group) decided to formulate a sugarless gum that tasted as good as sugared gums, yet protected teeth at the same time. Regular chewing gum had been a popular snack item since the late 1880s when several men began to develop a way of adding flavor to chewing gum made from a type of tree resin, chicle. Prior to that time, in 1869, New York photographer and inventor Thomas Adams had been working with chicle to see if a commercial product could be developed from the ingredient. The idea came to him one day while watching a young girl buy a piece of paraffin chewing wax, a popular snack in those days; Adams knew that Mexicans had been using chicle as chewing gum, and figured that there was a good market for the product in the United States as well.

Adams believed that chicle could replace the wax, and rolled chicle into round pellets, packing them 200 to a box. Adams also experimented with giving chicle flavor and developed what became known as Adams Black Jack. In 1879 John Colgan of Louisville, Kentucky, was selling a gum that was extracted from the balsam tree. He blended it with powdered sugar and also began to experiment with chicle. The end result was Colgan's Taffy Tolu Chewing Gum, which was chicle with a sweet flavor. The gum became an immediate success.

Also working independently with blending ingredients with chicle was Dr. Beeman of Ohio. Beeman blended a pepsin compound, which he had been using to aid digestion, with chicle. His aim was to create a product that would offer not only health benefits but pleasant taste. Beeman's bearded face was printed on the pepsin gum wrappers and became one of the trademarks of the chewing gum industry.

Another discovery by William White, a popcorn salesman from Cleveland, was that any flavor could be blended with corn syrup, which could then be blended with chicle. White developed a peppermint gum, called Yucatan, which was a wide success. In 1899 most of the leading gum makers, including Adams, White, and Beeman, organized themselves into the American Chicle Company.

By the end of World War II, the demand for chicle to be used in chewing gum exceeded supply. Researchers at American Chicle were looking for new resins made of food-approved materials that could replace chicle yet be its equivalent. Also, improvements were being made in the taste and texture of chewing gum.

At that time modern medicine and dentistry were making people aware of how sugar caused tooth decay. The American Dental Association suggested to manufacturers of products containing sugar that they should support research to develop procedures or agents that would prevent and control dental caries (cavities) that can result from using their products. Of special concern was young people's excessive intake of sugared snack products. The prime users of chewing gum were people aged 8 to 24. Other articles supported this view that sugar contributed to the development of dental caries, and scientists called for the development of non-cariogenic foods that would provide an alternative for consumers.

With this suggestion in mind, the researchers at American Chicle wondered if a good-tasting gum could be developed to serve some health benefit. Taking note of the pleasure that people get from the act of chewing itself, and the possible harm from consuming sugar, Trident's researchers wanted to develop a gum that tasted sweet but did not coat the teeth with sugar. Chewing is said to be natural, instinctive, and relaxing, also making the mouth feel clean and refreshed, especially if the gum has a minty flavor. Sugars that do the most dental damage are those with frequent or prolonged contact with the teeth.

However, creating a gum with a sweet flavor without the use of sugar, which adds not only taste but texture, was a technological hurdle. In 1959 a breakthrough occurred when researchers discovered that a unique combination of gum acacia solution and gum acacia powder could replace the corn syrup binder used in regular sugar gums. These ingredients supplied texture, fiber, and chewiness to sugarless gum, properties that were unattainable in earlier formulations.

First Sugarless Gum, Early Marketing Strategy

After nine years of research, Trident Sugarless Gum was introduced in 1962. The flavor, called Original, was developed with a unique mint flavor combination, and a formula that contained 0.1 percent sodium saccharin. In order to give sweetness to the gum, sorbitol was used as a sugar substitute. Sorbitol is a white, crystalline powder that occurs naturally in apples, cherries, mountain ash berries, pears, and plums, and is about 50 to 60 percent as sweet as sugar. Research studies suggested that sorbitol is broken down by bacteria so slowly that it doesn't harm the teeth.

In 1964 Trident Sugarless Gum was distributed nationally in its Original flavor. From the beginning, the gum was promoted as a product that tasted as good as sugared gum yet, because it did not contain sugar, was a cavity-fighter. This unique strategy aimed to show consumers that a product could both taste good and be good for them.

Product Changes and Package Variations

Throughout the years, flavors were added to the Trident line, and a new technology to sustain flavor was developed. In 1966 spearmint and fruit flavors were introduced, followed by cinnamon in 1969. Later two more flavors, bubble gum and orange, were added to the line.

In 1990 Freshmint flavor was added to the line. Freshmint, made with natural mint flavors that gave it a wintergreen taste, was developed with a new technology. Consumers were asking for longer-lasting flavor, so researchers developed a patented "encapsulation" method that allowed the release of flavor over a longer period of time. The encapsulation process steadily releases flavor and sweetness. By the early 1990s, the Trident line also included soft sugarless bubble gum, in flavors that included grape and strawberry.

In addition to being introduced in new flavors, the Trident gum line has appeared in a variety of packages. Each flavor has a different colored flag on the package, such as blue for Original and green for Spearmint. When Freshmint was introduced, it was packaged in light blue with a yellow flag announcing "Great New Flavor."

Flavor and color of packaging are not the only elements distinguishing Trident gum. A consumer may opt for three different sizes of Trident gum. A single pack contains 5 sticks, a Val-U-Pak contains 18 sticks, and an 8-Pak contains 8 packages consisting of 5 sticks each. A special foil-pouch package was developed, known as the Finseal, which is designed to lock in flavor, freshness, and the gum's soft texture.

Advertising Innovations

When Trident was introduced in the 1960s, its health benefits were advertised so that consumers would understand the gum was a different type of product. Several research studies with consumers had convinced dentists that Trident was safe for teeth because it did not promote tooth decay, and actually reduced the acids that form in plaque. Trident was the first sugarless gum to undergo extensive long-term clinical testing. In several controlled investigations with children and adults, Trident consistently demonstrated that it did not contribute to the development of cavities.

To communicate these findings to consumers, the tagline "4 out of 5 dentists surveyed recommend sugarless gum for their patients who chew gum" was developed. The phrase was based on a survey showing that 93 percent of the estimated 1,000 dentists representing a geographical cross-section of the nation made such a recommendation.

In 1986 a campaign to further educate consumers about Trident gum's ability to fight cavities was initiated, making advertising history in the process. Recent research studies had suggested that Trident may help to prevent cavities after people ate sugary snacks. The studies showed that chewing gum promoted saliva production that helped wash away mouth acids that cause cavities.

Trident spent $15 million to create a cavity-fighter image, the first time a product of its type made such a claim. A promotional and educational campaign was directed toward both dentists and consumers, and a toll-free phone number was made available for anyone wishing to obtain additional information from the company.

Advertising More than Health Benefits

A shift from focusing mostly on health benefits took place as the market heated up with competition from other sugarless gums. Moreover, tooth decay had become preventable with other measures, such as fluorinated water and more effective dentrifices. Consumers were demanding more from their chewing gum. They wanted not only flavor, but flavor that lasted longer, as well as a gum that produced fresh breath. New Trident ads stressed flavor plus the benefits of chewing sugarless gum, using the tagline, "All That Good Stuff and Great Taste, Too."

In 1990 Trident TV commercials took a humorous turn. A series of TV spots, called "Walk and Chew," created situations around a familiar description of an inept person—someone who couldn't walk and chew gum at the same time. People would take a stick of Trident and then fall or collapse to the ground. The commercials called attention to Trident's new fruitier flavor, and still reminded viewers that Trident was good for their teeth.

When the new Freshmint flavor was launched in 1990, the company implemented its largest marketing support program for a single flavor. The program included trade incentives, TV and radio ads, outdoor billboards, free-standing inserts, and extensive sampling. One TV commercial, called "Duet," was a computer animation that stated Freshmint had "The Coolest Cool and the Freshest Mint." The target markets were adults aged 18 to 34 years who were the prime gum chewers and most interested in fresh breath. More than 20 million samples were distributed, one of the largest efforts ever for the confectionery industry. Sampling was offered through in-store promotions, point-of-purchase displays, on-pack giveaways, and special events.

One special event that was promoted was recreational biking tours that took place across the country in such key cities as New York, Washington, D.C., Detroit, St. Louis, Phoenix, and San Diego. The promotion suggested that both Trident and bicycling were fun, refreshing, and relaxing. A Trident/AYH Capital City Bike Festival in Washington, D.C., was the showcase event, combining a 4,000-cyclist touring event with a full day of Trident product sampling, workshops, and entertainment.

As the 1990s progressed, Trident makers revisited the message communicated in its highly successful 1986 campaign. Advertisements delivered an oral hygiene message within a fun and relaxed setting, encouraging consumers to prevent tooth decay by chewing Trident after consuming meals in locations where they could not brush their teeth afterwards. The commercials used the slogan, "Chew on This!"

International Market, Performance, and Future Predictions

Outside of the United States, Canada is a prime market for Trident. Freshmint flavor was first introduced there two years before it made its debut in the United States. Within two years, Freshmint became the third most popular Trident flavor with Canadians. The most popular flavor in North America is Original, followed by Cinnamon.

Since Trident was introduced, many competitors entered the sugarless gum market. In 1991 alone, 21 new gum products were introduced, many of them of the sugarless variety. About 50 percent of all chewing gum sales are estimated to be for sugarless gum. Estimates vary for Trident and its competitors, but in 1992 Trident reportedly had 32 percent of the total sugarless gum market and nearly 12 percent of the total chewing gum market. Through the years, Trident producer American Chicle strove to keep pace with competitive chewing gum makers and satisfy consumer demand with new flavors and new gum properties. It can be expected that the company will follow this pattern in the future in order to maintain market share.

Further Reading:

Applebaum, Cara, "Trident Seeks to Shed Its Lab Coat," *Adweek's Marketing Week,* May 14, 1990, p. 5.

Dagnoll, Judith and Julie Liesse, "Chicle Shows Gumption after a Distasteful '91," *Advertising Age,* April 27, 1992, p. 50.

Davis, Sue, "Candy Charisma," *Prepared Foods,* mid-April 1992, pp. 69-71.

Garfield, Bob, "Trident Commercial Stumbles onto Concept that Sticks Out," *Advertising Age,* November 26, 1990, p. 64.

Pioneering the Confection Industry, Morris Plains, NJ: American Chicle Group.

"Securing a Foothold for Confectionery," *Candy Industry,* July 1992, pp. H2-H10.

Stern, R. J., Tucker Anthony, and R. L. Day, *Company Report of Warner-Lambert,* Morris Plains, NJ: Warner-Lambert Company, October 26, 1992.

Trident Sugarless Gum Fact Sheet, American Chicle Group.

Trident Sugarless Gum Launches New Freshmint Flavor (press release), June 7, 1990.

Trident Sugarless Gum: Meeting the Research Challenge, 1953-1987, American Chicle Group.

The Trident Sugarless Gum Story, Great Neck, NY: Resourcebook.

Winters, Patricia, "Trident Gum Tries Cavity-Fighter Image in $15M Campaign," *Advertising Age,* June 9, 1986, p.1.

—Dorothy Kroll

TROPICANA®

Tropicana is the leading brand of juice in the world. Tropicana Products, Inc. has distinguished its products in the $11.8 billion juice and juice drinks marketplace and has set many standards for the chilled fruit juice industry with its innovations in processing, packaging, and marketing. Tropicana has weathered attacks from such formidable competitors as Procter & Gamble and Coca-Cola and has profitably survived freezes and fluctuations in commodities prices.

The Origin of Tropicana

Tropicana Products, Inc. springs from a company called Fruit Industries, Inc. founded in 1947 by Anthony T. Rossi, a native Sicilian who emigrated to America in the early 1920s. Rossi and a few of his friends had come to New York as youths planning on only staying until they made enough money to finance an expedition to Africa for filmmaking and adventure. However, Rossi was so impressed by democracy and the possibilities for social mobility that he stayed, working a variety of blue collar jobs and running a grocery in Queens, New York.

After running this grocery for 13 years, he moved to Bradenton, on the gulf coast of Florida, where he started a cafeteria. He later opened a restaurant in Miami Beach, but this venture was thwarted as World War II diminished tourism.

Rossi began selling boxes of oranges and grapefruits to department stores. This venture proved surprisingly successful, gaining Rossi clients nationwide. He soon expanded this venture to include selling jars of chilled fruit sections, using a process he developed in the restaurant business. Rossi wondered what he could do with the oranges that were too small for his gift boxes. First he shipped them to a grocer in New York to juice and sell, then he bought a machine for making concentrate.

In 1954, five years later, he began packing 100 percent pure, pasteurized, not-from-concentrate juice under the name "Tropicana," using a method similar to the one he had developed for the chilled fruit sections. Before this, fresh juice could only be kept a few days unless it was pasteurized, which would extend its life to several weeks. Rossi's method allowed his juice to keep for up to three months. This method of delivering juice that was 100 percent pure and not made from concentrate to New York, always the center of Rossi's business, set him apart from other producers offering only reconstituted juice made from concentrate.

In 1951, Rossi conceptualized "Tropic-Ana," a girl wearing a grass skirt and lei and balancing a large bowl of oranges atop her head. She has remained Tropicana's trademark ever since. In 1955 Fruit Industries, Inc. changed its name to "Tropicana Products, Inc."

"Control"

"Control," Rossi told Wayne King of the *New York Times* in 1974, "that is the most important thing in business." To *Forbes* in 1971 he added that "if you lose control, you lose everything. We're a sort of a do-it-yourself company." That self-reliant attitude has been reflected in nearly all areas of Tropicana's business. Rossi designed many of the machines used in processing at Tropicana, which were made in Tropicana's own machine shop and installed by Tropicana personnel. To fuel all of this production and processing, in the late 1980s the company began construction of a 45 megawatt power plant which would re-use the energy from the steam required in its processing.

An obvious place to control production of orange juice is in its taste. Rossi is reported to have had both a very sharp sense of taste and an acute understanding of how to squeeze the oranges based on their particular chemical content, which changes according to such variables as their degree of ripeness and the amount of rainfall they have received. The squeezing action must be adjusted according to these factors in order to minimize the amount of bitter oils released into the juice from small globules visible just under the skin of the fruit.

Rossi's sense of taste once led him and his company into an extremely embarrassing situation, however. "In a weak moment," as he told *Fortune* in 1973, he added sweetening syrup to a batch of orange juice. This caused the U.S. Department of Agriculture to temporarily prohibit Tropicana from using their inspection shield on their packaging. The Florida Citrus Commission also suspended the company's Florida operations for a month.

In keeping with its philosophy of self-reliance, Tropicana designs and manufactures its own packaging, including the boxes the other products are shipped in. It has led the way in introducing new types of juice containers. In the 1970s it introduced specially designed barrier-lined cartons and introduced consumers to 32-ounce cans for concentrated orange juice. In the early 1980s it developed a plastic cap for its glass bottles, replacing the metal

AT A GLANCE

Tropicana brand of juices and juice beverages founded in 1947 in Bradenton, FL, by Anthony T. Rossi; originally called Fruit Industries, Inc., the company changed its name to Tropicana Products, Inc. in 1955.

Performance: *Market share*—12.8% dollar share of refrigerated, shelf-stable, and frozen juices and juice drinks. *Sales*—$1.5 billion (retail sales of refrigerated, shelf-stable, and frozen juices and juice drinks).

Major competitor: Coca-Cola's Minute Maid; also, Ocean Spray.

Advertising: *Agency*—Leo Burnett USA, Chicago, IL, 1986—. *Major campaign*—Actors sticking straws into fresh oranges, with slogan, "Tropicana—you can't pick a better juice" (1989).

Addresses: *Parent company*—Tropicana Products, Inc., P.O. Box 338, Bradenton, FL 34206; phone: (813) 747-4461. *Ultimate parent company*—The Seagram Company Ltd., 1430 Peel Street, Montreal, Quebec, Canada H3A 1S9; phone: (514) 849-5271.

ones. However, this proved unpopular since the cap shrank when refrigerated, making it difficult to remove. The company introduced a specially lined 96-ounce plastic jug in the late 1980s, which prompted rival Minute Maid to introduce its own 64-ounce version, which it said featured better aesthetics and ergonomics than the "industrial"-looking Tropicana container. In 1991 Tropicana captured the Clear Choice Glass Award for the 64-ounce Tropicana Twister. Tropicana has also introduced single serving packs for its Pure Premium pasteurized not-from-concentrate juice, first with six-packs of single serving, 6-ounce plastic cups and later with 8-ounce cartons packaged in groups of three called "Triplets," each packaged with its own telescoping straw.

Another area in which Tropicana has taken control of operations is in transportation of its products. This is important for Tropicana's competitiveness because its chilled juices are bulkier and more expensive to transport than concentrates. In fact, transportation figures second only to the juice itself as the company's largest cost factor in producing the juice. The company has at various times used trains, trucks, and ships to transport its products. The Tropicana train, unique to the food industry, began operating in 1970 and supplies product to the Northeast two to three times weekly. In 1962, after a disastrous crop in Florida, Tropicana equipped a ship with processing equipment and anchored it off the coast of Mexico, but problems with the Mexican government soon scuttled that venture.

Freezes and Squeezes

Despite the company's passion for self-reliance, Tropicana buys its oranges from outside growers. Its fortunes have been affected by the availability and price of oranges. When freezes hit Florida, as in 1957, quality oranges were scarce and Tropicana could face a lack of juice to process and distribute to market. However, this situation could also be profitable: in 1977, Tropicana profited from an increase in commodities prices that greatly increased the value of its inventory.

Tropicana has, of course, been affected by other trends affecting the orange juice industry. After spending millions of dol-

lars on advertisements associating orange juice with the breakfast table, in the mid-1960s the commission began a campaign to encourage consumption of the juice throughout the day.

Before 1968, these ads promoted chilled juices, canned juices, and concentrates separately. In 1968 a generic approach was tried by the commission in their campaign featuring actress Anita Bryant. The Florida Citrus Commission's symbol for Florida orange juice, "The Sunshine Tree," has been used for decades in Citrus Commission ads and on packages of all sorts of Florida orange juice, including, of course, Tropicana's.

The Florida Department of Citrus has also reacted along with processors such as Tropicana to the juicing fad of the early 1990s—a wave of books and "infomercials" touting the benefits of squeezing one's own fruits at home with juicing machines. In 1992 the Citrus Department felt it necessary to issue a statement to reassure consumers that packaged orange juice did not lose all its nutritional value in processing, as the media blitz had led some to believe. Tropicana also dispensed nutritional information to the public through its six-physician "Beverage Panel of Experts." However, according to a Tropicana spokesperson, Tropicana has felt little impact from the juicing phenomenon due to consumer demand for convenience, which Tropicana provides with its chilled juices.

The Orange Juice Wars

Competition for Tropicana's chilled juices entered a new era in 1960 as giant beverage marketer Coca-Cola bought Tropicana's old concentrate rival, Minute Maid. In 1973, Minute Maid introduced a chilled juice made from concentrate to compete with Tropicana's chilled juice. Also in 1973, Tropicana, under the direction of Anthony Rossi, began selling again the frozen concentrate it had dropped in the 1950s while expanding its fresh juice markets.

Since then these two companies have been in direct competition. In the chilled juice category, both have claimed to have the superior product. Tropicana has argued essentially that less is more; the less that is taken out or put in, the better. But Minute Maid declares that since it can store its concentrates and blend them, it can make a more consistently superior juice that is not so easily affected by seasonal fluctuations in orange quality and taste. However, Minute Maid itself introduced a not-from-concentrate juice in 1988 called Premium Choice to compete directly with Tropicana's Pure Premium. Both companies claimed to have the superior product and better, more convenient packaging.

Besides Minute Maid and a number of much smaller, private label juices, Tropicana was also faced with competition from a Procter & Gamble brand, Citrus Hill, which placed third in the chilled juice category until the fall of 1992, when Procter & Gamble took it off the market. Citrus Hill introduced a carton with a screw cap and had offered its from-concentrate juice fortified with calcium. In 1988, according to the *Wall Street Journal*, Tropicana led the pack with a 26.9 percent market share; Minute Maid had 17.9 percent, and Citrus Hill followed with 9.4 percent.

One of the smaller contenders entered the fray with an ironic twist for Tropicana. In 1991, Vero Beach Groves brought its Honestly Fresh Squeezed juice to market on a limited scale, supported by ads showing a carton of their product sitting on a block of ice and a carton of Tropicana's Pure Premium, which is pasteurized, sitting over a Bunsen burner. The Food and Drug

Administration in 1991 had prevented such brands as Citrus Hill from using the word "fresh" in describing products that were pasteurized. However, in May of 1992 Tropicana sued Vero Beach Groves for allegedly misleading consumers with its ads, which said Tropicana's pasteurized juice was "cooked." A federal judge from Boston ruled that Vero Beach Groves must discontinue their advertising, which portrays Pure Premium in a misleading way. The judge said that "the commercial creates and . . . was deliberately designed to create, a false impression" about Pure Premium. Tropicana's process gently pasteurizes the juice before packaging.

The freshness question was a key point of contention for Minute Maid as well. In 1982 it won a ruling against Tropicana for describing its product as "juice as it comes from the orange." As part of the settlement of the suit, both Tropicana and Minute Maid agreed not to show juice being squeezed from oranges in their advertising.

Minute Maid was in turn sued by Tropicana in 1988 for describing its not-from-concentrate but pasteurized Premium Choice as coming "straight from the orange." Coca-Cola Foods agreed to remove the line from the packaging and advertising. In 1990 Minute Maid Premium Choice had 11.7 percent of the not-from-concentrate, ready-to-serve orange juice market.

Brand Development

Tropicana itself has been aggressive in entering new markets. Tropicana's flagship brand, Pure Premium, has been expanded to include Pure Premium Original, Pure Premium Homestyle (with juicy bits of orange), and most recently Pure Premium Grovestand (with a fresh-squeezed flavor and texture). Besides challenging Minute Maid with an encore of its concentrate in 1973, it has also marketed a from-concentrate chilled juice, particularly when oranges were in short supply. Tropicana expanded its line of shelf-stable drinks in 1988 with the introduction of Twisters, four different blends of fruit juices in flavors billed as "flavors Mother Nature never intended," such as orange-strawberry-banana. This brought Tropicana into competition with other brands, notably Ocean Spray. In 1990 Tropicana dove into the thriving sparkling juice market with its Tropicana Juice Sparklers, taking on New Era Beverages' Sundance and others. Sparklers were introduced in four flavors: tropical orange, golden grapefruit, cranberry orchard, and wild berries. In 1991 Tropicana introduced a low calorie version of Tropicana Twister—Twister Light—available in four flavors: pink grapefruit cocktail, orange strawberry banana, orange raspberry, and orange cranberry. The Twister line has been expanded to include a frozen concentrate version of many of the flavors of the original Twister. In 1991 Twister sales totalled over $170 million.

Tropicana has also marketed a line of chilled 100 percent juice blends such as Orange Peach Mango and Orange Kiwi Passion, called Tropicana Pure Tropics. Robert Soran, president of Tropicana at the time, told *Business Week* in 1988 that the company would endeavor to introduce a new product every three to four months, a strategy the company continued to follow until 1991.

Many other of Tropicana's marketing innovations have since been forgotten. In 1959, Tropicana put forth its "Tropicana instant orange concentrated drink," a concentrated fruit beverage packaged in aerosol cans that was intended to compete with artificial orange drinks such as Tang. It was also intended to be useful as a syrup for waffles and ice cream. Tropicana developed the dispenser for this but did not patent it. Tropicana has also tried

marketing a concentrated coffee in a similar container, but, according to A. T. Rossi, the coffee was excellent but the valve was not accurate enough. The company also had plans to market other citrus beverages, such as lemonade and limeade, in this container.

Performance Evaluation

From 1966 to 1970, Tropicana nearly doubled its net sales from $39.6 million to $76.4 million. In 1973, its sales were $121 million. From 1985 to 1990 the company increased its share of the total $3 billion orange juice market from 14.8 percent to 22.3 percent, while Minute Maid declined from 22.9 percent to 22.2 percent. In 1991 Tropicana had a 10.1 percent gallon share of frozen concentrate and an 11.4 percent dollar share on frozen concentrate sales of $109 million.

Changes in Ownership

In the 1970s, Kellogg Co. made several offers to buy Tropicana, each of them being rejected by Rossi. In 1978, Beatrice Foods Co. acquired Tropicana for $490 million in cash and stock. Beatrice was ordered to sell Tropicana by an administrative law judge of the Federal Trade Commission in 1980. However, in 1983 the FTC overturned the administrative law judge's decision, and found that the 1978 acquisition of Tropicana by Beatrice was not illegal. Beatrice was not forced to sell Tropicana in 1980, nor forced to pay profits to the federal government. The reasoning behind this controversial suit was that Beatrice, which controlled less than 1 percent of the chilled juice market before buying Tropicana, would be potentially creating less competition in the chilled juice market, since it had the experience in producing and distributing refrigerated foods to develop its own brand, rather than buying the leading one. Beatrice's intention had been to develop Tropicana, whose primary market at the time was the northeast, into a national brand.

In 1988, The Seagram Co. bought Tropicana from Beatrice for $1.2 billion. Tropicana has since benefited from Seagram's international distributing experience. Under Seagram, Tropicana Products, Inc. produces and markets the leading brand of juice in the world. Tropicana products are sold in North America, Europe, Asia, and Latin America.

Further Reading:

Angrist, Stanley W., "The Squeeze on Orange Juice," *Forbes,* May 1, 1977, pp. 106-107.

Berman, Phyllis, "Orange Crush," *Forbes,* January 13, 1986, pp. 42-50.

"Beatrice Foods: Adding Tropicana for a Broader Nationwide Network," *Business Week,* May 15, 1978, pp. 114-116.

"Beatrice Foods Must Sell Unit, FTC Officer Says," *Wall Street Journal,* December 1, 1980, p. 2.

"Coca-Cola Invades Tropicana's Market," *Business Week,* December 1, 1973, pp. 26-27.

Cox, Meg, "Beatrice's Great Expectations for Tropicana Tempered by Host of Unforeseen Problems," *Wall Street Journal,* December 15, 1980, p. 27.

Dagnoli, Judann, "A Little Squirt Puts 'Fresh' Back in OJ," *Advertising Age,* March 9, 1992, pp. 1, 47.

Dagnoli, Judann, "Ocean Spray Splash: $30 Million Campaign Will Support Refreshers Juice," *Advertising Age,* June 17, 1991, p. 60.

Dagnoli, Judann and Patricia Winters, "Tropicana Rolls Out Sparkling Juice," *Advertising Age,* June 25, 1990, p. 3.

Danzig, Fred, "L & N Unveils Florida Citrus Drive Promoting Frozen Orange Concentrate," *Advertising Age,* September 12, 1966, pp. 3, 152.

"Florida Freeze Thaws Out New Juice Tricks," *Business Week,* January 11, 1958, pp. 32-34.

Freedman, Alan, "Seagram Plans a Tropicana Move into Canada's Fragmented Market," *Wall Street Journal,* May 27, 1988, p. 22.

Freedman, Alix M., "An Orange Juice War Is Growing as Makers Vie for Fresh Markets," *Wall Street Journal,* April 27, 1988, p. 32.

Freedman, Alix M., "Tropicana, Coke Reach Settlement over Juice Ads," *Wall Street Journal,* July 13, 1988, p. 28.

Freedman, Alix M., and Ed Bean, "Seagram to Buy Beatrice Unit For $1.2 Billion," *Wall Street Journal,* March 11, 1988, pp. 2-12.

Giges, Nancy, "Tropicana Plants Full-Line Strategy," *Advertising Age,* March 1, 1982, pp. 1, 74.

Giges, Nancy, "Tropicana's Jenner Spots Run into Coke Suit," *Advertising Age,* March 22, 1982, p. 78.

Hwang, Suein L., "Seagram Ousts President at Tropicana, Seeks New Course as Juice Unit Sours," *Wall Street Journal,* October 5, 1992, p. B1.

Kadri, Henry V., "Orange Juice Traders Keep Weather Watch," *Barron's,* September 18, 1967, pp. 35-36.

King, Wayne, "Tropicana's Boss Finds His 'Crazy' Ways Work," *New York Times Biographical Edition,* New York: Arno Press, 1974, pp. 881-883.

Liesse, Julie, "Ready To Build Tropicana: Healthy Choice Marketing Chief Tries New Challenge," *Advertising Age,* October 12, 1992, p. 48.

Lublin, Joann S., "More Chiefs Find Revolving Door at Top," *Wall Street Journal,* October 7, 1992, pp. B1-B6.

MacDonald, Stephen, "Form + Function," *Wall Street Journal,* October 12, 1988, p. B1.

McCarthy, Michael J., "Squeezing More Life into Orange Juice," *Wall Street Journal,* May 4, 1989, p. B1.

McCoy, Charles, "Tropicana Intends To Put the Squeeze on Electricity Costs," *Wall Street Journal,* September 22, 1988, p. 42.

Morgan, Hal, *Symbols of America,* New York: Viking, 1986.

Morris, Betsy and Alix M. Freedman, "Seagram's Tropicana Sues Unit of Coke over Orange Juice Ad," *Wall Street Journal,* July 6, 1988, p. 30.

"The New Rich," *Fortune,* September 1973.

O'Connor, John J., "Minute Maid, Tropicana 32-oz. O.J. Cans Debut," *Advertising Age,* January 27, 1975, p. 4.

Pacey, Margaret D., "Chilled or Frozen: Orange Juice Is Steadily Winning Fresh Adherents," *Barron's,* December 30, 1974, pp. 11-28.

Prince, Greg W., "What's the Deal with These Juicers?" *Beverage World,* November 1992, pp. 24-31.

Recio, Irene, and Zachary Schiller, "They're All Juiced Up at Tropicana," *Business Week,* May 13, 1991, p. 48.

The Seagram Company Ltd. Annual Report, Montreal: The Seagram Company Ltd., 1992.

Sfiligoj, Eric, "The Beverage Market Index for 1992," *Beverage World,* May 1992, pp. 30-49.

Silverman, Vera, "Tropicana Set To Enjoy Fresh Gain in Profits," *Barron's,* October 19, 1970, p. 27.

Smith, Timothy K., "Coke Will Challenge Tropicana's Juice in New York and Philadelphia Markets," *Wall Street Journal,* June 15, 1988, p. 30.

"U.S. Charges Tropicana Juice Was Sweetened," *Advertising Age,* April 25, 1960, p. 3.

"What Makes Rossi Run?" *Forbes,* November 15, 1971, pp. 50-51.

—*Frederick C. Ingram*

TWINKIES®

Few brand names are more synonymous with Americana than Twinkies, the nation's best-selling snack cake, and one of its oldest. Twinkies are a creme-filled yellow sponge cake sold either as a two-to-a-pack snack, or in boxes of ten individually wrapped cakes. According to Continental Baking Company, maker of Hostess products, over 500 million Twinkies were consumed nationwide in 1989. Approximately 40 billion Twinkies have been sold since their introduction in 1930, making Twinkies the top seller in Continental's Hostess line. Continental has 37 bakeries in 27 states and is the leading wholesale baker of bread and cakes in the United States.

Brand Origins

Twinkies were created in 1930, the same year Continental Baking introduced sliced bread to a then-skeptical public. Due to the depressed economy, overall sales of Continental's Hostess cake products were slow at that time. The late James A. Dewar, then a regional manager for Continental Baking Company, was looking for a way to boost company sales. He noticed that the pans used to make "little short cake fingers" were collecting dust for most of the year except during the six-week strawberry season. Dewar decided to inject the cakes with a banana cream filling and market them year-round.

Production

The first Twinkies were filled one at a time, using a hand-held piston-type filler. Today, "they don't so much bake Twinkies as assemble them," said *Denver Business Times* reporter Michael Booth. Twinkies are made assembly-line style in enormous bakeries that also produce Wonder brand bread and hamburger buns, and Hostess Ho Ho and Cupcakes. Continental officials are tight-lipped about the amount of flour and sugar used in production of Hostess goods, although it is said that over 52,000 Twinkies are made nationally every hour.

Continental's products are mixed, baked, and packaged in enormous quantities all in the same building. "Where you would use a measuring cup, we use a scale," Denver plant manager Floyd Calaway told Booth. Production is organized, mechanized, and efficient. While a person in the middle of the assembly line is supervising the air-injection of creme into the middle of Twinkies, another at the beginning of the line might be getting ready to make

Suzi-Q's while the baker at the end of the line is packaging fruit pies.

Meanwhile, hamburger buns are being plucked from their baking tins, loaves of bread pass over head on conveyor belts, and donuts are dropped eight at a time into huge vats of hot oil. The work is highly regulated and monitored for compliance with a corporate "spec book," which states standards for every facet of production. "Every point in this entire assembly line has a crucial time and temperature factor," said Calaway. "Wonder Bread has to be exactly the right temperature when it rolls into the slicer or the slice will tear every time." All Continental products are shipped daily to ensure freshness.

Product Development

The shape and size of Twinkies have changed little since their introduction, although the content of the snack cake has been modified slightly over the years. During World War II, when bananas were hard to come by, Twinkies' banana cream filling was replaced by a vanilla flavored filling. Other changes were minimal until 1970, when Continental, following food industry trends, began adding vitamins to the snack cake.

Continental Baking's biggest change in its Twinkies line occurred in 1988 with the introduction of Fruit and Creme Twinkies: traditional sponge cake with a strawberry and vanilla cream swirl in the center. "The strawberry and creme combination is tied to the roots of Twinkies—strawberry shortcake. It is a natural combination of a popular flavor with our traditional sponge cake and creme filling," said Greg Falk, associate product manager, upon its introduction. Another break from Twinkies tradition occurs during the slow summer months when devils food Twinkies are sold in selected markets.

Following another industry trend to provide "healthy" snack cakes, Twinkies Lights were introduced in 1991; in addition to finding vitamins in the cakes, customers could also enjoy these Twinkies that were 94 percent fat-free. First year sales of Twinkies and other Hostess Lights products were deemed favorable.

Marketing Strategies

The name Twinkies was coined by Dewar during a business trip to St. Louis, Missouri, where he saw a billboard advertising "Twinkle Toe Shoes." As the economy was tight, Dewar decided

AT A GLANCE

Twinkies brand snack cakes introduced in 1930 by Continental Baking Company, maker of Wonder breads and Hostess Cup Cakes; James A. Dewar developed Twinkies product using cake tins for "little shortcake fingers," which lay dormant outside of the six-week strawberry season; in 1968 Continental Baking Company purchased by ITT Corp., which changed its name to ITT Continental Baking Co.; Ralston Purina Company purchased the baking company from ITT, 1984, and the name reverted back to Continental Baking Company.

Major competitor: Little Debbie brand snack cakes.

Advertising: *Agency*—W. B. Doner & Company, Baltimore, MD. *Major campaign*—Series of television commercials with young children hypothesizing as to how the creme gets in the middle of Twinkies.

Addresses: *Parent company*—Continental Baking Company, Checkerboard Square, St. Louis, MO 63164; phone: (314) 982-2790; fax: (314) 982-2267. *Ultimate parent company*—Ralston Purina Company (address same as above); phone: (314) 982-1000; fax: (314) 982-4031.

to market Twinkies as a low-priced, convenient snack. He packaged them "two-to-a-pack for a nickel," and targeted the cake's advertising to children. Soon after their introduction, Twinkies became the top seller among Hostess products. "Twinkies was the best darn-tootin' idea I ever had," Dewar is quoted as having said. "Kids bought them, all right, and those same kids still buy them today, and so do their kids, and their kids."

Continental Baking's marketing strategy has changed little since the introduction of Twinkies. Efforts continue to focus on selling the product to children, using conservative but effective marketing strategies. In the 1950s, Twinkies sponsored the *Howdy Doody Show* where Buffalo Bob, Clarabell the Clown, and Howdy Doody touted Twinkies to a young public.

When Continental began adding vitamins and iron to Twinkies in the early 1970s, the newly fortified snack cakes were introduced in a joint television ad for Hostess Fruit Pies and Twinkies, created by Ted Bates & Co The ad contained the plug: "A major nutritional advance from Hostess. Snack cakes with body building vitamins and iron. Look for the big 'V' on every package." The 'V' stood for vitamins, and the ad closed with, "For the good taste kids love and the good nutrition they need."

In 1971 the Federal Trade Commission accused Continental of misleading the public, saying that the fortification of Twinkies with vitamins and iron did not amount to a nutritional advance above and beyond what is available in other baked goods for children. The big 'V' was removed from packages.

In the mid 1970s the official spokesperson became Twinkie the Kid, an animated cowboy Twinkie character wearing a bandanna, cowboy hat, and boots. When Continental removed the Twinkie the Kid character from Twinkie packages in 1988, they received a flood of protest letters. Among them was a petition signed by 135 members of the "Save the Twinkie the Kid Foundation" in New Jersey. Led by 15-year-old Judd Slivka, the foundation announced a boycott of Twinkies until the Kid's image was reinstated on the packages.

All the hullabaloo over the loss of Twinkie the Kid happily coincided with the 60th anniversary of the snack cake. "Kids of all ages know who Twinkie the Kid is, and they want their children to know him, too," Hostess spokesman Kerry Lyman told the *Detroit News* in 1990. "This was the perfect time for a reunion." A slightly more modern Twinkie the Kid was thus re-introduced to his public at a special birthday dinner at Continental's headquarters in St. Louis. Judd Slivka was invited to the birthday party as a special guest.

Tarnished Image

Although Continental stays on top of industry trends to fortify their products with vitamins and to reduce fat and cholesterol contents, the image of Twinkies has become a bit tarnished since the late 1970s. Twinkies enjoy, for better or worse, a reputation as the ultimate junk food, full of sugar and chemical additives. Despite a negative connotation and a rising health consciousness in the United States, Continental officials maintain that Twinkies sales have remained steady throughout the years.

In a study of the nutritive value of 32 possible snack items ranging from oranges to doughnuts, Twinkies earned a −20, the same value as homemade chocolate chip cookies, pretzels, and plain graham crackers. (Oranges were given a +80, the highest nutritive value; popsicles came in last with a nutritive value of −50.)

"It's just good, wholesome, fun food," Harry Pierce, a Continental vice president told *Advertising Age* in 1986, "made from ingredients you'd find in your own kitchen." In descending order of quantity, Twinkies are made from: sugar, enriched flour, corn syrup, water, partially hydrogenated vegetable oil and/or animal shortening, eggs, skim milk, leavening, whey, starch, salt, mono- and diglycerides, sodium caseinate, polysorbate 60, lecithin, xanthan gum, natural and artificial flavors, artificial colors, and sorbic acid.

Perhaps most damaging to Twinkies's image was its use as a defense for Dan White, a San Francisco city supervisor accused in the 1979 murder of San Francisco mayor George Moscone and city supervisor Harvey Milk. The defense employed a psychiatrist's statement that White's diet of Twinkies, Coca-Cola, and potato chips created extreme variations in his blood sugar level. This in turn worsened his existing manic depressive state, leading to the murder. The press labeled it the "Twinkies Defense."

American's attitudes towards Twinkies remain ambivalent. The snack cake has been served at the White House, and was the official cake at Superman's 50th birthday party. Television character Archie Bunker proclaimed them "white man's soul food" in the series *All in the Family*. They've been dubbed the "quintessential junk food" and an "icon of American junk food." Twinkies have allegedly been used to bribe votes from elderly people in Minneapolis, Minnesota, and to lure a gorilla back into his cage in Kings Mill, Ohio.

Future Predictions

Continental claims the growing trend in healthy snacking has had no adverse effect on Twinkies sales. However, despite Continental's claim of favorable Hostess Lights sales, including Twinkies Lights, industry analysts say the company's competitive market and lackluster marketing efforts led Continental's owner, Ralston Purina, to consider a spin-off of Continental in April 1992.

"There's enormous competition now with private-label baked goods that are cheaper than trademark names, and there is frankly an image problem with some of the products that [Continental] could have done a lot more and didn't," Ellen Barnes, a securities analyst with Duff & Phelps, concluded. "They could have marketed Wonder as a healthier product but they didn't—and when they tried something like Hostess Lights, it didn't work."

According to a company spokesperson, Ralston determined that spin-off costs for Continental were higher than anticipated, and decided to hold on to the baking company as a wholly owned subsidiary.

Continental seems to be staying slightly ahead of competition. A June, 1992, *Snack Food* magazine survey of the baking industry puts Continental as the nation-wide leader in breads and sweet baked goods sales. Company-wide sales in 1991 were $1.966 billion, up from $1.957 billion in 1990. No break-down is given on a product-by-product basis.

Further Reading:

Booth, Michael, article in *Denver Business Times,* 1988.

Colborn, Marge, "Twinkie, Twinkie, You Little 60-Year-Old Star," *Detroit News,* 1990, p. 1C.

"Continental Baking Builds on Twinkies Tradition with Strawberry Variation," *Milling and Baking News,* November 1, 1988, p. 19.

Donlon, Ted, "Food Men Warily Consider Promoting Nutritional Values," *Advertising Age,* October 19, 1970, p. 1.

Field, David, "Ralston Purina Dieting, Cuts Wonder Bread, Twinkies, Etc.," *Washington Times,* April 23, 1992, sec. C, p. 12.

"FTC settles with Profile, but Wonder, Hostess Next," *Advertising Age,* September 6, 1971, p. 3.

"Keep on Snackin,' " *Snack Foods,* March 1992, p. 24.

"Nabisco, Continental Fortify Snack Wares," *Advertising Age,* September 21, 1970, p. 4.

Super, Kari E., "Twinkies: 50 Years of 'Fun,' " *Advertising Age,* October 13, 1986, p. S-29.

—Maura Troester

TYSON®

Tyson Foods, Inc. is the world's largest poultry marketer and processor, and Tyson brand chicken is the number one selling brand in the United States. The brand's origins can be traced back to the late 1920s, when John Tyson had been making his living hauling apples, grapes, and other fresh produce throughout the southern tier of states about six months out of each year. It was not an especially profitable enterprise, so to provide income in slack months, he started hauling live chickens in this part of the country where the poor growing soil made poultry more profitable.

John's son, Don, described the founding of Tyson Foods to Phyllis Rice in the *Northwest Arkansas Times:* "Dad arrived in Springdale [Arkansas] in 1930 with a load of hay, a truck my granddaddy had given him, and a nickel. He was headed for Fort Smith, but he didn't have enough money so he had to stop here." Not a propitious start, but by 1935, John Tyson had founded Tyson Feed and Hatchery to provide chicks and feed to local growers, and then haul the grown birds to area processors. It was only logical that the next expansion would be to hatching the chicks himself and mixing his own feed.

Incorporated in 1947, John Tyson's company opened its first plant in Springdale on August 18, 1958. In 1963, the year Tyson went public, the company bought a second plant in Rogers, Arkansas, and changed its name to Tyson's Foods, Inc. That year, Tyson's Foods had sales of $16 million. In 1992, the company had sales greater than that every day.

Don Tyson was an infant when his father arrived in Springdale. He took over leadership of the business in 1967 when his parents were killed in a car-train collision. When he first joined the company in 1952, he was newly graduated from the University of Arkansas with a degree in agriculture. The company had 50 employees, but with growth came the pain of expansion. As Tyson explained to Rice, "We were short of capital. A lot of times we'd push ourselves a little bit too far. There'd be times when I didn't want all the checks to come back to the bank the same day.

"I caught Dad out of town one time and borrowed $80,000 [from the bank]. I thought he was going to fire me. Dad came through the Depression and he'd got debt-free and he didn't want to borrow any money. . . . Like most companies that are struggling and starting to grow, you go through a lot of growing pains . . . learning what you want to do and how you want to do it. . . .

"My first eleven years I never did take a day off, and that was seven days a week. My Dad didn't either. All I'd do was just follow him around. I called it the 'monkey do, monkey see' training program."

Leadership Status Came Early

In 1972 the company name made one final change to Tyson Foods, Inc., and Don Tyson continued his aggressive leadership to propel Tyson Foods into its enviable position as the number one food producer in the United States in 1992.

Acquisition of 20 companies over 25 years is credited with being the key to Tyson's continuing success. According to Pamela Bowers in *Poultry Processing* magazine, Tyson's philosophy on profits is that if you take care of employees first and customers second, your stockholders will be very pleased. In a period of rapid growth, he did just that, and from 1980 to 1990, the company was rated among the top ten American Companies for return to stockholders.

From 1981 to 1992, sales increased eight-fold, and the company posted annual 20 percent increases in compounded earning. Magazine articles and market analysts continued to explore Tyson's road to success. Total sales in 1992 were $4.2 billion. As Arkansas' largest employer (47,000 employees), the company owned 61 major facilities in 18 states and Mexico, produced 25 to 30 million chickens per week in 34 company-owned hatcheries, and processed 1.3 billion chickens yearly. To put that figure in perspective, Donald Woutat in the *Los Angeles Times* reported that all the California (the nation's biggest consumer of chicken) poultry producers combined turned out only 250 million birds a year. In addition, Tyson birds moved from hatchery to slaughterhouse in 28 days compared to the three or four months it used to take, and processing plants produced 100 pounds of chicken using eight minutes labor versus five hours in 1949.

To maintain a production and distribution flexibility that has been compared to that of Japanese car and technology companies, Tyson utilizes a fleet of 606 tractors and 975 refrigerated trailers that traveled more than 87 million miles a year in the United States. Their geographical territory includes 65 percent of the country. Twenty-three feed mills, 35 hatcheries, and 950 breeder farms support the operation.

AT A GLANCE

Tyson brand of chicken founded in 1935 by John Tyson, president of the Tyson Feed and Hatchery; company incorporated, 1947; company changed name to Tyson's Foods, Inc., 1963, and to Tyson Foods, Inc., 1972.

Performance: *Market share*—22% of U.S. chicken market. *Sales*—$4.2 billion in 1992.

Major competitor: ConAgra, Inc.'s brands of chicken; also, Gold Kist and Perdue.

Advertising: *Agencies*—Saatchi & Saatchi, New York, NY, 1988—; and Blackwood & Martin, Fayetteville, AR, 1988—. *Major campaign*—"Feeding You Like Family."

Addresses: *Parent company*—Tyson Foods, Inc., P. O. Box 2020, Springdale, AR 72764-2020; phone: (501) 756-4000; fax: (501) 750-4641.

In August 1992, Bob Ortega reported in the *Wall Street Journal* on efforts of chicken farmers in nine states to organize in opposition to the massive consolidation of poultry processors, with Tyson, their major competitor ConAgra, Gold Kist, Inc., Perdue, and Pilgrim's Pride Corporation holding 46 percent of the market.

Brand Development

"Nearly 85 percent of our poultry is value-enhanced. We're not in the chicken business. Chicken is the raw ingredient in the food we produce," Don Tyson said in *Poultry Processing* magazine. "Value-enhanced" is another term for further-processing or preparing the original birds so that they are available roasted, breaded, deboned, flavored, frozen, prepared in dinners, and processed as hot dogs or as McDonald's McNuggets and Kentucky Fried Chicken's Hot Wings. According to Baie Netzer in *Money* magazine, those products carry 20 percent gross profit margins, double those of unenhanced poultry.

Tyson credits that strategy as the primary reason that his company has been the world's leading chicken processor. Changes in the cost of feed affects profitability less for a value-enhanced product because those fluctuations are a smaller proportion of the final selling price. And as the country's largest buyer of corn to feed the birds, for Tyson that is an important part of the profit equation. So, Don Tyson explained, "we got to finding a few products that wouldn't vary in price, and we liked that so we started doing more and more."

A fortuitous interest in nutritious, high protein, low-fat meals by the nation's increasingly health-conscious families of the 1970s and 1980s helped to boost annual per capita consumption of chicken in the succeeding ten years by 55 percent from 40 to more than 70 pounds. Don Tyson was quoted in *Parade Magazine* as maintaining that "chicken is the perfect product—high in protein, low in calories, low in cholesterol, and it costs less than other meats." Americans got the message.

Soon this savvy chicken farmer was chairing the board of a company ranked 118th of *Fortune*'s 500 top U.S. corporations and acknowledged by *Forbes* as "the best managed, most profitable food processing company in the United States."

Marketing Strategy

"We don't do *more* chickens. We do more *to* chickens." Don Tyson said it frequently. "In three years, Americans will eat half of all their meals away from home," he added, defining his marketing strategy to "follow the stomach." Tyson saw that the average consumer doesn't know how to cut up a chicken so he did it for them: "We try to sell time to our customer, whomever that customer may be, whether it's the retail customer who takes it home to prepare it, or the fast food people who want it to be further processed so all they have to do is reheat the product." In fact, in 1992, 90 percent of their production was pre-cut and 87 percent value added. Not surprisingly, 55 percent of Tyson's sales were to the food service industry: restaurants, hotels, schools, military, and hospitals.

The umbrella theme supported by a $120 million marketing budget has been "Feeding you like family." Wendy Kimbrell in *Refrigerated & Frozen Foods* quotes Tyson senior vice president of sales and marketing, Bob Womack: "We feel we can fit a lot of different ideas and products under that theme. When you consume food, we want it to be a pleasurable experience. Being treated like family is a nice experience for anybody to have."

Product Changes

As a result of its commitment to value-added products, Tyson produces more than 2,100 different poultry items. In 1992 they introduced more than 130 new products: crepes, pasta salads, cornish hen products, new chicken breading flavors, fajitas, tempura battered, stir-fry, and boneless poultry, each item specifically targeted to identified consumers.

Jack Dunn, vice president, sales and marketing, told Kimbrell that "We invented the roasted chicken category about six years ago [1986] . . . it's a rapidly growing business." The company's roasted chickens are distributed across 65 percent of the United States.

A new test kitchen was completed in 1992 at corporate headquarters in Springdale, Arkansas. Tyson explained to Pamela Bowers in *Poultry Processing*, "It's bigger than that first processing plant I built 33 years ago, yet just one piece of R & D machinery for the kitchen costs more today than that entire plant!"

The story of Tyson's eight-month battle with ConAgra for the purchase of Holly Farms, Inc. in 1989 is an industry legend. The price tag made industry analysts nervous: $70 per share or $1.29 billion, leaving Tyson $1.4 billion in debt. But the company's rapid growth, especially as provider to the expanding fast food industry, meant that it desperately needed Holly's chickens. Initial skepticism faded as the company renegotiated its repayment schedule and has paid back the loan at twice the rate demanded by creditors.

That acquisition made Tyson the top chicken company in the world, with production nearly equal to that of Japan and Great Britain combined, according to *Refrigerated & Frozen Foods*. It also added beef and pork products to the Tyson line-up through Holly's subsidiaries.

Several product diversifications occurred in 1992. In October of that year, Tyson acquired Louis Kemp Seafood Co. from Oscar Meyer for $21 million and soon after that, Seattle-based Arctic Alaska Fisheries Corporation for $240 million. Mexican food sales, principally corn and flour tortillas, are also exceeding expectations.

International Market

According to Thomas C. Hayes in the *New York Times*, Tyson exported about $400 million a year in chicken products, and exports accounted for about ten percent of Tyson's sales in 1992. Japan, where Tyson has shipped chicken since 1968, contributed the major portion of sales among the 56 countries that purchased Tyson food products, including Japan, Hong Kong, Puerto Rico, Canada, Great Britain, British Columbia, China, Russia, and Indonesia.

Don Tyson traveled extensively in search of opportunities for international acquisitions or joint ventures. Sixty percent of export sales came from the Far East, and he looked for further expansion there as well as in the European community, not an easy task since European consumers eat far less poultry per capita than Americans.

Future Growth

Don Tyson set a goal for the company of achieving $8 billion in sales by 1995, and past performance would imply that acquisitions play a large role in that growth. Thomas C. Hayes in the *New York Times* said, "Tyson is preparing a war chest of cash, stock, and bank credit lines that within a year could finance $2 billion in acquisitions."

Expanded sales to fast-food restaurants that traditionally do not feature chicken were a top growth priority, as was increased attention to warehouse clubs, which had aggressive growth plans of their own. As number two in the kid's meals category, Tyson looked for more opportunity there. But it was the supermarket deli area that appeared to offer extraordinary growth opportunities for Tyson, considering the broad variety of food items already available in their product line and their history of double-digit growth in that segment of the market.

"Meal kits" including chicken, beef, and pork with the appropriate other ingredients met Tyson's vision of expanded convenience meals. Already on the market are kits for chicken stir-fry and beef fajitas. A pasta and chicken salad kit were tested. Tyson's Jack Dunn is quoted in *Refrigerated & Frozen Foods:* "Our objective is to penetrate as many different areas of the store as possible where people are going to be looking to spend food dollars."

Every division of the company had expansion plans. Tyson invested $150 million in its plants in 1992 and plans to invest $165 million in 1993.

Company Culture

When independent presidential candidate Ross Perot made fun of "chicken pluckers" during the 1992 campaign, he was making a jab at fellow candidate and Arkansas native Bill Clinton. However, the real "Super Chicken" in Arkansas was not the former governor, but rather Don Tyson. Tyson supported Clinton in the presidential race, and he had supplied funding and political connections for the governor for many years. Their political and personal association became a topic for discussion in the press during the campaign. Tyson, however, was proud of their mutually

beneficial relationship, and, having something of a reputation for enjoying a party, he was prominent among the partygoers during Clinton's inaugural celebration.

In spite of being ranked among *Forbes* magazine's list of richest Americans, Tyson is known for his unassuming manner, and at work he wears the standard khaki uniform with his first name embroidered on the pocket, just like everyone else. He leads Tyson Foods from an office that is a replica of the presidential Oval Office in Washington, D.C. Tyson headquarters feature a few differences, however. A rooster is carved in the wood-framed fireplace, and door knobs are egg-shaped. Half-eggs are carved into the ceiling border, and a bronzed egg carton graces a neighboring office.

Don Tyson's only hobby is deep-sea fishing. He was included in *Power and Motor Yacht* magazine's list of ten best American fisherman in 1991. The 1,100-pound black marlin he caught is prominently displayed in the Tyson Foods boardroom—smaller catch were returned to the sea.

Tyson's family have assumed prominent roles in company, including John, president, beef and pork division; Cheryl, who heads the family's Tyson Foundation; and Carla, employed in the company marketing department. Company representatives credit Don Tyson's ability to find the right people and inspire them to work hard, and an uncanny ability to acquire companies that are the right fit, as essential to Tyson Foods' success.

Further Reading:

Amey, David, "Profile: Tyson Foods, Inc.," *Broiler Industry*, December 1991, p. 98.

Anderson, Stephanie, "Tyson Is Winging Its Way to the Top," *Business Week*, February 25, 1991, pp. 57, 60.

"At Last, You'll Love What's Good For You," *Parade Magazine*, November 15, 1992.

Bowers, Pamela, "Can Don Tyson Beat the Odds?" *Poultry Processing*, December/January 1992, pp. 22-28.

Broiler Industry, December 1992.

Hayes, Thomas C., "Mr. Chicken Goes to Washington," *New York Times*, January 17, 1993, sec.3, p. F11.

Kelly, Kevin and Dean Foust, "Don Tyson Wins Holly Farms, But His Debts Aren't Chicken Feed," *Business Week*, July 10, 1989, pp.29,30.

Kimbrell, Wendy, "Selling Value," *Refrigerated & Frozen Foods*, August 1992, pp. 14-26.

Maraniss, David and Weisskopf, Michael, "In Arkansas, the Game Is Chicken," *Washington Post*, March 22, 1992, p. 1.

Netzer, Baie, "Tyson Goes Fishing for New Profits," *Money*, November 1992, p. 60.

Ortega, Bob, "Pecking Order Being Challenged in Chicken Industry," *Wall Street Journal*, August 12, 1992, Eastern edition, p. B6.

Pitts, Lee, "Here Comes Tyson," *Livestock Market Digest*, January 25, 1993, pp. 6, 7.

"Poultry's Down-Home Potentate," *Fortune*, January 1, 1990, p. 72.

Rice, Phyllis, "Tyson Remembers Humble Beginnings in Industry," *Northwest Arkansas Times*, October 1, 1992, section A10.

Stewart, D.R., "Tyson Foods Working Hard on Full Menu," *Arkansas Democrat Gazette*, November 22, 1992.

Tyson Foods, Inc., "Tyson Foods' Commitment to the Environment," brochure, 1992.

Woutat, Donald, "Ruler of the Roost," *The Dallas Morning News*, February 1, 1993, p. 1D.

—Margo MacInnes

UNCLE BEN'S®

Since 1942 the smiling, grandfatherly face of "Uncle Ben" has beckoned customers and denoted high quality and convenience in rice preparation. Uncle Ben's rice was the first raw commodity to be given a brand name and is among the top brands in North America and Europe. Uncle Ben's parent company, Mars, Inc., which also owns such leading brands as Milky Way candy bars, M&M's candies, Dove ice cream bars, and Pedigree dog food, is the largest private industrial company in the United States with annual sales of more than $9 billion. Recently Uncle Ben's has benefited from the public perception—reinforced by scientific evidence—that rice and rice bran play a significant role in cholesterol reduction and are an important part of a healthy diet.

Brand Origins

Although the Uncle Ben's brand was created in 1942, the history of its namesake actually dates back much further. The role model for the Uncle Ben portrayed on the product's packaging was a black Texas rice grower who, at some time in the past, perfected his trade to the extent that he was well known in and around Houston for the quality of his rice. Because this now legendary farmer's rice won many awards, other rice growers used it as a standard of comparison and often boasted that their rice was "as good as Uncle Ben's." In 1942 Forrest Mars, son of Mars, Inc. founder Frank Mars, teamed up with a Texas businessman who had invented a process for "converting" rice. Conversion prolongs shelf life, makes it easier to cook, and enhances nutritional value. The businessman remembered the legend of the original Uncle Ben and hoped to capitalize on his fame and reputation by naming the rice after him. While dining in a Chicago restaurant, Gordon L. Harwell, the first president of Converted Rice, Inc., asked the maitre d', Frank Brown, to pose for Uncle Ben's portrait. Mr. Brown agreed, thereby accepting a place in American popular culture as the well-known face of Uncle Ben.

Today the company is headquartered in Texas, the fourth ranking rice production state in America after Arkansas, California, and Louisiana. Texas rice producers like Uncle Ben's are responsible for supplying rice to more than 68 million Americans per year and account for that state's $1 billion rice industry.

Since the inception of Uncle Ben's rice, the line has expanded greatly. From the original Uncle Ben's Long Grain and Wild Rice, the line has branched off in several directions, also featuring such varieties as Specialty Blends Rice Mix, Country Inn Recipe Rice Dishes, and Fast Cook Converted Rice. Many of the varieties are microwaveable. In an effort to leverage the strength of the Uncle Ben's brand, in 1991 Mars introduced Uncle Ben's Meal Makers, a line of sauces and rice to which the consumer adds meat for a complete entree.

Brand History

Although the history of rice is probably as old as the history of food itself, American versions of the grain differ from their Asian relatives. Asians' use of chopsticks necessitated a stickier rice that clumped together and was easily picked up with the utensils.

Native Americans, on the other hand, ate rice with their hands, and so Americans have come to have a negative perception of "sticky rice," preferring rice to separate. Because of this preference, Uncle Ben's earliest advertising capitalized on its unique "converted" quality that rendered the outside of the kernel hard and prevented it from sticking to other kernels. In addition, conversion made it ideal for the novice cook because it was virtually impossible to overcook, as indicated by the brand's advertising claim that it "cooks up perfect every time." Conversion also reduced cooking time, an increasingly important factor in the post-World War II era. Convenience foods were born in the late 1940s and early 1950s, and Uncle Ben's quick-cooking fool-proof rice fit in perfectly with new items like TV dinners and cake mixes.

Although rice has had a presence in what is now the United States for centuries, it only became an important agricultural product during World War II, shortly before Uncle Ben's was created. Prior to the American Civil War, rice had been grown in the southern United States, especially the Carolinas, but the end of slavery signalled the end of the rice industry in that region, and the United States began importing rice from Asian countries. During World War II, however, the U.S. government began offering price supports to rice growers, a strong incentive for many Texas farmers.

Like many historic product logos, the portrait of Uncle Ben has received its share of criticism. In the January 30, 1993 edition of the *Toronto Star*, Alan Holliday, an assistant professor of mass communications at Boston University's College of Communications, said "When I see a box of Uncle Ben's, you can't help reading Uncle Tom, but they keep doing it." Although the Quaker Oats Company updated its Aunt Jemima character in response to outcry from the African American community, Uncle Ben has remained the same throughout his 50-year tenure as the company trademark. The Uncle Ben picture *was* removed from packages for a brief time during the 1980s, but this was done as a marketing test rather than as a response to consumer concerns. The removal of Uncle Ben was an attempt to weaken the link in consumers' minds between rice and Uncle Ben's, in order to extend the brand's name into other food categories. The portrait was, of course, restored, and the company has no plans to remove it again.

International Growth

Uncle Ben's rice was introduced into Great Britain soon after the end of World War II and has dominated that market ever since. This leadership has become increasingly important as recent studies indicate a significant rise in rice consumption among the British. Uncle Ben's is also the top-selling rice in France and has recently entered the Australian market as well. The brand's participation as Worldwide Sponsor of the 1992 Winter Olympics and the British Olympic Association (requiring between a $10 and $35 million fee) are a solid testament to its commitment to the international market. Parent company Mars, Inc. currently conducts business in more than 30 countries.

AT A GLANCE

Uncle Ben's brand of rice founded in 1942 by Gordon L. Harwell, president of Converted Rice, Inc., and Forrest Mars, son of Frank Mars, founder of parent company, Mars, Inc.

Performance: *Market share*—24% of dry rice/rice category. *Sales*—$863.9 million.

Advertising: *Agency*—Baker Spielvogel Bates, New York, NY.

Major competitor: Golden Grain Company's (division of The Quaker Oats Company) Rice-a-Roni brand.

Addresses: *Parent company*—Uncle Ben's, Inc., P.O. Box 1752, 5721 Harvey Wilson Drive, Houston, TX 77251; phone: (713) 674-9484. *Ultimate parent company*—Mars, Inc., 6885 Elm St., McLean, VA 22101; phone: (703) 821-4900; fax: (703) 448-9678.

Although the brand has a strong track record in Europe, the greatest foreign sales potential lies ahead as experts predict an opening up of the Japanese rice market to imports. Despite Japan's current policy prohibiting rice imports, a December 1992 CNN story reports that Japan is being pressured by the international community to open its markets, and that Uncle Ben's in particular is being analyzed in Japanese laboratories as a possible American import. According to the report, Uncle Ben's president, James Webb, "expects to help U.S. exporters crack the Japanese rice market, but he warns it will not be easy." Entering the $32 billion rice market would indeed prove lucrative to Uncle Ben's and other U.S. rice manufacturers, especially since analysts expect imports to eventually comprise 5 to 6 percent of the market.

Rice and Health

In 1990 a study conducted by Louisiana State University pointed to rice bran as a possible factor in the lowering of harmful cholesterol levels in humans. Another study at the University of Lowell revealed that rice bran oil reduced "bad" cholesterol in monkeys. Following the example of oat manufacturers, rice companies were quick to capitalize on these new findings and Uncle Ben's introduced Rite-Bran, pure rice bran for use in cooking and baking.

In September of 1991 Americans celebrated the first annual "National Rice Month." According to the U.S. Department of Agriculture's 1992 food guide *Pyramid*, the largest part of the American diet should consist of rice, bread, cereal, and pasta. The guide recommends six to eleven servings per day from this food group. Rice's versatility and ease of preparation fit in well with these new recommendations, which may be one reason that rice consumption in the United States has doubled since 1979 and is still climbing. Per capita consumption now stands at an estimated 20.5 pounds annually.

Uncle Ben's currently holds the number two spot among rice brands behind Quaker Oats' Rice-a-Roni. Although rice is Mars' smallest business unit, it is the company's number one brand, with 25 percent of the $900 million category. In fiscal year 1991-92, the company dramatically changed its advertising spending, concentrating on Uncle Ben's Wild Rice.

Future Predictions

In the March 15, 1993 *New York Times Magazine*, food columnist Molly O'Neill said that "rice is now rivaling pasta as both backbone and canvas for a main dish." Rice is the predominant food for six out of every 10 people in the world, and, although the United States lags behind in that statistic, recent trends indicate that it is catching up with the rest of the world. Quick-fix side dishes, like rice, are the fastest growing convenience food categories. The strength of parent company Mars, the resurgence of rice's popularity in general, and the power of the brand indicate continued vitality for Uncle Ben's.

Further Reading:

Beckett, Jamie, "Advertisers' Olympic Gold," *San Francisco Chronicle*, January 20, 1992.

Brenner, Joel Glenn, "Life on Mars," *Independent*, July 26, 1992, p. 14.

Criswell, Ann, "Meet a Very Rice Family," *Houston Chronicle*, November 4, 1992, p. 1.

Louis, Arthur M., "The U.S. Business Hall of Fame," *Fortune*, April 2, 1984, p. 106.

Meyer, Ann, "Mission from Mars," *Prepared Foods*, March, 1992, p. 49.

Morgan, Dan, "The Rice Connection," *Washington Post*, August 7, 1977, section B1.

Oishi, Nobuyuki, and Naomi Ono, "Politicians, Farmers Prepare to Accept Limited Rice Imports," *Nikkei Weekly*, June 8, 1991, p. 1.

Siegel, Martin, "Classic Trademarks Put Best Faces Forward," *Marketing News*, July 6, 1992, p. 17.

"100 Leading National Advertisers," *Advertising Age*, September 25, 1991, p. 47.

—Kate Sheehan

UNDERWOOD®

The Underwood label is easily identified by its Red Devil trademark, which grins and waves from every can as if to salute the consumers who made it the oldest food trademark in the United States. But just as the devil changed shape since its 1867 creation, the Wm. Underwood Co. evolved from its origins as a local cannery in 1822 in Boston, Massachusetts, to a pioneer in food preservation, to an international distributor of canned goods, specializing in meat spreads and baked beans. After a history of strategic acquisitions of its own, Underwood was acquired in 1982 by Pet Incorporated, at the time a subsidiary of IC Industries, which later was called Whitman Corporation. Underwood's substantial overseas market represented an important step in Pet's push to expand internationally. And Pet's experience as a powerful marketer of niche grocery items contributed to further growth potential for Underwood. By the 1990s, several new products had been introduced, including Honey Ham Spread in 1992.

Origins in Canning

Underwood's early history overlaps with the early history of commercial food preservation in canning. Discovery of the process is generally attributed to Nicholas Appert, a French winemaker and food supplier who discovered in 1809 that heated foods could be preserved in sealed jars. Initial use was reserved for the military—namely, for Napoleon's troops in France and the British Admiralty in England. Commercial applications soon followed, crossing the Atlantic and spawning new canneries in the United States. Business thrived mainly in port cities, where traffic flow and supplies of goods could ensure not only year-round business, but ready distribution. Baltimore, New York, Boston, and Portland, Maine, were some of the port cities in which canneries thrived in the mid-nineteenth century. The Wm. Underwood Co. was one such business.

In 1821 William Underwood emigrated from England to Boston, where he and his brother James opened a shop on Russia Wharf by the harbor in 1822. They began preserving such indigenous foods as cranberries, currants, onions, tomatoes, and cabbage. Early products were processed exclusively in glass bottles. Though a method of preserving foods in tin canisters, or cans, was developed in England shortly after Appert's discoveries, the process was inefficient and expensive, requiring the expertise and time of skilled tinsmiths. But the growing canning business coin-

cided with developments in machine cutting and soldering, so tin cans quickly became the norm for the Underwood enterprise.

Tin cans were imminently more practical to transport than glass, an important fact for the Underwood brothers, who had started an import-export business buying spices and other imported food items from merchants and selling their fruits and vegetables in return. Sailors bought Underwood goods for their own use and also sold them on commission in ports along the Atlantic coast and, eventually, around the world. By the mid-1800s Underwood preserves were being traded in the West Indies, South America, the Far East, and around the Mediterranean. In the United States, the company began national marketing by sending goods to gold miners working up appetites, if not gold fortunes, in California. Later Underwood, along with other canners, supplied Civil War armies and found greater demand in the postwar population boom.

Canning Innovation

Having benefitted from canning science in its early years of business, Underwood returned the favor by contributing research that changed the food preservation industry. William Lyman Underwood, the grandson of the company founder, worked in conjunction with Dean Samuel Cate Prescott of the Massachusetts Institute of Technology to investigate and better control spoilage in canned goods. During ten years of research at the end of the nineteenth century, the team isolated bacteria and developed new methods of sterilization. They discovered that the common practice of boiling sealed cans in water did not guarantee success in preservation. Pressure cookers and other tools were needed to ensure higher, more constant temperatures that, if monitored, could eliminate guesswork in canning. In honor of their research, the university established the Underwood-Prescott Professorship in Food Science.

Introduced the Red Devil

Better technology facilitated the introduction of new types of canned foods and helped old favorites survive and grow. Underwood meat spreads, for example, would benefit from canning advances to become Underwood's flagship line. In 1867 the Underwoods introduced a line of highly seasoned canned products, including chicken, turkey, ham, and lobster. The key to their recipe was a secret process marketed as "deviling." The

AT A GLANCE

Underwood brand of canned meat founded in 1822 by William and James Underwood, owners of the Wm. Underwood Co., a canning operation on Boston's Russia Wharf; first products were local food items, including cranberries, currants, onions, tomatoes, and cabbage, preserved in glass bottles; Wm. Underwood Co. became an import-export business; company began pioneering use of cans and diversified to include canned seafoods and meats; introduced a line of deviled canned products, including chicken, turkey, ham, and lobster; the Red Devil trademark established in 1867; company acquired Richardson & Robbins Co., 1959; Burnham & Morrill Co. and the Chevallier-Appert label, 1965; Ac'cent International, 1971; and C. Shippam Ltd., 1975; Underwood acquired by Pet Incorporated, a subsidiary of IC Industries, which was renamed Whitman Corp.; Pet was spun off from Whitman Corp. and reemerged as an independent public company, 1991. Underwood label now includes exclusively canned meats and sardines.

Performance: *Market share*—4.8% of canned meat category.

Advertising: *Agency*—D'Arcy Masius Benton & Bowles (D.M.B.&B.), St. Louis, MO, 1991—.

Addresses: *Parent company*—Pet Incorporated, 400 S. 4th Street, St. Louis, MO 63102; phone: (314) 622-7700; fax: (314) 622-6525.

Underwoods recommended that these deviled foods be used as sandwich spreads, even though the concept of the sandwich had not yet caught on in the United States. Thus, the success of the new products depended in large part on introducing the novel idea of the sandwich: a time-efficient, easy-to-prepare snack. In order to attract consumers' attention, the company designed a catchy trademark, the Red Devil.

Though its lineaments changed with time, the devil itself remained a consistent reinforcer of Underwood brand recognition. The first Red Devil, used on Original Deviled Ham and other spreads in 1867, was a stocky character, facing directly forward with arms and legs open as if ready to embrace the consumer. Its features were almost comically evil: enchanting eyes, a frightful grin outlined by a pointed moustache, clawed fingers, and one cloven foot. The tip of the tail branched to form a W, which was graphically worked right into the company name, written on the can as Wm. Underwood Co. In 1870, when the U.S. Patent Office registered its first trademarks, the Red Devil was assigned No. 82.

Over the next 150 years, the original Red Devil would be updated six times, but would retain its historical place in the trademark roster. In 1883, for example, it lost considerable weight, along with the W on its tail. It was turned sideways and given a slipper to cover its cloven left foot and a spear-type pitchfork, which it held over its shoulder like a javelin. By 1937 the Red Devil was turned forward again and lost its weapon and left slipper to reveal the cloven foot. Its lines were appreciably simplified; crosshatch and shading were replaced with a monochromatic print.

In 1959 the Red Devil was incorporated right into the Underwood brand name to create a clean and visually simplified logo. Furnished with a harmless-looking trident and a playful grin, it was changed from fiend to friend. A 1966 *Business Week* article outlining Underwood's new marketing strategies explained the new countenance: "The devil's main selling point is conve-

nience—and he's happy to be of service." The customer-oriented devil survived Pet's 1982 acquisition of the brand.

Early Advertising

To assist the Red Devil in developing strong brand recognition, Underwood increased its domination of the market through strong and innovative advertising support. The first magazine advertisement for Deviled Ham, placed in the January 3, 1895, edition of *Youth's Companion* magazine, played off the good nature and good sandwich taste of the Red Devil, who afforded its users "distinguished hospitality." Other early Underwood advertising typically appeared in such magazines as *Ladies' Home Journal*, *Woman's Home Companion*, and *Harper's*, which drew an audience of food buyers and food preparers.

Other ads evolved to accommodate wider audiences interested in fast, easy, and long-lasting food. Many print ads offered a free Underwood cookbook with recipes requiring little other than a can opener. Around the turn of the century, a memorable slogan described deviled products as "branded with the Devil but fit for the gods." Another popular slogan first appearing in 1909 coaxed the consumer to "taste the taste."

Around the same time, Underwood sent promotional cards to retailers and distributors. The cards depicted a celestial, colorful scene in which the Red Devil, emanating rays of light, faced a complete product list: "Wm. Underwood Co.'s Deviled Turkey, Chicken, Ham, Tongue, Lobster. Original Deviled Entremets." A 1912 ad in the *Saturday Evening Post* described a "spicy . . . not hot, just hungrifying" appeal to Deviled Ham and supplied a recipe for "A Delicious Sandwich." In addition to taste, the ad appealed to budgets, noting that a small can made 12 to 24 sandwiches.

Other ads exaggerated the plentiful contents and flavor of a small can by superimposing reduced human figures alongside oversized cans with the slogan, "You'll fight for the big taste." The sandwich spreads were also targeted at automobile travelers, for whom extensive roadside amenities did not yet line the highways. "Try this for motor trips," suggested a 1911 ad with a drawing of a smiling man, goggles hoisted on his forehead, with one hand spreading a layer of deviled ham on a slice of bread held in the other. The ad's copy directed the reader to "Mix together thoroughly one can of Underwood Deviled Ham, an equal quantity of mayonnaise dressing, and a very small onion chopped fine." In 1933 repackaging of the deviled ham can produced a new overlapping wrapper that not only inhibited rust, but provided the distinctive appearance of a specialty food. After market success, the wrapper was also applied to other Underwood spreads and sardines.

International Growth

From its beginnings on Russia Wharf, Underwood was linked to overseas markets. Before its international business could expand substantially, however, the company needed a strong domestic base. George C. Seybolt, the first Wm. Underwood Co. president not related to the founder, focused his energies on developing national brands in the 1960s. "Regional brands are very vulnerable," he commented in a June 18, 1966, *Business Week* article. "And supporting local brands requires management time and money; it just doesn't fit into the business we are developing." From 1961 to 1966 Seybolt sold off nearly $5 million worth of regional business, including some strong local brands. Moose-abec sardines, for example, was a best-seller in New York City, but Underwood sold it because the Maine fish supply would not have accommodated national distribution.

Seybolt also set in motion a series of acquisitions and overseas expansions to strengthen Underwood. In 1959 the company acquired Richardson & Robbins Co. (R&R), of Dover, Delaware. Though R&R marketed items to an East Coast market, Seybolt recognized broader potential for some of its canned chicken products. R&R Chicken Spread, for example, was transferred to the Underwood label and marketed nationally. Other acquisitions included Burnham & Morrill Co. (B&M), a producer of brown bread and baked beans, in 1965; Ac'cent International, producer of flavor enhancers, in 1971; and C. Shippam Ltd., in 1975. The company's ownership since 1965 of the Chevallier-Appert label in France associated it with the world's first cannery and with the earliest techniques of canned food preservation that Underwood brought to the United States in 1821.

From sales of $50 million in 1966, Underwood grew consistently to arrive at sales of $228 million in 1981. Approximately 45 percent of sales came from international operations in Canada, the United Kingdom, Mexico, Venezuela, Costa Rica, and Australia. Such success caught the attention of IC Industries, the parent of Pet Incorporated.

Pet Devil

In 1982 Pet acquired the Wm. Underwood Co. in a $150 million cash transaction. Once part of the Pet family, the brands of the Wm. Underwood Co.—Underwood, B&M, and Ac'cent—were operated separately. The Underwood brand appeared exclusively on canned meat spreads and sardines. William B. Johnson, chairman and CEO of IC Industries, said in a 1982, *PR Newswire* report, "Underwood's strong market position in the United States and other countries fits well with two of IC Industries' strategic goals: to add growth from high-margin consumer products, and to expand internationally."

The stakes were high, as Underwood had achieved annual sales growth for the previous 32 consecutive years and held an unbroken record of earnings growth for the previous 18 years. With an eye on fully exploiting Underwood's international potential, Pet formed an international group shortly after the acquisition. Early in 1984, the company brought the Old El Paso line of canned Mexican food to England and distributed it through Underwood's Shippams meat products operation there.

Whether the Underwood brand, like Old El Paso, would benefit from increased marketing efforts on a national and international level remained to be seen in the early 1990s. When Pet Incorporated assumed ownership, Underwood already commanded appreciable brand recognition and the respect that comes with brand maturity. In addition, Pet specialized in marketing and selling specialty items in specific markets. "What sets Pet apart is that we're not a general grocer to all consumers," said the then-Pet president and chief executive officer in a 1989 *Advertising Age* article. "But we try and understand our niches better than anyone else and be there with the right products."

In April of 1991 Pet was spun off from Whitman Corporation and reemerged as an independent public company. Its philosophy shifted from an earlier emphasis on growth through acquisition to development of such already established brands as Underwood. In 1988 and 1989 Pet devoted 90 percent of its marketing budget to promotions, according to Seth Lubove in a 1992 *Forbes* article. "Pet 'pushed' its goods on consumers with store displays and coupons, rather than attempting to 'pull' with advertising," he explained. For the 1990s, the company projected a larger budget for advertising and product development. By 1992 Underwood had already introduced a new Honey Ham Spread. Beyond that, Pet would have to find the niches in which the smiling Red Devil, "happy to be of service," could serve or be served best.

Further Reading:

Carey, David, "The IC Story: Master Plan Success," *Financial World,* February 19, 1985, p. 102.

Erickson, Julie Liesse, "New Pet Chief Sets Shelf-Stable Line," *Advertising Age,* September 11, 1989, p. 33.

"Highlights From 155 Years of Company History," Pet Incorporated Annual Report, 1992.

"IC Industries Acquisition," *PR Newswire,* June 1, 1982.

Lubove, Seth, "On Their Own," *Forbes,* March 16, 1992, p. 68.

Morgan, Hal, *Symbols of America,* New York, NY: Penguin, 1986, p. 105.

" 'Red Devil' Bites off a New Market," *Business Week,* June 18, 1966, p. 66.

"Wm. Underwood Acquired by IC," *PR Newswire,* May 11, 1982.

—Kerstan Cohen

V-8®

Since 1936, V-8 100 percent vegetable juice has been America's best-selling vegetable juice. Developed during the Great Depression, the product clearly dominates the vegetable juice market, with over 90 percent of sales. V-8, owned by the Campbell Soup Company, stands to benefit from recent trends emphasizing the nutritional qualities of vegetables in general and vegetable juice in particular. Four varieties of the beverage are available: Regular, Low Sodium, Spicy Hot, and Light 'n Tangy.

The Quest for Health

The Great Depression of the 1930s heralded an unusual nutrition paradox in the United States. Whereas many people endured poverty-induced malnutrition, members of the upper and middle classes strove to lose weight. In the wake of the androgenously skinny "flapper" of the 1920s, slimness remained the ideal body type. This ideal evolved as a result of fashion and new studies linking obesity and early death.

From the 1930s to the 1960s, nutritionists also emphasized the need to consume the right amount of nutrients, especially vitamins. By the end of the 1920s, vitamin awareness was widespread, and it was commonly held that these tasteless and invisible dietary components were indispensable for the maintenance of good vision, vitality, and even life itself. Some experts recommended the consumption of enormous quantities of green vegetables to combat calcium and vitamin A deficiencies.

Brand Origins

W. G. Peacock and three investors founded the New England Products Company, Inc. in 1933 in Evanston, Illinois, to capitalize on the health craze. With the help of his son, Peacock developed bottled and canned juices from a wide variety of vegetables, including carrots, spinach, lettuce, and celery.

But, as individual drinks, the juices were unappetizing. Even the most health-conscious consumers usually did not become repeat customers. This serious marketing problem inspired Peacock and his son to combine vegetable juices for a tastier product. After almost a year of experimentation, father and son formulated a unique combination of eight vegetable juices: tomato, celery, carrot, spinach, lettuce, watercress, beet, and parsley.

Peacock and son developed a label for their product and called it Veg-min, evoking the dual healthy images of vegetables and vitamins. The label design incorporated a large "V" and a predominant "8" listing the vegetable juices. When Peacock took samples of his new product to an Evanston specialty grocer, a clerk at the shop noticed the label and suggested that the name be simplified: V-8. His comment led to the adoption of V-8 Vegetable Juices as the brand name.

Early Marketing Strategy

The company started production in early 1936 and sold to several grocery chains, including Chicago's Stop and Shop Store and the First National Stores in New England. Within just two years, demand for V-8 had exhausted Peacock's ability to meet it. The Loudon Packing Company, the firm that supplied canned tomato juice for V-8, acquired the New England Products Company in April 1938.

In 1939, the Loudon Packing Company undertook a marketing campaign to promote V-8. The company designed a new label, which won the National Award for Attractive and Descriptive Label that year.

At the time, production of V-8 was very labor-intensive. Vegetables were washed partially by hand, trimmed, and passed through a grinder. They were juiced separately, using a household-sized cider press, then heated, filtered, bottled, and chilled in an ice house. After being blended in small nickel kettles, the juice was canned, sealed, labeled, and packed by hand. The cases were distributed directly to wholesale groceries, chain stores, and large independent stores. The painstaking process limited the company's production to just 25 cases per day, with 24 ten-ounce cans per case.

Brand Development

The Loudon Packing Company was purchased by Standard Brands, Inc. in 1943. Standard Brands was one of the largest food conglomerates to emerge from the Great Depression. Some economists surmised that giant food processors were inevitable because their size allowed economies of scale that enabled them to cut prices and drive smaller competitors out of business. V-8 would remain a brand controlled by large food conglomerates henceforward.

World War II heralded a renewed emphasis on vitamin-rich foods. The federal government's home front propaganda included

AT A GLANCE

V-8 brand vegetable juice formulated by W. G. Peacock and son in Evanston, IL, in 1934; brand first owned by New England Products Company, Inc., which was acquired by Loudon Packing Company in 1938; Loudon purchased by Standard Brands, Inc. in 1943; V-8 brand and properties acquired by Campbell Soup Company in 1948.

Performance: Market share—91.6% of vegetable juice category. Sales—$9.6 million.

Major competitor: Motts brand of vegetable juices.

Advertising: Agency—FCB/Leber Katz Partners, New York, NY. Major campaign—"Drink your vegetables," and "Have you had your vegetables today?"

Addresses: Parent company—Campbell Soup Company, Campbell Place, Camden, NJ 08103-1799; phone: (609) 342-4800; fax: (609) 342-5213.

the theme "the U.S. needs US strong," which was incorporated into V-8 advertisements. V-8 marketers also utilized wartime rationing to promote its product in much the same way that companies touted environmental packaging in the 1990s: a 1942 advertisement noted that V-8's larger can helped conserve tin for the Allied cause.

By the end of World War II, the V-8 brand and its production facilities were acquired by the Campbell Soup Company, which continued to control the trademark into the 1990s. In the postwar era, V-8 was produced in Saratoga, Indiana, at a modern plant built exclusively to manufacture the juice. About 600 acres of tomatoes were raised at the plant, and 12,000 tons of tomatoes were processed each year.

In 1975, Campbell consolidated its tomato operations by moving V-8 production to its tomato soup plant at Napoleon, Ohio. That year, Campbell advertisers launched the widely recognized "WOW, I could have had a V-8" campaign. The spots featured characters smacking their foreheads (with a distinctive "bonk" sound) upon realizing that they just drank a nutritionally empty beverage instead of a healthy and tasty V-8.

The V-8 recipe remained unchanged for over 50 years, until a Spicy Hot version was introduced in the late 1980s. In January, 1992, Campbell began national distribution of its newest V-8 variety, Light n' Tangy. The line extension had 50 percent less sodium than original V-8. That year, Low Sodium V-8 replaced a failing No Salt Added version. Low Sodium contained 75 percent less sodium than the original product, yet was tastier than the No Salt version. Low Sodium V-8 got a boost in early 1993 when Jenny Craig Inc., a national weight loss program, endorsed the product as a vegetable option for dieters.

"V-8's Time Has Come"

The 1990s saw a renewed popular interest in, and nutritional emphasis on, vegetables and vegetable juice. National mania for juice-making appliances was fueled by "infomercials"—30-minute advertisements—that extolled vegetable and fruit juices as

health aids. Also in 1991, the United States Department of Agriculture's Human Nutrition Information Service announced its new Food Pyramid Guidelines to encourage increased consumption of cereals, fruits, and vegetables. The guidelines urge Americans to eat as much as five servings of vegetables each day.

In addition to "juice mania" and governmental recommendation, convenience had become one of the biggest influences on consumer food purchases. The combination of these trends created a climate that naturally promoted V-8. The product was healthy, convenient, and practically endorsed by the U.S. Federal Government: The pre-canned, 35-calorie, no-fat, no-cholesterol drink provided 100 percent of the U.S. Recommended Daily Allowance (USRDA) of vitamin C and 30 percent of the USRDA of vitamin A. An executive of V-8's advertising agency, FCB/Leber Katz Partners (New York), went so far as to proclaim that "V-8's time has come" in a 1992 *New York Times* article.

Promotions by FCB/Leber Katz capitalized on the health-conscious trends. A television promotion played on the Food Pyramid Guidelines by asking, "Have you had your vegetables today?" Another tag line urged customers to "drink your vegetables." The commercials featured lively men and women who made quirky, but memorable remarks about V-8's qualities like, "Its a zippy kind of thing."

A campaign through the food service division of Campbell Soup Company, entitled "Wow," strove to market V-8 to commercial and noncommercial segments in restaurants and cafeterias. The campaign utilized buttons, posters, menu stickers, table tents, and cash register cards during the spring and summer of 1992.

Performance Appraisal

In many respects, V-8 has come full circle. Created at the dawn of vitamin consciousness in America, the product has once again benefited from nutritional trends in the 1990s. Health awareness concerning food products shows no sign of waning, and as the beverage industry overall responds to consumer demand for lighter, healthier, and more natural drinks, V-8's sales will continue to grow.

There is no sign that the brand's nearly 60-year domination of the vegetable juice market will waver. Its closest competitor, Motts Vegetable Juice, holds only 4 percent of the market; V-8 has captured over 90 percent.

Further Reading:

"Campbell Rolls Operator Campaign for V-8," *Nation's Restaurant News,* March 16, 1992, p. 38.

"Campbell Soup Co.," *Advertising Age,* January 6, 1992, p. 23.

Elliot, Stuart, "Vegetable Juices: Having Their Day?," *New York Times,* August 17, 1992, p. D7.

Levenstein, Harvey, *Paradox of Plenty: A Social History of Eating in Modern America,* Oxford University Press: New York, 1993.

Sinisi, John, "Food: Bursting with Health," *Adweek (Midwest Edition),* (Supplement to *Adweek, Brandweek,* and *Mediaweek*), 1992, pp. 80-87.

—April S. Dougal

VAN DE KAMP'S®

Van de Kamp's®
frozen seafoods

Van de Kamp's Frozen Seafood, which virtually pioneered the battered fish stick in the 1970s, fared the turbulent waters of the frozen seafood industry to become number one in its category by the early 1990s. From Van de Kamp's beginnings as a potato chip stand in the early 1900s, it grew into a line of bakeries, then into a line of restaurants. Under the parentage of General Host Corp., Van de Kamp's frozen foods business replaced restaurants as its core of business. By the late 1970s, the brand controlled a sizeable share of the frozen dinner and seafood industries, offering an increasingly diverse line, including halibut, fish fillets, fish & chips, and fish sticks. Pillsbury Co.'s 1984 acquisition of Van de Kamp's further improved national sales. When Pet Incorporated acquired the brand in 1989, Van de Kamp's ranked third in its category. By 1991, having become the category leader, Van de Kamp's saw renewed marketing support as well as line expansion, including the addition of Crisp and Healthy Fish Fillet/Fish Snacks.

Brand Origins

Van de Kamp's first established its name in the baking business. In 1915 Theodore J. Van de Kamp and his brother-in-law Lawrence L. Frank started a family business selling Saratoga Chips in downtown Los Angeles. Early marketing played off ethnic origins and cleanliness: The Van de Kamp sisters, Marion and Henrietta Frank, designed traditional Dutch costumes. The store window read, "Fresh Every Minute," and "Made—Kept—Sold—Clean Clean Clean." Before long, macaroons and pretzels were added to the menu, and a windmill trademark was designed to embellish the packages. A selection of beverages became available for on-premises consumption, representing the first step into the restaurant business.

In 1921 the Van de Kamp's trademark also became a landmark, as the first retail bakery store was built in the shape of a windmill, even sporting turning arms. By 1931 a Van de Kamp's central bakery supplied bakeries throughout the Los Angeles area. Throughout the 1930s Van de Kamp's capitalized on the growing popularity of supermarkets: bakeries were set up just beyond checkout counters, eventually migrating, with franchises, right into the markets.

1956 marked a transition from baked goods to big-scale food processing, from family run business to corporate control. After the death of Theodore Van de Kamp and because of Lawrence

Frank's physical disability, the business was sold to General Baking Company, which was later renamed General Host Corp. The bakeries had evolved into full-fledged restaurants specializing in batter-fried halibut and Mexican dishes, especially enchiladas. In 1959 the company experimented with frozen restaurant specialties for take-home business. Positive results prompted the 1960 construction of a $500,000, two-building processing plant for frozen foods, including french fried northern halibut, enchiladas, chicken pies, macaroni and cheese, and shrimp. Taking after the Van de Kamp windmill concept, the frozen foods plant was built in the shape of a giant ice cube. Despite change and growth, the company had retained its knack for setting itself apart from its competition.

Frozen foods were popular enough to warrant the formation of a separate frozen food division, which quickly became the focus of business operations. By 1965 plant and storage facilities were doubled. Further experimentation and consolidation resulted in even more emphasis on the core specialties of battered haddock and frozen Mexican dinners, especially beef, chicken, and cheese enchiladas. After a strong push in the direction of frozen baked goods—11 products, including baked and unbaked breads and desserts—the line was discontinued in 1970. In addition, all 18 coffee shops/restaurants were sold to the Tiny Naylor group in 1973. By the following year Van de Kamp's Frozen Foods had expanded to 11 states and generated approximately $13 million in sales. General Host recognized a need for more aggressive expansion, and in the 1970s, the company plunged into a sea of competition and emerged with a sizeable catch.

Better Batter—Growth in the 1970s

With new management direction and product innovation, General Host catapulted Van de Kamp's into the upper end of the frozen seafoods market by the early 1980s. Progress began with the hiring in 1974 of Steve Pokress, a management supervisor at Van de Kamp's advertising agency in Los Angeles who became president of Van de Kamp's Frozen Foods in May 1976. Pokress's strategy involved diversification of product line and expansion of the geographic area of sales and distribution. Emphasis was placed on Van de Kamp's battered fish, which had gained wide popularity and had undergone real-world testing during the restaurant years. Not only was the batter a proprietary mixture unavailable to other processors, but commercial equipment had not yet been developed

AT A GLANCE

Van de Kamp's brand of frozen seafood founded in 1915 by Theodore J. Van de Kamp and Lawrence L. Frank, as part of a Los Angeles potato chip stand selling Saratoga Chips; by 1920s, expanded to Van de Kamp's Holland Dutch Bakers, selling macaroons, pretzels, breads, and cakes from 80 shops housed in miniature windmills; company sold to General Baking Company, which was later renamed General Host Corp.; Van de Kamp's evolved into local restaurant chain specializing in batter-fried halibut and Mexican food; after developing substantial take-home business for frozen restaurant specialties, company sold the restaurants to focus on frozen food line, which was nationally distributed in 1979; brand sold in 1984 to Pillsbury Co., which was acquired by Grand Metropolitan PLC in 1988; Van de Kamp's sold to Pet Incorporated, a subsidiary of Whitman Corp. (formerly called IC Industries), 1989; Pet spun off from Whitman Corp. in 1991 and reemerged as an independent public company.

Performance: *Market share*—30.6% (top share) of frozen seafood category. *Sales*—$167.4 million.

Major competitor: General Mills' Gorton's; also, Campbell's Mrs. Paul's.

Advertising: *Agency*—D'Arcy Masius Benton & Bowles (D.M.B.&B), St. Louis, MO, 1991—.

Addresses: *Parent company*—Pet Incorporated, 400 S. 4th Street, St. Louis, MO 63102; phone: (314) 622-7700; fax: (314) 622-6525.

to produce it for a mass market. "The time, effort and money that went into trial-and-error research and building of special equipment and systems to mass produce a batter-coated fish product that matched up to our batch-produced restaurant favorite represented an epic of business determination," Pokress recalled in a 1979 article for *Quick Frozen Foods.*

Van de Kamp's began its foray into the battered fish market by introducing batter-coated cod fillets and fish-and-chips and then, after confirmed success, moving on to other popular species, such as haddock, perch, and sole. For each type of fish, General Host developed custom-formulated batters. By the late 1970s, the company generated enough volume to justify unlimited geographical marketing expansion. By 1979, Van de Kamp's was represented by 70 brokers and boasted sales of more than $75 million.

Better battered fish translated into success and diversification of other Van de Kamp's lines as well. In 1979 General Host introduced Country Seasoned Seafood, featuring a new type of seasoned breaded coating with crunchy crumbs and blended herbs and spices. The first varieties featuring the "old fashioned flavor" of the new coating were fish fillets, fish kabobs (individual coated balls of fish), and scallops. The company also continued development of its Mexican foods, which accounted for roughly 25 percent of shipments in 1979.

In 1983 Van de Kamp's launched a line of Chinese Classics and Italian Classics, which were marketed as unusually high-quality items in the already flooded frozen dinner market. Harking back to Van de Kamp's restaurant experience, advertising campaigns stressed the "restaurant quality" of the new lines, while Pokress described most competitors as "stomach stuffers" in an October 1983 *Business Week* article.

Going National

Though pioneering the battered fish market provided the materials needed for national growth, Van de Kamp's could not expand beyond its regional hold without an aggressive marketing strategy. Jack L. Casotti, vice-president of sales and distribution, and Ernest W. Townsend, vice-president of marketing, worked as a team at the center of an overall effort to fill markets across the nation. One problem they faced was choosing brokers who were not tied up by conflicting contracts with other producers trying to sell similar goods. Van de Kamp's tried sharing brokers who handled other styles and types of fish but whose emphasis on Van de Kamp's battered specialties would work in tandem. By employing brokers dealing in similar fish products, Van de Kamp's hoped to gain niche share by occupying shelf space with products representing other niches. Such cooperative brokering represented a new direction in retail marketing, according to a May 1979 article in *Quick and Frozen Foods.*

Van de Kamp's also overcame distribution obstacles by resourceful use of relatively new refrigeration technology. Benefitting from the so-called Total Distribution System of Arctic Cold Storage, a local low-temperature warehouse, Van de Kamp's tailored storage, inventory, and shipping of its frozen inventories. When operations expanded to a national level, Van de Kamp's contracted Total Distribution Plan for America, Inc. (TDP), eventually operating from Termicold, Inc. in Portland, Oregon; Continental Freezers out of Chicago; Alford Refrigerated Warehouses in Dallas, Texas; and Empire Freezers of Syracuse, New York. Distribution was thus achieved throughout the United States.

To accommodate new growth, Van de Kamp's developed new sources of raw material. As Van de Kamp's did not own a fishing fleet, all of its fish came from outside sources. In the brand's early commercial frozen food business, roughly one million pounds of halibut and a half million pounds of cod were used annually. By 1979 such quantities would not have lasted a month. General Host made new, reliable procurement contacts in countries as diverse as Norway, Denmark, Canada, Argentina, Japan, Korea, and Russia. In June of 1977 Van de Kamp's also began production of battered fish products at its new processing plant in Erie, Pennsylvania, facilitating distribution throughout the eastern half of the country.

Advertising Support

Gearing up for an anticipated push in market share and national expansion, Van de Kamp's devoted unprecedented funds to advertising and promotional spending in 1979. General Host launched a series of television advertisements playing off the batter's reputation, which dated back to its restaurant days. In one 30-second commercial, for example, a man who had just bitten into a batter-coated fillet asked, "Hey, who puffed the batter on this fish?" A fillet frying in oil was then shown and a voice answered, "Van de Kamp's fries fish just enough to give it the puff." The theme continued through several takes, culminating in an endearing older woman exclaiming, "I 'luff' the Puff!"

A newspaper promotion accompanied the ad, offering 25 cent coupons and a printed recapitulation of the slogan "Van de Kamp's fries fish just enough to give it the puff." For consumers not snagged by that series of ads, other 30-second commercials were built around the theme "Van de Kamp's, the fish that catches people. Take a delicate, tender flaky fish, puff it up with a light coat of tasty batter and what do you get? A fish that catches people." Additional bait appeared as 15 cent coupons in leading newspapers. And, another promotional campaign relied on full-color newspaper inserts cooperatively promoting Minute Maid Lemon Juice as a great fish accompaniment.

Brand Development

Just as Van de Kamp's original potato chips evolved into battered fish sticks, the fish sticks and other line extensions followed market trends to yield new products. Increasing concern over the healthfulness of batters and fatty foods in the late 1970s and early 1980s spawned a variety of low-fat, low-cholesterol alternatives. A February 1987 article in *Supermarket News* reported a swelling demand for fresh seafood and a steep drop in the popularity of traditional batter-dipped items. Sales of frozen raw fish were up 25-50 percent, while sales of the heat-and-serve items were down, according to the article. Van de Kamp's was ready for the changes, having introduced in 1983 a line of fish called Today's Catch, packed fresh without any coating or batter. The company offered a free recipe folder, "Fresh Ideas From Van de Kamp's," to buttress sales of its new freshly frozen fish.

To support less healthy items, Van de Kamp's developed a microwaveable line appealing to the convenience market—and, in certain products, to healthfulness as well. In order to preserve crispness and browning, the microwave selections depended on the use of devices called susceptors. By 1990, however, susceptors were still under investigation for possible hazardous effects. The Susceptor Microwave Packaging Committee—a collaboration between the Society of the Plastics Industry and the National Food Processors Association—had not yet submitted its final report on susceptor safety to the U.S. Food and Drug Administration (FDA).

To avoid consumer alienation, marketers replaced technical references to susceptors with user-friendly terms such as "silver dish" and "crisping tray." In 1992 Van de Kamp's introduced a fish stick negotiating the differences between health trends and traditional breading taste: Crisp and Healthy Fish Fillets, 97 percent fat free, were baked instead of fried. The product contained 2 grams of fat and 120 calories per serving. Results of a taste test reported in the March 4, 1992, *Seattle Times,* however, noted that the fish had a grayish hue and the breading was too thick, masking fish flavor. Other sources lauded the product as a healthy tribute to an old favorite.

Controversial Ad Claims

While many of Van de Kamp's brand developments appealed to health-conscious consumers, they also caught the attention of health specialists and media experts interested in the legal and ethical aspects of health claims in advertising. A case in point was the seemingly contradictory implications of frozen fish marketed as fresh ("fresh frozen"). The 1983 introduction of Today's Catch, for example, attracted customers with the catchy slogan, "possibly fresher than fresh." Ernie Townsend, vice-president of marketing for Van de Kamp's Frozen Foods, explained the claim in a press conference: "Fish that's called fresh can sit on ice on the boat for days and could be as much as a week old by the time it gets to market."

An article in *Marine Fisheries Review* by Louis J. Fonsivalli, former director of the National Marine Fisheries Services, stressed that "fresh-caught fish that are used immediately and held in ice thereafter will remain of high quality (US Grade A) for eight to nine days and of edible quality for about two weeks. At the other extreme, if fish are properly packaged, brought to a temperature of -20 degrees Fahrenheit, and held at that temperature or below, they will retain their higher quality for more than one year and will remain edible for much longer." Increasingly innovative packaging techniques and designs lent greater credibility to many frozen fish businesses, including Van de Kamp's. From packages sized to optimize consumption, to special techniques controlling spoilage, to package graphics conveying a quality image, frozen seafood grew appreciably fresher.

Despite the real benefits of the freezing process, certain claims did not stand up to questioning. In 1984 a series of Van de Kamp's ads by the Benton & Bowles agency rated the product as "Grade A" even though government inspectors were not actually checking the catch. (The seafood industry was not subject to mandatory federal inspection as were meat and poultry.) The National Advertising Division (NAD) of the Council of Better Business Bureaus intervened, and even though the advertiser disagreed with the verdict, it dropped the claim. In a 1992 dispute, General Mills, marketer of Gorton's frozen fish products, challenged a TV commercial that said, "Extensive taste tests in cities across the country of hundreds of fish stick experts yielded something your kid could have told us: 'I like Van de Kamp's.'" Though General Mills argued that the commercial implied a taste preference that could not be substantiated, the NAD supported Van de Kamp's, and the ad remained unchanged.

The term "healthy" also came under fire with the 1992 introduction of Van de Kamp's Crisp and Healthy fish sticks, but the Van de Kamp's brand held its position. In a May 5, 1992, article for the *Chicago Tribune,* Nancy Ryan tied the 1992 proliferation of "healthy" brands to lax FDA definitions. She speculated that a new round of federal food labeling laws, expected to be more comprehensive than ever before, might remove those items from store shelves before long. Crisp and Healthy also met resistance by the New York State Consumer Protection Board, which conducted calorie tests that it said indicated more calories than were listed on the brand's label. Though the FDA allowed for a 20 percent margin of error on food labeling claims, the board test showed 37 percent more calories in Crisp & Healthy than noted on the label. Van de Kamp's results, after two separate tests, showed that the product met the calorie claims. "We're always monitoring our product performance," said Melissa Moulton, a spokesperson for Pet Incorporated, in a 1992 *Chicago Tribune* article. The Consumer Protection Board's Jeff Weinstock proposed warnings on labels to highlight the possibility of inaccuracy. Manufacturers and the FDA stressed that such variability resulted from the natural variability of foods.

Performance Appraisal

Though Van de Kamp's Frozen Seafoods set sail in 1915, it caught the wind in the 1970s, with sales growing from $13 million in 1972 to $75 million in 1979. By 1989 it was third in the category of frozen seafood, holding 18.1 percent of the $1.1 billion market, trailing Mrs. Paul's 19.8 percent and Gorton's 23.8 percent. In an *Advertising Age* brand scorecard for 1992, Van de Kamp's led its category, with a 30.6 percent share, followed by Gorton's and Mrs. Paul's. Over the course of its growth, the brand has been owned by different parents: in 1984, General Host Corp. sold it to Pillsbury; in January of 1989, Pillsbury was acquired by Grand Metropolitan PLC; in a major reorganization effort, Pillsbury closed the Van de Kamp's fish processing plant in Santa Fe, California, to consolidate production in Erie, Pennsylvania; and in

August of 1989, Grand Met sold the brand to Pet Incorporated. Pet's strategy represented the clearest window on the future.

In 1991 Pet's objective to make Van de Kamp's "America's number one brand of frozen seafood" was met. The company increased item distribution in the brand's existing markets and geographically expanded it into the South and Southwest. In addition to Crisp & Healthy, Pet in 1993 introduced two lines for the value-conscious consumer: Value Pack Fish Sticks, Fish Portions, and Fish Nuggets; and Snack Pack Fish Sticks, Fish Fillets, and Fish Nuggets. In that same year Van de Kamp's, thanks to Pet's "back to basics" strategy and development of a balanced advertising, consumer, and trade promotion mix, was the number one brand in 38 of its 56 markets.

Further Reading:

Bivens, Terry, "Mrs. Paul's Fish Story Awaits Happy Ending," *Chicago Tribune,* July 24, 1989, p. N4.

"Brand Scorecard," *Advertising Age,* November 2, 1992, p. 16.

Brown, Larry, "A Cold Fact: Not All Fish Sticks Are Created Equal," *The Seattle Times,* March 4, 1992, p. E1.

Brunelli, Richard, "Pet Drops Buying Shop; Consolidates at D'Arcy; Pet Inc., D'Arcy Masius Benton and Bowles Inc.," *Mediaweek,* vol. 1, no. 17, p. 3.

Dagnoli, Judann, "Mrs. Paul's Casts for Brighter Future," *Advertising Age,* February 19, 1990, p. 63.

Dougherty, Philip H., "N.A.D. Resolves 9 Ad Complaints," *New York Times,* February 16, 1984, P. D24.

Erickson, Julie Liesse, "New Pet Chief Sets Shelf-Stable Line," *Advertising Age,* September 11, 1989, p. 33.

"Grand Met to Sell Two Pillsbury Food Units," *Reuter Library Report,* May 22, 1989.

Hanes, Phyllis, "The Freshest Fish Might Be Frozen," *Christian Science Monitor,* April 20, 1983, p. 16.

Harlow, Jay, "Breaded Filets: A Step Up From the Sticks," *San Francisco Chronicle,* March 14, 1990, p. 8.

Key, Janet, "Whitman Buys Frozen Seafood Company for $140 Million," *Chicago Tribune,* August 12, 1989, p. C7.

Millstein, Marc, "Demand for Fresh Fish Hurting Frozen Sales," *Supermarket News,* February 16, 1987, p. 43.

"Pillsbury Battle Ends; Fit Is Welcome," *Newsday,* December 20, 1988, p. 49.

"Pillsbury to Close California Fish Processing Plant," *United Press International,* March 27, 1989.

Ryan, Nancy, " 'Healthy' Is Hot New Food Label," *Chicago Tribune,* May 5, 1992, p. C3.

Sterling, Anthony, "Fishy Business; New Seafood Packaging," *Food and Beverage Marketing,* vol. 9, no. 11, p. 48.

Tanasychuk, John, "Don't Believe Everything You Read: 'Diet' Food Labels Legally Can Vary by as Much as 20 Percent," *Chicago Tribune,* October 1, 1992, p. C4.

"Van de Kamp's Cooks Up an Ethnic Formula," *Business Week,* October 24, 1983, p. 80.

"Van de Kamp's, the Frozen Food Line That Turns Light Users . . . " *Quick Frozen Foods,* May 1979, pp. 83-116.

Wilke, Michael, "Paintmaker Bristles at N.A.D. Decision," *Advertising Age,* August 31, 1992, p. 17.

—Kerstan Cohen

VELVEETA®

Velveeta

Velveeta, the pasteurized process cheese food of Kraft General Foods, Inc., was introduced to customers in the United States and Canada in 1928. The name Velveeta was coined by a company Kraft had acquired several years earlier, but the product was a completely new innovation. Velveeta was one of the first American cheese products to be developed scientifically through laboratory research.

Brand Origins

In 1927 the Kraft Cheese Company sponsored a study at Rutgers University to find a way to replace milk nutrients lost in the process of making cheese. In traditional cheese making, whey is drained out of cheese vats, taking with it many nutritional milk solids. Kraft's goal was to devise a method of adding those milk solids back into American cheddar cheese. The result was a new kind of cheese product—it was softer than most American cheeses, possessed a creamy, spreadable texture, and melted easily. Kraft introduced this new product in 1928 under the name Velveeta. That same year, Kraft merged with the Phenix Cheese Corporation, maker of Philadelphia Brand cream cheese, and adopted the name Kraft-Phenix Cheese Corporation.

Kraft continued funding the Rutgers University research project. Kraft researchers became pioneers in the study of cheese nutrition by analyzing the nutritional content of Velveeta. In 1931 Velveeta was submitted to the investigations of the American Medical Association (AMA) Committee on Foods. The committee studied the nutritional value of Velveeta as well as its manufacturing and distribution. Their conclusions supported claims made by Kraft that Velveeta was richer in calcium and phosphorous than cheeses without milk whey and also had more lactose than milk. Based on these findings, in 1931 Velveeta became the first cheese food to receive the AMA's seal of approval. Through extensive research over a period of about 20 years, Velveeta was also found to be a formidable source of riboflavin.

Marketing Strategies

Kraft's early marketing strategy for Velveeta capitalized on the product's uncommon origins. Half-pound packages of Velveeta displayed the slogan, "Velveeta, a delicious cheese food," a photo of Velveeta spread on a slice of bread, and a bucolic drawing of cows grazing in a country field. According to a 1945 company publication, Velveeta was termed a cheese food "be-

cause, although its principal ingredient was cheese, it possessed certain characteristics and compositions not ordinarily found in American cheddar cheese—characteristics which made it unique." Primary among the distinctive characteristics of Velveeta was its meltability, a trait continually capitalized on in ads and marketing campaigns. Because Velveeta also provided more milk minerals and vitamins than ordinary cheese, its healthfulness also became a top promotional strategy. After Velveeta received the AMA seal of approval, the seal was immediately included in advertising copy. By 1939 packaging for Velveeta included a descriptive label stating the product's exact ingredients, its moisture and butterfat contents, and the role of whey in enhancing the product's nutritional value. Kraft also positioned the product as a high quality cooking cheese and targeted Velveeta sales to middle-class American families with children.

Early Advertising

There was no media blitz to introduce Velveeta. One of the earliest mentions of the product appeared in a print ad for a variety of Kraft-Phenix products in a 1928 edition of the *Saturday Evening Post*. Two years later, Velveeta was accorded a solo ad in *Good Housekeeping*. One early ad displayed a milk jar, a package of Velveeta, and the simple slogan, "Digestible as milk itself!" Other advertisements capitalized on the product's scientific beginnings. "An amazing new food—a miracle wrought with milk," proclaimed a banner from a 1930s magazine ad. Several paragraphs followed touting Velveeta as "the contribution of science to the art of cheese making," that provided the "precious health-giving qualities of rich whole milk." Unlike other cheeses at that time, Velveeta, the ad noted, "spreads like butter. It can be sliced when chilled. It melts, dissolves and blends so readily with other foods that for cooking purposes its superiority is at once apparent." An address was also included so cooks could send for recipes using Velveeta.

Around the same time, Velveeta was targeted toward mothers with children. Ads emphasized the product's digestibility and mild taste (which appealed to children), focused on the high vitamin content of Velveeta (which pleased mothers), and featured photos of children cooking with Velveeta (to highlight the ease with which Velveeta could be used). "It's child's play to make a rich, cheese-flavored sauce with Velveeta!" proclaimed one ad that offered a recipe for such a sauce. In 1933 Kraft-Phenix expanded

AT A GLANCE

Velveeta brand of pasteurized process cheese spread developed at Rutgers University and introduced in 1928 by the Kraft-Phenix Cheese Corporation; Kraft-Phenix Cheese Corporation became a subsidiary of the National Dairy Products Corporation, 1930; Kraft-Phenix changed name to Kraft Cheese Company, 1940; Kraft Cheese Company named changed to Kraft Foods Company, 1945; National Dairy Products Corporation changes its name to Kraftco Corporation, 1969; Kraftco Corporation becomes Kraft Inc., 1976; Philip Morris Companies Inc. acquires Kraft Inc. in 1988 and combines it with General Foods Corporation in 1989, forming Kraft General Foods, Inc.

Major competitor: Cheez Whiz; natural cheddar cheeses.

Advertising: *Agency*—Leo Burnett & Company, Chicago, IL. *Major campaign*—"Velveeta Cooks Better" series of television ads demonstrating that Velveeta melts better than cheddar and other look-alike brands.

Addresses: *Parent company*—Kraft General Foods, Inc., Kraft Court, Glenview, IL, 60025; phone: (708) 998-2000. *Ultimate parent company*—Philip Morris Companies Inc., 120 Park Ave., New York, NY 10017; phone: (212) 880-5000.

its advertising into radio with sponsorship of the Kraft Music Hall. Kraft included a plug for its music program in most every print Velveeta ad. Listeners would then tune into the evening music program (stations and times were often printed on ads), during which ads introduced new Kraft products and new uses for its existing lines.

During World War II, Velveeta was served to U.S. soldiers in mess halls throughout Europe and the Pacific and, beginning in 1942, slogans such as "eat the foods that make America stronger" appeared in Velveeta ads. Kraft sponsorship of television programs began in 1947, with the weekly prime-time *Kraft Television Theatre,* on NBC-TV. During that hour, a variety of Kraft products were advertised. Kraft's kitchens constantly devised recipes using Velveeta. Favorites included grilled cheese sandwiches, tuna noodle casserole, and macaroni and cheese. Ads introducing new recipes were also frequently aired, and from 1947 to 1970, Kraft supposedly received more than 150 million requests annually for recipes aired during the show.

Product Innovations

Kraft introduced the two-pound loaf of Velveeta process cheese in 1933 and marketed it as a money-saving, convenient package. Not until the early 1980s, however, did Kraft began experimenting with Velveeta and manufacturing spin-off products. Introduced first in 1981 and nationally in 1982, individually wrapped segments of Velveeta called Velveeta slices were a way of combining "a well-known and well-liked brand name with the most convenient form of packaging." After the initial success of Velveeta slices, Kraft introduced extra thick Velveeta slices nationally in 1985 through direct mail coupons and newspaper ads. That same year, Kraft presented Velveeta Mexican process cheese spread with jalapeno peppers. Print ads were headlined "The hottest idea in cheese yet," and added, "So now you can have your Velveeta hot—if it's melted or not."

Convenience was the goal of new Velveeta products introduced in the 1980s. Kraft's most successful new product of that

time was Velveeta Shells and Cheese boxed macaroni and cheese dinner. Hoping to piggyback the success of Kraft's successful Macaroni and Cheese dinners, the Velveeta version contained a six-ounce pouch of Velveeta cheese sauce instead of a packet of powdered cheese. Kraft introduced the product without any test marketing, "since both our regular macaroni and cheese dinner and Velveeta products are popular," according to a Kraft spokeswoman. Sunday newspaper ads with coupons boasted that the new product was "complete with creamy Velveeta cheese sauce and enriched shell macaroni." Velveeta Shells and Cheese became number two nationwide in the dry package dinner category—second only to Kraft's Macaroni and Cheese.

In 1988 convenience-oriented packages of Velveeta shredded pasteurized process cheese food was introduced nationally in original, mild Mexican, and hot Mexican flavors. These eight-ounce packages were marketed as ready-to-use toppings for salads, baked potatoes, and casseroles. Shredded Velveeta was introduced through television commercials containing the plug, "the easy way to get the great taste of Velveeta."

Promotions: 1980 and Beyond

"Velveeta isn't an upscale product," brand manager Kevin Ponticelli announced in a 1988 Kraft magazine. "Our strength will continue to be in middle American households where children are present." As such households evolved over the years, however, Kraft repositioned its marketing to adapt to the changes. The

A historical advertisement for Velveeta.

rush to introduce new products in the 1980s coincided with a large change in American cooking habits. "Part of the reason for the boom in microwaves," noted a *Kraft Ink* writer, "is that today's woman, unlike her counterpart in 1928, is likely to work outside the home.'' In this climate, microwave ovens became popular and people had less time to prepare meals. By 1988, approximately 70 percent of American households used a microwave. Due to its easy meltability, Velveeta adapted well to microwave cooking. Many traditional recipes such as tuna noodle casserole and macaroni and cheese were as easily made in a microwave as a conventional oven.

According to some industry analysts, advertising expenditures for Velveeta surpassed $1 million in 1971, but dipped to $596,300 in 1979. There was a resurgence in the 1980s, however. Kraft's ''Bright Ideas'' magazine advertising series, begun during this time, was an updated version of early Velveeta ads. A larger banner introduced the new idea under various headings such as ''Velveeta Kid Stuff,'' ''Velveeta Sunrise'' or ''Velveeta Spuds'' followed by recipes. In 1988 Kraft began its ''Short Cut Chef'' marketing campaign promoting Velveeta as easily adaptable to microwave and introducing updated versions of popular older recipes and new uses for Velveeta products.

Also in 1988, Kraft launched a television campaign touting Velveeta as a superior cooking cheese. ''Velveeta cooks better,'' was the simple slogan for these ads which demonstrated how Velveeta melts better than cheddar cheese and look-alike brands. One 1988 ad presents a father and his little boy testing which melts better: Velveeta versus butter, Velveeta versus cheddar, and finally, Velveeta versus a snow pop. Velveeta won every time. Another 1992 television ad uses the familiar song ''La Giaconda'' with parody lyrics touting how much better Velveeta cooks.

Future Growth

''Cheese industry sales will double over the next ten years,'' predicted a New York-based research firm in a 1986 *Dairy Foods* survey of the cheese industry. Another 1986 study predicts annual per-capita consumption of cheese to reach 49.9 pounds by 1995, double the 1985 level. How this bodes for Velveeta is less certain. Forty-five percent of the manufacturers polled expect sales to rise in the early 1990s; the remainder expect sales to remain unchanged. However, the late 1980s saw a rush among cheese manufacturers to create and market ''healthy'' cheeses with reduced fat, lower cholesterol levels, and higher fiber. In 1989 Kraft Food Ingredients built a technical center in Memphis, Tennessee designed to develop innovations in food processing, focusing primarily on cheese. Kraft has always considered Velveeta a healthy cheese product. With a well-focused marketing campaign, Velveeta should remain prominent in the market.

Further Reading:

''Cheese Food Champion,'' *Kraftsman,* August 1945, p. 19.

''Cheese Industry Survey,'' *Dairy Foods,* July 1986.

''A Chronological History of Kraft General Foods,'' Glenview, Illinois: Kraft General Foods Archives Department, August 1992.

Duxbury, Dean D., ''U.S. Domestic Cheese Trends, Continued Market Growth Encourage Cheese Technology Research,'' *Process Foods,* November 1989, p. 34.

Freeman, Laurie, ''Velveeta, Macaroni Mixed,'' *Advertising Age,* September 17, 1984, p. 76.

Green, Chester R., ''TV Users,'' *Advertising Age,* November 2, 1970, p. 92.

''Hall of Fame,'' *Kraftsman,* January 1953.

Kittrell, Alison, ''Velveeta: Still Going Strong after 60 Years,'' *Kraft Ink,* 1988, p. 10.

''New Product Briefs: Shredded Velveeta,'' *Dairy Foods,* April 1988, p. 26.

''Presstime: Other Late News,'' *Advertising Age,* November 1, 1984, p. 59.

Sweda, Gerry, ''Our Golden Oldies,'' *Kraft Ink,* 1978, p. 19.

''Velveeta Now 'Accepted' by A.M.A Committee,'' *CheeseKraft,* April 1931, p. 1.

—Maura Troester

VIRGINIA SLIMS®

Virginia Slims is a brand of cigarettes marketed towards women. As such, it became the first brand in the cigarette market successfully targeted to a single segment of the population. Through consistently modern, fashion-based image advertising, Virginia Slims has secured a position as the premier brand of cigarettes for the discerning, independent woman. Virginia Slims also represents a textbook case in successful image advertising; women in print ads do not smoke the brand as much as they seem to use it as a fashion accessory. The exclusivity of the brand accentuates its good taste and femininity, and reflects a rich, exciting lifestyle.

Brand Origins

The Virginia Slims concept was developed in the mid-1960s by Joseph Cullman, president of Benson & Hedges, a cigarette manufacturer that had recently been acquired by Philip Morris. At that time, the Benson & Hedges line had an established reputation for quality. Perceived as the preferred brand of affluent people, Benson & Hedges had also become known during the 1950s as a healthier alternative to other brands of cigarettes. Available only in a 100-millimeter length, Benson & Hedges was one of the few popular filtered brands in existence. Because some of the harmful tar and nicotine were obstructed from ingestion by the filter, doctors were known to prescribe Benson & Hedges to heavy smokers of unfiltered brands, in the hope that it would guide them toward quitting.

During the profound social changes that began during 1966 and 1967, Cullman saw an opportunity for a unique brand extension. As people began to challenge social conventions, they came to experience new forms of liberation and freedom. Under the leadership of bold and politically astute feminists, the women's "liberation movement" gained a very high public profile, enlisting a large population of American women who considered themselves newly liberated. Cullman, and many other marketers, reasoned that this new sense of identity could be exploited. Any product, if properly packaged and promoted, would garner favor with women as long as it was clear that the product was developed especially for them.

Early Marketing Strategy

Philip Morris reasoned that the brand created especially for women could not be represented as a mere extension of the Benson & Hedges brand. Furthermore, the concept of the brand depended heavily on its appeal to women. A cigarette for women carrying the Benson & Hedges name might threaten to drive male smokers away from the regular brand in search of something more "manly." Thus, a radically separate identity was necessary.

The new brand incorporated a more densely packed variation on the blend of Virginia tobaccos used in Benson & Hedges. Tests indicated that this blend appealed to a slightly larger proportion of women than the parent brand, which was already popular with women. The new cigarette measured 23 millimeters in circumference, slimmer than the 25-millimeter circumference of existing brands. The slimmer design was generally found to appeal to women, who associated the tall, slim cigarette with a tall, slim figure. By virtue of its blend and dimensions, the new brand was given the name Virginia Slims. Like Benson & Hedges, however, the new cigarette would be offered only in a 100-millimeter length with a white filter, and in regular and menthol variations.

Packaging

Virginia Slims was given a white package with a series of vertical lines in a scale of closely related colors indicating either regular or menthol. The vertical lines accentuated the slightly slimmer package design (a result of the slimmer cigarette), creating an illusion that the package was either slimmer or longer than it was. This package design, called the "purse pack," was developed by the Walter Landor Company. The lettering on the package was carefully chosen to avoid overpowering the lined design scheme. Indeed, the tall, thin, slightly pale letters used to spell the product's name reflected the entire package design. It was elegant and understated. Like many other brands, Virginia Slims were wrapped in a foil lining, covered in the white lined package, and sealed in cellophane to maintain freshness during shipping and to extend shelf life.

Advertising

Virginia Slims was introduced in July of 1968 in one of America's leading bastions of progressive thought: San Francisco. The Chicago-based Leo Burnett Company developed a provocative advertising theme that portrayed a series of fictional historical events involving women in the early suffrage period. In the first commercial, a manufactured sepia-tone film purported to show Pamela Benjamin who, in 1910, was caught smoking in a gazebo. "She got a severe scolding and no supper that night." The ad continued, "In 1915, Mrs. Cynthia Robinson was caught smoking in the cellar behind the preserves. Although she was 34, her husband sent her straight to her room. Then, in 1920, women won their rights." The ad concluded by turning to a modern color format, featuring a fashion model with a Virginia Slims cigarette and a musical theme singing the jingle "You've come a long way, baby." Subsequent television ads and print advertising followed this same format.

The appeal was bold and controversial. The ad drew upon the public's attention to social change by illustrating how injustice to women had been destroyed in America. Indeed, the ads satirized this injustice and borrowed directly from the current "women's lib" movement. The inherently sexist tagline, "You've come a long way, baby," was, apparently, lost upon many at the time.

Print ads immediately established the exclusivity of the brand, asking, "What is this new extra-long cigarette for Women?" The ads continued, "We tailor it for the feminine hand. Virginia Slims are slimmer than the fat cigarettes men smoke." There was no question that men were not to use this product. After a wildly successful introduction in San Francisco, Virginia Slims was introduced to the rest of the nation, with much the same effect upon the public. Millions of women were compelled to try this new brand, even women who did not smoke.

In 1970 Philip Morris introduced a new premium to Virginia Slims women. At the end of each year, women were offered a free Book of Days Engagement Calendar for the following year. From year to year, the 84-page calendar booklet contained brief stories and excerpts from old etiquette books, including the advice that, when entertaining your husband's employer, "do not offer opinions about anything." The saucy Virginia Slims ads were interspersed throughout the booklet, featuring displays of glamorous models adorned in the world's most fashionable designer garments.

The calendars—in effect, a 365-day-a-year advertisement—were planned a full year in advance, with photo shoots on the scale of leading fashion magazine covers. More than one million calendars were distributed each year on cartons of Virginia Slims. Retailers reported that their supply of calendars would run out after only two days. The highly successful advertising formula for Virginia Slims has remained basically unchanged since the brand was introduced. In fact, the formula is the same for all of Philip Morris' brands.

Advertising creates a clearly defined brand image, and every other element of the marketing mix vigorously supports that image. In the late 1970s, however, the slogan came under attack by feminist groups who had bemusedly endured Virginia Slims advertising for a full decade. The battle cry, "I haven't come a long way and I'm not a baby," appeared in literature and graffiti and on protest signs. While not intended as an anti-smoking message, the reworked slogan effectively drew on Virginia Slims' highly recognized tagline.

With the elimination of television advertising for cigarettes in 1971, cigarette brands were forced into other forms of promotion. Winston and Marlboro turned to sponsorship of male-oriented sporting events, such as car racing. Likewise, Virginia Slims needed to place its name at highly visible, televised events. With the rise in popularity of the tennis star Billie Jean King—particularly after a heavily promoted battle of the sexes against the self-proclaimed chauvinist pig Bobby Riggs—Virginia Slims found a sport popular with women and in keeping with its image. Over a period of years, the Virginia Slims tennis tournaments achieved an identity of their own. As one of the more important prizes a female tennis player can win, the events also ensured

placement of the brand name, if not the cigarette, on the lips of legions of the world's leading tennis stars.

Health Claims

Virginia Slims has never been promoted, even indirectly, as a less harmful brand of cigarette. Where low-tar brands such as Carlton have been advertised with bold type copy reading, "If you smoke, please try Carlton," Virginia Slims' sole message has remained, "You've come a long way, baby." However, during the 1980s, virtually every product on the market from cooking oil to cheese in a spray can became available in a "light" version. Similarly, as brands such as Carlton began to raise health consciousness in the cigarette market, manufacturers were compelled to introduce low-tar extensions to prevent wholesale losses in market share.

For Virginia Slims, the introduction of light brand extensions gained support, particularly after Carlton challenged the line with an elegantly packaged line of slim cigarettes targeted at women. The introduction of Virginia Slims Lights and Menthol Lights may have contributed to the eventual demise of Carlton's slim brand. Salem and Newport, however, later crowded the market with a similar line of slim light cigarettes in 1984 and 1992, respectively. Virginia Slims introduced an even lower tar and nicotine extension, Virginia Slims Ultra Lights, during the late 1980s. For women who would otherwise have switched to a low-tar brand, or quit entirely out of concern for their health, the light brand extensions served to keep women loyal to the brand.

International Development

As many world-traveling women loyal to Virginia Slims already know, the brand is virtually unavailable outside of the United States. This may be attributable to several causes. Faced with a declining population of smokers in the United States, many tobacco companies have targeted sales in foreign markets to maintain sales growth. While many governments are reluctant to accept the importation of a consumer product with deleterious health effects, fair trade agreements allow a trickle of brands to be imported.

Companies such as Philip Morris are likely to have decided to promote only one brand for export, rather than the myriad of others it produces, to maximize the value of its advertising and consolidate brand identity in foreign countries. Philip Morris, it seems, has chosen market-leading Marlboro as its flagship export brand. Additionally, much of the image-heavy hype behind Virginia Slims does not translate well to European countries or the developing countries that have been targeted as export markets. Women in these countries, by and large, do not appreciate the American women's suffrage and liberation movements which gave Virginia Slims its reason for being. In European markets, the "Virginia Slims woman" may be rather more commonplace, and in Asia and South America, by and large, she does not even exist.

Brand Development

The popularity of Virginia Slims was substantially challenged during the 1980s by an entirely new concept in cigarette images. R.J. Reynolds introduced a dark brown 120-millimeter slim cigarette called More. This highly distinctive cigarette was featured prominently in the hand of Alexis Carrington in the popular television show *Dynasty*. Alexis, the vicious scheming nemesis of her ex-husband, gave the brand a pronounced identity. To millions of viewers, More became identified with outspoken, independent women whose evil ways often succeeded.

Philip Morris already had a 120, Saratoga, on the market, but its position was weak, and its identity was poorly defined. Rather than remake that brand, the company decided in 1989 to offer a 120-millimeter version of Virginia Slims in both light and ultra light versions. Unlike More, which was available only in a soft package, the Virginia Slims line came in a crush-proof box—all the better for coat pockets and crowded purses. Furthermore, the dark brown wrapping of Reynolds' brand reinforced the fact that More contained more tar and nicotine. This, combined with the cancellation of *Dynasty,* limited More's ability to siphon market share from Virginia Slims.

A second challenge to Virginia Slims emerged in 1987, when Brown & Williamson introduced a new 100-millimeter cigarette even thinner than Virginia Slims. The brand, called Capri, measured only 17 millimeters in circumference. Packaged in a crush-proof box, and targeted directly at the very same market as Virginia Slims, Capri attracted women who were even more concerned about how a cigarette "looked on them." Capri, with a length to circumference ratio of 5.8 (as opposed to Virginia Slims' 4.3), had a highly distinctive appearance. The brand also was promoted with fashion models.

In response, Philip Morris developed yet another extension of Virginia Slims. Superslims, as thin as Capri, entered the market in 1989. This new brand incorporated a new technology intended to appeal to those who felt sensitive about ambient smoke in social situations. With nearly half as much tar and nicotine, Superslims incorporated porous and non-porous paper to reduce "sidestream smoke"—smoke from the lit end—by 70 percent over regular brands, and 60 percent over Capri. The brand enabled smokers to be less obtrusive in social situations. The technology did not, however, provide any related health benefit to the smoker. Brown & Williamson countered the introduction of Superslims with a 120-millimeter version of Capri, extending the length to circum-ference ratio to 7, and providing women with the tallest, skinniest cigarette on the market.

Performance Appraisal

Despite several attempts at raiding Virginia Slims' following, competitors have remained largely unable to shake the brand's three percent market share. Though seemingly minuscule, three percent places Virginia Slims ahead of all but about ten of the 175 brands on the market. The imagery associated with the brand, successful since its introduction, has remained unchanged. In fact, even the slogan, "You've come a long way, baby," continues. Only the models and their fashions have been updated.

Future Predictions

In a market where tenths of a percent of market share are fought over with millions of advertising dollars, Virginia Slims' stability will likely guarantee a continuation of the brand's original themes: fashion, independence, and taste. Only a sustained loss of customers is likely to change this formula.

Further Reading:

"Benson & Hedges Introduces New Cigarette for Women," *Advertising Age,* July 29, 1968.

Dagnoli, Judann, "PM Presses on with Superslims," *Advertising Age,* October 2, 1989.

Dagnoli, Judann, "Superslims Shortage Just Smoke?" *Advertising Age,* November 13, 1989.

DiGiacomo, Frank, "Slims' Grand Slam," *Marketing & Media Decisions,* April, 1990, p. 4.

O'Connor, John J., "Virginia Slims 120s and The Lady are Latest Philip Morris Test Entries," *Advertising Age.*

Robinson, William, A., "Virginia Slims Come a Long Way in 17 years," *Advertising Age,* May 30, 1985, p. 30.

"Virginia Slims Goes National with Heavy Multi-Media Backing," *Advertising Age,* September 20, 1968.

—John Simley

WEIGHT WATCHERS®

To gauge the success of Weight Watchers Food Company, one must first understand Weight Watchers International, Inc., the market leader in the weight loss industry. The Weight Watchers program is based on a sound nutritional program, emphasizes group support and accountability, and is both reasonable and widely available.

Jean Nidetch went to the New York City Board of Health's free obesity clinic in 1961, where she was handed a printed copy of a diet devised by Dr. Norman Jolliffe. Nidetch lost 20 pounds, then realized she had to do more to continue losing pounds and keep the weight off. So she talked about her struggles with friends, and she lost a total of 72 pounds. Overweight friends came to her house to talk, finding the mutual support a major factor in successful weight loss. Albert Lippert was one of those friends, and it was he who suggested Nidetch set up weekly classes in a business area. Four hundred people showed up at the first unadvertised session.

The company expanded rapidly; members completed the program, trained with Nidetch, and started franchises of their own. Lippert then broadened operations. In 1967 the company started manufacturing Weight Watchers frozen dinners and other food products, licensing the rights to various food producers. Weight Watchers began publishing cookbooks and a monthly magazine, then moved into recreation, running summer camps for overweight children. Business continued to grow, due in large part to Weight Watchers no-nonsense approach, which emphasizes self-discipline, portion control, and positive reinforcement through weekly meetings.

The Weight Watchers Image

To Nidetch and Lippert, weight reduction was a service business; the client's attitude, not "a diet," was the focus. Understanding and working with clients was high on the company agenda. Because Jean Nidetch had been overweight herself, she knew all the excuses in the book—and wouldn't let her clients use them.

Program members were urged to get a doctor's permission before enrolling. As Nidetch made speeches in the community, she asked various doctors to attend, who found the Weight Watchers program to be a sound one. Fees were a mere two dollars a week when the company started. Nidetch insisted on maintaining the weekly fees rather than having clients sign a contract. Client

retention was then based only on the strength of the program, which Nidetch considered appropriate.

As the Weight Watchers reputation spread, similar organizations surfaced. Nidetch shared her knowledge with competitors. As quoted in a *McCall's* article in 1981, Nidetch stated, "I offered to meet with them and tell them the right way to do it. Why not? There's no shortage of fat people." The founder added that if anyone got sick as a result of a bad diet, it would reflect badly on all weight loss programs. As Barbara Grizzuti Harrison, author of the *McCall's* article, summarized: "[Nidetch] started an empire out of the conviction that what she knew and what she had successfully practiced was too good to keep to herself."

Early Advertising

The word got out. Weight Watchers' early advertising was primarily just that, word-of-mouth. By 1969 the program was discussed in a variety of magazines such as *Reader's Digest* and *Sales Management.* A feature in the journal *Purchasing* connected upward mobility in business to a fit and trim image. The Weight Watchers plan was described not as a "diet," but as a process of re-education.

By the early 1970s Weight Watchers was selling itself; as reported in the September 4, 1969, *Purchasing,* "the best 'salesmen' Weight Watchers has are the thousands of men, women and teenagers who have succeeded in losing weight and keeping it off." At Madison Square Garden in 1973, 15,000 Weight Watchers members rallied in tribute to the program's success.

Heinz Takes Over

In the 1970s Lippert moved Weight Watchers into the restaurant business, opening one in New York and two in Toronto. Weight Watchers was running 12,000 weekly classes internationally by 1977. In late 1978, Pittsburgh-based H. J. Heinz Company bought both Weight Watchers and Foodways National Inc., the U.S. producer of Weight Watchers frozen entrees, for $121 million. The Heinz purchase illustrated that the potential in the low-calorie food market was worth a substantial price. Albert Lippert would remain as chairman and chief executive, assigned to help expand Weight Watchers through its franchises into restaurants and possibly health resorts. The goal was to have Weight Watch-

AT A GLANCE

Weight Watchers brand founded in May, 1963, by Jean Nidetch and Albert Lippert in Queens, NY; became a publicly held corporation in September, 1968; the H. J. Heinz Company bought Weight Watchers International in 1978, for $72 million, and created the Weight Watchers Food Company in 1991; company also produces a monthly magazine, cookbooks, exercise tapes, appointment calendars, and other weight control related merchandise.

Performance: *Market share*—12% unit volume share of frozen entree market; 36% (top share) of full- or reduced-calorie frozen desserts. *Sales*—$800 million.

Major competitor: (Frozen entrees) ConAgra's Healthy Choice; also Stouffer's Lean Cuisine; Ultra Slim-Fast foods; and (frozen desserts) Sara Lee.

Advertising: *Agency*—Ally & Gargano, New York, NY, 1992—; formerly DDB Needham, New York, NY. *Major campaign*—"Total Indulgence. Zero Guilt."

Addresses: *Parent company*—Weight Watchers International Inc., 500 North Broadway, Jericho, NY, 11753; phone: (516) 939-0400; fax: (516) 949-0699. *Ultimate parent company*—H. J. Heinz Company, P.O. Box 57, Pittsburgh, PA 15230; phone: (412) 456-5700.

ers appeal to new market segments in addition to its traditional audience of overweight women.

Heinz also planned to make the Weight Watchers brand a force in international markets. With the Weight Watchers consumer base at 11 million, Heinz had an advantage over competitors. The company set aside $4 million for the 1979 promotion of the Weight Watchers program and its products.

In the national arena, Paul Corddry, head of Heinz's Ore-Ida subsidiary (the market leader in frozen potato products and onion rings), had a new challenge: to make Weight Watchers lead the low-calorie frozen foods market. As quoted in the March 5, 1979, *Business Week,* Corddry was optimistic: "In an industry where brand recognition is key, Weight Watchers is the undisputed leader."

Competition Surfaces

Initially, Heinz had an advantage over other food producers. In the late 1970s and early 1980s Weight Watchers was a successful company, while competitors remained in the research stage where reduced-calorie foods were concerned. However, it was only a matter of time before competitor products were ready to be launched. By 1983 Weight Watchers frozen entrees were up against Stouffer's Lean Cuisine, introduced only the year before. Results of a taste-test sponsored by *Consumer's Digest* considering aroma, flavor, texture, quantity, quality, satisfaction, and price found the two product lines head-to-head. Of the twelve items tested, the two producers each had four entrees listed in the good-to-very-good range; Lean Cuisine had two products rated "fair," and Weight Watchers had one meal rated "fair" and one "poor."

Weight Watchers was poised for a fight. Minding the home store, the company placed a print advertisement geared at the company's core customer in the March, 1983, *Ladies Home Journal.* In it Weight Watchers emphasized the success of its reliable and trusted program. Starting with the phrase, "After two decades

of helping millions of people slim down," the ad went on to celebrate the organization's twentieth anniversary by offering potential members an improved version of Weight Watchers "famous behavior management program." In the style of founder Jean Nidetch, the ad shared two weeks of menus comprising three meals a day plus snacks and desserts, as well as seven "diet action cards" complete with tips on relevant topics such as "hunger versus appetite," "cooking without eating," and "establishing hunger-free times."

Customer Profile Evolves

Through a variety of strategies and the strength of its name recognition, Weight Watchers pulled ahead of Stouffer's Lean Cuisine in the mid-1980s, once again becoming the best-seller in low-calorie meals. Weight Watchers, praised for not pushing its brand in classes, reaped the benefits nonetheless. As reporter Brian O'Reilly put it in the June 5, 1989, *Fortune,* "the message gets across anyway. Handouts at lectures often include coupons, and staying on the complex diet can require such tedious calculations that many dieters just stock up on Weight Watchers food instead." Sales of the Weight Watchers brand increased 20 percent in 1988 from the previous year.

Aiding growth in the U.S. market was the aging population as a whole, and the baby boomer generation in particular, a fact noted by Weight Watchers and its competitors. In the words of Nutri/System CEO Donald McCulloch, quoted in *Fortune,* "The demographics are on our [the industry's] side. As you get older, it gets harder to lose weight."

As information regarding health and nutrition changed, so did the public perception of weight control. Rather than view a change in attitude as going on a diet, many Americans considered their new behavior a way of life. As stated by Molly Gee, spokeswoman for the American Dietetic Association quoted in the January 3, 1990, *New York Times:* "Diet is a four-letter word." Jean Nidetch's gospel about weight control had finally gotten out; the only problem was, Weight Watchers wasn't the only group espousing it.

To disengage its reputation from the pack of competing companies and products—like Nutri/System, Jenny Craig Inc., the Diet Center, Sandoz Nutrition Corporation's Optifast, and Ultra Slim-Fast—Weight Watchers once again played up its history of success. Lynn Redgrave, spokesperson for the company since 1982, was solicited to represent the program. The 1990 television ads featured footage of Redgrave in the 1966 role of "Georgy Girl," a heavy young woman gazing at herself in the mirror while putting food in her mouth. The before and after shots addressed the healthy integration of a person's former, heavier image with the newer, thinner one. Weight Watchers budgeted $20 million for the campaign. While the late 1980s showed an increase in weight-loss program attendance, the 1990s promised something different.

Niche Marketing

Not satisfied with any single market, Weight Watchers entered the convenience breakfast market in the effort to carve out a new niche. As the breakfast market grew, Weight Watchers hoped to do for frozen breakfasts what it did for frozen dinners; that is, swing the public demand from full-calorie to low-calorie choices. By mid-1989 reduced-calorie dinners sold better than full-calorie meals.

In October, 1989, Weight Watchers low-calorie microwaveable breakfasts were tested in seven markets in California, Texas, and Colorado. Some items available were pancakes with fruit toppings, blueberry muffins, and french toast and sausage; all meals, priced between $1.49 and $1.89, were in the 170-270 calorie range. A survey of retailers polled by the November 6, 1989, issue of the trade journal *Supermarket News* found that the Weight Watchers brand carried enough clout to convince them to confidently stock the products. In some cases, due to shelf-space limits, Weight Watchers' competition in other categories was knocked out of the running. One retailer, for instance, removed Sara Lee dessert items since the new Weight Watchers series included sweet items. Most merchants placed the new items between frozen breakfasts and dessert goods, thus giving the line prime exposure.

Another effort, launched in mid-1991, was a joint venture with Burger King, the nation's second-largest hamburger chain. As Heinz had moved into the low-calorie market by buying Weight Watchers rather than developing its own products from scratch, so Burger King opted to scrap its own low-cal products in favor of selling the Weight Watchers brand. The chain saved research dollars and time by offering an already advertised and well-known brand. Within several years Weight Watchers was offering its products in more than 300 Burger King locations.

Competition among weight-loss programs came to a head in 1991 when Weight Watchers and Jenny Craig Inc. both sued Nutri/System. The latter's advertisement, published in *Healthline* magazine, quoted a Stanford University professor rating Nutri/System as the best of 16 commercial diet plans. According to Linda Webb, general manager of corporate communications for Weight Watchers, as quoted in the *New York Times,* "It [the ad] claims that only Nutri/System has an exercise component. Weight Watchers has had an exercise component for 10 years."

A Change in Tactics

Clearly, the $33 billion-a-year weight-loss industry was no longer in Weight Watchers' hands only. As competition escalated, Heinz decided to consolidate the manufacturing and marketing of Weight Watchers various products into one organization. In June 1991 the Pittsburgh-based Weight Watchers Food Company was founded, uniting the production of frozen entrees and desserts with dairy items, yogurt, bread, and mayonnaise, which were formerly under two separate divisions.

Weight Watchers products were expected to outsell all other Heinz food items by the mid-1990s. Brian Ruder, named CEO, was responsible for making that happen. Some industry observers expected big changes in Weight Watchers advertising under Ruder. In July 1991 Weight Watchers chose Earle Palmer Brown to advertise its weight-loss system; by November, Ally & Gargano took over the frozen foods advertising.

What had worked to parent company Heinz's advantage in the late 1970s—taking over Weight Watchers as an up-and-running concern—worked to its detriment in the early 1990s. In general, consumers were demanding healthier low-calorie foods, not necessarily connected to a weight-loss regimen. Companies like ConAgra and Kraft General Foods, not hampered by an entire business devoted to the market, had time to gauge demand and develop specific products accordingly. With the consolidation of Weight Watchers Food Company, however, the company prepared to react.

Interestingly, as the company's food manufacturer geared up for the fray, Weight Watchers International—the weight loss centers component—pulled further away from competitors. Analysts suggest that this was due in part to the competitors' emphasis on quick weight loss, sometimes at the expense of the client's health.

New Products

The low-cal frozen food market reached $3 billion by 1991, and Weight Watchers was ready with new product lines. Entrees were reformulated to be lower in sodium, fat, and calories. A variety of sub-lines were created. Seven new stir-fry entrees were added. The "Ultimate 200" sub-line carried sixteen items—entrees and sandwiches—each with only 200 calories. The ten-item "Smart Ones" line had only 170 calories and one gram of fat.

The dessert line, always a good seller, was consistently reviewed and new items were added for variety and excitement. Weight Watchers reorganized its traditional ("white box") desserts and breakfast items, adding the new categories Sweet Celebrations and Breakfast on the Go. The 38-item line of traditional entrees all came in at 300 calories. All packages were redesigned to emphasize how the product would meet the consumer's needs; thus, Ultimate 200 equalled 200 calories. Smart Ones implied that the customer is choosing to eat smart, and the Stir-Fry package suggested strong flavors.

Dairy and related foods were reformulated as well, under the Country Cottage Farms name; a new yogurt was introduced under the name Ultimate 90. All new products were promoted in television, radio, and print ads, with a budget of $50 million allocated.

Contemporary Image

Weight Watchers promoted a contemporary image in the 1990s, offering a variety of weight-loss plans. Newly formulated plans included the Quick Control option, a menu plan using everyday foods available at home or when eating out, and the Full Choice option, which allowed the member to design his or her own menus. Members could also opt to switch back and forth between these two plans from week to week. The Weight Watchers overall theme emphasized empowerment of the individual, not a weight loss plan, to change his or her life.

International Moves

To maintain its leading market share in the weight loss industry, Weight Watchers used the ties with parent company H. J. Heinz, a strong presence in the food service market. The company targeted family restaurants, college campuses, hotels, and airlines (where its products were already offered) as growth areas. Weight Watchers also continued to build on its strongest resource: member loyalty. With 25 million current and former members, the Weight Watchers Food Company worked to maintain the highest consumer loyalty toward a brand in the reduced-calorie market segment.

Further Reading:

Dagnoli, Judann, "Heavying Up on Diet Ads," *Advertising Age,* December 23, 1991, p. 3.

Dagnoli, Judann and Julie Liesse Erickson, "New Niches for Breakfast," *Advertising Age,* June 26, 1989, p. 4.

Dagnoli, Judann and Patricia Winters, "Diet Giants Try Limited-Choice Meal Programs," *Advertising Age,* October 22, 1990, p. 59.

Fischman, Carol, "Low-Calorie Line of Breakfasts Is Called a Nice Fit," *Supermarket News,* November 6, 1989, p. 24.

Garrison, Bob, "Weight Watchers Food Company: Smart Moves," *Refrigerated and Frozen Foods,* September 1992, p. 22.

" 'Georgy Girl' Then and Now in Weight Watchers Spots," *New York Times,* August 3, 1990, p. D5.

Gibson, Richard, "Burger King Lets Diners Have it Weight Watchers' Way," *New York Times,* July 18, 1991, p. B1.

Hall, Trish, "And Now, the Last Word on Dieting: Don't Bother," *New York Times,* January 3, 1990, pp. 1, C6.

Harrison, Barbara Grizzuti, "The First Weight Watcher," *McCall's,* September 1981, p. 26.

"Heinz Leaps into Low Calories," *Business Week,* March 5, 1979, pp. 57-59.

Moreau, Dan, "Change Agents: Jean Nidetch," *Changing Times,* August 1989, p. 88.

Morgan, Richard, "Burnett May be Gaining Weight," *Adweek,* July 8, 1991, p. 9.

O'Neill, Molly, "In Fighting Shape, 3 Diet Companies Mix It up over Advertising Claims," *New York Times,* June 8, 1991, p. 9.

O'Reilly, Brian, "Diet Centers Are Really in Fat City," *Fortune,* June 5, 1989, pp. 137, 140.

Roth, June, "Weighing the Value of Frozen Diet Foods," *Consumer's Digest,* January/February 1984, pp. 33-34.

Schroeder, Michael, "The Diet Business is Getting a Lot Skinnier," *Business Week,* June 24, 1991, pp. 132-34.

Warner, Fara, "The Diet-Food Frenzy: Weight Watchers Focusses on Eating," *Adweek's Marketing Week,* August 19, 1991, pp. 4-5.

"Weight Watchers and the Heavy Executive," *Purchasing,* September 4, 1969, p. 90.

"Weight Watchers Food Company Puts R&D and Marketing Muscle Behind New Products and Promotions," *Heinz Quarterly,* Pittsburgh: Heinz USA, Spring 1992, pp. 1-7.

"Weight Watchers: Potatoes Are Now OK," *Newsweek,* April 25, 1983, p. 16, 18.

"Weight Watchers Think Thin and Grow Fat," *Nation's Business,* September 1978, pp. 98, 100.

—Frances E. Norton

WELCH'S®

Thomas B. Welch created what would become America's favorite grape juice in 1869, when he produced the first bottles of Dr. Welch's Unfermented Wine. Not only was he the first to make grape juice, but his innovative approach to preventing fermentation laid the groundwork for the evolution of the modern fruit juice industry. Though originally marketed as a nonalcoholic wine substitute, shrewd marketing efforts refocused the brand as a great tasting drink for the general public. The success of Welch's Grape Juice eventually led to its being managed under a unique corporate management structure. In 1956 the National Grape Co-operative Association, Inc., a coalition of grape growers, purchased the Welch Grape Juice Company, Inc., which was renamed Welch Foods Inc. Continuing to work as an affiliated cooperative, Welch Foods manages marketing and production while National Grape supplies raw material. Together, through separate boards of directors, they insure the continued quality and market prominence of the many products now marketed under the Welch's brand.

Brand Origins

Thomas Welch was a life-long Prohibitionist with a creative talent. He is credited with inventing successful dental alloys, a stomach soother, and a spelling system. When his Methodist church asked him to distribute Communion bread and wine during religious services, he began to focus on creating a nonalcoholic grape beverage. His boyhood experiences with a father who enjoyed sipping whiskey, along with his strong religious convictions, had given Welch an aversion to alcohol. In order to serve Communion with a clear conscience, he set out to create a wine with no fermentation.

Living in Vineland, New Jersey, as a practicing dentist, Welch often received grapes in exchange for dental services. In addition, he had his own supply of grapes grown at home. Welch applied Pasteur's technique of heating to kill the yeast microorganism. By boiling bottled filtered grape juice, Welch was successful in preventing the natural fermentation process and producing a nonalcoholic grape juice. Thomas Welch attempted to sell the first bottles of "Dr. Welch's Unfermented Wine" to church officials, whom he had expected would purchase the bulk of the "wine" he produced. Church officials balked, however, at substituting the sacramental wine with grape juice. Four years after producing the first batches of grape juice, Welch disappointedly abandoned the

project completely and concentrated his efforts on supporting the growing Prohibition movement.

Early Marketing Strategy

Like his father, Charles Welch, one of Thomas and Lucy Welch's seven children, was a practicing dentist with his own creative talent. Charles believed he had the solution to selling his father's grape juice—advertising. In 1875 he placed the first print ads for Dr. Welch's Unfermented Wine. The ads promised quality and promoted the "wine" as a beverage for "sacramental and medicinal use." The advertising created a small market following, and by 1879 Welch's sales necessitated the processing of four tons of grapes.

Charles recognized early on the need to expand the reach and appeal of his product. He changed the name of the juice in 1890 to Dr. Welch's Grape Juice, and in 1893 to the current Welch's Grape Juice. In an effort to extend brand awareness, "Welch's Grape Juice" was exhibited at the Chicago World's Fair in 1893. Gaining the first wide public exposure at the fair proved to be a key promotion tactic. Volume growth between 1889 and 1899 was immense, increasing from 10 tons to 660 tons of grapes.

Charles Welch continued to view advertising and publicity as the key to Welch's success. He expanded advertising beyond the original religious and medicinal focus to include acceptance as a fountain and home juice beverage. Print advertising grew beyond small circulation religious and medical magazines to national magazines. Charles also continued to promote Welch's where crowds gathered: the Atlantic City Boardwalk, conventions, expositions, and fairs. Favored advertising vehicles also included contests and calendars.

The Prohibition Influence

Both Thomas and Charles Welch had strong convictions regarding abstinence from alcohol. The Prohibition era complimented their beliefs and further spurred growth in grape juice consumption. Two incidents focused the nation's attention on the prohibitionist issue and provided a great deal of national exposure for Welch's Grape Juice. In 1913 U.S. Secretary of State William Jennings Bryan garnered an enormous amount of national attention when he asked his guests to refrain from drinking wine during a diplomatic dinner honoring the British ambassador. Instead of

AT A GLANCE

Welch's brand of grape juice founded as Dr. Welch's Unfermented Wine in 1869 by Thomas B. Welch; brand further developed by Charles E. Welch; company originally a proprietorship, re-established as Welch Grape Juice Company, Inc., 1892; became a wholly owned subsidiary of National Grape Co-operative Association, 1956, and renamed Welch Foods Inc., 1969.

Performance: *Market share*—Top share of grape juice category. *Sales*—(Entire line of Welch's products) $464.3 million.

Major competitor: Mott's; also, Ocean Spray and Hi-C.

Advertising: *Agency*—Jordan, McGrath, Case & Taylor, New York, NY, 1979—. *Major campaign*—"Take the time to taste the Welch's."

Addresses: *Parent company*—Welch Foods Inc., 3 Concord Farms, 555 Virginia Road, Concord, MA 01742; phone: (508) 371-1000; fax: (508) 371-2832. *Ultimate parent company*—National Grape Co-operative Association, Inc., 2 South Portage St., Westfield, NY 14787; phone: (716) 326-3131.

wine, Bryan had Welch's Grape Juice served. The press reported mixed reactions to but provided lengthy coverage of the "Grape Juice Diplomacy" incident. A year later, Josephus Daniels, the secretary of the Navy, prohibited the consumption of alcoholic beverages on naval property. He dispensed Welch's Grape Juice as a substitute for sailor's rum rations. The event stirred the press again and produced an upheaval similar to the Bryan incident. Both events gained wide publicity for Welch's Grape Juice and increased its popularity. Welch's advertising wisely utilized temperance themes to gain further attention.

By the time the Eighteenth Amendment passed in 1919, sales of Welch's Grape Juice, the only nonalcoholic fruit drink in the country, reached close to $3 million. One year later sales doubled.

Advertising Adaptability

Not only were Welch's advertising efforts extensive, but they were continually adapted to focus and capitalize on the trends of the times. By 1931 sales had sagged as support for Prohibition waned. Welch's needed a new focus, and it seized an opportunity to promote itself as a "thin" drink. Welch's used Irene Rich, a popular movie star, to promote the drink on radio shows the company sponsored between 1933 and 1945. She attributed her slender figure to drinking Welch's Grape Juice, and the result was another surge in sales. By 1945 revenue topped $10 million.

Television's immensely popular 1950s children's show *Howdy Doody* was the next major trend to which Welch's attached itself successfully. Welch's needed a big campaign to try to make inroads into the strong market share orange juice makers held. So, Welch's arranged to license Howdy Doody at the height of his fame and put the character's image on the juice bottles. Ads on the *Howdy Doody* program included selected "peanuts" drinking the juice and voicing their satisfaction. The response was remarkable; Welch's had succeeded in attracting the attention of young baby boomers. By the close of the Howdy Doody advertising campaign in 1955, sales exceeded $37 million.

Brand Expansion

Welch's expanded its product lines over the years, adding grape jelly in 1923 and frozen grape juice concentrate in 1949. During the 1960s Welch's product line grew extensively. To reflect Welch's product expansion, the corporate name was changed from Welch Grape Juice Company, Inc., to Welch Foods Inc. in 1969. As the century progressed, Welch's product line grew to include a variety of fruit juices, blended juice cocktails, jams, jellies, preserves, frozen fruit juice bars, and sparkling juice beverages.

The purple Concord grape juice has always been the classic Welch brand product. Since the early 1980s, however, the company has attempted to reposition Welch's as a fruit products company, adding other fruits, such as apples, raspberries, cranberries, oranges, and strawberries to the repertoire of flavors. The repositioning of the Welch's brand was initiated when the company found its inventory filled to capacity with grape juice in 1983. It became imperative to create new products for the grape juice to help diminish the excess inventory. A rush of new grape-based, fruit-blend products resulted.

Unfortunately, some of Welch's new products did not mesh well with the traditional image on which the brand had built its identity. Welch's needed a symbol to unify the products and represent the image of the company. Consumers were asked to define Welch's in interviews, and focus groups used terms such as "quality" and "heritage." Commercial artists created a new look for Welch's that was more modern and yet conveyed a rich heritage of quality. The result was a label concept for Welch's that was complete with a bountiful fruit basket as a unifying symbol for all of Welch's products—new and old.

Performance

In 1878 sales of Welch's juice amounted to $1,320. By 1913 sales surpassed $2 million and by 1972 reached $100 million. Between 1979 and 1983 Welch's sales volume declined, while industry sales were increasing one to two percent annually. In August of 1982 Everett N. Baldwin became the new president and chief executive officer of Welch Foods. Baldwin recognized Welch as an underutilized company and initiated the effort to increase sales and market presence by introducing new products and increasing Welch's brand equity with a new trademark. Early on, Baldwin's basic strategy of "building the market strength of the company" produced tangible results. Sales increased by $10 million to $239 million by the end of his first full year. By 1992 sales had increased to $464 million.

In addition, Welch's has paid considerable attention to distribution. In the early 1990s its products were being sold to more than 175,000 retail distributors and institutions within the United States. Through licensing agreements and international divisions, Welch's products were marketed in 30 foreign countries. In an effort to further increase the scope of its market, Welch's began vending distribution in 1989 and has since placed its products in thousands of vending machines. Sold in 11.5 ounce cans, the 100 percent fruit juices and juice cocktails have reached beyond the traditional vended juice markets such as health clubs and schools to include mainstream businesses as well.

Market Trends

In 1991 grape juice volume ranked a distant third as a flavor category with sales of 90.2 million gallons. Apple juice ranked second behind the leader, orange juice, at a volume more than triple that of grape. It appeared likely that grape juice would remain the third favorite flavor for some time.

The good news for Welch's was that the consumption of fruit beverages was growing, fueling a 6.6 percent industry increase in 1991 that was the strongest growth rate for any beverage category. In *Beverage World* Michael Bellas, president of Beverage Marketing, was quoted as saying, "Consumers' continued concern for healthy, nutritional beverages and all-natural products has further spurred the [fruit beverage] industry's growth." He also predicted continuing consumer health consciousness as U.S. demographics indicated an aging population. Even if its percentage of the juice market in the flavor category remains constant, Welch's would no doubt benefit from continued increases in the overall juice market.

The strongest trend within the juice category was the increasing strength of the fruit drink market. As opposed to fruit juices, which are 100 percent juice, fruit drinks contain added water content and may have added sugar. Fruit drinks are popular due to the wide variety of flavors at prices that tend to be more stable than fruit juices. Welch's has met this trend with an upscale twist. Welch's Orchard fruit juice blends contain a higher juice content than average fruit drinks and are available in a variety of flavor combinations and blends. By offering greater flavor selection with higher juice content than the traditional low-priced competition, such as Hi-C, Welch's was in a position to benefit from the more upscale segment of this consumer trend.

Welch's has positioned itself to benefit from another strong industry trend—vending distribution. In 1991 fruit juice vending volume grew 21.7 percent. In analyzing 1990s juice market trends, Eric Sfiligoj in the May 1992 *Beverage World* reported that "though vending currently accounts for only a fraction of fruit beverage distribution, its future looks bright."

Future Predictions

The modern fruit juice industry began with the introduction of Welch's Grape Juice more than 120 years ago. Since its introduction, Welch's has attracted a plethora of competitors, and trends indicate that the industry will attract even more competitive entries and marketing strategies. Aware of its challenges, Welch's could

be expected to continue to attend to the key elements that led to Charles Welch's original success: quality, advertising, market expansion, and the loyalty of growers and employees. A quote from the president's letter in the company's 1991 annual report envisions Welch's future: "As we look to the future, we expect the competitive environment for products in our category to grow even more intense. But with a solid business base and a progressive, loyal membership, we continue to adhere to our vision of the company—to grow, process and market high quality fruit-based products and, in so doing, continue to anticipate and satisfy consumers' changing needs."

Further Reading:

Chazanoff, William, *Welch's Grape Juice: From Corporation to Co-operative,* New York, NY: Syracuse University Press, 1977.

Cuff, Daniel F., "New Welch Foods Chief Was at Land O' Lakes," *New York Times,* August 23, 1982, p. D2.

Davis, Stephen, "Too Many Strings Attached," *Advertising Age,* December 7, 1987, p. 41.

Flint, Peter B., "Irene Rich, Silent-Screen Actress and Radio Personality Dies at 96," *New York Times,* April 25, 1988, p. D12.

Fucini, Joseph J., and Suzy Fucini, *Entrepreneurs: The Men and Women Behind Famous Brand Names and How They Made It,* Boston, MA: G. K. Hall & Co., 1985.

Gershman, Michael, *Getting It Right the Second Time,* Reading, PA: Addison-Wesley, 1990, pp. 84-88.

Jabbonsky, Larry, "The Answer Man," *Beverage World,* March 1992, p. 25.

"Movie, Radio Performer Irene Rich," *Chicago Tribune,* April 25, 1988, p. C6.

National Grape Co-operative Association, Inc. & Welch Foods Inc., A Cooperative, Annual Report, 1991.

Sfiligoj, Eric, "The Beverage Market Index for 1992," *Beverage World,* May 1992, pp. 30-36.; "Healthy Growth," *Beverage World,* May 1992, p. 30.

Stacy, John D., "The Future of Fruit Drinks," *Beverage World,* August 1987, pp. 26-30.

Taylor, Nick, "Question: Just What Is Welch's?," *Madison Avenue,* June 1985, pp. 50-57.

"Welch Test-Marketing Grape Juice Blends," *Supermarket News,* September 14, 1992, p. 46.

"Welch's Offers Juice Line to Bottlers," *Beverage Industry,* November 1989, p. 4.

Welch's, Since 1869: This Is Our Story, National Grape Co-operative Association, Inc. & Welch Foods Inc., A Cooperative, 1989.

—*Louise L. Groden*

WHEATIES®

For more than 70 years Wheaties has been known as "The Breakfast of Champions." The cereal has associated itself with myriad major sports stars in America over the years and has managed to turn those associations into a guiding marketing philosophy.

Wheaties didn't start out as the archetypical athlete's breakfast. Rather, the product began as something of an error. According to Michael Gershman in his book *Getting It Right the Second Time,* it was in 1921 that "a Minneapolis health clinician stirred a batch of bran gruel a tad too vigorously, scattering drops of it on a hot stove. After he scraped the thin wafers off, he discovered that cooking had transformed them into tasty flakes. The Breakfast of Champions was born. Sort of."

The bran cereal needed some refinement—and a distributor. That mantle was taken up by the Washburn Crosby Company, which would evolve into General Mills some years later. Washburn Crosby "tried to make a breakfast cereal of the bran, but the flakes kept crumbling until the company's head miller succeeded with his thirty-sixth variety of wheat," as Gershman points out. Washburn Crosby held a company-wide contest to name the new concoction. The winner was Jane Bausman, an executive's wife, who came up with the name Wheaties, because "there's nothing as endearing as a nickname," as Gershman quotes.

Early Promotions

By 1924 Wheaties had begun to appear nationally—but the cereal didn't exactly get off to a championship start. In fact, sales proved uninspiring until 1926. That's when the Washburn Crosby Company used radio station WCCO (for Washburn Crosby Company) in Minneapolis, the city in which the company was headquartered, to showcase "a municipal court bailiff, a printer, a businessman, and an undertaker [who formed] a male quartet called The Gold Medal Four," continues Gershman. The group made history when it performed radio's first singing commercial—for Wheaties: "Have you tried Wheaties?/They're the whole wheat with all the bran/Won't you try Wheaties?/For wheat is the best food of man."

That jingle essentially saved Wheaties from oblivion, although sales figures for the product remained mediocre. Other slogans of that era—"Make Your Child Love Whole Wheat" and "Eat Whole Wheat the Alluring Way"—didn't help the cereal's cause

either. It wasn't until 1931—four years after Washburn Crosby had joined with other millers to form General Mills—that the producer of Wheaties "decided to bypass parents and appeal directly to children," as Gershman notes.

In its quest to reach younger consumers, Wheaties became associated with "Skippy," a then-popular comic book character who had also starred in a movie based on his exploits. "Skippy had already made his radio debut on WMAQ in Chicago," adds Gershman, "but General Mills sponsored his first network broadcast." In an early, successful marketing tie-in campaign, Wheaties sponsored one of the first "radio clubs," the Skippy Secret Service Society. Explains Gershman: "Youngsters sending in two Wheaties box tops became members, received certificates, buttons, and a secret code and handshake; more than half a million responded. The response validated the pitch to youth, and by 1932 the Gold Medal Four were off the air."

By 1933 Wheaties was ready to expand its consumer base to include both children and their parents, and General Mills searched for the appropriate marketing angle. Baseball seemed to fit the bill. General Mills bought sponsorship of the Minneapolis Millers, a minor-league club. "As a bonus, they also got the sponsorship of a signboard on the centerfield fence of the Millers' ballpark," Gershman relates. "When a Millers' executive asked what to put on the signboard, Knox Reeves, the head of Wheaties' ad agency, quickly drew the phrase 'Breakfast of Champions' across a Wheaties box, and that became the signboard message; every time a Miller hit a home run, the company would give a case of Wheaties to charity."

Little did General Mills know that both the promotion and the slogan would set imaginations blazing. When a Millers batter, Joe Hauser, set a league record with 69 home runs, local kids started referring to their own playground hits as "a case of Wheaties." "Breakfast of Champions" started "taking on richer and richer meaning," as Gershman notes. "While it hadn't been planned, the slogan became one of the slickest pieces of positioning strategy ever created; when commercials identifying Wheaties as the 'Breakfast of Champions' were broadcast on stations outside Minneapolis, impressionable young boys, convinced of Wheaties' sympathetic magic, ate it by the carload."

As the 1930s progressed, Wheaties expanded its baseball association, sponsoring 95 different broadcasts nationwide in both the

AT A GLANCE

Wheaties brand created in 1921 by a Minnesota health clinician; recipe and rights purchased by Washburn Crosby Company; product first distributed nationally in 1924; Washburn Crosby incorporated into General Mills, Inc. in 1927.

Performance: *Market share*—1.4% of dollar share among all ready-to-eat cereals (1991 figures).

Major competitor: Kellogg's Corn Flakes (Kellogg Company).

Advertising: *Agency*—DDB Needham, Chicago, IL, 1980—. *Major campaign*—"Breakfast of champions," 1933--; also, "Better eat your Wheaties," 1989—.

Addresses: *Parent company*—General Mills, Inc., One General Mills Blvd., Minneapolis, MN 55246; phone: (612) 540-2311; fax: (612) 540-4925.

minor and major leagues. Endorsements for Wheaties burgeoned, and featured stellar sports performers of the era such as Babe Ruth, Joe DiMaggio, Hank Greenberg, and Red Grange. By the time of the 1939 Major League All-Star Game, 46 of the 51 participating players endorsed Wheaties.

But Wheaties hadn't lost its affiliation with children's radio. With General Mills sponsoring the network series "Jack Armstrong, the All-American Boy," Wheaties appealed to an older group than the "Skippy" crowd. The "Jack Armstrong" adventure series stayed on the air 18 years, providing Wheaties with maximum exposure. The success of this partnership was realized early, when "one of the first Jack Armstrong shows mentioned a 'shooting plane' in the script and offered it to the public for a boxtop and ten cents," as Gershman explains. "The resultant flood of orders depleted stocks of Wheaties around the country; it would be nearly six months before Wheaties was readily available again."

Wheaties, however inadvertently, also played a part in shaping American political history. In 1937 a young Des Moines-based play-by-play man was voted Wheaties' most popular radio announcer. As part of his prize, Ronald Wilson "Dutch" Reagan won a trip to California to visit the Chicago Cubs' training camp. While there he made a screen test for Warner Brothers pictures and subsequently began a career in film that, 40 years later, he would parlay into his election as the 40th president of the United States.

Wheaties contributed to other moments in history. In 1939 the cereal sponsored the first-ever televised baseball game. The August 29 contest between the Cincinnati Reds and the Brooklyn Dodgers was broadcast live for some 500 television owners in New York City, with the legendary Red Barber providing the voice-over.

The testimonials continued. Wheaties had become so closely associated with athletic excellence, according to company history, that both heavyweight boxer Max Baer and baseball's Lou Gehrig inadvertently blurted that they began their day with Wheaties—on broadcasts sponsored by competing cereals. A short list of other World War II-era spokesmen and spokeswomen included Bronco Nagurski, Otto Graham, Babe Didrikson, Patty Berg, Sam Snead, and Ben Hogan.

"Breakfast of Champions"

Wheaties sought out "champions" wherever they were found. Other testimonials came from circus performers, coaches, trainers, managers, a big-game hunter, an airline pilot, parachute jumpers, and even a "champion" railroad engineer. One man's remark stands out in Wheaties history. In 1950 a bodybuilder made headlines by hoisting both an elephant and its trainer on his back. As quoted by *The Modern Millwheel*, a General Mills magazine, the man—who was not sponsored at that time—told reporters, "I guess there's only one thing I eat every day—Wheaties."

Sponsorship of sports teams had served Wheaties well for two decades, but by the end of the 1940s such activity was no longer economically feasible. Wheaties began to rely solely on testimonial commercials to get its name across—and the emerging medium of television seemed an ideal venue to pursue this course. This time, however, Wheaties' strategy failed: the testimonials were lost amid all the other television commercials, and sales dropped further when General Mills tried to recoup by more closely targeting young children. "Trading in Mickey Mantle for Mickey Mouse, the brass in Minneapolis changed Wheaties' package and brand image in an effort to get in on the heavy per-capita consumption that characterizes dry cereal," notes Gershman. "In this unfortunate replay of the Skippy experience, General Mills got the six-to-ten-year-olds back but lost the boys and men who had identified with the Breakfast of Champions theme. Sales slumped immediately, as much as 10 percent in a single year."

So in 1956 the famous slogan returned, as did a close association with sports—and this time, Wheaties made sure youngsters had their own identification. In the first of three marketing strategies, General Mills searched for a Wheaties spokesman, a role model to inspire athletic excellence and moral goodness. After screening 500 candidates, the company chose two-time Olympic track-and-field champion Bob Richards. Secondly, Wheaties plunged back into sports sponsorship on television, where they helped to pioneer such innovations as pre- and post-game shows.

Third, General Mills established the Wheaties Sports Federation. Working in association with such organizations as the President's Council on Youth Fitness, the Federation produced instructional films on all aspects of sportsmanship; the films were made available free to the public. Bob Richards served as director for the next 14 years.

"Look at That, Dora!": Advertising Themes

With this reestablished identity clearly in place, Wheaties used its advertising to drive home the message. Since the days of the Gold Medal Four, Wheaties had relied on innovative advertising efforts. As far back as 1933, print ads aimed at children presented a comic-strip vignette of spokesman Babe Ruth pitching the cereal to adoring children. In one strip, young "Jerry" and "Joe" find a home-run ball hit by Ruth. The ball player delivers the Wheaties benefit message ("there's nothing like them to give you energy and pep"), and the boys are subsequently seen devouring bowls of the cereal. After they send away a Wheaties boxtop for a Babe Ruth "moviebook"—a flip book demonstrating Ruth's swing—they become great hitters themselves. "Look at that, Dora!" exclaims their father. "I tell you these youngsters are getting so husky I can hardly believe it." "Thanks to the Babe Ruth moviebook that started them eating Wheaties," replies Dora. (In a surprising tilt away from the expected sexism of that era, the moviebook trumpeted: "Boys! Girls! How would you like to be able to step up to the plate and sock the old ball over the fence for a home run like Babe Ruth?'')

With the advent of television commercials, the ads became more creative and even humorous. The cereal's "most notable campaign, in the early '70s, gave the Wheaties sports heritage a flip side," notes Steve Wulf in a *Sports Illustrated* profile of the product. "In one commercial, [Cincinnati] Reds catcher Johnny Bench would fall, run into a screen and strike out. While he was stumbling around the field, a singer . . . would wail, 'Hey, John, you didn't have your Wheaties . . . ' It was a catchy tune and a catchy commercial, and similar ones were made with Henry Aaron and Tom Weiskopf."

The cereal's image suffered a blow during that same era, however, when consumer advocate Robert Choate "went after the ready-to-eat cereals, saying that they were little more than empty calories," Wulf wrote. "Choate called Wheaties the 'Breakfast of Chumps.' After the attack, General Mills started fortifying Wheaties with more vitamins." Ironically, according to the *Sports Illustrated* piece, General Mills' Total cereal, which the company acknowledges is Wheaties with an extra spray of nutrients, ranked lower on the nutritional scale than did Wheaties. (Wheaties did regain nutritional respectability in 1988, when the Surgeon General's report on the health benefits of whole grain led General Mills to remind consumers that Wheaties was one of the few cereals with this attribute.)

To further counter this smear of their honor, Wheaties brought in newly crowned Olympic decathlete Bruce Jenner as the second director of the Wheaties Sports Federation (Bob Richards had retired in 1970). From 1976 to 1980, Jenner starred in a series of commercials, the most memorable of which replayed his triumph in Montreal. As the image cut from Jenner's victory lap to Jenner at the breakfast table, he reminded viewers that on the road to a gold medal, "I logged a lot of miles . . . and downed a lot of Wheaties."

Unfortunately, Jenner's appeal was not as long-lived as Richards'; sales of Wheaties began to drop again in 1980. General Mills switched its advertising to DDB-Needham, the agency that devised the odd-sounding Eaties for Wheaties campaign. Commercials showed a woman swatting at a tennis ball while singing, "Before a day of breaking servies, I get the eaties for my Wheaties." Another commercial depicted a referee who "sings that before he whistles pass incompleties he gets the eaties for his Wheaties . . . you get the idea," said Wulf.

That campaign was replaced in 1984 with a new crop of sports heroes to carry on the Wheaties image. Among them was gold-medal gymnast Mary Lou Retton, who leaped and twirled her way through a routine, while a singer provided the message, "Now go tell your mama what the big boys eat!" (Retton, defiantly slurping up the last spoonful of cereal, fit the "big boys" image as much as

any of her male counterparts.) In 1987 General Mills announced that tennis ace Chris Evert was the recipient of its first Wheaties Champions Award. Superstar athletes Walter Payton and Michael Jordan joined the Wheaties lineup in the late-1980s, starring in their own commercials with the theme "Better Eat your Wheaties." Jordan, especially, provided prime promotion effectiveness with a "shoot hoops with Michael Jordan" action game on the back of specially marked boxes. General Mills also sponsored a Michael Jordan Flight (Fan) Club, producing the expected calendars and posters as premiums. Jordan remained a centerpiece of Wheaties' promotional strategy in the early 1990s.

The Inspirational Cereal

Wheaties themselves have changed a little since their introduction in the 1920s. The original formula, as Wulf's *Sports Illustrated* article relates, "which called for processing Wheaties a kernel at a time, remained untouched for 34 years. In 1958 'Redintegration' was introduced. Flakes were made from a more uniform mixture, and they became crispier, crunchier and more consistent." Studying the cereal further, Wulf's impression is that "the flakes themselves appear fairly innocuous. They come in different shapes and sizes, although they are uniformly butterscotch in color. Up close, they look a little ugly, with little hills and valleys." To Wulf, though, there's nothing ugly about the Wheaties box. "Wheaties deserves a permanent spot in the American cupboard, if only for the beauty of its box," he writes. "The dominant color can only be described as Wheaties orange; it has no place in nature. The hue cries out at shoppers and pries open the lids of drowsy breakfasters." Others, too, have found artistic inspiration in Wheaties; the box appears in the films *The Graduate* and *Pennies from Heaven*; and Kurt Vonnegut named one of his novels *Breakfast of Champions*.

Although Wheaties isn't General Mills' biggest seller—that honor belongs to Cheerios—it holds a special place in the heart of its manufacturer. Paul L. Parker, the company's chief administrative officer in 1981, explained it like this to *Sports Illustrated*: "There's something very special about Wheaties, something intangible. You could say the Wheaties ideal took over the entire company."

Further Reading:

Gershman, Michael, *Getting It Right the Second Time,* Reading, MA: Addison-Wesley, 1990, pp. 11–16.

Wheaties: 63 Historic Years (press release), Minneapolis, MN: General Mills, Inc., February 1987.

Wheaties and Sports Since 1933 (press release), Minneapolis, MN: General Mills, Inc., December 1992.

Wulf, Steve, "Famous Flakes of America," *Sports Illustrated,* April 5, 1982.

—Susan Salter

WHISKAS®

When England's Pedigree Petfoods founded the Whiskas cat food brand in 1959, it quickly became one of the major brands of cat food in Europe, Australia, and Japan. In fact, Pedigree's most famous slogan was "8 out of 10 owners said their cat preferred it." The Whiskas brand—owned in the United States by Kal Kan Foods, Inc., a subsidiary of Mars, Inc.—was available in the United States for years, but did not become a national brand until the late 1980s.

Canned cat food brands in the 1960s were considered a novelty if not a luxury for table scrap-fed felines. The pet food business grew in part out of the grain-based livestock feed business, and the first pet foods were dry and lacking in palatability for cats and dogs. The first canned foods were often made with meat substitutes like vegetable and soy proteins. Products made of meat by-products had a high fat content and had an unappealing smell; they were not very attractive to pet owners who had to dish out the odious mass to their finicky pets. When the cat began its reign as the preferred pet, the pet food industry deferred to kitty tastes. In a mad scramble since the 1980s, pet food producers have been vying to serve this burgeoning market with a selection of healthy menus. Pet food companies Kal Kan and Pedigree soon made their marks in the industry by developing healthy meat-based pet food brands.

Brand Origins

British Whiskas was the first brand to offer different varieties, a special food to meet the nutritional needs of kittens, and the Whiskas Cat Healthcare Insurance Plan. According to the *World's Greatest Brands,* Whiskas in the United Kingdom outsells its nearest competitor by 3 to 1 and garners a 50 percent share of the £455 million market. Pedigree Petfood officials attribute the brand's success to nutritional expertise and manufacturing efficiency, which allowed the company to offer the best possible cat food for a reasonable price.

Kal Kan brand of cat food had been a market leader before its Whiskas makeover in late 1988. Both brands were based on the same recipes with varying contents, depending on the availability of local ingredients. Mars, Inc., which owns Vernon, California-based Kal Kan Foods and Pedigree Petfoods, renamed its Kal Kan brand Whiskas in an attempt to gain more market share and make the brand as competitive and as popular as its English cousin. Kal Kan changed its cat food label to include a cat mask logo superimposed with the name Whiskas (the Kal Kan name now appeared in smaller print). Since then, American Whiskas has tried to maintain Kal Kan's dominance as a leading cat food in the United States.

Brand Development

The Whiskas brand introduction in the United States was designed to enable Mars to realize tangible global advertising and media efficiencies and consolidate advertising, marketing, and promotional campaigns. Focus group sessions held before the name change revealed that consumers preferred the name Whiskas over Kal Kan, which was traditionally associated with dog food. Besides, Mars had used the same strategy years earlier to much success when the company renamed its Kal Kan canned dog food and Mealtime dry dog food Pedigree brand and Pedigree Mealtime, respectively.

In launching the Whiskas brand to American shoppers, Mars augmented its advertising budget, the bulk of it targeted to television commercials that announced, "The cat food your cat prefers is now called Whiskas." Testimonials and ads featuring cat owners declaring their newfound allegiance to Whiskas were also used to promote the brand. Whiskas food for cats was packaged with new pull-tab lids and, in addition to 6-ounce cans, came in 13- and 22-ounce cans that attracted owners of one or more pets to the new brand. At the same time, Kal Kan Foods converted its Crave cat food line to Whiskas Dry, while the gourmet Sheba cat food line retained its name. Crave ranked fourth in dollar sales among dry cat foods, according to Wheat First Securities of Richmond, Virginia.

Kal Kan Foods' vice-president of sales, John Murray, said a major focus of the company's marketing strategy was upgrading quality and increasing pet food palatability. Kal Kan introduced foods that were based on meat, rather than on vegetable proteins, and adopted manufacturing techniques that made the food much more acceptable to pet owners. The products were no longer high in fat with an unpleasant odor, Murray stated in a 1991 *Supermarket Business* advertisement.

"We felt that to take on existing leaders with similar products was unlikely to be successful," Murray explained. "And from the retailer's standpoint, for us to go for a share without enlarging the market would be to swap pieces of the pie. As far as we were concerned, the name of the game was trying to enlarge that pie." He added, "Whiskas was expected to do $300 million in sales."

AT A GLANCE

Whiskas brand of cat food founded in 1959 in England by Pedigree Petfoods; became one of the major brands of cat food in Europe, Australia, and Japan; became a national brand in the United States in the late 1980s, when Kal Kan Foods, Inc., a subsidiary of Mars, Inc., renamed its cat food Whiskas.

Performance: *Market share*—15.8% of canned cat foods category; 8.34% of dry cat food category. *Sales*—(Canned varieties; 1989) $250 million; (dry varieties; 1989) $80 million.

Major competitor: Heinz's 9-Lives; also, Carnation's Friskies and Ralston Purina's Purina pet chows.

Advertising: *Agency*—D'Arcy Masius Benton & Bowles, Los Angeles, CA, 1992—. *Major campaign*—Television commercial launched in September of 1992 featuring a small colorful bird advising cats, "Read my beak: no more birds."

Addresses: *Parent company*—Kal Kan Foods, Inc., P.O. Box 58853, Vernon, CA 90058; phone: (213) 587-2727; fax: (212) 586-8347. *Ultimate parent company*—Mars, Inc., 6885 Elm Street, McLean, VA 22101; phone: (703) 821-4900.

The strategy of moving from marketing pet food to marketing "foods for companions," combined with Kal Kan's mixed-meal concept of providing meat and grain-based food, enabled the company to more than triple the average expenditure per pet, according to Murray.

Product Changes

In 1990 Kal Kan expanded its Whiskas brand by introducing pricier Whiskas Select Entrees, which joined Mars's Sheba brand. Whiskas Select and Sheba sold for the same price of between 60 and 73 cents for a three-and-a-half-ounce serving. Both featured the same square, single-serving package with a pull-tab top, except Whiskas Select Entrees contained minced meat, while Sheba was composed of chunks of meat.

In an attempt to offset slow supermarket sales and capture a piece of the $1 billion specialty veterinarian market, Kal Kan established a super premium Whiskas Expert Diet for cats and a companion expert diet product for dogs. In 1991 Kal Kan became the third company to use an in-store nutritional center concept, similar to such competitors as Hill's Science Diet. At the same time, Kal Kan's other competitors—Ralston Purina Co. and Quaker Oats Co.—followed suit by launching super premium pet food lines, Purina O.N.E. and Advanced Nutrition Formula, respectively. These high-price lines were targeted to consumers desiring life-stage nutrition for their pets.

International Market

The international market for pet foods, which had been growing by leaps and bounds, also experienced erosions in market share due to the recession of the early 1990s. Mars is the international leader in the pet food market, with shares of more than 60 percent by value and 60 percent by volume. The company sells pet food in more than 30 countries and in addition to owning best-selling cat food brands Whiskas and Sheba, which are marketed worldwide, sells Kit-E-Kat cat food in Europe. Pedigree's Whiskas is the number one cat food brand and is available in six countries.

In 1990 Pedigree launched Whiskas kitten food, which remains the only major specialty canned kitten food available on the market, according to a 1991 report by *Key Note Publications Ltd.* of Middlesex, England. The following year, Pedigree Petfoods launched in the United Kingdom Whiskas CatMilk, a low-lactose milk for cats, and had plans for a European rollout in France and Germany.

In the United Kingdom Pedigree Whiskas features 18 varieties of Whiskas canned cat food in 3 can sizes; Whiskas Crunch, a crunchy topping for canned food; Whiskas Cocktail dry cat food; and Whiskas Exelpet cat care accessories. The brand expanded in 1992 to include six varieties of Whiskas Select Cuts, which experienced a successful product launch establishing a £30 million value in four months, Pedigree Petfood officials said. Whiskas Select Cuts was one of the four contenders for a 1992 U.K. Marketing Society New Product of the Year Award. In addition, the Whiskas brand offers the Whiskas Cat Healthcare insurance plan that affords pet owners protection from the rising costs of veterinary care by granting such benefits as £1,500 for veterinary fees and services, hospital care, death benefits from illness or accident, recovery costs, boarding fees, and use of acupuncture and other homeopathic medicines.

Performance Appraisal

Americans own 110 million cats and dogs, making the pet food business a lucrative industry. Supermarket sales of pet food increased from $3.7 billion in 1979 to $5.9 billion in 1988. In the early 1990s the top six pet food companies controlled 81.1 percent of sales, up from 69 percent in 1985, according to Wheat First Securities analyst John Maxwell, Jr.

However, stiff competition and a downturn in the economy as a whole has affected petfood industry sales and increased competition among the brands. The popularity of cats as the pet of choice helped boost cat food sales volumes, although those margins have increased slightly. Cat food sales volume increased only one percent in 1989, with dry cat food leading in sales. Whiskas was the third best selling dry cat food in 1989 and fourth in canned meat cat food. The brand's ranking reversed in 1990: Whiskas was the third best selling canned cat food (15.8 percent of market share) and the fourth best selling dry cat food brand (8.34 percent market share).

Advertising Innovations

Customer testimonials have been a tried and true advertising ploy developed by the firm of Backer Spielvogel Bates of New York. Kal Kan has also sponsored charity campaigns, including its 1991 venture titled "Help Keep Animals in Our Lives." Once redeemed, Kal Kan coupons were used as donations to the World Wildlife Fund coinciding with World Animal Day.

But one of the most memorable advertising gimmicks was conceived in 1992, when Kal Kan switched to the Los Angeles-based advertising firm D'Arcy Masius Benton & Bowles (D.M.B.&B.). The firm introduced television viewers to Whiskas spokesanimal, a small colorful bird who speaks about the compelling reasons for pet owners to feed their cats Whiskas—the most important of which, from the bird's point of view, is that cats definitely prefer Whiskas to birds. The bird advises cats, "Read my beak: no more birds."

The spokesanimal sparked commentary by comedians, the television show *Entertainment Tonight,* and *People* magazine. According to *AdWeek,* the ads took two days and 14,000 feet of film to shoot because the bird kept flying away from the set. The crew got the bird to move its beak by feeding it peanut butter. They later used special effects to match beak, eye, and tongue movements to a voiceover.

Future Growth

By diversifying its product and expanding internationally, Mars, Inc., the second leading cat food manufacturer, stands to maintain Whiskas' brand dominance. In the United States the Whiskas brand is available in 29 varieties in chunky, minced, and choice cuts textures. Whiskas dry cat food is available in three varieties. In May of 1993 the U.K. arm of Mars began selling its wares, including Whiskas canned and dry cat food, in Russia. By continuing to diversify its product lines and geographically expand its market, Mars, Inc., will no doubt maintain Whiskas' brand prominence.

Further Reading:

Ackerman, Stephen J., and Judith Levine Willis, ''Pet Cuisine; Feeding Galloping Gourmets,'' *FDA Consumer,* March 1991, p. 28.

''Bullish Outlook for Animal Health and Nutrition Market?'' *European Chemical News,* March 23, p. 29.

Garry, Michael, ''Scratching out a Niche,'' *Progressive Grocer,* November, 1992, p. 89.

Klepacki, Laura, ''Animal Magnetism: Supermarkets Are Using Specialty Products and Deals to Win Back Pet Food Sales From the Competition,'' *Supermarket News,* September 21, 1992, p. 17.

Larson, Melissa, ''New Packages Herald Year of the Cat,'' *Packaging,* April 1989, p. 8.

McKay, Betsy, ''How to Sell Pet Food in Russia,'' *Advertising Age,* May 17, 1993.

Otto, Alison, ''It's Raining Cat and Dog Food,'' *Prepared Foods,* April 1989, p. 40.

Schifrin, Matthew, ''Mom's Cooking Was Never Like This,'' *Forbes,* August 19, 1991, p. 50.

Toor, Mat, ''Pedigree Chums Bounds to the Top as Whiskas Fails to Land on Its Feet,'' *Marketing,* July 25, 1991, p. 15.

World's Greatest Brands, New York: John Wiley & Sons, 1992, p. 48.

—Evelyn Dorman

WINSTON®

Winston is one of the few brands to enter the 1990s with a respectable market share after nearly forty years in a highly competitive market that is saturated, shrinking, and populated by more than 175 competitors. Unlike brands that are marketed for their image, Winston has consistently claimed only to be a full-flavor filtered cigarette. As a result, it is favored neither by sophisticates, fashionable women, or people who are trying to quit. But even among its core constituency, the blue-collar average Joe, Winston is locked in a battle for survival against Marlboro and perhaps against changing times.

Brand Origins

In 1951, Edward A. Darr, vice-president of sales for R. J. Reynolds, returned from a vacation in Switzerland with a startling observation: nearly half the cigarettes sold in that country were filtered brands. At the time, the few filtered brands for sale in the United States were bland imitations of "straight," or non-filtered, brands. Filtered cigarettes were purchased mostly by women, who did not smoke as much as men and who favored a lighter brand. But Switzerland, respected for its high standard of living and sophisticated lifestyles, indicated to Darr that a market was emerging for a significant variation on an established product. Until that time, all brands of cigarettes were virtually the same size and were differentiated only by the blends of tobacco they contained.

The following year, Darr was promoted to president of R. J. Reynolds. Under his direction, the company's research department began searching for a proper blend of tobaccos for a filtered brand that might appeal to the mass market. More than 250 combinations were tested when, after two years, someone tried blend number 736 and cried, "This is it!" The brand was named Winston, after the city in which the company was headquartered.

Early Marketing Strategy

True tobacco aficionados disliked filters because they masked the character of the tobaccos and took away their strength. Reynolds manufactured the number one brand in the nation: Camel, a straight brand blended with rich foreign and domestic tobaccos. Conscious of the gamble it was taking by rolling out a filtered brand, Reynolds made a conscious effort to distance Winston from its popular flagship cigarette.

The Winston filter, pressed from a cotton-like mixture of fibers, was wrapped in a printed beige cylinder that was intended to look like a cork. The first filtered brands, introduced over a decade earlier, initially incorporated corks as filters. The cork tip became a signature of filtered brands. Even after these brands switched to pressed fiber, manufacturers continued to print the image of a cork on the filter wrapping. Wishing to clearly identify Winston as a filtered brand, and to differentiate it from Camel, Reynolds gave its new cigarette this printed filter.

To further ensure that the public properly understood the relationship between Camel and Winston, Reynolds introduced the new brand to the public with the line, "Made by the makers of Camels." Demographically, the brand caught on with a wide variety of smokers, including women, laborers, and professionals. Soon, demand outstripped production capacity.

The production bottleneck was made worse by a dockyard strike that prevented the shipment of the special British-made devices that assembled the filters. Unable to unload the machines in New York, the ship returned to Europe, where ten were sent to Reynolds by air. Still unable to meet demand, Reynolds took delivery of an additional 114 German assemblers as quickly as they could be manufactured. At one point, the machines were turning out Winstons in the United States only four days after leaving Germany.

In the nine months of its first year, Winston sold 7.5 billion units. In 1955, sales climbed to 22.2 billion, and to 31 billion the following year. Winston set a record for new brand growth and became the nation's number one selling filter cigarette only a year after it was introduced.

Packaging

The Winston package is credited for boosting popularity of the brand. Originally designed as a gray package with red lettering, it was made over at the last minute by Royal Dadmun, a manufacturing design specialist with no previous experience in cigarette packaging. The new design took a much bolder approach, using red packaging with bright red letters on a white band across the center of the pack.

While the basic design has remained unchanged, two variations later were made in the packaging of Winston. Crush-proof boxes,

AT A GLANCE

Winston brand of cigarettes introduced in 1954 by R. J. Reynolds Tobacco Company, now a subsidiary of RJR Nabisco, Inc.

Performance: *Market share*—6.8% (second-largest selling American brand).

Major competitor: Philip Morris's Marlboro.

Advertising: *Agency*—FCB/Leber Katz Partners, New York, NY, 1989–. *Major campaign*—"Winston Tastes Good Like a Cigarette Should."

Addresses: *Parent company*—R. J. Reynolds Tobacco Company, 401 North Main Street, Winston-Salem, NC, 27102; phone: (919) 741-5000; fax: (919) 741-7674. *Ultimate parent company*—RJR Nabisco, Inc., 1301 Avenue of the Americas, New York, NY, 10019; phone: (212) 258-5600.

long a feature of arch-competitor Marlboro, were introduced in 1967. In 1992 Winston introduced FlavorSeal packaging, an airtight foil cover that replaced the traditional cellophane wrapper and promised to better maintain the freshness of its contents.

Advertising

The William Esty advertising agency created the famous tag line "Winston tastes good like a cigarette should" for the brand introduction in March 1954. Repeated relentlessly in print and billboard advertising, and reinforced musically with a jingle for radio and television, the slogan remains familiar to many even 20 years after it was discontinued. Grammarians, however, objected to the use of the word "like" as a conjunction, and petitioned the company to change the tag line to "Winston tastes good as a cigarette should." The matter was debated in newspapers and on television and radio talk shows, providing the brand with invaluable publicity.

In one notorious incident, the jingle was discussed by a panel on the television show *The Last Word*. After more than 20 minutes of heated discussion, the noted author and critic John Mason Brown declared that the slogan caused him physical pain. Brown then retrieved a pack of Winstons from his pocket, lit a cigarette on camera and added—before an audience of millions—"But I think the cigarette is great."

Shortly afterward, a group of teachers entered the fray. Eager to placate their concerns, and faced with the potentially explosive danger of gaining a reputation for undermining the cause of education, Reynolds was forced to act. Rather than change the slogan, Reynolds simply added a new tag line to the slogan, "What do you want? Good grammar or good taste?" This good humored response from the company effectively put the debate to rest. It did, after all, succeed in educating the American public on the proper use of conjunctions—a result that was not lost on the nation's educators.

After the voluntary ban on broadcast advertising for cigarettes took effect in 1971, Reynolds dropped the popular slogan. Esty created two new tag lines for the brand, "Winston and Me" and "How Good It Is." Dancer Fitzgerald Sample took the account in 1974, providing such lines as "If it wasn't for Winston, I wouldn't smoke." Esty regained the account in 1979 with "Big Red" and "America's Best," but was replaced again in 1985 by McCann-Erickson, which introduced the "Men of America" and "Real

Taste, Real People" slogans. In 1989, these were followed by "Winning Taste," drawing upon Winston's long-standing sponsorship of NASCAR automobile racing and other sporting events.

Low-Tar Extensions

Reynolds has never promoted Winston with any kind of health claim. When low-tar versions—Winston Lights and Winston Ultra Lights—were introduced in 1974 and 1980 respectively, these cigarettes were promoted only as full flavor low-tar brands. They did, however, find favor with regular Winston smokers who may have felt concerned about the effects of tar and nicotine on their health. The low-tar extensions of the brand also appeal to those who smoke only occasionally or who, faced only with full strength brands, would not smoke at all.

The package emblems on these brands were based on the original Winston package, but incorporated different colors. Winston Lights were wrapped in a gold package, and Ultra Lights appeared in a white package, both with red lettering. In addition, the light brands replaced the beige faux cork filter of the regular Winston brand with a plain white filter. This was intended to reinforce consumers' perception that the brands are, in fact, lower in tar and nicotine.

International Development

In the United States, sales of cigarettes have stagnated. As a result, cigarette manufacturers have turned to export markets, which have much greater sales growth potential. Many foreign governments, however, are opposed to increases in smoking by their people, citing the possible health risks. These governments also fear the loss of valuable foreign exchange to a consumer product. Despite this, export sales of Winston continue to grow measurably, although not as significantly as Marlboro, whose popularity is based on the uniquely popular American symbol of the cowboy.

Brand Development

As a result of Winston's strong growth, and the surprising popularity of a new menthol brand called Salem (also named for Reynolds' home town), the company constructed a massive new production facility, called the Whitaker Park plant, in 1961. Sales of Winston continued to grow, but not as fast as Philip Morris' Marlboro. Originally a "lady's" brand, reintroduced as a cigarette for men in the mid 1950s, Marlboro benefited greatly from an unrelenting advertising campaign that relied heavily on frontier cowboy images. Similarly packaged, Marlboro contained a slightly different blend that proved more successful than Winston in winning over smokers of straight brands.

In 1974, Reynolds began spending heavily on promotion of Winston in an attempt to maintain its nine-year record as the nation's number one selling cigarette. But Philip Morris, eager to steal the mantle from Winston, matched the effort. The following year, Marlboro surpassed Winston in sales, permanently relegating Reynolds' brand to the number two spot. The company experimented a great deal with extensions of the Winston brand. Versions of Winston were marketed in 80-, 85-, and 100-millimeter lengths, in boxes and soft packs, in light variations, and, briefly, as a menthol brand.

Performance Appraisal

Winston is an example of a consistently high-quality product that is losing market share due to changes in the market. Winston is favored most loyally by older, more discerning smokers who are eventually replaced in the market by younger smokers, who are more heavily influenced by the image-heavy advertising of other brands. By the late 1980s, after years of declining sales, Winston's market share had fallen to 10 percent.

Future Predictions

In 1992 Reynolds introduced another variation of Winston, a premium brand called Winston Select. Ostensibly for tobacco connoisseurs, the new brand was wrapped in a solid red Flavor-Seal package and adorned with gold lettering and the highly American symbol of an eagle. Winston Select borrows the established reputation of quality enjoyed by the original brand. It remains to be seen, however, whether the regular Winston will be perceived as a relatively lower quality brand as a result.

Winston remains the number two selling cigarette in the United States, outselling more than 175 other brands. The Winston name is highly recognized and continues to carry considerable value. With continued promotion, declining sales are likely to stabilize as a fairly static number of consumers establish their loyalty to the brand.

Further Reading:

Cleary, David Powers, *Great American Brands,* New York: Fairchild Publications, 1981, p. 46.

Dagnoli, Judann, and Gary Levin, "Reynolds to Get Lean, Mean," *Advertising Age,* July 31, 1989.

Furst, Sydney, *The Strategy of Change for Business Success,* New York: Clarkson Potter, 1969.

Miller, Barry, *History of Winston Cigarettes,* unpublished company document, 1992.

O'Connor, John J., "Winston Spending Big to Keep No. 1 Position," *Advertising Age,* May 29, 1974.

Tilley, Nannie M., *The R. J. Reynolds Tobacco Company,* Chapel Hill: University of North Carolina Press, 1985.

—John Simley

WISE®

If longevity in the marketplace is any indicator of success, there is more to Wise Potato Chips than meets the eye. Having survived for more than 70 years in what has become a fiercely competitive snack food market, Wise ranks as Borden, Inc.'s oldest and largest snack food unit. What sets Wise apart from other chip manufacturers is the chip's distinctive quality. This unique difference arises from a special proprietary cooking method that bypasses the more conventional blanching process utilized by most chip producers. The result is that much of the "natural potato-chip flavor" is retained. This special process, coupled with the fact that no artificial additives or preservatives are used, explains why the appearance and taste of Wise Chips differs from that of their competitors.

Borden, Inc., Wise's parent company, has consistently pursued a regional brand marketing strategy for Wise, which is notable for its trademark array of two-tone teal color schemes and owl eye logo. Wise brand potato chips are available in most of the eastern region of the United States, stretching from Maine to Florida east of the Appalachians.

Potatoes used for producing Wise chips are of a special variety, carefully selected and then harvested to ensure their high quality chipping characteristics. Wise Foods contracts with potato growers up and down the Atlantic coast, as well as suppliers in Ohio, Michigan, and North Dakota. In early spring potatoes arrive from Florida. As the growing season permits, potatoes arrive from more northern climates, moving through the Carolinas and reaching as far north as Maine. The potatoes enter the plants by truck or rail and are then quality inspected and test-fried. At this juncture they either go into storage or curing facilities or enter the production process. Upwards of 300 million pounds of potatoes are annually processed.

Wise has pioneered several product and packaging innovations. In the early 1930s it first introduced cellophane as a food-packaging material. It was also the first snack food company to introduce a continuous processing method while other companies still used the batch production method.

Brand History

The Wise Potato Chip brand was created in 1921, under circumstances that were a combination of accident, entrepreneurial perseverance, good luck, and down-home common sense. The chip's creator, Earl V. Wise, who operated a small fruit and vegetable store in Berwick, Pennsylvania, found himself with an unanticipated surplus of potatoes. Fearing for the loss of his investment, Earl carted several bushels of potatoes home. Inspired by a homemade potato chip recipe of his mother's, Earl hand peeled and then sliced the potatoes on an "old time" cabbage cutter. Using his mother's coal-fired stove, Earl experimented with several different cooking oils until he produced what he hoped would be a marketable product. He packaged the chips in characterless brown paper bags and began to sell them from his store.

The chips were an instant success with his customers. Not long after, area grocers noticed the chips' popularity and began to carry Earl's product. Noted for being one of the first processed foods offered for sale in a grocery outlet, Earl's chips became so popular they soon outgrew the production facility he had established in his mother's kitchen. To meet the growing demand, Earl remodeled a garage and expanded his base of operation.

A major expansion occurred in 1925 with the construction of a new facility in Berwick. Throughout the 1930s and early 1940s, the buoyant demand for Wise Chips encouraged the plant's continued expansion to dimensions that eventually exceeded 40,000 square feet. In 1944 a fire severely damaged this facility; in 1946 a new plant opened that was more than triple the size of the destroyed facility. Additional expansions over the years have made the Berwick-based plant one of the largest potato-chip-producing facilities in the United States today. Company documents published in the early 1990s referred to the facility as having achieved the efficiency status of a "hyper-plant." In addition to this facility, Wise operates a snack food plant in Spartanburg, South Carolina, and a pretzel plant in Denver, Pennsylvania.

The Wise Potato Chip Company was purchased by Borden, Inc., in October 1964. It was renamed Wise Foods in 1969, a change that would eventually reflect Wise's foray into the production and marketing of new flavors of potato chips and other snack food-related items. Several years later the Borden affiliate, Old London Foods, was merged with Wise Foods, until Borden's divestiture of the Old London Foods unit in 1986.

According to Borden, Inc.'s, *1992 Annual Report,* Wise Foods plays a leading role within its snack food group despite its regional brand marketing status. Snack food sales industrywide exceeded $10 billion in 1991. As reported by Michael McCarthy in *Adweek,* Borden controls an estimated eight percent of market share and ranks as the number two player within the industry. Its chief rival, Frito-Lay, has an estimated 35 percent share of the market, while the number three player, Eagle Snacks, registered an estimated 6 percent market share.

Early Marketing Strategy

Earl V. Wise first marketed his chips in ordinary brown paper bags. His rise to success in the potato chip industry was matched by a parallel effort to market a packaged product designed with visual appeal. If properly done, Earl reasoned that his customers would be struck with a lasting impression that would inspire a sense of brand name recognition. In the early 1930s, Wise became a packaging pioneer in processed foods when he began to market his chips wrapped in cellophane bags. Around this same period the advertising firm of Lynn-Fieldhouse in Wilkes-Barre, Pennsylvania, first introduced "Peppy the owl" as the brand's logo mainstay. At that time, a circular framed inset containing a head-to-claw rendition of Peppy graced the upper portion of the cellophane-packaged chips. Peppy stares out at the consumer wide-eyed, with serious intent, vigilantly motionless, erect with both claws firmly secured to the branch on which he is perched. Apparently, Peppy's presence was meant to convey a sense of assurance to the consumer in the wisdom of their choice and impart a sense of confidence in the quality of the packaged contents.

Since the time the cellophane wrap packaged chips were first introduced, Wise has switched to a packaging process that utilizes the lamination of numerous packaging films. Inner layers preserve the product, while the outer lawyer allows printing that conveys a colorfully modest yet strikingly sparkling effect.

Throughout its history, Wise Foods has followed a strategy that prioritizes the development of its distribution system over that of consumer brand advertising. Most Wise products leave their production sites within 24 hours to ensure their freshness. Wise's own tractor-trailer fleet, augmented by more than 100 leased trucks during the peak season, delivers potato chip shipments to over 80 independent wholesalers that specialize in snack food products. The size of these distribution outlets varies from "one-truck master distributors" to a huge operation in the metropolitan New York area that comprises almost 300 routes.

The extent of retail accounts ranges across chain and independent supermarkets to neighborhood stores and delicatessens, work place lunchrooms, video rental stores, and quick-stop gas stations.

Institutional venues include schools, chain and independently owned restaurants, and hospitals.

Without question, the Wise Food distribution network has come a long way from the days when Earl Wise used to peddle his specially designed bicycle from store to store to deliver, sell, and promote the product first conceived on his mother's coal fired stove.

Brand Development

In step with snack food industry trends, the potato chip segment has undergone considerable product diversification. Various new flavors appear constantly; some exhibit staying power, while others vanish almost as quickly as they are introduced. The size, shape, texture, and content mix of these different flavors, their other qualities in the realm of nutrition and taste aside, also appear to be factors that influence consumer choice.

To stay current with these trends, Wise distributes a product line in the 1990s that most consumers within its regional market easily recognize. Besides a standard chip, marketed as the "Natural Flavor" potato chip, Wise's product line also features onion and garlic, barbecue, salt and vinegar, and lightly salted flavored chips. Wise's Ridgies brand product line features a standard rippled chip, called "Regular," along with cheddar and sour cream, onion and sour cream, and mesquite-style barbecue flavored chips.

The dizzying speed with which new potato chip flavors are introduced in the 1990s is indicative of a potato chip industry that seems caught up in the throes of constant change. Adding fuel to this fire is a fickle public that seems to desire more health-related snacks, yet at the same time shows no intention of abandoning its taste for potato chips. If Wise is to successfully navigate these forces, the industry trend toward continued change and potato chip brand diversification can be expected to influence the development of Wise's product line.

Logo Changes Over Time

Since first being introduced as the Wise chips logo symbol in the 1930s, Peppy the owl and the success of Wise chips seem synonymous. However, the logo rendition of Peppy in the 1990s bears little resemblance to its 1930s image. Sandwiched between these two contrasting logo changes was a major logo overhaul undertaken in the early 1950s. Gone was Peppy's stoically calm and motionless posture and in its place whisked a more animated figure. With the "Wise Potato Chips" brand stamped conspicuously on its breastplate, Peppy is cast as a jovial owl in motion, stepping confidently upward with wings unfolded. A posture no longer vigilant but celebratory and carefree, its facial appearance and body movements were redrawn to suggest a more human than animal-like appearance.

In 1967 the Peppy logo was once again dramatically altered and reduced to a single owl's eye that dots the "i" in Wise. Focused on the consumer, its penetrating glance conveys an empathetically stern wisdom. Around 1980, Wise initiated an ad campaign that featured an elderly, fun-looking, bespectacled professor Peppy who lectured prospective customers to "Get Wise!" and urged them to "Make the Wise choice!" In recent times, however, observers have called into question Peppy's continued presence in any form. In 1992, as reported in *Adweek's Marketing Week*, a market research survey conducted by the New York-based design firm of Gerstman & Meyers revealed that "the Wise name actually had more recognition than the logo.'' Serious thought was given to dispensing with the logo altogether. Nevertheless, out of deference to the brand's tradition and the memory of Earl Wise, the logo was retained.

Packaged snack foods in the early 1990s have tended to feature hot, bright neon color hues and schemes. In early 1992, Wise repackaged its entire potato chip line in an effort to strengthen its second place market share. In a departure from this trend, however, Wise opted for a relatively sedate teal packaging design to set it apart from its competitors. All of Wise's different chip types are packaged and identifiable by their flavor-specific color scheme. At the same time they all share an easily recognized solid band of yellow that cuts across the midsection of their package, on top of which the chips' different flavors are identified to the consumer.

Future Trends

The snack food industry during the 1990s has undergone a protracted period of intense competition. The Snack Food Association reported in the *Progressive Grocer* that the twin effects of price cutting wars and falling profit margins have exacted a toll on all major players. An aggressive scramble has ensued as industry giants like Frito-Lay Inc., Borden, Eagle Snacks Inc., and Keebler Co. initiated new marketing strategies and introduced new product lines and advertising campaigns meant to increase their market share.

Potato chips and tortilla chips, the principal products that have traditionally dominated the salty-snack food industry, find a stiff challenge has arisen from pretzel sales, which have increased approximately 10 percent during the early 1990s. The *Progressive Grocer* attributes this growth in consumption to the pretzel product's low-fat content, an appealing benefit that reflects a shift in preferences by more health-conscious consumers away from fatty foods. Because they are fried in oil rather than baked like pretzels, chips understandably face an uphill battle when it comes to competing with healthier snack substitutes.

The *Progressive Grocer* also reported that many in the industry predict that Multi-grain chips, a baked health snack made from wheat, rice, corn, and other grains, will continue to be the rising snack food growth star for the 1990s. In response to this, Fara Warner has noted in *Adweek's Marketing Week* that Borden has begun to market ''Graingers,'' a multi-grain chip.

In the summer of 1993, Borden broke from its traditional emphasis on regional brands and began a pilot program in Michigan marketing potato chips and other snacks under the company's namesake. To promote the success of the chips, television and print advertising campaigns were launched to coincide with coupons and a sampling campaign. The Borden chip is formulated differently than the company's regional brands. It was made to be marketed alongside Borden's regional brands and to replace some of the company's smallest volume regional brands. In the May 24, 1993, issue of *Brandweek,* Betsy Spethmann reports that Peter J. Cline, Borden's Group Vice President, North American Snacks, says ''it would be silly to abandon our strong regional brands just because we have a national strategy.'' In Spring 1993 Borden began a radio advertising campaign for Wise and its other regional brands.

Further Reading:

Borden, Inc., Annual Reports, Columbus, OH: Borden, Inc., 1986-1992.

''Borden's Wise Choice,'' *Adweek's Marketing Week,* June 15, 1992, p. 30.

Morgan, Hal, *Symbols of America,* New York: Penguin, 1986, p. 141.

McCarthy, Michael, ''No.2 Borden Launches Snack Foods Attack,'' *Adweek,* January 6, 1992, p. 5.

Shapiro, Eben, ''Crisper Chips, Fresh Slogans,'' *New York Times,* May 8, 1992, sec. D, p. 16.

''Snacks,'' *Progressive Grocer,* July 1992, pp. 66-68.

Warner, Fara, ''Borden Salts Its Snacks as Profits Plunge,'' *Adweek's Marketing Week,* May 18, 1992, p. 9.

Zbytniewski, Jo-Ann, ''A Snack Food Free-For-All,'' *Progressive Grocer,* September, 1992, pp. 121-22.

—Daniel E. King

WONDER® BREAD

The Wonder brand of bread, in its traditional bright polka-dot packaging, has been the leading white bread in America for over 50 years. Wonder bread's glossy wrapping has remained virtually unchanged since 1925, so that an eye-catching design that was once ahead of its time now has the appeal of an old standard. The bread itself, except for the addition of supplemental nutrients in the 1940s, remains much the same today as in its early years: a soft, square loaf with a smooth, uniform texture and striking whiteness. Though consumer interest veered away from white bread beginning in the 1970s, Wonder has remained a best-selling brand. It is produced by the Continental Baking Company, which also makes another classic American bakery product, Hostess Twinkies. And though Wonder seems the quintessential white bread, it also comes in rye and whole wheat varieties, an Italian loaf, and a low-calorie version called Wonder Light.

Brand Origins

Commercial bread baking was not big business in America until the early years of the twentieth century, when technological innovations opened a whole new era. Until World War I, most bread was made at home or in small neighborhood bakeries. Because of the perishability of its ingredients, bread had to be made in small batches and sold immediately. Typically, commercial bread was wrapped in plain paper and tied with string at the time of purchase. But in 1914, a bread-wrapping machine was invented by Henri Sevigné. With this machine, bread could be wrapped and sealed in waxed paper soon after baking, and the product would keep fresh for 48 hours. And with the advent of motorized delivery vehicles, far more bread could be made and distributed than had been possible with slow, horse-drawn trucks. So the opportunity was there for a large wholesale bakery to produce a bread that could be delivered fresh over a wide area, stay fresh for two days, and of course, bear a shiny brand logo on the wrapper.

The Taggart Baking Company of Indianapolis had great success just after World War I with a one-pound wrapped loaf called Mary Maid. An intensive ad campaign fixed Mary in the minds of Indianapolis bread consumers, and the brand was so popular that Taggart executives were eager to introduce a new product, a jumbo one-and-a-half pound loaf. In 1921, Taggart Vice-President Elmer Cline was given the task of coming up with a design theme for the new loaf. While watching a balloon race over the Indianapolis Speedway, Cline was inspired with the name "Wonder." The bright colored balloons in the sky became the polka-dots that graced the new loaf's packaging.

The first promotion of Wonder bread featured Taggart's delivery trucks distributing helium balloons to children across Indianapolis. With the balloons, the children received a letter to their mothers, inviting them to try new Wonder bread. Wonder bread soon eclipsed all other brands in Indianapolis, including its sister Mary Maid.

In 1925, Taggart Baking Company was bought by a larger conglomerate, the Continental Baking Company. Wonder bread was then marketed as a national brand. Elmer Cline became a vice president and director at the new firm. By 1938, Wonder bread was the top-selling brand in the United States, and Continental had made it through the Great Depression without once going into the red.

Several men were responsible for the Continental Baking Company's early growth and success. One was William B. Ward, the first president of Continental and a remarkable entrepreneur. Ward was heir to the sprawling $30 million Ward Baking Company, but he had ambitions that took him beyond his family empire. He formed the United Bakeries Corp. in 1921, which in 1924 became Continental Baking. In Continental's first six months, the company bought up twenty smaller bakeries. In 1925, William Ward also gained control of General Bakery, and began to expand this company also. With Ward, Continental, and General, the businessman had control of the three biggest bakeries in the country. But in 1926, the Federal Trade Commission forced Mr. Ward to disband this bread monopoly, and he nominally severed his connections with Continental. Though he still had some behind-the-scenes influence over Continental's board of directors, others in the company were afraid of Ward's financial hijinx, and an executive revolt in 1927 left the company in the more conservative hands of M. Lee Marshall and Milton L. Livingston.

Early Marketing Strategy

Marshall and Livingston significantly reduced Continental's debt and streamlined its corporate structure. They also saw the wisdom of concentrating on making a standard, staple product that consumers all across the country had a need for. Wonder bread was that product. But because the bread market was relatively inflexible—consumers tended to buy a fixed amount of bread regardless of circumstances—the company needed intensive advertising in order to grab as much of that market for Wonder as possible. Therefore much of the credit for Wonder bread's early success went not to top executives Marshall and Livingston, but to vice president of sales George Gottfried and advertising manager Cedric Seaman.

Seaman made wide use of radio and newspaper advertising to promote Wonder bread. Many ads ran on radio shows directed toward children, such as "Renfrew of the Mounted" and "Uncle Neil." Ads directed toward housewives appeared during morning soap operas. Newspaper ads featured a movie star in a bathing suit, looking thin and glamorous. These ads implied that Wonder bread could make women thin, though the actual text stated only that Wonder gave you energy without making you gain weight while you dieted.

Besides marketing directly to the consumer, Continental aimed a campaign at grocers as well. Realizing that many customers asked only for "a loaf of white bread, please," leaving it up to the grocer which brand he handed over, Vice-President of Sales George Gottfried came up with an in-store Wonder promotion called the "1-2-3 test." A 1938 *Fortune* article noted that Continental hired girls ("preferably starry-eyed," according to the

AT A GLANCE

Wonder brand of bread first produced in 1921 in Indianapolis, IN, by Elmer Cline, vice-president of the Taggart Baking Company; became a national brand when Taggart was bought by the Continental Baking Company, 1925; Continental became ITT Continental Baking Company, 1968, after a merger with International Telephone & Telegraph Corp.; renamed Continental Baking Company, 1984, when it was bought by Ralston Purina.

Advertising: *Agency*—Tatham-Laird & Kudner, Chicago, IL, 1986—. *Major campaign*—"Just a little taste of America, Wonder bread."

Addresses: *Parent company*—Continental Baking Company, Checkerboard Square, St. Louis, MO, 63164; phone: (314) 982-2790; fax: (314) 982-2267. *Ultimate parent company*—Ralston Purina Company (address same as above); phone: (314) 982-1000; fax: (314) 982-4031.

instruction manual) to stand in grocery stores with a display of six slices of different white breads on a black tray. Customers were invited to "pick the best bread" by the 1-(look) 2-(feel) 3-(smell) test. The significance of the black tray was that any bread with large air holes in it would tend to look grayish against the dark background. Wonder's smooth, spongy texture gave it an advantage in the look and feel segments of the test. The smell step of the test could be skipped if the customer had already picked Wonder as the best bread, and 90 percent of those polled did pick Wonder. Though it is difficult to assess the impact of any particular ad campaign, Wonder bread sales rose steadily through the 1930s and 1940s. Later advertising continued these early successes with television advertising on such popular children's shows as *Howdy Doody.*

Pre-sliced bread was introduced in 1930. The only change in the bread's packaging came in 1935, with a slight alteration of the design. Graphic artist George Switzer reduced the size of the polka-dot balloons and removed the word "wonder" from them, to make a less cluttered design. In 1941, Continental added vitamins and minerals to Wonder bread, in line with a government-supported bread enrichment program. The nutritive value of Wonder bread became the product's biggest—and most controversial—selling point.

Nutritional Claims

In 1968, Continental Baking Company was acquired by International Telephone & Telegraph Corp. for $281 million, and was renamed ITT Continental Baking Co. The next year marked a change in consumer awareness when a White House Conference on Food, Nutrition, and Health convened. Shortly after, close government scrutiny began to plague Wonder bread, in the form of repeated false advertising charges brought by the Federal Trade Commission.

The charges against ITT Continental revolved around two main issues. One was that Wonder bread ads misled children. The other, broader issue concerned the right to advertise a so-called "parity" product such as enriched bread, which by law must conform to federal standards, as actually unique and better than other brands. Wonder advertising since the 1950s had heavily emphasized the nutritive properties of the bread. The FTC wanted

to know if Wonder was actually any *more* nutritious than its competitors. This kind of case was also brought against manufacturers of other "parity" products, such as baby food and cranberry juice.

In 1971, the FTC challenged one of Wonder's longest-running themes: "Helps build strong bodies twelve ways." According to *Business Week,* these ads claimed that children needed to eat Wonder bread during the " 'Wonder Years'—ages one through twelve—the years when your child grows to 90 percent of his adult height. How can you help? By serving nutritious Wonder Enriched Bread. Wonder helps build strong bodies twelve ways." This ad, with variations, had run on television since 1961. Along with the text, the ad showed a time-sequenced picture of a small child growing rapidly into a 12-year-old. Part of the FTC suit alleged that young children could interpret the time-sequenced growth image literally, and would believe that Wonder bread had fantastic properties. The suit also alleged that this ad made a deceptive claim regarding the nutritional value of the product.

ITT Continental responded to these charges in one way by bringing out a new ad campaign that emphasized only Wonder bread's squeezably soft freshness. Then the company was partially vindicated when in January 1973 FTC administrative judge Raymond J. Lynch recommended that the case against ITT Continental be dropped. Some surprising things arose from the judge's ruling. Relying on expert testimony, Judge Lynch found that even young children aged five to seven did not believe literally everything they saw on television. He also found that there was little data to suggest that children had any influence at all over what bread their parents bought for them. Judge Lynch also agreed with testimony that showed that Wonder's ads did little to convince adults that the bread was nutritious. According to *Advertising Age,* the judge wrote that only 5 percent of housewives perceived Wonder bread as standing out on nutrition, and only "a small and insignificant percentage of consumers exposed to Wonder bread tv commercials understood those commercials to make any claim" to extraordinary nutritional value. Another expert witness had testified that "95 percent of all advertising is a big waste of time anyway," and the judge seemed to concur.

In spite of Judge Lynch's recommendation that the FTC drop its suit against ITT Continental, the case was eventually reviewed by the full Federal Trade Commission at the end of 1973. Most of the complaint was finally dropped, but one charge of deceptive advertising was upheld. ITT Continental was ordered to stop its ads showing the time-sequenced growth of a child. Yet the case still dragged on, through appeals by consumer groups that sought to force the company to run corrective advertising. The FTC suit ended with neither a clear victory nor clear loss for either side, but one result was that Wonder bread gathered much publicity that was not exactly flattering.

A variety of other charges unrelated to advertising also dogged ITT Continental through the 1970s. In 1972, the *Wall Street Journal* reported that ITT Continental pleaded "no contest" to federal charges of conspiring with three other large bakeries to "fix, raise, maintain and stabilize" bread prices in the New York area. In 1974, the FTC charged the company with engaging in illegal pricing practices to monopolize markets for Wonder bread. The next year, the Supreme Court ruled against the bakery in an antitrust case that went back to 1962, and ITT Continental had to pay heavy fines. None of this was good news for the company.

Another ad became the subject of controversy in 1980. This television commercial showed children singing about Wonder bread while a mother said, "Nutrition that whole wheat can't beat." A consumer group petitioned the FTC to stop the ad, claiming that it was misleading and based on government statistics taken out of context. Rather than fight, ITT Continental dropped the commercial, while still defending the ad's claims. The issue of how a "parity" product could be advertised was never clearly delineated, but one result of these repeated claims against ITT Continental was that the company could not be careful enough in its ads for Wonder.

Brand Development

White bread sales declined overall in the 1970s, partly through consumer demands for whole wheat breads, which were perceived as healthy. Ads such as the one comparing Wonder's nutritional value to that of whole wheat were one way of fighting for a declining market share. Product innovations were another. In 1976, ITT Continental experimented with a new product, called Fresh Horizons, to compete in the health bread market. Fresh Horizons contained 400 percent more fiber than whole wheat bread, and its advertising suggested that the bread could be useful in the prevention of serious diseases because of this high fiber content. The Food and Drug Administration found these claims so extravagant that it threatened to classify the product as an untested medicine. The company immediately agreed to alter its advertising. Three years later, Fresh Horizons was in trouble again, this time for not declaring in its ads that the fiber source in this high-fiber bread was wood pulp.

Though a flood of new products was making the bread market ever more competitive, the safest thing ITT Continental seemed able to do was to play up kids' liking for the fresh, soft, good taste of Wonder. This ad, as quoted in a 1979 *Advertising Age*, stated, "If your child throws away the lunch you made today, send Wonder—kids eat it up! There are cheaper brands, but they aren't always this fresh and soft, the way kids like bread." But even this claim drew fire, this time from the National Advertising Review Board, for disparaging cheaper brands. The Review Board eventually backed off, but again, negative publicity had been drawn to Wonder. By the time ITT sold Continental Baking to Ralston Purina in 1984, it was the Hostess cake side of the baking company that seemed to make the deal attractive to the new owner. Continental's bread division was seen as increasingly threatened by stiff competition.

Under Ralston, Continental severed Wonder bread's 45-year connection with Ted Bates Advertising in New York, and moved the account to a Chicago firm, Tatham-Laird & Kudner. A big turnaround came in September 1986, when Continental introduced a new low-calorie Wonder product, called Wonder Light. Wonder Light had only a little more than half the calories of regular bread. It contained no cholesterol, came in wheat, white, Italian, and sourdough varieties, and contained fiber derived from corn and soybeans. By 1991, Wonder Light was the top-selling brand in the reduced calorie bread category, and represented about one-third of total white bread sales.

Other innovations introduced under the Wonder name included Wonder Bread Chippers in 1990, a crunchy bread snack item, and Wonder Stoneground 100 Percent Whole Wheat bread in 1991. A new WonderKids bread was also test marketed in 1991. This was a

white bread that contained, according to company sources, "the fiber and important nutrients of wheat." But Continental curtailed Wonder advertising, and in the 1990s the company was running no significant national media campaigns for Wonder bread.

Performance Appraisal

From its introduction in 1921, Wonder bread was an immediate hit. Consistently clever marketing and the swift growth of Continental Baking meant that sales of Wonder expanded easily for many years. In 1946, Continental's sales were $26.6 million; in 1967, sales had soared to $621 million. But new consumer health consciousness in the 1970s, combined with increased government regulation of advertising, led to declining markets for white bread. In the 1990s, though Continental's sales reached almost $2 billion, operating profits slumped. Ralston's 1991 annual report explained that they expected conditions in the baking industry to continue to be tough. While Continental remained the nation's largest wholesale baker, and Wonder bread America's leading brand, a highly competitive market cut into profits. As for the future, Ralston Purina's 1991 annual report claimed that growth opportunities for the bakery "will depend on the success of our efforts in new product development, continuous cost control programs, and more efficient bakery and distribution operations."

Further Reading:

Annual Report to Shareholders, St. Louis, MO: Ralston Purina Company, 1991.

Cohen, Stanley E., "Wonder Bread Decision Stalls FTC Drive for Corrective Ads," *Advertising Age,* January 1, 1973, p. 1.

"Continental Baking Focus Includes New Products and Cost Controls," *Milling and Baking News,* January 14, 1992, p. 37.

"Continental Hedges Bet with New Wonder Ads," *Advertising Age,* July 26, 1971, p. 3.

"FTC Rules Wonder Bread Ads Deceptive but Drops Other Charges against ITT Unit," *Wall Street Journal,* November 6, 1973, p. 7.

Gibson, Richard, "Ralston Purina Plans to Spin Off Big Baking Unit," *Wall Street Journal,* April 23, 1992, p. A4.

"Ralston Chief Sheds Little Light on Baking Unit Spinoff," *Wall Street Journal,* April 24, 1992, p. B3.

"How Big Does the FTC Want to Be?" *Fortune,* February 1972, p. 107.

"ITT Bakery Unit Gets FTC Order on Bread Product," *Wall Street Journal,* March 26, 1979, p. 13.

"I.T.T. Cancels Wonder Bread Ad after Protest by Consumer Group," *New York Times,* October 19, 1980, p. 55.

"ITT Continental Baking Is Backed by Examiner on Wonder Bread Ads," *Wall Street Journal,* December 29, 1972, p. 22.

"ITT, Continental Baking on Accord on Merger Plan," *Wall Street Journal,* May 20, 1968, p. 2.

McGrath, Molly Wade, *Top Sellers, U.S.A.,* New York: William Morrow and Company, Inc., 1983, pp. 130-131.

"Ruling by Supreme Court Stirs Antitrust Question," *New York Times,* February 20, 1975, p. 43.

"Washington's Diet for Food Companies," *Business Week,* March 20, 1971, p. 28.

"What a Free-standing Continental Means," *Milling and Baking News,* June 2, 1992, p. 7.

"Why ITT Is Healthier without Continental Baking," *Business Week,* September 17, 1984, p. 43.

"Wonder Bread," St. Louis, Missouri: Continental Baking Company.

"Wonder Bread and Circuses," *Fortune,* July 1938, p. 66.

"Wonder, F-310 Cases Sent to FTC Judges," *Advertising Age,* October 2, 1972, p. 34.

—*A. Woodward*

WRIGLEY'S®

The name Wrigley has become virtually synonymous with chewing gum. Through its main brands, Doublemint, Spearmint, and Juicy Fruit, and their extensions, the Wm. Wrigley Jr. Company controls nearly half of the U.S. market for chewing gum. Originally given away as a premium for other products, the brand identities were strictly managed. Founder William Wrigley Jr. instilled as the corporate mantra, "We are a five-cent business, and nobody in this company can ever afford to forget it." As such, the company resisted price increases for nearly 80 years, maintained a narrow brand line, and made product quality its defining characteristic. The company's dedication to quality was extended to the images it created in advertising and promotion. Wrigley print ads featured almost no written copy, and its broadcast ads almost no narrative. The company's product was featured with shiney-clean kids with broad, perfect smiles. Wrigley considered the act of chewing gum to be socially sensitive issue, and did not feature gum chewing in its ads until the 1980s.

Brand Origins

William Wrigley Jr., who never punctuated his name with a comma, began his career in business during the 1870s as a delinquent teen-age firebrand in Philadelphia. After running away from home at age eleven, and being expelled from school every few weeks upon his return, his father leveled with him. "Your school life," the senior Wrigley said, "hasn't been a success." Wrigley's father sentenced the boy to work in his soap factory, where he was to stir massive soap vats with a paddle, ten hours a day, for $1.50 per week.

After a year at hard labor, Wrigley won a promotion to sales. Equipped with a horse drawn wagon, Wrigley plied the streets of many Eastern cities, hawking his father's soap. He learned to make friends, influence people, and subdue them with expert, honest charm.

At the age of 29, Wrigley moved to virgin territory: Chicago. The soap, however, remained unpopular with merchants. Priced at only five cents, it provided them with virtually no profit margin. Wrigley convinced his father to raise the price to ten cents a box and to include cheap umbrellas as a dealer premium. While all 65,000 umbrellas bled red dye with the first raindrop, they moved a lot of soap out the door and confirmed to Wrigley that premiums were effective sales aids.

Wrigley established his own company, selling soap as a wholesaler, providing free baking soda as a premium, and promoting it with a cookbook. In time, however, the baking soda grew more popular than the soap. By 1892 Wrigley left the soap business to concentrate on baking powder and began to search for a new premium.

He settled on chewing gum which, at that time, was made from spruce gum and paraffin. After some research, Wrigley asked his supplier, Zeno Manufacturing, to make gum with chicle, a coagulated latex extract from tropical evergreen trees that was used in the rubber industry. Again, demand for the premium outstripped demand for the product. In 1909 Wrigley consolidated his company with Zeno and created the Wm. Wrigley Jr. Company.

Wrigley introduced two brands: Vassar, a brand targeted at women, and Lotta Gum, a sugary licorice brand for the general market. Soon after, Wrigley introduced Juicy Fruit, a sweet gum that worked well with the chicle, and Wrigley's Spearmint. While the latter varieties grew in popularity, Vassar and Lotta Gum were phased out.

Juicy Fruit was eventually wrapped, five sticks to a package, in a deep yellow wrapper with red trim. This scheme suggested a lemon/orange flavor combination, although the extracts used to flavor the gum were derived from neither fruit. Wrigley's Spearmint, also five sticks to a package, appeared in a clean white wrapper. The package was intended to suggest to consumers freshness and purity. Both packaging schemes featured the trademarked Wrigley arrow, which carried the brand name. Wrigley's gum was an immediately recognizable brand, each a variation of the other, each able to benefit from the image of the other.

Advertising

From his soap peddling days, Wrigley was aware of the price sensitivity of his product. As a wholesaler, he recognized that his job was to help the retailer, without whom there could be no sales. Still beholden to the belief that "Everybody likes something extra, for nothing," Wrigley provided dealers with free coffee grinders, cash registers, scales, lamps, and a wide variety of other appliances and implements. To promote the brands specifically, Wrigley supplied retailers with display cases. Despite the premiums, Wrigley was unable to achieve the sales growth he desired. Wrigley's philosophy of advertising was, "Tell 'em quick and tell 'em

AT A GLANCE

Wrigley's brand of gum introduced in 1893 by William Wrigley Jr., who created the Wm. Wrigley Jr. Company in Chicago, IL.

Performance: *Market share*—47% (top share) of gum category. *Sales*—$993 million.

Major competitor: Warner-Lambert's brands of chewing gum.

Advertising: *Agency*—BBDO Chicago, Chicago, IL. *Major campaign*—"Pure Chewing Satisfaction"; Doublemint Twins; Wrigley's as an alternative to smoking.

Addresses: *Parent company*—Wm. Wrigley Jr. Company, 410 North Michigan Avenue, Chicago, IL 60611; phone: (312) 644-2121.

often.'' He launched two massive advertising campaigns, each costing in excess of $100,000 and leaving Wrigley broke.

The Panic of 1907, a financial crisis that caused a lingering economic recession, dried up virtually the entire promotional market. Advertising rates were deeply discounted. Still without money, Wrigley borrowed $250,000 and, within three days, purchased ad space that would otherwise have run him more than $1.5 million.

With his competition quiet, Wrigley piggybacked the ad campaign with a retailer promotion, sending them coupons for free boxes of Wrigley's Spearmint, redeemable from Wrigley distributors. Thus, retailers identified themselves to distributors—to whom Wrigley's advice was to always be pleasant, always be patient, always be on time, and never argue—who were given an opportunity to convince the retailer to stock Wrigley gum. The strategy proved highly successful. Within weeks, Wrigley had grown from a local product to a firmly established national brand. Sales increased from $170,000 to more than $3 million. By 1910, Wrigley's Spearmint was the largest-selling brand in the nation.

This wave of popularity enabled Wrigley to introduce a third major variety, Doublemint, in 1914. Packaged almost identically (the arrow on the package had two arrowheads), the Doublemint wrapper was green and was, almost without exception, promoted with twins or double images. Minor brands, including Sweet 16, Licorice, Pepsin, Blood Orange, Pineapple, Banana, and Lemon Cream, were phased out.

Subsequent promotions included large public billboard campaigns and an ambitious mailing of complimentary samples to, at the time, all 1.5 million telephone subscribers in the United States. As part of its sponsorship of the radio show The Lone Wolf, Wrigley's promoters created a fictitious Indian tribe in which more than 100,000 children were members. Before his death in 1932, Wrigley had acquired the Chicago Cubs baseball team and California's Catalina Island resort.

Under the stewardship of Wrigley's son, Philip K. Wrigley, the company entered an extremely difficult period during World War II. Quality ingredients were in short supply, restricting the volume of Doublemint, Juicy Fruit, and Wrigley's Spearmint that could be produced. The full production of these products was earmarked for the armed forces. Left only with inferior quality ingredients for the civilian market, Wrigley introduced Orbit. Admitting that the

brand did not meet the company's standards, Wrigley packaged Orbit under a label different from the regular brands.

By 1943 Wrigley was unable to keep its regular brands in production even for the military. For the next two years, Wrigley's only product was Orbit. During this time, the company ran ads showing an empty Wrigley's Spearmint wrapper, carrying the tagline "Remember this wrapper!" This maintained the identity of the regular brands and, in fact, built up demand for them. After the war, when the brands were reintroduced, sales exceeded prewar levels.

In later years the company, seeking a simple key message, dreamed up the slogan "pure chewing satisfaction" for its Wrigley's Spearmint brand. The "pure chewing satisfaction" line, along with such staples as the straight-as-an-arrow Doublemint twins, gave Wrigley a reputation for conservative advertising.

From its earliest days as a spruce bark extract, used by Native Americans, gum has been known to relax gum chewers by exercising facial and related muscles. The addition of flavors and the use of more durable ingredients have improved the ability of chewing gum to reduce tension and stress. In 1990 the company scored a brilliant advertising coup by positioning its Wrigley's Spearmint gum as an alternative to cigarettes in instances where smoking was not permitted. Voice-overs and captions explained, "When I can't smoke, I enjoy pure chewing satisfaction."

International Growth

Wrigley began exporting its brands to Canada in 1910, to Australia in 1915, and to Great Britain in 1927. A special brand also was developed, and called P.K., not for Philip Wrigley's initials, as many have claimed, but for the company's slogan, "Packed tight, Kept right."

In England, where a strong social prejudice against chewing gum existed, Wrigley decided the public had never been educated about the social mores of the practice. In 1962 the company ran a series of ads over the tagline "Certainly not," illustrating instances in which it was socially unacceptable to chew gum. Barristers, businessmen, and students were depicted in situations where gum chewing would be offensive. Reacting to the ads, citizens wrote the company asking when and where they could chew gum. The campaign was altered to depict acceptable gum chewing situations.

Brand Development

In 1921 William Wrigley Jr. was asked what single policy had been his most profitable. He responded, "Restraint in regard to immediate profits. That has not only been our most profitable policy, it has been pretty nearly our only profitable one." By holding constant the price of his products at five cents, Wrigley built strong dealer confidence in his product, and held his raw materials suppliers to more stable prices. This Wrigley could manage only because of his company's dominant position in the market. Still, as competitors increased prices with inflation, Wrigley's price held constant. This won his brands greater loyalty from his customers, and convinced others to try his product. Finally, in 1971, after considering numerous pricing and packaging schemes, Wrigley increased its 5-stick pack retail price from five to seven cents. Subsequent price increases inevitably followed.

By 1974, Wrigley faced steadily slower growth at the hands of the sugar-free brands Trident and Dentyne. In 1975, after much consternation, the company added a new brand called Freedent, which was touted for not sticking to dental work. A year later, Wrigley rolled out Big Red, a hot cinnamon brand. Both were packaged in variations of the original brands.

The company reintroduced the Orbit brand in 1977, but this time as a sugar-free gum. The brand did not keep pace, perhaps due to findings that its artificial sweetener, saccharine, might be linked to cancer, and was withdrawn. Seeking to rob market share from the bubble gum market, Wrigley introduced Hubba Bubba in 1979, and in 1984 added Extra, a sugar-free line.

Performance Appraisal

The conservative, time-tested ideals that made Wrigley brands number one in the United States have yet to prove outdated. The company has never yielded on quality or consistency, and continues to resist pricing its products as premium brands. While its reaction to upstart competitors has often been slow, these ideals have enabled the company to meet these challenges with great success.

Because public gum chewing still carries a slight social stigma, Wrigley, through its advertising agency BBDO Chicago, has kept presentation of its brands squeaky-clean. As a result, Wrigley brands tend to be considered rather old fashioned. While they have remained almost exactly the same as the day they were introduced, with the recent national penchant for all things nostalgic, Wrigley's image should stand the gum in good stead.

After 100 years, and now under the leadership of William Wrigley III, the company has made no attempt to diversify into widely different product lines. While it produces some confectionery extensions such as suckers and baseball cards through its Amurol subsidiary, it has not ventured into the food, consumer products, or chemicals industries where its major competitors, RJR Nabisco and Warner-Lambert, do business.

As a result, the company, like its gum, can be expected to remain essentially the same as it is today for quite some time: stable, predictable, and successful. As William Wrigley Jr. once said, "It's not that we have a closed mind on diversifying, it's just that you're better off doing what you know how to do best."

Further Reading:

Cleary, David Powers, *Great American Brands,* New York: Fairchild Publications, 1981, pp. 287-294.

Gershman, Michael, *Getting It Right the Second Time,* Reading: Addison Wesley, 1990, p. 163-165.

Morgan, Hal, *Symbols of America,* New York: Viking, 1986.

—John Simley

WYLER'S®

Since the 1930s, Wyler's powdered drink mixes let consumers make their own flavored drinks by simply adding water and stirring. After Wyler's 1935 "Kold Kup" drink joined the mix-it-yourself soft drink market that Kool-Aid had pioneered in 1928, the two brands remained contenders and market leaders for over forty years. During that time, Wyler's underwent fundamental changes, all the while adhering to the original concept of a less expensive, easy-to-store alternative to pre-mixed drinks. In the mid-1950s, Wyler's introduced Lemonade flavor mix with its low calorie variation. Even as carbonated soft drinks, particularly Coca-Cola, overran the beverage industry, Wyler's established a competitive niche for ready-to-mix powdered drinks. Emphasis was placed on advertising and marketing innovations, including pre-assembled retail display racks and product canisters, new sugar substitutes, and an emphasis on children's drinks over the next thirty years. Despite such efforts, Wyler's market share began to decline in the early 1980s, and in 1985 the brand experienced substantial losses, prompting Borden, its owner since 1961, to sell it to the Thomas J. Lipton Company the following year. Under Lipton, the brand was revitalized and diversified, entering the canned soda market in 1990 with lightly carbonated lemonade and tropical punch. Nevertheless, its 1992 share of less than 2.3 percent of the powdered-mix category paled in comparison to the 40 percent share of its 1976 heyday. In 1992, Lipton announced joint ventures with the Pepsi-Cola Company in order to energize sales. Once limited to presweetened, powdered beverages, Wyler's was catapulted into new alliances between leading companies that tried to mix the old mix into new business solutions.

Brand Origins

Wyler's drink mixes date back to 1931, when Swiss-born Silvain S. Wyler, Anna Wyler, and J. H. Hildbrandt started a business in the United States importing chicken and beef bouillon from Europe. The company, called Wyler Foods, hired its first food broker in 1932. After three years of continued growth and expansion, Wyler and Company incorporated in 1935. That same year, the company introduced a new concept in beverage refreshment: Wyler "Kold Kup," the prototype for its later line of drinks.

Early Marketing

Wyler's "Kold Kup" was the first powdered drink mix that was presweetened. But novelty alone did not account for active sales. The product's name referred to the well-established market for refreshing drink preparations, or "cups," which formerly required time and expertise to concoct. As early as the mid-nineteenth century, books described, in almost scientific exactness, various recipes for quenching thirst. In London of 1869, for example, William Tarrington published a book entitled *Cooling Cups and Dainty Drinks,* marketed as "a collection of recipes for 'cups' and other compounded drinks, and of general information on beverages of all kinds." Informed by that tradition, Wyler's "Kold Kup" grew in popularity until 1945, when production was discontinued due to wartime sugar shortages.

Following the war, however, production resumed along with growth, and in 1954 the company introduced lemonade flavor drink mix, which experienced an increase in popularity that would lead to its becoming the best-selling flavor in the 1970s, despite the availability by that time of a wide variety of other flavors. In 1956, a low calorie lemonade was added to the line.

Borden and Marketing Innovation

Marketing efforts increased substantially under the parentage of Borden, which acquired Wyler Foods in 1961. In 1973, the company supplemented product envelopes with canisters, which had plastic resealable lids and a free scoop that measured the recommended amount of drink mix to make one quart. These family-size containers of drink mix available in grape, lemonade, and orange flavors held large enough quantities of mix to allow the consumer fewer trips to the store and a savings of money when compared to traditional canned flavored beverages. Wyler's offered a 45-oz. container that made 15 quarts of drink, costing just over half the price of a 46-oz. can (less than 1-1/2 quarts) of the average prepared drink. That same year, a series of advertising campaigns were designed to promote the soft drink mix category from October through March, a season that had been neglected in favor of generally thirstier summer months. The selling concept was called "the Second Season." By the 1980s, efforts had paid off. A February 1983 article in *Supermarket News* noted that cold beverages still peaked in summer—with 30 percent of their volume generated from Memorial Day to Labor Day—but were not nearly as seasonal as in the past.

Borden also changed in-store merchandising, emphasizing pre-assembled displays that reduced retail labor and product handling costs. In 1969, the company offered only one size display which held 16 cases of soft packs; in 1971, it began supplying 24- and 48-case racks; and in 1972, the two available sizes held 60 and 120 cases. By 1976, the powdered drink market had risen to $450 million, divided between three primary brands: 40 percent each to Kool-Aid and Wyler's, and 10 percent to Pillsbury Company's Funny Face. Under Borden, Wyler's had become a market share leader.

Growing Competition

Between 1974 and 1977, sales of powdered soft drinks grew rapidly. Industry sources estimated that the presweetened market totaled $165 million in 1974, surged 98 percent to $327 million in 1975, increased to $370 million in 1976 and to $377 million in 1977. By 1977, the market stabilized, so that the annual growth rate had slowed to a more modest 13 to 15 percent, according to a *Business Week* article. Powdered drinks had stolen a sizable share of their market from canned and bottled soft drinks. But such growth had its down side, especially for Wyler's. The surge in demand for powdered soft drinks swelled the number of companies in the field and tightened competition. In 1976, RJR Foods, Inc., the R. J. Reynolds Industries subsidiary, introduced a powdered version of its canned Hawaiian Punch. By 1977, the company had spent $10 million for advertising, winning the $70 million share of the market in under a year. In an article for *Business Week*, Robert L. Remke, chairperson of RJR Foods, explained that "many people who abandoned soda pop when prices soared have stayed with the mixes even though soda prices have since settled." Coca-Cola, which lost some of its soda share to powdered drink mixes, responded by introducing a mix brand of its own, in 1977 announcing a six-flavor line of powdered versions of it's Hi-C fruit juice and a powdered lemonade mix to be sold under the Minute Maid label. By 1978, Wyler's market share had declined to about 14 percent, and it had lost its position as market leader alongside Kool-Aid.

Sweet Controversies

The sweetening agent in presweetened powdered drink mixes represented not only a key ingredient, but a key factor in overall marketing strategies. In the 1970s, an increase in the popularity of diet foods spawned a wide variety of sugar replacements in sweet-

ened foods of all kinds. Ironically, Wyler's lag in the sugar substitute market served it well in the early 1970s, when a ban on cyclamate—the most commonly used sugar substitute at the time—knocked all other brands off the shelf. Wyler's, which used only sugar, remained to gain an advantage that would help it dominate the market over the next four years. By the summer of 1983, however, Borden introduced a line of Wyler's Sugar-Free drink mixes, sweetened with aspartame, a substitute 200 times stronger than sugar, according to Betty Barrett, manager of Borden's division of communications in a 1983 *Supermarket News* article. Aspartame was produced by G. D. Searle & Co., which marketed it under the trade name NutraSweet and in packets under the Equal brand. "It's a real innovative sweetener, and the only one since cyclamate that sweetens with no aftertaste and 95 percent fewer calories than sugar," Garrett said. The low calorie Wyler's mix was introduced in four flavors and in packages of two different sizes: envelopes yielding two quarts each and boxes yielding eight quarts. The introduction was supported by free trial offers during the month of April, followed by a three-month promotional blitz in which 200 million coupons were distributed. These measures, accompanied by a heavy television advertising schedule, were designed to set Wyler's apart from the growing list of competing products sweetened by Searle's product, including Swiss Miss presweetened hot chocolate, Lipton's presweetened tea, and various foods.

In late June of 1983, when the Food and Drug Administration approved the use of aspartame in all soft drinks—in addition to powdered soft-drink mixes—the sweetener sparked bitter debate. First of all, Dr. Richard Wurtman, a scientist at the Massachusetts Institute of Technology, cited health concerns. Experiments with both humans and rats indicated that drinking aspartame-sweetened Kool-Aid with a carbohydrate-containing snack might have induced a change in brain chemicals, according to a July 1983 article in the *Washington Post*. But the findings were not alarming enough to prevent FDA approval. Furthermore, aspartame showed no carcinogenic tendencies in tests, and the cancer-warning labels that were mandatory for products containing saccharine would not be required for the new sweetener. Health concerns related to aspartame had little affect on Wyler's sales.

Wyler's other concerns centered around aspartame's sweetening stability and cost. The sweetener's shelf life, across various time and temperature gradients, caused worries that sodas might go bad if not properly shipped and stored. But these concerns caused little discussion in the powdered-drink sector, where the aspartame was not in solution and was, therefore, stable. Less stability, however, characterized price. While saccharin's wholesale price was $3 a pound in 1983, aspartame went for around $90 a pound. In addition, aspartame provided less sweetening power, so that 50 percent more product was required to equal the sweetening strength of saccharin. With time and appreciable marketing efforts, however, aspartame overcame these obstacles to become the sugar substitute of preference—for Wyler's and its competitors—by the 1990s.

Fruitless Controversies

In August of 1983, the Department of Agriculture announced new labeling restrictions requiring beverages to list their percentages of fruit. These rules, which became effective by July of 1984, also prohibited fruit or vegetable drinks containing no fruit or vegetables from identifying themselves as juices or from using the 'ade' suffix, as in lemonade. Only drinks containing at least ten percent fruit or vegetables would have access to those terms. In an August 8, 1983, United Press International release, Jerome Schildler, representing Borden, Inc., said the rules ''would have a severe adverse impact on several food products that have been widely sold nationwide for ten years.'' Schildler's examples of such products included Wyler's, Kool-Aid, Country Time, Lemon Tree, and Hawaiian Punch brands.

Brand Decline

By 1985, Wyler's market share had declined to 15 percent of presweetened powdered drink mixes, while Kool-Aid claimed 70 percent. Wyler's forecast looked bleak, and a headline in a 1986 *Advertising Age* article read, ''Borden Pumps up Consumer Products . . . Though it's not Wild about Wyler's.'' The article quoted Romeo Ventres, president-CEO of Borden, as considering the possibility of selling the brand if the company could not turn it around. In an attempt to do just that, the company consolidated production plants—discontinuing its Lite Line powdered drink mix—and expanded its children's segment with Wyler's Bugs Bunny & Pals. That mix, made with NutraSweet, was supported through a licensing agreement for Warner Brothers' Looney Tunes characters, via Licensing Corp. of America, as well as network television, print, and coupons from Doyle Dane Bernbach, New York. A year later, not only was the Bugs Bunny line discontinued, but Wyler's, still not revitalized under Borden, had been sold.

Wyler's and Lipton

On December 30, 1986, Borden announced an exchange of assets with Thomas J. Lipton, Inc., whereby a Lipton subsidiary would acquire the Wyler's powdered soft drink business from Borden in exchange for the Pennsylvania Dutch Noodle business. The exchange left Borden in first place among U.S. pasta producers and left Lipton with another brand to buttress its profile as an international beverage giant. The timing was ripe, as Lipton introduced a new line of fruit tea mixes in 1986, signifying an attempt to gain a foothold in powdered soft drinks. That year, Nestlé Foods and General Foods also nationally introduced fruit teas, combining iced tea and juice or fruit flavors. Despite an estimated $24 million in ad spending for all three brands, fruit teas accounted for only 10 to 12 percent of the $400 million iced tea market by 1987, according to a 1987 *Advertising Age* article. Though these figures fell below Lipton's expectations, it would make numerous other attempts at beverage innovation with the newly acquired Wyler's brand.

After acquiring Wyler's, Lipton tried to improve its market share by reformulating the taste, adding flavors, repackaging with new graphics, and initiating new marketing campaigns. In March of 1988, Lipton commissioned Rodale Press to publish *Kidsmart,* a children's magazine available through on-pack coupons from Wyler drinks and other Lipton brands. Subtitled, ''An After-School Food, Fun and Safety Guide for Parents,'' the publication was printed biannually for two years and carried four pages of Lipton advertising in each issue. In April of the same year, Lipton introduced Wyler's FruitSlush, a fruit juice ''slush'' stored on dry-grocery shelves, away from the packed supermarket freezers. The product was packaged in four-pack plastic cups resembling yogurt containers and was available in five flavors: cherry, fruit punch, grape, orange, and strawberry. Advertising focused on Saturday morning television, targeting children as the main consumers of the ''freeze & eat'' snack, as described on its packaging. The

product signaled a new direction—beyond presweetened powdered mixes—for Wyler's.

FruitSlush was just one of many moves that set Wyler's on a new course. In 1989, Lipton introduced Wyler's Big Squeeze Fruit Drinks, available in Fruit Punch, Orange, Grape, and Cherry flavors and made with 10 percent fruit juice. The drink was sold in 6-packs of 8-oz. plastic bottles, which were designed to be twisted open and squeezed to facilitate drinking from the bottle. By the summer of 1990, Wyler's had advanced into the soda market as well, with lightly carbonated, canned variations on Wyler's Lemonade and Wyler's Tropical Punch, competing respectively against Hawaiian Punch and Country Time Lemonade. And in 1991 Wyler's went pink, offering pink lemonade mixes in both sweetened and unsweetened varieties. That year also marked the hundredth birthday for the Thomas J. Lipton Co. The party fare included a centennial tea tin offer requiring the universal product codes from five Lipton products, including Wyler's drinks. Whether Lipton would continue to diversify the Wyler's brand or focus anew on its powdered soft drink business remained unclear.

Future Predictions

In a 1976 *Business Week* article, a Borden spokesperson distinguished between two types of brands, according to their benefits for the company: ''The pullers are the ones pulling the company forward. Draggers are holding the company back. So if we have a dragger, we tell the man in charge to make it a puller.'' At that time, Wyler's was a ''puller.'' Its share of the presweetened powdered drink market had risen from 7 percent in 1967 to over 23 percent in 1972 and 40 percent in 1976. By the late 1970s, however, the brand began to slide, so that by 1986, with a market share of less than 5 percent, it had become a ''dragger.''

By 1990, under Lipton, the brand held approximately 2.3 percent of the powdered mix category. Yet the ''puller/dragger'' distinction was not easy to determine, particularly because the brand's product line was in flux. Before its market success could be measured, a specific market would have to be assumed. Nevertheless, Lipton was still attempting to revitalize it, crossing product categories if necessary. In December of 1991, Lipton announced a joint venture with Pepsi-Cola Company to develop and market new tea-based beverages and to expand distribution of existing Lipton ready-to-drink products. In connection with the agreement, Pepsi-Cola International and Lipton's parent company, Unilever Corp., would explore international affiliations on a market-by-market basis, according to a December 31, 1991 *PR Newswire* report. Prospects for Wyler's remained unclear, but hopeful.

Further Reading:

Dagnoli, Judann, ''Borden Pumps up Consumer Products,'' *Advertising Age,* November 10, 1986, p. 4.

Dagnoli, J., ''Fruit Teas Fail to Juice Sales,'' *Advertising Age,* July 20, 1987, p. 25.

Dagnoli, J., ''Lipton to Push New FruitSlush,'' *Advertising Age,* March 14, 1988, p. 85.

Dougherty, Philip H., ''Rodale Prepare a Magazine for Lipton,'' *New York Times,* February 29, 1988.

Lazarus, George, ''2 Wyler Flavors Go Soft Drink Route,'' *Chicago Tribune,* August 3, 1990, p. C2.

''The Mix it Yourself Boom in Soft Drinks,'' *Business Week,* May 17, 1976, p. 58.

"Pepsi-Cola and Thomas J. Lipton Company for Strategic Alliance," *PR Newswire,* December 3, 1991.

Pfaff, Dennis, "If Life Gives You Lemons . . . ," *United Press International,* August 8, 1983.

Rowan, Tom, "Wyler, Solid No. 2 in Drink Mixes, Also Plans for Soup, Sauce Growth," *Advertising Age,* September 4, 1972, p. 44-5.

"Searle Nutrasweet Contract with Royal Crown," *PR Newswire,* August 8, 1983.

Sease, Douglas, "Coca-Cola Enters Expanding Market for Powdered Soft Drinks," *Wall Street Journal,* January 6, 1978, p. 5.

Sugarman, Carol, "Controversy Surrounds Sweetener; Aspartame Approval & The Soft Drink Industry," *Washington Post,* July 3, 1983, p. D1.

Terrington, William, *Cooling Cups and Dainty Drinks,* London: George Routledge & Sons, 1869.

Winters, Patricia, "Nestle, GF, Lipton All Introduce Fruit Teas," *Advertising Age,* May 26, 1986, p. 24.

"Wyler's Brings Innovation to Beverages," nonexclusive release, New York: Borden, Inc., August, 1984.

—*Kerstan Cohen*

YOPLAIT®

Yoplait yogurt is the second-best-selling yogurt in the United States. The brand originated in France with the Sodima company, and is sold in the United States through Yoplait USA. It was first marketed in America by a small Michigan dairy company, then was picked up by General Mills, Inc., in 1977. Yoplait has a distinctive creamy texture and unique tapered packaging that sets it apart from other brands. Unlike Dannon, the leading yogurt brand, which comes in 8-ounce cups with fruit on the bottom, the original Yoplait came in 6-ounce containers with the fruit smoothly mixed throughout. Yoplait has brought out other varieties of yogurt targeted to meet specific market needs or trends, such as Breakfast Style yogurt and frozen yogurt, and the original recipe itself has been reformulated since its 1977 debut. Besides this original style, Yoplait is available in Custard Style; a fat-free version; artificially sweetened Yoplait Light; a two-flavor blend called Parfait Style; and Yoplait Trix for kids, all in a variety of flavors.

First Marketing Attempt

Yoplait yogurt began in France in 1964, marketed by the Parisian dairy cooperative Sodima. Americans had not traditionally been big yogurt eaters, and even in the 1980s after yogurt's popularity had risen sharply, a consumer survey placed yogurt in the top three most disliked foods category, right behind liver and lima beans. But dieters and health food enthusiasts had fueled the yogurt market in the 1970s, and Dannon, the only nationally distributed brand, was growing rapidly. Bill Bennet, the owner of the Michigan Cottage Cheese Company in Otsego, Michigan, guessed that consumers in America might prefer a creamier, less tart French-style yogurt to the native product. He tried to develop his own French-style brand in the 1970s, then found that Sodima was looking for an American franchise for Yoplait. Bennet's company became the first licensed U.S. Yoplait distributor in 1974.

Bennet had several key ideas about how Yoplait should be marketed. The French product included stabilizers, as did the American leading brand Dannon. But Bennet removed all Yoplait's artificial ingredients so he could proclaim it "all natural." Dannon sold in 8-ounce cups, and Yoplait sold in Europe in 4-ounce containers. Bennet settled on 6 ounces. He kept the French packaging, which tapered in at the top, and he had the printing done in French on one side, English on the other. This gave Yoplait a unique silhouette and a European aura that set it apart from anything else in the U.S. market at that time. And since the yogurt was actually quite different from its American counterparts—creamier, richer, with fruit blended throughout—Bennet believed his product would be a great hit. Unfortunately, after two years of development, Bennet could not get his Yoplait to the public. Having taken out the yogurt's stabilizers but keeping the French packaging, which was made of pressed wax, Bennet was faced with a product that leaked on his warehouse shelves. As he pondered changing the packaging, the Michigan Cottage Cheese Company was bought out by cereal giant General Mills. General Mills acquired the Yoplait franchise rights and formed a subsidiary company called Yoplait USA. The new company kept most of Bennet's ideas, but changed the wax cup to plastic. General Mills brought out Yoplait in 1977, and the brand soon had sales of over $50 million.

Early Marketing Strategy

General Mills backed its introduction of Yoplait with Yoplait bicycle races and Yoplait hot air balloons. A national television ad campaign featured celebrities such as Loretta Swit and Jack Klugman tasting Yoplait and proclaiming "Yoplait est fantastique!" When Yoplait was introduced to the New York–Philadelphia market, more than 200,000 cups of free yogurt were given away at community events and at a 50 kilometer Yoplait Bike Challenge. Free samples and television ads where actors were shown enjoying yogurt were important aspects of yogurt marketing, since only a relatively small percentage of Americans had even tried yogurt. Though the yogurt market experienced double-digit growth in the 1980s, and had sales of nearly $1 billion by 1985, by that year only 30 percent of the of U.S. population ate yogurt. Yoplait tried to entice consumers by emphasizing its Frenchness. After "Yoplait est fantastique" came ad campaigns such as "Vive la difference" and "Let Yoplait teach you French." The "Vive la difference" campaign reminded consumers of Yoplait's origins in the French countryside. "Let Yoplait teach you French" used print ads that translated phrases related to a cowboy's and a sunbather's garments into French (e.g., "lunettes de soleil" for sunglasses). Television advertising showed people eating Yoplait and bursting into French. And in 1985 General Mills recruited a dozen Yoplait Mimes to add a French theatrical touch to Yoplait promotions at local festivals.

AT A GLANCE

Yoplait brand yogurt first marketed in France in 1964 by the Sodima dairy cooperative; brought to the U.S. market in 1974 by Bill Bennet's Michigan Cottage Cheese Company; Michigan Cottage Cheese Company and Yoplait franchise rights acquired by General Mills, Inc., in 1977; Yoplait USA formed as subsidiary of General Mills.

Performance: *Market share*—19% of yogurt category. *Sales*—$175 million.

Major competitor: BSN-Gervais Danone's Dannon.

Advertising: *Agency*—DDB Needham, Chicago, IL. *Major campaign*—Television ads of active women, with theme "Yoplait. Do it for you."

Addresses: *Parent company*—Yoplait USA, P.O. Box 1113, Minneapolis, MN 55440; phone: (612) 540-2311; fax: (612) 540-4925. *Ultimate parent company*—General Mills, Inc., One General Mills Boulevard, Minneapolis, MN 55426; phone: (612) 540-2311; fax: (612) 540-4925.

Yoplait's French theme created imitations. Dannon introduced a 6-ounce package called Melange in 1981, and the Johanna Farms Company came out with La Yogurt. These copycat products mixed fruit into the yogurt like Yoplait, and had a smoother, lighter texture than the conventional fruit-on-the-bottom style. Because Yoplait was richer and less acidic than other brands, when food writer Mimi Sheraton reviewed Yoplait and other so-called "Frenchy" yogurts for the *New York Times* in 1981, she concluded that "the less one likes yogurt, the more one will like Yoplait." More people were eating more Yoplait by the mid-1980s. Yoplait's market share grew to roughly 15 percent by 1986, second only to Dannon's 26 percent.

Market Conditions

Yoplait had become more successful than General Mills was prepared for. After Yoplait's introduction in 1977, General Mills found itself under pressure to get its two yogurt processing plants to produce enough Yoplait to meet burgeoning consumer demand. In 1979 Yoplait USA won a Gold Cup award from Sodima of France as the franchise with the greatest annual increase in sales. Yoplait USA took the Gold Cup in 1980 and 1981 as well. In fact, Yoplait soon outsold General Mills' flagship brand, Cheerios.

Nevertheless, competition in the rapidly expanding U.S. yogurt market was stiff. Yoplait had captured the number two spot behind Dannon, and ahead of Kraft's Light & Lively and Breyer's brands, which had an 8 percent combined market share in the mid-1980s. Two other leading national brands, Kellogg's Whitney's and Beatrice's Mountain High, each had a 2 percent market share nationally, but in some regional markets they claimed between 8 and 10 percent. More than 125 brands of yogurt were being sold across America, as yogurt moved out of the health food category and became a mainstream grocery item.

Yoplait spent heavily on advertising to keep the brand in the forefront. Its ad expenditures were more than double Dannon's in 1984, at close to $13.5 million, and led the industry again the next year at almost $16 million. As more people tried yogurt, it became more difficult to define the typical yogurt consumer. In the 1970s the yogurt-buyer had been a dieter who was particularly health-conscious. In the 1980s the typical yogurt consumer might be a child under twelve or a college-educated woman between the ages of 18 and 49. This was a much broader spectrum than before. Yoplait explored this market by bringing out new products to suit more specific consumer tastes.

Brand Development

The first departure from the original Yoplait recipe was Yoplait Custard Style, which General Mills introduced in 1981. Custard Style was thicker than original Yoplait, with a smooth, delicate texture. The next year, General Mills brought out a special Yoplait line targeted for consumers who ate their yogurt early in the day. Breakfast Style Yoplait combined the original yogurt with five new fruit flavors and a blend of wheat grains, raisins, walnuts, and fruit chunks. Breakfast Style Yoplait was the first of its kind, though Dannon soon brought out a similar product, its Hearty Nuts & Raisins.

Then Yoplait ventured onto Dannon's turf with a new product, Fruit on the Bottom. General Mills saw this as a step toward displacing Dannon from the top spot in the yogurt market. However, Fruit on the Bottom lasted only two years, being discontinued in 1986. A less acidic yogurt called Yoplait Extra Mild was also tried in 1986 and quickly discontinued.

Yoplait changed its packaging somewhat, starting with Fruit on the Bottom. Fruit on the Bottom sold in two-packs of two different flavors. A Snack-Pack of four four-ounce containers followed. These sold well, and when market research showed many consumers commonly bought two Snack-Packs as a time, Yoplait brought out an eight-pack in 1989. The original single six-ounce containers remained available.

Yoplait explored many different segments of the potential yogurt market, and manufactured Yoplait products for all kinds of tastes. Several new Yoplait recipes were marketed not as snacks, breakfast, or diet food but as indulgent desserts. Premium desserts were a hot growth area when YoCreme Yoplait came out in 1986. YoCreme was a rich, mousse-like yogurt made with real cream. It came in a six-ounce cup mounted on a pedestal leg. The names of its five flavors added to YoCreme's elegant appeal: Strawberries Romanoff, Cherries Jubilee, Amaretto Almond, Chocolate Bavarian, and Raspberries with Cream. The frozen yogurt market grew even faster than the premium dessert market, with sales surging 200 percent in 1990, and Yoplait introduced both a soft and a hard frozen yogurt. Yoplait Soft Frozen had the consistency of the popular soft-serve ice cream, but fewer calories: only 90 per three-ounce serving. Yoplait's hard-packed frozen yogurt followed, backed by $3.5 million in advertising. It was targeted to a broad audience, but particularly to upscale women. Two other Yoplait dessert products came out in the 1990s. Yoplait pudding, which debuted in 1991, was the first refrigerated pudding that contained live yogurt cultures. It was sold in single cups or in four-packs. The four-pack packaging targeted children by featuring a cartoon character from a popular children's book series called *Where's Waldo?* Television advertising used the theme, "We gave pudding a good name." General Mills introduced a variant of Yoplait pudding the next year, a three-layered product called Parfait Style. This was a low-fat yogurt with a vanilla middle layer, surrounded by a top and bottom of strawberry, peach, blueberry, or cherry. 40 percent of the refrigerated puddings already on the market came in layers, so Parfait Style was marketed as a low-fat alternative to these.

Yoplait's dessert yogurts blended consumer desires for a sweet treat on the one hand and for a healthful and dietetic product on the other. Several other Yoplait introductions gave more emphasis to yogurt's low-calorie appeal. Original Yoplait was reformulated in 1987 to be thicker and creamier, and at the same time, Yoplait 150 came out. 150 was a non-fat yogurt with only 150 calories per six-ounce serving. Unlike Original Yoplait, it had fruit on the bottom. It was the first non-fat yogurt of this style on the market. Both the new Original and Yoplait 150 were advertised by a campaign that emphasized the brand's over-all good taste. Several television and movie actresses sponsored the new products, giving their opinions why Yoplait tasted better than other brands. Next came Yoplait Light, which captured the largest market share of any yogurt introduction in the 1980s. Yoplait Light was made with the artificial sweetener aspartame, and was targeted for Yoplait's calorie-conscious customers. It came on the market in January, 1989, to catch the post-holiday diet season. The use of the artificial sweetener was a departure from Yoplait's original "all natural" tag, yet consumer response was enthusiastic. In the first three months of Yoplait Light's introduction, Yoplait's market share surged to a record high of 21.8 percent. Yoplait Fat-Free was another yogurt for diet-conscious consumers. General Mills introduced it in 1991, and within a year it had become the fastest-growing product in the Yoplait line.

Performance Appraisal

Yoplait established a strong presence in the American yogurt market soon after General Mills began distributing it in 1977, and the brand's sales increased as the market as a whole grew. By 1992 Yoplait had retail sales of $175 million, and its market share was 19 percent. But sales had become sluggish in the late 1980s. The yogurt market had experienced a slump, and General Mills had cut back its television advertising for Yoplait. The company had instead concentrated its advertising on trade promotions with supermarkets. This in turn had caused problems. During a special promotion, Yoplait's price would be deeply discounted, and to meet the surge in demand, the company had to increase its production volume quickly. And a good balance between the regular shelf price and the discounted price was difficult to maintain. In the spring of 1991, Yoplait turned back to television advertising. Its previous advertising had left consumers with an image of Yoplait as a premium product for slim, beautiful women. The campaign that began airing in 1991 was instead geared toward the average, active woman. The ads, with the theme "Yoplait. Do it for you," tried to show Yoplait as a healthy, down-to-earth food for every day. The campaign aired for only eight weeks in 1991, but was broadcast nationally for a full 36 weeks the following year.

General Mills continued to innovate, bringing out new products such as Yoplait Trix, a layered, low-fat yogurt for children, in August 1992, and Yoplait Light Custard Style in January 1993. The Trix product seemed a particularly good direction for Yoplait, since children made up 25 percent of all yogurt consumers in the United States, and Yoplait believed that percentage would increase. Yoplait also believed it could increase consumer awareness of yogurt's health and nutritional benefits by using the National Yogurt Association Seal on its packaging. This seal guaranteed that the product it appeared on contained live yogurt cultures. These live cultures had many positive health benefits.

Yoplait's growth had slowed some in the late 1980s, but the brand's marketers predicted that the yogurt market would continue to expand, with Yoplait a driving force. By 1992 only 60 percent of the U.S. population ate yogurt, so that still left significant room for growth. Yoplait had demonstrated its ability to adapt to the evolving trends in the vibrant 1980s yogurt market by bringing out many new product introductions. With the company geared toward more effective advertising in the 1990s, and a renewed commitment to marketing and product innovation, Yoplait seems sure to remain a force in the yogurt market for a second decade.

Further Reading:

Carter, Kim, "Growing Yogurt Culture Warms Sales," *Advertising Age,* October 13, 1986, p. S-35-36.

Franz, Julie, "To-Fitness Hopes for Instant Yogurt Success," *Advertising Age,* October 14, 1985, pp. 74-76.

General Mills Family, 1981-1985.

General Mills Review, 1986-1993.

Gershman, Michael J., *Getting It Right the Second Time,* New York: Addison-Wesley, 1990, pp. 104-108.

Kimbrell, Wendy, "Good Balance," *Dairy Field,* January 1993, pp. 20-28.

Levitt, Alan, "Yoplait USA," *Dairy Foods,* April 1990, p. 62.

Liesse, Julie, "Pudding Push," *Advertising Age,* January 14, 1991, p. 6.

McDermott, Michael J., "Fat-Free-for-All," *Food & Beverage Marketing,* July 1990, p. 16.

Sheraton, Mimi, " 'French' Yogurts: Vive la Not-Much-Difference," *Minneapolis Tribune,* June 18, 1981, p. 11C.

Weinberger, Betsy, "Executive Goes from Hot (Bringer's) to Cold (Yoplait)," *Minneapolis/St. Paul cityBusiness,* October 23, 1992, p. 2.

—A. Woodward

INDEX TO BRAND NAMES

Listings are arranged in alphabetical order under brand name. Brand names appearing in bold type have historical essays on the page numbers appearing in bold.

INDEX TO COMPANIES AND PERSONS

Listings are arranged in alphabetical order under the company name; thus Philip Morris Companies Inc. will be found under the letter P. Definite articles (The) that precede the name are ignored for alphabetical purposes.

INDEX TO ADVERTISING AGENCIES

Listings are arranged in alphabetical order under the first letter of the agency name; thus Leo Burnett Company Inc. will be found under the letter L.

INDEX TO BRAND CATEGORIES

Brand categories are arranged alphabetically; listings beneath each category in turn are arranged alphabetically. This index contains only brand names that have individual historical essays in the series.

BABY FOOD

Gerber

BAKING

Arm & Hammer
Baker's
Betty Crocker
Bisquick
Carnation
Crisco
Domino Sugar
Duncan Hines
Fleischmann's
Gold Medal
Land O Lakes
Mazola
Morton Salt
Parkay
Pillsbury
Quaker Oats Oatmeal

BEER

Bass Ale
Beck's
Budweiser
Busch
Coors
Corona
Guinness Stout
Heineken
Miller
Molson
Old Milwaukee

BOTTLED WATER

Evian
Perrier

BREAD

See GRAINS

BREAKFAST FOOD

Aunt Jemima
Bisquick
Cap'n Crunch
Cheerios
Chex
Cream of Wheat
Eggo Waffles
Kellogg's Corn Flakes
Kellogg's Frosted Flakes
Kellogg's Pop Tarts
Kellogg's Raisin Bran
Kellogg's Rice Krispies
Log Cabin
Nabisco Shredded Wheat
Post Grape-Nuts
Quaker Oats Oatmeal
Total
Wheaties

CANDY

Brach's
Cadbury's

Certs
Hershey's
Life Savers
M&M's
Nestlé Chocolate
Reese's Peanut Butter Cups
Snickers
Tootsie Roll
Trident
Wrigley's

CAT FOOD

See PET FOOD

CEREAL

See BREAKFAST FOOD

CHEWING GUM

See CANDY

CHOCOLATE

See CANDY

CIGARETTES

See TOBACCO

COFFEE

Folgers
Maxwell House
Nescafé
Sanka
Taster's Choice

CONDIMENTS, JAMS, AND SAUCES

French's
Grey Poupon
Heinz Ketchup
Hellmann's
Lea & Perrins
Miracle Whip
Ragú
Smucker's
Tabasco

DAIRY

Borden Dairy
Breyers
Carnation
Dannon
Kraft Cheese
Háagen-Dazs
Land O Lakes
Philadelphia Brand Cream Cheese
Velveeta
Yoplait

DESSERTS

See SNACK FOOD: SWEET

DOG FOOD

See PET FOOD

FROZEN FOOD

Banquet
Birds Eye
Green Giant
Healthy Choice
Ore-Ida
Sara Lee
Stouffer's
Swanson
Van de Kamp's
Weight Watchers

FRUITS AND VEGETABLES

Birds Eye
Chiquita
Del Monte
Dole Pineapple
Green Giant
Ore-Ida
Sunkist
Sun-Maid

GRAINS: BREAD, PASTA, RICE

Chef Boyardee
Rice-A-Roni
Uncle Ben's
Wonder Bread

JUICE AND FRUIT-FLAVORED BEVERAGES

Gatorade
Hawaiian Punch
Hi-C
Kool-Aid
Minute Maid
Ocean Spray
Tropicana
V-8
Welch's Grape Juice
Wyler's

LIQUOR (also see BEER and WINE AND CHAMPAGNE)

Absolut
Bacardi Rum
Baileys
Canadian Mist
Dewar's
Di Saronno Amaretto
Gordon's
Grand Marnier
J&B
Jack Daniel's
Jim Beam
Johnnie Walker
Jose Cuervo
Kahlua
Seagram's
Smirnoff
Southern Comfort
Tanqueray

MARGARINE AND COOKING OIL

Crisco
Fleischmann's

Land O Lakes
Mazola
Parkay

MEAT

Butterball
Healthy Choice
Louis Rich
Oscar Mayer
Perdue
Spam
StarKist
Tyson
Underwood
Van de Kamp's

PASTA

See GRAINS

PEANUT BUTTER

Jif
Skippy

PET FOOD

Alpo
Friskies
Kal Kan
Mighty Dog
Milk-Bone
9-Lives
Purina Pet Chow
Whiskas

RICE

See GRAINS

SOFT DRINKS

A&W
Canada Dry
Coca-Cola
Dr Pepper
Hires
Mountain Dew
Pepsi-Cola
RC Cola
Schweppes
7UP
Shasta
Slice
Sprite

SOUP

Campbell's Soup
Progresso Soup

SNACK FOOD: SALTY

Doritos
Fritos
Keebler
Lay's
Orville Redenbacher's
Pepperidge Farm
Planters

Ritz
Rold Gold
Ruffles
Wise

SNACK FOOD: SWEET

Barnum's Animals Crackers
Breyers
Cracker Jack
Entenmann's
Fig Newtons
Háagen-Dazs
Jell-O
Keebler
Little Debbie
Oreo
Pepperidge Farm
Sara Lee
Twinkies

SUGAR AND SWEETENER

Domino Sugar
NutraSweet

TEA

Lipton
Nestea
Salada
Tetley

TOBACCO

Benson & Hedges
Camel
Kool
Lucky Strike
Marlboro
Newport
Salem
Virginia Slims
Winston

VEGETABLES

See FRUITS AND VEGETABLES

WINE AND CHAMPAGNE

Almaden
Beringer
Dom Pérignon
Gallo
Glen Ellen
Inglenook
Richards Wild Irish Rose
Sutter Home

NOTES ON CONTRIBUTORS

BARNSTORFF, Virginia. Free-lance writer. Special assignment writer and mathematics correlator for Silver Burdett Ginn (Simon & Schuster), 1989-91. Contributing writer, *HSPT Success: Work-A-Text Study Program for Writing,* 1991.

BROWN, Susan Windisch. Free-lance writer and editor.

BILAS, Wendy Johnson. Free-lance writer with 8 years of professional marketing experience; MBA in marketing, Wake Forest University; director of marketing for the Charlotte Symphony Orchestra.

BOYER, Dean. Former newspaper reporter; free-lance writer in Seattle area.

BRENNAN, Carol. Free-lance writer in Chicago.

COHEN, Kerstan. Free-lance writer and French translator; editor for *Letter-Ex* poetry review, Chicago.

DARLINGTON, Joy. Free-lance writer and author of five books; life-style writing, ranging from biographical profiles to reporting crime stories.

DORMAN, Evelyn. Free-lance journalist, public relations, French teacher, tutor, and graduate student. Contributor to *Brides Today,* the *Chicago Sun-Times, Lerner-Pulitzer* newspapers, and St. James Press' *International Directory of Company Histories.*

DOUGAL, April S. Archivist and free-lance writer specializing in business and social history in Cleveland, Ohio.

DUBOVOJ, Sina. History contractor and free-lance writer; adjunct professor of history, Montgomery College, Rockville, Maryland.

GOLD, Maxine. Free-lance writer, editor, and communications consultant. Managing editor, *Women Making History: Conversations with Fifteen New Yorkers,* March, 1985. Editor, *Status Report,* quarterly newsletter, New York City Commission on the Status of Women, 1980-91. Copyeditor, *Business Latin America,* weekly newsletter published by the Economist Intelligence Unit.

GOLDSWORTHY, Joan. Free-lance writer and editor. Contributor to *Newsmakers, Contemporary Black Biography, Contemporary Musicians,* and *Contemporary Authors.*

GRODEN, Louise L. Free-lance writer and MBA student at the University of Michigan.

HALL, Janet Reinhart. Free-lance writer.

HOFFMAN, Gary. Free-lance writer.

HUGHES, Anne C. Free-lance editor, writer, and desktop publisher in Chicago. Editor, *Maintenance Executive, Legal Information Alert,* and *Business Information Alert.*

INGRAM, Frederick. Free-lance writer.

JACOBSON, Robert R. Free-lance writer and musician.

JOE, Radcliffe A. New York-based writer.

JOHNSON, Anne Janette. Free-lance writer based in Philadelphia.

KING, Daniel E. Free-lance writer working on doctorate in economics at the New School for Social Research.

KROLL, Dorothy. Free-lance business writer, journalist, and industry analyst.

LEWIS, Scott M. Free-lance writer and editor; contributing editor, *Option.* Staff editor, *Security, Distributing and Marketing,* 1989-90.

MacINNES, Margo. Free-lance writer, editor, photographer. Listed in *Who's Who in American Women* and *World's Who's Who of Women.* Exceptional Achievement Award from the Council for Advancement and Support of Education in Washington, D.C. Articles have appeared in commercial and academic publications.

MAXFIELD, Doris Morris. Owner of Written Expressions, an editorial services business. Contributor to numerous reference publications. Editor of *Online Database Search Services Directory,* 1983-84 and 1988, and of *Charitable Organizations of the U.S.,* 1991-92 and 1992-93.

MOGELONSKY, Marcia K. Free-lance editor and writer; contributor to *American Demographics,* the *Numbers News, Modern Women,* and other magazines.

NEWMAN, Laura. Free-lance business and medical journalist; correspondent for medical trade press and news publications.

NORTON, Frances E. Free-lance writer; contributor to *Evanston Arts Review* and *Helicon.*

PATTI, Nicholas. Free-lance writer. Master's degree in English from the University of Michigan, Ann Arbor.

PATWARDHAN, Ashish. Free-lance writer enrolled in doctoral program in accounting/finance at the John Olin School of Business at Washington University. MBA in Finance from Carnegie Mellon University.

PAUL, Katherine J. Free-lance journalist; contributing editor, *Crain's Tire Business.* Senior reporter, Crain Communications Inc., 1989-1992. Editor, *Record News,* 1988-89. Assistant editor, *Record Courier,* 1987-88.

PEDERSON, Jay P. Free-lance writer and editor.

PENDERGAST, Sara. Free-lance writer and graduate student in business administration at Purdue University.

PENDERGAST, Tom. Free-lance writer and graduate student in business administration at Purdue University.

RIGGS, Thomas. Free-lance writer and editor.

ROSEN, Isaac. Free-lance writer and editor living on Cape Cod, MA.

SALTER, Susan. Writer/contributor to several reference series, including *Contemporary Authors, Newsmakers,* and *Major Authors and Illustrators for Children and Young Adults.*

SARICH, John A. Free-lance writer and editor. Graduate student in economics at the New School for Social Research.

SHEEHAN, Kate. Free-lance writer in Chicago.

SHERMAN, Francine Shonfeld. Free-lance writer and editor. Assistant editor, *Compton's Encyclopedia,* 1986-92. Contributing editor, *Britannica Book of the Year,* annual.

SIMLEY, John. Professional researcher and corporate issues analyst. Former research editor for *International Directory of Company Histories.*

SMITH, Caroline. Free-lance writer specializing in medical, social, and business issues; contributor to newspapers, magazines, and corporate journals.

SUN, Douglas. Assistant professor of English at California State University at Los Angeles. Contributor to *International Directory of Company Histories.*

TROESTER, Maura. Chicago-based free-lance writer.

TUDAHL, Kim. Executive assistant/travel consultant, Oriental Tours & Travel, Cambridge, MA. Free-lance writer; contributor to the *Harbus News,* Harvard Business School, and the *Rochester Post-Bulletin.*

WALTON, Dorothy. Free-lance writer with a specialty in business and legislative topics. Author of *A Guide to Managing REO and Receivership Properties* and *ADA Title III: Compliance Made Practical.* Writer for the *Journal of Property Management* and for the University of Chicago Press.

WANKOFF, Jordan. Free-lance writer; coeditor of *Vice Versa* literary magazine; museum editor, *California Art Review,* 1989.

WOLF, Gillian. Free-lance writer. Author of "The Ultimate Slingshot," 1989, and "Akh, Odessa!," 1990, both for *Jewish Affairs.*

WOODWARD, Angela. Free-lance writer.

YOUNG, Shannon. Ph.D. student in education at the University of Michigan. Free-lance writer and editor.